HOLLYWOOD BABY BOOMERS

Garland Reference Library of the Humanities
(Vol. 1295)

Also of Interest from Garland

Hollywood Songsters: A Biographical Dictionary
by James Robert Parish and Michael R. Pitts

Encyclopedia of American War Films
by Larry Langman and Edgar Borg

Encyclopedia of American Spy Films
by Larry Langman and David Ebner

Black Arts Annual
edited by Donald Bogle

Blacks in American Films and Television: An Illustrated Encyclopedia
by Donald Bogle

Encyclopedia of American Film Comedy
by Larry Langman

HOLLYWOOD BABY BOOMERS

by
James Robert Parish
and
Don Stanke

GARLAND PUBLISHING, INC.

New York & London 1992

Library of Congress Cataloging-in-Publication Data

Parish, James Robert.
    Hollywood baby boomers / by James Robert Parish and Don Stanke.
      p. cm.—(Garland reference library of the humanities: vol. 1295)
    Includes index.
    ISBN 0-8240-6104-7 (alk. paper)
    1. Motion picture actors and actresses—United States—Biography
Dictionaries. I. Stanke, Don E. II. Title. III. Series.
PN2285.P333 1992
791.43'028'092273—dc20
[B]   91-38768
                                      CIP

Book design: Barbara Bergeron
Cover design: John Röblin

Printed on acid-free, 250-year-life paper
Manufactured in the United States of America

71792

In Tribute to
Gilda Radner (1946–1989) and John Belushi (1949–1982)
Who Gave Us Joyous Memories

CONTENTS

Introduction   ix

Keys and Notes   xi

Acknowledgments   xiii

Richard Dean Anderson	1	Whoopi Goldberg	191
Dan Aykroyd	7	Jeff Goldblum	200
Alec Baldwin	14	John Goodman	208
Ellen Barkin	22	Melanie Griffith	215
Roseanne Barr	28	Steve Guttenberg	222
Kim Basinger	39	Arsenio Hall	229
Tom Berenger	45	Harry Hamlin	236
Candice Bergen	52	Tom Hanks	243
Bruce Boxleitner	62	Mark Harmon	250
Jeff Bridges	69	Gregory Harrison	259
Cher	77	Gregory Hines	268
Glenn Close	88	William Hurt	275
Kevin Costner	97	Timothy Hutton	283
Billy Crystal	106	Ann Jillian	291
Jamie Lee Curtis	113	Don Johnson	297
Willem Defoe	119	Tommy Lee Jones	305
Jeff Daniels	126	Diane Keaton	312
Ted Danson	134	Michael Keaton	319
Tony Danza	142	Perry King	327
Richard Dreyfuss	149	Kevin Kline	336
Sally Field	157	Christine Lahti	344
Richard Gere	165	Jessica Lange	352
Mel Gibson	174	Shelley Long	360
Danny Glover	182	Madonna	366

Contents

John Malkovich	375	Jaclyn Smith	500
Kelly McGillis	383	Jimmy Smits	508
Bill Murray	389	Sissy Spacek	514
Mandy Patnikin	396	Sylvester Stallone	521
Sean Penn	405	Meryl Streep	531
Michelle Pfeiffer	413	Patrick Swayze	541
Dennis Quaid	421	John Travolta	549
Christopher Reeve	428	Kathleen Turner	557
John Ritter	436	Lindsay Wagner	566
Mickey Rourke	444	Sigourney Weaver	574
Kurt Russell	452	Robin Williams	582
Susan Saint James	459	Treat Williams	591
Susan Sarandon	466	Bruce Willis	598
Arnold Schwarzenegger	474	Oprah Winfrey	607
Jane Seymour	483	Debra Winger	614
Cybill Shepherd	491	James Woods	622

Index 633

INTRODUCTION

THE GENERATION OF THE AMERICAN BABY BOOMERS IS COMPRISED of those born in the years from 1946, following the return home of soldiers who had fought in World War II, through 1964. It has been estimated that the Baby Boomers of America at present constitute one-third of the nation's population, or about seventy-six million persons. For purposes of brevity, this book includes Hollywood luminaries born between 1946 and 1960.

Many of the multi-talented superstars of today's Hollywood are of the Baby Boom generation; these actors, musicians, and comedians have made it to the top without the aid or protection of a major studio to serve as a safe harbor and launching pad of careers. Most of the successful members of this generation have formed their own production companies, thereby making themselves self-sufficient in dealings with the major film companies. They are, for the most part, an intelligent, self-sufficient group.

In the hope of delaying the aging process, the Baby Boomers frequently turn to skin preparations to repair the ravages caused by stage makeup and to deter nature's course. They often have had cosmetic surgery as well as injections of collagen to create voluptuous lips; they have substituted pectoral implants for regular visits to a gymnasium; and they have introduced their bodies to steroids. Church and God play a big part in their complex lives; they have strong beliefs in reincarnation and the existence of ghosts as well as the devil, and one in ten states that he or she has had a conversation with the latter. Astrology and telepathic experiences are also popular with the group.

Privacy is extremely important to today's Hollywood stars; many refuse interviews or, if they do sit for a printed or televised talk, steer clear of mentioning their offspring or where they reside. National tabloid publications have a field day with this generation in headlining and exploiting their (mis)adventures. Well-paid, muscular bodyguards surround these celebrities to keep away an adoring, clawing public, which in a few cases has included love-starved sociopaths who feel that it is their right to communicate one-on-one with the objects of their obsessive adoration. Many of Hollywood's Baby Boomers have chosen not to make Los Angeles their home; instead, they prefer to live as far away as possible, commuting when necessary to a film site.

While displaying their God-given or acting-class-derived talent—whether on huge movie screens or on stage in front of hundreds or thousands—they feel that the public (especially their fans) should recognize that they are working at what they love best and that they should be left alone, like bankers or any other successful business executives. However, the public needs and enjoys having idols to admire. The Baby Boomers' complaints about the tragedy of fame and the strains that status puts on a celebrity were ridiculed recently by Frank Sinatra, a superstar of an earlier generation. In a letter to the *Los Angeles Times* he wrote, in part, "you're on the top rung of a tall ladder called Stardom, which in Latin means thanks-to-the-fans who were there when it was lonely."

In earning salaries far in excess of what an average person might realize within two or even three lifetimes, Hollywood's Baby Boomers spend, spend, spend—not only on themselves, families, and friends, but also in generous donations to various causes, such as AIDS research, the environmental movement, relief for the homeless, and advocacy of reproductive freedom and free expression in the arts.

Most Baby Boomers of the entertainment industry who have now reached middle age have typically undergone a mellowing process, becoming introspective and recognizing their own mortality.

In this volume we celebrate Hollywood's Baby Boomer generation. While space limitations prevented us from including all its members, we strove to present a representative group. If one of your favorites has been omitted, we would appreciate your communication to the publisher, as well as any additions and corrections you may have to the text. Information in the text is accurate as of March 1991.

James Robert Parish
Don Stanke

JAMES ROBERT PARISH, Studio City, California–based direct-marketing consultant and freelance writer, was born in Cambridge, Massachusetts. He attended the University of Pennsylvania and graduated Phi Beta Kappa with a degree in English. A graduate of the University of Pennsylvania Law School, he is a member of the New York Bar. As president of Entertainment Copyright Research Co., Inc., he headed a major researching facility for the film and television industries. Later he was a film reviewer-interviewer for the trade newspapers *Motion Picture Daily* and *Variety*. He is the author of over seventy-five volumes, including *Prostitution in Hollywood Films*, *The Great Cop Pictures*, *Prison Pictures from Hollywood*, *The Fox Girls*, *Good Dames*, *The Slapstick Queens*, *The RKO Gals*, *The Tough Guys*, *The Jeanette MacDonald Story*, *The Elvis Presley Scrapbook*, *The Hollywood Beauties*, and *The Great Combat Pictures*. Among those he has co-written are *The MGM Stock Company*, *The Debonairs*, *Liza!*, *Hollywood Character Actors*, *The Hollywood Reliables*, *The Funsters*, *The Best of MGM*, *Black Action Pictures from Hollywood*, and his ongoing series, *Complete Actors' Television Credits* with Vincent Terrace. With Michael R. Pitts, he has co-written such works as *Hollywood on Hollywood*, *The Great Western Pictures* (base and companion volumes), *The Great Gangster Pictures* (base and companion volumes), *The Great Spy Pictures* (base and companion volumes), *The Great Science Fiction Pictures* (base and companion volumes), *The Great Detective Pictures*, *Great Hollywood Musicals*, and *Hollywood Songsters*. Mr. Parish is adviser for Greenwood Press's Bio-Bibliography in the Performing Arts series. His entertainment research collection is archived at Kent State University in Kent, Ohio.

DON STANKE, born and educated in St. Paul, Minnesota, resides in Reno, Nevada. He is a past president of San Francisco's prestigious Insurance Personnel Management Association. Don has contributed player biographies, many based on personal interviews, to various cinema publications including Leonard Maltin's *The Real Stars*, *The Real Stars #2*, and *Hollywood Kids*. With James Robert Parish, he is the co-author of *The Glamour Girls*, *The Swashbucklers*, *The Debonairs*, *The All-Americans*, *The Leading Ladies*, *The Forties Gals*, and *The Hollywood Beauties*, as well as a contributor to Parish's *The Tough Guys*.

KEYS AND NOTES

Filmography Key

AA	Allied Artists Pictures
ABC-TV	American Broadcasting Corporation
AIP	American International Pictures
Aust	Australian
Avco Emb	Avco Embassy Pictures
Br	British
BV	Buena Vista Distribution
CBS-TV	Columbia Broadcasting System
Cin	Cinerama Releasing
Col	Columbia Pictures
Emb	Embassy Pictures
Fr	French
HBO	Home Box Office–Cable
It	Italian
MGM	Metro-Goldwyn-Mayer Pictures
MGM/UA	Metro-Goldwyn-Mayer/United Artists Pictures
NBC-TV	National Broadcasting Corporation
NG	National General Pictures
Par	Paramount Pictures
(s)	Short subject
Sp	Spanish
Synd-TV	Syndicated
20th–Fox	Twentieth Century–Fox Films
UA	United Artists Pictures
Univ	Universal Pictures
Unk	Unknown distributor
WB	Warner Bros. Pictures

Notes

- Film titles in brackets are alternate release, reissue, or British release titles for the given film.
- Made-for-television feature films (telefilms) telecast over one or two evenings are listed in the filmography; miniseries (three parts or more) are listed under television series.

Television Key

ABC	American Broadcasting Corporation
Can	Canadian
CBS	Columbia Broadcasting System
HBO	Home Box Office–Cable
NBC	National Broadcasting Corporation
NN	Non-network
PBS	Public Broadcasting System
Synd	Syndicated

Discography Key

Only long-playing albums are included. The catalogue number given is for the LP album. For newer releases, where no LP was pressed, the compact disc catalogue number is provided.

OC	Original Cast
ST	Soundtrack
ST-TV	TV Soundtrack

ACKNOWLEDGMENTS

Barry Ayers
Jack Barnich
Kathy Bartels
David Bartholomew
Jerry Bentsch
Beverly Hills Public Library
James Brown
Beverley Bare Buehrer
Grace A. Catalano
John Cocchi
Howard Davis
Steve Eberly
Eddie Brandt's Saturday Matinee Shop
Steve Erb
Karin J. Fowler
Charlene George
Alex Gildzen
Marilyn Glasgow
Kim Holston
Carol A. How
Jane Klain
Laser Perceptions (Eldon Chan)
Limelight Book Store (Roy Johnson)
Lee Mattson

Doug McClelland
Marge Meisinger
Nancy Mendoza
Jim Meyer
Allen Mitchem
Bro. Gerald Molyneaux
The New York Public Library
  for the Performing Arts
Bob O'Neill
Michael R. Pitts
Barry Rivadue
Jerry Roberts
Bob Rusk
Margie Schultz
Arleen Schwartz
Edward Shreve
Steve Skjelstadt
Kevin Sweeney
Vincent Terrace
Evelyn Stanke Thompson
Jack Trafton
Brenda Wilson
Bill Wine

Editorial Consultant: Allan Taylor

HOLLYWOOD BABY BOOMERS

RICHARD DEAN ANDERSON

"Many times I've felt a little less than confident about my acting qualitatively so I've always tried to have as much fun as possible."
—*Drama-Logue*, December 11–17, 1986

RICHARD DEAN ANDERSON IS BEST KNOWN AS AN ATHLETIC TELEVI-sion hero, "a thinking man's adventurer" who leaps instantly to the aid of distressed victims. His hit TV show "MacGyver" (1985–) projects him as a rugged modern Robin Hood who employs wholesome, weaponless methods of dealing with his adversaries. This show has provided a superior forum for this 6' 2" sandy-haired, brown-eyed TV warrior, who, after concluding his on-screen heroics each season, has gone into seclusion, far from cameras, make-up, and scripts.

He was born on Monday, January 23, 1950, in Minneapolis, Minnesota. He was the first of four sons of jazz musician Stuart Anderson, who supplemented his income by teaching at Columbia Heights School, and his artist wife. Called Ricky Dean by his father, he was introduced to jazz music at an early age when he learned to play guitar and to sing. When he was twelve, he formed his own small rock band, Ricky Dean and Dante. Influenced by his father, who was a solid bass player, Ricky Dean made a 45-rpm recording for the Emmy label, singing "Little Girl"/"Blue Tears."

Also at an early age, he acquired a wanderlust, and it became common practice for him to hop onto freight trains for a quick ride to another town or state. In school he was active in various sports, with hockey his chief interest. His hopes of becoming a profession-al hockey player as star-wing were dashed when he was sixteen: in the quick-action game, he broke first one arm, then the other arm three weeks later. While in traction for three-and-a-half months, he concluded that hockey was not to be his profession. (As part of physical therapy after traction, he was required to swim. He volunteered for the school's swim team, but gave that up, too, when he cut his head on the edge of the diving board.)

On graduating from high school in 1967, he and two friends took a 5,600-mile bicycle excursion through Canada to Alaska. On returning to Minnesota, he enrolled at St. Cloud State College, where he studied humanities, with an emphasis on theater. A few months later, his drama professor, John Dennis, left the college to relocate to California. Richard Dean decided he did not wish to remain on campus without the man's stage guidance. He quit school to spend a few months in San Francisco, where he lived among the free spirits of the Haight-Ashbury district. "Drugs were rampant," he said later, "and I was living in the middle of it." His brief experiments with drugs ended when he elected to return east to enroll at Ohio University at Athens, Ohio, to study acting. After three years, as he was about to begin his senior year with a role in the drama department's production of Shakespeare's *Much Ado About Nothing*, he went to San Francisco to visit his father, who had by this time divorced his mother.

While in the Bay City, Richard learned that John Dennis, his acting mentor from Minnesota, was holding open auditions in Los Angeles for his upcoming production of *Superman in the Bones* at the Pilgrimage Theatre. Anderson went south, won a part in the play, and officially quit college. Although the production quickly closed without being reviewed, Richard decided to make Los Angeles his new headquarters. He worked at the Broadway Department Store selling curtains and shoes, then performed as a street mime and juggler. Later, he sang at a Renaissance-type cabaret and then stage-managed for the Improvisational Theatre Company. Next, he got a job at Marineland, a then-popular sea animal park, where he performed with the whales as well as wrote some of the choreographic scripts (one of which had a whale snapping a mackerel from Richard's mouth!).

In 1976 he received his first TV break when he was cast in the daytime drama "General Hospital" (ABC) as Dr. Jeff Webber. He earned a spot in the hall of live bloopers in a 1978 segment when, as Dr. Webber, he encountered a colleague in a hospital corridor and exclaimed, "Well, aren't you a sight for sore ears!" After three years, with the ratings slipping, Richard wanted out of his commitment and told his agent to demand a lot more money. The ploy backfired: the network met his salary ultimatum and he was forced to remain on the soap through 1981. By that time the inclusion of new characters, including Luke (Anthony Geary) and Laura (Genie Francis) had generated sufficient on-camera lust and love to send the drama soaring to the top of the rating scale. Richard was scheduled to appear in a cameo role, along with other TV soap opera doctors, in YOUNG DOCTORS IN LOVE (1982), but lost his chance to be seen in his first feature film with his departure from "General Hospital."

Instead, on March 25, 1981, he was featured in a thirty-minute episode, entitled "Brian and Sylvia," of the NBC-TV sitcom "The Facts of Life," intended as a possible series spin-off. Later, on November 29, 1981, he was in "The Fugitive" episode of "Today's FBI" (ABC-TV).

SEVEN BRIDES FOR SEVEN BROTHERS, based on Stephen Vincent Benet's story "The Sobbin' Women," had been a deliciously rousing MGM musical in 1954, starring Howard Keel and Jane Powell. In 1982 the premise was adapted as a television series by CBS with Richard in the Keel-originated role of "Adam" and Terri Treas as his wife, "Hannah," changed from "Milly" as played by Powell. For television, the setting was altered from the frontier to a present-day ranch in northern California to which the macho eldest brother, twenty-seven-year-old Adam, takes his new bride to face a ranch inhabited by his six unruly younger brothers (including Peter Horton and River Phoenix). Richard confided to Kay Gardella (*New York Daily News*) that the series "is the perfect vehicle for me right now, since I get to sing and dance and ride horses. Dancing is my weakest suit, but I manage to get through it." The series premiered at 8 p.m. on Sunday, September 19, 1982, and *Variety* acknowledged that Anderson "came off rather well in the opener." The action of the first few episodes was interlaced by songs written especially for the series by Jimmy Webb, including "Country Roads" and "Eggs." Despite being moved to other nights on the network, the show floundered. It was placed on hiatus in March 1983, and on its return in June the musical numbers were cut to a bare minimum, but even this failed to save the series, which was last telecast on July 2, 1983, without even one of the six unmarried brothers finding a bride.

In his third television series, a prime-time soap opera, "Emerald Point N.A.S.," which premiered on CBS-TV on September 26, 1983, Richard had a supporting role as the good-guy ace pilot Simon Adams, whose father (Patrick O'Neal, followed by Robert Vaughn) and sister (Sela Ward) were unscrupulous manipulators. Created by Richard and Esther Shapiro, who had brought the series "Dynasty" to network TV prominence, "Emerald Point N.A.S." languished for several weeks until its eventual demise on March 12, 1984.

Off camera, Richard and twenty-three-year-old Sela Ward became constant companions. Although they did not share a home, they lived a few blocks apart in West Hollywood, and both claimed they were not ready for marriage. Pictured in *People* magazine as half of a loving couple, Ward insisted that he was "sensitive, sexy and intelligent, but not a real macho type of guy." Their relationship would have an on-again, off-again status for several years.

Richard made his first theatrical motion picture appearance in ODD JOBS (1984) in the supporting role of Spud. Featuring comedians Paul Reiser, Robert Townsend, and Scott McGinnis, it was a lame comedy about college men working for a moving company during summer vacation. The minor film went into limited distribution in 1984, and was rereleased in March 1986. While searching for a teleseries suitable to his talents, he auditioned for the part of a hockey player in a futuristic pilot, "Generation." "I would've loved that one," he said, "but they said I came across so strong in the reading they thought I was doing *Hamlet*." Ironically, Drake Hogestyn, his former co-star in "Seven Brides for Seven Brothers," won the role in the two-hour film, shown on May 24, 1985, on ABC-TV.

The co-executive production team of John Rich and Henry Winkler had interviewed close to one hundred actors to star in their new action-adventure TV series "MacGyver" when they called Richard in to read for them. Of the meeting, producer Rich recalled, "One of the first things Anderson did was ask if we minded him reading with his glasses on. Henry and I looked at each other. After seeing so many macho types we appreciated his willingness to show a vulnerable side of himself. At that moment we knew we had found our man." "MacGyver," whose hero relies on science and ingenuity rather than guns and fists in resolving his assorted man-for-hire assignments, premiered on the ABC-TV network at 8 p.m. on Sunday, September 22, 1985. *Variety* judged that the program was "a fairly well-crafted adventure show, beautifully shot and edited, but that's about as far as it goes." From the beginning, the amiable, dashing hero had no first name, at least none that was used on the show. However, in the original script, written as a ninety-minute pilot but edited to a one-hour episode, MacGyver's given name was Stace.

Sources close to the show say that that name has been discarded and that another, selected by Anderson, may one day be revealed.

In its first season, "MacGyver" ranked #31 in the ratings, having been #2 and #1 some weeks during the season. *TV Guide* credited it as "entertaining, suspenseful and generally good fun" despite the show's "far-fetched premise." The premise was the star's using such items as a paper clip to short-circuit a nuclear missile or a chocolate bar to stop an acid leak. The production staff maintained direct contact with nearby colleges, whose students came up with some of the plot ideas. "Of course," Anderson admitted, "when we're putting together formulas for explosives, we leave one ingredient out, so kids aren't going to make bombs or flame throwers at home out of everyday objects." On the set every day with Richard was his ten-year-old Australian Shepherd dog, Whiskey.

During the September 1986 shoot of an episode for the second season of "Mac-Gyver," which had moved to Monday nights, at the Indian Dunes location in southern California, Richard traumatized his spinal cord after tripping and falling into a hole. In pain, he underwent medical treatment, including acupuncture to quicken the healing, which was "too slow for my level of patience." A short time before this accident, he had broken some fingers in a local hockey game, which did not prevent him from participating in the Special Olympics program at Park City, Utah, where he had earlier lensed ORDINARY HEROES. Originally geared as a theatrical release, the project was edited into a telefeature for ABC-TV. Telecast on October 19, 1986, ORDINARY HEROES was an updated remake of the well-regarded Warner Bros. World War II film PRIDE OF THE

Mary Beth Barber and **Richard Dean Anderson** in "MacGyver" (1986).

MARINES (1945), which had starred John Garfield. Opposite Valerie Bertinelli, Richard was a Vietnam War soldier blinded in combat three days before his scheduled discharge from service. *Variety* was unimpressed: "Anderson and Bertinelli are not compelling thesps, and they never breathe life into their cardboard characters or into the great love they're supposed to feel for one another."

For its third season (1987–1988), the "MacGyver" production company moved to Vancouver, British Columbia, where it was far less expensive to film. Because there was no facility large enough to accommodate the operation, Paramount renovated an old factory where San Francisco's Golden Gate Bridge had been fabricated in the mid-1930s. Continuing as a union shop, the Vancouver-based production crew consisted of eleven Americans heading key departments, assisted by 169 Canadians. Anderson, who had always wanted to return to Canada, was pleased with the change of locale as well as weather. He said, "I'm from Minneapolis and there's a northern work ethic I think is born of our heritage—the environment you have to deal with. Minnesota is extremely harsh in its winters and there comes a kind of stoic strength of mind and body and I find that almost paralleled here." In a *Variety* study, the show ranked tenth for the week of March 27, 1989, for the number of violent acts—and all committed without benefit of guns or fists. In August 1989 Richard's dog, aged fourteen, died. In December 1989, during the fifth season of "MacGyver," it was reported that Anderson had, at least temporarily, found a "secret love" in Vancouver when he was seen socially with forty-one-year-old actress Marcia Strassman. For the week ending February 11, 1990, "MacGyver," according to the A. C. Neilsen Company's ratings, ranked #35 with a 13.7 audience share. The show reached a milestone on March 5, 1990, when its one hundredth episode was televised. In a letter to "the MacGyver family," producers Henry Winkler and John Rich celebrated the occasion: "We feel so lucky to have Richard Dean Anderson as our Star Performer. His efforts, energy and level of cooperation—above and beyond the call of duty—have done much to cement the feeling of 'one-ness' that characterizes our set." One of Richard's favorite episodes was that of April 30, 1990, in which MacGyver, in an injury-induced coma, was reunited with his dead parents aboard a ship, a celestial type of waiting room. The series was renewed for a sixth season, which premiered on September 17, 1990, with an announced intention to offer several issue-oriented segments. Rick Sherwood (*Hollywood Reporter*) observed, "What once was new soon becomes old, and ABC's 'MacGyver' and star Richard Dean Anderson are starting to show their age. . . . The action-adventure series . . . seems to have lost the technological edge that won it a following." Later in the season, when the show's producers were considering adding a recurring love interest for Anderson's character, the actor responded, "I am definitely looking forward to seeing how they handle it. I do not necessarily have things so together in my real life that I can dictate the way the scripts should go."

Under his Gecco Productions banner in partnership with Michael Greenburg (supervising producer of "MacGyver"), Richard reportedly had several projects in development in mid-1990, one of which was a TV movie about G. Gordon Liddy. When Anderson is not recuperating from injuries incurred one way or another, he plays hockey with the Los Angeles Celebrity All Star Team, of which he is a co-founder. In matches played during periods of television-production hiatus, the team has raised more than $1 million for charitable causes. In April 1990 Richard entered the political arena by submitting written testimony to the House Ways and Means Committee hearing in Washington, D.C., in support of the Drug War Bond Act.

Mostly, when Anderson is on vacation from "MacGyver," he wants to enjoy himself during his series break. He has stated that he would like to have two children. "I'm almost jealous that I can't have a baby myself," he said jokingly.

Filmography

Odd Jobs (Tri-Star, 1984)
Ordinary Heroes (ABC-TV, 10/19/86)

Television Series

General Hospital (ABC, 1976–81)
Seven Brides for Seven Brothers (CBS, 1982–83)
Emerald Point N.A.S. (CBS, 1983–84)
MacGyver (ABC, 1985–)

DAN AYKROYD

"There's proof that laughter causes a reaction in the endocrine system.
There's a whole theory that laughter really *is* the best medicine."
—*Moviegoer* magazine, February 1986

THIS NATURALLY FUNNY AND WILD GUY IS FILLED WITH A RESTLESS-
ness (not impatience). It has shaped the man, who is best known for his enthusiasm and
optimism, qualities that flow into his writing as well as his acting. Average in appearance,
the slack-jawed Dan Aykroyd is able to walk along a busy street, shop for groceries, or
pump his own gas without immediate recognition. "I have the best of both worlds," he has
said, "because when I want to turn it on and want people to know who I am and what I'm
associated with, it's there." On another occasion the laconic performer assessed, "I have
this kind of mild nice-guy exterior, but inside, my heart is like a steel trap. I'm really quite
robotic."

Of the original repertory cast members of "Saturday Night Live" who became film
stars, Dan Aykroyd's feature films during the 1980s grossed $789.4 million at the
domestic box office, $45 million more than those of his closest contender, Bill Murray.
While Aykroyd is not 100 percent successful at selecting the best properties for himself, he
is close to it. Lorne Michaels, the creator of "Saturday Night Live," the landmark late-
night TV program that brought initial fame to Dan Aykroyd, has called him "the Alec
Guinness of the show. He's mutable. More than anyone else, he defined the range of
acting on the show." Unlike Steve Martin, Bill Murray, and Chevy Chase—his male
confreres from that comedy teleseries—Aykroyd has been able effectively to shift his
talents to the dramatic arena, where his peers have honored him with the ultimate
accolade: an Academy Award nomination for his performance in DRIVING MISS DAISY
(1989).

Daniel Edward Aykroyd was born on Tuesday, July 1, 1952, in Ottawa, Ontario,
Canada, to Samuel Cuthbert Peter Hugh Aykroyd, a government official whose father had
been a Canadian Royal Mounted Policeman, and Lorraine Gougeon Aykroyd. Both
parents were blessed with a sense of humor, and laughter reigned in the Aykroyd home
whose locale changed periodically from Quebec to the country hills of Ottawa and to bush
camps. Samuel, who had become the deputy minister of transport, was responsible for
overseeing the construction of highways in the rural areas. Between the ages of six and
fifteen, Dan changed schools several times as the family relocated. In preference to the
classroom, the young Aykroyd enjoyed hanging around the construction camps as well as

outside the barrooms while the crew drank beer and listened to rhythm-and-blues music. A rebellious youth, he would often slip inside and consume beers that were bought for him by his older friends. (As an adult, Dan has been known to drink sixteen to eighteen beers a day.) Nurturing his fondness for music, his parents bought him a drum set when he was thirteen, and by the time he was ready for college, Dan was also playing the harmonica.

In 1970 Aykroyd enrolled at Carleton University in Ottawa, where he studied criminology but had many other interests as well, including motorcycles, cars, aeronautics, and mysticism. At the age of twenty, in 1972, after performing bits on radio in Ottawa, he quit the university to relocate to Toronto where he joined the Toronto improvisational comedy company Second City. Also in the group was a young woman named Gilda Radner. Along with earning a regular slot on a children's comedy television show on the Canadian Broadcasting Company (CBC), he also managed an after-hours club in Toronto known as Club 505. He maneuvered a job as a fast-talking pitchman on a Toronto cable TV variety show, "Greed," then did a series, "Coming Up Rosie," on the CBC as well as working in the network's "The Hart and Lorne Terrific Hour" and "Today Makes Me Nervous."

On May 10, 1974, at the age of twenty-two, he was married to Maureen Lewis before moving south to Chicago to join the original Second City troupe. With Maureen he would have three children: Mark, Lloyd, and Oscar. The couple would divorce not long after the birth of their third son. In 1975 Lorne Michaels, the twenty-nine-year-old writer/ producer of a new late-night Saturday show to be telecast from New York, added Dan to his TV repertory company, named "the not ready for prime-time players." Others in this original group (sometimes called "the Beatles of comedy") were John Belushi, Chevy Chase, Jane Curtin, Garrett Morris, Laraine Newman, and Gilda Radner. "Live from New York, it's Saturday night" was first echoed through the corridors of 30 Rockefeller Plaza on October 11, 1975. The premiere edition of the ninety–minute "Saturday Night Live" was hosted by George Carlin; each show had a $200,000 budget. For the next four seasons, Dan's impersonations on the popular show included characters Beldar Conehead, Elwood Blues, E. Buzz Miller, and, with Steve Martin, the two wild and crazy Czech brothers. When each weekly show was over, the cast members would immediately begin preparing the next edition or spend hours at Elaine's, the trendy Manhattan restaurant hang-out for show business people. It was a fast-paced existence permitting hardly any social life. In 1976 the "not ready" players visited the White House at the invitation of President Gerald Ford, the man most frequently made fun of on the network show. Also in 1976, the entire company of "Saturday Night Live" made a comedy recording on the Arista label, *NBC's Saturday Night Live*. On September 12, 1977, Dan, along with thirteen others, won an Emmy Award for "Outstanding Writing" of the series' March 12, 1977, episode, which had been hosted by Sissy Spacek.

In 1977 Dan was seen in his first motion picture, LOVE AT FIRST SIGHT, a Canadian-made comedy in which he played a blind groom-to-be. *Variety* rated the film "lame" and reported, "It is hamstrung by heavy-handed acting by Dan Aykroyd." In 1978 the entire company of "Saturday Night Live" made a comedy recording on the Arista label and on March 22, 1978, he joined a large cast for NBC-TV's ninety-minute music/comedy/variety special "All You Need Is Cash," a Beatles parody created by Eric Idle. In September 1979 Dan and other cast members of the show appeared in the feature film MR. MIKE'S MONDO VIDEO, executive-produced by Lorne Michaels. Also that year, Dan and Belushi left the TV series to take their characters The Blues Brothers, the deadpan singing duo in dark suits, fedoras, and sunglasses, on a cross-country tour. They finished in Los Angeles where they starred in Steven Spielberg's zany screen comedy 1941 (1979). As The Blues Brothers, Elwood and Jake, Aykroyd and Belushi made three records for Atlantic, *A Briefcase Full of Blues*, of which *People* magazine observed, "This self-indulgent album is an insult to serious blues musicians," but which sold three million copies. It was followed by *The Blues Brothers—Made in America* and *Best of the Blues Brothers*. The albums earned them three Grammy nominations.

With John Landis, Dan co-wrote the screenplay for the expensively mounted ($30 million) THE BLUES BROTHERS (1980), a nutty, off-the-wall comedy which starred Aykroyd and Belushi as the deadpan duo who attempt to raise money for an orphanage and almost destroy Chicago in the process. *Variety* noted, "few pictures have ever been crammed with so much action, music, noise and general running around." The following year, the two friends starred in NEIGHBORS, and then Dan was one of the co-narrators of IT CAME FROM HOLLYWOOD (1982), primarily a compilation of clips from good and bad old movies. On March 5, 1982, John Belushi was found dead at age thirty-two of a drug overdose, the result of a habit that Dan did not realize had developed as far as it had. ("I would have slapped all this stuff out of his hands," the grieved Aykroyd said.)

Dan provided the voice of Beldar in the NBC-TV animated pilot film "The Coneheads" in 1983, soon after he married actress Donna Dixon on April 19, 1983. The next month he was seen in two theatrical releases, the abysmal DOCTOR DETROIT, in which he was a mild-mannered college professor taking over a stable of prostitutes, and the skillful TRADING PLACES, in which he played an affluent executive who switches roles with a fast-talking ghetto hustler (Eddie Murphy). *People* magazine observed, "Just when you might have given up on Dan Aykroyd . . . along came this satisfying comedy. TRADING PLACES made it respectable again to enjoy one of our truly gifted comedians." In June 1983 TWILIGHT ZONE—THE MOVIE was unveiled amid much notoriety, stemming from the deaths of three actors during the filming. Dan played a "passenger" in "The Prologue" segment as well as an ambulance driver in "Nightmare at 20,000 Feet."

Off screen, Dan Aykroyd had bought a home in Massachusetts, owned a trailer parked in the wilds of Ontario, Canada, and maintained apartments in both New Orleans and New York City. In addition, he was co-owner of Crooks, a Toronto bar, as well as part proprietor of the Hard Rock Cafe in Manhattan. In 1983 he was honored for his writing by the Writers Guild of America for "Steve Martin's Best Show Ever" (NBC-TV).

With funny man Harold Ramis, Aykroyd co-wrote the script of GHOSTBUSTERS (1984), in which a trio of paranormal investigators (Aykroyd, Bill Murray, Ramis) in New York City hire themselves out to get rid of ghosts and spirits. The blockbuster comedy went on to earn more than $220.8 million in U.S. box-office dollars, making it the #2 moneymaking film of 1984. Meanwhile, Dan jumped from the position of #25 box-office star in 1983 to #9 for 1984. In INDIANA JONES AND THE TEMPLE OF DOOM (1984) he had a cameo role as Weber, but the viewer looking for him must be quick of eye. To cash in on the popularity of both Dan and Bill Murray, MGM/UA released, in September 1984, the Lorne Michaels–produced NOTHING LASTS FOREVER, filmed in 1981, and Dan co-hosted with Bette Midler the first annual MTV Video Music Awards show on NBC-TV.

Dan had originally co-written the story on which SPIES LIKE US (1985) was based for John Belushi and himself, but it came to the motion picture screen with Chevy Chase in the role intended for Belushi and co-starred Aykroyd's wife, Donna Dixon. *Variety* rejected this "half-baked" comedy, noting, "Though Chase and Aykroyd provide moments, the overall script thinly takes on eccentric espionage and nuclear madness, with nothing new to add." Aykroyd was executive producer of ONE MORE SATURDAY NIGHT (1986), one of his obvious mistakes. However, he did better (at least according to critic Roger Ebert, who wrote, "Listening to him talk in this movie is a joy") with DRAGNET (1987), which he co-wrote. For this updated spoof of the venerable Jack Webb teleseries, Aykroyd also co-sang on the soundtrack with Tom Hanks the rap song "City of Crime." After twenty weeks of domestic release, the new DRAGNET had grossed $57.2 million.

The year 1988 was Aykroyd's busiest in movies up to that time, with four pictures in release. In THE COUCH TRIP, he was John Burns, a not-so-crazy inmate of a California

Eddie Murphy, Jamie Lee Curtis, and **Dan Aykroyd** in TRADING PLACES (1983).

correctional facility for the criminally insane who impersonates his psychiatrist and then takes over as host of a medical call-in radio show. THE GREAT OUTDOORS had him as a loudmouth relative who invades John Candy's peaceful vacation. This film was much better than the feeble CADDYSHACK II, an inept sequel to 1980's CADDYSHACK. Aykroyd's fourth film of the year, MY STEPMOTHER IS AN ALIEN, sounds like a 1930s Saturday serial. However, it is actually a funny movie with Dan as a radar astronomer whose overamplified Klystron beam attracts the chief extragalactic probist (Kim Basinger) from another planet. Dan wisely turned down an offer to star in VIBES (1988), a bomb that was taken on by Jeff Goldblum.

He and Harold Ramis teamed again for the screenplay for GHOSTBUSTERS II (1989), which had four exorcists (Aykroyd, Ramis, Bill Murray, and Ernie Hudson) again ridding Manhattan of slimy spooks. Called "dull" by *Time* magazine and "a lot of wasted time" by Roger Ebert, the derivative, uninspired sequel was nevertheless ranked as 1989's #6 top box-office movie (with a domestic gross of $111.7 million). Providing Aykroyd with a base salary plus 10 percent of the studio take, GHOSTBUSTERS II made Aykroyd an even wealthier performer.

Gary Groomes played Dan Aykroyd in WIRED (1989), based on the book by journalist Bob Woodward about the death of John Belushi. Not only did the feature film do poorly, it was also deeply frowned upon by most of the Hollywood community, including Dan. He was featured in the September 24, 1989, tribute, "Saturday Night Live 15th Anniversary" on NBC-TV, at which time Lorne Michaels reportedly was discussing a movie version of "Saturday Night Live" with original cast members. In November 1989 Dan and other celebrities lent their names to the antifur crusade by signing a statement promising never to wear furs. On November 18, 1989, Dan and wife Donna became parents of a daughter, Danielle Alexandra.

A month later, in December 1989, DRIVING MISS DAISY was in general release with Dan in the role of the son Boolie, a part for which no one considered him until he asked to read for it. *The New Yorker* magazine found, "This may be the first time Aykroyd has stayed within the limits of a screen character that wasn't shaped for his crazy-galoot style of comedy" and concluded that "He's quite wonderful." By mid-March 1990 the film had grossed $69.6 million domestically as well as earned nine Academy Award nominations, including one for Dan as Best Supporting Actor. Although the winning name announced in his category on March 26, 1990, was not his, Dan Aykroyd's performance in this warm drama greatly enhanced the industry's perception of his acting range.

While DRIVING MISS DAISY was a major hit as well as an Oscar winner as Best Picture of 1989, Dan's next movie, LOOSE CANNONS (1990), was, according to *Rolling Stone*, "a witless cop comedy" and *Entertainment Weekly* racked Dan mercilessly by saying, "someone made a very grave mistake in thinking his little act was an entire movie." The picture disappeared from theater screens quickly.

In 1990, after film earnings during the previous decade were tallied, Dan's earnings of $871 million ranked second only to Harrison Ford's, a truly Herculean feat from the youth who had sneaked beers in a barroom in Canada twenty-four years earlier. (The self-analytical Aykroyd has also admitted, "I have yet to perform a solo role that works.") At the February 7, 1990, NATO/Sho West '90 convention in Las Vegas, Dan, Chevy Chase, Tom Hanks, and John Candy provided impromptu stand-up comedy when the Warner Bros. sound system accompanying its product reel went out. When the presentation was finally ready, it revealed just one Christmas 1990 film release, VALKENVANIA (subsequently retitled NOTHING BUT TROUBLE), a comedy written and directed by Dan, and co-starring him (as a lawyer) with Chase, Candy, and Demi Moore. (The film's release was later rescheduled, to mid-February 1991, amid industry rumors that it was not a strong enough picture for the competitive holiday release season.) On March 16, 1990, Dan offered tributes to the British members of the Monty Python comedy troupe on Show-time-Cable's "Life of Python," along with Chevy Chase and Jane Curtin. On September 8, 1990, Dan, along with Bruce Willis, John Travolta, John Candy, and Vanessa Williams, was a guest on CBS-TV's "Phil Collins" as the rock star devoted an hour to showing excerpts from his recent concert tour. On October 17, 1990, at the New York Friars Club, Dan served as master of ceremonies for a roast of his pal Chevy Chase.

MASTERS OF MENACE (1991), a satirical biker comedy, boasted Dan Aykroyd in a cameo role along with John Candy and Jim Belushi. When screened at the Cinetex Film Festival in Las Vegas in September 1990, *Daily Variety* reported, "Exploring the bodily functions of the already socially unacceptable is not a great step forward . . . and hardly inspiration for whimsy." Aykroyd appeared as a gang member-turned-stunt rider who suffers from noisily creaking joints. This guest appearance was done as a favor to the film's writer, Tino Insana, a friend from the comics' Second City days. Meanwhile, Aykroyd and his wife, Donna Dixon, contracted with Revlon to cavort in that company's elaborate autumn 1990 advertising campaign, just as Melanie Griffith and Don Johnson had done previously. In late January 1991 Dan began MY GIRL, co-starring with Jamie Lee Curtis and young Macaulay Culkin.

Although Dan continues to concentrate on writing, directing, and starring in comedy features, because of his success in DRIVING MISS DAISY, it can be predicted that he will veer off occasionally into serious or serio-comic movies. With his bankable reputation within the film industry, his presence in future productions, regardless of their genre, is ensured.

Filmography

Love at First Sight (Quadrant Films/Movietime, 1977)
1941 (Univ/Col, 1979)
Mr. Mike's Mondo Video (New Line, 1979)
The Blues Brothers (Univ, 1980) (also co-screenplay)
Neighbors (Col, 1981)
It Came from Hollywood (Par, 1982)
Doctor Detroit (Univ, 1983)

Trading Places (Par, 1983)
Twilight Zone—The Movie (WB, 1983)
Ghostbusters (Col, 1984) (also co-screenplay)
Indiana Jones and the Temple of Doom (Par, 1984)
Nothing Lasts Forever (MGM/UA, 1984) [made in 1981]
Into the Night (Univ, 1985)
Spies Like Us (WB, 1985) (also co-story, co-screenplay)

One More Saturday Night (Col, 1986)
  (executive producer only)
Dragnet (Univ, 1987) (also co-screenplay)
The Couch Trip (Orion, 1988)
The Great Outdoors (Univ, 1988)
Caddyshack II (WB, 1988)

My Stepmother Is an Alien (Col, 1988)
Ghostbusters II (Col, 1989) (also co-screenplay)
Driving Miss Daisy (WB, 1989)
Loose Cannons (Tri-Star, 1990)
Nothing But Trouble (WB, 1991) (also director,
  screenplay)
Masters of Menace (New Line, 1991)

Future Releases

My Girl (Col, 1991)

Television Series

Coming Up Rosie (Can, 1973)
Saturday Night Live (NBC, 1975–79)

Album Discography

Best of the Blues Brothers (Atlantic)
The Blues Brothers—Made in America (Atlantic
  16025)

A Briefcase Full of Blues (Atlantic 19217)
NBC's Saturday Night Live (Arista ALB6-8435)

ALEC BALDWIN

"People ask me where I get all my energy. I don't do drugs or drink at all. I'm just always wired in the morning. It's gladiator-movie time. I get up stomping. I put on my breastplate, my helmet, my saber. I say 'Okay, let's go!'"   —*Rolling Stone* magazine, April 5, 1990

ALTHOUGH BY 1987 RASPY-YET-SEXY-VOICED ALEC BALDWIN HAD reached a career level in television as a "hot" commodity, his ambition was to make motion pictures "because that's where the work was being done that was most interesting to me." For a time, it appeared that he might forever be relegated to small roles in big films as best friend or boyfriend—a latter-day Ralph Bellamy, a second banana. Although the ingredients for stardom were all there—a strong voice, good looks with ice-blue eyes, and exceptional talent—the lead parts he coveted generally went to better-known stars such as Mel Gibson or Kevin Costner, with whom he has often been compared physically. Baldwin worked hard in the smaller acting assignments, was noticed, and waited. The patience saw fruition when he was selected to star as the hero in THE HUNT FOR RED OCTOBER (1990), an important movie version of a best-selling novel. As in the typical "overnight" success story, he became the darling of the press, who found his easy candor a delight, with such revelations as, "Well, I've gotten that leading man thing out of the way . . . and I won't have to wait in line for actors A, B, and C to say no to a project."

Alexander Rae Baldwin III was born in Amityville, Long Island, New York, on Thursday, April 3, 1958, to high school teacher Alexander Rae Baldwin, Jr., and his wife, Carol Martineau Baldwin, of Irish and French extraction, respectively. His birth was preceded by that of sister Beth (1956) and followed by Daniel (1961), Billy (1963), Jane (1965), and Stephen (1966). The children were raised as Catholics by the Kennedy Democrat parents in Massapequa, Long Island. The eldest son was called "Xander," who got his "get-up-and-go" from his father, whom he has called "the greatest man I ever knew. He did everything in the world for his children and never a damn thing for himself." Although Alexander acted in a few school plays, he grew up convinced he would like to pursue a political career, even to the point of one day being elected President of the United States. At the age of ten, with his father, he attended the funeral mass held for Robert Kennedy at St. Patrick's Cathedral in Manhattan, where he endured his first radio interview, which he found disgusting. During his high school summers he was employed as a lifeguard at Long Island beaches. After graduation in 1976 from Alfred G. Berner High School, he enrolled as an undergraduate at George Washington University in

Washington, D.C., as a pre-law major in order to prepare his way for a public service career.

After his third year at George Washington University, he visited a friend at New York University in Manhattan who introduced him to individuals at NYU's drama school. They told him of a program combining study at the Lee Strasberg Theatre Institute with academic classes at NYU. This plan intrigued him since he had a growing desire to try acting. He enrolled at NYU in 1979 to work on his double major of law and political science while taking classes at the Strasberg Institute taught by Marcia Haufrecht and Geoffrey Horne, as well as sessions with acting coach Mira Rostova. During this period he lived in the home of an NYU professor who was away in Africa, paying $150 a month and sharing the five-bedroom apartment with numerous cats, to whom he was allergic. To survive financially, he served as a waiter at a disco club (Studio 54) for two months before trying his hand at driving a limousine, then selling shirts, and, finally, working as a waiter/lifeguard at a health club in the Lincoln Center area.

It was the summer of 1980; Alex fully intended to return to NYU in the fall to complete his important final year of schooling and was even offered a scholarship to do so. However, at this juncture he was introduced to Susan Scudder of NBC-TV's casting department. The meeting changed his life. Asked to do a recurring part in the daytime soap opera "The Doctors," he acquired an agent, Michael Bloom, shortened his name to Alec, and began working on the soap as Billy Allison Aldrich. He earned $400 a day, making him feel like a Rockefeller. In retrospect, he has said that the salary was "peanuts" because he was unknown. Through Bloom, he obtained work in summer stock to gain experience—including *A Study in Scarlet* at the Williamstown Theatre—and in New York portrayed Lysander in *A Midsummer Night's Dream* at the Strasberg Theatre, performed the part of Soldier in *Summertree* at the Vandam Theatre, and had a role in *The Wager*. This stage work helped him gain confidence and made him less wooden and tense in front of TV cameras. "I was terrible," he has said of his early TV work. "A guy who's a good friend of mine . . . used to come out of the control room and say, 'Can't you scratch your nose or lick your lips or something to break the monotony?'"

In mid-1982, when his work on "The Doctors" came to an end, he was offered a lead in a promising television pilot at CBS in Hollywood. He moved West, into an apartment in West Hollywood, north of Sunset Boulevard. The pilot, "Cutter to Houston," was picked up as a network series, premiering at 8 p.m. on Saturday, October 1, 1983, with Alec as Dr. Hal Wexler, an internist on probation for writing unethical drug prescriptions and exiled to a small hospital in Cutter, Texas (population 5,231), which had a computer hookup to the Houston Medical Center. *Variety* complained of the premiere episode, "It was formula stuff all the way. And the main plot . . . is so unconvincingly melodramatic it sinks everybody." The hour-long series faded after seven episodes, putting Baldwin out of work.

Baldwin considered returning to NYU. However, he had friends at CBS in the talent and casting departments who assured him he would have another acting assignment soon, because "he has a face that you like to spend an hour with." Meanwhile, his father died of cancer in late 1983, necessitating a return East for several weeks to take care of details. Upon his return to the West Coast, he appeared in a second CBS-TV pilot, "The Sheriff and the Astronaut" (May 24, 1984), in the role of Sheriff Ed Cassaday. The hour program failed to materialize as a series.

His CBS pals then arranged for him to audition for the part of a new character to be introduced in the September 1984 return of the prime-time soap "Knots Landing." Lisa Hartman, who played Cathy in "Knots," was asked to read with him. She recalled the incident to *TV Guide* magazine: "when I saw this guy in the lobby, I thought, 'Boy, he's good looking. I hope he's the one.' It went fine and afterward he walked me to my car and I kept watching him in the rearview mirror as I drove away. Well I rear-ended another car and there were these people jumping up and down and screaming at me and I was still watching Alec in the mirror." Alec won the role of Joshua Rush, a conniving TV evangelist, who became increasingly evil with each episode after marrying Cathy and beating her. This inglorious character came to an end, a season later, with his death from a fall down an elevator shaft. During the time not occupied with "Knots," Alec did a CBS-TV movie, SWEET REVENGE (October 31, 1984) with Kelly McGillis and Kevin Dobson (also of "Knots Landing").

When not working, Alec's almost constant female companion was actress Holly Gagnier, of the TV soap opera "Days of Our Lives." "I'm a lonely guy," he admitted, "so I date women in the business who approximate to me—actresses mostly, so I don't remain lonely for long." He admitted to being close to marriage in the summer of 1985, but refused to divulge the lady's name. Instead of nuptials, however, he accepted the male lead in the NBC telefeature LOVE ON THE RUN (October 21, 1985), co-starring with Stephanie Zimbalist. She was a criminal lawyer who helps her lover (Baldwin), a convicted felon, break out of jail. *Variety* was not overly impressed with the production, but acknowledged that "Baldwin does a good job of persuasion."

Back in 1979, Gore Vidal had fashioned a film script from the novel *Dress Gray*, by Lucian K. Truscott IV, which flip-flopped from studio to studio and then was abandoned. In 1985 Warner Bros. Television resurrected the project, believing that the subject matter—homosexuality in a military academy, notably West Point—was acceptable material for a TV movie. Vidal was asked to lengthen his script to four hours. To avoid possible problems with West Point authorities, the setting was changed to a fictional military academy, called U.S. Grant, in an unspecified locale, but actually filmed at the New Mexico Military Academy at Roswell. Supported in featured roles by veteran actors Lloyd Bridges, Hal Holbrook, Alexis Smith, and Eddie Albert, Alec had the lead role of platoon leader cadet Rysam Slaight, prime suspect in the rape-murder of another cadet (Patrick Cassidy). The movie was shown on NBC on March 9 and 10, 1986, and *Variety* complimented Baldwin for "turning in a steadfast perf[ormance] as the beleaguered heroic cadet sergeant." *TV Guide* critic Judith Crist found Alec "impressive" and stated that there was "small doubt that homosexuality is way out of the TV-movie closet."

In December 1985 Alec had moved back to New York because "in Los Angeles I was being offered a pilot for my own show and a lot of TV work, and I began to worry that if I stayed, I would get caught up in . . . pursuit of money." Back on the East Coast, he did voiceovers for radio and TV commercials and took a supporting role in a revival of Joe Orton's *Loot*. The English black comedy opened at the Music Box Theatre on April 3, 1986, Alec's twenty-eighth birthday, and played one hundred performances and gained him the Theatre World Award for best performance by a newcomer. While on stage at night, he starred in a low-budget movie (FOREVER LULU, 1987) during the day because "I hadn't done a film, and I was beginning to think that Harrison Ford and Jeff Bridges were going to do all the movies I would be considered for." The confused murder mystery, which featured a cameo by Dr. Ruth Westheimer, was released in April 1987. It led *People* magazine to suggest, "Let's all just pretend this film never happened." Perhaps that is why Alec's publicity biographies ignore it as his film debut. In the film he portrays a Manhattan policeman named Buck who rescues the film's star, German actress Hanna Schygulla. It was also the film debut of rock vocalist Deborah Harry, who had third billing and very little dialogue.

Prior to the release of FOREVER LULU, Alec had gone to Brackettville, Texas, for the making of the NBC-TV movie THE ALAMO: 13 DAYS TO GLORY. This battle of 181 patriots against 6,000 Mexican soldiers for a Catholic mission was shot on the set built by John Wayne and company for his big-budgeted feature THE ALAMO (1960). At three hours, including commercials, the NBC effort was forty-eight minutes shorter than Wayne's. In the telefilm, shown on Monday, January 26, 1987, Alec was Colonel William Travis (played by Laurence Harvey in the Wayne film), known as "the tin soldier." In May 1987 *Rolling Stone* magazine published a photographic parody of the chronological career of mythical screen star Bluff Wheeler, with Alec hamming it up as Bluff.

The less-than-stellar domestic comedy SHE'S HAVING A BABY (1988), considered by some to be a prequel to MR. MOM (1982), has Alec as Kevin Bacon's brooding cad of a best friend who seduces Elizabeth McGovern. Alec later complained that much of his work wound up on the cutting-room floor: "These were some of the best scenes I ever did in my life, and I had this great speech, and then Kevin picks me up and throws me through a china closet, but all this stuff was cut because they tested the movie and audiences hated Elizabeth's character because she had slept with me. So they had to make it simple." Baldwin was given top billing in BEETLEJUICE (1988), but it was Michael Keaton in the title role, with special billing and Oscar-winning makeup, who was showcased in the best scenes and received better exposure. Adam Maitland (Alec) and his wife, Barb (Geena Davis, who is taller than Alec), emerge from their watery deaths as ghosts who hire the bizarre Beetlejuice to exorcise their home of its new inhabitants. The popular film was tenth in the year's tally of box-office receipts, with a gross of $73,326,666.

Alec returned to Broadway on February 9, 1988, for fifteen performances as the ruthless broker in Caryl Churchill's *Serious Money*, produced by Joe Papp. The role required him to affect a British accent. Of this professional experience, he said, "Loved it! Hated doing it until the bitter end and realized . . . how challenging it was. I was overwhelmed by it."

Now considered to be serious about his craft, he was the recipient of supporting roles in several big films, directed by top names. The first was the serio-comic MARRIED TO THE MOB (1988), directed by Jonathan Demme, in which Alec was mob hit-man Frankie "The Cucumber" DeMarco, husband to Angela (Michelle Pfeiffer). Frankie is killed on the edge of a bathtub by his boss, Tony "The Tiger" Russo (Dean Stockwell), in the film's first fifteen minutes. In spite of plot gaps, *Newsweek* magazine thought the movie was "a lot of fun." In Mike Nichols's WORKING GIRL (1988), Baldwin was cast as Mack, Melanie Griffith's Staten Island fisherman boyfriend, astounded by her decision to embark on a course of self-improvement. A nude love scene with Melanie was cut from the final release print at her insistence. Oliver Stone directed TALK RADIO (1988), based on a book (*Talked to Death: The Life and Murder of Alan Berg*) and a play (*Talk Radio*), in Dallas, Texas, with Alec in the role of a radio producer with ink-black hair who talks a lot—and fast.

Director Jim McBride, of THE BIG EASY (1987) fame, helmed GREAT BALLS OF FIRE! (1989), a biographical look at the early life of rock 'n' roller Jerry Lee Lewis (Dennis Quaid) termed "laughable" by the *San Francisco Chronicle*. As Lewis's cousin, religious revivalist Jimmy Swaggart, Alec devoted much of his on-screen time to clutching a prayerbook and gazing upward, imploring the heavens to cleanse Lewis's tarnished soul while denouncing the 1956 sound as "the devil's music." Expected to be a big hit of the summer, the disappointing picture disappeared after only a few weeks.

Alec was a top candidate of director Jeff Kanew to star in DEAD POETS SOCIETY (1989). But when Kanew was replaced by Peter Weir, the pivotal role went to Robin Williams. Baldwin was up for the part of Sonny Corleone's illegitimate son who returns to steal the family fortune in THE GODFATHER, PART III (1990), but lost the role to another up-and-coming actor, Andy Garcia. In January 1990 Baldwin rejected a $1 million offer to advertise cigarettes in Japan, although he is a smoker. The elaborately produced THE HUNT FOR RED OCTOBER (1990), based on the best-selling thriller novel by Tom Clancy, found Alec Baldwin in his first starring role, a part originally offered to Kevin Costner. Baldwin, as CIA analyst Jack Ryan, boards a state-of-the-art Russian nuclear submarine where he must come to terms with a maverick Soviet veteran nautical captain (Sean Connery). The film's producer, Mace Neufeld, said of Baldwin during production, "He has all

Alec Baldwin in TALK RADIO (1988).

the equipment to be a very big male leading man. He's good-looking without being pretty. He's very facile with dialogue. He's very analytical. He's got great eyes . . . a very natural style of acting" and is "drop-dead gorgeous." Gene Siskel (*Chicago Tribune*) predicted that the film would "make him a star" because of his "terrific performance"; *Variety* celebrated his "intelligent and likeable performance"; and *The Hollywood Reporter* found that he "plumbs the inner sparks of a man who triumphantly discovers he is never in water over his head." Opening March 2, 1990, in 1,225 theaters across the nation, the film realized $17.2 million in domestic ticket sales its first week, with $113.5 million after fifteen weeks.

Made before THE HUNT FOR RED OCTOBER, but not released until the next month (April 1990), was MIAMI BLUES, in which Alec again worked with Jonathan Demme, who served as co-producer of this low-budget thriller. (To prepare for the role, Alec took up boxing, noting, "Boxing is a no-frills situation. . . . You go in, the bell rings, you work out. The bell stops, you stop. I like to get there, do it, and go home.") In MIAMI BLUES, as the psychotic but likeable ex-convict Frederick J. Frenger, Jr., known as Junior to his friends and enemies, his modus operandi was to rob crooks who had robbed other people until he ultimately exploded in fury. He received second billing to Fred Ward, who owned the screen rights to the Charles Willeford novel on which it was based, but Alec's star status was ensured by *Playboy* magazine's comment that his "hot performance" served as "a star-of-tomorrow showcase for the smiling, gruff-blue-eyed Baldwin" and *Rolling Stone* magazine's observation of his having given "a funny-sexy-dangerous performance that jumps off the screen." *Time* magazine's Richard Corliss thought the movie "Handsomely made, wonderfully acted. . . . [It] is the kind of picture Hollywood ought to be making more of." In its first nine weeks of distribution, MIAMI BLUES grossed a respectable $9,654,290 in domestic distribution. With two successive critical hits, Alec's salary per film escalated to $2 million.

Meanwhile, on March 14, 1990, Alec returned to the stage, opening off-Broadway at the Circle Repertory Company in Manhattan in Craig Lucas's romantic fantasy *Prelude to a Kiss*, with Mary-Louise Parker and Barnard Hughes. A complete sellout for its off-Broadway limited run, the play co-starred him as Peter, the love-driven hero who, following his wedding, discovers that his bride has switched personalities with an old man who has kissed her. Critic Edith Oliver (*The New Yorker*) declared that all three actors "so inhabit their roles that one can't imagine anyone else playing them." However, she was given the opportunity to see another actor in the role when Alec, who departed on March 31 to fulfill a film commitment, was replaced by Timothy Hutton for the play's move to Broadway.

On April 21, 1990, Alec hosted "Saturday Night Live" on NBC-TV and at a May 7, 1990, New York City rally, he protested, as a member of the Creative Coalition, the ban against obscenity in federal grants to the arts. On June 10, 1990, he stood as best man at the marriage of his brother Stephen to model Kennya Deodata in Southampton, New York. He formed his own company, Meadowbrook Productions, in partnership with former ICM agent Hildy Gottlieb in July 1990, signing a two-year agreement with Orion

Pictures. Independent of this pact, he was featured in the Woody Allen–directed movie ALICE (1990) as a ghost who, along with William Hurt and Cybill Shepherd, figures prominently in the midlife crisis of a wealthy married New Yorker (Mia Farrow).

It was during the filming of THE MARRYING MAN (1991) that Alec and co-star Kim Basinger, fresh from her romance with singer Prince, began a relationship that was much publicized on both coasts. On Earth Day 1990, at a Central Park concert, they were photographed kissing each other, oblivious to those around them. In THE MARRYING MAN, a Neil Simon comedy, Baldwin plays a lecherous millionaire who becomes involved with a Las Vegas lounge singer (Basinger) on the eve of his marriage to another woman. During production of THE MARRYING MAN, both Baldwin and Basinger were at odds with the film crrew, and the resultant film was badly panned by the critics and not much attended by the public.

Aside from contractual commitments to Orion on behalf of Meadowbrook Productions, Baldwin was considered by Paramount to star in one or both of two Tom Clancy stories adapted for film, CLEAR AND PRESENT DANGER and PATRIOT GAMES. Definitely forthcoming for him is THE FUGITIVE, a suspense drama to be directed by Walter Hill. The thriller is based on the popular ABC-TV series of 1963–1967, with Alec cast as Dr. Richard Kimble, an innocent man who escapes prison after being wrongly convicted of killing his wife. Also in development is BUDDY BOYS, taken from Michael McAlary's novel about a true-life gang of cops operating on the night shift as a precinct, as well as the film version of PRELUDE TO A KISS and FELLOW TRAVELERS. Meanwhile, Baldwin could be heard as the voiceover spokesman for the J. C. Penney Company.

In September 1989, his brother Billy, formerly a model, starred as Robert Chambers in THE PREPPIE MURDER (ABC-TV), while brother Stephen was one of the stars of the ABC-TV series "The Young Riders." Alec continued to live in Manhattan on the Upper West Side but for tax reasons established his legal residence as Amagansett, Long Island. He no longer wished to be President of the United States, but he did confess (in October 1989) that he might quit acting at age forty and become involved in someone else's candidacy. He explained why he did not want to pay New York City income taxes with, "Why should I pay another set of taxes to a government that isn't doing what I want it to do with the money?" With his stardom, he was compared to Tyrone Power and was asked questions about his single status. "If I were marrying someone," he replied, "I wouldn't mind talking about it. But until then, I don't understand why people want to know."

Remaining strongly individualistic, the confident Baldwin assesses an actor's life this way: "Most directors rent actors. You're like a puppet. They put their hand up your sleeve, and you do what they want." As far as stardom is concerned, Alec insists, "It's all luck. . . . For a newcomer in movies, the train pulls out at 12:01. You're on it or you're not. The greatest plateau in Hollywood is when they hold the train for you."

A hot sex symbol, as well as a good actor, Alec admits that "Women come up to me at parties and tell me they like my butt." Although rejecting the symbolism, he seems to be enjoying the adulation.

Filmography

Sweet Revenge (CBS-TV, 10/31/84)
Love on the Run (NBC-TV, 10/21/85)
Dress Gray (NBC-TV, 3/9/86–3/10/86)
The Alamo: 13 Days to Glory (NBC-TV, 1/26/87)
Forever Lulu (Tri-Star, 1987)
Beetlejuice (WB, 1988)
She's Having a Baby (Par, 1988)
Married to the Mob (Orion, 1988)
Working Girl (20th–Fox, 1988)
Talk Radio (Univ, 1988)

Great Balls of Fire! (Orion, 1989)
The Hunt for Red October (Par, 1990)
Miami Blues (Orion, 1990)
Alice (Orion, 1990)
The Marrying Man (BV, 1991)
Guilty by Suspicion (WB, 1991)

Future Releases

Prelude to a Kiss (20th-Fox, 1992)

Television Series

The Doctors (NBC, 1980–82)
Cutter to Houston (CBS, 1983)

Knots Landing (CBS, 1984–85)

Broadway Shows

Loot (1985) (revival)

Serious Money (1988)

ELLEN BARKIN

"When I first started to make movies, I guess I had what one might
call an attitude problem, though a lot of it was grounded in reality. I
was treated badly, but I also came to it with my dukes up."
— *Vanity Fair* magazine, February 1990

WITHIN FIVE YEARS, THIS LADY WITH A TOUGH-AS-NAILS REPUTATION
went from "queen of the cameo" (*New York Sunday News* magazine, August 5, 1984) to
"killer actress" (*Time* magazine, October 23, 1989). On camera, she of the myopic hazel
eyes, slightly crooked nose, and lopsided smile effectively uses her throaty voice and lithe
body in much the same way as Anne Baxter and Lauren Bacall did in Hollywood movies of
the 1940s and 1950s. In France, Ellen has been termed "wildly sexy"; in the United States,
Stanley Kaufmann (*The New Republic* magazine) pronounced her "a professional sex
bomb" and Laura Morice (*US* magazine) termed her a "simmering screen siren," although
it was never her intention to become a sex symbol. At the early age of twenty-nine Barkin
was a recognized character performer, which was fine with her as long as she was acting.
She devotes a tremendous amount of research, study, and energy, to preparing for each
role, regardless of its size, to the point where some directors have considered her "a pain."
Like Debra Winger, also Jewish, Ellen Barkin has major star qualities.

Ellen Barkin was born on Saturday, April 16, 1955, on Longfellow Avenue in the
South Bronx, New York City, to middle-class Jewish parents who, although not devoutly
religious, observed all Jewish holidays with huge dinners. Her father was a chemical
salesman; her mother was a hospital administrator. Her older brother George was her
protector until she was big enough to hit back when other kids picked on her. Of her
South Bronx days, Ellen once recalled, "I remember it as quite pleasant except for the
mice." When she was six years old, the family moved to Kew Gardens Hills in Queens,
where she soon announced that she wanted to become an actress. Her mother called her
"Sarah Bernhardt," while her classmates quickly discovered that she was a fighter when
they chided her for her lack of good looks and, in the seventh grade, for having a flat chest.
During her eighth-grade year, however, her bosom began to expand, causing her to put
aside her Barbie dolls in exchange for boyfriends. She occasionally smoked marijuana with
most of her relatives, her mother being the last hold-out. Her father told Ellen, "Ah, we did
this in the '40s, you know. You kids think you've found something new."

At age fifteen she auditioned for, and was accepted by, New York's High School of
Performing Arts, the institution made famous in the movie (and TV series) FAME.

According to Barkin, "It was three years of torture. They were very mean to me. I guess I didn't fit into their mold." The instructors constantly reminded her that she was not pretty enough to become an actress and that the world is cruel. However, she refused to leave. During this period she had very few friends and appeared in just one play. In 1973 she entered Hunter College in New York City, but departed after half a day to go to work as a waitress at a bagel restaurant in Manhattan to earn money to pay for acting lessons with coach Marcia Haufrecht. She remembers a young, aggressive Jewish customer who repeatedly attempted to pick her up at the restaurant, but whose amorous advances she rebuffed successfully. His name was Jeff Goldblum, and they would meet again years later under more professional circumstances.

After two years, Ellen reenrolled at Hunter College as a student of ancient history and theater, studying acting under coach Lloyd Richards. However, she did not appear in any college theatrical productions. In 1978, six months before graduation, she left Hunter "mostly because of not being able to complete anything" and resumed acting classes with Haufrecht. One evening in 1979 a stage director was seated near Barkin in the audience of an off-Broadway play at the Ensemble Studio Theatre. He liked her looks and coaxed her to work for him as a teenage murderer in his production of *Irish Coffee*. It was her first professional stage appearance and she found it to be not as frightening as she had contemplated. This initial job was followed by playing a disturbed teenager in *Shout Across the River* off-Broadway at the Phoenix Theatre in January 1980 and *Killings on the Last Line* at the American Place Theatre in October 1980. Of her performance in the latter production, in which she was one of seven women working on a factory production line which processed chemicals for reactor parts, Mel Gussow (*New York Times*) enthused, "Miss Barkin seems to have a thoughtful affinity for her working class teen-ager. Because of her performance, we believe that the character is a potential Norma Rae." These assignments boosted her confidence to the point where she could walk into agent David Guc's office with the announcement, "I'm going to be a movie star."

After accepting Ellen as a client, Guc could find no work for her in commercials. However, he negotiated for her a short stint in the CBS-TV soap opera "Search for Tomorrow," as well as a supporting part in the CBS-TV movie PAROLE, filmed in Massachusetts in 1980, but not telecast until April 20, 1982. Also for CBS-TV she performed the fourth-billed role of Chris in a series pilot film about New York's Guardian Angels, WE'RE FIGHTING BACK, shown April 28, 1981, after having had a walk-on part in the NBC network telefeature KENT STATE (February 8, 1981). Looking back on this period, Barkin would observe in 1990, "Picking and choosing is something I did from the beginning. It could be a choice as simple as whether to take a part on 'Search for Tomorrow' or 'Ryan's Hope.' But choice is a priority for me."

Agent Guc also obtained for his client an audition with Ellen Chenoweth, casting director of DINER (1982), for the part of Beth, the young bride whose husband (Daniel Stern) berates her for misfiling one of his records, causing her to tell her ex-boyfriend (Mickey Rourke), "I don't have any sense of myself any more. I don't know if I'm pretty." In a man's movie, she was outstanding in a small role. During the 1982–1983 New York theater season, she was on stage off-Broadway as the British-accented Terry in *Extremities* while seen on film, at age twenty-eight, as the headstrong eighteen-year-old Sue Anne in TENDER MERCIES (1983). The latter performance led critic Pauline Kael to acknowledge that Ellen has "something rare in a young actress: power." A few months later Ellen had small roles in DANIEL (1983) and EDDIE AND THE CRUISERS (1983). (Of the latter film, Barkin would recall years later, "The only movie I've made that really upsets me is EDDIE AND THE CRUISERS. I hate it. And now it's out in video, so it never dies. People come up to me and say, 'You were great in EDDIE AND THE CRUISERS.' And I say, 'Sorry, that wasn't me.'") In the unsold series pilot "Murder, Ink," aired on September 6, 1983, on CBS-TV, Daniel Hugh-Kelly starred as a New York City police inspector married to mystery bookstore owner Tovah Feldshuh. Barkin was cast as Ellen Gray.

Barkin's meatiest role during this period was as the change-of-heart granddaughter in CBS-TV's TERRIBLE JOE MORAN (March 27, 1984), in which she appeared opposite two formidable actors, James Cagney and Art Carney. On motion picture screens, beginning in March 1984, she played Joanne Woodward's pregnant daughter in HARRY & SON, followed in August by the comedic role of heroine Penny Priddy in the science fiction spoof THE ADVENTURES OF BUCKAROO BANZAI: ACROSS THE 8TH DIMENSION, with her former bagel restaurant pursuer, Jeff Goldblum, also in the cast.

In 1984 Ellen's fairly steady date was actor Val Kilmer. She also purchased a large loft condominium in New York's Greenwich Village. She was beginning to gain nation-wide press interviews with writers who appreciated her naturalness, and she was quickly becoming the darling of film critics. Off-Broadway in 1985 she starred in *Eden Court*, and critic Frank Rich (*New York Times*) praised, "If it really were possible to give the kiss of life to a corpse, the actress Ellen Barkin would be the one to do it."

Three stories by Grace Paley provided the substance for ENORMOUS CHANGES AT THE LAST MINUTE (1985), and Ellen starred in the segment "Virginia's Story," which had been shot in 1982. In the unsatisfying thriller TERMINAL CHOICE (1985), filmed in Canada, she was one of those caught in hospital misdealings. Barkin wore a padded bra for her role as Starr, the sexy sister, in the underrated DESERT BLOOM (1986). She had a supporting role in Charles Bronson's cable movie ACT OF VENGEANCE (April 20, 1986) on HBO and had only one scene, but a memorable one, in DOWN BY LAW (1986), a moody black-and-white feature shot in Louisiana. For cable network Showtime's "Faerie Tale Theatre," on August 11, 1986, Ellen had the title role of "The Princess Who Never Laughed."

Ellen remained in Louisiana for the filming of THE BIG EASY (1987), in which she appeared as an uptight assistant district attorney in New Orleans. She played opposite Dennis Quaid, as a cocky, unorthodox police lieutenant with whom she finds sex and love. The well-liked THE BIG EASY earned $7,761,555 in domestic film rentals paid to the distributor, providing Ellen with a popular showcase. One of the movie's best scenes—showing Ellen, fully dressed, enjoying lovemaking with her co-star—enhanced her growing status as a sex symbol. Dennis Quaid told interviewers, "She's very smart and very giving. She'll challenge your personality, your intellect, your wit." Her part as Louise in

MADE IN HEAVEN (1987) was a cameo. However, in the arty SIESTA (1987), she received top billing as Claire, a skydiving stuntwoman ending up (semi)nude in Spain. This experimental film co-starred Irish actor Gabriel Byrne as her former lover. She and the thirty-eight-year-old Byrne, finding that they laughed at the same type of things, fell in love for real and were married in 1988. (Byrne would later say of his wife, "Ellen is not a Hollywood person, at all. In fact, one of the reasons I like her is that she's not actressy in that way.")

Classified as "everyone's choice for dream date of the year" by *Continental Choice* magazine in May 1988, Ellen starred as a sultry, classy (ex)hooker opposite Andy Garcia as a small-time smuggler of exotic birds who becomes involved in a scheme to bring guns to the Nicaraguan Contras on cable in HBO's CLINTON AND NADINE (May 28, 1988), later released on home video as BLOOD MONEY.

"I would have done that movie if they would have handed me the Yellow Pages, directed by a chimp," Ellen said of co-starring with Al Pacino in SEA OF LOVE (1989), a slick cop thriller. She was Helen, a murder suspect who initially walks out on a veteran Manhattan police inspector (Pacino), but later, after making love, causes him to admit, "I'm going to have to get air-lifted out of this bed into a standing position." The great chemistry between the two co-leads added good word of mouth to Universal's multimillion dollar advertising campaign. As a result, the film grossed $37.7 million domestically within a month of its release and $49 million after seven weeks on 1,419 movie screens nationwide. *US* magazine hailed Barkin as the "sexy bad girl of 1989" who "has finally hit stardom by letting her incendiary eroticism burn up the screen."

Two weeks after SEA OF LOVE premiered, JOHNNY HANDSOME (1989) was issued. Ellen had second billing to Mickey Rourke in the title role of this New Orleans–set gangster tale. "Barkin creates one of the ugliest femme characters seen in recent films," noted *Variety* of her performance as underworld denizen Sonny Boyd, while Jeffrey Lyons on TV's "Sneak Previews" warned, "Ellen Barkin will astonish you." When the film was previewed on September 6, 1989, at the Venice Film Festival, *Variety* predicted that it "faces an uphill battle for the box office dollar," a prophecy that proved cor-

Ellen Barkin and Mickey Rourke in JOHNNY HANDSOME (1989).

rect; although the film took in $2.4 million during its first week of distribution, it lost momentum thereafter.

While America was aglow in the discovery of Ellen Barkin as a sexy leading lady, she became a mother in Manhattan on October 18, 1989, with the birth of eight-pound son Jack. Insistent on breastfeeding her baby, she found the experience professionally beneficial to her cleavage. "I didn't have these before," she laughed, but seriously added, "Having the baby makes everything else seem sort of inconsequential." In an interview with Glenn Collins (*New York Times*), headlined "At Long Last, Glamour Comes to Ellen Barkin," ten days before the baby's birth, she reflected on her new screen image: "Suddenly, I've been perceived differently by the powers that be. I'm perceived as this glamorous, sexy leading lady. No, they see me as *the sex goddess!* It's amazing to me. . . . Hilarious! I'm doing the same thing I always did, and now they're saying *I'm a hot babe!*" Commenting that she had never been asked to play a dumb gal on screen, she declared, "Actually, it would be fun to play a bimbo. I mean, not just some character who's a pair of breasts attached to the leading man—but a great *ditzy* bimbo. You know?"

Following a year of maneuvering to get SWITCH (1991) into production, partners Blake Edwards and Tony Adams were finally able to get their fantasy comedy financed by Home Box Office with filming starting in Los Angeles in April 1990. In this project, at one time planned as a vehicle for Michelle Pfeiffer, Barkin was cast as the sexy reincarnation of a Madison Avenue male chauvinist (Perry King) murdered by a wealthy/wicked woman (JoBeth Williams). He/she is permitted to return to Earth in order to learn how it feels to be a woman in a world dominated, professionally and sexually, by men. His/her best friend (Jimmy Smits) becomes the romantic partner of the female incarnation.

Ellen and her husband own a house in Ireland where she escapes from industry pressure. She reflected recently, "Acting is intensely personal. And that's the personal side of me that I'm willing to give up. . . . I don't define my existence by being an actor. . . . I really have a pretty normal life, and I don't like to be away from my family. . . . I've figured out that I'm dedicated to the *work*, not to the career. I'd have a problem being devoted to Hollywood's idea of success. I don't understand what that's all about."

Filmography

Kent State (NBC-TV, 2/8/81)
We're Fighting Back (CBS-TV, 4/28/81)
Parole (CBS-TV, 4/20/82) [filmed in 1980]
Diner (MGM, 1982)
Tender Mercies (Univ, 1983)
Daniel (Par, 1983)
Eddie and the Cruisers (Emb, 1983)
Terrible Joe Moran (CBS-TV, 3/27/84)
Harry & Son (Orion, 1984)
The Adventures of Buckaroo Banzai: Across the 8th Dimension (20th–Fox, 1984)

Enormous Changes at the Last Minute (TC Films International, 1985) [Barkin's segment, "Virginia's Story," filmed in 1982]
Terminal Choice [Deathbed] (Almi Pictures, 1985)
Act of Vengeance (HBO–Cable, 4/20/86)
Desert Bloom (Col, 1986)
Down by Law (Island, 1986)
Made in Heaven (Lorimar, 1987)
The Big Easy (Col, 1987)
Siesta (Lorimar, 1987)

Clinton and Nadine [Blood Money] (HBO–
    Cable, 5/28/88)
Sea of Love (Univ, 1989)

Johnny Handsome (Tri-Star, 1989)
Switch (WB, 1991)

TV Series

Search for Tomorrow (CBS, 1980)

ROSEANNE BARR

"I think that's what my life is all about: that you can take anything—
anything—that's supposedly bad and turn it."
                                    —*People* magazine, October 9, 1990

ROSEANNE BARR HAS EMERGED AS ONE OF THE MORE UNLIKELY ROLE
models of the latter twentieth century. Her catchphrase is, "Hi. I'm a housewife, domestic
goddess." She is a dedicated feminist whose comedic personae as a working mother reflects
her troubled childhood. ("I wouldn't be making a lot of money and be very happy now if
I had grown up content and sheltered.") Much of her humor revolves around her
perception of the mistreatment of women in today's still male-dominated society. Her
jokes, told in a deadpan, nasal style, are typical put-downs of male intelligence ("Like they
think the uterus is a tracking device") and behavior ("You may marry the man of your
dreams, ladies, but fifteen years later you are married to a reclining chair that burps").

Developed on the comedy club circuit and then showcased on television, Roseanne's earthy, smart-mouthed character has become a celebrated part of American culture.
Roseanne takes her inspiration and cue from such past show business celebrities as Mae
West, Martha Raye, Fanny Brice, Marjorie Main, Bette Midler, Gilda Radner, and Selma
Diamond. With her very stocky frame, the very visible Barr has suffered the same barrage
of fat jokes that used to haunt vocalist Kate Smith. But unlike Smith, Barr fights back with
sharp-tongued witticisms, flaying her detractors with barbs or off-putting acceptance of
her build. ("It's OK to be fat. So you're fat. Just be fat and shut up about it.") Roseanne is
frequently rash and always brash. Her off-stage behavior is often crude. Some observers
insist that her persistent and amazing exhibitionism is a manifestation of a highly self-
destructive personality. But, jokes Barr, "As long as I bitch and get paid for it, I'm the
luckiest person in the world."

Roseanne Barr was born on Monday, November 3, 1952, in Salt Lake City, Utah,
the daughter of Jerry and Helen (Davis) Barr. There would be three other children:
Geraldine, Stephanie, and Ben. Jerry Barr was a door-to-door salesman of blankets/
jewelry/religious goods, and Helen was a sometime cashier and bookkeeper. Jerry and
Helen were eccentric Jewish liberals in a city noted for its conservative Mormon population. The family lived in a large tenement slum on Park Street. Roseanne recalls, "I was just
a real weird woman from the day I was born." For example, when she was two years old,
she snuck out into the busy street in front of her home, bent on keeping cars from moving
too fast. Although her mother spanked her for this prank, she went outside and did it

again. When Roseanne was three years old, she fell on a leg of the kitchen dinette table, which resulted in temporary paralysis of one side of her face. The distraught Mrs. Barr called in the rabbi, who said a prayer. Nothing happened. The next day, she summoned Mormon ministers, who offered special blessings. A day later, the paralysis disappeared and Mrs. Barr took this as a religious sign. Thereafter, on Friday, Saturday, and Sunday mornings, Roseanne was raised as a Jew; on Sunday, Tuesday, and Wednesday afternoons, she was instructed as a Mormon. Jerry Barr, an atheist, acquiesced in this split religious training. Roseanne would say years later, "My whole life was a total dichotomy."

As a youngster, Roseanne had as role models her baby-sitter Robbie, a large Appalachian woman from Tennessee, and her widowed maternal grandmother, Bobbe Mary, who managed the apartment building where the Barrs lived. At an early age, Roseanne discovered the pleasure of gaining attention by performing impromptu skits from the big windowsill of her grandmother's apartment after the special Friday night supper. The family called her "Sarah Bernhardt." It was Barr's father, an avid enthusiast of comedy, who introduced Roseanne to the works of the great comedians of the day. He had a large collection of comedy albums that he would play for the family, and he would explain some of the jokes to the impressionable youngsters. It was a Sunday night ritual for the Barrs to gather around the TV to watch "The Ed Sullivan Show," especially such famous guest comedians as Jack Benny, Jackie Vernon, Totie Fields, and Henny Young-man, all of whose routines made a great impression on Roseanne. By now the Barrs had a small house on Salt Lake City's Lincoln Street.

At age eight, Roseanne saw a hobo jump off a train. Suddenly, she was overcome with a tremendous sense of the possibilities of freedom. She promised herself, "When I get big, I'm going to be a hobo." In her adolescent years, she always felt "on the fringe . . . my God-given mission [was] to shock and upset people." In particular, she was embarrassed and confused by her repressive, dual religious background. When Barr was fifteen, she discovered in a medical dictionary that what she had suffered at age three was Bell's palsy, a temporary paralysis that usually lasts forty-eight hours. Now realizing that her sudden cure had not been a Mormon miracle, as her mother had interpreted it, Roseanne underwent a sudden and deep rebellion and depression. To vent her anger, the next day she smoked marijuana, got drunk, and had sexual relations.

When Roseanne was sixteen, she and a girlfriend were badly injured in a car accident when they jaywalked while on their way to East High School one morning. Barr was thrown in the air, cracked her skull, and was dragged thirty feet by the vehicle. As a result, she had to have skin grafts and plastic surgery on her legs. The emotional injuries she suffered were even greater. She began experiencing nightmares and became afraid to sleep. In addition, she was unable to remember things and suffered possible convulsions. The "new" Roseanne did not care about anything; her grades dropped. Because her distraught family was unable to cope with the bizarre transformation in her, in December 1969 seventeen-year-old Roseanne was committed to the Utah State Hospital in Provo. As Roseanne later described the experience: "It was a horrifying place and I was very heavily drugged, so I saw everything through a pretty intense fog. It was a place where you came out of and you became something else, or else you died. I came out."

It was a very "different" Roseanne who was released from the Utah institution. It would be years before the embittered young woman forgave her parents for committing her, but, ironically, she finally felt in touch with herself. "I was me. . . . Not the clone-Mormon princess everybody wanted me to be. That was when I welcomed myself and got on with it." Returning home, Roseanne almost immediately dropped out of high school. For a time she worked as a salad girl at the Chuckarama Restaurant in Salt Lake City. Meanwhile, she had become pregnant. She left Salt Lake City, giving birth to the child on May 16, 1971, at the Salvation Army's Booth Memorial Home in Denver, Colorado. She gave up the baby girl to the Jewish Family and Children's Service in Denver. (In 1989, as the result of a tabloid newspaper's investigation, Brandi was discovered to have been adopted by Stanley and Gail Brown of Denver, and the girl, then eighteen and living in Dallas with her mother, had a reunion with Roseanne in Los Angeles.)

Deciding to continue on her own, Roseanne traveled westward to the mountainous town of Georgetown, Colorado. She moved into a commune with newly made friends and held an assortment of part-time jobs, including being a dishwasher at the Silver Queen Restaurant. Soon she met Bill Pentland, the night clerk at the local motor inn. He was an avid admirer of the comedic arts, played the guitar, and was a painter, all of which attracted Roseanne. Then, too, she was impressed that "He had the only bathtub in the area of our county. So everyone went over to have big dinners and take [Saturday night] baths." It was also at this time that Roseanne became more aware of the women's movement in the United States and developed a growing, but still unformulated, desire to become a writer. After years of living together, on February 4, 1974, she and Bill Pentland married. They purchased a six-foot-wide trailer and moved to Manitou Springs, a suburb of Colorado Springs, and, still later, to Denver. Bill found jobs first as a sanitation worker and then as a postal worker. In 1975 Roseanne gave birth to daughter Jessica, followed in almost yearly succession by the births of Jennifer and Jake. During this period of being a housewife and mother, Roseanne listened to the radio a great deal, in particular, to a talk show hosted by Alan Berg. She called in one day and haltingly read something she had written. The host/DJ responded on the air, "That's very funny. You make a very good point there. Please call in again. I enjoyed talking to you." It was a turning point in Roseanne's life.

In 1980, frustrated at being a passive homemaker and angry at her husband for having let her become one, Roseanne, who had always been heavy, went on a crash diet. She trimmed down from 205 pounds to 105 pounds, becoming a size six, a situation that did not last long. By now, the Pentlands were living in a tiny house in Denver's Harvey Park section. Because of financial necessity, she took a part-time job as a window dresser in an apparel shop, planning to become a buyer in the clothing industry. One day she visited the Woman to Woman Bookstore in Denver; it proved a revelation, leading to Roseanne's liberation as a woman. She joined a feminist collective in hopes of becoming a published writer. However, there were more and more bills at home that had to be paid. In February 1981 she abandoned her $40-a-week position at the clothing shop and took a job at

Bennigan's bar/restaurant in Denver as a cocktail waitress. To handle the sometimes rowdy and randy male customers, she developed a routine of abrasive retorts and wisecracks. This made her a hit with the clientele, who encouraged her in her tart-mouthed dialogue.

Roseanne's younger sister Geraldine was now living with her. She encouraged Barr to try out her "act" at the local Comedy Works. Rebelling against the typical male chauvinist comedians, Roseanne delivered a feminist-point-of-view comedy performance. ("Based on a brand-new theory that we women have our own way of thinking, different from the way men think, and really different from the way they think we think.") However, the club owner found her routine "offensive," and she was not asked back. Determined to hone her act, she began appearing in local biker and punk clubs. Many evenings her performance was not favorably received by the audiences, but the experiences allowed her to improve her delivery. She developed her own brand of comedy, called "funny womanness." As she explained it, "I am a housewife! I'm not gonna go outside myself and say what I should be, I'm gonna say what is. . . . I suddenly knew I could do what Richard Pryor did for himself—get inside the stereotype and make it three-dimensional from within." So, on stage, she became the domestic goddess, a funny spokesperson who could say, "Hey, fellas. You've had it wrong all these years, we women are not the funny ones. We women are not the jokes. You are the jokes." Her act focused amusingly on daily routines familiar to any parent and especially to any housewife. It became Barr's goal to help untrap women from household drudgery.

Remaining faithful to her feminist point of view, Barr organized a women's comedy showcase which performed at the University of Colorado in Boulder. As the months passed, she negotiated appearances outside of Colorado, traveling, for example, to Kansas City, where for a twenty-minute performance she was paid $500. She also played engagements in Oklahoma and Texas. Barr would say of her new, assertive self: "I learned so much from stand up. I learned about discipline, which I'd never had in my life. I learned about language, communication, and writing. I was validating my existence on the stage."

In 1985 Roseanne won the Denver Laff-Off contest, competing against sixteen male stand-up comics. Roseanne's sister Geraldine encouraged her to go to Los Angeles, in particular to audition for the Comedy Store there. This famed emporium of laughs was operated by Mitzi Shore, noted for fostering the careers of many stand-up comics, including Robin Williams. It took only a six-minute audition for Roseanne to impress Shore, who hired her to appear at the club. While Roseanne was establishing herself on the West Coast, her husband and her children remained in Denver. Within a few weeks of her debut at the Comedy Store, Barr was hired to be on the ABC-TV special "Funny," co-produced by Mitzi Shore. A talent scout for Johnny Carson's "Tonight Show" spotted Roseanne at the Comedy Store and signed her for several appearances on the late-night talk show. She toured as the warm-up act for singer Julio Iglesias for four months, appeared on David Letterman's talk show, and, in Las Vegas, served as the opening act for the Pointer Sisters.

On September 6, 1986, Roseanne appeared on the HBO cable special "On Location: Rodney Dangerfield—It's Not Easy Bein' Me," starring bombastic comedian Rodney Dangerfield, an experience she would prefer to forget. She was embarrassed by her "dumb and dirty" lines and thought the exposure was a setback to her career. By now, her husband and her children had joined her in Los Angeles, as had her sister Geraldine. She continued to tour on the road and to build her reputation. For two months in the summer of 1987 she and Geraldine rented a house in the French Quarter of New Orleans. Roseanne's offspring were in summer camp and her husband was traveling around to comedy clubs working on his own comedy routine. On September 19, 1987, she had her own comedy special on HBO, called "On Location: The Roseanne Barr Show." Not only did she perform her own stand-up routines, but one part of the program presented her in a domestic setting in which she performed with a "husband" and "children." The show won two ACE (cable's version of the Emmy Awards) awards: one for best special and one for best female in a comedy.

Especially after the Rodney Dangerfield fiasco, Roseanne was determined to shape how she should be showcased on television, intent on retaining her feminist point of view. About this time, Matt Williams, a one-time writer for TV's "The [Bill] Cosby Show," was developing a new sitcom for ABC-TV to deal with a group of rough-edged blue-collar working mothers. However, after seeing Barr perform and meeting with her, he decided, along with Marcy Carsey and Tom Werner (the producers of "The Cosby Show") to change the concept to star Roseanne Barr.

"Roseanne" debuted on Tuesday, October 18, 1988, on ABC-TV. In format, the show's antecedents were Jackie Gleason's "The Honeymooners," Carroll O'Connor's "All in the Family," and the more recent "Married . . . with Children." The new series eschewed a fantasy type of TV family, instead focusing on the daily tribulations of a blue-collar family: Roseanne (Barr) and slothful Dan Conner (John Goodman) who have three smart-mouthed children (Sal Barone, Sara Gilbert, Lecy Goranson). She works in a plastics factory, along with her sister (Laurie Metcalf), and her husband is a frequently unemployed independent contractor. The two hefty, down-to-earth parents are shown facing life optimistically, despite the constant pile of unpaid bills, unwashed dishes, and a very hectic, often unkempt household. It was the type of show in which star Roseanne could toss off (always with a grin) such remarks as "Now I know why some animals eat their young" or remark sarcastically about friends who are getting divorced: "They shoulda stuck it out in the trenches, dodgin' that shrapnel with the rest of us that believe in true love." Regarding household finances, her character says, "You pay the ones [bills] marked final notice, and you throw the rest away."

The critics and public alike responded positively to "Roseanne." *TV Guide* magazine enthused, "Sharp-tongued comedienne Roseanne Barr brings her particular brand of humor to one of the season's most promising new sitcoms." *Variety* praised the show for capturing "the frantic, scattered rhythms of modern suburban families. Audiences should embrace the series with easy identification. . . ." As for Roseanne, the trade paper decided, "Barr has expert timing and a dry, whiny, nasal delivery that is unique; she's also got a strong personality that could put off a lot of people, but will probably attract even more." "Roseanne" was the first show since "The Cosby Show" in 1984 to go to #1 in the ratings in its debut year. Barr perceived that the show's popularity was due to its special point of view. "It's a voice I feel I've never heard in the media, a voice that tells the truth and doesn't worry. It's like having coffee with your neighbor—the way you talk before the husbands come in."

"Roseanne" made its star the darling of the press and the public. She was earning $30,000 a week and owned 15 percent of the program. Barr and her family lived in an Encino, California, home. Bill Pentland wrote comedy situations/lines for the weekly show (later becoming a staff writer and executive consultant), and her sister Geraldine was responsible for Roseanne's makeup. By the end of 1988, there were widespread rumors of unrest on the highly rated comedy show. As she became increasingly protective of her vehicle, Barr admitted great unhappiness with Matt Williams. She alleged that he was not only distorting her characterization in the scripts but humiliating her in front of the cast and crew. With the help of her husband, Roseanne began rewriting the show's scripts. By Christmas time, Barr gave the network an ultimatum: either Williams goes or she goes. Williams left the program, and she was given creative control. Williams's departure in January 1989 was the first of several publicized changes that occurred in the production team for the hit series.

In May 1989 Barr appeared on NBC-TV's "Friday Night Videos." That same month she was judged the funniest female performer in a leading role in a TV series at the American Comedy Awards. However, that fall she was conspicuously ignored by the Emmy Awards. Kay Gardella (*New York Daily News*) wrote: "It's poor judgment—the academy has snubbed mainstream America."

Roseanne went to New York City in the early summer of 1989. She was filming SHE-DEVIL, a comedy feature film teaming her with highly regarded dramatic actress Meryl Streep. The movie was directed by Susan Seidelman, best known for her successful han-

John Goodman and **Roseanne Barr** in "Roseanne" (1988).

dling of Madonna in DESPERATELY SEEKING SUSAN (1985). By now, Barr's elder daughter Jessica had entered a Westwood, California, treatment center for alcohol abuse. Roseanne and Bill Pentland had separated and the comedienne's constant escort was thirty-year-old Tom Arnold, a 6' 2", 240-pound fledgling comic she had met a few years earlier on one of her road tours.

Long anxious to demonstrate her ability as a writer, Roseanne had contracted to write her autobiography. *Roseanne: My Life as a Woman* was published by Harper & Row on August 30, 1989, and spent four months on the *New York Times* best-seller list. This offbeat, frank book had a special dedication: "For my Sister, Geraldine, for being intense, passionate, committed, brilliant, fierce—for creating a large part of me, my career, the world. Where do you end, where do I begin?" In reviewing the book, *People* magazine determined, "In her intimate, rambling style, Barr gives a humorous, sometimes wrenching account of the potholed path that led to her big break as a comic." If there were discreet gaps in reporting all the episodes of her life in her book, the supermarket tabloid newspapers made sure the public was aware of them. This led to an escalating battle between Barr and such publications. Meanwhile, Roseanne continued to be profiled frequently in mainstream publications. In a July 1989 article, James Brady (*Parade* magazine) asked: "What turns on America about Roseanne Barr, a frequently troubled woman who certainly doesn't go out of her way to charm anyone and who can, in fact, be as uncooperative and prickly as any of the longer established show-business super-egos?" Brady went on to answer his own question: "She is inarguably plump, undeniably dumpy, she has a big mouth. And we love her."

On September 12, 1989, "Roseanne" returned for its second season on ABC-TV. Miles Beller (*Hollywood Reporter*) enthused that the program "continues exalting the banal and elevating the gross. . . . Here slovenliness is next to godliness. . . . The utter inconsequentiality of everyday existence has been made into ring-around-the-collar entertainment." During the second season Roseanne's character quit the plastics factory and later became a beauty salon worker, while her character's sister, quite a man's lady, left the factory to become a police officer.

SHE-DEVIL was released in mid-December 1989. In this big-screen comedy, Roseanne was cast as an East Coast housewife (with a very noticeable facial mole) and mother of two whose self-centered accountant husband (Ed Begley, Jr.) is wooed away by an extremely wealthy and unreal romance novelist (Meryl Streep). Within the farce, geared as a feminist tract, the angered Roseanne sets about destroying her husband's world while gaining her own self-esteem and establishing an employment agency for unskilled, undesirable females. Not surprisingly, it was Streep, with her highly stylized, campy performance, who proved to be the highlight of this spiritless feature. As for Roseanne, Duane Byrge (*Hollywood Reporter*) summarized, "Barr lumbers through her part with such methodical dispatch, she might as well have ridden through on a golf cart. . . . [A]fter a while, her phlegmatic, monotonal voice-overs are dozers also." The expensively produced SHE-DEVIL garnered only $14,997,150 in its first thirteen weeks of domestic distribution. It was a career setback for Barr, who had proclaimed before the movie's release that she might well abandon TV to concentrate on making motion pictures.

Meanwhile, Barr's contretemps with the "Roseanne" production staff continued. She had heated disputes with executive producer Jeff Harris, especially after he fired Tom Arnold (who had been undergoing treatment for substance abuse) as a writer from the TV sitcom. Roseanne was also at odds with another of the show's producers, Danny Jacobson. By March 1990 Harris and others would be gone from the show, replaced by producer Jay Daniel, a friend of Bruce Willis's (in turn a friend of Barr's) who had been a producer on Willis's "Moonlighting" TV series.

When not reporting on the political tussles on her TV series, the tabloids focused on Roseanne's on-again, off-again romance with Tom Arnold. In mid-December 1989, amid rumors of physical abuse from her substance-addicted fiancé, Roseanne cancelled her planned January wedding to Arnold. (Later, he publicly admitted and apologized for the fact that he had sold information about his checkered romance with Roseanne to the tabloids.) He checked into the alcohol/drug rehabilitation clinic of the Century City Hospital. On January 17, 1990, Barr's divorce from Pentland was finalized. (He filed for custody of the three children, but the petition was not granted. Later he would file a $15 million palimony suit against Roseanne and her new husband.) Three days later, on January 20, Roseanne and Arnold were married by California Superior Court Judge Bert Glennon in her Benedict Canyon home. During the five-minute ceremony, helicopters filled with press members hovered over the house, eager to report on the nuptials. That night, before registering at a $1,000-a-night bungalow at the Beverly Hills Hotel, the newlyweds stopped at the Improv Comedy Club to tell a few blue jokes to the audience. Then the couple honeymooned in Acapulco. En route back to Los Angeles, they stopped in Austin, to visit Roseanne's daughter Brandi, now a freshman at the University of Texas.

In December 1989 Roseanne had been scheduled to play a limited engagement at the Circle Star Center Theatre in San Carlos, California. She had cancelled due to "exhaustion." As compensation, she appeared there in five performances from February 22 to 24, 1990. It was her first live stage appearance in three years. Part of her act was a mock tribute to Elvis (she tossed scarves out to members of the audience as Presley had done). Another segment was a conglomeration of established routines she had performed over the years, and another part of the show was a satirical sketch about a Las Vegas lounge performer making a comeback. The show allowed Tom Arnold to perform on stage and Barr to vocalize. Neither the press nor audiences were impressed by the production. Lawrence Christon (*Los Angeles Times*) observed, "Once she steps beyond domestic issues and the topic of having to deal with men, her observations aren't very sharp. . . ." Mike LaSalle (*San Francisco Chronicle*) was less charitable: "It wasn't only that the material was bad; it seemed tossed-off, as if Barr didn't care or was under the impression that people would laugh no matter what she did up there. It was the laziest excuse for a show . . . I'd ever seen by a major comedian."

Sensing that her constant battles with her show's creative team and the tabloids were causing a backlash, Roseanne undertook a flurry of appearances on TV shows. In March 1990 she taped appearances for the American Comedy Awards, the People's Choice

Awards, and a segment of Marsha Warfield's new NBC-TV daytime talk show. In May 1990 she and Arnold purchased (for around $3 million) a Tudor-style seventeen-room home on an acre in Brentwood, California. The two-story four-bedroom home behind gates boasted a wine cellar, guest house, and tennis court. It was quite a step up for the one-time trailer park resident. Still on summer hiatus from her TV series, Roseanne appeared—for a nearly seven-figure salary—in a two-week engagement at the Las Vegas Hilton Hotel in June 1990. *Variety* reported of her not-well-received act, "She seems irascible and indulgent, going into a screaming act instead of thoroughly conceiving and developing her funny routine as a Las Vegas lounge singer in her 'comeback' act." One of Barr's frequent targets in her act was TV talk show host Arsenio Hall, who had often made fun of Barr's weight and vulgarity on his television program.

Not since the baseball scandals of the early twentieth century had there been such an uproar as there was over Roseanne's special appearance at the San Diego Padres baseball game in San Diego. On Thursday, July 26, 1990, Tom Werner (executive producer of "Roseanne" and co-owner of the Padres) had arranged for Roseanne to sing the national anthem at "Working Women's Night" before the double-header between the Padres and the Cincinnati Reds. What followed went beyond even the unbridled antics of Barr and Arnold at the World Series in San Francisco the previous fall when they had mooned the crowd, revealing love tattoos on their buttocks. Barr appeared on schedule at the Jack Murphy Stadium to sing the anthem, but did so in a very scratchy, nasal voice, which caused some spectators to boo. She concluded her "performance" with unexpected shtick: she rubbed her crotch and spit on the ground before leaving the playing field. (She later claimed these gestures were suggested by Padre players, who told her it would be a funny parody of what baseball players do on the diamond.) The episode, interpreted by many as a disparagement of American patriotism, was captured by the (inter)national media. "She's done more damage to baseball than Pete Rose," opined Mike Nolan of Los Angeles's KFI radio. Reeling from the adverse reaction, Barr's husband, Tom Arnold, told the press, "They knew what kind of singer she is. She's just an average singer. She's not an opera singer. She did the best she could." Even the President of the United States, George Bush, went on record as being upset by her performance at the ball park. At the center of the maelstrom, Roseanne confided to the press, "I did the best I could under the circumstances. I don't want people to run me out of town on a rail." A few days later, she appeared on TV's "The Sally Jessy Raphaël Show," along with Tom Arnold, to reiterate her apology for any misinterpretation of her stadium singing, to repeat that she would continue to sing the national anthem since she was an American too (in fact, she joined the audience in a sing-along of the patriotic song), and to state that she intended to sue one of the more blatant tabloid newspapers for its continued harassment of her and her new spouse. An aftermath of the brouhaha was that several episodes of her high-rated series received poor ratings during the summer rerun season.

On September 18, 1990, Roseanne returned for her third year of "Roseanne." For the new season, her character underwent a career change (she became a waitress at a mall restaurant), and Barr's off-camera husband, Tom Arnold, became head writer on the series and has been scheduled to make several guest appearances. (By now, Barr and Arnold had become co-producers of the program.) *Daily Variety* reported, "Television's most notorious offscreen personality returns to what she does best. . . . By the Fall's early light, 'Roseanne' still looks a winner." The trade paper also noted, "there's been an apparent effort to soften the Roseanne persona, showing off a sensitive and human side without detracting from her acerbic wit. . . . Barr is also a better actress than she's given credit for in addition to her nasal comic delivery." Although the series's novelty wore off and the backlash from Barr's baseball stadium singing caused viewership of the sitcom to drop, the show remained in the top ten overall and was first in popularity with adults aged twenty-five to fifty-four. If TV watchers were tiring a bit of "Roseanne," Barr was still a remarkable prime-time newsmaker. She and Arnold announced plans to resettle in 1991 in the Minneapolis–St. Paul area (where the couple had a pleasant stay in August 1990 during a concert appearance) and to move production of the show to rock star Prince's Paisley Park Studios there by the 1991–1992 season. A few days later, however, the projected relocation was retracted as being too costly, at least for the time being. Meanwhile, Barr signed to cut her first album of ballads. In early October 1990 Barr and Arnold filed a multimillion dollar lawsuit alleging that two tabloid newspapers had stolen four love letters Roseanne had written to Arnold and had published them without permission earlier in 1990. Besides claiming invasion of privacy, the suit, filed in federal court, took a unique approach by seeking relief under the Racketeer Influenced and Corrupt Organizations Act (RICO), alleging that the defendants participated "in a scheme to obtain the private papers and effects of celebrities by inducing and paying persons and entities to steal such information and transport it in interstate commerce."

For the 1990–1991 TV season, Barr was the inspiration for a Saturday morning cartoon series, "Little Rosey," a program about a ten-year-old Roseanne (minus the brashness). Kathleen Laskey provided the voice for the title character of this show, which premiered on September 8, 1990. On the other hand, Roseanne was persuaded by Bruce Willis to provide the off-camera voice of Mikey's little sister Julie in LOOK WHO'S TALKING TOO (1990), the sequel to the surprise box-office hit LOOK WHO'S TALKING (1989). For this, her second motion picture role, Barr was paid a reported $850,000. In an extension and expansion of her ABC-TV network pact, Roseanne, partnered in Barnold Productions with her husband, agreed to appear in a forthcoming TV special and TV movie as well as to produce (but not star in) a new teleseries. Meanwhile, she and Arnold appeared together on a spate of talk shows to discuss her image; she starred for two nights in the late fall of 1990 at Universal's Amphitheater; and on January 5, 1991, she starred in the HBO–Cable special "Roseanne Barr Live from Trump Castle." Rick Sherwood (*Hollywood Reporter*) criticized the special: "[it] is a little bit like her TV series; it's an act that's getting old before its time. . . . This one-hour special is really little more than an exercise in ego, and it's just not funny." Lawrence Christon (*Los Angeles Times*) was equally unimpressed by the indulgent outing, but observed, "as artless and crude as she is, she's managed the unequivocal feat that's the first rule of artistic success: She's forced people to accept her on her own terms."

Ensconced as an icon of the late twentieth century, the 5' 4", 212-pound Barr remains outspoken. Regarding her position in show business, she says: "I want to be a voice for working women. . . . I'm trying to show that there's a lot more to being a woman than being a mother, but that there's a hell of a lot more to being a mother than most people suspect." Regarding her stocky frame, she observes: "To me, being fat isn't a negative. Being fat is a response. If you eat, you're choosing to be fat. Fat is a great friend. It's a cushion, very comforting at times. I feel sexy when I'm fat, but then I feel sexy when I'm skinny too. Being fat, for a woman, also means you take up more space, so you're seen—and probably heard—more easily. It's real ironic." About her future, she said a few years ago: "I think about growing older . . . when you're in your mid-thirties, you start to realize that this is your life. And it don't belong to nobody else. . . . This is my life."

Filmography

She-Devil (Orion, 1989)
Look Who's Talking Too (Tri-Star, 1990) (voice
   only)

Backfield in Motion (ABC-TV, 11/13/91)

Television Series

Roseanne (ABC, 1988–)

Album Discography

The Best of Comic Relief 2 (Rhino
   R11H-70707)
I Enjoy Being a Girl (Hollywood 61000-2)

KIM BASINGER

"Let's face it, we all got big egos. And we need to have 'em fed. It helped me tremendously, the security factor of my looks. . . . I'm going to use these looks the best way I know how."
— *Vanity Fair* magazine, June 1989

BLONDE AMBITION. TWO WORDS THAT HAVE FORMED A BUZZ PHRASE of the 1990s, used most frequently in reference to two of Hollywood's currently most active and popular women: Kim Basinger and Madonna. Of the two, Kim, the natural blonde, is a ravishing beauty with or without makeup. She began her career as a New York model and, as she became increasingly in demand, moved into television work. It quickly became obvious that she could also act. Then she was revealed to be a gifted comedienne— in the tradition of Carole Lombard—who could at times be Fifth Avenue elegant, at other times red-light-district trampy. Because of her sexiness, Basinger has been compared to France's Brigitte Bardot; because of her comedic talents, Kim has been heralded as another Judy Holliday. At present, she ranks at the top alongside Michelle Pfeiffer as one of the screen's two most beautiful women. Unlike Pfeiffer, Basinger and her off-screen love affairs have proved a treasure trove of material for the supermarket tabloids. Everything she does, including getting injections of collagen in her lips, is told and written and read about. And the more that is revealed about Kim Basinger, the more popular she becomes.

She was born on Tuesday, December 8, 1953, in Athens, Georgia, of Cherokee Indian ancestry to Donald Basinger, a loan company manager who had been a big band musician in Chicago before his marriage, and Ann Basinger, a former model and expert swimmer who had performed in water ballets on screen with Esther Williams. The Basinger household on Chestnut Lane included five offspring: the two eldest, sons Skip and Mick, and daughters Kim, Barbara, and Ashley. Kim's unusual reticence and shyness were thought at first to be the result of autism. However, medical tests indicated that she was simply withdrawn, possibly because of the marital tension between her parents and her father's criticism of her—nothing she did seemed to please him. (Ironically, at the age of two, the painfully shy little girl announced that someday she would be a great actress.) At school, her terror at the thought that the teacher *might* call on her would cause her to faint. Each year, Mrs. Basinger would phone Kim's new teachers to request that they not expect Kim to recite in class. Mrs. Basinger gave extra time to her daughter, enrolled her in ballet class and gymnastics, and encouraged her to sing in the church choir, all of which helped. Meanwhile, Kim hated school, preferring to closet herself in her bedroom, listening to music or writing poetry. Nonetheless, she attended parties happily by the time she was ten. Whenever a boy kissed her, she responded by slipping her tongue into his mouth, believing it was the thing to do. The other children taunted her as "rubberlips."

At Clarke Central High School, realizing it was critical to overcome her fears, she auditioned for the cheerleading squad. Although desperately frightened by the tryouts, she performed well and was accepted. At sixteen, she entered the Athens Junior Miss Contest, partly on a dare from her father, and sang "Wouldn't It Be Loverly" from *My Fair Lady*. Of winning, an accomplishment she considers her greatest to this day, she has said, "They didn't know I could talk, much less sing." Although she subsequently lost the Georgia state Junior Miss competition held in Atlanta, she was selected by Breck Shampoo as a contestant in its national hairstyling contest for high school seniors held in New York City. Winning this distinction as a "Breck Girl," she appeared with her mother in an advertisement for Gold Formula Breck Shampoo in 1970 that carried the inscription: "Ann and Kim share many interests: dress design, cooking, modeling in local stores, long walks on the beach, a love for animals." During her stay in Manhattan, Kim met Eileen Ford of the prestigious Ford modeling agency, who offered the newcomer a modeling contract. However, Kim turned it down to enroll at the University of Georgia, but stayed there less than two semesters. She returned to New York City under contract to Ford.

At the age of nineteen, the blue-gray eyed, 5' 7" young lady with long blonde hair became a top fashion model earning $1,000 a day for Clairol, Revlon, and Maybelline advertisements, along with gracing the covers of many major magazines. "She was the all-American girl," said Eileen Ford. But Kim found modeling to be a lonely existence, and she detested New York City. Years later, Basinger would observe of her modeling years: "It was very hard to go from one booking to another and always have to deal with the way I looked. I couldn't stand it. I felt myself choking." As a distraction, she took acting lessons at the Neighborhood Playhouse and sang under the *nom de chant* of "Chelsea" at Greenwich Village nightclubs and occasionally at a West Side church.

In 1976 Kim quit modeling when she relocated to Los Angeles with her dog and her then boyfriend, model Dale Robinette, to pursue an acting career under the guidance of agent Martin Gage. Capitalizing on her looks and modeling reputation, Gage quickly obtained assignments for her, first in an episode of "Starsky & Hutch" (ABC-TV), followed by a segment of "Charlie's Angels" entitled "Angels in Chains" (October 20, 1976) in which she was an inmate at a prison farm. Next she was in installments of "McMillan and Wife" and "The Six Million Dollar Man," both telecast on January 2, 1977. Beginning March 5, 1977, she co-starred as Officer J. Z. Kane—described as "bright," "sexy," and "competent"—on ABC-TV's "Dog and Cat," an hour-long police drama series which ended its run on May 14, 1977. The pilot film for that failed series was televised on July 22, 1977, *after* the show's demise.

In THE GHOST OF FLIGHT 401, a two-hour world premiere movie on NBC-TV on February 18, 1978, based on a true story, Kim was fourth-billed as Prissy. The same network's KATIE: PORTRAIT OF A CENTERFOLD, telecast October 23, 1978, presented her in the title role of a naive Texas beauty queen. This assignment, for which she did not need to conceal her southern drawl, is considered her first breakthrough role as a sex symbol. In the NBC-TV miniseries version of the James Jones novel *From Here to Eternity*, she played Lorene Rogers, the good-hearted whore played on screen by Donna Reed in the 1953 movie. The six-hour, three-part February 1979 video drama received high ratings and prompted the network to bring it back as a regular weekly series in March 1980, a mistake that lasted less than a month. (In August 1980, previously unaired episodes were telecast as NBC-TV "specials.")

Kim made her theatrical film debut in HARD COUNTRY, released in April 1981, as Jan-Michael Vincent's Texas girlfriend. *Variety* rated her "terrific." Also involved with this modest feature was Ron Britton, the makeup artist son of Allan "Whitey" Snyder, who had done Marilyn Monroe's burial makeup in 1962. Falling in love, Kim at age twenty-seven married Ron, fifteen years her senior, in 1980. Describing their union as "Toys 'R Us, we are *it*!" Kim said that they were "joined at the hip." The couple purchased a home in Woodland Hills, California, where Kim wrote songs, poetry, and screenplays, while a reported menagerie of nine dogs and seventeen cats cavorted nearby. Meanwhile, she screentested for the role of Cora in the remake of THE POSTMAN ALWAYS RINGS TWICE (1981), but lost out to Jessica Lange.

In the Charlton Heston–directed MOTHER LODE (1982), Kim, the obligatory love interest of Nick Mancuso, is wasted, as is Heston in a dual role. In 1982 Kim suffered from agoraphobia, a fear of public places and crowds, when she could not bring herself to leave the Britton home for a period of four months. After successful therapy with a Santa Monica, California, specialist, she undertook an eight-page nude layout for a 1983 issue of *Playboy* magazine, including its cover. She did the assignment against the advice of her agent and lawyer, because "I needed something that would remind the industry of me, something that would wow them. I considered the spread almost a silent film for myself."

As Domino in NEVER SAY NEVER AGAIN (1983), a supporting role, she is well remembered for her scant costuming as lover to James Bond (Sean Connery). *Newsweek* magazine observed that Kim "shows signs of being more than a Bond bimbo with her flashdance physicality and golden-eagle elegance." Her initial screen comedy role was in THE

Kim Basinger in HARD COUNTRY (1981).

MAN WHO LOVED WOMEN (1983), as a nymphomaniac in pursuit of compulsive lover Burt Reynolds. She stole the limelight from everyone else in this Blake Edwards–directed misfire, which nevertheless proved to be another career break for her. She was back to drama as a femme fatale in the baseball drama THE NATURAL (1984). Critic Rex Reed enthused of Basinger, "In sleek gowns and a peroxide pageboy, she combines the sultry goofiness of Marilyn Monroe with the cornfed sweetness of Carroll Baker." Following the release of this feature, which grossed more than $48 million, her name was linked romantically with that of co-star Robert Redford. Writer/actor Sam Shepard chose her as the female lead of his FOOL FOR LOVE (1985), about the romance between a rodeo rider and his half-sister. Although Jessica Lange chose to watch Kim's love scenes with her paramour, Shepard, from the sidelines, Kim managed to overcome the unnerving experience. FOOL FOR LOVE was quickly forgotten by moviegoers.

Although a critical flop, the much-edited 9 1/2 WEEKS (1986) was a big moneymaker in Europe. Kim claims to have detested her part as Elizabeth, the sexual slave of sadist Mickey Rourke. However, the film established her as a bankable international star with the power to command $1 million in salary for her next film, the thriller NO MERCY (1986). In this film, which co-starred Richard Gere, she proved, as an uneducated Cajun involved with the underworld, that she can act. (*People* magazine noted, "her lips may be the poutiest and most provocative in screen history.")

She reverted to comedy for her next three pictures. ("I love comedy and think it's the most powerful thing we have in the entertainment industry.") She first co-starred as Bruce Willis's BLIND DATE (1987), as a woman incapable of tolerating alcoholic beverages. Her next co-star, Jeff Bridges, likened her to "ripe fruit—something you just want to pick up." In NADINE (1987) she was a manicurist frantically attempting to retrieve nude photos of herself with help from her estranged husband (Bridges). She also had the title role in MY STEPMOTHER IS AN ALIEN (1988), as a beautiful creature from space, at a reported salary of $2 million. Although she received solid reviews for her performances, none of these pictures was well received at the box office.

Her marriage to Ron Britton was dissolved on December 14, 1988, when she filed for divorce stating that the union had been "very, very, very smothering." She began paying him $8,000 per month in alimony as well as continuing payments on their home, where he continued to reside. It was rumored that Kim was on the threshold of marrying her Australian personal fitness trainer, Phil Walsh, after the divorce became final, but that did not happen.

Replacing injured Sean Young in the role of Vicki Vale in the over $30 million production of BATMAN (1989), Kim flew to London for filming; there her much-publicized romance with producer Jon Peters fizzled when she met Prince, commissioned to write songs for the movie. With BATMAN in blockbuster moneymaking release during the summer and autumn of 1989, Kim moved to Minneapolis in October to be with Prince. There she did a rock video with him, "Scandalous Sex Suite," with moans and sighs, which doubled for his song "Steamy Lover's Dialogue" from the BATMAN soundtrack. She announced that she planned a solo recording with him as producer: "I was singing long before I was an actress. Now people will be able to see what I can do." She and Prince also announced that they would make a movie together, GRAFFITI BRIDGE (1990), similar to his PURPLE RAIN (1984). In February 1990, however, Kim's sudden split from Prince's influence put an end, at least for the moment, to her venture into recordings, and she was replaced by Ingrid Chavez in his $7.5 million film.

By the conclusion of 1989 Kim had appeared in a Fox Network TV special, "Inside the Summer Blockbusters" (June 3, 1989), to help publicize BATMAN—the hit drew over $251.2 million at the domestic box office alone—and she had dismissed her entire management team, agent, and attorney. Also during 1989, Kim, with reputed assets of $50 million, found time to appear in advertisements for The Gap clothing chain as well as negotiated for the purchase of the 1,728-acre town of Braselton, Georgia (population: 500). On January 24, 1990, in Atlanta, she signed the purchase documents with her investment company partners, American Information Technologies of Chicago. Paying $20 million for 80 percent ownership, she quipped, "I'm Barbara Stanwyck in 'The Big Valley.'" Her plans for Braselton, founded in 1876, included establishment of a major film studio and a recording studio.

At almost the same time, Kim negotiated to film a sequel to 9 1/2 WEEKS with Mickey Rourke in France; reportedly purchased an Italian restaurant in Santa Monica, California, with Tony Danza as her partner; and was named the world's sexiest woman by US magazine. She rejected the starring role in SLEEPING WITH THE ENEMY (1991), which went instead to Julia Roberts, and then was listed by fashion designer Mr. Blackwell as one of the worst-dressed women of 1989. ("This parading peep show should be banished to the back cave," he said.) On March 12, 1990, she wore, according to *Newsweek* magazine, "a tiny skirt and a pair of very long legs" to the office of Georgia's Secretary of State to receive a plaque honoring her as an "outstanding Georgian." As she once said with regard to her status in filmmaking, "You have to be a little unreal to be in this business." At the March 26, 1990, Academy Awards ceremonies in Los Angeles she was a first-time presenter, wearing a bell-bottomed gown of her own design, which prompted *San Francisco Chronicle* TV critic John Carmen to decide that she should have won an award as "Outstanding Achievement in Costume Design."

THE MARRYING MAN (1991), with Alec Baldwin as a Hollywood millionaire, enabled Kim, as a Las Vegas lounge performer, to display her singing abilities. (As a result of her on-screen vocalizing in THE MARRYING MAN, she has signed a recording contract with the Los Angeles–based Giant Records.) Off camera, the beautiful couple engaged in a romance and were reported by those close to them to be inseparable. At an Earth Day, 1990, concert in New York City's Central Park, they were photographed kissing while attempting to hide their identities behind smoked glasses; they later spent a Sunday afternoon testing futons at a futon shop in the trendy SoHo district of Manhattan.

It was announced in July 1990 that "the entire cast" (excepting Jack Nicholson) was to be re-assembled for the simultaneous filming of two Warner Bros. sequels to BAT-MAN—BATMAN II and BATMAN III—with Basinger and Michael Keaton reprising their original roles; however, Kim later dropped out of the projects. *Esquire* magazine in July

1990 reported the results of a reader poll to determine the perfect woman: she would have "the hair of Kim Basinger," along with the legs of Jamie Lee Curtis, the eyes of Elizabeth Taylor, and additional contributions from other famous beauties.

In the late fall of 1990, Kim earned a reported $1 million for appearing in a pantyhose commercial for Italian TV. At the same time, she sold (for more than $800,000 unfurnished) her 1,700-square-foot Hollywood Hills hideaway, purchased in May 1990 for nearly $1 million furnished. The animal rights activist Kim once said, "All I know about acting is, you just do it. God bless Stanislavsky, but I can't even pronounce his name." Of her buying habits, she has acknowledged, "I'm the world's maddest spender. I'll go into an antique shop, buy everything in sight, have it delivered home and then change my mind." Regarding her success, she has said, "I've always known that one day I'd succeed. I've always known what I wanted. It's as simple as that. It's a question of confidence. You've got to accept yourself for what you are." On another occasion, she remarked, "Sometimes I have this dream that I'd like to walk naked down the street and leave all my fame behind." More recently, the ambitious actress predicted, "In the next two years, you're gonna see somebody emerge that you had no idea about."

Filmography

Dog and Cat (ABC-TV, 7/22/77)
The Ghost of Flight 401 (NBC-TV, 2/18/78)
Katie: Portrait of a Centerfold (NBC-TV, 10/23/78)
Killjoy (CBS-TV, 10/22/81)
Hard Country (Associated Film, 1981)
Mother Lode (Martin Shafter–Andrew Scheinman, 1982)
The Man Who Loved Women (Col, 1983)
Never Say Never Again (WB, 1983)

The Natural (Tri-Star, 1984)
Fool for Love (Cannon, 1985)
9 1/2 Weeks (MGM/UA, 1986)
No Mercy (Tri-Star, 1986)
Blind Date (Tri-Star, 1987)
Nadine (Tri-Star, 1987)
My Stepmother Is an Alien (Col, 1988)
Batman (WB, 1989)
The Marrying Man (BV, 1991)

Television Series

Dog and Cat (ABC, 1977)
From Here to Eternity (NBC, 2/14/79; 2/21/79; 2/28/79) [miniseries]

From Here to Eternity (NBC, 1980)

TOM BERENGER

"There better be something other than this. You've got to have
another life. You're always learning something or picking something
up, either consciously or unconsciously. Because all your arts are really
about life."   —*Fame* magazine, April 1990

TOM BERENGER IS DEFINITELY CHAMELEONIC. ONE IS HARD-PRESSED
to distinguish the real-life Berenger from an assortment of his sharply etched on-camera
roles: the prison-made homosexual (LOOKING FOR MR. GOODBAR), the handsome,
moustached TV star (THE BIG CHILL), the scarred, evil battle sergeant (PLATOON), or the
complacent, round-faced police sergeant (SOMEONE TO WATCH OVER ME). Like contemporaries William Hurt and Kevin Kline, he performs a variety of screen types, but each
with a different face or voice. At times the talented Berenger looks like the young Albert
Finney; on other occasions he resembles a thicker-lipped Richard Gere or a laid-back Lee
Horsley. While Berenger's public image is that of a man of action, privately he prefers to
remain at home and write, a sedentary avocation that he finds more enjoyable than acting.
Although his peers seem bent on being cinematic stars, Tom has stated, "I don't care about
being a star. I can do a supporting role; I don't have to be a lead."

This man of many faces, who remains very private about his childhood, was born on
Wednesday, May 31, 1950, on the south side of Chicago to a printer and his wife. Of his
parents, Tom would one day reflect that they "were Depression kids, and they had a
defeatist attitude about life. They believed you should just try to get through life one day at
a time until you die. I've fought that philosophy all my life."

In September 1968 he enrolled at the University of Missouri at Columbia as a
journalism major. In his junior year, the university's drama department experienced an
upsurge in popularity through a sudden campus enthusiasm for theater. As a lark, Tom
auditioned for the school's production of *Who's Afraid of Virginia Woolf?*, the dialogue-
heavy four-character play. He got the part of Nick, the ambitious professor, the role played
by George Segal in the 1966 film version of the Broadway hit. The production was entered
in the annual Iowa College Theatre Festival, held at Iowa City, and his performance was so
well received by college critics that he determined to make drama his secondary scholastic
interest. Thereafter, he appeared in more plays. He was to recall later, "it was amateur
stuff. I really thought of it more as a hobby than a profession. Then I realized how seriously
a lot of these people took what they were doing and thankfully some of them made me
serious about it." The acting "bug" had bitten hard. He went to New York City.

There he studied for a short time at HB Studio, run by Uta Hagen and Herbert Berghof, before involving himself with Marshall W. Mason's Circle Repertory Company as well as the Ensemble Studio Theatre, Playwrights Horizons, and the Lion Theatre Company. For the next four years, through these professional connections, he learned about theater while perfecting the craft of acting in regional productions and off-off-Broadway presentations of plays such as *End as a Man* (as Jocko), *The Rose Tattoo* (as Jack), and *Electra* (as Orestes). *A Streetcar Named Desire* (in which he played Stanley Kowalski), staged by the Milwaukee Repertory Company, made a tour of Japan.

Television daytime soaps are ever on the lookout for the young and the handsome. When he was approached to play a part in the ABC daytime drama "One Life to Live," he readily accepted, for the experience as well as for the steady salary. In the five-day-a-week, forty-five-minute show, from September 1975 to September 1976 he was Tim Siegal, a wheelchair-bound young man who marries an ex-nun but then dies. Of this period in his life, he has said, "It was tough, but I learned a hell of a lot in the process."

During this time, Tom was married to Barbara, a union that produced two children, Allison, born in 1977, and Patrick, born in 1979. The couple would divorce in 1980.

He next earned the supporting role of Billy Sutton in the two-hour TV movie JOHNNY, WE HARDLY KNEW YE, filmed on the East Coast and shown on NBC on January 27, 1977. With a teleplay by Lionel Chetwynd, it was taken from the best-selling book about John F. Kennedy's campaign for a seat in Congress in 1946. This job was closely followed by one in California at Universal Studios in a small role, for which he was billed as "man at end," in THE SENTINEL (1977), a poor entry in the haunted-house genre. This film even had thickset, one-time glamour queen Ava Gardner bumping through it as a real estate agent.

Although THE SENTINEL was in release eight months before LOOKING FOR MR. GOODBAR (1977), the latter is considered Tom's official screen debut. MR. GOODBAR is a long (135 minutes), sordid account of the sexual appetite and wanderings of a liberated schoolteacher (Diane Keaton). As an ex-convict fighting his homosexuality, Tom appears in the final twenty minutes of the drama in drag while fighting off a group of New Year's Eve gay bashers. He sheds the feminine garments in the street, dons Levis, and heads for a singles bar where he meets Keaton. He easily charms himself into her bed where she laughs and makes a statement that he construes as an affront to his manhood. Psychologically over the edge, he repeatedly stabs her to death. A brutal ending to a long movie, this was not a terribly auspicious role for a screen "debut." Tom remarked about the role, "I had nightmares after I finished shooting. I felt dirty." However, *Screen World,* the annual chronicle of movies, pictured Tom as one of the Promising New Actors of 1977, along with Meryl Streep, Richard Gere, William Katt, and Lily Tomlin.

It was not until February 1979 that he really got noticed, partly because of the earthy language and partly because of generous amounts of nudity, in IN PRAISE OF OLDER WOMEN. Filmed in Canada and shown at the Toronto Film Festival in September 1978, the film presented Tom as Andras Vayda, an Austrian youth introduced to sex at age eleven by an older woman. Thereafter, he finds mature women more appealing in his quest for sex, and he is snubbed by girls his own age. *After Dark* magazine decided that "Attractive Tom Berenger tries hard to bring grace to the role he plays" and that, in spite of "unfocused direction," the film was "sexy, provocative." *After Dark* often photographed Tom in 1978–1979 in wide-stanced poses in tight pants. From time to time, his name was misspelled as Ber*i*nger.

Twentieth Century–Fox had a popular hit with its 1969 release BUTCH CASSIDY AND THE SUNDANCE KID, starring Robert Redford and Paul Newman. A decade later, Fox decided to do a prequel, BUTCH AND SUNDANCE: THE EARLY YEARS (1979), with Tom and William Katt as the boisterous partners in the Old West. Katt received billing over Tom, as Butch, in this summer release, which, although lacking the music of Burt Bacharach, had nice location photography and decent performances. *Variety* rated this entry as "standard sagebrush material" and noted that "Tom Berenger and William Katt acquit themselves admirably, but they simply can't compete with the ghosts of two superstars," although there are moments in the film when Tom easily resembles the young Newman.

In his first important television role, Tom starred as Bobby Fallon in CBS-TV's two-part (October 14 and 16, 1979) FLESH AND BLOOD. He played a streetwise boxer who indulges in an incestuous relationship with his mother (Suzanne Pleshette) while continuing a romance with a TV reporter (Kristin Griffith). The promos insisted, "Sometimes a man can fight too hard. Sometimes a mother can love too much," and advised viewers to exercise "parental discretion." (This made-for-television feature is not to be confused with the 1985 theatrical release of the same name starring Rutger Hauer.) Berenger's performance in FLESH AND BLOOD prompted Leslie Halliwell in his *Filmgoer's Companion* to list Tom as a "brooding leading man in the John Garfield mould."

Tom Berenger in THE DOGS OF WAR (1980).

He did a lot of brooding, too, in THE DOGS OF WAR (1980), a British-financed film for United Artists release, shot in the 100+ degree weather of Central America, as well as in locations in London and Africa. Tom played second fiddle to Christopher Walken, as the leader of a group of mercenaries who stage violent skirmishes when necessary. As the mercenary Drew, Tom was tough in battle, but dubious of the motives of his boss. Most critics found this to be a fascinating premise which devolved into dull entertainment.

Tom rejected the lead role of the homosexual Zack in MAKING LOVE (1982)—a part accepted by Michael Ontkean—but appeared in a confused Italian-made feature, BEYOND THE DOOR (1982), as an American engineer caught up in the complex relationship between a father (Marcello Mastroianni) and his daughter (Eleonora Giorgi). *Variety*, in reviewing the "rampaging melodrama," shown out of competition at the Venice Film Festival (September 1982), decided, "The actors barely cope with their abstract roles that dangerously skirt caricature."

Publicity biographies of the elusive Tom Berenger invariably included mention of his "almost fanatical devotion to physical fitness" and noted that he "never missed a daily work-out with his Bullworker muscle toner and his skipping rope." One bio revealed that his mood swings ranged from aloofness, when he chose to be remote, to friendliness and conviviality.

The success of his next release, THE BIG CHILL (1983), was a surprise to all concerned. He was Sam Weber, the macho star of a television series, "J. T. Lancer," who joins his former classmates from the University of Michigan at the funeral of their friend. Spending the weekend together, the seven people (the others were Glenn Close, Jeff Goldblum, William Hurt, Kevin Kline, Meg Tilly, and JoBeth Williams) reevaluate their lives. *Time* magazine observed that the "star actors deserve one big Oscar." As Sam, Tom was handsome, with blow-dried hair and moustache. EDDIE AND THE CRUISERS was released the same month (September) of the same year, with Tom in the role of Frank, the song-writing collaborator of rock 'n' roll singer Eddie Wilson (Michael Pare). In February 1985 Tom returned to motion picture screens for a short time in the low-budget actioner FEAR CITY, with a plot involving a police hunt for a Times Square slasher. Three months later, in a broad spoof of western movies called RUSTLERS' RHAPSODY, he was a singing cowboy dressed in white (for goodness) with a matching palomino horse named Wildfire. "It took me a week to get over my saddle sores," Tom remarked after spending four months on the range. The picture was a flop. Sidney Sheldon's big seller *If Tomorrow Comes* was adapted as a seven-hour TV miniseries, shown on CBS on March 16–18, 1986. Tom was the male lead, Jeff Stevens, a big-time con man and thief who joins forces with a former bank clerk (Madolyn Smith) in romance as well as heists. *Variety* reported, "As a jewel-thief caper, 'If Tomorrow Comes' comes off paste. . . . As for glamor, Smith and Berenger, playing at it, don't light any screen with their low-wattage perfs."

On July 29, 1986, in Beaufort, South Carolina, Tom married Lisa Williams, a brunette real estate salesperson he had met there while filming THE BIG CHILL. Later that year, they became parents to their first child, Chelsea, who was followed in June 1988 by a sister named Chloe. For six weeks each summer Tom had custody of his two older children, in what he has termed "a real intense" time with four kids in the house.

Writer-director Oliver Stone chronicled his Vietnam experiences in PLATOON (1986), the best in a series of movies depicting that terrible time in history. Lensed in the teeming jungles of the Philippines, the picture captures the truths of both sides of the war. Berenger, as the ruthless Sergeant Bob Barnes, wore what *Premiere* magazine termed "the best glamour scars since Joan Crawford's in A WOMAN'S FACE [1941]." Within the drama, Berenger is despicable; he is the top sergeant you love to hate, but the reasons for his behavior are not provided. "I am reality," he informs a small group of men before embarking on a final killing spree that ends in his own death at the weapon of one of his men. Garnering four Academy Awards, including Best Picture, PLATOON, with grosses in excess of $137 million, was the biggest moneymaker to win the Oscar since THE STING (1973). Both Tom and Willem Dafoe were nominated in the Best Supporting Actor category, although they were billed above the title. They lost to Michael Caine (HANNAH AND HER SISTERS). However, for Tom, this feature marked the apex of his career. He admitted to enjoying bad guy roles, and of Sergeant Barnes he said, "I actually liked him and, at times, felt sorry for him." For his PLATOON performance, Berenger won a Golden Globe Award.

For Columbia Pictures, in SOMEONE TO WATCH OVER ME (1987), he went on to portray blue-collar police detective Mike Keegan, assigned to protect a chic Manhattanite (Mimi Rogers) who is a material witness in a homicide case. He tells her in a Brooklyn/Queens accent, "Hey, I'm not going to let anything happen to you," then falls in love with the sophisticate while his wife and young son wait at home. Tom was next heard in voiceover in DEAR AMERICA: LETTERS HOME FROM VIETNAM (1987), comprised of stock footage from the NBC Video Archives. SHOOT TO KILL (1988), originally titled MOUNTAIN KING, paired Tom, as a taciturn wilderness guide, with Sidney Poitier, as an FBI agent in pursuit of a killer. The murderer has kidnapped Tom's girlfriend (Kirstie Alley) during his climb in the Canadian wilds. When asked her reaction to working with Berenger, Alley confessed, "Tom is very sexy . . . but he's sort of dangerous . . . he just has the ability to look at you real dangerously which I think is hot." He was Gary Simmons, a leader of a right-wing terrorist group, in BETRAYED (1988), which the *San Francisco Examiner* labeled "the dumbest movie of the year."

To help Tom in preparing for the role of a priest in LAST RITES (1988), director Don Bellisario sent him a Catholic priest's roman collar because "he totally immerses himself in a role. I'm sure he went out dressed as a priest; for all I know, he's probably married some people." Tom appeared as Father Michael, a dedicated, streetwise priest, whose father is a Mafia don. The priest's vows are put to the test when an appealing dancer (Daphne Zuniga) comes to him for protection. The routine drama was quickly relegated to home video.

In June 1988, to ready himself for the role of a rugged, aging catcher for the Cleveland Indians in MAJOR LEAGUE (1989), Tom went to Savannah, Georgia, to study the art of baseball spitting and self-scratching and to talk to pitchers from the minor-league Savannah Cardinals and Greensboro Hornets. Promoted as a "comedy with bats and balls," this baseball movie teamed Tom, Charlie Sheen (his PLATOON co-star), and Corbin Bernsen as three players who go on a winning spree because they do not want their team to be relocated to Miami. *People* magazine found that "Berenger and Sheen relax a bit from their usual stratospheric intensity levels," but that "the script oozes obscenities, which pointlessly makes the film an offense against younger children." MAJOR LEAGUE scored with $49 million at the domestic box office.

On November 22, 1988, Berenger returned to the stage in New Haven, Connecticut, when he appeared in the Long Wharf Theatre's production of *National Anthems*, which ran until January 28, 1989. In the underrated LOVE AT LARGE (1990), Tom was a private investigator hired by Anne Archer to follow her lover (Neil Young). As a result of her inadequate description of him, the investigator tails the wrong man (Ted Levine). Meanwhile, Tom is followed by a novice female detective (Elizabeth Perkins), with whom he falls in love. Although intended as a spoof of the *film noir* mysteries so popular in the 1940s, LOVE AT LARGE failed to amuse most critics, including Roger Ebert (*Chicago Sun-Times*), who found it to be "very confused" and "a parody in search of a genre." Of her co-star, Elizabeth Perkins was quoted as saying: "He is probably one of the most egoless actors I've ever worked with. It is very refreshing to work with someone where it's all about the work." Director Alan Rudolph said that Berenger "reminds me very much of Spencer Tracy or Paul Muni, the classic actors . . . a guy who understands the subtlety but won't celebrate it, doesn't do anything tricky. He understands the essence of things."

Due for release in late 1990, THE FIELD was filmed in Ireland and directed by Jim Sheridan, fresh from his success with MY LEFT FOOT (1989). Starring with Richard Harris and John Hurt, Tom played a wealthy Irish-American from Boston who returns to Ireland in 1939 where he runs afoul of locals when he becomes obsessed with buying a plot of land that he plans to exploit for its natural resources. Reviewing the film at the Toronto Film Festival in September 1990, *Variety* judged: "Superb acting and austere visual beauty are offset by a somewhat overheated screenplay in this tragic tale." Filming began in January 1990 in San Francisco for SHATTERED (1991), in which Tom portrayed a man suffering from amnesia. Directed by Wolfgang Petersen of West Germany, the thriller was adapted from Richard Nelly's novel and co-starred Bob Hoskins and Greta Scacchi. Within five months, with little time to spend with his family, Berenger was whisked off to Brazil in mid-1990 for AT PLAY IN THE FIELDS OF THE LORD (forthcoming, 1991), joining a cast consisting of Aidan Quinn, John Lithgow, Daryl Hannah, and Kathy Bates under the direction of Hector Babenco. The $28 million production concerns the efforts of developers, missionaries, and soldiers-of-fortune to pressure the Indians out of the rain forest. Tom's plane had barely landed in Brazil before he was asked by Paramount to co-star with Corbin Bernsen in a sequel to MAJOR LEAGUE, tentatively scheduled to be released in 1992.

Tom was among the stars who turned down the lead in the film version of THE FRONT RUNNER, based on Patricia Nell Warren's 1974 novel of a gay relationship, which may never see the light of day. He has admitted to writing a script about the Irish rebellion of 1920, which "is a fascinating period and place for me. I guess if I weren't an actor, I'd be a history professor." He stated that he had included a part in it for himself, "the bad guy or at least the insensitive one." His wife, Lisa, is a real estate salesperson near their home in South Carolina, where Tom prefers to live. "Sometimes I get off the plane in Savannah and then I drive 40 miles through the country and by the time I get there it's aaahhh? Great! My fantasy is just staying at home. That's where I go on my vacation." Although he has never revealed the exact location, it is thought that his home is in the area of Buford, South Carolina, the locale of THE BIG CHILL. One thing he has learned in his career to date is to "keep my mouth shut when dealing with reporters." If he had his life to live over, "I wouldn't be an actor. This life is too disruptive and manic, with crazy time schedules and no privacy. It's not a normal way to live."

Filmography

Johnny, We Hardly Knew Ye (NBC-TV, 1/27/77)

The Sentinel (Univ, 1977)

Looking for Mr. Goodbar (Par, 1977)

Flesh and Blood (CBS-TV, 10/14/79; 10/16/79)

In Praise of Older Women (Avco Emb, 1979)

Butch and Sundance: The Early Years (20th–Fox, 1979)

The Dogs of War (UA, 1980)

Beyond the Door [Oltre la Porta/Beyond Obsession] (Film Ventures International, 1982)

The Big Chill (Col, 1983)

Eddie and the Cruisers (Emb, 1983)

Fear City (Zupnik–Curtis, 1985)

Rustlers' Rhapsody (Par, 1985)

Platoon (Orion, 1986)

Someone to Watch over Me (Col, 1987)

Dear America: Letters Home from Vietnam (HBO–Couturie, 1987) (voice only)

Shoot to Kill (BV, 1988)

Betrayed (MGM/UA, 1988)

Last Rites (MGM/UA, 1988)

Major League (Par, 1989)

Born on the Fourth of July (Univ, 1989)

Love at Large (Orion, 1990)

The Field (Avenue, 1990)

Future Releases

Shattered (MGM–Pathe, 1991)

At Play in the Fields of the Lord (1991)

Television Series

One Life to Live (ABC, 1975–76)

If Tomorrow Comes (CBS, 3/16/86–3/18/86) [miniseries]

CANDICE BERGEN

"It takes a long time to become a person. Longer than they tell you. Longer than I thought. I am grateful for my past; it has given me the present. I want to do well by the future."
—from *Knock Wood* (1984) by Candice Bergen

IN THE MID-1960s CANDICE BERGEN, THE EX–IVY LEAGUE COLLEGE student daughter of a show business celebrity, emerged as a successful model, a jet set devotee, a dilettante motion picture performer, and a far-reaching advocate of contemporary causes. As in the case of the slightly older Ali MacGraw, critics vied with each other to write contemptuous bon mots about the state of Bergen's nonacting on camera. Seemingly immune to the jibes, Candice professed that photojournalism was her true artistic calling; she made films only for the money. At the time, her slapdash forays into motion pictures appeared to be a shameful waste of time for one so beautiful and so intelligent, and for an individual who had inherited so many enviable entrees into the entertainment business. However, periodically, Candice surprised everyone by turning in a respectable performance, notably in CARNAL KNOWLEDGE (1971) and STARTING OVER (1979).

By 1980, having reached early middle age and now taking a more mature approach to life, she focused on enhancing her private life (marriage, motherhood) and shaping a new career for herself. She emerged late in the decade as the darling of the media and the public—the bright, confident star of a hit TV comedy series, "Murphy Brown." It was a dramatically long path from her childhood, when she had had to play second fiddle to her father's tool-in-trade, the adored dummy Charlie McCarthy.

Candice Bergen was born on Thursday, May 9, 1946, in Beverly Hills, California, the daughter of ventriloquist Edgar Bergen and former model Frances Westerman. Edgar, of Swedish ancestry (his actual surname was Berggren), had grown up on a farm in Michigan. He later used his skill at "throwing voices" to develop a show business career, first on the stage and then, beginning in 1936, on radio as the star of the popular "The Chase and Sanborn Hour." With his dummy stooge—the irrepressible, wisecracking Charlie McCarthy—he gained tremendous success on the airwaves (and in several motion pictures), a national prominence which peaked in the 1930s and 1940s. In June 1945, Bergen and Frances Westerman (known professionally as Frances Westcott) married. It was the first marriage for each; he was forty-two, she was twenty.

When Candice (known for many years as Candy) was born, newspapers nationwide made much of the fact that the beloved Charlie McCarthy now had a baby sister. Indeed, for many years there was an actual rivalry between Candice and her father's wooden alter ego, the latter having his own room (bigger than hers) at the Bergens' Bel Air estate, Bella Vista, and being far more famous than she was. Later, Candice would recall times when the moody, reserved Bergen would place both of his "offspring" on his knees and squeeze their necks, doing the talking for each of them. With such a prominent father and "brother," it was only natural that Candy's playmates as a youngster should include the children of celebrities (Judy Garland's daughter Liza Minnelli; Dorothy Lamour's son Richard), that the visiting Santa Claus at Bella Vista one year might be David Niven and the next Charlton Heston, and that, for amusement, Candy would visit "Uncle" Walt Disney for a ride on his famous miniature train, which puffed through the filmmaker's back yard.

In 1952 Candice made her film debut in a Columbia Pictures short subject, YOUNG HOLLYWOOD, and that Christmas she made her bow on her father's radio show. Carefully coached by Edgar, she was instructed to allow appropriate pauses for the laughs, all of which were allotted to her nemesis, the monocled Charlie McCarthy. It was a telling experience for Candice, who would admit later, "I guess that was the beginning of my frustration at not being able to do comedy." Later, under her father's guidance, she learned to throw her voice too, but instead of employing the art professionally, she played pranks on her peers and sometimes on her teachers.

As a young Hollywood princess, Candice attended the prestigious Westlake School for Girls in nearby Holmby Hills, where, according to her, "The only poor people we knew were our teachers." At the age of fourteen, she sensed that her burgeoning social life was getting out of hand, and she begged her parents to allow her to join a young girlfriend at an expensive boarding school in Switzerland. (Another account states that her parents, anxious to keep their very independent daughter under more control, made the decision.) Candice was enrolled at the Montesano School in Gstaad, Switzerland, where she discovered quickly, "If I thought life was fast at home, here it made your head spin." When her parents visited her that Christmas (1960), the shocked Mrs. Bergen queried, "Candy, is that *all* you've learned here in three months. Smoking and drinking and bleaching your hair?" (She had also improved her French accent and her skiing.) By that spring, Candy had returned to California and to local schooling. That fall (October 12, 1961), Mrs. Bergen gave birth to a son, Kris, a real-life brother with whom Candice could relate and for whom she felt no jealousy. (As an adult, Kris would become a film editor.)

Initially it was thought that after high school Candice would attend Northwestern University in Evanston, Illinois, from which Edgar Bergen had graduated. However, she did not want to follow in his footsteps and be compared constantly to him. Instead, in browsing through an issue of *Holiday* magazine that featured a spread on Ivy League schools, she became fascinated with the University of Pennsylvania, a very traditional school whose tree-lined campus was situated in the midst of Philadelphia. Scarcely had she enrolled there, in the fall of 1963, than she was chosen Homecoming Queen and escorted onto the football field at halftime. The next day, the *Philadelphia Inquirer* published a photograph of her captioned, "Charlie's Sister Homecoming Queen—No Dummy She."

Despite or because of her show business background, Candice had no real interest in pursuing an acting career, opting instead for journalism. Attracted to photojournalism in particular, her role model was Margaret Bourke-White. One of Candice's campus friends was Mary Ellen Mark, an ardent photographer and graduate student who taught Bergen a great deal about the art of photography. However, with her pedigree, Candice could not entirely escape show business. On one trip home to California she appeared on the TV variety show "The Hollywood Palace," in a walk-on as part of her father's skit with Charlie McCarthy. On campus, she appeared in a student production of Tennessee Williams's *Summer and Smoke*, cast against type as the spinsterish Alma. For her surprisingly professional performance she received the school's award for Best Actress.

By the end of her sophomore year at college, Candy had grown bored and was making frequent trips to New York City. There, being tall (5' 8"), lithe, and blonde, and by using the luster of her family name, she quickly found modeling assignments, including posing for a national campaign for Revlon cosmetic products. By her junior year at school, Bergen was a student almost in name only, and she failed several classes. This led the University's Executive Committee to drop her from its rolls.

Slightly humbled but undaunted, Candice immediately accepted a role offered her by director Sidney Lumet in THE GROUP (1966). The film was based on Mary McCarthy's best-selling novel about eight Vassar graduates and how they fare during the Depression. In a cast of professionals (including Joan Hackett and Shirley Knight), Candice was cast as a chic lesbian. This offbeat role, plus being Edgar Bergen's daughter, got Candice the major share of the movie's publicity, which annoyed both her show business peers and film critics. This antipathy was to last for years, unhelped by Bergen's then unprofessional attitude (she insisted she was dabbling in films only to earn money to support her photojournalism career) or her rash statements. (She told *Time* magazine that "playing the part of a lesbian was the kind of rebellious gesture I enjoyed then.") When the Manhattan-filmed THE GROUP opened, most of the cast received complimentary reviews. However, Candice, acknowledged to be coolly beautiful (in the Grace Kelly tradition), was severely criticized for her wooden characterization as the haughty Lakey. Pauline Kael (in *Life* magazine) assessed, "She doesn't know how to move, she cannot say her lines." Kael added that Candice's only flair for acting was in her nostrils.

After making THE GROUP, the now New York–based Candice went off on a European lark with a thirty-seven-year-old Austrian count with whom she was involved briefly. Meanwhile, through the publicity generated by THE GROUP, Candice came to the attention of Oscar-winning filmmaker Robert Wise. He hired her to play a missionary schoolteacher romanced by a U.S. Naval machinist's mate (Steve McQueen) in THE SAND PEBBLES (1966). This epic of political/military turmoil in 1926 China was shot largely in Taiwan. When released, the grossly overlong motion picture (198 minutes) was praised more for its cinematography and music score than for its storyline or performances. While Bosley Crowther (*New York Times*) perceived Candice to be "beautiful and flawless," the majority agreed with William Wolf (*Cue* magazine), who determined that her appearance had in it "nothing resembling acting." In April 1967 Candice made her professional stage debut co-starring with Edgar Bergen (playing her father) in the comedy *Sabrina Fair* at the Westbury Music Fair in Long Island, New York.

During the shooting of THE GROUP, Candice had written an article for *Esquire* magazine about the making of the movie. This led to other such assignments, which were likely obtained more through her celebrity name than for her journalistic experience. However, they satisfied her need to do something more meaningful than posing in front of a camera. Actually, she much preferred to be on the other side of the lens. She would say later, "I took my camera and photographed everything. I found that it was a great way of disappearing and getting to know other people."

After THE SAND PEBBLES, she visited a friend in Rhodesia and then went on to South Africa to research articles for *Esquire* and *Vogue*. On this trek, she encountered Greek filmmaker Michael Cacoyannis who, having initially wanted Julie Christie for his next film, hired Candice to co-star in THE DAY THE FISH CAME OUT (1967). The bizarre picture, with strong homosexual overtones, was a "comedy" based on an actual occurrence in the 1960s when the U.S. Air Force lost two atomic bombs off the coast of Spain. Candice accepted the part of an anthropologist because it meant a free visit to Greece. Next, she went to Paris where Claude Lelouch hired her to fill in (again) for Julie Christie, this time as part of a love triangle in VIVRE POUR VIVRE [LIVE FOR LIFE] (1967). The romantic drama starred Yves Montand and allowed Bergen to journey to locations in East Africa and Amsterdam, as well as to Paris and New York City. In the poorly received THE MAGUS (1968), based on John Fowles's enigmatic novel and starring Anthony Quinn and Michael Caine, she played a patrician nymphomaniac schizophrenic. What attracted her to the project was the on-location shooting in Majorca.

During this phase of casual film-making, Candice continued writing articles and doing photo essays for *Esquire, Vogue, Cosmopolitan,* and other magazines. She still insisted that she had no real desire to be a performer: "It's not what I am or want to be. It's so contrary to what makes me happy, and I honestly don't know what I'm doing. I'm not an actress." Also in this period, her play *The Freezer* appeared in the collection *The Best Short Plays of 1968.*

Candice Bergen in THE MAGUS (1968).

After nearly two years abroad as part of the jet set, Candice returned to the United States in time to join the counter-culture society so prevalent on the West Coast. Her live-in romance at the time was Terry Melcher, the record producer son of Doris Day, who introduced her to revolutionist Huey Lewis and others. She rebelled against her family's tradition of Goldwater Republicanism and became involved in several social/political causes. Meanwhile, after Melcher's stepfather, film producer Marty Melcher, died in April 1968, Terry determined to take responsibility for helping to settle the huge debts Marty had left Doris Day. Therefore, he and Candice eventually moved out of the Hollywood Hills home they were sharing, relocating to Day's Malibu beach house. Thereafter, director Roman Polanski and actress Sharon Tate moved into the hill home, where, on August 9, 1969, Tate and several others were murdered by Charles Manson and his family of disciples. (Allegedly, that night Manson and his followers had been searching for Terry Melcher, whom he considered an enemy.)

After two years away from filmmaking, Candice had three 1970 releases. She went to Rome for the big-budgeted THE ADVENTURERS, based on Harold Robbins's popular trash novel. In dismissing this "classic monument to bad taste," *Variety* credited Candice as "the only principal to salvage anything from the film, playing a fabulously wealthy girl who marries the hero [Fakim Fehmiu], but loses their baby in a swing accident, becomes barren, and eventually turns lesbian." She went to Oregon to shoot GETTING STRAIGHT, a comedy about college protest. For a change, she was pleased with her assignment, which allowed her, as a student activist, to perform "in a reasonably honest context." Establishment critics were put off by this exploitative film, which co-starred Elliott Gould as a freewheeling, radical professor. For SOLDIER BLUE, set in the 1860s West, she was a tough easterner captured by the Cheyenne Indians and helped to safety by a soldier (Peter Strauss). While this feature was promoted for (but equally criticized for) its excessive violence, Candice received a few respectful reviews. Roger Greenspan (*New York Times*) acknowledged that she had "begun developing a film personality of grace, power, and intelligence." Bergen looks back on the R-rated SOLDIER BLUE with a mixture of horror (for its gratuitous violence) and amusement (she had to wear specially constructed falsies for her role as the buxom heroine).

It was in this period that Bergen received much attention for participating in a sleep-in at the former Alcatraz Prison to protest the predicament of American Indians. She was also a pro-abortion advocate, a board member of Friends of the Earth, and campaigned for anti–Vietnam War candidates.

Candice flew to Spain to co-star in the throwaway film THE HUNTING PARTY (1971), appearing as the wife of a Texas cattleman (Gene Hackman) who is kidnapped by a bandit chief (Oliver Reed) with whom she falls in love. Much more important to her career was a featured role in Mike Nichols's controversial CARNAL KNOWLEDGE (1971). In this study of two college pals (Jack Nicholson and Art Garfunkel) who experience assorted amatory relationships with the opposite sex from the repressive 1950s through the free-loving 1960s, she was the girl Garfunkel beds not knowing that she has already been seduced by his Amherst College roommate (Nicholson). Although Ann-Margret rightly received most of the critical attention for her surprisingly effective performance, Bergen's work did not go unnoticed. Vincent Canby (*New York Times*) observed, "Candice Bergen projects so much intelligence, humor, and feeling that the time has come to stop worrying about whether or not she's a good actress." T. R. BASKIN (1971) gave Bergen her first starring role, as a small town young woman seeking independence, romance, and excitement in Chicago. Most reviewers found the contrived yarn awful, with judgment on Bergen's performance mixed: "Ludicrously bad" (Pauline Kael, *The New Yorker* magazine); "[has] moments of sensitivity and deep emotion" (Judith Crist, *New York* magazine).

Then, for the next three years, she abandoned filmmaking, returning to her career as a freelance photojournalist. As such, she interviewed film celebrities (Paul Newman, Lee Marvin, Charles Chaplin) and international figures (Ethiopia's ruler Haile Selassie, animal behaviorist Jane Goodall), and prepared sociological photo essays (on, for example, the Masai tribe of Kenya). With her latest romantic interest, film producer Bert Schneider, she embarked on a three-and-a-half-week trek to the People's Republic of China.

Bergen returned to movies with the London-filmed 11 HARROWHOUSE (1974), in which she played a zany heiress involved in a diamond heist. For the preposterously cast but mildly popular THE WIND AND THE LION (1975), shot in Almería, Spain, she was the widow of an American diplomat kidnapped by a Berber chief (Sean Connery) and rescued by Theodore Roosevelt (Brian Keith). In the Western BITE THE BULLET (1975), lensed in New Mexico, she performed as an ex-prostitute who is one of several participants in a 700-mile horse race marathon. It was working with such accomplished co-players as Gene Hackman in BITE THE BULLET that convinced Bergen that she should take her craft more seriously. No longer wisecracking about moviemaking, she became a respectful pal of Hackman's during their third co-starring vehicle, THE DOMINO PRINCIPLE (1977). In this unsuccessful caper movie, she wore a brown wig and played a down-to-earth woman (leading some critics to note that she resembled a new generation's Shelley Winters).

Meanwhile, she pursued her other creative outlets. In 1975 she reported on her White House visit with President and Mrs. Gerald Ford for the *Ladies' Home Journal* and for the same magazine wrote a short story, "Dummy." She spent a week appearing on ABC-TV's news show "A.M. America." She was equally poised in her freelance assignments as a photojournalist for NBC-TV's "Today Show," in which she crisscrossed the country preparing photo layouts that she enhanced with verbal commentary. (She later rejected a co-hosting position on this news magazine program.) During the 1975–1976 premiere season of NBC-TV's late night comedy program "Saturday Night Live," Candice performed as occasional host, displaying a flair for comedy. Having now reached thirty, she displayed a new maturity: "My life didn't have a center, and I finally realized I was lonely." A very sobering experience was the death (on September 30, 1978) of her father, Edgar Bergen, at the age of seventy-five.

Candice won out over Kathleen Turner to play opposite Ryan O'Neal in OLIVER'S STORY (1978), a sappy sequel to LOVE STORY (1970). Much more meaningful to Bergen, if not to reviewers or to filmgoers, was her appearance in Lina Wertmuller's THE END OF THE WORLD IN OUR USUAL BED IN A NIGHT FULL OF RAIN (1978). She was cast as an American photographer with feminist leanings wed to a Communist Catholic journalist

(Giancarlo Giannini) in a marriage that is going sour. By studying Berlitz tapes, she learned Italian sufficiently well to dub her own voice for the Italian-language version of this drama.

The prophetically titled STARTING OVER (1979) marked the turning point in Candice's acting career. She had originally wanted to play the role of Burt Reynolds's sympathetic new love interest (a part that went to then more popular Jill Clayburgh). Instead, Bergen was hired as Reynolds's ex-wife, an acerbic songwriter (who has a penchant for singing off key). David Denby (*New York* magazine) observed of Bergen's bright performance: "She seems finally to have understood what people have always resented in her—the glacé perfection—and she parodies herself mercilessly." For her effective characterization in STARTING OVER, Bergen was nominated for an Academy Award. However, she lost the Best Supporting Actress Oscar to Meryl Streep (KRAMER VS. KRAMER).

Now bound to her acting craft, Candice abandoned professional photography because she lacked the same dedication as her peers. In 1977, in Connecticut, she had first met French filmmaker Louis Malle, noted for such international successes as LES AMANTS [THE LOVERS] (1958), LE SOUFFLE AU COEUR [MURMUR OF THE HEART] (1971), and LACOMBE LUCIEN (1974). He was then in the United States preparing to film PRETTY BABY (1978) with Susan Sarandon and Brooke Shields. In 1980, Malle, who had just directed Burt Lancaster and Susan Sarandon in ATLANTIC CITY, met Candice again over a four-hour lunch at New York City's Russian Tea Room. At the time, they were each confirmed bachelors. He had been divorced years before and more recently had had two children by two different women. A romance quickly developed between Candice and Malle, and they were married on September 27, 1980, at his home in the southwest of France. She was thirty-four, he was forty-eight. They soon developed a routine of her spending summers in France, reuniting at other times of the year in New York City (where she owned a spacious Central Park South duplex apartment) or, if she was working in Hollywood and he was free, being together in Los Angeles.

Because of her preoccupation with her marriage, Candice's acting career became even more secondary in the 1980s. She joined with Jacqueline Bisset in a lively remake of OLD ACQUAINTANCE (1943) entitled RICH AND FAMOUS (1981). Bisset (in Bette Davis's old part) played the thoughtful writer, while Candice, as the magnolia-accented Merry Nole Blake (first played on screen by Miriam Hopkins), blithely consumed her husband, literary career, Malibu, New York City, the publishing industry, and her decades-old friendship with Bisset. *People* magazine noted of scene-stealing Candice, "Bergen has rarely been this good. STARTING OVER suggested she had hidden comic resources; RICH AND FAMOUS confirms it." Fifteen years before, her SAND PEBBLES co-star Richard Attenborough (with whom she also worked in 11 HARROWHOUSE) had asked her to play Margaret Bourke-White in his pending project GANDHI. It was not until the 1980s that he was able to finance the project, and Bergen readily agreed to impersonate the American photojournalist in the 1982 Academy Award–winning drama starring Ben Kingsley as Mahatma Gandhi.

For several years, Bergen had been working on her autobiography, *Knock Wood*, which was published in 1984 to both critical and reader enthusiasm. For Candice it was a therapeutic experience, laying to rest many ghosts of her past. She made her Broadway stage debut in December 1984 when, for two weeks at the Ethel Barrymore Theatre, she took over the role of Darlene (originated by Sigourney Weaver) in the Mike Nichols–directed comedy *Hurlyburly*. In the Burt Reynolds–helmed fiasco STICK (1985; made for 1984 release), a distortion of an Elmore Leonard underworld novel, Bergen was wasted as Reynolds's improbable love interest. Frankly admitting that she had been a snob about doing commercial TV, Candice made her acting debut in the medium in the CBS-TV movie ARTHUR THE KING (April 26, 1985; filmed in late 1982). She appeared as a most unprettified Morgan Le Fey to Malcolm McDowell's King Arthur. She next accepted the role of Elaine Conti, the long-suffering wife of a movie star (Steve Forrest) attempting a comeback in "Hollywood Wives" (1985). This ABC-TV miniseries was based on Jackie Collins's trashy best-seller. Looking ill at ease, Candice brought dignity to her assignment, but did not seem to be having fun (as did such co-stars as Stefanie Powers, Angie Dickinson, and Suzanne Somers). Much more substantial was her performance in MURDER: BY REASON OF INSANITY (October 1, 1985). This CBS-TV movie was based on the true story of a Polish couple (Bergen, Jurgen Prochnow), both engineers, who immigrate to the United States in the late 1960s. When his consulting firm fails, she supports the family. After their divorce, the crazed ex-husband threatens publicly to kill her and does so brutally. John J. O'Connor (*New York Times*) endorsed, "The gifted Miss Bergen gives a beautifully restrained performance as Ewa, capturing fully the kind of woman whose charm is always a bit inhibited, thin-lipped, shy." A month later (November 8, 1985), Candice gave birth to a daughter whom the Malles named Chloe.

Preoccupied as a new mother, it was two years before Candice returned to acting. In the CBS-TV movie MAYFLOWER MADAM (November 15, 1987) she played Sydney Biddle Barrows, the real-life New York City blue-blood who had operated one of Manhattan's more successful call girl services. *TV Guide* magazine noted, "Candice Bergen makes a classy 'Mayflower Madam' in this trashy TV movie." Eight days later (November 23, 1987), Candice appeared in "Moving Day," one of six segments in PBS-TV's "Trying Times" series. Within the thirty-minute comedy, her character moves to Albuquerque after twenty years in Vancouver and finds herself at the center of a maelstrom of eccentricity created by her family. *Variety* lauded, "Bergen, fresh from her 'Mayflower Madam' misadventure, turns in a quality performance."

In retrospect, it seems nearly impossible that anybody else could have starred in the CBS-TV sitcom "Murphy Brown." But at the time, it was a tough sell to convince the series's executive producers (Diane English, Joel Shukovsky), let alone the network, that Candice, whose most recent TV credits were in drama, could handle the focal role. The part called for her to be a peppery but lovable TV anchorwoman, a single person who is a sharpshooter with biting one-liners. (The character is based on such TV news personalities as Diane Sawyer and Linda Ellerbee.) After much effort on her part, Bergen was hired to star in the series, which debuted on November 14, 1988. In the opening installment,

Murphy, fresh from a month's stay at the Betty Ford Clinic for substance abuse, returns to her Washington, D.C.–based TV news magazine show ("F.Y.I."). There, she finds not only a new twenty-five-year-old executive producer (Grant Shaud) in power, but learns that she must share the on-camera limelight with a former Miss America (Faith Ford), as well as with the other program regulars: stuffy anchor Jim Dial (Charles Kimbrough) and overly earnest reporter Frank Fontana (Joe Regalbuto). The program was an immediate hit with viewers and critics alike and soon became a programming mainstay of third-place network CBS. Bergen said of her career-rejuvenating role, "It feels like they've set me free. I finally can shed the glacial identity that my looks steered me toward. There's nothing I wouldn't do for a laugh. I'm not afraid of making a fool of myself." In September 1989 Candice won an Emmy as best actress in a comedy series. Clutching her award, she said, "I was dying for this! I wanted it badly."

During its second season, "Murphy Brown" continued to be highly rated, which resulted in the increasingly high profile of its striking star. With a successful series to her credit, Bergen and Malle purchased (for $1,295,000) a 3,000-foot one-story colonial-style home in the Beverly Hills Post Office area. (As a child, she had lived nearby in the Bergens' walled hacienda overlooking the Beverly Hills hotel.) In December 1989 she was on the cover of *Playboy* magazine, which featured a lengthy coming-of-age interview with her. That same month she was among the winners of the 49th Annual Golden Apple Awards, presented by the Hollywood Women's Press Club, sharing honors with Billy Crystal and Meg Ryan, among others. For the concluding "Murphy Brown" episode (May 21, 1990) of the second season, Candice's mother, Frances (who had had a brief role in "Hollywood Wives"), made a guest appearance. At the 42nd annual Emmy Awards on September 16, 1990, Bergen won her second consecutive Emmy Award as lead actress in a comedy series for her characterization in "Murphy Brown." Candice said as she accepted the trophy, "'Murphy Brown' is one of the happiest and most gratifying professional experiences of my life." The successful show's third season, beginning on September 17, 1990, found Candice's Murphy Brown as feisty, cranky, and lovable as ever. Miles Beller (*Hollywood Reporter*) decided, "The 'Brown' gang hits home for fall '90 with a good, strong opener." *Daily Variety* agreed that even in its third season, this "freshly conceived" and "deftly executed" sitcom "offers viewers something they can look forward to week after week." As part of the ongoing "Murphy Brown" phenomenon, an original television soundtrack album (*The Sounds of Murphy Brown*) was released, featuring cast members Bergen, Joe Regalbuto, and Grant Shaud singing "You Keep Me Hangin' On," and Robert S. Alley and Irby B. Brown authored *Murphy Brown: Anatomy of a Sitcom* (1990), in which they claimed that this half-hour TV show is a "classic in the making." Meanwhile, in the fall of 1990 she became the corporate spokesperson for the long-distance company US Sprint.

Candice is now at the peak of her acting career; her new success is the result of her talent and *not* her heritage or her looks. She has come to terms with herself over her spoiled princess childhood, her early dabbling in feature films, and her more recent roles as a wife and mother. However, she has not lost her characteristic outspokenness and candor. She assesses today's entertainment industry: "The new Hollywood is so much about money and nothing else . . . it's just full of little tiny cutthroats in little tiny suits and they're really arrogant little guys and women, all-knowing and very humorless." Of her old self: "it's hard to break away from that image from twenty years ago, but I don't think I present myself any longer as a Scandinavian snow queen. Some of it was unconscious. . . . It's not behavior I'm proud of." Of her future: "getting older means being responsible. You acquire a sense of responsibility for your own behavior and you don't pass it off on other people—on your parents, your environment. . . . You should behave honorably. It's very important to me. It is *not* what Hollywood is about."

Filmography

Young Hollywood (Col, 1952) (s)
The Group (UA, 1966)
The Sand Pebbles (20th–Fox, 1966)
The Day the Fish Came Out (20th–Fox, 1967)
Live for Life [Vivre pour Vivre] (UA, 1967)
The Magus (20th–Fox, 1968)
The Adventurers (Par, 1970)
Getting Straight (Col, 1970)
Soldier Blue (Avco Emb, 1970)
The Hunting Party (UA, 1971)
Carnal Knowledge (Avco Emb, 1971)
T. R. Baskin (Par, 1971)
11 Harrowhouse (20th–Fox, 1974)
The Wind and the Lion (UA, 1975)

Bite the Bullet (Col, 1975)
The Domino Principle (Avco Emb, 1977)
Oliver's Story (Par, 1978)
The End of the World in Our Usual Bed in a
    Night Full of Rain (WB, 1978)
Starting Over (Par, 1979)
Rich and Famous (MGM/UA, 1981)
Gandhi (Col, 1982)
Arthur the King (CBS-TV, 4/26/85)
Murder: By Reason of Insanity (CBS-TV,
    10/1/85)
Stick (Univ, 1985)
Mayflower Madam (CBS-TV, 11/15/87)

Television Series

Hollywood Wives (ABC, 2/17/85–2/19/85)
    [miniseries]

Murphy Brown (CBS, 1988–)

Broadway Shows

Hurlyburly (1984) (replacement)

Album Discography

Getting Straight (Colgems COSO-5010) [ST]

The Sounds of Murphy Brown (MCA-10063)
    [ST-TV]

BRUCE BOXLEITNER

"When it all comes down to it, what am I in this business for? . . .
I want recognition. I'd like to experience it. . . . Fame is a lure."
— *TV Guide* magazine, February 5, 1983

AMIABLE, HANDSOME BRUCE BOXLEITNER IS A STAUNCH YANKEE DOO-
dle man, an American patriot in the old-fashioned mold. The Old West is the major study
of his life, with a minor in the history of the Civil War. When writer Chris Barnett (*Los
Angeles Times*) visited the Boxleitner ranch in southern California's San Fernando Valley
to interview Bruce for the newspaper's "Home Section," Barnett found the interior of
Bruce's house to replicate the lifestyle of Cheyenne, Wyoming, circa 1872, with a two-foot
sculpture of John Wayne in a corner of the living room. "I wasn't a fan of Wayne's
politics," Bruce told Barnett, "but he represented a kind of America, a hero, and we'll
never have that kind of hero again." Boxleitner collects western antiques, American Indian
art, any such artifact dating from long ago. At work, he has been recognized as a diligent,
reliable performer in television series, miniseries, and made-for-television movies—so
many, in fact, that he may be considered a crown prince of the industry, along with Perry
King. At a quick glance, Bruce may be confused with Hart Bochner or Barry Bostwick, but
place their photographs side by side and the differences are apparent. Held in high esteem
by Hollywood producers, writers, and actors, Bruce was described by one TV critic as
having "old-fashioned star appeal." The critic continued, "I could see him in the studio
days being groomed for romantic leads."

Bruce Boxleitner was born on Friday, May 12, 1950, in Elgin, Illinois, about forty
miles northwest of Chicago where his father, of German ancestry, was a certified public
accountant. His birth was followed in quick succession by that of three sisters. Bruce spent
a great deal of his time, including all of his summers, living with his paternal grandparents
on their farm outside of Elgin. His doting grandfather provided him with his own pony,
but young Bruce had to work too, by rounding up the cows twice a day at milking time.
Saturday afternoons were spent at the local movie theater—the westerns of John Wayne
and Gary Cooper were his favorites—while every Saturday night was devoted to watching
his television hero, Marshall Dillon (James Arness), harness law and order in 1880s Dodge
City, Kansas, in "Gunsmoke."

In both grade and high school, Bruce was a poor student. His attention span was
limited because of his dreams, which were realized in his sophomore year of high school
when he understudied as Henry Higgins in the school production of *My Fair Lady*; he was

the first 2nd-year pupil ever chosen to be part of a school play. After that, his focus on academics was even more abstract. In his senior year, he was selected to star in *A Man for All Seasons*. The experience convinced him that acting was to be his profession.

After graduating from high school in 1968, he commuted to Chicago where he studied not only acting, but also set design and lighting, at the Goodman Theatre. After three years, he starred in an avant-garde play (*Status Quo Vadis*) that was a hit in Chicago, but which subsequently closed after only one performance (February 18, 1973) in New York City. Bruce was cast as a brash young man from the wrong side of the tracks who is used and discarded by a wealthy young woman (Gail Strickland). (Also in the aborted Broadway production was Ted Danson.) Too impatient to devote years to struggling for recognition on the New York stage, Bruce went to Los Angeles later in 1973. His 6' 2" height, green eyes, sandy hair, and strong chin brought him instant work; walk-on television parts in "Hawaii Five-O" (CBS) and "Police Woman" (NBC) and five lines of dialogue in "The Mary Tyler Moore Show" (CBS) afforded him credentials for a Screen Actors Guild union card. Besides playing a disreputable character on "Baretta" (ABC), he won a small role in one of the last episodes (March 31, 1975) of "Gunsmoke" (CBS), wearing, of course, old western gear. The youth who had idolized James Arness not only had the opportunity to meet him, but also to work with him, an experience he described as "one of my biggest thrills." Boxleitner had supporting parts in the telefeatures THE CHADWICK FAMILY (April 17, 1974), starring Fred MacMurray, and A CRY FOR HELP (February 2, 1975) and then had a supporting role as Bobby Joe in his debut feature film, SIX-PACK ANNIE, released in December 1975. He briefly considered changing his surname to something more American, like Wayne (Bruce Wayne!) or Flynn, but "To tell you the truth, my grandfather was still alive—and he'd never have understood why I would be ashamed of my name."

Bruce's big show business break came with a 150-minute western movie for television, THE MACAHANS, telecast on ABC on January 19, 1976. Recommended, partly because of his height, by James Arness, he played Seth Macahan, the trouble-prone nephew of Zeth Macahan (Arness), a mountain scout who leads members of his family westward in 1860 to avoid the Civil War. In favorably reviewing the telefeature, *Variety* reported, "Boxleitner took a while to get through to the viewer, but by the end had etched a role capable of generating considerable viewer rapport." Also in the cast was Kathryn Holcomb who played Bruce's sister Laura and with whom he began a live-in relationship.

Out of western attire and with his long hair parted in the center, he was a psycho in the telefeature KISS ME, KILL ME (May 28, 1976) and a mentally disturbed Houston Astro baseball team reject in the ABC-TV movie MURDER AT THE WORLD SERIES (March 20, 1977). In May 1977 Bruce and Kathryn Holcomb, called "Kitty" by friends, were married. They agreed that she would eventually give up her career to be a full-time mother to the children they planned to have and that together they would concentrate on promoting his career. They purchased a ranch-style home situated on over an acre of land in the town of Hidden Hills in the San Fernando Valley where they each bought a horse,

"55" for him and "Rosie" for her, and slowly began to collect items depicting the Old West.

On February 12, 1978, ABC-TV's "How the West Was Won," adapted from THE MACAHANS and from the 1962 star-laden motion picture, premiered as a weekly Sunday night series, having already been a popular miniseries in February 1977. John Wayne, who had been in the MGM feature film, visited one of the location sites of the teleseries, thus making another of Bruce's dreams come true. The hour program ran into August 1978, but returned in January 1979 with eleven new two-hour segments. The final showing took place on April 23, 1979. Meanwhile, on break from "How the West Was Won," Bruce co-starred opposite Suzanne Somers in HAPPILY EVER AFTER (September 5, 1978). During the filming of this CBS-TV movie, Jay Bernstein, carrying a walking stick, was on the set as Somers's personal manager/promoter. Bruce, realizing he needed someone to promote him professionally, was impressed with this man and thought, "If only one day I could get somebody like that." NBC-TV's "The Last Convertible" (1979), a six-hour miniseries adaptation of Anton Myrer's novel, shown in three parts, traced the lives of five Harvard men (Perry King, Bruce, Edward Albert, John Shea, Michael Nouri) from 1940 to 1969 when they attend their twenty-fifth class reunion.

In 1980 Bruce and Kitty became parents for the first time with the birth of son Sam, at which time Kitty retired from acting. Their second son, Lee Davis, was born on November 16, 1985.

Also in 1980 Bruce was Vern Tyree in WILD TIMES, a two-part western adventure made for television syndication, which co-starred veteran actor Ben Johnson, with whom Boxleitner began a long friendship. Bruce then appeared in his second feature film, THE BALTIMORE BULLET (1980), receiving third billing, after James Coburn and Omar Sharif. Next he co-starred as Billy Montana in KENNY ROGERS AS "THE GAMBLER," a CBS-TV movie shown on April 8, 1980, which was one of the highest-rated shows ever, due to the popularity of singer Rogers.

"She turned the love of brother for brother, father for son, into hate" read the *TV Guide* magazine ad for the initial showing of the eight-hour miniseries "John Steinbeck's 'East of Eden,'" a more complete version of the Steinbeck novel (1951) than the 1955 Warner Bros. feature. Bruce appeared only in Part One, shown in three hours on February 8, 1981, as Charles Trask, brother of Adam Trask (Timothy Bottoms). Both of them are beguiled and seduced by a malevolent teenager (Jane Seymour) who arrives at their home. Because Charles is too much like her, she weds Adam, who takes her to California where she makes his life miserable during the remaining two segments of the miniseries. The third installment, shown on November 11, 1988, had a Neilsen rating of 25.7, making it the sixteenth most popular broadcast of all time. This hit was followed by ABC-TV's FLY AWAY HOME (September 18, 1981), with Bruce as a news cameraman in Vietnam. In his third theatrical film, TRON (1982), starring Jeff Bridges, Boxleitner had the title role. The overly ambitious science fiction entry, filled with expensive special effects, failed to find its niche at the box office.

Bruce disliked socializing in Hollywood, much preferring to vanish into the mountains or elsewhere. However, his wife insisted that they attend an important industry party in Malibu in 1981 where she knew he would gain visibility. He was the first to admit that few in Hollywood knew his name, let alone were able to pronounce it. One casting agent had assessed, "If you had a Christmas parade on Hollywood Boulevard, you'd have to hang a sign around his neck." Both he and Kitty believed that although he was working regularly, he was not gaining any career momentum. At the Malibu gathering, he was introduced to Jay Bernstein, who, at this time, promoted/represented mostly blonde female performers such as Farrah Fawcett. The next day, Bruce met with Bernstein and Larry Thompson, a prominent entertainment attorney/producer and Bernstein's partner. A deal was struck whereby they would supervise Bruce's career. In the meantime, ABC-TV offered Boxleitner the teleseries "Tales of the Gold Monkey," but he turned it down because of his commitment to Bernstein and Thompson. Stephen Collins inherited the series, which lasted one season (1982–1983).

Nine months later, Bruce starred in his own rival CBS-TV series, "Bring 'Em Back Alive," lightly and loosely based on the adventures of wild animal hunter Frank Buck, which premiered on September 24, 1982. Bruce owned a percentage of the hour-long show, thanks to his promoters, who set him up with a production company with investment tax credits and ownership in syndication. This prompted Kitty to admit, "Bruce always would have worked, but now Jay is making him a star, and Larry is making us very rich." But "Bring 'Em Back Alive" did not garner the important hoped-for ratings, and expired with its final showing of June 21, 1983. During the eight-month run of the series, he earned $2.6 million. Meanwhile, Bruce received star billing for BARE ESSENCE, a five-hour CBS-TV movie telecast on October 4 and 5, 1982. A short-lived NBC series based on this account of life among the high rollers of the perfume industry ran in the spring of 1983, but without Bruce. On January 10, 1983, he played the title role in I MARRIED WYATT EARP, a telefeature filmed two years earlier.

With the premiere on October 3, 1983, of the CBS-TV series "Scarecrow and Mrs. King," Bruce finally achieved a sustained success. As Lee Stetson, using the code name of "Scarecrow," he was a spy employed by a CIA-type organization known as "The

Bruce Boxleitner and Kate Jackson in "Scarecrow and Mrs. King" (1986).

Agency." The distaff member of the duo was played by Kate Jackson, also a financial backer of the series. Robert MacKenzie (*TV Guide* magazine) noted that Bruce "plays his spy breezily, with a slightly touchy ego that gets agitated when his inexperienced partner turns out to be right about something." MacKenzie accurately noted that "the stories won't be in serious competition if there's an Emmy for originality," but Bruce was steadily employed in this light-hearted hour series for four TV seasons, ending in 1987. Soon after the hit series premiered, he reprised his part of Billy Montana in KENNY ROGERS AS "THE GAMBLER"—THE ADVENTURE CONTINUES (1983), a four-hour sequel that proved to be just as popular as the original had been three years earlier.

During breaks from his fanciful spy series, Bruce took time to complete three additional TV movies: PASSION FLOWER (January 19, 1986), which periodically required him to remove his shirt; THE RETURN OF MICKEY SPILLANE'S MIKE HAMMER (April 18, 1986), in which he had a walk-on cameo as himself; and LOUIS L'AMOUR'S "DOWN THE LONG HILLS" (November 15, 1986), based on one of the author's best-selling western novels, in which Bruce played a widowed father.

In 1987 Bruce and Kitty separated after ten years of marriage. At the time, he commented, "You gotta go through the whole battle—and my God, we battled long enough. It's a rough thing." Two years later, in July 1989, they were divorced officially, with Bruce referring to his ex-wife as "my best friend." They threw a large party to celebrate the divorce decree, with guests blessing their nonunion by tossing handfuls of rice.

For the CBS-TV telefeature ANGEL IN GREEN (September 22, 1987), Boxleitner was in the Pacific tropics as a Special Forces captain in a bloody insurrection, but he was back in western gear for the television remake of RED RIVER as Matthew Gart, the role created in 1948 by Montgomery Clift, again working with James Arness (in the John Wayne part). Produced by Gregory Harrison's Catalina Productions, RED RIVER was telecast on CBS on April 10, 1988. *Variety* found the production "a faint echo but not an answer" to the big-screen original and said that Boxleitner "gives a run-of-the-mill interpretation of a 2-fisted run-of-the-mill interpretation Western hero—one who gets to play a shoulders-and-sheets scene with Laura Johnson, playing the Joanne Dru part." Also in 1988 he returned to civilian garb as the county prosecutor in THE TOWN BULLY, shown on ABC-TV. Bruce starred opposite Lindsay Wagner in FROM THE DEAD OF NIGHT, an NBC-TV contemporary "thriller" shown in two parts in February 1989, and entered the World War II–era South Pacific fighting the Japanese in THE ROAD RAIDERS (April 25, 1989), a juvenile action-adventure. In April 1989 he made a pilot for a prospective series called "Interceptor," which was not picked up by any television network.

Bill Mann, television critic for the Oakland, California, *Tribune*, wrote, "As Dan Quayle is to political satirists, so is a Judith Krantz miniseries to a TV critic: almost too easy a target." This was in reference to TILL WE MEET AGAIN (1989), the third Krantz adaptation for television. Bruce joined Barry Bostwick, Courtney Cox, and many others in this Krantz marshmallow tale, in which he is a World War II flier, one of aviatrix Cox's love interests. *USA Today* labeled Bruce "stodgy," but maybe that was because, as Krantz has often complained, TV takes the steamy sex out of her writings. Bruce admitted to *US* magazine that "It was a necessary movie to make because I was going through a divorce and I had financial needs." On January 28, 1990, he hosted the sixty-minute presentation "Love with a Twist" (ABC-TV), a collection of real-life love stories.

Bruce journeyed to Melbourne, Australia, to star as the lone American in the feature film BREAKAWAY (1989) as a Vietnam War veteran who breaks out of an Australian jail to find his wife. "I don't ordinarily get offered roles like this," he said. "I think it's one of the best things I've ever done . . . a big thing for me emotionally. It just unleashed things I never knew I had." By the end of 1989, Jay Bernstein's single client was Bruce Boxleitner, and it was announced that a new pilot for CBS-TV, called "Triangle" and featuring two Long Beach, California, policemen and a woman had been completed for showing in the spring of 1990. In early March 1990 the series was renamed "Ventana," and executive producers Phil DeGuerre and James Crocker described the new show as "a hipper 'Simon and Simon.'" It was scheduled to premiere on April 18, 1990. Bruce was to play a private detective with Jameson Parker as a police chief, both in love with the editor of a local newspaper (Daphne Ashbrook). The series, three episodes of which had already been filmed, was cancelled when CBS-TV underwent a change in the hierarchy and the new regime pulled the program because, they said, it lacked "some real romantic tension between the three people."

On April 25, 1990, Bruce was a performer/presenter on the "Academy of Country Music Awards" show on NBC-TV. In "Sporting Chance" (CBS-TV), an unsuccessful one-hour pilot film shown on June 20, 1990, he starred as a former football hero trying to live down his ten-year-old involvement with a college gridiron point-fixing scandal. *Daily Variety* decided "It was a wise exec decision" to drop the property as a possible CBS-TV series because Bruce "hasn't anything to work with except for a running gag about a bloody nose." Meanwhile, Bruce's plan to star in a TV biography of Donald Trump is on hold (events changed too fast); instead, he starred for USA-Cable in MURDEROUS VISIONS (February 20, 1991) in a change-of-pace role, playing a loose cannon—a tough, cynical cop. The hastily assembled TV movie garnered no favor with critics. Andy Klein (*Hollywood Reporter*) dismissed the venture with, "you've seen it before, you've seen it better." *Daily Variety* agreed that Boxleitner had a dumb role to play and that the entire production was "listless." For CBS, he has a two-picture deal (part of his aborted "Triangle" series agreement), which has yet to be fulfilled.

Now in his forties, Boxleitner is seeking to change his bland, good-guy persona. "I've been playing young men forever. Now there are roles that have some meat." Eager to expand his white-bread image by adding more dimension to future characterizations, Bruce hopes, "Maybe I'll even get off eight o'clock television. Wouldn't that be something?"

Filmography

The Chadwick Family (ABC-TV, 4/17/74)
A Cry for Help (ABC-TV, 2/12/75)
Six-Pack Annie (AIP, 1975)
The Macahans (ABC-TV, 1/19/76)
Kiss Me, Kill Me (ABC-TV, 5/28/76)
Murder at the World Series (ABC-TV, 3/20/77)
Happily Ever After (CBS-TV, 9/5/78)
Wild Times (Synd-TV, 1/24/80; 1/31/80)
Kenny Rogers as "The Gambler" (CBS-TV, 4/8/80)
The Baltimore Bullet (Avco Emb, 1980)
Fly Away Home (ABC-TV, 9/18/81)
Bare Essence (CBS-TV, 10/4/82–10/5/82)
Tron (BV, 1982)
I Married Wyatt Earp (NBC-TV, 1/10/83) [filmed in 1981]
Kenny Rogers as "The Gambler"—The Adventure Continues (CBS-TV, 11/28/83–11/29/83)
Passion Flower (CBS-TV, 1/19/86)

The Return of Mickey Spillane's Mike Hammer (CBS-TV, 4/18/86)
Louis L'Amour's "Down the Long Hills" (The Disney Channel–Cable, 11/15/86)
Angel in Green (CBS-TV, 9/22/87)
The Gambler III—The Legend Continues (CBS-TV, 11/24/87)
Red River (CBS-TV, 4/10/88)
The Town Bully (ABC-TV, 4/24/88)
From the Dead of Night (NBC-TV, 2/27/89–2/28/89)
The Road Raiders (CBS-TV, 4/25/89)
Till We Meet Again (CBS-TV, 11/19/89)
Murderous Visions (USA–Cable, 2/20/91)

Future Releases

Breakaway (Smart Egg Releasing, 1989)
Diplomatic Immunity (Frier Entertainment, 1991)

Television Series

How the West Was Won (ABC, 2/6/77; 2/7/77; 2/13/77) [miniseries]
How the West Was Won (ABC, 1978–79)
The Last Convertible (NBC-TV, 9/24/79–9/26/79) [miniseries]

John Steinbeck's "East of Eden" (ABC, 2/8/81; 2/9/81; 2/11/81) [miniseries]
Bring 'Em Back Alive (CBS, 1982–83)
Scarecrow and Mrs. King (CBS, 1983–87)

Broadway Plays

Status Quo Vadis (1973)

JEFF BRIDGES

"My main job in all my artistic endeavors is to get my ego, my fears,
my own image out of the way."—*US* magazine, September 5, 1988

VERSATILE JEFF BRIDGES GREW UP IN FRONT OF MOTION PICTURE
cameras, a fate, good or bad, that was thrust upon him at the early age of two. For the first
twenty-five years of his life/career, he was referred to in the media as "son of Lloyd; brother
of Beau." Before establishing his own professional identity, he performed a succession of
juvenile roles, good ol' boys, bewildered and naive young men. It was not until 1984, at
the age of thirty-five, that he evolved into a cinematic symbol of desire in AGAINST ALL
ODDS. In that *film noir* he bared his chest a good deal of the time and swapped deep kisses
with leading lady Rachel Ward. His well-defined torso, pleasing smile, and deep-set blue-
gray eyes helped to cement his new-found status, bringing his screen charisma to the fore.

Rugged Jeff has been called the Joel McCrea of this era. This implies that either he
can be relied upon to provide solid performances in drama, comedy, or mystery, *or* that he
is merely a part of the scenery, depending on how one views Joel McCrea. Jeff Bridges's
three Academy Award nominations, to date, would seem to indicate that the former is the
case.

The younger of the movie brothers named Bridges, whom *Newsweek* magazine (in
1973) found to be "the most promising, talented and appealing . . . since Groucho, Harpo
and Chico," was born on Sunday, December 4, 1949, in the Los Angeles suburb of Mar
Vista, California, near the beach. During the birth, he and his mother both nearly died
from negative reactions to medication, but both survived the ordeal through the actions of
quick-thinking hospital attendants. His father is actor Lloyd Bridges; his mother is
Dorothy (Simpson) Bridges. Jeff was preceded in birth by Beau (1941) and followed by
Lucinda (1953). At Jeff's christening, actor Larry Parks and his actress wife Betty Garrett
acted as his godparents. The first years of the boys' lives were spent in a modest home in a
housing development, where they were reportedly happy. They later resented a move to
their father's newly acquired "estate" in Westwood. As father Lloyd was often away from
home on location for pictures, it was mother Dorothy who saw to the children's upbringing.

Lloyd has said, "I guess that I must have wanted the boys to be actors," a statement
substantiated by his early attempts to find performing jobs for his youngsters. By his
second birthday, Jeff had earned his first "acting" salary with his appearance in the arms of

Jane Greer at a railway station in RKO's THE COMPANY SHE KEEPS (1951), directed by the Bridges's friend John Cromwell.

In the mid-1950s, during Senator Joseph McCarthy's Communist witch hunt, Lloyd Bridges's name appeared on the notorious Hollywood blacklist. For close to three years he was unable to work in the industry. After his name was cleared, what followed almost made up for the lost years. He accepted the athletic role of Mike Nelson in the television series "Sea Hunt" (1957–1961), which grossed more than $10 million. When Jeff Bridges was eight years old, his father asked, "You wanna do something and make some money?" Jeff, who wanted more toys, replied in the affirmative and found himself in an episode of "Sea Hunt," with his mother playing his TV mother. He was not particularly fond of this type of employment, but found it better than attending school. His great love was music, and he soon purchased a guitar on which he strummed out tunes of his own composition. Brother Beau attempted to interest him in sports, but Jeff preferred his music. He later discovered that he also liked art better than sports. He appeared in two episodes of the CBS-TV series "The Lloyd Bridges Show," and in the summer of 1963, when he was fourteen, he made his stage debut by co-starring with his father in an East Coast summer stock tour of *Anniversary Waltz.*

Jeff began his high school years at a military academy to learn self-discipline, but soon left in favor of University High School in Los Angeles. While there, he became acquainted with marijuana and did more than experiment. He spent several sessions in psychiatric consultation and then entered the school's drug program. After graduation, he went to New York with his father, who was appearing on stage in *Cactus Flower.* Jeff enrolled at the HB Studio where he studied acting. While in New York, he toyed with the idea of becoming a model, but instead returned to California where he dabbled in EST and meditation under the guidance of Swami Muktananda. He left home suddenly to enlist in the U.S. Coast Guard Reserve, feeling that he did not want to remain in show business, where he saw himself as competing with his father and brother Beau. Jeff once said, "I think during those early years I felt guilty for having a father who could . . . push buttons and get me parts on his show." Lloyd was quoted in 1971 as saying, "there was never a burning desire in either of the boys to act. They couldn't have cared less."

Jeff concentrated on music, making a few guitar-strumming appearances in the Los Angeles area. Then, in 1969, he sang "Lost in Space," his own composition, on the soundtrack of JOHN AND MARY, a feature film starring Dustin Hoffman and Mia Farrow. Jeff had reportedly written more than seventy songs by this time. On December 16, 1969, Jeff, the actor, was seen in the NBC network telefeature SILENT NIGHT, LONELY NIGHT, starring his father and Shirley Jones.

At this juncture, through his father's professional contacts, Jeff was signed by one of Hollywood's biggest agents. This connection garnered Jeff fourth billing in HALLS OF ANGER (1970), a film about the desegregation of a black high school. A young actor named Barry Brown had a small role in the feature. Barry wrote of Jeff: "he wasn't a stuck-up, deluded phony" and "he understood his craft intuitively—the sort of gift that makes for the rare hybrid called good actor—movie star." Also in 1970 Jeff acted in a film written and directed by actor Burgess Meredith, called THE YIN AND YANG OF MR. GO, an arty drama that had only a brief release in 1973.

When his agent sent him to audition for Peter Bogdanovich's THE LAST PICTURE SHOW (1971), Jeff has said, "I walked in and Bogdanovich did kind of a double take. 'That's the guy!,' he said. I was the first person cast." Jeff won the role of Duane, a troubled young guy in the dying town of Anarene, Texas (in 1951), who gets his sexual initiation before going off to the Korean war in a state of disillusionment. *Newsweek* magazine called the drama "a brilliantly cast ensemble" and determined that Jeff had "the look of a young Elvis Presley." Jeff was Oscar-nominated as Best Supporting Actor but lost to Ben Johnson, also in the cast. In the ABC-TV movie IN SEARCH OF AMERICA (March 23, 1971), Jeff was a college dropout who convinces his family to take a cross-country trek in a 1928 Greyhound bus. He was a "warm-hearted scoundrel" in BAD COMPANY (1972), set in the Civil War era out West, and a pugilist in FAT CITY (1972), directed by John Huston. *After Dark* magazine found that Jeff "hits the nail on the head as an inarticulate young boxer." In LOLLY-MADONNA XXX (1973) Jeff was embroiled in a feud between two Tennessee mountain families; in THE LAST AMERICAN HERO (1973) he was a rum-running race-car driver; and in the adaptation of Eugene O'Neill's moody and philosophical THE ICEMAN COMETH (1973), he was among an ensemble that included Fredric March, Lee Marvin, and Bradford Dillman. Working with these talented men led Jeff to realize that "this is something I really did love," and he firmly decided to commit himself to the craft of acting.

Having made nine successive motion pictures, plus one TV movie, Jeff confessed to *Newsweek* magazine that "I'm trying to breathe between pictures." He did some of his off-screen relaxing by purchasing a house in Malibu which he began renovating, and by sharing digs with a succession of lady friends, the most enduring of whom was actress Candy Clark. He said at the time, "I don't think I'll ever get married; if you put a contract on something, you dampen that fresh love and it causes you a lot of pain trying to hold onto it." When the reluctant Jeff granted interviews, he was asked repeatedly if there were problems caused by having three established actors in the family. Jeff responded, "There's a tremendous humor in my family that saves everything. Any of the small ego problems . . . are vented in humor. We just laugh about it. . . . We have other bonds that are much tighter." *Newsweek* magazine, in comparing Jeff and Beau, stated, "The broad-shouldered Jeff conforms more closely to the classical leading man and projects a strength that can survive commercial failures."

His next film, THUNDERBOLT AND LIGHTFOOT (1974), was definitely *not* a failure. He was Lightfoot, a fast-talking kid who joins forces with a professional heist artist nicknamed Thunderbolt (Clint Eastwood). During the unrolling of the action film, Jeff did a few hilarious scenes in drag. Critics endorsed his performance in this money-earner: "one of the most personable young actors on the screen today" (Kevin Thomas, *Los Angeles Times*); "very touching" (Bridget Byrne, *Los Angeles Herald-Examiner*). Jeff received his second supporting actor Oscar nomination, but lost to Robert De Niro (THE GODFA-THER: PART II). In 1974 he went on location to Montana for RANCHO DELUXE (1975), about cattle rustlers who go on a binge and wind up in jail. While there he met North Dakota photographer Susan Geston. They would live together for three years before marrying.

His next vehicle was HEARTS OF THE WEST (1975), in which he played a naive Iowa farm boy who winds up in Hollywood in B-pictures. The movie was a flop, as was his next, STAY HUNGRY (1976), a peculiar blend of drama and comedy, set in Alabama and co-starring Sally Field and the emerging Arnold Schwarzenegger. These two failures were followed by an unnecessary remake of KING KONG (1976), in which, as zoologist Jack Prescott, he declares, "The natives will miss Kong; he was the mystery and magic of their lives," as the giant ape is kidnapped from his island by cunning Charles Grodin. The critics roasted the embarrassing rehash.

Jeff was off the screen during 1977, the year in which he married Susan Geston. He came back with a beard in SOMEBODY KILLED HER HUSBAND (1978), filmed in Manhattan with Farrah Fawcett-Majors. It was an unsuccessful blend of suspense and romance. WINTER KILLS (1979), focusing on a presidential assassination, found Bridges billed above the likes of John Huston, Richard Boone, and Tony Perkins. This was followed by an inept comedy, THE AMERICAN SUCCESS COMPANY (1980), with Jeff as a sometimes bewildered loser attempting to change his image. The film was twice reedited and reissued, the second time as SUCCESS. He returned to another of his loves in life as the host of the television special "Heroes of Rock 'n Roll" (1980) at about the same time that he and Beau rejected an offer to portray the outlaw Ford Brothers on screen. (THE LONG RIDERS [1980]

Jeff Bridges in WINTER KILLS (1979).

featured Christopher and Nicholas Guest as the Fords.) Jeff took a small role in the fiasco epic western HEAVEN'S GATE (1980), directed by Michael Cimino, who had helmed THUNDERBOLT AND LIGHTFOOT. The job served a purpose for Jeff at least. He bought a log cabin in Montana that had been used in the movie as a bordello set. It became his retreat.

His next film, CUTTER AND BONE, was first released in April 1981 and then rereleased in August of the same year as CUTTER'S WAY. Jeff was a gentle Ivy League type who is an eyewitness to what may have been the murder of a seventeen-year-old hitchhiker. The *San Francisco Chronicle* reported that Jeff "is a remarkably effective foil, demonstrating his maturity as a performer." TRON (1982), a $12.5

million electronic science-fiction fantasy, cast Jeff as a video game jockey/computer genius. For the animated musical fantasy THE LAST UNICORN (1982) he provided the voice of Prince Lir. (Others heard in this cartoon feature were Alan Arkin, Mia Farrow, and Tammy Grimes.) KISS ME GOODBYE (1982), a dismal remake of the hit Brazilian farce DOÑA FLOR AND HER TWO HUSBANDS (1978), saw Jeff third-billed as a man whose marriage (to Sally Field) is disrupted by the ghost of her departed spouse (James Caan).

During 1982, Jeff's daughter Isabelle was born, followed eighteen months later by daughter Jessie. In "Rapunzel," a sixty-minute "Faerie Tale Theatre" (Showtime–Cable) presentation in February 1983, Jeff was the prince plotting the rescue of the imprisoned maiden (Shelley Duvall).

The dramatic upswing of Jeff's already lengthy career came in March 1984 with his first romantic leading role in AGAINST ALL ODDS, a loose remake of the *film noir* classic OUT OF THE PAST (1947). He was the football player benched due to injury and hired by a big-time bookie (James Woods) to locate his missing mistress (Rachel Ward). In December of that year, Jeff was the winsome, flat-footed STARMAN, an extraterrestrial who accidentally lands in northern Wisconsin at the home of Karen Allen. She watches as he evolves from a single-cell bit of protoplasm into a physical replica of her dead house painter husband. From her he quickly learns English as he gently induces her to drive him to Arizona. For his touching, charming performance, Jeff was again honored with an Oscar nomination, this time as Best Actor, but he lost to F. Murray Abraham (of AMADEUS). A TV series, "Starman," emerged in 1986 with Robert Hays taking over the title role.

It was back to drama for Jeff's next motion pictures. In the very commercial JAGGED EDGE (1985) he was a wealthy San Francisco publisher accused of murdering his even wealthier wife. During the proceedings he has a love affair with his attorney (Glenn Close). The unliked 8 MILLION WAYS TO DIE (1986) found him as an alcoholic cop in a grim crime story. Then, in a holiday TV movie, "The Thanksgiving Promise" (November 23, 1986), he had an unbilled cameo in a warm drama starring three generations of Bridges (Lloyd, Beau, and Beau's son Jordan). In THE MORNING AFTER (1986), Jeff was cast as an ex-cop who is a steadying influence on a boozy actress (Jane Fonda) who believes she may have murdered a man in her bed while drunk. NADINE (1987) was a romantic comedy that had Kim Basinger stumbling into a murder and an elaborate land scam, with Jeff as the estranged husband who aids her in tracking down the culprits.

US magazine in 1988 acknowledged Jeff as a reluctant sex symbol and asked him about his cinematic couplings with the likes of Jane Fonda, Glenn Close, Kim Basinger, and the rest. He responded, "Sex is a weird deal, man. It changes everything. Kissing all those pretty girls up on the screen has got to be tough on Sue, though she says it's not so bad. It makes me love her all the more that she understands."

TUCKER: THE MAN AND HIS DREAM (1988) was director Francis Ford Coppola's paean to auto entrepreneur Preston Tucker. Set in the late 1940s, it is a creative biographical film about the maverick who dared to compete with the biggies of the auto industry. Critic David Ansen (*Newsweek* magazine) wrote, "Bridges excels at playing middle-range roles; he makes normalcy intriguing." Pauline Kael (*The New Yorker* magazine) penned that Jeff "is enough to make a picture worth seeing. He may be the most natural and least self-conscious screen actor who ever lived." Jeff repaid something of a debt to his father by suggesting him for the role of a malevolent senator in TUCKER. On December 3, 1988, Jeff became the youngest star ever to be honored by the London National Film Theatre with a three-week, eighteen-film retrospective held to coincide with the release in Britain of TUCKER.

The nonsensical SEE YOU IN THE MORNING (1989) was a soap opera that offered Jeff as a psychiatrist who divorces his wife (Farrah Fawcett) and leaves their two children to wed another woman (Alice Krige), who has several very troubled kids of her own. For the first time, Jeff and brother Beau teamed in a major motion picture in THE FABULOUS BAKER BOYS (1989), as piano-playing lounge lizards (for six months, they took lessons from pianists Joyce Collins and Lou Forestieri) whose relationship is confused by the hiring of sultry songstress Michelle Pfeiffer. In twenty-two weeks of domestic distribution, the highly acclaimed picture grossed only $18,073,375. *Time* magazine headlined its review "Finally, a True Character Comedy" and noted, "the Bridges boys are better than fabulous in it," while David Denby (*Cosmopolitan* magazine) gave it a top rating, writing that the film "is a bloody miracle . . . both hard-nosed and lyrical, both bluesy and exhilarating. . . . Jeff Bridges gives a classic performance." Jeff played the hip brother and Beau the square one, and Mick LaSalle (*San Francisco Chronicle*) thought that the "nice thing" about the Bridges boys was that neither "goes out of his way to make his character appealing. . . . They're not likeable. They are unremarkable characters living a bleak existence." In the western COLD FEET (1989), starring Keith Carradine, Jeff had a cameo as a small-town bartender.

Beginning August 15, 1989, in the Wichita Falls area of Texas, Peter Bogdanovich finally commenced filming the sequel to THE LAST PICTURE SHOW, entitled TEXASVILLE (1990), for which he was fortunate in getting many original cast members to reprise their roles. Jeff, at a salary of $2 million, headed the list, which included Cybill Shepherd, Timothy Bottoms, Cloris Leachman, Randy Quaid, and Eileen Brennan. Jeff gained thirty-five pounds in preparation for the role. In a plot described by Bogdanovich as "the complicated variations of love and romance," Jeff, as Duane, having returned from fighting in Korea, has become a successful oilman with a spunky wife (Annie Potts). Having attained great wealth, he has a beautiful home with jacuzzi and pool. However, by 1984 (when the new film takes place), he is deeply in debt. He needs someone to understand him, and he thinks it might be the rich girl (Shepherd) who broke his heart before Korea. She has recently returned to Anarene after a failed acting career and a bad marriage in Europe, as well as the tragic death of her son. Andy Klein (*Hollywood Reporter*) observed, "TEXASVILLE, while not THE LAST PICTURE SHOW by any means, is an excellent piece of work by any other yardstick." The tradepaper added, "Bridges, looking convincingly 50, quietly carries the film." David Ansen (*Newsweek* magazine) observed, "Bridges, slovenly handsome, makes a deft foil for this rueful farce." Perhaps the best assessment of Bridges's work in TEXASVILLE came from co-star Annie Potts: "I never worked with the like of him as an actor, he's completely focused on the work. You never see a seam—it's like Spencer Tracy." In its first week of limited domestic distribution, TEXASVILLE grossed a modest $1,575,078 at the box office.

On February 8, 1990, in Las Vegas, at the National Association of Theater Owners (NATO)/ShoWest convention at Bally's Hotel, Jeff was named Male Star of the Year. Immediately following this accolade, he embarked on a public appearance tour in Europe on behalf of THE FABULOUS BAKER BOYS. During the trek, a tribute was given in his honor at London's National Film Theatre.

With location shooting beginning in New York City on May 21, 1990, Jeff played a loud-mouthed radio disc jockey whose life spirals downward after a debilitating personal shock in THE FISHER KING (1991). In the course of the movie he befriends a homeless man (Robin Williams) in the hope that by helping someone less fortunate, the oppressive curse that has been put on him will be lifted.

On behalf of a major California environmental initiative on that state's election ballot in November 1990, Jeff joined other celebrities in donating his appearance in a television advertising campaign called "Big Green."

Through the years, Jeff has continued with his oil painting and his music. His canvases have been shown in Montana galleries, but his music remains a hobby, although his compositions have been considered marketable. He has formed his own production company, through which he has spoken of developing a film about world hunger (he is a founding member of the End Hunger Network). He claims that he is not "a real driven person . . . I sort of like to get pulled along." In an interview on TV's "Entertainment Tonight," he revealed that there is still a touch of insecurity within him: "I don't like feeling too confident. I always like coming from the underdog position. It's very scary when everything is going well." Regarding being a celebrity and a screen actor, he says, "Sometimes I find this flattering, that people will want to know what I think about things, especially if they're things I'm interested in. But I also like that the audience is never sure what I'm capable of. They see me in JAGGED EDGE or BAKER BOYS or TEXASVILLE, and they're not sure who I am. I like that. Sometimes after I finish a movie . . . I think that I never want to do it again. . . . Then, after I go home and I'm with my family, either in L.A. or, if we get to take some time, at the ranch in Montana, then somehow I get horny to work." Of his acting method, he says, "It's the 'erection principle.' . . . When you're rehearsing a scene, it's like you get a hard-on for the character. Then they keep rehearsing, and you start losing your erection. Sometimes it comes up again, but then it's gone. And ultimately, acting is all about this: You have to summon the erection up at will. You have to force your mind to get it up. And that's the challenge."

Filmography

The Company She Keeps (RKO, 1951)
Silent Night, Lonely Night (NBC-TV, 12/16/69)

John and Mary (20th–Fox, 1969) [voice only]
Halls of Anger (UA, 1970)
In Search of America (ABC-TV, 3/23/71)

The Last Picture Show (Col, 1971)
Bad Company (Par, 1972)
Fat City (Col, 1972)
The Yin and Yang of Mr. Go (Sunset International, 1973) [made in 1970]
Lolly-Madonna XXX [The Lolly Madonna Wars] (MGM, 1973)
The Last American Hero [Hard Driver] (20th–Fox, 1973)
The Iceman Cometh (American Film Theatre, 1973)
Thunderbolt and Lightfoot (UA, 1974)
Rancho Deluxe (UA, 1975)
Hearts of the West (UA, 1975)
Stay Hungry (UA, 1976)
King Kong (Par, 1976)
Somebody Killed Her Husband (Col, 1978)
Winter Kills (Avco Emb, 1979)
The American Success Company [Success] (Col, 1980)

Heaven's Gate (UA, 1980)
Cutter's Way [Cutter and Bone] (UA, 1981)
Tron (BV, 1982)
The Last Unicorn (ITC, 1982) (voice only)
Kiss Me Goodbye (20th–Fox, 1982)
Against All Odds (Col, 1984)
Starman (Col, 1984)
Jagged Edge (Col, 1985)
The Thanksgiving Promise (ABC-TV, 11/23/86)
8 Million Ways to Die (Tri-Star, 1986)
The Morning After (20th–Fox, 1986)
Nadine (Tri-Star, 1987)
Tucker: The Man and His Dream (Par, 1988)
See You in the Morning (WB, 1989)
The Fabulous Baker Boys (20th–Fox, 1989)
Cold Feet (Avenue Pictures, 1989)
Texasville (Col, 1990)
The Fisher King (Tri-Star, 1991)

Album Discography

John and Mary (A&M SP-4230) [ST]

CHER

"After all, this is my one and only life; it's not a dress rehearsal for anything else. This is the only one I know about, and it's more important to me what I think of me than what other people think of me."
—on "The Barbara Walters Special," April 11, 1988, ABC-TV

STEPHEN SONDHEIM LYRICALLY CHRONICLED THE ACCOMPLISHMENTS of a long-lasting living legend in his 1971 Broadway musical *Follies* in a song that began: "Good times and bum times, I've seen them all and . . . I'm here!" While obviously not composed with Cher in mind, the song still fits her like one of her body-hugging costumes.

Cher is a flamboyant survivor of twenty-plus years in show business. She rose to fame first as the taller, more deadpan half of the Sonny and Cher pop rock singing team; then, solo, she became a glamorous 1970s television sex symbol who displayed an engaging flair for comedy. Later, she unleashed her natural talents into the competitive arenas of rock music on stage and disc and, thereafter, in the big business of fashion and fragrance. She surprised everyone by evolving into a *serious* actress who won an Academy Award for MOONSTRUCK (1987). Along the way, Cher remained dedicated to looking good in her consistently outrageous designer creations, almost inevitably exposing either her navel or tattooed buttocks, or both. This never-boring woman, infused with a rechargeable magic, has an estimated annual income of more than $6 million. However, she is not known to hoard her earnings; she loves to spend money. But beneath the glitter and feathers and leather lies a vulnerable, honest, down-to-earth lady who, like chanteuse Hildegarde of several decades earlier, is absolutely incomparable.

Cherilyn Sarkisian was born in El Centro, California, on Monday, May 20, 1946. Of Armenian, Turkish, French, and Cherokee Indian ancestry, she is the daughter of blonde Georgia, a former fashion model/occasional actress, and John Sarkisian, a compulsive gambler. (As a result of medication prescribed for an intestinal dysfunction, he was to become addicted to drugs, specifically heroin.) When Cherilyn was six months old, her father disappeared. Because Georgia was unable both to hold a job and to raise a baby, she committed her infant girl to an orphanage and, later, to a foster home. Cherilyn remained there until the age of three, when John Sarkisian returned to his family. However, he departed again soon thereafter and Georgia obtained a divorce. In 1949 Georgia and Cherilyn appeared together in a live TV commercial, but Georgia "retired" a year later to marry John Southall, by whom she had a second daughter, blonde Georgeanne, in 1951.

Over the years, Georgia would have a total of six husbands, and would remarry Sarkisian but divorce him a second time, for a grand total of eight marriage ceremonies to date. As a result, Georgia and her daughters moved frequently, to various parts of the country, with her various spouses. At one point, between marriages, Georgia placed Cherilyn in a Catholic charity home.

Cherilyn's formative years were miserable ones for her. A shy child, she believed herself ugly because she was not fair-haired or fair-skinned like her mother and sister. In school—and there were many of them—she had difficulty with reading, spelling, and addition. However, she had a terrific memory and learned by retaining lessons she had heard. Early in life, she decided to become someone famous: if not an actress, then the revered discoverer of a new medical cure or some similarly renowned figure. To prepare for the day when fame would come, she studiously perfected her autograph. In 1957, when she was eleven, John Sarkisian again returned, this time to stay a year. She has recalled days of deprivation when she had to attend school with rubber bands on her shoes to keep the soles from falling off and claims to have lost her virginity to a married man when she was fourteen. Beginning in 1960, having been adopted by Georgia's then-husband, Gilbert LaPiere, a bank manager, both girls used his surname.

Because high school was not easy for her, Cherilyn developed into a belligerent, sarcastic student, to the point where "people kept away from me." (Regarding her elder daughter, Georgia would recall "always being called into the principal's office about something she was doing. She would never conform, ever.") In the second week of her junior year, Cherilyn dropped out of high school, moved to a Sunset Strip apartment in Los Angeles with a friend, and studied drama with character actor Jeff Corey. One night in 1962, she was picked up by actor Warren Beatty, then America's latest heartthrob. However, she remembers their sexual experience as a "disappointment" because "I didn't feel anything."

On another night, on a double date, Cherilyn met musician Salvatore "Sonny" Bono, eleven years her senior. He was newly separated from his wife and recently arrived in town from Detroit where he had worked with Phil Spector, creator of "the wall of sound" on the Philles record label. "She was kind of a waif and real lost as a person," Bono said later, "and I was kind of a waif and real lost as a person, so I told her she could stay with me." Persuading her to concentrate on singing rather than acting, Bono took full charge of her life. Her trust in him was complete. She would sign whatever paper he placed before her, allowing him to arrange their bookings at small Los Angeles clubs or as background vocalists for the Righteous Brothers, the Crystals, and the Ronettes. At first, the duo called themselves Caesar and Cleo because they had been told of their resemblance to Julius Caesar (his long hair) and Cleopatra (her regal appearance). They later changed the name of their act to Sonny and Cher. Their first single recording ("The Letter," backed with "String Fever," on the Vault label), however, was as Caesar and Cleo. This was followed by "Love Is Strange" (with "Do You Want to Dance") as Caesar and Cleo on Reprise Records. In 1964 Cher recorded "Ringo, I Love You" (backed with "Beatle Blues") under the name Bonnie Jo Mason on the Annette label, as well as "Dream Baby" (backed with

"Stan Quetzal") on Imperial, using the name Cherilyn.

Realizing that Bono's intervention in her elder daughter's life was more than professional, Georgia thwarted their advances toward obtaining a marriage license. However, on October 29, 1964, they eloped to Tijuana, Mexico; she was eighteen, he was twenty-nine. Between September 1964 and January 1966, the couple were frequent guests on ABC-TV's "Shindig," a popular thirty-minute teen rock 'n' roll show, and performed on "Hullabaloo," its one-hour counterpart on NBC-TV. They made their motion picture debut in WILD ON THE BEACH (1965), a low-budget comedy with songs written by Bono. In 1964 they had recorded "Baby Don't Go" for Reprise. However, because Bono did not like that version, he reputedly borrowed $168 to do a second recording of the song in July 1965 for Reprise, which became a top ten single. "Just You" followed on Atco, but it was the next recording on Atco that sent them over the top. "I Got You, Babe" remained on the *Billboard* magazine charts for fourteen weeks in the summer of 1965, for three of those weeks in the #1 position, replacing the Beatles. This recording alone has been estimated to have sold close to four million copies. In the autumn of 1965, they had five recordings on the "Best" lists, attracted large crowds to their rock concerts, and Cher's wide bell-bottom pants and Bono's fur vests and bell-bottoms set a fashion standard for the rock music world that soon spread to mainstream America. Some of the trademark costumes, designed by Cher, were successfully marketed bearing her label.

In 1966, when the British-made feature ALFIE was distributed in the United States by Paramount, Cher sang the title song on the soundtrack, having been asked to record over the voice of British singer Cilla Black. Also during 1966, Sonny and Cher embarked on a four-week European tour; they represented young love and marriage to teenagers in that part of the world. For Paramount, they starred in a kooky, lightweight feature, GOOD TIMES (1967), in which they were supported by George Sanders and sang "I Got You, Babe" on screen. Vehemently opposed to the use of drugs, the couple made an educational short film for the U.S. government extoling the advantages of not using marijuana. It was shown in high schools. They guest-starred in a tongue-in-cheek episode, "The Hot Number Affair" (March 10, 1967), on NBC-TV's "The Man from U.N.C.L.E." series.

In 1968 Cher made a statement that she would later contradict: "There's no sense trying to shock people with the way you dress. They don't shock easily anymore." The Bonos' daughter, Chastity, was born in March 1969. That same year Cher starred in the motion picture CHASTITY, which Sonny, as producer, also scripted, and for which he wrote songs, but in which he did not appear. The story of a waif (Cher) failed to thrill audiences; the film did not recoup its estimated $2 million cost. In fact, the Bonos came out of the venture $180,000 in debt, including back taxes owed.

Early in 1970, when Cher's recording of "Superstar" was a dud, but Karen Carpenter's version of the same song on another label became a hit, Mr. and Mrs. Bono realized that it was time to make a professional change. They contracted for nightclub appearances, discarding their former hippie attire for more conventional dress. (Cher appeared in low-cut gowns.) In these one-night stands, their on-stage patter included put-downs of Sonny. Audiences enjoyed the staged insults at such spots as the Empire Room at New York City's

Waldorf-Astoria Hotel and the Ambassador's Now Grove in Los Angeles, and at the Sahara Hotel in Las Vegas, where they were the warm-up act for headliner performers. On January 15, 1971, they appeared on ABC-TV's "Love, American Style" in the "Love and the Sack" episode, followed by an NBC-TV special, "The First Nine Months Are the Hardest" (January 21, 1971).

In June 1971 Sonny and Cher substituted successfully as hosts on "The Merv Griffin Show" (CBS-TV), which led to a commitment from the network for six one-hour shows for CBS during the summer of 1971. The limited series, "The Sonny and Cher Comedy Hour," began its run on August 1, 1971. Proving popular, the variety program was brought back as a midseason offering on December 27, 1971. Having obtained the talents of designer Bob Mackie, Cher was showcased in a different $10,000 costume on each show. Mackie has said, "Dressing Cher is like dressing a mythical figure. . . . She has a perfect body, she doesn't seem to age, she's theatrical, but no one else is like her." In Mackie's creations, bolstered by ideas of her own, Cher became a qualified sex symbol. The popular "The Sonny and Cher Comedy Hour" lasted through May 1974.

Meanwhile, the couple gained further audience exposure with engagements at the Fairmont Hotel's Venetian Room in San Francisco in May 1972, followed by an appearance as headliners at the Hotel Sahara in Las Vegas, where they were to play often. In 1972 Cher alone recorded *Gypsies, Tramps & Thieves*, which was a hit, as was the next year's *Half-Breed*. When the team was not traveling, they resided in a twenty-five-room mansion in Bel Air in Los Angeles with several servants and a variety of vehicles.

Suddenly, in the autumn of 1972, Cher, weighing ninety pounds and totally lacking a sense of self-worth or independence, asked Sonny for a marital separation. "America will hate you," he said. However, she claimed that she did not care. To the press she admitted that she owed much to Sonny, who "was more of a mother to me than my own mother," but "now I have to break out." Legal separation papers would not be filed by Sonny until February 19, 1974, and their divorce was finalized on June 27, 1975. (Their professional/contractual entanglements would not be unraveled until July 3, 1979.) Fifty-eight hours after Sonny's filing, they taped their last TV show.

She starred solo in her first TV special, appropriately called "Cher" (February 12, 1975), as a warm-up for her own musical variety program of the same title, which premiered on CBS-TV on February 16, 1975. Although she played host to many noted celebrities, including daughter Chastity, the show was not a success, and it ended on January 4, 1976. Following the demise of her series, she teamed with Bono in a revival of "The Sonny and Cher Comedy Hour" on CBS-TV, beginning February 8, 1976. Although the program survived through August 29, 1977, it lacked the magic of their earlier joint series.

During this period, she had been declared one of America's ten worst-dressed women by Mr. Blackwell, the self-ordained arbiter of such matters. He thought she looked "like a Hawaiian bar mitzvah." Her constant companion had been music/record producer David Geffen—until she met rock musician Gregg Allman, nineteen months her junior. On June 30, 1975, three days after her divorce from Bono, she married Allman in Las

Vegas. Nine days later, Cher sought to annul the union, but the couple reconciled when Cher discovered she was pregnant. She gave birth to a son, Elijah Blue, in the spring of 1976. It was also in 1976 that Cher learned that not only was Chastity dyslexic, but that she, too, had weathered the affliction during her lifetime. (This learning disability was the reason for her difficulties in school and later inability to read or dial a telephone number properly.) In 1977 she recorded "Love Me" using Allman & Woman as the artists' names. However, after a series of marital problems to which Allman's drug use was a major contributor, they divorced in 1978. Soon, Gene Simmons, the rocker of the group Kiss, supplanted Allman in Cher's affections.

Her second TV special, "Cher and Other Fantasies," was telecast on NBC on April 3, 1979, but her singing over the main credits for ROLLER BOOGIE (1979) did not enhance that film's chances for success. In 1980 she had a "holiday" home in Aspen, Colorado, which was inhabited, at times, by her then-boyfriend, Les Dudek, a rock guitarist, when she was not working as the unbilled lead singer with the hard-rock group Black Rose. Also reported to have been seen in the company of hockey player Ron Duguay, actor John Heard, and singer John Loeffler, she said, "I've loved all the men I've ever been with. They're really wonderful people. I still am friends with every man I've ever been with."

On March 17, 1980, she was on "Tom Snyder's Celebrity Spotlight" on NBC-TV, before packing for a move to New York City. Having seen Linda Ronstadt on the Broadway stage in a revival of *The Pirates of Penzance*, Cher decided that she, too, would attempt to expand her professional opportunities. This she did when director Robert Altman added her to the touring company of *Come Back to the 5 & Dime, Jimmy Dean, Jimmy Dean*, after which the play was seen off-Broadway before moving uptown to Broadway on July 29, 1982. Earning minimum salary for her stage work, Cher lived at the Mayflower Hotel with her children and staff in an $8,000-a-month suite. Prior to its Broadway run, the play was adapted to film for a November 1982 release. Cher was Sissy, one of six women who reunite twenty years after forming their James Dean fan club. Roger Ebert (*Chicago Sun-Times*) noted that "Cher is the one I watched the most because her performance here is a revelation." For her screen work, for which she was paid $25,000, Cher received a Golden Globe nomination as Best Supporting Actress. In July–August 1982 she performed in what would be her last Las Vegas revue for almost eight years at Caesar's Palace, with Showtime–Cable taping the event. (It was aired on April 21, 1983, as "Cher—A Celebration at Caesar's Palace.") In 1983 the new man in Cher's life was actor Val Kilmer, fourteen years her junior.

Impressed with her on-stage emoting in 1982, director Mike Nichols had visited Cher in New York to offer her the role of the lesbian friend of Meryl Streep in SILKWOOD (1983), set in a nuclear plant and based on a true story. Having done the feature for a $150,000 salary, Cher said she liked the experience because "I didn't have to wear makeup or care if I looked good." She received an Academy Award nomination as Best Supporting Actress but lost the Oscar to Linda Hunt (THE YEAR OF LIVING DANGEROUSLY). Cher did, however, win a Golden Globe Award in the supporting category. Wearing a black bikini skirt to the latter festivities, she was overwhelmed and at a loss for words. "Look at my dress," she said, "until I can think of something to say." Meanwhile, her romantic allegiance switched to ABC Films executive Joshua Donen (ten years younger than she), then to actor Eric Stoltz (sixteen years her junior). She appeared in advertisements for Jack LaLanne Health & Tennis Enterprises, stepping in for the company's first choice, Joan Rivers, who had refused to be seen in leotards. Cher stated that she took the job because she needed the money. At the last minute, Cher rejected the lead in GRANDVIEW, U.S.A. (1984), for an offered salary of $625,000. The role went to Jamie Lee Curtis. On February 14, 1985, Cher was named Woman of the Year by Harvard University's Hasty Pudding Club.

Jane Fonda was the initial choice to play Rusty Dennis in MASK (1985), but it was Cher who made the role memorable on screen, thereby further establishing her reputation as a serious actress. She was the motorcycle-riding, drug-dependent mother of sixteen-year-old Rocky (Eric Stoltz behind grotesque foam-rubber makeup), born with craniodiaphyseal dysplasia, a disfiguring condition involving calcium deposits that creates the appearance of a mask that is permanent. *People* magazine observed that "even her admirers may be astonished by the heat and bite she brings to the role." The film, adapted from a true story, was directed by Peter Bogdanovich, with whom Cher did not get along. (Bogdanovich would say later, "She was edgy and distrustful with me. I think she is a bit dubious about male authority figures in general, and a male director can't help being that.") After she was named best actress at the Cannes Film Festival in mid-1985, it was expected that Cher would also be Oscar-nominated. However, this was not the case. At the

Cher in MASK (1985).

April 1986 Academy Award ceremonies, in retaliation, she showed up in a large feathered headpiece and revealing, beaded costume that *Newsweek* magazine called an "X-rated impersonation of a 1956 Pontiac hood ornament."

Cosmetically, it was revealed that Cher had five tattoos (two on her buttocks, and one each on a shoulder, forearm, and ankle). All would eventually be exposed for public viewing. Also, she admitted to having had her nose and teeth re-done, along with having had breast surgery after the birth of each of her children.

Cher looked gorgeous in mink for a Blackglama "What Becomes a Legend Most" fur advertisement in 1986, the same year she met "the most beautiful man," Rob(ert) Camilletti. He was an aspiring actor eighteen years her junior whose past occupations included bagel maker, doorman, and bartender. Their live-in relationship would last well over two years, during which time their every noteworthy move was recorded in detail by the tabloids. In 1987 Cher formed Isis Productions, operated by Bohden Zachary, at Warner Bros. studios. The company would later move to Paramount and then to Columbia, where Cher had an office next to Madonna's. (In the fall of 1990, Cher would move Isis Productions to Tri-Star Pictures for a one-year, first-look pact.)

The first of Cher's three 1987 movies was THE WITCHES OF EASTWICK. She played one of three housewives in Eastwick, a New England hamlet. One is widowed (Cher), one divorced (Susan Sarandon), and one deserted (Michelle Pfeiffer). The women are too lonely to notice that they are capable of witchcraft until they conjure an ideal man who comes to them as Mephistopheles (Jack Nicholson). None of the actresses had anything good to say about the filming. (Cher commented that "It was like filming a movie on Friday the 13th in the middle of a hurricane.") Everything started off badly, with Sarandon angry with Cher, whom Sarandon was led to believe was responsible for a last-minute switch in roles. Nevertheless, the end product was highly entertaining. THE WITCHES OF EASTWICK grossed $63.7 million in worldwide distribution.

Released on October 23, 1987, SUSPECT starred Cher as a Washington, D.C., public defender assigned the case of a mentally disabled, deaf, mute, homeless Vietnam veteran (Liam Neeson) accused of robbery and murder. The detective work of a smug juror (Dennis Quaid) helps Cher clear the man's name, but uncovers a high government conspiracy. The script was flawed, but the thriller held one's attention, largely because of Cher's sincere performance.

However, it was MOONSTRUCK, which opened on December 16, 1987, that provided an Oscar for Cher. As Loretta Castorini, a drab young widow living in Brooklyn with her parents, she upsets her plan to marry a respectable dullard (Danny Aiello) by falling for his rebellious younger brother (Nicolas Cage), a baker, under the romantic full moon hovering over Brooklyn. Pauline Kael (*The New Yorker* magazine) wrote that Cher "is right at home in the screwball ethnic comedy" as well as "devastatingly funny and sinuous and beautiful." Cher won a Golden Globe Award as Best Actress and on April 11, 1988, at the Academy Awards she was named Best Actress. In her speech she said, "I've never won anything before from my peers. I'm really, really happy."

Meanwhile, Cher was seen with her mother, Georgia (now bearing the last name of Holt) on ABC-TV's "Super Stars & Their Moms" (May 3, 1987). Cher appeared with Sonny Bono on NBC-TV's "Late Night with David Letterman" (November 13, 1987) where they reprised "I Got You, Babe." She also had her first album (*Cher*) in six years in distribution and owned two pieces of property: a $7 million contemporary Egyptian-style Beverly Hills mansion, and a cooperative apartment in New York City's East Village. In demand following MASK, Cher had turned down several screen offers, including FATAL BEAUTY (1987), taken over by Whoopi Goldberg; BABY BOOM (1987), which went to Diane Keaton; and the co-starring role in BLACK WIDOW (1987), which went to Theresa Russell. After winning her Oscar, Cher was offered the female lead in THE WAR OF THE ROSES (1989), but rejected it because she felt she would lack the necessary chemistry opposite Michael Douglas. Kathleen Turner inherited the role. On the night of the Oscar telecast of April 11, 1988, Cher was interviewed on ABC-TV by Barbara Walters, who disclosed that Cher was one of her favorites.

In 1988 Cher did advertisements for Holiday Spa Health Club and opened in late 1988 at the Sands Hotel in Atlantic City, reportedly earning $150,000 per show during a ten-day stint. In November 1988 a new fragrance, "Uninhibited," was unveiled under Cher's name. This pricey perfume and eau de toilette garnered $10 million in retail sales during its first two months on the market. (Not permitted by Bono to wear a fragrance during their marriage, Cher had made another strike for personal independence.) Cher's 1988 earnings were reportedly $6 million, not including the "Uninhibited" royalties; her per-movie salary had escalated to somewhere between $1 million and $2 million.

The year 1988 wound down with her performance on CBS-TV's "Pee-wee's Playhouse Christmas Special" (December 21, 1988) and early in 1989 she broke up with Rob Camilletti. On March 18, 1989, she helped raise funds for America's homeless on HBO–Cable's "Comic Relief III." On June 3, 1989, she faced her first live concert audience in almost eight years at an outdoor amphitheater in Mansfield, Massachusetts. In July she performed at an AIDS benefit in Washington, D.C., prior to embarking on a concert tour called *Heart of Stone*, also the title of her popular June 1989 album on the Geffen label. Opening at Atlantic City's Sands Hotel on August 16, 1989, for five nights at $150,000 per show, she dazzled audiences in costumes created by Bob Mackie, Michael Schmidt, and Marlene Stewart. Cher's new love was now Richie Sambora, a guitarist with the group Bon Jovi, thirteen years her junior; their romance ended in August 1990.

At the sixth annual Video Music Awards (September 6, 1989) in Los Angeles, presented on MTV–Cable, she sang "If I Could Turn Back Time" wearing a diaphanous leotard that exposed her backside except for a thin strip of jumpsuit down the middle, topped by a leather jacket. (The video was shot aboard the U.S.S. *Missouri*, using sailors as extras.) MTV decided to show the video for "If I Could Turn Back Time" only between the hours of 9 p.m. and 6 a.m. because of "negative feedback" concerning her scant costume. The single recording of the song was on *Billboard* magazine's top twenty list for several weeks, while her album enjoyed similar popularity, selling over one million copies. She contributed to a book on nutrition written by Robert Haas, and sold her Beverly Hills home to Eddie Murphy for $6.4 million. Never staying long in one place, she moved into an eighteenth-floor duplex in Los Angeles. On November 9, 1989, Fredericks of Hollywood displayed in its new museum lingerie worn by Cher, Madonna, Judy Garland, Lana Turner, and other celebrated women.

Cher's song "Just Like Jesse James" had, as of January 12, 1990, been charted for fourteen weeks by *Billboard* magazine as one of America's top twenty singles. Beginning March 31, 1990, in Dallas, Texas, she embarked on a national forty-one-city tour—on bus, due to her fear of air travel. Meanwhile, daughter Chastity signed a recording deal with Geffen Records and formed her own band with singer/guitarist Heidi Shink. It was also rumored that CBS-TV was considering a morning talk show to be co-hosted by Georgia Holt and Jacqueline Stallone, two outspoken Hollywood mothers. On tour with

Cher was son Elijah Blue, aged fourteen, as rhythm guitarist. This tour, with three background singers and a seven-piece band, was Cher's bid to be taken seriously as a contemporary pop vocalist. When the tour played Oakland, California, Joel Selvin (*San Francisco Chronicle*) described Cher as "not only a gritty survivor, but still a credible competitor." In June 1990 Cher returned to Las Vegas, appearing at the new Mirage Hotel at $150,000 per show; CBS-TV taped her performance for airing on February 4, 1991. She was a presenter at the MTV Awards ceremony on September 6, 1990, and on September 13, 1990, she sang a medley of her hits at the Greek Theatre in Los Angeles on behalf of the environment. This show was telecast on ABC-TV as "An Evening with . . ." (September 19, 1990). The same night she was in Washington, D.C., to initiate a round of fundraising events for the International Craniofacial Foundation. After hosting a private dinner, in the company of a number of afflicted youngsters, she met with the Russian ambassador who gave her a gift from Soviet children. She then toured the White House with her charges.

Several screen projects had been reported to be in the works for Cher: MRS. CALIBAN for Paramount, ROAD SHOW for Twentieth Century–Fox, and John Carpenter's PIN CUSHION for Columbia. (In addition, during this period Cher had rejected the Charles Grodin part in MIDNIGHT RUN [1989], had dropped out of the running to play Morticia Frump Addams in a feature film based on the TV series "The Addams Family," and had lost out to Roseanne Barr to play opposite Meryl Streep in SHE-DEVIL [1989].) However, Cher chose to take a role as a mother (with Winona Ryder as one of her daughters) and romantic lead to Bob Hoskins in MERMAIDS. Plagued with "creative differences" and the illness of cast members, MERMAIDS was finally released in December 1990. *Daily Variety* was unimpressed, complaining that the picture was "confusingly titled, leisurely paced and dramatically unfocused," but acknowledging that Cher was "fine as the cavalier, self-centered mom." Duane Byrge (*Hollywood Reporter*) was more enthusiastic, judging the production a "warm and lively mother-daughter saga" and ranking Cher's performance as "magical, electric yet credibly restrained." For the film Cher recorded two songs, "Baby, I'm Yours" and "The Shoop Shoop Song (It's His Kiss)," with the latter being used for a music video. Her next announced screen venture was ANGRY HOUSEWIVES (1992). Another future project is TABLOIDS (1992), a comedy about a reporter and a celebrity who become close friends. Meanwhile, in a different medium, Cher did a reading of *The Ugly Duckling* for Random House's home video series. In late 1990 Cher purchased Jeunesse, a firm which manufactures skin care products, and in January 1991 Cher's health and exercise book *Forever Fit* was published by Bantam.

Now in mid-life, the in-demand, versatile, but controversially dressed Cher has publicly given thought to the aging process: "I do keep wondering about how much longer I'll be able to dress the way I want to dress and get away with it. Will I be able to have long hair when I'm 60 and wear it really weird and can I wear miniskirts if my legs are still good?" On being difficult, she notes, "Look, I'm only difficult if you're an idiot. If you don't know more than I know, then I'll be really difficult." Regarding the men in her life to date, Cher acknowledges that Sonny Bono still has a strong hold on her: "He is the most interesting person I've ever met. I've never met anyone that even comes close." Like Madonna, Cher insists that she is not a role model. "But trust me," she says, "if I could accomplish this thing that seemed impossible, you can accomplish anything you want to do. It's not me, it's just people need symbols along the way to remind them, '*Yes, I can do this.*'"

Filmography

Sonny and Cher

Wild on the Beach (20th–Fox, 1965) (also songs by Sonny)
Good Times (Par, 1967) (also songs by Sonny)

Chastity (AIP, 1969) (also produced, scripted, and music written by Sonny, who did not appear in this feature)

Cher Alone

Alfie (Par, 1966) (voice only)
Roller Boogie (UA, 1979) (voice only)
Come Back to the 5 & Dime, Jimmy Dean, Jimmy Dean (Cinecom International, 1982)
Silkwood (Par, 1983)
Mask (Univ, 1985)
The Witches of Eastwick (WB, 1987)
Suspect (Tri-Star, 1987)

Moonstruck (MGM/UA, 1987)
Mermaids (Orion, 1990)

Future Releases

Angry Housewives (BV, 1992)
Tabloids (Orion, 1992)

TV Series

The Sonny and Cher Comedy Hour (CBS, 1971–74; 1976–77)

Cher (CBS, 1975–76)

Broadway Plays

Come Back to the 5 & Dime, Jimmy Dean, Jimmy Dean (1982)

Album Discography

Sonny and Cher

All I Ever Need Is You (Kapp 3660, MCA 2021)
Baby Don't Go (Reprise 6177)
The Beat Goes On (Atco 11000)
The Best of Sonny and Cher (Atco 233-219)

Good Times (Atco 33-214) [ST]
Greatest Hits (Atco A2S-5178, MCA 2117)
In Case You're in Love (Atco SD-33-203)
Look at Us (Atco SD-33-177)

Sonny and Cher Live (Kapp 3654)
Sonny and Cher Live in Las Vegas, Vol. 2 (MCA 2-8004)
The Two of Us (Atco SD-2-804)

Wild on the Beach (RCA LPM/LSP-3441) [ST]
The Wondrous World of Sonny and Cher (Atco SD-33-183)

Cher Alone

All I Really Want to Do (Imperial 12292)
Backstage (Imperial 12373)
The Best of Cher (EMI E21K-91836)
The Best of Cher, Vols. 1–2 (Liberty 10110/11)
Bittersweet White Light (MCA 2101)
Black Rose (Casablanca NBLP-7234)
Chastity (Atco 302) [ST]
Cher (Geffen 6HS-24164)
Cher (Imperial 12320)
Cher Backstage (Imperial 12373)
Cher Superpak, Vols. 1–2 (UA 88, 94)
Cherished (WB 3046)
Comic Relief 3 (Rhino R21k-70893)
Dark Lady (MCA 2113)
Foxy Lady (Kapp 5514)
Golden Greats (Imperial 12406)
Greatest Hits (MCA 2127)
Gypsies, Tramps & Thieves (Kapp 3649)

Half-Breed (MCA 2104)
Heart of Stone (Geffen GHS-24239)
I Paralyze (CBS 38096)
I'd Rather Believe in You (WB 2898)
Mermaids (Geffen GHS-24310) [ST]
Prisoner (Casablanca 7184)
Roller Boogie (Casablanca NBLP-2-7194) [ST]
The Sonny Side of Cher (Imperial 9301/12301)
Stars (WB 2850)
Take Me Home (Casablanca 7133)
3614 Jackson Highway (Atco SD-33-298)
This Is Cher (Sunset 5276)
Two the Hard Way (WB K-3120) [Cher billed as Woman]
The Ugly Duckling (Windham Hill WH-0705)
The Very Best of Cher (UA 377)
With Love (Imperial 12358)

GLENN CLOSE

"There are certain characters who are incredibly cathartic to play.
You get to pull out all the stops, run the gamut of emotions.
It's thrilling because you can go way over everything you've done.
You can surprise yourself."

—*The Cable Guide* magazine, January 1990

EARLY IN HER ACTING CAREER, GLENN CLOSE WAS SAID TO BE INTELLI-
gent, aristocratic, courageous, stalwart, and consistent—affirmative adjectives, but none of
them indicating that she would set the world afire. In May 1984 *Newsweek* magazine
called her a "very talented actress," but cautioned that she "is in danger of becoming the
Norma Shearer of the '80s" because "a little of Close's selfless nobility goes a long way." In
the same month of the same year, on Broadway, she strode out of that brief Shearer
typecasting by playing the part of the "highly sexed, funny, idealistic and boisterous"
Annie in *The Real Thing*. The next year she was seen on screen as the devilish, flamboyant
MAXIE (1985). The goody-goody image was dissolved permanently with the release of
FATAL ATTRACTION (1987), in which she played a predatory soul hell-bent on revenge.

"Glennie," as she is known to friends, has gone from both on and off-Broadway to
films, back to Broadway, to television, and back to movies, where in 1988 she was voted
one of the top ten box-office draws of the year. Personally, she has moved from a
"morbidly shy" little girl to a "pleasing machine," and finally to the seemingly self-assured
woman of today. However, when asked on TV by interviewer Barbara Walters, "Who *is*
Glenn Close," her reply was, "The essence of me is still that little girl who was running
around in the country—pretending."

Glenn Close was born on Monday, May 19, 1947, in Greenwich, Connecticut, to
Dr. William Close and his wife, Bettine, both of whom were twenty-two years old. She
was the second child of four and was raised on her grandfather Close's large estate in
Greenwich. Because their ancestors had been instrumental in founding Greenwich late in
the seventeenth century, the Closes were considered members of the town's aristocracy.
The family's wealth also had much to do with the family's position. Glenn spent much of
her growing-up time by herself. Because of her extreme shyness, she played alone for hours
at a time, pretending she was someone or something else. Sometime between the ages of
five and seven she decided she wanted to become an actress.

When she was seven years old, Glenn's parents joined a quasi-religious organization
called Moral Rearmament, composed of affluent and socially conservative members. In

1960, when Glenn was thirteen, her father, a Harvard-educated surgeon, opened a clinic in the Belgian Congo (now Zaire) with the help of his wife. Their children lived with them briefly in Africa, but were soon sent to boarding schools in Switzerland and, later, in Connecticut. Glenn was enrolled at Rosemary Hall, an exclusive girls' boarding school in Greenwich. In school plays there, she opened up and "would do anything as a performer." With five other students she formed "The Fingernails, The Group with Polish," which did takeoffs on the popular songs of the day. They not only performed at Rosemary Hall but gave shows at other prep schools as well.

By 1965, when she graduated from Rosemary Hall, she was considered to be a talented lyric soprano. Then, at the age of eighteen, having decided against going to college, she joined a group called Up with People. She traveled around the world with this singing troupe, preaching old-fashioned values through song. During the Vietnam War, the group visited as many U.S. military bases as possible. "I wrote songs from the depths of my heart," she has said, "and sang them with great enthusiasm."

In 1969, while on the road, she married rock guitarist Cabot Wade. Together they dropped back into life and enrolled at the College of William and Mary in Williamsburg, Virginia, where Glenn majored in drama. The couple soon separated and were divorced in late 1971. Glenn emerged "spiritually bereft" and disillusioned from the experiences of marriage and traveling as a reactionary minstrel. She refers to the period between 1965 and 1970 as her "lost life."

In her senior year at college, she learned of a series of national stage auditions to be held in New York City, but did not think of herself as a likely candidate. Then, one afternoon while backstage painting scenery, she saw Dick Cavett interview Katharine Hepburn on TV. Hearing the legendary actress talk about her acting career inspired Close to decide positively, "If you want to do that, do it." She went to the head of the theater department and asked him to nominate her for the national auditions. He did. Later, she admitted, "I've always thought of that moment backstage watching Hepburn; it was like a penny dropped in my mind."

Glenn Close took part in the annual auditions held by the Theatre Communications Group for promising young thespians. She reached the final rounds, but did not win the competition. However, Broadway producer/director Hal Prince saw her tryout and offered her the job as understudy to Mary Ure in the New Phoenix Repertory Company's production of *Love for Love*, a Restoration comedy. On November 11, 1974, just prior to the final preview of the show at the Helen Hayes Theatre, Prince informed Glenn that Mary Ure had left the cast and that Glenn was to take over the role of Angelica. At the age of twenty-seven, suddenly, Glenn Close was on Broadway.

During the 1974–1975 Broadway season, after the close of *Love for Love*, Glenn remained with the New Phoenix company in revivals of Pirandello's *The Rules of the Game* and Carson McCullers's *The Member of the Wedding*, each of which ran for twelve performances. From there, she moved to regional theater productions—at such theaters as the Milwaukee Rep, Princeton's McCarter, New Haven's Long Wharf, the Yale Rep— where she appeared in a steady succession of parts in such plays as *King Lear, The Rose*

Tattoo, Uncle Vanya, and *A Streetcar Named Desire.* Off-Broadway she was in such shows as *Uncommon Women and Others.* In 1976 she appeared in her first Broadway musical, Richard Rodgers and Sheldon Harnick's *Rex,* which was a dismal failure and closed after only forty-one performances. That same year, her parents completed their medical missionary chores in Africa and returned to Greenwich.

During this time, Glenn became friendly with other actors who were making their way in the theater such as Mary Beth Hurt and William Hurt, Kevin Kline, John Lithgow, Christine Lahti, and Swoosie Kurtz. She would say later, "I feel like my generation is an exciting generation; I think that my peers are an exciting group of actors." Despite her crowded résumé, Glenn claims there were dry periods professionally when she was not working and "almost went crazy waiting for something to happen."

In January 1978 she auditioned at the Studio Arena Theatre in Buffalo for the role of villainess Irene St. Claire in Paul Giovanni's lighthearted mystery *The Crucifer of Blood,* based on Sherlock Holmes and other characters from the Arthur Conan Doyle stories. She won the part in the play, which opened on September 28, 1978, at the Helen Hayes Theatre on Broadway. The special effects by Bran Ferrin received the best notices, but the show ran for over two hundred performances. In 1979 she acted in two short-lived off-Broadway productions: *Wine Untouched* and *The Winter Dancers.* That same year she was in two made-for-television feature films. In NBC-TV's TOO FAR TO GO (March 12, 1979), she was seen as Rebecca Kuehn in the story of the dissolution of a twenty-year marriage; it was adapted from a series of stories by John Updike. In CBS-TV's ORPHAN TRAIN (December 22, 1979), she played the role of Jessica in a recreation of the true-life account of New York City slum orphans who in 1894 were taken to the Midwest in search of new families and lives.

Then, on April 30, 1980, Glenn embarked on what she later acknowledged to have been the turning point in her career. She opened at Broadway's St. James Theatre in *Barnum,* a musical about the life of Phineas T. Barnum (played by Jim Dale). In this razzle-dazzle production about the quintessential American showman, Glenn was cast as Barnum's wife, Charity. John Simon (*New York* magazine) reported that Close was "a splendid Mrs. Barnum, with the ambiguities of a passionate Puritan etched into the wily, pinched prettiness of her face, her very presence exuding the sour-sweet joys of circus lemonade." She was nominated for a Tony Award for Outstanding Performance by a Featured Actress in a Broadway Musical, but lost to Priscilla Lopez (*A Day in Hollywood/A Night in the Ukraine*).

In March 1981, after over three hundred performances as Charity Barnum, Glenn left the musical to go to Hollywood. Film director George Roy Hill, then preparing to shoot the screen adaptation of John Irving's comic novel *The World According to Garp,* had seen her in *Barnum.* He recalled later, "I noticed in Glenn a remarkable quality, a combination of dignity, warmth and extremely rare serenity." He cast her as the no-nonsense Jenny Fields who mates with a brain-damaged, bed-ridden paraplegic World War II gunner. From this pairing comes Garp, who was played as an adult by Robin Williams. In the course of the 136-minute THE WORLD ACCORDING TO GARP (1982),

Glenn's character ages thirty years, beginning as a young nurse, then becoming a single mother, and then authoring a book (*A Sexual Suspect*). The fame that follows makes her the unwitting idol of a group of radical feminists, among whom is the transsexual Roberta Muldoon (John Lithgow). The film, rated shallow and overlong, did not do well at the box office. However, Glenn received solid notices. *Variety* reported, "Stage actress Glenn Close proves a perfect choice as Jenny Fields, a woman of almost ethereal simplicity who achieves a certain greatness despite a total lack of ambition." Glenn was Oscar-nominated as Best Supporting Actress, but lost the Academy Award to Jessica Lange (TOOTSIE). During the filming of GARP, Glenn became involved romantically with John Starke, a production manager. This relationship dissolved when she returned to the East Coast to play the title role at the Manhattan Theatre Club in an adaptation of a short story, *The Singular Life of Albert Nobbs*. For her performance as a young woman of the 1860s who masquerades as a man to find employment, Glenn received an Obie Award for distinguished off-Broadway performance. However, the drama closed after a run of just four weeks, on July 10, 1982.

Lawrence Kasdan, the director/screenwriter/co-executive producer of THE BIG CHILL (1983) was so impressed with Glenn's work in GARP that he sent her the script of his forthcoming production and asked her to look at two parts. It was agreed that she would play Sarah, another earth mother type, while Mary Kay Place would be Meg. THE BIG CHILL concerns seven longtime friends who attend the funeral of another friend, who has killed himself. During the weekend spent at the home of Harold and Sarah Cooper (Kevin Kline, Close), they reexamine their past, explore the present, and hope for the future. Close's character, a physician who had had an extramarital affair with the deceased man, offers her husband as stud to Meg (Place), a single woman who has decided it is time for her to have a baby. Somewhat unexpectedly, THE BIG CHILL grossed over $50 million at the domestic box office. It helped launch the screen careers of Kevin Kline, Jeff Goldblum, and Meg Tilly; it further advanced the careers of Close, Tom Berenger, and William Hurt. For her second theatrical film, Glenn was again nominated for an Oscar as Best Supporting Actress. She lost this time to Linda Hunt (THE YEAR OF LIVING DANGEROUSLY). A bit of dialogue softly spoken by Glenn's character in THE BIG CHILL later seemed to have been prophetic of a drastic and sudden change in her own career: "Sometimes I wonder if maybe I was sick of being such a good girl. I could always be counted on to do the right thing. It's a disgusting curse."

On January 9, 1984, an estimated sixty million people watched the controversial, highly publicized television drama about incest SOMETHING ABOUT AMELIA. In this two-hour ABC-TV movie, Glenn was Gail Bennett, who slowly and devastatingly realizes that her husband (Ted Danson) is having sex with their teenaged daughter (Roxana Zal). At the time, SOMETHING ABOUT AMELIA earned the distinctions of being the second most popular TV film of all time (the most popular had been 1983's THE DAY AFTER) as well as jumping the hurdles of the medium's last taboo: incest. *Variety* noted that Glenn played her difficult part with "beautiful control." Both Close and Danson were nominated for Emmy Awards, but neither won.

THE STONE BOY (1984), a touching family drama, did not fare well commercially.

Close and Robert Duvall played a married couple struggling with a seemingly unremorseful son (Jason Presson) who has accidentally killed his older brother (Dean Cain). Eventually, the grandfather (Wilford Brimley) breaks through the boy's wall of silence. Glenn withdrew from the role of Verena Tarrant in the screen adaptation of Henry James's THE BOSTONIANS (1984) so that she could accept a role in THE NATURAL (1984), starring Robert Redford. Madeleine Potter took over Close's part in THE BOSTONIANS, while Glenn went to Buffalo for location shooting on THE NATURAL. Glenn was seen as the young girl who loves Nebraskan Roy Hobbs (Redford), who leaves her pregnant when he departs for a sports career. Years later, they meet just as he is resuming his baseball career and they reaffirm their love. Filled with baffling fantasy, the movie was not well understood by moviegoers, but because of Redford's box-office appeal, the perplexing movie was a moderate success. Glenn received her third Oscar nomination, but lost the Best Supporting Actress Award to Peggy Ashcroft (A PASSAGE TO INDIA).

Having played so many noble women, Glenn chose to break this pattern by appearing, with an English accent, as Annie in Tom Stoppard's play *The Real Thing*. She played a woman who has an adulterous affair with the already married Jeremy Irons, who is then divorced and weds her. Later, each of them is unfaithful to the other. Directed by Mike Nichols, *The Real Thing* premiered on January 5, 1984, at the Plymouth Theatre. Among the many Tony Awards won by the production was a Best Actress accolade for Glenn. Meanwhile, Glenn had dubbed the voice of Andie MacDowell (who had a South Carolinian drawl) as the aristocratic Victorian Jane Porter in GREYSTOKE: THE LEGEND OF TARZAN, LORD OF THE APES (1984). After leaving *The Real Thing*, Glenn starred on stage with William Hurt in Arthur Honegger's oratorio *Joan of Arc at the Stake* (1985), and with Sam Waterston and Mary Beth Hurt in Michael Frayn's *Benefactors* (1985). She also sang the national anthem at Shea Stadium before the New York Mets' first game of the baseball season. Meanwhile, on September 1, 1984, she married New York venture capitalist James Marsalis in a ceremony on Nantucket Island, Massachusetts.

MAXIE (1985), set in present-day San Francisco, offered Glenn a dual role. She played a staid and proper church librarian whose marriage (to Mandy Patinkin) is disrupted when the ghost of a 1920s flapper takes over her mind and body. There are several delightful moments in MAXIE,

Glenn Close in THE NATURAL (1984).

especially when Glenn shimmies and sings "Bye, Bye, Blackbird," much to the chagrin of a party room filled with librarians. Through no fault of Close's, MAXIE was not a success, its whimsy failing to find a wide audience. On the other hand, JAGGED EDGE (1985) was a major success. Glenn played the San Francisco corporate attorney asked to defend a playboy businessman (Jeff Bridges) accused of murdering his wife and maid. Soon she is beguiled by her charming client, who, she discovers, is not innocent, which prompts her to take drastic action. *Variety* observed, "Triple-Oscar nominees Bridges and Close play a balancing act that is both glossy and psychologically interesting."

Based on a forty-five-minute film (DIVERSION) that Britisher James Dearden had written/directed in 1979, FATAL ATTRACTION (1987) was conceived originally as a starring vehicle for French actress Isabelle Adjani. Later choices for the role included Debra Winger, Barbara Hershey, Kate Capshaw, and Mimi Rogers. Finally, Glenn, who had wanted the role, was hired by director Adrian Lyne. She worked with a trainer to lose fifteen pounds to look more sinister, while consulting with several psychiatrists to help her diagnose her character's compulsion. Glenn is the aggressive woman who seduces willing married man Michael Douglas. When he tries to sever the relationship so that he can return to his normal home life with his wife (Anne Archer) and six-year-old daughter (Ellen Hamilton Latzen), she refuses to be cast aside and obsessively pursues him. In the final showdown, it is Archer who defeats the demented, murderous Close. The crafty thriller struck a responsive chord in filmgoers and it grossed more than $150 million at the domestic box office. The ending was shot twice: in the first version, Close committed suicide to an aria from Puccini's *Madama Butterfly*; the second ending is the one seen in U.S. theaters and in the video release. *People* magazine termed Glenn "The antiheroine of the year" in "a performance of slamming energy and emotional precision." Glenn was Oscar-nominated, this time in the Best Actress category. However, she lost to Cher (MOONSTRUCK). Perhaps in commemoration of the screen role that provided her with such a reversal in screen characterizations, Glenn had the butcher's knife so prominently wielded in FATAL ATTRACTION framed and displayed on a wall of her den.

During the spring of 1987, Glenn and husband James Marsalis were divorced. Thereafter, in the summer of 1987, she began a relationship with producer John Starke, by whom she had a child, Annie Maude, born on April 26, 1988. When asked why she and Starke, aged thirty-seven, had not wed, she replied, "I've failed at two marriages and I don't want to get married until that's the best thing for us to do." Meanwhile, she was heard but not seen in LIGHT YEARS (1987), an animated science fiction tale written by Isaac Asimov. She provided the voice of Ambisextra. On CBS-TV, Glenn starred in STONES FOR IBARRA (January 29, 1988), a Hallmark Hall of Fame production. She and Keith Carradine co-starred as an American couple who move to a small village in Mexico into a house abandoned by the husband's grandfather in 1910. They achieve a blissful existence until the husband dies of leukemia. *TV Guide* magazine called the production a "haunting drama." Also in early 1988 Glenn was nominated for a Grammy for her spoken word recording of *The Legend of Sleepy Hollow* for Windham Hill. She also recorded an album of lullabies. For the PBS-TV series "The American Experience," Glenn narrated the segment "Do You Mean There Are Still Real Cowboys?"

Derived from Pierre Choderlos de Laclos's 1782 novel and Christopher Hampton's 1985 play, DANGEROUS LIAISONS (1988) was a superior retelling of sex and seduction among the aristocracy in eighteenth-century France. Glenn was the regally bosomy Marquise de Merteuil who matches power and wits with her ex-lover, the dandified Vicomte de Valmont (John Malkovich). He in turn falls in love with a married woman of quality (Michelle Pfeiffer). *Time* magazine opined that Glenn "secretes contempt under her frozen smile" and added that she was "wanly handsome." The *San Francisco Chronicle* named her the "most memorable" in the cast, observing, "When Merteuil finally lets loose and gives way to complete animal despair, Close is horrifying." For the fifth time, Glenn was Oscar-nominated. Again she lost the award—this time for Best Actress—to Jodie Foster (THE ACCUSED). In spite of glowing reviews and sumptuous settings and costumes, the period picture did not do well financially. Almost a year later, in November 1989, Orion released another version of the story, entitled VALMONT, in which Annette Bening, a relative newcomer, attempted the complex role of the seductive Marquise de Merteuil. Unfortunately for Bening, her performance, under Milos Forman's direction, paled in comparison to Glenn's interpretation.

Generally not political, Glenn attended a benefit for People Taking Action Against AIDS in Bellport, New York, as well as joined the 500,000 persons who converged on Washington, D.C., in April 1989 in support of women's right to abortion. She emerged a feminist, telling the *London Daily Mail*: "[Women] are emotionally and spiritually stronger than men, and sometimes we are more ruthless whether it's in sex, politics or whatever. Men, I think, are more vulnerable. . . . I have never wanted to be a man. I feel sorry for them."

As a change of pace and seemingly to demonstrate that she could play a very sympathetic, smiling character on screen, she accepted the co-lead in IMMEDIATE FAMILY (1989). She is a childless married woman who, with her husband (James Woods), invites a pregnant teenager (Mary Stuart Masterson) into their home, hoping to arrange to adopt the baby. The picture was called a "three-tissue heart-tugger" (by the *San Francisco Chronicle*). *Variety* observed, "Clever as she is, Close keeps her potentially cloying part understated." The movie was not an audience-drawer.

Glenn was honored on December 13, 1989, at the annual luncheon of New York Women in Film where she was handed the "Muse" for outstanding achievement. Later, students at Harvard University gave her the 1990 Woman of the Year distinction on February 13, 1990. On May 16, 1990, she appeared briefly in the PBS-TV tribute to songwriter Joe Raposo, "Sesame Street Remembers Joe Raposo."

REVERSAL OF FORTUNE (1990), set in privileged Newport, Rhode Island, reunited Glenn with Jeremy Irons. The movie had its unofficial world premiere at the September 1–3 (Labor Day weekend), 1990, Telluride Film Festival in Telluride, Colorado. Glenn portrayed real-life Sunny von Bulow in the story of the events leading up to and following Sunny's entrance into an insulin-induced coma in 1980, after she was allegedly injected with an insulin overdose by her husband, Claus (Irons), who sought to gain a $14 million inheritance. The film is told from the point of view of Sunny (and narrated by Glenn). The *Christian Science Monitor*, on hand at Telluride, reported that the wife was "brilliantly played" and that "Though the film lacks substance, each performance is as fascinating and intricate as a Swiss watch." *Daily Variety* reported, "Glenn Close is typically excellent in the smaller but pivotal role of Sunny von Bulow. . . . Except for one brief scene of flowering love, Close is obliged to play Sunny as a haggard, emotionally damaged woman whose fate may or may not have been the outcome of an impulse toward self-destruction." (During Glenn's marriage to James Marsalis, when the couple had lived on Fifth Avenue, she had attended several dinner parties at which Claus von Bulow was also a guest.) In its first seven weeks of release, REVERSAL OF FORTUNE grossed $9,653,227 at the domestic box office.

To qualify for Oscar consideration, HAMLET, filmed in England with Mel Gibson and Britishers Alan Bates, Paul Scofield, Ian Holm, and Helena Bonham-Carter, was released in New York, Los Angeles, and Toronto in December 1990. Under Franco Zeffirelli's direction, Glenn was seen as Gertrude, Hamlet's tormented mother.

For the third TNT cable special honoring three leading ladies from Hollywood's Golden Age, Glenn was the host of "The Divine Garbo" (December 3, 1990), following Kathleen Turner's tribute to Myrna Loy and Jessica Lange's to Vivien Leigh. Meanwhile, Glenn and her REVERSAL OF FORTUNE co-star Jeremy Irons co-starred on the home video release *Saint-Saëns Carnival of the Animals*, in which they narrated verses by Ogden Nash to accompany the score.

During the 1990–1991 season on CBS-TV, Glenn was in the turn-of-the-century pioneer drama SARAH PLAIN AND TALL (February 3, 1991). She had the title role of the mail-order bride of Christopher Walken, a Kansas widower with two children. She does not consider the TV movie, a "Hallmark Hall of Fame" presentation, which she co-executive produced, a comedown after HAMLET, nor does she condone such "snobbery."

Long discussed, a sequel to JAGGED EDGE was shelved during 1990, while Glenn returned to Europe (Budapest and Paris) to star as an internationally famed opera soprano in MEETING VENUS (1991), for which her singing voice was dubbed by Dame Kiri Te Kanawa. A comedy, it told of the chaos involving the efforts to stage an opera with a multinational company.

Regarding her chosen profession, Close says, "I'm a very competitive person, but I don't believe in competing with individual people because it's destructive. The best piece of advice I got on the first job I had was: 'Never compare your career with anybody else's. You'd jump out a window.'"

Filmography

Too Far to Go (NBC-TV, 3/12/79) [released theatrically in altered version by Zoetrope in 1982]
Orphan Train (CBS-TV, 12/22/79)
The World According to Garp (WB, 1982)

The Big Chill (Col, 1983)
Something About Amelia (ABC-TV, 1/9/84)
The Stone Boy (20th–Fox, 1984)
The Natural (Tri-Star, 1984)
Greystoke: The Legend of Tarzan, Lord of the

Apes (WB, 1984) (voice only)
Maxie (Orion, 1985)
Jagged Edge (Col, 1985)
Fatal Attraction (Par, 1987)
Light Years (Miramax, 1987) (voice only)
Stones for Ibarra (CBS-TV, 1/29/88)
Dangerous Liaisons (WB, 1988)
Immediate Family (Col, 1989)

Reversal of Fortune (WB, 1990)
Hamlet (WB, 1990)
Sarah Plain and Tall (CBS-TV, 2/3/91) (also co-executive producer)
Meeting Venus (WB, 1991)

Broadway Plays

Love for Love (1974) (revival)
The Rules of the Game (1975) (revival)
The Member of the Wedding (1975) (revival)
Rex (1976)

The Crucifer of Blood (1978)
Barnum (1980)
The Real Thing (1984)
Benefactors (1985)

Album Discography

Barnum (Columbia JS-36576) [OC]
The Emperor & The Nightingale (Windham Hill WH-0706)
The Legend of Sleepy Hollow (Windham Hill WH-0711)
Rex (RCA ABL1-1683) [OC]

KEVIN COSTNER

"Calling me 'the sexiest man' is just nonsense. It's just not true, and it gets in the way of everything else I'm trying to do as an actor."
—*Playgirl* magazine, January 1988

PRIOR TO 1987, THE GENERAL PUBLIC WAS NOT PARTICULARLY AWARE of Kevin Costner. He had appeared in a handful of low-budget movies with limited distribution and in a few grade-A features, either in the background, much like an extra with dialogue, or in undemanding roles. In 1985 he was noticed as something of a nut on camera in a comedic western, but it took playing Eliot Ness on screen to really bring him to the attention of viewers. Next—in a steamy, graphic love scene played in the back seat of a chauffeured limousine—he gained worldwide recognition as a hunk, a sex symbol. Almost instantly he was at the top of his profession in movies. He has been called the box-office king, Hollywood's most sought-after leading man. Much of the film industry does not know what to make of him, since he turns down very commercial projects in favor of making a lower salary for films he cares about and for which he wants to be remembered. All successful actors are inevitably compared with actors of the past. In Kevin's case, he is the new Gary Cooper or James Stewart or Clark Gable. *Vanity Fair* magazine analyzed his charisma this way: "Just standing there and delivering his lines Costner projects a fascinating volatility. You don't know what he might do next: grab the gun, grab the girl, or do a backflip. He is something the movies haven't seen for a while . . . a leading man."

Kevin Michael Costner was born on Tuesday, January 18, 1955, in Compton, California, a small town to the south of Los Angeles. His father, Bill, worked for Southern California Edison; his mother was with the department of social services. He was preceded in birth by brother Dan, in 1951. The Costners, of German and Irish descent, with a touch of Cherokee Indian blood, had moved west after losing their Oklahoma farmland. Since the senior Costner was constantly transferred throughout southern California in connection with his work, the sons never developed roots in any one place. Kevin was forced to change schools each time they moved. He remembers seeing HOW THE WEST WAS WON (1962) over and over as a youngster until he could recite much of the dialogue from memory. This was perhaps the beginning of his strong attachment to the Old West. He also grew up loving baseball. In school he sang a bit and was in a few plays, but never gave a thought to acting as a profession. He remembers his contented childhood with, "I didn't always have this egotistical desire to be the center of attention 'cause it wasn't tolerated in our family. No one was special."

Kevin grew up shy around girls, possibly due to his height. When he completed high school, he was still just 5' 2". When he was eighteen, he left Los Angeles to travel. He acquired a canoe and followed the trail taken by expeditioners Lewis and Clark, hunting for food and pitching a tent or sleeping out in the wilds. He visited the locale where Custer made his last stand. Later, he would admit, "I love that existence. I often feel I was born thirty years too late for the movies and a hundred years too late for real life."

Thereafter, he enrolled as a business major at California State University at Fullerton. At this point, he began to grow, eventually achieving his current height of 6' 1". During his college years, in 1975, he met co-ed Cindy Silva. They dated during the school year, but during the summer, she worked at Disneyland portraying Snow White, while he worked at odd jobs or headed north on fishing trips. In 1977, after both graduated from college, they were married. After honeymooning in Puerto Vallarta, Mexico, they flew back to Los Angeles on the same flight as actor Richard Burton. When Kevin asked his advice on becoming an actor, Burton told him to "make up your mind to let nothing . . . stand in your way." Cindy went to work for Delta Airlines. Kevin took a marketing job, but quickly became bored. One day he saw an advertisement for the South Coast Actor's Co-op in Los Angeles, which was producing *Rumpelstiltskin.* On the spot he made up his mind to become an actor, and he soon quit his job. "I never looked back," he would say. "I never breathed an easier breath. I relaxed. Then all I had to do was learn."

Part of his training was at the Actor's Co-op Workshop, where he appeared in a few community theater productions, including *Waiting for Lefty* and *A View from the Bridge.* At the same time, he took a job as stage manager at Raleigh Studios, across the street from Paramount Studios. Raleigh specialized in commercials and inexpensively mounted independent films. In 1979 a Raleigh director and Kevin's acting coach, Richard Brander, was casting an exploitation entry entitled MALIBU HOT SUMMER. Rather than ask for an audition, Kevin mailed in his photograph and a résumé. He was given the part of a wealthy cowboy who falls in love with a large-breasted lady. The film's producer, Eric Louzil, later recalled, "He had to do a scene where he's making love to the director's wife in front of a fireplace. He was real nervous. . . . He kissed her, but it was like he wasn't into it." Kevin received no salary for this nonunion work, which he claims he did for experience. The picture received scant distribution in 1980–1981, but was rereleased in May 1987 to capitalize on Costner's rising star status. Years later, Costner would say of this early filmmaking experience, "it taught me a valuable lesson. It changed me, not so much because of the low budget, but because of the filmmakers' low-budget thinking. And that's stayed with me ever since."

For the next six years, Kevin devoted himself to "studying intensely." To gain ease in front of the camera and to earn money, he worked for a modeling agency that put him to work in an ad for Gianfranco Ferre tuxedos. In the spring of 1981 he performed in a slasher drama, SHADOWS RUN BLACK, playing the minor role of a man accused of being the "Black Angel" serial killer. The tawdry picture sat on the shelf until it was released in 1986 directly to video, at which time *Variety* reported, "Tech credits are weak and acting, apart from Costner, only semi-pro." For Warner Bros. he was an extra in NIGHT SHIFT

(1982), as a frat man in a group that visits the morgue where Michael Keaton and Henry Winkler work. In FRANCES (1982) Costner can be spotted standing outside the stage door of Broadway's Belasco Theatre where Frances Farmer (Jessica Lange) is appearing in *Golden Boy*. In his "role" as the real-life actor Luther Adler, Costner had a line of dialogue consisting of three words—"Good night, Frances"—to be uttered as they leave the theater. Kevin, though, refused to say the words, insisting that it was not in character for Adler to say that. After four takes and still no words from Kevin, a body microphone was placed on him, in hopes he might say something. On the next take, the sound man verified that Kevin had indeed said the three required words, although they were barely audible. The scene of Lange waving and Kevin saying good night does not appear in the final print of FRANCES. However, the sound man's confirmation was enough to warrant Kevin's membership in the Screen Actors Guild. Years later, Kevin recalled, "I walked to the bus—the extras' bus—and sat there, all by myself. . . . I felt like crying. I said 'What is wrong with you? What was so fucking hard about saying that line?'"

Sometime in 1982 he worked, again without pay, in a low-budget picture, CHASING DREAMS, which was released in 1985 by producer David Brown of Nascent Productions. His character in this baseball story is on camera for about the first two minutes and then disappears, going off to medical school. After Kevin became a star, this unremarkable film was released by Prism Entertainment on videocassette in mid-1989, with a huge picture on the box of Costner wearing a baseball uniform.

TABLE FOR FIVE (1983), starring Jon Voight, was a class-A drama that did only modest box-office business. Kevin was twelfth-billed as the "newlywed husband" aboard the Norwegian Lines' *Vistafjord*, bound for the Near East. He and his on-camera wife (Cynthia Kania) had inconsequential dialogue that was deliberately out of range of the microphone and had nothing to do with the main proceedings. STACY'S KNIGHTS, another shoestring-budgeted offering, was released by Crown International in June 1983. Kevin received second billing as Will, who is tossed off a bridge and drowned in the waters below. That year Costner lost to Michael Nouri the lead part of Nick in the very successful FLASHDANCE.

Convinced it was to be his really big break in the movie world, Kevin eagerly accepted the role of Alex in THE BIG CHILL (1983), a major movie directed/produced/co-written by Lawrence Kasdan. Earlier, Kevin had agreed to a role in WARGAMES (1983), but withdrew in order to work with the likes of Glenn Close, Kevin Kline, William Hurt, and the rest of the impressive cast in the Kasdan feature. It is at the funeral of suicide victim Alex that seven friends from the 1960s meet and reevaluate their lives. Kevin was to be shown in the casket as well as in a flashback scene dressed in bell-bottoms and with ponytail. However, both scenes were excised for the sake of continuity and to shorten the long film. All that remains of Costner—if indeed it is Kevin—is a shot of an arm with stitches in the wrist while the credits unfold. Kasdan, who referred to Kevin as "a smart actor," promised to make it up to him for having his part cut.

Kevin tried out for a supporting part in the PBS-TV "American Playhouse" production of TESTAMENT as Phil Pitkin, who leaves Hamlin, California, with his wife

(Rebecca DeMornay) after their baby dies of the effects of nuclear fallout. The somber but well-regarded film was released theatrically by Paramount in 1983, prior to being shown on TV in November 1984.

In 1984 he turned down a role in the big-budgeted MRS. SOFFEL, but instead became involved in a twenty-four-day shoot in Canada on THE GUNRUNNER. In this cheapie, set in 1926, he played a man returning home to Montreal from China to launch a one-man vendetta against corruption while running guns to back a revolution in China. This aborted project finally saw distribution in a 1989 home video edition, distributed by New World Pictures and Video Voice. In January 1985 Costner was seen in FANDANGO as one of five 1971 college graduates who embark on a final fling before facing the world as adults. The quickie had been shot in mid-1983. *Variety* recorded that Kevin, as the irresponsible ringleader, is "charismatic enough to hold both the fictional group and the pic together, he has the sort of dangerous unpredictability that makes for topflight film performers." In limited release for one week, FANDANGO grossed just $50,347 domestically.

Lawrence Kasdan proved to be a man of his word when he included a part for Kevin in SILVERADO (1985). This comedic western was a surprise hit of that summer, grossing more than $32.2 million in domestic distribution. It is the movie that brought Kevin to the attention of filmgoers and filmmakers. In it he played Jake, the younger brother of Scott Glenn, a cackly laughing, wild cowboy in full command of a six-shooter. *Newsweek* magazine remarked on his "seductive flash" and predicted that his performance was certain to "win a lot of fans." In its July 1985 issue, *GQ* magazine turned most of the male cast members, including Kevin, into models, photographing them in western-style "high noon of men's fashion."

Kevin sought the part of the biker in MASK (1985), but lost it to Sam Elliott. He was considered not well-enough known to handle the lead in AIR AMERICA, which changed production hands several times before being filmed for 1990 release with Mel Gibson. Costner claims to have turned down the male lead in JAGGED EDGE (1985), which went to Jeff Bridges. He did star in AMERICAN FLYERS (1985) as Marcus, who is suffering from a fatal illness but spurs his brother (David Grant) to join him in competing in and winning a cross-country bicycle event. In *The Andy Warhol Diaries* (1989), Andy's entry for September 3, 1985, includes: "And for Kevin Costner, he'll have a big career."

During 1985, the professionally busy Kevin became a father for the first time when Cindy gave birth to daughter Annie. Two years later, a second daughter, Lily, was born, and in 1988, a son, whom they named Joe. (As the years passed, the Costners would divide their time between three California residences: an unpretentious home in a middle-class neighborhood near Pasadena, a beach house in Santa Barbara, and a condominium in the California Sierras.) Costner capped the year on November 3, 1985, on NBC-TV with the role of the cigar-chomping captain of a World War II bomber in a one-hour special edition of "Amazing Stories," the short-lived Steven Spielberg series.

Costner vetoed an offer to take the role of Sergeant Barnes in PLATOON (1986) because his brother, Dan, had served in Vietnam. "I didn't even meet with him [Oliver

Stone]," Kevin has said, "because . . . I was reluctant to do a film about something that had such impact on . . . life. In a way I regret not doing it; it was a wonderful film. But my consciousness was with my brother." It was Tom Berenger who played the role of Barnes, which garnered him an Oscar nomination. In 1986, without his having appeared in a feature film that year, *Screen World* chose Kevin as one of twelve "promising new actors" of the year. He did, however, appear in a silent short subject called BAD DAY, which saw limited release. He was voted a "Star of Tomorrow" by the National Association of Theater Owners in 1986.

One of the summer hits of 1987 was THE UNTOUCHABLES, the Brian De Palma–directed mega-gangster feature, which cost an estimated $24 million and for which an entire block of Chicago's LaSalle Street was recreated on the Paramount lot; the set required sixty vintage automobiles of the 1930s. Opening in 1,012 movie houses across the nation in June, the action movie grossed $16 million in its first week, with an ultimate domestic box-office gross of more than $74.5 million. Producer Art Linson first thought of either Harrison Ford or William Hurt for the Ness role, but both were busy. "We needed someone with the right combination of naivete, earnestness and strength," Linson told the press. Linson had seen Costner in SILVERADO and asked him to audition. "I immediately thought he was a passionate young man who'd look good with a gun," Linson would recall. Critic Roger Ebert wrote that THE UNTOUCHABLES "has great costumes, great sets, great cars, great guns, great locations, and a few shots that absolutely capture the Prohibition Era, but it does not have a great script, great performances, or great direction." Of Kevin's interpretation of the incorruptible Eliot Ness, Ebert assessed, "Costner is fine for the role, but it's a thankless one, giving him little to do other than act grim and incorrigible." Kevin's estimated salary for the movie was $800,000. At this time he signed with agent Mike Ovitz, who also represented Sean Connery, who won an Academy Award as Best Supporting Actor for his role in the picture.

Kevin campaigned for the lead role in RAISING ARIZONA (1987), but lost that one to Nicolas Cage. On the other hand, he waged a successful battle to star as the double-dealing Naval officer in an updated remake of the thriller THE BIG CLOCK (1947), which Orion was to distribute under the title NO WAY OUT (1987). This movie firmly established Kevin as a "nouveau sex symbol" due to his well-etched graphic sex scene in the back of a limousine with Sean Young. NO WAY OUT, in its first weekend of release in August 1987, realized $4.3 million in domestic box-office receipts and $10.2 million in its second week. With these figures a new label was born: "Costner Charisma!" He was now a bankable screen hunk.

US magazine has claimed, "While Costner's star has been on the rise for some time, it was BULL DURHAM [1988] that turned him into a leading-man legend." The athletic actor chose to do a movie concerned with his favorite sport, baseball, rather than star in other 1988 releases: MISSISSIPPI BURNING (that role went to Willem Dafoe), BETRAYED (Tom Berenger starred), EVERYBODY'S ALL-AMERICAN (Dennis Quaid did it), and THE ACCIDENTAL TOURIST (William Hurt got the lead). In BULL DURHAM, it is Susan Sarandon with whom he has the hot love scene. Released in June 1988, BULL DURHAM was called "A major league romp" by *Newsweek* magazine, which found of Costner, "He's acquired that lived-in, understated sensuality, laced with bitter wit, that Clark Gable used to have and that Paul Newman acquired with age." Historically, baseball movies have not done well at the box office, but in 1988 BULL DURHAM changed that by earning $49.9 million, while EIGHT MEN OUT, a second baseball film (also from Orion Pictures), fizzled. During the 1989 baseball season, Kevin had his own baseball card as a star "switch-hitter" of the Durham Bulls, one of a twenty-nine-player card set sold by the team for $5.

In August 1988 Kevin went to Japan to test a side career by singing with a group called "Roving Boy." The group's single "The Simple Truth" was charted #1 on Japan's foreign record chart while it ranked #67 on the domestic pop list. Also in August he was headlined, along with Mark Harmon and Tom Cruise, by CBS-TV's "Evening Magazine" as one of the "Hunks of Summer." Costner continued to reject properties: he turned down the leads in such films as PRINCE OF TIDES (eventually taken by Nick Nolte), THE HUNT FOR RED OCTOBER (assumed by Alec Baldwin), PRESUMED INNOCENT (played by Harrison Ford), and THE BONFIRE OF THE VANITIES (Tom Hanks took the part).

FIELD OF DREAMS (1989) has been termed "supersentimental" (*People* magazine) and a "Male weepie at its wussiest" (*Time* magazine), and *Seventeen* magazine instructed its young readers "to avoid this one." However, by September 1989 the movie, which *Variety* judged "Alternately affecting and affected . . . a fable about redemption and reconciliation," had grossed more than $63 million domestically. Another movie about baseball— Kevin's third—FIELD OF DREAMS was shot on location in Dyersville, Iowa. Kevin was featured as a college-educated Iowa farmer who, having inherited a passion for baseball from his father, a minor-league baseball player, now wants to make something special of his life. Costner listens to a mysterious "voice" that urges him to plow under his cornfields and create a baseball field. Soon the spirits of an array of deceased baseball greats arrive to play on the diamond, an occurrence initially seen by Costner and his family, but by no one else. Before the fantasy is completed, the revitalized Costner saves his farm from creditors.

On December 29, 1989, the women's group Man Watchers, Inc., of Los Angeles named Kevin Costner as their number one choice to watch, followed by Mel Gibson and Arsenio Hall.

With his salary now in the $3 million range, Kevin starred in REVENGE (1990). The Tony Scott–directed movie had him as a former U.S. Air Force pilot in Mexico who becomes romantically involved with the wife (Madeleine Stowe) of an elderly Mexican (Anthony Quinn), who then seeks revenge on the younger man. The picture was previewed in mid-July 1989 but was so poorly received that it was pulled for reworking. However, the expensive revamping did not help and the dramatic mishmash sank quickly from sight. Negative reviews—such as *New York* magazine's comment that "the movie just slides away from the audience into the pink dust" and *USA Today*'s observation that "If Costner's clout gets this 124-minute snooze even three weeks of business, dust off the Tom Cruise 'cocktail' award"—did not totally repel his fans. In two weeks of domestic release, REVENGE managed to gross $10.9 million.

In June 1989 Kevin and Orion Pictures entered into a long-term arrangement whereby Costner would produce and/or star in a number of pictures for the studio under his Tig Productions banner. The first project, DANCES WITH WOLVES (1990), cast Costner (who also served as director) as a Civil War Union Army officer stationed out west who is adopted by a Sioux Indian tribe and becomes involved romantically with a white woman (Mary McDonnell) raised by the tribe. Photographed near Rapid City, South Dakota, the finished film went over budget by $2 million (reportedly paid by Kevin) and ran over three hours. Orion did not, however, force Kevin to make cuts, but instead marketed the film as an "epic." At the time of its release in November 1990, Newmarket Press distributed a 192-page softcover book on the making of the picture. The epic itself met with almost universal praise: "Considering the scope and the ambitiousness of the material, the success of Costner and every one of his team seems monumental" (Sheila Benson, *Los Angeles Times*); "As a director, Costner is alive to the sweep of the country and the expansive spirit of the western-movie tradition" (Richard Schickel, *Time* magazine); "No dusty revisionist history . . . it's a wonderfully warm, rustling movie" (Duane Byrge, *Hollywood Reporter*); "In his directorial debut, Kevin Costner brings a rare degree of grace and feeling to this elegiac tale of a hero's adventure of discovery" (*Daily Variety*). In its first twenty weeks of domestic distribution, DANCES WITH WOLVES grossed an impressive $144,513,302 at the box office. However, the unorthodox Costner, more interested in producing creative art his way than in financial success Hollywood-style, is quick to note to industry observers, "I'm not in the hit business. To me, a flop is a bad movie, not one that fails at the box office."

DANCES WITH WOLVES would win a host of awards from various prestigious organizations in early 1991, climaxed by the film's earning seven Academy Awards at the March 25, 1991, Oscar ceremonies. Although Costner lost out to Jeremy Irons (REVERSAL OF FORTUNE) for Best Actor, he won as Best Director and saw his epic project win accolades for Best Picture and Best Adapted Screenplay among other awards. Said Costner when accepting his Oscars, "I will never forget what happened here tonight. My family will never forget. My Native American friends will never forget."

Meanwhile, in February 1990 Kevin was chosen by Harvard University's Hasty Pudding Theatricals as Man of the Year, and took time away from editing DANCES WITH WOLVES to appear with a host of

Kevin Costner in FIELD OF DREAMS (1989).

other celebrities in ABC-TV's "The Earth Day Special" (April 22, 1990). To attract the summer 1990 trade at New York's Stage Deli Restaurant, the management concocted the Kevin Costner sandwich. In October 1990, *US* magazine rated Kevin as among America's sexiest entertainers, reasoning, "No matter how hard he tries, Kevin Costner can't help being sexy. . . . Whatever his wardrobe, Costner always wears his sensitivity, modesty and integrity on his sleeve." (The typically modest actor once said of his much-touted physical appeal, "I've been told that the camera is really good to me, but sometimes when people meet me, they're baffled.")

Three projects, independent of one another, revolving around the legend of Robin Hood were on the drawing boards at the same time. However, Morgan Creek Productions jumped into the lead by signing Kevin at $7.5 million plus a percentage to star in its ROBIN HOOD: PRINCE OF THIEVES (1991). Filmed near Southampton, England, under the direction of Kevin Reynolds (FANDANGO), it co-starred Christian Slater, Morgan Freeman, and Mary Elizabeth Mastrantonio.

MICK, a product of Tig Productions scheduled for Orion Pictures release in 1991, stars Kevin as another legendary hero, Michael Collins, who led the fight for Irish independence early in this century. And while Costner pitched Suntory Malt in advertisements in Japan at a salary of about $1 million, he and Susan Sarandon and Tim Robbins were asked to reprise their original roles in BULL DURHAM II. Also forthcoming for Kevin is AMERICAN SPORTSMAN, a yuppie male-bonding drama co-starring Dustin Hoffman, as well as a possible co-starring role opposite Whitney Houston in THE BODYGUARD, scripted by Lawrence Kasdan. On the other side of the cameras, Kevin and Jim Wilson's Tig Productions has CHINA MOON, a *film noir* vehicle starring Ed Harris and Madeleine Stowe, planned for release in 1991–1992.

Of his newly found star status and the attention it has brought from fans and media alike, the 6' 1", 170-pound Costner has said wistfully, "There's something in my life that's slipping away . . . that I'll never have again. It's like this threatening thing that's coming to envelop me." He also admits, "I don't offer up everything there is, on screen or in life. It's not guile, but conversation is supposed to be a two-way thing, and generally people want to know more about me than they want to reveal about themselves. So, of course, I hold back. I'm not dying to tell people my story." Regarding his career choice, Costner explains, "I don't think people have a clue how I approach my work. . . . They think 'Leading actor, good times, good life,' and they don't realize that probably the most fun for me is being in my office and writing. . . . I like getting dirty with film and that is my life—the movies and how they work."

Filmography

Sizzle Beach, U.S.A. [Malibu Hot Summer] (Troma Team, 1987) [made in 1979; initially released ca. 1980]
Night Shift (WB, 1982)
Frances (Univ, 1982) [scene deleted]

Table for Five (WB, 1983)
Stacy's Knights (Crown International, 1983)
The Big Chill (Col, 1983)
Testament (Par, 1983)
Silverado (Col, 1985)

Fandango (WB, 1985) [made in 1983]
American Flyers (WB, 1985)
Chasing Dreams (Nascent Productions, 1985)
[made in 1982]
Shadows Run Black (Media Gallery, 1986)
[made in 1981]
Bad Day (Unk, 1986) (silent short subject)
The Untouchables (Par, 1987)
No Way Out (Orion, 1987)
Bull Durham (Orion, 1988)
The Gunrunner (New World Pictures, 1989)
[made in 1984]

Field of Dreams (Univ, 1989)
Revenge (Col, 1990)
Dances with Wolves (Orion, 1990) (also
director)
Robin Hood: Prince of Thieves (WB, 1991)

Future Releases

Mick (Orion, 1991)

BILLY CRYSTAL

"How many people like doing what they do in life? I remember
feeling, when I was doing 'Faerie Tale Theatre,' what a great joy to
sit in wardrobe and hear, 'What size hoof do you think you are?'"
—*American Film* magazine, July/August 1989

SHOW BUSINESS WAS BILLY CRYSTAL'S DESTINY. HE WAS BORN OF PAR-
ents committed to acting and music, descended from a grandparent heavily involved in
Yiddish theater, and was enveloped by singers and musicians from the time he toddled out
of his crib. Added to this heritage is the huge talent that propelled him to eventual
stardom. Very early in life, he drew upon good-natured imitations of those around him in
creating costumed characters with ethnic accents. Later, in his involvement with stand-up
comedy, the "Jewish leprechaun" became more famous for his off-the-wall characterizations than for his one-liners. His delivery of self-written words, although not intended to
offend, has incurred indignation from such diverse persons as Esther Williams (former
MGM swim queen) and The Sons of Italy. As with Dana Carvey, like Crystal a "Saturday
Night Live" cast member, the word "elfin" is frequently used to describe his 5' 6", 130-
pound physique. However, more like Robin Williams, Crystal eagerly shares his unre-
strained love for fun with appreciative audiences.

William Crystal was born on Friday, March 14, 1947, the third son of Jack and
Helen Gabler Crystal in Manhattan. The son of a Yiddish actor, Jack was the manager of
his brother-in-law's Commodore Music Shop on 52nd Street as well as the producer of
jazz concerts held on the Lower East Side. Helen Crystal, a great lover of theater,
performed in plays held at the family temple, while her brother, Milton, founder of
Commodore Records in the late 1930s, headed Decca Records. Forebears from both sides
of the family had immigrated to the United States from Russia.

After living the first two years of his life in the Bronx, Billy moved with the clan to
Long Beach, Long Island, which became headquarters for visiting jazz musicians from all
around New York. Billy and his brothers, Joel and Richard, grew up with W. C. Handy,
Billie Holiday, and Pee Wee Russell as friends; the latter taught Billy to play clarinet.
Helen Crystal encouraged her offspring to act or play instruments. When she uncovered
Billy's talent for imitating jive talk and Jewish accents, she helped him stage shows at home
as well as introduced him to comedy recordings. Billy's favorite was an LP by Bill Cosby
relating funny family stories, which Crystal emulated by tales of his own relatives. With his
brothers, Billy lip-synched to records by Spike Jones, Mel Brooks, Ernie Kovacs, and

others. He loved movies, with SHANE (1953) being his special favorite, and he never missed an Academy Awards show on the Crystals' black-and-white DuMont TV set. During the on-air commercials he would imitate the master of ceremonies, using a toothbrush as his make-believe microphone. It was all amusing diversion. However, he insists that he was never the class clown in school. "I was the class comedian. There's a difference. The class clown is the guy who drops his pants and runs across the field at half-time. The class comedian is the guy who talked him into doing it."

By the time Billy entered Long Beach High School, he had few, if any, longings for show business. A serious student, he specialized in sports. Baseball was his first love, with football, soccer, and wrestling close behind. On the wrestling mat he was known as "the brute," and he was captain of the baseball team as well as star shortstop. On a baseball scholarship, he was admitted to Marshall University in Huntington, West Virginia. However, by the time he registered at the school, there was no team, due to lack of funding. During his single year at Marshall, he turned to comedy for distraction and became a host of a campus call-in radio show.

In September 1966 he transferred to Nassau Community College at Garden City, Long Island, closer to home as well as to his show business pals. There he met a freshman student, Janice Goldfinger, who would become his wife in 1970. At Nassau, Billy delved into acting on a big scale, spending three summers with the school's alumni theater group, for which he directed the musical *The Apple Tree*. This led to his enrolling in 1968 at New York University in lower Manhattan as a major in television and motion picture direction, with Martin Scorsese as one of his instructors. While there, Crystal was house manager of the theater where the off-Broadway hit *You're a Good Man, Charlie Brown* was playing; he also formed an improvisational trio consisting of himself and two Nassau alumni. The trio, called at various times "We the People," "Comedy Jam," and "Three's Company," played Greenwich Village clubs and coffee houses in addition to small eastern colleges. He graduated from NYU with a bachelor's degree in 1969. The following year he and Janice were married. She became a secretary/counselor to help pay household bills, and he, in addition to his work with the trio, taught part-time at Long Beach Junior High School. In 1972 their first daughter, Jennifer, was born, to be followed in 1977 by Lindsay.

In 1973 Billy disbanded the trio to embark on a solo act. His first job, at an NYU fraternity party, paid him $25 for a twenty-minute monologue, which developed into an hour. He took his act to a Manhattan comedy club called Catch a Rising Star, and then did a tour of Playboy clubs in the East. In 1975, scheduled to perform a seven-minute monologue on NBC-TV's "Saturday Night Live," he walked out when the producer tried to cut his spot to two minutes. However, he bounced back on January 17, 1976, with a performance on ABC-TV's "Saturday Night Live with Howard Cosell." In April 1976 he was invited back to the NBC show, where he performed "Face," a monologue consisting of a composite of old black musicians.

Meanwhile, Billy had moved his small family to Los Angeles. He immediately headed for The Comedy Store, where television producer Norman Lear spotted him and tagged him for an appearance as a friend of Meathead (Rob Reiner) in an episode of the

CBS-TV sitcom "All in the Family" entitled "New Year's Wedding" (January 5, 1976). This marked the slow start of a friendship with Reiner, which eventually resulted in their becoming best friends.

Billy was a guest performer on "Dinah!" in January 1977 and on February 25, 1977, was seen as wise-cracking David, a passenger aboard this nation's first supersonic transport flight in the ABC-TV telefeature SST—DEATH FLIGHT. Next he became a cast member on ABC-TV's "Soap," which premiered September 13, 1977, remaining with the satirical show for the next three-and-a-half years. Because of its sexual situations, "Soap" was controversial from the beginning, and Billy's character, Jodie Dallas, was the first open homosexual to be portrayed on a continuing basis on any American network television series. Along with being comedic in his performances, Billy had many poignant moments as well; some of the best were during his hospital stay after a suicide attempt, in scenes with a nonrecurring character played by the talented Harold Gould.

In his debut motion picture, RABBIT TEST (1978), directed and co-scripted by Joan Rivers, Billy had the starring role. He was cast as Lionel Carpenter, who is raped on a pool table by a mystery woman (Sheree North) and becomes the first pregnant male. Although the cast included such well-known laugh-makers as Paul Lynde, Alice Ghostley, and Imogene Coca, the offbeat script could not keep up with them. When the film opened at the Lido movie theater in Billy's hometown, the marquee boasted "Long Beach's own Billy Crystal," which he found humorous.

In HUMAN FEELINGS, telecast by NBC on October 16, 1978, as a series pilot with laugh track, Billy was second-billed as an angel sent to Las Vegas by God (Nancy Walker) in search of six good people. The telefeature was rerun in 1980 without the canned laughter. Billy appeared on ABC-TV's "The Kissing Bandit" episode of "The Love Boat" on October 21, 1978, and appeared on such TV game shows as "The $20,000 Pyramid" later in the season. He was one of six buddies spending a summer at a Malibu, California, beach house after divorcing their respective wives in the two-part ABC network telefilm BREAKING UP IS HARD TO DO in September 1979.

The animated spoof "Animalympics: Winter Games" (NBC-TV, February 1, 1980) featured the voices of Billy Crystal, Gilda Radner, and others as sports announcers and reporters who interview athletic cartoon animals. The half-hour spoof was melded together with its unaired companion piece, "Animalympics: Summer Games," plus additional footage, to form the theatrical release ANIMALYMPICS (1983). Billy set comedy aside in taking the role of Lieutenant Jake Beser, one of the crew members of the plane that dropped the first atomic bomb on Hiroshima, in the NBC network telefilm ENOLA GAY: THE MEN, THE MISSION, THE ATOMIC BOMB (November 23, 1980). The final "Soap" installment was telecast on April 20, 1981, but its ninety-four episodes have since been seen in syndicated rerun and have a strong cult following. The following January, Billy was given his own comedy-variety show on NBC-TV, "The Billy Crystal Comedy Hour," on which he did celebrity impersonations, monologues, and skits with well-known guest stars. Despite his multitalented, congenial presence, the show proved to be short-lived, running only a month, from January 30 through February 27, 1982.

Over the next two years, Billy did club comedy routines, joined the twenty-first anniversary celebration "An Evening at the Improv" (Showtime–Cable, February 19, 1984), and made guest appearances on established TV comedy and talk shows. After hosting "Saturday Night Live" on March 17, 1984, he became a regular on the long-running comedy fest, doing striking impersonations of Grace Jones, Tina Turner, Sammy Davis, Jr., and Prince. One of his best-liked characterizations, in a blond wig, was Fernando, who he admitted was "loosely" based on late screen personality Fernando Lamas. Fernando, a fading Latin matinee idol/lothario, hosted a mock morning talk show whose advice included, "Remember, it's better to look good than to feel good, and, dahling, you look *mahvelous*." "Mahvelous" became a catch-word throughout the nation with Billy making a record, *You Look Mahvelous!*, and later a short video. Lamas's widow, Esther Williams, objected publicly, saying, "Billy had the best year of his life on my husband's charm, personality and character. . . . I just wish it weren't my husband. . . . I'm awfully tired of people coming up to me and saying, 'You look mahvelous, dahling.' I just wish he would knock it off." Crystal did knock it off, but not before receiving an Emmy nomination for his work on "Saturday Night Live" and a Grammy nomination for his recording. Also during 1984 he was seen in a guest shot in the mock rock documentary THIS IS SPINAL TAP, directed by and starring Rob Reiner. Billy was a regular attraction in Atlantic City at the Sands Hotel, as well as at the Bottom Line Club in Greenwich Village. He took time out to do a "Faerie Tale Theatre" episode, "The Three Little Pigs" (Showtime–Cable, February 12, 1985), as the pig whose house was made of brick.

TV Guide magazine alerted its readers that Billy would *not* return for the "Saturday Night Live" 1985–1986 season, because of a desire to pursue a motion picture career. In the June 1986 release RUNNING SCARED, Billy appeared with Gregory Hines as "Chicago's funniest cops." Before this action picture, though, Billy co-wrote and hosted "A Comedy Salute to Baseball" on NBC-TV in July 1985 and teamed on cable with Whoopi Goldberg and Robin Williams in HBO's first "Comic Relief" (March 1986), a show benefitting the homeless. He took his club act on tour in the summer of 1986 before taping a comedy special, "Don't Get Me Started," which was televised on HBO in August 1986. That September he took over Johnny Carson's hosting seat on NBC-TV's "The Tonight Show" as a summer replacement, at the same time that his semi-autobiographical book, *Absolutely Mahvelous*, was being read by his fans. In this book he wrote of his impersonations: "I'm comfortable being old . . . being black . . . being Jewish." For three years running he hosted the CBS-TV Grammy Awards presentation, for which he received an Emmy nomination in 1987 for his sterling 1986 work.

Resumption of his theatrical film career came in the form of his characterization, unrecognizable in old-age makeup and wig, as Miracle Max in THE PRINCESS BRIDE (1987), a delightful, wild adventure movie directed by Rob Reiner. This hit was followed three months later by THROW MOMMA FROM THE TRAIN, Danny DeVito's debut as a feature film director. Of Billy's impressive performance in this Christmas 1987 bonanza, *Variety* recorded, "Crystal's talents as a stand-up comic come through as it appears he got away with a fair amount of ad-libbing that wisely was retained in the final cut." Far less liked was MEMORIES OF ME (1988), a maudlin film directed by Henry Winkler, produced by the picture's stars (Crystal and Alan King), and based on a script co-authored by Billy. The *San Francisco Chronicle* decided that Crystal "is smooth-faced and wooden, working too hard not to slide into comedian-schtick." It was a box-office loser. On March 18, 1989, Billy co-hosted "Comic Relief III" on HBO, which claimed that $5 million had been raised for the homeless as a result of the previous two specials.

In his *Variety* column of April 18, 1988, Army Archerd reported, "Billy Crystal and Rob Reiner will team their friendship in BOY MEETS GIRL which Reiner will direct for his Castle Rock banner." The project reached movie screens on July 21, 1989, as WHEN HARRY MET SALLY . . ., based on a superlative script by Nora Ephron, with Billy as Harry and Meg Ryan as Sally, friends who eventually fall in love. Of the 446 feature films released in the United States during 1989, this one rated tenth at the nation's box offices, with gross earnings of more than $91 million. It garnered a Golden Globe Award nomination for Billy (a prize which he lost), but both he and Ryan were named "funniest" at the fourth annual American Comedy Awards ceremonies, held in Los Angeles on March 10, 1990.

Added to Billy's laurels was an Emmy for his hosting of the 1988 Grammy Awards show. As early as October 1989, Hollywood columnist Marilyn Beck reported that Billy was "hot to trot" with a sequel to WHEN HARRY MET SALLY . . ., which might take the couple into marriage and parenthood. Interviewed by Barbara Walters on ABC-TV on September 26, 1989, Billy talked of his impersonations and told how he had developed his Sammy Davis, Jr., impression by saying, "You just can't help but leave a room talking like him," along with revealing the calm normalcy of his domestic life. Yet another honor was bestowed upon him on October 18, 1989, when he received the thirteenth annual Jack Benny Award from the University of California at Los Angeles.

Meg Ryan and **Billy Crystal** in WHEN HARRY MET SALLY . . . (1989).

On October 21, 1989, on HBO–Cable, U.S. viewers saw his comedy special, "USSR, Midnight Train to Moscow," taped at the Pushkin Theatre in Moscow during his highly publicized trek to the homeland of his forebears. Billy had studied the complex Russian language for two months prior to the outing. "I was getting laughs in Russian," he boasted. (The special was nominated for four Emmy Awards, and won one for makeup and another for Crystal's scripting of the program.) Two more awards came to him in December 1989: he was named "Artist of the Year" by the Anti-Defamation League of B'nai B'rith and selected by the Hollywood Women's Press Club as recipient of a "Golden Apple" as male star of the year. On New Year's Eve, 1989, he starred in a major Pepsi-Cola TV ad campaign as both himself and a new character, "Uncle Lou."

On March 26, 1990, ABC telecast the sixty-second annual Academy Awards show from the Dorothy Chandler Pavilion in Los Angeles, with Billy as its sole host. This was for real—there was no toothbrush pretending to be a microphone. When the applause died down at the beginning of the show, his first words were: "Is that for me, or are you just glad I'm not Snow White?" (a reference to the previous year's disastrous opening production number). It was not his fault that the proceedings were, for many viewers, all too frequently dull. *Newsweek* magazine called him "irrepressibly irreverent" for a joke linking Italians with the Fifth Amendment. The comment led the Commission for Social Justice of the Order, Sons of Italy, and fifty-two members of the U.S. Congress to demand an apology. In February 1990 he was master of ceremonies for a benefit at the Los Angeles estate of producer Ted Field that raised $1.2 million for the Rainforest Foundation and the Environmental Media Association. As m.c., he quipped, "This tent looks like something Joan Collins would wear to the Golden Globes." She did not demand an apology.

While Billy and Eddie Murphy engaged in a publicized feud generated by Crystal's comment in a *Playboy* magazine interview that "I don't think he's a good comedian," Billy, Whoopi Goldberg, and Robin Williams showcased "Comic Relief IV" (HBO–Cable) on May 12, 1990, which garnered an additional $4.7 million for the cause of the homeless. On the PBS-TV network on December 2, 1990, Crystal joined Joan Rivers, Alan King, Milton Berle, and others as proponents of "The World of Jewish Humor."

For Rob Reiner's Castle Rock Entertainment, he co-starred with Daniel Stern and Bruno Kirby as three New York City pals who take time from their stressful jobs to participate in a week-long cattle drive from New Mexico to Wyoming in CITY SLICKERS (1991). Billy was also executive producer on this project. In development at Castle Rock in August 1990 was MR. SATURDAY NIGHT, to star Billy as a comedian experiencing highs and lows in a career spanning several years. The character (Buddy Young, Jr.) was based on one created by Crystal. On March 25, 1991, at the Shrine Auditorium in Los Angeles, Billy hosted the sixty-third annual Academy Awards ceremonies, making his entrance on a horse (to promote his CITY SLICKERS project). Once again, he proved to be the entertaining mainstay of the overlong awards show.

Although short, skinny, and talkative, Billy has found himself, in recent years, on several rosters of America's ten sexiest men. Squirming in embarrassment, he said: "What did I do? What did I say? It could be the other nine guys were like Bob Dole and

Refrigerator Perry." Funny without resorting to profanity, Crystal can always be trusted to give a good performance, whether as a master of ceremonies, in a stand-up comedy routine, or in a screen role. However, he never performs without first having a conversation with himself in front of a mirror, followed by at least thirty sneezes or a gagging session, after which he *knows* he is ready to go to work.

Filmography

SST—Death Flight (ABC-TV, 2/25/77)
Human Feelings (NBC-TV, 10/16/78)
Rabbit Test (Avco Emb, 1978)
Breaking Up Is Hard to Do (ABC-TV, 9/5/79; 9/7/79)
Enola Gay: The Men, the Mission, the Atomic Bomb (NBC-TV, 11/23/80)
Animalympics (Lisberger Films, 1983) (voice only)

This Is Spinal Tap [Spinal Tap] (Emb, 1984)
Running Scared (MGM, 1986)
The Princess Bride (20th–Fox, 1987)
Throw Momma from the Train (Orion, 1987)
Memories of Me (MGM/UA, 1988) (also co-producer, co-script)
When Harry Met Sally . . . (Col, 1989)
City Slickers (Col, 1991) (also executive producer)

Television Series

Soap (ABC, 1977–81)
The Billy Crystal Comedy Hour (NBC, 1982)

Saturday Night Live (NBC, 1984–85)

Album Discography

Animalympics (A&M 4810) [ST/TV]
The Best of Comic Relief 2 (Rhino R11H-70707)
Comic Relief '90 (Rhino R215-71010)

Comic Relief—The Best of Comic Relief (Rhino RNIN-70704)
Comic Relief 3 (Rhino R21K-70893)
You Look Mahvelous! (A&M SP-5096)

JAMIE LEE CURTIS

"My 20s were very hard; very, very hard. And I never thought I'd make 30. I didn't think I was going to live that long. I really think that's why now I'm, like, blossoming."
—*Movieline* magazine, April 1990

BORN INTO THE FANTASY WORLD OF MOVIE MAKING, JAMIE LEE Curtis resolved to join its acting ranks without assistance from anyone remotely connected with the industry, beginning on the big screen in 1978 as a latter-era Evelyn Ankers of peril. The professional path swathed by Curtis, utilizing determination as her scythe, led her through a career permutation from queen of teenage horror to sex queen to slut to art house figure to comedienne. In the latter category she has found the niche to which she seems best suited: "I've got a great figure, a low voice and I come off very self-assured."

However, beneath Jamie Lee's gloss of toughness is a fragility revealed only to those closest to her. Like Shelley Long, she can be difficult in her demands for perfection, but she is also known for her friendly, un-Hollywood, down-to-earth behavior. Added to this is the zany sense of humor that led TV talk show host/actor Arsenio Hall to list Jamie Lee Curtis as one of his favorites. In the chain of Hollywood evolution, Curtis has been replaced by Linnea Quigley in low-budget horror pictures, while Jamie Lee has stepped into the area of comedy left vacant by the departure of Myrna Loy.

Six-pound, twelve-ounce Jamie Lee Curtis was born at 8:37 a.m. on Saturday, November 22, 1958, in Los Angeles, the second daughter of screendom's golden couple, handsome Tony Curtis (born Bernard Schwartz) and beautiful Janet Leigh (born Jeanette Morrison). Her designated godparents were influential Lew Wasserman of MCA Corporation, later the head of Universal Studios, and his wife, Edie. Her sister, Kelly Leigh, whose outgrown clothes were handed down to her, had been born two years earlier, on June 17, 1956. Although the Curtis home, available by means of a road winding into the Hills of Beverly, was often filled with movie stars, young Jamie Lee knew them only as family friends and had no conception of their public status.

When Jamie Lee was three years old, her parents separated and she and her sister lived with their mother. In 1962 Janet married Robert Brandt on September 15, the day after she got a quick Mexican divorce from Tony. A Los Angeles businessman/real estate broker, Brandt became a convivial replacement for their real father, whom they never saw. Among the students at John Thomas Dye School, Jamie Lee was known as Tony Curtis's daughter, although her peers were the offspring of parents uninvolved with the film industry. Her favorite television shows were "The Brady Bunch" and "The Partridge Family"; the latter's David Cassidy was her idol. She recalls that as a youngster, "I didn't want to be an individual; I just wanted to fit in and be normal. . . . I learned early to be a chameleon, to turn whatever color was needed." When she was twelve, in 1970, Tony was arrested at a London airport for possession of marijuana, which prompted her schoolmates to chant, "Your father's Tony Curtis and your mother's Janet Leigh/Your father just got busted and your mother is free." She claims that all this did not bother her very much since, at that time, she really could not relate to him.

After graduating from Choate–Rosemary Hall boarding school in Wallingford, Connecticut, in 1976, she enrolled at the University of the Pacific at Stockton, California, where she took drama classes for three months before dropping out. Back in Los Angeles, she obtained an audition at Universal Studios, doing a scene from *Butterflies Are Free*. She was given a short-term contract, unknown to Lew Wasserman, head of the facility, who was then in Europe. Upon his return, she called him, identifying herself as his new employee. She made appearances on "The Match Game," "Hollywood Squares," and "The Second Annual Circus of the Stars," and had acting jobs on NBC-TV's "Quincy, M.E." (in the February 18, 1977, episode, "Visitors in Paradise") and ABC-TV's "Nancy Drew Mysteries" (in the April 17, 1977, episode, "Mystery of the Fallen Angels"). Now that she was earning her own living, she moved into an apartment, frosted her hair, and hid much of her face behind huge sunglasses. Her mother advised, "They aren't going to want you to be thirty-two. Just be Jamie at eighteen."

ABC-TV's pilot film OPERATION PETTICOAT was based on Universal's 1959 feature, which had co-starred Tony Curtis with Cary Grant. The pilot was shown on September 4, 1977, and the series began on September 17, with Jamie Lee in the one-season role of Lieutenant Barbara Duran. She was one of the five nurses aboard the dilapidated World War II submarine rover *Sea Tiger*, skippered by John Astin. For CBS-TV she joined "Festival of the Stars: Mexico," televised on May 18, 1978; played a golf pro in a "Charlie's Angels" episode aired on ABC-TV on October 18, 1978; and did a segment of ABC-TV's "The Love Boat" on November 11, 1978. Shortly thereafter, after experiencing double vision, she was diagnosed with multiple sclerosis, a neurological condition that could limit her ability to enjoy life fully. Determined to prove the diagnosis wrong, she plunged forward as the pursued heroine of director John Carpenter's HALLOWEEN (1978), a low-budget independent horror picture that attracted teenagers to box offices in droves. (The "classic" earned $18.5 million in domestic film rentals paid to the distributor.) This was followed by her participation in the 1979 version of "Circus of the Stars" and in November 1979 segments of NBC-TV's "Buck Rogers in the 25th Century" and ABC-TV's "The Love Boat."

During 1980, in quick succession Jamie Lee starred in three profitable horror films. She began the year with THE FOG, John Carpenter's follow-up to HALLOWEEN, in which both she and Janet Leigh were fleeing ghosts of an old shipwreck. Much of this scare movie's publicity was focused on the mother-daughter teaming, noting that Leigh had gained her greatest screen fame by starring in Alfred Hitchcock's horrific PSYCHO (1960) and that her daughter was now following in her cinematic footsteps. However, neither Leigh nor Curtis had that much to do in the popular picture, the bigger female role going to Adrienne Barbeau (Carpenter's wife) as the local radio station deejay. In PROM NIGHT, at age twenty-two, Jamie Lee played a high school student in flight from a slasher, and in a fraternity-hired TERROR TRAIN, made in Canada, she escaped brutalization by a disguised ex-frat man. *Variety* noted, "Jamie Lee Curtis runs around and screams a lot . . . so the film should make a lot of money. . . . Her acting fits a narrow groove that teen viewers evidently find easy to identify with, though adults might wish for more emotional range and clearer diction."

She traveled to Australia for the making of ROAD GAMES (1981), yet another horror entry, in which she is a hitchhiker picked up by Stacy Keach, a truck driver in hot pursuit of a murderer. As a break from screen scream roles, Jamie Lee co-starred with Kathleen Quinlan and Melanie Griffith as U.S. Army enlistees in the bland service comedy SHE'S IN THE ARMY NOW, telecast on ABC on May 20, 1981.

Because so many other people in the movie industry were doing it, she embarked on a period of drugs, parties, and alcohol that would last close to three years before she recognized the overall negative effects of this indulgence. During 1981 she attempted a reunion with her father, which did not work out at that time, nor when they met again as friends (not father and daughter) who did cocaine together. In 1984 Tony would admit himself to the Betty Ford Clinic in Palm Springs for its drug/alcohol dependency treatment. In 1981 Jamie Lee dated actor Robert Carradine and was then engaged to be married to another man, whose name she has not divulged. (In any case, the wedding never took place.)

What turned out to be her final horror film of the period, HALLOWEEN II (1981), is a same-night continuation of the original, with the depraved maniac still stalking her. *Variety* reported, "Stars Jamie Lee Curtis and Donald Pleasence are again quite convincing even if the script . . . isn't." At the same time, on November 1, 1981, she had her first starring role in a TV movie in DEATH OF A CENTERFOLD: THE DOROTHY STRATTEN STORY, which displayed her good body. Although Jamie Lee states that her physique is god-given, aided only by aerobics and other exercise, the publication *Woman's World* has reported that she is one of the more than two million American women who have had surgical breast implants. (Jamie Lee's retort to the press's preoccupation with her anatomy was, "I've worked so hard to find my identity. Now all they want to know is where I got my body.")

She appeared in "Callahan," a thirty-minute pilot for an unsold comedy-adventure series, which aired on ABC-TV on September 9, 1982. Hart Bochner (her co-star in TERROR TRAIN) played the globe-trotting curator of a historical foundation, with Jamie Lee as his attractive research assistant. For the TV movie MONEY ON THE SIDE (September 29, 1982), Jamie Lee was a suburban housewife who joins a prostitution ring. Now having graduated from movies about psychologically disturbed slashers, she looked back on those experiences as "good exercise" for allowing her "to play a lot of emotions."

Her return to theater screens was as a sexy lady in TRADING PLACES (1983), the Dan Aykroyd–Eddie Murphy comedy, which became that year's fourth highest grossing film with a box-office take of $90.4 million. *People* magazine judged that Curtis played the hooker "with disarming appeal." In the arty LOVE LETTERS (1984) she was a confused young woman who becomes the mistress of a married man (James Keach), and in the absurdist action spoof THE ADVENTURES OF BUCKAROO BANZAI: ACROSS THE 8TH DIMENSION (1984), she did a walk-on as Dr. Sandra Banzai. In GRANDVIEW, U.S.A. (1984), rated R for profanity, nudity, and violence, she was an independent soul running a small-town business. *People* magazine praised her as having "the kind of body cameras understandably worship, and her fierce intelligence shakes out every grain of truth she can find in the script." However, these attributes were unable to save PERFECT (1985) from a dreadful demise. Co-starring with John Travolta, whose career was badly faltering, Jamie Lee found it "a very public failure" because the project appeared on most critics' lists of the worst films of the year.

On December 18, 1985, she was married to thirty-seven-year-old actor/writer/director Christopher Guest, whose picture she had first seen in *Rolling Stone* and whom she considered "just the most beautiful man." She aggressively called his agent, but got nowhere until they later met in a restaurant. Then they began dating. Because she is unable to bear children, Jamie Lee and Christopher adopted a newborn child in 1986 whom they named Annie and "I happened to end up with a very beautiful little girl." Two days after her wedding, Jamie Lee was seen on Showtime–Cable as "Annie Oakley" in "Shelley Duvall's Tall Tales & Legends."

Jamie Lee Curtis and John Travolta in PERFECT (1985).

AS SUMMER DIES, an HBO cable feature, was filmed in Valdosta, Georgia, and co-starred Jamie Lee with Scott Glenn and Bette Davis; Jamie Lee played Davis's niece. She had a supporting role in AMAZING GRACE AND CHUCK (1987), an unsuccessful nuclear disarmament fantasy, and did a guest turn in A MAN IN LOVE (1987), an arty feature lensed in Rome. For the sentimental DOMINICK AND EUGENE (1988), she received third billing after Tom Hulce and Ray Liotta, two fine actors, in the title roles. She played the romantic interest of Eugene (Liotta), the medical intern, who must care for his childlike twin brother (Hulce). It is predicted that this teary, un-Hollywood picture will one day enjoy cult status among buffs.

After three years during which she became convinced that her work was judged more by her body than by her abilities, she next appeared in A FISH CALLED WANDA, released in July 1988. *Newsweek* magazine called the British-made comedy a "sleeper hit," critic Gene Siskel rated it "very funny," and *Newsday* judged it "the zaniest, sexiest adult movie entertainment of the summer." For the first time, Jamie's comedic talents were realized, and John Cleese, co-star, writer, and co-executive producer, observed, "I'm definitely a member of her fan club. The whole reason I cast her in the film was that I'd seen her act and she could be three things—funny, wicked and sexy. Actually, make that *four* things—she's very likable too." A FISH CALLED WANDA would earn $29,766,000 in domestic film rentals paid to the distributor. On December 19, 1988, on PBS-TV she joined "Sesame Street" for an outing, and on May 8, 1989, in a mother's day salute on TBS–Cable, she and Janet Leigh were among the "Superstars and Their Moms."

Prior to WANDA's release, Jamie Lee had done a series pilot for ABC-TV with stand-up comic Richard Lewis, which had been shelved. However, following the quick success of WANDA, the thirty-minute series debuted for a limited run on March 7, 1989, as "Anything But Love." *People* magazine extolled, "It would be hard to find a neater combination of sitcom co-stars." It was then picked up by the network as a regular series commencing September 17, 1989. Jamie Lee relinquished part of her salary in exchange for a commitment that it be filmed, rather than taped. "That's the first thing I did to take control," she told *TV Guide* magazine, adding, "I worked to get the rest of the cast in order and to get the sets looking right and to get the scripts funny and smart." On January 20, 1990, at the Beverly Hilton Hotel in Beverly Hills, her efforts paid off with a Golden Globe Award as Best Actress in a TV Series, Musical or Comedy, which she accepted with "Boy, oh, boy, oh, boy," but forgot to acknowledge her co-star in the acceptance speech. Afterward she told press members, "I really didn't think I was going to win; that's why I sounded bizarre on stage." Unfortunately, the generally intelligent "Anything But Love" was a victim of the ratings wars and was dropped by the network after the March 28, 1990, episode in which Hannah (Jamie Lee), celebrating her thirtieth birthday, left viewers in "cliffhanging" wonderment concerning her relationship with Marty (Lewis). The show went into summer reruns starting July 18, when ABC-TV ordered nine segments as a backup midseason replacement series for the 1990–1991 season. The show returned on February 6, 1991, to generally favorable reviews, especially for Curtis.

On January 30, 1990, from Park City, Utah, it was reported that "the hottest ticket at the Sundance United States Film Festival was BLUE STEEL," starring Jamie Lee as a New York City rookie cop. When the film opened to the public on March 16, 1990, critic Roger Ebert labeled it "a more complicated and psychological version of HALLOWEEN," but added that Jamie's character was "tough and smart." Sheila Benson (*Los Angeles Times*) did not like the action movie, but noted that Jamie "survives all this with a strong, honest and winning performance." In four weeks of domestic distribution, BLUE STEEL grossed an unremarkable $7,701,707 at the box office.

After hosting the Los Angeles premiere of *Shout and Twist*, produced by her sister and playwright Scott Morfee, whom Kelly had married on September 14, 1989, Jamie confided that she preferred doing a television series to movie work. She told Steve

Weinstein (*Los Angeles Times*), "I don't have a desperate need anymore to be on screen every year" and admitted that she was in love with the Guests' modest log cabin, purchased with five acres of land in the mountains of Idaho. Nevertheless, during a hiatus from her television work, Jamie Lee was on location in New York City for QUEENS LOGIC (1991) with Kevin Bacon and John Malkovich. For the home video *Help Save Planet Earth*, released in September 1990, Jamie Lee was among the celebrities (including Milton Berle, Beau Bridges, Ted Danson, Whoopi Goldberg, and John Ritter) making a plea for ecology practices. In January 1991 she began work on MY GIRL (forthcoming, 1991), co-starring Dan Aykroyd and directed by Howard Zieff.

Jamie Lee's legs received notice in *Esquire* magazine in July 1990. A reader poll to determine the ideal woman indicated that she would have Jamie Lee's legs, Kim Basinger's hair, Melanie Griffith's nose, and so on.

"I really don't like it here," she now says of Hollywood/Los Angeles. Feeling financially tethered to the land of lotus, she finds it "frightening" and wistfully hopes for the time when she might move permanently to Idaho. "I'd like to be able to work freelance from up there," she says. Admitting that "I've never been very popular or wanted by the powerful" in Hollywood because "maybe I'm considered pushy," she, who has gone from scream queen to comedy, would receive only her own echo from the Idaho mountains.

Filmography

Operation Petticoat (ABC-TV, 9/4/77)
Halloween (Compass International, 1978)
The Fog (Avco Emb, 1980)
Prom Night (Avco Emb, 1980)
Terror Train (20th–Fox, 1980)
She's in the Army Now (ABC-TV, 5/20/81)
Death of a Centerfold: The Dorothy Stratten Story (NBC-TV, 11/1/81)
Halloween II (Univ, 1981)
Road Games (Avco Emb, 1981)
Money on the Side (ABC-TV, 9/29/82)
Trading Places (Par, 1983)
Love Letters [My Love Letters] (New World, 1984)
The Adventures of Buckaroo Banzai: Across the 8th Dimension (20th–Fox, 1984)

Grandview, U.S.A. (CBS Theatrical Films, 1984)
Perfect (Col, 1985)
As Summer Dies (HBO–Cable, 5/18/86)
Amazing Grace and Chuck (Tri-Star, 1987)
A Man in Love (Cinecom, 1987)
Dominick and Eugene (Orion, 1988)
A Fish Called Wanda (MGM/UA, 1988)
Blue Steel (MGM/UA, 1990)
Queens Logic (New Visions, 1991)

Future Releases

My Girl (Col, 1991)

Television Series

Operation Petticoat (ABC, 1977–78)

Anything But Love (ABC, 1989–)

WILLEM DAFOE

"I always get a sense that by acting you can create a history that
will intertwine with your life."
　　　　　　　—*Continental Choice* magazine, September 1988

HIS DEEP, MELLIFLUOUS VOICE IS THE LAST THING AN ADVERSARY
hears before a bullet splatters his brain onto the carpet in TO LIVE AND DIE IN L.A. (1985).
This screen villain's voice, with a touch of the Bronx, is comforting and caressing, not at all
like the voices of such other movie bad guys as rapid-fire-talking Humphrey Bogart or
whining Richard Widmark. This is a self-assured, ugly/handsome villain, more like today's
James Woods, the type that is alternately admired and feared by the occupant of the seat in
the darkened movie house. What is remarkable is that Willem Dafoe went on to play Jesus
of Nazareth on screen. Other actors who have portrayed the Christian savior over the years
have found themselves later unable to further their careers after having trod the biblical
hills in robe and sandals. That was not the case with Dafoe, who was sought for just about
every movie produced after appearing as the humanized Jesus in THE LAST TEMPTATION
OF CHRIST (1988).

Willem has said, "I never act. I simply bring out the real animal that's in me." The
movements of his slight, sinewy body have been likened to those of the jack rabbit and the
cat. He admits that if he had not attained a degree of success as an actor, he would have
considered dance as a career.

He was born in Appleton, Wisconsin, on Friday, July 22, 1955, the seventh of eight
children of Flemish ancestry. His father was a gastrointestinal surgeon and his mother a
nurse. He was named William after his father. His formative years were spent playing in
nearby farm lands or going to movies. He particularly liked the monster films of Boris
Karloff and Peter Lorre as well as combat films. Since his workaholic parents were at the
hospital most of the time, the children led independent lives. They often did their own
cooking, except on holidays, when the family was together. William developed a talent for
mimicry, earning himself a reputation among his peers as a practical joker. In high school,
the precocious teenager acted in plays and wrote several of his own, as well as joined a
community playhouse group, the Attic Theatre. He admits he gravitated to the theater to
help him find his identity. ("When you come from a large family, you have to find . . . your
turf.") While in his teens, his friends and family began calling him "Willem," which was
fine with him since he preferred that to the more common diminutive "Billy."

Following high school, he became a student of drama at the University of Wisconsin at nearby Madison, but finding the curriculum too slow and disappointing, he dropped out. He joined a traveling children's theater, which played engagements throughout the South. In 1973, at age eighteen, he relocated to Milwaukee rather than return home to Appleton. He obtained a job on the graveyard shift in the binding operation for the magazines *Penthouse* and *Playgirl*. However, this, too, was short-lived and he quit to join other young people in an experimental theater group called Theatre X. "The money I made was enough to live on," he has recalled, "but it was really hard work." It was as much a lifestyle as anything else. The group became associated with a producer who took them to Europe, where they did most of their work, which consisted of performing a series of vignettes written especially for them.

Willem was with Theatre X for two years. While in Europe he met Richard Schechner, a radical leader in the off-off-Broadway movement and the founder of The Performance Group. Schechner persuaded Willem to join him in Manhattan to take the part of the killer in a play called *Cops*. However, the company's artistic director, Elizabeth LeCompte, vetoed this decision. While he took other jobs (such as figure modeling) to keep bread on his table, he always gravitated back to various theater groups. By 1977, Schechner had moved on to other pursuits and LeCompte had taken over the company, now known as the Wooster Group, whose playhouse was located in a converted garage. Willem hung around The Performing Garage, as the theater was known, doing odd jobs to endear himself to the outspoken director. He finally made his stage debut with the group in *Nayatt School*, playing "a huge, devouring chicken heart taking over the world."

In 1981 the Wooster Group carved a niche in theater history when it produced a commentary on the division of the races in America called *Routes 1 & 9*. It consisted of a version of Thornton Wilder's *Our Town* with an interpolated minstrel show, and a production called *L.S.D.* containing fifty minutes of Arthur Miller's *The Crucible*. Miller threatened legal action and so LeCompte dropped both shows. Willem was in most of the group's presentations during this period. Meanwhile, he and Elizabeth LeCompte, eleven years his senior, had become lovers. In 1982 they became parents with the birth of their son, Jack Frank. "We don't need a contract to stay together," he said, "and the child—he doesn't need it."

In the fiasco HEAVEN'S GATE, Willem was an extra. Also in 1980, Kathryn Bigelow and Monty Montgomery asked Willem to play the mean biker in their move THE LOVELESS. Dressed in black leather, Willem had little to do in this movie, which was released in Britain in 1982. (It would see only a very limited U.S. release in January 1984, when it was called simply LOVELESS.) Dafoe's presence was hardly noticed in THE HUNGER (1983), which concerned an ambisexual vampire (Catherine Deneuve) who seduces Susan Sarandon to the strains of "Lakmé." Willem's brief role was as one of two "phone booth youths." He blended into the background of a scene in NEW YORK NIGHTS (1984), but had a substantial role, again as the leader of a motorcycle gang, as the villainous Raven in STREETS OF FIRE (1984). A highlight of this action drama is the climactic showdown with sledge hammers between Willem and the film's hero (Michael Pare). Janet

Maslin (*New York Times*) found little to praise in the film, but singled Willem out as a "perfectly villainous punk heavy." His screen work for the year concluded with ROAD-HOUSE 66 (1984), in which he played a hitchhiker who thumbs a ride from an affluent motorist (Judge Reinhold). They are then stranded in a dusty Arizona town when the car gives out.

Although Willem had only one 1985 release, it proved to be his breakthrough film, and led him to get an agent to handle the abundance of offers that subsequently came his way. The movie was TO LIVE AND DIE IN L.A., directed by William Friedkin of THE FRENCH CONNECTION (1971) fame. Called "The French Connection of the West" by many, TO LIVE AND DIE IN L.A. is fast paced and well acted and includes one of the most exciting car chases ever filmed. Willem was cast as the ruthless, evil Rick Masters, an artist-turned-counterfeiter of $20 bills. With his pals he is understanding, almost kind, but to his enemies he is a real slimeball. His first words on camera—"Buddy, you're in the wrong place at the wrong time"—are spoken just prior to his blowing away the face of a federal agent. This notorious lawbreaker has eluded the authorities for years, but before the slam-bang film's finale he meets his demise, being burned to death. *People* magazine compli-mented Dafoe's "sinister verve." Don Minifie (*Films and Filming* magazine) recorded that Dafoe turns in "a performance of ice-cool nastiness." As a result of this spate of villainous assignments, which featured his maniacal grin, he was much in demand within the industry to play screen heavies.

Back in 1984, while filmmaker Oliver Stone was casting PLATOON (1986), he had met Willem and liked him but had nothing for him professionally. The role of Sergeant Elias in PLATOON was intended for an American Indian, but when Stone could not find the right actor for the role, his wife suggested that he take another look at Dafoe in TO LIVE AND DIE IN L.A. She felt he would make a perfect Elias if the part was rewritten. "Willem is sort of ugly," Stone has said, "but there's a sensuality about him that lends him a sense of danger." PLATOON was shot in 120+ degree weather in the Philippines. Stone admitted that Willem was "willing to do anything . . . the more obstacles the better. Nothing would stop the man."

In this film, set during the Vietnam War, Willem is the heavy drug-using but good man who cannot accept the need for the war, while his fellow infantryman, Sergeant Barnes (Tom Berenger), is the opposite. They fight not only the Viet Cong, but each other, and Barnes kills Elias while he scouts the jungle for the Asian enemy. The emotion-laden PLATOON cashed in, with a box-office gross of $137.9 million, making it the third-highest-grossing movie of 1986. *Variety* insisted that Dafoe "comes close to stealing the picture." It won the Academy Award as Best Picture and earned Best Supporting Actor bids for both Dafoe and Berenger, who lost to Michael Caine (HANNAH AND HER SISTERS). Willem confided to *Rolling Stone* magazine that he was not comfortable with the renown gained from playing the part of a combat soldier since he had not endured the real thing. "The vets who haven't responded to the film aren't gonna talk to me, of course. But I've gotten some very moving letters from vets who say, 'I knew Elias,' or 'I wanted to be like Elias,' or 'I *was* like Elias.' And, yeah, it's only a movie, and I'm only an actor, but that makes me very happy." Additional sources of happiness for Dafoe were that after PLA-TOON, his salary per picture escalated to $500,000 and that the film showed Hollywood that he could play nonvillains.

For the next year, Willem devoted his energies to the Wooster Group ("This place is where I fuel up") and to his family. On stage in New York at The Performing Garage he was part of the ensemble's retrospective trilogy entitled *The Road to Immortality*. He also edited a video by one of the group's collaborators, called *Flaubert Dreams of Travel But the Illness of His Mother Prevents It*, which was included in the production. At the age of four, Dafoe's son was already showing a proclivity for show business by dancing in hour-long impromptu solo performances. Willem enjoys his son but has admitted, "I still don't have a good image of myself as a father, but I still get a pleasurable little titillation when he calls me 'daddy.'"

The documentary DEAR AMERICA: LETTERS HOME FROM VIETNAM (1987) com-bined film clips of the war with voiceovers by a cast of film celebrities to give an account of the Vietnam War. Willem was one of those who read letters from combat soldiers written to their families in the United States. In June 1987 he went to Bangkok to co-star with Gregory Hines in OFF LIMITS (1988), an integrated buddy-cop picture. This time he was cast as a plainclothes military policeman, partnered with Hines to investigate the murder of six Vietnamese prostitutes who also happen to be the mothers of children sired by American servicemen. The setting was Saigon, 1968, which pre-release advertisements called "a city of killings, corruption and cover-ups." *Variety* dismissed the project as "mildly entertaining, if clearly derivative of more thoroughly executed actioners," but acknowledged the "macho posturing done well by the duo of Willem Dafoe and Gregory Hines."

Since 1971, director Martin Scorsese had been bent on making a film of *The Last Temptation of Christ* (1955), a novel by Nikos Kazantzakis, which had been banned by the Vatican. In late 1983 Paramount finally gave Scorsese the go-ahead, with Aidan Quinn set to star as Jesus. However, after dispatching a pre-production crew to Israel, the studio suddenly withdrew from the project in early 1984. Universal took up the project with Scorsese continuing as director, but they had not agreed on a star. Since Scorsese had not seen PLATOON, he had no sure way of knowing that Willem could play such a gentle hero. He chose him to portray Jesus based on the lean look and soft, commanding voice of the counterfeiter in TO LIVE AND DIE IN L.A. From the day filming began in October 1987, the long-standing controversy surrounding the book carried over to the film, because of its depiction of Christ's "merciless battle between the spirit and the flesh," because of his carnal desires, and because of his fantasies about being a normal individual who fornicates, fathers children, and grows old with two wives.

Universal announced its intention to release THE LAST TEMPTATION OF CHRIST in September 1988. Weeks before, it was vociferously condemned by various religious denominations, while fundamentalist groups demanded its destruction and offered to compensate the filmmakers for its production cost (the final figure was reported to be $7 million). The release date was moved up to August 12, and many theater chains, mostly in the South, refused to book it. *Newsweek* magazine gave the movie a two-page spread, stating, "[It] is far from a great movie, but it is one of the few truly religious movies Hollywood has bothered to finance in the past decade." Despite the publicity, or because of it, the picture grossed an estimated $16 million. While most reviewers stressed the contributions of director Martin Scorsese or novelist Nikos Kazantzakis, the *San Francisco Chronicle*'s Judy Stone declared that Willem's portrayal "is strongest when he is most pained by his own split feeling." However, Stone noted that when he "glows with a beatific smile, he is more likely to evoke discomfort in a viewer than an image of 'gentle Jesus,' meek and mild." In October 1989, when the much-discussed film was scheduled to be shown on cable TV, prefaced by a disclaimer as it had been in theatrical release, several U.S. cable companies refused to air it. That same month it was released on home video, and *Video Review* magazine decided it was "a wrenching experience longer on pain and guilt than on inspiration and redemption."

On completion of his work as Jesus, Willem rejoined the Wooster Group for a brief stage tour in Israel. After a few weeks he was back in the United States, specifically in Jackson, Mississippi, and Lafayette, Alabama, sporting a well-trimmed look to co-star with Gene Hackman as an FBI agent in 1964 in search of three missing Civil Rights workers in MISSISSIPPI BURNING (1988). The film generated controversy for its depiction of blacks, who claimed that the actual historical incidents were not clearly defined in the screenplay and that the film gave the FBI far more credit for aiding the Civil Rights struggle in the South than the facts merited. *People* magazine described the film "as a stinging reminder of a civil rights war still far from won . . . a film to rank with the year's best and boldest," and noted that Willem, as the idealistic northerner, gave a "tightly coiled" performance. (However, it was Hackman, not Dafoe, who was nominated for an Academy Award; he lost to Dustin Hoffman of RAIN MAN.)

Willem Dafoe in OFF LIMITS (1988).

As a favor to director Oliver Stone, Willem took a supporting role in the large-cast BORN ON THE FOURTH OF JULY (1989). The movie was based on the book by Ron Kovic (played on screen by Tom Cruise), the story of an idealistic patriot who returns from the Vietnam jungles as a wheelchair-bound paraplegic. Willem played a disillusioned paraplegic veteran hiding out in a Mexican beach town. He was credited by *Daily Variety* with giving "a startling, razor-sharp perf[ormance], brief but brilliantly authentic." After thirteen weeks in domestic release, the feature had grossed more than $63.7 million.

In the book *The New Breed* (1988), Dafoe told interviewer Kevin J. Koffler, "I respond to exotic locations and interesting people" and "I look for fun stuff to do, and to some degree, a character I feel an affinity for." For his next film, shot in the spring of 1989, the location could not have been more "exotic" than Auschwitz, the infamous Nazi prison camp, the site of thousands of Jewish deaths, nor the character more interesting than Salamo Arouch, a Greek-Jewish middleweight boxing champion. To play the man nick-named the Ballerina because of his footwork in the ring, Willem lost between ten and twenty pounds, bringing his weight down to 145 on his 5' 9" frame, and shaved his head, which made his sharp facial features even more prominent. Released as TRIUMPH OF THE SPIRIT (1989), the somber study met with little enthusiasm from filmgoers. While Janet Maslin (*New York Times*) thought the extermination camp was trivialized in the film, she judged Dafoe's performance "harrowingly good." Julie Salamon (*Wall Street Journal*) praised Willem with bringing "remarkable clarity of emotion" to a difficult part. Mean-while, Dafoe had found time to participate in worthwhile causes such as the September 1989 AIDS walk in Los Angeles, for which he was master of ceremonies. The walkathon raised $1.8 million.

Again as a favor, this time to John Waters, Hollywood's unorthodox moviemaker, Willem took a cameo as a really mean prison guard in CRY-BABY (1990). Other fun cameos were provided by Troy Donahue, Joey Heatherton, Polly Bergen, David Nelson, Iggy Pop, and Patty Hearst, but none of them managed to keep audiences from nodding off.

In third billing, after Nicolas Cage and Laura Dern, Willem showed up late in the unreeling of WILD AT HEART, directed by the innovative David Lynch. In the film, released August 17, 1990, in the United States, Willem was the "black angel," Bobby Peru, with fake gums and rotting teeth and a pencil moustache, who menaces a pregnant woman (played by Dern) in a motel room. Later in the picture, his head is blasted off his shoulders by a shotgun volley. *Entertainment Weekly* magazine discovered that Willem "proves a master of leering, fish-faced villainy." Laura Dern also discovered something unusual about Dafoe, which she divulged to *Exposure* magazine: "He does the most fabulous tongue tricks you've ever seen. Amazing ones. Like, he can make animals and shapes with it." In its opening week on 532 movie screens, the offbeat movie took in just $2.9 million domestically.

Dafoe walked off a Miami set after nine days of shooting on the comedy ARRIVE ALIVE, scheduled for Paramount distribution. His role was a scam artist hotel detective. He felt that "the feature was not developing as planned." With his departure as star, the movie was shelved indefinitely. Instead, Willem joined a European/U.S. tour of the Wooster Group that began in Amsterdam on June 20, 1990, with a stopover at the Los Angeles Theatre Center. Prior to the tour, he videotaped *Frank Dell's The Temptation of Saint Antony* for the Wooster Group, playing a man who, after leaving his important corporate job, starts making movies. Later in the year, Willem could be heard reading Stephen King's *Four Past Midnight* on audio cassette.

FLIGHT OF THE INTRUDER, whose release had twice been postponed, was released in January 1991 to coincide with the Martin Luther King, Jr., birthday observance, said to be the biggest box-office weekend prior to Memorial Day. Speculation had run high within the industry that all was not well with the production, which completed principal photography in Hawaii in the spring of 1990. In the $35 million movie, Willem co-starred with Brad Johnson and Danny Glover as an ace navigator/bombardier of an A-6 bomber that conducts an unauthorized raid over Hanoi in 1972. FLIGHT OF THE INTRUDER garnered a modest $14,156,622 in seven weeks of domestic release. Willem next made a cameo appearance for Oliver Stone in THE DOORS (1991), a biography of rocker Jim Morrison.

Future screen work includes roles as the American lover of a Cuban woman (Greta Scacchi) in FIRES WITHIN (1991) and as the hunchback in yet another version of Victor Hugo's *Notre Dame de Paris*, tentatively entitled THIS WILL KILL THAT. With the death of Andy Warhol and the publication of his diary in 1989, the iconoclastic artist was suddenly a hot property. With director Gus Van Sant lined up to direct and script a film biography, both Willem and John Malkovich were eager to play the white-haired cultural entrepreneur.

While Willem has become one of filmdom's busiest performers, his private life remains unchanged. "There's no story there," he has said of his family life, based in New York City's SoHo district. "I keep my life simple so I can keep the work exciting." He explains that he likes to be professionally vital: "I don't want to get boxed into a corner and feel like stuff is happening to me." On the other hand, the very serious-minded Dafoe insists there is a lighter side to his personality. "There's a side of me that has this very youthful, basic desire to have fun, to play, to pretend. I may be serious about what I do, but I often feel like a child. I'm an easygoing, good-time kind of guy. I think I'm well adjusted."

Filmography

Heaven's Gate (UA, 1980)
The Loveless [Loveless] (Mainline, 1982;
   Atlantic, 1984)*
The Hunger (MGM/UA, 1983)
New York Nights (Bedford Entertainment,
   1984)
Streets of Fire (Univ, 1984)*
Roadhouse 66 (Atlantic, 1984)
To Live and Die in L.A. (MGM/UA, 1985)
Platoon (Orion, 1986)
Dear America: Letters Home from Vietnam
   (HBO–Couturie, 1987) (voice only)
Off Limits (20th–Fox, 1988)

The Last Temptation of Christ (Univ, 1988)
Mississippi Burning (Orion, 1988)
Triumph of the Spirit (Nova International,
   1989)
Born on the Fourth of July (Univ, 1989)
Cry-Baby (Univ, 1990)
Wild at Heart (Samuel Goldwyn Co., 1990)
Flight of the Intruder (Par, 1991)
The Doors (Tri-Star, 1991)

Future Releases

Fires Within (MGM-Pathé, 1991)

As William Dafoe

JEFF DANIELS

"I've never been one of those twenty-four-hour-a-day, get-out-of-my-way career people, ever. I love acting, but to hell with all the rest of it, you know?"   —*GQ* magazine, October 1987

EVERYDAY NORMALCY IS WHAT JEFF DANIELS STRIVES FOR IN HIS LIFE at the risk of forfeiting a stellar film career. Being with family and the friends he grew up with is more important to him than prowling the in spots of Los Angeles in search of good screen roles. Typically all-American in appearance—tall, blond, blue-eyed, likeable—he has played himself more than a few times on camera. However, after he played the faithless spouse of a winsome cancer victim in TERMS OF ENDEARMENT (1983), he was long-remembered and identified in public as "that weasel, Flap Horton."

Any young actor who does comedy and drama with equal aplomb is automatically hailed as a new Cary Grant, as was Jeff Daniels, a comparison he views as ridiculous. It would make better sense to call him the new Joel McCrea or the next James Arness. A man of conviction, whose personal values come before all else, he has said, "You're up on the screen, bigger than life. Fall into that trap of believing you are. Pretty soon you can't tell a story without standing up. I don't want to be one of those guys."

Jeffery Daniels was born on Saturday, February 19, 1955, in rural Georgia to Robert Daniels and his wife. Soon after his birth, the Daniels family moved north to Chelsea, Michigan (population: 4,000), where Robert assumed control of the family lumber business. Jeff grew up in a bungalow near a lake. In the Boy Scouts he "learned how to build fires and camp out, but you also learned to drink Boone's Farm wine." Beginning with his last year in grade school, he worked summers in his family's lumberyard. He soon came to the conclusion that, no matter what, he did not want to devote his life to lumber. At Chelsea High School he was on the "B" Division championship football team, but his first love was baseball—he was obsessed with the game. On winter evenings when it was too dark or too cold to play sports, the town put on dramas and musicals, and most of the younger people performed in them. Jeff recalled, "For some reason, I could get up in front of 600 people and not be nervous, but I didn't seriously consider a career in acting."

In the fall of 1973, feeling that his future most likely lay in becoming an athletic coach, he enrolled at Eastern Michigan University, located thirty miles from home at Ypsilanti. The first years of college were mostly spent on the football and baseball fields or hanging out with his beer-loving cronies. However, in 1975 he discovered acting through Al Pacino's performance in DOG DAY AFTERNOON. He saw the movie repeatedly until he understood "that there's more to acting than reciting the lines and singing a song." He then slowly shifted his focus to the university's drama department and appeared in several campus productions.

Near the end of his four years at Eastern Michigan, in 1976, Marshall Mason, the longtime artistic director of New York City's creative Circle Repertory Company, was invited by the university to direct its production of *Summer and Smoke*. Mason cast Jeff, whom he described as a "football-player type covered in baby fat," in the lead role of the young doctor. Mason liked Jeff's approach to acting so much that he soon invited him to join the Circle Repertory Company in New York. "I had never before encouraged anyone to become an actor," Mason said, "but he had such an extraordinary talent."

After graduation, Jeff accepted Mason's invitation and moved to New York City, taking a small "fleabag" apartment on 23rd Street. "I wanted to leave the minute I got there," he later recalled, "and had one foot in Michigan the whole time I was there." He subscribed to his hometown newspaper but "stayed because I knew if I walked away I'd never go back and try it again." His first two acting tasks at Sheridan Square in Greenwich Village, where the Circle Repertory staged its productions, were in *The Shortchanged Review* and *The Farm*. After appearing in *Feedlot* in October–November 1977, the next month he attracted attention as the midwestern college student nephew in *Brontosaurus*, a one-act play written by the company's resident playwright, Lanford Wilson.

However, the play that made Jeff Daniels more visible in the eyes of producers was Lanford Wilson's *The 5th of July*, in which from April to September 1978 he was Jed, the quiet lover of a paralyzed Vietnam veteran. By this time, Jeff had slimmed down to 160 pounds. The veteran was first played by William Hurt, brought into the group by another of the company's playwrights, Corinne Jacker, who felt that Hurt had great promise. "It was obvious that he was this megastar about to happen," Jeff remembered. "Some of us had spent two or three years learning the workshops, getting ready to start carrying plays, and now suddenly seasons were being built around Bill Hurt. I shut the door on him." Jeff and Hurt would eventually become friends, but it would take several years. When Hurt went on to bigger projects, he was replaced in the role by Christopher Reeve and later by Richard Thomas in the Broadway production of the play, now called *The Fifth of July*. Jeff steadfastly aided all his co-stars by helping them walk with a cane and carrying them on stage, as set forth in the script. Later, Jeff and Reeve reprised their roles on stage in a Los Angeles production (1982) as well as in a live-on-tape showing for Showtime–Cable on October 14, 1982.

To offset his living expenses in Manhattan, Jeff did television commercials, which came his way easily because of his wholesome looks and "cracked-wheat" tenor speaking voice. In one of the commercials, for Butterball Turkeys, he and John Goodman were two of five sons seated at the family Thanksgiving dinner table with Jeff gushing, "Oh, isn't the turkey good. Umm-umm." With sports still in his blood, Daniels joined the Broadway Softball League, wearing the #13 jersey. "Some say I was the best first baseman in the league," he once said. "It should be a hobby. It's not. It's a sickness." Because of his outstanding work in *The Fifth of July*, he received two movie offers. However, before accepting them, he returned to Chelsea to marry a woman he had known most of his life, Kathleen Treado. Since the number thirteen was lucky for him, they chose July 13, 1979, as their wedding day. Jeff was twenty-four; Kathleen was nineteen.

He and his new bride settled in Manhattan, where they rented a nicer apartment and Jeff went to work, first in the supporting role of a chaplain in the two-part CBS-TV movie A RUMOR OF WAR (1980). His second role was larger. In the theatrical movie RAGTIME (1981), shot on the East Coast, he was a turn-of-the-century policeman named O'Donnell who is called upon by Coalhouse Walker, Jr. (Howard E. Rollins), to intercede when his new automobile is defiled by a group of bigoted firemen.

On January 3, 1982, NBC-TV aired "Catalina C-Lab," a sixty-minute pilot for an unsold series. It dealt with a scientific team based at an underwater research laboratory off Catalina Island. Jeff was among the cast supporting the star, Bruce Weitz. Back at the Circle Repertory, as of August 3, 1982, Jeff appeared in the one-actor production *Johnny Got His Gun*, the sad, often depressing antiwar script taken from the Dalton Trumbo novel about a World War I soldier who is physically dead except for his brain. Mel Gussow (*New York Times*) applauded Daniels because he "lends variety as well as conviction to his horrific role. . . . [He] is especially adept at conveying quiet heroism." For his work, Jeff was awarded an Obie for best male performance of the year in an off-Broadway play. After trying to obtain, but losing to John Lithgow, the part of the transsexual, Roberta Muldoon, in THE WORLD ACCORDING TO GARP (1982), Daniels auditioned with Diane Keaton for the role of her lover in SHOOT THE MOON (1982). At the conclusion of their meeting, when she asked his age, he was convinced she did not want him, which turned out to be correct. The part went to Peter Weller, eight years his senior and nearer Keaton's age.

His third movie was CBS-TV's AN INVASION OF PRIVACY (1983), which starred Valerie Harper. It was set in a small town off the coast of Maine but was filmed at Long Island Sound in New York. His fourth screen assignment is the one that earned Jeff his first real prominence. Receiving fifth billing for TERMS OF ENDEARMENT (1983), he played Flap Horton, a college English professor married to Emma (Debra Winger), with whom he has three children. Flap is seldom at home, because of his extramarital affairs with various co-eds. In one scene, to alibi his staying away from home overnight, he tells his wife that he fell asleep in the school library. For this scene, director James Brooks instructed him, "Convince her. Convince us. Be a brilliant liar." After the wife dies of cancer, he gives up custody of their children, thus proving to be a totally unsympathetic character. *People* magazine judged his performance "first rate." The tearjerker and two of its stars (Shirley MacLaine and Jack Nicholson) won Academy Awards, and the film was the year's #2 top box-office hit with $108.4 million in domestic grosses. Daniels returned to the New York stage in November 1983 in an off-Broadway production of *The Three Sisters* produced by the Manhattan Theatre Club.

The Danielses' first son, Benjamin, was born in November 1984 in New York City. He would be followed by a brother, Lucas, born in late 1987. While continuing to work with the Circle Repertory Company, Jeff kept his options open for possible screen work.

He did not want a television series of his own, nor was he anxious to make guest appearances in existing shows. About TV, he reasoned, "The way the media are—and this is particularly true of television—you're nothing more than the flavor of the month."

Woody Allen was a week into directing his screenplay THE PURPLE ROSE OF CAIRO (1985) when he fired his male lead, Michael Keaton, whose performance he considered too contemporary for the role of a 1930s movie star. The call went out for auditions for a replacement, and Jeff responded. Although he admitted nervousness in the presence of Allen, his reading won him the part. Obviously inspired by a 1924 Buster Keaton feature, SHERLOCK, JR., in which Keaton walks onto a movie screen to solve a mystery, THE PURPLE ROSE OF CAIRO works in reverse. The star (Daniels) of a society comedy walks off the theater screen to reply in person to the remarks from the audience of a mousy, abused housewife (Mia Farrow) whose sole joy in life is going to the movies. Because her movie hero knows nothing of the world except what is in the script of the movie he departed from, he is forced to return to the screen, leaving her behind to resume her Depression-era life of drudgery. Critic Roger Ebert called the picture "delightful from beginning to end" and credited Jeff and Farrow with exploring the problems of their characters with "clarity and charm." THE PURPLE ROSE OF CAIRO made *Variety*'s list of top fifty grossers for twenty-one weeks, with an overall domestic intake of $29 million. Woody Allen said of

Troy Bishop, **Jeff Daniels**, Megan Morris, Huckleberry Fox, and Debra Winger in
TERMS OF ENDEARMENT (1983).

Jeff that he "has got that quality that Robert Montgomery had when he was younger, that William Powell had, and Melvyn Douglas and Cary Grant. He's got that sophisticated comedic style. . . . Will there be sufficient literature to accommodate him?"

MARIE (1985), the account of a real-life crusader (Sissy Spacek), found Jeff co-starring as her college friend who has become the far-from-honest legal counsel to the governor of Tennessee. *People* magazine judged that he played with "oily charm" another unsympathetic role in a film that did not generate audience interest. Due to the editing of the final print of HEARTBURN (1986), in Jeff's words, "I wound up as a guest at the wedding." Based on Nora Ephron's book about her marriage to and divorce from Watergate reporter Carl Bernstein, the picture belongs to its stars: Meryl Streep and Jack Nicholson.

SOMETHING WILD of 1986 had nothing in common with the 1961 film of the same title. The later movie, co-starring Jeff opposite Melanie Griffith, indicated that he was certainly capable of being a leading man. In this instance, he was yuppie corporate vice-president Charlie Driggs, who obtains a ride back to his office from a black-haired wild thing (Griffith). She later lures him to a motel where she handcuffs him to a bed for a sexual experience he finds fascinating. After more comedic adventures, the movie suddenly turns serious when her ex-convict husband (Ray Liotta) tries to kill them both. It is a wild and wonderful film, which, although it failed at the box office, is developing minor cult status in home video. Reunited with Woody Allen's large ensemble of players for RADIO DAYS (1987), a nostalgic glimpse of the role that radio played in the early 1940s in the lives of residents of Rockaway Beach, New York, Jeff had what amounted to a cameo as radio G-man Biff Baxter. In the limited-run PBS-TV anthology series "Trying Times," Daniels teamed with Julie Hagerty in the segment "The Visit" (November 16, 1987) as a couple whose house is invaded by a nutsy one-time girlfriend (Swoosie Kurtz) of the husband. The half-hour segment was directed by actor Alan Arkin.

Never having acclimated to New York City living, in 1987 the Danielses left their Upper West Side apartment for a move back to Chelsea, Michigan. They purchased a house next to his younger brother, John, and his family, not far from their parents. Jeff financed a slow-pitch softball team called the Clams, which figured prominently in a circuit of sixteen teams. Determined to remain in Michigan, Jeff explained, "When I go off on movies, my family comes for a while, then they come back, to friends that are normal. Obviously, what I do isn't normal. And I refuse to drag my family through that kind of life-style. If living here costs me a career, it costs me a career. I don't care."

"I don't feel like a leading man yet," he informed the *Los Angeles Times* in March 1988 as THE HOUSE ON CARROLL STREET was released. Co-starring with Kelly McGillis, he played an FBI agent from Kansas who hates New York, where the action takes place in the 1950s during Senator Joseph McCarthy's witch hunt for American communists. Jeff is assigned the job of convincing a witness (McGillis) to help him uncover a plot to smuggle Nazi war criminals into the United States. *Premiere* magazine critiqued the would-be thriller as "never a boring story, but it's not very believable, either." The publication credited Jeff and McGillis with creating "some nice low-key chemistry."

In the CBS-TV dramatization of THE CAINE MUTINY COURT-MARTIAL (1988), Jeff was Lieutenant Maryk, on trial for having relieved his captain (Brad Davis) of command of the minesweeper U.S.S. *Caine*. *US* magazine judged that the presentation "crackles with tension" and "has the look and feel of a big-screen film." Jeff was resourceful in a role that had been played in the 1954 theatrical movie version by Van Johnson. Back in movie theaters, Daniels next received third billing for SWEET HEARTS DANCE (1988) as Don Johnson's carefree best friend, a high school principal who falls in love (with Elizabeth Perkins) just as married Johnson is falling out of love (with his wife, Susan Sarandon). As *Variety* analyzed, "under Robert Greenwald's uncertain direction, actors flounder through their roles before hitting their strides about halfway through."

Jeff's movie career needed a good jolt, which he hoped would be provided by his next vehicle, indicated by his saying that it "might put me over the top . . . it's perfect for me." CHECKING OUT (1989) proved, however, to be less than ideal for either audiences or critics. As a man obsessed with the fear of death, Jeff visits heart specialists, buys health-testing equipment, has a glimpse of heaven, and drives his frustrated wife (Melanie Mayron) to take up cigarettes. "This movie is one limp strand of spaghetti," judged the *San Francisco Chronicle*.

Daniels's career did receive a boost, but it came through a made-for-TV movie shown on CBS on December 3, 1989. NO PLACE LIKE HOME (originally called HOMELESS) was an accurate depiction of a family forced to go on welfare after the family's apartment building burns downs and the father (Jeff) loses his job as the building's superintendent. After several other misfortunes, they end up homeless. As Mike Cooper, a stubborn man who refuses to acknowledge the family's plight until it is too late, Jeff was "achingly effective," according to *USA Today*. Richard Zoglin (*Time* magazine) decided, "Daniels, though too fresh-faced as the blue-collar father, brings hot-tempered passion to the role." As his wife, Christine Lahti, too, was superb in this disturbing but haunting film directed by Academy Award winner Lee Grant.

Steven Spielberg chose Jeff to star as a doctor with a fear of spiders in ARACHNO-PHOBIA (1990), directed by first-timer Frank Marshall. Heralded as a "Thrill-omedy!" about creatures with "Eight legs, two fangs and an attitude," it is not a parody but a recreation of the 1950s-type monster films, with comedic touches provided by John Goodman as the local bugbuster. The *Hollywood Reporter*, in terming the picture "A good, old-style genre piece," also thought Jeff "credible and sympathetic" fighting his fear of the crawlies while battering them with baseball bats. Considered a disappointment in some financial circles, ARACHNOPHOBIA took in a respectable $52.8 million in nineteen weeks of domestic distribution, earning $15.7 million during its first week on 1,831 movie screens.

Jeff had spent eight weeks during the spring of 1989 in Waxahachie, Texas, making a film entitled LOVE HURTS. Unable for months to find a distributor, the producers finally showed the results in Las Vegas on September 8, 1990, at the Cinetex '90 film convention. *Daily Variety*, in its review, praised director Bud Yorkin for extracting "a lot of laughs with an eye for the absurd." As Paul, Jeff was newly divorced from Nancy (Cynthia Sikes) who, with their two children (Thomas Allen, Mary Griffin), attends the wedding of Jeff's sister (Amy Wright). There, although he wants to reconcile with his ex-wife, Paul's philandering ways are readily repeated with Susan (Judith Ivey). *Daily Variety* gave Jeff's comedic performance a rating of "superb."

In WELCOME HOME, ROXY CARMICHAEL (1990), Daniels played his hometown's biggest celebrity except for Roxy Carmichael, who has become a movie star. Winona Ryder co-starred as a troubled teenager. When released in October 1990, the low-keyed movie met with generally unfavorable critical reaction: "has a bit too much whimsy and archness for its own good" (Abbie Bernstein, *Drama-Logue*); "the problem with this movie is that it never feels at home with itself" (Jeff Menell, *Hollywood Reporter*). Most of the scant attention the film received went to rising star Winona Ryder, with Daniels largely left on the sidelines: "Jeff Daniels is persuasive as poor, doubly-abandoned Denton, but there's not much for him to do here besides mope" (Bernstein, *Drama-Logue*); "Daniels does a serviceable turn" (*Daily Variety*); "Jeff Daniels, being very Jeff Daniels–like" (Ella Taylor, *LA Weekly*). The picture disappeared quickly from theaters.

Scheduled for 1991 release is THE GRAND TOUR, in which Jeff stars as an earthling visited by time-travelers from the future who come to a small town only to find death and destruction. Filmed in Oakland, Oregon, by screenwriter David N. Twohy in his directorial debut, it is based on a science fiction novella, *Vintage Season* by Henry Kuttner and C. L. Moore. For this picture, Jeff's salary was $600,000. Daniels is on his way, if all continues to go well, to advancing to the "A" list of actors who earn $1 million or more per feature film. He was next signed to co-star with Demi Moore and Mary Steenburgen in THE BUTCHER'S WIFE (1991) for Paramount Pictures. Daniels portrays a New York City therapist who tangles with a North Carolinian psychic (Moore) when she moves to the Big Apple.

Despite the various successes of his acting career, Jeff Daniels continues to profess a steady love for softball. He "immortalized the sport" in a song he wrote and plays on his guitar, in which he sings, "Oh softball and the girl that I love." Described by the *Los Angeles Times* as "the guy with the face like a $100 cotton-flannel shirt," Jeff not only has mischief in his eyes, but truly likes to have fun. Regarding his frequently offbeat career decisions, Daniels admits, "I took chances. I always took them for good reasons. But if it doesn't work, then you move on to the next. Luckily, people kept calling." Looking back on ARACHNOPHOBIA, he has said, "Yes. OK, film is art and all of that, and you do those occasionally, that's fine. But I'd get bored doing those all the time. This was a lot of fun, a lot of fun. A lot of fun to go to work, three and a half months of sometimes 15-hour days. I'm a big believer in entertaining people on a Saturday night. Don't blow it for them; there are too many bad movies out there."

Filmography

A Rumor of War (CBS-TV, 9/24/80–9/25/80)
Ragtime (Par, 1981)
An Invasion of Privacy (CBS-TV, 1/12/83)
Terms of Endearment (Par, 1983)
The Purple Rose of Cairo (Orion, 1985)
Marie (MGM/UA, 1985)
Heartburn (Par, 1986)
Something Wild (Orion, 1986)
Radio Days (Orion, 1987)
The House on Carroll Street (Orion, 1988)
The Caine Mutiny Court-Martial (CBS-TV, 5/9/88)

Sweet Hearts Dance (Tri-Star, 1988)
Checking Out (WB, 1989)
No Place Like Home (CBS-TV, 12/3/89)
Arachnophobia (BV, 1990)
Love Hurts (Vestron, 1990)
Welcome Home, Roxy Carmichael (Par, 1990)
The Butcher's Wife (Par, 1991)

Future Releases

The Grand Tour (1991)

Broadway Plays

The Fifth of July (1980)

TED DANSON

"What acting really is, is pretending, while you're pretending you're not pretending." —*American Film* magazine, November 1984

ADVERTISEMENTS FOR BARBARA WALTERS'S ABC-TV SPECIAL OF NO-vember 1, 1989, announced that she would interview "a duchess, a movie queen, and a prince of a guy." The prince was Ted Danson, who, although overtly nervous at being questioned by the Great Lady of contemporary interviewers, came across to audiences as exactly what everyone has described him to be—a sincere, nice man. He related that he had been raised "to be very sensitive and caring," and that upbringing comes through in his voice. It also shows on that well-known, square-chinned face, which, when observed closely, looks as if it might have been molded by Dr. Frankenstein. He does not have the handsomeness of a Mel Gibson or a Robert Urich, but behind those Paul Newmanesque blue eyes is a brain that relays intelligent messages of compassion.

Before he began starring as Sam Malone on the teleseries "Cheers" in 1982, Ted Danson did not think he had sex appeal on camera. However, he realized that he must have it or something equal to it to prompt such favorable reactions from so many fans. Shelley Long, his "Cheers" co-star for several seasons, has said that he "has such great style, wit and class. . . . I think he's our next Cary Grant." Actually, Danson is cut more from the Gregory Peck pattern—if he is to be compared with any of his predecessors—or from that of Tom Selleck in the present. Danson's wife has said that the most important things to him are his family, his career, the planet, and the environment, elements of his life which he is determined to make better through work and humor.

Edward Bridge Danson III was born on Monday, December 29, 1947 (some sources state 1949 or 1952), in Flagstaff, Arizona. His father was an archaeologist and former director of the Museum and Research Center of Northern Arizona, located across the street from the Danson home three miles outside Flagstaff. His mother, an avid reader, would not permit a television set in the home so Ted grew up reading books and playing cowboys and Indians with real Indian children from the nearby Navajo and Hopi Indian reservations, as well as making frequent visits to Grand Canyon National Park to the northwest of them. During the first twelve years of his life, he came to love and care about the wonders of his natural environment. At the age of thirteen he stood six feet tall, weighed 120 pounds, was uncomfortable and shy around girls, and was self-conscious because none of his clothes fit him well because he outgrew everything so quickly.

In 1960 he was enrolled at a strict boarding school, Kent, in western Connecticut where he saw his first television and claims to have "devoured" the programming. Because of his height, he was assigned to play basketball, although he knew nothing about the game or, for that matter, any other sport. By the age of nineteen he had reached his full height (6' 2") and he entered California's Stanford University at Palo Alto. There, during his second year, he was intrigued by a classmate who cut short their conversation by stating that she had to audition for a Bertolt Brecht play. He tagged along and won a nonspeaking part in the production. He later recalled, "The first time I went before an audience, it just knocked my socks off." Before the end of his sophomore year, he had arranged a transfer to Carnegie-Mellon University in Pittsburgh, noted for its drama school. In acting he had found what he wanted to do with his life.

Danson was married in 1970. Whether his wife was the same person he accompanied to the Stanford audition is not known because he will not speak of her. All he has said in interviews is, "I don't really want to bring her into this. That wouldn't be fair. She's a nice lady. It just didn't work out." They divorced in 1972, by which time he had graduated from Carnegie-Mellon and moved to New York to pursue an acting career.

After taking a one-room apartment on West 90th Street, Ted interviewed with the Wilhelmina modeling agency, but was rejected as being too tall. Off-Broadway he became an understudy in the Tom Stoppard comedy *The Real Inspector Hound*, eventually gaining a small speaking part. He also found work in TV commercials, including one in which he wore yellow tights and a yellow box around his waist as a walking lemon-chiffon pie mix. Danson made his Broadway debut in the short-lived *Status Quo Vadis*, which opened and closed at the Brooks Atkinson Theatre on February 18, 1973. The avant-garde play about young men on the make starred Bruce Boxleitner and Gail Strickland. In late 1973 Ted read for the role of a womanizer on NBC-TV's daytime drama "Somerset," a thirty-minute spin-off from "Another World." "I was so nervous and crazy," he has said, "that instead of coming across as terrifier of women, I came across as terrified of the camera. They gave me the role of a sleaze instead." For two years, from September 1974 through December 31, 1976, when the show left the air, he was Tom Conway, a lawyer with dishonest intentions. He has compared this job to "walking in cement shoes."

In 1977 he determined that changes had to be made in his life. "I was going through this period when I would have to take a vote to cross the street." Friends of his who had subscribed to the EST workshops "came back somehow different. I thought maybe it would help me." Also an EST enthusiast was brunette Casey Coates, an environmental designer. "He used to get up in seminars," she has said, "and share his feelings with such sincerity and sweetness that I thought, either he's really terrific or he's a big nerd." They met one night over coffee and were immediately romantically hooked. Nine months later, in 1977, they were married. He was twenty-nine, she was thirty-nine.

The newlyweds moved to Los Angeles in 1978 where they both went to work for Dan Fauci, a fellow advocate of EST, as teachers at the Actors Institute, while Ted also studied his craft. He earned his first movie role as a Scottish-American Los Angeles policeman who plays bagpipes in THE ONION FIELD (1979). Adapted by Joseph Wambaugh from his own fact-based novel, the engrossing film had Ted fourth billed as Ian

Campbell, whose hideous murder in a Bakersfield ditch at the edge of an onion field set in motion the plot, involving the convolutions of the judicial system which cause the trials of the murderers (James Woods, Franklyn Seales) to devour seven years' worth of taxpayers' dollars and drive Danson's surviving cop partner (John Savage) to near insanity. On October 15, 1979, Ted appeared in an episode entitled "Love on Instant Replay" of the short-lived NBC-TV detective drama "Kate Loves a Mystery," which starred Kate Mulgrew as Kate Columbo, the wife who was never seen in the "Columbo" show.

Ted's career was now gaining momentum. In quick succession he made two television movies, but before their release, Casey, who had been ordered to bed in her seventh month of pregnancy because of abnormally high blood pressure, went into labor on December 24, 1979. In the hospital, during delivery of her daughter, Katherine MacMaster Danson, Casey suffered a massive stroke. The baby was fine, but the left side of Casey's body was totally paralyzed. Doctors prognosticated that "she will probably walk but won't use her arm." For almost a month, she lay paralyzed in her hospital bed, determined to overcome this disability, supported by Danson's understanding and determination. She went home in a wheelchair and began the physical therapy that would continue for the next two-and-one-half years. After eight months, both she and baby Kate were learning to walk. After her eventual and miraculous recovery, the Dansons bought a two-story home in Santa Monica which was remodeled after her designs.

Ted's first TV movie was ABC's THE WOMEN'S ROOM (1980), which cast him as the insensitive Norm, who leaves his wife (Lee Remick) after she has financed his medical school education. *Variety* rated the three-hour production "more than worth the viewer's time. The cast was first rate." Five days later, on September 19, he appeared in ONCE UPON A SPY (1980), an ABC-TV pilot for a projected series. The half-page ad for the show in *TV Guide* magazine exclaimed, "Attention, James Bond fans! This is your kind of movie!" Ted was Jack Chenault, a computer genius who also excels as a chess player. He is recruited by Eleanor Parker to eliminate a mad scientist (Christopher Lee). The series failed to materialize, but Danson was kept busy by appearing in a segment of CBS-TV's "Magnum P.I." (March 28, 1981) as well as in "Dear Teacher," another pilot for a thirty-minute series that did not sell, which was shown on a summer filler series, "Comedy Theater" (NBC-TV), on August 28, 1981.

In August 1981, the 1940s-style *film noir* BODY HEAT, which made a sex symbol and star of Kathleen Turner, was in release. Ted had the fourth-billed supporting part of Peter Lowenstein, the bespectacled district attorney friend of Ned Racine (William Hurt) who becomes suspicious of Ned's affair with the luscious Matty Walker (Turner) and forces Ned to reveal the truth. In this, his second theatrical picture, Ted gave a natural and respectable performance. The following month, on September 20, 1981, he co-starred in yet another series pilot for ABC-TV, OUR FAMILY BUSINESS, as the police-informant son of a crime syndicate boss (Sam Wanamaker). TV's first look at organized crime from the syndicate's viewpoint, this show also failed to develop into a series. Shortly after these two assignments, Ted signed a $40,000 one-year contract with Aramis to do sophisticated commercials as the Aramis Man, featuring him in exotic settings with beautiful women. A second year's contract with the advertiser earned Danson $60,000.

In 1981 the NBC network gave a thirteen-week guarantee to the creators of "Taxi" to develop a series. Good writers put together the concept of a bar owned by an ex-football player, and the search began for male and female stars. Co-producer/director James Burrows had seen Ted in BODY HEAT and had employed him on a "Taxi" episode (February 25, 1982) and decided that he had "just the right blend of humor and character." However, according to Burrows, Danson was the most unathletic man he auditioned for the pivotal role of the womanizing bartender. Out of the more than three hundred men and women tested for the leads, the choice was narrowed down to three sets of actors: William Devane and Lisa Eichhorn, Fred Dryer and Julia Duffy, and Ted Danson and Shelley Long, with the latter pair being selected. The owner's former occupation was altered to relief baseball pitcher for the Boston Red Soxs to better fit Ted's persona. The man became known as Sam "Mayday" Malone, an ex-alcoholic who says, "I quit because of elbow trouble. I bent it too much." Malone wears around his neck as a good luck charm the bottle cap from the last bottle of beer he ever drank. The series was named for the bar, "Cheers." Ted read a book on baseball and NBC sent him to bartending school, but he claims that he still cannot mix a drink properly. "Cheers" premiered on Thursday, September 30, 1982, from 9:00 to 9:30 p.m. *Variety* recorded that Danson "played the role straight, and will no doubt serve as a calming influence to the bizarre characters and plots which will make up the series." During its first season, it finished only 71 out of 124 programs, but it was nevertheless renewed for the 1983–1984 season for a final try at improving its ratings. In the spring of 1983, the cast members embarked on a promotional road trek around the country to drum up interest in the show. Ted, with Nick Colasanto, who played the bartender Coach, went to Boston. The ratings improved slowly during 1983–1984, but when the writers played up the sexual tension between Sam Malone and Diane Chambers (Long), they rose one week to a 23 percent share of the audience.

Ted Danson and Kirstie Alley in "Cheers" (1988).

During the first two seasons of "Cheers," Ted also appeared in an episode of "Tucker's Witch" (October 6, 1982). In the Warner Bros. theatrical release CREEP-SHOW (1982), he was a rotting zombie seen briefly in one of five of Stephen King's "fantastic tales." The CBS-TV movie COW-BOY (April 30, 1983) had him in the sixth-billed spot as Dale Weeks, a disabled ex-rodeo performer hired by James Brolin to help run his ranch. "Allison Sidney Harrison," a series pilot made earlier, was finally aired on NBC-TV on August 19, 1983. The hour-long show, directed by actor Richard Crenna, featured Ted as a private-eye whose young daughter helps him solve mysteries. He had an unbilled cameo in the CBS-TV movie QUARTERBACK PRINCESS (December 3, 1983), starring Helen Hunt as a teenager who in 1981 became a quarterback on a boys' football squad in Oregon and led the team to victory. For his portrayal of a father having an incestuous affair with his daughter (Roxana Zal) in SOMETHING ABOUT AMELIA, seen by an estimated sixty million viewers on ABC-TV on January 9, 1984, Ted received a nomination for a Best Actor Emmy Award, but failed to win. (He did, however, take home a Golden Globe Award for his work.) His wife in this gripping movie was played by Glenn Close, who observed of Ted, "There is an ingenuousness about him, almost a childlike quality. There really is no ego at all." In 1984 Casey Danson gave birth to a second daughter, Alexis, in a delivery without complications.

Before "Cheers" began its third TV season, Ted starred with Burt Lancaster and Margot Kidder in his fourth theatrical movie, LITTLE TREASURE (1985), wherein, for the first time on the big screen, he won the girl in the finale. Bickering between Lancaster and Kidder during filming was well publicized, and neither of these more veteran actors outshone Ted, who was singled out as having given the best performance.

Ted had been Emmy-nominated for his acting in "Cheers" during the second season, but he did not win. The third season saw the loss through death of cast regular Nick Colasanto, whose character was replaced by that of a much younger bartender, Woody (Woody Harrelson). Ted would continue to be Emmy-nominated throughout the run of "Cheers," but wound up a gracious loser until, at the September 16, 1990, Emmys, Ted finally won an Emmy in the Lead Actor, Comedy Series category. Appearing without his toupee, Danson acknowledged that it felt good to win the coveted award at last. He also admitted, "It's new to my body; it feels funny."

It became commonplace for Danson to use the summer hiatus from his series to appear in movies. During 1986 he co-starred with Mary Tyler Moore and Christine Lahti in JUST BETWEEN FRIENDS as Moore's husband who has an affair with Lahti. In A FINE MESS (1986), a frantic Blake Edwards comedy, Ted and Howie Mandel co-starred as two bumblers. The movie, unfortunately, was just what its title said—a mess! Ted was co-executive producer, with Dan Fauci, of WHEN THE BOUGH BREAKS (October 12, 1986) for NBC-TV, starring Danson as a psychologist who teams with a police detective (Richard Masur) to solve the murders of a number of wealthy men. Early the next year, Fauci and Ted co-produced a second telefeature, WE ARE THE CHILDREN, for ABC-TV (March 16, 1987), this time starring Ted as a TV journalist helping with relief efforts for the Ethiopian famine.

In 1987 Shelley Long left the cast of "Cheers" to pursue a full-time film career. In the plot, her character, Diane, and Sam are poised at the altar of matrimony when he suddenly realizes that marriage is not for them and points it out to her. She agrees, and quietly leaves the bar, determined to write her novel and return in six months. As the door closes behind her, he says softly, "Have a good life." Long's replacement was Kirstie Alley, who joined the show in the 1988–1989 season as Rebecca Howe, "a corporate vamp." The series maintained its position at or near the top of the hit show list.

Ted's next major motion picture established him as a box-office draw. Ted, Tom Selleck, and Steve Guttenberg were three New York City bachelors coping with a baby left on their doorstep in THREE MEN AND A BABY (1987). Directed by Leonard "Star Trek" Nimoy, it was an American remake of a 1985 French movie comedy. Selleck received the best notices of the trio and the picture went on to become the #1 grosser of 1987 with more than $170 million. In 1988 sales of videotapes and discs of the feature set an all-time high, with sales in excess of 535,000 copies. The producing studio announced that a sequel was in the works, but it would not be made until 1990. Meanwhile, Danson maintained his big-screen momentum with a remake of another French film, COUSIN, COUSINE (1976), entitled simply COUSINS (1989). Called by *Newsweek* magazine "a clever, glossy refurbishing," it is the tale of distant cousins, a dance instructor (Ted) and a legal secretary (Isabella Rossellini) who have an adulterous love affair. Syndicated columnist Liz Smith credited Danson as coming across "brilliantly as a romantic leading man." In ten weeks at the domestic box office, COUSINS grossed a respectable $21,707,236.

On April 21, 1989, Ted was a "special guest" on NBC's "The Jim Henson Hour," and "Cheers" swung into its eighth season on September 21 with the introduction of a new character, a megamillionaire (Roger Rees) with whom Rebecca would fall in love. Danson warned *TV Guide* magazine readers that the series would fold at the end of its ninth season. (He had similarly vowed to leave the show at the completion of the fifth season.) "Cheers" remained in the top clusters of hit TV shows. Kirstie Alley told *US* magazine that Ted is "funny, and that makes him sexy." She also revealed that "I only kissed him [once]. Ted's a good kisser."

Professionally, he ended the decade with DAD, released in October 1989. *Variety* predicted that the drama would "reinforce Ted Danson's status as a major bigscreen star." The title character is Jack Lemmon, aged to his early eighties through makeup, whose adult son (Ted) is called home when the mother (Olympia Dukakis) has a heart attack. While there, he learns that "Dad" has cancer, so the once-independent son sticks by him through successive ordeals, having never before been a good son. *Daily Variety* praised Ted's dramatic, albeit stiff, performance in acknowledging that he "brings tremendous depth to this big-league assignment, pulling off the film's one truly great moment." The syrupy and sentimental film earned a relatively modest $10 million in domestic film rentals paid to the distributor, its serious overtones being apparently too somber for many younger filmgoers.

Ted and Casey in 1987 founded the American Oceans Campaign, with its dedication to preserving clean and plentiful seas. To raise "consciousness and cash" for the program, Danson attended the 1989 National Governors Association convention in Chicago to promote a resolution to protect American beaches and waterways from pollution. His fast-growing group raised $140,000 for the drive with a celebrity golf tournament on the island of Kauai late in 1989, and he appeared on cable TV's "Earthbeat" on October 21. He was also a performing member of the Los Angeles Classic Theatre

Work (LACTW), which focused on presenting radio dramas.

Ted was a speaker at the largest environmental fundraiser ever held in the United States at the Los Angeles estate of producer Ted Field on February 13, 1990, on behalf of the Rainforest Foundation and the Environmental Media Association. With close to nine hundred persons in attendance, the event raised $1.2 million. He took part in the April 22, 1990, "The Earth Day Special" (ABC-TV), while on the same date he began hosting the twenty-six-part series "Challenge of the Seas" on cable's The Discovery Channel. Later in the year, at Dana Point Resort in California, Danson served as host at a weekend benefit for the American Oceans Campaign where accommodations and activities ranged from $600 for one person to $1,000 for two. In September 1990 a videotape, *Help Save Planet Earth*, with Ted's commentary and featuring appearances by Jamie Lee Curtis, Whoopi Goldberg, John Ritter, and others, was in distribution.

While "Cheers" was high in the television ratings during the summer 1990 reruns, it was announced that an album of theme music, songs, and extended bits of dialogue from the show would be marketed. The longest-running comedy series currently on television opened its ninth year on September 20, 1990, with Danson once again the owner of the bar and Rebecca (Kirstie Alley), with whom he has finally made love, now reduced to being a waitress at the establishment. *Variety* noted of the veteran comedy program, "'Cheers' remains a sitcom for the ages, looking ageless in its ninth-season premiere." To celebrate the approaching two hundredth episode of "Cheers," NBC gave the show an hour on November 8, 1990, to present a retrospective and a question-and-answer period between the cast, executive producers, creators, and studio audience. Shelley Long was on hand to participate in this special telecast. Also debuting on NBC-TV during 1990 was "Down Home" starring Judith Ivey, a new series for which Danson and Dan Fauci served as executive producers.

While the *National Enquirer*, provided with information from Clare Meeks, a former Danson household nanny, loudly hinted that either separation or divorce was imminent due to Casey's jealousy over her husband's on-camera love scenes with younger women, Ted was at work on THREE MEN AND A LITTLE LADY (1990), reunited with Tom Selleck and Steve Guttenberg. The three bachelors are joined in the comedy hi-jinks by a five-year-old girl (Robin Weisman). Filmed in Los Angeles, New York, and Stratford-on-Avon, England, the sequel was released in November 1990 in time to attract lucrative holiday business. As with most sequels, it proved not to have the freshness of the original, leading *Variety* to report: "Thinking people will be hard-pressed to find a single interesting moment in this relentlessly predictable fantasy." The trade paper added, "Only Danson seems unable to play it straight-faced, with flashes of mischief and mockery lighting up the edges of his delivery." Nevertheless, despite many critics' carping, THREE MEN AND A LITTLE LADY grossed a very healthy $29,771,815 in its initial two weeks of domestic release. For the future, Danson hopes to produce WHALE SONG, based on a play about a thirteen-year-old girl who learns to communicate (through music) with a whale. As for continuing with "Cheers" into a tenth season, he remains uncommitted at present, explaining, "It's tough to say goodbye to it."

On the eve of his forty-second birthday in 1989, Danson told Barbara Walters, "I'm just beginning to get weight as an actor, as a man, as a husband," and declared that he was looking forward to the future. "Fifty will be fine with me," he grinned, and concluded by stating that everything that had thus far happened to him represented "The most fascinating ride of my life."

Filmography

The Onion Field (Avco Emb, 1979)
The Women's Room (ABC-TV, 9/14/80)
Once Upon a Spy (ABC-TV, 9/19/80)
Our Family Business (ABC-TV, 9/20/81)
Body Heat (WB, 1981)
Creepshow (WB, 1982)
Cowboy (CBS-TV, 4/30/83)
Quarterback Princess (CBS-TV, 12/3/83)
Something About Amelia (ABC-TV, 1/9/84)
Little Treasure (Tri-Star, 1985)

When the Bough Breaks (NBC-TV, 10/12/86) (also co-executive producer)
Just Between Friends (Orion, 1986)
A Fine Mess (Col, 1986)
We Are the Children (ABC-TV, 3/16/87) (also co-executive producer)
Three Men and a Baby (BV, 1987)
Cousins (Par, 1989)
Dad (Univ, 1989)
Three Men and a Little Lady (BV, 1990)

Television Series

Somerset (NBC, 1974–76)
Cheers (NBC, 1982–)
Challenge of the Seas (Discovery, 1990) (host only)

Down Home (NBC, 1990–) (co-executive producer only)

Broadway Plays

Status Quo Vadis (1973)

TONY DANZA

"My big dream was to be a popular guy. . . . My big ambition was to walk down Fifth Avenue like it was, you know, the neighborhood."
—*The Washington Post*, November 8, 1978

IT IS THE DELIGHTFUL SMILE OF A GUY HAVING FUN, A GUY WHO IS not taking things too seriously, seemingly unbothered by stress. It is an infectious smile that illuminates the printed page, the television or motion picture screen. Tony Danza is uninhibited, robust, exuberant, vastly energetic with an oversized memory bank for the storage of jokes. Katherine Helmond, Mona of the teleseries "Who's the Boss?," has quipped of her gregarious co-star, "I'll bet Tony was a premature baby. No one could have kept him in one place for nine months," adding, "When Tony's unhappy you know it; when he's happy *everybody* knows it."

He was something wild from the concrete jungles of a claustrophobic metropolis who was tamed by the love of a woman. That may sound like the teaser line for a 1940s Warner Bros. melodrama, but it is also the real-life story of Tony Danza.

Ann and Matty Iadanza immigrated to Brooklyn from Italy soon after World War II. There, on Saturday, April 21, 1951, their first son, Anthony, was born, to be followed by a second son, Matty, a year later. The elder Matty was a sanitation worker who took pride in his work; Ann was a homemaker who had hoped for a daughter to help her with domestic chores, but decided to make the best of the situation by teaching these essentials to her elder son. Both parents were stern but loving and proud of their children and tried to provide them with happiness. Tony's playground was the streets of Brooklyn, and he has admitted to having been a "hoodlum" there whose chief ambition was to stay out of jail. On Saturdays he was not permitted out of the apartment until he had thoroughly cleaned it; he referred to himself as "Mr. Goodmop." Sent to twelve years of schooling at Brooklyn's Blessed Sacrament Catholic School, he was often suspended for not attending to the business of learning, for his major interests were not contained in books. Primarily he loved wrestling and girls, followed closely by baseball and football. In his final years at Blessed Sacrament, he participated in school musicals, playing roles in *South Pacific* and *Guys and Dolls*.

In 1969, after finishing high school, he won an athletic scholarship, based on his wrestling prowess, to the University of Dubuque in Iowa. There he underwent a major cultural change in the midwest corn fields, such a contrast to the asphalt of his native habitat. His college majors were history and fun-making, but he also was introduced to something new—boxing. Each summer he returned home to Brooklyn where in 1970 a love affair with a girl named Rhonda resulted in her pregnancy. They were married, and their son, Marc Anthony, was born in 1971 and they lived together that summer. By the time he resumed his studies in Iowa that September, they had separated. However, they did not divorce until 1974. As a kind of celebration in the fall of 1971, he went across the Iowa state line to Geneva, Wisconsin, where he had his right arm tattooed with "Keep on Truckin'," an act he has since regretted, calling it "the worst thing I ever did."

After graduating with a B.A. in history in the spring of 1973, Tony returned to Brooklyn, thinking he might become a history teacher. His first job was tending bar, followed by working for a moving company. Meanwhile, prank-minded friends submitted his name and credentials to the Golden Gloves amateur boxing competition. He soon received a letter of acceptance and decided to try boxing, turning professional with the New York Circuit after a few months. At 5' 11" and weighing in at 160 pounds, he was classed as a middleweight to light heavyweight. It was at this juncture that he dropped the "Ia" from his surname, and boxing billboards extolled his pugilistic talents as "Tough Tony Danza" as well as "The Italian Bull." When not boxing or working out at Gleason's Gym in Manhattan near Madison Square Garden, he sold jeans out of the back of his car.

Of eleven fights, Tony won eight because "I had a good knockout punch." His aspirations of becoming a boxing champion ran high. "I was white, I was Italian and I could talk," he would later say; "that's a lot going for you in the fight business." However, everything changed with the appearance at Gleason's Gym of Stuart Sheslow, an independent TV producer, who picked Tony to audition for him for a TV series pilot inspired by the movie ROCKY (1976). Sheslow directed him to an acting teacher around the corner from Gleason's who greeted the newcomer in "the most relaxing voice I ever heard." The acting class consisted of students lying on the floor, rolling their heads, with the teacher urging, "Relax, let each part of your body drain of tension." Tony fell asleep. This action ended his acting lessons.

Nevertheless, Sheslow escorted Tony to Hollywood to star in his pilot project about young boxers, first known as "The Warriors," later changed to "Fast Lane Blues." No TV network was interested, however, and the film was never shown. But in the interim, Tony had met James Brooks, the creator of a definitely scheduled new TV comedy series for ABC-TV called "Taxi." In it was the uncast role of an Irish boxer. Since Tony neither looked nor sounded Irish, the part was revamped as Italian and the character of Tony Banta was created for him. He was a part-time cab driver for the Sunshine Cab Company of New York City who was also a boxer, but who had never won a fight. The thirty-minute sitcom was first telecast on September 12, 1978. Tom Shales (*Washington Post*) declared it, "The only intelligent comedy show on ABC and one of the season's biggest hits." "Taxi," which co-starred Judd Hirsch, Danny DeVito, Christopher Lloyd, Jeff Conaway, and Marilu Henner, was destined to enjoy five TV seasons, winning several Emmy Awards. (After the fourth season, when the ratings dropped drastically, ABC gave it up to NBC, which aired it for one more season, until July 27, 1983.)

Although Tony found Hollywood "mind boggling," he immensely enjoyed his new-found popularity. He found that female companionship was never lacking, and he got a kick out of being photographed for *GQ* magazine wearing a $700 wardrobe, while posed beside Clark Gable's original Duesenberg car. With a personal loan of $50,000 from "Taxi" co-producer Ed. Weinberger, he purchased a Hollywood Hills home. During this time, he was involved romantically with actress Teri Copley.

Not one to idle away his free time, Tony made his theatrical film debut in May 1980 as "Duke," the leader of a group of 1965 high school hellions, in THE HOLLYWOOD KNIGHTS. Meant to be funny, this picture had few laughs. That same month, on May 21, 1980, he was third-billed as Pony Lambretta in the ABC-TV movie MURDER CAN HURT YOU!, an unsubtle spoof of TV detective series such as "Kojak," "Ironside," and "Baretta." For Paramount in April 1981, Tony had the lead in GOING APE!, as a man who will inherit $5 million if he is able to raise a trio of orangutans. *Variety* reported of this lazy comedy, "As for the apes, they seem to realize this vehicle is really not worth the effort and pretty much walk, (or more accurately, lumber) through the picture."

By 1983, his former wife, Rhonda, had relocated to New Mexico, where they had a brief reconciliation. She became pregnant and in 1984 a daughter, Gina, was born. Tony ended 1983 with a guest appearance on ABC-TV's "The Love Boat," shown on November 15.

In February 1984 Tony took Teri Copley back East to meet his mother, who then lived on Long Island. (His father had died the previous year.) On February 4, he and a friend visited the bar-restaurant of Manhattan's Mayflower Hotel where they became loud and playfully tossed food at each other. A plainclothes security guard challenged them and reached inside his jacket. "I thought he was some nut reaching for a gun," Tony explained, "so what am I gonna do?" He slugged the man. The incident was recorded on the front page of the *New York Post* with the headline "'Taxi' Star Arrested in Drunken Brawl." The guard sued Tony and his pal for $16 million in damages; in New York's civil court, both defendants were pronounced guilty. Along with paying an undisclosed fine, Tony was given three years' probation plus 250 hours of community service, which he fulfilled as a bookkeeper at Bellevue Hospital and as an activities director at Harlem's Jewish Home and Hospital for the Aged.

Meanwhile, Rhonda agreed to Danza's taking custody of their thirteen-year-old son, who temporarily lived with Tony's mother until the court case was settled. As for Teri Copley, she faded out of Tony's life.

Back in southern California with son Marc Anthony, Tony began work on "Who's the Boss?," a new sitcom for ABC-TV, in which he starred as Tony Micelli, an uninhibited, streetwise ex-athlete who moves from New York City to suburban Connecticut, which he considers a better place to raise his motherless young daughter, Samantha (Alyssa Milano). He is the live-in housekeeper for attractive advertising executive Angela Bower (Judith Light), her son, Jonathan (Danny Pintauro), and Mona, her outspoken mother (Katherine Helmond). Before this new series premiered, however, Tony was one of many television and movie personalities to make cameo appearances in CANNONBALL RUN II (1984), in the hopes of making this sequel as attractive a box-office hit as the original

CANNONBALL RUN (1981). However, the movie failed. For the ABC-TV made-for-television movie SINGLE BARS, SINGLE WOMEN (October 14, 1984), Tony was one of several habitués of a disco bar, in his case the swaggering macho man attracted to an English teacher (Christine Lahti).

From the moment "Who's the Boss?" was first shown on Thursday, September 20, 1984, the American Broadcasting Company received oral and written laurels for having created a major hit. *Variety* acknowledged that Tony gave the series "a lift with his tough-with-a-heart portrayal of a New York ex-jock." In the Nielsen-rating wars, it steadily registered as the nation's #12 show, with an average rating of 17.5. This was sufficient to keep the program alive for several years.

On April 14, 1985, Tony drove for the first time in a pro-celebrity auto race at Long Beach, California, where he was asked whether he intended to expand his sporting activities to the race course. He replied, "Yeah, I'm gonna try to be aggressive. I'm not cocky, just confident." The race was shown on NBC-TV's "Sportsworld" on April 20. He was also the star pitcher on weekends for Lamonica's Pizza softball team, which was #1 in the Entertainment League. ABC-TV, on May 7, 1985, had him and Susan Lucci giving advice to the loveless on "99 Ways to Attract the Right Man" and on November 20, 1985, he hosted the fourth annual American Video Awards ceremonies, which were taped by ABC-TV for viewing on November 22. He will not discuss or reveal his salary for "Who's the Boss?," but he has stated that he is "thrilled" by it. About his acting career, he told an interviewer from the *Los Angeles Times*, "What's amazing is how much I've retained. I learned from the best. If I had retained this much from college . . . I'd be teaching school someplace."

On June 29, 1986, he married blonde Tracy Robinson, an interior designer eight years his junior. He sold his Hollywood Hills home and moved to the San Fernando Valley to what he called "a nice, warm house, not a fortress," which included a sauna, pool, workout room, and nursery because Tracy immediately became pregnant. "I work fast, man," he kidded, but added seriously, "She has made my life a hundred percent better. Make that 200 percent. . . . How much longer can I hold off this maturity stuff?" Three months after his marriage, on September 23, 1986, he starred in the NBC-TV movie DOING LIFE, described in press releases as his "all-dramatic debut." He played Jerry Rosenberg in this real-life story of a small-time Brooklyn crook who is spared the electric chair to become one of America's top jailhouse lawyers and, later, the spokesperson for Attica Prison convicts during their uprising. Danza, who served

Tony Danza in "Who's the Boss?" (1988).

as co-executive producer for this Canadian-filmed venture, turned in a surprisingly thoughtful characterization. *Daily Variety* enthused, "it's Danza's energetic, concentrated performance that pulls the vidpic together; as the centerpiece, he's terrif."

Katharine Anne Danza was born on May 8, 1987, and quickly became the focus of the household since son Marc Anthony would soon be leaving home to attend college. By mid-1987, Tony, who was taking increasingly strong control over his teleseries, had directed three episodes of "Who's the Boss?" "I love it," he admitted. "It combines the two things I like to do best—act and tell other people what to do." Blake Hunter, one of the creators and co-producers of "Who's the Boss?," has praised Tony, known on the set as "the original man in motion," in these words: "[He] is undersung in many ways. As a comedian, he has a very good sense of timing, but he keeps a strong emotional line going too. He makes it look easy, so he doesn't get the recognition more trained actors get." At the televised Emmy Award presentations in September 1988, Tony was designated to accept the statues for those winners who were not present. With eight in his arms, he joked, "I got kinda used to that lady, Emmy. I'd like to take her home one night." On November 21, 1988, Tony received a star on the Hollywood Walk of Fame on Hollywood Boulevard, and on November 27 he was Grand Marshal of Hollywood's fifty-seventh annual Christmas parade.

Danza had gone to West Berlin to film FREEDOM FIGHTER, an NBC-TV movie shown on January 11, 1988. Among the mostly British cast and crew, he was an American soldier who finds himself separated from his East German girlfriend when the Berlin wall is erected. *Variety* assessed, "Tony Danza . . . proves to be a surprisingly effective dramatic lead in FREEDOM FIGHTER, itself an unexpectedly powerful film." In another attempt at success on the bigger theatrical screen, Tony starred in SHE'S OUT OF CONTROL (1989). Released during the potentially lucrative summer box-office period, it told the story of a Los Angeles radio executive (Tony) who returns from a business trip to find that his fifteen-year-old daughter has undergone a transformation from a gawky teenager to the sexual object of the obnoxious local boys. The picture was not popular, and *Variety* noted that Danza "plays too many scenes on a one-note level rather than weaving his character's changes into the stuff of more complex comedy."

He was thirty-eight years old, but he retained the exuberance of a teenager at the Ringling Brothers Circus benefit for Variety Children's Charities in Los Angeles in August 1989 when he exclaimed, "I'd love to parade around the tent on an elephant." A different note, however, was struck on the set of "Who's the Boss?" in its sixth season when Robert Culp guest-starred as a con artist. An "insider" to *TV Guide* magazine reported that Tony was "yelling and screaming and making demands" because, it was surmised, he felt upstaged by veteran Culp and because Tony's character was not the focal point of the episode. In the fall of 1989, Tony entered into a partnership with actress Kim Basinger to open an Italian restaurant in Santa Monica, California.

During the 1989–1990 season it was announced that two "Who's the Boss?" spin-off series were being planned, one of which, "Samantha," was Tony's idea for giving more exposure to Alyssa Milano and possibly unseating NBC-TV's top teen comedy, "A Different World." Neither offshoot series materialized.

At 7 p.m. on February 4, 1990, on ABC-TV, Tony hosted "Disneyland's 35th Anniversary Celebration" on "The Magical World of Disney" for sixty minutes, and an hour later on ABC-TV he was among the many who paid tribute to Sammy Davis, Jr., in "Honoring a Show Business Legend" when he danced. On June 25, 1990, Danza was a presenter on ABC-TV's "All-Star Pro Sports Award Show." A survey conducted for the makers of Glass Mates Glass Cleaning Wipes in July 1990 revealed that Tony was first runner-up to "Mom" as the best housekeeper in America.

Continuing to clone films for television presentations, ABC-TV adapted LOOK WHO'S TALKING (1989) as a series to be called "Baby Talk," to premiere in September 1990 with Tony as the voice of the baby narrating the action. In August 1990, however, ABC announced that it had delayed the series' debut when Connie Sellecca left the project (she was replaced later by Julia Duffy and then by Mary Page Keller). The series finally bowed on March 8, 1991, to unenthusiastic reviews.

After a screening of THE WHEREABOUTS OF JENNY, an ABC-TV dramatic movie which Tony executive-produced, he got up on stage at the Twenty/20 Restaurant in Los Angeles and did an impromptu tap dance routine to show his pleasure at the finished product. When asked by "Entertainment Tonight" why he chose another drama as his third behind-the-scenes movie, he responded, "I'm just trying to get an education." In this telefeature, broadcast on ABC on January 14, 1991, and starring Ed O'Neill as a San Francisco saloon keeper battling for custody of his young daughter, Tony had a cameo as a bar brawler.

When "Who's the Boss?" began its seventh season on ABC-TV on September 18, 1990, the storyline had altered to have Tony and Angela (Judith Light) agree to date other people while Tony's daughter (Alyssa Milano) joins dad in college. Later in the season, Tony adopts a five-year-old boy (Johnathon Halyalkar) from his old neighborhood. In analyzing the series' continued success, *Daily Variety* observed, "The best that can be said about it is that it provides 30 minutes of mindless (if not mind-numbing) entertainment in a predictable, unimaginative, time-tested sitcom fashion that viewers seem to find comforting and charming. . . . The key to 'Boss' is Tony Danza . . . there's nothing pretentious about him, and he comes across as so sweet it's almost impossible not to like him. Danza may never win an acting award, but he certainly can win over viewers."

Although nearing the dangerous age of forty, Tony continues to look like a kid, probably because he is blessed with the ability to think young. Seemingly without cares, he exudes the youthful vibrance of a man twenty years his junior. After his disastrous attempts at starring in motion pictures, he is wise to remain with the medium in which he excels and with which he is most comfortable. However, the nonstop actor/director/producer will undoubtedly find further means to release his creative energies.

Filmography

Murder Can Hurt You! (ABC-TV, 5/21/80)
The Hollywood Knights (Col, 1980)
Going Ape! (Par, 1981)
Single Bars, Single Women (ABC-TV,
    10/14/84)
Cannonball Run II (WB, 1984)

Doing Life (NBC-TV, 9/23/86) (also co-
    executive producer)
Freedom Fighter (NBC-TV, 1/11/88) (also co-
    executive producer)
She's Out of Control (Col, 1989)
The Whereabouts of Jenny (ABC-TV, 1/14/91)
    (also co-executive producer)

Television Series

Taxi (ABC, 1978–82; NBC, 1982–83)
Who's the Boss? (ABC, 1984–)

Baby Talk (ABC, 1991–) (voice only)

RICHARD DREYFUSS

"I won an Academy Award in 1978, and the moment Sylvester
Stallone said my name, I walked up onto the stage, and I turned
around to a sea of strangers. It was a very sad moment for me. It
wasn't their fault. I had been afraid to connect. I had been unwilling
and unable, and I didn't know who they were."
                                    —*Esquire* magazine, November 1987

EPITOMIZING THE "ME GENERATION" WITH ARROGANCE, CONCEIT,
and a desperate need for ego satisfaction, but with abundant versatile talent, Richard
Dreyfuss, neither macho nor handsome, soared to the highest peak of film stardom. Short
in stature at 5' 6", teddy-bear chubby, and generously charged with energy, pushiness, and
intelligence, his loquaciousness on any subject has become legend. By his own admission
he was an egoist, unemotionally claiming to have the I.Q. of a genius. ("Behind all art is
ego," he has reasoned, "and I am an artist and I am unique.") Feeling guilty for having
achieved so much so quickly, he was uncomfortable at the top. He offset his emptiness
with cocaine and alcohol, at the same time alienating friends and sabotaging his career
progression. In late 1982 he had a change of heart, after which he disappeared from the
industry scene temporarily, got married, became a father and developed humility. He
miraculously received a second chance at playing leading character parts in the pattern of
Spencer Tracy and James Cagney. A few writers have stated that Dreyfuss sometimes
resembles Paul Newman through the lens of the proper cameraperson. However, of the
upcoming crop of male performers, only Timothy Busfield with beard can be closely
compared in appearance to Richard Dreyfuss.

He was born on Thursday, October 29, 1947, in Brooklyn, the son of Norman
Dreyfuss, recently returned from two years in a military hospital following service in
World War II, and his wife, a Jewish feminist-activist. A Zionist and a corporation lawyer,
Norman moved his family, consisting of three children, from Brooklyn to a veterans tract
in Bayside, Queens, in 1950. Then, suddenly, one day in February 1956, Mr. Dreyfuss
announced that they were going to sell all their possessions and go to Europe. After
traipsing around the Continent for six months, they returned to New York long enough to
purchase an outdated Cadillac in which to drive to Los Angeles. There, moving in with his
parents, Norman went on to become a successful restaurateur.

Richard had always been in competition with his brother Lorin, three years his
senior, as well as with his many cousins. He would do or say almost anything to gain

attention. At age nine, he blurted out to his parents that he intended to become an important actor. "Just don't talk about it," was his mother's response. She took him to the West Side Jewish Center on Olympic Boulevard and to Temple Emanuel in Beverly Hills where, over the next few years, he acted in various productions. By the time he was twelve, his confidence was high. He was certain that he was outshining his brother in his parents' eyes. At the age of fifteen, at Beverly Hills High School—the school attended by children of high-echelon movie parents—he joined the drama group, Thespians. He received parts in *U.S.A.* and *The Skin of Our Teeth*, among other plays. Also at fifteen, he became a regular with the Gallery Theatre troupe; his first professional role, in the Jewish family drama *In Mama's House* as the bar mitzvah boy, was followed by roles in *Journey to the Day*, *People Need People*, *Incident at Vichy*, and other works. Rob Reiner and Albert Brooks became his best friends and with them he loved to see old movies. Through contacts at the Gallery Theatre, he won the supporting role of David Rowe III in the thirty-minute NBC-TV sitcom "Karen," which premiered October 5, 1964, three weeks before his seventeenth birthday. The trite series vanished after its episode of August 30, 1965.

On graduating from high school in 1965, Richard enrolled at San Fernando Valley State College to study theater arts. However, Dreyfuss was soon ejected from the drama department for arguing with a professor about the acting of Marlon Brando (whom Richard worshipped). Therefore, he switched his major to political science, since his second love was politics. (One of his ambitious enunciations early in life had been that he wanted to become an actor, then retire to become a senator from New York or California, then retire to teach history.) In 1966, with Rob Reiner (son of comedian/filmmaker Carl Reiner), Larry Bishop (son of comedian Joey Bishop), and Phil Mishkin (son of Meyer Mishkin, who would later become his agent), he formed an improvisational comedy group called "The Session." They played a few minor engagements in Los Angeles as well as in San Francisco, but were unsuccessful.

In Richard's sophomore year in college, he applied for admission to London's Academy of Music and Dramatic Arts as well as to Yale University, both of which accepted him. However, before he could decide between them, he came to the attention of the U.S. draft board. Immediately claiming to be a conscientious objector, he was given two years of alternative service as a file clerk on the midnight shift at Los Angeles County Hospital. To help sustain him through the boring and tedious work, Dreyfuss began taking amphetamines, to which he soon became addicted. At the same time, he spent six months in psychoanalysis because he thought he was impotent. However, this ended abruptly when he met a thirty-four-year-old woman who cured him.

Under the guidance of agent Meyer Mishkin, he won bit parts in THE GRADUATE (1967) and VALLEY OF THE DOLLS (1967), as well as on ABC-TV in such series as "The Mod Squad," "Room 222," "Judd for the Defense," "Peyton Place," and "The Big Valley." In 1968, for MGM, he had a more substantial role as a cocky auto thief in THE YOUNG RUNAWAYS, followed by a supporting part in the lackluster comedy HELLO DOWN THERE (1969).

In February 1969 he returned to New York City for a very short time to appear in the Broadway play *But, Seriously . . .*, at Henry Miller's Theatre. It closed after four performances. Back in Los Angeles in June, he joined the New Theatre for Now, with whom he did a number of plays at the Mark Taper Forum through May 31, 1970. He was back in Manhattan in February 1971 at off-Broadway's Theatre de Lys, appearing in thirty-one performances of two one-act plays, *Acrobats* and *Line*. On May 3, at the McAlpin Rooftop Theatre, he starred in *And Whose Little Boy Are You?*, after which he again tried stand-up comedy as part of a trio at Manhattan's Playhouse Club, but he was dismissed the first night for insulting patrons. His New York sojourn concluded with an appearance in Central Park in *Aesop* for the New York Shakespeare Festival.

Back in California, on February 26, 1972, in the ABC-TV movie TWO FOR THE MONEY, he played a supporting role to such top-notch character performers as Mercedes McCambridge, Anne Revere, and Walter Brennan. Joining the Center Theatre Group's Plumstead Playhouse, he was Dudley in *The Time of Your Life*, starring Henry Fonda, which opened at the Huntington Hartford Theatre before going on a national tour for four months. He played gangster Baby Face Nelson in the theatrical release DILLINGER (1973), and was back on stage at the Mark Taper Forum in *Major Barbara*. While emoting in the George Bernard Shaw work, he was spotted by producers from Universal Studios who offered him a key role (as a would-be loner) in AMERICAN GRAFFITI (1973), the first rung in his ladder to movie stardom. After two years, the film had grossed $50 million, while its star added alcohol to his regular intake of amphetamines. He returned to TV briefly to co-star in ABC's pilot film of "Catch-22," telecast on May 21, 1973. The hoped-for series never materialized.

Richard starred in the title role of THE APPRENTICESHIP OF DUDDY KRAVITZ (1974), filmed in Canada, in which he pretty much played himself—a kid from a Jewish ghetto determined to make it big. *Variety* reported that he "comes across effectively and with force and ignites the storyline." In the Gene Barry–produced, low-budgeted THE SECOND COMING OF SUZANNE, completed in 1972 but not released until October 1974, Dreyfuss supported Sondra Locke and Paul Sand. After rejecting it three times, he finally accepted the offer to co-star as the ichthyologist Matt Hooper in the Steven Spielberg–directed JAWS (1975). Dreyfuss reasoned that the thriller, based on the best-selling novel about shark-hunting, would be the flop of the decade. Costing a then-sizable $8 million, the movie grossed $70 million in its first three months in domestic release, eventually becoming one of Hollywood's most financially profitable features, with ticket sales of more than $130 million. It more than made up for the failure of his next movie, INSERTS (1975), an arty British-made study of a Hollywood movie director reduced to shooting pornography.

On December 13, 1976, Dreyfuss was featured, as were Kirk Douglas, Elizabeth Taylor, and others, in VICTORY AT ENTEBBE on ABC-TV. In 1976 he appeared on a Los Angeles stage in *The Tenth Man*, while filming back-to-back movies, CLOSE ENCOUNTERS OF THE THIRD KIND and THE GOODBYE GIRL, both released in November 1977. In the former, reunited with director Steven Spielberg, he was Ray (a role originally slated for Jack Nicholson), a man obsessed by an oddly shaped Wyoming mountain and UFOs.

After Dark magazine credited him with playing the role with "intense brilliance." His appearance as Elliott Garfield in THE GOODBYE GIRL was another replacement situation, this time for Robert De Niro, who left after two weeks of shooting. Essentially playing himself, but doing it quite nicely, Richard co-starred with Marsha Mason, who said "There's some kind of chemistry that happens" between them. She played a former actress with a precocious nine-year-old daughter (Quinn Cummings) who becomes entranced with her newest actor-boarder (Dreyfuss). *People* magazine commended, "His verbal jabs coupled with a pleasantly rumpled demeanor produce an enchanting, cuddly leading man." On January 28, 1978, he was awarded a Golden Globe as Best Actor of 1977. On April 3 he became the youngest actor—at age thirty—to win an Academy Award as Best Actor. At the ceremony he appeared emotionally at a loss for words. He was also honored for this performance by the British Academy.

Dreyfuss then entered into his Shakespearean period. From March 29 to April 23, 1978, he played Cassius to George Rose's emperor in *Julius Caesar* at the Brooklyn Academy of Music. Douglas Watt (*New York Daily News*) reported, "But if Richard Dreyfuss' chunky and vital Cassius has a lean and hungry look, it is only in his small, sharp eyes." Somewhat more favorable was Richard Eder's assessment in the *New York Times*: "Mr. Dreyfuss puts real power into the role of Cassius. When he is in action . . . Mr. Dreyfuss is moving and invariably interesting. What he lacks so far, is a measure of stage skill." Reportedly, the mixed reaction to this production sent Richard into a temporary emotional decline. Nevertheless, he returned to the Bard to play Iago to Paul Winfield's Othello at the Alliance Theatre Company of Atlanta during the 1978–1979 season. In late summer 1979 he was again Iago to Raul Julia's Othello for the New York Shakespeare Festival in Central Park.

Meanwhile, Dreyfuss co-produced THE BIG FIX (1978), in which he starred as a former campus activist turned Los Angeles private eye. He hoped that this would be the first of several Moses Wines celluloid whodunits. However, this competent movie failed to generate audience enthusiasm, perhaps because its detective character was too ethnic (Jewish) for general consumption. In 1978 Dreyfuss purchased a Beverly Hills mansion and maintained a New York City apartment. In addition, he owned a $30,000 Mercedes, earned $1.5 million per film, and consulted regularly with a psychoanalyst about his guilt feelings over his quick success. While remaining a voracious reader, he ate too much, drank too much, and was deep into cocaine use. He walked out during preproduction on ALL THAT JAZZ (1980), to be hastily replaced by Roy Scheider, a career move that cost Richard $350,000. He chose instead to star in THE COMPETITION (1980), with Amy Irving as a fellow pianist, and fought to play the paraplegic in WHOSE LIFE IS IT ANYWAY? (1981), which *Rolling Stone* magazine described as having "been made for twelve-year old cynics." Neither movie was a success.

During 1981–1982, his weight increased from its normal 149 pounds to 183 pounds. His voracious consumption of alcohol and cocaine turned away most of his friends except for Carrie Fisher, a then-constant drug companion. When he told her, "We're cut from the same piece of cloth," she knew what he meant, but also realized "It wasn't a great piece." The suicidal course he had unwittingly chosen had to end one way or another, and it did on October 16, 1982. While driving home from an all-night party in his Mercedes 450-SL, he struck a palm tree on Benedict Canyon Drive and flipped over, pinning him inside. He awoke in a hospital, miraculously uninjured, where he was cited by the police for possession of cocaine and Percodan, a prescription painkiller. "I fell down," he has said of the moment. "I was in a void and it began to occur to me that I had no allies." Released from the hospital, he abandoned drugs and alcohol cold turkey and entered a counseling program. The drug charges were dismissed, with a judge ruling that he had made satisfactory progress.

He was not heard of again until March 30, 1983, when he was married to Jeramie Rain (born Susan Davis), a CBS-TV producer/writer, in a Jewish ceremony followed by dancing to Cole Porter music on stage 26 at the Burbank Studios. "Getting married never seemed appropriate until I met Jeramie," he explained. A victim of a form of the lupus disease, Jeramie was said to be allergic to herself and often in pain from skin lesions. (Some years later, Richard would reveal to "Entertainment Tonight" that despite her physical problems, Jeramie actually "has terminal cheerfulness.") In November 1983, their daughter Emily was born, followed three years later by son Benjamin, born with Peter's Anomaly, a rare defect of the left cornea which necessitated twenty-seven operations by his third birthday.

In April 1983 Dreyfuss appeared on the Broadway stage as a single father in *Total Abandon*, which survived for just one performance. In January 1984 he was seen by limited audiences on movie screens in THE BUDDY SYSTEM opposite Susan Sarandon in a low-keyed comedy that was too reminiscent of THE GOODBYE GIRL.

Michael Hershewe, Danny Gellis, and **Richard Dreyfuss** in THE BIG FIX (1978).

In 1984–1985 Richard Dreyfuss was on the Los Angeles stage as a recovering alcoholic stage director in *The Hands of Its Enemies*, followed by the Los Angeles premiere of *The Normal Heart*, a play about AIDS whose script called for him to kiss co-star Bruce Davison on stage nightly. Dreyfuss had signed to co-star in the ambitious CBS-TV miniseries "Kane and Abel" (1985), but dropped out and was replaced by Peter Strauss. Instead, he responded favorably to an offer to read for the role of the bum in Paul Mazursky's DOWN AND OUT IN BEVERLY HILLS (1986), but ended up playing the nouveau-riche spouse of Bette Midler. It was a move that rejuvenated his career, but now as a leading man in character roles. He followed this success as the narrator/writer in STAND BY ME (1986), directed by pal Rob Reiner. He enjoyed further phenomenal resurgence with the bittersweet comedy TIN MEN (1987), opposite Danny DeVito, the thrilling action movie STAKEOUT (1987), opposite Emilio Estevez, and then the Barbra Streisand–produced NUTS (1987), in which he was the Legal Aid attorney representing in a competency hearing a prostitute (Streisand) accused of manslaughter. About the latter movie he has said that he would again work with Streisand, but *not* in a film over which she had control. On television he joined the star-studded tribute to Martin Luther King, Jr. (January 20, 1986), on the NBC network, and hosted the ABC-TV commemorative of the American Constitution, "Funny, You Don't Look 200," in December 1987, a project which he also produced and wrote.

Newsweek magazine wondered, "How many laughs can be wrung out of a fake mustache gone askew" in its critique of MOON OVER PARADOR (1988). Richard's now-gray hair was dyed brown for him to play an American actor strong-armed into assuming the place of Parador's dead dictator. This comedy, written and directed by Paul Mazursky, was not in the same league as his and Richard's former joint screen venture. In May 1989 Richard was one of several stars to make brief appearances with comments on the talents of supermodel Beverly Johnson in the four-minute clip of Michael Jackson's "Liberian Girl" video. He also joined a repertory company that included Ted Danson, Amy Irving, and Harry Hamlin and focused on radio acting, called Los Angeles Classic Theatre Work (LACTW). His first movie release during 1989 was LET IT RIDE, in which he played a compulsive Florida racetrack gambler whose streak of luck doubles and even redoubles an initial $50 bet. Released on August 18, the comedy, whose racetrack theme had been done often and better in earlier Hollywood films, disappeared from theaters within a week. The Christmas week 1989 release of ALWAYS, however, played a different cash-register tune. A Steven Spielberg remake of the Spencer Tracy–Irene Dunne MGM release A GUY NAMED JOE (1943), it was updated from World War II to pilots fighting fires in the wilderness. With Richard, according to *Variety*, "stepping into Tracy's shoes without strain," the movie got off to a slow financial start, but grossed a semi-respectable $42 million in domestic ticket sales. Of his third professional teaming with Spielberg, Dreyfuss has said, "Steven and I are good friends and tend to think a lot alike. . . . The best thing about working with Steven is we have a creative shorthand. . . . At times we tend to complete each other's thoughts because we're so aware of how the other is thinking."

In March 1990 Richard formed a production concern, Dreyfuss/James Productions, in partnership with Judith James. It was located on the Disney Studio lot when they entered into a long-term deal with Touchstone Pictures, the company through which his latter-day successes (DOWN AND OUT IN BEVERLY HILLS, STAKEOUT, and TIN MEN) were produced.

At Cedars-Sinai Medical Center in Los Angeles on August 9, 1990, Jeramie Dreyfuss gave birth to the couple's third child, who was named Harry Spencer.

On September 8, 1990, on the Fox television network, Richard narrated the first in a series of thirty-minute travelogues, called "American Chronicles," conceived by David Lynch and Mark Frost, co-creators of "Twin Peaks." *Entertainment Weekly* magazine dimly viewed the series as a "hack documentary" and termed Richard's narration "banal." Dreyfuss took a cameo role, along with Dennis Quaid, Gene Hackman, and others, in POSTCARDS FROM THE EDGE (1990), based on Carrie Fisher's novel, directed by Mike Nichols, and starring Meryl Streep and Shirley MacLaine. Richard was a doctor who pumps the stomach of a movie actress (Streep) after a drug overdose and later tries to court her. Off camera, Dreyfuss has been sponsoring Imagining the Peace: Alternative Futures for the Middle East, an organization devoted to exploring solutions to the Israeli-Arab discord.

His romantic co-star in ALWAYS, Holly Hunter, was selected to work with Dreyfuss again in ONCE AROUND (1991), a comedic fable about family life, co-starring Danny Aiello and Gena Rowlands. Once more Richard served as a replacement—this time for Sean Connery—as the Player in ROSENCRANTZ AND GUILDENSTERN ARE DEAD (1991), filmed with Gary Oldman and Tim Roth in Toronto and Yugoslavia, and directed by Tom Stoppard who wrote the original play. (The film won the top prize at the September 1990 Venice Film Festival.) Dreyfuss also starred in the Manhattan- and Virginia-filmed comedy WHAT ABOUT BOB? (1991), in which he co-stars as a psychiatrist opposite patient Bill Murray; Julie Hagerty is cast as Richard's wife. In mid-1990 Dreyfuss was set to star in RANDALL & JULIET, a remake of a French movie, in which he would be cast as a powerful businessman learning of corruption in his corporation through his black cleaning woman (Sheryl Lee Ralph). However, he dropped out of the project due to "creative differences." Forthcoming is THE PROUD AND THE FREE, an American Revolutionary War period piece taken from Howard Fast's novel in which Richard plays the leader of the Citizens Army of the Pennsylvania Line during a mutiny toward the end of the war for independence.

Currently in his fourth decade of moviemaking, Dreyfuss observes, "success can often be as destructive for a filmmaker as failure. At least with your failures you can generally learn what you did wrong. When you're an actor with a hit movie, Hollywood looks at you as the owner of a valuable secret that they need to have. The key for me is not getting emotionally off-balance by either extreme." In a fickle industry where memories are short, even an actor with a recent hit often wonders to himself, "Why are Kevin Costner's fingerprints on every script I'm being sent?—or Alec Baldwin's—or Jason Patric's—or the newest hot star." Having literally grown up in the business, Richard has been forced to hide cynicism with a healthy Jewish sense of humor.

Filmography

The Graduate (Emb, 1967)
Valley of the Dolls (20th–Fox, 1967)
The Young Runaways (MGM, 1968)
Hello Down There (Par, 1969)
Two for the Money (ABC-TV, 2/26/72)
Dillinger (AIP, 1973)
American Graffiti (Univ, 1973)
The Apprenticeship of Duddy Kravitz (Par, 1974)
The Second Coming of Suzanne (Barry, 1974) [made in 1972]
Jaws (Univ, 1975)
Inserts (UA, 1975)
Victory at Entebbe (ABC-TV, 12/13/76)
Close Encounters of the Third Kind (Col, 1977)
The Goodbye Girl (WB, 1977)
The Big Fix (Univ, 1978) (also co-producer)
The Competition (Col, 1980)
Whose Life Is It Anyway? (MGM, 1981)

The Buddy System (20th–Fox, 1984)
Down and Out in Beverly Hills (BV, 1986)
Stand by Me (Col, 1986)
Tin Men (BV, 1987)
Stakeout (BV, 1987)
Nuts (WB, 1987)
Moon over Parador (Univ, 1988)
Let It Ride (Par, 1989)
Always (Univ, 1989)
Postcards from the Edge (Col, 1990)
Once Around (Univ, 1991)
Rosencrantz and Guildenstern Are Dead (Cinecom, 1991)
What About Bob? (BV, 1991)

Future Releases

The Proud and the Free (BV, 1991)

Television Series

Karen (NBC, 1964–65)

Broadway Plays

But, Seriously . . . (1969)

Total Abandon (1983)

SALLY FIELD

"I think on some level I must be monumentally unsophisticated.
There must be something ordinary about me. I look like people you
might have grown up with."—*Playgirl* magazine, December 1985

CARY GRANT EXPLAINED TO LORETTA YOUNG IN THE BISHOP'S WIFE
(1947), "The world changes, but two things remain constant—youth and beauty." Grant
went on to add that "The only people who grow old were born old to begin with." This
dialogue passage clearly defines button-nosed Sally Field who, at 5' 2" and hovering at 100
pounds, has been described by the media as "pert," "cherubic," "diminutive," and so on.
With her dimpled cheeks, wide mouth, and slightly uneven teeth, she has a captivating
smile; one tends to smile back at her photograph.

Sally Field was born to act. She knew it from a very early age; television viewers
knew it when she was a teenager; but the hard-nosed critics did not acknowledge it until
shortly after her thirtieth birthday, when she was the "surprising revelation" of the 1976–
1977 TV season as a young woman with sixteen distinct personalities. Later, she proved
her skills to the world and won both international and national acting awards, including a
pair of Oscars. At one Oscar ceremony she made her now-famous acceptance speech,
which she has tried to live down since it was spoken that March evening in Los Angeles.
Time passes, even for those seemingly blessed with eternal youth, and before we knew it,
Sally Field was playing mother roles on screen opposite adult co-stars. She is handling
these new assignments with the same grace and exuberance she displayed in tackling the
hero-worshipping Gidget character soon after she was awarded her high school diploma.

Sally Field was born on Wednesday, November 6, 1946, in Pasadena, California,
the second child and only daughter of druggist Richard Field and his wife, Margaret, an
aspiring actress. In 1950, when Sally was four, the Fields divorced and Margaret married
Jock Mahoney, a muscular Hollywood stuntman who went on to play Tarzan in two
movies. The family took up residence in Van Nuys, California, in the San Fernando
Valley, and Sally's mother, using the name Maggie Mahoney, became a Paramount
Pictures starlet. She also took acting lessons from Charles Laughton and, when there was
no time to arrange for a babysitter, toted Sally with her to readings of classic plays. Left to
her own devices a great deal of the time, Sally would shut herself off in a room with her
mother's makeup and clothes and act out movie scenes in front of a mirror. She confessed
later, "I was very reclusive and always highly emotional. I didn't feel I was allowed to
express it, so I would cry and scream in front of the mirror and be very sexy. Acting was the
place where I could be me."

At the age of seven, she wrote plays and staged them, using neighborhood children as her cast. She took part in school plays at William Mulholland Junior High School in Van Nuys and devoted extracurricular hours to cheerleading and drama at Birmingham Senior High School. Before her graduation from high school in 1964, she had played leads in *Suddenly Last Summer*, *The Miracle Worker*, and *The Man Who Came to Dinner*. Sally's graduating class voted her "Most Gullible."

During the summer of 1964, Sally enrolled in the Columbia Pictures Workshop, a branch of the studio which hoped to develop fresh talent. Eddie Foy III, a friend of the Mahoneys, was the casting director for Screen Gems, the TV arm of Columbia. He encountered Sally one night on the lot and suggested she audition for a new series planned for ABC-TV called "Gidget," based on the movie character created on screen by Sandra Dee in 1959. She auditioned and six months later was awarded the role. At a weekly salary of $450, she signed a Screen Gems contract for "Gidget," which premiered on September 15, 1965. In the half-hour sitcom she was a giggly fifteen-and-a-half-year-old Santa Monica, California, girl rescued from the ocean by a surfer (Steven Miles) when she gets a cramp. He gives her the nickname of "Gidget" because of her 5' 2" height: she is not tall, but she is not a midget either. The series was commonly referred to as "silly," but the younger set loved it and protested when it was cancelled after only one season.

Sally was not idle for long. She was a recurring character in three episodes of NBC-TV's "Hey, Landlord!" in early 1967. After seeing her in "Gidget," film director Andrew McLaglen asked her to play Mercy McBee, a sixteen-year-old wagon train traveler on the Oregon Trail of 1843 in THE WAY WEST (1967). ABC-TV producer Harry Ackerman approached her about starring in a new situation comedy, "The Flying Nun." She rejected the part because she wanted to do more serious roles. However, Ackerman was persistent and she eventually accepted the part of ninety-pound Elsie Ethington, who dedicates her young life to helping the poor by joining a convent where she is known as Sister Bertrille. In San Juan, Puerto Rico, at the Convent San Tanco, she finds that she can fly when the trade winds catch the cornets of her habit in just the right way; but her landings sometimes are difficult. At a weekly salary of $4,000, she premiered as "The Flying Nun" on September 7, 1967, playing the role in eighty-two episodes over three seasons. *Cue* magazine called her "enchanting," "sunny," and "hoydenish without being tough," while *Variety* thought that "Miss Field has talent, but she is so busy being the cutesy comedienne that she has overlooked being the actress." During the first two years of the series, Sally sang on three 45-rpm recordings and one album, all on the Colgems label. Released on November 18, 1967, "Felicidad"/"Find Yourself a Rainbow" was on the *Billboard* magazine charts for four weeks at #94, her biggest "hit." This was followed by "Golden Days"/ "You're a Grand Old Flag" and, with Madeleine Sherwood (The Mother) and Marge Redmond (The Sister), "Months of the Year"/"Gonna Build a Mountain." The album was entitled *Sally Field (Star of "The Flying Nun")*. During the summer of 1968, after narrating an ABC-TV special, "California Girl" (April 26, 1968), Sally enrolled at Lee Strasberg's Actors Studio in Manhattan where she performed in *The Respectful Prostitute*, among other plays.

On September 16, 1968, at the start of her second season as "The Flying Nun," she was married to Steven Craig, a young man she had known most of her life. At the age of twenty-one, she immediately became pregnant with son Peter, born in 1969. The nun's costume concealed her pregnancy during the latter days of the series. When the show had run its course (it was last seen on September 18, 1970), she was offered a new sitcom, tentatively entitled "The Sally Field Show," but declined because she was now more interested in pursuing dramatic endeavors. She guest-starred in 1970 in an episode of NBC-TV's "Bracken's World," set within the movie industry, followed by an ABC-TV movie, MAYBE I'LL COME HOME IN THE SPRING (February 16, 1971), in which she played a troubled teenager. In the fall of 1971 she guest-starred on "Marcus Welby, M.D." and "Night Gallery" and was a free-spirited heiress in the NBC-TV movie MARRIAGE: YEAR ONE (October 15, 1971). On November 17, 1971, she appeared for the first time as Clementine Hale, a recurring character on ABC-TV's "Alias Smith and Jones," set in 1890s Kansas. The year ended for Sally with MONGO'S BACK IN TOWN (December 10, 1971), a CBS-TV movie in which she received second billing to Telly Savalas as a pre-"Kojak" police lieutenant.

In 1972 Sally gave birth to her second son, Elijah, after which she co-starred in an ABC-TV movie as one of three daughters called HOME FOR THE HOLIDAYS (November 28, 1972) by their father (Walter Brennan), who suspects that his wife (Julie Harris) is trying to poison him. After playing a teenaged newlywed in the old west in HITCHED (March 31, 1973) on NBC-TV, she returned to New York to resume studies at the Actors Studio. However, she returned west to Los Angeles for the NBC-TV comedy series "The Girl with Something Extra," which premiered September 14, 1973, and lasted one season. She was "the girl" of the title, and the "something extra" was her possession of E.S.P., which placed her attorney husband (John Davidson) in precarious situations.

Following the demise of this series fluff, Sally admitted, "The truth was that nobody around had any respect for me; to them I was a joke. So I took the plunge and changed everything at once—I got rid of my agent, my business manager, my house, and my husband." She went back to the Actors Studio to study under David Craig, the theatrical coach husband of Nancy Walker. For the next two years she devoted her time to learning, which included a stint with the Kenley Players stock company in Ohio, reemerging briefly in 1974 to host the Miss Teenage America Pageant on CBS-TV.

She came back to theater screens in STAY HUNGRY (1976) as a health spa reception-ist, causing the *New York Post*'s reviewer to write, "While not movie-star gorgeous, this actress is a powerfully sexy comedienne." In September 1976 she was among those involved with a legendary mountain man in BRIDGER on ABC-TV. Two months later, on November 14 and 15, 1976, Sally displayed her true talents as SYBIL, a young woman who develops sixteen distinct personalities as the result of disturbing childhood experiences. Reviewing this four-hour NBC-TV movie, the *New York Times* declared that Sally was "incredibly riveting" in her characterization and that she moved through the personalities "in a dazzling tour de force." For her work, Sally won an Emmy Award as Outstanding Lead Actress.

SYBIL was expected to change Sally's career, and it would, but not immediately because in 1977 she met Burt Reynolds. She fell in love with the hunk star, embarking on a relationship that would last several years with her acting in four of his feature films. The first was SMOKEY AND THE BANDIT (1977), in which she was Carrie, the girlfriend of rambunctious bootlegger Bandit (Reynolds). She took a break from Reynolds to co-star in HEROES (1977), in which, en route by bus from New York to California, she meets a disturbed Vietnam veteran (Henry Winkler). She then returned to Reynolds, appearing with him in two successive pictures. In THE END (1978) she played second fiddle to him as his girlfriend who does not want him to commit suicide although he is terminally ill. In HOOPER (1978) she had a smaller role, watching him do his Hollywood stunts. All three of these Reynolds–Fields movies were popular—especially SMOKEY AND THE BANDIT, which was the number two money-maker of 1977—but they did little for Sally's career. During the winter months of 1978 she aided Reynolds by appearing in *Vanities* at his dinner theater in Jupiter, Florida, along with co-starring with him in a production of *The Rainmaker.*

Of screen director Martin Ritt, Sally has said, "The most important thing that Marty did was to give me the opportunity to show what I can do." After being turned down by Jane Fonda, Jill Clayburgh, and Faye Dunaway, Ritt offered the role of Norma Rae Webster to Sally. At first she hesitated, but Reynolds convinced her to do it. Based in part on a true story, NORMA RAE (1979) told of an uneducated, underprivileged southern textile mill worker who becomes inspired to unionize her fellow workers. In the process, the spunky miss provides herself with dignity. Critic Gene Siskel called her "one of our most underrated actresses," while *New Republic* magazine exclaimed, "cheers—cheers from the heart—for Sally Field." In its first six weeks of domestic release, the drama took in $8 million. Sally received a standing ovation at the Cannes Film Festival in May 1979, where she was named Best Actress. Later, she won the Best Actress laurels from the New York Film Critics. When nominated for a Best Actress Academy Award, she said of the ceremonies, "I think it's exploitative, overcommercialized, frequently offensive and shouldn't be televised," but added, "Sure, I'll be there!" On April 14, 1980, she won the Oscar. As she walked to the podium, she shook her fist and accepted with: "I'm going to be the one to cry tonight, I'll tell you that right now. They said this couldn't be done."

Two months after winning the Oscar, she appeared in the boring BEYOND THE POSEIDON ADVENTURE (1979) as Michael Caine's love interest. She admitted to *Look* magazine, "It was God's way of giving me one final kick in the behind. I'll never do anything like it again." As a favor to Reynolds, she reprised her role of Carrie in SMOKEY AND THE BANDIT II (1980), a distillation of the original. In BACK ROADS (1981), again directed by Martin Ritt, she was a hooker who hitchhikes west from Mobile, Alabama, meeting a fellow wanderer (Tommy Lee Jones) along the way. Later in the year she was a tough, ambitious newspaper reporter with a habit of making up details in ABSENCE OF MALICE (1981). When asked by an interviewer if members of the press had ever personally hurt her, she responded, "Not really, but that's because I've been open to the press for eighteen years, so it's a way of life with me."

In 1981 she broke with Burt Reynolds, after which she said, "Getting over him was no fun." Although she detested dating, she began seeing Johnny Carson and Kevin Kline, among others. On December 21, 1981, she starred as Mary Follet in the NBC-TV "Live Theatre" presentation of "All the Way Home" with William Hurt, telecast from the campus of the University of Southern California. Off movie screens for over a year, she lumbered back in the would-be comedy KISS ME GOODBYE (1982). It was a lame remake of the Brazilian hit DOÑA FLOR AND HER TWO HUSBANDS (1978). When director Martin Ritt became ill in 1982, pre-production on the comedy NO SMALL AFFAIR, co-starring Sally with Matthew Broderick (as her love-struck young admirer), was abandoned; the film was later re-started in 1984, teaming Demi Moore and Jon Cryer.

In June 1984 Sally met Hollywood producer Alan Greisman, known about town as a "ladies man." They lived together for six months until they were married in December. In moviedom, 1984 was the year of the suffering farm women, with COUNTRY (Jessica Lange), THE RIVER (Sissy Spacek), and PLACES IN THE HEART. The latter starred Sally as Edna Spalding who finds herself widowed and penniless within the movie's opening five minutes. Released in September, PLACES IN THE HEART outdistanced the others in domestic film rentals with more than $14 million by March 1985, the result, according to *Film Comment* magazine, of "Field's undeniable star stature." *Playgirl* magazine noted that Sally gave "the performance of her career," and critic Judith Crist wrote that she "is simply stunning in her portrait of a woman of courage and compassion." Lange, Spacek, and Sally were all nominated for Academy Awards.

Sally Field in BEYOND THE POSEIDON ADVENTURE (1979).

On March 25, 1985, the Best Actress presenter was Robert Duvall, who tore open the envelope to announce that Sally Field had won. She raced to the stage, giving director Robert Benton a raised-arms gesture of triumph. Her acceptance speech throbbingly concluded with: "I haven't had an orthodox career and I wanted more than anything to have your respect. The first time I didn't feel it, but this time I feel it and I can't deny the fact you like me— right now, you *like* me!" The speech was torn apart by such critics as Pauline Kael who stated that Sally's overwhelming need for approval would keep her from being a first-rate actress, while one-time boyfriend Johnny Carson made fun of it on his night-time TV talk show. Sally defended herself with, "As I was walking up to receive the Oscar, I thought, I'm not going to give this moment away. . . . It's mine!"

Following this second Academy Award win, she and her husband purchased a $1.5 million home in the Brentwood section of Los Angeles and she formed her own production company, Fogwood Films, Ltd., headquartered on the Columbia lot. The first property to be made by Fogwood was MURPHY'S ROMANCE (1985), in which she co-starred with James Garner as a tough and witty pharmacist who woos her. The pleasant but unmemorable picture was directed by her old friend Martin Ritt. (While based at Columbia, Field optioned MOONGLOW, a project that faded, only to be repackaged for Cher and retitled for 1987 release as MOONSTRUCK.)

In its May 1986 edition *Life* magazine devoted several pages to "The Movies," featuring the "five most powerful women in the movies today, mistresses of their own professional destinies." The five were Sally Field, Jane Fonda, Goldie Hawn, Jessica Lange, and Barbra Streisand. A few months earlier, Sally had told *People* magazine, "I'm one of the five best actresses in this country. I really am. I'm as accomplished as a person can get, and I say that with great pride in myself. . . . I've won two Oscars, there isn't anyone else in my age group who has."

Sally was inactive for almost two years, during which time she gave birth, in December 1987 at age forty-one, to a baby boy who was named Sam. Two months earlier, she was reunited on screen with Michael Caine in SURRENDER (1987). This second pairing did not do much for either performer. Sally played a confused woman trying to decide whether to wed Caine, who pretends to be penniless, or remain with her affluent attorney boyfriend (Steve Guttenberg).

"Dying is easy. Comedy is hard" read the ads heralding the arrival of Sally's second feature co-produced through Fogwood. PUNCHLINE (1988) found her as a frumpy, mousy New Jersey housewife and mother who is trying to be a stand-up comic, to the dissatisfaction of her fat husband (John Goodman) and the encouragement of a hard-driven fellow comedian (Tom Hanks). The film drew a range of reviews, from "bold, sneaky, brilliant" (*Los Angeles Times*) to "maudlin and predictable" (*San Francisco Chronicle*). Hanks said of his co-star, who gave him some of the better scenes, "Sally has the right to be regal and demanding and unapproachable, but she's not. That's refreshing."

On October 29, 1988, a private jet plane carrying Sally, husband Alan, son Sam, and her mother was taking off from their vacation spot in Aspen, Colorado, when it collided on ground with two other jets. The plane was a total loss. Shaking and exhausted, she said later, "all I was thinking was 'hold on to Sam! . . .' I didn't care if I broke every bone in my body. Nothing flashed before my eyes except Sam."

STEEL MAGNOLIAS (1989) was based on the off-Broadway smash hit play from Robert Harling, who put into dialogue the tragic story of his diabetic sister who gave up her life in order to have a child. On the film's release in mid-November 1989, *Rolling Stone* magazine noted, "Just stand back and watch these ladies set off sparks," referring to the cast line-up of Sally, Dolly Parton, Shirley MacLaine, Olympia Dukakis, Julia Roberts, and Daryl Hannah. Sally and Roberts had the pivotal roles of the tightly wound southern mother and the pregnant, ill daughter, respectively. *Newsweek* magazine decided that Sally "dutifully restrains her natural exuberance and is rewarded with a big Oscar-mongering third-act explosion, which she milks for all it's worth" but considered that the total film "is so busy celebrating" the cast ladies that "it doesn't have time to stop to get acquainted." In its first twenty-eight weeks in domestic release, the tear-jerker grossed $82 million. Speculation ran high that Sally would be nominated for an Oscar in the Best Actress category, especially for her emotional cemetery scene, but her peers were apparently not sufficiently impressed. Julia Roberts, however, received a Best Supporting Actress nomination, but lost. Prior to the Academy Awards ceremonies, Sally was one of the film's stars to attend a Royal Command Performance showing of the film in London as well as a screening at the Berlin Film Festival. A teleseries pilot based on STEEL MAGNOLIAS failed to win CBS-TV's approval as an ongoing series; it had Cindy Williams in the role originated in the movie version by Sally.

Meanwhile, Sally had headed a cast that included Ed Asner, Rue McClanahan, and Bronson Pinchot in a special staged reading of *Twelfth Night* at the Balcony Theatre of the Pasadena Playhouse on January 6, 1990, presented by the Los Angeles Shakespeare Festival.

In NOT WITHOUT MY DAUGHTER (1991), Sally was a mother whose marriage to an Iranian doctor (Alfred Molina) fails, whereupon he holds the wife and daughter (Sheila Rosenthal) hostage in Iran. Released in January 1991 at the height of "Operation Desert Shield" against Iraq, NOT WITHOUT MY DAUGHTER was branded by Sheila Benson (*Los Angeles Times*) as "unbalanced polemic," even though it was based on a true story. Benson conceded that "Field is fine as the initially naive and always fiercely protective mother." *Variety* judged that "It is certainly as propaganda that the film is most successful, for its artlessness in all other respects will be noticeable even to those who may be convulsed by the cental dilemma." The trade paper acknowledged that Sally provided "an earnest, suitably emotional performance as a rather typically sincere, middle-class American." In eight weeks of domestic distribution, NOT WITHOUT MY DAUGHTER earned a weak $13,993,018. In CONUNDRUM (forthcoming, 1991), touted as a "psychological thriller," Sally was a Minneapolis police investigator caught in a "twisted tale of betrayal." In SOAPDISH (1991) Sally is cast as a fading TV soap opera star, with Carl Reiner as an absent-minded TV network boss and Whoopi Goldberg as a daytime soap opera writer. For DYING YOUNG (1991), starring Campbell Scott and Julia Roberts, Sally and Kevin McCormick served as producers.

Sally is straightforward in assessing "I'm a product of my time" and calls herself a bankable Hollywood commodity. Her sense of humor comes to the fore often, especially in such comments as "I look like a tree stump" in comparing herself to other beauties of the world.

Filmography

The Way West (UA, 1967)
Maybe I'll Come Home in the Spring (ABC-TV, 2/16/71)

Marriage: Year One (NBC-TV, 10/15/71)
Mongo's Back in Town (CBS-TV, 12/10/71)
Home for the Holidays (ABC-TV, 11/28/72)

Hitched (NBC-TV, 3/31/75)
Bridger (ABC-TV, 9/10/76)
Sybil (NBC-TV, 11/14/76–11/15/76)
Stay Hungry (UA, 1976)
Heroes (Univ, 1977)
Smokey and the Bandit (Univ, 1977)
The End (UA, 1978)
Hooper (WB, 1978)
Norma Rae (20th–Fox, 1979)
Beyond the Poseidon Adventure (WB, 1979)
Smokey and the Bandit II (Univ, 1980)
Absence of Malice (Col, 1981)
Back Roads (WB, 1981)
Kiss Me Goodbye (20th–Fox, 1982)

Places in the Heart [Colours of the Heart] (Tri-Star, 1984)
Murphy's Romance (Col, 1985)
Surrender (WB, 1987)
Punchline (Col, 1988)
Steel Magnolias (Tri-Star, 1989)
Not Without My Daughter (MGM, 1991)
Soapdish (Par, 1991)
Dying Young (20th–Fox, 1991)
   (co-producer only)

Future Releases

Conundrum (MGM/UA, 1991)

Television Series

Gidget (ABC, 1965–66)
The Flying Nun (ABC, 1967–70)
Alias Smith and Jones (ABC, 1971–73)

The Girl with Something Extra (NBC, 1973–74)

Album Discography

Sally Field (Colgems CO 106/COS-106)

RICHARD GERE

"I had an amazing vision one time. It had to do with seeing my whole male lineage behind my father lined up through a field and over a hill. It went back hundreds of generations. I had this tremendous sense that I was the outcome of all of that work and my connection to that was very emotional and very powerful."—*Vanity Fair* magazine, May 1990

BEDROOM BODY. PIN-UP. POSEUR. POSTURER. THESE ARE BUT A FEW of the terms used by journalists in describing moody, darkly handsome, 5' 9" Richard Gere. They have compared his on-screen behavior with that of just about every male symbol of sexuality in Hollywood's history, except perhaps Victor Mature. Some comparisons are justified, like those to Robert De Niro (Richard's idol) or John Garfield, while others are nonsensical, like those to Errol Flynn and Tyrone Power. All comparisons focusing on the physical incurred Gere's terrible scorn when, for a time, he carried on a running battle with the press. Blessed with a ruggedly handsome face and having acquired the talent of body language, he is actually one of a kind. When he is in full gear, he bears a likeness to no one, past or present. Future comparisons may be made with Richard Grieco and Todd McDurmont, who have his looks; Sasha Mitchell has his cockiness.

Richard Tiffany Gere was born on Monday, August 29, 1949, the second of five children, to French-Irish Methodist insurance salesman Homer and his wife, Dolores, in Philadelphia. While Richard was still a baby, the "sweet, honest, straight, church-going" Methodist family relocated to Syracuse, New York, where the children were raised. Richard's first taste of the stage occurred in the third grade, when he was Santa Claus in a school skit. The entire family was musical, with each member playing one or more instruments. Richard learned the trumpet, piano, guitar, banjo, and the Indian sitar. At the age of fourteen, he gave a trumpet solo in "The Messiah" with the Syracuse Symphony Orchestra. "I was a child prodigy," he has said. As a junior in high school he acted in the comedy *The Mouse That Roared* as well as composed the scores for a few high school productions. He was proficient in the school gym, but did not do well in his academic studies. Music was more important to him. He played trumpet in a local dance band and a marching band, and performed at weddings and bar mitzvahs.

In 1967 he graduated from high school feeling "pretty confused." He enrolled that autumn at the University of Massachusetts at Amherst on a gymnastics scholarship. He chose philosophy as his major, but after his sophomore year, he and a classmate decided to audition for the famed Provincetown Playhouse on Cape Cod. Gere got a salaried job in summer stock; his friend did not. Thus ended Richard's college days.

His first play was Eugene O'Neill's *The Great God Brown,* for which he wore a plastic mask; it was followed by *Rosencrantz and Guildenstern Are Dead, The White Lies, Everything in the Garden,* and *Camino Real.* The director at Provincetown was also a set designer for the Seattle Repertory in Washington state. He took Richard with him for one season of stock, during which Richard wrote music for a production of *Volpone* as well as acted in it. At Seattle he also acted in *Once in a Lifetime, The Three Sisters,* and *The Initiation.* He found repertory work a grueling, 'round-the-clock endeavor, however, and returned to the East Coast in the winter of 1970. He joined a group of musicians to form a rock band called The Strangers. After a few weeks of rehearsal in Vermont, the band members found that they disliked each other and parted company, with strong-minded Richard going on to New York City.

In Manhattan, Gere lived in a fifth-floor, roach-infested walk-up on the Lower East Side. He learned to play drums and to speak Spanish. Rock operas such as *Hair* were in vogue then and Richard was to remember later, "I played instruments and sang and had long hair, so I fitted right in and started working immediately." He landed a lead role in *Soon,* a rock opera starring Barry Bostwick which opened at the Ritz Theatre on January 12, 1971, but closed after three performances. This stint was quickly followed by a starring role in an evening of Richard Farina's songs and poetry called *Long Time Coming and a Long Time Gone* at the Lenox Hill Theatre. This theatrical appearance, too, was short-lived. Richard played with club bands as well as understudied Barry Bostwick in the leading role in the musical *Grease.* During this period he was cast in an unsold ABC-TV series pilot—starring Frank Converse—called "D.H.O.," which finally aired on June 17, 1973. Gere went to London under the auspices of director Frank Dunlop, head of The Young Vic, who asked him to portray the Pedant of Mantua in his production of *The Taming of the Shrew.* This was followed by his starring as Danny Zuko in the London production of *Grease.*

Gere was back in New York by early 1974, and that March he recreated his *Taming of the Shrew* role at the Brooklyn Academy of Music for twelve performances. During this time he also appeared in a New York City–filmed episode of "Kojak" for CBS-TV. On April 12, 1975, on NBC-TV he received third billing in a second series pilot, STRIKE FORCE, as a New York state trooper who joins a New York City detective (Cliff Gorman) and a federal agent (Donald Blakeley) to crush a narcotics ring. Also in April, he starred for thirty-four performances in a Sam Shepard one-act monologue, *Killer's Head,* at the American Place Theatre, in which he was strapped to an electric chair. The director of this venture was Wynn Handman, who also became Richard's acting teacher, guiding him through *Henry V* and other productions. Gere played Demetrius in *A Midsummer Night's Dream* at Lincoln Center's Newhouse Theatre, followed in the fall of 1975 by a gloriously vulgar British sex farce, *Habeas Corpus,* in which he was a falsies fitter. The show ran for ninety-five performances at the Martin Beck Theatre on Broadway. He then played the pivotal role in a revival of Clifford Odets's *Awake and Sing!* at the McCarter Theatre in Princeton, New Jersey, and traveled to Lake Forest, Illinois, to star in *The Farm* at the Academy Festival Theatre.

Finding television work "a humiliating, disgusting experience" and theater in an unhealthy state because "a lot of what theatre is doing is what it has been doing for centuries . . . the movies do that better now," Richard chose to move on to motion pictures. He was intrigued with the medium after his first taste in a small, twelfth-billed role in REPORT TO THE COMMISSIONER (1975), also known as OPERATION UNDERCOVER. He was seen as a street-wise Puerto Rican pimp and looked very swarthy, with his high cheekbones, deep-set brown eyes, dark brown hair, olive skin, and streetfighter-type nose, qualities that would suit him in future roles as well. *Variety* rated his appearance as Billy as "very good."

He received eighth billing in BABY BLUE MARINE (1976) as a blond, shell-shocked Marine raider of World War II who switches clothes with a would-be Marine (Jan-Michael Vincent) who has been dismissed from training camp. But it was LOOKING FOR MR. GOODBAR, filmed in 1975 but not released until October 1977, that established Richard as a very sexy on-screen presence. As the hustler Tony Lopanto, he momentarily captivates the attention of sexually insatiable schoolteacher Terry Dunn (Diane Keaton), both in bed and in a knife-wielding dance wearing a jockstrap. *After Dark* magazine found him "arresting, sure-footed, and strangely appealing." His next picture, too, was delayed in release after completion. DAYS OF HEAVEN (1978) underwent considerable editing and re-editing before it reached the screen, earning its cinematographer (Nestor Almendros) the

Richard Gere in BLOODBROTHERS (1978).

position as the movie's true star. In this vehicle, Gere and Sam Shepard compete for the love of Brooke Adams in 1917 Texas after escaping the steel mills of Chicago. For his role, with slight dialogue, Richard was given the David Donatello Award by the Italian film industry for Best Actor of the year. (On the other hand, *The New Yorker* magazine's Pauline Kael complained, "Gere, with his post-50s acting style and the associations it carries of Brando and Dean and Clift and all the others who shrugged and scowled and acted with their shoulders, is anachronistic.")

Gere departed the off-Broadway rehearsals of Albert Innaurato's *Earthworms* to make BLOODBROTHERS (1978). He played a sensitive Italian Bronx construction worker who breaks free of the yoke of his family's three interests in life: work, the union, and the neighborhood bar. *After Dark* magazine judged Richard a "superb talent" and "the best of the new breed of brooding young men." YANKS (1979) took a year to film at a cost of $7 million in the English village of Staleybridge. There director John Schlesinger, British by birth, recreated the 1943 invasion of feminine British hearts by American servicemen. Richard was U.S. Army cook Matt, who falls in love with Jean (Lisa Eichhorn), a country lass from a puritanical background. The listless feature was unpopular with critics and the public. Meanwhile, in 1978, Gere, who had become intrigued with Buddhism, made a visit to Tibetan refugee camps in Nepal, which deepened his interest in this Far Eastern religion.

Richard moved his living quarters to uptown New York City where, in 1979, he lived with actress Penelope Milford, a liaison that had begun in 1973. In 1980 he began a long-term live-in relationship with Brazilian painter Sylvia Martins, who signed herself "Silvinha" and who escaped the harsh Manhattan winters each year by returning to Brazil. In the March 19, 1980, entry of *The Andy Warhol Diaries* (1989), she is quoted as confessing to friends, "I don't know what to do about Richard; we stay out till 4:00 and then sometimes we have sex and then sometimes we don't, and I want to expand his mind and take him to art galleries." Years later, she would add, "He is also the most ambitious person I've ever met. I could never understand why he would want to be such a success and then act the way he did in public at the beginning. He was Sean Penn before Sean Penn was." Later, after they had broken off their affair, she called him "a real drama queen" because he took off his clothes in public in order to shock people, but she explained it as a means of covering up "how afraid he really is. He is so afraid of being hurt."

It was John Travolta whom producer Freddie Fields and director Paul Schrader wanted to play Julian Kay, the $1,000-a-visit Los Angeles hustler in AMERICAN GIGOLO (1980). However, the narcissistic role was inherited by Gere when negotiations with Travolta broke down. (DAYS OF HEAVEN had been another Travolta hand-me-down.) "Gigolo" is a nicer-sounding word than "prostitute." By advertising himself as the former, Julian wins favor with older women as well as young, and occasionally with other men. In one very funny scene, in order to confuse a friend of one of his clients, he affects a German accent along with the mannerisms of a gay decorator. In another scene, while Lauren Hutton lies in bed, Richard stands at a window nude. Most critics did not appreciate the film, and Vincent Canby (*New York Times*) insisted that Gere brought "no charm or interest" to his role, adding, "Like Dracula, whose image is unreflected by a mirror, Mr. Gere stands in front of the camera, but when the film is developed, the essential image has vanished." Despite the harsh reviews, the controversial feature garnered $11.5 million in domestic film rentals.

While his sensuality and nakedness were being exploited on screen in AMERICAN GIGOLO, Gere returned to the Broadway stage at the New Apollo Theatre in December 1979 as Max, the homosexual prisoner in Nazi Germany in *Bent*. With his co-star, David Dukes, he fantasizes an oral sex act through explicit dialogue until they both reach orgasm. The generally harsh New York critics found his performance "controlled," "magnetic," and "arresting." He was honored with the Theatre World Award as best actor before leaving the production in April 1980.

The puzzling Richard Gere did not like to do interviews. If somehow forced to do so, he would provide false answers to questions, especially those relating to his family or to his personal life, which he considered no one's business. He admitted disdain for the "publicity stuff" and told columnist Rex Reed, "I will not become Flavor of the Month. I will not become a piece of meat just so some jerk will pay $5.00 to look at an image on a screen." When a female writer from the *Ladies Home Journal* magazine mentioned his sex-object status and questioned him about his sexual preference, he dropped his pants and his blue Jockey shorts and retorted, "This is what I call a sex object." An interviewer from the *Washington Post* found that Richard "would clearly rather be somewhere else—perhaps at his dentist's having a little root-canal work," while a *Soho News* reporter termed him "pigheaded, stubborn, brooding, recalcitrant, obstreperous, intense, and just plain difficult." Remarking on his solid reviews for *Bent*, he received worldwide press exposure by stating that he would have actual oral sex on stage with a man if the role called for it. *Esquire* magazine, at the conclusion of a feature on "lusty" women, offered a list of the "other side of the meat market: 100% prime brute," with Richard receiving highest honors.

Before editing, AN OFFICER AND A GENTLEMAN (1982), shot mostly in Seattle, Washington, received an X rating for its motel scene, in which co-star Debra Winger, with tears streaming down her face, achieves orgasm while astride the supine Gere. Richard, again substituting for an uninterested John Travolta, was Zach Mayo, an enlistee at the Naval Aviation Officer Candidate School on Puget Sound, whose cockiness is knocked out of him by a determined drill sergeant (Louis Gossett, Jr.). *Newsweek* magazine endorsed the drama as "a genuinely satisfactory Hollywood love story" and noted that "Gere gives his best, least-mannered performance." On the other hand, *Time* magazine labeled it "nonsense" and "junk food that somehow reaches the chortling soul." The public loved it to the tune of $130 million at the box office, and Andy Warhol wrote that Richard "has gotten to be a really good actor." *People* magazine found it surprising that Richard was not Oscar-nominated and elicited from the film's director, Taylor Hackford, the comment that "People might see Richard as a matinee idol, that all he can do is look pretty." Both Winger and Gossett were nominated, with the latter winning in the Best Supporting Actor category. Rumors of an off-screen romance between Gere and Winger were dispelled by her calling him "a brick wall." Later in 1982 Richard was seen in a French documentary entitled THE REPORTERS. Quigley Publications, in its annual listing of top-rated box-office stars, placed Richard as #8 for both 1982 and 1983.

Regarding BREATHLESS (1983), *Playgirl* magazine observed that "the love scenes in this film will make AN OFFICER AND A GENTLEMAN look like a Disney film." Richard, as an amoral, frenetic punk, starred opposite nineteen-year-old Valerie Kaprisky, who was chosen after doing a nude test with him. This remake of the acclaimed 1959 French film switched its locale from Paris to the seedy gangster underworld milieu of Los Angeles. The *Hollywood Reporter* found the seamy movie "postured and pretentious," while Andy Warhol grunted, "he just drops his pants every chance he gets. But, it's strange seeing someone that age doing that." (In 1990 Richard would state, "I had no qualms about showing my body. I think America is weird about this. In Europe—where my sensibilities lie anyway—this is pretty parochial stuff. I don't have the need to do that stuff now. There are other actors who are prettier who can do that.") For BEYOND THE LIMIT (1983), also known as THE HONORARY CONSUL, Richard affected a British accent for the role of a doctor who involves himself with Central American rebels. During the filming in Mexico, Richard informed Andy Warhol that he had been hooked up to an I.V. unit for dysentery throughout the filming between takes. Based on the Graham Greene novel, and co-starring Michael Caine, the murky BEYOND THE LIMIT was not a box-office success. However, the political subject of the film caused Gere to become sympathetic to the plight of the people of Nicaragua, Honduras, and El Salvador, to which he made a fact-finding trek in 1986. Thereafter he became a supporter of the El Rescate legal/social service organization for Central American refugees in Southern California.

THE COTTON CLUB (1984) went before the cameras without a final script in August 1983, when Francis Coppola was summoned to save the project with around-the-clock writing. Richard has said that "there were levels of madness there that will never be surpassed in movie-making." As Dixie Dwyer, he goes from musician to gangster's gofer to silent screen star in just 127 minutes. The 1920s feel in the production was wonderful, as were fleeting appearances by Vincent Jerosa as James Cagney, Diane Venora as Gloria Swanson, and others. It was not a good film, but on some levels it affords a good deal of fun. Despite the huge promotional campaign, the enormously expensive production (it cost an estimated $51 million) grossed only $12.9 million in domestic film rentals. Richard's salary for this fiasco was $3 million plus $450,000 in earned overtime. Years later, Gere would admit that after this experience he went through a midlife crisis and wanted to leave filmmaking to become a rock 'n' roll star.

About the unsuccessful biblical entry KING DAVID (1985), Richard thought that "the movie was important as an examination of what makes a leader, because we live in a time where there are no great leaders." However, filmgoers felt different, as did critics. In the title role, Richard, according to *People* magazine, "plays David as a mumbly lech who seems to have left his charisma in the shepherd's hut." It was at this time, as his career was on a downhill roll, that Gere revealed that he had chosen to become a Buddhist in support of the plight of Tibet during its repressive rule by the Chinese. His next motion picture, POWER (1986), was no more powerful at the box office. He had stepped into the leading role as a political media consultant after Burt Reynolds turned it down. The plot concerns the packaging of political candidates by media wizards. Richard claims through the film to have finally learned how to deal with the press. Sidney Lumet, who directed POWER, said of his star, "I hired him because the film was about a business in which appearance *is* substance. Richard has wonderful technique. But when an actor is as beautiful as he is it's difficult to be taken seriously, especially early on in your career."

In preparation for his role of a Chicago cop in NO MERCY (1986), Richard went undercover for several days with narcotics detectives in Chicago wearing a bullet-proof vest. Most of the action was shot in the Louisiana swamps and on the streets of New Orleans where, as Eddie Jilette, he searches for the killer of his partner. Of this disappointing movie, he says, "We were surprised it wasn't received better. I think it's unlikely I'll do another film like that." It was two years before his next project. MILES FROM HOME (1988), set in Iowa, was a very personal project for Gere, who took a salary of only between $125,000 and $150,000. The "artistic" low-budget project was inspired by the Bruce Springsteen song "Highway Patrolman." Belatedly following in the wake of COUNTRY (1984), PLACES IN THE HEART (1984), and THE RIVER (1984), it dealt with family farm foreclosures, with vindictive Frank Roberts (Gere) and his younger brother (Kevin Anderson) becoming popular heroes after they lose their land because of overdue bank loans. *Variety* noted, "Gere is characteristically somber, remote and troubled." The picture received scant distribution.

On the personal side, in the 1980s, while Sylvia Martins wintered in Brazil, Richard was romantically linked with actresses Barbara Carrera, Tuesday Weld, Diana Ross, and Lauren Hutton, who referred to him as "a sexpot." Another with whom he had a "fairly little fling" was designer Diane Von Furstenberg, who has remembered: "Richard was never really a rotten boy. He looked like one and felt like he should be one. But it was all an act." His good friend and neighbor in New York was Susan Sarandon, and they have been known to open their doors at Halloween for costumed children. He has been an active supporter of South African freedom leader Nelson Mandela, as well as a companion to Tibet's exiled leader, the Dalai Lama, who was awarded the Nobel Peace Prize in October 1989. (Gere is the chairman and co-founder of the Tibet House New York, which promotes Tibet's cultural/religious heritage.) Gere was a supporter of presidential candidate Michael Dukakis in 1988 while simultaneously stunning diners at a posh Los Angeles restaurant by leaping to his feet in a spontaneous rendition of a rock 'n' roll song (he was asked to sit down or leave).

In jeopardy of becoming a has-been, Richard needed a healthy career jolt. Luckily, it was provided by two films released within one month of each other. The first, released February 12, 1990, was INTERNAL AFFAIRS, in which he was Dennis Peck, a wheeling/dealing street cop up to his neck in corruption, who comes under investigation by Raymond Avila (Andy Garcia) of the Los Angeles Police Department's Internal Affairs Division. Avila, obsessed with exposing Peck, takes on some of his nasty characteristics. A slick production, INTERNAL AFFAIRS received positive reviews from both Gene Siskel of the *Chicago Tribune* ("solid entertainment . . . raw sexuality") and Roger Ebert of the *Chicago Sun-Times* ("I was fascinated by this film."). Susan Granger of *American Movie Classics* magazine declared, "Gere has never been better," while Michael Wilmington in the *Los Angeles Times* proclaimed that Richard was "perfect casting for the sexy bad cop." In its first week, INTERNAL AFFAIRS took in $5 million at the domestic box office and within four weeks had earned $19.5 million, a decent showing for a midwinter release. Adding to Richard's appeal for the first time on screen was his graying hair, which he told *US* magazine had begun as far back as 1979. "It's not a problem for me," he said. "Maybe if the girls didn't like it. . . ."

The second film, PRETTY WOMAN, was revealed to movie audiences on March 19, 1990, following a wide advertising campaign showing Richard's hair without the gray. In this feature, a romantic comedy and a change for him, he was Edward Lewis, a super-wealthy corporate raider, who stops to ask directions from Vivian Ward (Julia Roberts), a Los Angeles street prostitute whom he hires at a fee of $3,000 to be his companion for a week; he then falls in love with her. Although some critics found the movie "slow, earnest, and rhythmless" (*Entertainment Weekly* magazine), *Daily Variety's* critique observed, "Despite its flaws [it] hits the right emotional targets to shape up as a monster hit." *People* magazine credited Richard with being "astonishingly subdued—and astonishingly effective." The *Hollywood Reporter* predicted that his return "to conventional leading man status . . . might add considerably to box-office punch and more than mollify female audience goers." Everyone was right, of course. During the first week, the pictured realized $16 million in domestic revenues. After sixteen weeks, in summer competition with the action releases, PRETTY WOMAN had climbed to $153.6 million, and by October 1990, in its twenty-seventh week at the box office, it had taken in $173,530,841, and would rank as the second biggest moneymaker of 1990, outdistanced only by the phenomenal GHOST. The movie's soundtrack album had been high on the top fifty chart for twenty weeks as of October 4, 1990. There is talk of a sequel to the hugely successful PRETTY WOMAN, to reunite stars Gere and Julia Roberts and director Garry Marshall.

Once again in demand for magazine cover interviews and films, Richard was mentioned for several screen projects, including one about the life of Buddha, which he claimed was not true, but he did admit to an interest in playing Alexander Pushkin, the nineteenth-century poet. Even *Playgirl* magazine leapt upon his bandwagon by naming him—for the first time—one of America's sexiest men, saying, "at 40, he just gets better with age (love that gray hair)."

His independent filmmaking company, Gere Productions, originally installed at Columbia Pictures during the presidency of Dawn Steel, moved to Tri-Star after Steel's departure in June 1990. Although no films had been produced during his Columbia pact, IMAGINING ARGENTINA, written by Christopher Hampton of DANGEROUS LIAISONS (1988) fame, was in development, with Richard to star as an Argentinian in search of his wife after the government has abducted her.

Forthcoming for Gere are a thriller, THE FINAL ANALYSIS (1991), in which he plays a psychiatrist who becomes romantically involved with the sister of a patient, and RHAPSODY IN AUGUST (1991), the latter made in Japan for Akira Kurosawa. The sole American in the cast, Gere has a cameo as the Japanese-American son of a pineapple grower. The all-Japanese dialogue, including Richard's, will be subtitled when the film is released in the United States. He is also considering starring in a remake of A FACE IN THE CROWD (1957), in the role of the heel/entertainer played by Andy Griffith. Meanwhile, on November 30, 1990, Gere, along with Whoopi Goldberg, Carrie Fisher, and Kyle MacLachlan, hosted the ABC-TV special "Red, Hot & Blue," a 1990s video tribute to Cole Porter's music as well as an AIDS informational special.

Richard Gere continues to be a conundrum although the once-petulant personality has mellowed with time. He no longer fights actively with the press. Rather, he seems content with himself in his quest for worldwide peace. (He says, "There's a major click one makes in one's brain and one's heart through this process of Buddhist practice. One begins to transform how one sees the other; not as a potential enemy, but as a loved one.") Currently owning a country house on the New York–Connecticut border, as well as a newly acquired $2.5 million Hollywood Hills home, he can now laugh at the posturings of the young Richard Gere. "I was an incredible brooder. I was a world-class brooder. I could chill out any room. It comes of deep insecurity and shyness." His companion for the past few years has been supermodel Cindy Crawford. Regarding his place in the spotlight, he insists, "I don't care too much about fame, I never did really. . . . I'm more interested in being a human being than an actor."

Filmography

Report to the Commissioner [Operation
  Undercover] (UA, 1975)
Strike Force (NBC-TV, 4/12/75)
Baby Blue Marine (Col, 1976)
Looking for Mr. Goodbar (Par, 1977)
Days of Heaven (Par, 1978)
Bloodbrothers (WB, 1978)
Yanks (Univ, 1979)
American Gigolo (Par, 1980)
An Officer and a Gentleman (Par, 1982)
The Reporters (Fr, 1982)
Breathless (Orion, 1983)
Beyond the Limit [The Honorary Consul] (Par,
  1983)

The Cotton Club (Orion, 1984)
King David (Par, 1985)
Power (20th–Fox, 1986)
No Mercy (Tri-Star, 1986)
Miles from Home (Cinecom, 1988)
Internal Affairs (Par, 1990)
Pretty Woman (BV, 1990)

Future Releases

The Final Analysis (WB, 1991)
Rhapsody in August (Orion Classics, 1991)

Broadway Plays

Grease (1972) (understudy)
Habeas Corpus (1975)

Bent (1979)

MEL GIBSON

"Being a star is being a target. It's like having your pants down around
your ankles and your hands tied behind your back. You become a
good opportunity for some parasite to throw darts into your chest."
—*Redbook* magazine, August 1990

EACH REPORTER, MALE OR FEMALE, WHO ENCOUNTERS MEL GIBSON
has something to say about his eyes in the published interview. They are, of course, blue or
azure. They are also, from article to article, "piercing," "opalescent," "intelligent," "smoky,"
"dewy," with "vagrant beams of light glancing from the corneas." Mention is then made of
his dark brows and "lashes so thick they would make Loretta Young envious," his square
jaw, and the "heart-melting smile that features a perfect set of white teeth." No wonder
actress Sigourney Weaver called him "the handsomest man I've ever met." No wonder
People magazine gave him the title of the "Sexiest Man Alive," which he initially thought
was ridiculous, but later found humorous. He is unpredictable, zany, as well as a vocal
mimic of John Wayne, Henry Fonda, and The Three Stooges. He has a unique fondness
for the English language. When told of his handsomeness, he will frequently twist his
features into a comical face, in defiance of his good looks. His acting is not from the
schools of method or manner; he is simply himself, a natural who has been accused of
working hard at not seeming like a movie star. Director Robert Towne calls him a real guy
with "an intensity that can translate into a kind of ferocious innocence." Because of that
trait, he is a modern-day Gary Cooper. Because of his looks, he is another Clark Gable.
Above all, he is a man's pal and a woman's heartthrob.

Mel Columbcille Gibson was the sixth of eleven children born to devout Irish
Catholics Hutton and Ann Gibson in the town of Peekskill in upstate New York on
Tuesday, January 3, 1956. He received his first name from St. Mel, an Irish saint, while his
middle name, derived from the Irish, means "dove of the church." When Mel was five, his
father, a well-educated brakeman with the Penn Central Railway, moved his clan to Mt.
Pleasant, New York, where Mel spent the next seven years of his childhood. He was taught
to remember the Ten Commandments plus an additional one which his father said was the
eleventh, "Thou shalt not kid thyself." Mel remembers that in those formative years the
family didn't have much money, "but we had a happy childhood, lots of snow, lots of trees,
lots to do."

In 1968, when Mel was twelve, his eldest brother was of draft age for the Vietnam
War, which their father felt was an unjustified conflict. With funds derived from an at-

work injury, the senior Gibson immigrated with his family to Sydney, New South Wales, Australia, the birthplace of his mother, opera singer Eva Mylott. The relocation was Gibson's way to spare his six sons the possible fate of jungle warfare. Mel was enrolled at a Catholic school run by Christian brothers where he was made to wear a uniform and where he was "bagged" (teased) by the other kids as a Yank. His peers soon got used to him. He was an altar boy at the family church or, "more aptly, a falter boy. I used to trip over my cassock or light myself on fire." He was not an extroverted youth; rather, he was quiet, never volunteering for anything. At the age of sixteen, however, he did join a "footy" (rugby) club, an association which introduced him to beer drinking. He was shy around girls, preferring to go to the movies, which he loved. One of his sisters prompted him to join the high school dramatic club, but he felt out of place with Shakespeare.

After graduation from Catholic high school in 1974, he considered being either a journalist or a chef. However, his sister on his behalf sent a scholarship application to Sydney's National Institute of Dramatic Art at the University of New South Wales. They requested that he audition. He did it, "figuring I'd never get in because they took so few," but "they made me do all these silly things—improvise, sing, dance." He was accepted after the auditioning committee asked why he wanted to become an actor. He responded with, "I've been goofing off all my life, I thought I might as well get paid for that." At the Institute, along with acting, he learned fencing, acrobatics, and gymnastics, all of which were to prove helpful later in doing bits of his own movie stunts. Among his roles at the Institute was Romeo to Judy Davis's Juliet in a school rendition of the bard's romance. While still a student, he made his motion picture debut in SUMMER CITY (1977) as a nineteen-year-old surfer who "simply surfed and acted dumb." He shot the film during summer vacation for the money, but never got paid. SUMMER CITY received scant distribution outside Australia. After graduating from the Institute in 1977, Mel joined the State Theatre Company of Southern Australia in Sydney, where he played small parts in *Oedipus, Henry IV*, and *Cedoona*.

Filmmaking in Australia during the 1960s and early to mid-1970s was nearly dormant due to the great number of importable, good American and British movies. Then, in the mid-to-late 1970s, the Australians began to make their own films, many of which were quite good. One of the directors involved in the upswing was George Miller, who was planning a low-budget futuristic film called MAD MAX (1979) set in a nuclear wasteland. Miller had seen SUMMER CITY and saw something in Gibson's performance which prompted him to ask Mel to audition for the lead role of the scurvy vigilante. The night before his test, however, Mel suffered a beating by three disgruntled drunks. After spending hours in a hospital having his face sewn back together, he reported for the audition looking "like a pound of raw hamburger." Nevertheless, his appearance was just what Miller wanted for Max Rockatansky, the highway patrolman who avenges the murders of his wife and child by a band of ugly marauding bikers. The violent film did well in Australia, Japan, and Germany. However, when it was released in the United States in June 1980 with dubbed American voices, it failed to find an immediate audience. But worldwide ticket sales soared beyond the $100 million mark for the production, which had cost only an estimated $300,000.

TIM (1978) was adapted from Colleen McCullough's first novel by Michael Pate, an Australian who had migrated to Hollywood as an actor in many films, then returned home. Pate also produced and directed the film, about a mentally retarded, childlike man who is hired by a middle-aged woman (Piper Laurie) as a gardener. In the title role, Mel tended the flowers in bathing trunks, thereby stirring the sexually repressed yearnings of his employer as well as feminine moviegoers. For his acting, Mel was awarded the Australian Film Institute's equivalent of an Academy Award, along with a "Sammy" from *TV Times* magazine as that year's best new talent. The movie was not released in the United States until September 1980, when the *New York Post* critiqued his portrayal as "a thing of beauty in its subtle shading of an adult with a very young mind." In ATTACK FORCE Z (1980), Mel was among a group of commandos assigned to rescue plane crash survivors on a Japanese-held atoll during World War II. This entry quickly disappeared from Australian screens, but shows up occasionally on U.S. late-night TV.

On June 7, 1980, Mel married Robyn Moore, a toothsome, attractive brunette nurse's aide, who shared his thoughts about ignoring birth control. In rapid succession they became parents to Hannah (born in January 1981), twin sons, Christian and Edward (born in 1982), son Will (born in July 1984), and son Louis (born in May 1988). Mel, the farceur, once quipped to the *London Sunday Mirror* magazine, "Every time Robyn gets pregnant, I feel like running away and joining the navy."

Peter Weir, an Australian director who had made an international name for himself with PICNIC AT HANGING ROCK (1975) and THE LAST WAVE (1977), cast Mel, without an audition, in GALLIPOLI (1981). Mel was Frank Dunne, a runner who was caught in World War I trenches in Turkey in a disastrous campaign that cost the lives of seven thousand Australian soldiers. Weir's prediction was that Mel would become a star because "he's got Factor X . . . the first person I'd seen in Australia who had it." The Australian Film Institute gave the film nine awards, including one to Mel, his second, as best actor.

Director George Miller decided to cash in on the success of MAD MAX by doing a sequel, known in Australia as MAD MAX II (1981), but released in the United States as THE ROAD WARRIOR (1982). Mel reprised his hard-living role in the film, which took up where the first installment ended, with Max Rockatansky as the lone defender of a group of homesteaders in the terrible wasteland. In its first seven months of release in North America, the action movie, without American-dubbed voices, grossed $24 million. It established Mel as an international star, a status which Metro-Goldwyn-Mayer/United Artists soon accepted when the studio underwrote the cost of his next Weir-directed feature, THE YEAR OF LIVING DANGEROUSLY (1983). Shot mostly near Manila in the Philippines, this feature is set in Indonesia at the time of the 1965 overthrow of its president, Sukarno. Mel, in the leading role of a broadcast journalist, was accompanied everywhere on location by a large Filipino bodyguard toting a .38-calibre pistol because death threats had been received from Moslem militants who insisted that the film was anti-Moslem. (The cast finally had to return to Sydney, Australia, to complete the production.) In his scenes with inches-taller co-star Sigourney Weaver, Mel (5' 8") wore platform shoes.

People magazine stated that they were "wonderful to watch," while *Playgirl* magazine found them "an electrifying pair." *Variety* ranked his new film as "perhaps his finest performance to date."

Mel turned down offers to star in THE LORDS OF DISCIPLINE (1983) and ONCE UPON A TIME IN AMERICA (1984), roles filled respectively by David Keith and James Woods. Instead, he chose to fulfill a commitment to play Biff, the older son, in a Sydney stage production of *Death of a Salesman*. Publicly, he stated that theater "still gives me a buzz." During this period, he also did TV roles in Sydney in the series "The Sullivans," "The Oracle," "Tickled Pink," and "The Hero."

Somehow, during this active period, he and Robyn found the time to purchase an old boarding house in the beachside community of Coogee, near Sydney. When he was asked why he retained his American citizenship, he replied that he would not give it up because of "pride of birth and all that sort of stuff." Meanwhile, on stage with the State Theatre Company of South Australia, he performed in *Romeo and Juliet* and *Waiting for Godot*, and filled in one night for an ill actor in *No Names, No Pack Drill*. He acknowledged his sudden recognition as a worldwide sex symbol with, "After all, it's good for business, now, isn't it?" This convivial behavior, however, would soon change when he was dubbed "Sexiest Man Alive." He became rude and orally abusive to reporters, a modus operandi with the press that would last three years until "I woke up one day and said, 'life's too short. You gotta roll with it . . . you don't have to have bad feelings unless you want them.'"

Mel embarked on a filmmaking spree that would take him away from Australia for more than a year. First was the latest remake of *Mutiny on the Bounty*, called THE BOUNTY (1984). It was shot in Tahiti, England, and New Zealand by producer Dino De Laurentiis with $20 million from New Zealand backers. As mutineer Fletcher Christian, Mel followed in the steps of Errol Flynn, Clark Gable, and Marlon Brando, who had portrayed this role in earlier versions. Mel is better than Brando, but not quite as good as Gable, in this edition, which failed to draw in moviegoers. The attentive viewer will note, in some scenes, that one side of Mel's face is swollen, the result of a barroom fight during off-work hours. His next movie, THE RIVER (1984), was his first to be backed by an American company and was lensed at Kingsport, Tennessee's Holston River locale. Over the film's opening credits is seen a seemingly endless rain storm, which sets the gloomy tone of the entire film, about a farmer (Gibson) and his wife (Sissy Spacek) who fight to hold onto their soggy land. Their adversary is Scott Glenn, who intends to dam the valley, which will put their property forever under water. The third and least of a trio of similar projects (including PLACES IN THE HEART and COUNTRY, both also 1984), THE RIVER was unsuccessful, with *Variety* noting of Gibson's restrained role, "He is a character without passion and the film suffers because of it."

His third film back-to-back was MRS. SOFFEL (1984), shot partially in Toronto in the snowy Canadian cold. Diane Keaton was cast as the repressed wife of a prison warden in 1904 who is attracted by and protects Mel, who, with his brother (Matthew Modine), escapes from the prison where they are being held on a homicide charge. During one lull in the Toronto shoot, Mel was arrested for driving while intoxicated, running a red light, and hitting another car. Soon thereafter, he swore to cut back on his consumption of alcohol. The dour MRS. SOFFEL opened to unenthusiastic reviews and poor box-office receipts. (Gibson had been scheduled to do a thriller, RUNNING MAN, for director Stuart Rosenberg, but when MGM dropped the property, he had agreed to substitute MRS. SOFFEL.)

Following this filmmaking marathon, all the films of which were considered financial failures, Mel was asked why he did this rash of three projects. He replied, with blue-eyed innocence, "I was hungry. Now I'm full. I'm bloated in fact. . . . My eyes were too big for my stomach." He was inactive for just seven months, though, and was next seen in mid-1985 in yet another sequel to MAD MAX, called MAD MAX III in Australia and MAD MAX BEYOND THUNDERDOME in the United States. This episode was shot in 125° summer weather in Adelaide, South Australia, by director George Miller. This time around, Max Rockatansky befriends a pack of wild children in the nuclear waste, and all of them find themselves at the mercy of sadistic Aunty Entity (Tina Turner). Roger Ebert (*Chicago Sun-Times*) judged this sequel "the best of the three MAD MAX movies . . . one of the best films of 1985." It grossed $41 million in U.S. domestic receipts by the end of 1985.

And then Gibson rested—for a while, at least—before buying and moving to an eight-hundred-acre cattle ranch in Victoria, Australia, five hundred miles from Sidney.

Shane Bailey, **Mel Gibson**, and Sissy Spacek in THE RIVER (1984).

From books he learned and practiced the art of ranching, while off the screen for two years. During this period, another Australian (this one by birth) became popular with American audiences, first through TV commercials and then by way of film. His name was Paul Hogan, of whom Mel said, "He's a charming, funny guy and he earned his success. Good luck to him!"

Professionally, Mel needed a boost, and he found it with LETHAL WEAPON (1987), which grossed more than $70 million in the United States alone during the summer of 1987. He was cast as Martin Riggs, a maniacal undercover cop in Los Angeles who has suicidal tendencies brought on by the death of his wife. His thrills in life are catching dope pushers and watching The Three Stooges on TV. He becomes partner to the aging Roger Murtaugh (Danny Glover), who brings a degree of stability to his existence. Because he does not care if he lives or dies, Riggs takes big chances, much to the chagrin of Murtaugh. As such, Riggs is *the* walking lethal weapon. The cop/buddy film is nonstop action throughout, except for a back nude shot of Mel. After this box-office bonanza, Gibson returned to his ranch, saying, "I do acting for the money, and the ranch for fun. . . . It's preferable to weaving baskets." In 1987 he established his own producing company, but developed no projects at the time. (In 1989 Mel formed Gibson Productions, Inc., which optioned the book *Deadline Salonika* as a starring vehicle for himself. He would play CBS News correspondent George Polk, who was killed in 1948 while covering the Greek Civil War.) Gibson was in TV commercials shown in Japan, where the salary for a few hours' work is reported to be anywhere from $200,000 to $1 million.

The plot of TEQUILA SUNRISE (1988) is so convoluted that it requires two viewings to begin to sort it out, but the viewer will notice immediately the blue eyes of its three stars: Gibson, Michelle Pfeiffer, and Kurt Russell. Within the plot, Mel and Kurt are boyhood friends, one a semi-reformed drug dealer, the other a cop; both of them are romantically entangled with a lovely restaurant owner (Pfeiffer). Gibson and Pfeiffer have a steamy sex scene in a hot tub, one which the *San Francisco Examiner* noted "goes straight to your head." Speaking of heads, Mel's cranium was so much smaller than Kurt Russell's and Michelle Pfeiffer's that it had to be enlarged 7 percent for advertising posters showing the three standing together. On November 3, 1988, on ABC-TV, Mel made a guest appearance on a sixty-minute offering, "The World's Greatest Stunts," a tribute to Hollywood's stunt artists, hosted by Christopher Reeve.

After two successful motion pictures in a row, Mel's salary jumped to $4 million per picture. His first expenditure was to pay $3 million for Rick Springfield's home in Malibu with its own beach so his family would have a nice place to stay while he was making movies. But he still retained his commitment to Australia. "Why should I move when Australia is only a phone call away from the rest of the world?" he asked.

The initial film at his increased salary was LETHAL WEAPON 2 (1989), which in many ways is a prequel rather than a sequel, with both Gibson and Glover repeating their Los Angeles policemen roles. This time they have a looney sidekick (Joe Pesci), whom they are asked to protect. Released nationwide in July 1989, the action-loaded adventure grossed $141.9 million domestically within thirteen weeks. Mel's salary reportedly now took a giant leap to $7 million per picture. Meanwhile, on March 25, 1989, Mel hosted "Saturday Night Live" on NBC-TV, just before he went to Vancouver, Canada, to begin filming BIRD ON A WIRE (1990). In the latter vehicle, he played a former 1960s activist on the run from drug smugglers, accompanied by his former lady friend lawyer (Goldie Hawn). Directed by John Badham, the production was touted as a takeoff on Alfred Hitchcock's NORTH BY NORTHWEST (1959) because it was all chases except for another scene featuring Gibson's famed bare buttocks. *US* magazine did not like the movie because "the spins and turns and hairbreadth action scenes lack conviction. And that's largely the fault of Gibson and Hawn, who don't believe in them." In one scene, in an effort to hide his character's true identity, Mel pretended he was a gay hairdresser, which immediately prompted the Gay and Lesbian Alliance Against Defamation to voice a strenuous objection. Despite the film's shortcomings, it grossed $15.3 million during its first week of release in May 1990 on 1,944 movie screens. It went on to do very well financially abroad, where both Gibson and Hawn are popular. In response to his bare-bottom scene, Gibson said, "I didn't realize I was that furry on my back end. My bum's got a fair carpet, doesn't it?"

Meanwhile, Mel became a father for the sixth time in December 1989 with the birth of his fifth son, Milo, and he joined Glenn Close in London to announce the winner in the art direction category on the March 26, 1990, Academy Awards show seen on ABC-TV.

To help publicize AIR AMERICA, in general release August 10, 1990, Gibson appeared on "The Tonight Show" on August 8, attended the American Film Institute premiere of the film on August 9, and was interviewed on "The Arsenio Hall Show" on August 10. Gossip columnist Liz Smith noted that it was almost "unheard of to be booked on competing talk shows so close together, but Mel, right now, is the proverbial five thousand-pound gorilla. And he'll chat wherever he wants to."

In AIR AMERICA, advertised as "The Few. The Proud. The Totally Insane," Gibson was Gene Ryack, a cynical expatriate pilot of the not-so-secret CIA C-123 airline that transported everything from pigs to heroin in the 1970 fight against the Communist menace in Southeast Asia (Laos). Filmed in the jungles of Thailand, the movie reportedly cost $35 million, with $10 million going to Mel in salary and percentages. *Newsweek* magazine's summation was that "AIR AMERICA should have been grounded." The *Los Angeles Times*, while finding that Mel "gives a cocky, assured performance—a star performance," felt that "the filmmakers got so high on the exhilarating possibilities in the material that they just let the cameras run, waiting for it to all come together in the editing room." Opening on 1,902 screens nationwide, it took in just $8.6 million in its first week, and by its seventh week had accumulated a relatively mild total of $29,708,418 in domestic box-office grosses.

While the Stage Deli in Manhattan added a new Mel Gibson sandwich to its menu at the request of its patrons, Mel wound up shooting in England on the title role in HAMLET (1990), with forty-two-year-old Glenn Close as Gertrude his mother, Paul Scofield as the ghost, and Alan Bates as Claudius. With his hair bleached blond to look

Danish, Mel was not intimidated in acting with the mostly British cast of veteran actors. "I can manage," he said. "You see, I take things as they come, play it by ear, and refuse to worry." Because he wanted the experience of working with director Franco Zeffirelli doing Shakespeare, he accepted scale salary.

Playgirl magazine in its September 1990 issue named Mel to its "Hall of Fame" as one of the ten sexiest men in America with the notation: "Those dazzling blue eyes! That gorgeous grin! That touchable hair! And, of course, those amazing buns! He's the one man we can never get enough of." Any response he may have had to this acclaim would undoubtedly contain words of disgust since he hates being called "the sexiest" anything. After making four motion pictures in a row without a break, he announced that he was taking a leave from filmmaking for a year. "It gets to a point where your work suffers," he explained. "I've got to go away and learn some new tricks. I've got to replenish my creative energy because I'm out of it." He plans to spend the off-time with his family at his cattle ranch in Australia. He was approached by Twentieth Century–Fox to play Robin Hood in one of a sudden rash of films about the legendary Sherwood Forest hero, but Mel's decision was in the negative. On November 14, 1990, he was among the latest celebrities to be interviewed by Barbara Walters on her ABC-TV special. During the hour program he reflected on his Catholic upbringing, his "dark period" of alcohol abuse in the mid-1980s, and his reason for tackling Shakespeare on screen ("when the gauntlet gets thrown down like that . . . I felt I should have a bash at that").

Regarding his mixed "nationality," Gibson admits, "I think it's good to be a hybrid. You can be more objective. If you get shifted from one culture to another, you look at something unusual and say, 'What is this?'"

Mel Gibson will continue to grace magazine covers while interviewers will continue to ask inane questions such as, "What about the many actresses you've worked with? How do they approach their roles?" He is a normal-acting man who happens also to be handsome, the idol of millions, and an individual who knows what he wants out of life. "I knew I was going to be successful," he has said in retrospect. "I didn't know at what. But I knew I'd find my own way and be good at something."

Filmography

Summer City (Aust, 1977)
Tim (Aust, 1978)
Mad Max (Aust, 1979)
Attack Force Z (Aust, 1980)
Gallipoli (Par, 1981)
The Road Warrior [Mad Max II] (Aust, 1981)
The Year of Living Dangerously (MGM/UA, 1983)
The River (Univ, 1984)
Mrs. Soffel (MGM/UA, 1984)

The Bounty (Orion, 1984)
Mad Max Beyond Thunderdome [Mad Max III] (WB, 1985)
Lethal Weapon (WB, 1987)
Tequila Sunrise (WB, 1988)
Lethal Weapon 2 (WB, 1989)
Bird on a Wire (Univ, 1990)
Air America (Tri-Star, 1990)
Hamlet (WB, 1990)

DANNY GLOVER

"The other day, I shocked myself. I was thinking about taking on a role, and I found myself questioning, 'Is this a part for a black man?' Then I realized that's crazy. This is a role for a human being. That's what's important."   —*Parade* magazine, May 6, 1990

RISING OUT OF THE FLOWER PETALS STREWN IN PROTEST IN SAN Francisco's Haight-Ashbury district in the 1960s, Danny Glover did not begin acting full-time until he was thirty-three. Then, making up for lost time, he etched a brief, but respected, stage career in the plays of a noted South African playwright before moving into television and movies. While not in the top-salary-commanding league of Bill Cosby or Eddie Murphy, Glover progressively cut a route to stardom in three film box-office hits and a critically acclaimed trio of special television movies. A black actor never has it easy, for reasons that are apparent, but he has remained with his chosen profession. He accomplishes his work with determination and gusto combined with the innate qualities of kindness, love, and compassion. Danny Glover acknowledges that "I'm driving down a road that others built": the liberalism that followed World War II made it possible for black men, such as Academy Award winner Sidney Poitier and Harry Belafonte, to be accepted in leading screen roles. Further advancements during the 1960s, 1970s, and even 1980s procured highly esteemed positions for other black actors—including Bill Cosby, Mr. T., and Carl Weathers. Unlike Eddie Murphy and Arsenio Hall, Danny, who has the potential to earn as much money as they do, places others before himself. His is not "me first" behavior.

Danny Glover was born in the Haight-Ashbury district of San Francisco on Tuesday, July 22, 1947, the eldest of five children. His parents were U.S. postal employees who wanted their children to be happy and encouraged them always to do their best. As a youngster, the gawky Danny was frequently a loner ("I never had any real running partners") and from age twelve to sixteen had a paper route. Danny's arrest by police for shoplifting when he was a teenager was a major disappointment to them, but it was a learning experience for him, and he vowed never to make that mistake again. At the age of seventeen, he was appointed babysitter to a newborn baby brother, and "I used to pretend that I was his father." Through this experience, he grew to love children, something that would be with him forever.

In 1965, having graduated from Washington High School, he lived for a time in a commune on Fillmore and Page and then entered San Francisco City College, earning tuition money through a night job washing dishes at a hospital. During the summer of 1966 he spent his days working with children at San Francisco State University, where he became a student of economics in 1967. He was also a student activist, protesting the Vietnam War among other issues, and landing in jail for two weeks on a charge of inciting a riot as leader of an unruly protest march. He was acquitted of the charges, but gained another lesson—that any future campaigning for causes would be done by him in a more peaceable manner. While at college, he discovered a new self-identity, bolstered by participation in the Black Student Union. "A new image of the black man had come in and I fit the mold. That really improved my self-esteem." In 1971, with a degree in economics to his credit, he went to work for the San Francisco City Planning Department. However, within a matter of months he began deriving pleasure and satisfaction from performing with San Francisco and Oakland community theater groups as well as non-Equity theaters in the area. Acting "was unquestionably something I wanted to do," he said years later. "I refused to allow myself to stay pat and not take that chance." He appeared in Sam Shepard's *Suicide in B-Flat* at San Francisco's Magic Theatre as the jazz musician, and acted in *Macbeth*, *The Island*, and *Sizwe Bansi Is Dead* both at the Eureka Theatre in San Francisco and at the Actors' Theatre in Los Angeles.

In 1975 he married a jazz singer named Asaka, which in African means "favorite one." The following year, their only child, a daughter, was born; she was named Mandisa, meaning "sweet" in African. Danny purchased a three-story Victorian house a few blocks from his parents' home, which he repaired himself and where he and his family have continued to live. (In late 1990, he would enthuse of his roots, "I can go around the corner here on Central Street and still see a number of people I grew up with. . . . And because of what I do, I'm able to go see other places and come back home, which is a great luxury."

Growing disenchanted with "pushing papers and working on case studies," he resigned his job with the city in 1979 to devote all his time to acting, a decision supported by his wife. He drove a cab by day while training at night in the Black Actors Workshop at San Francisco's American Conservatory Theatre (ACT). He did a few days' work as a bit player in ESCAPE FROM ALCATRAZ (1979), a Clint Eastwood movie filmed in and around the San Francisco Bay area. When South African playwright Athol Fugard, on a visit to ACT, asked Danny to join him in New York City to perform in one of his plays, he and Asaka, with their baby, flew East.

Starring off-Broadway from January to April 1980 in Fugard's two-character drama *Blood Knot*, set in South Africa, Danny was brother to a light-skinned man, passing as white, born of the same mother. The *New York Times* judged it the "best play of the year" and the *Times* reviewer, John Corry, found, "Mr. Glover's Zachariah is battered and brutish . . . and when he is overwhelmed by the awareness of what his black skin means, Mr. Glover sees to it that we are overwhelmed too. It is a fine piece of acting."

Before going to New York, Danny had done a sixth-billed role in his second movie, CHU CHU AND THE PHILLY FLASH, photographed in San Francisco, in support of Carol Burnett and Alan Arkin. Released in August 1981, it proved to be a waste of time. In 1982

Fugard cast Danny as Willie, the family friend/servant, in *Master Harold . . . and the Boys*, the first of Fugard's plays to premiere outside of South Africa. It was first presented at New Haven's Yale Repertory Theatre and then moved to Broadway on May 4, 1982. Clive Barnes (*New York Post*) endorsed, "Danny Glover is marvelously ragamuffin yet decent as the simple-minded Willie." For his performance, Glover received a Theatre World Award.

Film director Robert Benton, impressed with Danny's stage presence, suggested that he make a move to Los Angeles and promised him a major role in a movie he was preparing for Tri-Star. His wife and daughter returned to their home in San Francisco while Danny went to Los Angeles. While waiting for Benton to fulfill his promise, he did bit parts in the television series "Lou Grant" and "Hill Street Blues." For ABC-TV he had the eighth-billed role in THE FACE OF RAGE (March 20, 1983), a two-hour movie about rape victims who enter a therapy program with convicted rapists. A week later, on March 27, 1983, he was seen in an early look at the starving homeless in "A Place at the Table," an hour-long TV drama designed to give American seventh-graders a glimpse of what some of their classmates may be enduring. "Chiefs" (1983) was a six-hour CBS-TV miniseries shot in Chester, South Carolina, which chronicled the attempts of three generations of police chiefs to solve the murders in 1924, 1945, and 1962 of transient youths. Danny appeared in part two, the 1945 episode, in the role of Marshall Peters.

Glover had completed the Robert Benton film, but was first seen on screen as a security officer, seventh-billed as Loomis in ICEMAN (1984). The film dealt with an Arctic Neanderthal (John Lone) who is thawed from his 40,000-year imprisonment in ice when some mysterious antifreeze within his system permits him to resume life. PLACES IN THE HEART (1984) was written for the screen by Robert Benton, based on his Texas childhood, as well as directed by him. Danny was sixth-billed in this account of a 1935 widow (Sally Field) struggling to retain her farm land and children. He was Moze, an itinerant farm worker who teaches her to raise cotton, although he is at risk due to the ever-present Ku Klux Klan. *People* magazine lauded, "Danny Glover brings amazing directness and gallantry to what might have been a clichéd part as a black farmhand." Released in September 1984, the picture was honored with seven Academy Award nominations, with Oscars going to Field as Best Actress and to Benton for his screenplay.

With several film offers coming his way, Danny took a large apartment in Los Angeles where his wife and daughter spent time with him when he was shooting in the area, with all three intermittently returning home to San Francisco. The 6' 4", 220-pound actor liked to jog along ocean beaches in San Francisco. "Since we're part water, I feel right about running there," he said. Too, he could relax because his struggling days seemed at an end.

Professionally, the year 1985 began for Danny with the February release of WITNESS. He was eighth-billed as McFee, a corrupt, murderous cop, who is first seen at a Philadelphia train station urinal before he slits the throat of an honest plainclothesman. The film placed eighth in 1985 box-office hits by grossing $65.5 million in domestic distribution. The experimental video feature THE STAND-IN had first been shown at the 1984 Mill Valley film festival. It then received a special showing at San Francisco's

Exploratorium Theatre in April 1985. Danny played a low-budget movie director who becomes accidentally enmeshed in homicide and false identity. Made on a budget of $85,000, the movie was produced/directed/scripted by Robert N. Zagone, an established San Francisco freelance TV artist. In June's SILVERADO, a buddy western produced and directed by Lawrence Kasdan in a period when western movies had lost their popularity, he was seventh-billed as Mal, who walks into a bar-eatery with "I haven't had a drink of whiskey or slept in a bed in ten days—gimme a bottle." To the rousing musical score of Bruce Broughton, Danny joins forces with Kevin Kline, Scott Glenn, and Kevin Costner to rid the town of its menacing leader (Brian Dennehy) and cohorts. For *GQ* magazine, Danny joined other members of the SILVERADO cast to model western apparel; he was pictured in "Black suede teamed with silver and brass."

Steven Spielberg's THE COLOR PURPLE, a December 1985 release, had Danny top-billed as Albert, also known as Mister, who takes as his wife the much-abused Celie (Whoopi Goldberg) whom he continues to mistreat, emotionally and physically. Beautifully photographed by Allen Daviau, with music by Quincy Jones, the picture captured eleven Academy Award nominations. Glover, however, was not nominated, and THE COLOR PURPLE did not win in any category. Despite this, it was the year's number four box-office giant, with domestic receipts amounting to $94.2 million. Allegations, however, were made that the movie portrayed the black man as "a sadistic, sexually abusive ogre" and the Los Angeles opening was greeted by pickets reading, "Are white producers trying to destroy black men?" In support of the movie, Danny said, "Mister was an adequate representation of one particular story. He's a product of his past and his present and I think we showed that he has some capabilities of changing. It was a complex, multidimensional role." Glover felt that the debate was good for black actors and for the black community in general. "It's important for the NAACP and other organizations to question the film. It makes us actors more conscious of what we're doing. And that's all positive."

Danny Glover in THE COLOR PURPLE (1985).

In March 1986 Danny was on stage in Chicago in a revival of Athol Fugard's *A Lesson from Aloes*, which had won the New York Drama Critics Circle Award in 1980 as best play of the year.

Released in March 1987, LETHAL WEAPON, a slam-bang action film with a multiple-climax ending, was one of the most popular entries of the year. At the domestic box office during 1987 it grossed over $65 million, but with foreign release and homevideo sales, it is estimated to have earned more than $100 million. Danny was second-billed as Roger Murtaugh to

185

Mel Gibson's Martin Riggs, Murtaugh's suicidal partner on the Los Angeles police narcotics detail. Murtaugh's well-balanced home life offsets Riggs's bizarre behavior. At age forty, Danny played a police veteran who celebrated his fiftieth birthday in the film. For his solid work in LETHAL WEAPON, Glover was honored with the NAACP Image Award. Co-star Gibson told Roger Ebert in an interview, "He's a strange man, Danny. You know him, and yet you don't know him. He was bloody good to work with."

Danny traveled to Zimbabwe, Africa, to star as MANDELA in the literate HBO–Cable movie that premiered on September 20, 1987. Alfre Woodard appeared as his wife, Winnie. Both were cited by critic Judith Crist for bringing Nelson Mandela and his spouse "to impressive and appealing life." Glover was Emmy-nominated for his performance, but did not win.

Opening nationwide on October 21, 1988, his next film, BAT 21, had been shot in Borneo. He played Captain Dennis Clark, who hijacks a helicopter in order to find Colonel Iceal Hambleton (Gene Hackman), who is lost in the jungles of Vietnam. Jeffrey Lyons of TV's "Sneak Previews" stated that "Danny Glover is superb," while *Cosmopolitan* magazine thought that both he and Hackman "give citation-worthy performances." Coming in the wake of so many other war pictures, the film was not a success. Also during 1988 he was co-starred with Peter Coyote in OUT, a road odyssey from the 1960s to 1980s that had been made six years earlier. On December 10, 1988, Glover was a presenter at the twenty-first annual NAACP Image Awards ceremonies, taped in Los Angeles for viewing on NBC-TV on January 14, 1989.

For PBS-TV on February 1, 1989, he co-starred as Walter Lee in the three-hour "American Playhouse" presentation of Lorraine Hansberry's 1959 drama, *A Raisin in the Sun*, playing opposite Esther Rolle as the mother trying to decide how best to spend the $10,000 from her late husband's insurance policy. *People* magazine felt that Danny played the son (a part played on stage and film by Sidney Poitier) "with overdone movement and melodrama." A few days later, Glover was among the large cast of "Lonesome Dove," the sixteen-hour ABC-TV miniseries adaptation of Larry McMurtry's Pulitzer Prize–winning novel about a 2,500-mile cattle drive from Texas to Montana. Filmed in New Mexico at a cost of $20 million, the miniseries was aired nightly, February 5–8, 1989. Danny was Joshua Deets, described as a loyal friend of thirty years, the best hand on the ranch as well as "a peerless tracker" with "a mystical sense of what lies ahead." *US* magazine urged its readers, "Do not, repeat, do not miss this one." Because the show had received many Emmy Award nominations, including one for Danny as Best Supporting Actor in a Limited Series, most of the cast of "Lonesome Dove" attended the presentation ceremonies later that year, when Danny showed up in a flowing blue African robe which he called a "Bubu." (Glover lost the award, which was won by Derek Jacobi for "The Tenth Man.")

Television critic John Carman (*San Francisco Chronicle*) wrote, "DEAD MAN OUT is an unusually juicy actors' piece with a strong off-Broadway flavor." He continued, "As written, the roles make no reference to ethnicity. It's a happy accident of casting that the parts fell into the hands of two powerful actors, one black and one Hispanic." Shown on HBO–Cable on March 12, 1989, DEAD MAN OUT, a ninety-minute original teledrama shot at Laval and Bordeaux prisons in Montreal, had Danny co-starring as a death row psychiatrist sent to "cure" an inmate (Ruben Blades) gone crazy in prison, so he can be electrocuted for having committed murder during a diner holdup years before. On location, Danny was reminded of his youth, when he had been incarcerated in San Francisco: "I heard the clang of that gate being locked behind me, and it hit home all over again. It's a brutal sound."

On NBC-TV on May 12, 1989, he was one of many who paid farewell tributes to retiring basketball star Kareem Abdul-Jabbar. During much of his free time, Glover has given lectures on art, lobbied for sanctions on South Africa, and spoken on behalf of the National Association for Sickle Cell Anemia. At the Oakland–San Francisco nineteenth annual National Educational Film and Video Festival, May 19–29, 1989, Danny was heard narrating *Halfway to Hell*, a documentary short dealing with the involvement of a workers' union in the building of the Golden Gate Bridge. Then, nationwide on July 7, 1989, with an advertising campaign boasting "the magic is back," LETHAL WEAPON 2 was released. The sequel not only showed on camera how Danny Glover (again as harassed policeman Roger Murtaugh) looked on a toilet seat while earning a salary of $1.5 million, but showed skeptics that the Gibson-Glover team worked well for moviegoers, who by October 1, after the film's first thirteen weeks in domestic release, had spent $141.9 million on tickets. LETHAL WEAPON 2 ranked third for the year, with ticket sales amounting to $147 million at the domestic box office. *People* magazine estimated that Danny "probably wins the film on points. That's partly because he seems so human, partly because he has some nice lines and, as a black, has poetic justice on his side when he goes after the drug dealers (who are all white and blatant racists)." With two such hugely successful LETHAL WEAPON features behind them, it seems natural that Danny and Gibson will soon be called upon to make a third. Asked about Gibson's sex-symbol status, Danny commented, "Who's to say some women don't come to the movie and think about sleeping with me?"

While seen by millions in movie theaters in July 1989, Glover attended the NAACP's eightieth annual national conference in Detroit, "to talk about kids, the hazards of drugs and the importance of education." In October 1989 he joined homeless rights advocate Mitch Snyder and dozens of show business celebrities in a "Housing Now" march in Washington, D.C. In mid-October he signed to narrate "How the Leopard Got His Spots" for Showtime–Cable's "Storybook Classics," also made available on homevideo. On January 6, 1990, he was again a presenter at the NBC-televised twenty-second annual NAACP Image Awards ceremonies.

TO SLEEP WITH ANGER, a low-budget feature for which Danny was co-executive producer and in which he starred as Harry Mention, was lensed in the Adams Heights district of Los Angeles. Wearing a partial hairpiece but aged by makeup for the role, he was an evil outsider who intrudes upon a solid family, à la Sheridan Whiteside (of THE MAN WHO CAME TO DINNER), and soon upsets their placidity. Premiered at the U.S. Sundance Film Festival for independent filmmakers at Park City, Utah, in January 1990, the movie was honored with the Special Jury Award for excellence. *Daily Variety*, in reviewing

Danny's performance, praised him for displaying "chilling meanness" and found "his husky voice spellbindingly appropriate." David Ansen (*Newsweek* magazine) enthused, "Glover, in what may be the best role of his film career, makes him an unforgettable trickster, both frightening and a little pathetic." The picture went into limited general release in October 1990 and proved to be an artistic if not commercial art-house success. Of this positive filmmaking experience, Glover said, "The role the [black] community played in this was unlike any other project I have been involved with. . . . Maybe, some young kid watching [the production being shot] might think, 'I want to get involved in making films. My community has encouraged me to dream.' . . ."

At the Los Angeles Theatre Center in February 1990, Danny alternated with Carl Lumbly in the lead role in *Viva Detroit* by Derek Walcott. On February 17, 1990, Glover was the narrator of "Port Chicago Mutiny: A National Tragedy" on NBC-TV in San Francisco, in association with "Black History Month." On February 25, 1990, he was inducted into the Black Filmmakers Hall of Fame at the seventeenth annual Oscar Micheaux Awards ceremony held at the Paramount Theatre in Oakland, California. A few days later, on March 1, 1990, he gave a "spirited reading" (*People* magazine) of "Br'er Rabbit and the Wonderful Tar Baby" on Showtime–Cable's "Storybook Classics." On March 7, 1990, MANDELA was broadcast on the Fox TV network, edited to fit a two-hour commercial timeslot. As a result of the cuts, *TV Guide* magazine now described the film as "less a coherent drama than . . . a series of episodes." Author Alice Walker, Danny, playwright Ntozake Shange, and jazz musician John Handy were among the San Francisco Bay–area artists who appeared in *Social Change and the Fruits of Culture*. The event (held April 1, 1990, at the Lorraine Hansberry Theatre in San Francisco) celebrated African-American contributions to culture and benefited the Vanguard Public Foundation.

Danny and Jesse Jackson co-hosted a one-performance presentation, at the Oakland, California, Calvin Simmons Theatre on May 6, 1990, of a gospel show featuring gospel singer Tramaine Hawkins. On May 12–13, 1990, Danny narrated the Oakland Ballet's world premiere at the Paramount Theatre of its new presentation of Prokofiev's *Peter and the Wolf*. Next, he was among several celebrities to offer safe-driving tips to viewers on CBS-TV's "National Driving Test" (August 28, 1990), the second in a series of two.

PREDATOR 2, released in November 1990, was a sequel to the Arnold Schwarzenegger screen thriller of 1987, but with Danny now as the hero and the setting changed from the jungle to the urban chaos of 1997 Los Angeles. Of the switch, Glover said, "I hope that will continue to change some people's perceptions of blacks. It's not a black or white part, it's just a good role." *Variety* gave the slam-bang science fiction film a backhanded compliment, noting, "This overproduced sequel is so relentlessly paced that it's extremely entertaining even with its spaceshipful of shortcomings." Kevin Thomas (*Los Angeles Times*) observed, "We can be grateful that PREDATOR 2 has first-rate actors, even if the demands placed upon them are mainly physical." In its first week of domestic release, PREDATOR 2 grossed a powerful $19,720,520 at the box office. FLIGHT OF THE INTRUDER, long in production, and beset by casting problems and editing and re-editing, was finally released in January 1991. Reportedly having cost $35 million, it told of an unauthorized A-6 Intruder bomber raid over Hanoi in 1972, for which the squadron leader (Brad Johnson), pilot (Danny), and navigator/bombardier (Willem Dafoe) were responsible.

In A RAGE IN HARLEM (1991), Danny had a cameo role as Easy Money, a Harlem kingpin with connections for fencing stolen gold. Unable to recreate the 1956 period in Harlem today, the movie was shot in Cincinnati, Ohio. Glover next starred with Martin Short in the comedy thriller PURE LUCK (1991), a remake of the 1985 French film LA CHÈVRE. Glover is a detective teamed with accident-prone Short to rescue the world's most accident-prone woman. Directed by Nadia Tass, the feature was shot on location in Atlanta and Acapulco. And, of course, with the supercolossal success of the two LETHAL WEAPON films, plans are under way for yet another action tale centering around Mel Gibson and Glover.

Like Whoopi Goldberg, Danny Glover wants to work in quality material, not so much to make money as to prove his worth and to grow as a person—not a black person, but as a human being. "People search to reaffirm themselves through media stars," he says, "whether it's Tom Brokaw or Mel Gibson. But, I don't live in isolation as a black man. I live among people, a community. We should respect each other's cultures within that." A looming, benevolent advocate for civil rights, Glover told *Fame* magazine for its summer 1990 edition: "It's not enough for me to just run around and be an actor making some money; it's more important than that. If there was a theme in LETHAL WEAPON 2 about apartheid and South Africa, and some people remember that, then, man, that's a heavy statement about this industry, and about what I do."

Filmography

Escape from Alcatraz (Par, 1979)
Chu Chu and the Philly Flash (20th–Fox, 1981)
The Face of Rage (ABC-TV, 3/20/83)
Iceman (Univ, 1984)
Places in the Heart (Tri-Star, 1984)
Witness (Par, 1985)
The Stand-In (Stand-In Productions, 1985)
Silverado (Col, 1985)
The Color Purple (WB, 1985)
Mandela (HBO–Cable, 9/20/87)
Lethal Weapon (WB, 1987)

Bat 21 (Tri-Star, 1988)
Out (Cinema Group Home Video, 1988) [made in 1982]
Dead Man Out (HBO–Cable, 3/12/89)
Lethal Weapon 2 (WB, 1989)
To Sleep with Anger (Samuel Goldwyn, 1990) (also co-executive producer)
Predator 2 (20th–Fox, 1990)
Flight of the Intruder (Par, 1991)
A Rage in Harlem (Miramax, 1991)
Pure Luck (Univ, 1991)

Television Series

Chiefs (CBS, 11/13/83; 11/15/83; 11/16/83) [miniseries]

Lonesome Dove (ABC, 2/5/89–2/8/89) [miniseries]

Broadway Plays

Master Harold . . . and the Boys (1982)

Album Discography

Br'er Rabbit and the Wonderful Tar Baby
(Windham Hill WD-0716) [ST-TV]

How the Leopard Got His Spots (Windham Hill
WD-0715)

WHOOPI GOLDBERG

"It's pretty hard to top the hoopla of THE COLOR PURPLE and
that time. That I'm still around is astounding. That nobody has
crucified my acting is astounding to me."
                    —*US* magazine, September 14, 1988

"SHE'S WARM. SHE'S WONDERFUL. SHE'S WHOOPI." IN SIX WORDS, *PRE-miere* magazine gave a concise and accurate summation of the petite, lovable package called Whoopi Goldberg. This lady, a happy-faced welfare mother in 1983, rose to million-dollar status as a serious actress in just three years. She accomplished this with her award-caliber, bravura screen performance as Miss Celie in THE COLOR PURPLE (1985), sweeping the entertainment world into a state of "Whoopimania." Preferring to be considered a character performer, an identification manifest in the array of individuals of various sorts that she portrays in her one-woman stage shows, she also does not want to be labeled by a color, saying, "They don't write for black actors. They *do* write for actors."

When harshly criticized by outspoken black filmmaker/actor Spike Lee for wearing blue contact lenses, indicating, he claimed, that she wanted to be white, she quickly put this charge to rest by pointing to her hair, styled in what she calls "do-do" braids and for which she predicts she will be best remembered. She shaves her eyebrows because they itch, is involved in sixty-three charitable organizations at one time, has two honorary doctorates, and says, nonbraggingly, "I can play anything from a male to a speck of dust." She has assumed screen roles written or designated for white (and sometimes even male) actors and transformed them into a Whoopi characterization. Many of her films, although showing respectable grosses, have not been bonanza-type hits. Her taking on a television series as well as less-than-leading roles in motion pictures caused some to raise their eyebrows, but she insists that her goal is to be an actor, not a star. In comedy she ranks alongside contemporaries Billy Crystal and Robin Williams, with whom she has raised millions for the cause of America's homeless.

She was born Caryn Johnson in New York City on Sunday, November 13, 1949, to Emma Johnson and a father who later abandoned his family. Raised in a housing project in the Chelsea section of Manhattan with a younger brother, she began acting in children's programs at the Helena Rubinstein Children's Theatre at the Hudson Guild at the age of eight. She was a lonely child, who preferred watching movies on television to playing with other children because she felt that she did not fit in with them. Her preferences in old movies ran to Carole Lombard and Claudette Colbert films, with Colbert's IT HAPPENED

ONE NIGHT (1934) being her all-time favorite. She also adored horror films of the 1950s, especially the performances of the supporting character players. The annual Academy Awards show was not to be missed, and during the telecasts she drove her mother and brother from the room with her improvised acceptance speeches. She studiously observed every nuance of an actor's demeanor, and would say later, "I'm a real sponge in terms of seeing things and absorbing them."

She was educated by the nuns of Congregation Notre Dame at the parish of St. Columbia Church, but dropped out of high school in the 1960s. She became involved in political causes such as civil rights marches and the student demonstrations at Columbia University. She participated in the drug rituals of the hippie movement, but suddenly asked herself, "Am I going to keep doing drugs and kill myself or figure out what I'm going to do with my life?" Thus she embarked on a series of drug-counseling sessions with a man named Martin whom she married in 1971, and thereafter she got work singing in the Broadway choruses of *Hair*, *Jesus Christ Superstar*, and *Pippin*. In 1973 she divorced Mr. Martin, but then discovered herself pregnant with daughter Alexandrea, born in 1974.

Soon after the birth of Alexandrea, she and her daughter flew to Los Angeles on a one-way ticket given to her by a friend. From there she was offered a ride to San Diego, where she would spend the next six years. She started professionally by co-founding the San Diego Repertory Theatre and appearing in such diverse plays as *The Grass Is Greener*, *Mother Courage*, and *Getting Out*. She also joined an improvisational troupe known as Spontaneous Combustion, as well as partnered in stand-up comedy with Don Victor, a local comic. It was during this period that she changed her name, first considering "Whoopi Cushion," a takeoff on the prankster's gimmick. She finally settled on Goldberg because of the lunacy attached to the idea of a black woman with a German/Jewish surname. Between cash-paying stage jobs, she was also a bricklayer and a bank teller, and managed to graduate from a beauty school, thereby acquiring a cosmetician's license with which she secured work in a mortuary dressing the faces and hair of corpses.

In 1980 she and Don Victor negotiated an engagement to perform in San Francisco, but at the last minute Victor dropped out. Whoopi went north, nevertheless, with Alexandrea where she partnered with David Schein in Berkeley, California, in an experimental theater troupe called Blake Street Hawkeyes. With Schein she wrote *The Last Word*, a two-character satirical show which they performed in Berkeley in 1981. For the production she created an on-stage character called "Surfer Chick," a thirteen-year-old Valley girl who has performed an abortion on herself with a coat hanger. In support of women's abortion rights, Whoopi took time to picket a Berkeley hospital. During parts of 1981 and 1982, she was a single-parent recipient of state welfare benefits. However, in 1983, with the creation of her one-woman *The Spook Show*, she quickly rose to standing-room-only prominence in the San Francisco Bay area. *The Spook Show* consisted of four characterizations: Fontaine, a comically cynical male college graduate strung-out on drugs; a nine-year-old black girl who does not want to be black because "You have to be white to be on 'The Love Boat'"; a grotesquely crippled woman who gains normalcy through dreams; and the coat hanger-wielding California Valley miss.

After entitling her presentation *A Broad Abroad* or *Whoopi Goldberg Variations*, she took the characterizations on tour briefly in this country and abroad before ending in New York City in February 1984 at the Dance Theatre Workshop as part of the series "Character and Confession: New Experience in Narrative Theatre." At sellout performances, critics applauded her as "uncanny," with the ability to "transform her face and body, as well as her voice." Director/producer Mike Nichols was so impressed that he offered to produce her show on Broadway. However, she chose to return to Berkeley to appear as the late black stand-up comedienne Moms Mabley, in *Moms*, which she co-wrote. After winning the Bay Area Theatre Award for her efforts, she returned to Manhattan to belatedly accept Nichols's offer, opening October 24, 1984, at the Lyceum Theatre in *Whoopi Goldberg*. Her repertoire had by now expanded to include two additional characters: an old male panhandler and a Jamaican domestic involved with an eighty-year-old millionaire. Frank Rich (*New York Times*) complimented her sketches, which "walk a fine line between satire and pathos, stand-up comedy and acting." Rich added, "Miss Goldberg is a warm, almost childlike performer with a sweet clown's face, an elastic body, a sensitive social conscience and a joyous stage name." Her then-mentor Mike Nichols extolled, "She is one part Groucho [Marx], one part Ruth Draper, one part Richard Pryor, and five parts never before seen." In a contemporary interview, the new Broadway star explained, "The characters I play on the stage have been on a long voyage of discovery." Her efforts, which won her a Theatre World Award, were taped for HBO–Cable as "Whoopi Goldberg—Direct from Broadway" (January 20, 1985) and were also recorded as an album.

When Whoopi learned that Steven Spielberg intended to produce and direct a screen adaptation of Alice Walker's Pulitzer Prize–winning novel *The Color Purple* (1982), Goldberg joked, "Honey . . . I'd play the dirt." However, she was truly honored when Spielberg approached her to play the lead, Celie, although she preferred the supporting role of Sophia (which went to Oprah Winfrey) because "it had more spirit, more heart." Accepting his offer at a salary of $250,000, she roasted during the 1985 summer on location in North Carolina. However, when THE COLOR PURPLE was released in December, her reviews were laudatory. *Newsweek* magazine judged her a "riveting presence," adding, "This is powerhouse acting, all the more so because the rage and the exhilaration are held in reserve." For her first screen assignment, Whoopi was awarded a Golden Globe and received an Academy Award nomination as Best Actress. Honored with eleven Oscar nominations, THE COLOR PURPLE won no awards (Geraldine Page won the Best Actress award for THE TRIP TO BOUNTIFUL), but received monetary consolation at the box office with a domestic gross of $94.2 million, making it the #4 moneymaker of 1985.

Whoopi Goldberg was now an in-demand movie property, commanding a salary of $1 million per picture. *People* magazine selected her as one of the twenty-five "most intriguing people of 1985." She chose to live in New York City in a new apartment in a brownstone with her daughter and dog, Otis. She took over the lead role in JUMPIN' JACK FLASH (1986) when Shelley Long dropped out of the project, playing a computer operator receiving online messages from a secret agent caught behind the Iron Curtain. Considered a disappointment, the movie nevertheless grossed $26 million in domestic release. On May 13, 1986, she played a con artist on the "Camille" episode of "Moonlighting," for which she was Emmy-nominated. She found love with cinematographer David Claessen, nine years her junior, whom she married in 1986. With and without Claessen, she was seen at major openings on both coasts, with columnists reporting each as a "Whoopi Sighting." She said, "Someone even wrote that I'd go to the opening of an envelope. That hurt very deeply. I guess no one realized how new all of this was to me." The year 1986 also marked the first "Comic Relief" HBO–Cable telecast with Billy Crystal and Robin Williams to raise money for health care and related services for more than 150,000 homeless Americans.

TV Guide magazine heralded the February 10, 1987, ABC-TV telecast of "A Carol Burnett Special" with, "A very special hour of laughter and song with four of the funniest people on earth." The four were Burnett, Whoopi, Robin Williams, and Carl Reiner. For BURGLAR (1987), Whoopi stepped into the lead to replace the departing Bruce Willis as a redeemed cat burglar framed for a murder she did not commit. Although *Continental Choice* magazine said that she "steals the stage" in the title role, the action movie took in a relatively meager $16 million at domestic theater box offices. FATAL BEAUTY (1987), a project originally slated for Cher, fared even worse, grossing a poor $11 million domestically, with Goldberg's salary an estimated $2.25 million. For this integrated cop-buddy film in which she co-starred with Sam Elliott, she received the Best Actress NAACP Image Award on December 10, 1988. A potential screen remake of BORN YESTERDAY (1950), with Whoopi in the Judy Holliday role, failed to materialize during 1987. She ended the year professionally in December by joining creator Richard Dreyfuss on the ABC-TV special "Funny, You Don't Look 200."

Taking a reduction in salary to $500,000 plus 10 percent of net profits, she starred in the bizarre THE TELEPHONE (1988), as an unemployed actress with psychological problems. She later fought, but lost, a court attempt to block its release because of her dissatisfaction with director Rip Torn's editing job. Later, in very limited exposure, THE TELEPHONE failed badly at the box office. About her run of unsuccessful pictures, she told a press person, "Yes, I'm disappointed, but I take no responsibility for them. The studios take this nice, gritty script and turn it into pabulum."

She participated in ABC-TV's "Second Annual American Comedy Awards"

Whoopi Goldberg in JUMPIN' JACK FLASH (1986).

(May 17, 1988) and revived her one-woman stage show on July 7 and 8, 1988, at the Universal Amphitheater in Universal City, California, now calling it *Living on the Edge of Chaos.* The *Los Angeles Times* reviewer asked, "How many other entertainers send you home feeling like a human being?" (This theater work led to Whoopi's receiving the twelfth annual California Theatre Award for Outstanding Achievement on stage.) She was hoping for a hit with the October 1988 release by Warner Bros. of CLARA'S HEART. Whoopi's performance as a Jamaican maid/surrogate mother to a bewildered fifteen-year-old boy (Neil Patrick Harris) was praised by some critics ("she reaches new heights as a dramatic actress of substance and strength"—Rex Reed), but the comedy/drama was not judged as kindly ("just awful"—*People* magazine). This, too, was a financial disaster.

Turning to television, she guested on the syndicated series "Star Trek: The Next Generation" in the 1988–1989 season as "Guinan," the alien humanoid hostess who served advice with colorful drinks to the off-duty crew aboard the spacecraft. Her explanation for the assignment was that she had been a fan of the original "Star Trek" series, appreciative of the fact that program creator Gene Roddenberry had used a black actress (Nichelle Nichols) as a cast regular. (Whoopi would make return visits to the series in subsequent seasons, repeating her characterization.) She next starred in the ABC-TV special "Free to Be . . . A Family" (December 14, 1988) and appeared on CBS-TV's "Pee-wee's Playhouse Christmas Special" (December 21, 1988). Many observers wondered why she was spreading herself so thin professionally. She began the new year by accepting token payment for starring on CBS-TV's "Schoolbreak Special" in the segment "My Past Is My Own" (January 24, 1989). Through "hypnotic regression" she takes her nephew and niece back to a 1961 nonviolent black struggle to achieve civil rights in a small Georgia town. She participated in the ABC-TV special "The 75th Anniversary of Beverly Hills" (February 26, 1989), "The Debbie Allen Special" (ABC-TV, March 5, 1989), and HBO–Cable's "Comic Relief III" (March 19, 1989) with Cher, Arsenio Hall, and other celebrities volunteering for the homeless cause. In March 1989 she was named Humanitarian of the Year by the Starlight Foundation for her many contributions to charitable causes.

In the homevideo market, Karl-Lorimar released *The Best of Comic Relief* as well as a tape entitled *Whoopi Goldberg.* She also hosted both a twenty-minute and a longer version of *AIDS: Everything You Should Know,* distributed by Aims Media. Her TV-movie debut occurred on April 11, 1989, in KISS SHOT, in which she played an unemployed single mother who becomes a pool shark to earn money. *TV Guide* magazine called it "fluff," but added that "the stars are undeniably charming." The NBC-TV special "The All Star Tribute to Kareem Abdul-Jabbar" (May 12, 1989) merely featured Whoopi, but she was the undeniable focus of "Whoopi Goldberg Live" (August 6, 1989) on HBO–Cable. She hosted/narrated the TV documentary "The Truth About Teachers," nationally syndicated between September 7 and September 24, 1989, and repeated in December.

Grandmotherhood was awarded Whoopi on her fortieth birthday, November 13, 1989, when fifteen-year-old Alexandrea gave birth in Berkeley to Amarah Skye Martin. Whoopi, who had divorced David Claessen in late 1988, lived with her fiancé, Eddie Gold, a Hollywood camera operator, but was also reportedly involved with Brent Spiner, a West Coast business executive. After it had sat on a studio shelf for a year, HOMER & EDDIE was released on February 9, 1990. Although prerelease advertisements stated: "During the next 1200 miles, their lives will be turned upside down, inside out, and right side up," the *Los Angeles Times,* claiming that the film "lifts liberally" from LA STRADA (1954), branded it "cornball squishiness." Jim Belushi, as Homer, who had been hit in the head with a baseball as a kid, sets out from Arizona to Oregon to find his parents. On the road he meets Eddie (Whoopi), on the run from a mental institution. This was another of Whoopi's movies that failed to make any critic's list of recommendations.

According to the *San Francisco Chronicle,* Whoopi "hit the dusty comeback trail" in the CBS-TV half-hour series rendition of the 1988 sleeper hit movie BAGDAD CAFE, as Brenda, the role originated on screen by CCH Pounder. The series premiered on March 30, 1990, and the *Hollywood Reporter* found fault with the comedy script about two suddenly single women, but pointed out that Whoopi and co-star Jean Stapleton, "have the potential of sending electricity across the airwaves." The series was picked up for the 1990–1991 season. In April 1990, the always-working Whoopi was performing at the Circus Maximus club at Stateline, Nevada, while simultaneously appearing in Gap clothing advertisements, alone as well as with her mother, daughter, and granddaughter. She co-hosted the AIDS benefit TV show "That's What Friends Are For" (April 17, 1990). The May 9, 1990, CBS-TV "Happy Birthday, Bugs" tribute to Bugs Bunny's fiftieth anniversary year included Whoopi's salute to the late Mel Blanc, who created the cartoon character's voice. On May 12, 1990, "Comic Relief IV" was telecast on HBO–Cable and another $4.7 million was raised for the nation's homeless. (The first three shows were put on record by Rhino Records; the fourth, *The Best of Comic Relief '90,* was available from Rhino on CD, cassette, and home video. Proceeds from sales benefitted the homeless.) A Whoopi highlight of the proceedings was her Queen Elizabeth II of England spoof wherein she transformed into Tina Turner singing "Proud Mary." From May 21 through June 26, 1990, she took her latest one-woman show, *The Thundering Ho Down Under,* on tour to Australia, New Zealand, and Tasmania where she met, almost face-to-face, a following of ardent new fans.

On August 8, 1990, on CBS-TV's "This Morning," Whoopi talked of how it feels to be out of work. "It's like having a period all the time," she said, matter of factly. She joined Bruce Willis and the McGuire Sisters in a late-night tour of Los Angeles hot spots guided by the Pointer Sisters on Lifetime–Cable on August 4, 1990, in the sixty-minute "Pointer Sisters ('Pointers on L.A. Nightlife')."

In GHOST (1990), released *after* the July 4 holiday, Whoopi was a supporting co-star (to Patrick Swayze and Demi Moore) as a fake psychic through whom a ghost (Swayze) communicates with his sweetheart (Moore) after his untimely death in a street shooting in Manhattan. The *Hollywood Reporter* probably said it best: "As the squirrely psychic, [she] has garnered a part that stretches even her farfetched talents. It's one of the best kook parts in recent years and Goldberg cranks it up . . . she's a hoot." David Ansen (*Newsweek* magazine) enthused, "thank God Whoopi finally has a part that lets her strut her best stuff." Released in competition with big action films like DIE HARD 2, TOTAL

RECALL, ROBOCOP 2, and DICK TRACY, GHOST became the big surprise hit, and deservedly so. By early December 1990 it had taken in more than $197,954,919 in domestic box-office receipts, to become the year's top-grossing film. Although she finally had a megahit, Whoopi was still skeptical: "I got very few offers after THE COLOR PURPLE," she said. "Scripts do not come to me." Regarding her "comeback," Whoopi said, "I didn't know my career was so far down the toilet until I read the reviews for GHOST."

In September 1990 she was one of many, many celebrities at the Wiltern Theatre in Los Angeles to greet guests attending the AIDS Project Los Angeles's *Commitment to Life IV.* The TBS–Cable cartoon series "Captain Planet and the Planeteers" premiered September 15, 1990 (in syndicated release; on September 16, 1990, on TBS). It features a blue-skinned, green-haired hero (David Coburn), the answer to environmental threats. Whoopi provided the voice of Gaia, the spirit of the Earth, awakened from her sleep by global pollution. Others whose voices were heard as evildoers included Jeff Goldblum, Martin Sheen, Ed Asner, Dean Stockwell, and Meg Ryan. Miles Beller (*Hollywood Reporter*) noted, "a program constructed of animation that's just a bit better than the run of the mill cartoon, agitprop can get onerous even when outfitted in the tights of a campy superhero." *Daily Variety* observed, "While Edward Asner and John Ratzenberger do okay voicing as the villains, the rest of the cast is generally too listless or too typically cartoonish to click." On September 28, 1990, "Bagdad Cafe" returned for its second season. *Daily Variety* reported that the revamped program "has improved but still lacks the spark to make it a first-rate comedy. . . . During the more dramatic moments, Goldberg and [Jean] Stapleton shine brightest. Unfortunately, the program was conceived as a comedy, and there are few funny moments." For Nickelodeon–Cable, Whoopi created a new character, Hotrod Brown, Class Clown, who made appearances on two thirty-minute specials for children in the fall of 1990 filmed under the umbrella title "Tales from the Whoop." She was the guardian angel giving advice to a junior high school boy. Meanwhile, Goldberg was among the celebrities (including Milton Berle, Jamie Lee Curtis, Ted Danson, Sally Kellerman, and John Ritter) appearing in the home video *Help Save Planet Earth*, released in September 1990.

The tireless Whoopi next played Odessa, the maid to a middle-class Montgomery, Alabama, family, in THE LONG WALK HOME (1990), set during the 1955 black bus boycott. Odessa walks from her home in the poor part of town to do work for her spoiled employer (Sissy Spacek), who eventually gains a new perspective from her maid's act of courage. The film premiered at the seventeenth Telluride Film Festival in Telluride, Colorado, on Labor Day weekend 1990 and opened nationally in December 1990. The earnest film did very little business and quickly disappeared. However, it was re-released in March 1991, with an extensive ad campaign to promote its sincere subject and its two famous stars. For SOAPDISH (1991), starring Sally Field as a fading soap opera star and Carl Reiner as a harried daytime TV executive, Whoopi was cast as a soap opera writer. Possibly forthcoming is a remake of the British classic THE LADYKILLERS (1955), with Whoopi and Bob Hoskins in the Alec Guinness and Peter Sellers roles, respectively. Another possible role announced for Goldberg was as the demanding bureaucrat in the film version of Peter

Shaffer's London and New York stage hit comedy *Lettice and Lovage*. Thereafter, however, in late November 1990, Whoopi signed an exclusive agreement with Paramount Pictures.

Meanwhile, during the fall of 1990 "Bagdad Cafe" faltered badly in the ratings. While the CBS network was debating whether to cancel the failing show, Goldberg announced she was quitting the series, which ended its run abruptly on November 23, 1990. Her career undaunted by this setback, the much-in-demand Whoopi garnered several honors. She received a special tribute on October 27, 1990, at the Sixth Annual Women in Film Festival in Los Angeles, with her award of excellence presented by fellow comedian Robin Williams. (Previous winners of the award include Julie Andrews, Sally Field, and Kathleen Turner.) On December 1, 1990, she was named Entertainer of the Year at the twenty-third annual Image Awards ceremonies held at the Wiltern Theater in Los Angeles and sponsored by the Beverly Hills/Hollywood chapter of the National Association for the Advancement of Colored People. Among those participating in honoring Goldberg were past co-stars Patrick Swayze, Bob Goldthwait, and Jean Stapleton. On November 21, 1990, Whoopi was one of the ringmasters for the fifteenth annual edition of CBS-TV's "Circus of the Stars." On November 30, 1990, Whoopi joined Richard Gere, Carrie Fisher, and Kyle MacLachlan as hosts of the ABC-TV special "Red, Hot & Blue," a 1990s music video tribute to the music of Cole Porter which was also an AIDS informational program. Concurrently, FLY AWAY HOME, a live-action short film written, produced, and directed by Ashley Tyler and co-starring Whoopi, Rain Pryor, Esther Rolle, and Garrett Morris was being touted for Academy Award consideration.

At the height of her new-found fame in the mid-1980s, Whoopi Goldberg admitted, "It's a Cinderella dream come true. It's a gas. . . . Everyone should have this luck. . . . This is the last thing I expected to happen." More recently, in assessing her very full career to date, Whoopi has observed, "I haven't lived up to the expectations that everybody slapped on me when all of this began. I think a lot of people wanted me to be a female Eddie Murphy." She added, "If I sat and waited for what was the 'right role,' I would never work. COLOR PURPLEs don't come along that often." On another occasion, she observed, "One thing I'm not is a flash in the pan. Things have not always turned out the way I wanted, but I did the best job I could. . . . As a girl from the projects, I'm not at all disappointed in the way things are going. This is what I've always dreamed about. And I'm still here, which is the phenomenal thing." When, on March 25, 1991, Whoopi won an Academy Award as Best Supporting Actress for her role in GHOST, she stated in her tearful acceptance speech, "Ever since I was a little girl, I wanted this [Oscar]. . . . I'm so proud to be here. I'm proud to be an actor, and I'm gonna keep on acting."

Filmography

The Color Purple (WB, 1985)
Jumpin' Jack Flash (20th–Fox, 1986)
Burglar (WB, 1987)
Fatal Beauty (MGM/UA, 1987)

Clara's Heart (WB, 1988)
The Telephone (New World, 1988)
Kiss Shot (CBS-TV, 4/11/89)
Homer & Eddie (Skouras Pictures, 1990)

Ghost (Par, 1990)
The Long Walk Home (Miramax, 1990)

Fly Away Home (Firstborn Productions, 1990)
  (short subject)
Soapdish (Par, 1991)

TV Series

Bagdad Cafe (CBS, 1990)
Captain Planet and the Planeteers (TBS–Cable,
  1990–) (voice only)

Star Trek: The Next Generation (Synd-TV,
  1988–)

Broadway Plays

Hair (ca. 1971) (replacement)
Jesus Christ Superstar (ca. 1971) (replacement)

Pippin (1972) (replacement)
Whoopi Goldberg (1984) (also script)

Album Discography

The Best of Comic Relief 2
  (Rhino R11H-70707)
The Best of Comic Relief '90
  (Rhino R215-71010)
Comic Relief—The Best of Comic Relief (Rhino
  RNIN-70704)

Comic Relief 3 (Rhino R21K-70893)
Whoopi Goldberg—Direct from Broadway
  (Geffen GHS-24065)
Why Am I Straight? (MCA MCA-42243)

JEFF GOLDBLUM

"I am a lucky fellow. It's a pretty good life. You get a trailer,
a nice lunch."   —*GQ* magazine, July 1985

TALL AND LANKY AT 6' 4", WITH A NOSE THAT IS TOO PROMINENT TO BE acceptable on a leading man, Jeff Goldblum is acknowledged for what he is: a sometimes serious, sometimes bizarre actor with a penchant for eclectic roles. According to director Lawrence Kasdan, he is "obsessive" in creating his characters. In one of Kasdan's ensemble-cast movies, Jeff Goldblum became a composite of the many magazine writers he studiously observed in action, while in another Kasdan film, as a mysterious gambler of the Old West, he wore cowboy boots every day from the instant he won the part and attached a device to his arm to enable him to stealthily slip a derringer into his hand. Another Hollywood director in the mid-1980s assessed, "Jeff Goldblum is talented but he's not a leading man. His career will never be bigger than it is right now." However, the actor was briefly considered top star material with his superior performance as a man whose molecules become intermixed with those of a housefly. He resembles comedian Howie Mandel and, under the guidance of a good studio makeup artist, is able to come close to handsomeness, a ploy that works also for James Woods. A master at staccato, articulate delivery of dialogue—sprinkled with sarcasm—Goldblum, as the unnamed director observed in 1985, "will work until he is in the grave."

Jeffrey Goldblum was born on Wednesday, October 22, 1952, in Pittsburgh, Pennsylvania, the oldest of four children born to an affluent Jewish doctor and his wife, the latter a former tap dancer and Pittsburgh radio talk show hostess. They lived in a large home and took long, elaborate vacations; the parents provided well for their children. Jeff has recalled that the first time he thought about acting was when his parents bought him a cowboy outfit, which he put on to surprise some guest who "got a big kick out it." He added, with a straight face, "I suppose I was pretty cute." At an early age, he and his sister Pamela took piano lessons together, which resulted, he has said, in his playing with his hands, she with her nose. The elder Goldblums were avid theater- and moviegoers who took their children with them whenever they went. As a sixth-grader, Jeff starred in a spoof of Gilbert and Sullivan operettas at the Chatham Music Day Camp in Pittsburgh. This experience cemented his desire to associate himself with show business.

At the age of fourteen, while a freshman in high school, Jeff played piano in cocktail lounges, and his summers were devoted to theater programs at Pittsburgh's Carnegie-Mellon University. In 1969, after graduating from high school, he applied to the University's drama department. When he was rejected, his understanding parents not only provided moral support, but also paid for him to spend two years at Sanford Meisner's Neighborhood Playhouse in New York City. The financial allowance also provided for an Upper East Side apartment plus expenses. By this time, Jeff was seventeen.

During his tenure at the Neighborhood Playhouse, a telephone call came from Joseph Papp's New York Shakespeare Festival, inquiring if there might be someone at the theater school who was sufficiently tall to play a guard in Papp's upcoming production of Shakespeare's *The Two Gentlemen of Verona*, as transformed into a musical by Galt MacDermot, John Guare, and Mel Shapiro. At 6' 4", Jeff was plenty tall enough, and when it was discovered that he could sing and dance as well, he was also placed in the chorus. The show opened at the Delacorte Theatre on July 27, 1971, for twenty-seven performances and was so successful that it reopened on Broadway at the St. James Theatre on December 1, 1971, for 614 additional performances. Jeff next appeared in a subordinate role in the unorthodox musical *El Grande de Coca-Cola*, a high-spirited small-cast show. He was a manic piano player in the cabaret within a cabaret setting. The show began at the Mercer Arts Center on February 13, 1973, but had to be moved to the Plaza Hotel when the original theater collapsed. One night, during a driving blizzard, Hollywood director Robert Altman and his casting agent were forced to take refuge within the hotel and they caught the show. Altman offered Jeff small parts in two feature films he was preparing, while the casting agent thought him physically perfect to play one of three rapists seen in the early scenes of DEATH WISH (1974). In the first Altman movie, CALIFORNIA SPLIT (1974), Jeff was a gambler, while in NASHVILLE (1975) he was a weird magician-motorcyclist. Between these minor screen roles, he continued his stage work with such off-off-Broadway shows as *Our Late Night* and *City Sugar*. In the former, he played opposite Patricia Gaul as his wife. They lived together beginning in 1975, and in 1980 they were married.

His next screen job was in Paul Mazursky's New York–filmed NEXT STOP, GREENWICH VILLAGE (1976) in the small part of a neurotic actor named Clyde. This was followed by a quick appearance as a bank robber who gets caught in the comedy–heist caper SPECIAL DELIVERY (1976) and an even faster appearance and disappearance in ST. IVES (1976). Before heading for the West Coast in 1976, Goldblum did a few days' work for Woody Allen in ANNIE HALL (1977) as a meditator who finds it necessary to phone his guru when he forgets his mantra. "I know I was pretty lucky," Jeff recalled some years after his early good fortune. "I didn't have all that struggling and suffering that actors are supposed to go through. I don't remember being hungry."

He had a role in one of the final episodes of TV's "The Blue Knight," entitled "Upward Mobility." He achieved third billing as Max, a rock critic forced to sell his collection of free promotional discs in order to pay his rent in BETWEEN THE LINES (1977), after doing a walk-on part in THE SENTINEL (1977). He was a disco owner in THANK GOD IT'S FRIDAY (1978) and worked again for Robert Altman in the moody REMEMBER MY NAME (1978). His most important assignment during this period was as poet/part-time mud pack therapist Jack Bellicec in the remake of INVASION OF THE BODY

SNATCHERS (1978). It was also his biggest role to date, as a man who is transformed into an alien replica of himself by way of pod plants.

The two-hour pilot for the projected ABC-TV series "Tenspeed and Brown Shoe" was so well received that the series was picked up as a midseason replacement, beginning January 27, 1980, with much advance fanfare. Ben Vereen was Tenspeed, a charming hustler, while Jeff was Brown Shoe, a term once used for bankers or stockbrokers. Together they form a detective agency in Los Angeles off Sunset Boulevard. *Variety* reported, "Goldblum has a goofy, zonked-out charm." The first few installments rated high by the A. C. Nielsen count, but the ratings steadily decreased to the point that the show was dropped after its telecast on June 27, 1980. On Halloween night, October 31, 1980, Jeff was appropriately seen as Ichabod Crane in the Washington Irving classic THE LEGEND OF SLEEPY HOLLOW, a two-hour CBS-TV presentation.

With no Hollywood roles in the offing, he returned to the stage in *The Moony Shapiro Songbook*, a musical burlesque which had enjoyed a 209-performance run at the Globe Theatre in London in 1979. Opening on Broadway on May 3, 1981, Jeff co-starred with Judy Kaye and Timothy Jerome. The intimate production lasted only one night, but Jeff received solid reviews: "personable and gifted Goldblum . . . also serves as narrator" (Douglas Watt, *New York Daily News*); "a delightful, off-center movie actor" (Frank Rich, *New York Times*); "I was surprised to find he could sing and dance. And most of the time so does he" (Joel Siegel, WABC-TV). The versatile Goldblum turned to drama as the biologist, Dr. Aldo Behring, who invents an artificial heart for human transplant in THRESHOLD, made in and released in Canada in 1981. This picture, with Jeff second-billed, would not be released in the United States by 20th Century–Fox International Classics until February 1983, when the first real-life artificial heart transplant was achieved. On January 19, 1982, Jeff adapted to pure slapstick comedy in the "Watch the Fur Fly" episode of "Laverne and Shirley," while on May 26, 1982, he was back into drama for the CBS-TV movie REHEARSAL FOR MURDER. He portrayed one of the cast members of a Broadway play whose leading lady (Lynn Redgrave) has been found dead. The year was capped with his appearance in the segment "The Absolute Monarch of Ward C" of the Rock Hudson–Jack Scalia NBC-TV series "The Devlin Connection," telecast on October 30, 1982.

After several years of jumping professionally in many directions, Jeff's real test as to whether or not he was film star material came as part of the ensemble cast in Lawrence Kasdan's THE BIG CHILL (1983). He was Michael, the sardonic writer for *People* magazine who, along with former college classmates, attends the funeral of a friend. A highlight of Jeff's performance was his quick, succinct delivery of lines of dialogue such as: "Don't knock realization. Where would we be without it? I don't know anyone who'd go through the day without two or three juicy realizations. They're more important than sex. . . . Have you ever gone a week without a realization?" *Newsweek* magazine praised his "brilliantly compulsive" performance. After fourteen weeks in domestic release, THE BIG CHILL had grossed $45.6 million. One month later, in another ensemble-cast film, THE RIGHT STUFF, Jeff had a small role as a NASA recruiter who vomits before the eyes of U.S. Navy test pilots. This somber, overly detached study of America's space program was not well received by filmgoers.

On February 14, 1984, Jeff appeared in the PBS-TV "American Playhouse" presentation of "Popular Neurotics," and three months later, on May 14, starred in the title role of ERNIE KOVACS: BETWEEN THE LAUGHTER, a two-hour telefilm about the genius comedian's early life and the period when his children were kidnapped. A Kovacs trademark was a cigar, always in his mouth, which Jeff adopted for weeks while doing the characterization. "He was much beloved," Jeff told *TV Guide* magazine about Kovacs, "and for good reason. He was wonderful." W. D. Richter, who had written the screenplay for INVASION OF THE BODY SNATCHERS, directed Jeff's 1984 feature film release, THE ADVENTURES OF BUCKAROO BANZAI: ACROSS THE 8TH DIMENSION. "I had confidence in his taste and sense of style," Goldblum said of Richter after the quirky action satire, starring Peter Weller in the title role, did not initially set box-office records. (It later earned status as a cult favorite.) Fourth-billed as "New Jersey," Jeff was the brain surgeon who lays down his scalpel to become a cowboy.

TV Guide magazine judged "The Three Little Pigs" "delightfully witty" and "arguably the best" installment of Shelley Duvall's "Faerie Tale Theatre," presented by Showtime–Cable on February 12, 1985. Jeff was the big bad wolf threatening the very existence of the trio of li'l pigs (Billy Crystal, Stephen Furst, and Fred Willard).

Goldblum's first starring role in a theatrical release was in the overly episodic INTO THE NIGHT (1985). He was the well-meaning nerd helping a lovely lady (Michelle Pfeiffer) escape from would-be killers. Directed by John Landis, the suspense film failed miserably with audiences but is distinguished by its cameo appearances by several Hollywood directors, among them Lawrence Kasdan and Landis himself. The *Boston Globe* criticized Jeff for seeming "to spend the entire film looking so ill-at-ease, so unhappy."

Jeff Goldblum in TRANSYLVANIA 6-5000 (1985).

Lawrence Kasdan once stated that he wrote the part of Slick in SILVERADO (1985) especially for Jeff. "The part has grace and is sleek and sexy," explained Kasdan. Slick is a mysterious, murderous gambler in the western film, made at a time when that genre was considered dead. However, the sprawling sagebrush tale proved somewhat popular, especially in its homevideo release, and furthered the careers of several in the cast, including such BIG CHILL alumni as Kevin Kline, Kevin Costner, and

Jeff. "Ensemble casts breed a sort of communal attitude and a spirit of cooperative acting," Jeff said in support of such casting; "life is lived in groups of people, not simply in pairs." TRANSYLVANIA 6-5000 (1985), filmed in Yugoslavia, was a critical flop, with Goldblum as a tabloid reporter sent to Romania to verify reports that Frankenstein's monster was afoot. However, at the end of 1985, *Variety* reported that the spoof had been on the top fifty list for five weeks, eventually earning a total of $4.5 million in domestic film rentals paid to the distributor. Also in the cast, headed by Jeff, was newcomer Geena Davis, with whom he initiated a live-in relationship followed by filing for divorce from his wife of five years. He and Davis married in December 1987 in Las Vegas. He was thirty-five and the Massachusetts-born actress was thirty.

On the CBS-TV special "Bugs Bunny/Looney Tunes All-Star 50th Anniversary" (January 14, 1986), Jeff was one of the guest stars, along with Candice Bergen, Mel Blanc, Chevy Chase, Steve Martin, Bill Murray, and many others. Lensed in Toronto, Canada, "The Town Where No One Got Off" was the second installment of HBO–Cable's "Ray Bradbury Theatre," a series designed to startle the viewer with tales of nightmares, visions, and magic. The February 22, 1986, episode starred Jeff as a stranger passing through small-town America. However, rather than finding a quaint village, he encounters only one person, a psychotic old man.

Twentieth Century–Fox's THE FLY (1958) had ended with David Hedison's head on the body of a fly caught in a spider's web, screaming "Help me! Help meeeee!" The 1986 remake from the same studio went several giant steps farther in the area of makeup and special effects when Goldblum, as Seth Brundle, who has just fallen in love, experiments with teleportation at the instant that a housefly enters the chamber. The results are grotesque and eventually fatal, and his lady love (Geena Davis) is powerless to help him. *Premiere* magazine decided that this science fiction film came "close to making a star out of Jeff Goldblum." Other reviews were more emphatic: "one of the most sympathetic man-monsters ever seen on screen" (*Los Angeles Times*), "brilliant performance" (*Video Review* magazine). *Time* magazine, in naming the best movies of the 1980s, declared that THE FLY was "the decade's scariest" and "the most affecting." Gene Siskel (*Chicago Tribune*) was deeply disappointed when Jeff did not get an Oscar nomination, and wrote, "a witty, heartbreaking performance delivered from behind a mass of ever-evolving makeup has been ignored." Both the National Society of Film Critics and the Directors Guild named Goldblum runner-up as Best Actor of 1986. Jeff, in 1988, when asked about his seminal performance as the obsessive scientist, said, "Well, I was just *very* touched. I felt terribly sorry for me. By the end I was just wailing uncontrollably!" In 1989 the sequel, THE FLY II, starred Eric Stoltz as the mutant's offspring, who continues with his father's experiment. But as often happens, this follow-up fell far short of the mark with both critics and viewers.

BEYOND THERAPY (1987) had been a 1981 stage play focusing on a bisexual man who cannot decide between his girlfriend and his male lover. With direction by Robert Altman (who had lost professional esteem in recent years), the film version was a "severe disappointment," according to *Time* magazine, with the cast moving "like clubfooted puppets; they would be more fun if they had been photographed watching the Weather

Channel." On September 14, 1987, the ever-working, ever-reaching Jeff portrayed Dr. James Watson, the Nobel Prize–winning scientist who uncovered the structure of DNA, on the Arts & Entertainment cable TV network in THE RACE FOR THE DOUBLE HELIX (also known as LIFE FORCE). The film, produced by and shown earlier on the British Broadcasting Corporation, was later screened during the weekend of May 19–21, 1989, as part of the nineteenth annual National Educational Film and Video Festival at the Oakland, California, Museum and the following weekend at the San Francisco Exploratorium in an extension of the festival. The "science thriller" film was awarded the festival's Crystal Apple as one of the best.

In EARTH GIRLS ARE EASY (1988), three furry aliens (Jeff, Jim Carrey, Damon Wayans) land their spacecraft in the swimming pool of a California Valley girl (Geena Davis). After their transformation into human-lookalikes at her Curl Up and Dye Beauty Salon, they go out on the town while their ship dries out. While that movie was cute, likeable, and a lot of fun, Jeff's next, VIBES (1988), was dumb and overwrought. He accepted the role after Dan Aykroyd's chemistry failed to mesh with that of the female star, Cyndi Lauper. Unfortunately, Goldblum and Lauper just could not bring it off as a medium and a psychometrist in search of Ecuadorian treasure. Opening in a thousand theaters in August 1988, the picture had realized only a paltry $1,883,811 in domestic box-office dollars by January 1989. On the Fox-TV network on November 20, 1988, Jeff was in the "Go, Go, Goldblum" episode of "It's Garry Shandling's Show."

For several previews and seventeen performances (opening officially on July 9, 1989), Jeff played Malvolio, steward to the grieving countess Olivia (Michelle Pfeiffer), in producer Joseph Papp's open-air, free admission all-star presentation of *Twelfth Night* at the Delacorte Theatre in New York's Central Park. Critics did not take kindly to it ("the most depressing offering yet" in the New York Shakespeare Festival's Shakespeare marathon, insisted *The New Yorker* magazine), and *Newsweek* magazine blasted Jeff for having "no clue about his character." Made in Britain, THE TALL GUY, Jeff's next film, was released in that nation and in Canada in September 1989, when it was labeled "a devastatingly funny comedy" by the *Hollywood Reporter*. The movie was named Best Picture at the first Cinetex International Comedy Awards, held in Las Vegas on September 27, 1989. Jeff starred as a struggling American actor hoping to hit the big time in London, especially after he wins the title role in *Elephant!*, the musical version of *The Elephant Man*. Added the *Hollywood Reporter* in its critique, "the film's considerable charm belongs to Jeff Goldblum, whose endearingly lanky frame is stretched to its full comedic potential." When the R-rated film was released in the United States in September 1990, Peter Rainer (*Los Angeles Times*) found the comedy lacking in several respects, but decided that Jeff Goldblum was in top form as the nerd and has "never been funnier. . . . With the exception of Steve Martin, Goldblum is probably the best physical comic actor in the movies. It's not just that his movements are a surprise to us. They look like they're a surprise to him, too."

Shot in Paris, FRAMED, released as a feature film overseas, was telecast on HBO–Cable on June 24, 1990. Jeff stars as an artist talked into painting forgeries, for which he goes to prison. Two years later, out of confinement, he again encounters the woman

(Kristin Scott Thomas) who enticed him into the forgery business. A light, clever script by Gary Rosen was directed by Dean Parisot with a heavy, slow hand, causing *Daily Variety* to observe that the "understated performances end up blunting instead of building the sense of deadpan farce."

The French-made psychological thriller MR. FROST, lensed in the fall of 1989 and released in Paris in April 1990 (and in the United States briefly in November 1990), co-starred Jeff as a mass murderer whose arresting officer (Alan Bates) is positive that his prisoner is the devil incarnate. At an upscale asylum Goldblum's character wreaks havoc while two psychiatrists (Kathy Baker, Roland Giraud) attempt to analyze him. The offbeat film itself received little critical praise, but reviewers were impressed by Jeff's performance: "Goldblum brings an eerie, epicene majesty to his satanic post" (Duane Byrge, *Hollywood Reporter*); "It's too bad that the film isn't remotely as witty as Goldblum, who has lots of fun playing an insinuating, sexy tempter" (Kevin Thomas, *Los Angeles Times*). Early in August 1990 in TWISTED OBSESSION, which received limited theatrical release, Jeff starred as a screenwriter with an offer to script an art film. He is doubtful about the project until he sees the sixteen-year-old sister (Liza Walker) of the director (Dexter Fletcher). Then, he desperately wants the assignment and is soon obsessed with the girl. The film was shot in Paris and Madrid. According to the *Hollywood Reporter*, "If anything holds the nonsense together, it's Goldblum's sensitive performance." Kevin Thomas of the *Los Angeles Times* rated it as "sleek and sophisticated but . . . too elusive to be either convincing or satisfying." It disappeared from sight within a matter of days.

In the TBS–Cable animated teleseries "Captain Planet and the Planeteers," debuting September 15, 1990 (in syndicated distribution; on September 16, 1990, on TBS), on behalf of helping to save the earth, Jeff joined Meg Ryan, Ed Asner, Martin Sheen, James Coburn, and others in lending their voices to animated figures of ecological bad persons who threaten the planet's existence. Jeff gave voice to Verminous Skumm, a nonrecurring character. *Entertainment Weekly* reported of the series, "Like most popular art conceived as propaganda, 'Captain Planet' is dull and didactic. The dialogue is preachy. . . . When you add thin characterizations and stiff animation, you get one boring bit of noble programming."

Forthcoming for Jeff is THE FAVOR, THE WATCH AND THE VERY BIG FISH (1991) with Bob Hoskins and Natasha Richardson. Between acting assignments, Jeff has taught acting at the Playhouse West in Los Angeles and devoted as much attention as he can to boxing, a new-found activity for him.

Jeff admits that he is a "fitness nut" who devotes much of his free time to exercising in one fashion or another. He took up karate and boxing in 1989 and became an earnest spokesperson in the campaign to end world hunger. When his wife, Geena, won the Academy Award for her performance in THE ACCIDENTAL TOURIST (1988), the wryly humorous actor acknowledged that these days he might be best known as "Husband of the Year." (In mid-October 1990, Goldblum and Davis would file for divorce, citing irreconcilable differences as the cause.)

Jeff Goldblum has not yet found his niche in movies. An intelligent actor capable of fast delivery, he is not a typical Hollywood romantic leading man. "In my work," he has said, "I think individuality and unconventionality and unpredictability and spontaneity are good qualities. That's the kind of acting I like to see and like to do." He added quickly, "But nothing weird, because I'm not." He admits that for him "acting is very much like a form of therapy—a very healthy form. To be a good actor takes a great degree of health, yet one acts as a result of certain deprivations in their life. In order to act, you have to be open, receptive, sensitive and intuitive enough to get what another person is saying. That's a fabulous model for living."

Filmography

Death Wish (Par, 1974)
California Split (Col, 1974)
Nashville (Par, 1975)
Next Stop, Greenwich Village (20th–Fox, 1976)
Special Delivery (AIP, 1976)
St. Ives (WB, 1976)
Annie Hall (UA, 1977)
Between the Lines (Midwest Films, 1977)
The Sentinel (Univ, 1977)
Remember My Name (Lagoon, 1978)
Invasion of the Body Snatchers (UA, 1978)
Thank God It's Friday (Col, 1978)
The Legend of Sleepy Hollow (NBC-TV, 10/31/80)
Threshold (Can, 1981)
Rehearsal for Murder (CBS-TV, 5/26/82)
The Big Chill (Col, 1983)
The Right Stuff (WB, 1983)
Ernie Kovacs: Between the Laughter (ABC-TV, 5/14/84)
The Adventures of Buckaroo Banzai: Across the 8th Dimension (20th–Fox, 1984)

Into the Night (Univ, 1985)
Silverado (Col, 1985)
Transylvania 6-5000 (New World, 1985)
The Fly (20th–Fox, 1986)
The Race for the Double Helix [Life Force] (Arts & Entertainment–Cable, 9/14/87) [made for British TV]
Beyond Therapy (New World, 1987)
Vibes (Col, 1988)
Earth Girls Are Easy (Vestron/De Laurentiis Entertainment Group, 1988)
The Tall Guy (Miramax, 1989)
Framed (HBO–Cable, 6/24/90)
Mr. Frost (Triumph Releasing, 1990)
Twisted Obsession [El Sueño del Mono Loco/ The Crazy Monkey's Dream/The Mad Monkey] (Ive Films, 1990)

Future Releases

The Favor, the Watch and the Very Big Fish (1991)

Television Series

Tenspeed and Brown Shoe (ABC, 1980)

Broadway Plays

Two Gentlemen of Verona (1971) (musical adaptation)

The Moony Shapiro Songbook (1981)

JOHN GOODMAN

"I used to get a kick out of watching people, but now I'm the one who is stared and pointed at."—*Philadelphia Inquirer*, January 15, 1989

IN A REMARKABLY SHORT TIME IN THE LATE 1980s THIS REGULAR TYPE of guy who happens to carry extra poundage on his 6' 3" frame became one of the entertainment industry's hottest actors. Audiences relate to him because he is an average, blue collar-looking American who would probably turn his back on quiche and caviar in favor of meat and potatoes. Sally Field, a co-star in PUNCHLINE (1988), was one of the first to call him "a great big sexy man." *USA Weekend* soon proclaimed him to be "The Sexiest Man Alive" and *People* magazine declared that Goodman was "the sexiest big guy." John Goodman views all of this as "just too cute," much preferring to be liked because he epitomizes the guy next door—the playful guy who makes fun of himself by mugging in home movies or dancing around the kitchen in a display of happiness. "I'm a grunt," he admits freely, "I'm a character actor." However, unlike heavyset screen predecessors such as Sydney Greenstreet or Burl Ives, this guy is a lovable, huggable cherub. Unlike his contemporary John Candy, John Goodman is truly *cute*.

John Goodman was born on Friday, June 20, 1952, in Affton, Missouri, a suburb of St. Louis, to letter carrier Leslie Goodman and his wife, Virginia. A brother, Leslie, Jr., was twelve years older; a sister, Betty, was born later. Shortly before John's second birthday, his father died of a heart attack, leaving Virginia pregnant with Betty and in full support of the children. She found a job as a drugstore clerk while Leslie, Jr., who took a part-time job after school, soon became a father figure to his younger brother and sister. John was not an exceptional student, but he liked football and spent a good deal of his teen years with his buddies driving around St. Louis pursuing girls. Big-boned and heavyset, he was the class clown, "always goofing around trying to get some laughs and attention." In his senior year in high school he played defensive tackle and offensive guard on the Affton High School football squad, but was not especially gifted athletically. After acting in a few school plays, though, "I thought I was a neat guy." He graduated from high school in June 1970.

John obtained admittance to Southwest Missouri State University at Springfield on a limited athletic scholarship. But when he failed to take a required scholastic aptitude test, he was disqualified from football. Nevertheless, he remained in school to study speech and theater, although he has admitted, "I majored in beer." A steady ingestion of malt, hops, and junk food led to a further increase in weight, which he tried to level off with crash diets. During his years at SMSU, he nurtured a love for theater. On graduating in 1975 with a bachelor of fine arts degree and a $1,000 gift from his brother, he and a girlfriend went to New York City. He arrived there on August 14, 1975, a "hot, depressing, and scary" day.

His female friend found steady work, while John, unsuccessful in his initial endeavors, made the rounds in search of acting assignments. Out of desperation he took a job as a bouncer at a West Side night spot called Adam's Apple. However, when he was shown "all these cruel ways to beat up guys, like gorging their eyes out," he called in sick the next day and never returned. He involved himself with children's theater work, participated in a few off-off-Broadway plays in walk-on or very small supporting roles, and played Thomas Jefferson in a Springboro, Ohio, dinner theater production of *1776* for a few weeks. Until 1979, he was almost solely dependent on his girlfriend for support, existing mostly on macaroni-and-cheese dinners.

In late 1979 he earned his first role on Broadway as a three-week Christmas season replacement in *Loose Ends*, a serious comedy starring Kevin Kline, a fellow Missourian. Kline introduced Goodman to a bar on Manhattan's Upper West Side called Cafe Central, an actors' hang-out. There John became acquainted with Dennis Quaid and Bruce Willis, performers also "between assignments," who became his constant drinking buddies. During this time his weight ballooned. Professionally, he did several television commercials (for Coors beer, Crest toothpaste, and 7-Up). Although the pay was good, he did not view commercials as serious work, nor did he go out of his way to obtain such assignments. When called for a commercial, he would arrive with a hangover and/or nonchalant behavior, but would get the job anyway. His break from commercials—"which I *hated*"— and from Cafe Central came when he signed a contract to go on a road tour of *The Robber Bridegroom*. This engagement led in turn to supporting roles in four 1983 movies, as well as a television miniseries. The first film, for ABC-TV, was THE FACE OF RAGE (March 20, 1983), starring Dianne Wiest as a rape victim. This outing was followed by EDDIE MACON'S RUN for Universal, THE SURVIVORS at Columbia, a role in the six-hour, three-part TV miniseries "Chiefs," and the fifth-billed part of Raymond in HEART OF STEEL (ABC-TV, December 4, 1983), a drama about steelworkers caught in a plant shutdown that starred Peter Strauss.

Goodman was a frustrated coach in the puerile comedy REVENGE OF THE NERDS (1984), had one of those "look quick or you'll miss him" parts in the slimy C.H.U.D. ("Cannibalistic Humanoid Underground Dwellers") (1984), and was seen briefly in MARIA'S LOVERS (1985). Then he was cast by the American Repertory Theatre of Cambridge, Massachusetts, in *Big River*. Based on Mark Twain's *The Adventures of Huckleberry Finn*, *Big River*, after its regional premiere, opened on Broadway at the Eugene O'Neill Theatre on April 25, 1985, during a theatrical season in which only seven new musicals had opened, four of which had closed by June when the thirty-ninth annual Tony Awards were presented. Nominated for ten awards, *Big River* won seven, and it became the hottest ticket on Broadway despite its earlier lukewarm reviews. John had the role of Pap, Huck Finn's boozed-up father, who sings the anti-authority anthem "Guv'ment." During the time that *Big River* was enjoying Broadway popularity, John was seen on theatrical screens in the featured role of Otis, the big, rowdy buddy to Ed Harris in SWEET DREAMS (1985), the biography of country-western songstress Patsy Cline.

John left the cast of *Big River* to accept David Byrne's offer of the top-billed role in Warner Bros.'s TRUE STORIES (1986) as a lonely lovelorn Texan turning to personal ads for a companion. *Variety* characterized Goodman as a "loveable 'dancing bear' of a man" and noted that he and the cast (which included Swoosie Kurtz and Spalding Gray) "turn in affecting and fun turns that help to distract from the film's lack of narrative depth."

In March 1987 Goodman was seen on theater screens in two diverse productions. He was an escaped convict drenched in mud in RAISING ARIZONA, called a "comic joy ride" by *TV Guide* magazine. In the second film, BURGLAR, he was a police detective trailing a cat burglar (Whoopi Goldberg); *People* magazine observed that "nobody gets much funny material." A few months later, in August, he was reunited with his pal from the New York City days, Dennis Quaid, now a major film star, in support as a crooked cop in the suspenseful THE BIG EASY, appropriately filmed in New Orleans.

Although John had by now appeared in a total of thirteen theatrical and television films, most people were unable to identify him by name. Like M. Emmet Walsh, he was seen and generally applauded, but was merely referred to as "that big guy." Anonymity had its advantages, however, when he escaped press coverage for late-hour partying on Los Angeles city streets with his buddy Bruce Willis. During the summer of 1987, while on stage in Los Angeles in the supporting role of Enobarbus, a burly lieutenant, in *Antony and Cleopatra*, he was spotted by an ABC-TV producer as a possible contender for the male

Michael O'Neill, Al Pacino, and **John Goodman** in SEA OF LOVE (1989).

lead in a new sitcom series in preparation for the 1988–1989 season. He read for the part, instinctively knowing afterward that he had it in his pocket. Meanwhile, he was among the cast of "After Midnight," an hour-long pilot shown on ABC-TV on April 30, 1988, which became the genesis for the series "Midnight Caller."

"Roseanne," co-starring bulky stand-up comic Roseanne Barr in the title role, premiered on October 18, 1988, with John as her husband, Dan Conner, a flannel-shirt–clad, sometimes unemployed contractor and father of three. *Variety* judged that the new program "has a slobby, sarcastic point of view that's all its own" and that "One of the major plusses of the show is John Goodman—absolutely terrific as her husband." By its fourth week, the thirty-minute series had risen to the #2 spot in the Nielsen ratings, giving the long-popular "The Cosby Show" on NBC-TV a run for its money. "I don't know why people are tuning in," Goodman said unassumingly; "maybe it's just to see two fat people yelling at each other." Of her co-star, the not-easily-pleased Barr acknowledged, "John is a lot of fun. He puts us on the floor."

Meanwhile, on the big screen, Goodman was seen in support of a group of stand-up comics (Richard Lewis, Louie Anderson, Richard Belzer, Franklyn Ajaye) in THE WRONG GUYS (1988), a forgettable, stupid picture. However, he almost stole the show as Sally Field's confused insurance salesman spouse in PUNCHLINE (1988). He had earlier returned to Louisiana, to Baton Rouge, for the fourth-billed role of Dennis Quaid's gridiron buddy-turned-compulsive gambler in the lovely-to-look-at but overlong EVERYBODY'S ALL-AMERICAN (1988). *Empire* magazine credited John with being "in riveting form," while longtime friend Quaid revealed that he "is intense when he works." Quaid added, "We're good friends, but when he's doing a take, I don't want to be within ten feet of him, because there's a volcano bubbling down there . . . he gets very inside himself; he really shrinks away from other people, but when the cameras roll he's there a hundred percent." During location shooting, John met Anna Elizabeth Hartzog, a fine arts student at Louisiana State University. After returning to Los Angeles, he flew back to see her at regular intervals although he was terrified of flying "unless I've had a couple of belts."

By January 1989, all was not serene on the set of "Roseanne." Barr had had the show's creator and original executive producer, Matt Williams, fired, and then asked for the removal of his successor, Jeff Harris. "When I've freaked over stuff with the show," Barr said, "John has helped me out, and I've helped him. . . . Who knows what's going to happen?" Soon thereafter, the director, Ellen Falcon, left the show, and Barr separated from her husband (Bill Pentland) and was charged with allegedly paying $50 to have a bothersome photographer beaten up. All of this provided ample fodder for the tabloids, but John's comment was, "It's none of my business. I don't get involved." Months later, Barr was reportedly secretly arguing with the ABC network over replacing John in his $30,000-per-week job with her soon-to-be husband, Tom Arnold. This might have been inspired by jealousy on her part because she was ignored by the Academy of Television Arts and Sciences and the Hollywood Foreign Press Association while John was nominated for both an Emmy and a Golden Globe Award, although he failed to win in either contest. Despite the bizarre publicity generated by Barr, "Roseanne" was the #1 show for the week ending October 29, 1989, with a rating of 24.9, and ranked #1 overall for the season.

The year 1989 was a very busy one for John Goodman. In September he was teamed with Al Pacino and Ellen Barkin as the former's New York police detective sidekick in SEA OF LOVE, in which, according to *Drama-Logue*, he "is an unqualified delight" due to his "genial demeanor and perfect timing." Eight weeks after its release, the action drama had earned $53 million at the domestic box office. In October, on his mother's birthday, John was married at the St. Charles Avenue Presbyterian Church in New Orleans to Anna Elizabeth "Annabeth" Hartzog. He was thirty-seven; she was twenty-one. "John makes me laugh all the time," the bride said. "This is the first time I've been in love." John quipped that she was simply looking "for a gravy train." Eager to pick on someone new, the supermarket tabloids chose John, undoubtedly because of his close professional association with controversial Roseanne Barr. One of the publications ran a story with his byline headed "My Wonderful Wacky Wedding." "The last time I used 'wacky' in a sentence," he said in refuting the article, "I was in the sixth grade." As for the implication that he had written the piece, he said, "I haven't received a check for my efforts."

At a salary of $750,000, Goodman traveled to deforested acreage in Libby, Montana, to co-star as Richard Dreyfuss's firefighting buddy Al in ALWAYS (1989), a Steven Spielberg remake of A GUY NAMED JOE (1943), in which Ward Bond had played Al. Despite the generally unfavorable comparisons to its source, ALWAYS grossed $41,843,630 in fourteen weeks at the domestic box office. On December 2, 1989, Goodman served as host of NBC-TV's long-running "Saturday Night Live."

STELLA (1990), another updated remake, gave John second billing to Bette Midler in the role of Ed Munn, her drunken bartender admirer. *Variety* found him to be more effective than she was in his characterization and continued that John, "throwing in his role in ALWAYS, has the distinction in recent months of carving out memorable performances in two otherwise-lame remakes." Despite such remarks about the sappy feature, STELLA grossed $20,062,347 in its first thirteen weeks of domestic release.

In New Orleans for Mardi Gras in February 1990, John and Dennis Quaid reigned over two of the most popular parades, and John was grand marshal of the Krewe of Endymion on February 24. John's per-movie salary was rumored to be $1 million after his participation in three box-office hits. However, he told the *Los Angeles Times*, "For me, the reward is the work itself, and getting to work with the best people who love it as much as you do. And then if you're successful, that's gravy . . . on second thought, that's chicken-fried steak with gravy!" At the same time, he swore he was going to diet to lose at least seventy pounds.

On March 10, 1990, at the fourth annual American Comedy Awards in Los Angeles, he was named the funniest male in a TV series. At the ceremonies, televised on ABC-TV (March 19, 1990), Roseanne Barr lost the funniest female honor to Tracey Ullman, star of her own Fox Broadcasting show. At Los Angeles's popular China Club on April 2, 1990, John "wowed the crowd" (*Hollywood Reporter*) by performing a blues song with Bruce Willis, Sheila E., and Taylor Dayne.

In release July 18, 1990, was "A Thrill-Omedy!" entitled ARACHNOPHOBIA, described by Joel Siegel of ABC-TV as "JAWS With Legs." An update of the 1950s monster-film genre, it concerns a small town doctor (Jeff Daniels) with a deadly fear of spiders. A poisonous variety from South America finds its way into his backyard and mates with a native American spider. As a result, thousands of baby spiders hatch in the doctor's garage. Called to the scene is the local bugbuster/exterminator (John) who, in a bit of overacting, attacks the unpleasant spiders with spray guns holstered to his belt like Old-West six-shooters. *Rolling Stone* magazine credited John with being "hilarious," but the *Los Angeles Times* recorded that his "presence very nearly pulls the picture out of whack." Despite its several shortcomings, ARACHNOPHOBIA grossed over $52.8 million in nineteen weeks of domestic distribution.

"They don't usually hire great big fat guys to do leading men," Goodman said in 1990. However, this statement was soon proved incorrect when he was selected to star as KING RALPH (1991). The only living, but distant, relative of a royal family that was electrocuted while posing for a family photograph, Ralph, a former lounge lizard, takes the throne of England. No sooner had he completed filming this project in London than he went to work in BARTON FINK (1991), another comedy, in which he plays a traveling salesman. This venture was produced by his friends Ethan and Joel Coen, who had cast him previously in RAISING ARIZONA. Meanwhile, on September 18, 1990, he returned as co-star of "Roseanne" for its third season. *Daily Variety* reported, "John Goodman remains the spine of the show, which is simplicity in itself: a sitcom that speaks to blue-collar folk, with better-than-average writing and strong personalities."

On December 2, 1990, Goodman hosted the TBS–Cable special "Tom & Jerry's 50th Bash," a tribute to the enduring cartoon series. Enthused Rick Sherwood (*Hollywood Reporter*), "John Goodman . . . is a perfect choice to tie the package together. He mugs his way through the show, providing historical fact and perspective, re-enacting some of the schtick that animators borrowed from vaudeville, blending a slapstick humor and apparent love for the colorful duo. Goodman seems the incarnation of Lou Costello and Larry of the Three Stooges—a kind of a cartoon-like character unto himself."

When KING RALPH opened in mid-February 1991, Michael Wilmington (*Los Angeles Times*) judged the comedy "a majestic misfire for Goodman," reasoning that "KING RALPH . . . is a movie about a lovable boor at a royal tea party. But there's no real boorishness to it, little royalty and not much love. . . . It's an empty, puffed-up blob of a comedy, so devoid of humor that when star John Goodman does his show-stopper—a rousing, belly-flop-on-the-piano rendition of Little Richard's 'Good Golly, Miss Molly'—it's a blessed but only temporary relief." Nevertheless, in its first six weeks of domestic distribution, KING RALPH grossed a strong $28,930,605 based on the marquee allure of star Goodman.

Forthcoming for John is perhaps the co-starring role of Barney Rubble in THE FLINTSTONES (1992), a "real-people movie version" produced by Steven Spielberg, and definitely BABE (1992), a Universal movie based on Robert Creamer's book about Babe Ruth, the immortal big league baseball player. Lawrence Lyttle, producer of the latter project, felt that John was a perfect fit for the role of the man who "was bigger than baseball, a man with a voracious appetite for food, for women and for hitting home runs."

Now residing in a Hollywood Hills home, John and his wife became parents of Molly Evangeline, born August 31, 1990, at Cedars-Sinai Medical Center. Having risen from playing the hero's sidekick to being a character star, he remains modest about the fulsome praise he regularly receives. (*Time* magazine lauded him as having "the nimble, dancer-like grace of such portly clowns as Oliver Hardy and Jackie Gleason, anchored by a straight-from-the-heartland believability.") The insecure part of Goodman fantasizes that his now stable life could be shaken if "I fall hopelessly out of fashion and have to work in a carnival." Laughingly he adds, "Ten years ago, I was doing regional theater in Baltimore, and 10 years from now I'll probably be back there. Gladly. Five years from now, I could be a trivia question." At one point in 1990, rumors were rampant that the temperamental Roseanne Barr might leave her TV series, thus leaving the way open for John to continue alone in a re-named replacement show. "I would not be interested in carrying on alone," he told columnist Marilyn Beck. On the other hand, his "Roseanne" contract concludes at the end of the 1990–1991 season, and there is speculation that if he does not return, Barr's real-life husband, comedian Tom Arnold, might replace Goodman in the sitcom. Meanwhile, Goodman (who usually wears a size 54 suit) continues to battle with his weight, careful not to lose too much and thereby disappoint his fans and talent agents.

Filmography

The Face of Rage (ABC-TV, 3/20/83)
Heart of Steel (ABC-TV, 12/4/83)
Eddie Macon's Run (Univ, 1983)
The Survivors (Col, 1983)
C.H.U.D. (New World, 1984)
Revenge of the Nerds (20th–Fox, 1984)
Maria's Lovers (Cannon, 1985)
Sweet Dreams (Tri-Star, 1985)
True Stories (WB, 1986)
Raising Arizona (20th–Fox, 1987)
Burglar (WB, 1987)

The Big Easy (Col, 1987)
The Wrong Guys (New World, 1988)
Punchline (Col, 1988)
Everybody's All-American (WB, 1988)
Sea of Love (Univ, 1989)
Always (Univ, 1989)
Stella (BV, 1990)
Arachnophobia (BV, 1990)
King Ralph (Univ, 1991)
Barton Fink (20th–Fox, 1991)

Television Series

Chiefs (CBS, 11/13/83; 11/15/83; 11/16/83)
   [miniseries]

Roseanne (ABC, 1988–)

Broadway Plays

Loose Ends (1979) (replacement)

Big River (1985)

Album Discography

Big River (MCA MCAD-6147) [OC]

MELANIE GRIFFITH

"After working for 15 years then winning a Golden Globe and being nominated for an Academy Award, getting back with Don, getting married and having a baby—it's been too good to be true."
—*The Cable Guide* magazine, March 1990

IF THERE IS A "MELANIE GRIFFITH TYPE OF ROLE," IT IS THE SEEMINGLY defenseless, vulnerable heroine you want to hug reassuringly, but in whose innate, intelligent strength you bask. She is so convincing in such characterizations that they must reflect to some extent the complicated make-up of the actress herself. As such, the 5' 9" Melanie has been compared with similar-natured screen personalities: Jean Harlow, Judy Holliday, Jean Arthur, Marilyn Monroe. After playing occasional nymphet or ditsy-blonde roles and acquiring a reputation throughout Hollywood as a flaky, irresponsible actress with a hearty appetite for men, drugs, and alcohol, she was an "overnight sensation," clean of chemical and alcohol dependency, in one of the most honored performances of 1988. Bolstered by love and motherhood, the once indefatigable party girl has learned to place the cares of others above herself. She of the little-girl voice and off-balance face, who sometimes seemed such a kid, has also learned to ignore requests for nudity on camera, finding that smoldering physical intentions can be communicated just as easily through the eyes.

Born in New York City on Friday, August 9, 1957, Melanie is the daughter of Peter Griffith, real estate developer, and Nathalie Hedren, a statuesque blonde model who, as Tippi Hedren, would later be promoted by movie director Alfred Hitchcock as a replacement for filmdom's Grace Kelly (who had retired to become princess of the principality of Monaco). The Griffiths separated when their daughter was two years old, divorcing a year later. "I never saw them together," Melanie would remember years later. Hedren moved to Los Angeles in 1961 to pursue a career in TV modeling, married producer Noel Marshall, and raised her daughter on a suburban ranch, where Melanie was later joined by two half-siblings, Tracy and Clay. Melanie once described her early days as those of a typical movie industry offspring, appearing with her mother in Ivory Snow ads and visiting Universal movie sets while Tippi emoted in THE BIRDS (1963), under Hitchcock's direction. When Tippi refused her mentor's physical advances, he cunningly sabotaged his own discovery's career by making her look especially bad in their next project, MARNIE (1964).

In 1970 the entire Marshall clan, including Noel's brothers, went to Africa to make a film centered around the wild animals of the bush. There Tippi become personally involved in their plight, taking several back home with her to California. At age thirteen, Melanie had her own pet lion, named Casey, who would live to a ripe old age, dying in 1987. At the Marshall ranch over the course of several years there were 150 animals, ranging from lions and cougars to llamas. The film, which would have been Melanie's debut had it not been delayed in production by flood, fire, epidemic, and injury, ultimately cost $17 million. ROAR was not released until 1981.

While working as an extra in THE HARRAD EXPERIMENT (1973), Melanie fell madly in love with Don Johnson, eight years her senior. A non-Catholic student at a Catholic high school in the Los Angeles area at the time, she was expelled from the school for rebelliously questioning the religion. In 1974 she moved off the ranch and into a house rented by Don Johnson in the Laurel Canyon area. Johnson was well known for his sexual conquests as well as for his penchant for drugs and alcohol. She did not share the house long with Johnson, because the following year he married another woman, but in the interim he arranged an interview for her which she thought was about a potential modeling job. However, it was actually a reading for a role in NIGHT MOVES (1975), as a boy-crazy Hollywood child. In this film, at the age of seventeen, she was one of the youngest women ever to be photographed topless. Essentially playing herself, she at first detested movie making, but later learned to enjoy the process. Listed everywhere as her official screen debut, NIGHT MOVES was released in June 1975, a month *after* her screen job as an amoral beauty contestant, Miss Simi Valley, in SMILE (1975). In July she was seen in the sixth-billed part of Schuyler in THE DROWNING POOL (1975), starring Paul Newman, who encouraged her to take acting lessons with the famed coach Stella Adler in New York City. Adler, however, scared the somewhat bashful novice, who scurried back to the West Coast.

On a spring morning in 1976, she telephoned Don Johnson, who had just said goodbye to his overnight guest, Marjorie Wallace, the ex–Miss World. During their phone conversation they decided to get married. They flew to Las Vegas where they exchanged vows at 11:00 a.m. at the Silver Bell chapel with their cab driver as a witness. Immediately following the hasty nuptials, Melanie lowered her jeans while a tattoo artist decorated her left buttock with a pear, her nickname for the man she loved. The couple later posed for *Playboy* magazine where the artwork was revealed to readers.

While the marriage was shaky at best, she was a member of the large cast of "Once an Eagle," a nine-hour NBC-TV miniseries that began on December 2, 1976. Also acting in this saga of two contrasting soldiers from 1918 to World War II were Amy Irving, who became a friend, and Patti D'Arbanville, who would bear Don Johnson's child in 1982. Melanie had earlier journeyed to Israel to co-star in THE GARDEN (1977), a poetic fantasy. *Variety* complimented Griffith for playing "gracefully" her role as an angel-like creature. Melanie joined other movie star offspring such as Desi Arnaz, Jr., Robert Carradine, and Anne Lockhart in JOYRIDE (1977), and supported upcoming Robby Benson and Annette O'Toole in ONE ON ONE (1977) as a hitchhiker. For ABC-TV's "Starsky and Hutch" she did an episode shown on January 7, 1978; played the Girl in Hotel Room in the CBS-TV movie DADDY, I DON'T LIKE THIS (July 12, 1978); and in October 1978 became a recurring character—a cub reporter—in the ABC-TV Saturday night sitcom "Carter Country." She was fired from the series prior to its final telecast on August 23, 1979. On December 6, 1978, on NBC-TV she had a subordinate role in STEEL COWBOY, a forgettable movie starring James Brolin as a ranch trucker involved with rustled cattle.

With her marriage to Johnson ending in divorce in 1977, Melanie had already become well known for her alcohol and cocaine consumption, although she claimed that she used neither while at work. On an evening in 1980, while emerging drunk from Le Dome, a trendy Los Angeles night spot, she was struck by an equally inebriated motorist. The collision threw her twenty feet into the street. Knocked unconscious, she sustained a broken leg and arm, several hairline fractures, and a concussion. For two months she had to walk with crutches, and joined Alcoholics Anonymous during this period. However, when the crutches were finally discarded, so were her good intentions of remaining sober.

In January 1981 she was seen on a few movie screens in a dumb comedy, UNDER-GROUND ACES, that substituted profanity and nudity for a script. However, she had her best part to date in NBC-TV's THE STAR MAKER (May 11 and 12, 1981) as a victim of the "casting couch." A week later, on May 20, 1981, she was one of five women who join the ranks in SHE'S IN THE ARMY NOW, an ABC-TV pilot telefeature that did not evolve into a series. One thing she gained from this experience was a new lover, Steven "Rocky" Bauer, who was also in the film. GOLDEN GATE (September 25, 1981), an ABC-TV pilot for a prime-time soap opera about a publishing empire, found her seventh-billed as Karen.

In May 1982 she married Steven Bauer, who had persuaded her to again attempt acting sessions with Stella Adler. This second round of lessons proved much more successful, for she believed that Adler now liked her. Early in 1984, knowing that director Brian De Palma favored porn star Annette Havens for the character of Holly Body, a porno queen with a brain, in the planned BODY DOUBLE (1984), Melanie kept pestering him until he finally gave the role to her. Semi-clad, although several weeks pregnant, she had the full attention of audience members when she said, in the voice that was to become so familiar, "I do not do animal acts. I do not do S&M or any variations of that particular bent." The feature, with ideas generously borrowed from Hitchcock's REAR WINDOW (1954), has become a cult classic on home video.

On August 22, 1984, she gave birth to son Alexander. She would tell US magazine in 1989, "Having a child is the most amazing thing a woman can go through. It's like, 'Whoa! This is not about me.'" In early 1985 she was seen as a stripper in a sordid accounting of Manhattan's low life, FEAR CITY. For the May 5, 1985, telecast of ALFRED HITCHCOCK PRESENTS, NBC-TV recruited two of the great man's blondes, Kim Novak and Tippi Hedren, to appear along with John Huston, Melanie, and Steven Bauer in a new version of the 1960 creation "Man from the South," one of the telefilm's three episodes. Soon afterwards, Melanie and Bauer separated and divorced amicably in 1986. "For both of us," he has said, "it was really like going through an intense course in life."

The first motion picture role ever to be offered to her as a first choice was that of the marvelously unpredictable creature known alternately as Lulu and Audrey in Jonathan Demme's SOMETHING WILD (1986). She is the flamboyant troublemaker who kidnaps and teaches a hapless corporate figure (Jeff Daniels) sexual things he has never imagined. Starting as a fun comedy, the movie successfully switches gears in the hands of the underrated Ray Liotta as a murderous ex-husband. The video version remains a very popular rental item. "By Hooker, By Crook," the March 20, 1987, episode of NBC-TV's "Miami Vice," was directed by its star, Don Johnson, with Melanie cast as a brothel madam. A rekindling of their love occurred during the shooting, but it was short-lived, although Melanie maintained that Don Johnson was still the only man for her.

During 1988 Melanie was first seen with punk red hair as a real woman among robotic love slaves in CHERRY 2000, which quickly went into videocassette format and remains a cable TV favorite. In THE MILAGRO BEANFIELD WAR, shot on location in New Mexico in late August 1986 amid poor weather and changing seasons that delayed completion of the production, she had a supporting role as Flossie Devine. She took the assignment for the satisfaction of working with producer/director Robert Redford. STORMY MONDAY (1988), filmed in Newcastle, England, was a sexy, wobbly, dark look at American business shenanigans abroad with impressive performances from its leads (Melanie, Tommy Lee Jones, and Sting). The *Hollywood Reporter* extolled Melanie: "Speaking softly and doling out some manipulative little-girl mannerisms, Griffith is splendidly tough and vulnerable."

For the role of Tess McGill, a corporate Manhattan secretary with abundant brain power, Melanie auditioned and interviewed again and again in 1987 until she got what she wanted. A technical adviser on WORKING GIRL (1988) was Liam Dalton, a young vice president with a Wall Street firm and reportedly the inspiration for the Michael Douglas character in WALL STREET (1987). In researching her role, she and Dalton became live-in lovers for a year. In May 1988, upon completion of her scenes for the picture and at the urging of Don Johnson (who had done the same for himself in 1983), she volunteered to enter the drug/alcohol rehabilitation program at the Hazelden Foundation at Center City, Minnesota, a facility specializing in treating chemical dependency. Supported by regular telephone contact with Johnson, she left the foundation a month later with a clean bill of health. "I think we fell in love again on the phone," she explained, and went to Florida to live with Johnson, who was still starring in "Miami Vice." In September she presented the Best New Artist Video Award to Guns N' Roses at MTV's Video Awards and on December 17, 1988, while she was guest-hosting TV's "Saturday Night Live," John-

Melanie Griffith in WORKING GIRL (1988).

son surprised her on the air with a four-carat emerald-cut engagement ring. On December 26, they celebrated with an engagement party well attended by celebrities at his multi-million-dollar Aspen, Colorado, ranch.

Meanwhile, with WORKING GIRL in nationwide release during Christmas week 1988, Melanie Griffith became a top movie star. Even *The New Yorker* magazine, although not favoring the Mike Nichols–directed comedy, credited her as "very appealing" and with carrying "what there is of the picture." Although she was third-billed, after Sigourney Weaver, for initial box-office attention, but with her name still above the title, Melanie's role is much larger and more demanding than Weaver's. Reportedly not on friendly terms, the two actresses spoke well of one another in public, with Weaver saying, "She seemed so fragile, so insecure. I didn't immediately realize what a powerhouse she really was." Melanie was awarded a Golden Globe Award as Best Actress, as well as an Oscar nomination in the same category, while Weaver received a Best Supporting Actress nod. Neither won, but the popular movie earned $28.6 million in domestic film rentals paid to the distributor. On April 16, 1990, a short-lived NBC-TV series premiered with brunette Sandra Bullock as the "Working Girl."

After appearing with her mother in the Turner Broadcasting cable tribute to Mother's Day, "Superstars and Their Moms" (May 8, 1989), Melanie went to Aspen to prepare for her wedding on June 26. This time wearing white, although pregnant, she again became the bride of Don Johnson; it was her third time at the altar, his fourth. Due to pregnancy, she passed on the star role in THE GRIFTERS (1990), which went to Annette Bening. On October 4, 1989, at 2:49 p.m. at Brackenridge Hospital in Austin, Texas, near the film site of Johnson's THE HOT SPOT (1990), Melanie gave birth to a daughter, who was named Dakota Mayi in honor of a former Indian chief and a celebrated guru from India.

She appeared in a cameo role as a prostitute in Elaine May's IN THE SPIRIT (1990), and on April 17, 1990, co-hosted the AIDS benefit "That's What Friends Are For" on CBS-TV. In the spring of 1990, Melanie and Don were featured together in magazine advertisements for Revlon cosmetics. For HBO–Cable on August 19, 1990, she co-starred with James Woods in one of three half-hour stories in WOMEN AND MEN: STORIES OF SEDUCTION. Their episode, "Hills Like White Elephants," adapted from an Ernest Hemingway tale and set in Africa, was described by *Time* magazine as "a haunting brief encounter frozen in time by good acting and writing." With Matthew Modine as her husband in PACIFIC HEIGHTS (1990), she was menaced by their maniacal tenant (Michael Keaton). Filmed in hilly San Francisco, but not in the city's Pacific Heights district (rather, in Potrero Hill), pre-release advertisements warned: "They were the perfect couple, buying the perfect house. Until a perfect stranger moved into their lives." The *Hollywood Reporter* pinpointed the film's structural problem: "[the] script pays homage to the genre conventions of both horror and thriller without firmly staking a claim in either terrain. The house is not haunted nor is the tenant the Zodiac killer, but the movie tries to hint otherwise." The trade paper added, "Griffith at least gets to play the one character who evolves over the course of the movie. The way she subtly handles the woman's gradual realization of what they're up against shows what a gifted actress can do with even a modestly written role." Peter Rainer (*Los Angeles Times*) observed, "Melanie Griffith certainly knows how to work up a full-scale characterization out of dribs and drabs. She's an A actress with a knack for bringing out the resonance in B material." During its first week of domestic release, PACIFIC HEIGHTS grossed a strong $14,038,549, going on to earn $27,892,883 in seven weeks at the box office. Tippi Hedren took a small part (as Michael Keaton's next intended victim) in that psychological thriller, but turned down a similar cameo-type role in THE BONFIRE OF THE VANITIES (1990), directed by Brian De Palma, in which Melanie had the lead female role. SHINING THROUGH (forthcoming, 1992), produced for $25 million by Dolly Parton's movie company, featured Melanie as an ordinary secretary spying on the Nazis during World War II. The film co-starred Michael Douglas and Liam Neeson. Melanie and Don Johnson finally have opportunity to work together on screen in PARADISE (1991), a domestic drama.

In mid-1990, one supermarket tabloid had Don Johnson telling a friend, "When two actors are married, it's difficult. There's always friction, especially when one is doing better than the other. But, I'm not going to be pushed around by anyone—especially not a wife." However, Melanie does not seem the type to push him around, particularly when her career is now going better than his. She confided to *Vanity Fair* magazine that she considers them "the most fortunate people around." Obviously entranced with her spouse, she admitted: "Don was my first love and he's still my love—my best friend, my man, my partner. I've never had that ease, that specialness, with anyone else. And, we *both* feel that way, and it just keeps getting better and better."

Filmography

The Harrad Experiment (Cinerama, 1973)
Night Moves (WB, 1975)
Smile (UA, 1975)
The Drowning Pool (WB, 1975)
The Garden (Israeli, 1977)
Joyride (AIP, 1977)
One on One (WB, 1977)
Daddy, I Don't Like This (CBS-TV, 7/12/78)
Steel Cowboy (NBC-TV, 12/6/78)
The Star Maker (NBC-TV, 5/11/81–5/12/81)
She's in the Army Now (ABC-TV, 5/20/81)
Golden Gate (ABC-TV, 9/25/81)
Roar (Alpha/Filmways, 1981) [made in 1970]
Underground Aces (Filmways, 1981)
Body Double (Col, 1984)
Fear City (Zupnik-Curtis, 1985)
Alfred Hitchcock Presents (NBC-TV, 5/5/85)

[episode "Man from the South"]
Something Wild (Orion, 1986)
The Milagro Beanfield War (Univ, 1988)
Cherry 2000 (Orion, 1988)
Stormy Monday (Atlantic, 1988)
Working Girl (20th–Fox, 1988)
Women and Men: Stories of Seduction
    [episode "Hills Like White Elephants"]
    (HBO–Cable, 8/19/90)
In the Spirit (Castle Hill, 1990)
Pacific Heights (20th–Fox, 1990)
The Bonfire of the Vanities (WB, 1990)
Paradise (BV, 1991)

Future Releases

Shining Through (20th–Fox, 1991)

Television Series

Once an Eagle (NBC, 12/2/76; 12/9/76;
   12/16/76; 12/23/76; 12/30/76; 1/6/77;
   1/13/77) [miniseries]

Carter Country (ABC, 1978–79)

Album Discography

Can't Stop the Music (Casablanca NBLP-7220)
   [ST]

STEVE GUTTENBERG

"If you want it, really want it, you'll find a way to do it. My way was to run and climb and jump and scrape, do anything to meet people who might help."   —*New York Post*, January 15, 1987

A WRITER FOR THE *NEW YORK DAILY NEWS* IN 1978 LAMENTED THAT Steve Guttenberg was "brash, boastful, swaggering, sometimes obnoxious." At that time, Guttenberg referred to himself as "the Gucci of young actors" and "the best actor of my age in the world." A decade later, given experience mixed with maturity, he was described by the *Hollywood Reporter* as a "cute, kind, nice guy, soft-spoken," who revealed that "being Mr. Nice Guy has gotten me where I am today." His earlier behavior was explained with "I was confident, not cocky."

Whatever his methods, Steve Guttenberg rose from the rubble of early cinematic box-office bombs to become, by the late 1980s, one of the movie industry's most likable and bankable young actors, whose feature films have collectively grossed $750 million. Simultaneously, he transformed himself from a round-faced, round-bodied man who would not dream of taking off his shirt on camera to a trim, solid actor who was seen performing shirtless as often as Gregory Harrison. After years of vacillating between acting and dentistry, his fate was sealed with the release of DINER (1982), a sleeper hit that also launched the careers of Mickey Rourke, more the free spirit, and Kevin Bacon, more the thinker.

Steven Guttenberg was born on Sunday, August 24, 1958, in Brooklyn, the first of three children of a middle-class Jewish couple. His father, Jerome Stanley Guttenberg, a rookie cop, continued his off-duty education to obtain credentials as an electrical engineer and then moved his family to Massapequa, Long Island. His mother, Ann Iris Newman Guttenberg, was a surgical assistant. Growing up in a home that "leaned more toward television than books," Steve, the only son, was nevertheless expected to become a man of medicine, preferably a surgeon. Family friend Mike Bell, whose voice was heard in Parkay margarine commercials, helped Steve, at age sixteen, to obtain a summer job with a Long Island children's community theater which paid him $300 for the season. This was fine with Mr. Guttenberg, who had to agree that the boy should learn the value of working, but he objected strenuously when Steve enrolled at the High School of Performing Arts in Manhattan to concentrate on acting. Steve soon quit, giving the excuse that he had been dismissed because his residence was not within New York City. Returning to his Long Island high school, he graduated in January 1976 at the age of seventeen and then had a "terrible row with my father . . . about not going to college." He left home for the West Coast.

His first job in Los Angeles was at Farrell's Ice Cream Parlor while scouting the various movie studios for a means to slip through their security systems. Paramount was the easiest: he located an unused gymnasium there, rigged a telephone line into it, and made calls to casting agents representing himself as an assistant at Paramount describing the unlimited talents of an actor named Steven Guttenberg. Within two months he had a part in a Kentucky Fried Chicken commercial, which convinced him that "show business would be a piece of cake." A few weeks later he earned small parts in two CBS-TV series, "Doc" and "Police Story," as well as a supporting role in a CBS made-for-television movie, SOMETHING FOR JOEY (April 6, 1977). For ROLLERCOASTER (1977), a thriller set in various amusement parks, Guttenberg was an extra. In a low-budgeted, tasteless Phil Silvers feature, THE CHICKEN CHRONICLES (1977), Steve was third-billed as a high school student, circa 1969. *Variety* noted, "Guttenberg has, on a lower-order scale, the same nervous energy often projected by Tony Roberts."

With his acting résumé now containing legitimate credits, Guttenberg was, he claimed, "busy every hour of the day, but had no family or friends to talk to. It should have been fun, but I was lonely as hell." He returned home, a move undoubtedly designed to appease his parents. He immediately enrolled at the State University of New York at Albany in its dentistry program, which was shorter than the regular medical program. It was not long, however, before he left to study at the Juilliard School of Drama, headed by John Houseman. After appearing in an off-off-Broadway production of *The Lion in Winter*, he abruptly went back to Los Angeles to resume his dentistry studies at the University of California at Los Angeles (UCLA) because "I just couldn't keep telling my parents I was going to be an actor. I couldn't take the crying and the moaning." Reportedly dead serious about becoming a dentist, he was also bold in gaining the attention of TV and movie executives in their offices, in parking lots, doorways, and elsewhere, which proved successful when he obtained the part of the spoiled rich kid, Ludlum, in the NBC-TV thirty-minute pilot "Last Chance," shown on April 21, 1978. His character, Ludlum, was one of the juvenile delinquents working at a dude ranch.

For the filming of THE BOYS FROM BRAZIL (1978) in Portugal, Steven insisted that a dentistry tutor accompany him, a demand that was met. He then won his own TV series, "Billy," which premiered on CBS on February 26, 1979. In this spin-off from the British film BILLY LIAR (1963), he was a nineteen-year-old daydreaming clerk in a mortuary. *Variety* found him "merely acceptable as the young dreamer, with little developed by the script to give him the audience rapport that is vital to a premise of this sort." The sitcom faded on April 28, 1979. He informed Paramount casting agents that he was an excellent tennis player, which led to his gaining the part of a tennis hustler in PLAYERS (1979), a role originally intended for Robert Carradine. After feverish tennis lessons he was believable, although the Ali MacGraw movie was a disaster. He was billed for the first time as "Steve" in the starring role in CBS-TV's TO RACE THE WIND (March 12, 1980), a dramatization of the life of Harold Krents, a blind Harvard Law School student, which had also inspired the play (1969) and film BUTTERFLIES ARE FREE (1972).

CAN'T STOP THE MUSIC (1980), shot in New York City, was a multi-million-dollar musical production intended as a feature film showcase for the then-popular gay-oriented pop group The Village People. With a cast including a bizarre array of personalities, among them Steve, Valerie Perrine, Bruce Jenner, Altovise Davis, and June Havoc, the expensive outing was a gigantic box-office dud. Steve later said of this movie and of PLAYERS, "Sure I've got a few turkeys, everyone has. And it really hurts when a film comes out and it is not accepted by your peers."

By 1980 Guttenberg had abandoned the idea of dentistry and would confess some years later, "I was never actually going to be a dentist." On March 1, 1981, he was third-billed, after Karl Malden and Andrew Stevens, as a 1980 Olympic skater in ABC-TV's MIRACLE ON ICE. During 1981 he was involved in two projects, one for television, which did not succeed, and the other a feature film that was a surprise hit of 1982. For ABC-TV he starred as Roger, the manager of an Atlantic City hotel, in "No Soap, Radio," a thirty-minute sitcom that ran from April 15 through May 13, 1982. Neither the action nor the title made much sense. Also that April, DINER was released; it starred Steve as Eddie, one of a group of Baltimore friends who are in the process of growing up in 1959. *People* magazine termed it "a piercingly intelligent comedy." In this Barry Levinson–directed movie Guttenberg was the virgin who is about to be married, but first puts his bride-to-be through a horrendous football quiz. Several of the other cast members (Mickey Rourke, Kevin Bacon, Ellen Barkin) also went on to stardom.

After this turning-point picture, Steve embarked on a schedule of exercise to slim down for THE MAN WHO WASN'T THERE (1983). The plot required partial nudity in 3-D with Steve appearing as Sam Cooper, a protocol clerk with the U.S. State Department who accidentally stumbles onto a potion that makes people invisible. The movie was a flop. On the other hand, THE DAY AFTER (November 20, 1983) was the most publicized TV movie to that time, as well as a controversial one that received a hefty Nielsen share of 46 percent. The 135-minute ABC-TV movie dealt with the destruction of Lawrence, Kansas, in a nuclear explosion. The large cast was headed by Jason Robards, JoBeth Williams, and Steve.

When Steve signed to star in POLICE ACADEMY (1984), in which he would again remove his shirt, he began a weightlifting regimen to beef up his chest and arms. This episodic comedy about screwball recruits proved a surprisingly commercial bonanza, which by year's end was tallied as 1984's #6 box-office champion, with grosses of $81.2 million. Critics like Roger Ebert (*Chicago Sun-Times*) labeled it "the absolute pits," but obviously ticket buyers didn't care what was written about it, nor did Steve, who had a percentage of the profits and made a good deal of money from it. Warner Bros. quickly reassembled the same cast, plus San Francisco comic Bob Goldthwait as a gang leader, for POLICE ACADEMY 2: THEIR FIRST ASSIGNMENT (1985). *People* magazine wrote, "not many movies these days offer so many amiable, guilt-free guffaws." The picture was another major financial hit. Meanwhile, during the 1984–1985 TV season, Steve starred in a Blake Edwards–produced pilot for NBC entitled "The Ferret." He played a professional musician/amateur inventor whose father (Robert Loggia) is an antiterrorist agent. The concept never got beyond the pilot stage.

COCOON (1985) dealt with residents of a Florida retirement community who are rejuvenated by swimming in a pool containing the cocoons of alien beings. Steve played the owner of a boat that is rented by a crew from outer space. The picture is a joyful mixture of sentiment, optimism, fantasy, and wonderful performances by a cast of veteran performers (including Don Ameche, Hume Cronyn, Wilford Brimley, and Jessica Tandy). COCOON cost an estimated $17.5 million, but grossed $76.1 million in domestic ticket sales, making it the #6 moneymaker of 1985. On the other hand, the would-be comedy BAD MEDICINE (1985) was a near-instant failure. In it Steve was cast as a medical student in a Central American school ruled by Alan Arkin. In POLICE ACADEMY 3: BACK IN TRAINING (1986) he was a sergeant on the now screwball police force, and he then played the programmer of a robot in the science fiction comedy rip-off of E.T. (1982) known as SHORT CIRCUIT (1986). Amazingly, both movies were ranked in the top twenty of 1986: POLICE ACADEMY 3 was #17, while SHORT CIRCUIT was #19. (Steve chose not to appear in the sequel, SHORT CIRCUIT II [1989].) C. M. Fiorillo of *Films in Review* magazine found that Guttenberg's "sunny visage chokes up his act on more than one occasion" in THE BEDROOM WINDOW (1987). Steve's first dramatic feature, it was molded, said the releasing company, from the genius of Alfred Hitchcock. HIs performance and the film failed to impress either the critics or audiences. Meanwhile, on cable TV, Guttenberg had appeared on Showtime in both "Pecos Bill: King of the Cowboys" (May 12, 1986) and "A Star Spangled Celebration" (July 4, 1987). For "Gangs" (April 19, 1988), a CBS-TV "After-School Special," Steve served as co-producer.

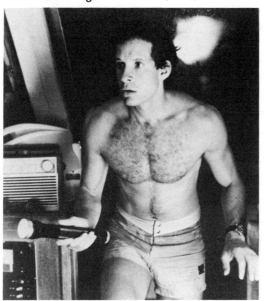

Steve Guttenberg in COCOON (1985).

Continuing to capitalize on the strength of its modern-day Keystone Kops series, Warner Bros. had POLICE ACADEMY 4: CITIZENS ON PATROL in release in April 1987. For this installment Guttenberg's participation deal included his services as a production associate. Ultimately, the four POLICE ACADEMY films starring Steve as Mahoney took in $500 million worldwide. Sequels V and VI would follow in 1988 and 1989, respectively, but without Steve, who had grown tired of the confining shenanigans of this declining series. In 1988, upon the release of HOT TO TROT, when the picture's star, Bob Goldthwait, was asked how he liked working with a talking horse, he responded, "Hey, I've worked with Steve Guttenberg—what's the big deal?"

Universal placed AMAZON WOMEN ON THE MOON on the shelf for a year before releasing it in September 1987, but the studio should have left it there. Consisting of several skits spoofing "the minor and major annoyances of contemporary living," the would-be comedy boasted a large cast. Steve appeared in skit #8, entitled "Two I.D.s," in which his blind date (Rosanna Arquette) asks for credit card information and a valid driver's license so that she can check him out in her computer before going out with him. The following month, Steve sported a moustache as a selfish, wealthy attorney competing with Michael Caine for the affection of Sally Field in SURRENDER. *Variety* correctly predicted of this faltering romantic comedy, "production runs out of steam early and probably will ditto at the boxoffice."

THREE MEN AND A BABY (1987), based on the 1985 French comedy TROIS HOMMES ET UN COUFFIN and directed by Leonard Nimoy, teamed Steve with TV megastars Tom Selleck and Ted Danson as three bachelor roommates who find an abandoned baby at their front door. Danson's character is the infant's father, but all three men are plunged into sudden and bewildering parenting. This surprise hit went on to become the #1 film of the year, with earnings in excess of $167.7 million. In 1988, on home video, it sold 535,000 copies, making it one of the all-time most popular video selections. Its tremendous success did a great deal to buoy the careers of each of its stars, including hyperbusy Steve, who had five releases in that year.

During 1988, Steve promoted Seagram's Golden Wine Coolers in TV commercials and was one of several spokespersons for the Will Rogers Institute. He had always managed to keep his private romances a secret, but the name of the lady about whom he had been so protective for the past three years was revealed when, on September 30, 1988, he married New York model Denise Bixler at her parents' home in Plymouth, Michigan. "She's very smart, very sensitive, and a marvelous cook" is all he would say. His favorite charitable organization was Greenpeace for its overall protection of the environment, to which he wholeheartedly subscribed.

Steve joined the ensemble cast in England and Ireland of HIGH SPIRITS (1988). His was the role of an American who becomes enchanted with the ghost of a beautiful eighteenth-century newlywed (Daryl Hannah) who had been murdered by her husband (Liam Neeson). The *San Francisco Examiner* decided that he gave a "bland performance" not "worthy of Hannah's friendly ghost." Twentieth Century–Fox was fortunate in obtaining all but one member (Brian Dennehy) of the original cast of COCOON for its sequel, COCOON: THE RETURN (1988). However, this follow-up, although it again provided the audience with extraterrestrial sex between Steve and Tahnee Welch and a geriatric basketball game, did not measure up to its predecessor. *Newsweek* magazine observed, "Nice as it is to see these actors again, the trouble with this less than necessary sequel is that it merely attempts to duplicate the experience of the original, with the inevitable loss of freshness."

In December 1989 producer Paul Maslansky reported that he hoped to reunite the entire original cast of POLICE ACADEMY for a sexier seventh installment, to be called OPERATION SCOTLAND YARD, but the project has yet to be finalized. DON'T TELL HER IT'S ME (1990) was written for the screen by Sarah Bird from her novel *The Boyfriend School* and filmed on location in Charleston, South Carolina. Steve starred as an introverted cartoonist who has lost his looks due to chemotherapy for Hodgkin's disease. His meddling sister (Shelley Long) determines to make him appealing to women by transforming him into a muscle-bound, long-haired New Zealander called Lobo. While *Variety* termed the misfire "a grotesquely unfunny comedy," Jeff Menell (*Hollywood Reporter*) acknowledged that Guttenberg "turns in an atypically low-keyed performance that would be credible anywhere else but here. He displays a sensitivity that has not surfaced before." In its first two weeks at the domestic box office, DON'T TELL HER IT'S ME earned a sluggish gross of $1,025,276.

The three stars of THREE MEN AND A BABY were reunited for THREE MEN AND A LITTLE LADY (1990), under the direction of Emile Ardolino, in which little Mary is now a five year old (Robin Weisman) with a mind of her own. The action centers around the mother's (Nancy Travis) decision to move to London, taking Mary with her. *Variety* perceived the follow-up film to be a "two-dimensional sequel . . . a project that proffers old-fashioned romance and family values while really ticking along with all the machine-like calculation of a modern-day presidential campaign." Michael Wilmington (*Los Angeles Times*) agreed that the sequel "plays less like a comedy than an evening gone wrong." Again playing the nationally syndicated cartoonist, Guttenberg received the least attention of the three male leads from reviewers; *Variety* described him as "a sweet, brotherly guy." Despite the creative disappointments of THREE MEN AND A LITTLE LADY, the comedy garnered $29,771,815 in its first week of domestic distribution.

In the works for Steve is PARADISE FOUND (1991), scripted by Jane Brownell, as a man on the run from the FBI and the mob who is mistaken for a child psychologist "in a wacky secluded cult somewhere in America's heartland." Meanwhile, in November 1990, Guttenberg was in London to make his dramatic stage debut in the West End in Tom Griffin's *The Boys Next Door*, a two-act play focusing on a young man (Steve) who attempts to guide a group of mentally troubled men. Steve made his Broadway bow in the spring of 1991 when he took over the male lead in *Prelude to a Kiss*, the fairytale comedy co-starring John Randolph and Ashley Crow.

In his scramble for show business recognition and success, the driven Steve Guttenberg once said, "If you get good reviews, your head gets big. Get a bad review and your head gets small. You wind up with stretch marks on your scalp." Although his pictures have for the most part made a profit, he still worries about the caliber of his various performances and what people think of him. "I want to become, in my own eyes, a real actor. Someone other actors look up to—like De Niro."

Filmography

Something for Joey (CBS-TV, 4/6/77)
Rollercoaster (Univ, 1977)
The Chicken Chronicles (Avco Emb, 1977)
The Boys from Brazil (20th–Fox, 1978)
Players (Par, 1979)
To Race the Wind (CBS-TV, 3/12/80)
Can't Stop the Music (Associated Film, 1980)
Miracle on Ice (ABC-TV, 3/1/81)
Diner (MGM, 1982)
The Day After (ABC-TV, 11/20/83)
The Man Who Wasn't There (Par, 1983)
Police Academy (WB, 1984)
Police Academy 2: Their First Assignment (WB, 1985)
Cocoon (20th–Fox, 1985)

Bad Medicine (20th–Fox, 1985)
Police Academy 3: Back in Training (WB, 1986)
Short Circuit (Tri-Star, 1986)
The Bedroom Window (DeLaurentiis Entertainment Group, 1987)
Police Academy 4: Citizens on Patrol (WB, 1987)
Amazon Women on the Moon (Univ, 1987)
Surrender (WB, 1987)
Three Men and a Baby (BV, 1987)
High Spirits (Tri-Star, 1988)
Cocoon: The Return (20th–Fox, 1988)
Don't Tell Her It's Me (Hemdale, 1990)
Three Men and a Little Lady (BV, 1990)

Television Series

Billy (CBS, 1979)

No Soap, Radio (ABC, 1982)

Broadway Plays

Prelude to a Kiss (1991) (replacement)

ARSENIO HALL

"I'm very special. I'm gifted. I was sent here to do this.
Now that sounds weird, but the bottom line is I sat back
and laughed because I planned this since I was twelve."
> —*US* magazine, September 18, 1989

"ARSENIOOOOOOOOOOOH!" AND THE STUDIO AUDIENCE GOES WILD.
When he undertook the post as a television talk show host—a goal he had dreamed about as a child—he quipped, "They called 1-800-Caucasian and no one answered." But he loves the job; he is a natural at it. Hall quickly became the first successful black male crossover host in the business, with a new generation of viewers estimated to be in the eighteen-to-thirty-four age group. His closest competitor, Johnny Carson, continues to attract the older, predominantly white audience, as he has done for nearly thirty years. Arsenio's questions to his guests, often blunt and irreverent, are not intended to offend them. After all, he is the host of the TV party, and why would he insult a guest? His appeal is to two different worlds, because he is fast, very funny, and hip. He is so hip that even some of his hip guests and audiences are not yet up on some of his terms. He has described his comedy style as "'brown bread' on the edge."

"I'm 'Mr. Happy,' I'm the 'Candy Man,'" he claims, and he is both when his party goes on the syndicated air. On the other hand, at home and in his office is a collection of more than 250 stuffed animals—most of the teddy bear variety—who do not talk during his studious viewing of tapes of his show or other hosts' programs. His inanimate, staring companions offer no distraction. "I'm the Rocky Balboa of the talk show circuit," he jokingly boasted to the syndicated "Entertainment Tonight." However, deep within this candy man is a loneliness, coupled with the fear that it may all end just as rapidly as it began.

Arsenio Hall was born on Tuesday, February 12, 1957, the only child of Reverend Fred Hall, a Baptist minister, and his wife, Annie, a healthcare worker. They lived in a rat- and cockroach-infested tenement on Kinsman Street in the black ghetto of Cleveland, Ohio. When Arsenio was five years old, his mother divorced the ultra-strict Mr. Hall. The rearing of Arsenio became the responsibility of his mother, his maternal grandmother, and his godmother. Annie Hall moved away from Kinsman Street to the Cleveland suburb of Warrensville Heights, where both she and her son would have better opportunities. At this time, Arsenio created a magic act with which he was featured on a local TV amateur show every Sunday morning; he also starred in a local special, "The Magic of Christmas."

Through many appearances on the program, he became a master magician. When he was eight years old, his mother gave him a Christmas gift of a stuffed toy dog which became his friend, a pal who was not jealous of his talents as were the older neighborhood boys, who taunted him, knocked him to the ground; and stole his school lunches.

At age twelve, Arsenio was a drummer for a while in a pop group, but spent a great deal of his spare time in front of a television, idolizing such personalities as Johnny Carson, Flip Wilson, and Dinah Shore. The latter's NBC-TV show always bore her signature on a title card. He devoted his seventh-grade study hall periods to repeatedly signing his first name in emulation of Dinah's. He informed classmates that he would one day have his own television interview show. They giggled. No one took him seriously. He also considered becoming a television weatherman. However, at home alone, he would sit at the center of a semicircle of empty chairs and pretend that he was Johnny Carson talking with celebrities. He earned money through his magic act as well as by playing drums and bass guitar in musical groups, while his mother also worked, banking as much as she could toward a college fund for her son.

At Warrensville Heights High School, Arsenio devoted a great deal of time to playing on the basketball team. After graduating from high school, he entered Ohio State University at Columbus, Ohio, but transferred in his sophomore year to Kent State University in Kent, Ohio, to be closer to home. He was a disc jockey on the campus radio station, and in his senior year won the role of Reverend Purlie in *Purlie Victorious*, staged by the Black Drama Workshop of the Institute for Afro-American Affairs. Through this experience he fell in love with the process of stage work, an interest that was reinforced by a campus visit from comedian Franklin Ajaye. Hall struck up a friendship with Ajaye, with the latter promising, if ever Arsenio came to Los Angeles, that he would introduce him to the Comedy Store, a showplace for stand-up comedians. Arsenio says that he graduated from Kent State in 1977 with a degree in speech and communications.

Annie Hall was apprehensive about her son's decision to pursue a career in show business because of its uncertainty and his possible exposure thereby to drugs and alcohol. To appease her, he briefly went into advertising sales in Detroit for the Noxema skin cream company. However, he also did stand-up comedy routines at clubs in and around Detroit and Chicago. In 1979 he left his full-time job in favor of doing comedy work. He moved to Chicago, performing first at the Maroon Raccoon Inn, followed quickly by becoming the opening act for Parliament Funkadelic. Singer Nancy Wilson hired him to be master-of-ceremonies for her club show. When she was twenty minutes late on opening night, Arsenio had to improvise. Not only did she like Hall's work, she also felt that he was an asset to her show. When her personal appearance schedule ended in early 1980, she asked him to join her in Los Angeles at her expense. He packed his belongings into his car and drove west.

Through contacts in Los Angeles, he obtained employment doing warm-up routines for appearances by Robert Goulet, The Temptations, Nancy Wilson, Tom Jones, Tina Turner, and others. At the Comedy Store he met Eddie Murphy, of whom he said, "Eddie's the brother I never had. We share intimate secrets. We cry together. There's no competitiveness between us." It was the start of a long, lucrative friendship. As a last-minute replacement for Nipsey Russell, Arsenio was hired by songstress Patti LaBelle to tour with her as her opening act. "What do you want me to do and what would you like me not to do?" he asked. Ms. LaBelle replied, "Honey, that's your act. You do what *you* want to do." Through this opportunity he achieved the recognition necessary to propel him into other areas such as television, and in 1983 he was chosen as co-host, along with Thom Sharp, of ABC-TV's "The Half-Hour Comedy Hour." The program, consisting of a grab bag of skits as well as one-liner bits of dialogue and gags, premiered on July 5, 1983. It had a repertory company of comics as well as comedic guest stars such as Henny Youngman, the master of one-liners. A month later, on August 9, the show died. With the money he earned from this brief stint, Arsenio bought automobiles for both his mother and himself. Also at this period he and British actress Emma Samms began a romance lasting several months, while his name was also linked romantically with actress Mary Frann.

In 1984 Hall became a regular on the syndicated television show "Thicke of the Night," a ninety-minute talk/variety show hosted by Canadian Alan Thicke. The program was expected to give competition to NBC-TV's "Tonight Show Starring Johnny Carson," but poor ratings forced it to be abandoned in 1984. The next year, Arsenio was on NBC-TV's "Motown Revue," which lasted from August 9 to September 13, 1985. He also gained popularity as co-host of the syndicated "Solid Gold" in early 1986.

In August 1987 the increasingly popular Arsenio Hall was hired by the Fox network as a replacement for talk show hostess Joan Rivers, who had been fired from her late-night program. His initial contract with Fox was for thirteen weeks, to fill in until another show, "The Wilton North Report," was ready as a permanent replacement. During the interim period (August 17, 1987–November 6, 1987) when he hosted "The Late Show," the ratings increased. When "The Wilton North Report" failed to generate enough interest to keep it on the air, Fox sought to rehire Arsenio with a financial offer of seven figures. By this time, however, he had signed a two-year deal with Paramount to make three pictures. Fox was reduced to airing "The Best of Arsenio Hall" repeats.

In September 1987, prior to fulfilling his Paramount commitment, Arsenio was seen in among the large cast in Universal's feature film AMAZON WOMEN ON THE MOON, which consisted of a series of unrelated blackout sketches spoofing everyday life. Arsenio opened the movie as a professional man physically abused by household appliances, including a VCR, that go haywire. The disjointed offering, made in 1986, was short-lived in theatrical distribution. It has enjoyed wider exposure on video, where, on a smaller screen, it makes better sense.

Hall's first Paramount offering was COMING TO AMERICA (1988), in which he played multiple roles opposite his buddy, Eddie Murphy, as an African prince in search of a wife of his own selection in the United States. Arsenio's contributions included playing the prince's deferential escort, a grizzled barbershop customer, a bombastic evangelist, and an extremely ugly girl. Said *Variety,* "Working their way through the streets, most of the time Murphy and Hall can do little but react. . . . The very best moments of the film are those when Murphy and Hall are out among other characters played by themselves. These are done so artfully, it's sometimes hard to tell which one of them is playing whom, if at all." The film grossed more than $128 million box-office dollars by November 1989, but with foreign distribution and video sales, it ultimately took in more than $300 million. On December 10, 1988, Arsenio was presented with an Image Award by the NAACP at its twenty-first annual awards ceremony, as Best Supporting Actor for his work in COMING TO AMERICA. Also during 1988 he was the solo host of the MTV Awards telecast.

Scheduled to star in a Paramount picture called THE BUTTERSCOTCH KID, which was cancelled, Arsenio entered a $2.5 million deal with Paramount Television as executive producer as well as star of his own syndicated talk show. At the same time, he established Arsenio Hall Communications to handle his affairs, and Eddie Murphy dubbed him "Little Money." "The Arsenio Hall Show" premiered on January 3, 1989. A bit stodgy and hesitant at first in his interviews, within only a few months Arsenio had improved his on-the-air technique to the point that his popularity, measured by the A. C. Nielsen Company, surpassed that of other TV hosts Pat Sajak and David Letterman, making Arsenio second only to Johnny Carson. His guests included both blacks and whites from various professions, such as Jesse Jackson, Howie Mandel, Julian Lennon, Brooke Shields, Dr. Ruth Westheimer, Magic Johnson, and Jamie Lee Curtis. His "we be having a party" and "woof woof, woof woof" became trademarks, as did the finger to his head that prompted immediate choruses of "hmmmmmmh" from the hip studio audience, which lined up for tickets as early as 8 A.M. for the 5:15 P.M. taping.

"My success isn't a race thing," Arsenio has said, "it's an age thing." His appeal is to a younger audience than Carson's. He is backed by the band The Posse, directed by Michael Wolff, with whom he would touch fingers as he walked on stage to deliver his monologue. Following his admonition, "Let's get busy," the band would then swing into action. He was sued for $10 million by Willis Edwards, head of the Beverly Hills–Hollywood NAACP, who claimed that Arsenio defamed him in January 1989 by calling him an "extortionist" in a Los Angeles radio station interview, which was also printed in the *LA Sentinel,* after. Edwards had accused Arsenio of not having enough black people on his staff. (The suit was dismissed by a Superior Court judge in March 1990.) On the air, Arsenio introduced his long-lost half-brother, "Chunkton Arthur Hall"—abbreviated to "Chunky A"—a

Eddie Murphy and **Arsenio Hall** in COMING TO AMERICA (1988).

three-hundred-pound rap singer, who was actually Arsenio with excessive padding and a bizarre costume. He later produced a comedy-music recording, "Large and in Charge," along with a video for MCA. A feud developed with filmmaker/ardent black activist Spike Lee, who contended that Arsenio was an "Uncle Tom" and who also ridiculed Oprah Winfrey for wearing blue contact lenses. Off camera, Arsenio's name was linked romantically with that of Dana Friedman, a twenty-four-year-old white woman who worked on the show. Arsenio did anti-drug commercials in 1989 and in December entered into an agreement to publicize Coca-Cola's Sprite soft drink.

HARLEM NIGHTS (1989), starring Eddie Murphy (who also produced, directed, and wrote the script), was Arsenio's second Paramount feature, at a salary of $900,000, while Murphy was reportedly paid $8 million. This lackadaisical depiction of an after-hours club in Harlem in 1938 which undergoes gangster problems was termed "deadly dull" by critic Gene Siskel, "marginally diverting" by *Newsweek* magazine, and "self-destructively primitive in tone and development" by *Time* magazine. *People* magazine tabulated that it contained 233 obscenities, something of a record even for Murphy. Yet by its second week of domestic release the film had grossed $34.9 million, and after ten weeks the grosses had climbed to $59,041,778, indicating that undemanding moviegoers did not mind a little cussing.

Along with Keenen Ivory Wayans, Robert Townsend, and Paul Mooney, Arsenio was named by Murphy as a member of his "Black Pack," an adaptation of Frank Sinatra's 1960s league of followers, who were known as the "Rat Pack." Arsenio was named best-dressed TV star by the Tailors Council of America, undoubtedly because of his $1,000 suits by Armani and Hugo Boss, and he was paired romantically with songstress Paula Abdul, who said, "I can talk to him about anything." As part of his celebrity status, Arsenio received death threats. He was chastened for revealing on the air the ending of THE WAR OF THE ROSES (1989). He ventured into the garment industry with sales of Arsenio Hall sleep shirts, T-shirts, sweatshirts, and hats, and led "The Force," a basketball team made up of the members of the Los Angeles Police Department, to victory over "New Edition," comprised of musicians, with the proceeds going to Target, a national anti-drug charitable organization. "You can't help most of the adults," Arsenio explained, "but tomorrow's future—the children—can be helped."

On March 11, 1990, at the sixteenth annual People's Choice Awards, he was chosen as the favorite late-night talk show host, and on March 14, 1990, he received the Sammy Davis, Jr., special award at the fourth annual Soul Train Music Awards ceremony where he said, "I've got a long way to go to deserve anything with Sammy's name on it." *TV Guide* magazine chose him as one of "The Top Stars of the '90's," stating, "There's no end to where Arsenio can go. He's probably going to become the biggest star of the '90s." Paul Junger Witt, producer of "The Golden Girls" and "Empty Nest," observed, "He has the ability to cross racial and cultural lines, transcending whatever hangups a white audience might have with sheer energy, talent and intelligence." When asked by *Woman's World* publication about the possibility of his ever marrying, he responded, "If I could find a girl who would watch television with me for the rest of my life, I'd get married in a flash."

When asked why, if he has perfect vision, he wears such a wide assortment of eyeglasses on his show, he responded, "It's a cosmetic touch," and that women have told him that glasses "are very sexy."

As Arsenio's late-night show continued, so did his various feuds with the likes of Roseanne Barr (about her figure), Spike Lee, Madonna, Keenen Ivory Wayans, Latoya Jackson, Public Enemy, and Andrew Dice Clay. *Entertainment Weekly* magazine wondered, "Arsenio Hall seems like such a nice guy. So, why are so many people so mad at him?" Spokespersons or publicists were not available for comment. On April 9, 1990, CBS-TV announced the cancellation of "The Pat Sajak Show," and it was reported that Arsenio had signed a long-term agreement with Paramount Pictures to develop and produce movies and television shows. On CBS-TV's "Face to Face with Connie Chung" (May 7, 1990), Hall spoke of his talk-show host image by saying, "I don't fit the mold at all," and of his desire to be known as "the Martin Luther King of comedy." Rumored to be in love with Janet Jackson (they were seen holding hands in May 1990), he was named the first national ambassador for "Drug Abuse Resistance Education" (DARE) in July 1990. On September 6, 1990, he hosted the seventh annual MTV Music Video Awards, during which Janet Jackson was presented with the Video Vanguard Award. (The show would be telecast over MTV–Cable on October 21, 1990.) On October 17, 1990, Hall was sued by former manager Robert Wachs (who still manages Eddie Murphy), who claimed in his Superior Court lawsuit that he had made Hall a superstar and thus is entitled to an allegedly promised 50 percent of the profits from Hall's popular talk show, as well as more than $75 million in damages. According to Wachs's suit, Hall will earn $12.5 million from "The Arsenio Hall Show" in 1990 alone.

Arsenio is most often seen wearing $1,000 Armani suits, and when Eddie Murphy gets something, like a golf car to drive around the Paramount lot, Arsenio gets one too. In September 1990, Hall bought the mountaintop home of the late crooner Rudy Vallee. This two-acre Hollywood Hills estate, purchased for $3.5 million, includes a five-bedroom, six-bath, 6,000-square-foot main house, with a tennis court, pool, game room, and theater. On the desk in Hall's production office are framed photographs of Murphy and Johnny Carson, who remains an idol. "I recently read," Arsenio told *TV Guide* magazine, "where [NBC Entertainment president] Brandon Tartikoff said I was going to burn out fast. I'm not just going to burn bright, Brandon," he added, "I'm going to burn long."

Regarding his current status, he reflects, "I've worked very hard all my life to educate myself, and now I get a chance not only to show the funny side of my personality, but the businessman locked inside me as well." Hall has very clear goals for himself: "I want to be an artist respected by other artists. . . . I want a person to look at me and be affected by my work."

Filmography

Amazon Women on the Moon (Univ, 1987)
Coming to America (Par, 1988)

Harlem Nights (Par, 1989)

Television Series

The Half-Hour Comedy Hour (ABC, 1983)
Thicke of the Night (Synd, 1984)
Motown Revue (NBC, 1985)
Solid Gold (Synd, 1986)

The Real Ghostbusters (ABC, 1986–87)
(Voice only)
The Late Show (Fox, 1987)
The Arsenio Hall Show (Synd, 1989–)

Album Discography

The Best of Comic Relief 2 (Rhino
R11H-70707)

HARRY HAMLIN

"Sexiness to me is something that's shared. You have to have the
emotional exchange."   —*People* magazine, March 30, 1987

LIKE HIS TWO PREDECESSORS, MEL GIBSON AND MARK HARMON, AS
People magazine's annual "Sexiest Man Alive," Harry Hamlin was embarrassed as well as
surprised that he would be so chosen. "Certainly, when I look in the mirror, I don't get
turned on," he said at the time. However, his Dick Tracy square jaw, full lips, sensitive
brown eyes, and dimpled chin obviously cause his host of admirers to think otherwise. His
acting is stiffer than Gibson's, without the latter's naturalness; his performing style is more
akin to that of the physically similar Steven Bauer. Hamlin is an intelligent conversation-
alist, which led *People* magazine to describe him as "the type who would talk afterward
instead of just rolling over or lighting a cigarette."

Harry Robinson Hamlin was born on Tuesday, October 30, 1951, in Pasadena,
California, to wealthy aeronautical engineer Chauncey Jerome Hamlin, Jr., aged forty-
nine, and his socialite wife, Bernice. Harry was the couple's second son as well as half
brother to two children from Chauncey's prior marriage, one of whom bore the name
Chauncey Jerome Hamlin III. Alone during most of his early years, Harry grew up with
books. Years later he would speak of the lack of camaraderie with his father, whose
sedentary ways at age sixty, when Harry was eleven or twelve, prevented them from playing
catch or touch football like other fathers and sons. While in junior high school, Harry
worked as a box boy at Hughes Supermarket in Pasadena, earning sizable tips from
matrons whose groceries he carefully placed in their cars. He attended one of the best
college preparatory schools in the nation, located in Pennsylvania. There, in school plays,
he obtained his initial taste of acting. The experience convinced him that he wanted to
become a performer, a decision that did not sit well with his parents, who expected their
sons to become doctors or lawyers, or at least to choose a profession more secure than
acting.

Thinking that he would change his mind, the Hamlins permitted Harry to enroll at
the University of California at Berkeley in the autumn of 1970 as a drama student with a
minor in psychology. He was on campus at the time when student antiwar demonstrations
were in full swing. He took part, but did not consider the causes to be anything more than
an excuse for partying. Popular with his peers, he was chosen president of his fraternity
after he advocated permitting women to live at the frat house. However, after an early
morning fire required evacuation of the building, a photograph of the coed inhabitants in

pajamas and other sleepwear appeared on the front page of the campus newspaper and was picked up by the press wire services. In the ensuing scandal, he later recalled, "The fraternity was called a brothel and I was called its pimp." Before this happened, however, he had already written to Yale University in New Haven seeking admission. When the University of California "encouraged" his departure, he became a student in Yale's drama department.

Upon graduation from Yale in 1974 with a degree in drama, Hamlin was offered a Fulbright grant to study theater in England, but declined it. Instead, in 1975 he became a student at the American Conservatory Theatre (ACT) in San Francisco, where he studied for two years before joining the troupe as a professional actor, performing in such productions as *Equus*. He next appeared with the McCarter Theatre in Princeton, New Jersey, in *Faustus in Hell* and other dramas. He left the stage when he received an offer to appear in a feature film, directed by Stanley Donen.

MOVIE, MOVIE (1978), a parody of 1930s/1940s-type double features, consisted of two stories, plus coming attractions. In the first episode, "Dynamite Hands," Harry is Joey Popchik, a boxer in a black-and-white–lensed spoof that was modeled on the boxing films done by John Garfield. The ill-conceived Warner Bros. feature was poorly received (*Variety* wrote, "MOVIE MOVIE is awful awful"), but Harry was noticed. The studio offered him a four-picture contract through superagent Sue Mengers, who sought to represent him. He turned down the bid in order to go his own way, which included starring in NBC-TV's six-hour miniseries "Studs Lonigan" (1979). Based on James T. Farrell's trilogy of novels, which had been banned during the 1930s for their frank sexuality, the expansive TV production was a remake of the 1960 theatrical movie, a failure that featured Christopher Knight as Studs, the sexually active young Chicagoan of the 1920s.

After these initial offerings, magazine writers began to preface his name with "handsome hunk," an indication that he was on his way to celluloid prominence. In 1979 he signed to co-star in the British production CLASH OF THE TITANS, to be filmed abroad with an international cast, including Laurence Olivier, Maggie Smith, Burgess Meredith, Claire Bloom, and Ursula Andress. With such a cast, the picture was expected to be a hit on both sides of the Atlantic, but Harry still remembers that after he signed the contract, his conscience screamed, "Let me out! I'm nauseous!" While on location, Harry, at the age of twenty-eight, began a highly publicized romantic liaison with Ursula Andress, aged forty-three, that would last three years and result in the birth of their son, Dimitri, in 1981.

While the trouble-plagued CLASH OF THE TITANS was undergoing further editing after its none-too-successful British premiere, Harry was seen on American movie screens in May 1981 in the forgettable KING OF THE MOUNTAIN. He played Steve, a beer-guzzling garage mechanic who joins his buddies in hotrod racing along Mulholland Drive in Los Angeles. A month later, CLASH OF THE TITANS (1981) was released in the United States, where the reception was chilly in spite of its cast and special animated effects by the famed (but old-fashioned) Ray Harryhausen. Set in mythological times, the film featured Harry as the athletic Perseus, the toga-clad son of Zeus (Olivier), who must face fearsome challenges in pursuit of his destiny. Ursula Andress, the former wife of actor/director John Derek, played Aphrodite, the goddess of love and beauty. The motion picture was lovely to look at, but at 118 minutes it was far too long, with pompous dialogue and stiff performances.

In November 1982 Harry appeared with the McCarter Theatre in Princeton, New Jersey, in *Hamlet*. Mel Gussow (*New York Times*) wrote of Hamlin's performance, "he offers a vigorous personification of Hamlet that to a great extent has been shaped in his image." In a change-of-pace role, Hamlin was next seen on theatrical screens as Bart, the homosexual writer who first pursues his doctor (Michael Ontkean) as his lover, then drops him, in the controversial MAKING LOVE (1982). "If you play a gay role, it sticks more than it does if an actor were to play a murderer or a psychopath," he later reflected. "There were a couple of producers that I heard through friends were convinced that I was gay and that if I was going out with a woman it was a front." Despite respectable box-office returns (the movie grossed $6.5 million in domestic film rentals) and solid reviews for the cast, Hamlin claims to have lost many potential job offers thereafter.

His only work in 1983 was the low-keyed BLUE SKIES AGAIN, about professional baseball from a woman player's viewpoint. The ranging nine-hour CBS miniseries "Master of the Game" was Harry's 1984 outing; it starred him as the weakling son of Dyan Cannon, the rich, power-hungry head of a family dynasty built on diamond trading. Filmed in Kenya, England, France, and New York, it was based on Sidney Sheldon's best-selling novel.

In March–April 1984, while at Broadway's Circle-in-the-Square Theatre in a revival of Clifford Odets's *Awake and Sing!*, Harry met Laura Johnson, a television actress then appearing in the nighttime drama "Falcon Crest," with whom he claims to have instantly fallen in love. In Los Angeles in March 1985, they were married and moved into a two-bedroom "cottage" in Laurel Canyon. "We're like Mutt and Jeff," he said. "We spend hardly any time apart." She said, "I was very much taken by this guy who was very nice, and very intelligent, and very articulate. Plus, he didn't ask me my sign." It was the second marriage for Laura.

Harry's next outing required nine months to film in various U.S. and European locations, at a hefty budget of $32 million, with a cast including several "bankable" stars, among them James Garner, Bruce Dern, Beau Bridges, and Michael York. Adapted from James A. Michener's 620-page novel of 1982, "Space" was a thirteen-hour miniseries shown in five parts on CBS-TV in April 1985. In this narrative of five couples whose lives intersect at the time of the Apollo moon landing, Harry was astronaut John Pope, whose wife, Penny (Blair Brown), is having an affair with a combat Naval officer (Garner). Stanley Marcus reported in *TV Guide* magazine that the stars "comprise an acting team second to none."

The two-hour pilot film for "L.A. Law," from Steven Bochco, the co-creator of the popular weekly series "Hill Street Blues," was telecast on NBC-TV on September 15, 1986, and the show began as a regular series on Friday, October 3, 1986. Centered in the high-power Century City (Los Angeles) law firm of McKenzie, Brackman, Chaney &

Kuzak, Harry was chosen to play Michael Kuzak, a white knight attorney who was less opportunistic than some of his colleagues (among them, Corbin Bernsen and Jimmy Smits). The series began where the pilot left off, with Kuzak setting his romantic sights on deputy district attorney Grace Van Owen (Susan Dey). Signing a five-year agreement, Harry was assured of steady employment if the series proved successful. At the end of its first season, "L.A. Law" ranked #21 in the ratings. In 1987 Harry wore a gorilla suit in the episode entitled "Simian Enchanted Evening," during which he also dropped his trousers (his own idea). "Great stuff, huh?" he mocked himself. "Real high-brow." But the fans loved it. In an ensemble cast like the one gathered for "L.A. Law," it is always difficult to single out individual cast members, but many in the cast received Emmy Award nominations before Harry was so honored. When Smits was one of six from the cast to be nominated, he noted, "Harry sent us all telegrams of congratulations." Smits also has said, "Harry's very intellectual. The other day while we were sitting in the conference room waiting for a shot, he talked for 25 minutes about anthropology and some rare fish."

During the 1987 summer break from "L.A. Law," after having been named "The Sexiest Man Alive" by *People* magazine, Harry made the moody but lumbering LAGUNA HEAT for HBO–Cable, a two-hour movie telecast on November 15, 1987. *TV Guide* magazine called it "video noir." Harry was cast as a police detective enmeshed in a darkly psychological relationship with his father (Jason Robards). It reminded Harry of his dealings with his own father, whom he had never known well but "had a moment when we came to an understanding. It was just two weeks before he died . . . we were finally able to say that we loved and respected each other." Also during 1987, Harry, along with Amy Irving, John Lithgow, and others, founded the Los Angeles Classic Theatre where they intended to stage presentations of the works of Shakespeare and other playwrights. During the 1987–1988 TV season, "L.A. Law" was America's eleventh most watched series.

Harry Hamlin in CLASH OF THE TITANS (1981).

In August 1988 Harry and Laura purchased a home in the Hollywood Hills at a cost of $1 million, then spent $500,000 to renovate and redecorate it to their tastes. His son, Dimitri, stayed with them during summer vacations from school in Rome, where he lived the rest of the year with Ursula Andress. At the same time, Laura was in a new ABC-TV medical series, "HeartBeat," which was scheduled opposite NBC's "L.A. Law." "Right now," said Laura, "we're remodeling a house, so of all things we have to argue about, it certainly won't be about our TV shows."

In addition to re-doing the new home, Harry starred in "Favorite Son" for NBC-TV, a six-hour miniseries shown in three parts beginning on his thirty-seventh birthday, October 30, 1988, a few days before the presidential election. In the political drama, Harry was Terry Fallon, the ambitious vice-presidential hopeful. Terry was a handsome, telegenic, but little-known right-wing junior senator whom the incumbent president (James Whitmore) was encouraged to select as a running mate. On October 26, the largest NBC-TV affiliate station in Indiana, the home state of Senator J. Dan[forth] Quayle, announced that it would not show "Favorite Son" because local Republicans saw potentially troublesome similarities between the fictional Terry and the real-life Quayle. Ads for the miniseries were dropped by the network, allegedly even before the Republican protests, in which Harry was depicted as "a handsome, young charismatic senator" campaigning with a sexy woman nearby (Linda Kozlowski), with the tag line, "You think a man should be vice president because he looks good on television?" While *Variety* said of the far-ranging, clichéd soap opera, "Only thing missing is the kitchen sink," the multipart offering was very popular with viewers, increasing Hamlin's status as an audience draw. On November 3, 1988, two days after the final installment of "Favorite Son," "L.A. Law" debuted for its third successful season.

Harry made a ten-minute videotape in early 1989 which contained a "personal message" to the subscribers of San Francisco's ACT, his original proving ground, telling them of the upcoming attractions to be staged in their Geary Theatre. On January 6, 1989, he acted in an episode of "The Hitchhiker," a suspense series on USA–Cable.

Although the Hamlins continued to be photographed cheek-to-jowl and smiling toward the camera, rumors persisted that all was not well in the newly renovated Hamlin home. Laura, it was reported, complained to friends that Harry was self-centered, and held the couple's purse strings too tightly. Then, in June 1989, they announced their marital separation, which Laura blamed on Harry's affair with blonde "Knots Landing" TV actress Nicollette Sheridan, twelve years his junior, who had had prior relationships with actors Scott Baio, Leif Garrett, and James Wilder. Although separated, Harry and Laura both continued to live in the house, eventually assigning to each and cordoning off sections, much as in THE WAR OF THE ROSES (1989). Laura's new boyfriend was Ray Liotta, whose then most recent screen role had been in FIELD OF DREAMS (1989). On September 1, 1989, Harry filed for divorce from the woman who had once said of him, "He is very romantic. Women spot Harry and make their way over to our table. You wouldn't believe the claws and fangs." Still, neither would move out of the house, a situation that became tabloid fodder.

During the fourth season of "L.A. Law," it was reported that Harry's and Susan Dey's characters "will continue to explore their relationship," but earlier Hamlin had suggested that his Kuzak was due for some excitement. NBC obliged him by introducing into the script a new vehicle for him to drive—a Harley-Davidson motorcycle. "I asked for a convertible," he said, and "they gave me a Harley. It's a highway patrol version, but I picked out the seats and accoutrements. It's very eclectic." He researched the change by taking bike-riding lessons for several weeks before driving in front of the camera in the series, a program designated by Dr. Joyce Brothers as a "mood buster," good for mental health. For the week ending December 10, 1989, "L.A. Law" was rated #9, with an 18.8 audience share.

DINNER AT EIGHT had been a classic film from MGM in 1933 with an all-star cast. It took chutzpah to do a remake, but that is exactly what TNT–Cable did on December 11, 1989. Harry took over the part of Larry Renault, originally created by John Barrymore as a boozing down-and-out matinee idol. In the new, updated rendition, Renault is a washed-out TV actor turned on to cocaine as well as alcohol. *USA Today* claimed, "You can almost smell the stench of day-old alcohol," while the *San Francisco Chronicle* complained that "Hamlin is too young to play someone who's described by another character as 'quite a hunk in his day.'" Despite the strands of gray distributed through his hair as an aging ploy, Harry did not project the strain the role called for, nor did his heavy-handed portrayal indicate any flair for comedy.

When asked by USA *Today* in December 1989 to comment on his complex personal life, specifically his pending divorce, he responded, "It's difficult enough for me to deal with it, without the help of all your readers."

Nominated for the first time for a Golden Globe Award as best actor in a TV series drama, Harry lost on January 20, 1990, to Ken Wahl of "Wiseguy." Scheduled to open May 2, 1990, in the American Conservatory Theatre's production of *Burn This* at the Stage Door Theatre in San Francisco, Harry withdrew from the project at the last minute, citing his shooting schedule for "L.A. Law." He was replaced by resident ACT performer Dan Reichert. Instead, Harry gave advice to viewers in "American Red Cross Emergency Test" (ABC-TV), hosted by John Ritter and televised June 7, 1990. DECEPTIONS, a telefilm he had made with co-star and lover Nicollette Sheridan, was aired on Showtime–Cable on June 10, 1990. Eager but unable to follow in the tradition of James M. Cain's *Double Indemnity*, this sordid murder mystery cast Hamlin as a hard-boiled detective with Sheridan as the prime suspect in a homicide case. *Entertainment Weekly* magazine noted, "At first, it's fun to watch this couple; Hamlin's perennial sneer forms an airlock with Sheridan's constant pout. But couldn't the filmmakers have built a real movie around these shenanigans." The publication rated the telefilm a "D."

The fifth season of "L.A. Law" began on October 18, 1990, with *Daily Variety* reporting that the veteran series is still "sometimes hilarious, sometimes maudlin, but overall a top-notch hour of entertainment." The trade paper noted of Hamlin's Michael Kuzak—involved in defending a white policeman who shot and killed a black teenager—"Hamlin is a bit inconsistent—he's strong in some scenes but appears a little uncomfortable in others." Also for the 1990–1991 television season, Harry starred as homicidal Dr. Charles Raynor in the ABC movie DEADLY INTENTIONS . . . AGAIN?, a four-hour sequel to the network's miniseries of 1987, which had featured Michael Biehn in the lead role. Both Hamlin and the two-hour TV film received mixed reviews. *Daily Variety* recorded, "Harry Hamlin now plays Raynor, whose medical privileges have been denied him. Raynor has an ability to charm the unsuspecting, a talent Hamlin doesn't manage. . . ." In contrast, Rick Sherwood (*Hollywood Reporter*) enthused, "This could have been a disaster, but instead it proves a carefully crafted story of suspense. . . . Harry Hamlin ('L.A. Law') as Raynor, and Joanna Kerns ('Growing Pains') as his devoted and trusting new wife, turn in terrific performances. . . . The film works because of Hamlin's forceful performance as a man bent on revenge."

On March 7, 1991, at the Los Angeles County Courthouse, Harry and Nicollette Sheridan (who earns over $1.24 million as co-star of the TV nighttime soap opera "Knots Landing") were married in a short ceremony. To avoid as much publicity as possible, the couple were wed at seven P.M., at a total wedding cost of $63.25.

Over the years, Harry Hamlin's personal life has received more serious press coverage than have his attempts at mastering the art of acting. However, television critic John Carman (*San Francisco Chronicle*) assessed him with, "Hamlin wants to act, yet he settles for posing. He's a fine piece of work as Michael Kuzak on 'L.A. Law,' but his outside efforts to stretch have produced torn ligaments." Perhaps Hamlin, who left "L.A. Law" at the end of the 1990–1991 season, should have, like Richard Dean Anderson, stuck to one television series if/when that program is successful.

Filmography

Movie, Movie (WB, 1978)
King of the Mountain (Univ, 1981)
Clash of the Titans (UA, 1981)
Making Love (20th–Fox, 1982)
Blue Skies Again (WB, 1983)

Maxie (Orion, 1985) (cameo)
Laguna Heat (HBO–Cable, 11/15/87)
Dinner at Eight (TNT–Cable, 12/11/89)
Deceptions (Showtime–Cable, 6/10/90)
Deadly Intentions . . . Again? (ABC-TV, 2/11/91)

Television Series

Studs Lonigan (NBC, 3/7/79; 3/14/79, 3/21/79) [miniseries]
Master of the Game (CBS, 2/19/84–2/21/84) [miniseries]

James A. Michener's "Space" (CBS, 4/14/85–4/18/85) [miniseries]
L.A. Law (NBC, 1986–91)
Favorite Son (NBC, 10/30/88–11/1/88) [miniseries]

Broadway Plays

Awake and Sing! (1984) (revival)

TOM HANKS

"I was very spoiled. . . . Suddenly, here was this tidal wave of
people saying very nice things about me and wanting me to be in
their films."   —*Premiere* magazine, April 1989

OVERNIGHT! METEORIC! TOM HANKS WAS RELATIVELY UNKNOWN TO
movie audiences before 1984, when he appeared in his second theatrical motion picture as
a boy-next-door–type of fellow who falls in love with a mermaid. By the end of the 1980s,
he was one of filmdom's biggest box-office draws, commanding a per-picture salary of
more than $3 million. There is nothing special about his looks; in fact, he admits that he
has a "goofy nose and geeky body." He is an average youngish man whose idea of a really
good time is going to a baseball game and having a Diet Coke with a hot dog. He is not a
stand-up comedian, like Michael Keaton; rather, he is touted as a "light comedy romantic
actor." This classification puts him in league with such all-time screen giants as Henry
Fonda, James Stewart, and Jack Lemmon.

So, what is so great about this guy? A co-star, Mare Winningham, says, "He's a
comedic genius," while producer/writer Daniel J. Petrie explains his popularity with,
"He's extraordinarily likable and people respond to him in real life." At the same time, he
bears a terrible burden, as writer/director David Seltzer attests: "Those who line their
pockets with his box-office receipts are going to want him to be a guy who makes
audiences laugh all the time." This expectation may not afford him latitude to expand into
straight dramatic acting, as did Michael Keaton. However, if Tom Hanks enjoys the
professional longevity of Tony Curtis—to whom he compares himself—he will be an
integral part of show business for several decades to come.

Thomas J. Hanks was born on Monday, July 9, 1956, in Concord, California, the
third of four children born to Amos Hanks, an itinerant cook, and his first wife, both
Catholics. When Tom was five years old, his parents divorced. He and his older siblings,
Larry and Sandra, went with Amos, while six-month-old Jimmy accompanied their
mother. Amos moved to Reno, Nevada, then to Redding, California, and later to several
other northern California locales. This transient life did not allow his children a chance to
make friends, for they never stayed long in any one spot. Amos married a Mormon woman
who instilled that religion in the trio of Hanks offspring. When that marriage did not last,
the children went to live with an aunt for two and a half years. She was a devout Nazarene,
and that belief was thrust upon them. Amos wed yet a third time, but in this marriage there
was no strong religious element; the family did finally settle down, however, in Oakland,

California, across the water from San Francisco. From then on, Tom called himself "an East Bay boy." Meanwhile, their mother remarried three times, having a child or two by each husband. Thus the Hanks children had several half brothers and sisters.

As a result of his childhood, Tom was shy and would not let anyone get too close to him. However, at Oakland's Skyline High School he participated in track meets and theater, activities which helped to open up his personality. He sang a role in the school's production of *South Pacific* and played in the school's Kazoo Marching Band. On his graduation from high school in 1974, his yearbook ranked him as "the class cut-up." He immediately enrolled at Chabot Community College in Hayward, California. One of his classes involved reading and then attending performances of such plays as *The Good Woman of Setzuan* and *Tiny Alice*. The play that affected him most was Eugene O'Neill's *The Iceman Cometh*, which he saw performed at the Berkeley Repertory Theatre, an experience which he said "was the most magical thing that had ever happened to me." After completing the two-year course at Chabot, Tom transferred to the California State University at Sacramento in 1976 to study acting, but found himself more interested in stage production and management.

A guest director at the university was Vincent Dowling, the artistic director of the Great Lakes Shakespeare Festival in Lakewood, Ohio, who was staging Chekhov's *The Cherry Orchard* in Sacramento. Tom auditioned for a part and, in getting it, so impressed Dowling that he invited Tom to intern (during the summer of 1977) with the Shakespearean group in Ohio, where he played Grumio in *The Taming of the Shrew*. After the summer, Tom returned to Sacramento, but quit college in favor of employment at a community theater as associate technical director. The next summer saw him back in Lakewood, Ohio, working on lighting and set design, along with acting in *Othello* as Cassio and in *The Two Gentlemen of Verona* as Proteus. As a result of these roles he received the Cleveland Critics Circle Award as best actor of 1978.

With a friend from the Great Lakes Shakespeare Festival as well as his actress girlfriend, Samantha Lewes, Hanks drove to New York City, arriving there in late November 1978. For several weeks they shared a small, cramped apartment with others. However, Tom and Samantha got their own apartment after their son, Colin, was born in December, at which time they were married at the Church of the Holy Apostles in Manhattan. "We were young and impetuous," he was to say later of this period when they lived as best they could through his meager jobs, unemployment payments, and a few dollars sent by his sister, raised by redeeming empty soda bottles. Hanks managed to appear in several plays (including *The Mandrake*) produced by the Riverside Shakespeare Company, but returned to Ohio to spend the summer of 1979 with the Shakespeare group there. Back in New York, he constantly auditioned for roles in theater, television, and motion pictures. He made $800 for a role in HE KNOWS YOU'RE ALONE (1980), a slasher movie in which prospective brides are murdered. Tom was eighth-billed as Elliot in this clumsy entry, shot mostly on Staten Island.

Spotted by an ABC-TV talent scout, Hanks was asked to go to Hollywood to audition for roles in several series in development for the network, one of which was

"Bosom Buddies." The thirty-minute situation comedy, about two New York City advertising agency men, Henry (Peter Scolari) and Kip (Tom), who are evicted from their apartment by a wrecking ball and move to the inexpensive Susan B. Anthony Hotel, a residence for women only, premiered on November 27, 1980. Living at the hotel while disguised as two young women named Hildegarde and Buffy, the young men had a fine time ogling the female occupants. *Variety* enthused, "Peter Scolari and Tom Hanks get a good chemistry going between them, buttressed by fine timing for young players." The show was especially popular with teenagers, but many critics did not share the overall enthusiasm. Tom's notices were good, however, with the word "appealing" popping up a lot. "Bosom Buddies" lasted two seasons, with the last new episode aired in June 1982.

Following the series' demise, Tom had little problem getting nonrecurring parts in episodes of "Taxi," "Family Ties," "The Love Boat," and "Happy Days." He was also selected by CBS-TV to star in its made-in-Canada movie RONA JAFFE'S "MAZES AND MONSTERS" (December 28, 1982). He was one of four college students who embark on fantasy game-playing against a medieval background. CBS then offered him a deal for a series pilot, providing that the right premise could be developed. Also in 1982, Tom and Samantha became parents for a second time, with the birth of a daughter, Elizabeth.

In early 1983 director Ron Howard and his partner, Brian Grazer, tried to talk every studio in Hollywood into producing their feature film about a mermaid. Finally the Walt Disney Studio agreed. For the male lead, Grazer said they "were looking for someone who had leading man qualities—he could kiss the girl and could drive a story. At the same time, we wanted someone who was funny, but not quirky or eccentric in his comedy." Michael Keaton, among several others, turned down the role before Tom, sent over by CBS-TV, auditioned. He appeared wearing Levis, construction boots, and a T-shirt. Grazer remembers, "And here's a guy who'd never had a major movie. I thought 'Why is this guy so calm?'" Both his apparel and his quiet manner helped to win Tom the role, at a salary of $70,000. SPLASH opened in theaters nationwide in February 1984 with Tom as a disillusioned bachelor whose faith is restored when he falls in love with a beautiful mermaid (Daryl Hannah). *New York* magazine credited Tom as "an expert comic"; *Newsweek* magazine considered his performance reminiscent of routines by Johnny

Tom Hanks in SPLASH (1984).

Carson and David Letterman, "all-American boys with mischief inside." By the end of 1984 the smash hit comedy had grossed more than $60 million, and Quigley Publications listed Tom as the #13 box-office star of the year. During the spring of 1988, a sequel would be telecast on NBC-TV, with Todd Waring taking over Tom's role.

In June 1984 Hanks starred as a bus driver who is given a BACHELOR PARTY by raunchy friends. This film earned an R-rating for profanity and nudity and $19,070,000 in domestic film rentals. It did nothing for his career, although doing it had been his own idea. A year later, in another error in judgment, he was seen as a musician mistaken for a spy in THE MAN WITH ONE RED SHOE (1985), in which his comedic abilities were kept too solidly under wraps. This remake of a French film, THE TALL BLOND MAN WITH ONE BLACK SHOE (1972), quickly disappeared from circulation. Released a month later, in August 1985, VOLUNTEERS featured Tom as a spoiled playboy gambler who flees to Thailand and the Peace Corps to avoid debt collectors. Gene Siskel (*Chicago Tribune*) decided that his portrayal, employing "a wildly inconsistent, imitation–Cary Grant voice," was not acceptable. Tom's leading lady in the feature was Rita Wilson, with whom he began a romantic relationship. During the making of his next picture, THE MONEY PIT (1986), he filed for divorce from Samantha.

THE MONEY PIT, a remake of sorts of MR. BLANDINGS BUILDS HIS DREAM HOUSE (1948), which had starred Cary Grant and Myrna Loy, presented Tom and his screen spouse, Shelley Long, with a great many more structural problems than Grant and Loy had had to face. Called a "miserable ripoff" by critic Gene Siskel, the comedy grossed over $30 million at the domestic box office thanks to Tom's increasing popularity coupled with Long's reputation from TV's "Cheers." Tom next co-starred with "The Great One," Jackie Gleason, in NOTHING IN COMMON (1986), a maudlin comedy drama about which *New York* magazine observed, "only Tom Hanks's virtuoso performance holds the piece in place." A brief 1987 TV series resulted from this movie, with Todd Waring again substituting for Tom. Hanks was a World War II American flyer in Jerusalem in EVERY TIME WE SAY GOODBYE (1986), a quickly forgotten sudsy tale. However, Hanks fared much better as the detective sidekick to Dan Aykroyd in DRAGNET (1987), an updated, slapstick send-up of the "Sergeant Friday" character created by Jack Webb on NBC-TV in the 1950s. Besides wanting to work with Aykroyd, another reason Tom gave for wanting to be in this major picture was "because I don't have to win the girl at the end . . . and I'm tired of that." Tom and Aykroyd also recorded a song, "City of Crime," for the film's soundtrack. The new DRAGNET grossed an impressive $30,920,130 in domestic film rentals.

On April 30, 1988, Tom and Rita Wilson were married in the Los Angeles area in Greek Orthodox services. Meanwhile, Hanks, who had hosted NBC-TV's "Saturday Night Live" (December 14, 1985) and had headlined a syndicated television special, "Just the Facts" (June 8, 1987), returned as guest host on "Saturday Night Live" (February 20, 1988).

"Hanks is an absolute delight," wrote Janet Maslin (*New York Times*), while David Ansen (*Newsweek* magazine) insisted, "Hanks has never been better." These were but two of the accolades for BIG (1988), a motion picture that is funny and fun, contains no profanity, and grossed $113.9 million at the box office, making it the #4 money-maker of 1988. It is the comedic tale of a thirteen-year-old boy (David Moscow) who suddenly finds himself grown up, in Tom's body, with improbable, amusing results. Tom was awarded a Golden Globe Award by the Hollywood Foreign Press Association as best actor in a comedy or musical and received an Academy Award nomination. He lost the Best Actor Oscar to Dustin Hoffman (RAIN MAN). PUNCHLINE (1988) was another movie he wanted to make, even though his character, a driven stand-up comic, is "not necessarily . . . redeemable." Playing opposite Sally Field, also one of the film's producers, Tom was Steven Gold, a gifted, self-destructive comedian. According to *US* magazine, Tom "turns in a wonderful performance," and Field stated simply, "Tom was brilliant." On January 24, 1989, for his work in both BIG and PUNCHLINE, Hanks was named best actor of 1988 by the Los Angeles Film Critics Association.

"Ozzie & Harriet Meets Charles Manson" is how Dana Olsen described his screenplay for THE 'BURBS (1989), in which an ensemble cast, headed by Tom, investigates the ghoulish house next door. *People* magazine panned this one with "Any episode of 'The Addams Family' or 'The Munsters' is sharper and funnier, not to mention an hour shorter." Nevertheless, the suspense comedy grossed $17,318,125 in domestic film rentals. TURNER & HOOCH (1989) got off to a bad start with the dismissal of its director, Henry Winkler, who was replaced by Roger Spottiswoode. However, this tale of a small-town cop, Turner (Tom), whose only witness to a murder is a large, beautiful/ugly Dogue de Bordeaux dog named Hooch (Beasley), was well received by critics; *Empire* magazine reported, "Tom Hanks once again brings his glorious physical comic talent to bear in an unlikely movie." Audiences agreed, to the cash-register tune of $68.5 million by its thirteenth week of domestic release, thereby ensuring Tom's per-picture salary of $3 million. In 1989 Hanks formed his own production company, which he named Clavius Base.

JOE VERSUS THE VOLCANO (1990), heralded by Bob Thomas of the Associated Press as "The First Comedy Hit of the 1990's," opened nationwide on March 9, 1990. Mick LaSalle (*San Francisco Chronicle*) found that it "has two substantial things going for it. One is Tom Hanks, whose naturalness and ease manage to smooth out some of the picture's bumps. . . . The other is the film's look." Tom was Joe, whose doctor (Robert Stack) gives him six months to live due to a "brain cloud." A business tycoon (Lloyd Bridges) asks Joe to sacrifice himself to a tropical volcano. In the course of the story, he meets three women, all played by Meg Ryan. Of her co-star, Ryan assessed, "He never stops making me laugh. A lot of comedians just turn it on and you can't get in there, you can't get close, but Tom is very available. That's what makes him good at what he does." In ten weeks of domestic release, JOE VERSUS THE VOLCANO grossed a sizable $36,707,420.

In Las Vegas, on February 7, 1990, at the NATO/ShoWest convention, Tom was among the stars—who also included Chevy Chase, Dan Aykroyd, and John Candy—who provided an impromptu stand-up comedy routine when a sound system glitch interrupted the unreeling of Warner Bros. product. In April 1990, when Tom was voted Entertainer of the Year by readers of *Cable Guide* magazine, his simple response was, "Wow! . . . It's a grand honor, what can I say?" The Stage Deli restaurant in New York City, known for its celebrity sandwiches, offered "the Tom Hanks" on its menu in response to its patrons' request in June 1990 that he replace "the Shecky Green." A series pilot based on TURNER & HOOCH was aired on NBC-TV on July 9, 1990, with Tom Wilson in Tom's original role as Scott Turner; *Daily Variety* rated it as "unbelievably boring."

On August 4, 1990, in Los Angeles, the Hankses became parents to their first child, a six-pound, four-ounce boy.

Traffic jams in the Bronx were incited by the filming of THE BONFIRE OF THE VANITIES (1990), starring three major stars, Tom, Melanie Griffith, and Bruce Willis, with Morgan Freeman in support. The inhabitants of the Bronx were concerned that their borough might be inappropriately pictured as a hovel, merely "a teeming sea of criminals and their victims." Adapted from Tom Wolfe's best-selling novel, the picture was produced and directed by Brian De Palma and was released in December 1990 in order to qualify for the Academy Awards. Tom played Sherman McCoy, a Wall Street bond trader who falls from grace. The film was a critical and financial disaster.

By his signing a three-picture deal with Walt Disney Studios, *American Film* magazine judged that Tom had "reached the point where he tells prospective directors how he sees a character." The publication wondered if, with his success and new-found confidence, Tom was "sexy enough, handsome enough to be a real leading man" in more serious work.

Upcoming for Hanks is his cameo and narration for RADIO FLYERS (1991), the production-plagued drama starring Adam Baldwin, John Heard, and Lorraine Bracco.

Tom claims he is a very normal type of man off screen. "I don't have one of those ranches in Alberta that I disappear to for months. When I'm not working, I wake up, drink some coffee, read the papers, and get on the phone to see what's going on." He would rather not attend chic Hollywood parties where tuxedos are de rigueur, because "I'm basically an average guy." Of his pre–movie-stardom years, he recalls, "I enjoyed working in television. Sure the pace is hectic, but the work has substance as long as you keep mentally stimulated." Like many of Hollywood's superstars of today, Tom is a private person, even refusing to divulge the name of his newly born son. He is polite, friendly, and completely at ease in interviews, but never interjects remarks or information of a personal nature.

Filmography

He Knows You're Alone (MGM/UA, 1980)
Rona Jaffe's "Mazes and Monsters" (CBS-TV, 12/28/82)
Splash (BV, 1984)
Bachelor Party (20th–Fox, 1984)
The Man with One Red Shoe (20th–Fox, 1985)
Volunteers (Tri-Star, 1985)

The Money Pit (Univ, 1986)
Nothing in Common (Tri-Star, 1986)
Every Time We Say Goodbye (Tri-Star, 1986)
Dragnet (Univ, 1987)
Big (20th–Fox, 1988)
Punchline (Col, 1988)
The 'Burbs (Univ, 1989)

Turner & Hooch (BV, 1989)
Joe Versus the Volcano (WB, 1990)
The Bonfire of the Vanities (WB, 1990)

Future Releases

Radio Flyers (Col, 1991)

Television Series

Bosom Buddies (ABC, 1980–82)

MARK HARMON

"I like to get better and have the opportunity to get better. . . .
I come from a background where repetition means getting better.
How I get there, it's a little bit insane."
—*Los Angeles Herald-Examiner*, August 23, 1985

MARK HARMON ONCE ADMITTED, "I'VE ALWAYS BEEN A LONER, BUT I'M no hermit." When he was loudly proclaimed in 1986 by *People* magazine as "The Sexiest Man Alive," his private life became nonexistent for a spell. "I never thought of myself as a sex symbol," he replied in the midst of the hoopla, "although it's quite flattering that others do." CBS-TV's "Evening Magazine" on August 8, 1988, more accurately pinpointed his image as a "very attractive boy-next-door, but with sex appeal." His handsomeness, which can easily be compared to that of the young Montgomery Clift, is nonthreatening, with a ruggedness shaded with softness.

Harmon has often been referred to as a "beefcake star." However, he has not been required, on camera, to remove his shirt as frequently as has Gregory Harrison or Mel Gibson. Mark's career has led gradually from walk-on TV parts in the mid-1970s to more recent showcasing roles ranging from a philandering surgeon to a serial murderer, from comedy to playing a gigolo. While top success has eluded him—he has won no awards and piled up no huge box-office grosses—he is, nonetheless, wholesome and capable as well as devoid of ego. "I'm not worried about image," he has stated. "I'm an actor."

He was born on Sunday, September 2, 1951, in Burbank, California, the only son of Tom and Elyse Knox Harmon, preceded in birth by sisters Kristin in 1945 and Kelly in 1948. Tom Harmon, a noted Los Angeles–area sportscaster in 1951, had been an All-American running back with the professional Michigan Wolverines and was the 1940 Heisman Trophy winner. Elyse Knox had had an acting career of sorts in Hollywood movies during the 1940s before retiring to become a full-time mother. While most youngsters sleep with a stuffed toy, Mark's nocturnal bed partner was a football given to him on a rare occasion when his father was not traveling to announce the latest plays. The popularity of Tom Harmon extended into the home, where the gridiron family was filmed at the breakfast table for cereal endorsements.

At the early age of five, Mark was called upon to model the latest in boys' fashions. Since he was alone a great deal of the time, his biggest thrill was tossing his football at mailboxes or going to the local school to wait for older boys to come out to play catch. His father was a powerful force in the family, a believer in strict discipline who did not overlook the childish pranks of his son. Mark was sent to a Catholic school where the nuns also administered severe discipline. He played Little League baseball, as well as football, and, when he was old enough, obtained odd jobs. In 1963, when he was twelve, his sister Kristin, aged seventeen, married Rick Nelson, the actor-musician son of Ozzie and Harriet Nelson, and from 1964 to 1966 played herself in "The Adventures of Ozzie and Harriet" on ABC-TV.

Since Mark was Tom Harmon's son, it was expected that he would excel in sports. When he was less than good, his father wordlessly walked away from him; when he was good, his father insisted he should have been better. It was a frustrating time for the youth. In 1965 Mark became a student at the exclusive military academy and college preparatory Harvard High School in North Hollywood, where he added rugby to his sports repertoire. In his first year there, his grades were so low that he voluntarily remained a freshman for a second year. In 1970, when he was nineteen, he enrolled at Pierce College in Woodland Hills, California, where he was named an All-American junior college football quarterback. His nickname was "Hormone." As a junior, he transferred to the University of California at Los Angeles (UCLA) to study communications, but earned further football laurels in 1972 as the starting quarterback for the winning UCLA Bruins. After post-game interviews lasting two hours, Mark found his father waiting for him outside the shower room. "Hey, great game," his father greeted him and hugged his son. "From that moment, I knew my dad," he later said. After another successful season of football in 1973, Mark won the National Football Foundation Award for all-around excellence.

During 1973 Mark was a lifeguard at South Laguna Beach, where he and frequent swimmer Ozzie Nelson became better acquainted. Mark confided that he was taking acting lessons on the side, maybe wanting eventually to become an actor. These were things he had told no one else. A short time later, Nelson contacted him to ask if he would fill in for an ill actor on his syndicated TV series, "Ozzie's Girls." Mark accepted the bit part of a guard dressed in a gorilla suit whose lines were, "Hi, I'm Harry King Kong. Which way's the Empire State Building?" Harmon recalls his TV debut of January 6, 1974, with "Nobody ever saw my face. It was a really great way to break in. I wasn't Mark Harmon." He put his college education on hold for a few months, during which time he appeared in a second episode of "Ozzie's Girls," without the gorilla suit, as well as in a bit part in an episode of NBC-TV's "Police Story."

The following September, having graduated cum laude from UCLA, he was promptly drafted by the New England Patriots with an offer of $40,000 to go to the NFL professional football camp. Since he had already incurred several on-field injuries, he turned down this offer in favor of taking a job selling athletic shoes, before accepting an entry-level job with an advertising agency. He continued with his acting lessons and appeared in an NBC-TV "Police Woman" episode in January 1975. While traveling on business for the ad agency, he had let his hair grow long and added a moustache; both the long hair and the moustache were rejected by veteran TV producer Jack Webb when Mark auditioned for him. Returning with a cleaner appearance, he earned parts in two of Webb's NBC-TV shows, which specialized in police action: "Adam-12" and "Emergency." The latter episode was actually the unsold pilot for a series to feature Harmon and Albert Popwell as members of the Los Angeles Bureau of Animal Control. By now, Mark was an advertising account executive with a seemingly solid future. However, on a flight back to Los Angeles after a sales trip, he decided to devote all his time to acting.

ELEANOR AND FRANKLIN (1976), a four-hour ABC-TV movie, had won several Emmy Awards, but had not covered the entire story of the lives of Eleanor and Franklin D. Roosevelt. A follow-up ABC-TV movie, ELEANOR AND FRANKLIN: THE WHITE HOUSE YEARS (March 13, 1977), covered their twelve years in residence at Pennsylvania Avenue. In this three-hour presentation, Mark had the role of Robert Dunlap, a disabled veteran of World War II. The program garnered seventeen Emmy Award nominations, including one for Mark in the Best Supporting Actor category. He did not win, but the telefeature was chosen Outstanding Special of the Year. He also appeared in segments of TV's "Laverne and Shirley" and "The Nancy Drew Mysteries."

Mark's six-foot, 170-pound frame, brown hair, and blue eyes publicly earned him the adjective "hunky" for the first time when he starred as Officer Mike Breen in the crime drama series "Sam," co-created by Jack Webb. It ran for just one month on CBS-TV from March 14 through April 18, 1978. The "Sam" of the title was Mike's partner, a yellow Labrador Retriever police dog. On May 17, 1978, on camera, Harmon was engaged to Bess Armstrong, who, in turn, was romantically pursued by Richard Thomas in the CBS-TV movie GETTING MARRIED, and on September 5, Mark was in the supporting cast of LITTLE MO, an NBC-TV movie about the life of real-life tennis pro Maureen Connolly (Glynnis O'Connor), who died of cancer.

He made his theatrical film debut in COMES A HORSEMAN (1978), starring Jane Fonda and James Caan, as a 1940s would-be cattle rancher. In Montana, where the film was shot, he obtained lessons from cowboys in the art of riding a horse, as well as branding, roping, and herding. He also acquired their habit of chewing tobacco, which he took with him back to Los Angeles. The year 1978 ended for him professionally when he appeared in two chapters of the expansive miniseries "Centennial" as John McIntosh, one role in a huge-cast drama depicting the history of the United States.

Harmon's second theatrical film was the superfluous sequel from Irwin Allen, BEYOND THE POSEIDON ADVENTURE (1979). He had twelfth billing as Larry Simpson, who does not survive the disaster depicted in the film. From August to December 1979 he had blond hair in the ABC-TV rescue series "240-Robert," co-starring as the husky Los Angeles County Sheriff's deputy Dwayne Thibideaux. During the same period he showed up in the September 15, 1979, episode of ABC-TV's "The Love Boat."

Mark received top billing for THE DREAM MERCHANTS (1980), the two-part adaptation of the Harold Robbins best-seller about the early days of silent movie-making. Although the syndicated telefeature was called "pedestrian" by critics, Mark was getting the film exposure he wanted. Lorimar Productions, with three CBS-TV prime-time adult serials, "Dallas," "Knots Landing," and "Secrets of Midland Heights," sold to NBC the idea of a nighttime soap opera based on the Robert Wilder novel and the 1949 Warner Bros. film FLAMINGO ROAD. After a two-hour pilot telefeature aired on May 12, 1980, the series premiered on January 6, 1981, and ran through July 13, 1982. Mark was Fielding Carlyle (played by Zachary Scott in the Warner Bros. movie), the politically ambitious deputy to the Florida town's scheming sheriff (Howard Duff). The character played in 1949 by Joan Crawford was renamed Lane Ballou; a sultry drifter who falls in love with Carlyle, she was played by Cristina Raines. Off screen, Mark and Raines began a love affair that would last several years. Soon after its first airing, Mark described the series this way: "It's really hot and racy, at least for television. It's definitely a ten o'clock show." In reality, the network shifted the show from 10 p.m. to 9 p.m. every few months in hopes of stirring viewer interest.

During the summer hiatus from "Flamingo Road," Mark starred in GOLIATH AWAITS (1981), a two-part syndicated telefilm. Lensed for the most part aboard the *Queen Mary* at Long Beach, California, it told the story of three hundred shipwreck victims discovered, still alive after forty years, by an oceanographer (Mark). The people have been living within a huge air pocket in a ship sunk during World War II. Although his performance as Fielding Carlyle had been called "stiff" and "immature," the *San Francisco Chronicle*'s TV critic thought he was "excellent" as the diving scientist in GOLIATH AWAITS.

At the conclusion of the run of "Flamingo Road," Harmon devoted the better part of a year to stage work. "After doing that series," he explained, "I didn't know whether I knew how to act anymore." In Toronto, he spent six months performing in *Key Exchange*, then returned to Los Angeles to appear in the Mark Medoff comedy *The Wager*. He bought an older home in Pacific Palisades which he renovated himself and took as roommates four dogs and a cat. He admitted to jogging several miles a day, and when asked about marriage replied, "I'm not big on catting around. I would like to get married once and want it to last."

Italian filmmaker Bernardo Bertolucci enticed him to Italy to star as TUAREG: THE DESERT WARRIOR (1984), a tribal hunter seeking revenge for the plunder of his village by murderous soldiers. This adventure feature was not released theatrically in the United States. On returning to Los Angeles, he auditioned for the lead in a new NBC-TV series, "Bay City Blues," about a minor-league baseball team. After eight readings, he was approached by the casting directors of "St. Elsewhere," an existing NBC-TV series in the throes of rewrites. The hospital-set program was planning to add new characters in an effort to raise its low Nielsen ratings. Mark's agent advised him to accept "Bay City Blues," which promised to be a winner. However, Mark said, "I watched 'St. Elsewhere' a lot last year and I liked the show. I really like these people." He fired his agent and went on, for more than two seasons, to play the charming, womanizing plastic surgeon, Dr. Robert Caldwell. His instincts served him well, since "Bay City Blues" survived less than a month, from October 25 through November 15, 1983. Before his debut on "St. Elsewhere," however, he co-starred with daytime soap stars Anthony Geary and Judith Light in INTIMATE AGONY (March 21, 1983), a TV movie dealing with the spread of herpes. Also, on November 19, 1983, he guested on another segment of "The Love Boat," called "Set Up for Romance."

In 1984 Harmon signed a lucrative contract with the Adolph Coors Company of Golden, Colorado, to film seven spot commercials a year for three years as the spokesperson for Coors Beer. He eventually filmed a total of twenty-nine endorsements, in which he was shown against Rocky Mountain vistas, leaping across streams, and casually walking through the brewery grounds. Coors's marketing director, Gary Naifeh, enthused, "Mark has established a credibility that is right up there with God and Walter Cronkite." Near the finish of his three-year agreement, which ended in November 1987, he was thrown from a horse while being photographed. He suffered a broken shoulder blade, whose repair required ten hours of surgery.

In August 1985, when interviewed by the *Los Angeles Herald-Examiner* with an open can of Coors at arm's reach, he said, "I look forward to a schedule where you work hard during the day and hustle to make the curtain." He was referring to returning to the stage in a new play, *Wrestlers*, written by Bill C. Davis, who also co-starred with Mark in the drama about two brothers. The play opened officially at the Cast Theatre in Los Angeles on August 25, 1985, for a limited run. About the Coors commercials, Harmon stated that they were "the closest that someone's paid attention to me and let me play someone like myself."

The lightweight telefilm PRINCE OF BEL-AIR (January 20, 1986) featured Mark as a smooth-talking Los Angeles pool man who chases after the ladies until falling for one (Kirstie Alley) who wants a serious commitment. Alley told *US* magazine, "He's very chivalrous; he runs over to the car and opens your door. If someone told you you were a bitch, he would, like, kill them." This ABC-TV movie, together with his exposure in the TV commercials, provided the basis for *People*'s naming him "The Sexiest Man Alive." His complete turnaround, in the role of the irresistible but sexually troubled serial killer Ted Bundy in THE DELIBERATE STRANGER, added fuel to the flame. Aired on NBC-TV on May 4–5, 1986, it was a true story, adapted from the book by the *Seattle Times* reporter who covered the 1974 murders of an estimated thirty-six young women in Washington, Utah, Colorado, and Florida. Of Mark's best acting job up to that point, critic Judith Crist wrote, "Bundy, played with deadly charm by Harmon, emerges as the ultimate sociopath, the enigmatic 'human monster.'"

Late in 1985 Mark had requested that his role in "St. Elsewhere" be made somehow more dramatic and more three-dimensional. However, when nothing changed in his role, he asked to leave the series to pursue other acting interests. The writers at first considered having his character suffer a nervous breakdown, but this idea was supplanted by having him contract AIDS from a prostitute. Dr. Caldwell then departed St. Eligius Hospital, presumably to work in an AIDS hospice. In February and March 1987 Mark turned up as astronaut Sam Crawford, a romantic yuppie challenger for the affections of Maddie Hayes (Cybill Shepherd) on ABC-TV's "Moonlighting." He returned to the big screen in LET'S GET HARRY (1986), branded a "turkey" by most critics, as a pipeline worker taken hostage in South America.

On March 27, 1987, thirty-five-year-old Mark was married to thirty-three-year-old Pam Dawber, the TV actress, whom he had met the previous year. A few weeks later he gave a UCLA extension course in Los Angeles focused on "Survival as an L.A.-Based Actor" or "Creative Waiting," which he admitted he was "not that great at" himself. He guest-hosted TV's "Saturday Night Live" on May 9, 1987. In July 1987 he co-starred with Kirstie Alley in what Paramount hoped would be a summer box-office smash, SUMMER SCHOOL. Mark was a laid-back gym teacher ordered to teach remedial English summer classes to the school screwups. The nonchalant feature fared modestly, garnering $15,748,562 in domestic film rentals.

Singer Rick Nelson, whom Mark's sister had divorced several years earlier, had been killed in a plane crash on December 31, 1985. In 1987 Mark went to court to obtain custody of the Nelson children because he felt the environment in which they lived with their mother was not healthy. He ultimately dropped the suit when the publicity became unbearable. He did better on film, in CBS-TV's AFTER THE PROMISE (October 11, 1987), as a Depression-era carpenter who regains custody of his four sons after they are made wards of the court following his wife's death. In November 1987 he was one of many Hollywood stars to provide voiceovers for the documentary DEAR AMERICA: LETTERS HOME FROM VIETNAM.

In January 1988 Mark starred as the cowboy in a Denver stage revival of *Bus Stop*. The play then moved to the Ahmanson Theatre in Los Angeles for a four-month run. It was during this time that a son, Sean Thomas Harmon, was born in Los Angeles to Mark and Pam, on April 25, 1988. THE PRESIDIO (1988), branded "a numbingly inane cop thriller" by *People* magazine, had all the ingredients of a standard action drama, including the car chase, partners who did not like each other, and the boy-girl love angle. Receiving second billing to Sean Connery, another (more mature) sex symbol, Mark was a street-smart San Francisco cop with an axe to grind. Fast-rising Meg Ryan played the feminine love interest. On the set, she found Mark a "forthright, funny man. It's great to work with him 'cause he has no secrets." STEALING HOME (1988) was an unsuccessful entry in the then current trend of baseball movies. Mark was Billy, responsible for finding a proper resting place for the ashes of the older woman (Jodie Foster, seen in flashback) to whom he had lost his virginity at age sixteen. With "Miami Vice" face stubble, Mark looked virile but his appearance alone could not save a movie with so convoluted a plot. On ABC-TV, he appeared with Mel Gibson and Patrick Swayze in a sixty-minute salute to Hollywood's stunt people, "The World's Greatest Stunts" (November 3, 1988), narrated by Christopher Reeve.

TV Guide magazine, in its issue of October 28, 1989, "cheered" Mark as "an actor who has honed his craft. Through hard work, [he] has made himself more than just another pretty face." The statement referred to his performance as Chance Wayne, the gigolo drifter in SWEET BIRD OF YOUTH, filmed in various southern California locales for the NBC-TV movie of October 1, 1989. "Youth fades. Only passion endures," insisted the ads touting the anticipated TV event, which showcased Elizabeth Taylor as the aging, alcohol- and drug-addicted actress, Alexandra Del Lago. *Variety* found few redeeming qualities in this adaptation of the Tennessee Williams drama, which had previously starred Geraldine Page and Paul Newman, both on the New York stage (1959) and in the movie version (1962). *Variety* stated that Mark "gives an ambitious college try" while "conveying none of the sensuousness and little of the heartlessness that both Chance and Alexandra share."

Magazine advertisements in late October 1989 asked, "Would you agree to marry this man?" Pictured below, in a reclining position, was Mark, in shirt, tie, suspenders, and beautiful smile. The movie was WORTH WINNING (1989), described in the ads as "An engaging comedy about a bachelor and three near Mrs." He was Taylor Worth, a TV weather personality who bets a friend (Mark Blum) that he can become engaged to three women (Lesley Ann Warren, Madeleine Stowe, Maria Holvoe) at the same time. The thin premise might better have served for an hour-long TV sitcom. The film flopped.

On Thursday, March 15, 1990, Tom Harmon (known throughout his lifetime as "old 98," the number he had worn on his football jersey), died of a heart attack at age seventy, shortly after playing eighteen holes of golf at the Bel-Air Country Club. Mark made the necessary telephone calls to around-the-country friends, reporters, and former gridiron colleagues of his father's.

It is obvious that Mark needs a solid box-office smash. His last good reviews had come for THE DELIBERATE STRANGER, back in 1986. In the summer of 1989 he went to Mexico and San Diego to film COLD HEAVEN (1991), co-starring with Theresa Russell. TILL THERE WAS YOU (1991), one of the biggest-budgeted features ever produced by the Australian film industry, was filmed at Vanuatu Island, south of Fiji, many of whose

Lesley Ann Warren, **Mark Harmon**, Madeleine Stowe, and Maria Holvoe in
WORTH WINNING (1989).

natives had never seen a white man. "The heat and humidity are beyond belief," Mark commented; "the smallest scrape could turn into a major infection."

In August 1990 Mark and Pam sold their home in Los Angeles's Mandeville Canyon, which they had bought in 1988 for $4 million, for a reported $7.9 million because they wanted a less hilly place for their children to play.

For ABC-TV Harmon enacted the American public enemy of the 1930s, DILLINGER (January 7, 1991). Filmed in Milwaukee, Wisconsin, it featured Sherilyn Fenn (of "Twin Peaks" fame) as his gun moll. The one-dimensional drama was not much liked by the critics or the public. The *film noir* THE FOURTH STORY, telecast on Showtime–Cable on January 19, 1991, featured Mark as a private investigator who becomes involved with a beautiful client (Mimi Rogers) while searching for her missing husband. For NBC-TV, the very active Mark was in LONG ROAD HOME (February 25, 1991), co-starred with Lee Purcell in a story of farm workers in 1937. This telefeature was shot in Gilroy, California, the garlic capital of the nation. *Variety* judged this two-hour film to be a "classy, likable vidpic with some top-notch performances and striking photography (but, alas, an abrupt, pure Hollywood ending that wouldn't have been out of place on 'The Waltons')." John Carman (*San Francisco Chronicle*) assessed, "It's refreshing to see a network movie of the idealistic GRAPES OF WRATH stripe, and equally refreshing to realize there may be more to Mark Harmon than a pretty face and bushy eyebrows." For CBS-TV's "Hallmark Hall of Fame" Harmon starred in the remake of Alfred Hitchcock's SHADOW OF A DOUBT (April 28, 1991), playing the smiling murderer that was portrayed by Joseph Cotten in the 1942 original feature. In the fall of 1991, NBC debuted "Reasonable Doubts," a weekly television series starring Harmon and Marlee Matlin. Forthcoming for Mark is the big screen release of SPITTIN' IN THE WIND (1991), with Mary Stuart Masterson, directed by Gary Devore.

Perennially handsome in the same vein as Tyrone Power, Mark, like Power, is not afraid to take chances in selecting roles. He has played psychos, criminals, and romantic and comedy heroes, and has serviced the lecherous wives of the wealthy around their Bel-Air pools. His repertoire has progressed and changed as often, probably, as Harry Hamlin has brushed his hair. When asked if there was a role or a moment in his work that gave him the most pride, Mark replied, "As an athlete, I never played a perfect game or thought, 'Wow, that's as good as it can get.' And as an actor, I find that same thing: there's always room to grow, room to change."

Filmography

Eleanor and Franklin: The White House Years (ABC-TV, 3/13/77)
Getting Married (CBS-TV, 5/17/78)
Little Mo (NBC-TV, 9/5/78)
Comes a Horseman (UA, 1978)
Beyond the Poseidon Adventure (WB, 1979)
Flamingo Road (NBC-TV, 5/12/80)
The Dream Merchants (Synd-TV, 5/12/80; 5/19/80)
Goliath Awaits (Synd-TV, 11/17/81; 11/23/81)
Intimate Agony (ABC-TV, 3/21/83)
Tuareg, the Desert Warrior (It, 1984)
Prince of Bel-Air (ABC-TV, 1/20/86)
The Deliberate Stranger (NBC-TV, 5/4/86–5/5/86)

Let's Get Harry (Orion, 1986)
After the Promise (CBS-TV, 10/11/87)
Summer School (Par, 1987)
Dear America: Letters Home from Vietnam
    (HBO–Couturie, 1987) (voice only)
The Presidio (Par, 1988)
Stealing Home (WB, 1988)
Sweet Bird of Youth (NBC-TV, 10/1/89)
Worth Winning (20th–Fox, 1989)
Dillinger (ABC-TV,1/7/91)

The Fourth Story (Showtime–Cable, 1/19/91)
Long Road Home (NBC-TV, 2/25/91)
Shadow of a Doubt (CBS-TV, 4/28/91)

Future Releases

Cold Heaven (1991)
Till There Was You (1991)
Spittin' in the Wind (1991)

Television Series

Sam (CBS, 1978)
Centennial (NBC-TV, 11/4/78; 11/11/78)
    [miniseries]
240-Robert (ABC, 1979)

Flamingo Road (NBC, 1981–82)
St. Elsewhere (NBC, 1983–86)
Reasonable Doubts (NBC, 1991–)

GREGORY HARRISON

"There aren't any rules I'm going to follow for the rest of my life
—then it's easier to forgive myself."
                              —*TV Guide* magazine, June 28, 1980

FOR CLOSE TO SEVEN YEARS, AS THE CO-STAR OF CBS-TV'S "TRAPPER
John, M.D.," Gregory Harrison was well known in television-watching homes in America.
Generally, if his real name was not on the tip of a tongue, he was identified as "Gonzo," the
handsome, fun-loving surgeon lothario at San Francisco Memorial Hospital. Having set
up a production company of his own, one of his initial undertakings was to star in a made-
for-television movie as a male stripper, a performance seen on thousands of TV sets, plus
thousands more when the videotape became available.

Publicly, Harrison was esteemed as a handsome golden boy spawned by TV. He
made occasional excursions into theater to prove to himself, as well as to critics, that he was
more than just a pretty face above a muscular trunk. It was an internal contest he shared
with such contemporaries as Mark Harmon and Tony Danza. Hidden behind it all,
however, was a terrible secret that would not openly emerge for eleven years: he was
addicted to cocaine. Ultimately, his drug problem cost Gregory Harrison in the neighborhood of three-quarters of a million dollars and severely hampered his career. The road back
has not been easy.

Gregory Harrison was born on Wednesday, May 31, 1950, to Captain Ed Harrison
and his wife, Donna, an accountant, both of Irish ancestry, in Avalon, the only city on the
island of Santa Catalina. A rugged, mountainous isle twenty-six miles from mainland Los
Angeles, Catalina is a popular resort and sport-fishing center; tourism is its principal
industry. "Cap'n Ed," as Gregory's father was known, ran a glass-bottom boat service, as
did his father before him. Everyone in Avalon knew everyone else, and Gregory, the
island's newest arrival, was bounced on all knees and gushed over by the ladies. When he
was old enough to walk, he would go out each morning to "watch the big ship coming in
with another load of crazy mainlanders." By the time he was five, he was supporting
himself by diving for coins for the tourists, making $8 to $10 a day. By age eleven, he had
added snorkeling and surfing to his outdoor life and his daily income from coin diving had
increased to $15 a day. Also when he was eleven, his brother Chris was born. Three years
later, his parents divorced and Donna left Catalina, taking her sons with her. After a few
months, Gregory returned to his father, who made it clear that he would be pretty much
on his own. Gregory got work on the island as he grew older as a deckhand, short-order

cook, and clothing salesman and buyer for Catalina's top men's shop. The island was often used as a location by movie companies, leading Harrison to observe, "I noticed no matter what kind of movie they were making, it took a lot of pretty girls and I decided that was a good business to be in."

He attended school in Avalon, acting in several plays and learning music composition. He wrote songs, which he played on a guitar. In September 1968, when he was eighteen, he enrolled at Saddleback Junior College on the mainland in Orange County. However, boredom set in—as it had with his various jobs—and he left after three months. In early 1969 he enlisted in the U.S. Army, thinking "I'd go kill for my country, simple as that." But after just a few days in basic training, he realized that he had made a mistake; he found that he did not want to kill another human being. His requests for discharge were turned down despite his refusal to take orders. He was stationed in Landshut, Germany, as a medic. Although he was far from the battlefields of Vietnam, he persisted in trying to get out of the Army, once by a suicide attempt, when "I took a whole bunch of pills and wound up in the hospital. . . . But I don't think I really wanted to die." After three weeks in a psychiatric ward, he was assigned to a cot—underground in an empty cryptography room—isolated from other soldiers. There he worked and lived for the remainder of his enlistment. His twenty-five months as a soldier came to a close when he was classified as a conscientious objector with an honorable discharge.

Back in Avalon, feeling insecure as well as uncertain about his future, he got a job as a doorman at a local nightclub. Within days he was on stage in the club's production of *The Fantasticks*. Actor Jason Robards, making a film at Catalina, saw him in the show and went backstage to tell Gregory that he could make a profession of acting if he was willing to work at it. The next day, Harrison quit his job, moved to Los Angeles, and began studying at the Actors Workshop, under the tutelage of veteran drama coach Estelle Harmon.

While studying drama, he supported himself with menial jobs plus an occasional little theater production, including *The Promise*. He worked in that show with a young actress, Christopher Norris, with whom he would cross paths again in a few years. He also appeared briefly in THE HARRAD EXPERIMENT (1973) and in a 1974 episode of CBS-TV's "M*A*S*H" and had a short role in the ABC-TV movie showcase for Karen Black, TRILOGY OF TERROR (March 4, 1975). In 1976 he was seen in an episode of ABC-TV's "Wonder Woman" as well as in a segment of "M*A*S*H." He then accepted the lead in a low-budget feature, entitled STORY OF A TEENAGER, put together by two high school boys and shot in Long Beach, California. Universal purchased the movie and released it in February 1976 as JIM, THE WORLD'S GREATEST. *Variety* reported, "Gregory Harrison is the lead, sympathetically playing a high school student living unhappily with alcoholic father . . . and young brother. . . ."

Charles Gary Allison was at the University of Southern California in Los Angeles in 1975 to earn his Ph.D. His thesis concerned the problems of a producer in making a movie. To research the subject, he decided to make a motion picture of his own. He used as the basis for his script an incident that had occurred during his college years, when a close friend of his strangled to death on an oil-soaked piece of raw liver during "Hell Week" hazing at a USC fraternity. The script was called OH, BROTHERHOOD, and to make the film he recruited help from USC students and faculty, and obtained actors from the university as well as from Estelle Harmon, who recommended Gregory. The movie was shot in forty-nine days in and around the USC campus. The results were initially shown on February 29, 1976, at USC, with major distributors in attendance at the screening. Paramount agreed to distribute the film, releasing it in April 1977 as FRATERNI-TY ROW. Gregory was Zac Sterling, the pledge who is stripped to his shorts, blindfolded, and forced to swallow the raw liver, on which he strangles. The *Los Angeles Times* critic wrote that Gregory "has genuine star quality."

Gregory had appeared in episodes of "The Nurses," "Barnaby Jones," and "M*A*S*H" on CBS-TV in October 1976 before his manager, Franklin Levy, arranged for him to star as Logan in the CBS-TV series "Logan's Run." Set in the year 2319, the futuristic story was based on the 1976 movie of the same name, which had starred Michael York. The fanciful teleseries premiered on September 16, 1977. Despite a change in timeslot, the series failed to catch on. The last episode was shown on January 16, 1978. A month before the series's demise, Gregory received seventh billing in the ABC-TV Christmas special THE GATHERING, telecast on December 4, 1977, as one of the sons called home for his father's (Ed Asner) last Christmas. A sequel, THE GATHERING II, would be shown two years later, with Lawrence Pressman in the role created by Gregory.

Unemployment after "Logan's Run" did not last long, for Harrison soon joined the big-name cast of "Centennial," an epic miniseries about the making of America taken from James Michener's hefty novel. The series was twenty-one hours long, not including commercial breaks, and was comprised of nine self-contained movies which could be shown separately. The story began in the late 1790s, and Gregory entered the picture in 1845 in Chapter 3, "The Wagon and the Elephant," as Levi Zendt, a Mennonite outcast on a wagon train heading west from St. Louis. Costing $25 million and composed of twelve chapters, which ran from October 1, 1978, to February 4, 1979, the impressive "Centennial" was the most expensive television project undertaken up to that time.

It was in 1978 that Gregory took his first snort of cocaine, after which, in retrospect, he said that he "felt more intelligent, more handsome, more creative, witty and charming." In the beginning he was only an occasional user of the drug, but within three years his drug use became habitual. "I'm not aware when the transition occurred," he has said. Also in 1978 he signed a five-year contract to co-star in a series for CBS-TV, "Trapper John, M.D.," a medical drama set at the fictional San Francisco Memorial Hospital. Starring in the title role was Pernell Roberts, whom Gregory had met during the filming of "Centennial"; they had decided then that they were both "idealistic" actors who "don't fit in." Roberts was Dr. John McIntyre, also known as "Trapper John," a character spun-off from "M*A*S*H," on which he had been played by Wayne Rogers for three years, from 1972 to 1975. Gregory was Dr. George Alonzo Gates, affectionately called "Gonzo," an impudent, satiric, woman-chasing, but talented, surgeon. Also in the cast was Christopher Norris as Nurse Gloria Brancusi, given the nickname "Ripples." Harrison's weekly salary was reported to be more than $10,000. The show debuted on September 23, 1979, and *TV Guide* magazine predicted that Harrison's "bedside manner and bedroom eyes are calculated to make female viewers swoon." In the two-part telefeature THE BEST PLACE TO BE (May 27–28, 1979), a glossy Ross Hunter–produced romantic drama, he was among the supporting cast (along with Mildred Dunnock, Betty White, Timothy Hutton, and John Phillip Law) backing star Donna Reed's return to television after twelve years' absence.

With the success of his new series, Harrison purchased a ranch-style home in the San Fernando Valley. Living with him was his brother Chris, nineteen, to whom Gregory was a sometime parent as well as older brother. In 1980, in partnership with Franklin Levy, he formed the Catalina Production Group, Ltd., named for his place of birth. Offices were first set up at the Burbank Studios, and then later moved to a shopping mall in Sherman Oaks, to be nearer his home. Also in 1980, at the annual "Battle of the Network Stars," he met pretty blonde Randi Oakes of TV's "CHiPs," with whom he became romantically involved.

"Once again in TV-Movieland, a woman literally lets down her hair and cavorts with a younger man," read Judith Crist's review of THE WOMEN'S ROOM, a three-hour ABC-TV presentation on September 14, 1980. The woman was Lee Remick; the younger man was Gregory, receiving special billing after the major cast members, with "and" before his name. The first production by his and Levy's company was ENOLA GAY: THE MEN, THE MISSION, THE ATOMIC BOMB, shown on NBC-TV on November 23, 1980, with Harrison in support of Patrick Duffy as the pilot colonel of the plane *Enola Gay*, which dropped the atomic bomb on Hiroshima during World War II.

While vacationing in Hawaii for a few weeks in the summer of 1980, Gregory was photographed beside the surf draped only in a towel. He and Levy had the photograph enlarged to poster size and sent it to NBC-TV, inscribed "For Ladies Only—Starring Gregory Harrison." The network responded favorably with a suggestion that they work up a teleplay. They hired writer John Riley, who had spent four months with male strippers at Los Angeles's largest club, Chippendale's, while writing an article for *New West* magazine. For more than three months, Gregory worked out every night with a bodybuilder, after filming "Trapper John" during the day. For two and a half months, he spent his weekends learning to bump and grind from both a choreographer and a professional stripper. While he was on hiatus from "Trapper John" in the summer of 1981, the movie was shot in New York City and in Atlanta at the Backstreet Disco, where two strip versions were filmed— one of them, far more risqué, was for foreign release. Under the Catalina banner, FOR LADIES ONLY was shown as a two-hour NBC-TV movie on November 9, 1981. Gregory headlined as an Iowan hankering to be a stage actor in New York City. When his money runs out, he takes a job at a male strip club, where he eventually becomes number one. The movie received a 30 share of the audience in the Nielsen ratings, ranking second in its timeslot to "Monday Night Football" on ABC-TV. Critic Judith Crist in *TV Guide* magazine, while not taking to it 100 percent because of "the screeches of drooling, lecherous women," did rate Gregory as "credible as both stud and untutored actor."

On November 8, 1981, the day before the airing of FOR LADIES ONLY, Gregory opened in his own stage production of *The Hasty Heart* at the Coast Theatre in West Hollywood, starring as the arrogant, terminally ill young soldier opposite Jennifer Salt as the nurse who befriends him. Later, the production moved to the larger, 2,100-seat Ahmanson Theatre in Los Angeles, and Cheryl Ladd took over the female lead. There it was taped for cablecast on Showtime, but would not be shown until September 1983. It was during 1981 that Harrison became a full-time user of cocaine.

On February 1, 1983, Catalina Productions featured rising young actor Rob Lowe in the telefeature THURSDAY'S CHILD. During that same TV "sweeps" month, on February 19, 1983, and also for Catalina, Gregory, with a thick, dark moustache, was THE FIGHTER. He starred as an unemployed millworker who hopes to regain his pride and the respect of his wife (Glynnis O'Connor) by earning money in the fight ring. During the course of the teleplay, Harrison had opportunity to exploit his 5' 11", 170-pound frame.

Despite the success of "Trapper John" and the large salary he earned as "Gonzo," Harrison was anxious for the end of his five-year contract in 1984. In 1983 he let it be known throughout the industry that he wanted to be in feature films, but he received no serious offers. An idea of his for a screen biography of Jim Morrison, late of the hard-rock group The Doors, failed to generate interest even though "I not only look like him, but I'm a musician." (The filmmaker Oliver Stone made a 1991 film about Morrison's life, with Val Kilmer starring as the late singer.) Gregory refused lucrative commercials and finally was rewarded with a feature film assignment for an Australian company. The shooting schedule required his presence in that nation's Outback for a period of time that would make him late reporting back to work on "Trapper John." The period of time was only nine days, for which he finally received approval from the network, but in exchange, a sixth season was added to his contract.

Gregory Harrison and Cybill Shepherd in SEDUCED (1985).

Braving the rugged Australian winter of 1983, along with a bite from a wild wombat, he survived the making of RAZORBACK (1984), about a giant terrorizing boar. *Variety* predicted that the JAWS-like feature "should bring home the bacon," but neither it nor Harrison was well received during its quick playoff dates in the United States.

Gregory and Randi Oakes were married on December 18, 1984. They took up residence in Sherman Oaks where, in February 1985, their first daughter, Emma Lee, was born. A second daughter, Lily Anne, would follow in 1988.

SEDUCED was a Catalina production for CBS-TV, shown on March 12, 1985. Gregory served as executive producer and co-starred with Cybill Shepherd in a tale of two former lovers who meet years later and become embroiled in the murder of her husband (Mel Ferrer). The one-third–page ad for "Trapper John, M.D." in *TV Guide* magazine for Sunday, January 5, 1986, read: "Gonzo says goodbye! Tonight: sad surprise, . . . a fond farewell." On that evening's episode Gonzo suffered a stroke, thus ending his workdays at San Francisco Memorial Hospital. Gregory was now free to pursue other acting endeavors as well as to devote more time to Catalina Productions. One of his first projects was as executive producer and star of OCEANS OF FIRE, televised in September 1986 and filmed in Mexico, off the Caribbean Sea. He was Ben Laforche, assigned to supervise a crew of disorderly former convicts in erecting an offshore oil rig.

Advertisements for the miniseries "Fresno" (1986) proclaimed: "A turbulent town tossed in a tempest of unchained passion . . . unspeakable greed . . . and unlimited parking!" The pivotal character, Charlotte Kensington (Carol Burnett), was a caricatured mixture of Jane Wyman's character in "Falcon Crest" and Joan Collins's predatory female in "Dynasty." Strolling into the midst of Charlotte's battle to gain supremacy over the raisin industry was bare-chested drifter "Torch" (Gregory). According to *TV Guide* magazine, his character was "the shirtless soap-opera stud with a restless, streetcorner sexiness." Before long, Torch awakens the sexual longings of just about every female in town. The labored multipart farce failed to generate audience interest. Also in November 1986, on the 10th, Showtime–Cable aired a taped version of *Picnic*, which had starred Gregory Harrison on the Los Angeles stage. He had the role of Hal the drifter, played on Broadway by Ralph Meeker and in the 1955 film by William Holden.

On May 18, 1987, ABC-TV presented a three-hour-long celebration of Hollywood's centennial, with Gregory portraying famed choreographer-director Busby Berkeley in a sketch featuring thirty celebrity chorines. Gregory had gone to Hawaii in the summer of 1986 to make his next feature film. In the forgettable NORTH SHORE (1987) he had a supporting role as a surfer who befriends a young surfing champion (Matt Adler) from Arizona. At about the same time that NORTH SHORE was released, in August 1987, Gregory drove himself to the Betty Ford Center in Palm Springs to undergo treatment for drug and alcohol dependency. After six years of substance abuse, his physical stamina was depleted. His wife had threatened to leave him, and his partner had temporarily walked out of their company. His life had become a series of lies to cover for his addiction. Sworn to sobriety after rehabilitation, he returned to the satisfaction of making movies for television, but it would be almost two years before he would speak publicly of his years as an addict. (At that time, he readily gave interviews regarding his former habit and did TV public service announcements in the hope of saving others from the same plight.)

MGM/UA, the owners of the rights to RED RIVER (1948), which had established screen credibility for both John Wayne and Montgomery Clift, asked Gregory and Levy to develop the western classic into a TV movie. Under the Catalina banner, with Gregory as co-executive producer, RED RIVER was shown on CBS on April 10, 1988, starring James Arness and Bruce Boxleitner in the Wayne and Clift roles. At the last minute, the actor scheduled to play Cherry Valance, a cocky gunfighter, quit and Gregory stepped into the part (it was played by John Ireland in 1948). A few weeks earlier, again for Catalina, Gregory and John Larroquette had co-starred as a pair of bumblers, who accidentally steal a priceless Renoir in the telefeature HOT PAINT (March 20, 1988). The *Chicago Sun Times* called it "a funny, stupid movie played solely for laughs." *TV Guide* magazine noted that it took Gregory "only 40 minutes of screen time to take off his shirt." He took off more than his shirt in the Pasadena Playhouse production in November 1988 of *Carnal Knowledge*, in which he appeared nude in silhouette.

Harrison made a deal with Lorimar Productions whereby he would join the cast of the CBS-TV nighttime drama "Falcon Crest" at the start of its ninth year in exchange for a series of his own when the right one came along. The pilot film of July 31, 1989, called "The Gregory Harrison Show," in which he was a career fashion photographer who tried to meet the demands of fatherhood, failed to make the grade. On September 29, 1989, he was introduced in "Falcon Crest" as Michael Sharpe, the wealthy, ruthless, slick business-man who assumes ownership of the Falcon Crest Winery while its matriarch (Jane Wyman) is in a coma. His return to series TV was noted by *TV Guide* magazine as his being "on the comeback trail." His salary was reported to be $60,000 per episode. Despite his presence, the sagging evening soap opera slowed down and ended its long run on May 17, 1990.

Meanwhile, on January 3, 1990, on PBS-TV, Gregory joined many other celebrities in a tribute to the Los Angeles County Music Center at the Dorothy Chandler Pavilion. In mid-January 1990 his Catalina Productions staged a revival of *Child's Play* at the Coast Playhouse. Gregory played Joseph Dobbs, the good teacher who refuses to believe ill of the students at St. Charles' School. Don Shirley of the *Los Angeles Times* felt that Gregory was "too young to play a man who's described in the stage directions as being in his late 50s," while *Daily Variety* credited him with mastering the role but failing "to carry off the later scenes, ultimately shortchanging an otherwise well-executed production." On February 14, 1990, he starred as a hired assassin in DANGEROUS PURSUIT, a USA–Cable movie, featuring Alexandra Powers, Brian Wimmer, and Scott Valentine, all of whom, according to *TV Guide* magazine, "manage to hold your attention."

Gregory returned to the CBS-TV network on Tuesday, September 11, 1990, in the preview showing of the Catalina-produced "The Family Man," a predictable half-hour sitcom, which then moved to its regular slot on Saturday night, beginning September 15, 1990. Originally called "Four Alarm Family" and proclaimed "Four-Alarm Fun" in the pages of *TV Guide* magazine, "The Family Man" starred Gregory as Jack Taylor, a widower/firefighter with four precocious children and a live-in father-in-law (Al Molin-aro). In the opener, Gregory did not once remove his shirt. Howard Rosenberg (*Los Angeles Times*) complained that the program was too derivative of Fred MacMurray's "My Three Sons" (1960–1972) and suffered by comparison, being charmless and too manipu-lative. In the initial Nielsen ratings for the new TV season, "The Family Man" fared poorly, finishing seventy-eighth. Meanwhile, Gregory could be seen delivering antidrug public service messages on TV. On October 2, 1990, Gregory co-starred with Jane Seymour in the CBS-TV movie ANGEL OF DEATH. He portrayed a mentally disturbed prison escapee who becomes fixated with an art teacher (Jane Seymour) and embarks on a new rash of murders. *Daily Variety* found the telefilm "as trite as its title" and claimed that it "wobbles from one cliché to another without looking back." As a psychotic hunk-on-the-run, Harrison had plenty of opportunity, as the trade paper noted, to "open his eyes wide." Once again the script called for Harrison to disrobe, this time to be a model in Seymour's art class. By early December 1990, it was evident that "The Family Man," sagging badly in the ratings—it was ranked 86—had bottomed out. CBS-TV put the comedy on hiatus. It returned briefly in the summer of 1991.

In BARE ESSENTIALS (January 8, 1991), a CBS-TV movie, Gregory co-starred as an American living on a South Pacific isle with his island love (Charlotte Lewis), and joined by New York public prosecutor Lisa Hartman and her corporate attorney significant other (Mark Linn-Baker). Laurence Vittes (*Hollywood Reporter*) dismissed the misadventure as "a forgettable romantic fantasy." *Daily Variety* noted, "What should be snappy dialog sags; Harrison, Linn-Baker and Hartman, working the dialog and situations for far more than they're worth, give the telefilm much-needed help." The telefeature was shot on location in the Virgin Islands at St. Thomas. When Gregory hosted the occasional CBS-TV variety entry "True Detectives" (March 29, 1991), a documentary show dealing with stories of real and amateur detectives, *Daily Variety* noted, "Harrison moves, sounds and acts like 'Unsolved Mysteries' host Robert Stack, but what makes this guy—best known for playing a bohemian doctor on 'Trapper John, M.D.'—the logical choice to front a crime re-creation show?" Meanwhile, on March 8, 1991, Gregory and his wife, Randi Oakes, became the parents of their third child with the birth of daughter Kate La-Priel, born at Cedars-Sinai Medical Center in Los Angeles.

With teeth the shade of polished pearls, finely dressed hair, handsome/rugged good looks, and a well-chiseled torso, Gregory Harrison is one of Hollywood's television hunks. There are many—Lee Horsley, Tom Selleck, Pierce Brosnan—who fit the same pattern, a type that has dominated the airwaves for close to a decade. (Encroaching on these established personalities is a new and different breed of young actor: Ken Wahl, Johnny Depp, Richard Grieco. They, in their earrings and leather, are establishing yet another image of the macho man.) While Gregory lacks the dramatic range to be a colossal actor, with the right role and proper direction, he is more than competent.

Filmography

The Harrad Experiment (Cinerama Releasing, 1973)
Trilogy of Terror (ABC-TV, 3/4/75)
Jim, the World's Greatest (Univ, 1976)
Fraternity Row [Oh, Brotherhood] (Par, 1977)

The Gathering (CBS-TV, 12/4/77)
The Best Place to Be (NBC-TV, 5/27/79–5/28/79)
The Women's Room (ABC-TV, 9/14/80)
Enola Gay: The Men, the Mission, the Atomic

Bomb (NBC-TV, 11/23/80)

For Ladies Only (NBC-TV, 11/9/81) (also co-producer)

The Fighter (CBS-TV, 2/19/83)

Razorback (WB, 1984)

Seduced (CBS-TV, 3/12/85) (also executive producer)

Oceans of Fire (CBS-TV, 9/16/86) (also executive producer)

North Shore (Univ, 1987)

Hot Paint (CBS-TV, 3/20/88) (also co-executive producer)

Red River (CBS-TV, 4/10/88) (also co-executive producer)

Dangerous Pursuit (USA–Cable, 2/14/90)

Angel of Death (CBS-TV, 10/2/90)

Bare Essentials (CBS-TV, 1/8/91)

Television Series

Logan's Run (CBS, 1977–78)

Centennial (NBC, 11/11/78; 12/3/78; 12/10/78; 1/14/79) [miniseries]

Trapper John, M.D. (CBS, 1979–86)

Fresno (CBS, 11/16/86–11/20/86) [miniseries]

Falcon Crest (CBS, 1989–90)

The Family Man (CBS, 1990–)

GREGORY HINES

"If there's anything I want, it's to be well rounded—to express
myself as an artist, a father, a husband, a friend."
—*American Film* magazine, December 1984

TAP DANCING NEVER REALLY DIES. PERIODICALLY IT IS SWEPT INTO
limbo until a current dance craze runs its course. Like four-inch neckties or pleated pants,
it always comes back. Tap dancing is a tremendous art requiring an enormous amount of
timing, energy, and improvisational ability. The most talented tapper of his time is
Gregory Hines. Like predecessors Fred Astaire, Bill "Bojangles" Robinson, Gene Kelly,
and Sammy Davis, Jr., he often makes it look easy. However, interspersed among those
debonair, nonchalant steps are many intricate and fast-moving motions that make the
viewer's jaw drop several inches in sheer admiration. The man is absolutely awesome.

Gregory Hines is also a good actor and has a not-altogether disagreeable singing
voice. Like Sammy Davis, Jr., of an earlier generation, Hines is remarkably gifted with a
multitude of talents. He has admitted, "It's difficult for me to consider myself an actor
because what I really think I am is a tap dancer." On another occasion, he explained,
"Most people don't know what tap dancing is today. They've never seen it in a contemporary light. The image of a tap dancer is still someone in a top hat and tails dancing up a
shiny black lacquer staircase. We need to shake that up."

Gregory Oliver Hines was born on St. Valentine's Day, Thursday, February 14,
1946, in New York City's Harlem, the second son of Maurice Hines, Sr., a soda salesman/
nightclub bouncer, and his wife, Alma Iola Lawless Hines. He was preceded in birth by a
brother, Maurice, Jr., born two years earlier, who was already enrolled in dance class. By
the time Gregory was three, his brother had taught him everything he had learned. Each
day Mrs. Hines escorted her two sons to Harlem's famed Apollo Theatre where they would
spend the day watching the stage show until she picked them up for supper. Their
playground and their school was the Apollo; their teachers were the array of talents who
performed there. This was Alma's way of providing a career for her children, to provide
them "an outlet . . . out of the ghetto."

Gregory, too, attended dance classes. However, he learned the most from masters of
improvisational tap such as Sandman Sims, Honi Coles, and Teddy Hale at the Apollo
who took the brothers under their wings. When Gregory was five, he and Maurice
performed locally for a week, and were held over for a second week at the Apollo. Two
years later, they went on tour during summer vacation from school, billed as The Hines

Kids. Another year went by, and when Gregory was eight, he and Maurice were cast as a shoeshine boy and a newspaper boy respectively in the Broadway musical comedy *The Girl in Pink Tights* (1954), which starred Jeanmaire. Their debut vehicle lasted 115 performances. Alma next arranged for them to study with Henry LeTang, who taught them spins, leaps, flips, and rapid-fire steps. Soon "the kids," looking cute in white collars and slicked-back, parted hair, were the opening act in ballrooms across much of the nation. In 1957, at age eleven, while performing in Miami, Gregory learned about "color lines." "I saw these two [water] fountains," he remembered. "One said 'white' the other, 'colored.' And I go right over to the white fountain 'cause I don't *want* any colored water. I got within a few feet, and about twenty of the black people in the show came running over and grabbed me. And I figured *the whole thing out.*"

By the late 1950s, tap had declined in favor of jazz dancing. The kids learned new steps and added dialogue and comedy to their routine, as well as a pantomimist named Johnny Brown. The trio, known as Hines, Hines and Brown, performed for a short time before Maurice, Sr., decided he wanted to go on tour with his sons and therefore learned to play drums. With Brown replaced by their father, the new act, called Hines, Hines and Dad, made appearances on TV on such variety shows as "The Ed Sullivan Show" and "The Tonight Show" and played the Palladium in London and the Olympia Theatre in Paris. Audiences responded enthusiastically to them, but they never quite attained stardom.

By the mid-1960s, according to Gregory, "Tap had died, and we were doing lounge routines. So I didn't dance for seven years. Didn't even own a pair of tap shoes." Their performances took place in slick nightclubs from Florida to Nevada. In 1970 Gregory married Patricia Panella, a white dance therapist; in 1971 their daughter, Daria, was born. A disagreement occurred between the brothers when Gregory decided that he wanted time off to write songs and perform rock music, while Maurice still preferred legitimate theater. The trio disbanded in 1973 at the same time that Gregory's marriage came to an end. He packed up and moved West with his daughter to the oceanside town of Venice in southern California where he led the life of a "long-haired hippie." He explained his actions years later with, "All my life, I'd had a buffer between me and the rest of the world—agents, managers, parents—I wanted to see what *I* wanted to do." As a new-wave hippie, he hung around the beaches, wrote songs, and played guitar. After a while, he borrowed money from Bill Cosby to start a jazz-rock band called Severence. To help make ends meet, he also worked as a waiter, a busboy, and an instructor in karate, another art he had learned along the way. He also met a woman named Pamela Koslow, who helped pay the rent.

Wanting to be closer to Daria, who had returned East to live with her mother, he too went back to New York City in January 1978. On the day he arrived, he won a $650-a-week tap-dancing role in the revue *The Last Minstrel Show*, which was Broadway-bound from Philadelphia. The production never made it to New York, but a month later both he and Maurice were signed to dance in *Eubie!*, an all-black tribute to composer Eubie Blake. Co-choreographed by their friend and former teacher Henry LeTang, it opened at the Ambassador Theatre on September 20, 1978. Both Gregory and Maurice were lauded for their singing and dancing, but Gregory received the lion's share of attention. The *New York Times* called Gregory's dancing "a kind of inspired graffiti." He was awarded an Outer Critics Award for his work, as well as a Tony nomination for Outstanding Performance by a Featured Actor in a Broadway Musical, but did not win. During the 439-performance run of the show, he performed a song-and-dance number, "Saturday Night Live," with the ninety-seven-year-old Eubie Blake. (In 1984 Warner Home Video released the eighty-five-minute *Eubie!*, edited from the cable-TV version of the musical. Gregory and Maurice Hines were among the cast reassembled for the project.)

Off the stage in 1979 he organized a group comprised of single parents in the theater to share experiences in the raising of children without benefit of a spouse. He received his second Tony nomination—this time for lead actor in a musical—for his portrayal of Scrooge in *Comin' Uptown* (December 20, 1979). It was his first try at acting, but this musical, based on Charles Dickens's *A Christmas Carol*, closed after forty-five performances. Off-Broadway in the spring of 1980, Hines choreographed *Blues in the Night*, a revue utilizing classic blues songs, which had a six-week run. In May 1980 at Town Hall, for twenty-four performances, he appeared in the *Black Broadway* tribute to past ethnic musicals. The cast included John W. Bubbles, Bobby Short, Nell Carter, and Honi Coles. Later in 1980, a pair of his tap shoes joined those of Fred Astaire, Ruby Keeler, and other dancers on the "Wall of Fame" at Manhattan's Roseland dancehall.

Sophisticated Ladies began in Philadelphia, moved to Washington, D.C., and, after several revisions, opened on Broadway on March 1, 1981. Gregory sang several of Duke Ellington's better-known songs, tapped up a staircase and danced down backwards, and performed a drum solo. For all his remarkable work in this musical, he received his third Tony Award nomination, again as lead actor, but again lost. While *Variety* was not satisfied with the musical as a whole, it did credit Hines's "remarkable variety of hoofing, singing, and slyly casual comedy."

Before embarking on the *Sophisticated Ladies* tour, Gregory made his motion picture debut in Mel Brooks's HISTORY OF THE WORLD: PART I, released in June 1981. It was not an auspicious screen beginning since the labored farce, referred to as "trash" by most critics, did so poorly that PART II was never made. In the sequences involving Madeline Kahn as Empress Nympho, Gregory was the libidinous slave Josephus, a part intended originally for Richard Pryor. On the heels of this disappointment, however, he had a major role in the South Bronx–filmed supernatural WOLFEN (1981), released a month later. He was a morgue technician who loses his throat to one of the huge wolves aprowl in New York City. Overall, Gregory's work in this horror thriller was praised by critics. (*Variety* noted that Hines was "excellent as a space-case coroner.")

On April 12, 1981, Gregory began a second interracial marriage with Pamela Koslow, whom he had met in California in 1975. They have a son, Zachary Evan, born in 1985.

In Los Angeles with the touring company of *Sophisticated Ladies*, Gregory learned of plans to make a movie about the legendary 1920s Harlem nightspot The Cotton Club, where his grandmother, Ora Hines, had been a showgirl performing for the wealthy white clientele. He also heard that producer Robert Evans was interested in casting him as Cab Calloway. However, after obtaining a copy of the script, he decided he would rather try for the black romantic lead, Sandman Williams, a tap dancer. To convince Evans that the switch should occur, Gregory visited the producer's offices and danced from the floor to a table and back again. This audition won him the larger part (originally conceived with Richard Pryor in mind), but the film-in-the-making had a long way to go—involving rewrites and financing difficulties—before its completion.

Meanwhile, Gregory was seen in an assortment of TV specials. In ABC's "I Love Liberty" (March 21, 1982) he was among those (including Jane Fonda, Burt Lancaster, and Barbra Streisand) saluting America; on CBS's "Shirley MacLaine's Illusions" (June 24, 1982) he was the star's sole guest; for ABC's "Parade of Stars" (May 22, 1983), a benefit for the Actor's Fund charity, he was among the many talents saluting the golden age of vaudeville. On theatrical screens, Hines appeared in DEAL OF THE CENTURY (1983), third-billed after Chevy Chase and Sigourney Weaver. He played an off-kilter test pilot involved in selling rejected airplanes to a Latin American country. *People* magazine suggested to its readers that they should see this rambling farce only if they felt "like being bored stiff for a couple of hours."

THE COTTON CLUB, released in December 1984, had required months to splice together due to behind-the-scenes squabbles, and it was finally tabulated to have cost at least $51 million. To date it has grossed only $12,931,284 in domestic film rentals, making it one of the all-time financial debacles of Hollywood filmmaking. Even with seventeen musical numbers cut, the release print was an overlong 127 minutes, and the public did not want to see it. However, the musical is captivating in its depiction of the Harlem of the 1920s and 1930s. The costumes and sets are authentic, and much of the acting is worth the price of admission. Critic Roger Ebert was among those who applauded it as, "quite simply, a wonderful movie." Maurice Hines was also in the cast, and according to Ebert, the brothers created "a wonderful moment of reconciliation when they begin to tap dance and end by forgiving each other for a lifetime's hurts." As expected, Gregory was more effective in the dance moments than as a romantic lead. Also in 1984, Gregory had what amounted to a cameo role, as one of those who help the Muppets to get their college show to Broadway in THE MUPPETS TAKE MANHATTAN.

He returned to the nightclub circuit in March 1985 with a seventy-minute solo act of dancing, singing, and playing the guitar. On May 4, 1985, he participated in the reopening of the Apollo Theatre with a six-hour taped tribute, shown in a condensed two-hour version on NBC-TV as "Motown Returns to the Apollo" (May 19, 1985). He won an Emmy nomination for this appearance. On November 5, 1985, he starred as "The Amazing Falsworth" in an episode of NBC-TV's "Amazing Stories." He completed the year by co-starring as a dancer who defects to Russia in WHITE NIGHTS (1985), filmed in Europe. His character's disillusionment with life, as well as with dancing, is dissipated through the rediscovery of his art with the help of a Russian dancer (Mikhail Baryshnikov). The movie's director, Taylor Hackford, described Gregory with: "At first you want to look at him and laugh, but there's a lot of pain and feeling back there. And that's what makes for good *actors*—not just comedians. I think Gregory is really a born movie actor."

NBC-TV honored the late Reverend Martin Luther King, Jr., on January 20, 1986, with an all-star celebration of the first observance of King's birthday as a federal holiday. The program was taped at Washington's Kennedy Center, New York's Radio City Music Hall, and Atlanta's Civic Center; Gregory danced in the Kennedy Center segment with the Alvin Ailey American Dance Theatre.

He was billed over comedian Billy Crystal, his co-star, in RUNNING SCARED (1986), in which they both played drug-busting, unorthodox Chicago cops who think it may be time to retire, but first pursue a small-time godfather of crime (Jimmy Smits). This buddy policeman comedy is fairly routine, but an obligatory car chase is one of its true highlights. *People* magazine regretted that "this song-and-dance master [Hines] is frittering away his formidable talents in a film that ignores them." Still, with Crystal as a relaxing catalyst, Hines seemed far more at ease on camera than he had in previous films.

"Gregory Hines. The Singer. A New Stage of a Brilliant Career" read the full-page magazine and newspaper ads heralding Hines's debut solo album on record, cassette, and compact disc. Released in February 1988 by Epic, a subsidiary of CBS Records, *Gregory Hines* included an earlier recording of "There's Nothing Better Than Love," sung in duet with the album's producer, Luther Vandross. In March 1988, also on Epic, he had a single recording and video, "That Girl Wants to Dance with Me." Also in March, his eighth motion picture was released. Shot in Thailand, OFF LIMITS (1988) has Gregory as a plainclothes military policeman investigating the murders of six Vietnamese prostitutes, all mothers of American servicemen's children. He was billed second, after Willem Dafoe. When the film was released on videocassette, *Video Review* magazine called it a "real sleeper" and "worth watching in its video version if you missed it theatrically, and odds are you probably did." In late 1988 Hines played "master" to Ben Vereen's cat in the Showtime–Cable presentation of "Puss in Boots" on "Faerie Tale Theatre."

Gregory Hines in OFF LIMITS (1988).

TAP (1989) hoped to update the art of tap dance for the 1980s. It starred Gregory as a disgruntled ex-hoofer fresh out of jail who is convinced by his aging tap mentor (Sammy Davis, Jr.) to exploit his talents and go straight. Gregory brought Henry LeTang into the movie production as choreographer, and several tap-dancing legends—Sandman Sims, Harold Nicholas, Bunny Briggs, Steve Condos, Arthur Duncan, and Jimmy Slyde—made appearances on screen. *Premiere* magazine lauded Gregory as "the magnetic center of a happy, uninhibited, tap-dancing world." Unfortunately, the picture did not attract action-hungry audiences. An adjunct to the picture was the March 17, 1989, hour-long PBS-TV presentation of "Gregory Hines' Tap Dance in America," a special taped at Billy Rose's Diamond Horseshoe in Manhattan in which Gregory did a tap duet with long-legged Tommy Tune. On July 9, 1989, at New York City's Delacorte Theatre in Central Park, he joined a Hollywood cast including Michelle Pfeiffer, Jeff Goldblum, and Stephen Collins, in the free New York Shakespeare Festival production of *Twelfth Night* for seventeen performances. Gregory played Feste, the jester to Sir Toby Belch (John Amos). *The New Yorker* magazine decided that "What the production expects of Hines—and expects the audience to expect—is that he be himself."

Hines began the new decade with the February 4, 1990, ABC-TV tribute to Sammy Davis, Jr., called "Honoring a Show-Business Legend." The dying Davis, who had undergone unsuccessful treatment for throat cancer, was celebrated in the two-hour show by many other celebrities such as Ella Fitzgerald, Frank Sinatra, and Nell Carter. Gregory was joined in a tap routine by Davis himself.

Off the screen for well over a year, Gregory was suddenly involved in the shooting of several productions. In the first, EVE OF DESTRUCTION, an action thriller lensed in February 1990 in the Santa Clarita Valley north of Los Angeles, he was an expert military marksman sent to terminate an android-gone-bad (Renee Soutendijk). Although his weight had risen to 182 pounds from his normal 150 pounds, he did most of his own stunt work. Originally slated for release in October 1990, its distribution was reset for early 1991. A RAGE IN HARLEM (1991) was a low-budget feature shot in Cincinnati, Ohio, in order to simulate the Harlem of 1956. He was cast as one of two brothers (the other was Forest Whitaker) in search of a woman (Robin Givens) with a trunk filled with gold. Termed a comedy thriller, it featured Danny Glover as a Harlem kingpin with connections for fencing the gold. In the late summer of 1990 it was announced that Hines and Martin Short would co-star in UNDERCOVER for Orion Pictures. In the Alan Rudolph–directed picture, Hines was to portray a traveling prosthetics salesman from Ohio who becomes involved accidentally in a police undercover drug operation. The picture was supposed to begin shooting in October 1990, but was delayed. Meanwhile, in October 1990, Gregory performed on a bill with singer Gladys Knight at Bally's Casino Resort in Las Vegas. Later in the same month, he teamed with the Los Angeles–based Rhapsody in Taps dance company for a new dance piece that was premiered on October 27, 1990, at the local Japan America Theatre.

Although Gregory had once held a black belt in karate and had studied the Korean martial art of Tae Kwan Do (consisting mostly of kicking techniques), Gregory has gotten out of the practice and no longer considers himself a black belt, simply because "I haven't maintained the discipline." Nowadays, he engages in weightlifting, introduced to him by Billy Crystal, in an effort to keep his weight down.

Based in New York City with his family, Gregory still has a primary goal: "Tap dancers for years have wanted respect for tap as an art. It's always been a struggle." Now in his mid-forties, Hines is more eager to concentrate his time and energies on making movies. "I'm starting to feel more confident as an actor with each part," he has said. "But it's difficult to find really good parts with enough dimension written for a black actor." He especially likes performing in action movies because of the opportunity to perform stunts. "I feel like everything I do stems from my ability as a dancer. So these kinds of roles, while it's not like dancing, it is choreography." Realizing that he has not been working enough in recent years, he adds, "If I did a few movies in a row, close together, that would be good."

Filmography

History of the World: Part I (20th–Fox, 1981)
Wolfen (Orion/WB, 1981)
Deal of the Century (WB, 1983)
The Cotton Club (Orion, 1984)
The Muppets Take Manhattan (Tri-Star, 1984)
White Nights (Col, 1985)

Running Scared (MGM, 1986)
Off Limits (20th–Fox, 1988)
Tap (Tri-Star, 1989)
Eve of Destruction (Orion, 1991)
A Rage in Harlem (Miramax, 1991)

Broadway Shows

The Girl in Pink Tights (1954)
Eubie! (1978)

Comin' Uptown (1979)
Sophisticated Ladies (1981)

Album Discography

Eubie! (WB HS-3267) [OC]
Gregory Hines (Epic OE-40671)

Sophisticated Ladies (RCA CPL2-4098) [OC]
Tap (Epic SE-45084) [ST]

WILLIAM HURT

"There are lots of gates through which you can race the race you raced
last time, all kinds of gates—and they come with checks on them."
—*Premiere* magazine, November 1987

WILLIAM HURT IS HANDSOME, TALENTED, AND INTELLIGENT, CUT TO
the pattern of a traditional leading man in the Robert Redford mold. However, his
height—6' 3"—leads to physical comparisons to the equally bulky Nick Nolte and French
star Gérard Depardieu. Hurt is quick to rebuff a leading-man label, stating that he "is a
character actor in a leading man's body." In conversation, he is verbose and prone to
abstruse, rambling discourses that have caused the likes of all-American Burt Lancaster,
accustomed to direct speech, to stare in gaping astonishment. Not since the convoluted
speeches of Jon Voight has the world experienced such flights of rhetoric as those of Hurt.
Despite his intense, ambiguous language, William is totally dedicated to his profession.
Even when running in a park he has gotten "this image of the actor who walks from city to
city and puts on a mask and loses himself and makes others find themselves. This is my
belief, my faith."

William McChord Hurt was born on Monday, March 20, 1950, in Washington,
D.C., to well-to-do parents, who were there awaiting a U.S. State Department posting.
His father, McChord Hurt, was an official who would be given the title Director of Trust
Territories—destination Hawaii and Guam. His mother, Claire McGill Hurt, had given
birth earlier to son Kenneth, with son James to follow William. William spent his first six
years growing up in the tropical South Pacific climate. In 1956 his parents divorced, and
William moved with his mother and brothers to New York City and a claustrophobic
four-room apartment on the Upper West Side. This culture shock was eased by summer
visits to his father, whose duty stations included Sudan, Somaliland, and Spain. But
William always had to return to New York and its street gangs, with whom he more than
once came into contact. Claire Hurt had been working at Time, Inc., publishers of *Time*
and *Life* magazines, where she met Henry Luce III, whose father had founded the august
publishing firm. In August 1960 they married and the family moved into a twenty-two-
room duplex on the Upper East Side, an exclusive area of Manhattan.

As a "short, fat, and uncoordinated" kid of fourteen, William was sent to Middlesex
School, a prestigious college preparatory academy in Concord, Massachusetts. There he
was neither athletic nor popular. "The transition was too great," he has said of this shift in
lifestyle, which required him to dress in herringbone jacket with tie. A teacher helped rid

him of some of the anger by suggesting that he become involved in school dramatics, an activity he found more fulfilling than anything else in his life to that time. However, he did not consider acting as anything but a part of the school work. Henry Luce III, a scholarly and deeply religious man, influenced William when the time for college came in the fall of 1968; William entered Tufts University in Medford, Massachusetts, as a theology major. In 1971, in the spring of his junior year, he married Mary Beth Supinger, eighteen months his senior, a graduate of New York University and an aspiring actress. Also during his junior year, under his bride's influence, his interest in theology waned in favor of acting, to which he devoted his extracurricular hours. In his final year of university studies he switched his major to drama, reasoning that "religion does not represent humanity anymore." His senior year was spent with Mary Beth in London studying acting under a student exchange program. In the spring of 1972 he obtained his bachelor's degree from Tufts.

He requested drama auditions for graduate acting study at Yale, New York University, and Juilliard's newly formed Drama School, but only the latter responded. His acceptance in the autumn of 1972 as a two-year student there settled his indecision over whether to train as an actor in England or the United States. In 1974, because of a traumatic and emotional crisis over the death of his mother, coupled with the fact that his marriage was foundering, he abruptly quit without graduating. Of Juilliard, he would remember, "I learned a tremendous amount . . . but I always was at odds with the institution and wanted to get away." He got even farther away by purchasing a Honda motorcycle in the spring of 1975 and embarking on a cross-country trek.

In June, he reached Ashland, Oregon, where he auditioned for and won the part of Edmund in the Oregon Shakespeare Festival's production of Eugene O'Neill's *A Long Day's Journey into Night*. "I had worked for years in complete darkness, complete doubt, complete confusion," he admitted later, "and then one day I walked out onstage and realized I had some craft. It was just there—and it felt so good." A year later he was back in Manhattan, furthering his stage training with the New York Shakespeare Festival in three small parts in *Henry V* at Central Park's open-air Delacorte Theatre, followed by a limited run at the Meadow Brook Theatre in Rochester, Michigan, in *Man and Superman*. He also did a stint in a 1976 episode of the New York–filmed "Kojak," the cop drama series starring Telly Savalas.

Hurt tried out for the lead in Corinne Jacker's new play, *My Life*, which the Circle Repertory Company world-premiered at its off-Broadway playhouse in Greenwich Village's Sheridan Square. About winning the role, William enthused, "It was like walking into my own home. All the things I had been thinking about for so long were in focus there." The *New Yorker* magazine found his acting to exhibit "quiet strength and emotion," and the *Village Voice* awarded him an Obie Award for giving one of the most distinguished performances of the 1977–1978 off-Broadway season. This was the start of an affiliation with the Circle Repertory Company that would last many years, with William returning periodically to its stage. Meanwhile, Corinne Jacker asked that he audition for "The Best of Families," a limited PBS-TV series about three late nineteenth-century American families, which premiered in a two-hour presentation on October 27, 1977, followed by seven subsequent sixty-minute episodes. William had the part of James Lathrop.

During the 1977–1978 season, Hurt starred in *Ulysses in Traction*, a revival of *Lulu*, and in *The 5th of July* as homosexual Kenneth Talley, Jr., a disabled Vietnam veteran. With him on stage in the latter play was the more delicately built Jeff Daniels, whose part required him to carry William in his arms. For his full season of work, William received a 1978 Theatre World Award, naming him one of the season's "outstanding new performers." On January 25, 1978, he was seen as Walter in the ninety-minute PBS-TV movie VERNA: U.S.O. GIRL, with Sissy Spacek in the title role. *Variety* noted, "the relationship between Sissy Spacek as the untalented U.S.O. girl in World War II and William Hurt as the soldier who falls for her never quite comes off—a key element that falls flat."

Although William and Mary Beth had reconciled in April 1978, their marriage failed for a second time and a final separation came in September; however, they would not divorce until December 3, 1982. Professionally Mary Beth retained the name Hurt.

In the early months of 1979 he played Father Rivard in Circle Rep's revival of *The Runner Stumbles*, a role that would be played on the screen the same year by Dick Van Dyke. In the last month of 1979 Hurt alternated in the title role in *Hamlet* and as secretary to Queen Elizabeth I in *Mary Stuart*. Of his noteworthy performance as the prince of Denmark, Clive Barnes (*New York Post*) wrote that it was "a marker stone in the career of a great actor." William has said that he received several movie offers as a result of his stage work. However, nothing appealed to him until he read a Paddy Chayefsky novel about a scientist whose experiments in sensory deprivation end in a reversion to his primal past. He accepted the role of the psychophysiologist, Dr. Eddie Jessup, in ALTERED STATES (1980), in a great deal of whose footage he is either philosophizing or semi-nude. Filming began in December 1979, but was interrupted many times by maddening disagreements between Chayefsky and director Arthur Penn. The latter finally quit and was replaced by Ken Russell. Critic Pauline Kael described the professional union of Chayefsky and Russell as "impossibly mismatched." However, of William she wrote, "The artful young stage actor brings nuances to his . . . role by acting slightly withdrawn and inhuman." Upon completion of ALTERED STATES and feeling "overwhelmed" by the experience, he started to rely on beer or wine for relaxation—a habit that would last more than six years and that would include his graduating to stronger alcoholic beverages, all of which took a noticeable physical and emotional toll.

His second film, the New York–lensed EYEWITNESS (1981), had him as a Vietnam veteran who works as a janitor, quietly doing his own thing until he meets a glamorous TV anchorwoman (Sigourney Weaver). To gain her attention, he says in what has been called his "low campus" voice, "Say, do your floors need buffing—or something? I shine it slowly, gently—until it beams" and smiles a boyish grin. *Newsweek* magazine found his "boyish romanticism endearingly real."

Also in February 1981 he returned to Circle Rep to portray Lord Byron in *Childe Byron* and remained to star, in 1982, in *Richard II*, as well as play two small roles in *The*

Great Grandson of Jedediah Kohler. That summer he performed in stock at Saratoga Springs, New York, where he met a New York City Ballet dancer named Sandra Jennings (real name Cronsberg). Thereafter, they shared his Central Park West apartment in Manhattan. Meanwhile, on December 21, 1981, he had a leading role as Jay Follet in the NBC-TV live presentation of "All the Way Home," telecast from the University of Southern California's Bing Theatre and co-starring Sally Field, Ned Beatty, Betty Garrett, and Polly Holliday. During the summer of 1982, Hurt played Oberon in the New York Shakespeare Festival's production of *A Midsummer Night's Dream.* A film, tentatively titled EAGLE OF BROADWAY, was scheduled for Hurt and James Cagney, but was cancelled due to the latter's ill health.

Meanwhile, Hurt made his breakthrough film, BODY HEAT (1981). He was seen as Ned Racine, the small-time Florida lawyer who is beguiled by manipulative, murderous Matty Walker (Kathleen Turner). At first she leads him on, then rejects him, but willingly gives herself to him after he crashes through her front window. If Hurt was not already considered a movie star, his sex-obsessed role in BODY HEAT gained him the title. First-time director Lawrence Kasdan, who also wrote the script, obtained from William, according to *American Film* magazine, "a rich, haunted performance." Hurt rejected an offer to play a married doctor who realizes he is gay and leaves his wife in MAKING LOVE (1982), but willingly joined Kasdan's cast of THE BIG CHILL (1983). He was the impotent, pot-smoking, cocaine-sniffing Vietnam veteran. Co-star Glenn Close commented, not unkindly, "His concentration is so extreme that he can make everybody around him tense."

William Hurt in GORKY PARK (1983).

Sandra Jennings joined William from December 9, 1982, to January 10, 1983, during the filming of THE BIG CHILL in Beaufort, South Carolina, one of the few states to recognize common-law marriages. On January 17, 1983, Sandra gave birth to their son, Alexander Devon Hurt, in New York City. William had little time to be with his son before he went on location the following month to Finland and Sweden to earn a $1 million salary as the lead in GORKY PARK (1983), also starring Lee Marvin, who was still smarting from his much-publicized, mudslinging palimony suit. The film was adapted from Martin Cruz Smith's engrossing thriller, and although William, with a British accent, did not immediately match the reader's conception of a Russian policeman, the viewer adapted to his characterization as the film wore on. Hurt was reportedly difficult during the shoot, to the point of provoking a punch in the jaw from one of the British actors, giving Marvin cause to snort, "Good, man, you saved me the trouble." Released in December, GORKY PARK grossed a disappointing $7,982,552 in domestic film rentals.

Like many actors of his generation, William did not like to give interviews because he preferred to keep his private life private. However, he would do so to promote one of his movies. His problem, though, was that he was often inebriated, making suggestive remarks to the ladies and swearing at the men of the press. To one journalist's compliments, he sneered, "Don't treat me like a god." Still, his drinking did not impair his acting, as evidenced by a nomination for a Tony Award as Outstanding Featured Actor in a Play for his work in David Rabe's *Hurlyburly*. The play premiered in Chicago in the spring of 1984, and after an off-Broadway stopover in June–July, the Mike Nichols–directed project transferred to Broadway in August 1984 for a run of almost a year. Although he lost the Tony to Barry Miller (*Biloxi Blues*), Hurt's next screen work would earn him several major awards.

Taking a substantial but undisclosed cut in salary, he went to Brazil to co-star with Raul Julia in KISS OF THE SPIDER WOMAN (1985). He was Luis Molina, an effeminate homosexual imprisoned for molesting a boy, living in a private movie fantasy world. His political prisoner cellmate (Julia), initially repelled by the newcomer, learns from him and vice-versa. *Playgirl* magazine termed William's portrayal "brilliant and unexpected," while the *New York Times* found that he made "the campy, flamboyant aspects of Molina's homosexuality seem credible and metaphorical in equal measure." For his memorable performance, Hurt won the best actor award at the Cannes Film Festival, was honored as best actor by the British Academy of Film and Television Arts, and won the Oscar as Best Actor. He almost did not attend the Academy Award presentations on March 24, 1986, because "artists don't compete," but was talked into attending by Steven Spielberg. When presenter Sally Field gave him his award, he whispered to her, "How do I deal with this?" She replied, "Go with it." He did, with an acceptance speech that included, "I accept this with Raul [Julia]. . . . I'm proud to be an actor."

After living together for three years, Hurt and Sandra Jennings had parted in 1984, with him paying her $65,000 a year in voluntary child support and "maintenance." His date at the Oscar ceremonies in March 1986 was a twenty-year-old hearing-impaired actress named Marlee Matlin, with whom he was living and co-starring in CHILDREN OF A LESSER GOD (1986). Based on Mark Medoff's Tony-winning play of 1980, it was a love story about an unorthodox teacher (Hurt) at a school for the deaf and an insulated, angry deaf woman (Matlin). They communicate through a mixture of lip-reading and sign language, which he learned for the role. Off camera, he told *Newsweek* magazine, "I've been waiting for her for a long time." On March 30, 1987, Matlin was presented with a Best Actress Academy Award by her lover, as Best Actor of the previous year. Although he, too, was nominated for an award, in the Best Actor category, he lost to Paul Newman (THE COLOR OF MONEY).

On the personal side, William revealed the existence of a select club known as "The

Bozos," whose members were required to have a "certain cool irreverence." He was a member in good standing, along with Robin Williams, Whoopi Goldberg, Kevin Kline, and Christopher Reeve. It was also reported that William had spent a month in 1986 at the Betty Ford Clinic in Palm Springs for alcohol-abuse rehabilitation and that Marlee had accompanied him for moral support. He joined Alcoholics Anonymous in 1987. Of his new-found sobriety, friend Glenn Close said, "He's in great shape; it's wonderful just to be around him. He's more accessible, more forgiving of himself. When you hate yourself, it's pretty hard to deal with other people."

"It's the story of their lives" read the movie posters for BROADCAST NEWS (1987), in which William was Tom Grunick, a handsome, not too smart, opportunistic newsman who uses people at the Washington, D.C., television news bureau to further his career as a network news anchorman. Written, directed, and produced by James L. Brooks, the incisive motion picture grossed $42.5 million domestically in its first sixteen weeks of release, between December 16, 1987, and March 1, 1988. William received yet another Academy Award nomination as Best Actor, but he lost again, this time to Michael Douglas (WALL STREET).

"Hurt looks shell-shocked throughout the movie, which is very understandable," observed one critic of A TIME OF DESTINY (1988), a colossal failure which had William bound for revenge during World War II against his brother-in-law (Timothy Hutton), whom he blames for the death of his father (Francisco Rabal). Released in April, it was on home video by October in the hope of recouping some of its cost. In May 1988 Sandra Jennings filed suit against Hurt in New York City, claiming that, compared with him, she was living at poverty level with their son. She wanted half of all his earnings since his divorce from Mary Beth in 1982.

The very cerebral THE ACCIDENTAL TOURIST (1988) reunited Hurt with BODY HEAT's Kathleen Turner and Lawrence Kasdan. It was released in Los Angeles and New York the last week of December to qualify for awards of 1988. Once again, William was cast as a bit of a repressed dimwit, this time a travel writer weary of traveling and unable to show emotion. *Newsday* claimed that his "portrait is a masterpiece," while *USA Today* decided his "performance is another triumph." Critic Roger Ebert noted that Kasdan had the ability "to employ Hurt's gift for somehow being likable at the same time he seems to be withdrawn." The movie was named best of the year by the New York Film Critics and received an Oscar nomination, but lost to RAIN MAN. Geena Davis, however, as a big-mouthed kennel worker who emotionally liberates the hero, was named Best Supporting Actress. Also in 1988, Hurt won the UCLA Spencer Tracy Award based on THE ACCIDEN-TAL TOURIST and his overall professional achievements.

After his divorce from Mary Beth, William had publicly stated that he would never again marry. His resolution was dashed on March 4, 1989, when the thirty-eight-year-old actor took as his bride twenty-seven-year-old Heidi Henderson, the daughter of bandlead-er Skitch Henderson, in Sneden's Landing, New York. On August 7, they became parents to son Samuel.

"He'd have one drink, and he'd have a personality change. He was abusive verbally and he used to spit at me and he used to throw things at me, but he never hit me until after Alex was born. I think he was jealous of Alex." This was typical of the testimony of Sandra Jennings about her turbulent existence with William in the six-day Manhattan court trial, which was partially televised and made headlines in almost every newspaper, tabloid, and magazine in the United States. During the palimony trial, which began on June 19, 1989, William's behavior, which he had hoped to keep private, was unveiled. He often lost his temper while under examination by Jennings's attorney, Richard Golub, who maintained that the couple had had a legal and spiritual marriage in South Carolina, where they lived together during the filming of THE BIG CHILL. *People* magazine reported, "Not since Michelle Triola socked the late Lee Marvin in the landmark palimony trial in 1979 has such private pain made broadcast news." Mary Beth Hurt took the stand, while Kevin Kline and Glenn Close signed affidavits on his behalf. William shunned reporters during the trial, but Sandra was more than willing to confide assorted domestic horrors. On October 3, 1989, New York State Supreme Court Justice Jacqueline Silbermann ruled in favor of Hurt, stating that he and Sandra did not have a common-law marriage and that Jennings had altered her signature on a photocopy of an original document. Jennings appealed the decision, but a five-judge panel of the Appellate Division of the New York State Supreme Court (in Manhattan) on April 24, 1990, unanimously upheld Justice Silbermann's verdict.

In July 1989 William outbid Hollywood production companies to obtain the dramatic rights to the life story of Portland, Oregon, cartoonist John Callahan, who is paralyzed from the chest down as the result of a Los Angeles auto accident in 1972. Hurt's plan included a one-man stage show, followed by a film of Callahan's autobiography, *Don't Worry, He Won't Get Far on Foot.* He joined Pamela Reed on stage at the Promenade Theatre in New York City on August 14, 1989, in reading A. R. Gurney's two-character play *Love Letters.* Beginning October 17, 1989, he returned to the Circle Repertory Company in New York in a supporting role as a UPS delivery man in *Beside Herself,* which the *Hollywood Reporter* judged "a laughably dreadful play," stating that William "intentionally mumbles his words, but he's no Marlon Brando. It's a professional performance, but he's too clean for the role [of a young man who has an affair with an older woman]."

Continuing to make news, William was back in court in early November 1989 when his former assistant, Diana Schiebel, filed for worker's compensation benefits based on an allegation that working for him had caused her "stress-related traumas" because he had hit his then-girlfriend Marlee Matlin. William denied abusing Matlin, but did admit there had been some "physical event." In Taipei, Taiwan, the weekend of December 9–10, 1989, at Taiwan's annual Golden Horse Awards, he was the recipient of the best actor prize, netting him a statuette and $4,000, for his work in THE ACCIDENTAL TOURIST.

In I LOVE YOU TO DEATH, in release April 6, 1990, Hurt took a supporting role as a favor to director Lawrence Kasdan and star Kevin Kline. With beard, long hair, and glasses, he was one of two drug addicts (the other was Keanu Reeves) hired by the wife (Tracey Ullman) and mother-in-law (Joan Plowright) of a philandering pizza maker (Kline) to murder him. *Daily Variety* slammed William for his hammy performance (he "pulls faces embarrassingly") and *Time* magazine rated him and Reeves with accomplishing "ostensibly hilarious results." The comedy proved to be a box-office dud.

Playgirl magazine in its September 1990 issue named William one of the ten sexiest men of 1990 because "he has melted our hearts in every role he's played. We especially loved him in BODY HEAT because it gave us ideas—and because he looked great with his clothes off. And that's not acting." Later in the month, on September 21, 1990, Hurt played the title role in Chekhov's *Ivanov* at the Yale Repertory Theatre in New Haven, directed by Oleg Yefremov, director of the Moscow Art Theatre.

While his participation in NAKED TANGO and SHINING THROUGH, both planned as 1991 releases, was cancelled for one reason or another, he appeared in ALICE (1990), a Manhattan-filmed comedy from Woody Allen co-starring Hurt with Mia Farrow, Alec Baldwin, and Joe Mantegna. William was the husband of a woman (Farrow) experiencing a midlife crisis. Hurt replaced Willem Dafoe in UNTIL THE END OF THE WORLD (1991), shot on location in eight countries, including Russia. The first feature film since LAW-RENCE OF ARABIA (1962) to be photographed in 65mm, it was set in post–cold war 1999 and had an international cast (Jeanne Moreau, Max von Sydow, Sam Neill) directed by Wim Wenders. William plays an American obsessed with tracing the journeys and discoveries of his father. In mid-1991 Hurt played the title role in THE DOCTOR, as a surgeon who becomes a patient when he diagnoses a cancerous tumor on his own vocal cords. Hurt was a replacement for Warren Beatty, who dropped out of the project because of "creative differences" with director Randa Haines.

The complex actor told an interviewer in 1987, "I always hold out the option that I'm gonna stop this [acting] and go fishing the rest of my life. . . . I think I discovered a long time ago, and rediscover sometimes, that I am alone—not that I'm lonely, but that I am alone."

Filmography

Verna: U.S.O. Girl (PBS-TV, 1/25/78)
Altered States (WB, 1980)
Eyewitness [The Janitor] (20th–Fox, 1981)
Body Heat (WB, 1981)
The Big Chill (Col, 1983)
Gorky Park (Orion, 1983)
Kiss of the Spider Woman (Island Alive, 1985)
Children of a Lesser God (Par, 1986)
Broadcast News (20th–Fox, 1987)

A Time of Destiny (Col, 1988)
The Accidental Tourist (WB, 1988)
I Love You to Death (Tri-Star, 1990)
Alice (Orion, 1990)
The Doctor (BV, 1991)

Future Releases

Until the End of the World (WB, 1991)

TV Series

The Best of Families (PBS, 1977)

Broadway Plays

Hurlyburly (1984)

TIMOTHY HUTTON

> "One thing about young actors like Sean [Penn] and me—we've got
> such a strong sense of where we're at. The whole breed of new actors
> is very confident, responsible, and mature; we're willing to take on
> the world."   —*Moviegoer* magazine, May 1984

IN 1981, MARY TYLER MOORE, HUTTON'S CO-STAR OF ORDINARY PEOPLE
(1980), said, "Timothy is nonarrogant and doesn't appear to be driven by desire for
success or ambition." The accuracy of this observation has altered little. Hutton is an
extremely laid-back individual with a natural ability to act, an innate talent that was
displayed, duly noted, and rewarded with honors when he was barely out of his teens. A
high-school dropout, he received his acting lessons on the job, while his knowledge of life
was achieved through research of all kinds—historical, biographical, and geographical—
into every movie locale, plot, and characterization with which he has been associated.

Although Hutton refused interviews following the release of his debut feature film
in 1980, he did become accessible to the press for a few years beginning in 1981. Later, he
developed a hands-off approach, much like that of his pal Sean Penn. At Oscar time in
1989, when he was asked, for the fun of it, where he kept his Academy Award, his publicist
answered coldly for him, stating, "He's not interested in sharing that information." Some
critics have hailed Timothy Hutton as the era's new Henry Fonda, a movie star to whom
he bears a physical resemblance. Yet so far, Timothy lacks Fonda's acting depth and
comedic gift, but this may change with the passing of time.

Timothy Tarquin Hutton was born in Malibu, California, on Tuesday, August 16,
1960, a year after the birth of his sister, Heidi. His parents were lanky Jim Hutton, known
in the entertainment industry as one of the screen's best new light comedians, and
Maryline Poole Hutton, a teacher. Tim did not speak a word until he was two, when his
words tumbled out in full sentences, causing his parents to consider him unusually
intelligent. When he was three, his parents divorced. Maryline and her children moved
first to Arlington, Massachusetts, and then to Cambridge, where they lived for five years.
Their new residence boasted a barn where Tim and Heidi spent considerable time dressing
up and acting in plays of their own invention. In 1968 the family relocated to Harwinton,
Connecticut, which was Maryline's hometown. There Tim played in Little League softball
and acquired a bent for acrobatics. During these growing-up years, the children saw their
father about once annually while he was between screen roles in such features as WALK,
DON'T RUN (1966), WHO'S MINDING THE MINT (1967), and THE GREEN BERETS (1968).

In 1973, when Tim was thirteen, Maryline moved the family once again, this time to Berkeley, California. Tim entered Berkeley Junior High School, where he devoted his energies to the basketball court as one of two white students on the school's team. For the next few years he focused totally on becoming a professional basketball player. However, after he entered Berkeley High in 1975 he discovered the institution's performing arts department. He auditioned for and earned the role of Dionysus in Euripides' *The Bacchae*. Enamored with the stage, he quit basketball in order to act in as many plays as he could manage. His friends changed from those inclined toward sports to aspiring musicians and actors. For two years he sang as a member of a barbershop quartet named Sput (Society for the Preservation of Us Teenagers). During his basketball phase, Tim ignored his book-worm sister, whose friends were mostly actors; when he switched interests and pals, it was her turn to do the ignoring. A rift developed between the two that would take years to mend. In 1981 Heidi stated that her brother was "a very charming person and when he was little or an adolescent, he knew very well that he was charming, so he could flash those baby blues at anybody and be all right. It's very annoying being his sister, because he's good at every . . . thing he tries."

He had spent the summer of 1975 with his father in Los Angeles at Jim's Laurel Canyon home; the two got along so well that Jim Hutton, whose career had faltered badly, suggested to his son that he live with him. Tim would say later, "The timing was perfect." As his mother was agreeable, Tim moved in with his father in 1976 and enrolled at Fairfax High School in Los Angeles. His first day there was the final day of tryouts for the school's production of the musical *Guys and Dolls*. Tim auditioned for the part of Nathan Detroit and won it, although he had never before danced. Father and son became close friends. They played poker, went to the race track often, listened to jazz, and played tennis, and "Hut" (as his father called Tim) would not think of having a party without including Jim. "My dad placed higher importance on us being friends than anything else," Tim has said in retrospect.

In 1977 Jim Hutton, whose screen career had died out, took to the road as Elwood P. Dowd in dinner theater productions of *Harvey*, beginning in Santa Cruz, California. Dropping out of high school, Tim joined the company of the comedy in the small part of a cabdriver. "It was very weird," Tim has said, "because we looked so much alike that, when we would come downstage, we could hear the audience gasping at the resemblance. It was a real show-stopper."

Now that he had acquired a taste for acting and applause, Tim obtained his high school equivalency diploma as well as an agent. The latter promptly got him a supporting part in the NBC-TV movie ZUMA BEACH (September 27, 1978). This part entitled Hutton to a Screen Actors Guild membership, and he briefly considered changing his professional name to "Tim Tarquin," a notion his father wisely discouraged. Meanwhile, to everyone in Hollywood he was known as "Young Tim Hutton." He acquired his own apartment in Westwood in late 1978. Soon thereafter he got a telephone call from his father, asking, "Hut, are you sitting down? I've got six months to a year to live." After experiencing pain following a game of tennis, Jim Hutton had seen his doctor, who diagnosed him as having cancer of the liver. "From that day on," Tim has remembered, "he was in the hospital. And it was hard to get used to the fact that my new friend, my father, would not be around anymore."

Tim appeared in two TV movies back to back. The first was FRIENDLY FIRE (April 22, 1979), as Carol Burnett's son, and was viewed by Tim and his father in the latter's hospital room. The second project was NBC-TV's four-hour THE BEST PLACE TO BE, shown on May 27 and 28, 1979, in which Tim was Donna Reed's rebellious son. Five days later, on June 2, 1979, Jim Hutton was dead at age forty-five.

To distract himself from his father's death, Tim immersed himself in reading as many books on acting as he could find, along with working in two additional telefeatures. In AND BABY MAKES SIX (October 22, 1979), he was one of three grown children of Colleen Dewhurst and Warren Oates, who find they are expecting another child. (A sequel, BABY COMES HOME, would be aired a year later, with Christopher Marcantel in Tim's role.) Hutton was the male lead in YOUNG LOVE, FIRST LOVE (November 20, 1979) as a California transplant finding love with Valerie Bertinelli. Learning by working, Tim told the *Los Angeles Times* in 1981, "On my second, I'd learned from the first, and on the third I could see where I'd been on the second. The thing about acting is that you learn so much about yourself, and about so much more than acting."

During the shooting of AND BABY MAKES SIX, Tim learned about Paramount's plans to make a movie of the Judith Guest novel *Ordinary People*, to be directed by Robert Redford. He read the book overnight and decided he wanted to audition for the part of the troubled son. Hundreds of young hopefuls read for the casting director and story editor, but both Tim and his partner, Dinah Manoff, were called back a second and then a third time. They were finally asked to meet with Redford to do a videotape. For the next three weeks, he waited for the call that finally came, informing him he had the third-billed role of Conrad, the guilt-ridden, suicidal son of Mary Tyler Moore and Donald Sutherland, in ORDINARY PEOPLE (1980). On location in Lake Forest, Illinois, the first thing Tim did was to obtain entrance under an assumed name to a group therapy session for troubled teenagers at a psychiatric hospital. Released in September, the movie was an immense success, tallying more than $52 million in box-office dollars, making it the ninth best grosser of the year. Hutton was well received in his big-screen debut, with *Variety* lauding, "Timothy Hutton, son of the late actor Jim Hutton, is up to the considerable demands of the central role." In January 1981 Tim received two Golden Globe awards: one as Best Supporting Actor and one as Best New Young Male Talent. At the same time, he earned the scorn of celebrity observer Andy Warhol by refusing an interview. Nominated for a Best Supporting Actor Academy Award, he attended the ceremonies at the Dorothy Chandler Pavilion in Los Angeles on March 31, 1981, with his mother and actress Diane Lane. The first trophy given that night was the one for his category, presented by Mary Tyler Moore and Jack Lemmon, who announced that Tim had won. His acceptance speech included the words, "I'd like to thank my father; I wish he were here." At the age of twenty, Tim was the second youngest person ever to win an Oscar for acting.

During the time between the making of ORDINARY PEOPLE and his winning the prizes, Tim had been on stage in Los Angeles in 1980 with Henry Fonda and George Grizzard in *The Oldest Living Graduate*, which was taped by NBC-TV for telecast on April 7, 1980. He had also co-starred as Hal Linden's son in the CBS-TV movie FATHER FIGURE (October 26, 1980). During his leisure hours, Tim had a much-publicized romance with Patti Reagan, daughter of the President-elect, and also appeared on the Hollywood social scene with Elizabeth McGovern. Hutton did not see ORDINARY PEOPLE in its entirety until June 1981, at which time he cried at the finale from a rush of memories about his father's death and the emotional support and help he had received from Redford, whom he chose as an actor role model.

After attending the European premiere of ORDINARY PEOPLE in London, he reported for work in TAPS (1981) on location at Valley Forge Military Academy in Pennsylvania. He had already read several biographies of military men. TAPS, adapted for the screen from the novel *Father Sky*, is the story of cadets at a military academy who take up arms against real estate developers who threaten to shut it down. Tim was the cadet leader, supported by Sean Penn and Tom Cruise. The movie was reviewed negatively by many critics, including one in *Time* magazine who remarked that it "never decides whether it has come to praise or bury the military tradition." However, Tim's work was reviewed positively, with *People* magazine declaring that he "brings the dignity of the early Henry Fonda to his part." TAPS reportedly became the box-office smash of the 1981 holiday season, with market researchers discovering that "children 15 to 21 were sitting through it two and even three times just to watch Tim." On December 6, 1981, Hutton starred in the ABC-TV movie A LONG WAY HOME, as a married teenager who searches for his brother and sister, both of whom had been placed in foster homes years earlier.

In 1982 Tim took up residence in a rented Malibu beach house where horseback riding with neighbors Kristy McNichol and Tatum O'Neal became his favorite hobby. By the next year, Tim was admitting to Andy Warhol's *Interview* magazine that in his career

Timothy Hutton and Dinah Manoff in ORDINARY PEOPLE (1980).

he had been "Really lucky. There's a whole new thing with young films and maybe if I had started ten years ago I wouldn't be as lucky as I am right now."

After his stint in the commercial TAPS, Tim was inundated with picture offers. He chose as his next venture DANIEL (1983), based on *The Book of Daniel* (1971) by E. L. Doctorow. It was a fictionalized account of Julius and Ethel Rosenberg, who were executed as Communist spies in 1953. Daniel, played by Tim, is the son of the pair, who, years after his parents' deaths, looks for answers to the questions surrounding his parents' actions. For the part, Tim read books about the Rosenbergs and spent time in synagogues to gain the feel of being Jewish. He grew a beard and let his hair grow long. Critics found the somber movie to be "ambitious" but "scrambled," but Tim was thought by *Newsweek* magazine to have given a performance "bristling with wounded intensity." DANIEL was a box-office failure. In ICEMAN (1984), Tim was a bearded anthropologist who fights to save a prehistoric man (John Lone) found frozen after centuries and thawed out for observation purposes. Critic Pauline Kael thought the offbeat movie was "very strange, elating" and noted that Tim and Lone "play off each other in a way that makes the film work, and this may be because of Hutton's slightly opaque, child-man quality."

While waiting for his next film project to develop, he took to the New York stage in the Circle in the Square Theatre's workshop production of Tennessee Williams's *Orpheus Descending* in the winter of 1984. At the same time, ink drawings by Tim were on display in an exhibition of art works at a Manhattan disco called Kamikaze, priced at $200 each. It was announced that Tim would join Jack Nicholson and Debra Winger in ROAD SHOW, a contemporary western, but the picture did not materialize. (Hutton sued MGM regarding the abortive ROAD SHOW and in February 1989 was awarded approximately $2.5 million in compensatory damages and $7.5 million in punitive damages, an award that was slightly reduced in a later 1989 settlement.) Instead, he and Sean Penn starred as Christopher Boyce and Andrew Daulton Lee, real-life Newport Beach, California, classmates who became Russian spies, in THE FALCON AND THE SNOWMAN (1985). His research for this role included visiting with Boyce in prison. Critic Roger Ebert liked both actors and wrote, "It's hard to say who gives the better performance." The moody thriller did only modestly at the box office.

Wanting to try his creative hand at something different, Tim directed a music video of the rock group The Cars performing the song "Drive," written by Ric Ocasek, as well as an episode of NBC-TV's "Amazing Stories." Enthusiasm ran high for his sixth theatrical movie, a comedy which he described as "really great, very off-the-wall, very humorous." It was called TURK 182 (1985) and had him starring as a New York graffiti artist who combats an uncaring city hall when his off-duty and intoxicated firefighter brother (Robert Urich) is injured while rescuing a fire victim. The anti-Establishment picture was a fiasco, and *People* magazine reported, "Nothing redeems TURK 182. . . . Not the acting performances. Though Hutton competently portrays the loony, impulsive boy-hero. . . ."

Hutton directed ex-Eagle vocalist Don Henley in a video of "Not Enough Love in the World" before marrying Debra Winger on March 16, 1986. She was five years his senior and they had already lived together for three months. She said there was "a lot of electricity" between them and, after honeymooning in Paris, exclaimed that "The sexiest thing in the world is to be totally naked with your wedding band on." Intent on starting a family, Debra became pregnant, but miscarried while on location in Seattle, Washington, for BLACK WIDOW (1987). A second pregnancy resulted in the birth of their son, Emanuel Noah, in April 1987.

In August 1987 it was announced that Tim would co-star with Scott Glenn in a screen version of Patrick Meyers's Broadway play *K2*, but things did not work out as planned (the film began production in 1990 with Michael Biehn and Matt Craven). In November his latest film, MADE IN HEAVEN, was in release, starring him opposite Kelly McGillis. This light-hearted fantasy presented him as a man who drowns in the late 1940s while saving another's life. In heaven he meets an unborn soul (McGillis) and falls in love. His guardian angel (played in male drag by Debra Winger in an unbilled cameo) agrees to send them to earth, where they will have thirty years in which to meet, but will have no memory of their meeting in heaven. Besides Tim's wife, Ellen Barkin and Ric Ocasek (of The Cars), among others, provided cameos. The bizarre love story was not liked by critics or audiences. "A story of love and revenge" were the words heralding the arrival in April 1988 of A TIME OF DESTINY, which had Tim second-billed to William Hurt as the latter's brother-in-law, who is blamed for the death of the family patriarch (Francisco Rabal). Hurt enlists in the same World War II Army unit as Hutton to seek his revenge. The *San Francisco Chronicle* labeled it "an interminable tale" that was "an ordeal to watch."

Tim repaid Debra's cameo appearance in MADE IN HEAVEN by donning an Uncle Sam costume on stilts while juggling three balls in her FBI thriller, BETRAYED (1988). In May 1988 the Huttons separated, which came as no great surprise to their friends, who had never considered them compatible. He chain-smoked, which she hated; she was aggressive and outspoken, while he was quiet and introverted. Debra publicly stated that some of their domestic problems resulted from Tim's closeness with Sean Penn, to whom he would go for advice after each spat. "Having Sean Penn as a marriage counselor," she said, "is like taking sailing lessons from the captain of the *Titanic*." Tim moved out of their Malibu home and in December 1988 filed for divorce, asking for joint custody of their son.

Rex Reed of TV's "At the Movies" was in the minority when he called EVERYBODY'S ALL-AMERICAN (1988) "a captivating and romantic film that gets under your skin and haunts you afterward." *People* magazine's critique was more in line with reality. It branded the movie a "turgid mess," adding, "Hutton, in a role he should have fired his agent for accepting . . . is saddled with absurd goatees, mustaches and hairstyles that are meant to show aging but only make him look like a kid playing grownup." Co-starring with Dennis Quaid and Jessica Lange, Tim was a 1950s high school student in Louisiana who survives the trials and tribulations of growing up, down to the present. All three stars needed a fresh box-office smash, but this feature was not it.

Tim was accused in April 1989 of engineering the beating, outside a Hollywood Boulevard bar (The Frolic Room), of aspiring actor Rene Diamante. The latter claimed that his nose was broken in three places and that he would require surgery to restore his face. While Tim's attorney denied that Hutton was involved, the bartender related that Tim had first attacked the victim from behind with open-handed slaps to the head.

From December 19 through 24, 1989, Tim was reunited with his friend and co-cast member of ORDINARY PEOPLE, Elizabeth McGovern, on the stage of the Edison Theatre in New York City as Andy and Melissa, reading *Love Letters*. The two-character A. R. Gurney play also had a company in San Francisco, with others planned for Chicago, Boston, Los Angeles, and London. In all the companies, the cast changed each week.

January 1990 saw the release and hasty departure from theater screens of the Italian-French produced TORRENTS OF SPRING, adapted from Ivan Turgenev's classic tale, and directed by Jerzy Skolimowski. Tim, as a nineteenth-century Russian aristocrat, was sought after by a married woman (Nastassja Kinski) as well as an Italian virgin (Valeria Golina), the daughter of a baker. Tim looked not only uncomfortable in period costumes but absurd as well. *Rolling Stone* magazine's simple critique of the film was that it was "crushingly insipid . . . these torrents barely amount to a drizzle."

Hutton fared a little better as an Irish-American assistant district attorney investigating a homicide case involving New York City's police force in Q & A, released in April 1990. In a cast that was headed by Nick Nolte and brilliantly assisted by underrated Armand Assante, Tim received mixed reviews: "lacks resonance" (*Entertainment Weekly* magazine), "at his sensitive best" (*US* magazine), "acts dazed" (*People* magazine). Directed by veteran Sidney Lumet, who has done better, the movie took in a paltry $10,738,946 during six weeks of domestic release.

At the same time, on May 1, 1990, Tim opened on Broadway at the Helen Hayes Theatre in *Prelude to a Kiss*, replacing Alec Baldwin, who had done the role off-Broadway, as a science writer whose bride (Mary-Louise Parker) undergoes a personality change after a kiss from an old man (Barnard Hughes). In comparing the performances of the two actors in the lead role, *Drama-Logue* concluded that although "Hutton is a fine actor with surprising glints of humor," he lacked "the expansive warmth with which Baldwin drew everyone inside his story." The play, written by Craig Lucas, was purchased for the movies by Twentieth Century–Fox and promptly offered to Alec Baldwin. Both the play and Parker were nominated for Tony Awards, but neither won. In the fall of 1990, Hutton left the cast of *Prelude to a Kiss* to star in George Romero's screen version of the Stephen King thriller THE DARK HALF (forthcoming, 1991), which was shot on location in Pittsburgh.

The young man who showed such promise more than a decade ago by winning an Academy Award has been engulfed since then (except for THE FALCON AND THE SNOW-MAN) in a less-than-successful screen career. In an industry focused intently on box-office receipts, Tim Hutton is badly in need of a hit movie. His good buddy Sean Penn seems to have mellowed and has moved into directing. Perhaps he will provide Tim's professional redemption in a friendship assignment of a screen role worthy of Hutton's boyish appeal and talents.

Filmography

Zuma Beach (NBC-TV, 9/27/78)
Friendly Fire (ABC-TV, 4/22/79)
The Best Place to Be (NBC-TV, 5/27/79–
    5/28/79)
And Baby Makes Six (NBC-TV, 10/22/79)
Young Love, First Love (CBS-TV, 11/20/79)
Father Figure (CBS-TV, 10/26/80)
Ordinary People (Par, 1980)
A Long Way Home (ABC-TV, 12/6/81)
Taps (20th–Fox, 1981)
Daniel (Par, 1983)
Iceman (Univ, 1984)

The Falcon and the Snowman (Orion, 1985)
Turk 182 (20th–Fox, 1985)
Made in Heaven (Lorimar, 1987)
A Time of Destiny (Col, 1988)
Betrayed (UA, 1988)
Everybody's All-American (WB, 1988)
Torrents of Spring (Millimeter Films, 1990)
Q & A (Tri-Star, 1990)

Future Releases

The Dark Half (Orion, 1991)

Broadway Plays

Love Letters (1990) (alternating cast)

Prelude to a Kiss (1990) (replacement for
    Broadway transfer)

ANN JILLIAN

"I've been a pudge-o at various times in my life. . . . I'm on a tough
diet and so far I've lost two dress sizes. I'm losing in some places I'd
rather not. How can I say this? . . . Well, it's my bust. Now, isn't that
a terrible thing for a *sex symbol* to have to go through?"
— *TV Guide* magazine, August 22, 1981

ANN JILLIAN, OF THE FAMED BLONDE DUTCH-BOY HAIRCUT, IS A VERY
lucky lady. Not only has she been blessed with an abundance of talent in all performing
areas—song, dance, comedy, drama—but she has the energy of two persons and seemingly
the courage of a dozen. Her luck includes having met and married Andy Murcia, the
compassionate, loving husband who remained unselfish through her darkest hour, when
she contracted breast cancer and underwent a double mastectomy.

Ann has compared her skills to those of Eve Arden, queen of the one-liners; to
Barbara Stanwyck, drama-comedy queen; and even to the unique Mae West. Hollywood
scribes, on the other hand, have, because of her platinum hair, inevitably drawn comparisons between Jillian and Loni Anderson. Like Stanwyck, Ann Jillian is beloved by scores of
genuine friends who are attracted by her lively, unpretentious nature.

Ann Jura Nauseda was conceived by Joseph and Margaret Nauseda aboard the
passenger ship S.S. *Mercy*, bound for America in April 1950. They had recently escaped
from their native Lithuania during the Communist takeover, sneaking out their infant son
in a basket. Settling in Cambridge, Massachusetts, they became parents a second time, on
Monday, January 29, 1951, when brown-haired Ann was born. At the age of four, she
appeared for the first time on stage in a Cambridge show in which she sang—even after the
music had stopped. That, along with remarks from the audience that the child had talent,
was all that stage-struck Margaret Nauseda required. Moving to Los Angeles, Margaret lost
no time in acquiring work for Ann, who by now had a new professional surname, "Jillian,"
and whose hair had been bleached. In rapid succession, the youngster did TV commercials
for Del Monte, Kraft, and Chevrolet. In 1961 Margaret obtained an audition for Ann with
the Walt Disney Studio, which was remaking Victor Herbert's operetta BABES IN TOY-
LAND. Winning the role of Little Bo Peep, Ann also acquired the lifelong nickname of
"Beep." The following year, she played "Dainty June" in GYPSY, the younger sister of the
stripper-to-be. On this occasion, she was billed as Ann Jilliann (with two n's).

On television, the well-liked, talented girl acted in a two-part episode of "The
Wonderful World of Disney" in late 1962 as well as in a segment of CBS-TV's "The

Twilight Zone" in early 1963. On November 14, 1963, she was in an episode of NBC-TV's "Hazel," starring Shirley Booth, as Millie Ballard, a character Ann would play again during the 1965–1966 season when the show switched to CBS. On stage at the Pasadena Playhouse in Pasadena, California, in 1964, she played the daughter in *Anniversary Waltz.* Among her several other TV appearances in this period were roles in two unsold series pilots: "The Dean Jones Show" (1965) and "Off We Go" (1966), the latter about a sixteen-year-old boy (Michael Burns) who becomes, by mistake, an officer in World War II.

Despite an active show business career, Ann continued her education at Taft High School in Woodland Hills, California, where she was termed "a real loner." Raised in a strict Roman Catholic home, she wore skirts and white gloves rather than the knock-about jeans and sweatshirts favored by her classmates. At age sixteen, Ann still had a somewhat baby face, but her body had developed into that of a voluptuous young woman and, having attained her final height of 5' 8", she was too tall to play juvenile parts anymore. She did voiceovers for children's records and was on stage at the Ahmanson Theatre in Los Angeles in *A Funny Thing Happened on the Way to the Forum.*

After graduating from high school, she entered Pierce Junior College in southern California as a psychology major, while also working as a department store clerk. After completing her two-year course, her self-confidence about reviving her show business career was at a low ebb. However, her friend Debra Shulman talked her into forming a singing duo, Jillian and Shulman, which became an opening act for headliners. Also in 1971, Ann received a trainee scholarship with the Los Angeles Civic Light Opera Association. She returned to TV on October 15, 1971, in a segment of "The Partridge Family," appearing as a singer. She also provided a voice for the animated cartoon "Scooby-Doo Where Are You?" on CBS-TV, and in the animated series "Sealab 2020" she was the voice of Gail, who had a pet dolphin named Tuffy. She was among many actors/actresses who did guest stints on "Kojak," her turn on the detective series being in the February 1974 episode "Die Before They Wake." Also during 1974 and into 1975, she sang in back-up groups on recordings and in nightclubs. However, wanting to do something different professionally, she joined the touring company of Sammy Cahn's *Words and Music,* winding up in Chicago in 1976.

The cast of *Words and Music* was housed at the Ambassador East Hotel where the moonlighting security director was an eighteen-year veteran of Chicago's police force, Andrew L. Murcia. Every night he saw this pretty blonde crossing the lobby to the elevator. Finally, one evening he struck up a conversation with her, and soon they started dating. "I had never had a steady boyfriend before," she was to say later, "and here was a guy who was protective, fun to be with, had a sense of humor. He was tender, but also tough." She starred with Mickey Rooney in Chicago's Drury Lane Theatre production of the farce *Goodnight Ladies,* and then was married to Andy Murcia in March 1977 in Georgia by a justice of the peace. Ann was twenty-six; the divorced Murcia was thirty-five.

At the time of their marriage, they made a pact that he would resign from the police force to be her manager if and when her career demanded it. However, for eighteen months Ann went into self-imposed "retirement" as a Chicago housewife, reemerging in 1979 for a brief Midwest tour in the musical *I Love My Wife*. Next she joined Mickey Rooney and Ann Miller in the summer of 1979 for a three-month pre-Broadway tour in *Sugar Babies*. In Los Angeles, San Francisco, Chicago, Detroit, and Philadelphia, Jillian mugged and camped her way through corny old burlesque routines with Rooney along with belting out a set of songs. When *Sugar Babies* opened on Broadway in October 1979 at the Mark Hellinger Theatre, *After Dark* magazine called Ann Jillian "a choice long-legged beauty . . . who scores a triumph in a number of scenes." Her part, though, was cut back after the Broadway bow because Ann Miller, not Jillian, was the show's star.

The ABC-TV network was conducting a talent hunt at that time, and scout Joyce Selznick, impressed by Ann's performance in *Sugar Babies*, took her on as a client and became her manager. In the spring of 1980 Jillian left the hit musical and moved back to Los Angeles with her husband, waiting for the network to develop a series for her. While biding her time, she auditioned for the role of Marilyn Monroe in ABC-TV's MARILYN: THE UNTOLD STORY (1980), a part that went to Catherine Hicks. Undaunted, Ann said, "I'm extremely proud of the . . . test. It shows what I can do with dramatic scenes." She did a "Love Boat" episode, broadcast on November 1, 1980, two days after her sitcom series about five waitresses, "It's a Living," debuted with Ann in the role of sexy Cassie Cranston, the brassy deliverer of one-line retorts. Said *Variety*, "Ann Jillian . . . kept the show on the fast track." On December 5, 1980, she was in the ABC-TV special "Battle of the Network Stars" and on NBC-TV was one of the "Women Who Rate a '10'" on February 15, 1981. Despite undergoing changes of time slots and nights, "It's a Living" did not do well its first season. It came back for a second try with a title change to "Making a Living" in the fall of 1981. It still failed to make the ratings grade and was dropped from the ABC line-up at the end of the season. In 1984, once again called "It's a Living," the show was revived in first-run syndication, with Ann returning for one more season.

Meanwhile, Ann worked in the CBS-TV special "Doug Henning's World of Magic" (February 14, 1982), along with singing in ABC's April 1982 special "Perry Como's Easter in Guadalajara." She won Emmy and Golden Globe nominations for her lively portrayal of MAE WEST (May 2, 1982) on ABC-TV. That stint was followed by an NBC-TV pilot for a series that did not materialize, "The Rainbow Girl" ("The Ann Jillian Show"), shown on June 4, 1982. She played a singer forced to work on a local TV show headlined by a penny-pinching bandleader (Cesar Romero). In the splashy but empty two-part ABC-TV movie MALIBU (January 23–24, 1983), she was a TV journalist. Her first feature film in twenty-one years was MR. MOM (1983), in which she was a sex-starved divorcée hankering after Michael Keaton.

NBC-TV introduced the cast members of its new fall series in an hour of film clips on "NBC All-Star Hour" (September 12, 1983). Ann did a production number to advertise her show, for which she had written the theme song, "Most Beautiful Ghost." "Jennifer Slept Here" premiered on October 21, 1983. As the show opened, a Hollywood tour bus driver sighed about the late movie star Jennifer Farrell (Ann), "When her star vanished, the heavens glowed a little less brightly." However, the legend's ghost refuses to leave her mansion, which is now occupied by new owners. *Variety* predicted, "One suspects 'Jennifer' has a slight chance of success, primarily because Jillian and her great sense of presence seem capable of sustaining the sauciness and sass of the ghostly lead character." The series vanished after one season. Ann next had a supporting role in NBC-TV's GIRLS OF THE WHITE ORCHID (November 28, 1983) about nightclub performers sold into white slavery in Tokyo. She then spent Christmas 1983 in Lebanon with Bob Hope, in a performance taped for the NBC special "Bob Hope's USO Christmas in Beirut" (January 15, 1984).

Ann earned a second Emmy Award nomination for her portrayal of an ambitious performer who marries a songwriter (Peter Riegert) to further her career in CBS-TV's "Ellis Island," adapted as a seven-hour miniseries from the fact-filled novel by Fred Mustard Stewart. The production boasted a huge cast, including Faye Dunaway and Richard Burton.

In January 1985, while in the shower, Ann felt a lump the size of a pea in her left breast; tests determined it to be benign. Meanwhile, she was seen in a small role in the ABC-TV movie THIS WIFE FOR HIRE (March 18, 1985). In March, a fresh examination disclosed that she had cancer; both breasts would have to be removed. On April 12, 1985, at age thirty-four, she underwent surgery, followed by chemotherapy. She was filled with doubts concerning herself, her husband, and her career as she lost her hair and her weight shot up to 160 pounds from her normal 128 pounds due to the treatments. Rather than opt for reconstructive surgery, Ann chose to wear prostheses.

Ann Jillian in THE ANN JILLIAN STORY (1988).

Eleven days after surgery, Ann was at work as the Red Queen in CBS-TV's two-part ALICE IN WONDERLAND, which aired December 9–10, 1985. The following month she faced the challenge of playing dual roles in a CBS television remake of the Bette Davis thriller DEAD RINGER (1964), telecast on March 31, 1986, as KILLER IN THE MIRROR. Also in 1986 she completed an album for Laurel Records, *Introducing Ann Jillian the Singer.* In NBC-TV's CONVICTED: A MOTHER'S STORY (February 2, 1987), she was a duped woman who suffers through a prison term for helping a conniving boyfriend and, after her release, must cope with her distraught children. In NBC-TV's PERRY MASON: THE CASE OF THE MURDERED MADAM (October 4, 1987), she had a substantial role as the ex-madam who becomes a public relations executive and then is found dead, with her jealous spouse (Vincent Baggetta) initially accused of the crime.

Ann had become a highly visible spokesperson for the American Cancer Society, promoting the early detection of breast cancer. She had also sold the story of her illness to NBC-TV, with the provision that she would portray herself on screen. Her story, appropriately titled THE ANN JILLIAN STORY, was telecast on January 4, 1988, with Tony Lo Bianco portraying her sympathetic husband. *TV Guide* magazine reported that the biographical drama "succeeds on a couple of levels: as a love story . . . and, more tellingly, as a source of inspiration to other women suffering from breast cancer." The program was reportedly the highest-rated telefeature of the 1987–1988 season, with Ann winning a Golden Globe as best dramatic actress.

In 1988 and 1989 Ann was among the guests appearing on Bob Hope's NBC-TV specials, and she co-starred with Charlton Heston in the NBC-TV movie ORIGINAL SIN (February 20, 1989). Another mob boss drama, it was described by *USA Today* with: "It's so much drivel that dribbles over two hours of prime-time television." She traveled to Rome to shoot NBC-TV's LITTLE WHITE LIES (November 27, 1989), a romantic comedy in which she plays a Philadelphia cop who lies about herself to a doctor (Tim Matheson) she meets, while he avoids revealing his true profession to her. Labeling it "preposterous," a *TV Guide* reviewer wrote that Ann "is always a treat to watch." Meanwhile, her husband, Andy, had written a book, *Man to Man*, which had been purchased by the Disney studio as the basis for a TV movie.

TV Guide, in its review of "The Ann Jillian Show," an NBC-TV sitcom that premiered on November 30, 1989, decided that Ann did not have "the kind of star power that would justify using her name as the title of a series. Cute and personable she is; Lucille Ball she isn't." She played a former Rockette dancer, now a widow with a teenaged daughter (Lisa Rieffel), who has migrated to California. After its January 20, 1990, telecast, the show was placed on hiatus. Ann told *TV Guide* backstage at the January Golden Globe Awards ceremonies, "I was a real good soldier for six episodes. People think of a star as someone who throws tantrums and locks herself in the dressing room, but I am definitely not that kind of person. I should have been." Stating that following the hiring of three new producers, she was invited to attend creative meetings, she said, "win, lose or draw, when we return to the air, I am going to give the audience a good family." The show returned to the airwaves on August 5, 1990, but after three weeks quietly disappeared.

Meanwhile, on April 9, 1990, Ann guest-starred in Bob Hope's "Fun in the Mexican Sun" (NBC-TV), in which she and Bob spoofed Donald and Ivana Trump by playing "the Frumps," a bickering couple with billions. On June 10, 1990, she hosted "a wet and wonderful evening of music, magic and miracles of the deep," "Sea World Summer Night Magic," on ABC-TV, taped at Florida's Sea World. Ann sang "Ebb Tide" and "The Music of the Night." Active in support of the Disabled American Veterans (DAV) organization by visiting patients in Veterans Administration hospitals throughout the United States, she opened the DAV Convention in Anaheim, California, on July 29, 1990, by singing the National Anthem backed by the U.S. Marine Corp band. An attendee reported that Ann's rendition was "much, much better, more reverent, and more professional" than Roseanne Barr's at a recent baseball game.

For the American Cancer Society's observance of Daffodil Days in March 1990, Ann's photograph appeared on the society's brochure with this comment from her: "Yes, there is life after breast cancer. And that's the whole point." This courageous woman begs other women to practice breast self-examination and to seek periodic mammograms. "Take it from someone who's been through it all," she says. "Life is just too wonderful to give up on." Jillian has continued to do what she enjoys most, acting and singing. Of her style of vocalizing, she says, "People aren't to hear Michael Jackson–type songs," and she praises Linda Ronstadt, who has "brought everybody's attention again to good solid songs with lyrics you can understand."

Filmography

Babes in Toyland (BV, 1961)
Gypsy (WB, 1962) (as Ann Jilliann)
Mae West (ABC-TV, 5/2/82)
Malibu (ABC-TV, 1/23/83–1/24/83)
Girls of the White Orchid [Night Ride to Osaka] (NBC-TV, 11/28/83)
Mr. Mom (20th–Fox, 1983)
This Wife for Hire (ABC-TV, 3/18/85)

Alice in Wonderland (CBS-TV, 12/9/85–12/10/85)
Killer in the Mirror (CBS-TV, 3/31/86)
Convicted: A Mother's Story (NBC-TV, 2/2/87)
Perry Mason: The Case of the Murdered Madam (NBC-TV, 10/4/87)
The Ann Jillian Story (NBC-TV, 1/4/88)
Original Sin (NBC-TV, 2/20/89)
Little White Lies (NBC-TV, 11/27/89)

Television Series

Hazel (CBS, 1965–66)
Sealab 2020 (NBC, 1972–73) (voice only)
It's a Living [Making a Living] (ABC, 1980–82; Synd, 1984–85)

Jennifer Slept Here (NBC, 1983–84)
Ellis Island (CBS-TV, 11/11/84; 11/13/84; 11/14/84) [miniseries]
The Ann Jillian Show (NBC, 1989–90)

Broadway Plays

Sugar Babies (1979)

Discography

Babes in Toyland (Buena Vista BV/BVS-4022) [ST]
Gypsy (Warner Bros. BS 1480) [ST]

Introducing Ann Jillian the Singer (Laurel Records LR-507)

DON JOHNSON

"I resented that part of it—looking pretty—when I had these
strong emotions inside of me that weren't matching what was
in my face. . . ."   —*Interview* magazine, September 1986

AT THE AGE OF TWENTY, DIMPLE-FACED DON JOHNSON THOUGHT HE
was at the top of the heap. He had a starring role in his first motion picture and a pact with
MGM. Within months, it all toppled. He would spend the better part of the next fourteen
years in supporting roles. Ten of those years were partially devoted to "finding the more
social forms of entertainment," while he was in various stages of inebriation or soaring on
marijuana or cocaine. Known in Hollywood as "Don Juanson" because of his seemingly
limitless sexual appetite, he finally sought treatment for substance abuse.

Later, Johnson became a television sensation in a hip detective series that was "a
cultural phenomenon." As the star of "Miami Vice" (1984–1989), he was a fashion
trendsetter, popularizing rumpled white Italian suits, no socks, slip-on shoes, designer
sunglasses, and three-day facial stubble. With his thick dark blond hair, dark eyebrows,
blue eyes, and gravelly voice, he was considered "the sexiest man on television." However,
he had also become an astute technician, with director Stuart Cooper comparing him to
megastars Paul Newman and Steve McQueen by saying, "Don's like Newman and
McQueen; he knows where the camera is and he puts his performance right in the lens."
Beloved by teenaged and older women fans who called him "drop-dead gorgeous," he
earned a less than favorable reputation with the press and members of certain groups
because of his arrogant and demanding behavior. At the same time, his personal life
became fodder for the notorious tabloids, which he seems secretly to enjoy.

Don Wayne Johnson was born on Thursday, December 15, 1949, in Galena,
Missouri, in his grandmother Johnson's house. He was the oldest of four children born to
Wayne Fred Johnson, a farmer, and his wife, sixteen-year-old Nell Wilson Johnson, who
would later become a beautician. Both parents were of American Cherokee Indian
heritage. When Don was five, his family moved to Wichita, Kansas, where Wayne Fred
worked for an aircraft manufacturer and where Don's maternal grandfather, a fundamentalist preacher, persuaded Don to sing in the church choir as well as at wedding banquets.
When he was eleven, Don's short-tempered parents divorced. He lived with his mother in
Kansas while his father returned to Missouri, where he bought a small country store with
a garage. A year later, at the age of twelve, Don had his first love affair, with a seventeen-

year-old baby-sitter. A few years later he was arrested for car theft. After spending two weeks in a juvenile detention center, he was released into the custody of his father and stepmother, Darlene. However, the quarrels and physical fights in their home were too numerous for him, and at the age of sixteen he returned to Wichita to resume his high school education.

Taking a part-time job in a meat packing plant, Don took up residence with a twenty-six-year-old cocktail waitress with whom he "studied anatomy by Braille." He played football, but at 5' 11" was not tall enough and at about 160 pounds was not heavy enough to be an outstanding player. While in the classroom, he slept much of the time. On the brink of flunking high school, he spoke to a guidance counselor who told him that he should concentrate on drama. When it was discovered that he could sing, he was given the lead role of Tony in the school's production of *West Side Story*. He would claim later that acting "struck something in me that was true and honest. . . . For the first time in my life, I felt that I belonged to something."

Graduating from high school in 1967, he auditioned for a full drama scholarship to the University of Kansas at Lawrence. Determined to obtain the grant, he nagged the authorities daily until it was awarded to him. For the next two years, he was an "insatiable" student of Shakespeare, Chekhov, and Ibsen. He lived with his twenty-nine-year-old female drama professor, who arranged for him to read *The Rake's Progress* for a visiting director from San Francisco's American Conservatory Theatre (ACT) in the hope of obtaining a grant to continue his studies with the group. Although his teacher left him for another man, Don was accepted by ACT.

In 1968 Johnson moved to San Francisco where, within a few weeks, he debuted professionally in *Your Own Thing*, a rock musical based on *Twelfth Night*. He earned $150 a week, an astronomical sum compared to what he had made in the past on any job. At this time, he also embarked on his first marriage, to a dancer in a road company cabaret group; the marriage was annulled after two months. Actor/producer Sal Mineo, in San Francisco in search of talent for his production of *Fortune and Men's Eyes*, a play about homosexuality in prison, selected Don to play the part of Smitty. The show opened in Los Angeles at the small Coronet Theatre on January 12, 1969, and *Variety*'s reviewer acclaimed Don's performance as "a powerful delineation of character by an excellent actor."

As Mineo prepared to move his production to New York's off-Broadway, Don was offered a deal by producer Martin Poll on behalf of MGM to star in THE MAGIC GARDEN OF STANLEY SWEETHEART (1970), with an option for a second movie. With possible screen stardom within his grasp, he withdrew from the play, but wound up in Manhattan anyway, because the movie was shot there. As Stanley Sweetheart, a part for which Poll had considered Richard Thomas before he met Don, Johnson was nude a great deal of the time as a college kid experiencing many psychedelic drug/sexual fantasy excursions. Of his screen debut, one critic, a woman, wrote that she loved his "wonderfully impish grin." However, others, such as the critic for *Women's Wear Daily*, called him an "obvious case of no-talent," and Judith Crist thought "his epicene looks suggest a lot of seamy living." When the picture failed at the box office, MGM chose to drop its option. "I felt my career was over," he remembered years later. "They had written me off. I took whatever I could find."

Before returning to California, he met a young entertainer named Patti D'Arbanville. She would reenter his life twelve years later, making an indelible impression. He also played a supporting role in the rock western ZACHARIAH (1971) and became friendly with several groups of musicians.

Johnson appeared in an episode ("The Combatants") of NBC-TV's "Sarge," telecast on September 21, 1971. He was chosen by Cinerama as the third-billed Stanley, again displaying a great deal of skin while communing with nature in THE HARRAD EXPERIMENT (1973). The female lead was Tippi Hedren, whose fourteen-year-old daughter, Melanie Griffith, working as an extra, took a particular liking to Don. In 1973 he married for a second time, to a wealthy young woman he referred to as a "bimbo." They annulled this union a few days later, after discovering they had made a mistake.

On November 8, 1973, Don was seen on ABC-TV's "Kung Fu" series. It was also at this time that he began to become more involved with drugs and alcohol. He mistakenly thought he was handling his drug use well enough that it did not interfere with his work. He was seen in February 1974 in an episode of ABC-TV's "The Rookies," but was thereafter dismissed by the powerful William Morris Agency, which had represented him. They claimed his "career was finished," words he vowed to make them one day retract.

Although his career was stalled briefly, Don was seen in A BOY AND HIS DOG (1975), which dealt with a punk youth and his dog who forage for food and women following a nuclear holocaust. This low-budget feature, shot in April–May 1973 in Venice and Barstow, California, earned him the Golden Scroll Award from the Academy of Science Fiction and Horror Films as best actor of the year. The movie, which was reissued in 1982, has since become a cult classic. He next co-starred with screen novice Nick Nolte in RETURN TO MACON COUNTY (1975), an inconspicuous sequel to the previous year's MACON COUNTY LINE.

On April 29, 1976, he co-starred with Jim Davis in LAW OF THE LAND, an NBC-TV movie/pilot about frontier lawmen. It was the first of several projects that failed to materialize as teleseries. In the spring of 1976, after returning home from a date with Marjorie Wallace, a former Miss World, he had a telephone conversation with Melanie Griffith. The talk climaxed in their decision to go to Las Vegas to get married. She was eighteen; he was twenty-six. He has since admitted that his lack of maturity matched her years. The union was ill-fated, and they would divorce in 1977. She left the marriage with a pear tattooed on her left buttock ("Pear" was the nickname she had given him).

Johnson acted in episodes of TV's "The Streets of San Francisco" and "Barnaby Jones" in December 1976 and was seen in a second series pilot, THE CITY (January 12, 1977), with his third series attempt, COVER GIRLS (March 18, 1977), following closely thereafter. In September 1977 he joined the cast of NBC-TV's "Big Hawaii" for the "Gandy" episode and was also in an installment of the same network's "Police Story." Johnson wrote two songs with Dickey Betts for the Allman Brothers' album *Enlightened Rogues*, released in December 1977. He showed up in a segment of "What Really

Happened to the Class of '65" on NBC-TV in January 1978, and traveled to Canada to film the exciting CBS-TV movie SKI LIFT TO DEATH (March 3, 1978). The ABC-TV Friday night movie of April 14, 1978, THE TWO-FIVE—about cops—was another failed series pilot. He was in the "Survival" episode of ABC-TV's "The American Girls" on October 21, 1978, and two nights later appeared in the NBC-TV movie KATIE: PORTRAIT OF A CENTERFOLD. Don rounded out 1978 professionally with a small assignment in the CBS-TV dramatic movie FIRST YOU CRY (November 8, 1978), starring Mary Tyler Moore.

During 1979, Don made just two television appearances, as "Cowboy" in AMATEUR NIGHT AT THE DIXIE BAR AND GRILL (NBC-TV, January 8, 1979) and his May 14 and 21 co-starring role as Judson Fletcher in the syndicated THE REBELS, a sequel to THE BASTARD (1978), both of them starring Andrew Stevens. "From Here to Eternity," taken from the James Jones novel, began as an NBC-TV miniseries in February 1979. Don entered the action of the regular weekly series in March 1980 as Jefferson Davis Prewitt, who replaces his brother (Steve Railsback) as the lover of a prostitute (Kim Basinger) and weds her. The weekly series died after only a month, but remaining filmed episodes were telecast as specials in August 1980. The southern plantation epic BEULAH LAND was a six-hour miniseries in October 1980. It was plagued with filming problems and was later criticized by blacks for its rough depiction of slaves. Don was Bonard Davis in a cast seemingly of thousands. Three nights later, on October 12, 1980, he was one of the suburban husbands who treat their wives as chattel in THE REVENGE OF THE STEPFORD WIVES.

Elvis Presley will apparently never die; television and his fans will not permit it. On March 1, 1981, Don, after gaining forty pounds, played the paunchy, drug-dependent entertainer in ELVIS AND THE BEAUTY QUEEN on NBC-TV, lip-synching to the vocals of Ronnie McDowell, who also did the vocals for Kurt Russell in the superior ABC-TV movie, ELVIS (1979). Unfortunately, this new account of Elvis's later years was not as popular. Don was again a policeman in THE TWO LIVES OF CAROL LETNER (October 14, 1981) on CBS-TV, and he then went to Canada to make MELANIE (1982), in support of Glynnis O'Connor as an illiterate Arkansas mother. For a short spell in April 1982 he was seen on movie screens in the unbelievably entitled feature SOGGY BOTTOM U.S.A., which will not be found on any list of the year's best films.

Earlier in 1982, in January, while on a date with singer Tanya Tucker, Don re-met Patti D'Arbanville at a Los Angeles nightclub. He abandoned Tucker and took Patti to bed, where they remained for seven nights and eight days, with food supplied periodically by a take-out service. When she later found that she was pregnant with his child, she willingly gave up drugs and alcohol, determined to have a healthy baby. Their son, Jesse Wayne, was born on December 7, 1982, with the parents agreeing not to marry. (Their relationship would end in 1986.) While she was sober and drug-free, Don continued to indulge. He recalled finding "the AA Big Book on my side of the bed night after night. I'd come home drunk and have to move it to go to sleep."

On July 24, 1983, he was seen in yet another series pilot, SIX PACK, an NBC-TV effort based on the Kenny Rogers movie (1982). He appeared in a "Matt Houston" episode that aired on September 16, 1983, five days after he had, with Patti's help, entered a forty-five-day detoxification program. By the end of October, clean but shaky, he vowed never again to use in drugs or alcohol. On November 15, 1983, he was seen in an episode of CBS-TV's "The Mississippi," and during that month he did a test for yet another projected TV series from NBC, entitled, at various times, "Dade County Fast Lane" and "MTV Cops," about a pair of really hip Miami vice squad law enforcers.

Meanwhile, Johnson earned the lead in CEASE FIRE (1985), as a Vietnam veteran plagued by nightmares. Before this drama was released, however, he had won a co-starring role in the first series for which he had tested back in November 1983. "Miami Vice" premiered on September 16, 1984. Within a year, almost all young American men were trying to emulate Sonny Crockett (Don Johnson), with his unshaven face, baggy linen suits, loafers, and sunglasses. Nominated for an Emmy Award as best actor, Don lost in 1985, but the show helped make NBC the #1 network.

Within months, Johnson was seen in an anti-drug TV commercial, had had dinner with first lady Nancy Reagan at the White House, had earned a reported $1 million for a diet soft drink commercial, was immortalized by Bloomingdale's department store in New York City with a seven-foot cut-out of his figure in Jockey shorts, and had acquired a home in Miami because of his dislike for the "parasitical elements" of Hollywood. Earning a salary of $50,000 per episode, Don Johnson was reportedly becoming increasingly difficult on the set and was fast becoming quick copy for the various supermarket tabloids.

NBC-TV filmed a remake of THE LONG HOT SUMMER at a cost of $6.6 million in 103° temperatures during June 1985 in Texas, with Don playing Ben Quick, the hunky drifter role made famous by Paul Newman in the 1958 movie adaptation. *TV Guide* magazine's Judith Crist decided that the two-part movie, which aired October 6–7, 1985, was "justified" with "a fine cast." *Variety* enthused, "We get a heavy dose of Johnson's pectorals . . . but we also get a character study of a man in wrenching transition, a part played with just the right amount of restraint and passion. It is his portrayal that puts it all together."

In 1986 Don won a Golden Globe for his "Miami Vice" work and had two single recordings in release, the first of which, "Heartbeat" on the Epic label, enjoyed popularity on *Billboard* magazine's charts for fifteen weeks. The second single, released November 22, 1986, was "Heartache Away," which spent eleven weeks on the charts. In between, his LP *Heartbeat*, for which he had written two songs, "Love Roulette" and "Can't Take Your Memory," was released and went on to sell over a million copies. *Rolling Stone* magazine applauded him as having a "semi-sweet tenor" voice. (A special, "Heartbeat," focusing on this album was aired on HBO–Cable on January 17, 1987.) For the October 3, 1986, episode of "Miami Vice," a coup of sorts was achieved by obtaining the services of G. Gordon Liddy (of Watergate infamy) in a guest role. Don directed his ex-wife, Melanie Griffith, in a guest appearance as a madam, aired on March 20, 1987. He provided one of the voices (as the womanizing Lieutenant Falcon) in the animated cartoon feature G.I. JOE—THE MOVIE (1987), which was released direct to video. He received further cartoon immortality through his depiction in the newspaper comic strip "Doonesbury." In January 1988 he and Barbra Streisand met in Aspen, Colorado, where he frequently skied. The encounter resulted in a love affair that lasted months while their activities were dissected by the media. They did a duet, the romantic ballad "Till I Loved You," which was included in her album of the same title. By the time the disc was released in January 1989, their romance was over.

Don gained twenty-five pounds for the role of Wiley Boon in SWEET HEARTS DANCE (1988), the story of a middle-aged small town couple (Johnson, Susan Sarandon) going through a marital crisis. *Variety*, which thought the film drifted badly, noted that Johnson "relies mostly on a cantankerous young man act, and is unconvincing." "Miami Vice" fans were not intrigued by this slow-moving domestic saga, nor by seeing their small-screen hero so out of shape.

In December 1988 Streisand was replaced in Johnson's heart by Melanie Griffith, whom the actor had earlier convinced to seek treatment for alcohol and drug abuse. They became engaged to marry with his gift to her of a four-carat diamond ring. The cop action thriller DEAD-BANG (1989), Don's second theatrical film in as many years, also failed to generate box-office excitement. Skeptics were now calling him a "flash in the pan." On May 21, 1989, "Miami Vice" went "out with a bang," according to *TV Guide* magazine, with a two-hour finale in which both Don and co-star Philip Michael Thomas appeared understandably weary.

Don Johnson and Penelope Ann Miller in DEAD-BANG (1989).

At the same time, Don decided to relocate back to California and purchased, for $3 million, a nine-room English colonial house on 1.3 acres in Beverly Hills, an estate once owned by comedian Bert Lahr. On June 26, 1989, at his Aspen, Colorado, ranch, he and Griffith were remarried in an event that received notoriety in the tabloids when his bodyguards shot at a reporters' helicopter hovering above, wounding two men. Melanie, thirty-one and pregnant, wore white. Their daughter, Dakota Mayi, named for an Indian tribe and a celebrity mystic guru, was born on October 4, 1989, at Brackenridge Hospital in Austin, Texas, seventy miles from Muldoon, Texas, where Don was filming THE HOT SPOT (1990).

In May 1990, Don joined other celebrities involved in a fundraising campaign to buy historic land (made famous in the writings of Henry David Thoreau) in Boston, Massachusetts, bordering Walden Pond, to save it from condominium or office park development. Also in May, with Kurt Russell as his navigator, Don piloted his fifty-foot white speedboat, *Team USA*, at more than one hundred miles per hour five hundred yards off Miami Beach into a second-place win in the Offshore World Cup regatta. Beating him was a novice racer, actor Chuck Norris. Don gave first-aid advice to viewers of "American Red Cross Emergency Test" (ABC-TV, June 7, 1990), hosted by John Ritter.

THE HOT SPOT, in general theatrical release in late September 1990, was reviewed at the Toronto Festival of Festivals by the *Hollywood Reporter* as a "steamy film noir romp." Directed by Dennis Hopper, and based on Charles Williams's novel *Hell Hath No Fury* (1952), the movie was laced with nudity and dangerous sex. Don was cast as a charming drifter who arrives in a small Texas town where he gets a job as a used-car salesman. He quickly becomes involved romantically with both his boss's wife (Virginia Madsen) and the attractive yet naive office accountant (Jennifer Connelly). The *Reporter* noted that Johnson "slips effortlessly into the role of ruthless charmer." The torrid love scenes between Johnson and Madsen were the highlight of the moody movie. John Powers (*LA Weekly*) judged that THE HOT SPOT provided Johnson with "his best performance since A BOY AND HIS DOG in 1975—for once, his greasy smirk is perfectly apt." *People* magazine thought that Don, "reminiscent of William Hurt in BODY HEAT, is convincing enough." Unfortunately, the turgid feature failed to find its audience and faded after three weeks in domestic release, during which it grossed only $1,158,836.

Johnson teamed with Mickey Rourke in HARLEY DAVIDSON AND THE MARLBORO MAN (1991). The co-stars played buddies who, after saving a friend's restaurant business, become mixed up in international drug trafficking. The project was shot on location in Arizona and Las Vegas. With his wife, Melanie Griffith, Don co-starred in PARADISE (1991), a soul-searching drama.

Don Johnson, when asked by *Rolling Stone* magazine what he wanted ultimately out of life, once responded: "To live it to the hilt. . . . I mean, get down and wallow in it— enjoy life and be happy. And for me to be happy, I want to pack this life full. I want it all." Toward this goal, he formed a company called DJ Racing which races powerboats, has a film production firm (which produced such properties as 1988's unsold TV sitcom pilot "Flipside"), and is a buddy of Donald Trump.

Filmography

The Magic Garden of Stanley Sweetheart
    (MGM, 1970)
Zachariah (Cin, 1971)
The Harrad Experiment (Cin, 1973)
A Boy and His Dog (LGJaf Films, 1975)
Return to Macon County (AIP, 1975)
Law of the Land (NBC-TV, 4/29/76)
The City (NBC-TV, 1/12/77)
Cover Girls (NBC-TV, 5/18/77)
Ski Lift to Death (CBS-TV, 3/3/78)
The Two-Five (ABC-TV, 4/14/78)
Katie: Portrait of a Centerfold (NBC-TV,
    10/23/78)
First You Cry (CBS-TV, 11/8/78)
Amateur Night at the Dixie Bar and Grill
    (NBC-TV, 1/8/79)
The Rebels (Synd TV, 5/14/79; 5/21/79)
The Revenge of the Stepford Wives (NBC-TV,
    10/12/80)
Elvis and the Beauty Queen (NBC-TV, 3/1/81)
The Two Lives of Carol Letner (CBS-TV,
    10/14/81)
Melanie (Emb, 1982)
Soggy Bottom U.S.A. (Gaylord, 1982)
Six Pack (NBC-TV, 7/24/83)
The Long Hot Summer (NBC-TV, 10/6/85–
    10/7/85)
Cease Fire (Cineworld, 1985)
G.I. Joe—The Movie (Celebrity Home
    Entertainment, 1987)
Sweet Hearts Dance (Tri-Star, 1988)
Dead-Bang (WB, 1989)
The Hot Spot (Orion, 1990)
Harley Davidson and the Marlboro Man
    (MGM-Pathe, 1991)
Paradise (BV, 1991)

Television Series

From Here to Eternity (NBC, 1980)
Beulah Land (NBC, 10/7/80–10/9/80)
    [miniseries]

Miami Vice (NBC, 1984–89)

Album Discography

Enlightened Rogues (Polydor 831589-2) (co-
    songwriter only)
Heartbeat (Epic EK-40366) (also co-songwriter)

Mega Hits (MCA 5985)
Till I Loved You (Columbia OC-40880)

TOMMY LEE JONES

"Movie star, hell. You get well known a little bit and that word crops
up. I don't want to be a movie star, I want to be a successful actor."
—*San Francisco Sunday Examiner & Chronicle*, March 15, 1981

A COUNTRY MAN FROM THE WARM ENVIRONS OF WESTERN TEXAS,
Tommy Lee Jones removed himself to the cold pavement of cities on both coasts in pursuit
of an acting career. Within ten years he had "come to terms with my own ethnicity," and,
just as eagerly as he had left home, he returned to Texas to live. Later, he went back to
California, this time as one of filmdom's fastest-rising leading men. By then, he had seven
movie roles to his credit, plus a critically acclaimed television portrayal of America's most
famous reclusive billionaire, Howard Hughes.

Jones's unorthodox, craggy face does not conjure the image of a pretty-faced Tyrone
Power or Robert Taylor. However, his sheer masculinity, muscular six-foot frame, direct
no-nonsense manner, and low voice with a touch of Texas make him a sexually appealing
actor. Like the Marlon Brando of the past, and Willem Dafoe of today, Jones does not
believe in movie stardom, nor does he search for it.

Tommy Lee Jones was born on Sunday, September 15, 1946, one hundred miles
from Austin in the small town of San Saba in western Texas. His father, Clyde L. Jones,
who had been a cowboy in his youth, worked on oil rigs; his mother, Lucille Marie (Scott)
Jones, was a policewoman. Tommy grew up around horses, learning to ride and rope at an
early age. At school he found that he enjoyed and was good at football, while in the
classroom he discovered literature. He became a voracious reader of classic tales of
heroism. During school vacations, he worked in the oil fields with his dad. However, in
1963, after performing in his first high school play, he became certain that acting was to be
his vocation.

In 1965, a year after graduating from high school, he left San Saba to study
literature at Harvard University in Cambridge, Massachusetts. It was a far cry from the
cowboy and Indian locales of the comparatively much younger American Southwest.
Tommy did not want to change his name, but to simplify matters and to sound older, he
became known as Tom Lee Jones. Within the ivy-covered buildings comprising the
campus, he studied drama along with literature, and on the university's football field he
played the position of offensive guard, and was named "all Ivy" and "All East." He was
introduced to the game of polo and became one of the team's best players. This was the
start of a life-long fondness for the sport. In 1969 he graduated cum laude from Harvard

with a degree in English. After receiving his first professional acting paycheck for his work in a movie filmed partially at Harvard, he quickly decided to go to New York in search of acting opportunities. In the tearjerker LOVE STORY (1970), which became a box-office bonanza, he played Hank, one of Ryan O'Neal's classmates.

In Manhattan, Jones devoted the next few years to gaining acting experience in a series of plays, the first of which was *A Patriot for Me* (1969), a drama of Tsarist Russia starring Maximilian Schell, in which Tommy played five walk-on parts. This short-lived production was followed by multiple roles in *Four on a Garden* (1970), starring Sid Caesar and Carol Channing. It was also during 1970 that he went to Canada to appear on screen in ELIZA'S HOROSCOPE, a mystical study of a young woman (Elizabeth Moorman) seeking to fulfill a prophecy that she will marry into wealth. In the process, her Canadian Indian lover (Jones) is shot while trying to blow up a bridge. The ambiguous feature did not see even limited distribution until late 1975.

In 1971 Tommy negotiated a continuing part in the daytime drama "One Life to Live" on ABC-TV. As Dr. Mark Toland, Tommy caused a stir in the heart of soap opera fans when on August 28, 1973, the character married his patient, the long-suffering, suicidal Julie Siegel (Lee Warrick). The entire cast joined in the wedding festivities and all other story-lines were set aside for the occasion. Also at this time, he appeared in his second feature film, LIFE STUDY, shot in New York City in 1972. However, it did not find even limited independent distribution until the next year. In this clumsy tale of young love, Jones was fourth-billed as Gus. Jones's stage work during this period included the off-Broadway *Blue Boys*, which lasted for one performance in November 1972.

It was at this juncture that Tommy was married to aspiring actress Katherine Lardner, daughter of writer Ring Lardner, Jr. The couple would remain married for seven years, during which time they would become parents to two sons (Austin and Leonard).

In 1974 Tommy departed the cast of "One Life to Live" and joined the Broadway cast of *Ulysses in Nighttown*, which opened at the Winter Garden Theatre on March 10, 1974. Under Burgess Meredith's direction, the irrepressible Zero Mostel starred as Leopold Bloom with Tommy cast as Stephen Dedalus. (Douglas Watt of the *New York Post* recorded, "Tom Lee Jones cuts an appropriately romantic figure as young Dedalus.") The revival lasted sixty-nine performances. Jones returned to "One Life to Live" on April 28, 1975, for a brief time before his character was permanently written out. Thereafter, he moved to Los Angeles to obtain television as well as feature film work, reverting to the use of his full name, Tommy Lee Jones. "I never thought of changing my name," he said. "I'm proud of my name—it's a regional name, an ethnic name. Don't ask me what *kind* of ethnic; it's just Ethnica, America."

His initial appearance from the West Coast was in the "Fatal Witness" episode of CBS-TV's "Barnaby Jones" on November 14, 1975, followed by the showing of the telefeature/series pilot for CHARLIE'S ANGELS (March 21, 1976), in which he was cast as an Armenian vintner suspected of murdering his wealthy employer. In JACKSON COUNTY JAIL (1976), his fourth theatrical feature film, he had the role of an inmate of a small town jail who escapes with a woman prisoner (Yvette Mimieux) after she has been raped by, and has killed, a guard. In reviewing this modestly budgeted actioner, *Variety* noted, "Jones doesn't act much but he has a strong, pleasing, easy-going screen presence." The property was later remade as a TV movie, OUTSIDE CHANCE (1978), with Mimieux repeating her role, but without Tommy. He was on the other side of the law as a California highway patrolman in SMASH UP ON INTERSTATE 5 (December 3, 1976), an ABC-TV movie in which thirty-nine autos pile up on a fog-shrouded freeway.

In THE AMAZING HOWARD HUGHES (April 13–14, 1977), a too leisurely two-part CBS-TV movie, Jones had the leading role, in which he aged from eighteen to seventy. While some critics thought he was lethargic and flat in the focal assignment, the showcasing brought him fully to the attention of Hollywood casting directors. As a Vietnam veteran helping his buddy (William Devane) to locate the killers of his family in ROLLING THUNDER (1977), Tommy further established his credibility as an actor. However, his abilities were smothered in THE BETSY (1978), the overblown screen adaptation of the Harold Robbins novel. He was the fearless racecar driver hired by a Detroit auto tycoon (Laurence Olivier) to build a trend-setting new car. In the course of the 125 minutes, Jones appeared partially nude, leading one critic to remark that his physique and looks were those of "a young Rudolf Nureyev." Of his acting, *Variety* observed that Tommy "plays his role with a mixture of edginess and offhandedness—a combination of Burt Reynolds and Harvey Keitel. His style—it's got a sense of humor and a campy quality to it—seems more to the point."

Tommy was back in New York City to shoot EYES OF LAURA MARS (1978), co-scripted by John Carpenter. Faye Dunaway's fashion photo camera provided some of the "eyes"; the others were her visions of grisly murders. Tommy was police officer John Neville, her protector, lover, and ultimately would-be murderer. *People* magazine endorsed this "slick murder mystery" and called Jones "perfect as the sympathetic detective."

Interviewed by Guy Flatley, a free-lance writer and managing editor of *Cosmopolitan* magazine in August 1978, Tommy said, "I'm proud to be an actor." He then elaborated on that pride with, "I've put a lot of time into sounding like a lot of people, and a whole zooful of animals. I can talk any way my role requires." He also revealed one of his tricks of the trade: "I don't

Tommy Lee Jones in THE BETSY (1978).

borrow from other actors. I *steal* whatever and whenever I can, the way all actors do. Acting is a communal profession; we contribute to one another."

With COAL MINER'S DAUGHTER (1980), Jones achieved Hollywood leading man status with his portrayal of Mooney Doolittle, the husband of thirteen-year-old Loretta Lynn (Sissy Spacek), the budding country western singer. His rising reputation was enhanced when this motion picture was honored with seven Academy Award nominations, including a win for Spacek as Best Actress, as well as grossed $79.9 million in domestic distribution, making it the fifth biggest moneymaker of the year. Next he appeared as Ben Quick (the character played by Paul Newman in THE LONG HOT SUMMER [1958]) on PBS-TV's "The American Short Story" in March 1980. Thereafter, Tommy, who had parted company with his wife, moved back to San Saba, where he would not feel "like a stranger in a strange land." Although he was now a celebrity, his Texas neighbors treated him no differently than they had before his New York and Hollywood sojourns; he was comfortable in a ten-gallon hat.

BACK ROADS (1981), filmed in southern Alabama, tells the story of a down-and-out boxer who meets a down-on-her-luck hooker (Sally Field) while hitchhiking West. With this role he was determined to destroy "the hillbilly stereotype" because "this country is full of regional prejudices. A lot of people up north think we're bigots in the south. A lot of people in the south won't give the time of day to no damn yankee." BACK ROADS, directed by Martin Ritt, was not a hit. On May 23, 1981, in Austin, Texas, Tommy was married to Kimberlea Gayle Cloughley, a photographer. "We're perfect for each other," Jones told the press. "We're both basically west Texas country people and artists." They purchased a ranch in San Saba where Tommy raised polo ponies, among other animals. In 1983 a son was born.

On October 22, 1982, Tommy starred in the Showtime–Cable special presentation of "The Rainmaker," teamed with Tuesday Weld and William Katt. As intense as he was in that John Frankenheimer–directed offering, he was more riveting as Gary Gilmore, the real-life convicted killer of an Orem, Utah, service station attendant and a motel manager in NBC-TV's THE EXECUTIONER'S SONG (November 28–29, 1982). Adapted by Norman Mailer from his best-selling book, the stark four-hour made-for-television movie led *Variety* to note, "It takes a strong stomach to watch the insidious Gilmore live out his squalid life and get what he wants—death by firing squad and a telefilm glorifying him." (Gilmore had in fact wanted Warren Oates to star in his life story on screen.) As for Jones, *Variety* rated his performance "electric." Jones won an Emmy Award for this compelling, hypnotic characterization. In November 1983 Jones returned to the big screen as the swashbuckling Hayes to Michael O'Keefe's Nate, both of whom seem to be having a great time in NATE AND HAYES. Sadly, Paramount threw away the adventure picture in double-bill program distribution.

While Jessica Lange was reportedly very demanding on the set of "Cat on a Hot Tin Roof," offered by Showtime–Cable, Tommy minded his own business and would make no comment for publication. Upon the telecast (August 19, 1984) of the remake of the

1958 movie, in which Paul Newman had played the part now undertaken by Tommy, *People* magazine announced that "Tennessee Williams would be proud of Tommy Lee Jones and Jessica Lange." He was back to playing a convict in THE RIVER RAT (1984), directed by Tom Rickman, who had scripted COAL MINER'S DAUGHTER. Jones's character returns home after serving thirteen years in prison for a crime of which he is innocent and attempts to establish a rapport with his young daughter (Martha Plimpton). The moody drama was not popular. In HBO–Cable's THIS PARK IS MINE (October 6, 1985) he was an embittered Vietnam veteran threatening to blow up Central Park.

Nudity was again exploited in BLACK MOON RISING (1986), in which Tommy unwittingly becomes involved with a ring of car thieves, and he was a CIA agent in the HBO–Cable movie YURI NOSENKO, KGB (September 7, 1986). Critic Judith Crist rated as "excellent" his portrayal of a parish priest who questions his faith in BROKEN VOWS (January 28, 1987) on CBS-TV. However, this presentation was unfortunately followed by the forgettable THE BIG TOWN (1987), set in 1950s Chicago, which was intended as a showcase for rising young actor Matt Dillon. Tommy was third-billed as a Windy City gambler.

In STRANGER ON MY LAND (January 17, 1988), shown on ABC-TV, he was top-billed, but again as a Vietnam veteran, this time one fighting to save his farm from a U.S. government takeover. *Variety* noted that much of the telefilm's credibility resulted from Tommy's "strong presence." He was again a smooth racketeer in STORMY MONDAY (1988), a convoluted motion picture that must be seen a second or even a third time if one wishes to fully understand what has occurred. The 157th installment of the "Hallmark Hall of Fame," APRIL MORNING, aired on CBS-TV on April 24, 1988, was based on a Howard Fast novel about the coming of age of a fifteen year old (Chad Lowe) during the American Revolution. Tommy was the youth's stern, independent father, a minuteman who is killed in battle. Shot on farm land outside Montreal, this production was disappointing. *People* magazine described Showtime–Cable's GOTHAM (August 21, 1988) as "beautiful but empty." Tommy disrobed for a bedroom sequence as a failing private detective entranced by a lovely ghost (Virginia Madsen). It was a comedy, a genre in which Tommy does not excel. Madsen told *TV Guide* magazine that Tommy is "definitely the strong, silent, intelligent and intense type. I was just a babbling idiot around him."

After the disappointing ratings for the "War and Remembrance" (1988) mega-miniseries, many industry observers declared that the era of the multi-part TV epic was dead. Nevertheless, it enjoyed a resurrection on February 5 through 8, 1989, when CBS-TV offered its version of the Larry McMurtry western novel *Lonesome Dove*. Made up with white hair and whiskers, Tommy was second-billed to Robert Duvall as former Texas Ranger Woodrow F. Call, one of those called upon to drive a herd of cattle 2,500 miles from Texas to Montana. The $20 million project, filmed near Austin, Texas, as well as north of Santa Fe, New Mexico, earned a Golden Globe nomination for Tommy as best supporting actor in a television series, miniseries, or made-for-television movie. (He lost to Dean Stockwell of "Quantum Leap.") Tommy, by this time, was well known for confronting directors and producers with ideas or actions to make his characters more believable. During the making of "Lonesome Dove," he insisted on doing his own (stunt) riding. "If I don't," he told producer Dyson Lovell, "you get half a performance." Tommy won the argument. *US* magazine credited Duvall and Jones as being "magnificent" in their roles.

THE PACKAGE (1989) was called "devastating" by Jeffrey Lyons of TV's "Sneak Previews" and "a top notch thriller" by Bob Thomas of the Associated Press, but a "plodding tale" by *US* magazine. The package of the title was Tommy, a trained assassin masquerading as a prisoner, who escapes from his custodian (Gene Hackman) while en route from Berlin to the United States. *Variety* observed, "In the brief but pivotal title role, Jones shows it's possible to play an out-of-control psychopath without turning into a gargoyle." The thriller grossed a modest $4.3 million in domestic film rentals.

"Let's full-tilt boogie for freedom and justice," Tommy shouted above sounds created by his AH-64 Apache helicopter in FIRE BIRDS (1990) as he aimed his craft at the vicious airborne mercenary of a drug cartel over an unnamed South American nation. In this picture, called a "lively B adventure movie" by *People* magazine, he was second-billed to Nicolas Cage. Jones played an overage macho warrant officer–pilot trainer whose "easy, self-deprecating style," according to *People*, "relieves some of the heavy mood cast by Cage." *Rolling Stone* magazine, on the other hand, considered that "Nothing saves this offensively stupid propaganda from disaster." In thirteen weeks of domestic release, FIRE BIRDS grossed a relatively unimpressive $14,719,622 at the box office, making it a failure.

Forthcoming in 1991 is BLUE SKY, with Tommy co-starring with Jessica Lange as her nuclear-physicist husband on a 1950s Army base in the South. In this drama directed by Tony Richardson, Lange's character is extramaritally involved with Powers Boothe.

Generally called an "extremely polite man," Tommy Lee Jones can be outspoken in his criticism of the Hollywood system in a manner that is often brusque. He is certain to take umbrage if probing interviewers ask that clichéd question: "What is your finest work?" or when queried about his leading man status. He clearly prefers to act and to be left alone, which is why he retreats so frequently to his open ranch land in Texas.

Filmography

Love Story (Par, 1970)*
Life Study (Nebbia, 1973)*
Eliza's Horoscope (O'Zali Films, 1975)* [made in 1970]
Charlie's Angels (ABC-TV, 3/21/76)
Smash-Up on Interstate 5 (ABC-TV, 12/3/76)
Jackson County Jail (New World, 1976)
The Amazing Howard Hughes (CBS-TV, 4/13/77–4/14/77)
Rolling Thunder (AIP, 1977)
The Betsy (AA, 1978)
Eyes of Laura Mars (Col, 1978)

Coal Miner's Daughter (Univ, 1980)
Back Roads (WB, 1981)
The Executioner's Song (NBC-TV, 11/28/82–11/29/82)
Nate and Hayes [Savage Islands] (Par, 1983)
The River Rat (Par, 1984)
This Park Is Mine (HBO–Cable, 10/6/85)
Yuri Nosenko, KGB (HBO–Cable, 9/7/86)
Black Moon Rising (New World, 1986)
Broken Vows (CBS-TV, 1/28/87)
The Big Town (Col, 1987)
Stranger on My Land (ABC-TV, 1/17/88)

*As Tom Lee Jones

April Morning (CBS-TV, 4/24/88)
Gotham (Showtime–Cable, 8/21/88)
Stormy Monday (Atlantic Releasing, 1988)
The Package (Orion, 1989)
Fire Birds (BV, 1990)

Future Releases

Blue Sky (Orion, 1991)

Television Series

One Life to Live (ABC, 1971–74; 1975)

Lonesome Dove (CBS, 2/5/89–2/8/89) [miniseries]

Broadway Plays

A Patriot for Me (1969)
Four on a Garden (1970)

Ulysses in Nighttown (1974) (revival)

DIANE KEATON

"I'm a tough observer. I'm looking for anything that has any kind of
life. If it's not the usual reaction I don't care. If people act like jerks
and they do something wrong, still that's better than being phony."
—*Newsweek* magazine, February 15, 1982

IT IS *NEARLY* IMPOSSIBLE TO FIND A DISPARAGING COMMENT FROM
anyone regarding Diane Keaton. Rex Reed adores her. Roger Ebert praises her. Woody
Allen, Warren Beatty, and Al Pacino love her. Alone stands celebrity observer Andy
Warhol's derogatory remark, "Who does she think she is!," entered in his diary not once,
but twice. Progressing from the comedic "La-di-da" girl of 1977 to one of Hollywood's
major dramatic actresses less than a decade later, Diane was classed with Meryl Streep in
the glowing *Newsweek* magazine cover story of February 15, 1982, as "a new kind of star—
a star without ego."

Keaton's unpretentiousness, exemplified by the thrift-shop wardrobe and Greta
Garbo–style hats she wears, is universally recognized. As Warren Beatty has observed,
"She's constantly in search of something that's true." Diane feels that she resembles Loretta
Young, considers Irene Dunne one of filmdom's all-time finest actresses, and has been
compared—physically and technically—with Rosalind Russell. Like these three major
stars of Hollywood's golden age, Diane Keaton has successfully varied her work between
comedy and drama.

She was born Diane Hall on Saturday, January 5, 1946, in Los Angeles to Jack Hall,
a civil engineer who later became wealthy through real estate investment, and Dorothy
(Keaton) Hall, an artist and photographer. The eldest of four children, with brother
Randy and sisters Robin and Dorrie following her in birth, Diane spent the first nine years
of her life in Los Angeles, where she sang in a Methodist church choir at age five. She
organized her siblings into an acting troupe as soon as they were old enough to wear
costumes and learn lines of dialogue. She liked to stage performances for her parents of
skits she had written herself with parts played by all the children.

When Diane was ten, the family moved south to Santa Ana in Orange County,
California. In junior high school, she initially failed to convince her teachers that she was
good enough to participate in talent shows, so she formed her own group, comprised of
neighborhood kids. At Santa Ana High School, she did not make the cheerleading squad,
but she sang with a girls' choir called The Debutantes, which led to top roles in school
musicals such as *Bye Bye Birdie* and *Little Mary Sunshine.* She has admitted that she did not

learn much, scholastically, in this period, as she devoted most of her time and energy to drama, with a bit left over for photography classes and for rebelling against Establishment dress codes. She was named "Miss Personality" by classmates at graduation time in 1964, the same year that her mother, who had gone back to college, earned a degree.

After spending less than a year at Santa Ana Junior College, Diane went to New York City, with financial support from her parents, to study with Sanford Meisner at the Neighborhood Playhouse School of the Theatre. While learning the craft of acting by day, she sang and danced by night with a rock 'n' roll band, The Roadrunners, at small out-of-town clubs. Upon completing the Meisner course in the spring of 1967, she spent the summer doing theater in Woodstock, New York. Back in Manhattan, she auditioned for the rock musical *Hair*, which opened on April 29, 1968, at the Biltmore Theatre. (It was during this period that she adopted the name Diane Keaton, since there was already an actress by the name of Diana Hall.) She won a minor part in *Hair* as a tribe member, along with understudying the female lead, Lynn Kellogg. When the latter left the production a few months later, Diane took over the role. The show's finale required that cast members remove their clothing, but her firm refusal to do so was accepted, thus making her the only garmented performer on stage for each closing.

In late 1968 she auditioned for the female lead in a new play written by a stand-up comedian named Woody Allen. He has said, "I thought she was great the second I saw her, but I thought possibly she might be too tall." Standing 5' 7", she steadfastly insists that they are the same height, while he just as stubbornly says that she is taller. (Judging from photographs and from their screen appearances together, it appears that he is correct.) After a Washington, D.C., tryout, *Play It Again, Sam* opened at Broadway's Broadhurst Theatre on February 12, 1969. It starred Allen as a fanatical movie buff in love with the wife (Diane) of his best friend (Tony Roberts). Martin Gottfried *(Women's Wear Daily)* judged, "Diane Keaton played his wife with confidence and charm which made up for the role's absence of character (other than being a good gal)." By the time the hit comedy closed on May 14, 1970, Diane and Woody were living together. She appreciated his wry humor, intelligence, and immense talent, much of which rubbed off onto her, including his many Yiddish expressions. "She's an honorary Jew," he once said. While their living arrangement lasted for only about a year, they would remain good friends.

Keaton earned a small part as the wife who wants a divorce in LOVERS AND OTHER STRANGERS (1970), filmed mostly in New York City. She did television commercials for Hour After Hour deodorant, which depicted her jogging around a kitchen, of all places, wearing a track suit, yelling, "This stuff is great!" On November 27, 1970, she had a part on ABC-TV's "Love, American Style," while continuing to appear as frequently as possible on East Coast–based talk shows, singing and chatting with the likes of Johnny Carson. More television roles came her way in 1971, on "The FBI," "Mannix," and "Night Gallery."

Director-writer Francis Ford Coppola selected Diane to play the young WASP girlfriend/wife of the Mafia chief's son (Al Pacino) in the 176-minute screen adaptation of Mario Puzo's blockbuster novel, THE GODFATHER (1972). According to Keaton, her role was little more than "background music" to those of Marlon Brando (who won an Oscar) and Pacino. Nevertheless, it provided more than decent exposure for the actress. She and Woody Allen reprised their earlier stage roles in the screen version of PLAY IT AGAIN, SAM (1972), which *Show* magazine found "flat and tiring—amusing at best." She auditioned for the Neil Simon–scripted movie THE HEARTBREAK KID (1972), but despite her fine test, director Elaine May hired her daughter (Jeannie Berlin) to play Charles Grodin's put-upon bride. In SLEEPER (1973), directed for the first time by Allen, she was given a broader opportunity to display her comedic abilities as a futuristic hostess. In 1974, after completing various dramatically charged scenes in THE GODFATHER, PART II, again as Pacino's wife, this time a neglected and rebellious one, she did a singing engagement at Reno Sweeney, a Manhattan cabaret. The enormously popular GODFATHER sequel went on to win the Best Picture Oscar, the first time a follow-up picture was so honored.

In LOVE AND DEATH (1975), a parody of *War and Peace* and other Dostoyevsky, Tolstoy, and Chekhov themes, written and directed by Woody Allen, Diane was simultaneously a lustful flirt and a woman of high intellect. *Variety* enthused of the comedy, "It is impossible to catalog the comedic blueprint; suffice [it] to say it is another zany product of the terrific synergism of the two stars." Having proved comedy to be her forte, Keaton worked without Allen in the little-seen I WILL, I WILL . . . FOR NOW (1976). In it she was teamed with Elliott Gould. On February 7, 1976, she returned to the New York stage at off-Broadway's Circle in the Square Theatre as the neurotic teacher in the comedy *The Primary English Class.* Before the show closed on May 16, 1976, she left the cast and was replaced by Jill Eikenberry. In June 1976 Diane was enjoyed on movie screens, along with James Caan, Elliott Gould, and Michael Caine, in the unsuccessful 1890s lark HARRY AND WALTER GO TO NEW YORK, as a militant journalist. Also in the cast were Carol Kane and Kathryn Grody (the real-life wife of Mandy Patinkin). Keaton and Grody became friends, with Grody saying, "She's the closest thing I've ever had to a sister." Diane sang at the downstairs club at the American Place Theatre in Manhattan as well as at the Ice House in Pasadena, California, before becoming nationally known in ANNIE HALL (1977), directed by Woody Allen from his co-written script.

The title character is a neurotic Minnesota-born aspiring singer taking lessons in life from an urban comic in New York. Finally, the once-stammering, insecure woman gains self-confidence and passes him by. Said to be the account of Diane and Woody's own melancholy, bittersweet love affair, the comedy became a major hit of 1977, and Diane adopted her character's Chaplinesque apparel in her own wardrobe. ANNIE HALL won a Best Picture Oscar, with Academy Awards going also to Allen as Best Director and to Allen and Marshall Brickman for Best Original Screenplay. Previously presented with a Golden Globe Award as Best Actress, Diane was also lauded by the National Society of Film Critics, the New York Film Critics, and the British Academy. On April 3, 1978, when presented with an Academy Award by Janet Gaynor, she sputtered, "It's simply terrific! This is something!" Along with gracing the cover of the September 26, 1977, issue of *Time* magazine, she was named by *Variety* as one of two women (the other was Barbra Streisand) calculated to be the year's top box-office draws.

LOOKING FOR MR. GOODBAR, in release in October 1977, also contributed to her growing popularity. In the role of Terry Dunn, a significant departure from anything she had done before, Diane was a teacher of the deaf who cruised Manhattan singles bars at night for sex. Terry is attempting by her angry psychological use of men to get even with her repressive father (Richard Kiley). For one of the first times on screen, Diane's beauty was revealed and her figure was not disguised under confining costumes. Years later, GOODBAR director Richard Brooks would recall warning womanizer Richard Gere, then being considered for the role of the psychotic killer, about how to deal with Keaton. "Don't fuck around with this girl because she's a very gentle, very shy, very nervous person and I don't want her injured psychologically or otherwise. . . . Get to know her. But don't monkey around."

In 1978 Diane chose to reside in Manhattan in a two-bedroom apartment on East 68th Street where a romance blossomed with actor/filmmaker Warren Beatty, who had taken particular notice of her in LOOKING FOR MR. GOODBAR. Since her chief avocational interest was photography, it was not unusual for her to be spotted, wearing a floppy hat, shooting pictures around New York City. She was featured as a top motion picture entertainer in a filmed sequence on January 9, 1978, in "Variety '77—The Year in Entertainment" on CBS-TV, as well as in a two-hour special on November 11, 1978, CBS's "Hollywood's Diamond Jubilee." In Woody Allen's offbeat, moody INTERIORS (1978), she gave "her best performance to date," according to *After Dark* magazine. Keaton appeared as a reclusive poet with a death complex, smothered by her warring parents (Geraldine Page, E. G. Marshall).

Her sixth movie with Woody Allen was MANHATTAN (1979), in which she played a homewrecker. While many thought it harkened back too much to ANNIE HALL, the film was a critical and commercial success. A John Schlesinger–directed project, FINAL PAYMENTS, did not materialize. On January 4, 1980, she was featured in the NBC-TV special "The Sensational, Shocking, Wonderful, Wacky '70s." During 1980, *Reservations* was published, filled with her photographs of hotel interiors throughout the country. (A showing of her camera work would take place in 1982 at the Castelli Graphics Gallery in New York City.)

She was next directed by and co-starred with Warren Beatty, her soon-to-be ex-lover, in REDS (1981), a sprawling (200-minute-long), expensive ($33.5 million) production, as the free-thinking Louise Bryant who flees to Russia in the 1910s. Diane was nominated for an Academy Award but did not win, although Oscars were given to Beatty as Best Director and Maureen Stapleton as Best Supporting Actress. In SHOOT THE MOON (1982), whose title derives from the card game Hearts, she was the Marin County, California, wife whose marriage and family crumble in divorce. A poignant moment in the drama finds her in a bathtub singing the Beatles song "If I Fell" in a cracked voice with tears streaming down her face. The Diane Keaton–directed seventeen-minute documentary, WHAT DOES DORRIE WANT?, comprised of interviews with her sister Dorrie, was a 1982 entry at the Filmex Festival in Los Angeles. In 1983 she co-edited with Marvin Heiferman a book of Hollywood publicity photographs, entitled *Still Life*.

John Le Carré's 1983 novel was a treat, but the screen version of THE LITTLE DRUMMER GIRL (1984), branded "a piece of psychobabble" by critic Pauline Kael, was far too long and much too confusing. *Playgirl* magazine thought Diane was "not exactly convincing" as the turncoat actress, and revenue from this project was minimal. MRS. SOFFEL (1984) was an overly gloomy picture shot in Canada with Diane as a prison warden's wife who falls in love with a convict (Mel Gibson). Once again, she was smothered by fashions of the early 1900s. CRIMES OF THE HEART (1986) co-starred her with Jessica Lange and Sissy Spacek as outlandish southern sisters. *American Choice* magazine decided that "the chemistry between Keaton, Lange, and Spacek is a joy to behold," but the offbeat movie did not fare well financially. Andy Warhol referred to Diane and Cybill Shepherd as "the wornouts."

Diane had a cameo performance as a singer in Woody Allen's wonderfully nostalgic RADIO DAYS (1987). It was during this time that she and craggy-faced Al Pacino became lovers. She was continuing her pattern of loving men older than herself: Allen was eleven years her senior; Beatty, nine years; Pacino, six years. She placed herself behind the camera to direct the documentary HEAVEN (1987), which was a distinct bomb. It caused her to state, "I don't think I really know anything about directing."

Rex Reed gave BABY BOOM (1987) a four-star rating, while the Chicago duo of Gene Siskel and Roger Ebert gave it two thumbs-up. *Premiere* magazine, calling it "stylish," credited Diane with being "at her comedic best" as the valium-popping yuppie management consultant who inherits a thirteen-month-old baby. Later she buys a Vermont farm, develops a flourishing baby food business, and romances a veterinarian (Sam Shepard). This hit movie, Diane's first in several years, was adapted later as a short-lived TV series in 1988 starring Kate Jackson. Anne Archer reportedly turned down the role of THE GOOD MOTHER (1988) before director Leonard Nimoy convinced the Disney producers that Diane was right for the part. Controversial in nature, the movie tells the story of a divorced woman (Diane) with a six-year-old daughter (Asia Vieira) who is allegedly abused by the mother's lover (Liam Neeson). *Newsweek* magazine found Diane "remarkable," although the

Diane Keaton in THE LITTLE DRUMMER GIRL (1984).

movie "leaves you both wrung out and puzzled," while Nimoy spoke of "her great technique." Meanwhile, in late 1987 Diane directed music videos of "I Get Weak" and "Heaven Is a Place on Earth," cuts from Belinda Carlisle's album *Heaven on Earth*, released in January 1988.

After spending the bulk of her adult life residing in New York City, Diane relocated to California in the autumn of 1988. She purchased, for more than $1.2 million, the former Hollywood Hills home of actor Ramon Novarro. Because the house had been the site, twenty years earlier, of Novarro's brutal murder, real estate agents had found it difficult to sell.

She was touted to produce yet another version of THE BLUE ANGEL (1930, 1959), but the project evaporated during 1989. She made her television directorial debut on January 30, 1990, with the hour-long CBS-TV "Schoolbreak Special" episode "The Girl with the Crazy Brother." *Variety* observed, "she is as skilled behind the camera as in front of it." Her big-screen movie THE LEMON SISTERS had been scheduled for a summer 1989 release, but it did not have distribution until September 1, 1990. With cast approval, Keaton chose friends Carol Kane and Kathryn Grody to join her as women who have been friends since childhood, and actor/musician Ruben Blades as her love interest. In the movie, the three women moonlight as singers in their hometown, Atlantic City, calling themselves "The Lemon Sisters" because Nola's (Grody) mother once told her, "Three lemons apart are just lemons, but three lemons together are a jackpot." Continuing to sing at a local club until it is slated to be torn down to make way for a new casino, they plan to buy their own place, but do not have the necessary $200,000. The second film about female bonding to be set in Atlantic City (following 1989's BEACHES, with Bette Midler and Barbara Hershey), THE LEMON SISTERS received unfavorable notices: "contrived, unbelievable and, at times, ridiculous" (*Hollywood Reporter*), "deserves credit just for being made, but the credit stops there" (*Rolling Stone* magazine), "Diane Keaton is still Diane Keaton, but watching them struggle is no fun at all" (*San Francisco Chronicle*).

While in Italy with Al Pacino filming the oft-discussed, long-awaited third GODFA-THER installment, THE GODFATHER, PART III (1990), she and her co-star continued their on-again, off-again romance, hampered by her desire for the couple finally to wed. By May 1990, as the film company departed Italy for final shooting in New York City, their relationship had reached the "serious falling-out" stage. In the film, Diane repeated her role of Kay, the estranged wife of the "godfather" (Pacino), at a salary of $1.75 million. This time around, godfather Corleone moves the family out of crime and gambling operations into legitimate corporate takeovers and international finance involving the Vatican while at the same time struggling to name an heir to his position as head of the clan.

Diane directed the "Fever" episode (November 3, 1990) of ABC-TV's "China Beach," the series revolving around the Vietnam war. Keaton's segment dealt with nurse Dana Delany's return to Kansas after the war. "I'm not sure why she decided to do it," said series producer Carol Flint, "I guess she just likes the show." Matt Roush (*USA Today*) lauded Keaton's "dazzling job behind the camera," adding, "Directing 'China Beach' means performing at the level of its complex scripts—no mean feat this season, as the stories echo with the chaotic memories of war against the equally dangerous traumas of stateside adjustment." She later directed an episode of ABC-TV's "Twin Peaks."

In assessing her life to date, the very analytical Keaton has said, "I wanted to be more than a nice girl. I felt I wasn't really interesting enough. I was a California girl—I mean *beach*. I think that's one of the reasons I went into acting." Of today's Keaton she says, "In my past I've done an awful lot of apologizing. I always liked to say I'm sorry before anything happened, but I don't do that as much anymore." Well-rounded in her screen interpretations from comedy to action to drama, Diane Keaton can be compared to Katharine Hepburn. However, as *Premiere* magazine noted a few years ago about Diane: "Now she faces the female movie star's principal problem in middle age (one that Bette Davis never solved): finding a male co-star who is her equal."

Filmography

Lovers and Other Strangers (Cin, 1970)
The Godfather (Par, 1972)
Play It Again, Sam (Par, 1972)
Sleeper (UA, 1973)
The Godfather, Part II (Par, 1974)
Love and Death (UA, 1975)
Harry and Walter Go to New York (Col, 1976)
I Will, I Will . . . For Now (20th–Fox, 1976)
Annie Hall (UA, 1977)
Looking for Mr. Goodbar (Par, 1977)
Interiors (UA, 1978)
Manhattan (UA, 1979)
Reds (Par, 1981)

What Does Dorrie Want? (Unk, 1982)
    (documentary short) (director only)
Shoot the Moon (MGM, 1982)
The Little Drummer Girl (WB, 1984)
Mrs. Soffel (MGM/UA, 1984)
Crimes of the Heart [Colours of the Heart]
    (DeLaurentiis Entertainment Group, 1986)
Baby Boom (MGM/UA, 1987)
Radio Days (Orion, 1987)
Heaven (Island, 1987) (director only)
The Good Mother (BV, 1988)
The Lemon Sisters (Miramax, 1990)
The Godfather, Part III (Par, 1990)

Broadway Plays

Hair (1968)

Play It Again, Sam (1969)

Album Discography

Hair (RCA LSO 1150) [OC]

MICHAEL KEATON

"There's something great about being a movie star . . . let's face it!
How many people get to be movie stars? Not a lot!"
—*Premiere* magazine, July 1989

WITH A FACE LIKE HIS—OPEN, FRIENDLY, MISCHIEVOUS—HE COULD easily double as a balding leprechaun somersaulting over Irish dales. It has been reported, however, that beneath Michael Keaton's cheerful exterior lies a "hair-trigger" temper which can erupt unexpectedly. Like passing thunderstorms, the outbursts are quickly forgotten. Comedy and satire established him as a movie star who was compared early on to fellow performer Jack Nicholson. More recently, Keaton has been been said to rank with Tom Hanks, an assessment with which he agrees, or Bill Murray, a comparison with which he disagrees vehemently. A sudden star with his first two motion pictures, Keaton spent the next five years floundering until he was rediscovered in back-to-back movies, in one of which he was hidden beneath weird, award-winning makeup. That is when he realized he did not always have to be a likable guy in movies: "you see something that scares you," he said, "that's what you go for."

The last of seven children, he was born in Coraopolis, Pennsylvania, on Wednesday, September 5, 1951, to an Irish-Catholic couple named Douglas. His father was a civil engineer-surveyor; his mother, Leona, was a housewife. Michael Douglas grew up in Forest Grove, Pennsylvania, a suburb of Pittsburgh. There, in school, he learned that comedy was just as big a tool of acceptance among his peers as fist fighting. He became the town's new young clown, always ready with a joke or a quick retort. His large family constituted a ready-made audience, for whom he would do imitations of Elvis Presley with candy wrappers attached to his ears to substitute for sideburns. He once recalled that "I was kind of a wild kid and I was ring leader in the sense that I was funny and could make the guys laugh." Taking playtime very seriously in early grammar school, he would force the other youngsters to rehearse before playing. In such a large family of children, he once said, "You were either getting smacked or hugged, but at least you were getting something."

Undergoing a strict Catholic upbringing, he was required to go to confession regularly, which was eased by making light of it: "I'd . . . confess I'd scored with a girl, figuring that if I had, I would have already confessed it and if I hadn't, then I'd have just got a credit. I have so much credit, I may never have to go to confession again." Although not academically astute, he survived his years at Montour High School in McKees Rocks,

Pennsylvania, where his major activity was the golf team. However, he preferred to attract attention rather than study. (One summer, he walked the length of the resort town Geneva-on-the-Lake, Ohio, on his hands.) In 1969 he entered Kent State University in Kent, Ohio, majoring in speech communications because it was "the vaguest thing I could major in." He appeared in several campus plays, including *The Odd Couple.* He soon found that he enjoyed writing his own material as well as acting in comedic plays. He also developed a talent for art, painting oils and water colors. However, as a lifelong friend once observed, "he never seemed to have any direction. You wanted to shake him and tell him to make up his mind."

In 1971, just before he was to begin his junior year at Kent State, he more or less did make up his mind. He quit school, moved to Pittsburgh, and took a job as a cab and ice cream truck driver by day, while performing in a local coffee house at night as a stand-up comedian. He earned $25 per evening for his act. The routine involved his strolling on stage with a guitar case and opening it to find it empty. Then he would strum the case. Later, he introduced into his stage business the character of Louis the Incredible Dancing Chicken, a rubber bird that he would extract from the guitar case. The unpolished stand-up comedy act ended for a spell when he took a job as a technician at Pittsburgh's public television station, WQED. He was soon in front of the camera as a ventriloquist called Señor Taco, with a live person as his dummy. He also was something of a regular on "Mister Rogers' Neighborhood" as Black-and-White Panda.

After almost three years at WQED, Michael decided it was time for a change. He told co-workers that he was relocating to New York City. Instead, because of the potential adventure, he went to New Mexico to work at the large Navajo Indian reservation near the town of Aztec. For several months, as part of a group which included hippies, missionaries, and archaeologists, he helped clear brush, chased after renegade horses, and organized plays for the children. More than anything else, it was the bad food that persuaded him to cut short his volunteer work. "I *know* I ate horse meat," he said later, "I just know it!"

At WQED Michael had worked with producer Charlie Hauck, who had since moved to Los Angeles to become story editor for the Bea Arthur sitcom "Maude." Arriving in Los Angeles in 1975, Michael took a job as a singing busboy that lasted two nights and then contacted Hauck. The latter said he would keep him in mind. Meanwhile, Michael got nocturnal employment parking cars at a nightclub, while waiting tables during the day. Whenever possible he performed comedy routines at clubs which offered "open-mike" or amateur nights. He spent a brief time dispensing draft beer at Magic Mountain Amusement Park, while gaining stage exposure at the Comedy Club in West Hollywood as well as at the Second City Improvisational Workshop on Sunset Boulevard.

During this period he managed to get a thirty-second bit as a burglar in an episode of "Mary Hartman, Mary Hartman" on syndicated TV. Through friend Hauck, Michael was hired to play a sports reporter in a segment of "Maude," and made brief appearances on "The Tony Randall Show" and "All in the Family." At this point, because there was already a Michael Douglas with a Screen Actors Guild card, Michael was forced to change his surname. He claims to have seen a picture of actress Diane Keaton in the *Los Angeles*

Times and to have decided on Keaton as a temporary show business name, thinking that "later on, I'll pick some really brilliant name."

In 1977 Michael joined the cast of CBS-TV's "All's Fair," a sitcom starring Richard Crenna and Bernadette Peters that had premiered on September 20, 1976. He was Lanny Wolf, known as a "super hip" aide to President Jimmy Carter. He did not have much occasion to prove himself because the show was cancelled at the end of its first season. At the Comedy Club in 1978 he met Harry Colomby, a former New York schoolteacher who had managed the career of jazz musician Thelonious Monk. On the lookout for comedy talent to manage, Colomby was impressed by Keaton: "What I saw in Michael," he was to say, "was something original. I also saw charisma on stage. Something about his look and timing was exquisite." He became Michael's partner/manager, a relationship that would last several years.

Colomby negotiated for Michael a role as a regular on Mary Tyler Moore's new CBS-TV variety show, "Mary," which premiered on September 24, 1978. After just three telecasts, however, the show was cancelled. Determined to try again, Moore came through with "The Mary Tyler Moore Hour" (not to be confused with her earlier, long-running comedy series). Michael was cast as Kenneth Christy, an ambitious page at a fictional network where Mary starred in a variety series. Premiering on March 4, 1979, this CBS-TV variety show lasted only eleven segments, despite having the likes of Lucille Ball, Bea Arthur, Nancy Walker, Dick Van Dyke, and others as guest stars. At the Comedy Club, Michael and Colomby met Jim Belushi, with whom they developed the concept for the TV series "Working Stiffs," which had its first CBS telecast on September 15, 1979. Michael and Jim were two Chicago brothers who worked as janitors but were determined to work their way up the ladder of big business, even though they were frightfully clumsy. This show, too, did not draw audience attention, and it was dropped after four segments. With four TV series failures behind him, Michael decided to concentrate, for the time being, on his comedy routines. He even turned down a role in CAVEMAN (1981), which then went to Dennis Quaid.

During 1982, Michael fared better, professionally, as well as on a personal level. He starred in a CBS-TV series, "Report to Murphy," as an inexperienced parole officer who becomes too involved with his clients. The situation comedy was first seen on April 5, 1982, with *Variety* reporting, "Keaton looks a trifle too young to be entrusted with parole officer duty, but no matter—he's a light comedian of considerable ability." Nevertheless, the program had a short life, ending on May 31, 1982. However, by this time he had completed a Ron Howard–directed feature film that would bring him favorable attention. In general theatrical release in July 1982, NIGHT SHIFT starred Henry Winkler as Chuck, the meek nighttime supervisor at the city morgue who yearns merely for peace and quiet. His solitude is broken by the loud arrival of his new, whacked-out assistant (Michael) who has some wild ideas, one of which is to operate a prostitution service through the morgue. Although the picture was earmarked as a big-screen triumph for Winkler, it was Michael who stole the show, becoming, according to most critics ("wonderfully deranged" enthused *Variety*), an instant star. This sleeper comedy hit grossed a very respectable $8.5

million in domestic film rentals.

In 1982, at age thirty-one, Michael married actress Caroline McWilliams, age thirty-eight, who during 1978–1979 was on TV's "Soap" as Sally and later played Marcy on "Benson" from 1979 to 1981. In 1983 they had a son, Sean.

Following NIGHT SHIFT, Michael's salary escalated from $60,000 to $300,000 for MR. MOM (1983), in which the husband/father (Michael) loses his job, requiring the wife/mother (Teri Garr) to work to support the family while he attempts to run the household and take care of their three small children. As *People* magazine noted, "it's Keaton's kinetic energy, ever-undulating eyebrows, and wise-guy humor that carry the whole potentially dismal project." MR. MOM grossed a substantial $32 million in domestic film rentals. On November 30, 1984, an unsold pilot for an ABC-TV series based on the movie was telecast with Barry Van Dyke as the unemployed father.

After MR. MOM established Michael as a hot box-office commodity, he was swiftly signed by Twentieth Century–Fox to star in JOHNNY DANGEROUSLY (1984). It was a spoof of the gangster movies of the 1930s with a screenplay co-written by Harry Colomby, who was also an executive producer on the project. The beginning was humorous, but the picture soon disintegrated into an embarrassment. Released in December 1984, JOHNNY DANGEROUSLY was chastised by critics and ignored by moviegoers. Prior to its release, though, the studio entered into a four-year nonexclusive contract with Michael to make one film per year for them. (The agreement would expire in February 1988 without his ever having appeared in a single project for the studio during that period.) Keaton's big mistake was turning down the offer from Touchstone Pictures to star in SPLASH (1984) in the role that then went to Tom Hanks. It became the #10 hit of the year, grossing $69.8 million at the domestic box office and ensuring stardom for Hanks.

Taking a cut in salary to $250,000 to work with Woody Allen, Michael started in the comedian's production of THE PURPLE ROSE OF CAIRO (1985). However, he was dismissed after a week, because his interpretation of the 1930s film star who walks off the screen was thought to be too contemporary. He was replaced by Jeff Daniels. Hoping to make up for turning down SPLASH, directed by Ron Howard, he reunited with Howard for GUNG HO (1986) as a cocky Pennsylvania auto assembly plant worker whose company is purchased by Japanese investors. Filmed partly in Argentina, the movie proved to be another semi-mistake, which was labeled by *People* magazine as "Not much of anything except two hours long." Nevertheless, the picture grossed $15.5 million in domestic film rentals. The property became a one-season TV series in 1987–1988 with Scott Bakula in the role created on screen by Michael.

TOUCH AND GO (1987), in which Michael was a Chicago pro-hockey star, was a critical and financial bomb that had languished on the shelf for almost a year before its release in January 1987. After THE SQUEEZE (1987), in which he was a con man involved in murder, proved to be another disaster, Michael wrote a friend back home, "Man, I'm dying out here." Unfortunately, he turned down an offer to star in STAKEOUT (1987), in the role that helped Richard Dreyfuss regain popularity. STAKEOUT became the #9 domestic grosser of the year.

Despondent as he was over four screen failures in a row, Michael's famed temper was at an all-time high, especially at home. In a trial separation from Caroline, he moved out. "I know I haven't been the perfect husband," he said publicly, "but I love my wife and son. There isn't anything I wouldn't do to get them back." The separation continued, although she was his frequent companion at Hollywood screenings and premieres. He now lived in a recently purchased Beverly Hills home, with his dog, a border collie named Dusty. Around Hollywood he was linked romantically with Michelle Pfeiffer and later with Kim Basinger. However, he claimed that all he really wanted was to be reunited with his family.

Tim Burton, a young film director who had begun in animation before tackling feature films, did not have a sizeable budget for BEETLEJUICE (1988). Nonetheless, he had faith in Michael Keaton, who he said only needed the right director to bring out his subtlety. Since he could not afford the then-big comedic screen names, he offered the title role in this film to Michael. However, Michael came close to turning it down, which would have been yet another error in judgment. Although he is in just nineteen of the movie's ninety-two minutes, and is buried beneath a fake nose and bizarre makeup, he steals the proceedings (abetted by special effects) as the unsavory "bio-exorcist." Opening in theaters nationwide on March 30, 1988, the picture had domestic grosses of over $74 million and emerged as the #10 box-office draw of the year. (In January 1990, ABC-TV would introduce an animated Saturday morning children's show bearing the same title, depicting a ghostly ghoul indulging in grossness.)

In August 1988 CLEAN AND SOBER reached American movie screens. Twice Michael had demurred from accepting the lead role, but Bruce Willis talked him into taking the assignment of the shifty executive who hides out at a Philadelphia detoxification center for cocaine addiction and remains to graduate. Tom Hanks was originally sought for the part, but director Glenn Gordon Caron preferred Keaton. By autumn, critics agreed that Michael had given an award-winning performance. He was honored in January 1989 by the National Society of Film Critics as Best Actor of 1988 for both BEETLEJUICE and CLEAN AND SOBER, but was ignored by the Academy of Motion Picture Arts and Sciences when it came time for Oscar nominations.

Keaton's career was now on the upswing after three years of being called "unbankable" by film producers. With Colomby, he formed a production company in conjunction with Warner Bros. Howev-

Michael Keaton in THE SQUEEZE (1987).

er, it was for Universal that he starred in what has been called a third-rate ONE FLEW OVER THE CUCKOO'S NEST (1975), this time a story about four mental patients (Keaton, Christopher Lloyd, Peter Boyle, Stephen Furst) at a New Jersey institution who are on the loose in Manhattan. THE DREAM TEAM was released in April 1989, with critic Rex Reed finding Michael "positively wonderful" while the *Los Angeles Times*, although stating that Michael was "good," thought the movie contained a "rambling story." THE DREAM TEAM grossed $14,384,108 in domestic film rentals, largely on the basis of Keaton's drawing power.

Meanwhile, moviegoers were waiting in great anticipation for the release of BAT-MAN (1989), the highly promoted new screen adventure of the comic strip hero, directed by Tim Burton. Just as there had been many published accounts of the on-set problems during filming of BATMAN (including script rewrites and the replacing of leading lady Sean Young with Kim Basinger), so Warner Bros. was now heavily hyping the picture in conjunction with saturation merchandising of Batman products (T-shirts, capes, coffee mugs, etc.). Michael was not everyone's first choice to play hero Bruce Wayne; the skeptics included Bob Kane, Batman's creator and a consultant on the London-made production. (Producer Jon Peters preferred Bill Murray.) However, after a few alterations to Keaton's hairline, accomplished partly by a frontal hair piece, it was decided he could be believable in the "dead-serious melodrama" about the schizophrenic Wayne. Keaton's up-front salary was $5 million, with an additional 8 percent of the studio box-office take to be paid only if it exceeded his initial salary. During the five-day Independence Day weekend of 1989 when it debuted, BATMAN grossed $43.6 million, which set a new record for any movie over that holiday period. By year's end, BATMAN had grossed $251.2 million domestically. But while Michael had the title role of the peculiarly melancholy playboy hero, it was co-star Jack Nicholson (receiving a higher salary and better percentage deal), as the extravagantly malevolent Joker, who stole the limelight. *Variety* noted, "Jack Nicholson's incandescent Joker overwhelms Michael Keaton's subdued title character." The trade paper added, "Keaton captures the haunted intensity of the character and seems particularly lonely and obsessive without Robin around to share his exploits." With such a hefty financial return from BATMAN, a sequel was immediately discussed, with Michael agreeing to repeat his role. Ultimately, it was decided to film two sequels at one time while the cast and sets were on hand, as had been done with BACK TO THE FUTURE II and III. With the Joker character out of the storyline, it was uncertain what characters would provide the nemeses for the "caped crusader."

In January 1990, after seven years of marriage, Michael and Caroline McWilliams filed for an amicable divorce, with Caroline asking for custody of their son. After purchasing a many-acred Montana ranch in 1990, Michael lived in a tent which he moved to various locations on the property before selecting a location on which to build a home. On April 22, 1990, he joined several other film celebrities in a two-hour ABC-TV ecology presentation, "Earth Day Special," dealing with remedies to repair the dying planet. Keaton was now being seen in public with his new pal, actress Courteney Cox.

The exterior shots for PACIFIC HEIGHTS, in release September 28, 1990, were made in San Francisco, not in its Pacific Heights district but in Potrero Heights, where parking is better but the views are different. While in the city, Michael stayed at the Huntington Hotel atop Nob Hill where he registered as Michael Douglas, intending to confuse the press. During filming, he devoted his free daylight hours to playing golf. In the movie, directed by John Schlesinger, he was the tenant from hell of "the perfect couple" (Melanie Griffith, Matthew Modine), a presumably friendly man until he begins psychologically menacing his landlords. David Ansen (*Newsweek* magazine) found the chiller disappointing ("slick but only semi-thrilling"), but noted, "There's always been something manic and mischievous in Michael Keaton's performances, but until PACIFIC HEIGHTS he hasn't had the chance to be flat out malevolent. It's not surprising he makes a superb psycho.... But he's not on screen enough." *Variety* noted that "Schlesinger never manages to convincingly meld the pic's schizophrenic halves—its sweet normality and bizarre menace." The trade paper added, "Keaton is a fine actor ... but he comes off as almost a parody of a creep, the way he sits around twisting razor-blades in the dark." Director John Schlesinger chose Michael to play the sociopath because "when I saw him in CLEAN AND SOBER, I realized what a really good actor he is." During its first week of domestic release, PACIFIC HEIGHTS grossed an impressive $14,038,549, and after seven weeks had taken in $27,892,883 at the box office.

Taking the celebrity slant a step further, the Ralston Purina Pet Food Company put out a 1991 calendar with a photograph each month of the dog of a star. Michael, with Bob Hope, Barbara Mandrell, Kirstie Alley, and others, coaxed his dog to "smile for the camera."

In ONE GOOD COP (1991), shot in New York City and Los Angeles, Michael portrays an honest cop "forced to compromise his ethics" in order to adopt the children of his widowed partner (Anthony LaPaglia), who is killed in the line of duty.

At one point during 1990 it was rumored in the film industry that a remake of SOME LIKE IT HOT (1959) was "in the talking stages," to star Madonna in the Marilyn Monroe role and Michael and Tom Cruise playing the Jack Lemmon and Tony Curtis parts in partial drag. The project has yet to materialize.

Highly excitable when situations do not come up to his expectations, Michael Keaton is known in the movie industry as someone who readily expresses his dislikes. "Hey, look, it's my face up there on the screen," he says in self-defense, "and it's me that's gonna take the knocks if the movie goes belly up." He refuses to feel stupid or untalented and "That's why I put all my creative energies—and opinions—into every movie I do." Reputed to be moodier than Dustin Hoffman, whose reputation is legend, Keaton comments, "I still try to get along with the people I work with. I don't want to intimidate anybody." Of all the productions with which he has been affiliated, he states unequivocally that fatherhood is the most important. "Hands down, it's the best thing I've ever done in my life," he says proudly.

Filmography

Night Shift (WB, 1982)
Mr. Mom (20th–Fox, 1983)
Johnny Dangerously (20th–Fox, 1984)
Gung Ho (Par, 1986)
Touch and Go (Tri-Star, 1987)
The Squeeze (Tri-Star, 1987)

Beetlejuice (WB, 1988)
Clean and Sober (WB, 1988)
The Dream Team (Univ, 1989)
Batman (WB, 1989)
Pacific Heights (20th–Fox, 1990)
One Good Cop (BV, 1991)

Television Series

All's Fair (CBS, 1977)
Mary (CBS, 1978)
The Mary Tyler Moore Hour (CBS, 1979)

Working Stiffs (CBS, 1979)
Report to Murphy (CBS, 1982)

PERRY KING

"An actor can expect to be in his prime to at least fifty-five
and in character roles till as long as he wants."
—*After Dark* magazine, January 1977

PERRY KING IS DESCRIBED AS "INCREDIBLY HANDSOME" WITH A "Camelot-like quality." He started out in show business at the same time as Sylvester Stallone, with whom he later co-starred in THE LORDS OF FLATBUSH (1974). King is an actor whose theatrical motion picture career was derailed in the late 1970s by, he claims, his playing a homosexual on screen during a period when the subject was not yet fully out of the closet. Turning to television as an alternative, he soon challenged Peter Strauss as prince of the miniseries. Later, when he co-starred with Joe Penny in TV's "Riptide," a mid-season replacement series with lots of action, boats, beaches, and scant clothing, at-home viewers responded very favorably. From the first showing of the lightweight series, which enjoyed two years of popularity, the muscular King was described quite simply as "a hunk." Conversationally articulate on many topics, Perry is a congenial interviewee with old-fashioned, polite manners. His patrician features, topped by a blond-to-brown mane, have served him well on camera, whether he was portraying a lover, an aristocrat, a daredevil, or a villain.

Perry King was born in Alliance, Ohio, on Friday, April 30, 1948. His father, a physician, was following in a long line of family doctors; his mother, like her mother before her, was known for her beauty. Perry is related, on his mother's side, to Maxwell Perkins, the editor/publisher responsible for putting the works of such authors as F. Scott Fitzgerald and Thomas Wolfe into print. Perry has one brother and two sisters, all of whom are often involved with or married to persons in the publishing business. At age four, Perry announced that he wanted to grow up to be a doctor like his dad. However, after discovering tin soldiers, with which he played endlessly, he decided he now wanted to be a military cadet. This phase passed too. At St. Paul's preparatory school in New Haven, Connecticut, he became interested in sports, including sailing and rowing. In 1966, during his final year at the school, he was an American Schoolboy champion rower whose crew won the world championship at the Henley Regatta in England and came in second, by half a length, in the competition for the Princess Elizabeth Cup.

It was also at St. Paul's that he appeared in his first stage play. When he entered Yale University in the autumn of 1966, he chose drama as his major. Once there, however, he found, "I didn't like their drama program for undergraduates and didn't think much of the

Drama School itself." Nevertheless, he remained with drama as a major study. He fulfilled the curriculum's requirements by spending three vacation periods doing summer stock. In 1968, at the age of twenty, he met and married Karen Hryharrow, a student at Albertus Magnus College, also located in New Haven. She had previously been a postulant in a religious order. When they bought their wedding rings, they entered a contest in which they won a new car. Since they had little money, they sold the vehicle and bought a used car (which he repaired), plus an old motorcycle with a sidecar. Motorcycles would become one of his passions, as would the restoration of old cars.

Following his graduation from Yale, Perry enrolled at the Juilliard School in New York City in 1970, studying drama under John Houseman. Within three months, though, his Juilliard studies came to an end when, through an acquaintance who worked for Broadway producer David Merrick, he auditioned for Merrick "as a lark, just to see if I could put into practice some of the wonderful things Juilliard was teaching me." (On the same day as his audition in February 1971, daughter Louise was born.) He got the part in *Child's Play*, as a replacement for Tony Award winner Ken Howard, who was leaving the drama. King signed with Jane Oliver of the CMA talent agency. She arranged immediately for a screen test for a feature film. When he won a small part in SLAUGHTERHOUSE-FIVE (1972), she sent him to test for another picture, in which he was cast in a co-starring role. Just when he began to wonder where he was going to find time to do three projects simultaneously, *Child's Play* closed without his having set foot on stage.

Shooting on THE POSSESSION OF JOEL DELANEY (1972) started first, in New York, but SLAUGHTERHOUSE-FIVE was the first of the two films to be released. As Robert, he played the teenage son. In THE POSSESSION OF JOEL DELANEY, filmed largely in New York City locations, he was a young man who becomes possessed by the murderously evil spirit of his dead best friend, a Puerto Rican (José Fernandez). King had to speak with an accent during the possession scenes. Perry credits the movie's star, Shirley MacLaine, with helping him adapt to screen work. "God, she was kind to me," he has said. The bizarre storyline received mixed reviews, but *Variety* noted, "Newcomer Perry King is fine." After completing these two back-to-back projects, he won a role in a Peter Ustinov feature shot in Israel, known as BIG MACK AND POOR CLARE and sometimes called POOR CLARE. The movie was never released, but King cherished meeting, working with, and learning from the multi-talented Ustinov, who, Perry has said, "was so superbly filled with so many aspects of life, so much knowledge and wit."

Upon returning to the United States, Perry and his small family moved to Los Angeles where they lived in two adjoining houses. When asked why, he replied simply, "because they're there." He visited Hawaii for an appearance in the CBS-TV series "Hawaii Five-O" in an episode entitled "The Banzai Pipeline" (January 1, 1974), then rushed back to the mainland to do the "Blood Money" segment (February 6, 1974) of CBS-TV's "Cannon." Prior to his move to California, he starred as one of four leather-jacketed street toughs comprising a gang, circa 1957, in THE LORDS OF FLATBUSH (1974). He received top billing over Sylvester Stallone and Henry Winkler, both of whom would go on to become major stars. Ray Sharkey and Armand Assante had bit parts in this flavorful, nostalgic exercise. Also in 1974, Perry made an appearance on CBS-TV's "Apple's Way," as well as in another "Hawaii Five-O" installment.

The year 1975 was his busiest to date; he was in demand for both movies and television and worked also on the off-Broadway stage. He was enthusiastically involved with producer Alan Belkin and director Paul Aaron in a potential movie project about a gay man and a lesbian who fall in love and parent a child. The idea was temporarily shelved due to lack of financing. Meanwhile, he appeared in an episode of the long-running CBS-TV series "Medical Center" and co-starred with James Mason and Susan George in MANDINGO (1975). In this adaptation of Taylor Caldwell's romantic historical novel, set in pre–Civil War days, he was Hammond Maxwell, the son of an aging Louisiana plantation owner (Mason). The Maxwells own many slaves, and Hammond provides stud service to the "wenches." King's character was the type who, before taking his pleasure with one of them (Debbi Morgan), kneels besides the bed in prayer, "Now I lay me down to sleep. . . ." His frontal nude scene apparently did not embarrass him in the least. Most critics used words such as "sleazy" and "trashy" in their critiques, but Perry defended the film: "I loved MANDINGO. What fascinates me is that it received angry, carping, incensed reviews, and yet it's an incredible success." It grossed a hefty $8.6 million in domestic film rentals, and the film's producer, Dino De Laurentiis, immediately scheduled a continuation, called DRUM (1976). De Laurentiis was eager to wait for Perry to unravel his commitments in order to reprise his role of Hammond. As it developed, however, Warren Oates substituted for Perry, with DRUM being derided as ultratrashy. It was a box-office failure.

THE WILD PARTY (1975) was a strange fabrication guided by American-born director James Ivory, who had made an international reputation with movies lensed in India, including THE HOUSEHOLDER (1962) and SHAKESPEARE WALLAH (1964). THE WILD PARTY was set in Hollywood in 1929. The silent film era has ended and a Fatty Arbuckle–like character (James Coco) is vainly struggling to save his worldwide comic career, while losing his glamorous mistress (Raquel Welch) to a vain actor/stud (King). Unintentionally verging on burlesque, this big-screen misfire was harmed further by having one of the characters (David Dukes) narrate the lurid storyline in rhyme. After this outing, on television Perry played Ernest Hemingway at age thirty in "The Hemingway Play" on PBS, as well as starred as one of two New York City police officers gunned down in an ambush in the CBS-TV movie FOSTER & LAURIE (November 3, 1975). His year concluded professionally with a three-week run off-Broadway at the Phoenix Theatre as Curley Delafield, who searches unsuccessfully for his sister in *Knuckle*.

As a favor to Dino De Laurentiis, to make up for not doing DRUM, Perry took the third-billed role in LIPSTICK (1976), a wretched exploitation film featuring two Hemingway sisters: Margaux and Mariel. As King termed it, he had "A somewhat dry, dead, functional part that at this point I wouldn't normally have taken." "Captains and the Kings," another adaptation of a sprawling Taylor Caldwell novel, was a nine-hour miniseries shown on NBC-TV each Thursday from September 30 through November 18, 1976. In a large cast that included many Hollywood names, Perry appeared in the last four episodes as Irishman Rory Armagh, a wealthy, tragic presidential hopeful. Because of its deliberate parallels with the Kennedy family chronicle, the miniseries was popular with viewers and brought Perry to the fore as a handsome actor. He was back in New York to co-star with Carroll Baker in ANDY WARHOL'S BAD (1977), a bizarre story, financed by the bizarre little man, about hired killers whose specialties are animals and children. He fared better in "Aspen" (November 5–7, 1977), a six-hour NBC-TV miniseries, in which he was an innocent drifter accused of murder. King's acting school mentor, John Houseman, had a guest-starring role in the proceedings. THE CHOIRBOYS (1977) is best remembered for its ribald sexual situations and its foul language as a group of Los Angeles policemen attempt to live it up as an antidote to their deadening, dangerous occupation. Perry was Slate, considered "overly educated" to be a cop (and who later kills himself), in this badly trivialized rendition of the Joseph Wambaugh novel.

In mid-1977 producer Alan Belkin and director Paul Aaron, whom Perry had known since 1975, resurrected their idea of a feature film about a gay man and a lesbian. King was cast as Albert, a Los Angeles–based gay fashion designer, with Meg Foster as the lesbian who becomes his wife and has his child (all of which turns an unconventional premise into a conventional love story). Released in June 1978, the low-budget A DIFFER-ENT STORY put off many mainstream critics, among them Richard Schickel (*Time* magazine): "There's something in A DIFFERENT STORY to turn off audiences of every sexual persuasion—and movie lovers most of all." Viewed today, this offbeat picture is more timely; it was obviously produced during an era when its controversial subject matter was not as readily acceptable or understandable. Ten years after A DIFFERENT STORY came and went, Perry told *TV Guide* magazine, "Because of that part, producers and casting directors in the motion picture industry didn't cast me in a lot of roles. I had a reasonable film career, and it began to stumble." From then on, his career was primarily in TV, with only a few, unsuccessful movie assignments.

In the ABC-TV movie THE CRACKER FACTORY (March 16, 1979), he was a psychiatrist assigned to unravel the depressions of alcoholic Natalie Wood. He returned to the costumes of the Old South in a sad rip-off of GONE WITH THE WIND (1939) in ABC-TV's LOVE'S SAVAGE FURY (May 20, 1979). Also in May 1979 he was on stage opposite Sandy Dennis in the Long Beach (California) Theatre Festival production of Tennessee Williams's *Eccentricities of a Nightingale*. A 1939 Packard was the focal point of "The Last Convertible" (September 24–26, 1979), an NBC-TV six-hour miniseries tracing the lives of five Harvard students from 1940 to 1969. In an interview with the Associated Press prior to the showing of this project, Perry said, "One of the reasons I work more and more in television is because they make movies of the 1930s [style]." He revealed that he had many offers for TV series employment, but, he explained, "I want to play a lot of roles . . . playing in a series would be like waking up every morning and playing the same game."

In 1980 Perry and Karen separated. Now an attorney, she received custody of their nine-year-old daughter, with liberal visitation rights awarded to King. NBC-TV's CITY IN FEAR (March 30, 1980) had Perry as a police lieutenant, while in ABC-TV's INMATES: A

LOVE STORY (February 13, 1981) he was a former accountant serving time in an experimental co-ed prison where he finds romance with a petty thief (Kate Jackson). During 1981 he also starred as a reporter in a theatrical release, THE CLAIRVOYANT, in which he becomes involved with an artist (Elizabeth Kemp) who is able to sketch homicide victims before the crimes occur. Also known as THE KILLING HOUR, the suspense yarn was quickly sold off to TV. Another motion picture made for the large screen was SEARCH AND DESTROY (1981), filmed in 1978 but shelved for three years, in which he was an American G.I. involved in South Vietnamese intrigue. On September 25, 1981, he starred in an ABC-TV series pilot/feature, GOLDEN GATE, as the scion of a San Francisco publishing family. CLASS OF 1984 (1982), a theatrical movie, was reminiscent of THE BLACKBOARD JUNGLE (1955) but did not fare as well; Perry was a victimized high school teacher resorting to violence.

Contrary to his earlier remarks about not wishing to do a teleseries, Perry agreed to star as a photojournalist in ABC-TV's "The Quest," a farfetched escapist concept about four Americans (King, Noah Beery, Jr., Karen Austin, Ray Vitte) inheriting the throne of a Mediterranean kingdom called Glendora. Premiering on October 22, 1982, the show faded a month later with its November 19 episode. In the September 1983 Showtime–Cable special "The Hasty Heart," Perry assumed the role performed by Ronald Reagan in the 1949 movie version, as a sympathetic American soldier who befriends a dying but arrogant young Scots soldier (Gregory Harrison).

"Riptide," a mid-season NBC-TV replacement series that premiered January 3, 1984, was called "James Bondian in spirit" by *TV Guide* magazine. By February 10, 1985, "Riptide" had a 20.1 Nielsen rating, second only to TV's hit series "The A-Team." With such viewer response, it was natural that the program would return in September as a regular Tuesday night hour offering, in which two robust beach bums, Cody Allen (Perry with moustache) and Nick Ryder (Joe Penny), decide to go into business as private detectives. They live aboard Cody's trawler (*Riptide*) in a southern California marina next to a charter boat, whose all-female, bikini-clad crew is headed by Mama Jo (Anne Francis). No one wore much clothing in the series, except the nerdy electronic genius (Thom Bray) recruited by the womanizing Cody and Nick to work with them. The action series would endure through the 1985–1986 season.

Perry King in "Riptide" (1985).

While "Riptide" was gaining early popularity, Perry played an editor with whom Helen Keller (Mare Winningham) becomes enamored but who marries Helen's companion/teacher, Anne Sullivan (Blythe Danner) in the two-hour syndicated TV movie HELEN KELLER: THE MIRACLE CONTINUES (April 23, 1984). During the summer of 1986, Perry went to Tahiti to co-star with Loni Anderson for NBC-TV as rival advertising executives who get STRANDED (September 22, 1986) on a deserted island. This ninety-minute comedy was a first for him, aside from the often comedic touches of "Riptide."

Judith Krantz's *I'll Take Manhattan* (1986) sold more than 3,790,000 copies in both hard- and soft-cover editions. The story of sex, greed, and manipulation was brought to the television screen by CBS in a four-part miniseries, estimated to have been seen by 20.3 million households on March 1 through 4, 1987. Perry was the villainous Cutter Amberville, brother to the founder (Barry Bostwick) of a publishing empire. Judith Krantz, whose novels have to be toned down in their televised adaptations, liked Perry as the hated man of the plot. "His face is just built for this," she said. "He has those marvelous, sensual but cruel lips." *TV Guide* magazine's critic described him as "so delicious a villain that [producer] Aaron Spelling should cast him in [the nighttime soap opera] 'The Colbys' tomorrow."

Following that successful TV outing, he and Lauren Hutton teamed as a long-married couple who regenerate their figures and their personalities in ABC-TV's PERFECT PEOPLE (February 29, 1988). In CBS-TV's fact-based SHAKEDOWN ON THE SUNSET STRIP (April 22, 1988), he had a sympathetic part as a 1940s Los Angeles vice officer uncovering departmental corruption involving ties to prostitution rings. Later in the year, he co-starred with Michael O'Keefe and Dennis Weaver as an Air Force major striving to ward off a nuclear warhead that could wipe out the state of Texas in ABC-TV's DISASTER AT SILO 7 (November 27, 1988).

For syndicated television, he flew to Paris to join an international cast for the television version of A. E. Hotchner's novel THE MAN WHO LIVED AT THE RITZ. During his three months in France, King claims, he was cornered frequently "on the streets" by viewers of "I'll Take Manhattan" to "tell me they hated me. I took it as a compliment." In the two-part THE MAN WHO LIVED AT THE RITZ (November 28–29, 1988), he was Philip Weber, an American artist headquartered at the famed Paris hotel when the Germans occupy the city in 1940. Intent on remaining neutral, he is drawn into the war after the Gestapo murder his girlfriend (Cherie Lunghi). Thereafter, he spies for the French resistance while acting as an art consultant to Reichsmarshal Herman Goering (Joss Ackland). John Carman (*San Francisco Chronicle*) felt that Ackland stole the show because "Perry King couldn't act his way out of an almond croissant." While on location in France, Perry was visited by his seventeen-year-old daughter as well as by his steady girlfriend, Jamison "Jamie" Elvidge, whom he had met in 1986 and who tested motorcycles for a living. King admitted to the press that he missed working in a TV series and was in search of one in which to star. (He had headlined an ABC-TV series pilot, "Half 'n' Half," aired on September 1, 1988. In it he played a racecar driver who discovers that a black jazz musician [Dorian Harewood] is his half brother and that their mother had been murdered.

Variety tagged this "a shoo-in for dumbest idea of them all.")

People magazine stated, "Hunky Perry King plays Pete as a slightly nicer J. R. Ewing," while *Variety* credited him as "excellent, oozing malevolence and two-faced smarminess while at the same time exhibiting the charm that enabled him to seduce women." Pete is Herbert "Pete" Pulitzer of the publishing Pulitzers, who took as his second wife a woman (Chynna Phillips) twenty years his junior with whom he had twin sons, followed by a scandalous divorce suit in 1982. This was all brought to light by the woman in a best-selling book of 1987, which became NBC-TV's ROXANNE: THE PRIZE PULITZER (October 16, 1989). Because of Roxanne Pulitzer's connection with the making of the project (as both consultant and actress in a bit part), the narrative is biased in her favor. The most believable element of this specious offering was Perry, with graying hair as a middle-aged man attracted to a younger lass.

In early 1990, King and Dorian Harewood shot their second TV series pilot, "The Knife and Gun Club," about two doctors who are partners in ownership of an urban emergency hospital. The unsold pilot aired on July 30, 1990, on ABC, with the hour-long entry overstuffed with clichéd plotlines (missing drugs, a hostage situation) and not enough dimensional characterization. With no TV series commitment ahead, Perry was able to focus on his hobby of auto racing, entering a celebrity auto race in Los Angeles as well as competing in the 1,000-mile Mille Miglia rally in Italy. Influenced by his lover, Jamison Elvidge, King was also by now an avid motorcycle enthusiast.

At the Pasadena Playhouse Balcony Theatre, Perry and Sandy Duncan read the two-character A. R. Gurney play *Love Letters* on March 11 and 12, 1990. Perry repeated his role in the frequently changed cast on March 25 and 26 with Donna Mills.

On June 9, 1990, in Pismo Beach, California, Perry was married to Jamison "Jamie" Elvidge, now the editor of *American Woman Road Racing* magazine. "This is a beautiful woman," he said, "a woman who loves motorcycles and who can write beautifully." Following their wedding, he (aged forty-two) and his bride (aged twenty-five) boarded their individual Kawasaki motorcycles, one with a "Just" sign, the other with a sign reading "Married," and rode away to Canada for a three-week honeymoon.

For CBS-TV's second annual "National Driving Test" (August 28, 1990), hosted by Robert Urich, Perry was among several television celebrities, along with President George Bush, to offer driving safety tips. On September 7, 1990, at the Wiltern Theatre in Los Angeles, King was on hand to greet guests attending the AIDS Project Los Angeles's *Commitment to Life IV*. Perry returned to television with the NBC-TV movie DANIELLE STEEL'S KALEIDOSCOPE (October 15, 1990), in which he played a wealthy, handsome detective hired by a dying man to solve the mystery of three women (including Jaclyn Smith) separated as children following the strange death of their parents. *Entertainment Weekly* magazine rated the turgid offering a C–. John Carman (*San Francisco Chronicle*) complained, "'Kaleidoscope' would be described as a pure waste of talent, if only Smith and King had talent to waste." Some days later, on October 27, 1990, Perry was seen in ONLY ONE SURVIVED, a CBS telefeature in which he and Michael Beck were among four friends who embark from New York on a deep-sea fishing vacation at the port of San

Pedro in the Amazon and become involved in salvaging an abandoned craft filled with explosives. The production met with critical jabs. Andy Klein (*Hollywood Reporter*) complained, "It takes a noteworthy talent to make a two hour adventure movie . . . so utterly soporific. . . . None of the actors is well served by the clichéd exposition." *Daily Variety* sympathized, "Perry King works valiantly to give effective subtlety and shading to the central character Philip, fighting a script that gives him little of substance to build on." Forthcoming for Perry on theatrical screens is his first major motion picture since 1978, as a male chauvinist who dies in SWITCH (1991) and returns to life as a woman (Ellen Barkin). Then his best friend (Jimmy Smits) makes a play for her/him. This was also King's first comedy since the serio-comedic "Riptide" series.

On December 10, 1990, Perry made his Broadway bow in *A Few Good Men*, taking over the role of the villain previously played by Stephen Lang and Ron Perlman. Meanwhile, on Dove audio cassettes, King could be heard reading Erle Stanley Gardner's Perry Mason mystery *The Case of the Beautiful Beggar* and joined with Roddy McDowall and James Stacy in reading *Murder in Los Angeles*, a trio of stories by three Southern California mystery writers.

Still in his prime, Perry King continues to get occasional co-starring roles in films, but is primarily considered a television actor. Admittedly wanting another series, one that will provide him with status and longevity, he hones his acting craft with each miniseries or made-for-television movie. Now middle-aged, his handsomeness is unaltered except for the minute addition of a character line here or there. In an interview near the start of his career, he said, "In western thought, you are what you've done and, conversely, you exist for what you will be. And so there is no present." By living his present to the fullest, he maintains that the future never comes.

Filmography

Slaughterhouse-Five (Univ, 1972)

The Possession of Joel Delaney (Par, 1972)

Big Mack and Poor Clare [Poor Clare] (Br-Israeli, 1972) [unreleased]

The Lords of Flatbush (Col, 1974)

Foster & Laurie (CBS-TV, 11/3/75)

Mandingo (Par, 1975)

The Wild Party (AIP, 1975)

Lipstick (Par, 1976)

Andy Warhol's Bad (New World, 1977)

The Choirboys (Univ, 1977)

A Different Story (Avco Emb, 1978)

The Cracker Factory (ABC-TV, 3/16/79)

Love's Savage Fury (ABC-TV, 5/20/79)

City in Fear (ABC-TV, 3/30/80)

Inmates: A Love Story (ABC-TV, 2/13/81)

Golden Gate (ABC-TV, 9/25/81)

The Clairvoyant [The Killing Hour] (Landsbury-Berun, 1981)

Search and Destroy [Striking Back] (Film Venture, 1981) [made in 1978]

Class of 1984 (United Film Distributors, 1982)

Helen Keller: The Miracle Continues (Synd-TV, 4/23/84)

Stranded (NBC-TV, 9/22/86)

Perfect People (ABC-TV, 2/29/88)

Shakedown on the Sunset Strip (CBS-TV, 4/22/88)

Disaster at Silo 7 (ABC-TV, 11/27/88)

The Man Who Lived at the Ritz (Synd-TV, 11/28/88–11/29/88)

Roxanne: The Prize Pulitzer (NBC-TV, 10/16/89)

Danielle Steel's Kaleidoscope (NBC-TV, 10/15/90)

Only One Survived (CBS-TV, 10/27/90)

Switch (WB, 1991)

Television Series

Captains and the Kings (NBC, 10/14/76; 10/28/76; 11/4/76; 11/18/76) [miniseries]

Aspen (NBC, 11/5/77–11/7/77) [miniseries]

The Last Convertible (NBC, 9/24/79–9/26/79) [miniseries]

The Quest (ABC, 1982)

Riptide (NBC, 1984–86)

I'll Take Manhattan (CBS, 3/1/87–3/4/87) [miniseries]

Broadway Plays

A Few Good Men (1990) (replacement)

KEVIN KLINE

"I think every American actor wants, ultimately, to be a movie star."
—*Hollywood Reporter*, March 2, 1988

"CHARISMATIC" IS AN ADJECTIVE THAT HAS BEEN FREELY APPLIED TO actors of every generation. However, of all the male Hollywood Baby Boomers, it may be most suitably used to describe Kevin Kline. This magnetic actor has a preference for artistry in acting, rather than stardom. His top-quality work is that of an intelligent professional rather than that of a pretty-faced, macho-identified personality. Like his peers he sought fame, but after obtaining it he bemoaned his loss of anonymity.

Kline's six-foot height, curly brown hair, and blue eyes solicit comparison with Robin Williams or Bill Murray. However, his strong, resonant, and direct voice suggests Laurence Olivier and John Barrymore. His relaxed, effortless style invites analogies with Douglas Fairbanks and Errol Flynn. *US* magazine decided not long ago, "When he looks up he resembles Errol Flynn—when he looks down, it's Geraldo Rivera," then advised, "Keep that chin up, sweetheart!" Kevin, too, has an idol—Alec Guinness. Wherever he goes, Kline is superstitious enough to tote with him a good luck poster of Guinness's movie THE HORSE'S MOUTH (1958).

Kevin Delaney Kline was born on Friday, October 24, 1947, in St. Louis, Missouri, preceded in birth by a sister, Kate. His mother, whose family name was Delaney, was a Roman Catholic of Irish ancestry while his father, the owner of the largest toy store in St. Louis as well as of a record outlet, was a nonreligious German Jew. While supplying his children with all the latest toys, the father was also an opera buff and an amateur pianist who filled the home with music, from both records and his own piano playing, mostly of classical music. Raised a Roman Catholic, Kevin spent his grammar and high school years at the St. Louis Priory School, where he was educated by Benedictine monks. He liked athletics as well as the movies and concerts to which his parents took him. He preferred playing football to reading novels. However, his sister introduced him to art films because of her feeling that he was intellectually deprived. Influenced by his father, he took piano lessons and learned to play well, but did not harbor any interest in becoming a performer. Instead, he thought he might want to become a classical composer.

Throughout his high school years, Kevin participated in soccer and football and developed a reputation as a young womanizer and as the rebellious wit of his class. Because his family had no interest in theater, he had not been exposed to the stage. However, in his senior year he participated in the school play, which he was to describe later as a "peak experience," the same feeling, he said, that he had gotten from music. He was a pianist with a rock 'n' roll band during his final year at Priory before graduating and going to Indiana University at Bloomington to study music. By the beginning of his junior year in college, however, he realized that he had started in music too late to become a serious composer. He switched his major to drama and helped to form a student acting troupe, called The Vest Pocket Players. They performed once a week in topical satirical revues at an on-campus coffeehouse. During this period, he admitted to being a "wretched—repressed—inhibited" actor. He recalls that his instructors frequently advised him to "Stop thinking so much, you're too intellectual, you intellectualize everything." Unlike his politically committed peers during the late 1960s, Kevin was too busy to get involved.

In the spring of 1970, after graduating from the university, he moved to New York City where his first stage job was as a spear-carrier in *Wars of the Roses* at the New York Shakespeare Festival. He then enrolled at John Houseman's newly formed drama department at Juilliard in Lincoln Center, where, along with being taught everything else about the stage, he learned "the three most important things an actor must know: how to pick the right scripts, how to wait on tables, and how not to go crazy in between jobs."

Under the disciplined leadership of the seventy-two-year-old John Houseman, Juilliard's rigorous drama course was a two-year program, ending for the first graduating class in the spring of 1972. The eighteen "seniors" in the departing group presented a rotating repertory of classic plays in the school's small auditorium before an invited audience of New York directors, producers, agents, and critics, who responded enthusiastically. With this encouragement, Houseman formed, with his core of actors, a repertory group called the Acting Company, which became the only permanent professional ensemble in the United States presenting a regular repertory of the classics. In order to operate and to pay the actors a guaranteed modest salary, Houseman obtained funding largely through federal and state grants, with additional donations from private individuals and corporations.

That first summer of 1972, and in successive summers, they performed at the Performing Arts Center at the famed tourist spa at Saratoga Springs, New York. Each fall, the company returned to Manhattan, where it made its off-Broadway debut at Good Shepherd Faith Church in the autumn of 1972. In the fall of 1973 the troupe had a three-week run at Broadway's Billy Rose Theatre. Working a total of forty-eight weeks a year, the company members had by November 1975 traveled 50,000 miles on tour to twenty-two states, performing in fifty cities. During these years, Kevin honed his acting skills in such plays as *The Beggar's Opera, The School for Scandal, The Lower Depths,* and *She Stoops to Conquer.* One of the original eighteen company members was Patti LuPone, with whom Kevin became involved romantically. In 1974 Kline took a summer leave from the company to do stock work with the Bucks County Playhouse in Pennsylvania, where he starred in *One Flew Over the Cuckoo's Nest* and *The Promise.* In early November 1975 the company took over the Harkness Theatre in Manhattan for a limited engagement during which Kevin sang the lead in the world premiere of *The Robber Bridegroom.* He was the dashing Mississippi highwayman who beguiles a willing victim (LuPone). In March 1976, on PBS-TV, members of the company appeared in William Saroyan's *The Time of Your Life* in a two-hour presentation hosted by Hal Holbrook. Kevin played the role of McCarthy.

When it came time for Kevin to move on professionally, he looked back on his four years with the Acting Company by reflecting: "The general premise is that if an actor can play the classics well, he can do anything. The classics tend to stretch your ability and constantly test you." In 1976 he acquired a supporting part in the longest-running CBS daytime TV soap opera, "Search for Tomorrow." His part of Woody Reed required him to work just once or twice a week, thus permitting him ample time also to do TV commercials, along with other acting jobs. On March 20, 1977, he was Petruchio in the CBS-TV "Festival of Lively Arts for Young People," which was a compilation of excerpts from the works of Shakespeare, taped at the American Shakespeare Theatre at Stratford, Connecticut. In July 1977 he was on stage at the Hudson Guild Theatre in Manhattan in *Dance on a Country Grave.*

Kline left the soap opera in mid-1977 to accept the part of a flamboyant gigolo in the musical *On the Twentieth Century* (1978), about a manic train ride from New York to Chicago. Disagreeing with his agent, who advised him not to take the small part, Kevin chose to work with director Harold Prince and the musical team of Cy Coleman, Betty Comden, and Adolph Green. He added acrobatics to his character's actions, to the delight of Prince's team, and his part was expanded to include a duet written especially for him and star John Cullum. For his efforts, Kevin was awarded a Tony on June 4, 1978, as Outstanding Actor in a Featured Role in a Musical; later, he won a Drama Desk Award.

In 1979 he was cast as Paul, the male lead, by director Alan Schneider in the serious comedy *Loose Ends,* which became Kevin's second Broadway hit. Walter Kerr (*New York Times*) wondered if Kevin could act without employing acrobatics, but concluded, "He can, in spades, clubs, diamonds and hearts." Schneider commented that Kevin "can do anything . . . can become the finest actor in the American theatre." When the New York Shakespeare Festival decided to present a revival of Gilbert & Sullivan's *The Pirates of Penzance* at the open-air Delacorte Theatre in Central Park in the summer of 1980, Raul Julia was initially sought as the Pirate King. He was not available, but recommended Kevin, who had understudied him at Lincoln Center in *The Threepenny Opera* (1976). Taking the pivotal part, Kevin played it as a hammy swashbuckler who was dashing but a bit clumsy. The production thrived so well in Central Park that it transferred to Broadway in the fall for the 1980–1981 season. On June 7, 1981, Kevin was given his second Tony Award, this time for Outstanding Performance by an Actor in a Musical. The female star of *Pirates* was Linda Ronstadt, who failed to win a Tony but did win Kevin's romantic attention for a while.

Screen director Alan J. Pakula had auditioned several men for the role of Nathan in his adaptation of William Styron's novel *Sophie's Choice.* He had met with Kevin in the winter of 1980 but thought him too rational and therefore wrong for the part. However, Pakula later saw *The Pirates of Penzance* and realized that Kevin was not all that calm or rational when in character. "I can't see anyone else doing this role but you," he informed

Kevin as he offered him the co-starring role with Meryl Streep. In SOPHIE'S CHOICE (1982), set in 1947, Kline portrayed Sophie's sometimes angry, sometimes exhilarated lover, a schizophrenic who is a true romantic. Roger Ebert (*Chicago Sun-Times*) found the lengthy movie "perfectly cast and well-imagined," remarks that helped make the film a critical if not financial success. Universal, the producing studio, campaigned for Academy Award nominations for both Kevin and Streep, but only she succeeded in getting one, along with an Oscar as Best Actress.

In February 1983 Universal brought THE PIRATES OF PENZANCE to the screen with its original Broadway cast, plus Angela Lansbury. This comic opera about an apprentice pirate (Kevin) who falls in love with the shy daughter (Linda Ronstadt) of a general was first presented on stage in 1879. A century later, audiences seeing it on film were still smiling and laughing at its fun. Kevin returned to the New York Shakespeare Festival in the summer of 1983 as the deformed, ruthless *Richard III* at the Delacorte Theatre in Central Park.

THE BIG CHILL (1983) provided a showcase for seven baby boom generation actors playing radical college chums of the 1960s reunited in 1983 for the funeral of a fellow student. Kevin was Harold Cooper, who has become a success in the shoe business, and whom he described as "Potentially, the most boring of the group," but "I chose [the part] deliberately to show that I could do other things than taking center stage." *Time* magazine suggested that all the "star actors deserve one big Oscar," but only one was nominated— Glenn Close, who failed to win in the Best Supporting Actress category.

Kevin was back in Central Park in the summer of 1984 as Shakespeare's *Henry V.* In May 1985 he was Captain Bluntschli, the anti-romantic mercenary, in a revival of George Bernard Shaw's *Arms and the Man* at New York's Circle in the Square under the direction of John Malkovich. With the exception of Kline's performance, the production was not liked.

In an era when the Hollywood western movie seemed to be dead, Lawrence and Mark Kasdan put together a script called SILVERADO (1985), about four men who team up to eradicate the town's bad guys. Done tongue-in-cheek fashion, the film had Kline top-billed as Paden, spending the first minutes of the story in long johns, but later becoming manager of the town's bar. The film surprisingly became one of the summer's box-office hits, grossing in excess of $32.2 million. One of Kevin's co-stars in the movie, Scott Glenn, said that Kevin "is such a perfectionist, but he has a very low opinion of himself. You have to beat him into admitting that he's a good actor." Kline had now starred in four features, most of which were shot on location. "I never had to pursue a film career," he admitted. "I was well employed and busy on the stage, and I would have been content just to do that.... I wasn't hungry for a career in the movies." Columnists linked him romantically, from time to time, with Mary Beth Hurt, Barbara Hershey, Phoebe Cates, and others, prompting his publicist to remark, "He'd be dead by now if he'd done half of it." Kevin hated the loss of anonymity and blasted columnists who "will print pure lies." He added, "I think it's important not to know that an actor's favorite food is fish and that he likes to go skin diving."

During the 1985–1986 off-Broadway season, he starred in *Hamlet* at the New York Shakespeare Festival's Public Theatre. Summing up his Shakespearean performance, Frank Rich (*New York Times*) wrote, "Each of these appearances has been distinguished by Mr. Kline's restless, pungent wit, not to mention his balletic grace of body and speech." In May 1986 Kevin was honored at the *Village Voice*'s thirty-first annual Obie Awards ceremony for "sustained excellence of performance" in his off-Broadway work.

VIOLETS ARE BLUE (1986) paired Kevin and Sissy Spacek as former high school sweethearts who think they can pick up the pieces after many years, although he is married (to Bonnie Bedelia) while Spacek is a very busy career woman. *Variety* dismissed the modest production with: "Superficial romance fails to blossom." In CRY FREEDOM (1987), Kline was Donald Woods, the real-life white South African journalist who wrote books about his hatred of apartheid and about the struggle and death by beating of black activist Stephen Biko (Denzel Washington). *Premiere* magazine found the movie, which was pompously directed by Richard Attenborough, to have "the lumpish gracelessness of a political pamphlet" and criticized Kevin for trying "a little too hard, but look at what he has to work with."

Film critics Gene Siskel and Roger Ebert agreed by saying, respectively, "It's very funny" and "It's just funny from beginning to end—it's just plain funny" in their appraisals of A FISH CALLED WANDA (1988). The co-producer, writer, co-star, and

Denzel Washington and **Kevin Kline** in CRY FREEDOM (1987).

uncredited co-director, John Cleese of Monty Python fame, put the project together because "I felt it was time I did something for fish." The fish of the title is the pet of stutterer Ken (Michael Palin) but the lady who masterminds a $20 million jewel heist is *also* named Wanda (Jamie Lee Curtis). Kevin is Otto, the lady Wanda's boyfriend, whom the others believe to be her brother. Otto is a dim-witted, off-the-wall American in England who hates the English. At the end of the wacky film, his character is run over by a steamroller. *The New Yorker* magazine observed of Kline, "it's nice to see him enjoying himself [for once] onscreen" and noted that the movie "would be a lot duller without him." The film's director was seventy-seven-year-old Charles Crichton, who had previously helmed the British comedy classic THE LAVENDER HILL MOB (1951), starring Kline's beloved Alec Guinness. For his well-etched performance in A FISH CALLED WANDA, Kevin won an Academy Award as Best Supporting Actor. A FISH CALLED WANDA grossed $29,766,000 in domestic film rentals.

Shot in New York and Toronto, THE JANUARY MAN was released appropriately in January 1989, but the *San Francisco Chronicle* insisted that it "Will be forgotten by February." The movie begins on a serious note, with Kevin as an ex-cop who is reinstated to the Gotham police force by the chief (Rod Steiger) to solve a series of murders. During the last twenty minutes—without warning—the action turns comedic, which is disconcerting to the viewer. *Newsweek* observed that the end result "looks like a jigsaw puzzle whose parts have been forced to fit—it's not a pretty picture." The magazine condemned director Pat O'Connor for encouraging Kevin "to proclaim his cuteness from the first frame: the actor all but licks the camera. Instead of seeming charming . . . [he] seems smug and self-regarding." THE JANUARY MAN was a box-office failure.

In July 1989 Kevin returned to the New York Shakespeare Festival to star in *Much Ado About Nothing*. Earlier in the year, he had embarked on a short honeymoon with his actress wife, Phoebe Cates, whom he had married in New York City on March 5, 1989. Kevin was forty-two; Phoebe was twenty-five. She is the daughter of film/TV/stage producer Joseph Cates.

Downtown Tacoma, Washington, was invaded by director Lawrence Kasdan and his crew for the exterior filming of I LOVE YOU TO DEATH (1990). A black comedy, it was based on the true story of a philandering pizzeria owner named Joey Boca whose murder is plotted by his wife (Tracey Ullman) and her Yugoslav mother (Joan Plowright) with bungling assistance from two super-stoned hippie types (William Hurt, Keanu Reeves). Pre-release advertisements explained: "With these people trying to kill him, Joey Boca may just live forever." The picture was called "the weirdest misfire of the year" by *Time* magazine, and *Variety* concluded that it "wastes considerable acting talent." *Entertainment Weekly* magazine gave credit to Kevin for underplaying his accented Italian-born character, thus making him "easygoing and likable," but *Rolling Stone* magazine maintained that he was "a caricature." The film was not successful at the box office.

In the spring of 1990, after long resisting a demand from the National Stuttering Project that he apologize for his behavior to a stutterer in A FISH CALLED WANDA because he felt they had missed the humor in his role, Kevin wrote the organization a letter of apology. In part, he stated: "The character I portrayed . . . should not be considered a role model for any civilized person when talking to a stutterer."

Kevin starred again in *Hamlet* and directed the New York Shakespeare Festival's 1990 version of the classic at the Public Theatre in New York City, which opened on May 8, 1990. Frank Rich (*New York Times*) praised his performance, saying it had "intelligence, sardonic humor, verbal and physical virility," but wrote that his direction "lacks the spark that might make it deeply moving." However, *Drama-Logue* considered the modern-dress production "Straight-forward, strongly cast, smoothly paced." In July 1990 it was announced that the play would be telecast on PBS as an offering in its "Great Performances" series in late 1990. The original cast members (Diane Venora, Brian Murray, Dana Ivey, Josef Sommer, and Kevin) taped their work at the studios of WNET-TV in New York City in August 1990. The production, co-directed by Kline and Kirk Browning for television, aired on November 2, 1990, with David Hiltbrand (*People* magazine) deciding, "The contemporary costuming . . . and stark, stagey sets, are off-putting but, oh, that glorious Bardic language." As for Kevin, Hiltbrand judged, "Though better in dialogue than in the famous soliloquies, Kline primes the play most passionately with his prince. Viewers who are familiar only with his film work will be pleasantly surprised at what a good classical actor Kline is." *Daily Variety* added, "If there were ever a suffering yet well-rounded Hamlet, Kline has found him."

The Cox News Service reported that "Camera crews and congressmen turned out in hordes" on July 12, 1990, on Capitol Hill in Washington, D.C., when Kevin, Kathleen Turner, Morgan Freeman, and theater producer Joseph Papp arrived to lobby Congress not to place (censorship) restrictions on National Endowment for the Arts grants to artists. Following a luncheon of the Arts Caucus, Turner said that members of Congress "seemed to be very supportive."

Kevin co-starred with Sally Field, Whoopi Goldberg, and Elisabeth Shue in SOAP-DISH (1991), a comedy about the soap opera lives of a soap opera cast. He also is the narrator for "Merlin and the Dragons," an animated special to be telecast over PBS, based on a story by Jane Yolen, with music by Michel Rubini.

Shifting back and forth from leading roles to character parts does not bother Kevin, since he claims not to pay much attention to the matter. "I suppose if I only allowed myself to play leading-man roles, I wouldn't have played 'Otto' in WANDA, which was a lot of fun to do, and is, I suppose, a character part. To me, they're all characters." As for his alternating stage and screen work, "I get different things from each of them. . . . I went to see John Malkovich do *Burn This* three times and every time it was like getting a great shot of vitamins." On another occasion, he assessed his choice of profession this way: "Acting was a release for me. I'm much more expressive of emotion now than I used to be. . . . I feel actors are very fortunate because they can get this stuff out. You get to explore those things in yourself. . . . I love sensation. . . . I'm just a cheap sensationalist, is what it comes down to."

Filmography

Sophie's Choice (Univ, 1982)
The Pirates of Penzance (Univ, 1983)
The Big Chill (Col, 1983)
Silverado (Col, 1985)
Violets Are Blue (Col, 1986)

Cry Freedom (Univ, 1987)
A Fish Called Wanda (MGM/UA, 1988)
The January Man (MGM, 1989)
I Love You to Death (Tri-Star, 1990)
Soapdish (Par, 1991)

TV Series

Search for Tomorrow (CBS, 1976–77)

Broadway Plays

On the Twentieth Century (1978)
Loose Ends (1979)

The Pirates of Penzance (1980) (revival)
Arms and the Man (1985) (revival)

Album Discography

Merlin and the Dragons (Lightyear 15106 [ST-TV]
On the Twentieth Century (Columbia 35330) [OC]

The Pirates of Penzance (Electra VE-601) [OC]

CHRISTINE LAHTI

"I consider myself a feminist, and I think that women often struggle with things that men don't have to struggle with. Men have other problems. I think almost every woman I play is kind of dismissed in some way, and that adds a little juice for me."
—*American Film* magazine, April 1986

LIKE BETTE DAVIS AND JOAN CRAWFORD, FELLOW ARIES OF A PRIOR generation, Christine Lahti is independent, adventurous, aggressive, and a workaholic. From the start of her career, which began with a TV commercial, she has been unstoppable. She moves easily between the stage, movies, and television, doing what she loves best—acting. Rather than accept a role in a commercial venture in which she does not fully believe, she elects to work in less commercial projects because of the material or the part. "I think the way my career has gone has been absolutely right," she has said. "It's been slow and steady. Because I'm not a big star, I've been able to take risks." She looks like Jane Alexander and has been compared with Sigourney Weaver, probably since both are just under 5' 11". Lahti moves in a determined, take-charge manner that is quickly forgotten when her face softens with that dimpled smile.

Christine Lahti was born in Detroit, Michigan, on Tuesday, April 4, 1950, to Paul Theodore Lahti, a prominent surgeon, and Elizabeth Tabar Lahti, a former nurse turned painter. Both parents were of Finnish ancestry. (Lahti means "bay of water" and is also the name of a town north of Helsinki.) Christine was the third of six children who were raised in affluent Birmingham, about twenty miles from Detroit. As the middle child, she vied for her parents' attention through dramatics, earning her the family nickname of "Sarah Bernhardt," as well as "the funny one." She knew that she wanted to be an actress after playing the part of the Virgin Mary in a grade-school Christmas play that made her the center of attention. At the age of thirteen, in the seventh grade, she stood heads above her peers at 5' 10", but rather than allow her height to depress her, she made light of it. As a result, her classmates called her "the jolly green giant." In high school, she says, she was an "approval junkie" who struggled to be popular. "I was in the cool group," she has remembered, "but really on the edge—I had to work for it. I got in by being funny, by being the entertainer because the other women were gorgeous—knockout, kill-yourself gorgeous—and I couldn't compete on that level."

In the autumn of 1968, she entered the University of Michigan at Ann Arbor, initially as a language major. After a few weeks, she switched to speech and drama. "I thought it would be really romantic to work as an interpreter at the UN," she once said, but "then I got involved in a lot of plays and decided I had to do that." She was the first in her family to become interested in acting "unless you count my grandmother," she said, "who had a Finnish language news radio program on the upper Michigan peninsula." Christine also studied modern dance and voice and worked as a singing waitress one summer. Another summer, she took off to London and Edinburgh, Scotland, with some classmates where they performed in little theaters in *The Tempest.* She graduated in 1972 with a Bachelor of Arts degree and then enrolled at Florida State University at Tallahassee for graduate work. In 1973 she left school and went to New York City, taking up residence in Greenwich Village. Even after years of doing college plays, she was not sure she was cut out to be an actor because of her unconventionality. She realized she did not conform to what was expected of a leading lady.

Christine took a job as a waitress. In her free time she studied acting and improvisation at the Neighborhood Playhouse and with Uta Hagen and William Esper. Still, she felt that she was not accepted as an actress. "I felt that as a professional woman I had a lot to prove, and that was part of the reason I didn't want to go the sex-object route. I was determined to be respected." She refused to wear makeup, would not shave her legs, and did not care about her clothes. Then she happened to see THE APPRENTICESHIP OF DUDDY KRAVITZ (1974), wherein relative newcomer Richard Dreyfuss overcame his ethnicity and physical shortcomings to do an impressive star turn on camera. "He used his uniqueness," she said. "He was a little guy, and he just celebrated it. I was really inspired by that." With that stimulation and despite what she has called her "defensive feminist" behavior, she managed to perform in various off-off-Broadway productions by night. During the day, she either waitressed or made the rounds of casting calls or agents' offices. Her dream was to play all the great women's parts written by George Bernard Shaw or Henrik Ibsen. However, she was told all too frequently that she was too tall or too strong or that she should change her hair or have a nose job. A lesser individual would have been defeated, but not highly optimistic Christine Lahti.

Although it was not within her usual realm of artistic interest, Christine was attracted by a backstage notice which read: "Actors, get work in commercials." "Since I realized that waitressing isn't all it's cracked up to be," she has said with tongue in cheek, she applied to a gentleman who took head shots of her. The next day he called to say she had gotten a job, if she passed his special "audition." She refused to participate in his casting-couch regimen. "Listen," the man advised her, "you'd better do *something.* You have no connections, you're not that pretty, and you're not that special." In tears, she replied, "You're wrong." Later, through a more ethical agency, she obtained a commercial for a rug shampoo, Spray 'n Vac, followed by eight others for products including Sominex and Joy dishwashing liquid, for which she was paid $225 per day of shooting, plus occasional residuals. These chores enabled her to quit the restaurant job and devote all her energies to off-off-Broadway, where she estimates she appeared in fifteen productions.

In 1977, after two years of that routine, she won the female lead in the two-character David Mamet play *The Woods.* It opened on April 25, 1977, at Joseph Papp's

Public Theatre with Chris Sarandon co-starred. Her performance won her a Theatre World Award in 1978 as best actress in a dramatic play. She was chosen by Harvey Korman to play his daughter Maggie (replacing actress Susan Lawrence, who had appeared in the 1977 pilot) in a thirty-minute ABC-TV sitcom, "The Harvey Korman Show," about an actor who operates an acting academy in his home. The series previewed on January 31, 1978, but by the summer was off the air, a victim of low ratings. In the meantime, Christine starred with Nick Mancuso in the ABC-TV movie/series pilot DR. SCORPION (February 24, 1978), a James Bond–like espionage entry shot on location in Hawaii. She was also third-billed in the ABC-TV dramatic movie THE LAST TENANT (June 25, 1978), about a family's quandary over what to do with their aged father (Lee Strasberg).

After seeing her in THE LAST TENANT, producer/director Norman Jewison chose her for the seventh-billed female lead in his almost all-male cast of . . . AND JUSTICE FOR ALL (1979). In this, her theatrical film debut, she was Gail Packer, a lawyer serving on a U.S. Ethics Committee who investigates and becomes romantically attracted to a sensitive Baltimore attorney (Al Pacino). While the movie was a sometimes funny, sometimes overly serious muddle, *Variety* acknowledged that "Christine Lahti is wonderful in her screen debut." Christine was next seen in her third television movie, CBS's THE HENDER-SON MONSTER (May 27, 1980), as the Ph.D. assistant to a Nobel Prize–winning scientist

Christine Lahti in ...AND JUSTICE FOR ALL (1979).

(Jason Miller) who hopes to create a Frankenstein-like creature. Meanwhile, on the stage, Lahti succeeded Roxanne Hart, opposite Kevin Kline, in *Loose Ends* at the Circle in the Square Theatre during the latter part of 1979. As Maggie the Cat, she was seen in New Haven, Connecticut, in the Long Wharf Theatre revival of *Cat on a Hot Tin Roof.* "I love to play these crazy, neurotic and vulnerable women," she told the *New York Post* in 1980. She was on Broadway at the Ambassador Theatre in *Division Street,* co-starred with John Lithgow and Keene Curtis. The play, which opened on October 8, 1980, lasted twenty-one performances. Later, she was part of *Scenes and Revelations* (June 25, 1981) at Circle in the Square. She also went to England to do a BBC television miniseries, "Wolcott," in which she played a private detective. "It wasn't good," she said later; "I did it for the money and the chance to go to London."

Then she had the opportunity to act with the man who had given her inspiration back in 1974. In WHOSE LIFE IS IT ANYWAY? (1981), starring Richard Dreyfuss, she was Dr. Clare Scott (played on Broadway by Jean Marsh) who sympathizes with bedridden Ken Harrison (Dreyfuss), who shouts ironically, "This hospital will kill no quadriplegic before his time!" Described by *People* magazine as the "statuesque doctor" who "cries a lot," Christine gave as well-shaded a performance as the material allowed. She also acted the supporting role of Aunt Linda, an alcoholic housewife, in LADIES AND GENTLEMEN, THE FABULOUS STAINS (1981), a major studio (Paramount) picture that received scant distribution. "Some of my best work was in that movie; I would say maybe five people saw it." She was in a second vehicle about a man who wished to die, THE EXECUTIONER'S SONG, an NBC-TV adaptation of Norman Mailer's Pulitzer Prize–winning book about convicted murderer Gary Gilmore (Tommy Lee Jones), shown in two parts in November 1982. Christine played Gilmore's affectionate cousin, Brenda, and James Wolcott (*New York* magazine) observed that Christine "does what she does best—digs her heels into the carpet and sexily, sturdily refuses to budge." The *New York Times* called her "sexy in a wholesomely down-to-earth way."

Christine starred opposite George C. Scott in 1983 on Broadway in a revival of the Noël Coward comedy *Present Laughter*. On September 4, 1983, she was married to television director Thomas Schlamme, whom she had met at a New York party given by a mutual friend. Tommy, as he was known, had directed HBO–Cable specials for Whoopi Goldberg and Bette Midler and would move later into motion pictures. She was back on the off-Broadway boards in a 1984 revival of John Guare's *Landscape of the Body*, in the lead role of a woman who is afraid of not being loved. John Simon (*New York* magazine) praised her as "sincere and true as usual." Movie audiences really took notice of her in SWING SHIFT (1984), produced by and starring Goldie Hawn. It was a wavering comedy-romance about World War II women riveters on a bomber assembly line and their lives and loves during a turbulent time. Critic Roger Ebert noted, "The best performance is Lahti as Hazel—tough, vulnerable, cynical, a real pal." Before its release, thirty minutes of the feature were reshot, eliminating some of Christine's key scenes in favor of playing up the role performed by Kurt Russell, Hawn's off-camera lover. After seeing the cuts, Christine had dinner with Hawn. "We were still friendly," she has said, "but I told her I thought she had hurt the movie a lot. She thought she was saving it and making it more commercial." The resultant movie received weak reviews, but everyone applauded Christine. She was awarded the Best Supporting Actress plaque by the New York Film Critics Circle and received Golden Globe and Academy Award nominations, but lost the Oscar to Peggy Ashcroft (A PASSAGE TO INDIA).

After her SWING SHIFT success, Christine received a spate of film offers, all for best-pal roles, none of which interested her. Instead, she chose to appear in the ABC-TV movie SINGLE BARS, SINGLE WOMEN (October 14, 1984) as a thirty-five-year-old teacher who is single and lonely. This entry was followed by yet another ABC-TV movie, LOVE LIVES ON (April 1, 1985), in which Christine played a mother (to Mary Stuart Masterson) who rehabilitates her drug-abusing teenaged daughter, then finds out that the teenager has cancer. John J. O'Connor (*New York Times*) reckoned Christine to be "indeed convincing and touching against the formidable odds."

"Amerika," at fourteen hours, was a long, and for the most part tedious and pretentious, ABC miniseries, shown on seven nights beginning February 15, 1987. The setting was the 1990s in Nebraska, ten years after a nonviolent Soviet takeover of the United States. Christine was Alethea Milford, sister to the story's hero (Kris Kristofferson), and Janet Maslin (*New Republic* magazine) reported that Christine "gives the only worthwhile performance here." She won an Emmy nomination for this assignment. Next, she was Sandy Dunlap, who has an affair with Mary Tyler Moore's husband (Ted Danson) in JUST BETWEEN FRIENDS (1986), an unliked (melo)drama. One of Sandy's lines is, "I was good at my career but not at my life." Christine applied this to herself, acknowledging that in real life she is a workhorse, always trying to prove herself. She declared to the *New York Times* that she felt empty without an acting assignment and as such "was just an unemployed actress." Now known to journalists as "the scene stealing sidekick" or "the second banana," she protested to Hollywood reporters, "They were both good parts. It never occurred to me to turn one down. I can't afford to think like that, to build a career on fears instead of challenges." In giving credit to both Goldie Hawn and Mary Tyler Moore, she added, "If I'm good, it's because the people I work with are good. They give me something to work off."

For the Second Stage, she played Patsy in an off-Broadway revival of Jules Feiffer's wacky *Little Murders* in 1987. She turned down the role of Alex Forrest, the obsessed woman in FATAL ATTRACTION (1987), because she found it too misogynistic. Glenn Close substituted in this screen megahit. Instead Christine chose to star as a Montana farm woman of 1954 in STACKING (1987), in which *Premiere* magazine judged her to be "splendid . . . a woman in her prime, aching with frustrated ambitions." This picture was followed quickly in release a month later by HOUSEKEEPING (1987), in which she starred as the eccentric Aunt Sylvie, a drifter suddenly put in charge of two teenagers. It was a role originally planned for Diane Keaton, who dropped out just before filming began. Graham Fuller in *The Film Yearbook* (1988) declared it "a travesty of justice" that Christine was not nominated for an Oscar for her spacy performance. However, John Powers (*Premiere* magazine) wrote, "Terribly miscast, this tough, sexy, worldly-wise actress spends the movie drifting around and trying to grin with luminous pixilation." By a few votes, Christine lost the best actress citation from the New York Film Critics Circle to Holly Hunter (of BROADCAST NEWS).

Lahti chose to co-star in RUNNING ON EMPTY (1988) because the premise, as well as her character, Annie Pope, intrigued her. She portrayed a promising music student-turned-1960s radical who bombs a napalm plant, accidentally blinding and paralyzing a janitor. For the next two decades, she and her husband (Judd Hirsch) and two sons (River Phoenix, Jonas Abry) elude the FBI by setting up new "base camps" and establishing new identities each time their relentless pursuers get close. "What I love most about Annie," she has said, "is that she really changes from the beginning to the end. I play a seemingly numbed-out person who is reborn and gets to become heroic in her own way." *Newsweek* magazine found Christine "particularly moving" in her portrayal. Her best scene is the one where she visits her Manhattanite father (Steven Hill) to ask him to take care of her older son (Phoenix) so that he may be free to attend the Juilliard School to study music. For her work, Lahti received the best actress award on January 24, 1989, from the Los Angeles Film Critics Association.

Off-Broadway and later in the 1961 film, Geraldine Page etched an unforgettable portrait as Alma, the shy, frustrated, but proud spinster in Tennessee Williams's *Summer and Smoke*. However, audiences at Los Angeles's Ahmanson Theatre from February 19 through April 10, 1988, saw an entirely fresh interpretation of Alma Winemuller by Christine in the Center Theatre Group's production, co-starring Christopher Reeve. Christine was gutsy rather than waifish, in control rather than shy. *Drama-Logue* found her to be "more the love priestess offering comfort and warmth to whatever traveling salesman comes along and while she's at it maybe having a good time herself out at the Moon Lake Casino. There's life in the old girl yet and while there's life there's hope." *Drama-Logue* added that as the love-starved Alma, Christine "gives a world class performance of luminosity, tenderness, truth, strength—and humor."

Christine was set to play the role of Elain in MISS FIRECRACKER (1989), directed by her husband, when she found that she was pregnant. "I slept with the director, but somehow it backfired," she joked with the press. Mary Steenburgen took over the part of the selfish, preening cousin to the film's self-effacing southern heroine (Holly Hunter), while Christine gave birth to son Wilson ("Willie") on July 5, 1988, in Jackson, Mississippi, where MISS FIRECRACKER was on location. (Lahti would make a cameo appearance in the offbeat comedy-drama as a neighbor holding up a newborn baby—her own.)

On the lookout for a good commercial comedy in which she would feel at ease, she informed *Premiere* magazine that "even though I'm actively looking [for a comedy] if a serious, challenging character part came along, chances are I would take it. . . . So career move, career schmoove—it's very secondary, ultimately. I think it should be more primary, but I keep taking this path that is mine." Former co-star Al Pacino extolls her with: "The fact is, she's working; the fact is, she does get parts. And the excellence, that's real."

She found a comedy, albeit only "moderately amusing" according to the *San Francisco Examiner*, in GROSS ANATOMY (1989). She was a medical school professor who teaches a student (Matthew Modine) that medicine is not just about making money. Both Lahti and Modine, the *Examiner* judged, "give the kind of performances that belong in a sharper, more worldly movie." The feature grossed a modest $4.7 million in domestic film rentals. She was back on Broadway at the Plymouth Theatre when she took over the lead role in *The Heidi Chronicles* in September 1989. She played different ages in the life of a midwestern woman who undergoes many changes from high school days to becoming a determined feminist. Later, she softens in midlife after adopting a daughter and embarking on a new romance. Michael Sander (*Drama-Logue*) praised Christine as a "positive Heidi who adds force to the play and the relationships it depicts" by her "assertiveness as an actress, coupled with her apparent intelligence."

In celebrating its fiftieth anniversary in New York City at the Marriott Marquis Hotel on November 2, 1989, the 256-member Motion Picture Bookers Club presented the Female Star of the Year award to Christine. In 1985 the Club had voted Lahti the Female Star of Tomorrow.

Christine completed the year by co-starring with Jeff Daniels in the CBS-TV movie NO PLACE LIKE HOME (December 3, 1989), directed by actress Lee Grant. *Time* magazine raved, "A moving and eloquent film . . . about a working-class family that descends into homelessness, not only puts human flesh on an abstract problem but also transforms it into something approaching tragedy." *Time* said of the actress, "Lahti, possibly the best actress in America working in TV . . . is truly heartbreaking. She can convey both the despair lurking behind a brave comment to her husband and a pathetic joy at ever smaller victories." Director Grant observed of Christine, "she does have that whole middle-American ethos. . . . There's a comfort level about Christine. There's an ability to identify with her. She can be beautiful and still live on your block." Lahti was nominated for an Emmy Award as Lead Actress in a Miniseries or Special, but lost to Barbara Hershey ("A Killing in a Small Town").

Leaving her star spot in *The Heidi Chronicles* in January 1990 to fulfill a motion picture assignment with Gene Wilder, Christine was replaced on stage by Brooke Adams. Meanwhile, in Los Angeles on September 7, 1990, Lahti joined many other actors and musicians at the AIDS Project Los Angeles's fundraiser, *Commitment to Life IV*, held at the Wiltern Theatre.

Originally titled NEW YORK TIMES, FUNNY ABOUT LOVE was in release September 21, 1990, co-starring Christine with Gene Wilder and Mary Stuart Masterson in a comedy directed by Leonard Nimoy about a New York cartoonist (Wilder) torn between several lovers (including Masterson) after separating from his wife (Christine), a caterer. *People* magazine, which found the film derivative, acknowledged that Christine was "intelligent seeming and attractive." *Variety* termed the comedy a "Sappy combination of smiles and sentimentality" and acknowledged, "Both Lahti and Masterson remain most appealing actresses in search of challenging roles, not provided here." Peter Rainer (*Los Angeles Times*) found the movie lacking, but agreed that "Lahti is one of these amazing actresses who is doubly amazing for bringing out the best in her co-stars. She is a virtuoso team player." In its first two weeks of domestic distribution, FUNNY ABOUT LOVE grossed a tame $6,784,905 at the box office.

Since making FUNNY ABOUT LOVE, Christine has starred in Eugene O'Neill's *A Moon for the Misbegotten* in Williamstown, Massachusetts. Thereafter, at Vassar College she appeared in a workshop production of Beth Henley's new play, *Signature*, a comedy set in Hollywood in the year 2050. In the TNT–Cable film CRAZY FROM THE HEART (1991), she co-stars with Ruben Blades. In THE DOCTOR (1991), she is the passive, patient spouse of a surgeon (William Hurt) undergoing a life-changing experience.

Now based in a six-room New York City apartment (and an upstate New York farm) with her husband and son, Lahti says, "I got married—though there was a time I wasn't sure I ever would. I entertained the idea of buying a brownstone with a bunch of women and maybe raising children with them. It didn't work out that way. Thank God." She admits that having a husband and a child has opened up a whole new vista for her, making her less compulsive about her acting career. While not politically active ("because I work so much"), Lahti cares "deeply about equality for all people. I think being a feminist is being a humanist." An interviewer once pointed out that Christine's habit of beginning or ending statements with the words "to be honest" indicates deep-rooted honesty. That writer was undoubtedly correct, as was *Newsweek* magazine when it rated her a "super actress—who . . . can look forward to a future as an American Vanessa Redgrave." Christine has admitted, "I'm trying to carve out this niche. I want to play different parts— Lady Macbeth, Hedda Gabler, screwball comedies. I want to be a leading lady but also a character actress. All those labels make me crazy. Because *ultimately* we're all actresses."

Filmography

Dr. Scorpion (ABC-TV, 2/24/78)
The Last Tenant (ABC-TV, 6/25/78)
. . . And Justice for All (Col, 1979)
The Henderson Monster (CBS-TV, 5/27/80)
Whose Life Is It Anyway? (MGM, 1981)
Ladies and Gentlemen, The Fabulous Stains
   (Par, 1981)
The Executioner's Song (NBC-TV, 11/28/82–
   11/29/82)
Single Bars, Single Women (ABC-TV,
   10/14/84)

Swing Shift (WB, 1984)
Love Lives On (ABC-TV, 4/1/85)
Just Between Friends (Orion, 1986)
Stacking (Spectrafilm, 1987)
Housekeeping (Col, 1987)
Running on Empty (WB, 1988)
No Place Like Home (CBS-TV, 12/3/89)
Miss Firecracker (Corsair Pictures, 1989)
Gross Anatomy (BV, 1989)
Funny About Love (Par, 1990)
The Doctor (BV, 1991)
Crazy from the Heart (TNT–Cable, 1991)

TV Series

The Harvey Korman Show (ABC, 1978)

Amerika (ABC, 2/15/87–2/21/87) [miniseries]

Broadway Plays

Loose Ends (1979) (replacement)
Division Street (1980)
Scenes and Revelations (1981)

Present Laughter (1983) (revival)
The Heidi Chronicles (1989) (replacement)

JESSICA LANGE

"I really want to do different things in the next 10 years. I figure I've got maybe another good five years in film and then . . . the parts are gonna all go to those other girls—those younger ones."
—*American Film* magazine, August 1990

A SENSITIVITY TO THE SUPERNATURAL EXISTS WITHIN JESSICA LANGE. She is drawn to peaceful cemeteries for no reason other than their beauty, but will later find that a message was gained from such a visit. During the filming of FRANCES, she felt a presence that gave impetus for a certain action or helped her develop a perplexing screen scene. Lange is quiet, almost shy with strangers. She guards her privacy and that of her family with tenacity. She is *not* a southern California type of star. She prefers to live far from the Hollywood social scene, refusing even to name the region of the state where she resides.

Early in her career, Jessica was likened to Carole Lombard. However, she soon began to be compared to Jill Clayburgh and then to Meryl Streep. She and Streep have vied with each other for several screen roles, with Streep generally getting the parts, leaving Jessica neither jealous nor resentful. She is too classy for such behavior. Striving for perfection, and expecting it from others, she has been known to be very difficult on the set.

Jessica Lange was born on Wednesday, April 20, 1949, in the iron-ore area of Minnesota. Her father and mother, Albert and Dorothy, of Finnish and German-Dutch ancestry, moved eighteen times after their third daughter's birth. However, Jessica spent her later growing-up years in Cloquet, Minnesota, near Duluth. Albert Lange, who aspired to become a lawyer, drifted in and out of such occupations as salesman, miner, and railroad worker, until he settled on the latter with the Burlington Northern Railroad, for which he worked until his retirement. A son was born to the Langes after Jessica's birth. She grew up with the nickname "Jessie" in the cruel climate of northeastern Minnesota. From an early age, she dreamed of escaping. Mentally, she escaped through a love of art and by reading and rereading *Gone with the Wind.* She recalls, "It's not that . . . [my childhood] was horrendous—it was my way of removing myself."

She was an A student at Cloquet High School, a member of the National Honor Society, and chairperson of the decoration committee for Kiwanis Club school dances. She was to have played the lead in the senior class play, *Rebel Without a Cause,* but the production was cancelled when a student was found stabbed to death in the band room. The school's yearbook for May 1967, when she graduated, noted beneath her photograph:

"Artistic, dramatic, and fun is she; a new girl Cloquet was glad to see." Attending the University of Minnesota at Minneapolis on an art scholarship, she studied fine art there for two quarters until a handsome twenty-four-year-old Spaniard, Paco Grande, spoke to her class as a guest professor. "Swept off my feet" by him, she fell in love and abandoned her studies in order to accompany him on a tour of the United States in an old truck in search of Bohemian life. In May 1968 they were in Paris where they eagerly witnessed the demonstrations of radical students. Returning to the United States, they took up residence in an illegal loft in New York's Bowery where Jessica's specialty was painting formica boxes. The couple was married on July 29, 1970, at her parents' home, which was then at Lake Nebagamon, Wisconsin.

During this period, a filmmaker friend of Paco's, Danny Seymour, shot a short movie called HOME IS WHERE THE HEART IS, directed by Robert Frank and featuring Jessica. Jan Sarkisian, a colleague of hers in New York and Paris, would recall later, "you knew right away that she was special."

Hating what she called "Nixonian America," she returned to Paris in 1971, alone, with $300 in her purse. For the next two years she lived as a Bohemian in a garret five flights up with no heat or hot water. She studied mime under the tutelage of Etienne DeCroux, Marcel Marceau's teacher. She also danced with the Opéra Comique.

In late 1973 she returned to New York City to "the bleakest time of my life." She took a one-room place on Perry Street, earning rent money by waitressing at the Lion's Head pub. After her experiences in Paris, she had decided to turn to the stage, with a career in dancing. She joined the small, experimental dance company run by Ellie Klein. Through a fashion illustrator acquaintance, Jessica, who had lightened her hair, obtained modeling assignments from agents Zoli and Wilhelmina Cooper, solely for the salary.

Around this time, Italian film producer Dino De Laurentiis had launched a worldwide search for an unknown actress to appear in the remake of KING KONG in the role played in the 1933 version by Fay Wray. A friend in the talent department at the Wilhelmina Cooper agency sent Jessica's photograph to De Laurentiis, who contacted her for a screen test in Hollywood. A chauffeured limousine collected her at Perry Street as her friends waved goodbye. She was flown first class to Los Angeles—another first for her— and ensconced at the Beverly Wilshire Hotel. "The only reason I agreed to do the test in the first place," she has said, "was that my sister was sailing down the coast and had docked in San Diego. I wanted to see her, and I figured it was a free trip. The idea of actually doing KING KONG was totally abstract to me." It was Christmas time 1975. Trees around the hotel were ablaze with pink and blue lights, it was warm, there was sunshine by day, balmy breezes by night. It was fantasy land to the young woman who had escaped Minnesota, as well as the dreariness of her New York tenement.

KING KONG (1976), which ultimately cost more than $25 million, was a disappointing, almost laughable production that critic Judith Crist called "an overblown remake." In the months before the film's release, as part of the hoopla for the movie, huge posters of nearly nude Jessica in the giant ape's hand appeared all over America, even in department stores. "As for the work itself," she has said, "I had nothing to do. I was alone in this huge mechanical hand for months. I either had no dialogue or worked with the other actors only occasionally. It was quite awful." *After Dark* magazine's reaction was that Jessica's "naive charm makes her second only to Kong in appeal." Comments like that irked Jessica, who felt like a commodity rather than a person. De Laurentiis, who had signed her to a seven-year contract, generated publicity for his new star by claiming that she had been a high-paid, top magazine cover model who had made it big in movies. "That was bull," she said, "there were no covers. . . . I hated it, being lumped into that category of model-turned-actress." She unhappily fulfilled her agreement to help promote the film with personal appearances. She returned to New York in December 1976 with nothing to do. She tried for the part of Julia Tate in GOIN' SOUTH (1978) opposite Jack Nicholson, but lost out to Mary Steenburgen. Nicholson wrote her a letter stating that he was sure they would work together one day.

In 1977, compelled to overcome the stigma of being known as Kong's girl, she devoted her time to acting lessons while receiving a salary from De Laurentiis. At a party, she met Russian ballet star Mikhail Baryshnikov. This was the start of a love affair that would endure, on and off, for more than five years and which would produce a daughter, Alexandra (nicknamed Shura), born in 1981. In the early days of their romance, in his company, she would be identified mistakenly as his secretary.

Another womanizer, dancer/choreographer/director Bob Fosse, became infatuated with Jessica, even to the point of falling in love with her. He called her "the sexiest, funniest, cutest thing" that he had seen in a long while. He cast her as Angelique, the angel of death, in ALL THAT JAZZ (1979), an avant-garde autobiographical musical study of his professional and private life. Roy Scheider starred, while Fosse directed the venture. She considers the picture a "brilliant piece of work," although she was not a part of the total experience, having been cast late in the filming, by which time her contract with De Laurentiis had been terminated by mutual agreement. Her third feature was HOW TO BEAT THE HIGH COST OF LIVING (1980), about three housewives (Susan St. James, Jane Curtin, and Lange) who decide to commit a robbery at their local shopping center. It was a flat heist comedy, but Jessica received good notices. "Of the actresses, Lange comes off best, in no small measure because her character has it more together" (*Variety*). Following this box-office failure, Jessica chose to do summer stock in North Carolina. In her debut stage role she was Donna Peterson in *Angel on My Shoulder*, a romantic comedy by Stephen Levi.

For nearly a decade, Jack Nicholson wanted to star in a remake of THE POSTMAN ALWAYS RINGS TWICE (1981) in the role made famous by John Garfield in the 1946 original. Finally, in 1980, he convinced his friend Bob Rafelson to direct a new rendition. Jill Clayburgh, Meryl Streep, and Jessica were considered for the role of Cora, the erotic murderess of the older husband (John Colicos), played by a platinum-coiffed Lana Turner in the 1940s. Nicholson made his written prophecy come true with the selection of Jessica. This production differs from its predecessor in that the industry codes of 1981 were far more permissive than those of the 1940s. In this film, the sex scenes are far more explicit; at one point, on a kitchen counter covered with flour, the couple engage in a spontaneous act of intercourse while Lange's character, Cora, wantonly urges, "All right—come on, huh? Come on . . . come on." (The act was fully captured by the camera in one take, but no genitalia were revealed.) Ralph Novak and Peter Travers (*People Magazine's Guide to Movies on Video*, 1987) acclaimed Jessica: "whatever is worth stealing in this picture is purloined by Lange in the performance that finally made audiences forget she was the insipid blonde pursued by King Kong the Younger. . . . Bravos for Lange; boos for the picture." Nicholson went on record with another prediction: "Jessie's got the Eighties wrapped up already if she wants to."

Jessica next turned down the role of Suzy the prostitute as being too young for her in CANNERY ROW (1982). The part went to Raquel Welch, aged forty-two, who eventually was fired during production and replaced by Debra Winger, aged twenty-seven (six years younger than Jessica). Lange wanted SOPHIE'S CHOICE (1982), but lost out to Meryl Streep.

Since the 1970s, Jessica had been intrigued by the life story of actress Frances Farmer. She had read her autobiography, *Will There Really Be a Morning?* (1972), and had seen scenes from the book acted out during her years of acting study in New York. She mentioned her great interest in a film of Farmer's life to several directors. No one was interested until she talked to Graeme Clifford, the editor of POSTMAN, then in search of his first directorial chore. Clifford took the concept to Universal, which purchased it. When the project was announced, Goldie Hawn, Jane Fonda, and Diane Keaton all vied for the lead part. Another actress who wanted the role was Tuesday Weld, a close friend of Jessica's who also resembles her, but Clifford held true to Jessica. Before filming began on FRANCES, Jessica began divorce proceedings to dissolve her marriage to Paco Grande, with whom she had not lived for almost a decade. He countersued for $3,000 a month in alimony to supplement the Social Security disability income he received because of his failing eyesight as a result of retinitis pigmentosa. The divorce became final in January 1983 with a New York judge ordering her to pay him $300 per month. By then, she was in love with the Pulitzer Prize–winning playwright/actor Sam Shepard.

As FRANCES, Jessica says, "I see Hollywood as a stepping stone," but she behaves in so anti-social a manner that her domineering mother (Kim Stanley) considers her indeed crazy for not wanting a career in Hollywood and has her committed to an asylum in Washington state. The film is narrated by a fictional journalist/lover (Sam Shepard), a part reportedly written just for him. Jessica was the ideal choice for the role since she does look like the star of the 1930s and 1940s. *GQ* magazine found Jessica's performance to be "miraculous" and "a brilliant, intricately polished piece of work full of irony, pain and energy." Publicly, Jessica stated that she was certain of a spiritual presence on the set and, like Frances Farmer, had moments when she was difficult to work with. Her wise co-star, Kim Stanley, advised that she do a comedy as soon as possible in order to get over the problems of Frances Farmer.

Jessica took Stanley's suggestion by going to work immediately in TOOTSIE (1982). (Coincidentally, in FRANCES, the head of the studio, played by Allan Rich, had tweaked her cheek and called her "Tootsie.") This TOOTSIE is a New York actor named Michael

Dorsey (Dustin Hoffman) who cannot make it in show business until he dresses as a woman and changes his name to Dorothy Michaels. While working on a TV soap opera, he/she meets Julie (Jessica), who plays a nurse on the hospital show, and falls in love with her, after which she teaches him a few lessons in humility. In TOOTSIE's first three months of domestic distribution, it grossed over $126 million at the box office. For the year 1982, it was the second largest grosser, with $177.2 million. The *Village Voice*'s Andrew Sarris wrote that Jessica "lit up the screen with . . . beauty and intelligence."

For the third time in Academy Award history, an actress was nominated in both the Best Actress and Best Supporting Actress categories. As Best Supporting Actress for TOOTSIE, Jessica won the Golden Globe Award, the New York Film Critics Award, the award of the National Society of Film Critics, and, finally, the Oscar. Her parents, who seldom left Minnesota, were present at the Oscar presentations to see Jessica accept the statue with the statement that she was "very flattered to have had Dustin Hoffman as my leading lady." The Best Actress award that year went to Meryl Streep (SOPHIE'S CHOICE).

Having left his wife (O-Lan Johnson Dark) of several years, Shepard moved in with Jessica, bringing with him his fifteen horses. They chose to live near Taos, New Mexico, while also securing a lakeside "cabin" on 120 acres of land in Minnesota near her parents. Residing part time in Minnesota was now different for Jessica; she could leave whenever she chose, but it would always be by some type of ground conveyance since Shepard had a

Dustin Hoffman and **Jessica Lange** in TOOTSIE (1982).

fear of flying. In January 1984 she gave birth to her first child by Shepard, who was named Hannah, to be followed in February 1986 by a son, Samuel. Also in 1986 they moved from New Mexico to Virginia, to a farm near Charlottesville, because she had seen a photograph of the locale in a New York newspaper and reasoned that it looked like a nice area in which to live. When asked about the possibility of marriage to Shepard, she quipped, "The legality of it means absolutely nothing to me." She admitted that her parents did not really understand, but felt that her happiness came first. In May 1986 Jessica shared the cover of *Life* magazine with Sally Field, Jane Fonda, Goldie Hawn, and Barbra Streisand in its tribute to the movies as the five most powerful women in Hollywood at that time.

When Elizabeth Ashley was forced to drop out of the cable TV version of "Cat on a Hot Tin Roof," Jessica was asked to replace her in the lead role of the smoldering Maggie (which was performed in the 1959 film by Elizabeth Taylor and in a 1976 telecast by Natalie Wood). In the August 19, 1984, Showtime–Cable production, Tommy Lee Jones was Brick, the problem-ridden southern husband, coping badly with a tyrannical father (Rip Torn) dying of cancer, his sexually frustrated and perplexed wife (Lange), and his own confused sexuality. *People* magazine wrote that "Lange gets carried away with her southern accent, but nonetheless plays Maggie with sympathy and terrible sadness." As she had done with FRANCES, Jessica immersed herself totally in the role, to the point of exhaustion. She confided to *TV Guide* magazine, "Most of the time acting for me has been so painful; I've dreaded it." Aside from dialogue, she and Tommy Lee Jones had little to say to each other, and when he was asked later if he had had any sort of rapport with her, he replied, "I hope so. I like her very much, she's a wonderful actress, just loved working with her. I hope the answer to that question is yes." In 1984 she commanded a salary of $2 million for COUNTRY, an American farm story, which she also co-produced. As a tortured couple facing the possibility of losing their homestead, Jessica and Shepard co-starred; he received a salary of $1 million. *Playgirl* magazine thought the film "plays out its desolate drama under a cloud of collective impotence." Two other feature films about suffering farm people were released that year, with all the female leads nominated for an Academy Award: Sally Field for PLACES IN THE HEART, Sissy Spacek for THE RIVER, and Jessica for COUNTRY. Field received her second Oscar for her efforts.

While driving from New Mexico to Virginia in 1984, Jessica and Shepard stopped overnight in Winchester, Virginia. To relax, she went for a walk and wound up in the town's cemetery. "I felt this incredible kind of pull," she admitted. "I don't know why, but I do have a fascination with cemeteries." A few weeks later, she received the script of a film to be made about the life of country western singer Patsy Cline, called SWEET DREAMS (1985). It was then that she recalled that Cline was buried in that Winchester cemetery. *Playgirl* magazine called her performance as Patsy Cline "breathtaking," as well as "gaudy, gorgeous and raunchy." The review was capped with "she rips into the role like a prizefighter and never looks back, giving the most exuberant performance of her versatile career." Jessica, who lipsynched to Cline's recordings, was again Oscar-nominated, but lost to Geraldine Page (THE TRIP TO BOUNTIFUL).

Her next feature was CRIMES OF THE HEART (1986), made for her former contract mogul, Dino De Laurentiis. As one of the three quirky Magrath sisters (with Diane Keaton and Sissy Spacek) of Mississippi, she returns home after a failed Hollywood try as a singer. *People* magazine labeled the film a "mess" despite strong performances by the stars (all of whom were too mature for their roles). The prolific Shepard, who had had a supporting role in CRIMES OF THE HEART, had written a script for a TV movie, but it was changed to a theatrical release due to Jessica's reluctance to work again in that medium. Filmed near her hometown of Cloquet, Minnesota, FAR NORTH (1988) was also directed by Shepard. Critics lambasted the story of a kooky family, the head of which (Charles Durning) is near death as the result of a fall from his horse. As one of his daughters, Jessica wants the animal killed, while other family members do not. Richard Corliss (*Time* magazine) said, "The film should have been put out of its misery." In the same review, which included remarks about EVERYBODY'S ALL-AMERICAN (1988), Corliss found that Jessica "comes close to embodying everything a modern woman hopes to see in the mirror of her hard-earned self esteem." In EVERYBODY'S ALL-AMERICAN she is again a southerner, this time aging twenty-five years from the film's opening sequences, in which she appears as a high school beauty, to its conclusion, in which she has matured into the businesswoman wife of her ex–football hero husband (Dennis Quaid), who has reluctantly finally come of age. Gene Shalit of NBC-TV's "Today" show reported, "And not for nothing is Jessica Lange a leading actress." Jack Garnet of Gannett Newspapers thought that both Quaid and Lange "are wonderful in this rousing, sweeping saga." But despite the actors' performances, the overlong picture was not liked and it was a box-office failure.

In the Chicago-filmed MUSIC BOX, directed by Costa-Gavras, released in December 1989, she was dark-haired attorney Ann Talbot, who defends her own father (Armin Mueller-Stahl) in extradition proceedings when he is accused of having committed war crimes in Hungary during World War II. Jessica admitted that her character was "the furthest I've ever played from myself." *The New Yorker* magazine praised her for having "the will and the technique to take a role that's really no more than a function of melodrama and turn the movie into a cello concerto." Again nominated for an Academy Award as Best Actress, she lost to Jessica Tandy (DRIVING MISS DAISY). MUSIC BOX was too uncompromisingly somber a study to be a commercial success.

A few weeks later, starting February 2, 1990, Lange portrayed a suddenly widowed woman with two sons (Chris O'Donnell, Charlie Korsmo) in MEN DON'T LEAVE. She is forced to sell their suburban home and resettle in larger Baltimore to earn a living without skills. "It is Lange, more than anyone or anything," observed the *Hollywood Reporter*, "who keeps this rosey-hued vehicle on a solid human track." Once again she received favorable reviews, but in seven weeks the film took in only a meager $5,999,115 in domestic box-office receipts.

On the TNT–Cable network (October 22, 1990), Jessica narrated the second in a series of specials honoring leading ladies of Hollywood's golden age; her installment was entitled "Vivien Leigh: Scarlett and Beyond." *Entertainment Weekly* magazine rated the documentary a "sappy salute" because of "an annoying movie-star-magazine tone to the narration." By contrast, *People* magazine praised this outing as an "involving portrayal" filled with "touching, well-edited remembrances" and noted, "The narration is beautifully done by the beguiling Jessica Lange."

In 1990, joined by Nick Nolte and Robert De Niro, she began production under Martin Scorsese's direction of CAPE FEAR (1991), a remake of the well-regarded 1962 revenge thriller which starred Gregory Peck, Polly Bergen and Robert Mitchum. Coming up for Jessica is BLUE SKY, the first movie in a multi-picture pact between her Prairie Films (in partnership with Lynn Arost) and Orion. In this film, now scheduled for release in 1992, she is reunited with Tommy Lee Jones in the tale of a wife on a southern Army base in the 1950s who takes a lover (Powers Boothe). Location lensing took place in Florida and Alabama, close to home. Another upcoming Prairie/Orion production is THE EX-MR. WINFIELD, "a romantic comedy caper" starring Jessica as a writer brought together with her ex-husband. Jessica admits she would "*love* to play Madame Bovary. I would love to be able to track that kind of obsession, to play the passion in the obsession and the repercussions of it. I always thought that would be a great character. Or Anna Karenina. Any of those really romantic characters."

Jessica has been described as a "fine-boned" beauty, but she is unable to see far without her glasses. She has been affectionately nicknamed "Blinky" by Jack Nicholson, who claims that her poor eyesight is the reason for her lack of narcissism. She agrees with Shepard's comment about Hollywood: "All you have to do is to go to L.A. for a week to see the insanity it promotes." Despite her nonstop acting and film producing activities, she admits that she likes the role of motherhood best of all. She has written a screenplay, based on a novel about family life, and relaxes at home by painting, her foremost artistic pursuit.

Filmography

Home Is Where the Heart Is (Unk, ca. 1970) (short subject)
King Kong (Par, 1976)
All That Jazz (Col/20th–Fox, 1979)
How to Beat the High Cost of Living (Avco Emb, 1980)
The Postman Always Rings Twice (Par, 1981)
Tootsie (Col, 1982)
Frances (Univ, 1982)
Country (BV, 1984) (also co-producer)
Sweet Dreams (Tri-Star, 1985)

Crimes of the Heart [Colours of the Heart] (De Laurentiis Entertainment Group, 1986)
Far North (Alive, 1988)
Everybody's All-American (WB, 1988)
Music Box (Tri-Star, 1989)
Men Don't Leave (WB, 1990)
Cape Fear (Univ, 1991)

Future Releases

Blue Sky (Orion, 1992)
The Ex-Mr. Winfield (Orion, 1992)

SHELLEY LONG

"When I was four years old, when somebody asked me what I wanted
to be when I grew up, I didn't hesitate a beat and said, 'A clown!'
I don't know how I knew that. I don't even know that I had ever
been around a clown. I don't even know if I was aware I could make
people laugh." —*Continental Choice* magazine, May 1988

IF A PAIR OF WORN, AUTOGRAPHED SNEAKERS AUCTIONED BY *IN FASH-
ion* magazine is any gauge of popularity, Shelley Long at $150 ranks above Jane Fonda
($100) and Sean Penn ($50), but far below Madonna ($4,500). Long made her presence
known for five prime-time TV seasons as the verbally agile Diane Chambers of "Cheers."
Not always recognized by the public is that behind her slightly carnival doll–leprechaun
face is a shrewd, calculating mind; she even planned her pregnancy to occur conveniently
during series hiatus.

Like Lucille Ball, with whom she likes to be compared, Shelley Long is a perfection-
ist who cares about her work: "Anything I do I want to be absolutely the best." Presented
as a typical girl next door, with intelligent sophistication, she replaced Mary Tyler Moore
as America's new TV sweetheart in the 1980s. However, as also happened to Moore, her
career took a deep dip after she chose to leave an immensely popular sitcom. Said to talk to
supermarket vegetables and stuffed animals, she takes her own tape recorder to interviews
in order to analyze later exactly what she has said. Precise and filled with gusto, the
porcelain-skinned actress continually seeks to find a high-level niche in show business.

The only child of Presbyterian parents, both of whom were teachers, Shelley Long
was born on Tuesday, August 23, 1949, in Fort Wayne, Indiana, situated in "tornado
country." She grew up "a happy kid" in "a wonderful community." She was both a
Brownie (which she liked because of her brown uniform) and a Girl Scout (which she did
not like, because of the green outfit). She took part early in school plays and at home
entertained her parents with theatricals. As she approached high school graduation, they
hoped that she would study to become a teacher. However, an event in her senior year at
age seventeen changed that career direction. After she won the national title in Girls'
Extemporaneous Speaking (on the topic of sex education), a teacher encouraged her to
enroll in Northwestern University's summer program of drama and speech. That September (1967), she was accepted by Northwestern, located in Evanston, Illinois, as an
undergraduate in the drama department. Her campus roommate was Ann Ryerson, whose
life would run parallel with Shelley's for a few years.

She spent the summer of 1968 doing stock theater in the Chicago area. Back at Northwestern in the fall, boredom set in at the prospect of another year in the university's lecture halls with no acting. She lasted until the next spring when Ryerson, who had left school earlier to take up modeling, got her a job as a model. At 5' 7", Shelley was the ideal height. This job led quickly, again with Ryerson's help, to TV commercials, through which Shelley became Homemaker Furniture's TV and radio spokesperson. At the same time, she wrote scripts for, and appeared in, industrial and educational films. Also during these years she acted in plays at the Candlelight Dinner Theatre and the Ivanhoe Theatre in Chicago.

In 1974, at age twenty-five, she was hired by Chicago's WMAQ-TV as a writer/associate producer, as well as co-host with producer Bob Smith, of the daytime magazine program "Sorting It Out." During the next two years, she would win three local Emmy awards for her on-camera work. In 1975, again inspired by Ann Ryerson, Shelley joined a one-year improvisational workshop at Second City, the alma mater of, among others, Gilda Radner, Bill Murray, and John Belushi. After the year she was asked to become a member of the resident company, which prompted her to leave WMAQ-TV. Opening in August 1976 as a replacement for Ryerson (who had moved on to Los Angeles), Shelley debuted at Second City in the troupe's fifty-third revue, *North by North Wells*, the title referring to the showcase's address at 1616 North Wells in Chicago. At the time she told the *Chicago Tribune*, "I'm concerned about whether I'm a funny person—I hope I measure up." The group's director, Bernie Sahlins, said, "She's not a comic, she's a comic actress." It was during this time that Shelley subscribed wholeheartedly to Transcendental Meditation, saying, "It isn't foolproof, but it clears your mind and puts you in touch with the deeper self." Also during this period she married and divorced a man whom she refuses to discuss.

ABC-TV talent scouts enticed Shelley, among other comedians recruited across the nation, to move to Los Angeles in 1977. The incentive was "That Thing on ABC," the pilot for a proposed music/comedy/variety program. It aired on January 4, 1978, but failed to generate sufficient audience interest; nor did its sequel, "That Second Thing on ABC" (March 8, 1978). Between these stints, Shelley appeared in a segment of "The Love Boat." In February 1979 she guested on the prime-time drama "Family," then had a supporting role in ABC-TV's THE CRACKER FACTORY (March 16, 1979), about a suburban housewife (Natalie Wood) suffering a nervous breakdown. Striving to get situated in a permanent format, Shelley participated in two pilots: ABC-TV's "Young Guy Christian" (May 24, 1979), as a professor's daughter who helps the hero (Barry Bostwick) fight crime, and CBS-TV's "The Dooley Brothers" (July 31, 1979), as the put-upon daughter of a nearly blind sheriff (Dub Taylor) in the Old West. Lingering at CBS, she was seen in an episode of "Trapper John, M.D." in October 1979 as well as a January 1980 installment of "M*A*S*H."

Shelley's theatrical film debut was as a college student caught up in the campus unrest of the 1960s in A SMALL CIRCLE OF FRIENDS (1980), a well-intentioned drama that was forgotten within days. For ABC-TV she made yet another pilot, "Ghost of a Chance"

(July 7, 1980), based on the Brazilian comedy hit DOÑA FLOR AND HER TWO HUSBANDS (1978), in which her new husband (Barry Van Dyke) must compete for her attention with the ghost of her dead spouse (Steven Keats). That November she supported Valerie Bertinelli and Jameson Parker in the CBS-TV movie THE PROMISE OF LOVE (November 11, 1980). Her second theatrical movie, CAVEMAN (1981), was better received, mainly because of its lead, Ringo Starr. A crude takeoff on the twice-before-filmed story of ONE MILLION B.C. (1940), this satire is set in one zillion B.C. with Long as Tala who remains the love mate of her tribe's chief (Starr) in spite of the competition from buxom Barbara Bach. Next, Shelley again supported Valerie Bertinelli, in THE PRINCESS AND THE CABBIE (November 3, 1981), a CBS-TV movie.

In October 1981 Shelley was married in Santa Monica, California, to stockbroker/investment advisor Bruce Tyson, four years her junior. She had met him on a blind date in 1979. "Being married to Shelley," he said, "is like Cracker Jacks. Every day a new prize inside." The newlyweds took up residence in a home in Pacific Palisades, not far from Hollywood. That same year, she was on stage in Los Angeles as Rose, the daydreaming, innocent salesgirl, in *The Woolgatherer.*

NIGHT SHIFT (1982), directed deftly by Ron Howard, had Shelley as a "good-as-gold prostitute." Her performance as a happy hooker was a highlight of the popular comedy. This film, along with setting Michael Keaton on the road to stardom, established Shelley's comic talents. Her position as a funster was further enhanced by her signing a seven-year contract with NBC-TV to co-star in the new thirty-minute weekly situation comedy "Cheers," which premiered September 30, 1982. Into the Boston bar known as Cheers walks Diane Chambers (Shelley), a rather prissy, pretentious, snooty, upper-middle-class college graduate student on her way to being married. When she is jilted, she is hired by the bar's womanizing owner, Sam Malone (Ted Danson), as a waitress, the only position for which she is qualified. In the beginning she loathes Sam, but a volatile romantic relationship evolves over the months between the ex-alcoholic, ex-baseball player and the barmaid-poetess. Their courtship is punctuated by sarcastic barbs tossed by both. "Ah, yes, I should have known," she says in one episode. "As usual, Mr. Malone has his brains caught in his zipper." Receiving low ratings during its debut season, "Cheers" was nevertheless renewed for a second season, and in September 1983 it was awarded five Emmys, including one for Shelley as Outstanding Lead Actress in a Comedy Series. She also received a Golden Globe Award.

Prior to starting "Cheers," she had the fourth-billed role as Kathy, an unhappy housewife who drives a carload of teenagers to Tijuana, Mexico, in LOSIN' IT (1983). Once there she seduces a willing teen, Tom Cruise. Then, during the 1983 summer hiatus, Shelley co-starred with Ryan O'Neal in IRRECONCILABLE DIFFERENCES. When it was previewed in Phoenix in January 1984, the *Hollywood Reporter* noted that the word on the film "and Shelley Long is music to everyone's ears, further cueing the decision . . . to hold the film for a fall exposure." Upon its release in September 1984, Chicago critic Roger Ebert stoutly praised this bittersweet study of a feuding Hollywood couple (Long, O'Neal) sued for divorce by their ten-year-old daughter (Drew Barrymore). Ebert also called

Shelley "one of my favorite actresses."

On December 9, 1984, she helped pay tribute to one of her idols in the CBS-TV special "An All-Star Party for Lucille Ball." The following month she was handed her second Golden Globe as Best Actress, TV Comedy or Musical Series. She was seen in the NBC-TV salute "Second City 25th Anniversary Special" (April 13, 1985) before giving birth in June 1985 to daughter Juliana, having carefully planned the event to occur during series hiatus. "Maybe you find that a bit much," she told *People* magazine, "but I want to do it in a fair way—one that was fair to the show and to my family." During the 1985–1986 season of "Cheers," her per-episode pay was $35,000, low compared to Danson's $50,000 per-segment salary.

For PBS-TV she guest-starred in March 1986 in an "An American Portrait" episode. At the same time, she was seen on the big screen opposite Tom Hanks in THE MONEY PIT (1986), an updated version of MR. BLANDINGS BUILDS HIS DREAM HOUSE (1948), in which she and Hanks played a couple buying a rundown house. She described the Steven Spielberg–produced feature with, "It's a very simple love story with domestic special effects." The movie grossed over $30 million due to its stars' popularity.

Forced to drop out of JUMPIN' JACK FLASH (1986), which went to Whoopi Goldberg, Shelley joined the lineup of performers for the TV special "NBC's 60th Anniversary Celebration" (May 12, 1986). By then, she was already at work on OUTRAGEOUS FORTUNE (1987), "a refreshingly female 'buddy' picture" (*Films in Review* magazine). She and Bette Midler were a hilariously funny duo. As budding actresses, both in love with the same man (Peter Coyote), they are asked to identify a body believed to be his, but instantly reject it due to the size of the corpse's penis. Madcap mayhem ensues. Rumored to be in conflict with Midler during the shooting, Shelley denied any trouble except that which existed between their respective managers over billing, which resulted in the decision to place Shelley's name first in one-half of the nation, with Midler getting top billing in the other half. OUTRAGEOUS FORTUNE grossed a hefty $22,647,000 in domestic film rentals.

After signing a three-year film contract with the Disney studio, Shelley opted to withdraw from "Cheers." She reasoned, "Movies seem to be opening up for me now, and I want to take advantage of that." She added, "'Cheers' will do just fine without me." The reigning America's Sweetheart abdicated the title with her final episode of "Cheers," telecast May 7, 1987. Of the time she spent on the series, during which her character was almost married to a doctor, wound up in a nunnery, jumped off a boat, etc., etc., she admitted, "My vocabulary has increased tremendously. After five years there aren't too many words that Diane hasn't said." Rumored to be increasingly demanding and difficult on the set, Shelley was not defended by Danson, who told *TV Guide* magazine that he could not say anything that was not negative. To replace Long, a new character, Rebecca Howe (Kirstie Alley), was introduced in the fall of 1987 as the new manager of Cheers, now owned by a megacorporation, with Sam demoted to chief bartender. The chemistry between Danson and Alley lacked the snap and crackle that he had enjoyed with Shelley. (On November 8, 1990, to celebrate the approaching two hundredth episode of "Cheers,"

Shelley joined the cast of the long-running series for an hour special, which included both a retrospective and a question-and-answer forum between the creators, executive producers, cast, and studio audience.)

In 1987 Shelley formed a production company with her former manager, Marty Mickelson, in conjunction with her Disney pact. Mickelson co-produced HELLO AGAIN (1987), starring Shelley as a Long Island housewife who chokes to death but is resurrected by her witch sister (Judith Ivey) a year later. Neither critics nor audiences fancied the premise. Long was one of six stars interviewed by host Merv Griffin on NBC-TV's "Secrets Women Never Share" (December 14, 1987); helped Bob Hope observe his eighty-fifth on "Happy Birthday, Bob" on NBC in 1988; and joined Hope again in January 1989 for NBC-TV's "Bob Hope's Super Bowl Party."

To *Continental Choice* magazine, Shelley admitted to being in a position to pick and choose her film properties. She said, "Even when you're in the middle of a mess and you make a mistake, if you can laugh at it, you're already on the road to recovery." One hopes she was able to laugh at her next project, which was indeed a mess, grossing only $8,455,880 at the box office in five weeks of domestic distribution. TROOP BEVERLY HILLS (1989) found her as a rich, pampered Beverly Hills wife (to Craig T. Nelson) and mother (to Jenny Lewis) trying to rejuvenate her failing marriage by leading a troop of spoiled, bored, wealthy young members of the Wilderness Girls of America. A charitable *Variety* noted, "Overall, pic would not likely have flown without Long, whose airy, whimsical charm builds a winning momentum that prevails over a decidedly flat beginning and implausible story."

In April 1990 it was reported that Shelley and her husband had paid $3 million for the former home of architect Brian A. Murphy in Pacific Palisades. Originally built in 1963 on a half-acre of land, the 7,000-square-foot expanded two-story home boasted four bedrooms, seven baths, a paddle tennis court, a forty-foot pool, a spa, fountains, and views of the sea.

Shelley Long in TROOP BEVERLY HILLS (1989).

For the four-hour ABC-TV movie VOICES WITHIN: THE LIVES OF TRUDI CHASE (May 20–21, 1990), Shelley turned to drama. In this fact-based account, she played the title character, who had twenty-two documented personalities as the result of a childhood of severe abuse by a harsh stepfather. It was hoped that this film would do for Shelley what SYBIL had done for Sally Field back in 1976. The *San Francisco Ex-*

aminer found Long's performance "spellbinding" in "a spirited, grandly offbeat tragicomedy." However, this two-part production just did not generate the excitement of SYBIL.

For DON'T TELL HER IT'S ME (1990), adapted for the screen by Sarah Bird from her novel *The Boyfriend School*, Shelley had special billing: "and Shelley Long as Lizzie." Steve Guttenberg starred as an introverted cartoonist who, having recovered from a ravaging, near-fatal ailment, is given a new image (as a long-haired motorcycle devotee) by his meddlesome older sister (Long), a romance novelist, so that he can attract a girlfriend. Jeff Menell (*Hollywood Reporter*) dismissed the film as a "ridiculous comedy" filled with "implausible plot twists" and a plotline that "would embarrass a TV sitcom." Mostly because of the poor scripting and tasteless direction, Shelley's character emerged as crass and strange, rather than eccentric and lovably wacky. The only performer to receive good notices for this hodgepodge was Steve Guttenberg. DON'T TELL HER IT'S ME grossed less than $1 million in its first week of domestic distribution. From October 23 to 28, 1990, at the Canon Theatre in Beverly Hills, Shelley and Tim Matheson read *Love Letters* by A. R. Gurney. Soon thereafter, it was announced that Shelley had agreed to return to series TV in a half-hour CBS program being developed for the 1991–1992 season.

Back in 1976, Shelley Long had said of her several career gambles, "It's a risk, I know. But I want to find out. I want to know what I do best, and now is the time to learn that." To date she has taken many such risks; undoubtedly, she will continue professionally to surprise her public because that is the type of woman she is. A constant surprise is the hair color Shelley chooses for her various portrayals: she has gone from light brown to blonde to dark blonde to auburn to an almost garish color bordering on orange. "I pay careful attention to how things feel," she has explained, "but when it's not clear, I turn it over and let a larger power determine what it's going to be—call that God or the universe, or whatever. . . . I don't believe that we're cornered, that we have to do things in a certain way. I don't believe in predestination, even though I was raised a Presbyterian." In a position to pick and choose, Long takes only those parts that deeply appeal to her, comedy or drama. "I can play some real outrageous characters," she says.

Filmography

The Cracker Factory (ABC-TV, 3/16/79)
The Promise of Love (CBS-TV, 11/11/80)
A Small Circle of Friends (UA, 1980)
The Princess and the Cabbie (CBS-TV, 11/3/81)
Caveman (UA, 1981)
Night Shift (WB, 1982)
Losin' It (Emb, 1983)

Irreconcilable Differences (WB, 1984)
The Money Pit (Univ, 1986)
Outrageous Fortune (BV, 1987)
Hello Again (BV, 1987)
Troop Beverly Hills (Col, 1989)
Voices Within: The Lives of Trudi Chase (ABC-TV, 5/20/90–5/21/90)
Don't Tell Her It's Me (Hemdale, 1990)

Television Series

Sorting It Out (WMAQ, 1974–76) (Chicago local)

Cheers (NBC, 1982–87)

MADONNA

"I think the public is tired of trying to figure out whether I'm a
feminist or not. I don't think of what I'm doing as gender specific.
I am what I am, and I do what I do. I never set out to be a role model
for girls or women."   —*Cosmopolitan* magazine, May 1990

"CHAMELEON" IS AN ESPECIALLY APPROPRIATE DESCRIPTION OF
Madonna. On and off stage, she is capable of many faces, poses, and hair colors and styles.
Madonna arrived on the entertainment scene at a time when a new goddess was needed to
epitomize today's independent American girl/woman. Within months of gaining prominence, her teenaged followers were chanting, "I wanna be like Madonna." Loyal fans aped
her unique dress and style: exposed navels, beauty marks, merry widow corsets (corselets),
and a new creation, bustiers, became the rage.

Fortunately for Madonna, a medium for rapid exposure was available. Cable
television's MTV seemed to have been designed for her and she made the most of it.
Quickly, the ubiquitous, pouty, crotch-grabbing performer knocked Donna Summer and
Deborah Harry off the charts, becoming popular music's reigning female power. Said to be
a "punk" Mae West, a carbon copy of Marilyn Monroe with touches of Kim Novak,
Madonna has occasionally emulated her favorite actress, Judy Holliday, and has good-
naturedly sparred with Cher, a competitor in costumes and energy.

Like her or not (her acting, dancing, and singing skills are limited and she leans too
heavily on gimmickry), one must admire Madonna's shrewd mind and innovativeness.
Whether concertizing around the world, having a stormy marriage to actor Sean Penn, or
romancing Warren Beatty, her co-star/director of DICK TRACY (1990), she continually
fascinates an intrigued public. In short, Madonna is *the* woman of the current era.

With a first name inherited from her mother and grandmother, Madonna Louise
Veronica Ciccone was born in Bay City, Michigan, on Saturday, August 16, 1958. Her
father, Sylvio "Tony" Ciccone, a first-generation Italian-American, was a design engineer
for the Chrysler/General Dynamics Corporation, and a strict Roman Catholic. Her
mother, of French-Canadian ancestry, had given birth previously to two other children,
with a fourth to follow in 1961. Tony was proud of his dark-haired oldest girl, whom he
called "Nonny," for obeying his rule that no one in his household was to watch television,
because it was sinful, and for dutifully attending church every Sunday. Although she was a
flirtatious five year old, bouncing from one man's lap to another, she thought about
becoming a nun when she grew up. In December 1963 her mother died of breast cancer.

Tony moved his family to Pontiac, Michigan, where Madonna grew up wanting to be black because all her friends were black.

In 1966, after employing a succession of housekeepers, Tony married the latest of them, whom Madonna instantly disliked for stealing away her father's affections. Madonna was handy to baby sit for her two new stepbrothers, and "I couldn't wait to escape." While in junior high school, she took part in plays and made a home movie. However, she was best at dancing, which became her passion. At the age of fourteen, she met a dance instructor, Christopher Flynn, who took a particular liking to the precocious teenager and introduced her to the Detroit world of disco dancing. "I latched onto him like a leech," she would say later, "and took everything I could from him." Her father disapproved of this friendship and gave her a 1966 red Ford Mustang as a reward to stay away from Flynn.

At Rochester Adams High School in Pontiac, Madonna absorbed studies "like a sponge," receiving mostly A's on her report cards. She was a member of the Adams Thespian Society and was also a cheerleader. At age seventeen, in January 1976, she graduated from high school. She received a dance scholarship to the University of Michigan at Ann Arbor, where Flynn was a professor of dance. After one year, with confidence instilled by Flynn, she quit the university. In late summer 1978 she arrived in New York City with approximately $37 in her purse. (Her move alienated her father for many years.) She lived in a low-rent tenement building in the crime- and drug-ridden East Village. She took waitress jobs and earned money modeling (frequently in the nude) for artists and photographers. In 1979 she appeared in a softcore pornographic film, A CERTAIN SACRIFICE, as a dominatrix with three slaves at her beck and call. Auditioning for the Alvin Ailey American Dance Theater's third company—consisting mostly of Hispanics and blacks, all with ambitions of stardom—she was accepted, but left after a few months. Instead, she took classes with Pearl Lang, a former Martha Graham choreographer. This lasted even a shorter time due to a personality clash with the strong-willed Lang.

Meanwhile, Madonna found romance, along with an introduction to rock 'n' roll, with musician Dan Gilroy. From him she learned to play drums and guitar. This relationship was interrupted, however, when, after responding to a classified ad, she was selected as a backup singer for a minor disco star based in Paris. With all expenses paid, she was flown to Paris, where she worked for a few months until illness and homesickness took their toll. Returning to America, she lived with Dan Gilroy in an abandoned synagogue in Brooklyn, while performing as drummer/vocalist in his group, Breakfast Club. The romance ended when he refused to permit her to be lead singer. She moved back to Manhattan and with Steve Bray, a friend from Ann Arbor, formed her own band, which had several names before Emmy was settled on. In 1982 she was placed on salary by Camille Barbone, a promoter/manager, when Emmy was disbanded and a new band, Madonna, was organized to feature the new, funkier rap music.

Branching out to the newer sound of so-called funk or rap-dance, she made a demonstration recording of "Everybody" which she distributed to disc jockeys at various local discos. She became involved romantically with Mark Kamins, the d.j. at Danceteria, a fashionable and trendy musical night spot. Not only did he play her record frequently at the club, but through him she obtained a meeting with Seymour Stein, the president of Sire Records. Observing that "she had the drive to match her talent," Stein signed her to a recording contract.

On July 27, 1983, her first album, *Madonna*, was released on the Sire label. It was slow to catch on, but with the help of her wanton type of dancing at Manhattan dance clubs and of frequent radio showcasing, three cuts from the album made it to the pop charts. Both "Borderline" and "Lucky Star" were in the top ten by the spring of 1984, with "Holiday" resting at #16. A fourth offering from the LP, "Burning Up," was also her first video shown on MTV. It featured her writhing on hot pavement, "burning up for your love," presenting a lacy, sex-kitten image. The term "boy toy" (to refer to lovers) emblazoned on her belt buckles caused feminists to speculate that she was not on their side. However, she stated that if sensual male performers could perform sexist routines, so could she.

Madonna's second album, *Like a Virgin* (November 1984), was the first LP by a female artist to sell more than five million copies worldwide. While strutting her pouty stuff with bare midriff in the MTV video "Lucky Star" (from her *Like a Virgin* album), Madonna made her mainstream motion picture debut in February 1985 in VISION QUEST. Seen briefly in the movie as a singer with a club band, she sang "Crazy for You." The song was also recorded on the Geffen label and became one of the top ten American singles. On February 13, 1985, she had her first public date with brat pack actor Sean Penn, born August 17, 1960, two years and a day after her birth.

People magazine described the New York City–filmed DESPERATELY SEEKING SUSAN (1985) as "at times . . . the first punk sitcom" but still "fresh and funky." In this Susan Seidelman–directed comedy, Madonna had her first co-starring role. She played Susan, whose wild wardrobe resulted from shoplifting and who slept in a bathtub when not strutting through the madcap action involving a bored housewife (Rosanna Arquette) who wants to be like her. David Denby (*New York* magazine) thought that "Madonna looks confident enough to crunch boulders," while *Variety* found that she turned in "a rounded, interesting performance." Grossing $10.9 million in domestic rentals, the low-budget feature illustrated that Madonna was a competent actress. She recorded "Into the Groove," a song from the movie.

In the MTV video "Like a Virgin," Madonna wore a wedding dress of white lace. However, it was her next video, "Material Girl," that fully established her controversial reputation. Emulating Marilyn Monroe in a hot-pink strapless dress, she performed a clever rendition of "Diamonds Are a Girl's Best Friend." For the week of April 25, 1985, charts for the top ten singles, albums, and videos listed Madonna six times for both sides of the Atlantic Ocean. After attaining the coveted cover of *Time* magazine (May 25, 1985), she embarked on her first concert tour, *Like a Virgin*. For her performance on June 6, 1985, at the Radio City Music Hall in Manhattan, she earned entries in Andy Warhol's diary as "simple and sexy" and "so pretty."

She was now a super celebrity, and everything Madonna said or did or wore was chronicled. At her July 17, 1985, bridal shower, she wore black, and it was assumed that she was pregnant, a rumor that persisted until she finally denied it in November while hosting "Saturday Night Live" on NBC-TV. On her twenty-seventh birthday, August 16, 1985, on a Malibu, California, bluff overlooking the Pacific Ocean, she and Sean Penn were married. The peaceful scene was marred by hovering helicopters occupied by overeager media reporters and photographers. In January 1986 the couple purchased an $850,000 Central Park West apartment in Manhattan. However, their period of domestic bliss was interrupted on April 12, 1986, when Penn physically attacked songwriter David Wolinski, an old friend of his wife's, for publicly kissing her on the lips. (Penn was fined $1,700 and placed on probation.)

Madonna's third album, *True Blue*, was released on June 30, 1986. It was dedicated to Penn, "the coolest guy in the universe." Not only did the album sell 2.5 million copies, but four tracks ("Live to Tell," "Papa Don't Preach," "La Isla Bonita," and the title song) were released as singles and became very popular. Together, her first three albums had sold 15 million copies. Also in June 1986 she and Penn made headlines by quarreling at the Pyramid Club in Manhattan; later, crowds gathered on the sidewalk while they screamed at each other. In August 1986 the couple appeared together on stage in a limited-run Lincoln Center workshop production of David Rabe's play *Goose and Tomtom*. During the show's run, Penn once again gained notoriety for slugging a pair of photographers who were attempting to get him and Madonna on film. Meanwhile, two more Madonna videos captured the attention of MTV viewers: "Open Your Heart" (in which she sported chopped-off hair) and "Papa Don't Preach" (in which she wore orange lipstick, which clashed with her blonde hair).

Madonna rejected an offer to star in RUTHLESS PEOPLE (1986), which made Bette Midler a bankable movie star. Instead, she unwisely chose to co-star with Sean Penn in SHANGHAI SURPRISE (1986), financed by singer George Harrison at $15 million. This dismal production cast Madonna as a 1930s missionary in China with Penn as a necktie salesman seeking a shipment of opium. Despite its popular lead players, the period feature was a flop. Disgruntled producer Harrison would now say of Madonna that she "has to realize that you can be a fabulous person and be humble as well."

Amid rumors that she and Penn were contemplating divorce,

Sean Penn and **Madonna** in SHANGHAI SURPRISE (1986).

Madonna's single "La Isla Bonita," from her *True Blue* album, was #10 on American charts in May 1987 and #3 in Britain. By May 21, 1987, the album itself had risen within two weeks from #47 to #26.

Scheduled to star together in BLIND DATE (1987), Madonna and Penn were suddenly out of the comedy when Blake Edwards was assigned to direct; it became a Bruce Willis–Kim Basinger project. In June 1987 Madonna began her second two-month concert tour, *Who's That Girl*, beginning in the rain in Tokyo, followed by engagements in several cities in the United States. In Turin, Italy, the show was taped for MTV as "Madonna Ciao Italia: Live from Italy." The tour ended August 4, 1987, in London. The biggest female draw ever in the United Kingdom, she earned $6.4 million. Prior to the European tour, Madonna participated energetically in the July 13, 1987, benefit at New York's Madison Square Garden for AIDS research. Diane Keaton was eager to produce a remake of THE BLUE ANGEL, co-starring Madonna with Al Pacino for Twentieth Century–Fox release. However, this enterprise failed to materialize, as did a remake of SOME LIKE IT HOT and an Allan Carr production of Cheryl Crane's *Detour*, with Madonna cast as Lana Turner's daughter. Meanwhile, Sean Penn had been sentenced to sixty days in the Los Angeles County Central Jail for violating his probation when he attacked an extra on a movie set. He was released in August 1987 for good behavior after thirty-two days behind bars.

When WHO'S THAT GIRL opened in Manhattan on August 7, 1987, a crowd estimated at twenty thousand stopped traffic in hopes of getting near Madonna while she attended the premiere. Something of a remake of BRINGING UP BABY (1938) in that a tiger is featured in the thin plotline, the picture cast Madonna as a newly released convict out to clear her name. Supposedly a screwball comedy, it was "loutishly acted" (according to the *Hollywood Reporter*) and stood, according to the trade paper, as "unfortunate and irrefutable evidence of how far comedy has regressed in less than 50 years." Audiences agreed, but her single on the Sire label of the title song rose to #1 on the charts. In November 1987 Madonna ordered Penn out of their New York apartment and then filed for divorce. However, a few days later, they reconciled.

Speed-the-Plow, an eighty-five-minute play by David Mamet about Hollywood, opened at the Royale Theatre on Broadway, beginning May 4, 1988. With her hair a natural black, Madonna was Karen, a seemingly naive temporary secretary who becomes the sexual target of a mogul (Joe Mantegna). Because of her presence in the cast, audiences flocked to the presentation to see if she could really act. Edwin Wilson (*Wall Street Journal*) reported, "Though Madonna works hard to hold her own, she can not be blamed if she appears to be out of her depth." With Penn away in Thailand for location filming on CASUALTIES OF WAR (1989), her playmate became comedienne Sandra Bernhard, with whom she performed on stage at the Brooklyn Academy of Music on May 24, 1988, in a benefit for the preservation of the rain forest.

Penn, on stage in Los Angeles in *Hurlyburly*, expected his wife to be on time for his November 16, 1988, opening. However, she entered the theater with Bernhard after the curtain went up, thus provoking the famous Penn temper again. Early in December 1988

Madonna made a TV public service announcement (*You Can't Tell by Looking*) on behalf of AIDS research, which was telecast nationwide. On December 28, 1988, she filed an assault complaint against Penn, stating that he had drunkenly entered their Malibu estate in a rage and that he had hog-tied her with leather straps after slapping her around. She insisted that she was not able to persuade him to release her for hours thereafter. A few days later, she withdrew the complaint. However, on January 5, 1989, she filed for divorce.

On March 2, 1989, Madonna signed a highly touted $5 million contract with Pepsi-Cola calling for her to star in several elaborate two-minute commercials tied in with her new single, "Like a Prayer," the music video for which, in a dream sequence, she prayed before a church altar as a religious statue turned into a hunky man. To be shown in forty countries, the Pepsi commercial (which omitted the religious symbolism of the video) debuted on American TV in early April 1989 in several spots. By the following week, it was removed from the U.S. airwaves after the American Family Association and several religious organizations protested (on the basis of the video, not the Pepsi commercial itself) that Madonna was not a suitable spokesperson for the soft drink beloved by millions of young people. Her contract with Pepsi was cancelled on April 20, 1989.

Forbes magazine estimated in 1989 that Madonna had earned $43 million in the previous two years. It listed her as president of her own music publishing and video companies as well as the head of her film production firm, Siren Films, headquartered at Columbia Studios. Her album *Like a Prayer*, on which she and Prince dueted on "Love Song," remained on *Billboard* magazine's top pop album chart for twenty-six weeks, ranking twelfth for the year. A single ("Cherish") on the Sire label also was a top twenty pop hit. In October 1989 Madonna's likeness appeared on a seventy-five-cent postage stamp in Grenada, and on November 9, 1989, Frederick's of Hollywood featured lingerie worn by her in the company's permanent museum.

BLOODHOUNDS OF BROADWAY (1989) had originally been filmed for PBS-TV's "American Playhouse" series, but sat on the shelf for a year. After a premiere showing at the Seattle, Washington, Film Festival in May 1989, the movie, adapted from four Damon Runyon stories of the 1920s, had a short-lived theatrical release in November 1989. Madonna was Hortense, a singer/dancer in a riotous speakeasy who sang "I Surrender Dear" in duet with Jennifer Grey. So disconnected was the quartet of stories that during sixty-nine showings of the feature at Manhattan's Plaza Theatre, filmgoers were unaware that two entire reels were missing.

On MTV's "Video Music Awards" show, Madonna was named the Viewers' Choice for her "Like a Prayer" video. Madonna realized several million dollars by appearing in Mitsubishi ads in Japan, while 62,656 Belgians bought their copies of *Like a Prayer* and a bustier worn by her was sold at auction for $3,750 at Sotheby's in London. Dr. Joyce Brothers interpreted Madonna's popularity psychologically by saying: "She's independent and on her own two feet. Women like her because they don't feel she's a victim. Men like her because she's sexy."

Madonna's *Blond Ambition* tour was launched on April 13, 1990, for three weeks in Tokyo in a nation that adored her. Appearing in a silver corselet, she greeted her audience with, "Hi, Tokyo, genki desuka" (How are you, Tokyo) and then presented them with ninety minutes of nonstop dancing, interspersed with eighteen songs. (Audiences seemed unmindful that she lip-synched her songs so as not to risk any false notes during her athletic dancing.) The American leg of her tour started in Houston, Texas, on May 4, 1990, and included stops in Boston and Toronto, as well as assorted cities in New Jersey, Maryland, California, and Michigan. Meanwhile, on May 4, 1990, MTV programmed a thirteen-hour marathon of Madonna in backstage tour footage, on stage in Houston, and in highlights from her video library. In May 1990, a month before the release of DICK TRACY, in which she co-starred, Madonna's album *I'm Breathless: Music from and Inspired by the Film "Dick Tracy"* was released. *Entertainment Weekly* magazine critiqued it as a "brilliant re-creation of '30s and '40s musical styles, spiced with coy sexiness," adding that it was "10 times more accomplished than any record she had made before." Interlaced with her solos were duets with both Warren Beatty and Mandy Patinkin, the latter on a song written by Stephen Sondheim. By September 20, 1990, it had been on the album charts for eight weeks.

Following tremendous hype and a saturation merchandising campaign, DICK TRACY opened on 2,400 domestic theater screens on June 15, 1990, with a good deal of the publicity having been engendered by the on- and off-camera romance between Madonna and twenty-one-year-older Warren Beatty, who had conceived, directed, and starred in this new adaptation of the famed comic strip. Aided by luminous matte painting to create a big-city comic book world and excellent makeup for the various underworld characters, DICK TRACY proved to be a lot of fun, despite its slow first hour. Madonna played Breathless Mahoney, a brassy torch singer, as well as a deep-voiced thug with no face who gets her just desserts in the movie's final moments. However, as *Entertainment Weekly* pointed out, "she doesn't get nearly enough screen time." Not since DESPERATELY SEEKING SUSAN had Madonna excelled to such an extent on screen. Made at an estimated cost of $40 million, DICK TRACY grossed well over $100 million at the domestic box office.

As Madonna's *Blond Ambition* tour continued, she was met with criticism in Rome, as she had been in Toronto earlier, for her use on stage of crucifixes and other Christian symbols. In Rome, she was forced to cancel the July 11, 1990, performance, allegedly because of a pending strike, rather than as the result of denunciation from the Catholic Church for a display of "bad taste." "My show is not blasphemous," she stated emphatically. "On the contrary, it is entertaining and educational." Her final appearance in Nice, France, was telecast on HBO–Cable on August 5, 1990, and was seen by 4 million households. After the curtain rang down on the final act of *Blond Ambition*, she thanked the crew and musicians, saying, "I should pat you all on the back for surviving me, 'cause God knows I'm a bitch."

Madonna turned down the female lead in THE FABULOUS BAKER BOYS (1989) because of "Such a Wonder Bread cast. I think of all those people as being California people—blond and boring." (Michelle Pfeiffer took the part.) It was rumored that she was interested in starring in a remake of GYPSY (1962) in the role of Gypsy Rose Lee with Barbra Streisand as Mama Rose, but both the playwright (Arthur Laurents) and composer

(Jule Styne) of the Broadway musical original said they would not agree to it. For a while, it was thought that Madonna might be the Catwoman in a BATMAN (1989) movie sequel, but this concept fell through as well. Initially Meryl Streep was set to play Eva Peron in EVITA, the movie version of the Broadway hit musical of 1979, but later both she and director Oliver Stone dropped out of the project. Later, it was announced that Madonna would go before the cameras as the infamous first lady of Argentina, with EVITA set for 1992 theatrical release, but the project has again stalled. Meanwhile, another project, FRIDA AND DIEGO, to co-star her and Mickey Rourke, never materialized.

Nominated for eight Video Music Awards for her video "Vogue" and her album *I'm Breathless*, she performed in Louis XIV–era costume on the MTV ceremonies on September 6, 1990, hosted by Arsenio Hall. Her video won three awards, for best direction, best editing, and best cinematography. The following evening she was honored at the Wiltern Theatre in Los Angeles at the AIDS Project Los Angeles' *Commitment to Life IV* for her fundraising work on behalf of the spreading illness, which had raised more than $1 million. *Forbes* magazine in September 1990 listed Madonna as one of America's biggest wage earners within the entertainment field, at $62 million during the previous year. By October 1990 Madonna was being escorted in public by model-artist Tony Ward, a few years her junior, a romance that ended in early 1991.

A concert documentary movie produced by Propaganda Films featured taped performances of Madonna from her *Blond Ambition* tour as well as interviews and behind-the-scenes footage. Entitled TRUTH OR DARE, it was released in May 1991 by Miramax.

While speculation ran high that Madonna's on-again, off-again romance with Warren Beatty had run its course (and it had), she had been announced to appear in BLESSING IN DISGUISE, a picture to be made in association with him for Siren Films for release by Columbia Pictures. She was to star as a daughter returning to her midwestern family to attend a brother's funeral, during which time she redefines her familial ties. When this project evaporated, Madonna agreed to co-star with Demi Moore in LEDA AND SWAN as lady cops, but that was dropped too. For Woody Allen's new motion picture, SHADOWS AND FOG (1992), which began shooting in New York in late 1990 with Mia Farrow starred, Madonna was assigned to play an acrobat.

In typical Madonna fashion, when her newest album, *The Immaculate Collection*, was released in November 1990, it stirred a fresh wave of publicity for the iconoclastic singer. A compilation of her songs from 1984 to 1990, *The Immaculate Collection* contained two new numbers. One of them was "Justify My Love," for which she made an accompanying video. The suggestive footage—which became the most talked-about video of the year—featured Madonna with her current boyfriend, Tony Ward, in a bisexual fantasy set in a hotel room. When MTV refused to air the controversial video, claiming it was too steamy for its viewers, interest in the song and the album soared. This led Madonna (who said of the number, "It's a celebration of sexuality. What's wrong with that?") and her recording company, Warner Bros. Records, to release the single on home video, a marketing first.

Having risen to the pinnacle of her singing and dancing profession in a relatively short time, Madonna contends, "Nothing came as fast as I wanted it." Confessing that her worst fault is impatience, she has said, "I always want everything right away." At this juncture, it might seem she has acquired "everything" already. However, given her nature, it seems more likely that she will invent yet other gimmicks to keep her public intrigued. Over and over it has been said that Madonna loves just one person—herself. Perhaps proof of this are her words regarding ex-boyfriends who go on to have affairs with other women: "I have a little twinge of jealousy behind my knee. I secretly want to kill them. You get really territorial over people you spent years of your life with. You don't want anybody else to have them." Doubtless, she will outgrow this "little twinge."

Filmography

A Certain Sacrifice (Virgin Video, 1979)
Vision Quest (WB, 1985)
Desperately Seeking Susan (Orion, 1985)
At Close Range (Orion, 1986) (voice and co-
   songs only)
Shanghai Surprise (MGM, 1986)
Who's That Girl (WB, 1987) (also co-songs)

Bloodhounds of Broadway (Col, 1989)
Dick Tracy (BV, 1990)
Truth or Dare (Miramax, 1991)

Future Releases

Shadows and Fog (Orion, 1992)

Broadway Plays

Speed-the-Plow (1988)

Album Discography

I'm Breathless: Music from and Inspired by the
   Film "Dick Tracy" (Sire 26209)
The Immaculate Collection (Sire 26440)
Like a Prayer (Sire 1-25844)
Like a Virgin (Sire 1-25157)

Lucky Star (Sire 23867-1)
Madonna (Sire 1-23867)
True Blue (Sire 1-25442)
Vision Quest (Geffen 240063) [ST]
Who's That Girl (Sire 1-25611) [ST]
You Can Dance (Sire 1-25535)

JOHN MALKOVICH

"There's definitely a lack of good scripts offered to me—I did,
however, receive a 400-page Dutch script about Purgatory, but I'm
just not up to it now."—*Hollywood Reporter*, December 19, 1988

THE ACTING PROFESSION IS FILLED WITH HANDSOME LEADING MEN.
However, John Malkovich, with his receding hairline and slightly awry eyes, is not
considered one of them. Moreover, he does not care much about his looks, saying, "It's not
something I'm completely enthralled with, but it doesn't make me throw up." If he
possessed an inflated pride in his appearance, he would cover his head constantly with a
hairpiece and would shave regularly. But like Lee J. Cobb of a past era, Malkovich is an
actor not the least bit interested in what is thought of him personally. Like his peer Willem
Dafoe, he started in roles of an unpredictable and creepy nature before graduating to
playing a soft-voiced eighteenth-century sexual predator.

Malkovich admits to being a small town man who has never been tempted by drugs
or alcohol. "My idea of fun," he has said, "is to stay home and stain a piece of furniture."
He is an obstinate, chronic complainer whose only vice is chain-smoking unfiltered
cigarettes. Oscar-winning Sally Field finds him "gentle, kind and unpretentious, but he's
wickedly irreverent too and very funny." Playwright Arthur Miller calls him an acting
"thoroughbred"; actress Debra Winger says "he's very, very rich" in talent. Once proclaimed as a new Marlon Brando, he has a wardrobe of items from vintage clothing stores
that make him appear, by his own account, as though he belongs on a 1940s-era
oceanliner. Obviously able to poke fun at himself, he posed not long ago for a *Rolling Stone*
magazine fashion spread wearing a $50 T-shirt, a $615 jacket, $398 pants, and $180
shoes.

John Malkovich was born in Christopher, Illinois, on Wednesday, December 9,
1953, the second of five children and the younger of two sons. His father, Daniel, was an
environmentalist and writer, who later owned *Illinois* magazine. His mother, Jo Anne, was
secretary of her family's newspaper, the *Evening Herald*, published in the coal mining
community of Benton, Illinois, where John grew up. The children all inherited their
father's volatile temper, with John's being one of the worst. Often, as a child, he was locked
out of the family home until his tantrum passed, while Jo Anne turned up the volume on
the television to block out the noise he made. Looking back on his childhood, John would
assess, "Although my parents were bright and articulate and well-mannered, something
just went awry. We had a lot of freedom, too much freedom, it was always chaos." In

school, John was tentative, shy, and a loner until he found that he could gain attention by showing off; thus, he became the class clown. After he saw his first play, _Our Town_, at the age of seven, he could not forget it. He plagued his parents with questions about the characters, the story, the setting.

Always an overweight child, when he entered Benton High School, he was 6' 1" and weighed 230 pounds. In order to be accepted on the football squad, he went on a Jell-o diet for three months, losing seventy pounds. (Since his mother did not cook, it was up to him to boil and stir his own simple diet food, switching flavors each meal.) He played guard on the pigskin squad, played tuba in the school band, and taught himself to play the guitar. Not a good student, he was, however, an avid reader of fiction.

After graduating from high school in 1972, he remained in his hometown for a few years before deciding to attend Eastern Illinois University at Charleston to follow in his father's footsteps by majoring in environmental studies. Within a year, however, he switched to theater because of his romantic feelings for a girl in the drama class. Lucy Gabbard, one of his acting and directing instructors, had written about the works of playwright Harold Pinter. Pinter became John's obsession, and he read everything he could find by and about the man. In his junior year, John transferred to Illinois State University at Normal where he became the resident hippie actor, adopting a costume of platform shoes, sunglasses, and a cape. His classmates called him "tweety bird" because his head seemed too large for his torso. By night he performed at local coffeehouses, playing guitar and singing his own compositions. He had parts in such campus productions as _The Lover_, by Pinter, and _The Man Who Came to Dinner_. It was his interpretation of a visiting celebrity in the latter that brought him to the attention of Gary Sinise, a high school acquaintance who had ideas of forming an acting troupe. Fascinated by John's half-whispered stage voice in "the stupidest performance I'd ever seen," Sinise recruited him away from the university in the spring of 1976 as one of nine co-founders of the Steppenwolf Theatre Company (the name was taken from a Hermann Hesse novel), which had a budget of $2,000.

The ensemble group, all of whose members were under the age of twenty-five, gave its initial production (_Rosencrantz and Guildenstern Are Dead_) in the ninety-seat basement of a grade school on Deerfield Road in Highland Park, Illinois, on July 22, 1976. For the next six years, John served as actor, director, costume maker, set builder, and ticket seller, while supporting himself at various times as a bookstore clerk, a kitchen helper in a Chinese restaurant, and a school busdriver. At the same time, he still also managed to play third base with the Piersalls softball team.

The _Chicago Tribune_ of March 25, 1977, applauded John's direction of _The Sea Horse_, which he had shortened by forty-five minutes, with, "What remains is virtually a new play, one that shimmers with implications." Occasionally, John stepped outside the Steppenwolf arena, acting in such productions as _Ashes_ at Chicago's St. Nicholas Theatre, _Waiting for Lefty_ at the Apollo Theatre Center, and Sam Shepard's _The Curse of the Starving Class_ at the Goodman Theatre. The latter part required him to walk naked across the stage. Appearing in Shepard's play with John was a young actress named Glenne

Headly. When he played Tom in Steppenwolf's *The Glass Menagerie* (May 1979), the *Chicago Tribune* singled him out as "an amazing young actor whose performances always seem to teeter on the edge of danger."

After spending the summer and fall of 1979 in New York City where he saw *Evita*, his first Broadway show, he returned to Steppenwolf, which moved to Chicago. Its 1980 production of *Balm in Gilead* won seven Joseph Jefferson Awards, Chicago's equivalent of New York's Obie Awards, including one for John's direction of that production as well as that of *No Man's Land*. During the 1981–1982 theater season, he appeared in Sam Shepard's *True West*, giving a performance that a local critic found to be "fearsome and hilarious." For this appearance, he was awarded a Jefferson as best actor.

By now, Malkovich's abilities were recognized beyond Chicago and he won a supporting role in the CBS-TV movie WORD OF HONOR (January 6, 1981), in which a veteran reporter (Karl Malden) decides to go to jail rather than reveal his sources. John had the supporting role of Gary. In ABC-TV's AMERICAN DREAM (April 26, 1981), shot on location in Chicago, John was among those involved when a family relocates from the lush suburbs of Chicago to the grim inner city, where the father (Stephen Macht) grew up. AMERICAN DREAM became a short-lived series, but Malkovich was not involved. By now, John's hairline was receding.

On August 1, 1982, John, aged twenty-eight, married Glenne Headly, aged twenty-seven. They temporarily left Chicago, where it is estimated that he had been involved with more than sixty stage productions, to go to New York City, where he made his off-Broadway debut at the Cherry Lane Theatre in Greenwich Village on October 17, 1982, in *True West*. As the loutish slob, he was called "a comic original" by *The New York Times* "with perfect timing and inexhaustible expressiveness." He received the Obie Award from the *Village Voice*, a Theatre World Award, and the Clarence Derwent Award as New York's most promising male actor. *True West* was presented on PBS-TV as part of its "American Playhouse" series early in 1983. Next, John was hired through an audition to play Biff, the sensitive but neurotic athletic son, in Dustin Hoffman's stage revival of Arthur Miller's *Death of a Salesman*. Hoffman agreed to wait while John fulfilled two movie obligations—the first to be filmed in Thailand, the second in Texas.

Following previews first in Chicago, then at the Kennedy Center's Eisenhower Theatre in Washington, D.C., *Death of a Salesman* opened at Broadway's Broadhurst Theatre for a limited run on March 29, 1984. *Newsday* noted that "the delicate interplay between Hoffman and Malkovich lifts the production to grandeur." At the same time, John was directing an off-Broadway version of *Balm in Gilead* featuring several Steppenwolf actors, including his wife. It opened May 31, 1984, at the Circle Repertory Company, later moving to off-Broadway's then-new Minetta Lane Theatre. For this work, he added another Obie, a Drama Desk Award, and an Outer Critics Circle Award to his growing collection.

Although filmed after his Thailand assignment, PLACES IN THE HEART was released first, in September 1984. It was one of three pictures (along with COUNTRY and THE RIVER) that year to deal with the plight of the American farmer—in this case, a Depression-era sheriff's widow (Sally Field) who has children to support. For playing plucky Field's blind lodger, with his eyes open, John was nominated for an Academy Award as Best Supporting Actor. (To research his role he had gone to the Dallas Lighthouse to observe disabled people at first hand.) Ironically, however, he lost the Oscar to Dr. Haing S. Ngor, his co-worker in THE KILLING FIELDS. The latter movie, released in November 1984, dealt with the American invasion of Cambodia in the spring of 1971 and, in particular, with the bond that developed between a *New York Times* reporter (Sam Waterston) and a local journalist/translator (Ngor). Malkovich played a highly charged American news photographer, who, beneath his cynicism and druggie demeanor, was a practical, caring individual. For John's incisive performances in both motion pictures, Janet Maslin (*The New York Times*) credited him as "the best thing to happen to screen acting in a long while."

On September 15, 1985, CBS-TV telecast its three-hour DEATH OF A SALESMAN, reuniting most of the stage cast from the Broadway revival. Despite the plethora of commercial breaks, the Academy of Television Arts and Sciences found John's compelling work worthy of an Emmy as Outstanding Supporting Actor in a Miniseries or Special. The following month, an eighty-eight-minute documentary film, PRIVATE CONVERSATIONS (1985), was in limited theatrical release. It concerned the making of CBS's DEATH OF A SALESMAN, and featured Arthur Miller, the play's author, and cast members Dustin Hoffman, Malkovich, and Charles Durning. Also during 1985, John was in Chicago directing Steppenwolf's revival of Harold Pinter's *The Caretaker*, along with *Coyote Ugly* both in Chicago and at the Kennedy Center in Washington, D.C. In New York, at Broadway's Circle in the Square, he directed Kevin Kline, Raul Julia, and his wife in *Arms and the Man*. Earlier in the year, in June, the Steppenwolf Theatre Company had been awarded a Tony for excellence in regional theater. The year culminated with John's "creepy" portrayal of a newsman in Greece investigating his mother's political murder thirty years prior. The film, ELENI, was filmed in Spain with John's wife, Glenne, in a supporting role. While Malkovich was lauded for his portrayal of the real-life *New York Times* reporter Nicholas

John Malkovich in PLACES IN THE HEART (1984).

Gage, the movie was panned. *Variety*, for example, judged, "ELENI is as lofty in ambition as it is deficient in accomplishment." This, Malkovich's first co-starring film, was a financial flop.

Clifford Odets' searing drama *Rocket to the Moon* was brought to PBS-TV's "American Playhouse" series on May 5, 1986. John starred as dentist Ben Stark, seeking to free himself from a stifling life, marred by a nagging wife (Connie Booth). The *Hollywood Reporter* lauded the telecast for its "outstanding performances."

The *Los Angeles Herald-Examiner*'s banner headline above its review of MAKING MR. RIGHT (1987), John's first starring movie, indicated that it "is missing a few parts." In a dual role, Malkovich is Jeff Peters, an often crabby blond scientist, and Ulysses, his creation, a blond robot. According to Richard Schickel (*Time* magazine), "Malkovich gives a wonderful performance where we do not expect one, and it makes the rest of the film problematic." This comedic departure, while not a hit, remains John's favorite screen role to date. Critics applauded his portrayal of Joanne Woodward's wistful son in the Paul Newman–directed remake of THE GLASS MENAGERIE (1987) and full-page ads in industry publications strongly urged an Oscar nomination for him as Best Actor of the year. However, the arty film was not a commercial success. Wearing brown bangs, John, at thirty-four, looked ten years younger. Desmond Ryan (*Philadelphia Inquirer*) noted, "Malkovich's role has ripened into one of the major screen performances of the year—full of haunted passion and torment," while Joy Boyum (*Glamour* magazine) summed up his performance in one word: "Brilliant."

Burn This, a new play by Lanford Wilson, premiered at the Mark Taper Forum in Los Angeles in 1987 before moving to Chicago to 2851 North Halsted, the location of Steppenwolf's permanent theater. From there it went to New York's off-Broadway Circle Repertory Company, then to Broadway's Plymouth Theatre, where it debuted on October 14, 1987. In a long black wig, John starred as Pale, the psychopathic older brother of a gay man who has died in a boating accident. Clive Barnes (*New York Post*) credited Malkovich with providing "a stellar performance. Vivid and powerful enough to provide the stuff of Broadway legend." The word "brilliant" was again used to describe a Malkovich performance, this time by the *Hollywood Reporter*'s Morna Murphy-Martell. John would leave this production during its New York run to make DANGEROUS LIAISONS (1988), to be replaced by Eric Roberts and later by Scott Glenn.

Warner Bros.'s big Christmas 1987 release was EMPIRE OF THE SUN, directed/produced by Steven Spielberg in Shanghai, England, and Spain at a cost of $38 million. In a broad but impressive characterization, John, with second billing, was Basie, a rogue adventurer befriending an English boy (Christian Bale) in a Japanese prison in Shanghai during World War II. *Variety* pinpointed why this expansive (152-minute) production failed to appeal to a wide base of moviegoers: "length, sketchy characterizations, pronounced Britishness and lack of a strong narrative." As for Malkovich's opportunistic American, the trade paper observed that Basie "keeps threatening to become a fully developed character but never does, although the man remains interesting and the actor's sly, insinuating line readings frequently conjure up thoughts of Jack Nicholson." This epic suffered a production loss of $27.5 million, making it one of the top flops of the 1980s. On Christmas Eve, 1987, John gave his voice to the animated "SantaBear's Highflying Adventure" (CBS-TV), as the animal of the title. As a favor to friend Gary Sinise, who was directing MILES FROM HOME (1988), starring Richard Gere, John and other members of the Steppenwolf group took supporting roles. The picture, revolving around two farmer brothers rebelling against governmental autocracy, was unsuccessful.

Christmas 1988 revealed a much more memorable portrayal by John as the Vicomte de Valmont, the eighteenth-century upper-class Parisian. He was the viper who says, "She was astonishing. So much so that I ended by falling on my knees and pledging her eternal love. And, do you know, at the time and for several hours afterward, I actually meant it!" The role was played earlier on Broadway by Alan Rickman in the play, known as *Les Liaisons Dangereuses*. John's performance in the film (complete with dandified period costumes and powdered wigs) takes a little adjusting to. However, he soon becomes totally convincing as the handsome, sexy defiler of women in the screen version, entitled DANGEROUS LIAISONS, in which the wonderful Glenn Close plays his former mistress. British director Stephen Frears had this to say about John: "He's romantic when you expect him to be sinister, and then in casual moments he'll look just like Dracula. . . . I was thrilled to have him." A year later, the Miloš Forman version of the same story, VALMONT (1989), would star Colin Firth as the Vicomte, but would not create the stir of its predecessor. Off screen, John and Michelle Pfeiffer, another co-star in the film, were said to be engaged in a love affair.

In 1988 John had formed his own movie production company in partnership with his manager, Phyllis Carlyle. Their first endeavor was as executive producers of THE ACCIDENTAL TOURIST, another December 1988 film, which garnered an Academy Award for supporting actress Geena Davis. In January 1989 John displayed his sense of humor as host of NBC-TV's "Saturday Night Live," but temporarily misplaced it when he and Glenne separated a few months later. Said to be in a state of depression over the breakup, in May 1989 he quit the starring role in CRAZY PEOPLE (1990) after two weeks of shooting. He was replaced by Dudley Moore in this satirical study of American advertising.

In August 1990 Frank Rich of *The New York Times* reported, "by far the most talked-about actor in a London theater right now is . . . John Malkovich, who is re-creating his Broadway role of Pale in Lanford Wilson's *Burn This*." Along with heating up London's West End theater district, John revealed to British gossip columnist Baz Bamigboye that he was an expectant father with a child due in September 1990, whose mother was "a very private lady" whom "I met on a film set." He refused to give her name, but it was conjectured that the "private lady" had had some connection with his upcoming film THE SHELTERING SKY, which had been filmed in Morocco. He explained that the couple did not plan to marry and that he would move permanently to London. "I am putting the past away," he said, with possible reference to both Headly and Pfeiffer. "I don't see going back to America in the near future, not even to work."

THE SHELTERING SKY (1990), directed by Italian filmmaker Bernardo Bertolucci and set in 1947, cast John as the husband of Debra Winger. Along with Campbell Scott, they are Americans traveling through post–World War II North Africa where John's character contracts typhoid fever and is dying. When THE SHELTERING SKY opened in late December 1990, most reviewers acknowledged that the picture was visually stunning, intellectually complex, and filled with many meaningful stretches of silence. However, *Variety* prognosticated, "But those who haven't read the book—the vast majority of filmgoers—will be left bewildered, as [author Paul] Bowles' delicate achievement has simply not managed the transfer to celluloid." The trade paper added, "John Malkovich is an excellent choice as Port, his shifting, centaurlike physicality—sometimes fey and graceful, sometimes rooted and intransigent—filling in for the interior life the screen can't provide."

Producers Paul Heller and Rick Bloom, reportedly eager to put the Andy Warhol biography as written by Victor Bockris onto motion picture screens, were "close to a deal" with director Gus Van Sant to write the screenplay as well as direct the project. Both Malkovich and Willem Dafoe expressed interest in playing the silver-haired Warhol. Since Heller is from Britain, it is possible that if John is selected, the production might be lensed in London.

For QUEENS LOGIC (1991), an arty attempt at nostalgia, John played a New York fish business owner who is a dour homosexual. Others in the cast included Jamie Lee Curtis, Kevin Bacon, Ken Olin, and Joe Mantegna. Michael Wilmington (*Los Angeles Times*) insisted that director Steve Rash stages his drama with "lots of energy, warmth and detail" and that the "actors chomp into their roles like street corner pepperoni slices." However, cautioned Wilmington, "the overall effect is slight and skittery."

"It's great with John," said Andie MacDowell of her co-star in the comedy THE OBJECT OF BEAUTY (1991). As an American couple stranded in a luxury London hotel, they rely on his shady commodity deals for their livelihood. When THE OBJECT OF BEAUTY opened in the spring of 1991, Duane Byrge (*Hollywood Reporter*) observed, "Smartly idiosyncratic, this John Malkovich–Andie MacDowell starrer is, however, likely to alienate viewers as much as it entrances them—so cavalierly cretinous are the two major characters." *Variety* concluded, "THE OBJECT OF BEAUTY is a throwback to the romantic comedies of Swinging London cinema of the late '60s but lacks the punch of the best of that genre. . . . As in THE SHELTERING SKY, John Malkovich plays a drifting character. . . . Malkovich ably brings out the unsympathetic nature of his antihero, but the script doesn't help him much in balancing that with any impelling reason for identification—it is hard to care about someone whose future lies in produce sitting on a dock in Sierra Leone."

For Woody Allen's ensemble study SHADOWS AND FOG (forthcoming, 1992), Malkovich is among the star cast, which also includes Madonna and Mia Farrow.

In a recent *Playboy* magazine article, John described his acting technique: "You have to betray an audience or nothing really happens. . . . You have to convince people they're watching a certain thing that's easily identified—everything's fine, don't worry—and then you turn on them, betray them with something completely different." On another occasion, he admitted, "I try never to do any more research than is absolutely necessary . . . . I became an actor to exercise my imagination, not my research skills." When asked how he retains his perspective in the light of his acclaim, he once responded, "Well, I count on my good friends to treat me as they always do—like dirt."

Filmography

Word of Honor (CBS-TV, 1/6/81)
American Dream (ABC-TV, 4/26/81)
Places in the Heart (Tri-Star, 1984)
The Killing Fields (WB, 1984)
Death of a Salesman (CBS-TV, 9/15/85)
Private Conversations (Punch, 1985)
Eleni (WB, 1985)
Making Mr. Right (Orion, 1987)
Empire of the Sun (WB, 1987)
The Glass Menagerie (Cineplex Odeon, 1987)
Miles from Home (Cinecom, 1988)

The Accidental Tourist (WB, 1988) (co-executive producer only)
Dangerous Liaisons (WB, 1988)
The Sheltering Sky (WB, 1990)
Queens Logic (New Visions, 1991)
The Object of Beauty (Avenue Pictures, 1991)

Future Releases

Shadows and Fog (Orion, 1992)

Broadway Plays

Death of a Salesman (1984) (revival)
Arms and the Man (1985) (revival) (director only)
Burn This (1987)

KELLY McGILLIS

"I'm just an actress who appreciates the work she's had and who
was once very poor. I certainly don't get the star treatment at home.
I don't want to be any different. I do the laundry."
                                        —*Chicago Tribune*, October 8, 1989

IT REQUIRES A LONG STRETCH OF THE IMAGINATION TO VISUALIZE A
teenaged Kelly McGillis as too tall and too overweight to attract a date for her high school
junior prom. Today, lacking conceit or narcissism as a result of that earlier gawky period,
she finds it difficult to accept adulation. By her own admission, "the real Kelly McGillis is
boring." She is not a typical Hollywood glamour queen or a controversial figure whose
private life provides spicy items for weekly tabloids. She is a rarity in today's Hollywood.
Like the young Ingrid Bergman of the late 1930s, she is an actress who "would like to act
until I'm too old and feeble to do it anymore." Unlike Kathleen Turner, she is not a
method actress who takes her character or accent home from the movie set. Kelly McGillis
believes in retaining her individuality.

Born on Tuesday, July 9, 1957, in Newport Beach, California, she was the first of
three daughters to enter the meticulously maintained home of their physician father and
his wife. Later, in school, she towered above her classmates, who made fun of her. She
overate out of frustration and, by the time she started high school, carried close to 200
pounds on her 5' 10", broad-shouldered frame. Her insecurity about her appearance was
made worse when she failed to qualify as a cheerleader, a position of paramount importance with her Newport Beach peers. Imbued with tremendous energy, she was never
without a part-time job, which enabled her to be at least partially independent. In her
seventeenth summer, she developed a great interest in men. She also hung out at the beach,
surfing and sailing, which, along with careful dieting, helped her to lose weight. By now
she had abandoned any plans to follow in her father's footsteps as a physician, realizing
that she was far too sensitive for such a calling. (As a child she had gone on a house call with
her father and seeing the patient, who had severed his thumb, in tears, she began crying
too.) She had already acted in a school production of *The Serpent* and decided she wanted
to pursue acting as a profession. ("I was a pretty wild girl. My outlet was acting. I decided
not to do anything else. I didn't like anything else.") Propelled by her career desire as well
as teenage rebelliousness, she quit high school in the early spring of 1975, only a few
months before graduation.

During the next two years she worked largely as a waitress in local restaurants and bars, saving money so she could study to be an actress. Although vigorously discouraged by her parents, she enrolled at the Pacific Conservatory of the Performing Arts in Santa Maria, California, in 1977. After two years there, in 1979, a few weeks before her twenty-second birthday, she went to New York City, where she had been accepted as a four-year student at the famed Juilliard School of Drama where she specialized in classical theater. She paid her way by waitressing at all-night establishments. In 1980 she married writer Boyd Black, but the union did not last; they were divorced two years later. She was initiated into the cold detachment of big-city Manhattan life one night in 1981 when she was mugged at gunpoint near Lincoln Center. "I wasn't really frightened," she admitted some years later. "It seemed that everyone in New York got mugged."

A year later, in February 1982, she was traumatized by a much more severe incident. While she was at home alone (her roommate was out), two men forced their way into the apartment and proceeded to ridicule, abuse, and sodomize her. Calling her a "white bitch," among other racial slurs, and threatening her with kitchen knives, they forced her onto the bed and sexually assaulted her. "That 20 minutes of my life seemed to last 20 years," she was to tell *People* magazine more than six years later. "Then there was a loud banging on the front door and they both fled out the window." The new arrivals were the police, who had been summoned by someone who heard her screams. She later telephoned her parents, who flew to New York to be with her. Unable to convince her to return to California, they gave her financial support so that she could move to a better neighborhood in Manhattan. At the same time they finally accepted her decision to become an actress. "The first few weeks after the incident," she told *People*, "I couldn't eat or sleep. I twitched incessantly. I would gasp suddenly without being able to control it." Always a loner, she became more withdrawn and says that she probably would have committed suicide had it not been for her understanding friends and teachers at Juilliard. Two years later, in 1984, she sought psychiatric help, but would not speak openly of the rape until 1988.

During her years at Juilliard she appeared in productions of *Love for Love, Six Characters in Search of an Author, The Winter's Tale, The Three Sisters,* and other plays. During the summers she performed in Shakespeare in the Park, where producer Julius J. Epstein discovered her. In the film REUBEN, REUBEN (1983), adapted from a Peter deVries novel, he cast her as Geneva Spofford, a New England college student in love with a hard-drinking Scottish poet (Tom Conti) who is touring the campus lecture circuit. Now having graduated from Juilliard, she continued to wait tables at night while searching for acting jobs by day. "I was just a little kid that nobody ever heard of. I was pounding the pavement like a million other actors." Things became easier for her after the release in December 1983 of REUBEN, REUBEN, an unpretentiously joyous production. *Variety* judged her debut film performance "solid" and noted that her "chic blonde Vassar looks interestingly contrast . . . with her character's farmyard roots." Thereafter, she obtained occasional work in a few daytime TV soap operas taped in New York and played one of the patients of a New York psychiatrist (Mike Farrell) in an NBC-TV pilot film, PRIVATE

SESSIONS, which was not telecast until March 18, 1985. By then she had already co-starred with Kevin Dobson and Alec Baldwin in the well-crafted CBS-TV movie SWEET RE-VENGE (October 31, 1984). *Variety* recorded, "Kelly McGillis, poised actress . . . delivers the goods as Katherine, purposeful woman mixed up in love for her husband, hate for the colonel."

Despite her already solid film and TV credentials, Kelly continued to think of herself as a stage actress and had little ambition of becoming famous. She took a job as a waitress at Jimmy Ray's, a New York show business restaurant on Eighth Avenue in the theater district. However, three days later she received an offer from Australian director Peter Weir to co-star opposite Harrison Ford in Weir's first American feature, WITNESS (1985). To prepare for her role as Rachel Lapp, a Pennsylvania Dutch widow, Kelly lived for a time with an Amish woman to study the mannerisms and speech of this strict sect of Mennonite followers of Jacob Amman, who had settled in America in the eighteenth century. WITNESS made a star of Kelly McGillis. She played the mother of a young boy (Lukas Haas) who has witnessed a brutal killing in the men's room of a Philadelphia train station. When a police detective (Ford) is assigned to the case, he not only uncovers departmental corruption, but also falls in love with McGillis. This leads to a romantic interlude on her family farm in Lancaster County before the inevitable showdown with the gone-bad cops. Surprisingly for a mainstream production, WITNESS avoids a fairy tale Hollywood ending. It realistically has the two lovers sadly acknowledge that their different cultures are too alien for them to co-exist happily together. WITNESS was praised as "a knockout police story" by critic Judith Crist and earned several Academy Award nominations. It became the year's eighth top grosser, taking in $65.5 million at the domestic box office.

In 1985, while patrons were lining up at the box office to see WITNESS, Kelly joined the cast of TOP GUN (1986) after her role of Charlie was changed from a leotard-clad gymnast to an astrophysics instructor at a naval aviation training school. Her reason for accepting the part was to demonstrate to the industry that she could do something more glamorous after her performance as a simply dressed Amish widow. Released in May 1986, TOP GUN is certainly one of the noisiest pictures ever made, but it also boasts the most outstanding aerial cinematography to date. Its crowd-pleasing

Kelly McGillis and Tom Cruise in TOP GUN (1986).

romantic adventure catered to young moviegoers but not to the critics. *Variety*, for example, noted, "TOP GUN is revved-up but empty entertainment" and added, "McGillis is blessed with an intelligent and mature face that doesn't blend that well with Cruise's one-note grinning." Nevertheless, the hugely popular action entry made a top star of Tom Cruise and further cemented the status of Kelly, who had lightened her hair for her role. TOP GUN became the top moneymaker of that year, with box-office grosses of more than $176.7 million.

In the supporting cast of TOP GUN, playing Wolfman, was actor Barry Tubb, with whom Kelly had moved to Los Angeles in the summer of 1985 and whom she would marry. By October 1986 she was in Washington, D.C., on stage in a production of Anton Chekhov's *The Sea Gull*, in the ingenue role of Nina. She remained with the play until January 1986. Meanwhile, on television she was the narrator of "SantaBear's First Christmas" (ABC-TV, November 22, 1986), a half-hour "Weekend Special" dealing with a young snow bear at the North Pole who is separated from his family. (She would also be heard in "SantaBear's Highflying Adventure" on CBS-TV on December 24, 1987.)

In early 1987 Kelly was awaiting the development of Jack Nicholson's long-anticipated THE TWO JAKES (1990), the sequel to CHINATOWN (1974). She was to play the part of the daughter. However, by the time the mystery went in front of the camera in 1989, the role was played by Meg Tilly. Meanwhile, her relationship with Barry Tubb had ended and she was involved romantically in New York City with actor Don Yesso. At the same time she bought a home in the Park Slope section of Brooklyn and told interviewers of little girls who rang her doorbell asking, "Is Tom [Cruise] here?" Later in the year she was seen on theater screens with darkened tresses as Annie Packert, a lost soul in heaven later reborn as Ally Chandler in MADE IN HEAVEN (1987), co-starring Timothy Hutton. The fantasy romance was unsuccessful.

She went to Israel to make a film in which she was top-billed for the first time. She played a 1920s Viennese doctor who takes up the pioneer life with other Jews in Palestine. Helmed by Israeli director Uri Barbarsh and co-starring John Shea, the movie was in limited release during 1987 as DREAMERS (it was also known as ONCE WE WERE DREAMERS). Later it would show up at Jewish film festivals and on video as UNSETTLED LAND.

In the spring of 1988 McGillis spent a few weeks in Washington, D.C., performing as Portia in *The Merchant of Venice* with the Folger Library theater company, considered one of the finest Shakespearean troupes in the world. At the time, she was engaged to marry French television producer Michel Thoulouze, but the liaison ended after a few months.

Because of its taut climactic scenes, THE HOUSE ON CARROLL STREET (1988) was often compared to Alfred Hitchcock's films. However, it was critiqued by *Premiere* magazine as being "only good enough to make us wish it were better." This thriller had Kelly top-billed, over Jeff Daniels, as a 1950s political activist discovering that Nazi scientists are being smuggled into the United States. To research her role, she read as much as she could find on the Senator Joseph McCarthy Communist witch-hunt period. Her performance in THE HOUSE ON CARROLL STREET is quite believable, but she and the cast were thwarted by the sluggish script. With modest box-office receipts, THE HOUSE ON CARROLL STREET was another cinematic failure in her stalled movie career.

For THE ACCUSED (1988), Kelly had the starring role of an ambitious, articulate assistant district attorney, defending a rape victim (Jodie Foster) with a troubled past. After the rapists receive light court sentences, the belatedly empathetic McGillis brings to trial several of the cheering onlookers to the crime. McGillis underplayed her part in deference to Foster's showier performance. The critically acclaimed feature won a Best Actress Oscar for Foster. Following the October 1988 release of this controversial movie, Kelly went public about her own harrowing rape experience of 1982. Thereafter, she spoke regularly at colleges and to women's groups about rape prevention and recovery.

"The whole world celebrates our anniversary," Kelly said after her New Year's Eve marriage, on December 31, 1988, to yacht broker Fred Tillman, off the coast of Miami. Their honeymoon was spent delivering a motor yacht from Florida to San Diego.

Shot partly in Banner Elk, North Carolina, WINTER PEOPLE (1989) paired Kelly, as an unwed mother with a secret, with Kurt Russell, as a widowed clock maker who falls in love with her amid an Appalachian blood feud. Although advertisements read, "A passion so strong it kills," the brooding character study did not attract movie theater audiences, and within five months it was relegated to home video. As a part of her continuing campaign (and self-therapy) to educate Americans about the effects of rape, she appeared on PBS-TV's "Late Night America" in "Crime Victims"; then hosted "Against Her Will," a Lifetime–Cable special shown on June 8, 1989; and was on the Fox network's "The Reporters" on June 10, 1989, in the segment "The Criminal Justice System." CAT CHASER (1989), a little-seen film that went almost directly to videocassette distribution, is a convoluted caper picture based on an Elmore Leonard novel. In the complex storyline, Peter Weller, who runs a seedy Florida motel, rekindles a romance with an old flame (McGillis) from Detroit, when they meet in the Dominican Republic. He has returned there to exorcise nightmares engendered when he served as a U.S. Marine during the American intervention of 1965. She did another children's special, "Thumbelina," which aired on Showtime–Cable on September 12, 1989.

In September 1989 Kelly revealed that she and Tillman were building a home in North Carolina because "I like it there a lot," having spent weeks in the southern state shooting both REUBEN, REUBEN and WINTER PEOPLE. Early in October 1989 she rejoined the Folger Library Repertory Company in Washington, D.C., intending to remain for its entire season of four classical plays, earning a weekly salary of $575. She began with *Twelfth Night*. The *Washington Post* praised her performance: "Plucky and precise, her voice musically varied, she makes a charming Viola." This production, which closed on November 19, 1989, was followed by *The Tempest*, in which she had a small role. Thereafter, her physician found that she was two months pregnant and recommended that she not proceed with the scheduled *Mary Stuart* and *The Merry Wives of Windsor*. Her condition also forced her to withdraw from Blake Edwards's comedy SWITCH (1991), in which she was replaced by Ellen Barkin. On December 14, 1989, in Washington, D.C., Kelly co-hosted the twelfth annual Kennedy Center Honors, a tribute to Harry Belafonte,

Claudette Colbert, Alexandra Danilova, Mary Martin, and William Schuman, telecast on CBS-TV.

While awaiting the birth of her child in 1990, she made plans to produce and act in GRAND ISLE (forthcoming, 1991). This romantic drama, set in early nineteenth-century Louisiana, was directed by Mary Lambert. "This isn't something I always strove to do," she explained of this career choice. "I turned to it out of artistic necessity. I got to the point where I wanted more control over my work." Shot in late 1990 in Thibodaux, Louisiana, with additional filming in New Orleans and Destin, Florida, the film is based on Kate Chopin's feminist classic, *The Awakening*. The cast includes Kelly, Adrian Pasdar, Ellen Burstyn, Julian Sands, and Glenne Headly.

On one occasion, Kelly told the press, "I would like to do something brand new that nobody's ever done before." She had her chance with BEFORE AND AFTER EDITH (1991), in which she played a murderess in 1918 Vienna pursued by police inspector Gary Oldman. As the killer, she castrates her victims.

Called an "alarmingly compulsive chain smoker" by one interviewer, Kelly McGillis, heralded by critic Roger Ebert as an "instant star" after WITNESS, is not a gregarious Hollywood type. "I don't run in that crowd," she says, preferring not to wear makeup off stage and driving a vintage Volkswagen Beetle convertible over the rugged roads of rural North Carolina.

Filmography

Reuben, Reuben (20th–Fox, 1983)
Sweet Revenge (CBS-TV, 10/31/84)
Private Sessions (NBC-TV, 3/18/85)
Witness (Par, 1985)
Top Gun (Par, 1986)
Made in Heaven (Lorimar, 1987)
Dreamers [Once We Were Dreamers/Unsettled Land] (Hemdale, 1987)
The House on Carroll Street (Orion, 1988)

The Accused (Par, 1988)
Winter People (Col, 1989)
Cat Chaser (Vestron, 1989)

Future Releases

Before and After Edith (1991)
Grand Isle (Turner Pictures, 1991) (also producer)

Album Discography

SantaBear's First Christmas (Windham Hill WH-0700) [ST-TV]

Thumbelina (Windham Hill WH-0712) [ST-TV]

BILL MURRAY

"I'm actually a better person when I'm making movies, because I'm
really trying to be there, be somebody all the time. But am I happy?
Nobody wants to ask me that. Nobody cares!"
                              —*Tower Video Collector*, December 1989

BEHIND THE SCRUFFINESS, LOOKING AS THOUGH HE HAS MISPLACED
both razor and comb, is a highly moral, well-mannered gentleman with a genuine sense of
unpredictable humor. "Anybody can get a laugh. I'm interested in making sense," he says.
Yet he tosses off good-natured barbs, like this one to the New York doorman at his former
posh East Side apartment building: "Hey, great shoes! You make those in prison?" Noted
for his deadpan face and zany irreverence, Murray gained initial experience at the Second
City comedy club and on TV's "Saturday Night Live," both of which spawned many
successful celebrities. In Hollywood, he became one of the screen's most bankable actors.
At the same time, he denounced Hollywood big shots, stating, "They're all on the decency
committees and they are the biggest thieves and crooks in the world."

A long, lucrative career has been predicted for Bill Murray. However, he views his
success as an accident, for he has never craved a niche in the acting profession. As with
Kurt Russell, it would surprise no one if he wore a bumper sticker across his broad
forehead reading, "I'd rather be baseballing." *GQ* magazine once described him as a "joint
reincarnation of Groucho Marx and Clark Gable": Groucho because of his manic energy,
Gable for his laid-back demeanor and sometimes almost handsomeness. He is a complex
performer, who settled on his forte in comedy after taking a risk in a drama that fizzled.
Along with fellow "Saturday Night Live" alumni—Dan Aykroyd, Martin Short, Eddie
Murphy—he is one of Hollywood's funniest stars.

William Murray, known for years as Billy, was born on Thursday, September 21,
1950, the fifth of nine children. His parents—Ed Murray, a lumber company salesman,
and his wife, Lucille—were lower-middle-class residents of Wilmette, Illinois, an affluent
suburb of Chicago. He considers himself to have been his family's black sheep for having
created more problems for his parents than all of his siblings combined. He grew up
surrounded by humor. Both his father and grandfather were considered very funny men,
but he did not realize that his mother shared this attribute until he became an adult and
took the time to really listen to her.

He received his basic education at St. Joseph's parochial school in Wilmette
through the stern tutelage of Franciscan nuns. He was ejected by the Boy Scouts, as well as
the Catholic Altar Boys Society, for his rebellious antics. Gradually he learned to mix

humor with his questionable behavior, thinking it might lessen any punishment he would receive. He played Little League softball, happy to get out of the classroom. His boredom with and dislike of studies ("I had no interest in getting good grades," he would say years later) carried over into high school, the Loyola Academy for Boys in Wilmette, operated by Jesuit priests. To help his parents pay for his Catholic education, he was forced to work as a golf caddy and later in a pizza parlor. He became intrigued with show business after playing the role of Lieutenant Keefer in the school's production of *The Caine Mutiny Court-Martial.* He auditioned for *The Music Man* as well, because there were girls from another school in the cast. He performed as a member of the musical's barbershop quartet.

In December 1969, while Bill was a high school junior, his father died of a heart attack. Money now was scarcer than ever; the older children worked at whatever jobs they could get. After graduating from high school in January 1970, Bill remained at home for a few months, considering whether to study medicine or to become a minor league ball player. He chose the former, enrolling at the Jesuit-run Regis College in Denver, where his activities focused more on experimenting with soft drugs than on the pre-med curriculum. Charges stemming from his arrest in Sterling, Colorado, for alleged possession of marijuana were dropped for lack of evidence, but he quit college at the end of his first semester. A few weeks later he was again arrested, this time at Chicago's O'Hare International Airport, for carrying a suitcase containing eight pounds of marijuana. Found guilty, he was placed on probation.

His brother Brian, five years his senior, was living in Old Town, Chicago's hippie district, and was involved actively with the Second City comedy troupe, where he was known as Brian Doyle-Murray. Through him Bill met John Belushi and Harold Ramis, also with Second City, and entered the group's workshop. In 1974, Belushi, who had gone ahead of them to New York, recruited both Murray brothers, along with Gilda Radner and Chevy Chase, for "The National Lampoon Radio Hour," taped in New York and heard nationally in syndication. As a lark, Bill hired on as an extra leaning against a barroom wall in the New York–filmed NEXT STOP, GREENWICH VILLAGE (1975), which is his motion picture debut, albeit in as inconspicuous a part as possible.

From radio, the cast members went into the cabaret stage revue *The National Lampoon Show,* produced by Canadian Ivan Reitman. After touring Philadelphia, Ontario, and Long Island, the show opened in New York at the New Palladium bar/ restaurant on March 23, 1975, where it played 180 performances. While Radner, Chase, and Belushi were chosen by another Canadian producer, Lorne Michaels, to help create NBC-TV's "Saturday Night Live," iconoclastic sportscaster Howard Cosell selected the Murray brothers to appear sporadically in his ABC-TV show "Saturday Night with Howard Cosell," which premiered on September 23, 1975. Upon the cancellation of Cosell's variety program in January 1976, Bill went to Los Angeles to provide a touch of comedy to TV documentaries.

Lorne Michaels asked him to return East, however, as a member of the "Not Ready for Prime Time Players" on "Saturday Night Live," as the replacement for Chevy Chase, beginning in January 1977. Murray would remain with the series through March 1980. In his three years on the show he created silly characters that included Nick the Lounge Singer, Todd DiLaMucca, a noogie-giving nerd, a hip movie critic, and a gossip columnist. Many of these people were sleazy and boorish. The most controversial sketch in which he participated was "The Nerds' Nativity," broadcast December 22, 1979, with Bill as Joseph and Gilda Radner as Mary doing a high school nativity pageant. It was not certain that the network would permit the sketch, but it was finally approved, with changes made to the dialogue up to the last second. Critic Pauline Kael likened the Bill Murray of "Saturday Night Live" to "something out of a swamp—cold-blooded and sweaty," but Lorne Michaels has called him "the best" and has praised his "athletic grace." Of his tenure on the hit show, Bill has said, "People think that working on 'Saturday Night Live' was fun. It was a *nightmare*—the most high-pressure job I ever had in my life."

During 1977 he began work on a film called COMING ATTRACTIONS, a spoof of movie reviews, which was not distributed until March 1979. It was subsequently rereleased a year later as LOOSE SHOES to capitalize on his name, which was by then well known.

Still not certain that show business was to be his destiny, Murray was in Oregon in the summer of 1978 playing third base with the Gray Harbor Loggers, a Class A Northwest League baseball team. After several attempts, his Canadian mentor, Ivan Reitman, was able to entice him away from the baseball diamond to star in MEATBALLS (1979), filmed in Ontario, Canada, on a $1.5 million budget. Released in June, it ultimately grossed $64 million at the domestic box office. Its success surprised Murray, who had approached the slapstick project with, "I figured at worst I could get free practice at being in movies" and "Ivan convinced me that if it was no good, it would never be seen in America." (Bill did not appear in any of the several MEATBALLS movie follow-ups.)

Cast members of "Saturday Night Live" joined forces with other New York–based actors for MR. MIKE'S MONDO VIDEO (1979). This was followed by SHAME OF THE JUNGLE (1979), an animated spoof of Tarzan movies, originally made by a Belgian cartoonist and rewritten for American audiences by "Saturday Night Live" writers with voices dubbed by Bill, John Belushi, Brian Doyle-Murray, and Johnny Weissmuller, Jr. As a favor to his pal Steve Martin, who had conceived the story, Bill took a cameo role in THE JERK (1979) as an effeminate Jewish interior decorator.

With his "Saturday Night Live" sketches behind him, in 1980 Murray starred as an underground journalist in WHERE THE BUFFALO ROAM, a comedy that was understood by few and quickly forgotten by all. At the same time, with Chevy Chase, Rodney Dangerfield, Ted Knight, and Brian Doyle-Murray, he was in CADDYSHACK (1980). Bill played a brain-damaged Vietnam veteran chasing gophers around the golf course of a posh country club. This "slob humor" comedy grossed a surprising $20.5 million at the domestic box office. (Bill was among those who refused to appear in the lackluster sequel in 1989.)

On January 21, 1981, in a civil ceremony, he married his high school sweetheart, Margaret "Mickey" Kelly, a television talk show talent coordinator. Two months later, on March 25, 1981, in a ceremony arranged by his nun sister, they were joined in holy matrimony in the eyes of the Catholic Church. The couple took up residence in two rented homes, at Sneden's Landing, New York (a popular hideaway for the theater crowd), and in a Manhattan apartment.

For his ninth motion picture, again teamed with Ivan Reitman and Harold Ramis, Bill had top billing in STRIPES (1981), in which he was a loser who joins the U.S. Army. Made for an estimated $10 million from a script co-written by Ramis, with rewrites contributed by Bill, the comedy grossed over $85.2 million domestically, making it the fifth biggest moneymaker of the year. As a result, Quigley Publications listed Bill as the #10 box-office draw of 1981.

In 1982 Mickey Murray gave birth to the couple's first child, Homer Bank William, named after the Chicago Cubs baseball player Ernie Banks. A second son, Luke, would be born in 1985.

For TOOTSIE (1982), in which he played the frustrated playwright roommate of Dustin Hoffman, Bill requested that his name not be used in any prerelease advertising, lest potential audiences be led to expect that the movie was another MEATBALLS or STRIPES. TOOTSIE went on to become Columbia Pictures' biggest box-office hit up to that time, with grosses of $177.2 million, and the #2 sensation of 1982. The following year, Bill struck a deal with Columbia to co-star in the Dan Aykroyd–Harold Ramis screenplay of GHOSTBUSTERS (1984), originally written with John Belushi in mind, if he would then be allowed to do a remake of W. Somerset Maugham's THE RAZOR'S EDGE (1946). The studio agreed reluctantly. Produced/directed by Ivan Reitman, GHOSTBUSTERS followed the misadventures of a trio of wacky "paranormal investigators" who help rid New York City of unwanted spirits and ghosts. The film's total income was tabulated at $220.8 million, making it the #2 smash of 1984. Bill Murray was now a top star in Hollywood.

In NOTHING LASTS FOREVER (1984), made in 1981, he took another cameo role, as a cruise director. Produced by Lorne Michaels and directed by Tom Schiller (also a "Saturday Night Live" behind-the-scenes figure), the gimmicky film had a cast that included Imogene Coca, Eddie Fisher, Mort Sahl, and Dan Aykroyd. This mishmash was only in brief release. After GHOSTBUSTERS, Bill could command $2 million per film, but he was so eager to do drama—not only as a change of pace, but also in an effort to thwart typecasting—that he took no salary at all for acting in THE RAZOR'S EDGE (1984). His fee was just $12,000 for co-writing the screenplay. His starring role, handled by Tyrone Power in the earlier film version of the story, was that of a World War I veteran undertaking an odyssey of self-discovery and constantly questioning the meaning of life. "I'm terrified," he admitted at the time, "but maybe when people see the movie, the possibilities for me as an actor will be different." On completing the film, he went to Paris where he spent a year studying French at the Sorbonne. Unfortunately for Murray, not many people bothered to see the new, anachronistic THE RAZOR'S EDGE, which featured his brother Brian in a supporting role. Those who did view the rambling drama, like critic Molly Haskell (*Playgirl* magazine), found it "gassy." *Variety*, in a kind review, acknowledged, "His essentially irreverent, iconoclastic attitude does bring unexpected and pleasant wrinkles to his characterization." However, most other critics found Murray inexpressive and overly glum on camera. Except for his cameo role as Arthur Denton in LITTLE SHOP

OF HORRORS (1986), Bill did not make another movie for four years. He was too embarrassed by the failure of THE RAZOR'S EDGE.

During 1985–1986 he became part owner of two minor league baseball teams: the Salt Lake City (Utah) Trappers and the Pittsfield (Massachusetts) Cubs. Following his teams' games, which he viewed from the dugout, he generally tended bar at local taverns as a form of unwinding. He appeared on a baseball card wearing uniform #29, identified as "Bill Murray Team Owner." In 1987 he filled in for regular Chicago Cubs play-by-play broadcaster Harry Caray for a game in the Windy City with the San Diego Padres. Meanwhile, he was one of the guest stars on CBS-TV's "Bugs Bunny/Looney Tunes All-Star 50th Anniversary," aired on January 14, 1986. LEGAL EAGLES (1986), a movie said to have been conceived for Dustin Hoffman and Murray, went instead to Robert Redford and Debra Winger, while DIRTY ROTTEN SCOUNDRELS (1988), intended for Bill and Steve Martin, became a Martin and Michael Caine vehicle.

Murray was finally enticed back to the screen by a script based on Charles Dickens's "A Christmas Carol." However, before the release of SCROOGED in November 1988, he joined John Candy, Mandy Patinkin, Ray Liotta, and Brian Murray in a reportedly "hilarious" reading of a one-act play about baseball at the New York Shakespeare Festival's Public Theatre in Manhattan. For the most part, SCROOGED received favorable notices. *People* magazine wrote, "Bill Murray, you nut, you've pulled it off." *US* magazine commended him "for his bravery and for this wry Christmas comeback." The too violent low point of the satirical comedy occurs when Carol Kane, as the Ghost of Christmas Present, kicks him in the crotch, smacks him across the head with a toaster, and socks him in the jaw.

Columbia Pictures waited too long in getting GHOSTBUSTERS II (1989) into movie theaters. Released nationwide in June, it was in fierce summer box-office competition with BATMAN and INDIANA JONES AND THE LAST CRUSADE and grossed a relatively soft $112 million. Again under Ivan Reitman's direction, the original cast members were reassembled to fight demon slime in Manhattan. Pauline Kael (*The New Yorker* magazine) noted that Bill "can perform casual miracles with a simple joke" and also mentioned that he had "mellowed" but was no less funny. Most found this follow-up to be disappointingly predictable and unspontaneous, with the cast looking bored. Bill took an up-front salary of $25,000 for repeating his role, with an additional deal to receive fifteen percent of net profit.

In August 1989, with Robert De Niro, Sean Penn, Mikhail Baryshnikov, and others, Bill financially backed the Tribeca Bar & Grill on the first floor of an eight-story building in Lower Manhattan converted by De Niro into his film production center. A few months later, for a reported $7 million, Murray purchased a mansion at Sneden's Landing, a home formerly owned by actress Katharine Cornell. He paid tribute to his comic beginnings in the New York–produced NBC-TV comedy special "Saturday Night Live 15th Anniversary" (September 24, 1989). At the time, it was mentioned that Lorne Michaels was talking with NBC about a theatrical movie with the show's cast that would be "the funniest movie of the '90s."

Murray was one of those who turned down AIR AMERICA (1990) as well as ONE GOOD COP (1991) in order to co-direct (with Howard Franklin) and co-produce QUICK CHANGE (1990), in which he and co-stars Geena Davis and Randy Quaid were three New Yorkers who rob a bank but find that the robbery was more easily accomplished than getting through New York City to an airport to escape to the Caribbean. They can't even find a cab driver who speaks English. The story was originally a 1983 best-selling novel by Jay Cronley entitled *Quick*, which had been adapted as the French film HOLD-UP (1985), starring Jean-Paul Belmondo. That film had been brought to Bill's attention by Frederic Golchan, who would be the new film's executive producer. Generally well received by critics ("a comfy lived-in feel," *Newsweek* magazine; "highly entertaining," *Hollywood Reporter*, "smart, sardonic and very funny," *Daily Variety*), the film appealed largely to adults. Released in the summer of 1990, the film had by September earned just $14.6 million domestically (it had cost about $15 million to make).

In WHAT ABOUT BOB? (1991), a comedy written by Tom Schulman (who provided the screenplays for 1989's DEAD POETS SOCIETY and HONEY, I SHRUNK THE KIDS), Bill plays an extremely neurotic man who drives his psychiatrist (Richard Dreyfuss) frantic.

Having achieved show business success, Murray has his own perspective on his achievements. "No one is raised by their parents to be prepared for what happens when you become famous. . . . It's bullshit to hear people whine and complain about their success, and I don't like to hear about it." When asked to differentiate between working in television and in movies, Murray says, "They're two different mediums and you can't

Sigourney Weaver and **Bill Murray** in GHOSTBUSTERS II (1989).

compare them. On TV, there's just not that much that can go wrong—you only have to be good for five minutes at a time. But in movies, there's a million things that can go wrong. It's a lot more complicated."

Filmography

Next Stop, Greenwich Village (20th–Fox, 1975)
Meatballs (Par, 1979)
Mr. Mike's Mondo Video (New Line, 1979)
Coming Attractions [Loose Shoes] (National-American, 1979) [made in 1977]
Shame of the Jungle (International Harmony, 1979) (voice only)
The Jerk (Univ, 1979)
Caddyshack (Orion, 1980)
Where the Buffalo Roam (Univ, 1980)
Stripes (Col, 1981)
Tootsie (Col, 1982)

Ghostbusters (Col, 1984)
Nothing Lasts Forever (MGM/UA, 1984) [made in 1981]
The Razor's Edge (Col, 1984) (also co-screenplay)
Little Shop of Horrors (WB, 1986)
Scrooged (Par, 1988)
Ghostbusters II (Col, 1989)
Quick Change (WB, 1990) (also co-producer, co-director)
What About Bob? (BV, 1991)

Radio Series

The National Lampoon Radio Hour (Synd, 1974)

Television Series

Saturday Night Live (NBC, 1977–80)

Album Discography

NBC's Saturday Night Live (Arista ALB6-8435)

MANDY PATINKIN

"... frankly I want to do it all. I want to be a character guy, I want
to play leading-man parts, I want to work in theater, I want to work
in film. And I'm lucky to have options open to me."
  —*Hollywood Reporter*, October 31, 1988

ADMITTEDLY A HIGHLY SELF-CRITICAL INDIVIDUAL, WHO BREAKS OUT
in hives before a performance, Mandy Patinkin aims to be less obsessive about acting, to
not dwell endlessly on the playing of a scene. Director Rob Reiner once told him, "Get out
of your way, man." It was good advice, and Mandy has resolved to follow it forever.
Marginally successful in feature films, he is a male counterpart to Meryl Streep in his use of
accents, employing them, along with full beards and bushy hair, as a mask. His enormous
reserve of nervous energy bursts forth in his singing, setting him apart from most other
singers in his concerts and spectacular solo recordings of one hundred years of American
show tunes. Stephen Sondheim calls his musical voice "brilliant," with "a working two-
octave range, up and down to G-sharp." In response, the self-effacing Mandy has said, "If
I knew what that meant it would really scare me. I don't read music. I just know when it
goes up and down."
  Mandel Patinkin was born on the South Side of Chicago on Sunday, November 30,
1952, to Lester Patinkin, a scrap metal dealer, and his wife, Doris Sinton Patinkin. Two
years later, a second child, daughter Marsha, was born. Called Mandy from the start, the
boy grew up surrounded by the music of the Beatles as well as the cantorial singing in the
synagogue his family attended. He went to private schools in Chicago but found that he
hated being confined to schoolwork. For a short while, to please his father, he played Little
League ball, but quit after getting hit in the face with a hard-driven ball. He turned to what
he loved most—singing and music. Between the ages of nine and fourteen, he sang in the
choir of Rodfi Zedek Temple, where he basked in the attention bestowed upon him by the
entire Jewish community for his God-given voice and his use of the "cry" to give dramatic
impact to the Hebrew liturgical music.
  During high school, partly to get away from studies, he joined a Chicago community theater group where he acted and sang in musical presentations. In September 1970, at
the age of eighteen, he enrolled at the University of Kansas at Lawrence to study acting.
However, after two years he decided he was not learning quickly enough and quit to go to
New York City, the hub of the acting universe. There he was a theater student at the
Juilliard School for two years. By 1974 he found the constantly demanding schedule of
classes, rehearsals, and performance too oppressive. He left Juilliard.

At the age of twenty-two, after having pulled himself free forever of classroom constraints, he went to work for Joseph Papp's New York Shakespeare Festival, at the same time doing double duty with the Hudson Guild Theatre. At Papp's Public Theatre, he performed in *Henry IV, Part I* as Hotspur, in the title role of *Hamlet*, in *Rebel Women* and *Leave It to Beaver Is Dead*. At the Hudson Guild he acted in *Savages*. In April 1977 he made his Broadway debut at the Morosco Theatre in Michael Cristofer's 1977 Pulitzer Prize–winning play, *The Shadow Box*, in the supporting role of the male lover of a terminally ill writer (Laurence Luckinbill). It proved to be a fortuitous debut because the drama was given a Tony Award as the Best Play of the 1976–1977 Broadway season.

In 1978 Mandy expanded his repertoire to include television by first appearing in "That Thing on ABC" (January 4, 1978), a sixty-minute variety special featuring comedians recruited from across the United States. *Variety* noted, "Of the group, [Denny] Evans and Mandy Patinkin showed the most versatility (both sticking out in the show's high spot sketch about two white guys applying for a job at a black record company)." He had a small role in NBC's "Hallmark Hall of Fame" sixty-minute dramatic special "Taxi" (February 2, 1978), in which Martin Sheen and Eva Marie Saint starred as a cabdriver and passenger. He was called back to ABC for its sequel to "That Thing," called "That Second Thing on ABC" (March 8, 1978). He was also among the supporting cast of "Sparrow" (1978), an unsold two-episode ABC-TV pilot for a detective series set in New Orleans. Meanwhile, Patinkin continued with stage work. He starred off-Broadway in *Split*, acting opposite Kathryn Grody, with whom he began a two-year live-in relationship. They would marry on June 15, 1980, and produce sons Isaac in 1983 and Gideon in 1987.

Mandy's first taste of filmmaking was in THE BIG FIX (1978), starring Richard Dreyfuss, as one of many in the crowd of 1960s campus radicals in a flashback scene. On the small screen, he received exposure in a large role in CHARLESTON (NBC-TV, January 15, 1979), a miniature rip-off of GONE WITH THE WIND starring Delta Burke. For the big-screen thriller LAST EMBRACE (1979), he received thirteenth billing as "a commuter." He played Sayyid in Paramount's theatrical release FRENCH POSTCARDS (1979), a comedy about college students who go to Europe for a year. *Variety* reported, "Supporting cast is especially good, particularly Mandy Patinkin as a lecherous Iranian." By the time this latter film was released, Mandy's career had taken a definite turn for the better.

Twenty-six years after the death of Argentina's Eva Peron, an opera-drama of her tumultuous life, entitled *Evita*, was developed by composer Andrew Lloyd Webber and lyricist Tim Rice. They took a chance that the theater-going public would be interested in the controversial woman who rose from whoredom and poverty to become Argentina's larger-than-life first lady before dying at age thirty-two from cancer. After the operatic show had opened successfully in London in June 1978, stager Hal Prince decided to take another chance by casting unknowns in the two leading roles for the American edition. Patti LuPone was transformed into a dazzling Eva Duarte Peron while Mandy, in his first public singing appearance since high school, became the revolutionary. As Che Guevara, he was a Greek chorus of one who smirks, rages, and slinks across the stage in indignation at Eva's manipulative ways. *Evita* premiered in Los Angeles at the Dorothy Chandler

Pavilion on May 8, 1979, for a nine-week engagement, moved north to San Francisco in July after the cast was recorded by MCA Records, and opened in New York City at the Broadway Theatre on September 25. Mandy was commended for his high tenor voice, with *After Dark* magazine crediting him with delivering "a smashing and polished performance that sends *Evita* smoothly through its intricate patterns." Jack Kroll (*Newsweek* magazine) complimented the "vigor and urgency of Mandy Patinkin's excellent performance." On June 8, 1980, in ceremonies held at the Mark Hellinger Theatre, he was awarded a Tony for Outstanding Performance by a Featured Actor in a Musical. The show itself received the Best Musical honor along with several other awards, including Outstanding Director for Prince. Patinkin and Prince were also cited for distinguished achievement by the Los Angeles Drama Critics Circle in June.

Early one morning in 1979, following his regular *Evita* performance, Mandy appeared on New York television's "Midnight Special," a ninety-minute show that aired from 1 a.m. to 2:30 a.m., featuring musical performers from the worlds of rock, pop, and soul. On film in 1980 he was seen as a cabdriver in NIGHT OF THE JUGGLER, a grim portrait of New York City. Cinematically he stood out in RAGTIME (1981), directed by Miloš Forman from the E. L. Doctorow novel. In RAGTIME, Mandy is first seen in the brilliantly recreated turn-of-the-century New York City doing silhouette cutouts while his daughter (Jenny Nichols) is tethered to his thigh so no one will steal her. Later in the narrative, he becomes a film director who takes a special liking to an attractive, not quite liberated housewife/mother (Mary Steenburgen). In the final scene, he is shown driving her away from her staid husband (James Olson), with members of her family in the back seat, presumably off to California to make movies. Disguised behind a beard and accented broken English that has him saying, "I can do everything what your heart desires," he is outstanding in his interpretation of a poor immigrant whose talents are eventually recognized.

Patinkin's next movie was also taken from an E. L. Doctorow novel. *The Book of Daniel* was based loosely on the lives of Julius and Ethel Rosenberg, executed on June 19, 1953, as American Communist spies. Entitled DANIEL (1983), the low-budget adaptation was too serious for the average moviegoer. Timothy Hutton was the Daniel of the title, the truth-seeking son of the first-generation-American-Jewish radicals who were accused of passing atomic secrets to the Russians. In flashbacks, Mandy was his father, Paul Isaacson, a thinly veiled characterization of Julius Rosenberg.

For ten years after acquiring the rights to Isaac Bashevis Singer's short story "Yentl, the Yeshiva Boy," Barbra Streisand attempted unsuccessfully to interest Hollywood in a movie version. Finally, after forming her own production company, she approached the project with full steam. She co-wrote the screenplay, along with co-producing and directing the screen musical. Mandy auditioned for Streisand at her New York apartment for the male lead of Avigdor, and "he totally surprised me with his original approach. He was unpredictable, emotionally volatile and very gifted and that was exciting for me as a director." Photographed largely in Czechoslovakia, YENTL (1983) was the account of an Eastern European girl in 1904, a time when books and studying were reserved for men.

Women were allowed to gaze at picture books, but to do nothing more cerebral. Yentl (Streisand) wants more, so she disguises herself as a boy of seventeen in order to enter a yeshiva, an orthodox Jewish school. There she meets handsome Avigdor who becomes her mentor and with whom she falls in love, not revealing her true identity to him until nearly the end of the 134-minute picture. By this point, she has married the girl (Amy Irving) he loves, in order to be near him. The overly long production is handled fairly well, although the focus is always on (the very mannered) Streisand. In January 1984, YENTL was honored by the Hollywood Foreign Press Association with Golden Globe Awards for Best Motion Picture—Musical or Comedy and for Streisand as Best Director—Motion Picture. Although Mandy was nominated for a Golden Globe Award in the Best Performance by an Actor in a Motion Picture Musical or Comedy category, he lost to Michael Caine for EDUCATING RITA. Except for two nominations in the Song and Score categories, YENTL was snubbed by the Academy of Motion Picture Arts and Sciences for the Oscars. This caused Streisand fans, on the night of the award ceremonies, to picket the proceedings with banners reading, "Oscar, Do You Hear Me?" Critic Roger Ebert credited Mandy (once again with a beard), along with the feminine leads, with possessing "cheerful high energy." *People* magazine endorsed Mandy's performance with, "Mandy Patinkin contributes a star-making performance as the student Yentl loves." Ironically, of the thirteen musical numbers that remained in YENTL, none featured Patinkin.

Continuing to balance his film and stage work, Mandy returned to the theater in May 1984 at Broadway's Booth Theatre in Stephen Sondheim and James Lapine's Pulitzer Prize–winning *Sunday in the Park with George*, produced by the Shubert Organization and Emanuel Azenberg. Patinkin portrayed the French artist Georges Seurat, whose painting "A Sunday Afternoon on the Island of La Grande Jatte" (1884–1886) was the inspiration for composer/lyricist Sondheim. Before starting rehearsals for the James Lapine–directed show, Mandy returned to Chicago, where Seurat's painting has hung for years in the Art Institute, and spent hours in front of the painting. He later told *The New York Times* that he felt inhabited by Seurat's ghost, and that at age thirty-one, he was the same age as the artist at the time of his death in 1891. He also noted, "I even look like the guy, too. I get a little freaked about how much I look like him." Both he and his musical co-star, Bernadette Peters, were nominated for Tony Awards, but lost out respectively to George Hearn and Chita Rivera. *Sunday in the Park with George* was taped for showing on television, first playing on Showtime–Cable on February 18, 1986. *People* magazine rated Mandy's video performance as "perfect." The production was rebroadcast in June 1986 on PBS-TV.

In critic Judith Crist's words, MAXIE (1985) was "pure pleasure," offering "fun, fantasy and charm." Mandy co-starred in this film as Nick, the patient, beardless loving husband of Jan (Glenn Close). Periodically she is possessed by a dead and mischievous spirit named Maxie, a 1920s Hollywood flapper. However, MAXIE failed to click with audiences. Mandy was next hired to play the leading male role of famed reporter Carl Bernstein opposite Meryl Streep's Nora Ephron in HEARTBURN (1986), a fictionalized account of their stormy marriage. However, due to "artistic differences," he was fired after the first day of shooting by director Mike Nichols and was replaced by Jack Nicholson.

On September 6 and 7, 1985, Mandy joined what has been called "a powerhouse cast" (including Barbara Cook, Lee Remick, and George Hearn) in concert at Avery Fisher Hall at New York City's Lincoln Center. The occasion was a special concert presentation, directed by Herbert Ross, of *Follies*, Stephen Sondheim's 1971 musical, which has become a cult classic. Seats for the benefit performances had a top ticket price of $500. Mandy sang the role of Buddy Plummer, a former stage door Johnny who went on to become a traveling oil salesman. Buddy has a girl in every town, although he is married to Sally (Barbara Cook). Standing stage center the first night to sing "Buddy's Blues," Mandy stopped the conductor of the New York Philharmonic Orchestra to confess "I'm a little nervous" to the audience, which gave him a big round of applause. "That helped," he has said, and he went on to give a powerful rendition of the song. A film based on the concert, to which rehearsal scenes and interviews were added, was shown for ninety minutes as "Follies in Concert" on PBS-TV on March 14, 1986, narrated by Roy Scheider. Later it was released on home video.

In January 1986 Mandy traveled to London to Henry Wood Hall for a closed-mike recording of tunes from Rodgers and Hammerstein's immortal Broadway hit *South Pacific*. Backed by the London Symphony Orchestra with the renowned Ambrosian Singers, he had the role of Lieutenant Cable and sang "Younger Than Springtime" and "Carefully Taught." Others in the newly assembled cast included José Carreras, Kiri Te Kanawa, and Sarah Vaughan, respectively handling the roles performed by Ezio Pinza, Mary Martin, and Juanita Hall in the original Broadway edition. A videotape of the recording session was released later in the year.

Mandy Patinkin in THE PRINCESS BRIDE (1987).

Mandy turned down the lead in the original London production of *Phantom of the Opera* (1986) because it would have meant relocating his family for a long period of time. Instead, after having been "ostracized" by Hollywood for a year after his dismissal by Mike Nichols, he returned to moviemaking with THE PRINCESS BRIDE (1987). This was an offbeat romantic comedy directed by Rob Reiner from the William Goldman fairy tale story. In second billing he was Inigo Montoya, a Spanish swordsman with long hair, drooping moustache, and an accent. *Premiere* magazine called his performance a "saving grace . . . truly one of the best in this fantasy tale." The movie grossed a decent $13.5 million in domestic film rentals. This was followed by THE HOUSE ON CARROLL STREET (1988), described by the *Hollywood Reporter* as "a surprisingly tedious, disappointingly dusty offering." It takes place in the 1950s when the Subversive Activities Control Act was the top priority of Joseph McCarthy's Senate Committee. With oil-slicked hair, Mandy was an anti-democratic Senate committeeman called "chillingly slippery, downright scary" by the *Hollywood Reporter*.

In June 1988, with pianist Paul Ford and musical director Paul Gemignani, with whom he had worked on "Follies in Concert", Mandy recorded for CBS Records twenty-four songs from theater and the movies, ranging from Gilbert and Sullivan's "Love, Unrequited, Robs Me of My Rest" (1882) to Stephen Sondheim's "No One Is Alone" (1987). The work is dedicated to his wife and sons, "who give me something to sing about." *Newsweek* magazine proclaimed of the album, called simply *Mandy Patinkin,* "No doubt of it, Patinkin has chutzpah" and "what's remarkable is Patinkin's straight, uncynical approach to music that went out with the rumble seat."

In October 1988, a few months before the release of his CBS album, he was definitely hidden behind makeup and veiny skull cap in ALIEN NATION. He was Samuel "George" Francisco, one of 250,000 aliens who crash land in the Mojave Desert from another planet. These "newcomers" are eventually accepted into the 1991 community of Los Angeles, some of them, like Samuel, a policeman, leading respectable lives, while others turn to crime. The *San Francisco Chronicle* gave Mandy what is probably his best review: "Patinkin is such a good actor that you could nail him into a fish crate and he'd act his way out of it—and superbly." This science fiction entry did not generate a lot of box-office business, but it was adapted for TV by the Fox network as a weekly series (1989), with Eric Pierpoint in Mandy's original role.

Also in October 1988, Mandy was slated to co-star with Al Pacino in CARLITO'S WAY, a project that was later shelved. That month, along with Bill Murray, John Candy, Ray Liotta, and Joan Cusack, Mandy read for Joseph Papp at New York's Public Theatre a one-act play by Marilyn Suzanne Miller, who wrote much of Gilda Radner's material for "Saturday Night Live." Of his screen work, Mandy in late 1988 said, "I hope that one day my range of choices increases, but if it doesn't, I'm not complaining either, because if I make one movie a year I'm OK." He also noted, "I never look the same and that is more interesting to me . . . I still try, no matter how I look, to put my own ideas, values and opinion in that character. . . . In a sense I'm only putting myself up there, but I like to wear a funny hat, have a little mask—it makes it easier for me." Oliver Stone and Meryl Streep had chosen Mandy to reprise his role of Che Guevara in a film adaptation of *Evita,* but this offer was cancelled when Streep withdrew from the project.

On February 27, 1989, Mandy acted off-Broadway at the Public Theatre for Joseph Papp in *The Winter's Tale* with Christopher Reeve. The latter found Patinkin "very self-effacing and humble." At the same time, Mandy undertook a series of six sold-out Monday-night concerts at the Public Theatre. The project, entitled *Mandy Patinkin in Concert: Dress Casual,* consisting of Broadway and Tin Pan Alley songs with Mandy accompanied by Paul Ford on piano, was such a hit that the revue moved to Broadway's Helen Hayes Theatre for a four-week engagement from July 25 through August 19, 1989. However, lovers of music and Patinkin on stage in sneakers and T-shirt demanded more, and the run was extended through September 12. *Drama-Logue* recorded, "It is thrilling to witness a major artist taking on a new dimension, and enriching both himself and the theatre to which he contributes." *The New Yorker* magazine called it "an evening of glorious song and good fun." In June 1990, when *Variety* listed the 1989–1990 Broadway productions that had thus far recouped their investments, Mandy's revue was one of five "hits" during the season.

On Christmas Day, 1989, on ABC-TV's "Today" show, Mandy joined the St. Thomas Boys' Choir of New York City in presenting Yuletide songs. In January 1990 he was back off-Broadway in rehearsals at The Second Stage for a new play with music by Steve Tesich, *Square One*. However, once again due to "artistic differences," this time with director Jerry Zaks, Patinkin was replaced. Richard Thomas opened in the show on January 26, 1990.

On June 15, 1990, the long-anticipated Warren Beatty (producer, director, star) film DICK TRACY, based on Chester Gould's comic strip characters, was in nationwide release. Beautifully re-creating the graphics of the comic strip with various optical effects, authentic sets and costumes, and fantastic makeup, the picture was credited by the *Hollywood Reporter* as being "more broadly entertaining and more thoughtfully conceived" than the megahit BATMAN (1989). However, by summer's end DICK TRACY had taken in only $100 million in domestic receipts, compared to BATMAN's $244 million for the same period a year earlier. As 88 Keys, the love-struck accompanist for sexy torch singer Breathless Mahoney (Madonna), Mandy sang in a movie for the first time. Beginning the Stephen Sondheim–composed song "What Can You Lose," he was joined in harmony by Madonna. Jack Mathews (*Los Angeles Times*) called the duet "lovely," while Eleanor Ringel (Cox News Service) observed that Madonna's singing was "fairly warped (especially compared to Mandy Patinkin's)." Patinkin was one of the few actors in the supporting cast not hidden by a prosthetic nose or rubber chin, lips, or ears.

Almost a month before the film's release, Madonna's album *I'm Breathless: Music from and Inspired by the Film "Dick Tracy"* was available to consumers; it included Mandy's duet with the blonde songstress. *L.A. Weekly*'s Arion Berger noted, "But at least *he* [Mandy] can sing," and the *Los Angeles Times* found that the song "nicely nails down the pretty side of things." The album enjoyed several weeks on the Top Ten Pop charts.

At the Hollywood Bowl on August 10 and 11, 1990, Mandy and Barbara Cook sang a program of songs by Rodgers and Hammerstein and other composers with Erich Kunzel conducting the Los Angeles Philharmonic Orchestra. Mandy, with beard and dressed in casual attire, took the stage during the first half to perform such songs as "Over the Rainbow," "Younger Than Springtime," and "Soliloquy" (from *Carousel*) in what *Daily Variety* noted "was musical theater at its best." After Cook's second-half presentation, the program ended in duets. The trade paper reported that "The sold-out audience response to the entire program was enthusiastic."

Mandy had a supporting role as a crooked real estate developer in TRUE COLORS (1991), a drama starring John Cusack and James Spader, with Richard Widmark and Dina Merrill in supporting roles. Although filmed in the fall of 1989, IMPROMPTU was not released until the spring of 1991. It provided a reunion with Bernadette Peters and with their *Sunday in the Park with George* director, James Lapine. The British-produced film was a new version of the story of the relationship between composer Frédéric Chopin (Hugh Grant) and freethinking novelist George Sand (Judy Davis). Patinkin was cast as jaunty poet Alfred de Musset. Duane Byrge (*Hollywood Reporter*) rated the movie "a diverting, parlor-like entertainment, a sugar and cookies and tea-type interlude. . . . Mandy Patinkin has fun with his role of loutish suitor, while Bernadette Peters fills out perfectly her seductress's role." *Variety* observed, "Bright playing, a bit broad at times but fitting the material, is pic's strongest suit. . . . Patinkin is adroitly used as plot catalyst." Meanwhile, Patinkin's new album, *Mandy Patinkin—Dress Casual,* devoted to a spectrum of American popular song, was released. In the Marsha Norman–Lucy Simon musical *The Secret Garden,* which bowed on Broadway in April 1991, Mandy had the leading male role. In THE DOCTOR (1991), Patinkin plays a slyly unethical pal of fellow physician William Hurt.

Back in 1979, when Mandy received so much attention and so many honors for *Evita,* he said that the acclaim came too soon, that he was not ready for it. Yet he admitted that he would like to become a Hollywood movie star. Years later, he seemed to have reassessed his career philosophy: "Take supporting parts, come back to New York and sing for a week, then do a play. In the end you'll be known for your body of work."

Filmography

The Big Fix (Univ, 1978)
Charleston (NBC-TV, 1/15/79)
Last Embrace (UA, 1979)
French Postcards (Par, 1979)
Night of the Juggler (Col, 1980)
Ragtime (Par, 1981)
Daniel (Par, 1983)
Yentl (MGM/UA, 1983)

Maxie (Orion, 1985)
The Princess Bride (20th–Fox, 1987)
The House on Carroll Street (Orion, 1988)
Alien Nation (20th–Fox, 1988)
Dick Tracy (BV, 1990)
True Colors (Par, 1991)
Impromptu (Hemdale, 1991)
The Doctor (BV, 1991)

Broadway Plays

The Shadow Box (1977)
Evita (1979)

Sunday in the Park with George (1984)
The Secret Garden (1991)

Album Discography

Evita (MCA MCA2-11007) [OC]
Follies in Concert (RCA HBC2-7128) [OC]
I'm Breathless: Music from and Inspired by the
    Film "Dick Tracy" (Sire 26209)

Mandy Patinkin (CBS FM-44943)
Mandy Patinkin—Dress Casual (CBS MK
    45998)
South Pacific (Columbia SM-42205)

Sunday in the Park with George (RC HBC1-
  5042) [OC]

Yentl (Columbia CK-39152) [ST]

SEAN PENN

"My animosity is a media-created thing. I've basically been able to
laugh it off. But an invasion of privacy is something else. At a certain
point you really get disgusted."—*American Film* magazine, April 1986

INITIALLY THROUGH CONNECTIONS WITHIN THE ENTERTAINMENT
industry, Hollywood doors were opened to Sean Penn. It is because of his great talent that
they have remained open. One of his generation's best actors, he stimulates those scenes in
which he appears. Through intense study of each character he portrays, he seems to
actually *become* the person he is enacting. Such craftsmanship leads to instant comparison
with Marlon Brando, James Dean, Montgomery Clift, and Robert De Niro. In 1985
Andy Warhol recognized him as another Dustin Hoffman who will "be around a long
time." Boasting thin lips, small eyes, and a fixed, brooding, pouting expression, Sean does
not possess the qualities of a romantic matinee idol. Rather, it is his arresting presence that
captures on-camera attention. On the other hand, his off-screen reputation has been
notorious, second to none. His bizarre behavior is founded in jealousy and a dislike for the
press. While co-workers claim that he is sweet, creative, and hard working, his public
image has been that of a surly, spoiled, temperamental, irascible, world-hating young man.
Like Kathleen Turner, he states that he owes the public nothing.

Preceded by brother Michael and followed by brother Christopher, Sean Penn was
born on Wednesday, August 17, 1960, in Santa Monica, California. His father was actor/
director Leo Penn and his mother was former actress Eileen Ryan Penn. In a climate
conducive to outdoor living, his early days were devoted solely to having fun. Surfing and
tennis were his major interests. Hating school, he continually got into minor scrapes with
the authorities, none of them amounting to much. He was introduced to movies at an
early age, seeing and liking everything that came along. He quickly decided he wanted to
become an actor. As a Christmas gift in 1976, Leo Penn gave his two younger sons a Super-
8 millimeter camera, which they immediately utilized to shoot violent cops-and-robbers
movies using anyone they could corral to act in them. Their most notable accomplishment
was an hour-long movie entitled LOOKING FOR SOMEONE, shot mostly at night in
deserted areas of Westwood with Sean performing what was considered spectacular stunt
work.

After graduating from Santa Monica High School in 1978, he was hired as a
production assistant (that is, a "gofer") with the Los Angeles Group Repertory Theatre,
where he also acted in *Earthworms*. He was permitted to direct a presentation of a one-act

play he had written, *Terrible Jim Fitch*, during the two years he spent with the company. As a favor to Leo Penn, director Kenneth C. Gilbert cast Sean in a 1978 episode of TV's "Barnaby Jones." He had one line: "Looks like she shoots horse to me, mainlining it." Sean did not want to face the camera, and Gilbert had to reshoot the bit after urging the young actor to look up. Thus, at the age of eighteen, Sean acquired his union acting card. After this TV debut, he negotiated a bit in "The Time of Your Life" (PBS-TV) as a singing newsboy, but was fired due to his lack of musical ability. In the CBS-TV movie THE CONCRETE COWBOYS (October 17, 1979), starring Jerry Reed and Tom Selleck, Penn had a small, unbilled role.

Peggy Feury, a renowned Los Angeles–based drama coach, was a friend of the Penn family. She did not like to take on students who were not college educated, but she dropped the requirement in Sean's case because "he already was really clear about what he wanted to do. . . . Just one little session, and I knew there was nothing to worry about." He was accepted as a student in her four-days-a-week, four-hours-a-day class. During this period, his mother advised him that, in order to feel a sense of strength during auditions for movies and TV, he should picture the producers as "not sitting at a desk, but sitting on a toilet." He got a small bit in the Leo Penn–directed CBS-TV movie HELLINGER'S LAW, telecast March 10, 1981, but had more to do the next evening in the same network's movie THE KILLING OF RANDY WEBSTER.

Finding commercials too disruptive of the flow of his television work, Sean bought a one-way ticket to New York City. He had an appointment, arranged by a mutual friend in Los Angeles, to audition with Art Wolff, the director of *Heartland*, due to open on Broadway. After a bad first attempt, he was permitted a second reading, again at the urging of the Los Angeles friend. The audition resulted in Sean's obtaining the important part of the psychotic son. The drama closed after three weeks. However, he had been spotted by a talent agent through whom he got the fourth-billed role of Alex Dwyer, a military academy student, in TAPS (1981), filmed in Pennsylvania. Because of his intensity on the set, his co-workers called him "Sean De Niro."

Returning to California, Sean contracted for the male lead in Amy Heckerling's FAST TIMES AT RIDGEMONT HIGH (1982), hailed by *Premiere* magazine as "the quintessential high school film" but denounced by critic Roger Ebert as "another one of those adolescent sex romps." Ebert did, however, find Sean "perfect" as surfer Jeff Spicoli, the long-haired student who has been stoned since the third grade. The film introduced into the English language the greeting, "Hey, dude, let's party." To better delve into his spaced-out role, Sean insisted that everyone connected with the project call him "Dude" or "Spicoli," a practice he would also follow on his next two films. Playing a minor role in FAST TIMES AT RIDGEMONT HIGH was Pamela Springsteen. Sean and Pamela became engaged, but did not marry, allegedly due to his higher dedication to acting. (When CBS-TV aired its short-lived series version of "Fast Times" in 1986, Dean Cameron inherited Penn's role of Jeff Spicoli.)

Sean next starred as an incarcerated hard-core juvenile delinquent in the Chicago-filmed BAD BOYS (1983). *Variety* raved, "Penn is nothing short of terrific in the key role, which . . . calls for him to rely primarily on his emotional and physical abilities. It's a subtle, studied performance that others might likely have played more broadly to much less effect." Also during 1983, he returned to the New York stage to co-star with Kevin Bacon as a Scottish teenage factory worker in *The Slab Boys*. Critics complimented him on his perfect accent. Later that year, he was on stage in Los Angeles as the American soldier in *The Girl on the Via Flamina*.

CRACKERS (1984), from distinguished French director Louis Malle, was a remake of the Italian movie BIG DEAL ON MADONNA STREET (1956). Malle would recall of Penn's audition, "When he came to my office to interview for CRACKERS, I nearly fell off my chair because in front of me was someone who had nothing to do with that character [the stoned airhead from FAST TIMES]. . . . Sean has exceptional talent for absorbing all sorts of different characters." Within CRACKERS, Sean was Dillard, a Texas rockabilly musician who can play harmonica and dance at the same time. He joins with three others in robbing their pawnbroker friend (Jack Warden). Somehow the remake did not gel as intended, leading *People* magazine to query, "Why did Malle bother?"

In RACING WITH THE MOON (1984), Penn was a World War II recruit living and loving his final days of freedom in a small California town. His performance in this nostalgic exercise ensured his reputation for versatility. Although Sean refused to help promote the feature (which grossed a mere $3.3 million), director Richard Benjamin forgave him with: "I find him quite exceptional and I'd much rather work with a talented actor than a bad one who likes to go on talk shows." Upon completion of RACING WITH THE MOON, Sean and co-star Elizabeth McGovern were involved romantically for a short time.

THE FALCON AND THE SNOWMAN (1985), based on the 1979 Robert Lindsey book, traces the adventures of true-life California boys, Christopher Boyce and Andrew Daulton Lee, convicted of spying for the Soviet Union. Sean portrayed Lee, a whining drug dealer who becomes a courier to the Russians for information submitted by Boyce (Timothy Hutton). For the role, he wore blue contact lenses, trimmed his eyebrows, wore a set of fitted dentures, grew a shaggy moustache, and used nose-spreaders to broaden his features. For some scenes he gained twenty pounds. For throwing himself into character as well as for his excellent, Robert De Niro–type performance, *Playgirl* magazine, among many others, considered him a shoe-in for an Oscar nomination, a tribute that did not materialize. Timothy Hutton, who had been the star of TAPS and had since become a close friend of Penn, called the actor "really, really great."

Following a brief love affair with Mary Stuart Masterson, Sean met singing sensation Madonna at a taping of her "Material Girl" video. Although she ordered him to "Get out!" three times, they had a first date in February 1985 in New York City. Never one to be photographed in public, Sean was charged with throwing rocks at two British photographers who tried to snap shots of him and Madonna jogging in Central Park in the spring of 1985. Amid much media-generated hoopla, the couple were married on August 16, 1985. It was Madonna Louise Ciccone's twenty-seventh birthday, and the day before Sean's twenty-fifth. They were united in matrimony in what they had hoped would be a private ceremony atop an ocean bluff in Malibu, California, but the proceedings were interrupted continually by press helicopters buzzing overhead. Rumored to have shot at the helicopters on the eve of his wedding, Sean, after the wedding, said, "I would have been very excited to see one of those helicopters burn and the bodies melt." Now the owners of a Malibu home, the Penns in January 1986 also purchased a Manhattan apartment on Central Park West at a cost of $850,000.

On the set of his pictures, Sean gave explicit instructions that if any journalists were to be allowed access, they were not to be permitted within his line of vision. On his dressing room was the sign "Never Enter Without Knocking. Never Knock Without Need." His salary for his next movie, AT CLOSE RANGE (1986), was reported to be between $1 million and $1.5 million, a major sum considering that none of his pictures to date had been box-office giants. He pumped up his muscles with weights for a role that seemed tailor-made for him: a bored, brooding punk talked into a life of crime by his father (Christopher Walken). Roger Ebert found him to be "one of the best actors alive," but he was now getting too old to play teenagers.

On April 12, 1986, Sean was arrested for assaulting songwriter David Wolinski in Los Angeles at Helena's nightclub. An old friend of Madonna's, Wolinski had kissed her,

Sean Penn in COLORS (1988).

whereupon Sean punched, kicked, and beat him with a chair. He was fined $1,700 and placed on probation. Two months later, at New York City's Pyramid Club, he and Madonna engaged in a screaming match during which he cornered her against a wall. Nevertheless, a few weeks later she dedicated her new album, *True Blue*, to him, calling him "the coolest guy in the universe." In late August they appeared together on stage at the Mitzi E. Newhouse Theatre in the Lincoln Center workshop production of David Rabe's play *Goose and Tomtom*. After a performance, Sean allegedly socked a photographer, with the couple's hefty bodyguards issuing the general warning "If you take one picture, we'll kill you." On September 19, 1986, Sean and Madonna's co-starring motion picture, SHANGHAI SURPRISE, was in release. *Variety* dismissed it as "a silly little trifle that wouldn't even have passed muster as a 1930s programmer." Madonna played a missionary in Japanese-occupied China in 1938, with Sean a down-at-his-heels aspiring adventurer who tries to help her. The foolish movie grossed a paltry $2.2 million in domestic distribution.

In June 1987 on the set of COLORS (1988), Sean attacked and beat a film extra who attempted to take a picture of him. On June 23 he was arrested for, and later convicted of, reckless driving while under the influence of alcohol. Since the offense was a violation of his probation, he was ordered to serve sixty days in jail, which he did on weekends while he completed work on COLORS. He was also allowed to serve the term in two parts and at a jail of his choosing. Before he went to California's Mono County jail at Bridgeport, Sean and Madonna spent four relaxing days at the Turnberry Club in Miami. On September 17, 1987, he was released from jail after serving thirty-three days; the sentence had been reduced due to good behavior. His probation, however, would continue for two years. For DEAR AMERICA: LETTERS HOME FROM VIETNAM (1987), Sean was one of many stars reading letters from G.I.s stationed in the war zone. As a November 27, 1987, Thanksgiving surprise, Madonna served him with divorce papers. However, they reconciled some days later with a relaxing stay at the Hotel Shangri-la in Los Angeles.

COLORS, released in April 1988, garnered huge publicity for the fear that this graphic study of Los Angeles cops versus streets gangs might engender riots. It teamed Penn with Robert Duvall, the former as a young, inexperienced police officer and the latter as a veteran officer looking forward to retirement. *Variety* approved of this Dennis Hopper–directed entry: "COLORS is a solidly crafted depiction of some current big-city horrors and succeeds largely because of the Robert Duvall–Sean Penn teaming as frontline cops. They're terrific together. . . ." For the modestly conceived JUDGMENT IN BERLIN (1988), directed by his father, Sean accepted a cameo role as Guenther X, demonstrating his convincing acting ability in a climatic courtroom scene.

Penn denied kicking a dent in a New York City photographer's auto on July 3, 1988. Thereafter, he was back in Los Angeles starring on stage at the West Theatre (from November 16, 1988, to January 15, 1989) in *Hurlyburly*, written and directed by David Rabe. His opening night joy was marred when he became furious with Madonna for arriving late with her good friend, comedian Sandra Bernhard. On December 28, 1988, Madonna called police to their Malibu home, charging that, in a drunken rage, he had beaten and gagged her, and tied her to a chair for nine hours. "His demons have totally taken him over," she said. On January 5, 1989, Madonna filed for divorce on the grounds of irreconcilable differences. However, she dropped the criminal assault charges due to lack of evidence, since no one else had been present at the time. Their divorce was settled out of court: he got the Malibu house, she got the New York City apartment.

Playwright David Rabe wrote the screenplay of CASUALTIES OF WAR (1989), based on a *New Yorker* magazine story of twenty years earlier about an actual incident that occurred during the Vietnam War. In what *Time* magazine called "an uncompromising performance," Sean, second-billed to Michael J. Fox, was the ruthless, tobacco-chewing sergeant who orders the kidnap/gang rape of a Vietnamese girl (Thuy Thu Le). The somber movie grossed $10.5 million in its first two weeks of domestic release in August 1989. However, it took a sharp dip after that to become one of the year's biggest flops, despite Brian De Palma's directing skills and Ennio Morricone's music score.

In late August 1989 Sean, along with Bill Murray, Christopher Walken, and others, bought into the Tribeca Bar & Grill, located on the street level of an eight-story building in Lower Manhattan converted by Robert De Niro to house his new film production company.

On camera, Penn got the opportunity to co-star with his **idol**, De Niro, in WE'RE NO ANGELS (1989), loosely taken from the same-titled Humphrey Bogart comedy of 1955. They played two convicts who disguise themselves as priests, hoping to cross over into Canada and find freedom. While both stars gave in-depth characterizations appreciated by reviewers, the premise was too thin to stretch into a satisfying feature film. Thus WE'RE NO ANGELS was his second box-office dud of the year. Ironically, Sean had been considered to star in BORN ON THE FOURTH OF JULY (1989), but it was Tom Cruise whom director Oliver Stone cast in this dramatic hit. For a charity event in December 1989, partly organized by his mother, Sean sculpted a welded steel "Christmas Tree Chaos" in his Malibu garage. It sold for $500 at a Santa Monica shopping mall, with the proceeds benefitting abused children.

With a blond ponytail and a variety of accents, Sean took a cameo role in COOL BLUE, distributed in February 1990. The plotline has Woody Harrelson, as a budding Los Angeles artist, falling for Ely Pouget after one night of love. For the rest of the film, he searches for her. In a bar scene, a customer (Sean) throws peanuts at him, then issues an accented philosophical dissertation and disappears. *Daily Variety* moaned that although Sean "livens up this otherwise trite 'finding myself' picture," he "unfortunately . . . takes a hike and the film returns to its plodding pace." In March 1990, Michael Penn, Sean's older brother, had a hit recording with "No Myth," soon followed by his first album, *March.* Meanwhile, Sean's younger brother, Chris, continued his own acting career, having appeared in such movies as RUMBLE FISH (1983), PALE RIDER (1985), and BEST OF THE BEST (1990).

STATE OF GRACE, in nationwide release on September 15, 1990, co-starred Sean with Ed Harris and Gary Oldman as members of an Irish mob in New York City's notorious Hell's Kitchen. *Newsweek* magazine's review included an accolade to Sean for giving "a superbly controlled portrait of a guy in over his head and slowly losing his grip" in this "kind of modern-day Western." Although Sheila Benson (*Los Angeles Times*) termed STATE OF GRACE a "wildly indulgent and artily self-conscious gangster melodrama," she had praise for Sean as the undercover cop who is now committed to undermining his boyhood-friends-turned-thugs: "Penn has one of the most complete and complex characters since his father-son partnership with Christopher Walken in AT CLOSE RANGE, and he is marvelous." While *Variety* termed STATE OF GRACE "ultimately overlong and overindulgent," it found Penn "excellent as Terry, who drinks too much and who ultimately gets too personally involved with his mission." Released at the same time as the far superior gangster chronicle GOODFELLAS, starring Robert De Niro and Ray Liotta, STATE OF GRACE suffered by comparison. In its first three weeks at the domestic box office (in limited release), STATE OF GRACE earned only $1,510,576.

Playing Penn's old flame in STATE OF GRACE was Robin Wright, with whom he became romantically involved at the same time that he was reportedly living with model Elaine Irwin in Los Angeles. (Penn and Wright had first met in 1988 when both were cast in the film LOON, from which he bailed out, to be replaced by Jason Patric, then Wright's boyfriend.) Early in September 1990, word leaked to the press that the twenty-four-year-old Wright was pregnant with Sean's child. His publicist announced, "He couldn't be happier, but they were hopeful the news wouldn't get out so soon." The baby, due in the spring of 1991, prompted the couple to state that they "will be getting married, probably after October [1990]." Interviewed on the syndicated "Entertainment Tonight" (September 14, 1990) to coincide with the opening of STATE OF GRACE, Wright said, "It's time to grow up for both of us" and revealed that Sean is "ultra sensitive" and has "a wonderful soul and it was destroyed in a way by the outside world." In November 1990 it was announced that Penn and Wright would marry in a Los Angeles church on November 18 with three hundred guests attending. However, at the last minute the ceremony was cancelled. Their daughter, Dylan Francis, was born on April 13, 1991.

Producer Thom Mount announced in May 1990 plans to finance and distribute a film from Sean's script, THE INDIAN RUNNER, about a middle-American family unit including a pair of brothers, with Sean in the director's chair. "Our feeling—and his—," Mount said, "is that it would be a fool's errand for a first-time director to also act in his picture." Shooting began on location in Omaha, Nebraska, on August 20, 1990. Mount, who displayed no doubts that Sean would be anything but exemplary in his behavior as a director, was undoubtedly relieved when the *Norfolk* (Nebraska) *Daily News* reported that Sean was "polite and quiet" and when the state's governor, Kay Orr, after a visit from Sean, stated that he was "very quiet and well-behaved." Starring in THE INDIAN RUNNER are Charles Bronson, Sandy Dennis, David Morse, and Patricia Arquette.

Said to be in a stage of development for Sean as star is SHE'S DA LOVELY.

Regarding his craft, Penn admits, "I like to spend my time researching my parts, the people I play because I feel a need and a responsibility to the people who live the life I'm portraying, so that they're not disappointed or feel misrepresented when they see the film. So they recognize something real." With Sean now seated in a chair marked "Director," it seems that he may have been predestined to follow in his father's footsteps. And his innate, ample talents may finally override his past bad publicity with the help of a supportive family, in the same way that Bruce Willis lost the "Bad Boy" stigma.

Filmography

The Concrete Cowboys (CBS-TV, 10/17/79)

Hellinger's Law (CBS-TV, 3/10/81)

The Killing of Randy Webster (CBS-TV, 3/11/81)

Taps (20th–Fox, 1981)

Fast Times at Ridgemont High (Univ, 1982)

Bad Boys (Univ, 1983)

Crackers (Univ, 1984)

Racing with the Moon (Par, 1984)

The Falcon and the Snowman (Orion, 1985)

At Close Range (Orion, 1986)

Shanghai Surprise (MGM, 1986)

Dear America: Letters Home from Vietnam (HBO–Couturie, 1987) (voice only)

Colors (Orion, 1988)
Judgment in Berlin (New Line, 1988)
Casualties of War (Col, 1989)
We're No Angels (Par, 1989)

Cool Blue (Cinema Corp. of America, 1990)
State of Grace (Orion, 1990)
The Indian Runner (Univ, 1991) (director, screenplay only)

Broadway Plays

Heartland (1981)

The Slab Boys (1983)

MICHELLE PFEIFFER

"I have such a fear of embarrassing myself that I will do anything
not to. . . . That's the key to my success."
                    —*Empire* magazine, February 1990

BACK IN THE GOLDEN DAYS OF HOLLYWOOD DURING THE 1930s AND
1940s, stars were manufactured by Hollywood studios. A beautiful young woman would
be quickly signed to a short-term contract, rushed into photo sessions, then acting classes,
and then be given a succession of film roles to determine whether or not she would click
with ticket buyers. MGM's Lana Turner was one such star; another was Ava Gardner. It
was the era of the screen goddesses: Columbia produced Rita Hayworth; Paramount
fostered Dorothy Lamour; Warner Bros. had Lauren Bacall; Twentieth Century–Fox
nurtured Betty Grable, Linda Darnell, Jeanne Crain, and later Marilyn Monroe; Republic
groomed Vera Hruba Ralston; RKO prepped Lizabeth Scott and Jane Russell. By the
1980s, the studio system was long gone; there were no more studio-groomed screen love
goddesses. However, actress Michelle Pfeiffer, beautiful and smart, groomed herself. She
selected her roles carefully, proved that she could act, and unwittingly contributed to the
revival of the long-dormant goddess status. With the style of Eleanor Parker and the
charisma of Susan Hayward, Michelle has a striking beauty (almond-shaped eyes, silky
hair, porcelain skin) that has been praised by the media: "a classic screen siren" (*Newsweek*
magazine); "her face a sculptured meadow of delight" (*People* magazine); "drop dead
gorgeous" (*Time* magazine); "the lady most men would kill for" ("Entertainment Tonight"). Yet she sees herself as having the face of a duck: "I should have played HOWARD
THE DUCK." She has elevated herself from being just another pretty Hollywood blonde to
being a Jean Harlow–like goddess whose every word or action makes news. Like Julia
Roberts and Jennifer Jason Leigh, with whom she shares a size six dress size, she is a very
popular and sought-after screen actress.

She was born on Monday, April 29, 1957, to Donna and Richard Pfeiffer, residents
of Midway City, California, in Orange County. She has admitted to being "a very typical"
Taurus. She was the second of four children and the eldest of three daughters who were all
taught the importance of the work ethic. Michelle was selected by her father, a heating and
air-conditioning contractor, for the dubious distinction of cleaning old refrigerators which
he would then recondition and sell. For this work, her first paying job, she received fifty
cents per unit. She did not like grammar school, preferring to stay home to watch old
Hollywood movies on television. The titles meant nothing to her, but of the acting she

413

thought, "I can do that." At the age of fourteen she began working part time in a clothing store and then had positions in an optometrist's office, in a printing plant, and at a jewelry manufacturer. Her free moments were spent at the beach with various boyfriends and in experimenting with all kinds of drugs.

At Fountain Valley High School she participated in one play, a day-long Christmas presentation written by students. She played one of two children waiting up for Santa's arrival. In her sophomore year, in world history class in a skit written by her teacher, she was a Hiroshima bombing victim testifying at the imaginary war-crimes trial of Harry S. Truman. In 1975 she obtained a high-school diploma by getting course credit for her after-school jobs. She matriculated at Golden West (Junior) College in Huntington Beach, California, but quit after a few weeks due to boredom. Instead, she was hired by the Vons supermarket chain as a grocery checkout clerk at store #50 in El Toro, where she would spend the next year. She took steno courses at a school in Garden Grove (also in Orange County) with the thought of becoming a court reporter. But again boredom caused her to leave.

For months Michelle's hairdresser had advised her to send photographs to modeling and talent agencies. However, she did not think she was pretty enough. But then the 1977 Orange County beauty pageant came along, and it was announced that Hollywood talent agent John LaRocca would be one of the judges. Deciding that it was time for her to think seriously about an acting career, she entered the contest. Her hope was to meet LaRocca, whose specialty was television. She was not only selected as Miss Orange County, she was also signed by LaRocca. He quickly found her work in a few TV commercials, which she did not like. These jobs were followed by a one-line part saying "Who is he, Naomi?" in a 1978 episode of ABC-TV's "Fantasy Island." At least the miniscule role entitled her to a Screen Actors Guild membership card. Meanwhile, she had become involved in a meta-physical, quasi-religious cult that she claimed "brainwashed" her and sidetracked her temporarily from her career.

After moving to Los Angeles, Pfeiffer took acting lessons with coach Peggy Feury. LaRocca soon got her steady employment in ABC-TV's "Delta House," one of three major network imitations of the enormously popular comedy NATIONAL LAMPOON'S ANIMAL HOUSE (1978). In the series, which premiered January 18, 1979, Michelle was Bombshell, the blonde bimbo, a part for which she wore a padded bra. Fortunately for her career, the derivative sitcom ended with its episode of April 28, 1979, the day before her twenty-second birthday. Thereafter, she had a small supporting role in CBS's THE SOLITARY MAN (October 9, 1979), a TV movie about the breakup of a family. Next she was enticed into a second TV series, "B.A.D. Cats" (Burglary Auto Detail, Commercial Auto Thefts) as lady cop Samantha Jensen. The ABC-TV show premiered on January 4, 1980. *Variety* rated the show "mechanical" and said of the cast, "The three young leads [Pfeiffer, Asher Brauner, Steve Hanks] show no discernible acting ability or personality draw." This screeching-wheels police drama was pulled after the fifth telecast, on February 8, 1980. Producer Everett Chambers would say, "I'm not putting this on my credits."

Later, after her show business success, Michelle's advice to neophytes would be to try to avoid involvement with a TV series that might come back to haunt them. THE HOLLY-WOOD KNIGHTS (1980), about fun-loving high school students on Halloween night in 1965, marked the inauspicious theatrical film debut of both Michelle (as a carhop) and Tony Danza. Her second big-screen appearance was in the little-seen FALLING IN LOVE AGAIN (1980). She was the young WASP princess seen in flashback sequences—standing in for the older Susannah York—and pursued romantically by Jewish Elliott Gould.

In 1980 she was married to aspiring actor Peter Horton, who would gain some prominence as one of the brothers in the teleseries "Seven Brides for Seven Brothers" (1982–1983) and later on "Thirtysomething" (1987–1991). The marriage would end in 1988, at which time Michelle would explain, "Looking back, I think I was just too young to get married." She was twenty-three at the time.

She was featured in CHARLIE CHAN AND THE CURSE OF THE DRAGON QUEEN (1981), as a debutante with the commanding name of Cordelia Farrington III. However, she was wasted along with the likes of Peter Ustinov, Lee Grant, Angie Dickinson, and Rachel Roberts. At this career juncture, she fired agent LaRocca, but left him with a photograph inscribed, "To John, who has taken me from crayons to perfume. Thank you for your hard work, never-ending faith and love." She signed with the prestigious William Morris Agency, with which she would remain until 1988.

During 1981, she was cast as a feminist student in a Los Angeles stage production of *Playground in the Fall.* In the CBS-TV three-hour movie CALLIE & SON (October 13, 1981), she was in support of Lindsay Wagner and Jameson Parker, and on October 26 of that year appeared in the NBC-TV scene-for-scene remake of the William Inge–written SPLENDOR IN THE GRASS (1961). Michelle had the role of the flapper sister, Ginny, played in the earlier version by Barbara Loden. Two months later, on December 5, 1981, she had her first leading role, in the CBS-TV movie THE CHILDREN NOBODY WANTED, which was filmed on location in Marshall, Missouri. It dealt with the true-life crusade of activist Tom Butterfield (Fredric Lehne) to create a family life for homeless children.

In 1978 Paramount had enjoyed great success with GREASE, the adaptation of the long-running Broadway musical. Hoping for equal success with a sequel, it cast Pfeiffer and Maxwell Caulfield in roles to parallel those handled by Olivia Newton-John and John Travolta in the megahit original. Michelle took singing and dancing lessons for her co-starring role as gum-cracking Stephanie Zinone, in which she soloed on "Cool Rider," dueted on "(Love Will) Turn Back the Hands of Time" with Caulfield, and harmonized with cast members on "Who's That Guy," "Girl for All Seasons," "Rock-A-Hula-Lua," and "We'll Be Together." Like most Hollywood sequels, GREASE 2 (1982) suffered by comparison to its lively predecessor. The songs were forgettable, the storyline thin, and the nostalgia too coy. *Variety* noted of the musical's leading lady, "Pfeiffer is all anyone could ask for in the looks department, and while her performance is mostly devoted to impatient pouting, she fills Newton-John's shoes and tight pants very well, thank you." But GREASE 2 was not popular, and its failure damaged Pfeiffer's standing in the industry.

Always resilient and learning from her errors, Michelle sought a far more dimen-sional role in the remake of SCARFACE (1983). After several auditions she was finally cast as the cocaine-sniffing bitch wife of Miami's new drug lord (Al Pacino). In this far cry from GREASE 2, she displayed great acting talent in a film that would be long remembered for its violence. *People* magazine noted, "Michelle Pfeiffer, undefeated by the fiasco of GREASE 2, makes one of the sexiest entrances in screen history as [Robert] Loggia's mistress, a hot number who'd rather powder her nose with cocaine than respond to Pacino's advances." Vincent Canby (*The New York Times*) observed that Michelle was "a beautiful young actress without a bad—or even an awkward—camera angle to her entire body." Despite the excesses of Pacino's energetic acting, the overabundance of gore, and the unflattering comparison to the original SCARFACE (1932), the lengthy (170 minutes) remake grossed $23,330,730 in domestic film rentals.

As a result of her personal success in SCARFACE, Michelle received numerous screen offers—all of the bitch variety—during the next year. In the hour-long ABC-TV entry "One Too Many Lives" (March 6, 1985) Michelle co-starred with Val Kilmer in a drama about teenage drinking and driving. The project was directed by Michelle's husband, Peter Horton. Not wishing to be typecast in any particular mold, Pfeiffer chose the fairy tale fantasy LADYHAWKE (1985), filmed on location in Italy. She was a short-haired medieval maiden who, with her moody knight (Rutger Hauer), is under the evil curse of a bishop (John Wood). *Variety* enthused, "Lovely Michelle Pfeiffer is perfect as the enchanting beauty who appears by night, always in the vicinity of a vicious but protective wolf." The

Al Pacino and **Michelle Pfeiffer** in SCARFACE (1983).

mock thriller INTO THE NIGHT (1985) had her second-billed to Jeff Goldblum as a woman with knowledge of stolen emeralds who is being hotly pursued by would-be killers. *People* magazine considered her "a knockout of the first order who here displayed a flair for comedy." Michelle's sole screen role during 1986 was in the little-liked farce SWEET LIBERTY, written and directed by star Alan Alda. She was Faith Healy, a sexy career-driven actress, and her performance, according to critic Roger Ebert, "uses some wonderfully subtle touches."

THE WITCHES OF EASTWICK (1987), boasting a marvelous cast and based on the John Updike book, was instrumental in ensuring stardom for Michelle. She was a local newspaper reporter, one of three man-hungry New England housewives (Pfeiffer, Cher, Susan Sarandon) who, in their boredom, utilize unsuspected supernatural powers to conjure up the devil (Jack Nicholson). Michelle claims that Nicholson held the production together when producers Neil Canton, Peter Guber, and Jon Peters, together with director George Miller, decided just before shooting began that Cher and Sarandon should switch parts and when the four men seemed to lose interest in the film. Cher and Michelle became close friends, and Cher has said, "When I met her, I thought she was very soft and maybe too sweet, too nice," adding, "but you know, it's all part of someone who has a definite purpose, who's a lot stronger than even she knows sometimes." THE WITCHES OF EASTWICK became the year's #10 box-office champion with domestic grosses of $63.7 million. NBC-TV made a thirty-minute series pilot based on the film, but it failed to materialize as a series.

After being shelved for a year, AMAZON WOMEN ON THE MOON, consisting of a series of middling skits spoofing contemporary living, was released in September 1987 with little fanfare or audience response. Michelle and her real-life husband, Peter Horton, were co-starred in the "Hospital" sequence. On November 6, 1987, for PBS-TV's "Great Performances," she starred in the title role of "Natica Jackson," an hour-long presentation of the John O'Hara story of a 1930s Hollywood actress who has an affair with a married chemist (Brian Kerwin). Kay Gardella (*New York Daily News*) noted that she played the role "to perfection." Later, in March 1990, an extended version was released on home video, entitled *Power, Passion & Murder.*

In 1988, the year that saw Michelle's rise to superstardom, her agent, Ed Limato, moved from the William Morris Agency to International Creative Management. He took her with him, saying, "She's very quiet. She doesn't show it, but she's no fool." *Newsweek* magazine called MARRIED TO THE MOB (1988) her "breakthrough performance." Wearing a black wig and using a heavy New York accent, she was gum-chewing Angela, the jittery widow of a hit man (Alec Baldwin). Called "THE GODFATHER on laughing gas" by the *Philadelphia Inquirer*, the script had her whining, "Everything we own, everything we wear, everything we eat fell off a truck." *Variety* complimented her as having "never been better than in showing this very different portrait of a mobster's wife than she displayed in SCARFACE." In 1989 a television sitcom would emerge from the story, but would not enjoy a long run. TEQUILA SUNRISE, released in early December 1988, paired Michelle with Mel Gibson and Kurt Russell, with Michelle playing a sophisticated restaurant operator. Called a "sensual and suspenseful thriller" by hard-to-please critic Rex Reed, this contemporary *film noir* boasted an extremely well-photographed, sexy hot tub scene with Michelle and Gibson. Of his co-star, Gibson said, "She was very firm about what she was doing and how she wanted to do it." Because of its trio of personable stars and despite its flawed storyline, the mediocre TEQUILA SUNRISE grossed $19.1 million in domestic film rentals.

Released in Los Angeles and New York in December 1988 in order to qualify for that year's awards, DANGEROUS LIAISONS was in general release nationwide in January 1989. Michelle was third-billed as pious Mme. de Tourvel. The scenario, set in decadent pre-Revolution eighteenth-century France, had her as the virtuous married woman who originally resists the game of love as played by the notorious Vicomte de Valmont (John Malkovich). However, she ultimately gives in to his wiles. She was required to weep a lot on camera, and Michelle's eyes seemed permanently reddened. Critic Roger Ebert noted, "for Pfeiffer, in a year which saw her in such various assignments as MARRIED TO THE MOB and TEQUILA SUNRISE, the movie is more evidence of her versatility—she is good when she is innocent, and superb when she is guilty." Both she and co-star Glenn Close were nominated for Academy Awards—Michelle in the Best Supporting Actress category—but neither won. She did, however, have an off-screen affair with Malkovich, as well as with Michael Keaton.

Michelle made her New York stage debut in the New York Shakespeare Festival's open-air Delacorte Theatre in Central Park on July 6, 1989, as Olivia in *Twelfth Night.* Mimi Kramer (*The New Yorker* magazine) wrote that Michelle "tries to remain beautiful while manifesting temperament—something she seems to confuse with acting." In the cast, which included Gregory Hines and Jeff Goldblum, was twenty-five-year-old actor Fisher Stevens (playing Sir Andrew Aguecheek) with whom Michelle, some six years his senior, began a love affair.

"What emerges here is a Hollywood rarity these days," wrote Richard Schickel (*Time* magazine) about THE FABULOUS BAKER BOYS (1989), "a true character comedy." Michelle earned praise also from critic Judith Crist: "The fabulous Bridges brothers [Beau and Jeff] and Michelle Pfeiffer at her sexiest, funniest best, make this romantic comedy a joy to watch." To play Susie Diamond, professional escort turned sultry lounge singer, Michelle took singing lessons for the second time in her life to help her render her torchy versions of "More Than You Know" and the sizzling "Makin' Whoopee" while slithering atop a grand piano. The scene was pleasantly reminiscent of Rita Hayworth's upright song in GILDA (1946). Michelle credits Jeff Bridges with teaching her how to have fun while acting. She explained, "Before, I could never let my guard down. I was very serious, concentrated, focused." Released in October 1989, the film grossed $18.1 million in domestic ticket sales. Not only had Michelle's status as an actress been raised from the "B" to the "A" list, but her per-picture salary had escalated to $2 million. This professional upgrade was sparked by her winning 1989 best actress awards from the Hollywood Foreign Press (Golden Globe Award), the Los Angeles Film Critics Association, the National Society of Film Critics, and the New York Film Critics Circle. Nominated for an Academy Award, she lost the Best Actress Oscar to Jessica Tandy (DRIVING MISS DAISY).

In December 1989, while it was being speculated that Michelle had had collagen injected into her lips, Blistex, Inc. placed her at the top of its list of the "most beautiful lips of 1989." Meanwhile, she had formed her own production company, which in tandem with Orion Pictures would create projects which she would produce and/or star in. By now, her two younger sisters, Dedee and Lori, had each become actresses. In March 1990, Michelle was engaged to marry songwriter Geoffrey Tozer and was honored by both *People* and *US* magazines as one of the world's most beautiful women. In July 1990 the readers of *Esquire* magazine designed the "perfect woman," choosing Michelle's body. Other actresses contributing to such perfection were Jamie Lee Curtis (legs), Geena Davis (mouth), and Kathleen Turner (voice). She was replaced by Jodie Foster in THE SILENCE OF THE LAMBS (1991) after allegedly demanding too high a salary. Instead, she traveled to Leningrad, Moscow, London, Lisbon, and Maine to co-star with Sean Connery in THE RUSSIA HOUSE (1990), based on John Le Carré's best-seller. She was Katya, a Russian book editor who becomes a cautious courier for a Soviet scientist smuggling secret military information to the West. (When the *glasnost*-era spy thriller opened in mid-December 1990, *Variety* observed, "Attractive as they are, Sean Connery and Michelle Pfeiffer are constantly upstaged by the fresh and arresting settings in which the stars play. . . . Pfeiffer's Russian accent proves very believable and one is drawn to the lovely actress, but she has limited notes to play here.") In FRANKIE AND JOHNNY (1991), directed by Garry Marshall and based on Terrence McNally's award-winning play *Frankie and Johnny in the Clair de Lune*, Michelle plays a diner waitress who becomes romantically involved with the establishment's cook (Al Pacino). After entering into a nonexclusive, first-look production pact with Orion Pictures, her first project there was LOVE FIELD (forthcoming, 1992), at a salary of $2.5 million. The film is an interracial love story—filmed in North Carolina—about a relationship with a stranger (Dennis Haysbert) begun on a bus trip following the assassination of John F. Kennedy in November 1963.

Having arrived at the top of the Hollywood ladder, Michelle Pfeiffer states that there will be no more boring screen or television parts for her . . . ever! "I've had enough of those to know I never want to do it again," she has said. "I mean, I'd rather go back to checking groceries." Regarding the industry that has fostered her career, Michelle notes, "I like the fact that I don't have to worry about money. I like that the projects that I'm being offered get better and better and the people I'm with are really interesting. But I don't like just about everything else about it."

Filmography

The Solitary Man (CBS-TV, 10/9/79)
The Hollywood Knights (Col, 1980)
Falling in Love Again (International Picture Show, 1980)
Callie & Son (CBS-TV, 10/13/81)
Splendor in the Grass (NBC-TV, 10/26/81)

The Children Nobody Wanted (CBS-TV, 12/5/81)
Charlie Chan and the Curse of the Dragon Queen (American Cinema, 1981)
Grease 2 (Par, 1982)
Scarface (Univ, 1983)

Ladyhawke (WB/20th–Fox, 1985)
Into the Night (Univ, 1985)
Sweet Liberty (Univ, 1986)
The Witches of Eastwick (WB, 1987)
Amazon Women on the Moon (Univ, 1987)
Married to the Mob (Orion, 1988)
Tequila Sunrise (WB, 1988)
Dangerous Liaisons (WB, 1988)

The Fabulous Baker Boys (20th–Fox, 1989)
The Russia House (MGM/UA, 1990)
Frankie and Johnny (Par, 1991)

Future Releases

Love Field (Orion, 1992)

Television Series

Delta House (ABC, 1979)

B.A.D. Cats (ABC, 1980)

Album Discography

The Fabulous Baker Boys (GRP GR-2002) [ST]

Grease 2 (RSO RS 1-3803) [ST]

DENNIS QUAID

"Well, I guess I could say I'm an actor, which I am, but that
sounds like I'm putting down being a movie star, which, let's face it,
is what I've become to many people."
— *Chicago Tribune*, November 6, 1988

NO ONE HAS EVER REVEALED WHETHER OR NOT DENNIS QUAID HAS A
two-way mirror on *his* bedroom ceiling, but in another way he is the Errol Flynn of 1990s
Hollywood. "He lives pedal to the floor, always in fifth gear," his good buddy, actor John
Goodman, has said, while a Montana bartender claims that "he's a crazy man, always very
front-and-center stage." The fast-living Quaid has created an alter ego for himself, another
identity for his partying moods. It was this "Buck Gibson" who invented the recipe for his
own martini: Stolichnaya vodka, four drops of bourbon and vermouth, a touch of olive
juice, and two good swipes of Tabasco—served straight up.

Dennis, the younger brother of respected character actor Randy Quaid, had been in
Hollywood twelve years and had twenty film credits before he was "discovered," with the
help of a memorable line of sexual dialogue to his leading lady, in THE BIG EASY (1987).
After that, *People* and *US* magazines vied to see which could place him more often on its
lists of "First Class Males" or "Who Turns You On" or "The Sexiest Man." Dennis is
outspoken, demanding, brash, and reportedly crude after too many of Buck Gibson's
special martinis. However, with his irresistible grin, dimples, and little-boy-lost demeanor
on screen, he has become one of Hollywood's better-liked leading men, although none of
his starring films has been a box-office smash.

Dennis Quaid was born on Friday, April 9, 1954, in Houston, Texas, the second
and last child of William "Buddy" Quaid, who had always wanted to be both an actor and
a singer, and his wife, Nita, the daughter of a Baptist preacher. Said to resemble actor Dana
Andrews, Buddy had been offered a screen test by a Columbia Pictures talent scout.
However, he had to decline due to his commitment to the U.S. Merchant Marines. Later,
back in civilian life, he became an electrician who entertained his family by singing and
dancing around the house. The interest in show business had been instilled in the Quaid
side of the family by Buddy's mother, a singer, dancer, and piano player whose father had
been in vaudeville. The Quaids were also distant cousins to Gene Autry.

Prior to Dennis' birth, four-year-old Randy was prince of the Quaid household. But
with the arrival of a brother came resentment. Because Dennis was smaller and skinnier, it
was easy for Randy to pin him to the floor by threatening to, and eventually spitting in his

face. At age four, Dennis began piano lessons, which he enjoyed; he eagerly learned to play guitar and mandolin as well. When he was twelve, his parents divorced. Their action began the "miserable" period in his life, when his best friend was his dog. He would spend hours considering whether he wanted to be a veterinarian or a forest ranger, both solitary professions. However, at Bellaire High School in Houston his shyness swiftly disappeared through acting in school plays. At the age of fifteen he created a nightclub comedy act, which he performed at Houston's Tideland Hotel and at other local spots. During the summers he was a clown at Astroworld, sold Fuller brush sets and encyclopedias door to door, and tried his hand at being a carpenter's apprentice.

Upon graduation from Bellaire High School in 1972, he enrolled as a drama major at the University of Houston, where he starred as the cowboy in *Bus Stop*. Midway through his junior year, he quit the university to join brother Randy, who was then in the process of launching his movie career in Hollywood. Dennis, too, wanted to be in movies. Arriving in Los Angeles in February 1975, he acquired an acting coach, but could not persuade any talent agent to represent him. On his own, he won a one-line bit in CRAZY MAMA (1975), which would end up on the cutting-room floor. Visiting the set of THE MISSOURI BREAKS (1976), a western in which Randy was at work, Dennis met fun-loving Jack Nicholson, whom he liked, and taught the more reclusive Marlon Brando to play the mandolin. During this period Dennis experimented with marijuana and cocaine, but was too ambitious to rely on these drugs for courage. Instead, he took up middleweight boxing, hoping to compete in the 1980 Olympics.

At the small $150-a-month apartment he shared with two roommates in West Hollywood, Dennis wrote songs which he played on his guitar. He wangled himself a bit in I NEVER PROMISED YOU A ROSE GARDEN (1977), an underrated study of a young woman (Kathleen Quinlan) coping with her schizophrenia. In *Variety*, Quaid read of a casting call for an upcoming film entitled 9/30/55 (1977), about the impact of James Dean's death on a sensitive Arkansas undergraduate (Richard Thomas). Dennis wanted to be in the production and repeatedly called the casting director until he won the sixth-billed part of Frank, one of Thomas' fellow college students. Then Dennis was a 1960s high school student in the derivative OUR WINNING SEASON (1978). Regarding his high-energy performance, *Variety* reported, "acting kudos go to Dennis Quaid as [Scott] Jacoby's manic buddy. In one of the few non-stereotyped potsmoking scenes of recent films, Quaid is outstanding." He was one of four collegians who propel a sex clinic into a million-dollar enterprise in THE SENIORS (1978). Also that year he was Phil Lawyer, in the CBS-TV fright entry ARE YOU IN THE HOUSE ALONE? (September 20, 1978). He had a tiny part in AMATEUR NIGHT AT THE DIXIE BAR AND GRILL, an NBC-TV movie shot early in 1978 but not aired until January 8, 1979.

Dennis had met actress P. J. Soles while they both were emoting in OUR WINNING SEASON. On November 24, 1978, at the age of twenty-four, Quaid married her. The union proved unstable, and they would divorce in 1983. "I think it was a question of being too young," he later analyzed. "I was looking to fall in love. I'd never really fallen in love before. I guess I just wanted to get married as a kind of way to put my parents back together."

He and his bride worked together in a second picture, BREAKING AWAY (1979), filmed largely in Bloomington, Indiana, in which Dennis was a surly ex-jock named Mike. Optimism surrounded this offbeat film, which went on to become a sleeper hit. After finishing his work on the film, Dennis went alone to New York City, where he spent a few weeks hanging out at the Cafe Central, where he met, among others, budding actor John Goodman. Returning to Indiana, he bought a 1954 yellow Chevrolet with a green top as a gift for himself to commemorate his birth year. He drove back to the West Coast via Montana, where he purchased two acres of land in Paradise Valley, intending one day to build his dream house there.

To fulfill his dream Dennis needed money, which he proceeded to earn from working in movies. Some of them, such as GORP (1980), involving drugs and summer camp, would be soon forgotten. In the western THE LONG RIDERS (1980), a more interesting entry, he acted for the first time on screen with brother Randy. Together they were the outlaw Miller Brothers. In the problem-plagued production ALL NIGHT LONG (1981), a comedy, he was cast as a slightly dimwitted individual who becomes Barbra Streisand's lover. CAVEMAN (1981), designed to display Ringo Starr's "comedic" talents, had Dennis as a prehistoric tribal outcast joining Starr's newly formed cave-dwelling family. Dennis next sang four of his songs in THE NIGHT THE LIGHTS WENT OUT IN GEORGIA (1981), in which he played Kristy McNichol's unbridled brother.

The CBS-TV movie BILL (December 22, 1981) co-starred Dennis as a filmmaker who at first views the mentally retarded Bill Sackster (Mickey Rooney) merely as the subject for a documentary. However, he becomes his best friend while helping Sackster cope with life in the outside world after forty-six years of institutionalization. Rooney was honored with an Emmy for his work. JOHNNY BELINDA had been filmed for motion pictures and television four times prior to its October 19, 1982, presentation on CBS-TV. In this version, Dennis was the local bully who rapes and impregnates the deaf-mute heroine (Rosanna Arquette). *TV Guide* critic Judith Crist rated Dennis' villain as "properly nasty." In May 1983 Quaid received top billing in TOUGH ENOUGH as an out-of-work country singer who goes into amateur boxing. Another of his songs was used for this project. JAWS 3-D (1983), shot in the gimmicky three-dimensional process, was the third in the series of films about the rampaging white shark. As the chief engineer at Sea World in Florida, Dennis, according to *People* magazine, was "more nondescript than heroic."

Astronaut Gordon Cooper had always been Dennis' idol. This admiration led him to ask to audition for the part of Cooper in Warner Bros.'s screen rendition of Tom Wolfe's THE RIGHT STUFF (1983), about the beginnings of America's space program. Initially he was considered too boyish-looking to play the thirty-two-year-old astronaut. However, the actor cut his hair, dyed it darker, and immediately took flying lessons. He also simulated Cooper's military stride and learned to hold his mouth like Cooper's. In an ensemble cast of virtual screen unknowns, including playwright/actor Sam Shepard, Dennis was fourth-billed. The ambitious saga was not popular with moviegoers. In CBS-TV's BILL: ON HIS OWN (November 9, 1983), the sequel to the acclaimed BILL, Dennis appeared briefly in a reprise of his original part.

Upon divorcing P. J. Soles in 1983, Dennis sold his Montana property and went to New York City to reevaluate his career. After working in a number of pictures just for the money, he was unhappy with the course of his career. "It was the most discouraging point of my life," he has said. He took acting lessons and, after a few weeks, co-starred off-Broadway (and later on the Los Angeles stage) with his brother in Sam Shepard's play *True West*, a dark comedy about a psychotic relationship between two brothers who try to kill each other. Dennis claims that this experience was a major turning point in his relationship with Randy, as well as in his career. During this period, his latest film, DREAMSCAPE (1984), was in release. In it he starred as a man capable of physically entering the dreams of others. By doing so, he manages to save the life of the President (Eddie Albert) of the United States.

ENEMY MINE (1985) proved to be one of the most trouble-plagued and overbudgeted feature films of the 1980s. For this futuristic survival story of two antagonistic space fighters downed on an alien planet and forced to coexist, Dennis and co-star Louis Gossett, Jr., went to the Canary Islands and Munich, Germany. The offbeat science fiction entry did not recoup its reported $56 million cost at the box office. *Cinefantastique* magazine found that Dennis, "ordinarily a very likeable actor, works *so* hard in fact that his character becomes strident and wild-eyed."

The year 1987 proved to be Dennis' best film year. It began with the release on the weekend of July 4 of INNERSPACE, in which he was cast as a hard-drinking, irresponsible Navy test pilot who is accidentally injected into the bloodstream of a meek supermarket clerk (Martin Short). The film had an intriguing premise (similar to that of the earlier FANTASTIC VOYAGE [1966]) and superior special effects, but the studio failed to promote it correctly and its title did not help. Whatever the reasons, the hoped-for summer hit did not materialize. Critic Roger Ebert assessed, "[The] plot is not only unbelievable, but almost unworkable. . . . Working inside Short in his tiny capsule, Quaid has a tougher role because he can't get physical. All of his actions have to be taken through the instrument of Short's body, and there are wonderful scenes where he uses rhetoric to inspire this nerd to act like a hero." Co-starring with Dennis in INNERSPACE was Meg Ryan, with whom he began a romantic relationship.

THE BIG EASY (1987), although completed almost a year earlier, followed INNERSPACE into release in August. For this cop action yarn he co-wrote the song "Closer to You," which he performed on the soundtrack. During filming in New Orleans, he played guitar with a blues band, while, on screen, he was the corrupt cop seducer of the prim assistant district attorney (Ellen Barkin). When she says, "I never did have much luck with sex," his character replies huskily, "Your luck's about to change." Their steamy bedroom scenes were instrumental in promoting Dennis into sex-symbol leading-man status, a perception that was abetted by a televised statement by actress Susan Saint James that Dennis "has the best abs" (abdominal stomach muscles) in Hollywood. When told that he was suddenly a heartthrob, he quipped, "But it's not like I wake up in the morning and go, 'Oh, you heartthrob, you! How are you today? Go out and throb some hearts!'" THE BIG EASY, which garnered tremendous publicity for itself and Dennis, grossed a very respectable $18 million in domestic ticket sales. His leading-man status was furthered by the October release of SUSPECT (1987), in which, as a jaunty juror, he helps the seductive public defender (Cher) close her murder case. *TV Host* magazine critiqued this thriller as "a spine-tingling, heart-chilling, intelligent suspenser." Of her co-star, Cher said, "He's like an imp . . . like a bad boy . . . makes dull work a lot of fun . . . adorable."

In 1987 Dennis bought another parcel of 175 acres of land in Livingston, Montana, formerly owned by director Sam Peckinpah and later by Warren Oates (Dennis' TOUGH ENOUGH co-star); Dennis and Oates had been friends before the latter's untimely death in 1983. On the front door of his cabin was the sign: "This house protected by shotgun three days out of seven. You guess which three." Also during the year, he formed a six-member rhythm-and-blues band called The Eclectics and was soon performing in various northern California clubs.

D.O.A. (1988), co-starring Meg Ryan, was a remake of the well-regarded 1949 *film noir* that had starred Edmund O'Brien. It was updated to feature Dennis as a cynical university professor poisoned with a slow-acting toxin. *Time* magazine rated him "charming even unto death," but the glitzy, high-tech rehash was a flop. Critic Gene Shalit credited Quaid as "sensational" in EVERYBODY'S ALL-AMERICAN (1988), in which he ages from a crew-cut high school football hero to a paunchy middle-aged has-been. Dennis was required to gain forty pounds for the role. The overlong, unconvincing melodrama drew few filmgoers.

Dennis Quaid in EVERYBODY'S ALL-AMERICAN (1988).

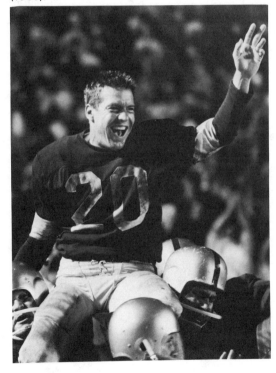

After bouncing around Hollywood for a number of years and once considered as a possible starring vehicle for Mickey Rourke, the bio-pic of rock 'n' roll great Jerry Lee Lewis emerged as GREAT BALLS OF FIRE (1989), filmed in Memphis, Arkansas, Mississippi, and London, with Dennis cast as the trend-setting singer. Dennis had hoped to do his own singing, but eventually was persuaded to lip-synch such trademark numbers as the title song, "Whole Lotta Shakin' Goin' On," and "Breathless" to Lewis' distinctive voice and phrasing. GREAT BALLS OF FIRE was released amid a great deal of fanfare. However, the cartoonish musical biography proved to be a major disappointment, with *US* magazine rating Dennis as "talented and hard-working," but as never getting "under Jerry's skin." It was Dennis' third starring feature to fail in a row and the film industry was loudly questioning his marquee power.

Also in 1989 singer Bonnie Raitt chose Dennis to appear in her music video "Thing Called Love" because "I had to sing for somebody, and he was the cutest guy I could think of." At about the same time, he signed with Capitol Records on behalf of The Eclectics. He also entered into a long-term, nonexclusive agreement with Orion Pictures to star in, develop, and produce features for the studio through his co-owned production company, Summers/Quaid, in partnership with Cathleen Summers, executive producer of D.O.A. (In July 1990 they would move their company to Tri-Star Pictures in a three-year development pact.) On October 5, 1989, in Santa Barbara, California, Randy Quaid was married to businesswoman Evi Motolanez, with Dennis and Meg Ryan as best man and maid of honor. Then, on November 21, Dennis and Meg announced their engagement to be married. Meg called him "as normal as they get—unpretentious, with great charm."

In May 1990 Dennis and fiancée Meg Ryan purchased a "showplace house" in San Francisco's Pacific Heights district at Pacific and Pierce Streets for $2,745,000. However, within months they found that the commute was "impractical" and placed the house back on the market in July, at an asking price of $3.2 million. On May 19, 1990, Dennis purchased a Montana resident fishing license near his place at Livingston, Montana, falsely stating on the application that he was a full-time inhabitant of the state. His lawyer, Joe Swindlehurst, was forced to post a $115 bond on August 13, 1990, when Dennis failed to appear in court for a hearing on the matter. Meanwhile, Dennis underwent a drug rehabilitation program at St. John's Hospital in Santa Monica, California, to rid himself of a dependency that allegedly began during the filming of GREAT BALLS OF FIRE.

In POSTCARDS FROM THE EDGE (1990), adapted for the screen by Carrie Fisher from her semi-autobiographical novel of the same title, Dennis was Jack Falkner, a Don Juan who has a one-night stand with Suzanne Vale (Meryl Streep), an actress/singer who passes out from a drug overdose in his bed and whom he takes to a hospital for detoxification. Largely a women's picture, directed by Mike Nichols, the *Hollywood Reporter* found it "sharp and witty." However, in the estimation of Judy Stone (*San Francisco Chronicle*), the film "doesn't get very believable in Suzanne's scenes with lover boy Quaid." Susan Linfied (*The New York Times*) observed that "Dennis Quaid seems to spoof all the sexy bad boys he has ever played."

In COME SEE THE PARADISE (1990) Dennis is the husband in an interracial marriage with Tamlyn Tomita. Written and directed by Alan Parker, the film was previewed at the May 1990 Cannes Film Festival where it was reported to be "the director's most romantic movie to date." Set between 1936 and 1948, it concerns the controversial subject of the U.S. Government's internment of Japanese-Americans in prison-like camps during World War II. On February 14, 1991, Quaid and Meg Ryan, aged twenty-eight, were married at Los Angeles City Hall in a no-frills ceremony.

Future projects for Dennis Quaid may include TROPPO, in which he would be a gun-running captain of a ship that inadvertently dumps toxic waste into the ocean off New Zealand, and 25-CENT ROMANCE, in which he would portray a jailed man who conducts a pen-pal relationship with a sexually repressed woman. Both potential films, if made, will be released by Orion, as arranged prior to his production company's move to Tri-Star.

Of his film stardom, which by 1990 was earning him a salary of $3 million per picture plus a $20,000 expense allowance when working outside Los Angeles, he admitted, "I like it. . . . I like wearing suits and getting the girl. . . . Limousines I don't mind so much. Saves you cab fare." Regarding nudity, he joked, "I won't show my wanker. There's got to be some mystery left." For the February 1990 Mardi Gras celebration in New Orleans, he was selected, along with John Goodman, to reign over one of the city's parades.

Like Jeff Daniels, Dennis prefers to be away from the spotlight, and like many others of his generation, he detests press interviews. That's why he created Buck Gibson. It is *not* Dennis one sees on the street or whom reporters meet—it is Buck. "He *enjoys* being a celebrity," Dennis says. "I've created a whole world for Buck. He's Glen Campbell's cousin. He has his own variety show on the Fox Network called 'Buck Gibson's House Party.' . . . Buck was born in Bakersfield, California, started out on 'Hee-Haw' and does personal appearances at shopping malls." Dennis claims that "Becoming Buck keeps it all in perspective and keeps me from being one of those angry young actors who shuns the public and the press and basically walks around all day thinking about how he can be more of an ass."

Filmography

Crazy Mama (New World, 1975) [scene deleted]
I Never Promised You a Rose Garden (New World, 1977)
9/30/55 [30 September, 1955] (Univ, 1977)
Are You in the House Alone? (CBS-TV, 9/20/78)
Our Winning Season (AIP, 1978)
The Seniors (Cinema Shares, 1978)
Amateur Night at the Dixie Bar and Grill (NBC-TV, 1/8/79)
Breaking Away (20th–Fox, 1979)
Gorp (Filmways, 1980)
The Long Riders (UA, 1980)
Bill (CBS-TV, 12/22/81)
All Night Long (Univ, 1981)
Caveman (UA, 1981)
The Night the Lights Went Out in Georgia

(Avco Emb, 1981) (also co-songs)
Johnny Belinda (CBS-TV, 10/19/82)
Bill: On His Own (CBS-TV, 11/9/83)
Tough Enough [Tough Dreams] (20th–Fox, 1983) (also co-song)
Jaws 3-D (Univ, 1983)
The Right Stuff (WB, 1983)
Dreamscape (20th–Fox, 1984)
Enemy Mine (20th–Fox, 1985)
Innerspace (WB, 1987)
The Big Easy (Col, 1987) (also co-song)
Suspect (Tri-Star, 1987)
D.O.A. (BV, 1988)
Everybody's All-American (WB, 1988)
Great Balls of Fire (Orion, 1989)
Postcards from the Edge (Col, 1990)
Come See the Paradise (20th–Fox, 1990)

Album Discography

The Night the Lights Went Out in Georgia (Mirage WTG-16051) [ST]

CHRISTOPHER REEVE

"To the extent that there are people out there who insist on seeing
me as Superman, there's nothing I can do about it. I think it's kind of
a bore at this point because there is so much else that I have to offer.
And I think it's just plain rude to limit anybody."

— *US* magazine, April 16, 1990

THE 6' 4" FRAME, THE BROAD SHOULDERS, THE CHISELED NOSE, THE
blue eyes, and the charming, boyish smile conjure a vision of an Adonis, or at least a
dashing gladiator of ancient Rome. These are the physical qualities of the man who,
literally overnight, became familiar to almost every moviegoing household in America
through the enactment (in four films) of a famed comic strip character who flies. In the
hope of avoiding being typecast as the caped crusader, he returns periodically to the
theater, where he may become many characters in the beginning-to-end continuity of
stage plays. Although he was among the top twenty movie box-office attractions two years
in a row, chiefly due to his comic-strip portrayal, he has never wanted to be a big movie
star. He prefers to be known as an actor—an actor constantly learning in order to perfect
his craft.

Christopher Reeve was born Thursday, September 25, 1952, in the borough of
Manhattan to Columbia University professor Franklin D. Reeve and his wife, Barbara
Johnson Reeve, a writer. His birth to the Episcopalian couple was quickly followed by that
of brother Benjamin. The boys did not grow up dependent for their entertainment on
Saturday morning cartoons, since television was not permitted in the Reeve household.
Instead, they were infused with the sound of classical music and the read-aloud words of
literary classics. Soon after he was able to walk, Christopher was introduced to both the
snow slopes and frozen ponds by his skiing- and skating-enthusiast father.

When he was four years old, his parents went through a bitter divorce. Both of them
wanted custody of the children, which ultimately was given to Barbara, with generous
visitation given to Franklin. With their mother, the boys moved to Princeton, New Jersey,
where she began writing for a local newspaper and eventually married a wealthy stockbro-
ker. That union resulted in two stepbrothers (Mark and Brock) and a stepsister (Allison).
Christopher entered the Princeton Day School and began piano lessons at age seven; he
would study piano for twelve years and owned his own Steinway by the time he was
sixteen. He was not particularly sports-minded, but discovered a love for sailing and,
through seventh-grade shop class, a bent for making things. His school also staged

numerous plays, in which he participated, and he joined Princeton's McCarter Theatre group for a singing part in the Gilbert and Sullivan operetta *Yeoman of the Guard.* Through acting, he found that he was able to forget the insecurities caused by his well-meaning parents, who each wanted him as their own.

During the summer of his fourteenth year, he studied stagecraft and makeup and had reached a height of 6' 2". He auditioned for a few Broadway plays without luck. However, the following summer he apprenticed at the Williamstown Theatre in Massachusetts, an important source of learning to which he would return during many summers in later years. At the Princeton Day School he was a letterman for four years as varsity goalie in ice hockey, was assistant conductor of the school's orchestra in his senior year, and sang high tenor in the glee club until his voice changed. The summers of these high school years were spent at the Loeb Drama Center in Cambridge, Massachusetts, the Boothbay Playhouse in Maine, and the Shakespeare Festival in San Diego. At sixteen he achieved his full height (6' 4") and became a member of Actors Equity and acquired an agent because, unlike many people his age, he knew exactly what he wanted in life.

In September 1970 Christopher enrolled at Cornell University, with major studies in English and music theory, with his summers again spent in or around theaters, one of which was the Old Vic in London and another the Comédie-Française in Paris. In 1973 he also enrolled at the Juilliard School in Manhattan, studying advanced drama under John Houseman. In the autumn of 1974 he received his B.A. from Cornell before going to work in the CBS-TV daytime soap opera "Love of Life," as an opportunistic bigamist named Ben Harper. He had intended that his salary from the soap would pay for his second year at Juilliard, but his TV character gained such popularity in the day-to-day storyline that his part was enlarged, leaving him no time to study at Juilliard. For the next eighteen months he was the heartless gold digger in "Love of Life" while on weekends he discovered the fun of glider flying and of piloting small planes. These avocations led Christopher to obtain a pilot's license. He also found time to do occasional stage work in New York with the Circle Repertory Company and the Manhattan Theatre Club.

In the winter of 1975 Christopher was chosen to play the grandson to Katharine Hepburn in Enid Bagnold's offbeat comedy *A Matter of Gravity.* After out-of-town tryouts, the show opened on Broadway at the Broadhurst Theatre on February 3, 1976, where it played through April, after which Christopher went to Hollywood to do a film. GRAY LADY DOWN (1978), starring Charlton Heston, was a tired melodrama in which Christopher had a bit part, with fifteenth billing, as Ensign Phillips aboard an endangered nuclear submarine. While in Los Angeles, Reeve also provided English-language dubbing for the Mexican-made SURVIVE! (1976), an exploitation drama about survivors of a plane crash who resort to cannibalism. (He would later do a similar English-language dubbing chore for the voice of Giancarlo Giannini in the Italian-made THE INNOCENT, finally shown in the U.S. in 1979.) Thereafter, nothing happened professionally. He contemplated his future on the beaches at Santa Monica, California, where "I was sponging off friends, sleeping on couches, turning into a vegetable and then one day I said 'this isn't right.'" He returned to New York City where he auditioned for a Woolite commercial, and then got a supporting part in an off-Broadway production of *My Life* for a limited run beginning in January 1977. This was followed by rehearsals for *Dracula*, but after two days he left that project to go to London where his life and career were to be altered greatly.

The invincible Superman began as a newspaper comic strip in 1938. Through the years it evolved into a perennial comic book feature and was further glorified by thirteen years on radio, as well as seventeen animated cartoon shorts, two movie serials with Kirk Alyn, and a TV series with George Reeves. In 1974 producers Alexander and Ilya Salkind purchased the rights to make a full-length movie of Superman's adventures. Thus began a quest to find the right actor to play the caped man of steel who fought for "truth and justice and the American way." Robert Redford, James Caan, and Clint Eastwood turned it down; Steve McQueen, Charles Bronson, Sylvester Stallone, and Bruce Jenner were all considered, then dropped for one reason or another. Because of his height and good looks, Christopher was suggested to the Salkinds as a possible candidate, and they and the actor conferred in December 1976. Christopher's initial reaction was, "Poor Hollywood. . . . Why can't they come up with something new and exciting?" However, he read the script and liked it. By this time, the producers had signed Marlon Brando and Gene Hackman as box-office insurance, so they now concentrated on finding an unknown for the title role.

By the spring of 1977, the Salkinds had failed to interview any better prospects when Christopher was flown to London for a screen test, which earned him the role. He signed a contract giving him $250,000 for five weeks of work plus $5,000 for each additional week with options for one or two sequels. Christopher began a ten-week course of weight lifting, plus a four-meal-a-day diet of high-protein food, which added 33 pounds to his 188-pound frame and two inches to his chest. Shooting began in March 1977 in London, with other location filming in New York City, New Mexico, and Alberta, Canada, over an eighteen-month period. Following a world premiere in Washington, D.C., to benefit the Special Olympics, SUPERMAN opened in 700 theaters in the United States on December 15, 1978. During its first week, it grossed $12 million, eventually earning $300 million worldwide, making it one of the all-time top money-makers.

The 143 minutes of SUPERMAN pass fairly quickly because it is a fun movie, beginning with the baby Kal-el's (seven-month-old Lee Quigley) ascent to earth from the doomed planet Krypton in a flight engineered by his parents (Marlon Brando, Susannah York). The child (Aaron Smolinski) who lands in Kansas is now five or six and displays his great strength to his adoptive earth parents (Glenn Ford, Phyllis Thaxter). Reeve enters the action as the thirty-year-old man from planet Krypton forty-seven minutes into the film when his Clark Kent applies for a job at the *Daily Planet* newspaper and is hired by harried editor Perry White (Jackie Cooper) because he is a "mild-mannered reporter" as well as the "fastest typist in the business." The remainder of the action feature deals with reporter Clark Kent's infatuation with reporter Lois Lane (Margot Kidder) and his battle with archrival Lex Luthor (Gene Hackman). Backed by John Williams's music score and sets by John Barry, the movie is a visual delight. The exceptional special effects by Colin Chivers earned him an Academy Award. At the conclusion of a long list of credits is the promise of "Superman II next year." *Variety* judged Christopher "excellent," and *After Dark* magazine found him "charming and genuine," noting that "he looks like Clark Kent should look—stern, eager, strong, virginal."

While in London, Christopher met Gae Exton, a twenty-seven-year-old models' agent, with whom he shared a flat. After completing SUPERMAN, the couple would shuttle back and forth between London and New York, eventually becoming parents to Matthew, born in 1980, and Alexandra, born in 1984.

Basking in his sudden SUPERMAN fame, he went through a "mandatory one-year idiocy period" of thinking that he was on top of the world. He also sailed a boat with a crew from Connecticut to Bermuda, bought his own plane, and taped an NBC-TV interview which was shown on "Hot Hero Sandwich," a show featuring the top heroes of American teenagers. To *People* magazine he confided, "Over the past two years I've decided I'm not a bad actor after all."

Reeve rejected a $1 million offer to replace John Travolta in AMERICAN GIGOLO (1980) because he found the movie's premise distasteful; the role then went to Richard Gere. Instead, against the advice of his agent, Reeve accepted a $500,000 offer to star in SOMEWHERE IN TIME (1980) because he responded to the story of a playwright in modern Chicago who travels back in time to 1912 to find a woman (Jane Seymour) with whose photograph he has become obsessed. Filmed for the most part at Mackinac Island, Michigan, the highly romantic tale failed to click with critics such as Vincent Canby (*New York Times*): "Unfortunately, his unshadowed good looks, granite profile, bright naivete and eagerness to please—the qualities that made him such an ideal SUPERMAN—look absurd here." John Barry's score was the highlight of the movie.

During the summer of 1980, Christopher returned to the Williamstown Theatre where he appeared in *The Front Page, Candida*, and *The Cherry Orchard*. In later summers he would do *The Greeks, Summer and Smoke, The Heiress*, and other plays there. On November 5, 1980, he opened at Broadway's New Apollo Theatre as the disabled Vietnam War veteran in *The Fifth of July*. He was replaced in April 1981 by Richard Thomas so that he could fulfill a commitment to co-star in the film adaptation of Ira Levin's stage thriller DEATHTRAP (1982). In this suspense yarn he was the young homosexual playwright caught in a deadly struggle with a burned-out dramatist (Michael Caine). *Newsweek* called it "a dandy little movie" in which "plot twists are everything" and gave Christopher credit with "getting to show new facets of his talent."

Before DEATHTRAP was released, SUPERMAN II lured moviegoers intent on finding out if the sequel would be as good as the original. For many viewers it was. Shown first in Europe in December 1980, the film was unveiled in the United States in June 1981, where in one day (June 20) it grossed more than $4.5 million. This time around, Clark Kent reveals his true identity to Lois Lane (Margot Kidder) when he makes love to her, an act that causes a temporary loss of his powers. David Denby (*New York Post*) observed, "Just as before, Christopher Reeve's little smile and charming modesty make the conceit work." Christopher's salary this time was $500,000.

As tabulated by Quigley Publications, he was #15 at the 1981 box office and #18 in 1982. His second motion picture of that year was MONSIGNOR, in which he played Father

Flaherty, a wayward Vatican priest with Mafia connections who seduces a nun (Genevieve Bujold). Audiences who bothered to see the movie found it laughable, and *People* magazine decided that director Frank Perry "has gone over the edge" by believing that "Reeve's popularity was enough to make audiences swallow two hours of staggering ineptitude."

After turning down the role of another priest, in the ABC-TV miniseries "The Thornbirds" (1983), which went to Richard Chamberlain, Christopher, who had previously insisted he would not do another sequel, was in SUPERMAN III in June 1983. This entry was found by critic Roger Ebert to be "a cinematic comic book, shallow, silly, filled with stunts and action, without much human interest." On July 7, 1983, he was the prince in Shelley Duvall's "Faerie Tale Theatre" Showtime–Cable episode "Sleeping Beauty." In THE BOSTONIANS (1984), a talky adaptation of the Henry James novel, he was the southern lawyer who travels to Boston where he battles with a nineteenth-century feminist (Vanessa Redgrave) for the affections and soul of a young woman (Madeleine Potter). This production did not sit well with non–art house moviegoers, nor did his next film, THE AVIATOR (1985), which permitted him to be paid for indulging in flying, one of his off-screen thrills. In 1984, prior to the release of this film, he was in London while Gae Exton awaited the birth of their second child. At the West End Theatre he appeared opposite Vanessa Redgrave and Wendy Hiller in a dramatization of Henry James's *The Aspern Papers.*

Always reticent in public regarding his relationship with Gae, he insisted that marriage "can't take the place of genuine trust." He also stated that he had more to offer moviemakers than his SUPERMAN image suggested. He got the opportunity to do romance in the CBS-TV movie adaptation of ANNA KARENINA (March 26, 1985). In the torrid Leo Tolstoy drama he was Count Aleksey Vronsky, who is irresistibly drawn to the title figure (Jacqueline Bisset). The *Chicago Tribune* commended Reeve as "the perfect Victorian hero; dark, handsome, self-indulgent and headstrong, exuding masculinity like a patina of sweat after a hard workout in the local gym." On November 5, 1985, he hosted a sixty-minute CBS-TV documentary, "Dinosaur!," and later narrated a tribute to the spectacular stunt-flying Blue Angels called "Touch the Sky." Off the screen for two years, Christopher returned as a magazine writer-turned-TV reporter in STREET SMART (1987). He was credible as the dishonest journalist, but acting laurels went to Morgan Freeman as the conniving pimp.

He was scheduled to star as THE RUNNING MAN (1987), but because of lengthy preproduction delays, he was forced to relinquish the role in order to fulfill another commitment. He was replaced by Arnold Schwarzenegger. In July 1987 the man of steel flew yet again in SUPERMAN IV: THE QUEST FOR PEACE. Christopher also received credits for co-writing the story and as one of the second-unit directors. The quest of the title referred to Superman's efforts to rid the world of nuclear arms and his squelching of a profiteer (Gene Hackman, returning as Lex Luthor). Critic Gene Siskel complained, "It's as if all the scenes are half-written to save money." This fourth entry in the series was a box-office disappointment.

During the summer of 1987, while at Williamstown, Massachusetts, in *The Rover*, he met a twenty-eight-year-old actress named Dana Morosini, who became his live-in partner after he and Gae Exton separated. Of this breakup with Gae, he has said that they remained "very good friends and have a very comfortable relationship." Although he had avoided marriage with Gae because "The impression I got of marriage as a child was that marriage is not a stable institution," he has said that there exist "strong possibilities" of a marital union with Dana.

From February 19 to April 10, 1988, Christopher was at Los Angeles's Ahmanson Theatre in the Center Theatre Group's revival of *Summer and Smoke*, opposite Christine Lahti. Polly Warfield (*Drama-Logue*) recorded that he "couldn't look more right" and "does what he does well enough, though rather woodenly." In March 1988, a fourth film version of Ben Hecht and Charles MacArthur's play *The Front Page* was released as SWITCHING CHANNELS. The classic newspaper story was updated to a Chicago cable TV station, with Kathleen Turner as a TV newscaster, Burt Reynolds as the boss, and Christopher (with hair dyed blond) third-billed as the filthy rich sporting-goods magnate engaged to wed Turner. This version was ill-received and disappeared in a few weeks after grossing just $8 million.

No longer able to pick and choose his acting assignments, he traveled to Yugoslavia to film THE GREAT ESCAPE II: THE UNTOLD STORY (November 6–7, 1988), a four-hour NBC-TV movie, which chronicled the fate of Nazi prison escapees. He played the character created by James Garner (but with a different character name) in THE GREAT ESCAPE (1963). In the sequel, Reeve returns to Germany after the war to search for the men who had murdered fifty escapees in defiance of the Geneva Conventions. Although *People* magazine criticized him for delivering his lines "as if they were the Boy Scout oath," the *San Francisco Chronicle* found that "his performance reflects the toned-down psychological nature of this treatment."

In New York in 1988 he helped raise $500,000 for the Design Industries Foundation for AIDS with a dinner and auction of art and furnishings. In February 1989 he acted off-Broadway in *The Winter's*

Christopher Reeve in STREET SMART (1987).

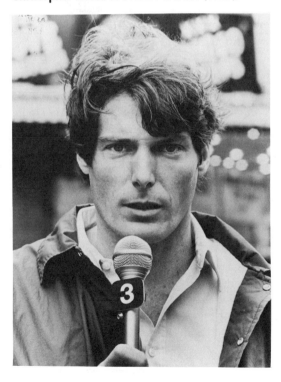

Tale with Mandy Patinkin for Joseph Papp's Public Theatre. On August 29, 1989, he hosted "National Driving Test" on CBS-TV. When asked why he had not been seen in a movie for some time, he responded, "I'm basically waiting for Harrison Ford to retire."

On November 18, 1989, on the Fox TV network he, Robert Wagner, and Olivia Newton-John gave reports on environmental issues on "Timebomb: Mother Earth," and on January 29, 1990, he hosted the Theatre Hall of Fame in New York City, a live award show. At a time when many actors were performing in the "revolving-door" cast of *Love Letters* on stage, Christopher was in the production in San Francisco with Julie Hagerty at Theatre-on-the-Square from February 6 to 18, 1990; in New York City with Dana Ivey at the Promenade Theatre the week of April 24, 1990; and in Los Angeles the week of May 9, 1990, again with Hagerty as his stage partner. For the San Francisco engagement, he flew his plane in from New York and, during his stay in the area, piloted the space shuttle simulator at Moffett Field where he landed safely from Hawaii at 80,000 feet. (He and Hagerty would again reprise their *Love Letters* roles in San Francisco from November 6 to 17, 1990.)

Having refused to pitch Japanese cigarettes in commercials in that country, Reeve became a spokesperson for Maidenform Bra in the United States because "I need money quick" to pay taxes owed to the British government. In the advertisements he said, "Women don't wear beautiful lingerie just for men. But thank you anyway." In March 1990, at a Washington, D.C., rally, he joined other celebrities in protesting a ban against alleged obscenity in federally funded arts projects. On the Discovery cable channel on March 18, 1990, he narrated "Black Tide," a documentary exposing the effects on the marine ecosystem resulting from the 1989 Exxon oil tanker spill in Alaska. *Daily Variety* rated his narration as a "stirring commentary."

In the TNT–Cable movie THE ROSE AND THE JACKAL (April 16, 1990), Christopher was detective Allan Pinkerton, who was instrumental in saving President Abraham Lincoln from a Baltimore assassination attempt in 1861, and then brought a charming Confederate spy (Madolyn Smith Osborne) to justice. Allan Pinkerton, of course, was the founder of the now-famous Pinkerton Detective Agency. *TV Guide* magazine's criticism of the Georgia-lensed movie noted, "Neither of the stars lives up to expectations, but if you've always wanted to see Reeve hiding beneath a big beard and speaking with a Scottish accent, this is your chance."

By the spring of 1990, Christopher had become one of Hollywood's most outspoken fundraisers for AIDS research. His long-time agent, Stark Hesseltine, had died of the disease in 1987, the first of twelve of Reeve's friends who succumbed. "People told me that a heterosexual movie star should be careful," he said, or "people would think I was gay. I told them to stuff it. When you see babies and middle-aged women die of AIDS, you realize the disease cuts across all segments."

The World's Greatest Stunts! A Tribute to Hollywood Stuntmen, a documentary hosted by Christopher, was in general homevideo release in August 1990 with "chat" provided by Arnold Schwarzenegger, Michael Douglas, and Charlton Heston.

For CBS-TV, Christopher co-starred in the TV movie BUMP IN THE NIGHT

(January 6, 1991). Meredith Baxter played an alcoholic journalist, with Reeve cast as a college professor who is also a crafty kidnapper and pederast. Next he became one of the first to travel, following the reunification of Germany, to Poland and the former East Berlin to film the theatrical release MIDNIGHT SPY (forthcoming, 1991). It is the true story of Polish count Adam Tarnowski, who spied against the Nazis prior to Germany's conquest of Poland in 1939. The movie co-stars Joan Severance and Mariel Hemingway. For Lifetime Cable's DEATH DREAMS (1991), Reeve plays a jealous husband to Marg Helgenberger, whose murdered stepdaughter (Taylor Fry) refuses to stay dead.

When asked why he had picked acting as a profession, he once analyzed, "If you look at pictures of me when I was a kid I never cracked a smile. Really grim. Acting was a way to help me loosen up, expose myself, relax, and I think I've made some progress. But I also think it takes twenty years to make an actor. I'm halfway there."

One of those rare actors who finds aging to be an agreeable biological event—to dispel the Superman connection—he predicts, "between 37 and 57 I think more opportunities will be coming up." With glee he stated in early 1990: "I'm too old to play Superman anymore. I'm looking for a brilliant role that pays tons of money." Finding the leading-man status a frustrating one, he now states, "It's the character parts, the quirky, offbeat, contradictory people surrounding leading men that I've always found more interesting. That's what I'm seeking." However, by late 1990, Reeve, in a seeming turnabout, admitted that he had been talking recently with producers Ilya and Alexander Salkind about a possible SUPERMAN V. "If it can be a wonderful movie with a wonderful script, I'd be happy to do it."

Filmography

Survive! (Par, 1976) (dubbing only)
Gray Lady Down (Univ, 1978)
Superman (WB, 1978)
The Innocent (Analysis Film, 1979) (dubbing only)
Somewhere in Time (Univ, 1980)
Superman II (WB, 1980)
Deathtrap (WB, 1982)
Monsignor (20th–Fox, 1982)
Superman III (WB, 1983)
The Bostonians (Almi, 1984)
Anna Karenina (CBS-TV, 3/26/85)

The Aviator (MGM/UA, 1985)
Street Smart (Cannon, 1987)
Superman IV: The Quest for Peace (WB, 1987) (also co-story, co–second-unit director)
The Great Escape II: The Untold Story (NBC-TV, 11/6/88–11/7/88)
Switching Channels (Tri-Star, 1988)
The Rose and the Jackal (TNT–Cable, 4/16/90)
Bump in the Night (CBS-TV, 1/6/91)
Death Dreams (Lifetime Cable, 6/25/91)

Future Releases

Midnight Spy (Axelia International, 1991)

TV Series

Love of Life (CBS, 1974–76)

Broadway Plays

A Matter of Gravity (1976)

JOHN RITTER

"Let's face it: there are people out there who think I'm a little too big for Mr. Camera. . . . Like I'm always playing scenes much too big for the camera. . . . Like all I can do is fall or drool. You wonder what you need to do to prove yourself?"

—*TV Guide* magazine, December 12, 1987

IF A TALLY WERE TAKEN OF THE NUMBER OF TIMES JOHN RITTER HAS been seen on worldwide television, including reruns, specials, variety shows, movies, and even a witless "All-Star Family Feud," the count would reveal that he is one of Hollywood's most-often-seen TV personalities. It is quite a record, considering that he has been at it only since age twenty-four, or less than twenty years.

Known for his charm, energy, and easy-going nature, he has seldom been photographed wearing anything but a very happy face. *Movie Life* magazine in 1979 aptly called it his "swallow the ears smile." In the early-to-mid-1970s, although playing the semiregular part of a Baptist minister on CBS-TV's "The Waltons," he was, in real life, well known for his serious drive to bed down every young, attractive woman who crossed his path. He viewed these women coldly as mere conquests. While the media have, at various times, referred to him as "impish," adorable," and a "cuddly stud," director Blake Edwards likens his comedic talents to those of Peter Sellers. Like Billy Crystal and Robin Williams, Ritter is a natural-born ham. However, he admits that he is not nearly as quick a wit as they, that he is not a comedian, but an actor who does comedy. He claims that that is more difficult than to act in drama.

Jonathan Southworth Ritter was born on Tuesday, September 17, 1948, in Burbank, California. He was the second son of Maurice Woodward "Tex" Ritter, the country singer who starred in scores of western movies, and his wife, former actress Dorothy Fay Southworth Ritter. He and his brother, Thomas (born in 1946 with cerebral palsy), led an insulated life, with much exposure to sound stages. Young John loved to pretend he was someone else. He learned to do impersonations in an attempt to be popular among his peers. His lip-synching, hip-swivelling imitation of Elvis Presley's "Hound Dog" was high on the list of his most-appreciated routines. Baseball was a favorite pastime. However, between the ages of twelve and fourteen, his attention was focused, with that of other neighborhood kids, on the making of a home-movie version of TV's "Bonanza," which they titled "Bananas." His father, a popular recording artist, thought John might have musical talent and bought him a guitar. But the instrument only gathered dust.

At Hollywood High School he was elected president of the student council in his senior year. By then, his attention had turned to politics. "I wanted to be junior senator from California by the time I was thirty-five, but I couldn't take myself seriously that long," he has said. After John graduated from school in 1966, his father, who had studied law at Northwestern University, hoped that John would do the same. However, at the University of Southern California in Los Angeles, John chose psychology as his major, planning to become a psychiatrist. Within two years, though, following the death of two of his idols—Robert Kennedy and Martin Luther King, Jr.—he felt a need to express himself and found that he could best do that through acting. Switching his interest to theater arts, he joined a college theater troupe in 1968, traveling to Edinburgh, Scotland, to participate in a summer program of plays. The following summer, he rejoined the group, which returned to Scotland and performed also in England, Holland, and Germany. Other college vacations were spent in Nashville, to which his parents had moved and where Tex Ritter ran unsuccessfully for the U.S. Senate in 1970.

Graduating from USC with a B.A. degree in drama in 1971, John took acting lessons in Los Angeles from both Stella Adler and Nina Foch. Finally convinced that his older son intended to pursue an acting career, Tex Ritter advised John to "Just keep your mouth shut and listen more." During his first year in the profession, John began assembling an impressive resumé. He debuted in an episode of ABC-TV's detective series "Dan August," starring Burt Reynolds. He had supporting parts in two Walt Disney screen comedies: THE BAREFOOT EXECUTIVE (1971) and SCANDALOUS JOHN (1971). In addition, he made several stage appearances in summer stock and regional theater. He performed in *Desire Under the Elms* with Eva Marie Saint at the Berkshire Theatre Festival in Stockbridge, Massachusetts. At Jean Stapleton's Totem Pole Playhouse in Pennsylvania he was in *The Glass Menagerie* and *Butterflies Are Free*, and he was in several productions with the First Los Angeles Free Shakespeare Festival. Also in Los Angeles, at the Mark Taper Forum Laboratory, he appeared in *Nevada*. He also joined the troupe of Harvey Lembeck's Comedy Workshop in Hollywood. There he spent several years learning and doing improvisational comedy as well as forming a friendship with fellow performer Robin Williams.

John played his first minister role in the NBC-TV movie EVIL ROY SLADE (February 18, 1972), a comedy western strung together from two unsold TV pilots. He had a small part in the supernatural drama THE OTHER (1972), and in the fall of 1972 he appeared in an episode of CBS-TV's "Hawaii Five-O." Beginning October 26, 1972, he took the occasional role of Baptist minister Reverend Matthew Fordwick in the immensely popular CBS-TV dramatic series "The Waltons." Over the next four years, he would appear in thirteen more segments. "Bachelor-at-Law" (June 5, 1973) was a CBS-TV pilot produced by Mary Tyler Moore's production company. It starred John as an idealistic young attorney who goes to work for an irascible older lawyer (Harold Gould). The would-be series failed to find a buyer. In August 1973 Ritter was seen on theater screens in a minor role as a Vietnam veteran in Charles Bronson's excessively violent THE STONE KILLER.

In Nashville in early January 1974, Tex Ritter, now dying, told John, "No matter how good you think you are, you're not—never rest easy and keep tuning the thing up." After Tex's death, John's mother would remain in Nashville, becoming the official greeter at the Grand Ole Opry; his brother, Thomas, would become an attorney. Returning briefly to the stage, John was one of several young comedians in a fast-moving one-act revue, *Break-Up*, at the Next Stage Theatre in Los Angeles. During 1975 he worked in a variety of TV series: "Mannix," "Petrocelli," "The Streets of San Francisco," "The Mary Tyler Moore Show," and "The Rookies." On Halloween night, 1975, John was among those in the ABC-TV movie THE NIGHT THAT PANICKED AMERICA, which depicted the nationwide fright resulting from the famous 1938 radio broadcast of "War of the Worlds" by Orson Welles and his Mercury Theatre players.

In March 1975, on the set of NICKELODEON (1976), in which he played a man involved earnestly with early Hollywood moviemaking, John met Nancy Morgan. She was an extra in the picture as well as a veteran of many commercials. Six months later, they moved together to a rented house in Benedict Canyon, Los Angeles, thereby putting an end to John's freewheeling bachelorhood. Later that year, he competed with fifty other actors in auditioning for the lead in a proposed ABC-TV sitcom to be called "Three's Company," adapted from the hit British TV series "A Man About the House." Programming chief Fred Silverman chose John for the part, with a pilot telecast in March 1976, followed by two more pilots, each trying out additional characters.

Ritter continued episodic television appearances in "Starsky and Hutch," "Rhoda," and "Phyllis" in 1976 and on "Hawaii Five-O" in February 1977, before "Three's Company" premiered as a series on March 15, 1977. The titillating premise of the show cast Ritter as Jack Tripper, a girl-chasing young Los Angelean who is an excellent cook. He pretends to be gay in order to save money by sharing an apartment with two attractive young single women (Joyce DeWitt and Suzanne Somers, the latter replaced in the final years by Priscilla Barnes). The comedy was deliberately raunchy and puerile. *Variety* noted, "The show flirted continually with double entendre possibilities and was often on the border of bad taste, but it did succeed in evoking a fair amount of laughs, mostly from the deft playing of John Ritter as the student, and Audra Lindley and Norman Fell, as the landlord and his wife." Audiences loved it, ABC's ratings went up, and it became a regular series beginning September 13, 1977. By February 1978 it was the most popular program on prime-time television. The series would run for seven years, ending with its final network (rerun) showing of September 18, 1984. John would receive an Emmy Award five days later, on September 23, 1984, following a Golden Globe win. To this day, the 174 taped episodes, including the 1984 special retrospective show hosted by Lucille Ball, are constantly televised somewhere in the world.

During the summer of 1977, John was in summer stock at the Westport County Playhouse in Connecticut before marrying Nancy Morgan on October 16 in Bel Air in a Methodist ceremony conducted by the Reverend Bob Watson, a celebrity minister. Ecstatic with happiness, Nancy said, "We expect to be together for the rest of our lives," while John informed the press, "If ABC said 'goodbye' and everybody else said 'he's a has-been,' it would be totally fine with me as long as we had each other." In July 1978 they purchased a two-story English country-style home in Brentwood where it was reported that their best friends were Ron Howard and his wife, Cheryl. In February 1980 son Jason was born, followed in 1982 by daughter Carly and in 1985 by son Tyler. Also in 1977, for the first time John hosted the annual United Cerebral Palsy Association telethon, a job he would accept eagerly during the years to come. By 1989, it was estimated that the fundraisers had garnered more than $130 million.

In 1978 he co-starred on the big screen in the little-seen BREAKFAST IN BED, the story of a disintegrating marriage. He received top billing in the ABC-TV movie LEAVE YESTERDAY BEHIND (May 14, 1978) in a dramatic role as a veterinary student paralyzed for life. On television in 1978, aside from "Three's Company," he was host or guest star on nine separate occasions in such shows as ABC's "Silver Anniversary Celebration" and CBS's "The Goldie Hawn Special." On theater screens he was the president of the United States with wife Nancy Morgan as First Lady in AMERICATHON (1979). He also made a guest appearance in "The Party" episode of "The Ropers," a series spin-off of "Three's Company," shown on September 15, 1979. That year, Ritter, seeking to gain greater inner peace, completed the Werner Erhard seminar training in EST.

In February 1980 he starred in HERO AT LARGE as a luckless actor who becomes a "Captain Avenger" in a tight-fitting, Superman-type costume. On April 11, 1980, in an ABC-TV movie, he was THE COMEBACK KID, a minor-league baseball pitcher coaching a gang of disadvantaged kids. For WHOLLY MOSES! (1980), a biblical comedy that *People* magazine termed "witless" and "tedious," he performed a cameo as the devil. He was in an episode of the religious-oriented syndicated TV series "Insight" in 1981 and joined Audrey Hepburn and Ben Gazzara as co-stars of THEY ALL LAUGHED (1981), filmed in New York City. Directed by Peter Bogdanovich, who had helmed NICKELODEON, the frenetic comedy was a failure. Once again John was a minister, this time dramatically involved with television evangelism, in the ABC-TV movie PRAY TV (February 1, 1982). However, he was back in romantic comedy in the CBS-TV film IN LOVE WITH AN OLDER WOMAN (November 24, 1982) as a cocky attorney tumbling romantically for a divorced mother (Karen Carlson) who has a daughter (Jamie Rose) his own age. ABC's "The Love Boat" claimed him as a guest star in a November 1983 episode, and he was abundantly charming as a comic forced to go to work driving the SUNSET LIMOUSINE (October 12, 1983), a CBS-TV movie. John became the 1,768th star to be honored with a star on the Hollywood

John Ritter in HERO AT LARGE (1980).

Boulevard Walk of Fame; it was situated next to the star honoring his father. In the Los Angeles Stage Company's production of *The Middle Ages*, John co-starred with Rue McClanahan beginning March 21, 1984. Two months later he and Penny Marshall starred in the ABC-TV movie LOVE THY NEIGHBOR (May 23, 1984) as next-door enemies thrown together when their spouses (Constance McCashin, Bert Convy) fall in love.

In 1984, with attorney Robert Myman, John formed Adam Productions, Inc., to produce television offerings, including series and telefeatures.

On September 25, 1984, ABC-TV introduced its continuing comedic situation spin-off "Three's a Crowd," with John reprising the part of Jack Tripper. This time he is living with his girlfriend (Mary Cadorette), but is constantly visited by her harassing father (Robert Mandan), who happens to own the building. *TV Guide* magazine's Cyra McFadden admitted, "By now it's hard to take [Ritter] seriously when he does a TV-movie and [plays] someone other than Jack." She credited him with holding "the spin-off together, as he held together the original. An accomplished and inventive physical clown, he hasn't yet exhausted the number of ways he can walk into a swinging door." Although McFadden predicted that "Three's a Crowd" would have "staying power," the derivative series lasted only twenty-two episodes, proving the truth of *Variety*'s contention that the series rehash had "more force than farce."

Meanwhile, John had co-hosted "The Secret World of the Very Young" on CBS-TV in September 1984 to help parents understand the way their children think. John said, "Kids are funny. They're also mysterious, adorable and surprising." He guest-starred in an episode of TV's short-lived "Pryor's Place" in November 1984 and was one of several guests (ranging from Bruce Jenner to Andy Warhol) on "Donald Duck's 50th Birthday" on CBS-TV. He co-starred with Sharon Gless in a screwball romance, LETTING GO (May 11, 1985), an ABC-TV movie packaged by Adam Productions. In the animated ABC-TV movie FLIGHT OF THE DRAGONS (August 3, 1986), he provided the voice of a young Boston writer who travels back in time to the era before the dawn of the age of science. On September 27, 1986, he was reunited with his good friend and admirer Lucille Ball in the "Lucy Makes a Hit with John Ritter" segment of TV's "Life with Lucy."

John could not have gotten further away from the slapstick Jack Tripper characterization than he did in UNNATURAL CAUSES (November 10, 1986), an NBC-TV movie in which he was a Vietnam veteran dying from the effects of the defoliant known as Agent Orange. For Dolly Parton's TV acting debut, he took the unbilled part of a sympathetic judge in the ABC-TV movie A SMOKY MOUNTAIN CHRISTMAS (December 14, 1986). Shifting back to comedy, he fell in love with Connie Sellecca who was engaged to marry another man (John Bennett Perry) in THE LAST FLING (February 9, 1987). This ABC-TV movie prompted *People* magazine to suggest, "If you can't guess how this trifle ends, then you must have just bought your first TV." He was again sympathetic, this time as a warden, in a relatively minor role in the CBS-TV movie PRISON FOR CHILDREN (March 14, 1987). In extremely limited release beginning in September 1987, the long-shelved REAL MEN starred him opposite James Belushi as a nerd about to meet extraterrestrials. This effort was soon relegated to home viewing, and *Video Review* magazine graded it as "an enjoyable if repetitive absurdist comedy."

Not wanting to "go down in history as 'Jack Tripper,'" John's Adam Productions developed a new teleseries for him. The result, "Hooperman," premiered on ABC on September 23, 1987. The show cast him as a San Francisco police inspector whose murdered landlady wills him her apartment building along with her yapping dog. *Variety* enthused of this blend of comedy and drama, "Not only does John Ritter . . . once again demonstrate his range and compassion, he leads an ensemble cast in a funny, even charming cop show; that doesn't happen often." The show survived two seasons, ending in the spring of 1989. (In 1988 he received the People's Choice Award for Best Male Performance in a New TV Program.)

Ritter was unbilled in a cameo appearance as Cindy Williams's unfaithful husband, who meets an early demise, in the CBS-TV movie TRICKS OF THE TRADE (December 8, 1988). His widow joins with the hooker (Markie Post) in whose apartment he is murdered to find his killer before the murderer gets them. On the environmental front, John took a trip through portions of the Amazon jungle in Brazil in August 1989 to witness firsthand the depletion of the rain forest. Accompanying him were Dr. Thomas Lovely of the Smithsonian Institution and actor Tom Cruise and his then-wife, Mimi Rogers. Also intent on preserving Santa Monica Bay in Southern California, John was a strong supporter of the organization Heal the Bay. During the summer of 1989 the environmental group held a "teach-in" on Santa Monica Beach which included a dramatization of the dangers of nonbiodegradable trash in the bay. Dressed as Toxic Man for the event, Ritter explained that it was a personal experience that had led him to get involved actively in the environmental movement. "It probably began when I bit into some Santa Monica fish and started to glow," he half-joked.

According to *Boxoffice* magazine's critique of SKIN DEEP (1989), "The condom scene alone will no doubt put a few extra million dollars in the bank." That scene has John as a hard-drinking writer with a great hunger for women doing phallic battle in the dark with a British rock singer, both of them naked except for glow-in-the-dark condoms. The Blake Edwards–directed comedy managed to attract a total of $19.7 million in domestic box-office receipts. Within a few months it was on video, and the *San Francisco Chronicle* wrote of Ritter, who seemingly could not cross over successfully from the small screen to the big screen, "This underrated actor from trivial TV shows surprises with his comic and dramatic range." *Daily Variety*'s review of MY BROTHER'S WIFE (December 17, 1989), an ABC-TV movie, was not as kind: "Ritter doesn't get a handle on the character's inferred charm, so the soufflé collapses." As a man in love with the wife (Mel Harris) of his brother (David Byron) for twenty-seven years, he had to age through makeup including a full beard with gray streaks. John's production company was involved in two 1989 TV series, "Have Faith" and "Anything But Love."

In February 1990 John was seen on TV promoting Professor Claude Olney's audio and video seminars for students hoping to achieve higher grades in school. Four months later, Ritter and his family were featured in the thirty-two-minute Hi-Tops videotape *Baby Songs Presents John Lithgow's Kid-Size Concert*. On June 7, 1990, John hosted the ABC-TV hour-long "American Red Cross Emergency Test," which offered tests and facts regarding accidents. *Entertainment Weekly* magazine predicted that PROBLEM CHILD (1990) "could be the sleeper hit of the summer" and that "It might do for Ritter what LOOK WHO'S TALKING [1989] did for John Travolta." It tells the story of a childless couple (Ritter, Amy Yasbeck) who adopt a seven-year-old boy (Michael Oliver), a charming monster who wreaks havoc in their lives and in the father's career. In general release on July 28, 1990, on 1,714 movie screens, the comedy grossed $10.03 million during its first week and by its ninth week of release had taken in more than $47.86 million domestically, a respectable showing. Critics were not as kind as ticket buyers, however. *People* magazine credited John with being "as usual, appealingly earnest," but said of the film that its "ugly moments can't help but leave a bad taste." *Daily Variety* called PROBLEM CHILD a "serious contender for the worst release of the year."

John was one of the notables (including Milton Berle, Jamie Lee Curtis, Ted Danson, Whoopi Goldberg, and Cheech Marin) who appeared in the home video *Help Save Planet Earth*, released in September 1990. THE DREAMER OF OZ, an NBC-TV movie tentatively scheduled for viewing on Easter Sunday (April 15, 1990) did not air until December 10, 1990. John starred as L. Frank Baum in this dramatization of the life of the author of *The Wonderful Wizard of Oz* and its many sequels. Charles Solomon of the *Los Angeles Times* labeled the production "A Mushy Story of the Wizard Behind 'The Wizard of Oz'" and criticized Ritter for "playing Baum as a one-dimensional bo-bo of such unfaltering goodness that he makes Mr. Rogers look like the Marquis de Sade." The more kindly *Variety* acknowledged that Ritter performed his role "enthusiastically . . . as a gentle, loving, uncomplicated man." From October 16–21, 1990, at the Canon Theatre in Beverly Hills, John and Annette O'Toole read *Love Letters* by A. R. Gurney. In the first few segments of "Anything But Love" (ABC-TV), a returning sitcom starring Jamie Lee Curtis and Richard Lewis, John helped spice the proceedings by guesting as a photographer in pursuit of Hannah (Curtis). The series began its new season on February 6, 1991.

John was to play the "debonair moneyman" in THE MARRYING MAN (1991) but backed out at the last moment; he was replaced by Alec Baldwin (teamed with Kim Basinger). In November 1990, John appeared in the adaptation of the 1986 best-selling *Stephen King's It* for ABC-TV. Said Ritter, "I always wanted to do a scary picture." Airing on November 18 and 20 in a four-hour production, STEPHEN KING'S IT told of seven children in Maine in 1960 who confront an evil spirit (it) and make a pact to reunite if the sinister force should ever reappear. Thirty years later it does, and architect John Ritter and his childhood pals (including Richard Thomas, Annette O'Toole, and Dennis Christopher) convene. The highly promoted telefeature received mixed reviews, with *Daily Variety* noting, "something's wrong when principal characters get in the way of the chills." *Entertainment Weekly* magazine rated the show a B– for its slow pacing, but added, "Once the adults are assembled, though, IT features a high level of ensemble acting rare for any horror film."

The NBC-TV movie MY FATHER GREW UP (March 3, 1991) found John as the father of an eleven-year-old boy (Matthew Lawrence). He has remarried, as has the boy's mother (Margaret Whitton). When the youngster goes through a coming-of-age trauma, his (step)parents are forced to readjust their values and lives as well. Laurence Vittes (*Hollywood Reporter*) found virtues in this made-for-television drama, but noted, "Ritter misjudges the energy he needs to create his character. As he shows at the end, with restraint he could be a fine actor." *Daily Variety* concurred: "John Ritter has a tough time coping as the father of an alienated preteen in his latest vidpic. A plodding, uneven script—which fails to define adequately his character's motivations and suffers from assembly line dialog—and a fairy tale ending exacerbate the problem."

Meanwhile, with the huge success of PROBLEM CHILD, John reunited with Jack Warden for a sequel, PROBLEM CHILD II (1991), which was shot in Orlando, Florida. Laraine Newman and Michael Oliver rounded out the cast of this comedy follow-up.

John once said of his heritage, "If I had grown up with just dad, I'd have become a good ol' boy and probably been a trucker. And if I'd been raised by mother, I'd be an interior designer. Between the two, I have a nice balance."

Filmography

The Barefoot Executive (BV, 1971)

Scandalous John (BV, 1971)

Evil Roy Slade (NBC-TV, 2/18/72)

The Other (20th–Fox, 1972)

The Stone Killer (Col, 1973)

The Night That Panicked America (ABC-TV, 10/31/75)

Nickelodeon (Col, 1976)

Leave Yesterday Behind (ABC-TV, 5/14/78)

Breakfast in Bed (William Haugse, 1978)

Americathon (UA, 1979)

The Comeback Kid (ABC-TV, 4/11/80)

Hero at Large (MGM/UA, 1980)

Wholly Moses! (Col, 1980)

They All Laughed (20th–Fox, 1981)

Pray TV (ABC-TV, 2/1/82)

In Love with an Older Woman (CBS-TV, 11/24/82)

Sunset Limousine (CBS-TV, 10/12/83)

Love Thy Neighbor (ABC-TV, 5/23/84)

Letting Go (ABC-TV, 5/11/85)

Flight of the Dragons (ABC-TV, 8/3/86) (voice only)

Unnatural Causes (NBC-TV, 11/10/86)

A Smoky Mountain Christmas (ABC-TV, 12/14/86)

The Last Fling (ABC-TV, 2/9/87)

Prison for Children (CBS-TV, 3/14/87)

Real Men (MGM/UA, 1987)

Tricks of the Trade (CBS-TV, 12/8/88)

My Brother's Wife (ABC-TV, 12/17/89)

Skin Deep (20th–Fox, 1989)

Problem Child (Univ, 1990)

Stephen King's It (ABC-TV, 11/18/90; 11/20/90)

The Dreamer of Oz: The L. Frank Baum Story (NBC-TV, 12/10/90)

My Father Grew Up (NBC-TV, 3/3/91)

Problem Child II (Univ, 1991)

Television Series

The Waltons (CBS, 1972–76) (semi-recurring role)

Three's Company (ABC, 1977–84)

Three's a Crowd (ABC, 1984–85)

Hooperman (ABC, 1987–89)

MICKEY ROURKE

"You could be mediocre and be a success in the movie business; it's not any big deal. Look around at who the stars are in the American film industry. Most of them can hardly call themselves actors. So I don't put much stock in 'success.'"

—*Interview* magazine, January 1988

THE MARLBORO MAN OF HOLLYWOOD IS NOT CLEAN SHAVEN, NOR does he wear a cowboy hat or ride a horse. He is dressed in black leather, drives a Harley-Davidson motorcycle, and chain-smokes cigarettes. Between puffs, he angrily criticizes the Hollywood establishment in the well-known, soft-spoken voice that frequently lapses into profanity. Although he has not had any major screen hits in the United States, he is considered a hot item, especially prized as a rough sex symbol by European and South American filmgoers. While friends revere him for his loyalty, generosity, and sensitivity, and perhaps love him for his raunchiness, he admits to disillusionment with the movie industry because "all that *really* matters is how much money your film makes."

Most often his screen work falls into the molds of Marlon Brando or James Dean, but contemporary comparison may be made with Ray Sharkey or Jack Scalia. Preferring not to shave unless he has to, he is happiest in the reckless company of his bandana-wearing biker buddies, careening along the well-tended boulevards of Beverly Hills. "At any second," he admits, "somebody could run through a red light and run you over. That's kind of exciting in a way."

He was born Philip Andre Rourke, Jr., in 1950 in Schenectady, New York, to unhappy Irish/Scottish Catholic parents who fought constantly. He, his older sister, and his younger brother escaped the parental bickering by frequently fleeing to the downstairs apartment where their grandmother lived, to watch TV and eat chocolate cake. Since his father, a caretaker/bartender at a country club, was also named Philip, the boy was called Mickey. When he was seven years old, his parents divorced, with his mother and grandmother relocating to Miami Beach with the children. Mickey, who wanted to remain with his father, embarked on several years of what he terms "a nightmare," but has studiously avoided providing details. They lived in the back of a launderette operated by the grandmother until Mrs. Rourke married a policeman with five sons. Said to be a violent man, the stepfather apparently made Mickey's life miserable to the point where he would lie in bed at night wondering, "Why me? Why is this happening to me?"

Mickey was not a good student. At school, his daydreaming constantly got him into trouble with teachers, from whom he refused to take direction. His problem with authority figures stemmed from his distrust of adults. When he was fourteen, he began to train as a boxer at Miami's Fifth Street Gym, where Muhammad Ali had gotten his early training. Rourke was unable to tolerate wearing protective headgear because of claustrophobia. During his stay at Miami Beach High School, an affluent school where students drove their own cars and had money to spend, Mickey bused tables during his free time to earn pocket money. He was a loner who did not fit in, but he did join both the football squad and the boxing team. When not working out at the Fifth Street Gym, he boxed at the Police Athletic League where, in his eighteenth year, he suffered a concussion. He quit the ring, but not because of the injury. In retrospect, he claimed that he abandoned boxing because "I didn't have the discipline. I didn't have enough guidance or respect for myself."

After graduating from high school he spent most of the next few years hanging out at the 48th Street Beach and smoking marijuana. He took time away from the beach to appear in an amateur stage production of the prison drama *Deathwatch*. Although he did not consider acting to be a masculine activity, he was enthralled with the potential of opening up emotionally through the use of a writer's words. In 1975, fed up with the beach as well as the drug scene, he borrowed money from his sister for a one-way ticket to New York City. There he lived at the Marlton Hotel in Greenwich Village, where he slept with a club for protection, and had a succession of jobs: dishwasher, attack-dog agitator, massage parlor bouncer, parking lot attendant, street pretzel vendor. For the most part, he existed on "sacks of potato chips and stolen Hershey bars." For a short time he studied cosmetology with Giuseppe Franco (who would later become a hairstylist to Hollywood stars), but abandoned that to study with drama coach Sandra Seacat. "It was like some crazy therapy," he has remembered, "and when I realized that I wanted more from acting than just a payday, that's when everything started to click." He also studied at the Lee Strasberg Theatre Institute and spent a year at the Actors Studio where, he claims, nothing ever happened.

Early in 1979, he went to Los Angeles where he got an unbilled job in Steven Spielberg's comedy 1941 (1979). Within months, the ambitious newcomer obtained TV movie work in ABC's CITY IN FEAR (March 30, 1980), fourth-billed as Tony Pate, a psycho murderer of young blonde women. In NBC's ACT OF LOVE (September 24, 1980), he was third-billed as a quadriplegic motorcycle accident victim begging his brother (Ron Howard) to end his life. On October 30, 1980, on CBS, he portrayed John Rideout, charged by his wife (Linda Hamilton) with rape in RAPE AND MARRIAGE—THE RIDEOUT CASE, based on the real-life Oregon criminal court case. In this, his third made-for-television movie, Mickey had top billing.

On theatrical screens Rourke had the supporting role of Richie in the abundantly violent FADE TO BLACK (1980) as well as a bit part in the ill-fated western HEAVEN'S GATE (1980), which set negative box-office records with losses in excess of $34.5 million. His sixth-billed role as Teddy Lewis in BODY HEAT (1981) is the one most film historians consider Mickey's big-screen "debut." It certainly is the production that gave him the most to do up to that time, along with sufficient cause for filmgoers to wonder, "*Who* is that guy?" Soft-spoken and streetwise, he teaches William Hurt how to make a fire bomb that will kill the husband (Richard Crenna) of Kathleen Turner (in her film debut). *Variety* acknowledged that Rourke, among the other supporting players, "vividly etched" his role as a punk. BODY HEAT became *the* movie of the summer of 1981. Also in 1981 Mickey completed EUREKA as the mob lawyer/mouthpiece brother-in-law of the superb Rutger Hauer, grasping to gain Gene Hackman's gold fortune. Scheduled for release in both 1982 and 1983, the film was finally given limited distribution in October 1984.

DINER (1982), with an ensemble cast of new young actors, was written and directed by Barry Levinson. Set in 1950s Baltimore, it tells of the last months of freedom before marriage and adulthood of a group of friends, male and female. The well-received feature was instrumental in paving career paths for Steve Guttenberg, Rourke, Kevin Bacon, Ellen Barkin, and Timothy Daly. Mickey played Boogie, the unkempt beautician attending law school at night, who has women and sex uppermost in his mind. His scene in a movie theater with a box of popcorn is a classic. The role was a forerunner to many future sex-symbol parts.

In 1982 Mickey was married to Debra Feuer, a Hollywood dancer/actress. Their marriage took place outdoors on a hilltop overlooking the Pacific Ocean, near Los Angeles. Debra has stated that it was his shyness and insecurity that attracted her to him, not his

Mickey Rourke, Daryl Hannah, and Eric Roberts in THE POPE OF GREENWICH VILLAGE (1984).

looks, because "he had no socks and his hair was dirty." Theirs would not be a conventional marriage in that they would seldom live together, Mickey reasoning, "I need my space and so does she." He would engage in extramarital affairs, but both insisted that they would never divorce. "I just can't imagine my life without Debra," he has said.

Mickey had auditioned for Francis Ford Coppola for THE OUTSIDERS (1983), but since there was not a suitable part for him in that youth drama, he was instead co-starred with Matt Dillon in Coppola's second feature that year, RUMBLE FISH (1983). Rourke was Dillon's older motorcycle-riding brother, a burned-out case who is half-deaf and color blind from too many street rumbles, but who is still the "hero" of the old neighborhood. Shot in both black-and-white and color, RUMBLE FISH was described by *Film Comment* magazine as "a legend of love, aspiration, and loss," but many critics found it too highly stylized and overwrought. It was not a box-office winner. In THE POPE OF GREENWICH VILLAGE (1984), a very moody piece, he and Eric Roberts are cousins in New York City's Little Italy. Rourke is a street hustler unable to break away from his erring relative. *Variety* rated this production a "near-miss" and reported that Mickey's performance "consists mainly of surface effects which pall upon repetition . . . or his overly Brando-inflected gimmick of punching walls and smashing furniture when irritated." Rourke was among those who turned down the lead in BEVERLY HILLS COP (1984), which made a wealthy star of Eddie Murphy. Screenwriter William Kennedy was working on a screenplay about racketeer Legs Diamond which Francis Ford Coppola was to direct with Mickey in the title role. To date, this project has not materialized.

During this period, Mickey was linked romantically with Tatum O'Neal and Lauren Hutton. For his screen roles, he insisted on choosing his own wardrobe, because "I know best what kind of clothes that character should wear and how he should look." However, it is not known if he also selected his many hair-color changes in YEAR OF THE DRAGON (1985), found by *New York* magazine to be "a mess, but it's easily the most exciting bad movie of the year." Filmed at a cost of $18 million by Michael Cimino (the director of HEAVEN'S GATE), it grossed less than $8 million in domestic film rentals. However, its stylized obliqueness was beloved in France and Britain, with London's *The Guardian* stating, "You won't see filmmaking of this calibre very often emanating from Hollywood." Rourke was cast as a very middle-aged (!) cop, a virtuous soul struggling amid departmental corruption and apathy, who single-mindedly (and almost single-handedly) combats a young crime lord (John Lone) in New York's Chinatown. In the process, his long-suffering wife (Caroline Kava) is killed, and he begins an affair with a Chinese-American TV newscaster (Ariane) who veers between hating and loving him. *People* magazine decided that "Cimino and screenwriter Oliver Stone turned a workable idea into a cinematic version of chop suey." They argued that Rourke played his stoic role "with noble but ultimately futile intensity" and that he "can hardly take a step without running into a wild shoot-out, knifing, garroting, or brawl. In his quieter moments he just discovers bodies."

Mickey isolated himself from his wife for three months while he filmed the controversial 9 1/2 WEEKS (1986) in order that he might immerse himself totally in his role as a Manhattan businessman who has a short, passionate, sado-masochistic affair with an art dealer (Kim Basinger). Americans knew of the movie for about eighteen months before it was finally released in the United States, after several scheduling changes and editing and reediting to avoid an X rating. Panned by critics, it became a blockbuster hit in Europe, especially in France, with worldwide grosses of $100 million. When co-star Basinger was asked if she was aware that in Europe Mickey was a huge sex symbol, she responded cooly, "Yes, I heard this," and added, "Shall we take a vote?" He was again sexy in ANGEL HEART (1987) as a seedy private eye investigating bizarre goings-on in New Orleans. His co-star was Lisa Bonet of "The Cosby Show" TV fame. The murky melodrama received an X rating, but was rerated as R after director Alan Parker edited a mere ten seconds of blood pouring from a ceiling. Roger Ebert, in reappraising the production for his *Movie Home Companion* (1989), observed, "Rourke occupies the center of the film like a violent unmade bed. No other actor, with the possible exception of France's Gérard Depardieu, has made such a career out of being a slob. He looks unshaven, unwashed, hungover, and desperate, and that's at the beginning of the film, before things start to go wrong."

A PRAYER FOR THE DYING (1987) had Rourke gallantly attempting an Irish accent as an IRA hit man. The film co-starred Bob Hoskins, who was miscast as a priest. This embarrassing movie, appearing in theaters in September, was all but forgotten by October, when BARFLY (1987) was in general release. Here Mickey and Faye Dunaway played a pair of Los Angeles skid-row drunks unable to abandon their addiction, although he does try to do so. This time critic Roger Ebert noted, "The dialogue scenes between Rourke and Dunaway . . . are never less than a pleasure. . . . Rourke and Dunaway take their characters as opportunities to stretch as actors, to take chances and do extreme things." BARFLY suffered at the box office because of the release of a similar-themed picture that year, IRONWEED, with far more popular stars, Jack Nicholson and Meryl Streep.

In 1987 Mickey was part-owner of a Beverly Hills beauty salon with his friend from beauty school days, Giuseppe Franco. With his brother, Rourke opened Mickey and Joey's, a 1950s-style soda shop in Beverly Hills. For ten years or more, Rourke had written and rewritten a story (HOMEBOY) about a boxer approaching the end of a less-than-illustrious career. Wanting to produce it as a movie with himself as its star, he was finally able to interest producer Elliott Kastner. When a theatrical distributor could not be found, the completed picture was made available on home video in the fall of 1988. *Video Review* magazine criticized the project as "an old-hat story," but found Mickey's "quirky charm" shining through in a "memorable" performance. In June 1989 the actor sued Kastner for close to $6 million, alleging that he had not been paid for either his acting or story writing services and was not given promised creative approvals.

At the Cannes Film Festival in May 1989, Mickey stated that he intended to give much of his fee for FRANCESCO (1989), a West German–Italian co-production he had made in Rome, in which he played Saint Francis of Assisi, to "certain causes in Ireland." The fee was estimated to have been between $1 million and $3 million. During the week beginning May 22, 1989, the London tabloids exploited his statement, calling him an IRA sympathizer, headlining him as "Mad Mickey," and urging a boycott of all his pictures. Fleet Street's top columnist, Jean Rook, wrote, "Mr. Rourke doesn't know what the hell Ireland is about." In August 1989 Mickey threatened to sue each and every newspaper. At the same time, in the London *Daily Mail,* Helena Bonham-Carter, his FRANCESCO co-star, was quoted as saying, "It was a case of whatever Mickey wanted, Mickey got. As soon as he'd finished shooting . . . he'd be surrounded by all his mounties [flunkies] who would flood the set to tell him how wonderful he was." *Variety* reported of this two-and-a-half-hour, ambling chronicle, "Mickey Rourke gives a likable if at times too contemporary performance as a mystical loner in search of God, and is pic's main audience draw." To date, the picture has not been released theatrically in the United States.

On October 1, 1989, on the syndicated television program "Siskel & Ebert," both critics had high praise for JOHNNY HANDSOME (1989), with Ebert commending the actor for taking "chances in roles" and Gene Siskel giving him a thumbs-up review for a "solid performance." *Rolling Stone* magazine complimented "an amazing piece of acting from Mickey Rourke." Mickey was cast as a facially disfigured convict given a new identity, including a handsome new face, upon release from prison. *Variety* decided that the movie "faces an uphill battle to get the audience on-side," a battle that was lost after a mere four weeks, during which only $6.6 million was realized in domestic box-office grosses.

With successive tepid viewer response to his movies, Mickey invested some of his substantial earnings in a Los Angeles nightclub called Club Rubber, catering, for the most part, to motorcyclists. *Woman's World* magazine in late 1989 named Rourke "one of the 10 sexiest men in America," declaring, "but who cares if [he] has nothing nice to say? Plenty of women out there would happily spend 9 1/2 weeks—or minutes—with him." The *New York Daily News* reported that Mickey, perhaps taking his JOHNNY HANDSOME role to heart, had undergone liposuction and other surgery to restructure his cheekbones and teeth.

Released in Italy in December 1989, WILD ORCHID, directed by Zalman King, who had co-produced and co-scripted 9 1/2 WEEKS, took in $1.1 million in its first three weeks and broke eighteen house records on forty movie screens. In the story, Rourke is a well-tanned, mysterious entrepreneur residing in Rio who has powers of seduction over a voluptuous innocent (Carré Otis). His dialogue was spiced with such phrases as "How could mere words express my soul?" The reedited version came to American screens in April 1990, and after eight weeks it had grossed a respectable $10,721,808. Mickey and his co-star, former model Carré Otis, reportedly had actually engaged in sex while doing their love scene, which was abbreviated for U.S. audiences in order to earn an R rating. *Rolling Stone* magazine described Mickey as appearing "comatose" during the big moment. In May 1990 both he and Otis sued Vision International, Vision P.D.G., Brazil Star Film, and others (Brazil Star negotiated the original agreements with Rourke and Otis; Vision was assigned all agreements in conjunction with the picture, including Rourke's contract) for breach of contract, stating that the production company did not obtain their permission to release their love-scene photographs to assorted magazines. The film companies countersued, alleging that during the movie's production in Rio de Janeiro, "Rourke's conduct was hostile and uncooperative" and he "made many demands for concessions additional to those negotiated in his contract, using his personal bodyguards to physically 'threaten' those who did not acquiesce to his demands." The cross-complaint against Otis was for her refusal to help promote the film. The conflict was settled out of court in the late summer of 1990.

Finding the remuneration high, Mickey (for anywhere between $1 million and $3 million each) appeared in advertisements in Japan for Daihatsu's Charade automobiles and peered over the smooth edge of a cocktail glass as he gulped Suntory Special Reserve Whiskey.

In October 1989 Mickey signed to star with Anthony Hopkins in DESPERATE HOURS (1990), a Michael Cimino–directed remake, filmed in Utah and Colorado, of the well-regarded Humphrey Bogart–Fredric March feature of 1955. Mickey had the Bogart role as an escaped convict who holds Hopkins and his family hostage. When the R-rated movie debuted on October 5, 1990, it was inevitably compared to the original. *Daily Variety* judged it "a coldly mechanical and uninvolving remake," while Michael Wilmington (*Los Angeles Times*) noted that because the movie attempts to blend the sensibilities of the 1950s (when the initial film version, based on a Broadway play, was made) with the "strange, garish, elegant fury in the '90s," the resultant new edition is "in limbo, trapped between eras, top-heavy with its own double psychic and social load." In contrasting Mickey's interpretation with Bogart's, Wilmington observed, "Rourke plays Griffin loose and mean and shaggily seductive . . . not the gruff menace of the still brilliant but aging Humphrey Bogart who . . . looked more tired, more played out." *Daily Variety* reported, "Rourke, though bringing some leavening jocularity to the role, has to work against his typecasting as a scuz and can't begin to compare with memories of Humphrey Bogart in the kind of mad dog part Bogie patented." In its first week of domestic distribution at 1,162 theaters, DESPERATE HOURS grossed only $1,200,883.

Shooting began October 20, 1990, in Arizona and Las Vegas on HARLEY DAVIDSON AND THE MARLBORO MAN (1991), starring Don Johnson and Rourke. It is described as "a buddy movie about two old pals who get together to save a friend's restaurant, which is threatened by drug dealers." Among possible upcoming motion-picture projects for Rourke is EL CORDOBES, directed by Luis Valdez, focusing on the early life of flamboyant matador Manuel Benitez.

A natural actor accused of narcissistic posing, Mickey Rourke has been called a "monosyllabic sex god." However, Rourke hates Hollywood and regards American critics as the lowest of abominations. He rates Hollywood as appreciative of "a certain type of serious acting" only when all political angles are covered. "There's a certain group of directors that, no matter what they do, or if they use a Michael Douglas, or this one or that one it's safe," he says. A bigger box-office attraction overseas than he is here at home, he wishes "they'd just release any movie I do over in Europe" because "I got the criticism, and I don't really give a . . . for the praise. It's at the point where it's too late. . . . I don't want it either. I'm just numb to it right now." In the same breath, he goes one step further, saying, "I have no respect for this profession [acting] at all."

Filmography

1941 (Univ/Col, 1979)
City in Fear (ABC-TV, 3/30/80)
Act of Love (NBC-TV, 9/24/80)
Rape and Marriage—The Rideout Case (CBS-TV, 10/30/80)
Fade to Black (American Cinema, 1980)
Heaven's Gate (UA, 1980)
Body Heat (WB, 1981)
Diner (MGM, 1982)
Rumble Fish (Univ, 1983)
Eureka (UA Classics, 1984) [made in 1981]
The Pope of Greenwich Village (MGM/UA, 1984)

Year of the Dragon (MGM/UA, 1985)
9 1/2 Weeks (MGM/UA, 1986)
Angel Heart (Tri-Star, 1987)
A Prayer for the Dying (Goldwyn, 1987)
Barfly (Cannon, 1987)
Homeboy (Ive Home Video, 1988) (also original story)
Francesco (West German–It, 1989)
Johnny Handsome (Tri-Star, 1989)
Wild Orchid (Triumph Releasing, 1989)
Desperate Hours (MGM/UA, 1990)
Harley Davidson and the Marlboro Man (MGM/Pathé, 1991)

KURT RUSSELL

"In my opinion, acting is a very low artform, if you can even throw it
in the category of art. That may sound like I don't care about what I'm
doing, but when I go to work I can't think of anything I'd rather do."
—*Arena* magazine, Winter 1989/1990

KURT RUSSELL PRACTICALLY GREW UP ON THE DISNEY STUDIO LOT.
He was the round-faced, dimpled boy actor/friend and ping pong partner of the chief
himself, Walt Disney. In boyhood, his classroom was a sound stage and his teachers were
veteran screen actors. From this background emerged the square-jawed, virile jock whose
dimples grew deeper with time and whose eyes turned bluer. While he enjoys acting, it is
secondary to his big thrill in life—baseball. If he were favored to win a top acting award on
the night a World Series game was to be played, he would be at the game. Along with not
viewing acting as art, he is not stimulated by associating with other actors. They in turn
joined together to publicly protest his Celebrity Shoot-Outs of wild animals. Like Jeff
Bridges, another star who was an all-American kid actor, Kurt is a family man, but unlike
Bridges, he prefers not to be married. Like Patrick Swayze, he is at home in the country in
cowboy boots, jeans, and flannel shirt; it is a lifestyle far more satisfying to him than
sipping cocktails in society in a suit and tie.

Kurt Von Vogel Russell was born on Saturday, March 17, 1951, in Springfield,
Massachusetts, of German and Native American ancestry to Bing Oliver Russell and
Louise "Lulu" Julia Crone Russell. The only son, he had three sisters (Jill, Jody, and
Jamie). He was introduced to baseball at a very early age by his father, who had been a
professional player. Kurt learned to appreciate the outdoors in the Ranger Lakes district of
Maine where he spent a great deal of time at a resort hotel owned by his grandfather. When
he was four years old, the Russells relocated to Los Angeles after Bing was forced to give up
baseball after a head injury. They lived for a while in the attic of a friend's home in
Pacoima, in the San Fernando Valley, before Bing Russell got work in western films,
eventually playing a sheriff for fourteen years in one hundred episodes of TV's "Bonanza."
After the family had moved to the more affluent Thousand Oaks, Kurt became a
champion go-cart driver and played Little League baseball.

At the age of nine, with baseball as his chief interest, he auditioned for the part of
the boy in SAFE AT HOME (1962), a Walt Disney Studios movie to feature Mickey Mantle
and Roger Maris, two New York Yankees baseball stars whom he hoped to meet. His
dream did not materialize since another Russell boy, Bryan, got the part. However, the

studio gave him a walk on in Fred MacMurray's THE ABSENT-MINDED PROFESSOR (1961). Competing in Las Vegas in the "Race of Champions" class modified go-cart stock, Kurt was named world champion. It spurred his dream of becoming a star baseball player, possibly one day playing in a World Series game. He attended a San Fernando Valley grammar school but hated it as well as the other kids, who considered him weird because of his movie connections.

In 1963, at age twelve, he had a small part in Elvis Presley's IT HAPPENED AT THE WORLD'S FAIR, playing a boy who kicks the star in the chin. This was followed by a small nonrecurring part in the ABC-TV sitcom "Our Man Higgins." Soon after this, he played the title role in the same network's series "The Travels of Jaimie McPheeters," which premiered on September 14, 1963, and lasted one season. *Variety* noted of the newcomer, "he plays with great charm and assurance." On theatrical screens, he was seen in GUNS OF DIABLO (1964), a low-budget MGM western. During the 1964–1965 TV season, Russell appeared in episodes of a variety of series: "Gunsmoke," "The Fugitive," "The Man from U.N.C.L.E.," and "Gilligan's Island."

When he was fourteen, he signed a seven-year contract with the Disney Studios, whose releasing company was Buena Vista. There he soon got to know Walt Disney, who became a surrogate grandfather; they played ping pong, and Walt offered Kurt professional and personal advice. When Disney died of cancer in December 1966, in his office was discovered a pad on which his final notation had been "Kurt Russell." Russell's initial contract film with the studio was FOLLOW ME, BOYS (1966). Fred MacMurray was the harassed Boy Scout leader who adopts an orphan (Kurt) to make his wife (Vera Miles) happy. On television he appeared in a segment of "Lost in Space" and in another episode of "The Fugitive" in 1966. For NBC-TV's "The Wonderful World of Disney," in January 1967, he successively had co-starring roles in "Willie and the Yank," "The Mosby Raiders," "A Matchmaker," and "Terror on the Trail." The next month he was in a "Daniel Boone" episode.

Too busy acting and playing baseball to attend a regular high school, Kurt was tutored on the Burbank lot. In GUNS IN THE HEATHER (1968), he was an American schoolboy in Ireland discovering that his brother (Glenn Corbett) is a CIA agent. He participated in THE HORSE IN THE GRAY FLANNEL SUIT (1968), which starred Dean Jones, another Disney favorite. In THE ONE AND ONLY GENUINE ORIGINAL FAMILY BAND (1968), he was surrounded by a cast of veteran actors. Also in this homey musical was a blonde dancer whom the sixteen year old ogled from afar. She was billed as Goldie Jeanne Hawn. Meanwhile, at the studio he obtained a high school diploma.

In 1969 Kurt appeared on TV in two more episodes of "Daniel Boone" as well as in a baseball-related episode of "Then Came Bronson." In 1970, after winding up work on THE COMPUTER WORE TENNIS SHOES, another comedy with Dean Jones, he was on segments of TV's "High Chaparral" and "Love, American Style." The studio cast him as a TV network page in THE BAREFOOT EXECUTIVE (1971); his co-star was a chimpanzee who could predict hit shows. *Variety* acknowledged, "Kurt Russell does yeoman service as the page who becomes the 'Wonder Boy of the Networks.'" Like his other wholesome

Disney excursions, this was a healthy box-office hit. For Columbia Pictures he played the absurdly named Johnny Jesus in the fifth-billed supporting slot in an equally absurd FOOLS' PARADISE (1971), starring James Stewart. For Capitol Records, Kurt recorded a single in 1971.

Since Russell had always considered acting a part-time, off-baseball-season type of job, it was no surprise to his family or friends when he signed with a minor league team, The Rainbows, of Bend, Oregon, in 1971. For the next two years, he played second base and outfield for the Walla Walla (Washington) Islanders and El Paso (Texas) Sun Kings, as well as for The Rainbows, all farm teams of the San Diego Padres and California Angels. As such, he achieved status as a Class AA lead-hitter. During the winter months he filmed Disney's NOW YOU SEE HIM, NOW YOU DON'T (1972), in which he played a science student discovering the secret of invisibility. He was also in the less-popular CHARLEY AND THE ANGEL (1973), which starred Fred MacMurray. In 1973, while playing ball with the Sun Kings, Kurt suffered a serious injury to the rotator cuff in his right shoulder. A physician advised him, "Well, now, you're a full-time actor." His baseball days were over, at least temporarily.

Although his Disney contract had expired in 1972, he did a comedy for the studio called SUPERDAD (1974), in which he played the fiancée of Bob Crane's daughter (Kathleen Cody). This was followed by his starring in the ABC-TV series "The New Land," as a Swedish immigrant searching for the American dream in Minnesota in 1858. In competition with the very popular "All in the Family," the new series premiered on September 14, 1974, and was off the air a month later. Also at ABC-TV Kurt starred in the movie SEARCH FOR THE GODS (March 9, 1975), while, continuing to be cast in student roles, he starred as THE STRONGEST MAN IN THE WORLD (1975) at Disney. In NBC-TV's THE DEADLY TOWER (October 18, 1975) he had a change of pace as Charles Whitman, the disturbed student who massacred thirteen persons from a tower at the University of Texas. Meanwhile, during 1974 and 1975 he had appeared on segments of "Police Story," "Gunsmoke," "Hec Ramsey," and "Harry O."

After serving a short stint with the California Air Naval Guard, Kurt purchased a mountain cabin one hundred miles from Los Angeles which he called "The Walled Off A-Story-A" and again sang for Capitol Records on an album entitled *Kurt Russell*. On May 13, 1976, he and Tim Matheson co-starred in a two-hour NBC-TV movie/pilot, THE QUEST, about two brothers searching for their Comanche-abducted sister. The series began on September 22, 1976. *Variety* branded the program "grossly violent, poorly written" and added, "Series stars Kurt Russell and Tim Matheson are workmanlike performers, but any chance to develop their characters is lost in a charge to the next episode of violence." The series was off the air by the end of December. Now undertaking more mature roles, Kurt was an Appalachian coal miner in the NBC-TV movie CHRIST-MAS MIRACLE IN CAUFIELD, U.S.A. [THE CHRISTMAS COAL MINE MIRACLE] (December 26, 1977). Earlier that year, in the spring, he returned to baseball, playing with the Portland (Oregon) Mavericks, which were owned by his dad, and earned $100 weekly as a Class A Northwest leaguer.

Prior to February 11, 1979, Kurt had acted numerous times in starring roles on TV and in motion pictures. However, *TV Guide* magazine referred to him as "relatively unknown" when he portrayed ELVIS on ABC-TV's three-hour "Sunday Night Movie." Lip-synching to the voice of Ronnie McDowell, Kurt based his portrayal of Presley partly on twenty-five viewings of LOVING YOU (1957) plus a clear personal memory of the legend, who had died in 1977. The movie was the sixth-most-watched show of the week, and of the several actors who would portray Presley on television, Kurt is the only one to have earned an Emmy nomination. Kurt's father, Bing, portrayed Elvis' father, with Season Hubley as Priscilla Presley. After ELVIS, Kurt at twenty-seven was finally recognized by the industry as an actor. On March 17, 1979, his twenty-eighth birthday, he and Season Hubley were married, a union that would last less than three turbulent years. Their son, Boston Russell, was born in March 1980. During the late 1970s, Kurt collaborated on TV movie scripts in short-lived partnership with screenwriter Michael McGreevey. He also became a member of Hollywood's Stuntman's Association.

Of ELVIS, Kurt said, "It was the first time I ever did a role one-hundred percent my way—that was a breakthrough." Thereafter, he was a cocky model in ABC-TV's AMBER WAVES (March 9, 1980) and an auto salesman in the tasteless but popular USED CARS (1980). In ESCAPE FROM NEW YORK (1981), directed by John Carpenter (who had directed ELVIS), he ran completely counter to his wholesome image by playing a scruffy, eye-patched muscular criminal recruited to rescue the kidnapped President (Donald Pleasence) of 1997 U.S.A. Then Kurt returned to Disney briefly as the voice of Copper the hound in the animated feature THE FOX AND THE HOUND (1981). Also that year, he was at the Los Angeles Music Center on stage co-starring with Gregory Harrison in a revival of *The Hasty Heart.*

Russell was united with director John Carpenter for the third time in the unnecessary remake of the 1951 classic THE THING (1982). In the high-intentioned SILKWOOD (1983) he played Meryl Streep's co-worker and lover. The movie, directed by Mike Nichols, was a far cry from Kurt's youthful excursions in Disney screen exercises. SWING SHIFT (1984), about World War II factory workers, was produced by and starred Goldie Hawn. At her insistence Kurt's part was enlarged, requiring that thirty minutes be reshot. He and the woman he had admired sixteen years earlier became instant lovers. He moved into her Pacific Palisades home, saying that she was "the most fun person I think I've ever known." One of Hollywood's most influential women, but in need of a hit movie, Goldie, six years Kurt's senior, was already the mother of Oliver (born in 1977) and Katie (born in 1980) from her six-year marriage to singer Bill Hudson, which had ended in 1982. Kurt would say, "I suppose my biggest regret is that, as life would have it, I didn't meet Goldie in my early twenties." Although SWING SHIFT was not a commercial success—it grossed only $4.6 million in domestic film rentals—he holds it in high esteem for having been responsible for his personal happiness.

Kurt flew to Italy as star of LADYHAWKE (1985), but finding it "too difficult a shoot," he dropped out of the production after a few days. He was replaced by Rutger Hauer. Known for its violence, nudity, and strong language, THE MEAN SEASON (1985) had Kurt as a crafty Miami newspaperman involved with Mariel Hemingway. THE BEST OF TIMES (1986) was a fiasco that paired him with Robin Williams as ex-high school football rivals who relive the big game twenty years later. Once again with John Carpenter as director, Kurt was a truck driver called upon to vanquish a 2,000-year-old villainous Chinese magician (James Hong) in BIG TROUBLE IN LITTLE CHINA (1986). This comic book tale of horror, comedy, and adventure was set beneath the streets of San Francisco's Chinatown and unsuccessfully forced Russell into the satirical heroic mold of Harrison Ford's INDIANA JONES screen trilogy.

In 1986 Kurt and Goldie purchased a seventy-two-acre spread, 7,000 feet above sea level at Old Snowmass, Colorado, which he named Home Run Ranch. In July 1986 he and Goldie became parents to son Wyatt, but neither was eager to marry after having gone through the pain of divorce from previous mates. On screen in the comedy OVERBOARD (1987), they co-starred with another former child actor, Roddy McDowall, who had created the idea for the picture. "I have so much fun working with Kurt," Goldie said in an interview. "We work very similarly in that there's not a lot of chaos . . . we sort of do it and move on. . . . I fall in love with him more every day." The antics of OVERBOARD had more appeal to moviegoers than SWING SHIFT had; it grossed over $12.7 million in domestic film rentals.

Kim Cattrall, **Kurt Russell**, Dennis Dun, and Suzee Pai in BIG TROUBLE IN LITTLE CHINA (1986).

People magazine, in its critique of TEQUILA SUNRISE (1988), noted, "Russell, freed from the restrictions of Goldie Hawn ding-a-ling comedies, realizes the dramatic potential he showed in SILKWOOD." The three stars (Mel Gibson, Michelle Pfeiffer, and Russell) "who infuse this movie with a heavy dose of old-fashioned star glamour" (*Newsweek* magazine) are perhaps the most attractive blue-eyed players ever to appear together in one motion picture. On the other hand, TEQUILA SUNRISE was a convoluted *film noir* of one-time pals, Los Angeles cop Russell and ex-drug dealer Gibson, who fight over drugs and sultry restaurateur Pfeiffer. WINTER PEOPLE (1989) advertised its stars, Russell and Kelly McGillis, as having "A passion so strong it kills." This may have been correct, but the film, set in 1930s Appalachia, was overwrought and slow, which helped to kill it at the ticket windows.

An unidentified crew member on TANGO AND CASH (1989) called it "the worst-organized, most poorly prepared film I've ever been on in my life." The cop actioner opened on 1,600 screens in the United States in December 1989 and grossed $60.1 million after eighty days in release. Cast opposite Sylvester Stallone, with whom he had immediate rapport, Kurt was a slovenly drug-busting Los Angeles cop with long hair and disheveled clothing; he resembled Mel Gibson in the more successful buddy picture LETHAL WEAPON (1987).

When Kurt's second annual Celebrity Shoot-Out was announced for the islands of Hawaii from August 29 through September 23, 1989, opponents took full-page ads in industry publications to denounce the killing of "beautiful animals." "We commend the many famous stars who refuse to participate in the Kurt Russell Celebrity Shoot-Out," the ads read. "*To you* we give our unending admiration and support." As a result of such adverse criticism, Kurt toned down the event. In May 1990, 500 yards off Miami Beach, Kurt was navigator to Don Johnson's piloting of the latter's fifty-foot white speedboat *Team USA* in a race that sent them soaring through the ocean's waters at a speed well in excess of 100 miles per hour. The duo finished second to their actor friend Chuck Norris, a comparative novice in the sport. "Obviously it's hazardous," Kurt said afterward, "but I like competing at the highest level in anything I do."

In 1991 Kurt starred in BACKDRAFT, with an ensemble cast that included Robert De Niro, William Baldwin, Scott Glenn, Jennifer Jason Leigh, and Rebecca DeMornay. Directed by Ron Howard, it is an action drama about two fire-fighting brothers (Kurt, Baldwin) involved in an arson investigation conducted by De Niro. In preparation for their roles, Russell, Baldwin, Glenn, and De Niro took a crash course from instructors at Chicago's Fire Academy. Prior to location filming in Chicago in July 1990, director Howard promised that the movie would have a lot of "very tricky, dangerous" fire segments. At the same time, Howard predicted that his effort would be much more realistic than THE TOWERING INFERNO (1974).

Kurt remains one of Hollywood's most quotable personalities, having been giving interviews and making statements for publication since he was a teenager. Not long ago, he said, "I don't understand *why* I'm admired. I think that in an emotional respect actors can have a great influence on people, but I have a hard time justifying admiration, I'm not fighting for admiration. I'm fighting for the same thing I wanted when I was nine years old and that's putting on a good show."

Filmography

The Absent-Minded Professor (BV, 1961)
It Happened at the World's Fair (MGM, 1963)
Guns of Diablo (MGM, 1964)
Follow Me, Boys (BV, 1966)
Guns in the Heather (BV, 1968)
The Horse in the Gray Flannel Suit (BV, 1968)
The One and Only Genuine Original Family Band (BV, 1968)
The Computer Wore Tennis Shoes (BV, 1970)
The Barefoot Executive (BV, 1971)
Fools' Parade (Col, 1971)
Now You See Him, Now You Don't (BV, 1972)
Charley and the Angel (BV, 1973)
Superdad (BV, 1974)
Search for the Gods (ABC-TV, 3/9/75)
The Deadly Tower (NBC-TV, 10/18/75)
The Strongest Man in the World (BV, 1975)
The Quest (NBC-TV, 5/13/76)
Christmas Miracle in Caufield, U.S.A. [The Christmas Coal Mine Miracle] (NBC-TV, 12/26/77)
Elvis (ABC-TV, 2/11/79)
Amber Waves (ABC-TV, 3/9/80)
Used Cars (Col, 1980)
Escape from New York (Avco Emb, 1981)
The Fox and the Hound (BV, 1981) (voice only)
The Thing (Univ, 1982)
Silkwood (20th–Fox, 1983)
Swing Shift (WB, 1984)
The Mean Season (Orion, 1985)
The Best of Times (Univ, 1986)
Big Trouble in Little China (20th–Fox, 1986)
Overboard (MGM/UA, 1987)
Tequila Sunrise (WB, 1988)
Winter People (Col, 1989)
Tango and Cash (WB, 1989)
Backdraft (Univ, 1991)

Television Series

The Travels of Jaimie McPheeters (ABC, 1963–64)
The New Land (ABC, 1974)
The Quest (NBC, 1976)

Album Discography

Kurt Russell (Capitol SKAO-492)
The One and Only Genuine Family Band (Bueno Vesta 5002/ST-5002) [ST]

SUSAN SAINT JAMES

"I know I'm always going to work. . . . I've had so many years on TV.
That's God smiling on me. But it's not hard work. There's this fallacy
that you have to suffer to produce great art."
—*Chicago Sun-Times*, December 2, 1984

SUSAN SAINT JAMES WAS ONE OF THE LAST STARS TO SIGN A STANDARD
major Hollywood studio seven-year contract. Initially she underwent the customary
glamorization treatment, but it failed to work for her. She literally auditioned on screen in
minor motion-picture roles before finding celebrity through television, not her medium of
first choice. But on television she could be herself, a bright free spirit not afraid to voice her
opinions or objections. In 1971 *Show* magazine labeled her the "elegant kook with the
wisecracking tongue." Later, this same speech organ earned her the uncomplimentary tag
of "instant mouth" from studio producers. But finally, from a meager-waged contractee
she developed into one of TV's natural comics. After a decade and a half of successful series
programming, a *Chicago Sunday American* description of her still applies a quarter of a
century later: "A star who will shine as long as she wants."

Susan Jane Miller was born on Wednesday, August 14, 1946, in Los Angeles, the
second child and first daughter born to the wife of an executive of a toy manufacturing
company. An Irish-Catholic, she dreamed of becoming a nun until she discovered the
movies. As a child she idolized Sandra Dee, while having a girlhood crush on Elvis Presley.
In 1957, when she was eleven years old, the family moved to Rockford, Illinois, where her
father was appointed chairman of the Testor Corporation, which made glue for model
airplanes.

Susan developed into a plump, precocious girl with braces on her teeth at Wood-
lands Academy of the Sacred Heart in Lake Forest, Illinois. She was a fast-learning student
who questioned *everything* she did not understand or agree with, but she was not a
problem student; rather, she earned high grades. After the braces were removed from her
teeth in her sophomore year of high school at Sacred Heart, she exercised and dieted to lose
weight until reaching an acceptable, to her, point of curvaciousness. She spent the school
term of 1961, her junior year, in France as an exchange student. She learned French
fluently and, according to her, "came back wriggling like Brigitte Bardot."

She obtained her high school diploma in June 1962 at the age of fifteen. She
immediately took a brief course in theater at Rockford College before leaving for Connecticut College for Women in New London. After one week at the college, selected by her

parents, she asked herself, "What am I doing here?" She promptly left the school. With the French-inspired name change to Susan Saint James, she went to New York City where her brother was newly wed to a model. Her sister-in-law helped her to obtain agents and she was quickly assigned to high-paying modeling jobs. However, after a year, despite liking the money she made, she became bored. Because of her fluency in French, her agents suggested she go to France, which she did in 1963. Over the next two years, she appeared on magazine covers in France, England, Italy, Germany, and Spain. This stopped when she met Edith Piaf's protégé, Charles Aznavour, a troubadour singer doing a one-man show at the Olympia Theatre in Paris. Walking away from a lucrative modeling career, she acquired a union card in order to get a job pulling curtains every night at the Olympia in order to be near him.

In late 1965 she followed Aznavour when he came to America. During their Los Angeles stay she broke a leg, prompting her to remain there rather than tag after him to his next destination, Hawaii. Their geographical separation helped to bring an end to their relationship. After taking six acting lessons, she visited several film studios in the hope of finding work, thinking nothing of barging into executives' offices demanding a reading. She was determined to become a movie star.

A vice-president at Universal, impressed with her uninhibited manner of speaking, signed her to a seven-year contract, thereby making her one of the last of the studio's contractees. From the start, because of her tendency to gain weight quickly, she forced herself to stick to a regimen of diets and diet foods, eventually choosing to become a vegetarian. The studio immediately cast her as a bright, ambitious, and slightly off-center editorial assistant working for a Los Angeles–based publication empire in FAME IS THE NAME OF THE GAME (November 26, 1966). This was one of Universal's first made-for-television movies.

During the next several months, while the studio pondered what to do with its twenty-year-old contract player with her waist-length hair, Susan involved herself with the Hollywood hippie crowd. She smoked marijuana, embraced several causes, and spoke out against the Vietnam War. Although she had told an interviewer that she and her boy-friend, writer Richard Neubert, had little in common, they exchanged marriage vows in 1967. During the one year they were married, they apparently failed to develop similar interests. They remained friends after their divorce, and she later said, "We were trying too hard to take over each other's lives." On December 21, 1967, she appeared in the "Girl in the Night" episode of "Ironside," followed by two successive segments of "It Takes a Thief" and then another installment of "Ironside." All of these were Universal-made TV series.

She was given a short dark wig and lots of glamour makeup for her eighth-billed role in George Peppard's detective caper P.J. (1968). She was loaned to Columbia for WHERE ANGELS GO . . . TROUBLE FOLLOWS (1968), in which she was one of the prankish Catholic School students challenging the authority of the mother superior (Rosalind Russell). *Variety* noted that Susan gave "a very good showing of screen promise." Two months later, back on the home lot, she was in support of Harry Guardino and others in JIGSAW (1968), a quickly assembled remake of the studio's MIRAGE (1965), which had starred Gregory Peck and Diane Baker. She was then cast in the heavy-handed comedy WHAT'S SO BAD ABOUT FEELING GOOD? (1968), starring George Peppard and Mary Tyler Moore.

Meanwhile, a weekly TV series evolved from FAME IS THE NAME OF THE GAME. It premiered on NBC on September 20, 1968, under the abbreviated title "The Name of the Game." It was actually three series under one title, each episode being self-contained and starring one of three male stars (Gene Barry, Tony Franciosa, Robert Stack). However, their editorial assistant, Peggy Maxwell (Susan), appeared in each ninety-minute segment. *Variety* judged the series "pulp fiction with electronic gloss," but observed that Susan "turned in a brightly flippant performance and should prove one of the series' main assets." For her work on the series, Susan was presented with an Emmy Award on June 8, 1969, for Outstanding Continued Performance by an Actress in a Supporting Role. The series would enjoy three years of air time, expiring at the end of the 1970–1971 TV season. During this period Universal kept her busy on other projects as well. She played in two more segments of "It Takes a Thief," and made one appearance each on "McCloud" and "Love, American Style." She also had the female lead in the ABC-TV movie/pilot ALIAS SMITH AND JONES (January 5, 1971).

With "The Name of the Game" dead, Universal was eager to find a new property for its contractee. She was assigned to the role of the unorthodox, meddlesome wife of Rock Hudson, a San Francisco police commissioner, in ONCE UPON A DEAD MAN, an NBC-TV movie/pilot telecast on September 17, 1971. Made with care and a hefty budget (since it was geared to launch Hudson on a TV series career), the two-hour TV movie was a hit. During the filming of ONCE UPON A DEAD MAN, in early 1971, she married her makeup man, Tom Lucas, by whom she would have two children: daughter Sunshine (born in 1973) and son Harmony (born in 1975). This marriage would end soon after their son's birth.

Susan's second teleseries, fast on the heels of the first, debuted on September 29, 1971, on NBC. *Variety* rated "McMillan and Wife" a successful updating of THE THIN MAN concept of a sophisticated husband-and-wife team solving crimes and enjoying a happy marriage. *Variety* report-

Susan Saint James in "McMillan and Wife" (1973).

ed, "Hudson plays it with the right flavor, as does Miss Saint James," citing as one of the show's successful ingredients "the basic humor inherent in the concept Miss Saint James brings to the role of his slightly cuckoo wife." As Sally McMillan, the pretty, long-haired spouse with a habit of involving herself and her husband (Hudson) in criminal cases, Susan, at twenty-five, was earning $1,500 per week under her Universal contract, while her co-star Hudson, at forty-seven, was making $50,000 per episode. She would be with the popular series for five years, but just before the start of the 1973–1974 season, she threatened to leave if a salary adjustment was not made. During contract negotiations, actress Susan Oliver was alerted by Universal to stand by as a possible replacement. The matter was resolved temporarily, although Susan was never happy with her situation. Initially, there was tension between her and Hudson, who was not convinced that she was right for the part of his wife, but the situation was smoothed over eventually as he got to know her. Because of her personal commitment to women's liberation, she often insisted that lines of dialogue be altered to reflect the changing times. In one instance, Hudson's character was to explain about a woman he had known years before, "But I never dated her." Knowing that the word "dated" was out of style, she declared emphatically, "It's a dated word. Change it." It was changed, and she told *TV Guide* magazine, "I am the trend expert." She finally departed the series at the conclusion of the 1975–1976 season, ending her working relationship with Universal, which she had at one point sarcastically described as a "Big Deal!" When the program returned in September 1976 it was called simply "McMillan," and her wacky character had supposedly been killed in an airplane accident. The series faded at the end of that season. Years later, when Rock Hudson went public in divulging his infection with the AIDS virus, the outspoken Susan said it should not matter if a star happens to be gay. "I mean, what the hell difference does it make?"

During her five years with "McMillan and Wife," she stepped away from the Nora Charles–type character just once. She went to Rome for Universal as the star of the ABC-TV movie MAGIC CARPET (November 6, 1972). She portrayed a Rome-based language student who becomes a tour guide and soon falls in love with a mystifying stowaway (Robert Pratt).

On October 13, 1976, she provided the feminine interest in an NBC-TV movie/series pilot that did not make it. SCOTT FREE involved a con artist (Michael Brandon) who is blackmailed into helping government agents expose a Mafia boss. Then Susan appeared in her first major motion picture role as a back-up singer in the pleasant comedic chase movie OUTLAW BLUES (1977). It starred Peter Fonda as an ex-convict who has talent as a country and western singer but who is pursued by the police. *Variety* recommended, "Saint James is a sexy knockout who ought to be on theatre screens more often." At loose ends professionally, she participated in the January 10, 1977, special, "The Second Annual Circus of the Stars," followed by another special in November 1977, "Celebrity Challenge of the Sexes." Early in the new year, she was a mother plagued by dreams of her dead child (Nichole Faustino) in NIGHT CRIES (January 29, 1978), an ABC-TV movie. She traveled down under for a guest-star appearance on "John Denver in Australia" (February 16, 1978). Finding Australian cocktails too much to her liking, she was forced to again watch her weight, which often escalated to 130 pounds, considered too much for her slight 5' 6 1/2" frame.

In DESPERATE WOMEN (October 25, 1978), an NBC-TV movie set in the Old West, Susan was one of three female prisoners abandoned in the desert. In THE GIRLS IN THE OFFICE (February 2, 1979), an ABC-TV movie, she was one of four female employees of a Houston department store who find that romance and a business career conflict. Initially considered not pretty enough to play a fashion model in LOVE AT FIRST BITE (1979), a spoof of the Dracula story set in Manhattan, she was finally hired as the Transylvanian's love interest who enjoys having her ankles licked by the debonair gentleman (George Hamilton). She played a dedicated career woman who said, "I hate housework, it killed my mother." She and Hamilton worked beautifully together in this lighthearted feature, which went on to gross $20.6 million in domestic film rentals. In the CBS-TV romantic comedy movie SEX AND THE SINGLE PARENT (September 19, 1979), she was a divorcée who falls in love with a divorced man (Mike Farrell). Each has parental responsibilities which hinder their romance.

S.O.S. TITANIC (September 23, 1979), a three-hour ABC-TV movie, combined accuracy, atmosphere, and lavishness in retelling the mystifying story of the great royal mail ship's final hours. Third-billed as second-class passenger Leigh Goodwin, Susan was but one of three Americans (along with David Janssen and Cloris Leachman) in an otherwise British cast. Too long for the large screen, this telefeature was sheared to 102 minutes for theatrical showings overseas. Following this outing, Susan received top billing as one of three financially strapped housewives who plan but bungle a caper to rob a shopping mall in HOW TO BEAT THE HIGH COST OF LIVING (1980). Her co-stars were Jane Curtin (who was to figure prominently in her life four years later) and Jessica Lange (who had the best-developed role of the trio).

Romantically during this period, Susan's name was coupled with that of rock musician Stephen Stills, filmmaker Bruce Lewis, and the Democratic senator from Massachusetts, Edward Kennedy. About the latter, she stated vehemently that it was merely a friendship. In 1981 she was the National Chairperson of the Special Olympics and was honored by Eunice Kennedy Shriver who presented her with the Caritas Society Saint Coletta Award for her work in the field of mental retardation. Also in 1981, while guest-hosting TV's "Saturday Night Live," she met the show's executive producer, dashing Dick Ebersol. "I knew I was going to take down my old boyfriends' pictures," she recalled later, "and ask him what he wanted for breakfast." They were married within six weeks of their meeting.

Not satisfied with her career, and relying on alcohol to have a good time, she bemoaned the path her professional life was taking. She told interviewer Roderick Mann, "I don't need to convince the public—they seem to like me—but I've got to convince those guys in Hollywood to give me a job. Their attitude seems to be, 'If Margot Kidder isn't free and Meryl Streep is tied up and Jackie Bisset isn't available then maybe we'll let you read for the role.' Honestly. That's where I am in the business today." In Avco Embassy's CARBON COPY (1981), she was George Segal's bigoted wife, and she was the mother of a mentally retarded youth (Ricky Wittman) in the NBC-TV movie THE KID FROM NOWHERE (January 4, 1982). On January 21, 1982, she made a pact with her father, also a heavy drinker, to stop drinking; they agreed that the first one to have a drink would be sent by the other to a sanitarium. To date, this agreement has not been broken by either party.

In mid-1982 she went to the Philippines to film the theatrical feature DON'T CRY, IT'S ONLY THUNDER (1982), in which she played an uptight woman who softens through exposure to children in a Vietnam orphanage. That November, having returned to the States, she and her husband purchased a sixteen-room home in Litchfield, Connecticut. They decided that if their marriage was to work, they must give up trying to juggle two residences (New York and Los Angeles) on opposite sides of the country. Both sets of the couple's parents also relocated to Litchfield. On January 5, 1983, she starred in I TAKE THESE MEN, a CBS-TV movie about a married woman fantasizing romance with three other men (Adam West, John Rubinstein, Brian Dennehy). On June 6, 1983, CBS-TV finally aired the year-old thirty-minute pilot "After George." She starred as a widow who discovers that her late husband has programmed his "personality" into the home computer that operates the household. Said *Variety* of the strained gimmick, "it was hard to believe anyone would let themselves be so dominated by an electronic gadget. . . . Susan Saint James played the comely widow with a sprightly touch." Susan gave birth to her third child, a boy who was named Charles, in 1983.

Finally, after years of show business stagnation, Susan's third teleseries debuted on March 19, 1984, on CBS. Called "a witty, distaff odd couple" by *Time* magazine, "Kate & Allie" paired Susan with Jane Curtin (formerly of "Saturday Night Live") as divorced women and longtime friends, both with children. They share an apartment in New York City's Greenwich Village. The sitcom was taped at the Ed Sullivan Theatre on Broadway. As Kate McArdle, Susan was the wise-cracking, truly modern woman, to Curtin's Allie Lowell, the practical, predictable one. At the end of its premiere season, "Kate & Allie" was the only situation comedy ranking in the top ten. The series lasted five years, during which time Curtin (who was generally given the scripts' wittiest dialogue) was awarded two Emmys. The ever-frank Susan admitted to being jealous. Of her co-star, Curtin has said, "Susan's one of the funniest people I've ever met" and "I think we'll always be friends." In 1985 the pregnant Susan's condition was concealed on camera by a bunny outfit, among other costumes, but she suffered a miscarriage in September. In 1986 she again became pregnant and her abdomen was hidden by bed sheets for four weeks while her character recuperated in a hospital bed with a broken leg. Her fourth child, a boy named Willie, was born that year. (The child was named in honor of her favorite sports heroes, Willie Mays, Willie Davis, Willie McCovey, and Joe Willie Namath.) On April 3, 1986, Saint James did the "Eunice Kennedy Shriver" episode of "An American Portrait" on CBS-TV, which comprised her extra-series work until January 4, 1989. On that date, with Susan as Kate and Curtin as Allie, they appeared in guest cameos on the short-lived "Tattinger's" on NBC-TV. Marking the one hundredth episode of "Kate & Allie" on May 23, 1988, both ladies stepped out of character to show their favorite scenes of the past years, plus some of their bloopers. The much-watched series ended its prime-time run on June 6, 1988. Meanwhile, in 1988 she narrated "Peter and the Wolf" at two New York Pops concerts conducted by Skitch Henderson.

In June 1990, from her Connecticut home, Susan announced her retirement from show business, stating, "I'm thinking of buying our local FM radio station, creating my own perfume, clothing—and I'm collating research for a book about my life." (During this period she did TV commercials for Diet Center.) She admitted, at the age of forty-three, to not being afraid to have another child. On June 10, 1990, in a Torrington, Connecticut, hospital, Susan gave birth to another son, Edward Bright Ebersol. No longer such an opinionated activist, she has said, "Having kids deradicalizes you a bit. I had a falling out with the Catholic Church in my radical days, but now I realize I can do more being active in the church. Plus it's the only way I know to pray. That gives a deeper sense to life." In the spring of 1991, Susan and her husband, Dick Ebersol (NBC Sports president), completed their newly built home in Telluride, Colorado, which cost the couple over $1.5 million. They still make their permanent home in Litchfield, Connecticut.

Filmography

Fame Is the Name of the Game (NBC-TV, 11/26/66)

P. J. [New Face in Hell] (Univ, 1968)

Where Angels Go . . . Trouble Follows (Col, 1968)

Jigsaw (Univ, 1968)

What's So Bad About Feeling Good? (Univ, 1968)

Alias Smith and Jones (ABC-TV, 1/5/71)

Once Upon a Dead Man (NBC-TV, 9/17/71)

Magic Carpet (ABC-TV, 11/6/72)

Scott Free (NBC-TV, 10/13/76)

Outlaw Blues (WB, 1977)

Night Cries (ABC-TV, 1/29/78)

Desperate Women (NBC-TV, 10/25/78)

The Girls in the Office (ABC-TV, 2/2/79)

Sex and the Single Parent (CBS-TV, 9/19/79)

S.O.S. Titanic (ABC-TV, 9/23/79)

Love at First Bite (AIP, 1979)

How to Beat the High Cost of Living (Filmways, 1980)

Carbon Copy (Avco Emb, 1981)

The Kid from Nowhere (NBC-TV, 1/4/82)

Don't Cry, It's Only Thunder (Sanrio Communications, 1982)

I Take These Men (CBS-TV, 1/5/83)

Television Series

The Name of the Game (NBC, 1968–71)

McMillan and Wife (NBC, 1971–76)

Kate & Allie (CBS, 1984–89)

SUSAN SARANDON

"It's not like we're trying to be brain surgeons or come up with a global peace plan. You work and you learn, you benefit by meeting other people, you pocket some cash, you go to a nice location—it's an extraordinary lifestyle." —*Premiere* magazine, May 1988

SUSAN SARANDON IS THE ACCIDENTAL ACTRESS, WHO INITIALLY HAD no professional training or inclination toward an acting career. She was thrust into the business unexpectedly by agents and producers excited by her potential. For years she was on the brink of stardom. However, reaching the top was made impossible by her refusal to participate in industry power games. Her great intelligence seemed to intimidate most directors and producers.

With expressive eyes that are among the largest, kindest, and sexiest in the business, she is comfortable in either comedy or drama. Like those of Lesley Ann Warren, her performances are saucy and naughty. On screen, Susan is a free spirit who has been seduced and has performed topless more often than most, yet she does it each time in a manner that is neither mechanical nor tiresome.

Born Susan Abigail Tomalin on Friday, October 4, 1946, she was the first of nine children of Phillip Leslie Tomalin, a band singer turned advertising man, and Lenora Marie Criscioni Tomalin. From New York City, the Catholic Welsh/Italian parents moved to New Jersey, first to Metuchen and later to Edison, where Susan grew up. Because she was the eldest, she was drafted at an early age to help care for her eight siblings. She had what she has termed a "not particularly happy childhood." Quiet and introspective, she escaped reality through literature and by writing children's stories as well as action scenes for backyard plays. After a sheltered elementary education in convent schools, she entered the public Edison High School where she was exposed for the first time to the varying cultures of classmates.

Because, as she admits, college was "the thing to do" in the 1960s, she enrolled at the Catholic University of America in Washington, D.C. She made this choice because she could live off campus with her grandparents. In her freshman year, while appearing in a college play, she was spotted by Chris Sarandon, a graduate student four years her senior. They lived together until her junior year when, because of family pressure, they were married on September 16, 1967. In her spare time, Susan worked as a switchboard operator, cleaned houses, and modeled for advertisements in the *Washington Post* as well as a brochure for the Watergate complex, which was then under construction.

After she graduated with a bachelor's degree in English in 1968, she and Chris moved to New York City where she registered with the Ford modeling agency while he pursued a stage career. When he needed someone to read with him at an audition, she accompanied him, which led to both of them being quickly signed by talent agencies. Five days later, she was called to audition for a part in a motion picture. Asked to improvise, she did not know what that meant. Nevertheless, she won the prominent role of the drug-addicted daughter of an advertising executive (Dennis Patrick) who kills her equally addicted boyfriend (Patrick McDermott) in JOE (1970). Saying, "Gee, this seems easy," she decided to try acting for a while, although her real interest lay in issues dealing with civil rights as well as protests against the Vietnam War.

With Chris already in the CBS-TV daytime soap opera "The Guiding Light," she got the part in 1970 of the seventeen-year-old adopted daughter, Patrice Kahlman, facing many perils in the new ABC-TV soap "A World Apart." She was now earning $1,000 per week. Aired opposite the extremely popular "Search for Tomorrow," "A World Apart" came to an end in 1971 with the episode in which Patrice's child is baptized, with viewers never learning whether or not the baby was mercury-poisoned. In 1971–1972, Susan made her stage debut in off-Broadway's *An Evening with Richard Nixon* and did local radio/TV commercials. In 1972 she made a sixteen-week commitment to playing the murderous drifter Sarah Fairbanks in CBS-TV's long-running soap opera "Search for Tomorrow." She was also seen briefly in her second feature film, partially shot in Manhattan. LADY LIBERTY (1972) was an Italian production released in the United States by United Artists and starring Sophia Loren with William Devane. On October 26, 1973, she was in an episode of James Coco's short-lived sitcom, "Calucci's Department," on CBS-TV. By then, her agents had persuaded her to move to Hollywood. Still not considering herself an actress, she looked upon the motion picture/television scene as a joke, whereby she was making more money than her husband, who continued to do theater work in New York.

Susan Sarandon in THE FRONT PAGE (1974).

In the third-billed role of a southern actress, she supported Richard Chamberlain and Blythe Danner in the ABC-TV movie F. SCOTT FITZGERALD AND "THE LAST OF THE BELLES" (January 7, 1974). Then she was featured in PBS-TV's "Theatre in America" episode "June Moon" (January 30, 1974) and was again in support of Danner and others in LOVIN' MOLLY (1974), about life and love in Texas. She was Peggy Grant in THE FRONT PAGE (1974), the third and most tasteless screen adaptation of the Ben Hecht–Charles MacArthur play. She bounced back to tele-

vision for the December 17, 1974, showing on CBS of a segment in "Lives of Benjamin Franklin."

One day in 1974 she visited a friend, British singer/actor Tim Curry, who was in Hollywood for discussions about his playing a mad transvestite scientist. Asked to read for the female lead in the planned project, she got the part. Immediately, friends urged her to reject the role due to the questionable taste of the whole concept. Ignoring her friends, she quickly completed her scenes as the hapless heroine who plummets from the wings of a biplane in Robert Redford's THE GREAT WALDO PEPPER (1975). Then she flew to London to film the Curry starring vehicle, THE ROCKY HORROR PICTURE SHOW (1975). Working for scale, she was Janet, who with boyfriend Brad (Barry Bostwick) on a stormy night enters the decadent den of alien transvestite Dr. Frank-N-Furter (Curry). She got to join in such song numbers as "Dammit Janet," "Over at the Frankenstein Place," "Touch-A, Touch-A, Touch Me," "Rose Tint My World," and "Super Heroes." Of the unique experience, she would later say, "It thrills me that one day my grandchildren may see their grandmother in her little half-slip and bra, seducing a monster." The film, a major financial disappointment at the time of its release, would within four years develop a subculture of its own, with ritualistic midnight showings in two hundred metropolitan and college towns. Ticket buyers, impersonating the screen characters in costume and makeup, would line up for hours outside theaters. Through its cult following, the offbeat feature grossed $60 million. While in London, stricken with pneumonia, Susan saw her weight decrease to eighty-five pounds. On top of that, she suffered a nervous breakdown because her marriage was disintegrating and she became depressed about the world in general. By dropping out for a short time, she regrouped and fought her way back.

Returning to America, she went on location in Danbury, Connecticut, for ONE SUMMER LOVE (1976), as a movie theater candy seller who befriends a mental hospital dischargee (Beau Bridges). In 1977, "B" movies were supposedly no longer made, but CHECKERED FLAG OR CRASH, shot in the Philippines, was nothing more than that, with Susan providing love interest to racing car driver Joe Don Baker. A distinction of sorts during this bleak period was her starring in a trashy bomb derived from the Sidney Sheldon novel THE OTHER SIDE OF MIDNIGHT (1977). It concerned a European femme fatale (Marie-France Pisier) who becomes a big Hollywood star. Susan was gorgeous as the wife of an established actor (John Beck). Sarandon co-produced the low-budget THE GREAT SMOKEY ROADBLOCK (1978) and appeared in it as one of several prostitutes. Even Henry Fonda in the lead role of an aging trucker could not save its pedestrian storyline.

French director Louis Malle came to America in 1977 to make his first English-language feature film, PRETTY BABY (1978). Malle had met with Susan for ten minutes while the project was still in the casting stage. However, by the time negotiations were under way for her to co-star, he was confused and thought it was Susan Blakely he would be directing. "I thought working with a small group in a community effort would be a total change from THE OTHER SIDE OF MIDNIGHT," Sarandon said. Set in Storyville, the red light district of 1917 New Orleans, PRETTY BABY cast Susan as the prostitute mother of a twelve year old (Brooke Shields). Because of its nudity, the movie created a sensation.

About her nude scenes, Susan said, "If you're making a movie about Storyville, you can't have people lying in bed with the sheets double-taped across their breasts the way they do in Doris Day movies." While columnists like Earl Wilson thought the movie was scandalous, critic Rex Reed liked it and wrote that Susan's "star is rising so fast the noise is deafening." She and Malle, once he knew who she was, began a love affair in 1977 that would last three years, with her commuting to Paris as often as she could to be with him. In tribute to him, she had "Lou" tattooed atop one of her breasts. In 1977 she and Chris Sarandon separated officially, with an amicable divorce following in 1979.

She was playwright Tennessee Williams' third choice, following Ann-Margret and Meryl Streep, to star as Blanche Du Bois in a remake of *A Streetcar Named Desire*. However, the project would not be done until seven years later, with Ann-Margret in the ABC-TV movie version. Instead, Susan co-starred in an odd story of power struggles within a Gypsy clan, KING OF THE GYPSIES (1978). As the fortune teller Rose, she wore a black wig and boasted an accent. With none of her recent pictures having emerged as a box-office success, Hollywood magazine columnist Toni Holt pondered, "With her great looks and acting ability, we can't understand why [she] doesn't have better luck." Susan completed her first decade in show business by appearing as a love-smitten magazine writer in SOMETHING SHORT OF PARADISE (1979), a blatant rip-off of ANNIE HALL (1977) which did nothing for her reputation. It was also during this time that two of her business managers, through her naivete and lack of financial sense, embezzled funds from her.

Entering the 1980s, she realized finally that acting was her forte. She co-starred with Eileen Brennan off-Broadway in what the *New York Daily News* proclaimed "a lighter than air comedy on female bonding," *A Coupla White Chicks Sitting Around Talking*. The audience's laughter and applause fortified her declaration, "Yes, I'm an actor. That's really what I want to do." On the motion picture screen in October 1980, she and Stephen Collins were one of the LOVING COUPLES, who swap mates with Shirley MacLaine and James Coburn. The tired formula picture did not do well.

She was again directed by Louis Malle in the French-Canadian production ATLANTIC CITY (1981). She was Sally, a clam bar waitress who attends dealer's school and listens to French-language cassettes because she aspires to be the first female dealer in a Monte Carlo casino. Starring opposite Burt Lancaster (as a small-time crook), she again bared her breasts. However, Richard Schickel (*Time* magazine) overlooked that in his complimentary review: "There is a core of strength in her, even when she is playing losers, a lack of guile and artifice that is extremely appealing." Since Lancaster refused to promote the movie, it was left to Susan, who did no fewer than thirty-five talk show appearances and interviews. *Esquire* magazine did a layout on her; *Playboy* magazine chose hers as "The celebrity breasts of the summer." After Paramount ran full-page industry ads urging a Best Supporting Actress nomination for Susan, it came as a surprise when she was nominated for an Oscar in the Best Actress category. Once the surprise passed, she admitted, "I felt like the chorus person who was finally moved into the ranks." She lost the award to Katharine Hepburn for ON GOLDEN POND.

On February 2, 1982, she starred in PBS-TV's "American Playhouse" presentation of "Who Am I This Time?" opposite Christopher Walken, with whom she was linked romantically. In this period she also dated Richard Gere and Tom Noonan. In order to work with director Paul Mazursky and actors John Cassavetes, Gena Rowlands, and Raul Julia, Susan took the part of Aretha in TEMPEST (1982). It was photographed beautifully in Greece, but lacked a cohesive storyline. THE HUNGER (1983), labeled a "Sexy sci-fi flick" by one critic, initially received an X rating before the love scenes between Catherine Deneuve and Susan were softened. A bisexual vampiress millions of years old, Deneuve's character requires fresh blood to survive and she seduces Susan to the strains of Léo Delibes' opera *Lakmé*. Again nude on screen, Susan quipped, "I don't think my breasts have been so much on display; they've just been in some fairly historic movies."

Cited as "A white-knuckle psychological thriller" by *USA Today*, *Extremities* (1983) by William Mastrosimone starred Susan off-Broadway as a woman, attacked in her apartment by a rapist, who overpowers and binds him in the fireplace. At New York City's Public Theatre, Susan formed an improvisational acting group with Richard Dreyfuss, Carol Kane, and others. Having rejected the lead in ROMANCING THE STONE (1984) to do *Extremities*, she chose to co-star with Dreyfuss in THE BUDDY SYSTEM (1984), a leaden romantic comedy. She was one of dozens of celebrities to take part in the 1984 documentary IN OUR HANDS, which recorded the June 1982 antinuclear rally in New York City. On Showtime–Cable's "Faerie Tale Theatre" she co-starred with Klaus Kinski in "Beauty and the Beast" (August 13, 1984). An active member of MADRE, a group consisting of American women working to relieve Central American suffering, Susan went to Nicaragua in 1984 to help deliver food and hospital supplies. She was also a vociferous proponent of worldwide disarmament. In the $30 million NBC-TV epic miniseries "A.D." (1985), filmed in Tunisia, she was Livilla. The large cast included four hundred speaking parts. She starred as a Long Island housewife in the sometimes black comedy COMPROMISING POSITIONS (1985) and played Edda Ciano in the made-in-Italy HBO–Cable two-night presentation MUSSOLINI: THE DECLINE AND FALL OF IL DUCE (September 8–9, 1985).

In 1985 Susan gave birth to a daughter, Eva Maria Livia Amurri, fathered by handsome Italian writer/director Franco Amurri. She made no demands on him and decided on her own to have the baby, which she stated was "really the only extraordinary thing I've ever done."

She portrayed Dolores Huertas in the "An American Portrait" series (March 3, 1986) on CBS-TV and managed to survive the brutality of a World War II Japanese prison camp in the CBS-TV movie WOMEN OF VALOR (November 23, 1986). For THE WITCHES OF EASTWICK (1987), she was hired to play Alex, the sculptress, but at the last moment that role was handed to Cher, with Susan switched to the part of Jane, the schoolteacher/cellist. More confusion followed on the project. She could either stay, or quit and risk getting blacklisted for a year. Her decision to remain was wise in that the feature, starring Jack Nicholson as the devil, summoned to a New England town by three restless residents (Sarandon, Cher, Michelle Pfeiffer), became the year's #10 box-office attraction with domestic grosses of more than $63.7 million. Commenting on her co-star, Cher said, "She lives in the real world. She really faced the challenge and decided to make the best of it. I think she's really good, she's very funny, and she's very smart."

"There's never been a ballplayer slept with me who didn't have the best year of his career." These are the words of Annie Savoy (Susan), ardent fan of the minor league Durham (N.C.) Bulls in BULL DURHAM (1988). Each season she chooses one player to instruct in the ways of the world. She teaches a rookie (Tim Robbins) to breathe through his eyelids and ties him to her bed while she reads from Walt Whitman. However, it is Crash (Kevin Costner) with whom she has the most sexual fun, including his painting her toenails. David Ansen (*Newsweek* magazine) found her "irresistible," while the *San Francisco Examiner* predicted that her performance gave her "a running start for the Hollywood Walk of Fame." BULL DURHAM grossed $49.9 million in domestic ticket sales. Off screen, Susan, aged forty-two, and Tim Robbins, aged thirty, were involved romantically.

Chicago critics Gene Siskel of the *Tribune* and Roger Ebert of the *Sun-Times* in their syndicated movie review show of July 31, 1988, included Susan as one of three of Hollywood's more underrated actors (Tommy Lee Jones and Melanie Griffith were the others). Siskel said that she had been ahead of her time for years. "I'm glad the movies are equal to her," he added. *US* magazine picked her as one of the "Top 20" movie stars of 1988. In New York City, where she maintained an apartment in the same building as Richard Gere, she was among 1,200 celebrities and socialites attending a $350 AIDS benefit for individuals from the interior design industry who were infected with the virus, and she strongly supported Jesse Jackson for the U.S. presidency.

She made a motion picture in Italy called DA GRANDE (1988), which did not surface in America. She sadly chose to follow up her BULL DURHAM success with SWEET HEARTS DANCE (1988), as Don Johnson's patient wife. While the *Los Angeles Times* found this tale of midlife crisis "annoying," it rated Susan as "one of the American movies' exemplars of mature female sexuality." The film's director, Robert Greenwald, observed that Susan has "gotten a whole generation of men and women turned on to the mind."

On Lifetime–Cable, Susan hosted "Postpartum: Beyond the Blues" (March 22, 1989) and in Manhattan, on May 15, 1989, she became a mother for the second time. Jack Henry Robbins was fathered by Tim Robbins. Sarandon told the press she was "one happy mommy."

Peter Travers (*People* magazine) criticized THE JANUARY MAN (1989), the black comedy account of a serial killer loose in New York City, as "a movie at war with itself: an amiable mess." Susan played the first bitch role of her career as a society woman married unhappily to Harvey Keitel, the brother of Kevin Kline, the film's star. In September she was seen in the cameo part of a jaded journalist in A DRY WHITE SEASON (1989), filmed in Africa and noteworthy for Marlon Brando's return to movie screens after almost a decade. Also in September, on the 25th, Susan performed in the syndicated TV episode "He'll See You Now" of the British teleseries "Oxbridge Blues." Later in 1989 she lobbied in Washington, D.C., for America's homeless with "Housing Now!" Returning to the nation's capital in March 1990 she joined Alec Baldwin, Christopher Reeve, and Ron Silver (the president of Creative Coalition) to protest a ban on alleged obscenity in federally funded arts projects.

In WHITE PALACE (1990), shot in St. Louis, Susan played a spicy-tongued waitress from the wrong side of the tracks who falls in love with an upscale young widower (James Spader). However, his mother (Renee Taylor) prefers that he continue to mourn his wife rather than indulge in a romance with an older woman from a questionable background. With such an intriguing premise, expectations for the project ran high, but a disappointed Richard Corliss (*Time* magazine) noted, "WHITE PALACE settles into stolid ordinariness, after flirting with being a handsome essay on the grandeur of reciprocal lust." Owen Gleiberman (*Entertainment Weekly* magazine) labeled the picture "a piece of 1970s-style whimsy" but granted that "Sarandon shows some of the comic vibrancy she had in BULL DURHAM. Her Nora is full of high spirits and low funk, a deeply pragmatic woman whose no-nonsense demeanor extends to sensuality. She knows what she wants and takes it; Sarandon makes Nora's very slatternliness seem radiant." *Variety* endorsed, "Bravely allowing herself to look the character's age, Sarandon nevertheless brings uncommon sensuality to the part—equaling, if not surpassing, her own standard in films like BULL DURHAM and ATLANTIC CITY." In its first seven weeks of domestic distribution, WHITE PALACE grossed a respectable $16,553,633.

On October 25, 1990, for one day only, videocassette retailers were permitted to order, for November 8 delivery, the homevideo version of THE ROCKY HORROR PICTURE SHOW. With a six-to-eight-minute prologue showing viewers what it is like to attend a screening of the classic, with live performances and audience participation, Fox expected to sell between 200,000 and 300,000 cassettes. Never shown on commercial television, the cult movie had grossed, worldwide, in excess of $100 million and reportedly continues to attract $1 million each year at theater box offices. At the same time, a revival of the play was on the London stage.

THELMA & LOUISE (1991), filmed in several states including Arkansas, Oklahoma, New Mexico, and California, co-starred Susan and Geena Davis in a female buddy movie.

In late June 1990 Orion Pictures gave the approval for a sequel to BULL DURHAM to producer Thom Mount, who immediately contracted Ron Shelton, who had written the original, to work up a screenplay. "I can't tell you the plot," Mount told the *Durham* (North Carolina) *Morning Herald*, "but . . . it involves the same three characters at later stages in their lives." It was hoped that Kevin Costner, Susan, and Tim Robbins would all agree to repeating their characters in a "sexy baseball saga" sequel.

Always off-handed about the art of acting, which she has mastered, the very natural Susan once analyzed that she emotes "from the gut. I've never learned to make this vein here pop out or to cry on cue. But, you know, in film you've only got to get it right once and you've got all day to do it. . . . Anybody can act. It's no big deal." Discussing some of the strange career choices she has made, she explains, "One of the reasons I've done the roles that I've done is that they frighten me so much." Regarding her films, she says, "I hope to get as many of these elements as possible: great script, great people involved, great location and a great salary, but the chances of getting all of these is slim. Now that I have children, the exotic location has become more of a complication than an asset. Above all, I like to have fun and finally, when the dust settles, I hope there is something left standing that I'm proud of."

Filmography

Joe (Cannon, 1970)
Lady Liberty [La Mortadella] (UA, 1972)
F. Scott Fitzgerald and "The Last of the Belles" (ABC-TV, 1/7/74)
Lovin' Molly (Col, 1974)
The Front Page (Univ, 1974)
The Great Waldo Pepper (Univ, 1975)
The Rocky Horror Picture Show (20th–Fox, 1975)
One Summer Love [Dragonfly] (AIP, 1976)
Checkered Flag or Crash (Univ, 1977)
The Other Side of Midnight (20th–Fox, 1977)
The Great Smokey Roadblock [The Last of the Cowboys] (Dimension, 1978) (also co-producer)
Pretty Baby (Par, 1978)
King of the Gypsies (Par, 1978)
Something Short of Paradise (AIP, 1979)
Loving Couples (20th–Fox, 1980)
Atlantic City [Atlantic City, U.S.A.] (Par, 1981)

Tempest (Col, 1982)
The Hunger (MGM/UA, 1983)
The Buddy System (20th–Fox, 1984)
In Our Hands (Almi Classics, 1984)
Mussolini: The Decline and Fall of Il Duce [Mussolini and I] (HBO–Cable, 9/8/85–9/9/85)
Compromising Positions (Par, 1985)
Women of Valor (CBS-TV, 11/23/86)
The Witches of Eastwick (WB, 1987)
Bull Durham (Orion, 1988)
Da Grande (It, 1988)
Sweet Hearts Dance (Tri-Star, 1988)
The January Man (MGM, 1989)
A Dry White Season (MGM, 1989)
Through the Wire (Nina Rosenblum,1990) (director/producer/co-writer only) (documentary)
White Palace (Univ, 1990)
Thelma & Louise (MGM/Pathé, 1991)

Television Series

A World Apart (ABC, 1970–71)
Search for Tomorrow (CBS, 1972)

A.D. (NBC, 3/31/85–4/4/85) [miniseries]

Album Discography

The Rocky Horror Picture Show (Ode OSV 21653) [ST]

ARNOLD SCHWARZENEGGER

"I don't say whether I think I'm any good. If I do say I'm good then people think I'm bragging and if I say I don't think I'm so good, people think I don't believe in myself. So, I leave the judgment to the people." —*Video Review* magazine, January 1989

HIS IS MUCH MORE THAN THE SUCCESS STORY OF A POOR IMMIGRANT who became a self-made American millionaire through tremendous aggressiveness and sustained motivation. Luck, too, has had a great deal to do with Arnold Schwarzenegger's spectacular accomplishments. Had he been born forty, even twenty, years earlier, he might well have been viewed as an oddity, a fad, perhaps a freak. He might well have come and gone on the celebrity scene, viewed as a pleasing physical specimen, like Johnny Weissmuller or Steve Reeves, but not as someone to be taken really seriously. Instead, Arnold emerged at a time when bodybuilding had gained worldwide popularity. He smartly took advantage of that, and of his charm, wry humor, and love of life, to help him become a major action movie star. Like Sylvester Stallone, Lou Ferrigno, and porn star Joey Sefano, Arnold was in the right place at the right time. Later, Dolph Lundgren and Jean-Claude Van Damme sought to cash in on the muscle craze, but so far have failed to fill Arnold's giant footsteps.

Arnold was born on Wednesday, July 30, 1947, in southeastern Austria in the small city of Graz. Although the surname Schwarzenegger translates as "black plowman," the father, Gustav, was chief of police rather than a farmer. He was also a one-time champion ice curler and a former member of the Nazi Party. The boy's mother, Aurelia, of solid Russian peasant stock, was a meticulous homemaker. Although Arnold's early years in the village of Thal were marred by illness, neither he nor his older brother, Meinhard, were given preferential treatment by their strict disciplinarian father, who permitted no talking during meals and who decreed that Arnold would be a champion soccer player while Meinhard would become an engineer.

Through diet and exercise at a local athletic club to develop a soccer player's legs, Arnold's health improved immensely and he began lifting weights. "I was a sculptor shaping the body," he has remembered of those early days. As Roman Catholics, the parents escorted their sons to church each Sunday morning; in Sunday afternoon outings Gustav dictated that his sons sit down and describe the services in writing. If their grammar, punctuation, or spelling was incorrect, he would demand that they rewrite their essays until they were perfect. There was no television in Thal, but there was one in Graz, two hours away by foot, as well as a movie theater where Arnold became captivated by the series of Italian-made Hercules films with musclemen Steve Reeves, Alan Steel, and Reg Park at various times in the title role. British bodybuilder Park especially became his hero, whom he tried to emulate by lifting weights six days a week. At the age of fifteen Arnold rebelled against his father's demand that he become a soccer player when Gustav established a curfew restricting the boy to just three nights a week at the gym. Arnold immediately set up his own training equipment at home in an unheated room, determined to be like Park and the others. He also planned one day to go to America to be in movies.

For three years in secondary school (high school), he studied business administration, with which he was enthralled. Upon graduation in 1965, he enlisted for three years in the Austrian army. After one month in the military service, at age eighteen, he won the Austrian Junior Olympic weightlifting championship. This was followed by his winning the Junior Mr. Europe title in Stuttgart, Germany. There he met Sardinian bodybuilder Francesco Columbu, with whom he would have a lifelong friendship. After winning both the Austrian and European curling championships, Arnold has admitted, "I thought I was King Kong."

After one year he was permitted to leave the army and went to Munich as the manager of a health/bodybuilding club where he developed innovative training techniques. Later he would admit to having been a bully in this period, intent on proving his masculinity and strength. In 1966 he was named the Best Built Man of Europe and Mr. Europe. In addition, he won the International Powerlifting Championship, which entitled him to compete in the National Amateur Bodybuilder Association's Mr. Universe contest in London, in which he placed second. In 1967 he won the amateur title and in 1968 was named Mr. Universe, the first of what would be five wins. In England he not only met his idol, Reg Park, but also teamed with him for an exhibition tour of England and Ireland.

In 1968 he was invited to the United States by California-based Joe Weider, known as the premier promoter of bodybuilding and publisher of several muscle magazines. After winning his second Mr. Universe contest in Miami, Arnold went to Santa Monica, California, under the patronage of Weider. The latter provided him with an apartment, an automobile, and $60 weekly for writing articles for his publications. Dubbed "The Austrian Oak" by Weider, Arnold began an affiliation with Gold's Gym in nearby Venice, where everyone immediately recognized him. He also enrolled in English classes at Santa Monica College, where he would study for more than a year. Meanwhile, he won the titles of Mr. World and Mr. Olympia; the latter competition was known as "the superbowl of weightlifting." Later he was a business administration and English student at the University of California at Los Angeles, where he obtained a bachelor's degree.

After winning three major competitions in a year—in London; Columbus, Ohio; and New York City—Arnold remained in Manhattan while Weider persuaded the makers of a low-budget spoof of the HERCULES movies that Arnold was their man. He failed to mention his protégé's heavily accented English. After the producers took one look at the big man, who allowed Weider to do all the negotiating, Arnold was hired at $1,000 per week for HERCULES IN NEW YORK (1970), also known as HERCULES GOES BANANAS. He played the strong man who, among other feats, steers a chariot along Manhattan's byways. Although his voice was dubbed, Arnold had realized his dream—he was in a movie. He was billed as Arnold Strong. Two years later, still not yet adept in the English language and continuing to use the name Strong, he was seen but not heard as a muscular hood in THE LONG GOODBYE (1973).

In the autumn of 1974, author Charles Gaines and photographer George Butler had their book, *Pumping Iron: The Art and Sport of Bodybuilding*, published by Simon & Schuster. Arnold was generously featured, again using the name Arnold Strong. To help promote the book, Arnold appeared on Merv Griffin's syndicated TV talk show, where he was permitted to speak. Gary Morton, Lucille Ball's producer husband, saw his interview and, finding him amusing, gave him a guest spot under his real name in Ball's CBS-TV special "Happy Anniversary and Goodbye" (November 19, 1974).

In 1975, after six wins as Mr. Olympia, Arnold retired from bodybuilding competition, explaining, "I had gotten the physical development I wanted and my ego wasn't being satisfied anymore from winning." With this portion of his life supposedly behind him, he reminisced, "I lost in my whole life three competitions," admitting, "I was upset about it for months." At the age of twenty-eight, he opened a new chapter of his life by taking acting lessons with drama coach Eric Morris in Los Angeles.

STAY HUNGRY (1976), starring Jeff Bridges and Sally Field, was based on a story by Charles Gaines, who recommended Arnold for a part. His role as Joe Santo, in which he spoke halting English, is considered to be his acting debut. Naturally, Arnold played a bodybuilder. *Variety* observed, "Schwarzenegger's cautious work comes across with a solid dignity." For his efforts, Arnold was awarded a Golden Globe for Best Acting Debut—Male.

In early 1977, PUMPING IRON, a documentary based on the Gaines–Butler book, was in release and featured a charming, witty Arnold, who likened the flexing of his muscles to having an orgasm. *After Dark* magazine ran a multi-page spread on Arnold that included a frontal-nude color photograph. He told the publication, "I see myself in the position of climbing up this ladder at the fastest speed possible. I'm anxious, perhaps overanxious, to get there, but I'm taking one step at a time—and I just can't wait." Later that year, his first book, an autobiography/training manual entitled *Arnold: The Education of a Bodybuilder*, was published by Simon & Schuster. The cover showed the bikini-clad Arnold standing atop the world. The 256-page book contained 290 photos of Arnold and sold 150,000 hardcover copies. In the text he advised young bodybuilders, "The meaning of life is . . . to move ahead, to go up, to achieve, to conquer." *Cosmopolitan* magazine selected him for a 1977 (mostly nude) fold-out photo. Through his publicist, he wangled an invitation to the Robert F. Kennedy Tennis Tournament held in Hyannis Port, Massachusetts, where he met twenty-two-year-old Maria Shriver, daughter of Eunice Kennedy Shriver, sister of John and Robert Kennedy. Maria, who would later become a television journalist, recalled the meeting with, "You sell people short when you attach labels to them. I met him as a human being, not a bodybuilder." Although Arnold had smoked marijuana in the final scene of PUMPING IRON, he now claimed it was just for show and that his real passion was the cigar.

He guest-starred in the "Dead Lifts" episode of TV's "The Streets of San Francisco" (May 5, 1977); was featured in the ninety-minute CBS-TV presentation "Variety '77— The Year in Entertainment" (January 9, 1978), inspired by the top names and stories from *Daily Variety*, and was a commentator on a telecast of "ABC'S Wide World of Sports." He was third-billed as Handsome, wearing a tight-fitting costume, in the superior Western spoof THE VILLAIN (1979). However, he is best remembered from that production for riding in a jiggling buckboard seated beside the buxom Ann-Margret. He also had a small part in the comedy misfire SCAVENGER HUNT (1979). In November 1979 his second book, *Arnold's Bodyshaping for Women*, was published by Simon & Schuster. At the same time, it was revealed that he had become a millionaire through his various enterprises: mail-order training courses in bodybuilding and physical fitness, a line of workout clothing and equipment, product endorsements for various food supplements, seminars and paid public appearances, sales of Arnold T-shirts, and real-estate holdings in California and Colorado. Schwarzenegger lived in Santa Monica, with a winter house in Palm Springs. By now, his father had died of a heart attack and his brother had been killed in 1968, at age twenty-three, while driving while intoxicated. He visited his mother in Austria, but insisted, "There's no place in the world where I feel as comfortable as in America." In 1979 Arnold met with influential Italian-born producer Dino De Laurentiis in Hollywood to discuss starring in FLASH GORDON (1980). However, he lost the part to Sam J. Jones when he unwittingly insulted De Laurentiis in later negotiations.

In 1980 he was lured out of bodybuilding retirement to compete in Australia for the Mr. Olympia title, which he won for the seventh time. He flexed his muscles for home viewers as Mickey Hargitay, the Hungarian-born bodybuilder, in CBS's one-dimensional biography THE JAYNE MANSFIELD STORY (October 29, 1980), opposite Loni Anderson. Arnold's first box-office success was CONAN THE BARBARIAN (1982), filmed in Spain under the auspices of Dino De Laurentiis. The producer was determined that anyone but Arnold would play the ancient slave hero who became a gladiator, but director John Milius refused to accept another actor. Arnold's English had vastly improved by this juncture, although when the super-muscular Conan is asked what is the best thing in life, he replies, "Crush your enemies—see dem driven before you and to hear der lamentation of dair vimen!" The action-laden adventure entry grossed $41 million in U.S. box-office ticket sales and took in another $60 million overseas.

The October 1982 issue of *Life* magazine included tips from Arnold to exercising women in his article, "A Beauty and the Best Show How It's Done," with photographs of him with his CONAN co-star, Sandahl Bergman. In 1983, with some fanfare, Arnold became an American citizen, at which time he spoke of his admiration for Ronald Reagan: "he's done the impossible—he's never gotten beaten in any election. He's really in touch with the people." Arnold formed Oak Productions with an office in Venice, California, adorned with a large American flag and a portrait of Reagan.

After the gigantic success of the initial CONAN, it would have been unthinkable for

De Laurentiis not to produce a sequel. Filmed in Mexico, the follow-up reached movie screens as CONAN THE DESTROYER (1984), in which Conan searches for a mystical gem with the help of his athletic buddy (Grace Jones). As in the first CONAN, Arnold's quick delivery of comic lines in between physical feats endeared him to audiences. CONAN THE DESTROYER grossed $31 million domestically with another $70 million derived from overseas box-office sales. Later that year he starred in THE TERMINATOR as a cyborg sent from the future back to the year 2029 to kill an innocent woman (Linda Hamilton). This nonstop action picture would set standards for many such genre entries to come. Arnold gave his best performance to date as the unstoppable robot killer. This led *People* magazine to backhandedly compliment the star: "The title character of this film speaks English with a terrible accent, never says more than one sentence at a time, is as expressive as a rhino, and moves as gracefully as an anvil with legs. In other words, he was born to be played by Arnold Schwarzenegger." Released to generally favorable reviews, the feature grossed nearly $17 million in domestic film rentals; in the opinion of much of Hollywood, the gross would have been far more had the distributor packaged and previewed the film better. Following this breakthrough role, Arnold's salary doubled, reaching the $5 million mark.

RED SONJA (1985), shot in Rome, was a regressive career step for Arnold and did not fare as well. Although Arnold did his best, he was tiring of the sword-and-sorcery plotlines; this time he was the only warrior who can match the strength of the Amazonian Sonja (Brigitte Nielsen). Nielsen, who prefers men big and brawny, to match her own size, reportedly seduced Arnold during the Italian location-shooting. The only way he could maneuver out of the relationship was to introduce her to Sylvester Stallone. RED SONJA turned out to be Arnold's first box-office disappointment. "The most important thing to me," he said, "is to sell tickets. Then you have the power to do the kind of projects you want."

COMMANDO, in its first three days of release in October 1985, grossed $7.7 million in 1,485 theaters. In this contemporary action picture, Arnold is the retired leader of an American special operations task force who is suddenly coerced into finding his daughter (Alyssa Milano), who has been kidnapped by the army of a no-good South American dictator (Dan Hedaya). Stripping off his shirt for action and box-office appeal, he ultimately shoots it out with the villains, saying to one, "You're a funny guy, Sully [David Patrick Kelly]. That's why I'm going to kill you last."

During 1985, Arnold was the national weightlifting coach for the Special Olympics, but laid down all gym equipment for his April 26, 1986, society marriage to Maria Shriver at St. Francis Xavier Church in Hyannis, Massachusetts. Facial analyst Sandra Jean Copperfield of Cranston, Rhode Island, noted in a tabloid that their facial shapes are a "perfect match," suggesting that they will be together forever.

He starred as a disgraced former FBI agent in RAW DEAL (1986). It contained a love scene with Kathryn Harrold. Arnold was not at ease in such romantic situations, nor did his fans accept him as a screen lover. Despite the action sequences (which found him almost single-handedly wiping out a crime ring) and his by-now-standard comic moments, the film floundered because of an inadequate storyline and uninspired direction. On the other hand, the science-fiction-oriented PREDATOR (1987) sustained his box-office power with domestic film rentals of $31 million. Short on dialogue but long on suspense and riveting action, the feature cast him as the lone survivor of a commando force in a Central American jungle who stalks an elusive, powerful alien being. THE RUNNING MAN (1987), originally scheduled to star Christopher Reeve and adapted from a Richard Bachman [Stephen King] short story, was set in the twenty-first century. In that future time, condemned criminals, guilty or not, are forced to compete on a deadly television game show. A highlight of the movie was the amusing casting of Richard Dawson (of TV's "Family Feud" fame) as the slimy host of the program-within-the-movie. Arnold's often-used line, "I'll be back," is found here, with Dawson's character replying with a sneer, "Only in a rerun." THE RUNNING MAN grossed $16 million in domestic film rentals.

In December 1987 Arnold's star was placed on the Hollywood Walk of Fame along Hollywood Boulevard. By then, Joe Gold, the owner of Gold's World Gym, had given Schwarzenegger a private terrazzo parking space outside the Venice gym with his name inlaid in brass as a fortieth birthday gift.

The February 21, 1988, headline of a British tabloid blazed "Hollywood Star's Nazi Secret." The piece alleged that Arnold was a "fervent Nazi with anti-Semitic views" and that he was a "secret admirer of Adolf Hitler." Arnold won a suit against the publication in December 1989 when he was paid undisclosed damages plus legal costs. During 1988 he toured with George Bush, the Republican candidate for President of the United States. Dubbed by the press as "Conan the Republican," Arnold said, "I can only play the Terminator in my movies, but let me tell you, when it comes to the American future, Michael Dukakis [the Democratic presidential candidate] will be the *real* Terminator." Schwarzenegger also won a libel suit filed against him by Freddie Ortiz, a former Mr. Universe who is mentioned in Arnold's co-authored book, *The Encyclopedia of Modern Bodybuilding* (1985), as having smoked cigarettes and drunk whiskey while in training. A New York judge ruled that Arnold's written comments were not libelous.

RED HEAT (1988), filmed in Moscow's Red Square and in Chicago, presented Arnold as a stone-faced, highly disciplined Soviet policeman teamed with a slovenly Chicago detective (James Belushi) in tracking Russian drug dealers. This tribute to the new Russian policy of *glasnost* was the first fully American-financed feature to shoot inside Communist Russia. *People* magazine ridiculed it as "mindless," but acknowledged that it was "hard action delivered with humor and flair." *Variety* decided that Schwarzenegger was "right on target with his characterization of the iron-willed soldier." RED HEAT grossed $16 million in domestic film rentals.

TWINS (1988) was a different story in more ways than one. In this, Arnold's first intentional comedy, he and short-statured Danny DeVito (who also directed) were identical twins (!), the result of a genetic experiment pooling the minds and sperm of six scientists with the body of a beautiful woman in the hope of creating a superior human. When two shockingly different babies emerged from the womb, they were separated. As adults, the disparate twins discover one another and go off together in search of their mother (Bonnie Bartlett). Of his co-star DeVito said, "His concentration is almost supreme when it comes to things he wants. But he does have a major weakness, which is vanilla ice cream." TWINS became the year's #5 box-office champion, with tremendous domestic film rentals of $57,237,170. Instead of his now usual $9 million fee, Arnold accepted a minimal up-front salary plus 17.5 percent of the studio's gross; his take-home pay was estimated at an eventual $16 million.

Beginning in 1989, Arnold appeared in TV commercials in Japan for Nissin Noodles showing him gaining rowing speed in a boat after sipping noodle soup. His salary for this chore was said to be close to $1 million. In September 1989 he stepped down as a judge of the Miss America pageant to avoid a conflict of interest, since his wife, Maria, was handling a television story about the event. In a *Playboy* interview, Arnold admitted to having taken steroids years earlier to build his muscles, but said that the limited intake had produced no side effects. On December 13, 1989, Schwarzenegger's daughter, named Katherine Eunice, was born in Santa Monica.

On March 26, 1990, on ABC-TV on Oscar night, Arnold was one of three celebrities interviewed on "The Barbara Walters Special." He disclosed that his philosophy was to "stay hungry." He said, "I really get hungry when people say you *can't* do it." It was revealed in Wendy Leigh's unauthorized biography, *Arnold* (1990), that he was supporting his late brother's son, Peter Knapp, whom he had brought to California from Austria.

Arnold Schwarzenegger in TWINS (1988).

Superstar Schwarzenegger turned director for the April 21, 1990, HBO–Cable airing of "Tales from the Crypt," comprised of three thirty-minute episodes. The second, "The Switch," directed by Arnold, starred William Hickey as an old man who swaps body parts with a young man in order to attract a younger woman (Kelly Preston). Arnold liked being behind the camera, saying, "I didn't want to start out with a big movie and fall on my face." Rejecting multipicture acting offers from several studios, Arnold, on May 1, 1990, was named by President George Bush as chairman of the President's "National Physical Fitness and Sports Month." Arnold quipped, "Read my lips, no more flab," and was not photographed for a month with a cigar in his mouth. His article "A Secret Tragedy," published in the May 21, 1990, issue of *Newsweek* magazine, urged children to exercise. That same month he posed doing mock dance steps with Sylvester Stallone at the Cannes Film Festival. In a poll conducted by Stolichnaya Vodka in Moscow, he was named one of the Muscovites' favorite screen stars.

A short story by Philip K. Dick, "We Can Remember It for You Wholesale," had bounced around film production companies since 1979. After it was acquired by filmmaker Dino De Laurentiis in 1982, preproduction began in 1984 in Italy with Richard Dreyfuss as the star. Work then stopped, with subsequent unrealized plans in Australia to start the movie again with Patrick Swayze in the lead. In 1988, with the De Laurentiis organization in need of cash, Arnold purchased the property for $3 million. The resultant science fiction thriller premiered on June 1, 1990, as TOTAL RECALL, shot in Mexico. It was Arnold's first motion picture release in nearly two years. Helmed by the noted Dutch director Paul Verhoeven, of ROBOCOP (1987) fame, the $50 million production, financed by a Dutch bank, boasted terrific makeup, tantalizing sets, and, as expected in an Arnold Schwarzenegger screen enterprise, nonstop action and humorous throwaway asides. The film is set in the year 2084, when Mars has become a colony of Earth. As Doug Quaid, he has nightmares and vague recollections of experiences on Mars, which he insists he has never visited. His wife (Sharon Stone) proves to be his mortal enemy as he embarks on high adventures to uncover his bizarre past, which lead ultimately to a showdown on Mars with the dictatorial forces of an oppressor (Ronnie Cox). "The movie is a cartoon, though a mammothly enjoyable one" was the critique of *Rolling Stone* magazine, which also stated that Arnold "has rarely looked as revved up for action." The *Hollywood Reporter* noted that Arnold is, "as usual, a terrific superhero," and *Newsweek* magazine, finding the film to be "decadent fun," insisted that Arnold's "charm, both guileless and knowing," once again established him as "the screen's most playful destroyer of human flesh." TOTAL RECALL, in its first weekend of release, set the year's record, with domestic box-office grosses of $25.5 million. After six weeks it had grossed over $99.2 million in ticket sales, and by the autumn months of 1990, it was the #1 screen attraction in London, Amsterdam, and Madrid. In November 1990 the movie was released on videocassette.

Arnold was a presenter on ABC-TV's "All-Star Pro Sports Awards" (June 25, 1990), and on July 21, 1990, in Seattle, he led a fitness workout as part of the welcoming ceremony for the 1990 Goodwill Games. In Las Vegas on August 8, 1990, he was honored as Video Star of the Year by a Homer Award, given by the 4,000 video store owners comprising the Video Software Dealers Association. Also in August, he spoke of Hollywood's stuntmen on the MPI-released documentary videotape, *The World's Greatest Stunts! A Tribute to Hollywood Stuntmen*, hosted by Christopher Reeve. *Forbes* magazine on September 16, 1990, listed the world's highest-paid entertainers; Arnold was #6, with an annual income of $55 million. The November 30, 1990, one-hour NBC-TV special "A Hollywood Tribute to Arnold Schwarzenegger," hosted by Milton Berle, was just that—a tribute, not a roast.

A movie developed for Arnold, SGT. ROCK (forthcoming, 1991), went to Bruce Willis because of a scheduling conflict, while Arnold instead journeyed to Oregon to shoot KINDERGARTEN COP (1990). In this comedy adventure he was an undercover cop substituting as a teacher in a kindergarten class in order to locate the child and missing wife of a jailed drug dealer (Richard Tyson). The Ivan Reitman–directed comedy-drama was in general release in time for the Christmas 1990 box-office business. In October 1990 Arnold began filming TERMINATOR 2 (1991), a sequel to his earlier hit action picture. On Sunday, November 25, 1990, a most convivial Schwarzenegger served as the grand marshal of the fifty-ninth annual Hollywood Christmas Parade.

Listed by *Forbes* magazine as one of America's ten wealthiest entertainers, the disarmingly intelligent and charming Arnold is constantly mentioned as having political ambitions, most often in connection with the California governorship. He neither admits to nor denies such aspirations, but he does have the financial wherewithal for such a race. Despite his affiliation by marriage with the staunch Democrats of Massachusetts, the Kennedy clan, he remains a devout Republican.

Filmography

Hercules in New York [Hercules Goes Bananas/ Hercules: The Movie] (RAF–United Films, 1970) (as Arnold Strong)

The Long Goodbye (UA, 1973) (as Arnold Strong)

Stay Hungry (UA, 1976)

Pumping Iron (Cinema 5, 1977)

The Villain [Cactus Jack] (Col, 1979)

Scavenger Hunt (20th–Fox, 1979)

The Jayne Mansfield Story (CBS-TV, 10/29/80)

Conan the Barbarian (Univ, 1982)

Conan the Destroyer (Univ, 1984)

The Terminator (Orion, 1984)

Red Sonja (MGM/UA, 1985)

Commando (20th–Fox, 1985)

Raw Deal (De Laurentiis Entertainment Group, 1986)

Predator (20th–Fox, 1987)

The Running Man (Tri-Star, 1987)

Red Heat (Tri-Star, 1988)

Twins (Univ, 1988)

Total Recall (Tri-Star, 1990)

Kindergarten Cop (Univ, 1990)

Terminator 2: Judgment Day (Orion, 1991)

JANE SEYMOUR

"I'm someone who comes up with the goods, someone who can
even survive bad material. I'm sure I'll always work."
—*European Travel & Life* magazine, November 1989

DURING A TWELVE-YEAR PERIOD THIS BRITISH-BORN, STRIKINGLY BEAU-
tiful lady played just one role in ten with an English accent; all her other roles were as
Americans. Like her countryman Bob Hoskins, she speaks flawlessly like an American
from any region, emulating a twang or a drawl she has heard only once or twice. She has
been known to telephone a geographical region simply to get the sound of the voice of the
directory-assistance operator. The ubiquitous Jane Seymour has been termed "the queen
of the miniseries," rivaled only by Jaclyn Smith. Like Smith, Seymour is a classic beauty,
but borders on the exotic like Merle Oberon of the 1930s.

In 1981, while performing as one of fiction's most heinous women (in the miniser-
ies "John Steinbeck's 'East of Eden,'" she said, "Let the others play the sweet young things.
What I like is the evil parts—just as Barbara Stanwyck, Joan Crawford, and Bette Davis
once did. . . . I hate perfection. That's why I'd never, never, never be a Charlie's angel."
Jane has played straight roles, but she is most memorable when her character is tainted.
Oddly, she has one green eye and one brown eye. In the seventeenth-century days of
Salem's New England witches, this would have been considered a sign of the devil and just
cause for burning at the stake.

Joyce Penelope Wilhelmina Frankenberg was born on Thursday, February 15,
1951, in Hilingdon, Middlesex, England, to Dr. John Frankenberg and his wife, Mieke.
Renowned in England as an obstetrician/gynecologist, Dr. Frankenberg was the son of a
Jewish immigrant from Poland who lost many relatives to the Nazi death camps during
World War II. His Dutch wife had spent three-and-one-half years in Indonesia in a
Japanese-run concentration camp during World War II and later became an official with
the international Red Cross. "I get my creative instincts from daddy," the most famous of
their three daughters once said, "and my toughness and drive from mum."

Joyce was enrolled in ballet classes at the age of two as a recommended cure for flat-
footedness. She did so well that her parents decided to permit her to continue for as long as
she liked. At the age of ten, because of problems in pronouncing her "r's," she also enrolled
in a voice class. She danced with the London Festival Ballet at the age of thirteen and was
admitted to the Arts Educational Trust, a school for talented children. Despite her early

performances on stage before audiences, she was a shy girl, obsessed with ballet. At the age of sixteen, she was chosen to dance in the Kirov Ballet's performances of *Cinderella* at London's Covent Garden. Because her surname might be confused with Frankenstein, it was suggested that she change it. She chose Jane Seymour, not because it was very British and the name of Henry VIII's third wife, but because "it scanned nicely and rolled trippingly from the tongue." A few months later, at age seventeen, while practicing knee-rolls for a jazz ballet class in school, she developed severe pains behind both knees. Physicians recommended serious knee surgery, if she wanted to dance again, or complete rest, which meant abandoning ballet. Jane chose the latter. In order to remain at the Arts Educational Trust, she switched her performing arts major to theater. The decision was unpopular with her parents, but Jane admitted, "I'm exceedingly stubborn and I made the move anyway."

In 1968, soon after graduating from school, she got a very small part in Richard Attenborough's satirical World War I film, OH! WHAT A LOVELY WAR (1969). During production, she met Attenborough's son Michael, a student to whom she was married in 1971 at the age of twenty. Meanwhile, in OKTOBER-DAGE (1970), a.k.a. THE ONLY WAY, she played the daughter of a Danish Jew, caught in the Nazi occupation of their homeland. Her acting career began to blossom with work in both BBC radio and television and small repertory theater companies playing the provinces. Her first major part was in the BBC-TV series "The Onedin Line," followed by stage parts in *Not Now, Darling* and *Young Winston.* She repeated the latter role in the 1972 film version of the biography of Churchill. BBC radio afforded her drama work in "Far from the Madding Crowd" and "The Silence of Saint Vierge."

Then, in 1972, thinking it might prove to be a breakthrough into American filmmaking, she accepted the role of Solitaire, the tarot card reader, in LIVE AND LET DIE (1973), playing opposite Roger Moore as James Bond. It was Moore who, during production, called her "Baby Bernhardt" because of her dedication to the part. Because of the travel requirements of the film's shooting, the young Mrs. Attenborough was seldom at home in London. Because he was often referred to as "Mr. Seymour," her husband, Michael, suffered an identity crisis. The ill-timed marriage ended in 1973. Soon afterward, she met businessman Geoffrey Planer, who persuaded her to broaden her scope by performing in works by Shakespeare and other classic playwrights. The two began living together while she made television movies for American viewing, including a dual role in FRANKENSTEIN: THE TRUE STORY (November 30–December 1, 1973) and the role of Bathsheba in THE STORY OF DAVID, shot in Israel and Spain but not aired until April 9 and 11, 1976.

Producer Howard W. Koch tested her for a part in JACQUELINE SUSANN'S ONCE IS NOT ENOUGH (1975), but she came across as too English; the role went to Deborah Raffin. In 1976, when they decided to move to the United States, Jane married Planer, with whom she had lived for two years. Ten days after the wedding, Jane left for the United States with $600 and a six-week return airline ticket. Planer intended to follow, but never did.

In Hollywood, Jane shared an apartment with British-born actress Jenny Agutter. While doing pre-telecast publicity on behalf of THE STORY OF DAVID, Seymour was offered a part in the nine-hour NBC-TV miniseries "Captains and the Kings" (1976). After she accepted this offer, her British agent fired her as a client. Meanwhile, she lost the NBC opportunity when a U.S. work permit failed to materialize. Opting for a temporary visa, she regained the role, as a member of a Boston Irish clan in quest of fame and fortune. Her acting, with authentic Boston accent, won her an Emmy nomination in the supporting actress category, but she did not win. By now, it had become apparent that her second marriage was not going to work. She filed for divorce, saying, "I'm wary of marriage—it ends relationships."

After straightening out matters with the immigration authorities, Jane got an abundance of work in Hollywood television, starting with the NBC-TV caper movie BENNY & BARNEY: LAS VEGAS UNDERCOVER (January 9, 1977). On the heels of that came an episode of "McCloud" and an appearance on the ABC-TV special "Battle of the Network Stars," both in January 1977. Her second miniseries was "Seventh Avenue" (1977), a six-hour miniseries shown in three parts. Third-billed as a fashion designer, she spoke like a native New Yorker. She was Patrick Wayne's vis-à-vis in the British-made SINBAD AND THE EYE OF THE TIGER (1977), an ill-conceived, childish sequel to THE GOLDEN VOYAGE OF SINBAD (1974). But, at least, her diaphanous costumes revealed her trim figure. In the NBC-TV movie KILLER ON BOARD (October 10, 1977) she had a supporting role as a passenger aboard a cruise liner who is struck by a deadly virus. On New Year's Day, 1978, she played the love interest, gowned in gorgeous 1880s costumes, in the fifth rendition of the haunting tale of THE FOUR FEATHERS, shot by NBC-TV in England. The following month, in "the saga of an American Woman," she was in sibling support of star Elizabeth Montgomery in "The Awakening Land" (1978), a seven-hour NBC-TV miniseries spanning twenty-seven years of frontier settlement in Ohio.

Jane supported Cliff Potts and Carrie Snodgress in NBC-TV's LOVE'S DARK RIDE (April 2, 1978), while receiving top billing as Bella Wilfer in the British-made "Our Mutual Friend," premiering on PBS-TV on April 16, 1978. She turned athletic for ABC-TV's sports special "Us Against the World II" (September 9, 1978) as a member of the World Team opposing the U.S. team at Magic Mountain amusement park in Southern California. She was back to drama again in the "Battlestar Galactica" episode "Saga of a Star World," telecast on September 17, 1978. THE DALLAS COWBOYS CHEERLEADERS (January 14, 1979), an ABC-TV movie, was the highest-rated TV film of the 1978–1979 season. It featured Jane as an ambitious magazine reporter assigned to uncover the inside story of the famous Astrodome cheerleading troupe.

With so many television jobs, plus a Universal film, BATTLESTAR GALACTICA (1979), based on the TV series, Jane required a financial manager to keep her personal affairs in order. Friends recommended Los Angeles–based David Flynn, who was at the time also managing Goldie Hawn and Warren Beatty. She remembers, "he's a strong man, the type that immediately makes you feel secure. . . . I liked David from the very first moment." Slowly, since he was going through a divorce, they became friends.

In the silly OH, HEAVENLY DOG (1980), Jane was Chevy Chase's paramour. She moved from the ridiculous to the sublime to play Mozart's wife, Constanze, in *Amadeus*, which premiered at the National Theatre in Washington, D.C., and then opened on Broadway on December 17, 1980, at the Broadhurst Theatre with Tim Curry as the famed composer and Ian McKellen as his archrival, Antonio Salieri. Meanwhile, on theatrical screens, she was in SOMEWHERE IN TIME (1980), a highly romantic fiction boasting John Barry's rich musical score. She played the lady/actress for whom lovestruck Christopher Reeve travels sixty-five years back in time. *Variety* noted, "Seymour is lovely and mesmerizing enough to justify Reeve's grand romantic obsession with her."

TV producer Barney Rosenzweig had never heard of Jane Seymour when it was insisted that she play the key role in ABC-TV's eight-hour miniseries "John Steinbeck's 'East of Eden'" (1981). He was not convinced after screening a few of her films. However, after a lengthy interview, he concluded that "she's an extremely beautiful, bright, and talented actress, capable of playing one of the most evil women in American literature—from puberty to decrepit middle age." Within the too leisurely production, Jane was cast as Cathy Ames Trask, who breaks "every law of man and God." For her outstanding work, she was honored with both an Emmy and a Golden Globe Award. The miniseries was classed by the A. C. Nielsen Company as the sixteenth most popular miniseries to that time.

In February 1981 David Flynn proposed marriage to Jane. Married that September, the bride was five months pregnant, with daughter Katherine born in January 1982.

TV Guide magazine found Jane "delicious" as Lady Blakeney in the CBS-TV movie THE SCARLET PIMPERNEL (November 9, 1982). Thereafter, she went to Hungary to film PHANTOM OF THE OPERA (January 29, 1983), a CBS-TV movie in which she was seen as an ambitious American singer with Maximilian Schell as the deformed, revengeful composer. (ABC-TV had tried unsuccessfully to buy her way out of these two assignments so that she might play the lead opposite Richard Chamberlain in "The Thorn Birds" (1982); that part went instead to Rachel Ward.) On the small screen, she starred in THE HAUNTING PASSION (October 24, 1983) as a radiant woman loved both by her sportscaster husband (Gerald McRaney) and by a handsome ghost (Paul Rossilli). By now, Jane could shine in such confections with a minimum of effort. While she was equally effective as a performer in theatrical releases, she did not seem able to negotiate important vehicles. For example, LASSITER (1984) cast

Jane Seymour in SOMEWHERE IN TIME (1980).

TV's Tom Selleck as a refined jewel thief in 1930s England who recruits the help of his lady love (Jane). In reviewing this formula picture, *Variety* noted, "As the girlfriend, Seymour is wasted. Her role is basically to stand-by as Selleck races about trying to grab the diamonds and run." The picture was not a moneymaker. Far more challenging was her dual role in ABC-TV's DARK MIRROR (March 5, 1984), in which she handled the bad and good sister roles previously performed by Olivia De Havilland in a 1946 feature film. Jane's younger sister, Sally, a London airline employee, doubled for Jane in long shots. During 1984 and 1985, Jane promoted Max Factor perfumes.

"She couldn't have the one man she loved . . . so she had them all," insisted ads in *TV Guide* magazine heralding the telecast of NBC's ERNEST HEMINGWAY'S "THE SUN ALSO RISES" (December 9–10, 1984), starring Jane as Lady Brett Ashley. Critic Judith Crist credited Seymour with underlining "Brett's appeal with a neurotic energy." On January 31, 1985, she starred in the "John Alexander" episode of CBS-TV's "An American Portrait" series. During the next months she starred in the title role of the ABC-TV movie OBSESSED WITH A MARRIED WOMAN (February 11, 1985), with Tim Matheson as the one obsessed. She tested for the lead in OUT OF AFRICA (1985), which went to Meryl Streep, but was consoled in July 1985 by the birth in England of son Sean. The new edition of Daphne Du Maurier's JAMAICA INN was seen on syndicated TV in June 1985, having been filmed three years earlier. In December 1985 she was sexy in the inane motion picture HEAD OFFICE, but was sexy *and* bad as Lee Horsley's spouse in ABC-TV's six-hour miniseries "Crossings" (February 23–25, 1986), wearing $2.5 million jewels loaned by Cartier.

In 1987 Jane and her family lived in Santa Barbara, but spent the summers at the fifteenth-century estate, comprised of a thirty-four-room castle on fifteen acres of land, that they had purchased in Bath, England, for $400,000. Declared a historic site, the estate was rented occasionally as a movie set, but was also where Jane wrote her immensely popular book, *Jane Seymour's Guide to Romantic Living* (1988). Professionally, 1987 was quiet compared to past years, consisting of just one televised appearance, on "D.C. Follies." She came back to the small screen with a splash as the notorious Wallis Simpson, opposite Anthony Andrews as the king who abdicated the English throne for THE WOMAN HE LOVED (April 3, 1988) on CBS-TV. On April 23, 1988, she was seen in another segment of the satirical "D.C. Follies" and narrated the PBS-TV documentary "Japan." She was in fine fiery form as Maria Callas (lip-synching to recordings by the famed diva) in CBS's ONASSIS: THE RICHEST MAN IN THE WORLD (May 1–2, 1988), filmed in Spain and Majorca. She won an Emmy in the Best Supporting Actress category, although her rambling acceptance speech startled fans. On May 19, 1988, she interviewed designer Christian LaCroix in Paris for the ABC-TV special "M & W—Men & Women" and revealed to the press that she had been covetous of playing either of the two leading female roles in DANGEROUS LIAISONS (1988), parts which went to Glenn Close and Michelle Pfeiffer. Instead, she participated in one of filmdom's more boring theatrical features, the Spanish-made EL TÚNEL (1988), in which she was photographed beautifully but was totally uninteresting.

She was a newspaper sketch artist in CBS-TV's JACK THE RIPPER (October 21 and 23, 1988), made in England with Michael Caine as the Scotland Yard investigator uncloaking the 1880s murderer (Armand Assante). Replacing the abrasive Ali MacGraw, who had been Natalie Jastrow in the miniseries "The Winds of War" (1983), Jane worked for twenty-one months in various European locations for its sequel, "War and Remembrance," set during World War II. The $110 million marathon-length miniseries began where "The Winds of War" had ended and was telecast in two clusters: eighteen hours in November 1988, followed by fourteen hours in May 1989. Jane was seen as Natalie Jastrow, a young American woman who travels to Italy to assist her uncle (Sir John Gielgud) in his scholarly research. Once there, she is swept into the complicated horrors of the Nazi infiltration of Europe, eventually becoming interned, because of her Jewish ancestry, at Auschwitz in Poland. Meanwhile, her handsome husband, Byron (Hart Bochner), fights the Battle of Midway in the Pacific war zone. Harry F. Waters (*Time* magazine) noted, "The thanks of an entire nation go to ABC for replacing princess-pouty Ali MacGraw with Jane Seymour, whose face is a radiant sunburst by comparison." Although the mammoth project was considered an overall disappointment and did not do well in the ratings, *TV Guide* magazine named both it and its predecessor as the #14 show of the 1980s, noting that they "should be remembered for their haunting chronicle of the Holocaust." It was speculated that Jane would win the Emmy, but she lost to Holly Hunter of ROE VS. WADE. Seymour did receive, on January 21, 1990, the Israel Cultural Award for her performance in "War and Remembrance."

Jane was hostess for ABC-TV's "All-Star Salute to the President" (George Bush) (January 19, 1989). *US* magazine's second annual readers' poll in May 1989 revealed that Jane was the public's choice to play Scarlett O'Hara in any remake or sequel to GONE WITH THE WIND, with Tom Selleck getting the most votes as the new Rhett Butler. At home in Santa Barbara that October, Jane was a gambling casino dealer in a charity evening benefitting the Society for the Prevention of Cruelty to Animals, and the next month was one of the hosts for CBS's "50 Years on Television." Costing $50 million, the forthcoming international co-production THE FRENCH REVOLUTION was shot twice—in English and French—to be released as two full-length companion features. Jane, as Marie Antoinette, enlisted her real-life children to play the royal offspring of the queen and king (Peter Ustinov) of France during the late eighteenth century. The 1989 Cannes Film Festival featured WESSEX (forthcoming) starring Jane with Aidan Quinn, Hugh Grant, Mare Winningham, Bryan Brown, and Uma Thurman. Jane went to Hong Kong to shoot KEYS TO FREEDOM (forthcoming) as a British surgeon, opposite Omar Sharif.

She returned to television in the CBS-TV movie ANGEL OF DEATH, shown on October 2, 1990. She starred as an art teacher who, with her overly protected young son (Brian Bonsall), is befriended by a psychotic escaped murderer (Gregory Harrison). *People* rated the thriller a "B+" with the magazine noting, "Even through the TV movie's draggy denouement, Seymour makes a terrific lady in peril." *Daily Variety* observed, "Seymour plays the frightened mother with surprising effectiveness." For use as props in ANGEL OF DEATH, Seymour contributed her own paintings, which she later donated to Southern

California Lithographics to be printed as greeting cards on recycled material to benefit Childhelp USA and City Hearts, a fundraiser organized in part by Max Factor Cosmetics (for whom she was a spokeswoman). Earlier, Jane had been named by President George Bush as the International Ambassador for Childhelp. In the made-for-television movie MATTERS OF THE HEART, shown on USA–Cable on December 26, 1990, Seymour played a heavy-drinking concert pianist whose pursuit of an eighteen-year-old music student (Christopher Garlin) is tearfully interrupted when she becomes terminally ill with cancer.

For her newly formed production company, Moonstar & Sons, Jane co-produced with Guber-Peters for CBS-TV a television movie version of GASLIGHT, based on the play *Angel Street*, for 1991 viewing. The *Hollywood Reporter* called this "one of her toughest acting challenges yet" in following Ingrid Bergman's superlative Oscar-winning performance in the MGM film of 1944. Meanwhile, by early 1991, Jane and her third husband, David Flynn, had embarked on a trial separation.

Jane Seymour goes one step beyond the status of queen of American television miniseries; she can easily be called goddess. Although she states publicly that her family comes above all else, she continually works and, with her husband, has bought homes in the Los Angeles area to renovate and resell. In Britain she is not beloved by television fans, who refuse steadfastly to condone her leaving England in pursuit of American riches. She has explained her heavy acting schedule, which during 1989 totaled forty-three hours of original prime-time TV, by saying, "My feeling is that you should always be onto the next one by the time the first one's out. You can't count on one thing and sit back smugly and say, 'This is it. This is the one that will make people think I'm a better actress.'" She also admits, "I'm just as driven trying to cook and to decorate my houses. . . . If I had more hours in a day, I'd probably be taking up piano again." She just does not waste time.

Filmography

Oh! What a Lovely War (Par, 1969)

Oktober-Dage [The Only Way] (Panamanian-Danish-U.S., 1970)

Young Winston (Col, 1972)

Frankenstein: The True Story (NBC-TV, 11/30/73–12/1/73)

Live and Let Die (UA, 1973)

The Story of David (ABC-TV, 4/9/76; 4/11/76) [made in 1973]

Benny & Barney: Las Vegas Undercover (NBC-TV, 1/9/77)

Killer on Board (NBC-TV, 10/10/77)

Sinbad and the Eye of the Tiger (Col, 1977)

The Four Feathers (NBC-TV, 1/1/78)

Love's Dark Ride (NBC-TV, 4/2/78)

The Dallas Cowboys Cheerleaders (ABC-TV, 1/14/79)

Battlestar Galactica (Univ, 1979)

Oh, Heavenly Dog (20th–Fox, 1980)

Somewhere in Time (Univ, 1980)

The Scarlet Pimpernel (CBS-TV, 11/9/82)

Phantom of the Opera (CBS-TV, 1/29/83)

The Haunting Passion (NBC-TV, 10/24/83)

Dark Mirror (ABC-TV, 3/5/84)

Ernest Hemingway's "The Sun Also Rises" (NBC-TV, 12/9/84–12/10/84)

Lassiter (WB, 1984)

Obsessed with a Married Woman (ABC-TV, 2/11/85)

Jamaica Inn (Synd, 6/3/85; 6/10/85) [filmed in 1982]

Head Office (Tri-Star, 1985)

The Woman He Loved (CBS-TV, 4/3/88)

Onassis: The Richest Man in the World (ABC-TV, 5/1/88–5/2/88)

Jack the Ripper (CBS-TV, 10/21/88; 10/23/88)

El Túnel [The Tunnel] (Sp, 1988)
Angel of Death (CBS-TV, 10/2/90)

Matters of the Heart (USA–Cable, 12/26/90)
Gaslight (CBS-TV,1991) (also co-producer)

Future Releases

Wessex (unscheduled) (made in 1988)
Keys to Freedom (unscheduled) (made in 1988–1989)

The French Revolution (unscheduled) (made in 1989)

Television Series

Captains and the Kings (NBC, 9/30/76; 10/7/76; 10/14/76; 10/28/76; 11/4/76; 11/18/76) [miniseries]
Seventh Avenue (NBC, 2/10/77; 2/17/77; 2/24/77) [miniseries]
The Awakening Land (NBC, 2/19/78–2/21/78) [miniseries]
Masterpiece Theatre: Our Mutual Friend (PBS, weekly, 4/9/78–5/27/78) [miniseries]

John Steinbeck's "East of Eden" (ABC, 2/8/81; 2/9/81; 2/11/81) [miniseries]
Crossings (ABC, 2/23/86–2/25/86) [miniseries]
War and Remembrance (ABC, 11/13/88–11/23/88) [miniseries]
War and Remembrance: The Final Chapter (ABC, 5/7/89; 5/8/89; 5/9/89; 5/10/89; 5/14/89) [miniseries]

Broadway Plays

Amadeus (1980)

CYBILL SHEPHERD

"I've always figured that if I'm out, I'm fair game. I think these people who bash photographers around and are so worried about having their picture taken should go to work for American Airlines or become plumbers."   —*Interview* magazine, November 1986

BLONDE, BLUE-EYED, COOL CYBILL SHEPHERD CONTINUES TO GRACE the covers of American magazines long after motherhood and even after reaching the "dreaded" age of forty. She is rare among the baby boom generation in that her life is openly catalogued on the inside pages of those same magazines. Desirous and unafraid of interviews, she is cooperative and candid.

In the early 1970s Cybill was whisked out of a modeling career into films by a Hollywood Svengali. Her career spiraled from being "this year's blonde" to movie star to ostracized, arrogant homewrecker to lounge singer. TV critic Gene Shalit informed his 1975 viewers, "Cybill Shepherd cannot sing, dance or act." So she went forth to learn, returning to the limelight a few years later as a far more self-assured and accomplished actress. The new Cybill was soon recognized as one of Hollywood's prized comediennes, likened to madcap Carole Lombard or the intelligently comedic Myrna Loy and Jean Arthur.

Born on Saturday, February 19, 1950 (some sources say 1949), the second of three children, her unusual name was derived from "Cy," her grandfather, and "Bill," her father. William "Bill" Jennings Shepherd, a former football player, managed the family-owned home appliance business in Memphis, Tennessee; his wife, Patty Shobe Shepherd, an attractive blonde, managed their home. Cybill Lynne was a tomboy whose first love was sports. She began singing at the age of eight in the Episcopal church choir. Her lack of self-confidence was shielded by fantasizing about swimming the English Channel or becoming a singing/dancing movie star. Although she has remembered that "being a teen-ager was the pits," her teenage years were the time when things began happening for her. Large-framed, with broad shoulders, she was active in swimming and softball at East High School in Memphis, was a champion distance jumper, and played center on the Memphis City Championship Girls Basketball team. Despite her athletic skills, she failed gym class for talking back to the teacher. In 1966 a cousin entered her name and photograph in the Miss Teenage Memphis contest. Urged on by her mother, she competed although she thought she was not sufficiently pretty. Nevertheless, she won. But in the Miss Teenage America competition that followed, in which she sang, she failed to win any major recognition, but did win the congeniality award. Years later, Shepherd admitted that during this time, she met and dated Elvis Presley. She even followed him to Las Vegas, but left soon after discovering his strong drug dependency.

Interested in art, her short-term goal was to attend Louisiana State University at New Orleans. Instead, after she visited the art museums of Europe in the summer of 1967, her focus shifted to possible college studies in Florence, Italy. But her plans changed soon after graduating from high school in 1968, where she was voted the most attractive in her class. She entered the Model of the Year contest, nationally televised on CBS. As the winner, she was awarded $25,000, which made her totally independent of her now-divorced parents. In New York City, through the Stewart Model Agency, she became an overnight cover girl sensation, appearing seventeen times on the cover of *Glamour* magazine alone. Ruth Whitney, *Glamour*'s editor, explained, "Cybill has a strong, open face. There's nothing cute or Kewpie doll about her." As one of America's most successful models, Shepherd was earning upwards of $500 per day and also appearing in national TV commercials for Breck shampoo, Ultra-Brite toothpaste, Coca-Cola, and Cover Girl makeup.

Despite the attention and the salary, Cybill claims to have "loathed" modeling and saved toward the day that she could begin studying in Italy. Meanwhile, she took night courses in art at Manhattan's Hunter College, spent a few vacation weeks at the suburban College of New Rochelle, and later enrolled in art, math, and French classes at New York University. Meanwhile, Hollywood moviemaker Peter Bogdanovich sought Cybill for a possible role in his new film, while French director Roger Vadim wanted her for a part in his English-language PRETTY MAIDS ALL IN A ROW (1971), to be shot in Hollywood. She found the Bogdanovich project more promising, with its offer to co-star as Jacy Farrow, the spoiled, fickle, oil-rich teenage bitch in THE LAST PICTURE SHOW (1971). Beautifully photographed in black and white by Robert Surtees in the Archer City/Wichita Falls area of the Lone Star state, the movie, based on Larry McMurtry's novel, emerged as a superior study of small town Texas life. The *Washington Post* credited Cybill with giving "the most convincing movie incarnation of a bitch in quite some time," while *Newsweek* magazine endorsed her performance, which "embodies every crummy value in town." The town is the fictional Anarene of 1951 where the adults (including Cloris Leachman, Eileen Brennan, and Ben Johnson) have no hope, but the teenagers (including Cybill, Timothy Bottoms, and Jeff Bridges) have some vitality. At first, Cybill rebelled against performing a nude scene atop a diving board, but acquiesced when Bogdanovich assured her that it would be done tastefully. "I was waiting for God to strike me dead," she has said of the moment her clothes came off on camera. Despite her lack of training, Cybill was suddenly Hollywood's golden-haired "Star of Tomorrow," her prominence enhanced when *Playboy* magazine published nude shots taken of her on the set. (A lawsuit, filed on her behalf in 1971, would take seven years to resolve.)

Concluding her first bout of moviemaking, Cybill returned to New York, but in January 1971 moved to Los Angeles to be with Bogdanovich. His wife of ten years, Polly Platt, a highly regarded set designer/writer, had, with their two daughters, moved out of their Bel-Air mansion. Although Bogdanovich insisted that he and Cybill were "friends," he was openly her lover, mentor, and, some said, her "puppet master." Hoping to be accepted as one of the industry's "golden couples," they were instead met with hostility from the movie community. A frequent house guest in Bel-Air was Orson Welles, who helped Cybill gain confidence.

Her second feature, with which Bogdanovich was not involved, was THE HEART-BREAK KID (1972), a superior Neil Simon comedy directed by Elaine May. As Kelly, a blonde goddess from Minnesota, she encounters a newly married young Jewish man (Charles Grodin) in Florida and, by flirting with him, causes the love-struck man to abandon his nerdish wife (Jeannie Berlin). *Variety* extolled Cybill as "luscious" in her man-baiting role. Off screen, Cybill studied with an opera coach and eventually took an apartment of her own. In 1973 she was taken to Italy and Switzerland to star as DAISY MILLER (1974), produced and directed by Bogdanovich. Set in 1870s Europe, it was adapted from the Henry James novella, which both Bogdanovich and Welles insisted might have been written just for her. Audiences and critics disagreed, however, and the period romantic drama was a major dud. Critic Pauline Kael disqualified Cybill as an actress, noting, "She's hard and snippy and artificially mechanical." In 1974 Bogdanovich produced her first record album, *Cybill Does It . . . to Cole Porter*, released by Paramount. The recording received unfavorable reviews, such as *Newsday*'s, which called Shepherd/

Eddie Albert, Audra Lindley, and **Cybill Shepherd** in THE HEARTBREAK KID (1972).

Bogdanovich "the Bonnie and Clyde of movies and records, getting away with murder in public. Cybill not only can't act or sing, she can't even talk."

Bogdanovich initially convinced Warner Bros. to produce a 1930s-style musical, which he would write, produce, and direct, using sixteen Cole Porter songs. Called QUADRILLE, it was to star Elliott Gould, Cybill, and Madeline Kahn. When Warners backed out of the deal, he took the package to Twentieth Century–Fox. However, since Gould was no longer available, he was replaced by Burt Reynolds. For the film, renamed AT LONG LAST LOVE, lyrics from the Porter songs served as much of the dialogue, while none of the "singers" was allowed to prerecord the numbers. The film was set in New York City, but filmed in Hollywood. The impressive sets and costumes, stylishly black-and-white, were two of several ingredients to like about the $6.5 million movie. Embarrassing in the extreme, the film received scathing reviews and the studio yanked it from circulation. AT LONG LAST LOVE grossed a mere $1.1 million domestically. Undaunted, Bogdanovich wanted Cybill to co-star in NICKELODEON (1976), but Columbia Pictures said absolutely not!

Cybill was now considered box-office poison, and the major studios agreed that she could do only supporting roles. She proved "adroitly cast" (*Variety*) as the presidential campaign worker in Martin Scorsese's TAXI DRIVER (1976), although most of the attention went to star Robert De Niro and young Jodie Foster. In SPECIAL DELIVERY (1976), a low-budget grade "B" heist story, she was the wacky love interest of a Vietnam veteran (Bo Svenson) and demonstrated a definite flair for comedy. This ability was reconfirmed in the comedy SILVER BEARS (1978), filmed in Switzerland and Morocco, in which she played the nutty wife of a junior bank executive (Tom Smothers). Had the latter film been a success, her career might have gone in a different direction. After making her television debut in the two-hour ABC-TV movie A GUIDE FOR THE MARRIED WOMAN (October 13, 1978) as a bored housewife, she left Bogdanovich *and* Hollywood, despite Cary Grant's advice, "Don't let 'em get you down. They don't give awards to people who look like you and me." It was at this juncture that she was awarded "a lot of money" from her suit against *Playboy* plus 50 percent of the film rights to Paul Theroux's novel *Saint Jack*, a property she had planned to film, which she gave to Bogdanovich, who had fallen on hard times.

Buoyed by the success in Japan of a record album (*Mad About the Boy*) she had done with Stan Getz in 1977, she went to New York City to sing at The Cookery for an indefinite engagement, but quit after "two devastating weeks." Going home to Memphis, she met David Ford, an auto parts manager for a Mercedes-Benz dealership, three years her junior. They were married in the autumn of 1978 in a thirteenth-century church in Gloucestershire, England, where she was filming a remake of Alfred Hitchcock's THE LADY VANISHES (1980). The undistinguished new edition was disliked for the intrusive screwball comedy interpretations of stars Shepherd and Elliott Gould. Also during this period she made THE RETURN (1980), a.k.a. THE ALIENS RETURN and EARTHRIGHT, with Jan-Michael Vincent.

In 1979 she gave birth to a daughter whom she named Clementine, for a character in her favorite John Ford movie, MY DARLING CLEMENTINE (1946). Thereafter, Cybill formed a jazz band, The Memphis All-Stars, with Phineas Newborn, Jr., at the piano. Husband Ford quit his job to play guitar, manage her singing career, and book the band on a tour. On her third record album, *Vanilla*, she sang live with the band, leading *GQ* magazine to gush, "She shines through the rhythm like a new sunflower . . . when she sinks her feet into that delta mud, the music really cooks." (The album was reissued in 1990, prompting *Los Angeles Times* music critic Leonard Feather to wonder, "Why doesn't she return now to the studios, to make the superior jazz session of which she is capable?")

Not satisfied with singing in hotel lounges, she contemplated taking acting lessons in order to restart her career in that direction. However, both Orson Welles and her friend Gena Rowlands advised her to "just do it." Beginning in Norfolk, Virginia, her first dinner-theater stage role was in the comedy *A Shot in the Dark*. This was followed by Midwest, South, and Southwest regional theater in such plays as *Picnic, Vanities*, and *Lunch Power* from which she "learned more about acting than in all the films I did in Hollywood."

In 1982 she returned to Los Angeles, accompanied by David and Clementine. But this time their marriage was nearly over. "We outgrew each other," she has said of the divorce, in which she paid him $15,000. After her former agent, Sue Mengers, told her, "Cybill, you've been in Memphis for four years, you might as well be dead," she got another agent. A guest spot on ABC-TV's "Fantasy Island" (February 26, 1983) led to a co-starring role (as a wealthy livestock owner) in a modern-day western-style soap opera, "The Yellow Rose," which premiered on NBC-TV on October 2, 1983. *Time* magazine, impressed with her acting, stated, "The irony with Cybill is that she could finally get what she almost got ten years ago—stardom." Generally liked by critics, but suffering in the rating wars, the show ended with the May 12, 1984 telecast. (In the summer of 1990, NBC would replay the series in prime time.)

Shepherd had appeared in the pilot episode of a short-lived foreign intrigue series, "Masquerade," shown on December 15, 1983. She received more exposure as a beautiful hooker in the NBC-TV movie SECRETS OF A MARRIED MAN (September 24, 1984), filmed in Vancouver, British Columbia. In 1984, with her career on an upward swing, she was signed to star in the new ABC-TV yuppie screwball comedy series "Moonlighting." Soon after its initial showing on March 3, 1985, Cybill and her co-star, Bruce Willis, were known in households throughout America. As Maddie Hayes, an ex-model turned private investigator and owner of the Blue Moon Detective Agency, Cybill, according to *Newsweek* magazine, was "Gorgeous, petulant, spunky, haughtily sarcastic and very much her own boss" and "the most formidable female ever to ignite the tube." Although slow in attaining popularity, by the summer of 1985 the program was in the top ten in the Nielsen ratings.

Cybill won a Golden Globe in 1985, at which time she devoted her speech to thanking Bogdanovich. (On another occasion, Shepherd would admit, "Only a handful of people in my life have seen me beneath the exterior and realized that my brain isn't blond. One of those people was Peter [Bogdanovich].") Cybill appeared on the cover of *Glamour* magazine for the eighteenth time, as well as on the cover of *Harper's Bazaar*. The

Hollywood Press Association named her the "Star of the '80s" and she guested on TV's "Late Night with David Letterman" wearing a huge bath towel. When she was on "The Tonight Show Starring Johnny Carson," her arrival caused him to spill coffee on his desk. "You should have spilled it in your lap," she flirted. "Then I could have cleaned it up." At the 1986 Emmy Awards she sported a black strapless evening gown with orange Reebok sneakers because, she said, they were more comfortable than heels. This free-spirited act earned her a place on Earl Blackwell's infamous "Worst Dressed" list of that year. She actively participated in a pro-choice group, Voters for Choice, becoming its national spokesperson in 1990. She appeared on the cover of *People* magazine, which called her "TV's Sexiest Spitfire." With a weekly salary of $45,000, her major comeback in the entertainment industry was well established.

The week following the premiere of "Moonlighting," she co-starred with Gregory Harrison in a dumb CBS-TV murder mystery movie, SEDUCED (March 12, 1985). It lacked the on-screen chemistry that was so evident between Shepherd and Willis. It was during shooting of SEDUCED that Beverly Hills chiropractor Bruce Oppenheim was called to the set to administer to Harrison's back problems. At the same time he relieved Cybill of headache pains and a romance began between them. Meanwhile, she also juggled a long-term on-again/off-again affair with writer Larry McMurtry, with whom she was developing a screenplay, SEPTEMBER, SEPTEMBER. She appeared in the ABC-TV "All-Star Spectacular" (September 15, 1985) before co-starring with Don Johnson and a top supporting cast in THE LONG HOT SUMMER (October 6–7, 1985), televised in four hours and two parts. Fireworks were expected on screen between two of television's hottest performers. However, the film proved to be a disappointment in that regard since the two shared no one-on-one scenes. About her, Johnson said, "She is an actress with depth that's never been tapped. If anybody ever does tap that source, the sky's the limit." *TV Guide* magazine named the movie one of the year's ten best. *Variety* noted that Cybill (in the role played by Lee Remick in the 1958 feature film version) "has never been better, bringing depth and subtlety to her part as the unruly daughter-in-law who tries to buy love with sex."

She rejected the starring role in Ryan O'Neal's TOUGH GUYS DON'T DANCE (1987), but accepted an offer from the American Beef Council to do TV commercials. Amid reported bickering on the "Moonlight" set, when she stated that the series "won't last, but I will," she found herself pregnant by Oppenheim. They married on March 1, 1987, at her San Fernando Valley home in a shoeless, no-ring ceremony. "Moonlighting" earned its highest ratings ever with the episode of March 31, 1987, showing Cybill and Willis in bed together. She appeared with her mother in the ABC-TV special "Superstars and Their Moms" (May 3, 1987). Ordered by her doctor to take a six-month leave of absence from the series due to a difficult pregnancy, she gained forty-five pounds. On October 6, 1987, she gave birth to twins (Molly Ariel and Cyrus Zachariah) at the new California Medical Center in Los Angeles.

By April 1988, Cybill was featured in extensive print advertisements and TV commercials for L'Oréal Hair Color. Continuing to be plagued by on-the-set problems, some of which were reportedly created by Cybill, "Moonlighting" lumbered along through the loss of its executive producer, Glenn Gordon Caron, who had quit in October 1988 after an unsuccessful ploy to introduce Farrah Fawcett into the program's storyline as a possible successor to Cybill. Meanwhile, Cybill was given a star on Hollywood's Walk of Fame and was prevented from buying a swank Memphis co-op overlooking the Mississippi River, because the building association was uncertain who might be living there during her absences. She and Oppenheim separated on January 31, 1989, and she filed for divorce on February 15 on grounds of "irreconcilable differences." She gave him a cash settlement because "I had money and he didn't." Immediately thereafter, she was involved reportedly with Michael Wolff, the bandleader on "The Arsenio Hall Show," whom she had known in high school. Later, she was linked romantically with Boston-based lawyer/political consultant Frank Smith.

In CHANCES ARE (1989), she was seen in her first theatrically released picture in nine years. The romantic comedy deals with the reincarnated spirit (Robert Downey, Jr.) of Cybill's deceased husband, who returns to earth to complicate her life and that of her daughter (Mary Stuart Masterson). It was only fitfully entertaining and not very popular. Earning a salary of $1.5 million for her work in this misfire, she was amazed to learn that her TV co-star/rival Bruce Willis had received $5 million for DIE HARD (1988), which had turned into a box-office megahit.

With the episode of May 14, 1989, "Moonlighting" ended, having greatly disappointed viewers in latter days with seemingly endless reruns and padded episodes focusing on supporting players. At the end of 1989, *TV Guide* magazine selected the series as the #8 show of the decade, calling it a "delight" with its "memorable flights of fancy," citing as highlights the take-off of *The Taming of the Shrew* and the black-and-white homage to the 1940s Big Band era in which Cybill sang. In retrospect, Shepherd admits that she was relieved when "Moonlighting" was cancelled. "It was like being trapped in a gilded cage together [with Bruce Willis]. I'm not saying the show wasn't a great opportunity for me. It was the part and break of a lifetime."

Frederick's of Hollywood in November 1989 opened its permanent lingerie museum with undergarments on display that had been worn by Cybill in various installments of "Moonlighting." She co-hosted the televised Golden Globe ceremonies with Sam Elliott on January 30, 1990, before celebrating her fortieth birthday in London. *US* magazine in April 1990 named her one of the "World's Ten Most Beautiful Women," prompting her to state, "Beauty is the spirit of the person. We're all beautiful in our own ways." On "Face to Face with Connie Chung" (CBS-TV), she discussed her role in TEXASVILLE on September 10, 1990. During the period leading up to David Souter's confirmation as a justice on the U.S. Supreme Court, Cybill said publicly, "I'm absolutely terrified" because of Souter's undeclared position on abortion. "It's a frightening time for women in our country," she said. "This appointment is a real problem."

She had joined members of the original cast of THE LAST PICTURE SHOW in Texas for its sequel, TEXASVILLE (1990), set in 1984. Peter Bogdanovich was reunited in directing Cybill, Jeff Bridges, Cloris Leachman, Timothy Bottoms, and Eileen Brennan in relating what had happened to their characters over the three decades after the earlier film ended. Shepherd played the former high school beauty queen who has had a spotty movie career in Italy and who has now returned to Anarene to recover from the tragic death of her son. Of the ensemble cast, Annie Potts, as Bridges' spirited wife, received the best notices. Regarding the sequel, David Ansen (*Newsweek* magazine) said, "Like any reunion, TEXAS-VILLE is filled with awkward moments. But it's a friendly gathering—funny, a little sad and worth the visit." Of Shepherd's delayed entrance into the TEXASVILLE storyline, *Variety* observed, "Shepherd adopts a no-makeup look and is unflatteringly photographed. . . . This does not produce the desired effect of aging her (the LAST teen characters are all pushing 50 here), but merely makes her look weatherbeaten, especially opposite the vivacious Potts." During its first week in limited release at the domestic box office, TEXASVILLE drew in a flat $1,575,078 in ticket sales.

In Woody Allen's New York City–filmed ALICE (1990) she was among the actors, including Alec Baldwin and William Hurt, who had cameo roles. In WHICH WAY HOME, a TNT–Cable movie shown January 28, 1991, Cybill starred as a nurse attempting to smuggle eight orphans out of Southeast Asia. She credited the eight children from China and the Philippines, ranging in age from four to fourteen, "for inspiring me to carry on" through hot days and long hours of night shooting in Thailand. "They remained stoic and patient," she said. "I told myself, 'If they can do it, so can I.' They provided a lesson in humility for me." MARRIED TO IT (forthcoming, 1992), shot in New York and Toronto, deals with three married couples and features Cybill, Ron Silver, Beau Bridges, and Stockard Channing.

After eight years of trying to get her screenplay SEPTEMBER, SEPTEMBER, based on the novel of the same title by Shelby Foote, into production, she was finally able to co-produce it with Larry McMurtry for TNT–Cable, with a title change to MEMPHIS (forthcoming, 1991). Shepherd plays one of a group of three white racists who capture a wealthy black boy. It is up to her to take care of him while he is in captivity. She described her character as "white trash." Next, Cybill joined Sean Young, Jim Belushi, Richard Lewis, Giancarlo Giannini, Ornella Muti, and John Candy in the caper comedy RETURN-ING NAPOLEON, shot in Rome and Monte Carlo in early 1991. The murder mystery is a remake of a 1960 Italian movie, CRIMEN.

Because of "The Yellow Rose," which revitalized her acting career, and the hit television series "Moonlighting," Cybill Shepherd is now accepted as a full-fledged actress unafraid of not looking pretty. "I'm sick of being perky," she told *Fame* magazine for its August 1990 edition. "If you don't think I can look cheap, you're wrong" as she bared her stomach over her miniskirt for the interviewer and shrieked, "Gonna show my stretch marks. My proud banners of childbirth, proud banners of love!" Commenting on her reputation for outspokenness and standing up for herself, she said, "It's absolutely still true what Bette Davis said: 'If a woman stands up for herself, she's a bitch. If a man stands up for himself, he's admired for it.' That's been *my* experience." Regarding her career to date, she has said, "I never asked myself how I was going to do it; I just went ahead and did it. Surviving is the best revenge." Of her professional future, she says, "I'm on the roller coaster; I've been up and down enough, and I'm not going to give up. . . . I'm stubborn."

She insists she does not want to undertake another TV series—at least not now. "I'm not ready to settle down with another job that could last for five years." Despite her recent nonstop filmmaking activity, she claims her life is at a slower pace. "I'm looking forward to enjoying a quiet life with my three children for a while." Looking forward to maturity, she is uncertain whether or not she will ever undergo cosmetic surgery to erase some of nature's cruelest processes. "You can always improve the product," she concludes, but "finally, though, is it going to matter when you die?"

Filmography

The Last Picture Show (Col, 1971)
The Heartbreak Kid (20th–Fox, 1972)
Daisy Miller (Par, 1974)
At Long Last Love (20th–Fox, 1975)
Taxi Driver (Col, 1976)
Special Delivery (AIP, 1976)
A Guide for the Married Woman (ABC-TV, 10/13/78)
Silver Bears (Col, 1978)
The Lady Vanishes (Group One, 1980)
The Return [The Aliens Return/Earthright] (O.F.M. Pictures, 1980)
Secrets of a Married Man (NBC-TV, 9/24/84)
Moonlighting (ABC-TV, 3/3/85)

Seduced (CBS-TV, 3/12/85)
The Long Hot Summer (NBC-TV, 10/6/85–10/7/85)
Chances Are (Tri-Star, 1989)
Texasville (Col, 1990)
Alice (Orion, 1990)
Which Way Home (TNT–Cable, 1/28/91)

Future Releases

Memphis (TNT–Cable, 1991) (also co-producer)
Returning Napoleon (Univ, 1991)
Married to It (Orion, 1992)

Television Series

The Yellow Rose (NBC, 1983–84)

Moonlighting (ABC, 1985–89)

Album Discography

At Long Last Love (RCA ABL2-0967) [ST]
Cybill Does It . . . to Cole Porter (Paramount 1018)
The Heartbreak Kid (Columbia S-32155) [ST]

Mad About the Boy (Inner City 1097)
Moonlighting (MCA 6214) [ST/TV]
Vanilla (Peabody/Gold Coast D215-71331))

JACLYN SMITH

"People ask me if I tire of hearing about my beauty. I *like* to hear it. It's flattering, but it comes as a surprise. I think I have more to offer than a pretty face; I'm not a sex symbol."
—*Ladies Home Journal* magazine, July 1979

FOR TWO DECADES, JACLYN SMITH HAS BEEN CONSIDERED ONE OF the most beautiful women in the world, if not the single most beautiful. She is the personification of elegance and sophistication, much in the pattern set years ago by Grace Kelly. Along with this, Jaclyn represents old-fashioned womanhood in that she has no contemporary vices, placing family, religion, and morality above all else. Her chief goal has been to achieve a contented home life, but that has eluded her thus far.

One of Hollywood's wealthiest women, Jaclyn has ignored the age-old doctrine that money cannot buy happiness. She purchased her way out of a third marriage to avoid a nasty court case and to protect her children. Highly structured, a worrier, and neat to a fault, she has emotional needs similar to Joan Crawford's. Today, Jaclyn, along with Jane Seymour, is queen of the multi-part TV movie. Like that of Linda Evans, Smith's radiance has worn well, gaining character in middle age.

Jaclyn Ellen Smith was born on Sunday, October 26, 1947, in Houston, Texas, to wealthy dentist Jack Smith and his green-eyed, dimpled wife, Margaret Ellen. With her older half brother, Tommy, she spent most of her early youth at the family's large farm in Luling, about one hundred miles west of Houston. Drinking, smoking, and swearing were not permitted in the Smith household, where her maternal grandfather (whom she called "Paw-Paw") also lived. A retired Methodist minister, Gaston Hartsfield, a friend of the family, who would live past his one hundred first birthday in 1976, greatly influenced the youngster and was hugely loved by her. Leading a sheltered life, Jaclyn entertained herself by dressing up in her mother's finery, pretending she was the star of GONE WITH THE WIND, even to the point of asking her family to call her Scarlett. At the age of three, she was placed in ballet class where she would spend the next eight years studying with Florie Olenbush, who said that "Jackie" was her best student. In the seventh grade, Jaclyn was voted Miss Beautiful by her classmates.

After graduation from high school, where she had appeared in several plays, she became a drama student at Trinity University in San Antonio in 1965. However, after two years she quit to join regional theater groups in Boston and, later, in upstate New York, appearing in such musical productions as *West Side Story, Gentlemen Prefer Blondes, Bye*

Bye Birdie, and *Peg*. Returning to Texas, she discovered that the state did not offer what she wanted in the way of a career path. She therefore convinced her father to finance her studies at George Balanchine's School of American Ballet in New York City. With a $1,000 a month allowance, she checked into the Barbizon Hotel for Women in Manhattan. However, at Balanchine's school she found that she was, at age twenty-one, one of the oldest students in the class. Later, she decided, "I wasn't cut out for dancing" and, homesick for her family, was about to leave for Texas. At this juncture, she was discovered by a modeling agent, who quickly negotiated jobs for her doing commercials for Listerine, Camay, and Wella Balsam. She turned down an offer to dance in Las Vegas at Caesar's Palace, instead accepting a lucrative Breck Shampoo contract.

While she was receiving national recognition as the Breck Shampoo Girl, she met television actor Roger Davis, who had appeared in two short-lived series in 1962–1963 and who would replace Peter Deuel in TV's "Alias Smith and Jones" in 1972–1973. She obtained a small screen role as a model in GOODBYE COLUMBUS (1969), billed, for the only time, as Jackie Smith. When she was asked to play a supporting part in THE ADVENTURERS (1970), a steamy adaptation of Harold Robbins' salacious novel, she agreed under the conditions that she not be required to swear or to pose in the nude. "I'm not a goody-two-shoes," she explained, "but on the other hand I don't mind being called a prude either." Continuing to work in commercials, she joined Davis in Los Angeles while he filmed a ninety-minute ABC-TV movie. She too got a job at ABC, in a segment (October 23, 1970) of "The Partridge Family." Because of her pronounced southern accent, screen/TV offerings were not plentiful, although she did appear briefly in an NBC-TV feature, PROBE (February 21, 1972), the pilot for the series "Search."

In 1972 she and Roger Davis were married, with her grandfather officiating at the Texas ceremony. Davis "was the first man I had physical love with," she would reveal later. With dreams of an ideal family life, she mostly abandoned her career to be Davis' wife. Nevertheless, she was seen in a January 1973 episode of TV's "McCloud" and had her biggest part to date in her third theatrical release, BOOTLEGGERS (1974). (*Variety* labeled the low-budget film a "Painful, amateurish look at Depression bootleggers in the Ozarks" and said of Jaclyn's appearance, "Smith makes a curiously glamorized hick-town ingenue.")

Within months, she realized her marriage had been a mistake, but stuck with it. Meanwhile she improved her speech by taking diction lessons. Resuming her acting, she was in "Fools, Females and Fun" (1974), the unsold pilot for an anthology series. In the segment "Is There a Doctor in the House?" she appeared with Barry Nelson and Barbara Rush. She worked in another "McCloud" segment in January 1975 and was on the distaff detective TV series "Get Christie Love" in March 1975. After playing in the CBS-TV feature/pilot SWITCH (March 21, 1975), which starred Robert Wagner and Eddie Albert, she guested on the series on September 16 and 23, and October 21, 1975. She showed up on "The Rookies" in December 1975, and then in the two-part "The Whiz Kid and the Carnival Caper" on the "World of Disney" in January 1976.

She and Roger Davis divorced in 1976, by which time he was more active in real estate than in acting. Soon thereafter, she became involved romantically with musician-turned-actor Dennis Cole. Eight years her senior and the father of a teenaged son, he was a veteran of several TV series and movies.

CHARLIE'S ANGELS was a ninety-minute ABC-TV movie/series pilot telecast on March 21, 1976. Jaclyn was third-billed as Kelly Garrett, a former showgirl who has "been around." With her two partners (Kate Jackson, Farrah Fawcett), Kelly was a shapely police-trained detective working for a wealthy private investigator named Charlie, who was never seen, only heard (the voice of John Forsythe). In the pilot, the three attractive women were dispatched by Charlie to discover where a vineyard manager (Tommy Lee Jones) had hidden the body of his rich employer, whom he had killed years before. Despite its resemblance to rival NBC's "Police Woman," starring Angie Dickinson, the project was picked up as a series, commencing September 22, 1976. Jaclyn signed a five-year contract at a starting salary of $5,000 per episode. Each of the three "angels" was asked to pose for individual posters that would be sold to help promote the program. Fawcett, the first to respond, was photographed with her thick blonde hair in the style that would be emulated by countless viewers and wearing a diaphanous costume that left nothing to the imagination. Jaclyn, choosing to pose wearing a satin robe, was said to be "Very old-fashioned, very sexy and very elegant." Although the series became a major hit in its first season, Fawcett elected to leave and was replaced in 1977 by Cheryl Ladd, with Jaclyn moving up to the second-billed spot.

During this period, Jaclyn realized supplementary income from the sale of posters, plus Kelly dolls and games, in addition to earning $500,000 annually from television commercials. Through contract renegotiations, her per-episode "Angels" salary escalated to $15,000 in 1978, $40,000 in 1979, and $50,000 in 1980. By then, she was the lone survivor of the original trio and she received top billing. With her mind for business, Jaclyn not only invested in California and Texas real estate, but also filled her home—which she referred to as Tara—with valuable antiques. Using her grandfather's initials, she formed GH Productions as a tax-credit investment. In addition, she agreed to make shows and movies for ABC-TV on a nonexclusive basis.

Along with appearing regularly in "Charlie's Angels," she did an NBC-TV special, "The Mad, Mad, Mad World of the Superbowl" (January 8, 1977), and an ABC-TV special, "Battle of the Network Stars" (February 28, 1977), as well as guested on three ABC-TV series in the fall of 1977: "San Pedro Beach Bums," "The Love Boat," and "Hardy Boys/Nancy Drew Mysteries." For the first time, she was given top billing in a dramatic TV movie, ESCAPE FROM BOGEN COUNTY (October 7, 1977), as the suppressed wife of a powerful political figure (Mitchell Ryan). She joined assorted ABC stars, past and present, in the four-hour tribute "ABC's Silver Anniversary Celebration—25 and Still the One" (February 5, 1978). In the network's movie THE USERS (October 1, 1978), based on gossip columnist Joyce Haber's best-selling account of Hollywood's social climbers, she was billed over Tony Curtis as the mastermind behind the resurrection of his faded screen career.

During the almost two years that Jaclyn had known Dennis Cole, she had insisted that they live separately. However, in October 1978 she and Cole were married in New York City. He was a strong believer in positive thinking and arranged an elaborate wedding at Marble Collegiate Church, headed by Norman Vincent Peale. Dennis' son, eighteen-year-old Joseph, lived with the couple in her ten-room Coldwater Canyon–area home in Los Angeles and called her "mom." Domestic problems began almost immediately when she wanted to adopt a child, an idea Cole vetoed.

In rejecting an offer from *Playboy* magazine to pose for its centerfold, Jaclyn said, "I couldn't believe they'd pay me a million [dollars] to take off my clothes." During 1979 she negotiated with Motown Productions to star in an ABC-TV movie based on 1940s movie star Gene Tierney's autobiography, *Self Portrait*. However, the film was never made despite Tierney's approval. Instead, Jaclyn traveled to Phoenix to co-star with Robert Mitchum and James Franciscus in NIGHTKILL, a muddled murder mystery financed by a German production company, which ended up on NBC-TV on December 18, 1980. During the filming in Arizona, she met British cinematographer/director Anthony Richmond, six years her senior. He would become her third husband in 1981, after she divorced Cole.

At the end of the 1980–1981 season she concluded her five-year run as luscious Kelly Garrett on "Charlie's Angels." The defunct series quickly became a rerun staple in syndication. Looking back on her career-molding role, she has said, "I don't regret 'Charlie's Angels.' We did get hyped and thought of as slick, empty-headed girls. Step by step we are all living it down." *TV Guide* magazine called her next project "A portrait of a living legend." It was the story of JACQUELINE BOUVIER KENNEDY (October 14, 1981) as portrayed by Jaclyn for ABC-TV. *TV Guide* advised, "it may not convince all viewers, but it has wit, charm, spunk, drive and an attempt to capture Jackie's charisma." She was featured in NBC's "Magic with the Stars" (January 17, 1982) as well as in the same network's "Television's Greatest Commercials" (May 22, 1982).

In March 1982 Jaclyn Smith Richmond became a mother for the first time, with the birth of a son, Gaston Anthony. A daughter, Spencer-Margaret, would join the family at their spacious Bel-Air home in November 1985.

"The minute I put down the book," Jaclyn told author Sidney Sheldon, "I called my agent and said, 'Get me that part!'" The part was that of lawyer Jennifer Parker who is almost disbarred through a staged frame-up but who survives to juggle two love affairs simultaneously in RAGE OF ANGELS (February 20–21, 1983). *TV Guide* magazine judged this four-hour, two-part NBC-TV movie to be "lush, lavish and irresistible." *Variety* acknowledged that it was a "commercial whizbang," but felt that "Smith, whose beauty is awesome, doesn't negotiate Jennifer's role with much credibility, but then Jennifer's not the deepest heroine to come along the pike of late." Undemanding TV viewers adored it. Jaclyn followed this with another ambitious production, "George Washington" (1984), an eight-hour CBS-TV miniseries. Jaclyn was cast as the unrequited love of America's first President (Barry Bostwick). Smith's husband, Tony Richmond, and Gary Morton (Lucille Ball's spouse), were co-executive producers of SENTIMENTAL JOURNEY (CBS-TV, October 16, 1984), a static remake of Maureen O'Hara's 1946 tearjerker, which had been redone in 1958 (as THE GIFT OF LOVE) with Lauren Bacall. Jaclyn (as a dying theatrical producer) and David Dukes (as a New York actor) were a Broadway couple who adopt a precocious little girl. The holiday season of 1984 prompted ABC-TV's three-hour THE NIGHT THEY SAVED CHRISTMAS, with Jaclyn as a young mother escorting her three children (Scott Grimes, Laura Jacoby, R. J. Williams) to meet the great Claus (Art Carney) and saving the North Pole from destruction. Richmond was again one of the producers as Jaclyn portrayed staunch British nurse FLORENCE NIGHTINGALE (April 7, 1985) in three hours on NBC-TV. He also directed her in a dual role in her fourth theatrical release, DÉJÀ VU (1985), which went into limited release. (*Variety* judged it "a lame thriller" and noted, "Smith gives a monotonous performance in both roles.")

During the 1980s Jaclyn continued to make television commercials, but in 1985 she turned author with *The Jaclyn Smith Beauty Book*, published by Simon & Schuster, and designed a line of clothing sold at K-Mart outlets because "It's a family store." She joined the ABC-TV special observance of "Texas 150: A Celebration" (April 28, 1986). Grabbing at a former success, she reprised her Jennifer Parker role in a $50,000 wardrobe in the $8 million, four-hour NBC-TV production RAGE OF ANGELS: THE STORY CONTINUES (November 2–3, 1986). More flashy than but as vapid as its predecessor, it continued the turgid drama of attorney Smith's romance with politician Ken Howard (reprising his earlier role), who is married to an alcoholic (Susan Sullivan). Meanwhile, Smith copes with the threatening brother (Michael Nouri) of her deceased Mafia attorney/ lover (played by Armand Assante in the original). Best liked in the sequel was Angela Lansbury as the scene-stealing Italian Marchesa. Jaclyn's only professional credit for 1987 was her appearance on ABC-TV's "Happy Birthday, Hollywood" on May 18.

Jaclyn was billed over Robert Wagner, whom she had supported in a TV movie thirteen years earlier, in yet another Sidney Sheldon whirlwind thriller. WINDMILLS OF THE GODS (February 7 and 9, 1988) was a four-hour CBS-TV movie, filmed in Romania, Chile, England, France, Morocco, and Yugoslavia. Of her work as a U.S. ambassador to Romania, *TV Guide* magazine observed, "Smith may not be our greatest actress, but she's certainly attractive." *Variety* reported that Jaclyn "has a way of putting herself across that makes her a good bet in any TV project. . . . Smith sashays prettily through the nonsense." Her costumes for this project were said to have cost $85,000.

The *Hollywood Reporter* of May 5, 1988, announced: "Together, ladies and gentlemen, right here on this miniseries stage for the first time . . . Richard Chamberlain and Jaclyn Smith in ABC's THE BOURNE IDENTITY." As the reigning monarchs of the medium, it was inevitable that the two should be co-starred. Shown in two parts of two hours each on May 8 and 9, 1988, and based on Robert Ludlum's best-selling novel, the story had Jaclyn as Marie St. Jacques, a Canadian economist involved in international intrigue with a deadly American amnesiac (Chamberlain) whom many global forces would prefer dead. *Variety* agreed that the telefilm "supplies lots of mystery (not entirely unravelled), atmosphere and suspense," adding, "Some of the chase scenes are terrific, but a car race through Paris in Part I goes on indefinitely, and gunshots perforate rather than punctuate the teleplay with their abundance." More harsh was John Carman (*San Francisco Chronicle*) who criticized Smith for being "her usual superficial drag." The following month, on June 10, 1988, she joined in the festivities on CBS-TV's "Sea World's All-Star Celebration."

US magazine on October 17, 1988, chose her and Kevin Costner as the third best-looking woman and man in America. In an interview with the same magazine, she remarked, "Things are not as picture perfect as they seem," in a veiled reference to her married life. In April 1989 she was selected by *Ladies Home Journal* magazine to pose, in a tribute to the Academy Awards, wearing costumes portraying four of Oscar's favorites, one of which was Scarlett O'Hara. During the summer of 1989, at Bloomingdale's department store in Manhattan, Max Factor introduced the Jaclyn Smith signature fragrance "California."

In September 1989 Tony Richmond filed for divorce, claiming that he could no longer tolerate her compulsive cleaning of the house, rearranging of his personal possessions, and her strict scheduling of their lives. Months earlier, supermarket tabloids had predicted an end to the marriage due to Richmond's alleged extramarital relationship with makeup artist Julie Parker. Smith settled with Richmond by paying him $4 million in order to shield her children from a potentially messy divorce action.

Her sole screen work in 1989 was the NBC-TV movie SETTLE THE SCORE. During its relatively exciting two hours, she portrayed Kate, a Chicago cop who returns home to Arkansas to seek revenge against an unknown man who had brutally raped her twenty years earlier. *US* magazine decided that "Smith has given some bland performances, but this isn't one of them." On November 6, 1989, Jaclyn's star was added to the Hollywood Walk of Fame. "When I got into show business," she quipped, "my friends said 'They're going to walk all over you.'"

After rejecting several teleseries offers, including one based on RAGE OF ANGELS, in the fall of 1989 she joined ABC's Saturday night rotation of Burt Reynolds ("B. L. Stryker"), Peter Falk ("Columbo"), and Telly Savalas ("Kojak") in its "Mystery Movie" series. She was "Christine Cromwell," a San Francisco attorney specializing in "crime styles of the rich and famous." The series had a colorful setting, plush interiors, and a lush wardrobe. *People* magazine observed that

Richmond Hoxie and **Jaclyn Smith** in "Christine Cromwell" (1990).

she "carries the lead with customary elegant aloofness." Like Reynolds' Florida-based segments, her installments never gained credibility or substantial viewership and the series faded from the TV line-up at the end of its first season. Meanwhile, for Christmas 1989 she presented each of her children with $10,000 mini-Mercedes, to match hers, with walkie-talkie car phones. In January 1990 she added Plus Project Literacy to her roster of TV commercials. In its summer 1990 issue, *People* magazine named her one of "The Fifty Most Beautiful People in the World," to which she responded, "I'm not a sex symbol. How could I be with these skinny bowlegs?" Even before her divorce settlement with Richmond was final in March 1990, she had begun seriously dating film industry figure David Niven, Jr., son of the late star. On October 15, 1990, Jaclyn returned to television in the NBC-TV mystery movie DANIELLE STEEL'S KALEIDOSCOPE, with Perry King as the detective hired to track down three sisters who, as children thirty years before, were separated after the bizarre death of their parents. Smith played one of the trio, a Manhattan TV executive trying to avoid her sordid past. *People* magazine judged the two-hour telefilm a "shallow saga that starts out streamlined but grows increasingly sappy and sluggish." *Entertainment Weekly* magazine noted that Jaclyn was "thin, tanner, and happier-looking than she was in 'Christine Cromwell.'" A less charitable John Carman (*San Francisco Chronicle*) observed, "Look at it this way. You know a movie is bad when it suffers during Jaclyn Smith's absences from the screen. And you know it's not aiming too high when it requires not one, but several establishing shots to tell you it's set in New York City."

In the CBS-TV movie LIES BEFORE KISSES (March 3, 1991), Jaclyn was cast as the determined wife of a wealthy publisher (Ben Gazzara) whose indiscretions lead her husband into a murderous plan. Laurence Vittes (*Hollywood Reporter*) decided, "once it picks up steam and its main character begins to feel her oats, LIES BEFORE KISSES turns into a surprisingly gripping psychological drama. . . . The show's success lies squarely on Smith's magnetic screen presence. Despite surprisingly sloppy production values . . . she lights all the requisite plot-thickening fires with her luscious radiance."

Jaclyn's chief ambition, which she has admitted many times, is to live to be 102 years old and to one day find a husband who will understand her. Of love she says, "When you're confident of being loved totally, then a natural sexiness comes out of that sureness. It's the sensuality of feeling desirable."

Filmography

Goodbye Columbus (Par, 1969) (as Jackie Smith)
The Adventurers (Par, 1970)
Probe (NBC-TV, 2/21/72)
Bootleggers [Bootlegger's Angel] (Howco International, 1974)
Switch (CBS-TV, 3/21/75)
Charlie's Angels (ABC-TV, 3/21/76)
Escape from Bogen County (CBS-TV, 10/7/77)

The Users (ABC-TV, 10/1/78)
Nightkill (NBC-TV, 12/18/80)
Jacqueline Bouvier Kennedy (ABC-TV, 10/14/81)
Rage of Angels (NBC-TV, 2/20/83–2/21/83)
Sentimental Journey (CBS-TV, 10/16/84)
The Night They Saved Christmas (ABC-TV, 12/13/84)
Florence Nightingale (NBC-TV, 4/7/85)

Déjà Vu [Always] (Cannon, 1985)
Rage of Angels: The Story Continues (NBC-TV, 11/2/86–11/3/86)
Windmills of the Gods (CBS-TV, 2/7/88; 2/9/88)

The Bourne Identity (ABC-TV, 5/8/88–5/9/88)
Settle the Score (NBC-TV, 10/30/89)
Danielle Steel's Kaleidoscope (NBC-TV, 10/15/90)
Lies Before Kisses (CBS-TV, 3/3/91)

Television Series

Charlie's Angels (ABC, 1976–81)
George Washington (CBS, 4/8/84; 4/10/84; 4/11/84) [miniseries]

Christine Cromwell (ABC, 1989–90)

JIMMY SMITS

"I always felt that I had to prove something because I'm Hispanic.
When I started studying acting, it wasn't good enough for someone to
say, 'For a Latino, he's okay,' so I studied twice as hard as anybody."
—*Parade* magazine, February 18, 1990

IN HOLLYWOOD'S EARLIER DAYS, IT WAS ALMOST MANDATORY THAT A
Latin actor/lover have an exotic name that emphasized his ethnicity, like Ramon Novarro,
Ricardo Montalban, and Fernando Lamas. The few with Anglo names, such as Anthony
Quinn and Gilbert Roland, were identified by an accent or dark-skinned appearance.
Historically, compared with their north-of-the-border counterparts within the entertain-
ment industry, the Hispanics to achieve star status in Hollywood were few and far
between.

Like Edward James Olmos, Jimmy Smits attained his high-profile status through
television, where he could be seen weekly as an "ethnic and elegant" high-cheekboned,
dark-eyed heartthrob. Said to be moody, Jimmy Smits is a very private person who abhors
talking about himself, which adds mystery to the brooding looks. "He does his work and
disappears," said Steven Bochco, co-creator and executive producer of "L.A. Law." Co-
worker Corbin Bernsen has observed, "He doesn't talk about himself at all. It's just not
something he's comfortable doing." Jimmy himself has said, "It's really difficult for me to
open up. It's probably why my creative outlet has been acting." In selecting him as one of
the ten sexiest men in America in November 1989, *Woman's World* magazine contended
that he "turns up the pilot light on the average female with his lethal combination of Latin
looks and an understanding of the opposite sex."

Jimmy Smits was born on Saturday, July 9, 1955, in a middle-income neighborhood of Brooklyn. He would be followed by two younger sisters. His father was of Dutch
and South American Indian parentage, originally from Suriname (Dutch Guiana) in
South America. His Puerto Rican–born mother Emeline preferred talking in Spanish. The
parents had met and married in New York where the father, a merchant seaman, later
became a plant manager in Brooklyn. During Jimmy's early life, the family moved a great
deal within Brooklyn, then to the Bronx, where he liked to sing with other children on
street corners. He also enjoyed impersonating Ed Sullivan for his father's poker-playing
buddies. When Jimmy was ten, the family moved to Puerto Rico, but were back in New
York within two years. Because of the frequent relocations, Jimmy was alone with his
sisters much of the time and was often left in charge of them. To escape this everyday

humdrum existence, he would pretend he was someone else—somewhere else. At the age of thirteen he was detained by a store owner for shoplifting model airplane parts. For this offense, his father disciplined him with a beating for having shamed the family. "I felt awful," he said later. "I never stole again."

After attending George Gershwin Junior High School, Jimmy became a student at Thomas Jefferson High School in Brooklyn where he played football, but he quit the sport when he joined the drama club. His first stage appearance was in the school's production of *Purlie Victorious*. At the end of one performance, his football squad, wearing their team jackets and occupying the first two rows, gave him a standing ovation, an assurance that he was still their friend. In 1973 he enrolled at Brooklyn College to study education with the intention of becoming a teacher. But he soon switched to a theater major, which did not please his parents, whose own lives were disrupted that year when they divorced. In 1974, when Jimmy was nineteen, his girlfriend Barbara told him that she was pregnant. He moved in with her and their first child, Taina, was born a few months later. After obtaining a bachelor's degree in fine arts from Brooklyn College in 1976, Jimmy began graduate studies on a scholarship at Cornell University in Ithaca, New York. (Many of his theater classmates from Brooklyn College tried to induce him to go to Hollywood with them in search of screen careers.) In 1978, with a Master of Fine Arts degree, he returned to Brooklyn where he married Barbara in 1979 and, for a time, worked as a community organizer.

For the New York Shakespeare Festival, he had small parts at the Public Theatre, off-Broadway, in *Othello*, *Hamlet*, and *The Ballad of Soapy Smith*, among others. At the American Place Theatre he played Buck in *Little Victories*. At the same time, he got small, nonrecurring roles in ABC-TV's soap opera "All My Children" (as a Tibetan monk), in NBC's "Another World" (as a bartender), in CBS's "Guiding Light" (as a Latin American soldier), and in ABC's "One Life to Live" (as a gunrunner). "I wasn't making a lot of money, but I could pay the bills," he remembered later.

In 1983, soon after the birth of his son Joaquin, Jimmy's agent got him an assignment in Miami as Don Johnson's policeman partner who is killed in the early scenes of the teleseries pilot episode of NBC's "Miami Vice" (September 16, 1984). In 1985, after playing at Baltimore's Center Stage in *Native Speech*, *Of Mice and Men*, and *Ariano*, Jimmy read for a role in the pilot for NBC's projected series "L.A. Law." He knew by the time he had left NBC's headquarters at Rockefeller Center that he had done poorly because of nervousness. His agent urged him to fly to Los Angeles for a second try. Arriving there in December 1985, he greatly impressed the producers of "L.A. Law," who were unaware of his initial New York reading. Meanwhile, he won a small role, as "2nd Policeman," in Valerie Bertinelli's CBS-TV movie ROCKABYE (January 2, 1986). He had a far more substantial, albeit one-dimensional, assignment as a would-be drug lord in RUNNING SCARED (1986), a Chicago-set theatrical movie starring Billy Crystal and Gregory Hines as two zany cops/buddies.

The pilot of "L.A. Law" aired on September 15, 1986, with Jimmy as Victor Sifuentes, an angry, defiant attorney with the upscale Century City law firm of McKenzie,

Brackman, Chaney & Kuzak. In the corporate boardroom, Sifuentes, who has no apparent private life, refuses to remove his earring before entering the courtroom. Off the air, in private life, Smits gladly removed the character prop, which he did not like. On October 3, 1986, the series kicked off where the pilot left off, with Sifuentes defending an enraged father who has killed his son's murderer. To his client he exclaims, "You're hiring a Chicano to do your dirty work for you!" As the television season progressed, Sifuentes became more upscale and less defiant, and the 6' 3", caramel-skinned character was even given the opportunity for tepid romance.

After eighteen months in Los Angeles, Smits admitted that he missed his children, who were back East with their mother from whom he had filed for divorce (which became final in 1987). "In L.A.," he complained mildly, "you just can't get away from 'the business.' It's everywhere. It's all anyone talks about. And it's not like I'm living the wild life, out in the clubs every night. We work long days on the show." Under prompting, he admitted that he was dating someone on a regular basis, but would not reveal the woman's name. She was Wanda De Jesus, a New York actress with whom he had lived in Los Angeles since arriving in town. In August 1987, during an argument between the couple, a neighbor called the police to intercede, and one officer claimed that Jimmy had struck him. Smits was charged with battery and resisting arrest, along with disturbing the peace. After the incident made headlines in Los Angeles, Jimmy pleaded "no contest" to all the charges. "I hated to do that," he explained, "but if I had fought the charges, it really would have been a zoo. The whole thing got blown out of proportion, but it taught me how the press and this business work." He and Wanda, confiding to friends that the incident had brought them closer together, never again permitted their private lives to be made public.

On September 20, 1987, in an NBC-TV movie/series pilot, Jimmy, as a guest star, was second-billed to Sam J. Jones who had the title role as THE HIGHWAYMAN, a Texas-type road warrior pursuing a crook (G. Gordon Liddy) with a big rig fitted with futuristic accoutrements. Smits played a volatile one-time war hero who, with motorcycle pack pals, has taken $14 million in cash from a bank's safety deposit boxes. Much more dimensional was Jimmy's role opposite Judith Light (another alumnus of "One Life to Live") in DANGEROUS AFFECTION (November 1, 1987). In this NBC-TV movie he was a sensitive police detective assigned to protect a pregnant woman (Light) from a killer; in the process, he falls in love with her. "The suspense-action romance-thriller that keeps everyone guessing," according to advertisements in *TV Guide* magazine, was similar in plot to SOMEONE TO WATCH OVER ME, the Tom Berenger feature film released just a month earlier. Also in 1987 Jimmy was seen in his second theatrical motion picture release, THE BELIEVERS, set in New York and starring Martin Sheen. Smits had the supporting role of Tom Lopez, a Manhattan detective afflicted with paralyzing pain by followers of the cult religion of Santeria, believers in the sacrifice of children. It is not long before the hysterical police investigator kills himself. The moderately successful scare thriller grossed $7,848,832 in domestic film rentals. For PBS-TV on May 11, 1987, Jimmy narrated its presentation "The Other Side of the Border," concerning the influx of Mexicans into California and Texas.

In 1987 Smits received the first of three Emmy nominations to date for his work on "L.A. Law." At that time he told interviewers, "I'm always getting asked for legal advice. And two or three bar associations have asked me to become a member. Actually I *am* a member of the Alaska Trial Lawyers Association. And I've been asked to speak at legal conventions."

Jimmy returned to Puerto Rico for partial filming of GLITZ (October 21, 1988). He had the starring role of Miami cop Vincent Mora, described in *TV Guide* magazine ads with: "He's a cop in search of a killer. Now the killer is searching for him." Diluted from the original gritty Elmore Leonard novel, this made-for-television movie was set also in Atlantic City. It is there that the cynical, fast-shooting hero becomes involved romantically with an attractive, going-nowhere lounge singer (Markie Post). *Variety* was unimpressed with this highly touted, slam-bang production: "The 'body count' initiated in the opening scenes dissipates as the story proceeds, but so does the suspense. . . . Viewers looking for a touch of Leonard's mastery on the screen will be disappointed. . . ." As for Smits' characterization, the trade paper analyzed, "Smits would seem to be a natural for the quick-triggered, detective-without-a-tie character, but he comes across unconvincingly due to a poor script that gives him lines like 'I slept with her, but I wouldn't marry her.' . . ." The third season of "L.A. Law," beginning November 3, 1988, included a "sizzling" relationship between Victor and a character named Joyce Huser (Alison Gottlieb), which syndicated columnist Marilyn Beck promised "will become even more intriguing in the weeks to come."

Reducing his appearances on "L.A. Law" only to boardroom sequences, Jimmy went to Mexico with Jane Fonda and company to film OLD GRINGO, released October 6, 1989. As soon as she had reached the proper age to portray the heroine of the Carlos Fuentes novel on which the film was based, Fonda fought hard and long to have the story brought to the screen. Termed "an exceptionally handsome period piece about the Mexican revolution" by *Drama-Logue*, the feature underwent many production traumas and postproduction editing delays. As the spinster schoolteacher who goes to Mexico in 1913, Fonda was the recipient of most of the unfavorable reviews, while her co-stars, Gregory Peck (as the septuagenarian writer) and Smits (as General Tomas Aroya, the youngish aide to Pancho Villa, who falls in love with the idealistic American woman), fared better. The *San Francisco Chronicle* called Jimmy simply "believable," but *US* magazine went much further in

Jimmy Smits in OLD GRINGO (1989).

emphasizing that his "electrifying sexuality dominates the screen." After three weeks in release, the $26 million epic had grossed just over $2.5 million in domestic ticket sales. By Thanksgiving weekend, it had vanished from theatrical distribution. Although rumors were rampant in the tabloids that Fonda and Smits had engaged in an off-camera love affair during the protracted making of this fiasco, it was reported in mid-November 1989 that the Oscar-winning actress's new beau was Italian actor Lorenzo Caccialanza.

The fourth season of "L.A. Law" began November 2, 1989, with Victor reluctantly defending a furrier (John Lehne) against angry animal-rights activists. *TV Guide* magazine listed "L.A. Law" as one of those teleseries whose honesty makes "thousands of men and women . . . more comfortable in their bedrooms. . . ." In addition, the *TV Guide* article cited medical experts as saying that "Crying with a character with whom we empathize can heal our wounds and bring relief, and it may even do more. There's evidence that the ability to weep may help prolong our lives."

During the summer 1989 hiatus from "L.A. Law," Smits filmed VITAL SIGNS (1990), in which he played a medical school instructor, Dr. David Redding, the third-year dean. He was the oldest in an ensemble cast of young actors. *Variety* underscored his "buoyant contribution" as "not much of a stretch" from "L.A. Law," but "still a choice performance, as he displays all the right instincts" as the glib but sexy doctor whose appreciation is sought by students Adrian Pasdar, Jack Gwaltney, Jane Adams, Tim Ransom, and Diane Lane.

On May 14, 1990, Jimmy was a guest on CBS-TV's "Face to Face with Connie Chung," discussing, among other subjects, obstacles Hispanic actors face in today's entertainment industry. The advertisement in *TV Guide* magazine for the segment touted, "JIMMY SMITS. . . . Tall. Dark. And Handsome. See the sexy side of the hottest actor on 'L.A. Law.'" Three days later, on May 17, 1990, Smits shone in the season finale of "L.A. Law," in which the mother (Carmen Zapata) of his boyhood friend (A. Martinez) convinces him to make an emotional appeal to the court to stay the execution of her convicted murderer son. On September 7, 1990, at the Wiltern Theatre in Los Angeles, Jimmy joined a host of other celebrities for the AIDS Project Los Angeles' *Commitment to Life IV* fundraiser. Nine evenings later, on September 16, 1990, at the Pasadena Civic Auditorium, and telecast live on the Fox network, Jimmy was awarded the Emmy as Best Supporting Actor, Drama Series, for his work in "L.A. Law." *Playgirl* magazine, meanwhile, had named Jimmy in its September 1990 issue as one of the ten sexiest men in America, describing him as "passionate, work-obsessed and looks great in a suit (or out of one)." The magazine's writers suggested, "Drop those [legal] briefs, and let's get down to cases!"

In 1991 Smits co-starred in SWITCH (1991) in which he plays Perry King's best friend. When King's character dies and comes back as a woman (Ellen Barkin), Smits does not realize it is his buddy and begins to pursue her/him. Directed by Blake Edwards, the film marked a departure for Jimmy from drama into comedy. After undergoing a couple of title changes (LITTLE HAVANA, DISTANT SHORES), FIRES WITHIN is scheduled to reach movie theater screens in 1991. Jimmy stars as a Cuban journalist serving a life sentence under the Castro regime. Escaping prison, he finds that his wife (Greta Scacchi) is in love with an American fisherman (Vincent P. D'Onofrio). Smits returned for the fifth season of "L.A. Law," which began on October 16, 1990. (In the spring of 1991, he announced that he would not return for the show's sixth season.)

With Jimmy Smits, the Latin lover has made a cinematic comeback in Hollywood, although finding a variety of choice acting assignments is still difficult in the WASP-oriented industry. Jane Fonda perhaps best described Smits after a lengthy search for an appropriate actor to co-star as the Mexican revolutionary of OLD GRINGO: "We wanted someone incredibly attractive, very sexy and with emotional intensity. Jimmy looks fantastic—and he has that heat on the screen."

Filmography

Rockabye (CBS-TV, 1/2/86)
Running Scared (MGM, 1986)
The Highwayman (NBC-TV, 9/20/87)
Dangerous Affection (NBC-TV, 11/1/87)
The Believers (Orion, 1987)
Glitz (NBC-TV, 10/21/88)
Old Gringo (Col, 1989)

Vital Signs (20th–Fox, 1990)
Switch (WB, 1991)

Future Releases

Fires Within (MGM/Pathé, 1991)

Television Series

L.A. Law (NBC, 1986–91)

SISSY SPACEK

"You have to know your own talent and keep plugging along. . . .
Of course, a lot has to do with luck and timing and you have to be
able to deal with it emotionally. . . . I'm lucky. I have a real strong
family and lots of security and love."—*Circus* magazine, July 21, 1977

THERE HAS NEVER BEEN ANY HINT OF SCANDAL IN HER PRIVATE LIFE.
Her face, pictured in tabloid-style distress, has not beckoned to supermarket shoppers. She
is not known for sitting for interviews, but it may be surmised that she is exactly as she
appears: a normal, drug-free, alcohol-free individual who comes out of self-imposed
hibernation to perform capably in a movie, then retreats soundlessly to her family when it
is done. *Playgirl* magazine (January 1986) named her as one of the three most gifted
actresses in Hollywood (the others were Glenn Close and Meryl Streep). This well-
deserved status is not likely to be reversed, even with her habit of absenting herself for too-
long intervals by so meticulously choosing her vehicles.

Mary Elizabeth Spacek was born on Sunday, December 25, 1949, to Virginia and
Edwin Spacek in Quitman, Texas, a small town whose residents were mainly of Czech
ancestry. With her father, the Wood County agent for the U.S. Department of Agricul-
ture, and two older brothers (Robbie and Ed), Sissy, as she was called by her family,
quickly became a diminutive creature of the outdoors, which perhaps accounts for her
abundant freckles. Along with hunting squirrels and frogs, she had her own horse, Buck,
which she learned to ride well enough to participate later in local rodeos, even skillfully
maneuvering him in square dances and barrel races. At the age of thirteen, she ordered a
$14.95 guitar from the Sears-Roebuck catalogue. She taught herself to play it by following
instructions in a pamphlet, and then took lessons from the town's Church of Christ
minister. She was soon singing and playing guitar in school programs as well as giving
instruction to others at a charge of fifty cents per lesson.

At Quitman High School, she was a cheerleader and drum majorette, sang in a
choral group, worked on the school paper, was active in 4-H, and was an officer in the
Spanish club. In her senior year she was voted homecoming queen, but was rejected for a
part in the class play. In 1966, during her junior year, her brother Robbie, known for his
athletic prowess, was struck down by leukemia. After her high school graduation in June
1967, Sissy's parents, not wanting her to witness the everyday debilitation of her beloved
brother's health, sent her to New York City to spend the summer with her cousin, Rip
Torn, and his wife, Geraldine Page. Exposed for the first time to the glitzy world of show

business, she decided to become a rock singer. She auditioned for several agents before she won a booking for three performances on NBC-TV's "The Tonight Show Starring Johnny Carson." However, because of stage fright, she made only two appearances. She was offered a long-term agent/management pact, but her father, whose approval was needed because she was still a minor, refused to sign the contract for her. He reasoned that it was for too long a period of time for a person of her age. Soon after she returned to Quitman, Robbie died. Devastated over the loss, Sissy said, "There isn't all the time you thought there was supposed to be."

She enrolled at the University of Texas at Austin in the autumn of 1967. However, she quit after a few semesters to return to New York to pursue a music career. Accompanying herself on a large twelve-string guitar, she sang country rock compositions, many of which were her own, in open-air sessions in Washington Square as well as at the Bitter End bistro in Greenwich Village. At the same time she did background vocals for airline and bubble gum commercials and on the recording of the theme song for Andy Warhol's 16mm film LONESOME COWBOYS (1968). Her finances were augmented further by clerking at a Madison Avenue boutique. Trying her hand as a photographer's model, Spacek appeared in one perfume ad in *The New Yorker* magazine. In 1969, at the urging of a record promoter, she sang—using the name Rainbo—on a seven-inch single for Roulette Records, "John, You Went Too Far This Time," the title referring to the nude photos of John Lennon and Yoko Ono on the cover of their 1968 album, *Two Virgins*. She was an extra in crowd scenes in the Andy Warhol–produced TRASH (1970) as well as in another of Warhol's 16mm films, WOMEN IN REVOLT (1971), before enrolling for six months of studies with the Lee Strasberg Theatrical Institute. Her free hours were spent visiting motion picture casting offices, which resulted in earning for her the role of a drugged teenager in PRIME CUT (1972), filmed in Canada. Of her efforts, critic Judith Crist noted, "The film's sole virtue is Sissy Spacek, a lovely twenty year old [sic] with an exquisitely appealing face."

Boosted by such kind words, Sissy felt that whatever career she might have would be in movies rather than music. Relocating to Los Angeles in early 1972, she was quick to obtain acting jobs on an episode of ABC-TV's "Love, American Style" (January 19, 1973) and as one of THE GIRLS OF HUNTINGTON HOUSE (February 14, 1973), an ABC-TV movie about unwed mothers. In rapid succession, she took parts in two segments of TV's "The Waltons" (March 8, 1973; September 20, 1973) as well as in "The Rookies" (December 17, 1973). On a few motion picture screens she was seen in the title role of GINGER IN THE MORNING (1973), in which she starred as a hitchhiker who finds romance. Co-starred in this minor release were Monte Markham and Susan Oliver.

On location during the 1973 filming of BADLANDS (1974), Sissy met motion picture art director Jack Fisk, with whom she began her first serious romantic liaison. (Together, later that year, they worked behind the scenes on the Brian De Palma–directed PHANTOM OF THE PARADISE (1974) with Sissy acting as set decorator.) She received third billing as an itinerant fruit picker in the Tennessee Williams–inspired THE MIGRANTS (February 3, 1974), a CBS-TV movie. BADLANDS, first viewed at the eleventh annual New

York Film Festival prior to its general release in March 1974, received critical acclaim. Vincent Canby (*The New York Times*) singled out Sissy for managing "the rather grand feat of being simultaneously transparent and mysterious, sweet and heedlessly cruel." As a disturbed fifteen year old, she aided in the murder of her dad before setting off on a cross-country spree of mayhem with her older boyfriend (Martin Sheen). Over the years, this stark drama has developed a cult following.

In Santa Monica, California, on April 12, 1974, Sissy and Jack Fisk were married in a chapel near the beach. His sheepdog was their sole witness. Fisk was thirty-nine; she was twenty-four. Moving to a "little tract house" in the Topanga Canyon area of Los Angeles, she maintained their home in an immaculate fashion, saying, "If I get hit by a car, I want to go out knowing I returned my neighbor's cake pan."

In KATHERINE (October 5, 1975), a highly touted ABC-TV telefilm, she was a wealthy young woman who becomes a militant activist in order to change society à la Patty Hearst. In this well-written drama of transformation, in which Art Carney and Jane Wyatt played her parents, she gave a well-etched characterization. For later viewings, the production was cut from one hundred minutes to seventy-eight minutes.

Jack Fisk was the art director on CARRIE (1976), based on Stephen King's novel. It was he who suggested to director Brian De Palma that his wife play the teenaged high school girl whose telekinetic powers are unleashed by a series of unpleasant events. De Palma, a disciple of Alfred Hitchcock, gave the name Bates to the high school where outcast Carrie (Spacek) is first tormented, but is then invited to the prom by the class jock (William Katt) at the urging of his girlfriend (Amy Irving). These good intentions are undone by another student (Nancy Allen), who hates Carrie, and by her beer-drinking pal (John Travolta). It is the latter who drops a bucket of pig's blood over Carrie's head. At movie's end, everyone is dead except Irving, including Carrie's mad, man-hating, Bible-quoting mama (Piper Laurie). This well-crafted horror entry was responsible for Sissy's rise to stardom. CARRIE grossed $15 million at domestic box offices, which constituted a hit by 1976 standards. In addition, Sissy was named Best Actress of the year by the National Society of Film Critics. She (in the Best Actress category) and Laurie (in the Best Supporting Actress category) were Oscar-nominated, but neither won an Academy Award. *Newsweek* magazine's issue of February 14, 1977, pictured Sissy, radiant and conventionally pretty, on its cover as the "most promising" new actress in movies. On March 12, 1977, she hosted NBC-TV's "Saturday Night Live," appearing in comedy skits, twirling a baton, and singing her own songs. This segment of the series won an Emmy for outstanding writing.

The R-rated WELCOME TO L.A. was completed before CARRIE, but not released until March 1977. Directed by Robert Altman's associate Alan Rudolph, it was an ensemble offering with a diverse array of talent, including Keith Carradine, Sally Kellerman, Geraldine Chaplin, Harvey Keitel, Lauren Hutton, and Viveca Lindfors. It offered Sissy as a topless maid making extra money as a hooker. A disgruntled *Variety* termed the arty production a "slack attempt to demonstrate the impermanence of contemporary sexual relationships." As for Spacek, the trade paper acknowledged that she "exhibits her quirky charm as a spaced-out maid." A much better feature was the bizarre THREE WOMEN (1977), written, produced, and directed by Robert Altman with Sissy as a lost soul from Texas who attempts suicide. She drifts into a coma, only to awaken and assume the name and personality of another woman (Shelley Duvall). This offbeat production, European in flavor and not a big-grossing entry, garnered Sissy a Best Supporting Actress award from the New York Film Critics. She was a guest star on the two-hour CBS-TV special "*Rolling Stone: The 10th Anniversary*" (November 25, 1977). VERNA: U.S.O. GIRL (PBS-TV, January 25, 1978) offered Sissy as an untalented Chicago dancer who entertains front-line troops during World War II. *Variety* reported that "the relationship between Sissy Spacek ... and William Hurt as the soldier who falls for her never quite comes off—a key element that falls flat." However, the reviewer acknowledged, "Spacek herself is marvelous, a truly appealing loser."

Sissy preferred to remain at home rather than accept just any role. It was not until country western singer Loretta Lynn selected Sissy to portray her in COAL MINER'S DAUGHTER (1980) that Sissy returned to the screen. Sissy once again developed successfully from an insecure adolescent—her frequent screen persona—to a powerhouse in this musical biography chronicle of the rise to national stardom of a backwoods girl. Doing her own singing as Lynn, Sissy was almost a one-woman show until Beverly D'Angelo's strong appearance as songstress Patsy Cline. Released in February, the picture had by year's end grossed $79 million in domestic box-office receipts. Additional earnings came from Sissy's seven-inch recordings of songs from the film, 45-rpm picture sleeves, and the soundtrack recording on the MCA label, plus an MCA single recording with D'Angelo. Once again, the New York Film Critics named Sissy Best Actress. After receiving an Academy Award nomination, Spacek said of Loretta Lynn: "She and I are the same size—five feet two and one-half inches and there is something so familiar about her. It was like meeting a long-lost friend." On March 31, 1981, Sissy, in accepting her Oscar from the stage of the Dorothy Chandler Pavilion in Los Angeles, thanked Lynn, "the lady who gave me all that hair," as well as her co-star, Tommy Lee Jones, and her "mama and daddy."

In April 1980 she co-starred on motion picture screens as Carolyn Cassaday in HEART BEAT, a disconnected script dealing with the 1950s lives of beat generation writers Jack Kerouac (John Heard), Neal Cassaday (Nick Nolte), and the latter's wife. The movie was too specialized to have mass appeal, but *People* magazine noted, "Sissy Spacek shows her remarkable range as the sophisticated Carolyn, traversing an emotional minefield between John Heard's sensitive, gentlemanly Jack and Nick Nolte's primal, self-centered Neal." Then Jack Fisk directed his wife in RAGGEDY MAN (1981), a minor but haunting story of a small town Texas switchboard operator trying to raise two children (Henry Thomas, Carey Hollis, Jr.) while a mysterious eccentric (Sam Shepard) guards them from afar. MISSING (1982), based on the nonfiction book *The Execution of Charles Horman*, was shot in Mexico. Politically oriented director Constantin Costa-Gavras featured Sissy as the wife of a young American (John Shea) who has disappeared in Chile during a junta takeover. With the man's stiff-willed, politically conservative father (Jack Lemmon), she searches for the dismaying truth. Two days prior to the movie's release, the U.S. State

Department denied any "possibility that U.S. government officials" were connected in any way with the real subject's disappearance and ultimate murder. Both the French-based Russian-Greek director (in his American film debut) and Jack Lemmon strained far too hard to project topical relevance, leaving it to Sissy to provide a needed touch of reality. Pauline Kael (*The New Yorker* magazine) complimented her for being "fresh and natural." For the third time, Sissy was nominated for an Academy Award, but she lost to Meryl Streep (SOPHIE'S CHOICE).

Sissy then was scheduled to star as Emma, the daughter in TERMS OF ENDEARMENT (1983). However, she was forced to withdraw due to pregnancy and Debra Winger won the pivotal role. (Sissy's daughter, Schuyler Elizabeth, was born on June 8, 1982.) Instead, during 1983 Sissy was heard, but not seen, as the voice of a brain in a jar in the Steve Martin comedy THE MAN WITH TWO BRAINS.

The year 1984 was the time of the distressed farmer and the distressed farmer's wife in motion pictures. Sissy and heartthrob leading man Mel Gibson co-starred as a couple struggling to save their land from THE RIVER. (Meanwhile, Jessica Lange suffered in COUNTRY, and Sally Field was brave in PLACES IN THE HEART.) Critic Roger Ebert, who, like many filmgoers, was satiated by the rash of these genre pieces, acknowledged, "The movie contains a heartfelt performance by Sissy Spacek as the Tennessee farm wife; an adequate performance by Mel Gibson as her husband; and a scene-stealing performance by Scott Glenn as the local financier who wants to buy up all the land in the valley. . . ." Sissy received her fourth Oscar nomination, with Oscar bids going to the other two ladies as well. It was Sally Field who won the honor. Made at an estimated cost of $21 million, THE RIVER grossed only $5,105,031 in domestic film rentals. MARIE (1985) was a true story about an abused wife (Sissy) who works her way through Vanderbilt University, goes to work for the parole department in the Tennessee state government, and then blows the whistle on corruption within the political structure, with murderous results. Confused by the well-intentioned narrative, Molly Haskell (*Playgirl* magazine) observed, "Sissy Spacek sits there under her visible halo, looking pale and saintly and determined, but how she got there we never understand."

Kevin Kline and **Sissy Spacek** in VIOLETS ARE BLUE (1986).

Kevin Kline was chosen as her co-star for VIOLETS ARE BLUE

(1986), a little picture directed by her husband, Jack Fisk. They played former high school lovers whose romance blooms years later, although by now he is wed to Bonnie Bedelia. *Variety* carped, "As an antidote to the epidemic of kiddie films, VIOLETS ARE BLUE is a commendable effort, but unfortunately, not the cure. . . . Performances are competent but don't do enough to flesh out the inner workings of these people." On April 26, 1986, Sissy was one of many performers marking the sesquicentennial of "Texas 150: A Celebration" on ABC-TV. With Anne Bancroft (who bears no resemblance to her) as her mother, Sissy was the suicidal daughter in 'NIGHT, MOTHER (1986), adapted for the screen from the 1983 Pulitzer Prize–winning play by Marsha Norman. The depressing drama soon disappeared from theater screens, to reappear on home video and television. At that time *TV Guide* magazine noted that Sissy "is just too vital to be believable as a woman who's going to kill herself at film's end." It was yet another box-office misfire for Sissy. Sheer chemistry between the stars of CRIMES OF THE HEART (1986) was largely responsible for whatever success the movie enjoyed. Diane Keaton, Jessica Lange, and Sissy—all too mature for their parts—were southern sisters with "lots of endearing quirks" who relive childhood memories in their old North Carolina home. As the unpredictable Babe, frustrated over a love affair, Sissy shoots her husband (Beeson Carroll), then asks if he would like a glass of lemonade.

Having taken up residence in the state of Virginia near friends (Jessica Lange and Sam Shepard), Sissy and Jack became parents to a second daughter, Virginia Madison Fisk, born in October 1988. She was off movie screens for four years, until she co-starred with Whoopi Goldberg in THE LONG WALK HOME (1990), dealing with the Montgomery, Alabama, bus boycott of 1955. During the boycott, Odessa Cotter (Goldberg) walks across town to her maid's job with the upper-crust white household controlled by Miriam Thompson (Sissy), who depends upon Odessa to keep everything running smoothly. Little by little, Miriam becomes more aware of, and sympathetic to, the cause of the blacks. In reviewing the feature on September 10, 1990, at the Telluride Film Festival, *Variety* judged that the movie's "historical sensibilities, while relevant, may be too remote for wide audiences," but that the "modest, worthwhile" film "is well suited for video, cable and foreign ancillary playoff." At the same time, the trade publication noted that "Spacek fills out the character with subtlety and insight" in what was called a "sturdy" performance. Syndicated gossip columnist Liz Smith was in Telluride too, and she penned her reactions to the showing where "sobs were heard throughout the theater—then applause and cheers as the final credits began to roll."

Forthcoming for Sissy in late 1991, under the direction of Martin Davidson, is HARD PROMISES, a romantic comedy in which she stars opposite William Petersen. Filmed in Texas, it is the story of a rogue (Petersen) who returns to his home town hoping to win back his ex-wife (Sissy) just as she is about to wed another (Bruce Kerwin).

Sissy, with her last substantial movie hit in 1980's COAL MINER'S DAUGHTER, seems content to rest on her laurels in Virginia, far from the hurly-burly of Hollywood. She once said that if she had to give up making movies, she would easily find many other interests to occupy her, among them writing poetry, screenplays, or children's books. Too, she stated that she would perhaps like to direct a feature film one day, but it would be something she would carefully select herself. When asked about her earlier aggressiveness in establishing her screen career, she reasoned, "I always had a secure life, always had such support from my family . . . maybe that makes it easier to focus on what you want. You can go farther out on a limb, because you know if you don't make it, it doesn't really matter."

Filmography

Lonesome Cowboys (Factory Films, 1968) (background vocals only)
Trash (Factory Films, 1970) (extra only)
Women in Revolt (Factory Films, 1971) (extra only)
Prime Cut (NG, 1972)
The Girls of Huntington House (ABC-TV, 2/14/73)
Ginger in the Morning (National Film, 1973)
The Migrants (CBS-TV, 2/3/74)
Badlands (WB, 1974)
Phantom of the Paradise (20th–Fox, 1974) (set decorator only)
Katherine (ABC-TV, 10/5/75)
Carrie (UA, 1976)
Welcome to L.A. (UA, 1977)
Three Women (20th–Fox, 1977)
Verna: U.S.O. Girl (PBS-TV, 1/25/78)

Coal Miner's Daughter (Univ, 1980)
Heart Beat (Orion, 1980)
Raggedy Man (Univ, 1981)
Missing (Univ, 1982)
The Man with Two Brains (WB, 1983) (voice only)
The River (Univ, 1984)
Marie (MGM/UA, 1985)
Violets Are Blue (Col, 1986)
'Night, Mother (Univ, 1986)
Crimes of the Heart [Colours of the Heat] (De Laurentiis Entertainment Group, 1986)
The Long Walk Home (Miramax, 1990)

Future Releases

Hard Promises (Col, 1991)

Album Discography

Coal Miner's Daughter (MCA 5107) [ST]
Hanging Up My Heart (Atlantic 7-90100-1)

SYLVESTER STALLONE

"I take a lot of crap, a lot of insults, a lot of humiliation. Some of it
is self-generated and some is promulgated by people who see only this
neolithic, primordial image."—*American Film* magazine, January 1990

ONCE UPON A TIME, IN A RAT- AND ROACH-INFESTED TENEMENT ON
Manhattan's West Side, there lived a puny, undisciplined kid deprived of sunlight and
Vitamin D. Slavishly he transformed his body and spirit into a #1 macho movie star
machine with an annual income estimated to be $63 million. Responsible for introducing
"Yo!" to our vocabulary, this sexy, sloe-eyed celluloid hero, acting with body, fists, and
automatic weapons, symbolizes the great American dream—rags to riches.

Like Victor Mature of a half-century earlier, Sylvester Stallone is the Latin proponent of strength. Like today's John Travolta and Al Pacino, Stallone is the smoldering
paisan on camera. As with Arnold Schwarzenegger, a shirt seldom covers Stallone's
bulging muscles on screen. Sylvester is a nonstop worker who within a fourteen-year
period wrote thirteen screenplays and directed five feature films, while acting in nineteen
productions that cumulatively grossed $2 billion worldwide. At a salary approximating
$25 million per film, the "Italian Stallion" is the highest-paid actor in Hollywood history.
His status and popularity require him to retain a coterie of muscular bodyguards to keep
away the tugging public that adores the screen persona he has created for himself through
two screen heroes—John Rambo and Rocky Balboa.

Sylvester Enzio Stallone was born on Saturday, July 6, 1946, in a charity hospital on
New York City's West Side near his parents' tenement residence at 50th Street and Tenth
Avenue in what is called Hell's Kitchen. While his father, Frank, a Sicilian immigrant,
studied hairdressing, his flamboyant mother, Jacqueline LaBeau Stallone, supported her
husband by working part time as a chorine at Billy Rose's Diamond Horseshoe Club. The
delivery of her first child proved difficult and resulted in a birth injury to the baby, leaving
Sylvester with a slight facial paralysis and, later, a speech defect. A second son, Frank, Jr.,
was born four years later, on July 30, 1950. A small, sickly boy with rickets, Sylvester spent
his first five years in foster homes from which he ran away as often as he could. When he
was five, his family was reunited by a move to Silver Spring, Maryland. There his parents
opened a small chain of beauty salons. Sylvester was disliked by the other children, who
made fun of his name and speech. He became a lonely, unruly boy who spent his time
fantasizing about becoming a famous writer.

In 1957 his parents divorced. At first the two children divided their time between their mother and father. Finally, they went to Philadelphia with their mother, who had married a pizza manufacturer, who set her up in a gymnasium/health spa business. By the time he was fifteen, Sylvester, who had changed his name to Mike to avoid torment from his peers, had been expelled from fourteen schools. "I had all the sensibilities of a Quasimodo," he has said of his earlier self. At sixteen, he was enrolled in Devereux Manor, a private high school in Berwyn, Pennsylvania, which provided counseling for children with behavioral problems. There, as means of exorcising his frustrations, he turned to weightlifting and oil painting along with playing fullback on the football team. He also developed a fondness for fencing and discus throwing, and what would prove to be a lifelong fascination with horses.

Although Sylvester liked acting in school plays, his grades were at the barely passing level. However, on his graduation in 1965, his mother obtained for him a work-study scholarship at the American College in Leysin, Switzerland, as athletic coach to the female students. There he developed a real interest in the stage, after performing in a satirical version of Arthur Miller's *Death of a Salesman*. On returning to the United States in 1967, he enrolled in drama courses at the University of Miami in Coral Gables, Florida. When the university refused to produce his own playscripts, he formed an independent acting group. Before graduation, he either quit or was ousted—depending on which of his accounts one accepts.

Arriving back in New York City in August 1969, Sylvester established his headquarters at a third-rate hotel where, each day before embarking on auditions, he practiced in front of a mirror. After several rejections, he finally got a part in *Rain*, produced by The Extension, a small off-off-Broadway troupe. This job was followed by a role in *Score*, a semi-nude off-Broadway production that ran for twenty-three performances at the Martinique Theatre. Between these stage engagements, he swept cages at the Central Park Zoo, did pizza demonstrations for his stepfather at food conventions, dressed fish for display, and was an usher at the Baronet movie theater on Manhattan's Upper East Side. There he met another usher, a young woman named Sasha Czack, whom he would later marry.

To help support himself, he undertook two jobs that would one day return to haunt him. He posed for nude photographs and starred in a pornographic 8mm film, A PARTY AT KITTY AND STUD'S (1970). (This feature would be transferred in 1985 to videocassette format by Electric Hollywood Home Video and distributed by Essex Video as THE ITALIAN STALLION.) After buying and studying a handbook on screenwriting, Stallone was able to sell several half-hour television scripts, causing his mother, a believer in astrology, to predict that her son would achieve success as a writer before becoming known as an actor.

In April 1971 Stallone made his official motion picture debut in BANANAS, as an unbilled ruffian who mugs Woody Allen in a New York City subway station. In 1973 he had a role in the independently made NO PLACE TO HIDE, released in a few theaters in 1975. He was billed as Sylvester E. Stallone and played a student radical. In 1988 the film was distributed to television, and two years later it was reedited as a parody for videocassette release as A MAN CALLED . . . RAINBO.

Also in 1973 he attended an audition with a friend and as a result won a leading role in the low-budget THE LORDS OF FLATBUSH (1974), which dealt nostalgically with a gang of tough Brooklyn high school boys circa 1957. Filmed in Brooklyn and containing some dialogue written by Sylvester, it was initially not well received. However, the feature went on to develop a cult following after having spawned several future stars. *Time* magazine thought that Stallone offered a "truly exceptional characterization" as the roughhouse but basically gentle Stanley. Perry King, one of the film's co-leads, has said of Stallone, "I assumed he was the dumb, sweet guy he was playing, but then he gave me a screenplay he had written about Edgar Allan Poe, and I think it may have been the best script I've ever read. I truly consider him a genius." Another cast member, Henry Winkler, later achieved renown as The Fonz in TV's "Happy Days," aping mannerisms learned by observing Sylvester on the set.

Early in 1974 Stallone packed an old car with scripts, and along with his girlfriend, Sasha, and his dog, drove to Los Angeles. There he hoped to sell his scenarios to Hollywood producers. On December 28, 1974, he and Sasha were married. Meanwhile, he won a small part in THE PRISONER OF SECOND AVENUE (1974), this time as a mugging victim. This outing was followed by several other small parts. He was a gun-toting thug in Robert Mitchum's remake of FAREWELL, MY LOVELY (1975). He fared better as the third-billed Machine Gun Joe, a futuristic auto racer, in the satirical DEATH RACE 2000 (1975), directed by Paul Bartel. In CAPONE (1975), a copy of many other features about the notorious mobster, Stallone played Frank Nitti, the infamous hitman and successor to the gangster kingpin. On television, he was featured in "The Cutting Edge" episode (September 15, 1975) of NBC's "Police Story" as well as in the "My Brother, My Enemy" segment (September 21, 1975) of CBS's "Kojak."

Although his screenplay about Edgar Allan Poe received attention from Hollywood filmmakers, no one was seriously interested in purchasing the property. Sylvester would continue rewrites of this project through the 1980s. Another script, called HELL'S KITCHEN, was optioned by Paramount Pictures, but never produced. Finding promise in a third script, a story about a Philadelphia boxer that he had written in three days, producers offered him as much as $310,000 for it as a possible starring vehicle for Burt Reynolds, James Caan, Warren Beatty, or Ryan O'Neal. However, Sylvester refused to sell it. Although he allegedly had just $106 to his name, and a pregnant wife, he envisioned no one in the focal role but himself. In the meantime, he took a bit part as a favor to his friend, director Paul Bartel, in CANNONBALL (1976). On May 5, 1976, Sasha gave birth to Sage Moonblood.

United Artists finally took a chance in acquiescing to Sylvester's demand, paying him $75,000 for his script about a small-time fighter who wins his big chance at immortality. He was to receive a $650 per week salary to star, as well as an assurance of 10 percent of the profits. Before filming began, Stallone underwent a strenuous five-month physical training course. He added to his credits on the production by choreographing the fight scenes and also provided small roles in the feature for his father, brother, and dog.

Completed in twenty-eight days at a cost of $1.1 million, ROCKY (1976) received mostly favorable reviews, such as that in the *New York Daily News*: "it's likeable and decent in a basic way that makes the heart glow." Pauline Kael (*The New Yorker* magazine) said of the actor's performance as the underdog boxer who gains self-respect while seeking the championship: "He's amazing to watch: there's a bull-necked energy in him, smoldering, and in his deep caveman's voice he gives the most surprising, sharp, fresh shadings to his lines." The deeply emotional, naive ROCKY was honored with a Golden Globe Award, shared the best picture award of the Los Angeles Film Critics with NETWORK, received awards from the Directors Guild of America and the American Cinema Editors, and was nominated for ten Academy Awards. Sly, as he was now affectionately called, was nominated in both the Best Actor and Best Screenplay categories. (He was the third person in Oscar history to be so honored, preceded by Charles Chaplin in 1940 and Orson Welles in 1941.) He failed to win either award, but ROCKY was named the Best Picture of 1976, and a Best Director Oscar went to John G. Avildsen. In the final box-office tabulations, the feature grossed $117 million domestically and Sylvester Stallone was an "overnight"

Sylvester Stallone in ROCKY (1976).

star. Adding to the glory of both ROCKY and Sly was the Ballantine Books paperback novelization of ROCKY plus *The Official Rocky Scrapbook*, written by Stallone and published by Grosset & Dunlap in 1977. More money was made on the sale of ROCKY posters and T-shirts. That same year, G. P. Putnam published Sly's novel, *Paradise Alley*, a reworking of his HELL'S KITCHEN scenario. Universal filmed this property in 1978, with Stallone directing, writing, and starring—and he sang the movie's title song. The primitive tale of three brothers from the tenements of New York City was severely roasted by the critics and grossed a disappointing $6.5 million in domestic release.

Meanwhile, he had co-authored the script of F.I.S.T. [Federation of Interstate Truckers] (1978), in which he starred as Johnny Kovak, a man of humble Hungarian origins who rises from rags to riches as a teamster boss. In the movie's later scenes, as the aged organizer, his stiff movements resemble those of Dr. Frankenstein's monster. Nevertheless, this overstated melodrama grossed $20 million domestically.

During this period, Stallone was quoted as saying, "I'm not handsome in the classical sense. The eyes droop, the mouth is crooked, the teeth aren't straight, the voice sounds like a Mafioso pallbearer, but somehow it all works." From his home in Los Angeles' Coldwater Canyon, formerly owned by Ernie Kovacs, Sylvester noted, "I make my living with my mind. My muscles I consider merely machinery to carry my mind around."

ROCKY II (1979), directed and scripted by and starring Sylvester in a reprise of his Rocky Balboa characterization, was essentially a rehash of the original, yet grossed $79 million domestically. Also during 1979, a second son was born to the Stallones, named Sergeoh Joseph (he was later diagnosed as autistic).

Off the screen for two years, Stallone returned in April 1981. He traded boxing shorts for a suit as a New York City undercover cop in pursuit of an international terrorist (Rutger Hauer) in NIGHTHAWKS. Unable to merely star in a picture, he spent one day directing during the absence of director Bruce Malmuth, causing him to be fined $50,000 in penalties by the Directors Guild. Even after the action movie was sneak-previewed to decent response in Washington, D.C., Stallone insisted he could have edited it better himself. To pacify him, producer Marty Poll incorporated his ideas into a print that was shown in Santa Monica, California, where it bombed. The final version, which grossed $14 million domestically, was Malmuth's cut. In VICTORY (1981), sometimes known as ESCAPE TO VICTORY, Sly and co-star Michael Caine were prisoners of war in World War II Germany who refuse a chance to escape in order to complete a soccer game. It was a mighty dumb premise that took in $10.4 million domestically.

Knowing that his fans liked him best as Rocky Balboa, Stallone wrote and directed ROCKY III (1982), which by year's end had realized $123 million in domestic grosses. During filming, again in Philadelphia, an 8' 6" statue of the actor as Rocky was placed outside the Philadelphia Art Museum but was later moved to an indoor area at The Spectrum sports arena. In October 1982, John Rambo, a decorated Vietnam veteran waging a one-man war against the police and National Guard in the Pacific Northwest, was unveiled in FIRST BLOOD. Stallone offered an uncredited assist in writing the violent, right-wing script, in which his Rambo took viewers on nonstop gory action through the wilds of Oregon. The hero, who has little dialogue, made an incomprehensible patriotic speech at film's bloody end. Many critics were aghast at the manipulative dramatics, but the public approved to the tune of $120 in domestic/foreign grosses. (By now, Stallone was an important international screen star, with strong audience loyalty in Japan, England, France, Italy, Scandinavia, and India.)

Stallone was director, co-producer, and co-writer of STAYING ALIVE (1983), the first feature film with which he was involved but in which he did not star. A disappointing sequel to the enormously popular SATURDAY NIGHT FEVER (1977), it again had John Travolta—this time with bulging muscles—as the Broadway dancer involved in romance and a ROCKY-like battle to succeed on the musical stage. It grossed $63.8 million domestically. Stallone next teamed with Dolly Parton in RHINESTONE (1984), a change of pace comedy/musical that he co-wrote. However, his "singing" failed to be a turn-on and the film took in only $21.5 million. *People* magazine, one of the film's few quasi-champions, noted, "Ordinarily, there's barely enough room on a movie screen for Sylvester Stallone and his ego, let alone anyone else. Well, Sly, meet Dolly Parton. Parton is such a powerful screen personality that her shimmery, sweet-natured energy more than matches Stallone's sullen, macho introversion. The contrast between them is fascinating." It was back to the mold for Stallone in RAMBO: FIRST BLOOD PART II (1985), which he co-scripted. As the one-man guerrilla army in Cambodia searching for Americans missing in action, he emerged as the screen's most incredible superhero. The sequel grossed $300 million in worldwide earnings. Continuing to play it safe in audience-pleasing roles, he directed and co-scripted as well as starred in ROCKY IV (1985). This time the patriotic American battled a Russian superhuman champion (Dolph Lundgren). Due to Stallone's box-office pull, the lackluster feature grossed $128 million domestically. The star admitted, "I'll just go on playing RAMBO and ROCKY. Both are money-making machines that can't be switched off."

His marriage to Sasha ended in September 1985, with him admitting that he was to blame for never being at home. He paid her between $20 million and $32 million as a community property divorce settlement, plus alimony and child support payments. Three months later, in December, he married Brigitte Nielsen, a six-foot Danish model-turned-actress (ROCKY IV). She was eighteen years his junior and claims to have pursued him, although Arnold Schwarzenegger (her co-star in RED SONJA) says that he introduced her to Sly in an effort to get rid of her.

During 1986 Sylvester was honored by Harvard University with its Hasty Pudding Club award as the Man of the Year. Hong Kong film baron Run Run Shaw offered the star $30 million to do a RAMBO III sequel. He formed White Eagle Enterprises in a production deal with United Artists, stipulating that during the next six years, Sylvester would star in five films and write, direct, produce, or act in another five. Sly's only film in 1986 was COBRA, written by him and co-starring his new wife. A conventional police action picture, it was a box-office failure compared with ROCKY and RAMBO, with a domestic take of only $59 million. His acting salary for the mawkish OVER THE TOP (1987) was $12 million, making him the highest-paid actor to date. He also co-scripted the saccharine tale about a truck driver—with an alienated son and a dying wife—whose stops always include a session in arm wrestling. After a disastrous opening in February 1987, the pre-release ads depicting Sly wrist-to-wrist with a huge shaven-headed man were redone to show him staring wistfully into space. The ploy failed; the film grossed only $16 million domestically.

In early 1987 Stallone completed the construction of his own polo field on the island of Kauai, Hawaii, near his home on Anini Beach. At the same time, he was building a horse ranch at Chatsworth, California, out of logs and headed a polo team known as White Eagle. In July 1987 he filed for divorce from "Gitte" Nielsen, charging the standard "irreconcilable differences." He also noted bitterly, "When I look at her, I see dollar signs in her eyes. And, when she looks at me, I think she sees the Bank of America." Before the divorce was final in January 1988, she had found solace with director Tony Scott and later with pro-footballer Mark Gastineau. During 1987 BEVERLY HILLS COP was released, starring Eddie Murphy in a role originally meant for Stallone before he rewrote that role into too expensive a script. The Murphy film grossed $153.6 million domestically.

During 1988 Stallone, who was honorary chairman for the New York March of Dimes, was linked romantically with socialite Cornelia Guest, as well as with TV personalities Mary Hart and Vanna White, singer Madonna, and also with twenty-two-year-old model Jennifer Flavin. In June 1988 the syndicated TV cartoon series "Rambo and the Force of Freedom"—which did not utilize Stallone's voice for the hero—left the air after a year's run. Also in 1988, production of the RAMBO doll was discontinued after two years of relative nonsales. Meanwhile, the much-touted and much-delayed RAMBO III (1988), using Sylvester's co-written script, was partially filmed in Israel. The newest sequel earned him a flat salary of $20 million and had the invincible one fighting the Russians almost singlehandedly in support of the Afghans. Released in 1,500 movie theaters in late May 1988, the tawdry action caper grossed just $54 million domestically, but collected an additional $96 million in foreign markets.

During the summer of 1988 he was seen in Japan in print ads for the Ito Ham Company, captioned in Japanese: "A delicious way to send our love." It was revealed that Sylvester had a large collection of modern art, that he owned real estate in Europe and the United States, that he loved Puccini operas, and that, like his mother, he believed in reincarnation. His friends no longer included Arnold Schwarzenegger and Eddie Murphy, but did include Mickey Rourke and Ray Sharkey. He began wearing glasses in public, saying, "I need them for distances, even though I think with some of the mistakes I've made in life, I could have used them for close-up endeavors, too." In late 1989 NAL published Jackie Stallone's *Starpower: An Astrological Guide to Supersuccess*, wherein she wrote that her womanizing Cancer-born son "suffers from a bad case of zipperitis." Stallone had been mentioned as one of the potential stars of THE GODFATHER PART III (1990), but negotiations fell through. However, he was signed by Carolco Pictures to make ten features for Showtime–Cable. Meanwhile, San Francisco's long-running stage revue *Beach Blanket Babylon* parodied his ROCKY figure.

As model prisoner Frank Leone in LOCK UP (1989), Stallone is told by the psycho warden (Donald Sutherland), "You are in hell," then proceeds to settle an old grudge. During the film's overextended 106 minutes, the camera focuses on his well-defined torso as he is beaten in the prison yard, stabbed in the back, tossed into solitary, and then tormented by sadistic guards. However, his inane dialogue was badly mumbled, which proved a blessing. Produced by his White Eagle Enterprises, this shoddy movie earned only $23 million in domestic box-office grosses. However, TANGO AND CASH (1989) did much better, perhaps abetted by the joint appeal of co-star Kurt Russell. This buddy cop story was found to be "one of the worst written" (*Los Angeles Times*); *People* magazine insisted that its scenarist (Randy Feldman) "seems to have jotted this one down on the way to the set." After eighty days this nonsensical action entry had grossed $60.1 million domestically.

In late 1989 Sylvester failed to interest yet another director, Stanley Kubrick, in helming his Edgar Allan Poe biography project, while denying rumors that he had been approached with a $2 million offer to write a book on physical fitness. In February 1990 a bronze statue of him called *The Age of Steel*, standing twelve feet tall and weighing 1,000 pounds, was placed atop the seventy-two steps leading to the Philadelphia Art Museum. The sculpture, commissioned by him in 1986, was originally to depict him with Brigitte Nielsen in his arms. Upon their break up, he dictated to the sculptor that her likeness be chiseled away. Recipient of the tenth annual Golden Raspberry Award, Sly was in Philadelphia with his ROCKY statue again out in the open air while he filmed his penned screenplay, ROCKY V (1990), under the direction of John G. Avildsen. This time, as a boxing trainer, he discovers a young fighter (Tommy Morrison, John Wayne's great-grandnephew) of whom he is determined to make a champion. Said to be "the final chapter in a great American story," the newest installment features Sly's son Sage, playing Rocky, Jr. (In an early draft of the screenplay, Stallone had Rocky die, but he was reportedly talked out of the idea by MGM/UA.) When asked if there might be a RAMBO IV in the future, Stallone replied that it might be a possibility "if it deals with ecology and the environment."

In April 1990 he unveiled in Los Angeles his interpretation of the Berlin wall in oils and announced that forty of his paintings would be on display in September in a one-person show at Hanson Gallery in Beverly Hills. Within days, all but four of his paintings had been sold, for more than $16,000 each. A portion of the proceeds of more than $500,000 was donated to help finance the campaign for California's Proposition 128, the "Big Green" ballot initiative in November 1990. In May 1990 he and Arnold Schwarzenegger—box-office rivals as top action stars—put past disagreements behind them at the Cannes Film Festival when they joined arms in a tango for press photographers. After going to Milan, Italy, to receive the Pelegotto Award from Italian television as "the world's most popular actor," Sly received the Dwight D. Eisenhower physical fitness distinction in Washington, D.C., which he said was "like winning an Academy Award."

Forbes magazine reported in September 1990 that Stallone was the fourth biggest entertainment earner of the previous year, with an income of $63 million.

The highly promoted ROCKY V opened in mid-November 1990, with Duane Byrge (*Hollywood Reporter*) judging, "Although the final bell hasn't sounded officially on Rocky, it's hard to imagine Stallone executing a more graceful or natural step from the ring for Rocky Balboa. . . . Stallone's performance is at its most powerful in his most underdog moments." Less charitable was *Variety*, which insisted, "this is the most dimwitted of the sequels, making all those associated with it seem punch-drunk. . . . Stallone again scripted and continues to rely on the same clichés . . . sinking to a new low with the ending, which seems inspired by championship wrestling." The trade paper concluded, "Rocky remains Stallone's most enduring, likable and unintelligible character. . . . It's no wonder he keeps returning to it, like going home to a place where one can be genuinely loved." The bottom line in Hollywood, of course, is always how a movie performs at the box office. In its first three weeks of domestic distribution, ROCKY V grossed a relatively mild $34,654,072, proving that filmgoers were finally tiring of the ongoing saga of the Philadelphia pugilist who, in this installment, has suffered brain damage, lost all his savings, and has returned to his old neighborhood roots. Interestingly, in the course of this 104-minute feature, it was Stallone's real-life son Sage (playing Rocky's fourteen-year-old boy) who provided the most sincere and compelling performance.

In December 1990 Stallone purchased for $5.7 million a Beverly Hills–area home, the 8,400-square-foot, two-story Spanish-style house he had been leasing for the past three years from financier Kirk Kerkorian. This made the fifth residence for Sylvester, who also owned residences in Malibu, Kauai, Maryland, and Hidden Valley. (The same month Stallone put his 23-acre ranch in Hidden Valley on the market at $7.9 million.)

OSCAR (1991), a comedy, starred Sly as a 1930s gangster trying to go straight, with Kirk Douglas as his dying father. The John Landis–directed feature had his character hosting a society party where everything goes awry. The film was a disappointment.

In an earnest attempt to dispel public opinion that he is a man lacking intelligence or wit, Stallone told *M* magazine recently that he reads "every morning" from the literary works of Robert Frost and Edna St. Vincent Millay. "I'm subject to the whims and perceptions of a fictional character," he said. "I am a verbal person and RAMBO is an Elizabethan dumb show, almost a mime. It isn't as if I'm in the gutter drinking Woolite, but it has jaded and distorted the image of who I am." On another occasion, he explained his show business success by saying, "Once in a man's life, for one mortal moment, he must make a grab for immortality. If not, he has not lived." As to the state of his psyche, he admits, "In the last few years, I've had a revelation in my life. It's blowing by and I don't want to be left with a bunch of film cuts, accolades, sunglasses and autographs. I'm going home. I'm taking my makeup off, shedding the tuxedo. I'm putting my house in order." Reasons Stallone, "Who needs the Hollywood Babylon syndrome, stars who wind up miserable, broken, shallow, frightened. . . ."

Filmography

A Party at Kitty and Stud's [The Italian Stallion] (Unk, 1970) [released in videocassette format in 1985]

Bananas (UA, 1971)

The Lords of Flatbush (Col, 1974)

The Prisoner of Second Avenue (Par, 1974)

No Place to Hide [Rebel/A Man Called . . . Rainbo] (Galaxy/American, 1975) [made in 1973] (as Sylvester E. Stallone)

Farewell, My Lovely (Avco Emb, 1975)

Capone (20th–Fox, 1975)

Death Race 2000 (New World, 1975)

Cannonball [Carquake] (New World, 1976)

Rocky (UA, 1976) (also script, choreography)

F.I.S.T. (UA, 1978) (also co-script)

Paradise Alley (Univ, 1978) (also director, script, title song vocal)

Rocky II (UA, 1979) (also director, script)

Nighthawks (Univ, 1981)

Victory [Escape to Victory] (Par, 1981)

Rocky III (1982) (also director, script, title song vocal)

First Blood (Orion, 1982)

Staying Alive (1983) (co-producer, director, co-script only)

Rhinestone (20th–Fox, 1984) (also co-script)

Rambo: First Blood Part II (Tri-Star, 1985) (also co-script)

Rocky IV (MGM/UA, 1985) (also director, co-script)

Cobra (WB, 1986) (also script)
Over the Top (WB, 1987) (also co-script)
Rambo III (Tri-Star, 1988) (also co-script)
Lock Up (Tri-Star, 1989)

Tango and Cash (WB, 1989)
Rocky V (MGM/UA, 1990) (also script)
Oscar (BV, 1991)

Album Discography

Rhinestone (RCA ABL1-5032) [ST]

Rocky III (EMI-Manhattan E21Y-46561) [ST]

MERYL STREEP

"Under anesthesia, I'm sure I'd talk in several strange tongues."
—*US* magazine, January 23, 1989

DUSTIN HOFFMAN HAS SAID THAT MERYL STREEP IS NOT JUST USING accents, "she's looking for the character." On the other hand, her severest critic, movie reviewer Pauline Kael, wrote that she "has used too many accents on us." True, on camera Streep has been Polish, British, Australian, Danish, and Oklahoman, but all the accents have been flawless, perfected by hours of practice. According to director Sydney Pollack, Meryl "can actually vanish into another person . . . in every role she becomes a totally new human being." As far back as 1977, during a busy two-year period of performing on and off Broadway, critics emphasized her "hypnotic appeal." In 1986 she was classed as "the finest actress of her generation," commanding a salary of $3 million per film, not as much as Jack Nicholson or Bruce Willis earns, but, as she observed unhappily, "It's a guy's game," this world of movies.

The critical Pauline Kael once raked Meryl in print for her seriousness in screen roles: "If only she would giggle more and suffer less—she keeps turning into the red-eye special." Streep defended herself with "I have a long nose; my face is wrong for comedy." (She proved herself wrong by providing a wonderfully comic performance that outshone the work of her funny lady co-star Roseanne Barr in SHE-DEVIL [1989] and another comic gem of a performance later in POSTCARDS FROM THE EDGE [1990].) Some have said that Meryl is haughty, superior, and aloof, but such behavior is a cover for her shyness. Studio photographers are intimidated by her burning a hole in a publicity-release slide or cutting her face out of it if she is not content with the results. This is because she does not like the way she looks; she thinks she looks like Sean Penn. At the start of her movie career, she was said to resemble Faye Dunaway, a comparison that died with the latter's MOMMIE DEAREST (1981), after which Dunaway's popularity waned for her having portrayed Joan Crawford on screen. Actually, with or without an accent, Meryl Streep is her own unique self. Director Robert Benton described her as "one of the most sensible, well-adjusted people I've ever met."

Mary Louise Streep was born in Summit, New Jersey, on Wednesday, June 22, 1949, to Harry Streep II, an executive with the Merck pharmaceutical firm, and Mary Streep, a commercial artist. The oldest of three children, she has two brothers. Almost from the day of her birth, she was called "Mar'L" by her mother, which evolved into Meryl. She grew up in Basking Ridge, New Jersey, a very unhappy little girl with glasses and braces on her teeth; her hair was always curled by permanent waves, unlike that of the other girls, who scampered about with straight hair. At the age of eight, she almost convinced herself that she was the Virgin Mary. She was a bossy child not liked by her peers. When she was twelve, she was asked to sing a solo of "O Holy Night" in the school's Christmas program. Her parents, marveling at her soprano voice, sent her to Beverly Sills' singing teacher in New York City for the next four years, once a week.

During her four years at Bernards High School in Bernardsville, New Jersey, she was selected to play the female lead in the annual presentations of the musicals *The Music Man, Li'l Abner*, and *Oklahoma!* By this time, she had shed her glasses in favor of contact lenses, outgrown her braces, and lightened her hair. With new-found confidence, she joined the school's cheerleading squad, participated on the swimming team, and was voted homecoming queen in her senior year.

In the fall of 1967 she enrolled at Vassar College for women in Poughkeepsie, New York, which she found to be a much less socially pressured atmosphere than that of her coed high school. She has recalled, "I remember feeling: I can have a thought. . . . I can do anything, because everything is allowed." In 1969, in her sophomore year, in an introduction-to-drama class she was asked to read a scene from *A Streetcar Named Desire*. She so impressed her instructor that he cast her in the title role in the campus production of *Miss Julie*. He later described her as playing the role with "a voluptuousness that was almost shocking." The following spring, while on break from classes, this same instructor directed her in an off-Broadway production at the Cubiculo Theatre of *The Playboy of Seville*, which marked her New York City debut. In her senior year, Meryl took part in an exchange program with Dartmouth College at Hanover, New Hampshire, where she spent one semester as a drama student, studying costume design, dance, and playwriting.

After graduating from Vassar in the spring of 1971, she joined the Green Mountain Guild, a stock company in Vermont where she spent the summer, fall, and winter acting in short plays presented in school auditoriums, ski resorts, bowling alleys—anywhere there was space. Now convinced that she wanted to act, she also felt that she required more training. She auditioned for entrance to Yale University's School of Drama at New Haven. She was accepted as a three-year student and worked as a waitress and typist to supplement her scholarship. During her years there, she acted in more than forty plays in roles of all types and ages, earning herself a reputation as utterly reliable. Several of her appearances were at the prestigious Yale Repertory Theatre, where one of her roles was Hallelujah Lil in the Bertolt Brecht–Kurt Weill musical *Happy End*. In the spring of 1975 she graduated from Yale with a Master of Fine Arts degree and spent the summer in Waterford, Connecticut, with the National Playwrights Conference acting in productions at the Eugene O'Neill Theatre.

After Labor Day 1975 she moved to New York City with an impressive resumé, which she presented immediately to Joseph Papp of the New York Shakespeare Festival. He hired her for the supporting part of Imogen Parrott in his first production of the season, *Trelawny of the Wells*, which opened on October 15, 1975, at Lincoln Center's Vivian Beaumont Theatre. *Variety* judged Meryl "convincing and attractive." It was suggested to her that she change her professional name to Merle Street because it would be easier to pronounce and to remember. However, she refused, reasoning, "Streep is a perfectly good Dutch name, like Rockefeller." Next, Meryl joined the New Phoenix Theatre in two one-act plays, *27 Wagons Full of Cotton* and *A Memory of Two Mondays*, which opened in late January 1976. In the first she was a "blowsy-blonde," while in the second she was a dark-haired and prim secretary. Many theatergoers were not aware that the same actress played both parts. For her work in *27 Wagons*, she received a Drama Desk Award nomination as well as a Tony Award nomination as Best Actress in a Featured Role in a drama, but lost to Shirley Knight for *Kennedy's Children*. Streep did win awards from the Outer Critics Circle and Theatre World, however.

Late in the spring of 1976 she was with the New Phoenix Repertory Company as Edith in *Secret Service*, a revival of the William Gillette play about Civil War espionage. This production was taped for PBS-TV's "Great Performances" series, where it was shown on January 12, 1977. She spent the summer of 1976 with the New York Shakespeare Festival at the open-air Delacorte Theatre in Central Park. She was Princess Katherine in *Henry V* and Isabella in *Measure for Measure*. In the cast of the latter play was John Cazale, who became Meryl's live-in lover until his untimely death of bone cancer at age forty-two on March 12, 1978. Meanwhile, she was among the off-screen voices in CBS-TV's "Everybody Rides the Carousel" (September 10, 1976), a three-part, ninety-minute animated study of psychiatrist Erik H. Erikson's eight stages of the life cycle. During the winter of 1977, she was Dunyasha in Chekhov's *The Cherry Orchard* at the Vivian Beaumont Theatre. On March 16, 1977, she suffered as Sharon Miller, wife of a professional hockey player (Michael Moriarty) charged with on-ice manslaughter in THE DEADLIEST SEASON, a CBS-TV movie. Three days before the opening of *Happy End* at the Chelsea Theatre Center, Meryl was called in as a replacement for Shirley Knight, fired reportedly because she could not properly sing the role of Hallelujah Lil, a Salvation Army woman caught in a frolic with Chicago gangsters. In April 1977 the production moved to Broadway, where it played for nine weeks, with Meryl's singing of "Surabaya Johnny" declared "a highlight of the season."

Her first theatrical film role was that of Anne Marie, the brunette, flighty Fifth Avenue friend of Lillian Hellman (Jane Fonda) in JULIA (1977), for which she was selected by *Screen World* as a "promising new actor" of 1977. She was asked to play Blanche DuBois in a proposed television production of *A Streetcar Named Desire*, but had to turn down the offer due to a previous commitment. The project was shelved, but was resurrected in 1984 when Ann-Margret took the role for ABC-TV.

The previous commitment was "Holocaust," a nine-and-a-half-hour miniseries for NBC-TV shown in April 1978, in which she joined a huge cast in the story of the systematic extermination of millions by the Nazis. Meryl, in the role of a Roman Catholic married to a Jew, won an Emmy Award along with a special accolade from the B'nai B'rith Anti-Defamation League. She rejoined the Phoenix Theatre group for the ninety-minute PBS-TV presentation (May 24, 1978) of "Uncommon Women and Others," as Leilah, one of a group of graduates of a women's college who meet years later to evaluate their lives. The summer of 1978 saw her at the Delacorte Theatre in *The Taming of the Shrew* as Katherine, opposite Raul Julia as Petruchio. *The New York Times* found her "hysterically funny."

In September 1978 Meryl married sculptor Donald Gummer, a friend of her brother, Harry III, in New York City. The union produced son Henry in 1979, daughter Mary Willa ("Mamie") in 1984, and daughter Grace in 1986. (In December 1990 Meryl announced that she was pregnant with the couple's fourth child, due in the summer of 1991. Louisa Jacobson Gummer was born on June 12, 1991.)

Streep was scheduled to star as Alice in a musical version of *Alice in Wonderland* at the Public Theatre on December 27, 1978. However, the show was canceled by Joseph Papp, so that further work could be done on its book. Instead, Meryl performed the singing role three times during Christmas week at the Public in concert form. During this holiday season, her second theatrical movie was in release—THE DEER HUNTER (1978). Her performance as a young woman living in a Pennsylvania steel town before, during, and after the Vietnam War prompted one critic to call her "pluperfect." Meryl was nominated for a Best Supporting Actress Academy Award, but lost to Maggie Smith (CALIFORNIA SUITE). However, she did win the approval of the National Society of Film Critics. In MANHATTAN (1979) she was the ex-wife of Woody Allen, turned lesbian and threatening to expose their married life in a book. In the spring of 1979 she was back with

Meryl Streep and Woody Allen in MANHATTAN (1979).

Joseph Papp and the Public Theatre in the all-female cast of *Taken in Marriage*, as the five-times-married and cynical Andrea.

American politics was the subject of Meryl's next feature, THE SEDUCTION OF JOE TYNAN (1979), scripted by Alan Alda. In it she was the southern lawyer mistress of the title character (Alda). Meryl claims to have patterned her drawl after Dinah Shore's. This was closely followed by KRAMER VS. KRAMER (1979), which dealt with the breakup of a marriage and the wife's (Streep) return eighteen months later to retrieve her son (Justin Henry) from her ex-husband (Dustin Hoffman), who prefers to fight for him in court rather than give him up. Critic Judith Crist summed up the movie with "Thanks to the stars . . . what might have been an old-fashioned tearjerker emerges as a sophisticated contemporary domestic drama." Meryl won Best Supporting Actress awards from the National Board of Review, the New York Film Critics, and the Los Angeles Film Critics, as well as a Golden Globe. Nominated for five major Academy Awards, the film won Best Picture, Best Actor for Hoffman, and Best Supporting Actress for Meryl. Her April 14, 1980, acceptance speech was "Holy mackerel!" However, backstage, later, she said, "I think the supporting actress category is the most spectacular one to get nominated in—because you support."

On syndicated television on January 10, 1981, she repeated her Katherine in *The Taming of the Shrew* in a special entitled "Kiss Me, Petruchio." Meryl crossed the Atlantic by ship with husband and child for the filming of THE FRENCH LIEUTENANT'S WOMAN (1981). Harold Pinter's adaptation of John Fowles' novel is actually two stories: one set in the Victorian period, the other contemporary, with Meryl and Jeremy Irons portraying characters of both eras. Critic Roger Ebert credited Meryl as "remarkable" in this double performance, in which she was "offhandedly contemporary one moment, and then gloriously, theatrically Victorian the next." Earning her third Oscar nomination, this time as Best Actress, she lost to Katharine Hepburn (ON GOLDEN POND).

On January 16, 1982, she reprised her Alice in Wonderland characterization on NBC-TV in "Alice at the Palace," ninety minutes of story and song. In December 1982 she had two motion pictures in release. The first, STILL OF THE NIGHT, was a failed murder mystery co-starring Roy Scheider as a psychiatrist with Meryl as the suspected killer of one of his patients. The second, SOPHIE'S CHOICE, cast Meryl as a Polish-Catholic woman who has survived internment in a World War II concentration camp. Having buried her past, she has relocated to Brooklyn where she encounters an anguished Jew (Kevin Kline), with whom she falls in love. For her telling portrayal in this overlong production, Meryl won several acting awards, including the Best Actress Award of the New York Film Critics. She also became the thirteenth actress to win a second Oscar, along with being the fourth to have won in both the Best Actress and Best Supporting Actress categories. Receiving the statuette from presenter Sylvester Stallone, she said, "I'm so incredibly thrilled, right down to my toes. I'm going to be one of those people who mention a lot of names"—and she did.

Her depiction of Karen Silkwood, who fought for better safety conditions at the Kerr-McGee plutonium plant and lost her life under mysterious circumstances, earned

Meryl yet another Oscar nomination as Best Actress for the fact-based SILKWOOD (1983). However, she lost to Shirley MacLaine (TERMS OF ENDEARMENT). Streep was reunited with Robert De Niro, with whom she had worked in THE DEER HUNTER, as a married woman who becomes involved romantically with a married man in FALLING IN LOVE (1984). It remains one of her simplest yet most effective characterizations. She was one of many stars to participate in IN OUR HANDS (1985), a ninety-minute film about the survivors of the Hiroshima and Nagasaki atomic bombings of World War II. On March 10, 1985, she narrated the PBS-TV special "The Velveteen Rabbit." (This was one of several children's stories that Meryl would narrate for videocassette and audiocassette release.) In PLENTY (1985), shot in England, she played a Britisher who had fought with the French Resistance only to find the moral climate of postwar Britain not to her liking. *People* magazine noted, "At first it's off-putting to hear Streep trot out the la-de-dah English accent she used with mixed results in THE FRENCH LIEUTENANT'S WOMAN to play a character meant to symbolize Britain's decline." PLENTY was not a box-office success.

Another six months were spent abroad, this time in the heat of Kenya, filming the $32 million OUT OF AFRICA (1985) with Robert Redford. (His salary was $6 million compared to Meryl's $3 million, although she has more screen time than he.) Based on the 1938 memoirs of Karen Blixen, published under the name Isak Dinesen, about her years as manager of a Kenya coffee plantation beginning in 1914, the film has breathtaking cinematography, excellent costumes, a beautiful John Barry score, and Meryl's authentic Danish accent. Meryl's second movie (KRAMER VS. KRAMER was the first) to rank as one of the top ten grossing films of its year, OUT OF AFRICA had domestic box-office revenues of $87 million. It also earned Streep another Oscar nomination as Best Actress, but she lost to Geraldine Page (THE TRIP TO BOUNTIFUL). Of her visit to the Kenya set, *Playgirl* magazine reporter Kathy Eldon wrote that Meryl "was admired by everyone who came in contact with her, delighting extras with her willingness to chat and her unfailingly pleasant manner" despite the heat.

In 1986 Meryl and her husband purchased a Connecticut farm and HEARTBURN opened. As far back as April 1984, *Esquire* magazine had wondered if Mike Nichols' choice of Meryl to play the "very funny, very Jewish heroine" in this picture was a wise one. Goldie Hawn, more adept as a Jewish American princess, was also in contention, but Nichols held out for the very busy Meryl, whom he had directed in SILKWOOD. The screenplay is based on the novel by Nora Ephron, said to be an accounting of her life with Carl Bernstein, the famed reporter who helped expose the Watergate scandal. Jack Nicholson replaced Mandy Patinkin—who was fired from the project—as Meryl's co-star. In her first attempt at screen comedy, critic Roger Ebert found Meryl to be "dowdy and querulous" and observed that with the names of Streep and Nicholson "on the marquee you'd figure the movie would have to be electrifying. But it's not." Wearing unflattering black wigs, Meryl may have appeared drab because she was pregnant during the filming.

"A must-see film" (ABC-TV's Joel Siegel); "The movie has no momentum—[it is] like a death sentence" (*The New Yorker* magazine's Pauline Kael). Such were the vastly conflicting reviews of IRONWEED (1987), which reunited Streep and Jack Nicholson as

Depression-era bums in Albany, New York. Despite conflicting opinions about the lengthy (144-minute), downbeat story, the critics were unanimous that the acting by the two leads was superb. As Helen Archer, a has-been singer, Meryl had a big bar scene in which she sang "He's My Pal," a 1905 Tin Pan Alley tune chosen by William Kennedy, who adapted his 1983 Pulitzer Prize–winning novel for the screen. Along with Nicholson, Streep was Oscar-nominated. However, she lost to Cher (MOONSTRUCK).

"I always look for something that grabs my heart," said Meryl after signing to portray Lindy Chamberlain in A CRY IN THE DARK (1988). After reading the book and determining how she would play her, she met the real Lindy, called by some "The Most Hated Woman in Australia." After the meeting, Streep admitted, "My whole approach will have to change. . . . [Lindy] is much harder than I imagined." Wearing a number of black wigs, Meryl gave perhaps the best performance of her career to date as the mother of baby Azaria who disappears from the family tent during a clear night in the Northern Territory. *Time* magazine found the feature "a hair-raising, excruciating story" because of "the uncompromising artistry of Streep and director Fred Schepisi." Although the picture was not popular with moviegoers, Meryl was honored with the New York Film Critics Award as Best Actress, as well as that given at the Cannes Film Festival. Nominated again for an Oscar, she lost to Jodie Foster (THE ACCUSED). This led *TV Guide* magazine to comment, "The Academy, over the past few years, has felt that nominating her is all it wants to do." The Australian film industry, on October 10, 1989, named Meryl best actress for her work in A CRY IN THE DARK.

Jerry Weintraub Productions, owners of the film rights to the Broadway smash hit musical *Evita*, commissioned director Oliver Stone to prepare the screen version. Stone first sought Madonna to star, but when she refused to audition, Meryl was asked to do the role, which she accepted without question. Streep became committed to the role, with the part of Che Guevara likely to be played by Mandy Patinkin, who had played it in the Broadway production. Meryl reported that she would do her own singing, saying she was "wild about the idea; I have wanted to play the part for ten years." Prerecording was set to start in Los Angeles in November 1989, with location filming to commence the following February in Seville, Spain. In September 1989, however, Meryl withdrew suddenly from the project because of "exhaustion." Plans for EVITA the film were shelved—temporarily—until 1990, when Stone too was out of the project and when Madonna was being seriously considered to portray the Argentinian.

In March 1989, although generally publicity shy, Meryl was in the nation's capital as spokesperson for the Natural Resources Defense Council on behalf of Mothers and Others for Pesticide Limits. She did a PBS-TV spot on the subject with daughter Mamie, and when asked if activism was to play a large part in her future, Meryl responded, "Oh, God, no. This is my first time—and my last. I just want to be able to go and shop with a clear conscience." In May 1989 she gained yet another award, this time from the National Mother's Day Committee, which named her "Outstanding Mother" of the year. (She claimed her mother was her inspiration.) In September 1989, on PBS-TV, she narrated a study of America's efforts to develop "energy choices that are safe, reliable, affordable, and environmentally sound." The November 1989 issue of *American Film* magazine reported on a critics poll that named Meryl the best actress of the 1980s. On November 23, 1989, *The New York Times* contained a full-page ad demanding a halt to U.S. military aid to El Salvador. Among the many celebrities who signed the declaration was Meryl.

Meryl had turned down an offer to star with Kevin Kline in the comedy I LOVE YOU TO DEATH (1990) in order to play Mary Fisher, the pink-clad authoress with a pink mansion who steals away the husband (Ed Begley, Jr.) of a chunky proletarian (Roseanne Barr). With two such diverse leading ladies, it was expected that SHE-DEVIL (1989) would be a major hit. Despite positive reviews for Streep's outrageously satirical performance (*Time* magazine applauded Meryl's "delicious style" and noted, "The great gray lady of movie drama brings her precise acting tools to a comedy of manners"), but far less positive ones for Barr in her screen debut, SHE-DEVIL proved a box-office disappointment. It grossed only $14,997,150 at the box office in its first thirteen weeks of domestic distribution. But at least SHE-DEVIL demonstrated that the versatile Streep was indeed adept at screen farce.

On February 21, 1990, on CBS-TV, Meryl presented a Lifetime Achievement Award to ex-Beatle Paul McCartney at the 32nd Annual Grammy Awards; *Daily Variety* commented on her "school girlish gushing." Streep narrated two Beatrix Potter tales for children on the April 9, 1990, Showtime–Cable presentation "Peter Rabbit and Mr. Jeremy Fisher" and gave of her time and energy to help save planet earth in ABC-TV's "The Earth Day Special" (April 22, 1990). On TBS–Cable she narrated the hour-long special "Arctic Refuge: A Vanishing Wilderness" (May 27, 1990), which investigated the threat posed to Alaska's Arctic National Wildlife Refuge by an oil development drilling plan. At the Greek Theatre in Los Angeles on September 13, 1990, Meryl joined Robin Williams, Goldie Hawn, Cher, and others in an evening of "music and comedy" to aid the environment and to benefit California's November ballot initiative 128, called "Big Green." The show was taped and shown on ABC-TV on September 19, 1990, as "An Evening with. . . ."

In POSTCARDS FROM THE EDGE (1990), adapted from Carrie Fisher's partly autobiographical novel, Meryl starred as Suzanne Vale, the actress daughter of Doris Mann (Shirley MacLaine), an overpowering, egotistical musical comedy movie star of the 1950s. Suzanne, in an effort to block out her mother and the tension of being in the spotlight, has turned to drugs and alcohol. Directed by Mike Nichols, Meryl got the opportunity within POSTCARDS FROM THE EDGE to sing "I'm Checkin' Out," her rendition of which *Rolling Stone* magazine called "surprisingly affecting." *Playboy* magazine gave the movie four stars and rated it "electric filmmaking, Academy Award quality," while David Ansen (*Newsweek* magazine) noted that "Meryl's too old to play Shirley's daughter, but they're both so good, you begin to forget that." *Daily Variety* praised Meryl for being "Refreshingly guileless and unaffected in a role that requires casual clothing and no accent." Richard Corliss (*Time* magazine) enthused of Meryl, "she proves again she is our finest comedienne; like the late Irene Dunne, she adds spin and sizzle to every bon mot. . . . And she can sing too, bringing her uniquely precise passion to ballads and down-home rave-ups." MacLaine, questioned about her co-star on the syndicated "Entertainment Tonight" (September 21, 1990), responded, not unkindly, "I'm not sure I ever met her; she comes to work as the character." Within its first three weeks of domestic release, POSTCARDS FROM THE EDGE grossed an impressive $27,477,417.

Sticking to comedy, Meryl next appeared in DEFENDING YOUR LIFE (1991), with Albert Brooks as director, writer, and co-star as a man who, in the afterlife, must defend his earthly ways. Meanwhile, Streep was seen as host of the ten-part PBS-TV series "Race to Save the Planet," which bowed on October 4, 1990. Based on the Worldwide Institute's *State of the World* reports, the weekly hour-long program probed the focal ecological concerns challenging Earth today. Roy Scheider narrated the series.

Reportedly now at a salary level of $4 million per film, Meryl Streep is at the top of Hollywood's list of actresses, and she bristles at the very mention of male names such as Bruce Willis, Sylvester Stallone, Harrison Ford, and others who command $10 million or more per project. Denouncing the money-making action films, she says, "I think we who don't go to DIE HARD II and ROBOCOP and DAYS OF THUNDER and THE TERMINATOR... need to make noise about what we do want to see. Until then, we'll get more of the same." She finds it uncomfortable as well as unbelievable that young women will go to see a Cinderella tale like PRETTY WOMAN (1990) four or five times. "There are a lot of women screenwriters and a lot of women in development, but I guess because those women want to make it past the glass ceiling, maybe they think they have to say, 'Do DIE HARD II. Now let me be vice president.'" She added, "If the Martians landed and did nothing but go to the movies this year, they would come to the fair conclusion that the chief occupation of women on Earth is hooking. And, I don't mean rugs." In summing up her criticism of today's movie industry, she says, "The crackling wit and stylish verbal surprise which characterized films of the past has been crushed under the wheels of blockbusters."

When asked about her acting style, Meryl has said, "I have no method. I've never read Stanislavsky. I have a smattering of things I've learned from different teachers, but nothing I can put into a valise and open it up and say, 'Now which one would you like?' Nothing I can count on, and that makes it more dangerous. But then the danger makes it more exciting." Regarding fame, Streep speculates, "It seems to me when you become famous, a lot of your energy goes into maintaining what you had before you were famous, maintaining your sense of observation, being able to look at other people. If they take away your observation powers, you're lost."

Filmography

The Deadliest Season (CBS-TV, 3/16/77)

Julia (20th–Fox, 1977)

The Deer Hunter (Univ, 1978)

Manhattan (UA, 1979)

The Seduction of Joe Tynan (Univ, 1979)

Kramer Vs. Kramer (Col, 1979)

The French Lieutenant's Woman (UA, 1981)

Still of the Night (MGM/UA, 1982)

Sophie's Choice (Univ, 1982)

Silkwood (20th–Fox, 1983)

Falling in Love (Par, 1984)

In Our Hands (Libra Cinema 5, 1985)

Plenty (20th–Fox, 1985)

Out of Africa (Univ, 1985)

Heartburn (Par, 1986)
Ironweed (Tri-Star, 1987)
A Cry in the Dark (WB, 1988)

She-Devil (Orion, 1989)
Postcards from the Edge (Col, 1990)
Defending Your Life (WB, 1991)

Television Series

Holocaust (NBC, 4/16/78–4/19/78) [miniseries]

Race to Save the Planet (PBS, 1990) (host only)

Broadway Plays

Trelawny of the Wells (1975) (revival)
27 Wagons Full of Cotton/A Memory of Two
    Mondays (1976) (revival)

Secret Service (1976) (revival)
The Cherry Orchard (1976) (revival)
Happy End (1977) (revival)

Album Discography

The Tailor of Gloucester (Windham Hill WH-
    0710)
The Tale of Peter Rabbit with The Tales of Mr.

Jeremy Fisher and Two Bad Mice (Windham
    Hill WH-0708)
The Velveteen Rabbit (Dancing Cat DC-3007)

PATRICK SWAYZE

> "The spoiler in life now is the isolation and loneliness. You wind up
> trying to create a world for yourself because you don't have the real
> one anymore. You can't go anywhere."
>
> —*GQ* magazine, February 1989

PATRICK SWAYZE'S TWO GREAT FEARS IN LIFE ARE LOSING HIS WIFE
and "that I'm not good enough for what's happening to me." The first concern can be
controlled only by himself. The other is up to his fans, many of whom have seen his
sexually charged hit dance movie, DIRTY DANCING (1987), a hundred times or more.
Women adore him; men are intimidated by him. With his musculature garbed in tight
jeans and T-shirt, Patrick was named by *US* magazine as Hollywood's "hardest-working,
most earnest sex symbol." He exudes a sensuality that seems quite natural. Because of his
swivel-hipped dance movements, he has been publicized as the Elvis Presley of the 1990s,
while his outdoorsy, cowboy-like face encourages comparisons to Kurt Russell's. Patrick
Swayze's many occupations include acting, singing, dancing, writing and performing
music, and breeding horses. According to Kenny Kingston, psychic to Hollywood stars,
Patrick's activities are guided "from the other side" by his late father. Patrick publicly
mourned his loss by crying involuntarily during a Barbara Walters interview on national
television. This display of human emotion, he feels, made him "a bigger star than anything
else I've ever done," establishing that this is a macho man of deep sensitivities.

Patrick Wayne Swayze was born on Monday, August 18, 1952 (some sources say
1954) in Houston, Texas, the second child of Jesse Wayne "Buddy" Swayze and his wife,
Patsy. He was preceded in birth by a sister, Vicki, and followed by brothers Don and Sean.
A fifth child, Bambi, a Korean orphan, was adopted by the Swayzes when she was four
years old. Jesse, a drafting engineer for an oil company, worked with bigoted rednecks, but
did not share in their denunciations of people who were different. Patsy Swayze, a dance
instructor, had her own studio where she gave lessons in ballet and would, in 1980,
choreograph URBAN COWBOY. She got Patrick into ballet as early as age two, later
involving him with violin and guitar lessons as well as children's theater. In school, because
he owned leotards and danced, "I was alienated from other kids. Being a dancer just didn't
work in redneck country." He was called a sissy by his bully classmates, and if it had not
been for his father, who called him "Little Buddy," which was printed on a jacket
matching his father's "Big Buddy," his life would have been spent in utter loneliness.

At the age of thirteen, while a student at Black Junior High School, he was ambushed and beaten behind a church by five boys. A few days later, in the school gym, his father arranged that he fight each boy individually with gloves. Patrick defeated all five, but was then taunted by others eager to determine if he was really that tough. Soon after the beating incident, he quit dancing to become involved in gymnastics, track, diving, swimming, karate, and football. At Waltrip High School, although he starred in whatever plays were produced, he was also the football team's star quarterback, as well as the recipient of trophies for his gymnastic prowess. His peers still picked on him, but he was able now to defend himself. He remembered these years later by saying, "Now when I go back to Texas, I see the same guys who used to beat me up, walking around in sweat-stained T-shirts with big beer bellies."

While in high school, he sustained a major injury to his left leg, and it was at first thought that the leg would have to be amputated due to staph infection in the knee. "My life was screwed at that moment," he has said. "I thought it was all over. That's when I started smoking." Through treatment, the leg mended. However, he still experiences problems with the knee; periodically, to relieve the pressure, he has to have it drained of fluid mixed with blood.

In 1970, when he was eighteen, Patrick entered San Jacinto College at Pasadena, Texas, on a gymnastics scholarship. There he acquired the nicknames "Crazy Swayze" (because of his Casanova-type activities in trying to juggle a bevy of girlfriends at the same time) and "Troph" (for his many trophies). When he was twenty, on a visit to his mother's studio he met a fifteen-year-old dance student named Lisa Haapaniemi, who became his confidante. Over the years, the friendship turned to love and they were married in June 1974. That same summer he joined the Disney-on Parade touring company for one year. Next, he went to New York City, where Lisa joined him within a short time. They both trained with the Harkness and Joffrey ballet companies. Patrick danced with the Eliot Feld dance company before joining the Broadway cast of *Goodtime Charley*, which opened at the Palace Theatre on March 3, 1975. This musical about the Dauphin of France (Joel Grey) and Joan of Arc (Ann Reinking) closed after 104 performances. (For this production, in which he was a chorus dancer, Swayze was billed as Pat Swayze.) This was followed by dancing the part of Riff in a short-run off-Broadway revival of *West Side Story*. In 1978 Swayze took over the part of Danny Zuko in Broadway's long-playing *Grease*. He was forced to leave the show when his leg began to give him problems. His most harrowing experience in Manhattan was a subway attack by two would-be muggers with knives, whom he beat off.

Early in 1979 Patrick and Lisa moved to Los Angeles, hoping to get into films. They both took acting lessons and Lisa shortened her name to Niemi. He found a supporting part in SKATETOWN, U.S.A. (1979), which *US* magazine dubbed "a bubble-brained ode to Seventies disco done on wheels." As Ace, the leader of the rink's bad guys, Patrick donned roller skates and a pair of very tight black leather pants. Through his mother, also in southern California at work on URBAN COWBOY, he met people within the industry but received little if any assistance in obtaining work. For the next two years, he and Lisa were forced to live spartanly, with just a few acting roles coming his way. During the 1980–1981 season of "M*A*S*H," Patrick appeared in the "Blood Brothers" segment. For an ABC-TV movie he supported baseball player John Ritter in THE COMEBACK KID (April 11, 1980). Eighteen months later, in the CBS-TV movie RETURN OF THE REBELS (October 17, 1981), he had another supporting role as a motorcyclist. Ten months after that, however, he was given second billing in an ABC-TV movies/series pilot, THE RENEGADES (August 11, 1982). He had the part of Bandit, one of seven streetwise toughs recruited as undercover investigative cops. "The Renegades" was picked up as a series in 1983, but lasted just a month. *Variety* dismissed the clichéd series as "'Mod Squad' Plus Four." Meanwhile, in 1982, back in Texas, Jesse Swayze died of a massive heart attack while jogging. Patrick has never gotten over having lost his best friend without being able to tell him goodbye and thank you.

Francis Ford Coppola's THE OUTSIDERS (1983), about warring street kids in mid-1960s Tulsa, Oklahoma, is best remembered for its cast of unknowns who went on to achieve individual, respectable screen renown. Fourth-billed Patrick, at thirty-one, was by far the eldest over Matt Dillon and Rob Lowe, both nineteen; Ralph Macchio, twenty-two; C. Thomas Howell, sixteen; and Emilio Estevez and Tom Cruise, both twenty-one. (In March 1990, a dramatic Fox Network series would evolve from the story, with Boyd Kestner as Darrel Curtis, the role created by Patrick.) At the end of 1983, Patrick was in support of veteran actors Gene Hackman and Robert Stack as a Vietnam veteran induced to join a Laos invasion task force in UNCOMMON VALOR. *Variety* acknowledged of this actioner, "On the plus side, the picture does resort to less foolishness than usually required to enlist a ragtag band of soldiers on an impossible mission."

In 1984 Patrick and Lisa performed in Los Angeles in their co-written autobiographical play, *Without a Word*, about their lives together as struggling ballet dancers. They hoped to produce it as a low-budget art film supported, at least morally, by Gene Kelly. On July 6, 1984, NBC-TV finally aired OFF SIDES, a TV movie completed four years earlier. It starred Tony Randall as a bearded guru (!), while Patrick was ninth-billed as a football player. On the big screen in the unappreciated GRAND-VIEW, U.S.A. (1984), audiences were treated to seeing Patrick as a macho construction worker in love with a very independent Jamie Lee Curtis. The small town romantic drama featured a musical dream sequence co-choreographed by Patrick and Lisa. The controversial RED DAWN (1984) presented the still-intriguing concept of a Russian/Cuban paratroop invasion of the

Patrick Swayze in RED DAWN (1984).

United States, but fell far short of suspenseful action. Patrick played the leader of a high school guerrilla force hidden in the Colorado hills. *People* magazine noted, "Patrick Swayze . . . and Charlie Sheen as his younger brother share one astonishing scene in which one of their group is executed for being a spy." One of the other young rebels in RED DAWN was played by Jennifer Grey, the daughter of Patrick's *Goodtime Charley* star, Joel Grey.

"North and South" (ABC-TV) earned a "Heartily recommended" rating from *TV Guide* magazine because "Love, sex, politics, virtue and depravity keep the pot boiling." The twelve-hour miniseries, telecast in two-hour segments over six nights in November 1985, was an adaptation of the best-selling John Jakes novel, made at a cost of $25 million. Patrick, as South Carolinian Orry Main, co-starred with James Read as George Hazard of Pennsylvania whose lives interweave during the restless period (1842–1861) leading to the Civil War. To boost the ratings for this mainstream costume vehicle, Elizabeth Taylor, Gene Kelly, Robert Mitchum, and other major stars provided splashy little cameos.

"He fought for what he believed in. He lived for the woman he loved." So read the ads announcing "North and South, Book II" (1986), the $28.5 million sequel that took the original characters, along with new guest stars (Olivia de Havilland, James Stewart, Linda Evans), through the war that divided the states. Another twelve-hour miniseries, it was shown on six nights that May. *Variety* reported, "Less florid than 'North and South, Book I,' with the melodrama soft-pedaled . . . second marathon settles for sudsy affairs, several stiff portrayals, some hokum and strenuous battle scenes. . . . [James] Read and Swayze as George and Orry continue their staunch play-acting, though the eccentrics are the ones that garner the attention." Prior to this sequel, he supported Rob Lowe, one of his THE OUTSIDERS sidekicks, as a hockey player in the mediocre YOUNGBLOOD (1986). On November 6, 1986, Swayze appeared in the "Life on Death Row" episode of NBC-TV's "Amazing Stories." A year earlier, Patrick and Lisa purchased a five-acre ranch in the foothills of the Los Angeles–area San Gabriel Mountains which they named Rancho Bizzaro. Complete with recording studio, the property also housed thirteen horses, two Rhodesian Ridgeback dogs, four cats, two poodles, and numerous chickens, peacocks, and peahens.

On the release of DIRTY DANCING (1987), New York City's vocal mayor, Edward I. Koch, was quoted as saying, "Swayze is only slightly better than my brother, who has a bum knee." Of course, Hizzoner did not know that Patrick too had a bad knee, which, during the course of filming at Mountain Lake (Virginia—representing the Catskills of 1963), required needle-draining at least once. Costing $5 million to produce, DIRTY DANCING was the sleeper hit of the year. Its premise focused on Baby (Jennifer Grey), the bright, well-bred daughter of a Jewish physician (Jerry Orbach) who, over the course of a summer romance with a gigolo dance instructor (Swayze) at an upstate New York resort, develops self-respect and maturity. For the street-tough dancer/stud, life now seems less vicious and offers more options. *Hollywood Studio* magazine reported elaborately: "Just as Elvis became a synonym for the smouldering sensuality of that wild, new beat known as rock 'n' roll, Patrick Swayze had come to epitomize the waist-clutching, groin-grinding intensity of touch-dancing that just doesn't get any hotter or 'dirtier.'" The musical romance earned more than $50 million in box-office grosses by year's end. By 1990, the worldwide take was estimated at over $120 million. The soundtrack album, containing Patrick's composition "She's Like the Wind," sold over three million copies, with his single recording of the song reaching the top five on the music charts. His singing voice was described by one critic as "molten honey." In addition, twenty-five thousand copies of a poster of him in dance repose were bought immediately after the movie's release. His salary for the picture was $200,000, a figure that escalated to $1 million the following year when he said, "Suddenly everybody in the world wants to be your buddy." For his performance as the macho heel-with-a-heart in DIRTY DANCING, Patrick was nominated for a Best Actor Golden Globe by the Hollywood Foreign Press Association. (In October 1988, CBS-TV launched a short-lived weekly series based on DIRTY DANCING with Patrick Cassidy inheriting the part of sexy Johnny Castle.)

STEEL DAWN (1987), filmed on location in Africa, followed the hit DIRTY DANCING three months later. Patrick and his wife co-starred as a futuristic warrior and the lady he protects. The abysmal adventure yarn died at the box office within two weeks.

In 1988 Patrick and Lisa formed their own production company, Troph. He was offered $10 million to promote an exercise video and a cologne called "Patrick," but turned the deal down. It was also in 1988 that he cried on camera during a Barbara Walters TV interview and starred as TIGER WARSAW (1988), a mixed-up junkie who returns home to sort out the shambles of his life. The *Los Angeles Times* found this flop "paced like a funeral." He made a guest appearance on ABC-TV's "World's Greatest Stunts" (November 3, 1988), a tribute to Hollywood stuntmen, and was courted unsuccessfully by Pepsi-Cola to plug its products (he had insisted that Lisa also appear in the ads, in which he suggested they dance).

Celebrity photographer Marc Raboy in January 1989 named Patrick as having the best body in his third annual list of Fabulous Features of Famous Faces. *Video Review* magazine's critic wrote: "Let's be blunt! ROAD HOUSE is corny, juvenile, exploitative, misogynistic, homophobic, brutally violent and just plain stupid. *But* I love it." Released in June 1989, this modern-day western contained a song ("Cliff's Edge") Swayze had written, as well as eight sustained sequences of his shirtless torso. He was Dalton, the best barroom bouncer in the business, who almost meets his match in a small Missouri town where he has been hired to bring "law and order" to the rough-and-tumble Double Deuce road house. (His motto is "It's my way or the highway.") In the process, he not only overcomes the local sadistic extortionist (Ben Gazzara) but also wins the love of a comely blonde doctor (Kelly Lynch). After six weeks, the senseless action picture had grossed $25.6 million domestically, considered only a modest sum in 1989.

During the summer of 1989, Patrick spent thousands of dollars recording songs from the Broadway musical hit *Evita* in the hope of being chosen by director Oliver Stone to co-star (as Che Guevara) with Meryl Streep in the long-announced film version. The project was later shelved yet again. In October 1989 the Swayzes bought a getaway home in Lake Arrowhead, California. That same month his latest entry, NEXT OF KIN (1989), was in release. Photographed in Chicago, it was a ludicrous tale of fearless city cop Swayze and some righteous mountain folk armed with bows and arrows combatting urban mobsters in a showdown! Critic Gene Siskel judged it "a truly boring film," while Siskel's TV critic cohort, Roger Ebert, labeled it as "Desperation time at the old movie factory." NEXT OF KIN grossed a disappointing $15,362,628 in its first five weeks of domestic release. The *Tacoma* (Washington) *News Tribune* observed of Patrick's faltering career, "First ROAD HOUSE and now this. And this makes ROAD HOUSE look like OUT OF AFRICA." In November 1989, when he was named by *US* magazine as one of the sexiest men alive, Patrick responded with, "You can't believe the hype for one second or you're a dead man. I don't wanna be a sex symbol. I wanna be an actor."

In February 1990 it was reported that Lisa had suffered a miscarriage, her first pregnancy since their decision a few years earlier to begin a family. Also in February, Patrick was a co-presenter with Paula Abdul at the thirty-second annual Grammy Award ceremonies. It was no surprise that there might be a forthcoming DIRTY DANCING II, with both Patrick and co-star Jennifer Grey reprising their original roles. This time his fee was estimated to be $5 million. Having held out for a year before committing himself to the sequel, he claims that it was actress Shirley MacLaine who convinced him that he "owed it to the public."

On May 6, 1990, in the "Roy Orbison Tribute" televised on Showtime–Cable, Patrick dueted with Larry Gatlin on "Love Hurts," and on July 5, 1990, on ABC-TV, viewers watched him honored as a recipient of The Gypsy Award for his DIRTY DANCING on the sixty-minute "America's Dance Honors." "I can't believe this is happening," he said, "there are finally awards. . . . Thank you for this."

GHOST, released in July 1990, became the surprise hit of the summer, surpassing blockbuster action movies like TOTAL RECALL, ROBOCOP II, DIE HARD II, and DAYS OF THUNDER. In GHOST, boasting excellent special effects and no four-letter words, Patrick was Sam Wheat, a rising investment banker on Wall Street who is murdered in the street by a would-be mugger (Rick Aviles) in the presence of the woman he loves (Demi Moore). However, Swayze's spirit is not yet permitted to go to heaven. Instead, he remains on earth in ghostly form unable to communicate with his lady love until he finds a fake psychic (Whoopi Goldberg) who, it develops, can actually hear but not see him. With her assistance, the mystery of why he was murdered is unravelled. The *Hollywood Reporter* viewed this fantasy tale of Yuppie romance as a blend "sweetly and skillfully stirred" along, and found that Patrick "exhibits an endearing nice-guy quality, fleshing out the cardboard role to a nicely sympathetic dimension." David Ansen (*Newsweek* magazine) noted, "The hunky Swayze may not be everybody's idea of a banker, dead or alive, but he and [Demi] Moore . . . make sweet chemistry together." Earning $199,942,490 in domestic box-office grosses by mid-December 1990, the movie also provided a much-needed resurrection of Whoopi Goldberg's sagging screen career, launched Demi Moore as a big-time contender, and gave Patrick his second box-office champion. "I can be 100% proud of this film," he told the syndicated "Entertainment Tonight."

While moviegoers stood in long lines to see Swayze's latest hit as well as his often-exposed torso, nude photographs of him taken years before as an artist's model turned up in various tabloids. His face graced the covers of several magazines, including *People*, which ran a six-page Swayze profile.

On September 7, 1990, in Los Angeles at the Wiltern Theatre, he joined many other celebrities in raising funds for the AIDS Project Los Angeles' *Commitment to Life IV*. With his Troph Productions, Patrick entered into a two-year, first-look agreement with Twentieth Century–Fox Studios. Janice Yarbrough, formerly a development executive for Sally Field's Fogwood Films, was named to head the new production company. Seemingly reaching in all directions, Patrick and friend Bobby Ochs are partners in the Mulholland Drive Cafe, an eatery located in New York City and North Miami Beach, Florida. In the fall of 1990, while wife Lisa joined the syndicated TV series "Super Force" in the recurring role of a no-nonsense cop, Patrick was announced to star in the forthcoming Troph production of a psychological thriller, DOUBLE FAULT, and was considering starring in VINNIE THE GIVER, about a New York City construction worker who saves a woman from being crushed by a crane. Swayze hosted the October 27, 1990, edition of NBC-TV's "Saturday Night Live," on which he and Lisa performed a Fred Astaire–Ginger Rogers type dance routine.

Released in 1991, POINT BREAK stars Patrick as a surfer (again having the opportunity to expose his body) suspected by the FBI of engineering a series of near-perfect bank robberies. The two FBI agents on his trail will be played by Keanu Reeves and Gary Busey. In choosing screen projects, Swayze says, "I look for power and passion in a script. Can I affect people's lives or make their lives lighter for a moment or make them understand something better through what I do."

In an industry that is notorious for remembering only a star's last production and whether or not it made a lot of money, Patrick Swayze is once again *hot*. He is an emotional man, filled with insecurities that were at one time temporarily healed by alcohol. He believes in living his life for the moment "because that's all you've got." He has said, "If you don't communicate with the people you love, you set yourself up for incredible pain if you lose them" (obviously referring to his father). Although Swayze professes to be "a romantic to the death," he would prefer to be diverse in his screen assignments. "I don't want to be Mr. Romantic Leading Man. I don't want to be the Dance Dude. I don't want to be the Action Guy. If I had to do any one of those all my life, it'd drive me crazy."

Filmography

Skatetown, U.S.A. (Col, 1979)
The Comeback Kid (ABC-TV, 4/11/80)
Return of the Rebels (CBS-TV, 10/17/81)
The Renegades (ABC-TV, 8/11/82)
The Outsiders (WB, 1983)
Uncommon Valor (Par, 1983)
Off Sides (NBC-TV, 7/6/84) [made in 1980]
Grandview, U.S.A. (CBS Theatrical Films, 1984) (also co-choreographer)

Red Dawn (MGM/UA, 1984)
Youngblood (MGM/UA, 1986)
Dirty Dancing (Vestron, 1987) (also co-song)
Steel Dawn (Vestron, 1987)
Tiger Warsaw (Sony, 1988)
Road House (UA, 1989) (also song)
Next of Kin (WB, 1989)
Ghost (Par, 1990)
Point Break (20th–Fox, 1991)

Television Series

The Renegades (ABC, 1983)
North and South (ABC, 11/3/85; 11/5/85–11/7/85; 11/9/85–11/10/85) [miniseries]

North and South, Book II (ABC, 5/4/86–5/8/86; 5/11/86) [miniseries]

Broadway Plays

Goodtime Charley (1975)

Grease (1978) (replacement)

Album Discography

Dirty Dancing (RCA 6408-1-R8) [ST]

Goodtime Charley (RCA ARL 1-1011) [O/C]

JOHN TRAVOLTA

"You are always dispensable in this business. Even at the height of my career, I was dispensable." —*US* magazine, November 27, 1989

"EVERYTHING CAME TOO EASILY TO HIM" WAS AN OBSERVATION MADE about Robert Redford's character in THE WAY WE WERE (1973). The same might be said of John Travolta. During the late 1970s discomania era, the twenty-two-year-old Travolta became the idol of the nation's teenyboppers. Entranced with his "Welcome Back, Kotter" TV image of the sympathetic underdog, his fans emulated him in dress and style, especially after he starred in the hit movie SATURDAY NIGHT FEVER (1977). By the time he was twenty-five, he was a megalomaniacal miniindustry, complete with managers, advisers, agents, employees, relatives—all bowing to his demands. *Time* magazine predicted that he would be "revered forever in the manner" of Elvis Presley, James Dean, and Marilyn Monroe. However, only four brief years later, he was no longer the celluloid underdog and his fans had outgrown their bell-bottoms. His career took a gigantic slide into the cellar. The process was abetted by his flaunting his costly possessions in an oversaturation of media coverage and by bad judgment in the selection of screen projects. Another six years would pass before, at the age of thirty-five, he made LOOK WHO'S TALKING (1989), which proved to be a sleeper hit. It showed him as a rather portly paternal figure, and suddenly he was "box office" again. Like Richard Gere, he had made a comeback; he was not as red hot as he had been twelve years earlier, but he was at least more than tepid.

John Joseph Travolta was born on Thursday, February 18, 1954, in Englewood, New Jersey, the sixth child of Salvatore "Sam" Travolta, of Italian ancestry, and Helen Burke Travolta, of Irish descent. Sam, a retired semi-professional football player, owned an automobile tire shop, while Helen, formerly a long-distance swimmer and actress, was a drama coach and director of high school stage productions. It was her wish that all her children—Sam, Joey, Ellen, Margaret, Anne, and John—should have careers in the entertainment field. To this end, she involved them early in their lives in working toward that goal. When John was five years old, he was studying with Fred Kelly, brother of Gene, who instructed him in the art of tap dancing. By the time he was seven, John was acting on stage with his mother and sister Ellen. Meanwhile, he also developed a love of airplanes, which would be an abiding interest throughout his life. In 1966, at the age of twelve, he appeared with the Actors Studio Workshop in its production of *Who'll Save the Plowboy?*

At Dwight Morrow High School in Englewood, he was, he has admitted, "only an average student," spending much of his time clowning around and learning all the new dances. His closest friends were drawn from the black community, where his dancing, he felt, was better appreciated. He had a variety of part-time jobs: in a supermarket, a furniture store, and his father's tire shop. However, at the age of sixteen, with his parents' approval, he quit school to pursue an acting career. When his sister was performing in a summer stock production of *Gypsy*, he hung around backstage observing and learning. Later he was in a stock company production of the musical *Bye Bye Birdie*, in which he was spotted by talent agent Bob LeMond. With his parents co-signing, he was put under contract by LeMond and his partner, Lois Zeller. They obtained work for him doing TV commercials in New York City. At age seventeen, he moved to Manhattan, living first with his sister Anne, then moving to his own Lower East Side flat. With earnings from commercials for Mutual of New York Insurance, BandAids, Honda motorcycles, and others, plus occasional small roles in a few TV soap operas, he paid for singing and dancing lessons. He next won a role in the off-Broadway production of *Metaphors*, then opened in *Rain* on March 23, 1972, at the Astor Place Theatre.

He traveled to the West Coast to appear in ABC-TV's "Owen Marshall, Counselor at Law," in the segment "A Piece of God" (December 14, 1972). After that, he was given the minor part of Doody in the first national touring company of *Grease*, one of Broadway's longest-running musicals. Beginning in Boston on December 23, 1972, the tour lasted nine months. During this period he auditioned for the important role of Meadows in the Jack Nicholson feature THE LAST DETAIL (1973), but lost the opportunity to Randy Quaid. He also took time in Los Angeles to film an episode of ABC-TV's "The Rookies," appearing on the segment "Frozen Smoke" (December 1, 1973). Concluding the tour of *Grease*, he took over as Doody on Broadway at the same time that Marilu Henner also played a part in the hit. This was the beginning of a lasting friendship. The chance to play a dancing soldier in the chorus of *Over Here!* was too tempting to reject, so he left *Grease* to open with Patty and Maxene Andrews at the Shubert Theatre on March 6, 1974. (Treat Williams was also in the chorus.) During the nine months of 348 performances, he took flying lessons in his time off and obtained a pilot's license. His agents advised that he reject an offer to act in *The Ritz* (1974) on Broadway in favor of going to Hollywood where he did the "Saturday's Child" episode (December 16, 1974) of CBS-TV's "Medical Center." Then he wore a mask as Danny in his debut motion picture, appearing in the embarrassing horror film THE DEVIL'S RAIN (1975), starring Ida Lupino and William Shatner.

The casting director of THE LAST DETAIL remembered John and recommended him as the dim-witted, blue-collar Brooklyn punk Vinnie Barbarino, leader of the street gang known as the Sweathogs in "Welcome Back, Kotter" (ABC-TV), co-created by the situation comedy's star, Gabriel Kaplan. Following the premiere on September 9, 1975, John gained immediate recognition by the preteen and teenaged viewers for his tough, cool interpretation, which was later changed to a more vulnerable, spiritual character unafraid to reveal his shortcomings. In love with him, young audiences lined up to buy posters of their six-foot, blue-eyed, dimple-chinned dreamboat. His admirers were further thrilled when he sang in a "Kotter" episode, a prelude to his first single recording, "Let Her

In," released May 1, 1976, by Midland International Records. Selling over 800,000 copies, the recording was on the charts for twenty weeks, ranked by *Cashbox* magazine as #5 and by *Billboard* as #10. On July 17, 1976, his album *John Travolta* was released by Midland. During the summer of 1976, while on hiatus from "Kotter," he toured New England as Bo Decker in a stock production of *Bus Stop*. In September 1976 he was a guest performer at the second annual Rock Music Awards ceremonies held at the Hollywood Palladium and telecast live on CBS. Beginning the following month, his Midland single "Whenever I'm Away from You" was charted for six consecutive weeks.

His second motion picture was CARRIE (1976), directed by Brian De Palma from the Stephen King story about a mousy high school girl (Sissy Spacek) with astounding telekinetic powers which are unleashed to the fullest by a cruel **prank** executed by Billy Nolan (John) and his friend (Nancy Allen). Starring in the title role of the ABC-TV movie THE BOY IN THE PLASTIC BUBBLE (November 12, 1976), Travolta played a teenager born without immunities and forced to live free of human contact. Diana Hyland, eighteen years his senior, played his mother in the drama, and the two began a romantic relationship. It was she who urged him to accept a $1 million three-picture pact with producer Robert Stigwood with plans to star him first as a disco dancer. This contract, along with the $1 million annual salary from "Kotter," plus recording royalties, made him a very wealthy young man at the age of twenty-three, but one without privacy. "That's part of the deal," he told *TV Guide* magazine at the time, "and there's no point in griping about it. Nobody, after all, made me become an actor." His Midland recording "All Strung Out Over You," released in February 1977, proved to be another popular single.

In March 1977, having received *Billboard* magazine's Newcomer Award, John was shocked by Diana Hyland's death, in his arms, of cancer, on March 27. "It was a disaster," he admitted later, "and it will always be a disaster. If I had not had the work, I might have gone crazy." He spent seven months in psychoanalysis, and then embraced the teachings of the Church of Scientology to give him confidence and direction. Following her death, he accepted on her behalf an Emmy Award for her performance in THE BOY IN THE PLASTIC BUBBLE. Handed the trophy, he raised the statuette and said emotionally, "Here's to you, Diana, wherever you are."

On September 10, 1977, along with the cast of "Kotter," he was in the thirty-minute ABC-TV comedy special "Sweathog Back-to-School Special" and made a cameo appearance in the October 23, 1977, hour-long special "Gabriel Kaplan Presents the Small Event" (ABC-TV). He was also featured on several occasions in the syndicated TV music broadcasts of "Don Kirshner's Rock Concert."

Called "Disco Heaven" by one critic, SATURDAY NIGHT FEVER premiered in December 1977, telling of a Brooklyn youth who has dreams of grandeur based on his flashy hoofing on the disco floor. Through his new partner (Karen Lynn Gorney) he not only develops a sensitivity to others, but also enlarges his goals beyond the confines of the borough of Brooklyn. John's character, Tony Manero, became a household name among disco lovers, who sought to emulate his style of dancing "The Hustle" while wearing a white suit with vest and open-collared black shirt. SATURDAY NIGHT FEVER became the third highest-grossing R-rated feature film in history, with worldwide grosses of $350 million; its soundtrack recording sold over twenty-five million copies. The film made a star of John Travolta, and its original, contemporary music by Maurice, Barry, and Robin Gibb—known collectively as the Bee Gees—made them the recording industry's biggest names and brought them $50 million. A short-lived ABC-TV series, "Makin' It," adapted from SATURDAY NIGHT FEVER would debut on February 1, 1979, with David Naughton as a hopeful dancer and Ellen Travolta cast in a supporting role in the hope of connecting the series with the hit movie. In February 1978 John was honored as the best actor of 1977 by the National Board of Review, and also received an Academy Award nomination in the same category. When he lost the Oscar to Richard Dreyfuss (THE GOODBYE GIRL), John's mother admitted that she was glad because her son, at twenty-four, was too young for such a victory and, had he won the accolade, he would have "nothing to look forward to."

In March 1978, after losing the lead in DAYS OF HEAVEN (1978) to Richard Gere due to "scheduling conflicts," he formed his own production company, with a two-picture agreement with Orion Pictures at $1 million each. Both AMERICAN GIGOLO (1980) and THE GODFATHER, PART III (1990) were slated for him, but neither would materialize as a Travolta project. *Time* magazine had him on its cover in April 1978, with a five-page spread devoted to "Travolta Fever," and he was photographed for the first of four *Rolling Stone* magazine covers.

The satirical/nostalgic musical *Grease* was still playing on Broadway when the motion picture version debuted in June 1978. Although Henry Winkler had been the producers' first choice, it was John who starred as Danny Zuko, the leader of the high school motorcycle gang who woos a pretty, wholesome new student (Olivia Newton-John). His second film for Stigwood Productions, GREASE eventually became the motion picture industry's #6 all-time box-office hit, grossing $400 million worldwide. The soundtrack recording was extremely popular, while Travolta's single with Newton-John "You're the One That I Want" was #1 on the charts for twenty-four weeks. "Summer Nights," another duet from the movie, reached #5 during its sixteen-week tenure on the charts. Meanwhile, John was pictured on bubble gum cards, GREASE posters, and hundreds of magazine covers, and was one of the first guests to be interviewed by David Frost on the latter's NBC-TV talk show, "Headliners." Michael Eisner, then president of Paramount Pictures, was quoted as saying, "Today, Travolta is the biggest star in the world, bar none. Just the mere fact that he's in a project, or might be in it, turns it into a major event." In October 1978 John dined at the White House with President Jimmy Carter and his family; young Amy Carter was a fan. By 1978 Travolta was seen only occasionally in "Welcome Back, Kotter," agreeing to return beginning in September 1978 for a series of well-publicized farewell appearances. (The sitcom went off the air at the end of the 1978–1979 TV season.)

John's third film under his Stigwood contract was MOMENT BY MOMENT (1978), in which he co-starred with comedian Lily Tomlin who had made a debut splash in NASHVILLE (1975). Written and directed by Tomlin's partner, Jane Wagner, the film cast Travolta as a streetwise hustler who falls in love with a sophisticated, mature woman

(Tomlin) in the plush environs of Los Angeles. He did not dance or sing in the production. Instead, he was pensive most of the time, deliberating on his attraction to the older woman. It was a change of pace that audiences found neither interesting nor believable. Not only did the two stars look enough alike to be siblings, but the script was overly talky and frequently boring. Its failure caused critics to predict that John was finished in motion pictures.

Deeply upset by the reaction to MOMENT BY MOMENT, John secluded himself from the Hollywood mainstream for eighteen months. He hoped to revive his faltering career with URBAN COWBOY (1980), a contemporary western set in Texas and featuring a very modern type of cowboy competition (the bucking mechanical bull at Gilly's dance bar in Pasadena, Texas). On the set, the once-cooperative Travolta surrounded himself with bodyguards to ward off press people and demanded that his dance numbers be videotaped. "I don't know what his personal problems are," said producer Bob Evans, "but he is scared to death." URBAN COWBOY overcame production problems and was released in June 1980. The critics were again unenthralled: "even Travolta, photographed with excessive attention and doing his damnedest to block a Stetson around his Brooklyn persona, cannot subdue all the pretensions of the screenplay" (*People* magazine). It was not a financial blockbuster as anticipated. PRINCE OF THE CITY (1981), a Travolta assignment dealing with urban police corruption, went to Treat Williams. Instead, John was reunited with

Brian De Palma and Nancy Allen in BLOW OUT (1981), playing a movie sound man who unwittingly records a murder. Although praised by critics such as Roger Ebert ("this movie is inhabited by a real cinematic intelligence"), the feature was not appreciated at the box office. Columbia Pictures purchased the screen rights to STAIRWAY TO HEAVEN (1946) as a remake for John, but dropped the project when his popularity sagged. He also lost the lead in AN OFFICER AND A GENTLEMAN (1982), again to Richard Gere, as well as the second lead in NIGHT SHIFT (1982), to Michael Keaton.

Under the debut direction of Sylvester Stallone, John reprised his Tony Manero role in STAYING ALIVE (1983) after seven months of gymnastic training supervised by Stallone. With a well-defined torso above muscular legs, his dancing could not have been better, but the film's dialogue was, at best, banal. The story became

John Travolta in MOMENT BY MOMENT (1978).

bogged down in anticipation of the ROCKY-like finale. Nonetheless, the film grossed $63.8 million domestically and $86.2 million overseas, where both Travolta and Stallone were popular.

John's follow-up to STAYING ALIVE was an unfortunate choice. He selected TWO OF A KIND (1983) with Olivia Newton-John, whose own brief movie career was fast fading. An old-fashioned whimsical romantic comedy involving divine intervention, TWO OF A KIND made little impression on critics or audiences and was a financial disaster. With his diminished status, he was passed over for the male lead in SPLASH (1984), which made a star of Tom Hanks, and turned down a $4 million offer to dance in the movie of A CHORUS LINE (1985) because the part was too small. The compilation documentary THAT'S DANCING! (1985) contained a disco sequence from SATURDAY NIGHT FEVER. In PERFECT (1985), opposite fast-rising Jamie Lee Curtis, Travolta played a reporter for *Rolling Stone* magazine who is investigating health clubs and the possibility of their becoming the disco clubs of the 1980s. *Variety* scoffed, "Set in the world of journalism, pic is guilty of the sins it condemns—superficiality, manipulation and smugness. . . . As an actor, Travolta never really gets a hold on the character and is unconvincing as a reporter or a man of feeling." It was the second consecutive movie defeat for John.

In 1985 Travolta owned three airplanes, a seventeen-acre ranch in Santa Barbara, and three foreign automobiles and a Cadillac, and continued to reject interview requests. He also acquired a new talent agent, Jonathon Krane of M.C.E.G. Agency, and was again invited to the White House in November 1985. This time the Reagans were the hosts and the invitation was at the request of visiting Princess Diana of Great Britain, who danced with Travolta while press photographers captured them for headline stories around the world. A comedy lead in RUNNING SCARED (1986) was offered to John but rejected, and went to Billy Crystal. Instead, John chose to co-star with Tom Conti in an hour-long TV adaptation of Harold Pinter's one-act play *The Dumb Waiter*, seen on ABC on May 12, 1987. Art Durbano (*TV Guide* magazine) was unenthusiastic, noting, "Conti chews the scenery shamelessly, perhaps to keep you from noticing how often Travolta forgets the British accent he's affected for this thing."

Unseen on motion picture screens in over three years, John agreed for some reason to star in THE EXPERTS, a spy spoof which opened briefly in January 1989 but was quickly relegated to home video by mid-summer. *Video Review* magazine warned of the preposterous plot, "you'll have to see for yourself (although you'll wish you hadn't)." Whatever saving grace this minor endeavor had was in the few dance sequences provided by John. In the spring of 1989 he rejected yet another offer—to announce the Academy Award winner for best music score—saying that he would rather introduce a major award, in keeping with his previous Oscar history of presenting awards in major categories. By now his weight was up to 190 pounds because he did not like to exercise, and he admitted to living alone in his new home at Spruce Creek, Daytona Beach, Florida, which had a landing strip for his Lear jet. (He had sold his Santa Barbara ranch a year earlier at a profit of $2.35 million.)

Time magazine called it the "baby-faced sleeper hit" of the autumn 1989 season, while *Variety* criticized it as a "Yuppie-targeted programmer . . . destined for a short life in theaters." LOOK WHO'S TALKING had its faults, but overall it was a fun and witty movie excursion about an unmarried career woman (Kirstie Alley) seeking a father for her baby. Into her life walks a laid-back cab driver (John) who proves to be *the* man for the job. The winning gimmick of the comedy was the use of Bruce Willis's voice for the wise-cracking fetus/child, plus outstanding support from Olympia Dukakis and Abe Vigoda. The comedy hit went on to gross over $133 million domestically. For the first time in twelve years, John enjoyed a box-office hit and was humble enough to grant promotional interviews. To the syndicated "Entertainment Tonight" he confided, "Nothing can compare to the joys I have known," and he confessed to *US* magazine, when it named him one of the top twenty screen stars of 1989, that he was relieved to be thirty-five and "no longer confined to available-hunk roles." In New York City, in early November 1990, John was named Male Star of the Year by the 256-member Motion Picture Bookers Club, celebrating its fiftieth anniversary with an awards luncheon at the Marriott Marquis Hotel. Because of Travolta's overseas drawing power, his salary was still high, at $1.75 million per picture, which increased to $2 million during early negotiations for LOOK WHO'S TALK-ING TOO (1990), which went into production on June 11, 1990, in Vancouver, British Columbia, reteaming Travolta with Kirstie Alley, and boasting the voices of Bruce Willis (as the little boy Mikey), Roseanne Barr (as his sister, Julie), and Damon Wayans (as Eddie, the kid next door). When it was released in mid-December 1990, Kirk Honeycutt (*Hollywood Reporter*) reported, "John Travolta and Kirstie Alley still make great straight men to these talking babies. . . . Travolta displays the charm and sparkle that once made him a teen idol. In a dance sequence . . . he also reminds you what a pleasure it still is to watch him move."

Meanwhile, two projects filmed before LOOK WHO'S TALKING floundered. THE TENDER cast him as the father of a young daughter, who becomes involved in the Chicago underworld. Completed in 1988, it was put back into post-production for further revisions and then disappeared. He filmed CHAINS OF GOLD in Miami with long-time friend Marilu Henner. CHAINS OF GOLD finally emerged on cable TV in the fall of 1991. The film proved to be a dull mess. There was talk of John's starring in yet another sequel to SATURDAY NIGHT FEVER, but it did not materialize. Plans for him to co-star in London in the stage musical *Zorba!*, in the role played by Alan Bates in the Anthony Quinn movie ZORBA THE GREEK (1964), also did not pan out.

In early 1990, in accepting the People's Choice Award for LOOK WHO'S TALKING as favorite screen comedy, he said, "This means a lot to me," and he seemed to mean it. In Las Vegas on August 8, 1990, at the Video Software Dealers Association, the RCA/Columbia Home Video of LOOK WHO'S TALKING was given a Homer Award as the association's favorite comedy movie. John made a guest appearance on CBS-TV's hour-long Phil Collins special (September 8, 1990) when the rock star showed excerpts from his recent concert tours. In mid-October 1990 Travolta began SHOUT (1991), co-starring Richard Jordan and Heather Graham and shot on location in Stockton, California. The film is a quasi-musical set in 1955 with John as a band instructor and James Walter as his wayward protege.

"Golly, it's just nice to have success again," John Travolta was quoted as saying in *US* magazine following the huge box-office tallies of LOOK WHO'S TALKING. However, his manager claims that he is no longer obsessed with his career. Instead, he participates in a low-keyed lifestyle in Spruce Creek, Florida, known as a "country club community," where a real estate developer has praised him, saying, "He's such a nice person . . . he fits right in." His frequent companion is actress Kelly Preston, whom was pregnant with their child when they wed in Paris on September 5, 1991. Back on the "A" list of Hollywood actors, he has no plans to return to California. "I will be eternally grateful for the opportunities the town has given me, but I wouldn't live there for anything."

Filmography

The Devil's Rain (Bryanston, 1975)
Carrie (UA, 1976)
The Boy in the Plastic Bubble (ABC-TV, 11/12/76)
Saturday Night Fever (Par, 1977)
Grease (Par, 1978)
Moment by Moment (Univ, 1978)
Urban Cowboy (Par, 1980)
Blow Out (Filmways, 1981)
Staying Alive (Par, 1983)

Two of a Kind (20th–Fox, 1983)
Perfect (Col, 1985)
The Tender (Triumph Releasing—Unreleased) [made in 1988]
The Experts (Par, 1989)
Look Who's Talking (Tri-Star, 1989)
Look Who's Talking Too (Tri-Star, 1990)
Chains of Gold (M.C.E.G., 1991) [made in 1988]
Shout (Univ, 1991)

Broadway Plays

Grease (1974) (replacement)

Over Here! (1974)

Television Series

Welcome Back, Kotter (ABC, 1975–79)

Album Discography

Can't Let You Go (Midland International BKL1-2211)
Grease (RSO RS-2-4002) [ST]
John Travolta (Midland International BKL1-11563)

Over Here! (Columbia KS-32961) [OC]
Travolta Fever (Midsong International 001)
Two of a Kind (MCA 6127) [ST]

KATHLEEN TURNER

"I'm an expert at presenting Kathleen Turner, capital K, capital T,
whether it's finding the right sentence to say, or the right way to say it.
I have a kind of carriage that projects the beautiful, powerful presence
of a woman. That's my job." —*Los Angeles Times*, April 8, 1990

KATHLEEN TURNER ADMITS TO BEING A SNOB, JUDGING PEOPLE BY
their accents or by their knowledge. She advises media persons to call her Miss Turner
rather than Kathleen inasmuch as they are not her friends. She claims that she does not
owe her fans a thing; that they should buy tickets to see her movies rather than expect her
to please them. Her dramatic screen premiere was in a superior *film noir*, in which she
slickly vamped a man into helping her murder her husband. After declaring her love in
throaty measures, she disappeared, leaving him to take the rap. Immediately, she was a hit.
Immediately, she was compared to those distinctive-voiced stars of the 1940s who did the
same types of willful things to men on camera: Barbara Stanwyck, Lauren Bacall, Susan
Hayward, Lizabeth Scott, Mary Astor, and others.

Turner has proved to be very smart in her selection of movie roles. Her judgment
has helped her to become one of the five most-sought-after and high-priced actresses in
today's Hollywood. She is a *star*.

Kathleen Turner was born on Saturday, June 19, 1954, in her mother's hometown
of Springfield, Missouri. She was the third of four children, all born within a six-year
period, to Allen Richard Turner, a U.S. foreign diplomat, and Patsy Magee Turner,
formerly with the United Nations in China. "Dick" Turner, who has been described as a
"tall, stiff Victorian" type of gentleman, had lived many years in China, spending World
War II in a Japanese prison camp. After the war and during his children's formative years,
Turner, in the line of foreign service work, moved his family many times, from Canada to
Washington, D.C., to Cuba to Venezuela. There, Kathleen learned to speak fluent
Spanish. However, when she was thirteen and admittedly something of a tomboy, the
family was uprooted again, this time to London, where she was enrolled at the American
School.

Because of the transient lifestyle, she had no chance to foster any friendships.
Within the Turner family itself, her relationships with her siblings were marked by rivalry.
A brother would say later that Kathleen was an "insanely jealous teenager" with a fervent
need to prove that she was worthwhile. A solution to this need unexpectedly presented
itself on their first night in London, when the family went to see Angela Lansbury perform

in *Mame*. From that moment on, Kathleen was in love with the theater and saw as many as two plays a week, traveling by train when necessary throughout England. She knew she wanted to be a *professional* actor (her emphasis). At school, she organized a group of students into a drama club, which gave presentations of *The Boy Friend* and *Lovers*. To further satisfy her thirst for acting, Kathleen took courses at London's Central School of Speech and Drama because "I thought it would be a great way to make a living, a great job. In England, it's quite a respectable profession." Here she learned that an actor can better become any character by changing the voice, so she concentrated on developing that aspect of her talents.

In 1972 she graduated from the American School, still without any really close companions. Ironically, in the annual yearbook, she was quoted as saying, "The measure of a man is his friends." A fellow graduate, Nina Cameron, would remember years later that at the time Kathleen was "the most determined person I had ever seen." Shortly before graduation, Turner's father had died of a heart attack. Patsy Turner moved the family back to Springfield, Missouri, where Kathleen entered Southwest Missouri State University studying drama, where John Goodman was a fellow student. "It was pretty strange," she has recalled. "Springfield was quite a cultural shock. I was scared and everything, so I made myself as absolutely English as possible—you know. 'I'm Kathleen Turnuh, I'm studying theatuh.'" She claims to have won all the Shakespearean leads in school productions and continued to work on her voice through exercises such as clamping eraser tips between her back teeth while speaking, in order to lower the tone. She was determined to have a voice that she could change at will, unlike most American actors who "will go to great lengths to gain weight or lose weight or dye their hair—and use the same voice." Tess Harper, who would also become a screen actor, was a student at Southwest. She remembered Kathleen as an "ice princess" who was "the most determined person I'd ever met. Unlike the rest of us, she had a game plan." Harper says that Kathleen "tricked up a plummy English accent and put on phony airs—all accent and legs."

Unhappy at Southwest Missouri because of dormitory living as well as the lack of experimental theater, she transferred as a senior to the University of Maryland at College Park. During her year there, she helped found the New Theater Festival while also auditioning with the Arena Stage in Washington, D.C. In May 1977 she graduated from college with a bachelor's degree in fine arts. She immediately went to New York City with a recommendation from the Arena casting director to talent agent David Guc. Guc remembered that her voice was "very strange—deep and accent nonspecific, somewhere between Taiwan and Bolivia." Through him she signed a contract with Bloom Associates to do television commercials. Although she looked sensational on film, her voice did not fit with her enactment of the happy housewife finding sparkle in her kitchen floor. As such, she was assigned to doing voiceovers. She also briefly waited tables, played off-off-Broadway, and began a live-in affair with Guc that would last almost five years. She auditioned for the role of Ryan O'Neal's new-found love in OLIVER'S STORY (1978), but lost out to Candice Bergen.

In February 1978 Kathleen agreed to a twenty-month commitment in the daytime soap drama "The Doctors" on NBC-TV, as Nola Dancy Aldrich, an "incompetent villainess." An advocate of stage work, she had to admit that she had found a new form of expression through the camera: "You could do things with the rate at which you open and close your eyes. Things that in a theatre would be lost except to the first ten rows, and things with your voice that you could never do on stage." During this same period, she acted on Broadway for nine months as a replacement in the role of Judith Hastings in *Gemini*. After the demise of her character in "The Doctors" in October 1979, she performed at the Manitoba Theatre Center in Winnipeg, Canada, in *Travesties* and *The Seagull*.

She received a call from Los Angeles for a screen test with Peter Falk for a Robert Aldrich–directed feature, ALL THE MARBLES (1981), about beautiful lady wrestlers. She thanked God that she did not get the part. Since she had never been to southern California before, she decided to linger to see if she could obtain an interview for a film she wanted to do.

For this important interview, she wore her highest heels, a slit skirt to better display her shapely legs, and makeup appropriate for a high-powered seductress. Tested by director/writer Lawrence Kasdan at the Burbank Studios, she was asked to appear intoxicated. She was convincing to the point of cascading into a low table, sending cigarettes flying across the sound stage. Kasdan liked her and especially found her voice exciting. However, he had hoped for a big-name actress to portray the conniving, sensual Matty Walker in his screenplay, which borrowed heavily from DOUBLE INDEMNITY (1944). Nevertheless, because of the high-voltage sexuality that Turner displayed in her audition, he decided to go with this unknown. The camera rolled on BODY HEAT (1981) in the winter of 1980.

Before the release of BODY HEAT in August 1981, few people had heard of Kathleen Turner. Within a year, everyone seemed to know her name; it was as though she had always been there. She made a smoldering characterization of conniving Matty Walker who, in the heat of summer in a southern town, dupes a gullible beau (William Hurt) into murdering her husband (Richard Crenna). (She half-telegraphs her plans in their first meeting when she says, "You're not too smart, are you? I like that in a man.") She is the sexy lady who informs Hurt: "My body temperature runs a couple of degrees higher than normal, around a hundred. I don't mind. I guess it's the engine or something. Runs a little fast." Critic Gene Siskel noted, "Her languorous naked body is on display throughout . . . but that—honest—isn't what is so impressive. . . . Rather, it's that she stays in character, albeit a quirky character." Barbara Stanwyck, who had played the prototype of Matty in DOUBLE INDEMNITY thirty-seven years earlier, said of BODY HEAT, "the only one who could have done it better is me." With Kathleen Turner's emergence, the world of cinema witnessed the birth of a movie star in a mold that was considered lost with the 1940s. Kathleen, however, found it difficult to cope with the loss of privacy that a screen star experiences. She began psychiatric sessions that would continue for several years.

After BODY HEAT, Turner rejected offers to repeat the same type of screen character. Instead, she returned to Washington, D.C., to the Arena Stage where she was Titania in *A Midsummer Night's Dream.* Eight months later, she sought the distaff lead in Carl Reiner's THE MAN WITH TWO BRAINS (1983) opposite Steve Martin. After auditioning for Reiner, she won the role of Dolores Benedict, a parody of her earlier Matty Walker. The usually harsh Pauline Kael wrote that Kathleen "comes alive in comedy," while *Newsweek* magazine described her as "not only sensationally glamorous but also stylish and hilarious."

Quite a bit of persuasion was required to convince producer/star Michael Douglas that she could successfully handle the role of a mousy writer who sobs over her own love stories and later rolls around in the muddy waters of Colombia in ROMANCING THE STONE (1984). Actually filmed for three months in Mexico, the comedy has shy, introspective writer Joan Wilder (Turner) leaving New York City for South America with a treasure map. There she meets a bedraggled soldier of fortune (Douglas) while pursued by others (among them Danny DeVito and Manuel Ojeda) who also want the map. En route, crawling reptiles play into the plotline. ROMANCING THE STONE caught the public's fancy and grossed $75 million in domestic release, making it the #9 financial hit of the year. She earned a Golden Globe Award as Best Actress for her performance in this comedy.

Rejecting an offer to co-star with Richard Chamberlain in the remake KING SOLOMON'S MINES (1985), which would have again dumped her in mud and slush, she opted to play the role of an Appalachian housewife named Stella who also owns a fish-supply store in A BREED APART (1984), which paired her with Rutger Hauer and Powers Boothe. *Variety* correctly predicted that this would be a box-office flop because it "lacks reason, dramatic tension or emotional involvement." She taped a children's TV special offering puppets in a spoof of ROMANCING THE STONE, called "Loving the Rock." For iconoclastic filmmaker Ken Russell she was a fashion designer named Joanna Crane who moonlights as a blonde hooker named China Blue for the attention, not the money, in CRIMES OF PASSION (1984). With explicit sex scenes, the film did not fare well in the United States. However, in Europe, with added footage, including China Blue's sodomizing a policeman with his night stick, it did quite well. *Time* magazine credited her portrayal as "a clever, daring, mad performance in a movie that is just as reckless."

Called "aloof" and "withdrawn" while on the sets of her pictures, she publicly announced that filming love scenes was "very exciting and . . . also frightening because you can't ever let yourself go completely. Everybody gets quite excited, not just the actors. You look around and the camera guys are all panting; you gotta take a walk in the cool air after a shot." She insisted on no nude scenes in her films and stated that she would have nothing to do with a film that might earn an X (now NC-17) rating. To critic Roger Ebert, she indicated that most filmmakers "don't know what the hell to do with me" but "they've never asked me to play one of those heroic farm women." She was outspoken in her criticism of Los Angeles, saying that "most people there are concerned with the product; they're only concerned with maintaining a business. I hope that the best of them want to make a good film, but the rest should be bank tellers." She took up permanent residence in New York City in 1984 with the help of real estate developer Jay Weiss, whom she married in the autumn of that year. Two years his senior, she felt protected in marriage and liked being called "Mrs. Weiss," with him making decisions about their joint lives. She has said that when she has gotten too pushy around their home, he has told her, "Get small. You are not the boss here. Am I getting a check from you?"

Professionally, on February 2, 1985, she headlined an episode of CBS-TV's "An American Portrait" entitled "Mary Henton Vorse" and co-starred opposite Jack Nicholson in the John Huston feature PRIZZI'S HONOR (1985). She played a freelance hit woman who performs three or four assassinations a year, but who claims, "It's not many if you consider the population." *People* magazine lauded her work in this dark comedy, stating that she played her offbeat role "with enough come-on carnality to singe the screen. Turner is glorious, the sexiest presence in movies of the '80s and a prodigious actress to boot." She was awarded her second Golden Globe Award, was named Star of the Year by the National Association of Theater Owners, and was listed as #13 at the box office by Quigley Publications. The latter honor was bestowed before her next film release, THE JEW-EL OF THE NILE (1985). It was a sequel to ROMANCING THE STONE, for which she had contracted with Michael Douglas back in 1984. Although the sequel was not as fresh or exciting as the original, it never-theless went on to gross over $65 million in domestic release, making it the #7 moneymaker of 1985. Turner, Douglas, and Danny De-Vito also appeared in a music video of the theme song from the comedy, which proved very popular. When Turner and Douglas were later ap-proached to make a third entry in the series, they stood firm on an asking price of $5 million each, which negated the project.

At one time, Debra Winger and then Penny Marshall were slat-ed to star in Francis Ford Coppola's feature PEGGY SUE GOT MARRIED (1986). Then Kathleen took over the title role of Peggy Sue Kelcher Bodell, an unwitting time traveler

Kathleen Turner and Jack Nicholson in PRIZZI'S HONOR (1985).

who returns to the time when she was an eighteen-year-old high school student. Without changing makeup or hairstyle, Kathleen called upon her innate talents to embody a forty-two-year-old woman momentarily reincarnated as a teenager. For her efforts, she received an Academy Award nomination as Best Actress but lost the award to Marlee Matlin (CHILDREN OF A LESSER GOD). In 1986 Kathleen was listed as the #9 box-office attraction by Quigley Publications.

In the fall of 1987 Kathleen gave birth to a daughter, Rachel Ann. Although Turner loved her offspring, she described her months of inactivity with "I wasn't crazy about being pregnant. I have talked to these women who said it was the most glorious time of their life and I thought, 'Haven't you ever played a good game of racquetball?'" That November, she was one of many stars to be heard in DEAR AMERICA: LETTERS HOME FROM VIETNAM (1987), consisting of stock footage from the NBC video archives. In February 1988 she was the star of JULIA AND JULIA, filmed in Milan, Italy. Julia (Giulia in Italian) is a travel agent who drifts back and forth between the world of now and a world of fantasy in which she has a wild affair with a zany photographer (Sting) as well as a relationship with her husband, alive in her fantasy but dead in actuality. Hailed as the first feature to be shot entirely on high-definition videotape and then transferred onto film, it emerged as a confusing, illogical mishmash. Of her experience of working with rock performer Sting, she commented, "I got real tired of the hundreds of little girls hanging around screaming, 'Oh Sting, oh Sting, oh Sting.'" As for his sex scenes with her, Sting countered with, "It's not arousing in the least."

SWITCHING CHANNELS (1988) proved to be an unsuccessful remake of THE FRONT PAGE, with Kathleen as a TV anchorwoman torn between her ex-husband/boss (Burt Reynolds) and her wealthy fiancé (Christopher Reeve). *Time* magazine labeled the labored comedy a "weakened update," but credited her "with percolating through that great womanly laugh" and "strut[ting] in high style." On March 22, 1988, she appeared at UCLA's Royce Hall in a Sundance Institute tribute to *A Night of Great Movie Music* in which the score of BODY HEAT was performed by the Sundance Symphony Orchestra. She was heard but not seen in commercials for Fab detergent; of the job, she said, "You work fifteen minutes and they give you an enormous amount of money." In June 1988 hers was the sultry voice of Jessica Rabbit, who says, "I'm not bad, I'm just drawn that way" in WHO FRAMED ROGER RABBIT, which became the #2 financial box-office draw of the year with domestic grosses of $154 million. Although Kathleen chose to receive no on-screen credit for the voice of the animated character in that blockbuster, actress Amy Irving did receive mention for providing Jessica's singing voice.

In THE ACCIDENTAL TOURIST (1988), Kathleen took a decidedly supporting role to William Hurt and Geena Davis, although she received second billing as Sarah. She played the wife who leaves husband Hurt, not to reappear until the film's end, when she tries to win him back but fails. She appeared to have gained weight, and her performance was summed up by the *San Francisco Chronicle* as "merely adequate in a part that doesn't offer much opportunity."

In January 1989 she was named by celebrity photographer Marc Raboy in his third annual list of Fabulous Features of Famous Faces as having the best voice, while in February she was given Harvard University's annual Hasty Pudding Award as woman of the year in Cambridge, Massachusetts, where she joined two male students in a sizzling rendition of "Wild Thing." When asked her age by a fan, she replied coldly, "Professionally, I have no age." On June 23, 1989, she again supplied the voice of Jessica Rabbit in the Disney cartoon short TUMMY TROUBLE. Disney decided to merchandise Jessica as a figurine and a key chain. Turner was scheduled to star at Columbia in HARDBOILED, which was postponed. Instead, she co-starred for a third time with Michael Douglas in THE WAR OF THE ROSES (1989). Slimmed down to her BODY HEAT look, Kathleen was one-half of the married Roses who battle each other throughout. A black comedy directed by Danny DeVito, who also co-starred, the film has Kathleen as Barbara Rose, who becomes bored with her marriage to Oliver (Douglas) after renovating their lovely home and raising their two children. Realizing that their marriage is empty and that her husband will never change, she sues for divorce, which turns into a nasty knock-down, drag-out fight over their possessions. *Daily Variety* was on target with its statement that the film "starts out winningly as a sharp, cynical and sexy romantic comedy, but it soon deteriorates into sordid tedious nonsense." The trade paper continued, "Despite it all, Turner has seldom been more stunning to watch." *Newsweek* magazine's David Ansen found that "she's both a powerful and unstable presence" who "with her breathless vocal ticks and unlocatable accent, is a strangely unsettling actress." After nine weeks in domestic release, the picture had taken in a very respectable $75 million.

She was *Camille* on stage at New Haven's Long Wharf Theatre in 1989. On October 21, 1989, she hosted "Saturday Night Live" on NBC-TV and the day before was host of the American Cinematheque's honor to celebrity photographer Douglas Kirkland at the Directors Guild of America in Los Angeles. On November 1, 1989, she was interviewed on ABC-TV by Barbara Walters. In her husky voice, Turner revealed that she intended to remain in acting for another fifty years or more because "It's the only profession they can't retire you from if you can walk and talk." She also professed to love being married to Jay Weiss, who, she said, will not watch her do a death scene, whether in a movie or on stage.

In March 1990, as Kathleen readied herself for a Broadway run, her husband was unwittingly involved in a complicated matter concerning ownership of an illegal social club in New York City called Happy Land that had been torched and in which eighty-seven persons lost their lives. Jay Weiss had leased the property to the social club's operator after having leased it from a major real estate broker.

Kathleen opened at the Eugene O'Neill Theatre on Broadway in a revival of Tennessee Williams's *Cat on a Hot Tin Roof* on March 21, 1990, for a limited run. Frank Rich (*New York Times*) rated her as "an accomplished Maggie, mesmerizing to watch, comfortable onstage and robustly good-humored." Playing Big Daddy was Charles Durning, who said, "I was prepared not to like her, but she's a terrific lady." Kathleen followed in the footsteps of several actresses (Barbara Bel Geddes, Elizabeth Ashley, Natalie Wood) who had played Maggie the Cat, but it was to Elizabeth Taylor's performance in the 1958 screen version that Kathleen's work was inevitably compared. Kathleen said, "Ms. Taylor is the one who comes to mind when you think of Maggie the Cat, but they cut the heck out of the play in the film to erase any suggestion of homosexuality, so they butchered the part. . . . I hope to put a stamp on this role for the stage."

Kathleen journeyed from the new family home at Amagansett, Long Island, to host the forty-fourth edition of the Tony Awards on June 3, 1990, at the Lunt-Fontanne Theatre, replacing her idol, Angela Lansbury, who had played host the previous three years. Although nominated as Best Actress in a Drama, Kathleen did not win, losing to Maggie Smith (of *Lettice and Lovage*).

When, in June 1990, *Variety* listed the 1989–1990 Broadway productions that had thus far recouped their investments, *Cat on a Hot Tin Roof* appeared on the list. As Kathleen exited the production after taking bows for the August 1, 1990, performance, plans were under way by ABC-TV to televise the play with the cast intact.

Meanwhile, on June 4, 1990, Kathleen hosted on TNT–Cable a tribute to Myrna Loy, entitled "So Nice to Come Home to." *TV Guide* magazine noted that Kathleen "is a fan of Myrna, and her enthusiasm is infectious." In this fine profile of Loy, utilizing film clips organized by *Time* magazine critic Richard Schickel, Kathleen termed her the "ideal of womanliness." On June 26, 1990, the custom-made slip that Kathleen wore on stage as Maggie sold for $1,200 at a black-tie-dinner auction in New York benefiting Easter Seals, a charity aiding people with disabilities. In July 1990 readers of *Esquire* magazine voted Turner's voice one of the embodiments of the "perfect woman," along with Kim Basinger's hair, Jamie Lee Curtis's legs, and Candice Bergen's heart. Kathleen was spokesperson for a group (Kevin Kline, Morgan Freeman, Joseph Papp) who went to Capitol Hill in Washington, D.C., to lobby against the proposed limitations by Congress on National Endowment for the Arts (NEA) grants to artists. On October 29, 1990, at the Regent Beverly Wilshire Hotel in Los Angeles, Kathleen, as well as singer Don Henley, received the Spirit of Liberty Award from the People for the American Way. Turner was acknowledged for her efforts to aid the NEA. Meanwhile, in voiceover, Kathleen could be heard doing commercials for Maxwell House coffee and Arrow shirts.

Although Turner has optioned the Robert Stone novel *A Flag for Sunrise*, about an American nun caught in Central American political upheaval, as a screen project for herself, nothing has occurred in this area to date.

On October 15, 1990, however, Kathleen went before the cameras as the star of V. I. WARSHAWSKI, adapted from Sara Paretsky's popular mystery novels. Kathleen plays the writer's "tough lady detective and heroine." Since Paretsky has (to date) written six stories about the New York City–based character, syndicated columnist Liz Smith opined that if the initial film is a hit, "Kathleen might find herself the new James Bond." Says Paretsky of the casting, "Turner doesn't look like the hazy character I envision when I write, but I like that under her soft good looks, there's a sexy gleam that captures the spirit of the character."

Still driven to excel, Kathleen is always striving to prove herself to herself. "I do not like failing," she once said. Of acting, she has commented, "all this is still a learning process for me. I don't know yet what I'm best at. What I want, ideally, is acting that's a jump. You can prepare as best you can, then jump—emotionally, physically or in whatever way is required." When actor Don Johnson was asked by *Penthouse* magazine to name the screen's top ten women, he listed Kathleen as #8 because "Even when she gained weight, she was sexy. She can act and she looks great. Of all the non-X-rated pictures I've ever seen, I think Kathleen Turner in BODY HEAT was one of the biggest turn-ons for me."

Filmography

Body Heat (WB, 1981)
The Man with Two Brains (WB, 1983)
Romancing the Stone (20th–Fox, 1984)
A Breed Apart (Orion, 1984)
Crimes of Passion [China Blue] (New World, 1984)
Prizzi's Honor (20th–Fox, 1985)
The Jewel of the Nile (20th–Fox, 1985)
Peggy Sue Got Married (Tri-Star, 1986)

Dear America: Letters Home from Vietnam (HBO–Couturie, 1987) (voice only)
Julia and Julia (Cinecom, 1988)
Switching Channels (Tri-Star, 1988)
Who Framed Roger Rabbit (BV, 1988) (voice only)
The Accidental Tourist (WB, 1988)
The War of the Roses (20th–Fox, 1989)
V. I. Warshawski (BV, 1991)

Television Series

The Doctors (NBC, 1978–79)

Broadway Plays

Gemini (1978) (replacement)

Cat on a Hot Tin Roof (1990) (revival)

LINDSAY WAGNER

"I would never take a part irresponsibly, knowing that the media
so strongly affects our society. Children are growing up watching
television, whether the programs are made for children or not.
For most kids, television is their babysitter."
—*Chicago Tribune*, November 1, 1987

TO BE FOREVER IDENTIFIED AS THE TV HEROINE WITH ELECTROME-
chanical enhancements has not been Lindsay Wagner's wish, although the science of
bionics provided her first stepping stone to success. In an endeavor to prove her seriousness
about acting she has selected meaningful subject matter for her TV movies, which have
dealt with such central subjects as child abuse, holistic medicine, and wife beating. These
are all issues with which she is personally concerned.

Wagner attained maturity at an early age. Her no-nonsense approach to performing, laced with a sense of humor, quickly made her a favorite among television producers;
viewers are attracted by her capacity to embrace characters from all walks of life. Like
Shelley Long, Jane Seymour, and Jaclyn Smith, Lindsay has established her niche in
television following undistinguished motion pictures roles. But like Lauren Bacall (for her
height and hair) and Anne Bancroft (for her eyes), Wagner actually looks more like a
movie star.

Lindsay Wagner was born in Los Angeles on Wednesday, June 22, 1949, to the
teenaged couple Billy Nowels Wagner, who became a professional school photographer,
and Marilyn Louise (Thrasher) Wagner. When Lindsay was seven, her parents divorced.
When she was eleven, her mother, with whom she lived, married a second time, to Ted
Ball, who was in the construction industry. Tall for her age at 5' 7", Lindsay brought
money into the home by babysitting for such show business people as the Glen Campbells
and Joby Best, a dance instructor, and her husband, Jim, a drama coach. Through a family
connection, Lindsay got a job modeling at $50 an hour for the newly formed Nina
Blanchard Agency and soon became a top model for the firm. Joby Best had persuaded
Lindsay to study dancing but because Wagner suffered from undiagnosed, untreated
dyslexia, she dropped out of classes because learning the precise routines was a problem.
However, in Jim Best's drama classes Lindsay displayed talent that showed that was where
she belonged.

At the age of thirteen, Lindsay starred in a showcase stage production of *This
Property Is Condemned.* An MGM talent scout offered her a lead in a forthcoming

teleseries, but she rejected the offer on the advice of Best, who explained not only the pitfalls of being a child actor, but also that she still had a lot to learn. During her first year at North Hollywood High School, she was seen on television in commercials for Diet Rite, continued to be photographed as a fashion model, and, meanwhile, developed stomach ulcers. A stepsister, Randall, was born when Lindsay was fourteen.

When Lindsay was sixteen, her stepfather moved the family to Portland, Oregon, where she entered David Douglas High School. She found enjoyment in acting in school plays directed by a drama teacher (Ramona Reynolds) who gave her needed encouragement. She also found time on weekends to sing with a traveling rock group. After graduation from high school in 1967, she went to France for two months with a student group. That fall she enrolled at the University of Oregon in Eugene to study drama and music. After two semesters, she transferred to Mt. Hood Community College in Gresham, Oregon, but left after one semester. (Because of her dyslexia, Lindsay found the study regimen too difficult.) During this period she sang with college rock groups at off-campus sites.

In January 1968 Lindsay, at the age of eighteen, returned to Los Angeles. During this period she modeled and for five months taught young children at the Founders School. Ignoring a doctor's advice that she undergo surgery for ulcers, she joined the Church of Religious Science where, through meditation and self-investigation, she regained her health, although she fought a battle against anemia.

Early in 1971 a friend introduced her to a casting director at Universal Studios, where she was placed under contract at $162 per week, with escalating salary clauses. Beginning her contractual obligations in June 1971, her first TV appearance was in the "Million Dollar Bluff" episode of NBC's "Adam-12," broadcast on September 22, the same month she was married to Alan Rider, a music publisher. During the remainder of that year she was seen on such TV series as "The Man and the City," "Night Gallery," "The Bold Ones: The Lawyers," "Marcus Welby, M.D.," "Sarge," and "Owen Marshall, Counselor at Law."

For her motion picture debut in the romantic drama TWO PEOPLE (1973), Universal sent Lindsay to France and Morocco to co-star (as a fashion model) with Peter Fonda (as a soldier who defects during the Vietnam War). Directed by the acclaimed Robert Wise, the badly paced movie was poorly received, especially because its topic was untimely (prisoners of war from Vietnam were then returning to the United States). Meanwhile, Wagner's marriage to Rider fell apart and they divorced in the fall of 1973. Her second theatrical film was THE PAPER CHASE (1973), made on loan to Twentieth Century–Fox. She was cast as the daughter of a Harvard Law School professor (John Houseman) who falls in love with a law student (Timothy Bottoms). Next Lindsay co-starred with James Garner in the NBC series pilot THE ROCKFORD FILES (March 27, 1974), returning as a guest on the series in January 1975. That same month, she returned to "Marcus Welby, M.D." in the two-part episode "Dark Fury."

At this juncture, Universal's casting directors fired her because, they decided, she was too tall, too thin, and too flat-chested. The programming department, however, was unaware of the move and hired her to co-star in two episodes of ABC-TV's "The Six Million Dollar Man," in which she co-starred opposite series lead Lee Majors. Her contract was extended when the error was discovered. As Jaime Sommers, the one-time girlfriend of Colonel Steve Austin (Majors), she was a former tennis star saved by bionics after a near-fatal skydiving accident. Given two atomic legs, an arm, and an ear, she joined Steve on dangerous missions for the Office of Scientific Information. The installments entitled "The Bionic Woman" aired on March 16 and 23, 1975, and helped the series' ratings, which had been slipping. In the second segment, the script had Jamie dying of bionic injection. However, the rash of letters from protesting fans forced Universal and ABC to re-hire Lindsay for two additional episodes, this time at a then-unheard-of salary of $25,000 for the two-parter. Resurrected from a frozen state of near death, she reappeared in "The Return of the Bionic Woman," aired on September 14 and 21, 1975, which shot the series to near the top of the Nielsen ratings with a 45 percent share of the audience.

The show's producers hired Lindsay to star in her own series, "The Bionic Woman," for which her manager, Ron Samuels, negotiated for her a salary of $500,000 per season, plus a guarantee of at least one feature film a year, plus 12.5 percent of proceeds from the sales of bionic dolls, T-shirts, and other merchandise that might be forthcoming. These figures surpassed what Majors was currently earning, thus generating hard feelings between the two stars. Premiering on ABC on September 14, 1976, "The Bionic Woman" would move to NBC-TV in September 1977, where it would remain until its final summer rerun episode, shown on September 2, 1978, thus outliving the Majors series, which left the air in March 1978. During these two years, Lindsay also guest-starred on "The Six Million Dollar Man" several times.

In 1976 the made-in-Canada motion picture SECOND WIND was released, in which she co-starred with James Naughton. Earlier that year, on January 19 at 10 a.m., the MGB car she was driving slammed into a tree near her home in the Coldwater Canyon district of Los Angeles. She suffered a deep gash in the forehead and a split lip, causing production on "The Bionic Woman" to shut down for two weeks. The passenger in her car, Michael Brandon, her live-in lover, required five hours of surgery. An actor/writer, Brandon had shared a home with her since 1974; they often spoke of marriage, but admitted, "We have such a nice relationship now, we wonder if marriage would mess it up." Nevertheless, they were married in December 1976; divorce would follow in early 1978. On September 12, 1977, Lindsay was awarded an Emmy as Outstanding Lead Actress in a Drama Series. Next, ABC-TV gave her her own special, "Lindsay Wagner—Another Side of Me" (November 7, 1977), in which she sang and danced.

She was one of several television personalities featured in what NBC-TV called an "adult comedy pilot," entitled "Windows, Doors & Keyholes," presented May 16, 1978. She then had a stint as a panelist exploring American heroes on PBS-TV's "You're Not a Hero Until You're Sung" (September 3, 1978). During 1978 Warner Bros. Television launched a nationwide search for the actress to portray Billy Ikehorn in a dramatization of Judith Krantz's best-selling novel *Scruples.* Meanwhile, Lindsay starred in the title role of the CBS-TV movie THE INCREDIBLE JOURNEY OF DOCTOR MEG LAUREL (January 2, 1979) as a modern doctor in Appalachia. In the same network's telefeature THE TWO WORLDS OF JENNIE LOGAN (October 31, 1979), she joined Marc Singer in a slickly executed study of love and murder set simultaneously in two centuries. In CBS-TV's six-hour, three-part miniseries "Scruples" (1980), Lindsay starred as the character who rose from rags to riches within the fashion industry.

In April 1981 Lindsay was seen on theater screens in the throwaway role of Sylvester Stallone's ex-wife in NIGHTHAWKS, while the next month she was at HIGH RISK in a South American drug caper. On October 13, 1981, she was asked to age thirty years during the three-hour CBS-TV teledrama CALLIE & SON. "The aging part was fun," she said, "especially when you can make yourself look like what you want to look like at that age." During 1981 she married for a third time, her new husband being Hollywood stuntman Henry Kingi. They would have two children: Dorian Henry, born September 25, 1982, and Alex Nathan, born September 7, 1986. The couple would later divorce.

Lindsay played a former mental patient in CBS-TV's MEMORIES NEVER DIE (December 5, 1982) and portrayed the wanton, possibly innocent Barbara Graham in ABC-TV's I WANT TO LIVE (May 9, 1983). In PRINCESS DAISY (November 6–7, 1983), another adaptation of a Judith Krantz novel (this time dealing with the cosmetics industry), she was a beautiful film star whose daughter (Merete Van Kamp) rises to success in the business world. On November 8, 1983, the night after that two-part movie concluded, she returned on CBS-TV in TWO KINDS OF LOVE, as a mother who dies, leaving her son (Rick Schroder) to fend for himself.

She joined "The Love Boat Fall Preview Party" on September 15, 1984, then premiered three days later in "Jessie," an hour-long ABC-TV drama series in which she played a staff psychiatrist for a California police department. *Variety* prognosticated, "'Jessie' is an uncomfortable and unsuccessful attempt to combine the cop and medico formats." As for Lindsay, the trade paper noted, "Wagner and [co-star Tony] Lo Bianco are earnest in their one-note characters, but neither has a chance with this material." The show's producers overruled her wish to make the show more informative on the medical side and insisted on sticking to standard cop action formulas. Consequently, "Jessie" was last telecast only two months later, on November 13, 1984.

Sylvester Stallone and **Lindsay Wagner** in NIGHTHAWKS (1981).

Cinergy Video Entertainment released Lindsay's first videotape, *Psychocalisthenics with Lindsay Wagner*, during 1984. It was high drama in CBS-TV's PASSIONS (October 1, 1984), in which, as the mistress of Richard Crenna, she is forced to face his wife (Joanne Woodward) after he dies. Returning to medicine, Lindsay was a doctor in the motion picture MARTIN'S DAY (1985), but in CBS-TV's THE OTHER LOVER (September 24, 1985), she was a married publishing executive unable to harness her attraction for a handsome author (Jack Scalia). The constantly working Wagner next played a parent involved in a court battle with Chris Sarandon over custody of their adopted child in NBC-TV's THIS CHILD IS MINE (November 4, 1985), found by *TV Guide* magazine to be "thought-provoking and touching."

On February 9, 1986, Lindsay starred as a social worker who suspects sexual molestation of a child (Taliesin Jaffe) whom she tries to help in CHILD'S CRY (CBS-TV). She had the title role in the "Antonia Stone" episode of "An American Portrait," shown in February 1986. Once again she had TV movies on consecutive nights, this time on the same network (ABC), beginning May 11, 1986, with YOUNG AGAIN as the old high school girlfriend of Robert Urich. The following evening she fought to free her postman husband (John Larroquette) of a false rape accusation in CONVICTED. *TV Guide* magazine decided that she and co-star Armand Assante "don't surmount the suds" as an amnesiac housewife and her husband in NBC-TV's STRANGER IN MY BED (January 12, 1987). As a change of pace, she guest-starred as a cooking school teacher on the January 20, 1987, segment of CBS's "Kate and Allie." For a time, the premise was considered for a potential spinoff series, but nothing further developed.

Wagner was called upon to reprise her Jaime Sommers characterization with Lee Majors in RETURN OF THE SIX MILLION DOLLAR MAN AND THE BIONIC WOMAN (May 17, 1987), an uninspired entry that nevertheless pleased devotees of the earlier series. STUDENT EXCHANGE (ABC-TV, November 29 and December 6, 1987) starred her in a two-part "Disney Sunday Night Movie." Also during 1987 she narrated the instructional video TOUCH for Media Ventures; concerning ways to recognize potential child abuse/molestation situations, it was shown to community groups and in schools. Known as an expert in the field of the healing arts, she had both a Lorimar video and a Prentice Hall book in release, both entitled *Lindsay Wagner's New Beauty: The Acupressure Facelift*.

She fought anti-Semitism in Canada in ABC-TV's EVIL IN CLEAR RIVER (January 11, 1988) and turned to mystery for USA–Cable in the "Prism" segment of "Alfred Hitchcock Presents" on February 20, 1988. Possibly Lindsay's most compelling performance to date has been as the airline purser striving to protect her passengers from terrorists in NBC-TV's THE TAKING OF FLIGHT 847: THE ULI DERICKSON STORY (May 2, 1988). Lindsay received some of her best reviews to date for this project: "Wagner keeps her character poised on the razor's edge of hysteria without toppling over into histrionics" (Michael Barb, *Hollywood Reporter*); "Derickson is superbly played, in the performance of her career, by Lindsay Wagner" (Tom Jicha, *Miami News*); "Wagner's performance is a tour de force" (Kay Gardella, *New York Daily News*). This was followed that same month by CBS-TV's NIGHTMARE AT BITTER CREEK (May 24, 1988), in which a weekend pleasure trip to the mountains becomes one of terror at the hands of a fugitive white supremacist. For Lifetime–Cable, she hosted the special "Once Upon Her Time" (June 22, 1988), then hosted a special on ABC-TV, "Scandals" (October 29, 1988). For ABC-TV's POLICE STORY: BURNOUT (November 29, 1988), Lindsay was a cop whose female partner kills herself, leaving the traumatized Wagner to sink into an alcoholic retreat. Eventually she regains her spirit to return to the police force. (This was a virtual remake of an April 1980 "Police Story" segment that had starred Karen Black.) In NBC-TV's two-part stylish thriller FROM THE DEAD OF NIGHT (February 27–28, 1989), she was a fashion designer who cheats death, only to be pursued by dead people insistent that she join them on the other side.

When contracted for a second reunion with Lee Majors for NBC-TV's THE BIONIC SHOWDOWN: THE SIX MILLION DOLLAR MAN AND THE BIONIC WOMAN (April 30, 1989), she said, "I get the numbers [high Neilsen ratings] and that's why they keep hiring me." For this go-round, the duo was teamed with a younger bionic (Sandra Bullock) to battle evil. She narrated the CBS-TV special "The Queen of the Beasts" (August 30, 1989), as a prelude to a new series, "The Peaceable Kingdom." In the series, which premiered on September 30, 1989, she and Tom Wopat were sibling directors of the Los Angeles County Zoo, filled with animals of every variety—some lovable, others predatory. Hoping to educate the public about zoos and conservation, CBS spent millions of dollars in creating its own zoo. The *Hollywood Reporter* noted, "It's the animals that provide the real excitement . . . all else being rather predictable." *People* magazine called the series "charming," but blamed the producers for making the stars siblings rather than "would-be lovers" because "What's left are shots of sweet gorillas, and a plot that can drive you ape." The show failed to attract sufficient viewers and it was cancelled after its November 15, 1989, episode.

Lindsay's annual income was enhanced by contracting with the Ford Motor Company as its television spokesperson in the autumn of 1989. Continuing to light up television screens by starring in movies, she played a beautiful, talented actress with a secret in VOICE OF THE HEART, adapted from Barbara Taylor Bradford's novel, which sold over seven million copies. It was telecast in syndication on April 23–24, 1990.

On May 6, 1990, she was married for a fourth time, to producer Lawrence Mortoff, in a garden ceremony in Los Angeles. Following a vegetarian buffet reception, the bride honeymooned in Bali with her groom, the father of three.

With Roger Gimbel, she was co-executive producer as well as the star of CBS-TV's SHATTERED DREAMS (May 13, 1990), based on the nonfiction book by Charlotte Fedders revealing that she had suffered ten years of marriage to a wife beater. The movie averaged a 16.4 Nielsen rating with a 26 percent share of the audience. The *Hollywood Reporter* recommended it for Lindsay's "restrained yet expressive portrait of a woman imprisoned in a marriage."

Off screen, Lindsay is not only ecology-minded, but campaigns against child abuse and domestic violence. For two years she was the national spokesperson for Shelter Aid, a support group for victims of domestic violence. In addition, in June 1990 her vegetarian cookbook, *The High Road to Health*, written with Ariane Spade, was in bookstores; published by Prentice Hall, it soon went into a third printing.

On September 17, 1990, Lindsay co-starred with Dinah Manoff and Marcy Walker in BABIES (NBC-TV), a two-hour movie about "babies (and how to make them)" (ads in *TV Guide* magazine). In the role of a single successful woman (a college department chair) whose biological clock worries her, Lindsay considers having a baby alone (by artificial insemination) but changes her mind by the end of the film. According to *TV Guide*, "an attractive cast is the appeal" of this outing about three friends contemplating pregnancy or the lack of it. In September 1990 Lindsay went to England to shoot TO BE THE BEST, based on Barbara Taylor Bradford's novel, and slated to be a four-hour syndicated movie in 1992. Her co-stars include Anthony Hopkins, Stephanie Beacham, and Christopher Cazenove. For the cop action film RICOCHET (forthcoming, 1991), Lindsay plays a tough district attorney dealing with police rookie Denzel Washington. In the CBS-TV movie FIRE IN THE DARK (forthcoming, 1991), Lindsay's character must cope with the needs of her aged widowed mother (Olympia Dukakis).

Along with Susan Saint James, Lindsay Wagner is one of the last among the Baby Boom generation to have had a major studio contract (with Universal) but to make her mark in television rather than theatrical films. Professionally active since the age of twelve, Wagner has carried the full weight of many TV movies and miniseries, but speaks of the medium with concern. "Women used to be portrayed in the kitchen with their aprons on," Lindsay has said. "We've advanced now, to the point where most of the women you see on dramatic TV shows are either being raped and beaten or are cold and heartless creatures. There's a lot of anger against women being shown, and a lot of people are buying it." Because Lindsay Wagner has excelled to such a degree as a dramatic actress, finding a suitable situation comedy TV series role for herself has become an ongoing challenge.

Filmography

Two People (Univ, 1973)
The Paper Chase (20th–Fox, 1973)
The Rockford Files (NBC-TV, 3/27/74)
Second Wind (Ambassador, 1976)
The Incredible Journey of Doctor Meg Laurel (CBS-TV, 1/2/79)
The Two Worlds of Jennie Logan (CBS-TV, 10/31/79)
Callie & Son (CBS-TV, 10/13/81)
Nighthawks (Univ, 1981)
High Risk (American Cinema, 1981)
Memories Never Die (CBS-TV, 12/5/82)
I Want to Live (ABC-TV, 5/9/83)
Princess Daisy (NBC-TV, 11/6/83–11/7/83)
Two Kinds of Love (CBS-TV, 11/8/83)
Passions (CBS-TV, 10/1/84)

The Other Lover (CBS-TV, 9/24/85)
This Child Is Mine (NBC-TV, 11/4/85)
Martin's Day (MGM/UA, 1985)
Child's Cry (CBS-TV, 2/9/86)
Young Again (ABC-TV, 5/11/86)
Convicted (ABC-TV, 5/12/86)
Stranger in My Bed (NBC-TV, 1/12/87)
Return of the Six Million Dollar Man and the Bionic Woman (NBC-TV, 5/17/87)
Student Exchange (ABC-TV, 11/29/87; 12/6/87)
Evil in Clear River (ABC-TV, 1/11/88)
The Taking of Flight 847: The Uli Derickson Story (NBC-TV, 5/2/88)
Nightmare at Bitter Creek (CBS-TV, 5/24/88)
Police Story: Burnout (ABC-TV, 11/26/88)
From the Dead of Night (NBC-TV, 2/27/89–2/28/89)

The Bionic Showdown: The Six Millon Dollar Man and the Bionic Woman (NBC-TV, 4/30/89)

Voice of the Heart (Synd-TV, 4/23/90–4/24/90)

Shattered Dreams (CBS-TV, 5/13/90) (also co-executive producer)

Babies (NBC-TV, 9/17/90)

Future Releases

Ricochet (WB, 1991)
Fire in the Dark (CBS-TV, 1991)
To Be the Best (Synd-TV, 1992)

Television Series

The Bionic Woman (ABC, 1976–77; NBC, 1977–78)

Scruples (CBS, 2/25/80; 2/26/80; 2/28/80) [miniseries]

Jessie (ABC, 1984)
The Peaceable Kingdom (CBS, 1989)

SIGOURNEY WEAVER

"I think my greatest asset as an actress has been my height because
it's forced people to think of me for distinctive roles."
—*New York Daily News*, January 23, 1981

SIGOURNEY WEAVER WAS NOT THE FIRST PERSON TO BE NOMINATED
for Academy Awards in both the leading and supporting acting categories in the same year.
However, she was the first person not to win either prize. An interesting aspect of the dual
nomination was that one was for drama, the other for comedy. As in the case of Jessica
Lange, this illustrates Sigourney's diversified adeptness. Called "a seamless fusion of beauty
and intelligence" by *Newsweek* magazine, she considers herself "an overeducated east coast
person," attributes which may have intimidated Academy voters. Once told that she was
too tall at 5' 11" for a particular part, she offered jokingly to "paint shoes on my feet and
play it barefooted." Instead, Mel Gibson was asked to stand on a box when they co-starred
in THE YEAR OF LIVING DANGEROUSLY (1983).

Because of Weaver's imposing physical stature, Hollywood has failed to fully tap her
natural flair for comedy. Instead, it has preferred to pit her on camera against intergalacti-
cal monsters or creatures of slime. Often compared with Meryl Streep, she has said, "I
think I get the roles Meryl's not doing." Despite much critical acclaim and several box-
office successes, she does not consider herself "one of the top people."

She was born Susan Alexandra Weaver in New York City on Saturday, October 8,
1949, to Sylvester "Pat" Weaver, at the time a top NBC-TV network executive, and
Elizabeth Inglis Weaver, a British-born actress and former Warner Bros. contract player.
Preceded in birth by brother Trajan, she later claimed to have been "a privileged,
pampered, sheltered child" as well as "a sweet, stupid little child." Summers were spent at
the family's colonial farmhouse on Long Island, while during the winters the family lived
in a luxury apartment on Manhattan's Upper East Side. A frequent visitor was Pat's
brother, Winston "Doodles" Weaver, a well-known comedian. Her early schooling took
place at exclusive institutions (the Chapin and Brearley Schools in Manhattan) where, at
various times, she wanted to be a marine biologist, a lawyer, a doctor, or to devote her life
to animals as Jane Goodall had done. Her first encounter with a creature of the jungle
occurred when she visited "The Today Show," created by her father and hosted by Dave
Garroway. There J. Fred Muggs, the NBC network chimpanzee, attacked her by taking
away her hat and smashing her coat. She later remembered the incident with, "I don't
think I thought of him as an ape—I thought he was a little boy. He was in clothes."

At the age of thirteen, having attained her full height of 5' 11", she became a "very successful clown" to hide her clumsiness. However, at fourteen she made the decision that she was too tall to be known as Susie and changed her name to Sigourney after a character in F. Scott Fitzgerald's *The Great Gatsby*. Not certain that she was serious about the name change, her family, for a year, simply called her "S." Her high school years were spent in Simsbury, Connecticut, at the Ethel Walker private boarding school. This was followed, after graduation, by her coming out in November 1967 at the age of eighteen at the Grosvenor Debutante Ball, held at Manhattan's Plaza Hotel. Engaged at the time to marry Aaron Latham, a writer, she was later said by him to have worshipped her father and to have had a rivalry with her mother.

After studying a year at Sarah Lawrence College in Bronxville, New York, she transferred to Stanford University in California as an English major. Her goal was to earn a Ph.D. degree and become a professor of literature. This lofty plan was discarded, however, when she became involved with a "guerrilla theater" group at Stanford, which participated in the anti-Vietnam War movement by staging political plays. In further protest, she often dressed herself as an elf and even lived in a tree. She aligned herself with a second theater company touring the San Francisco Bay area doing *King Lear* and other Shakespearean plays. She next spent three years at the Yale School of Drama in New Haven, a time she described as "joyless and negative" in a "pretentious and pseudo-serious" atmosphere. She did find a kindred spirit in classmate Christopher Durang. She worked in several of his improvisational stage plays, including *Better Dead Than Sorry* (singing the title song while receiving electro-shock therapy) and *The Marriage of Bette and Boo* (laughing while being beaten by a husband).

Immediately upon graduating from Yale in 1974, Sigourney returned to New York to pursue a stage career. Supported by her father for several months while she sought work, she was finally hired as an understudy by director John Gielgud for his Broadway revival of W. Somerset Maugham's *The Constant Wife*, starring Ingrid Bergman. While appearing in television commercials for Pepsi-Cola and Lowenbräu beer, she made her professional stage debut in Durang's off-Broadway production of *Titanic* as a homicidal schizophrenic, and then later starred off-Broadway in *Gemini* (1976), written by Yale classmate Albert Innaurato. Also during 1976, Sigourney landed the role of Avis Ryan, a television news reporter, in NBC-TV's soap opera "Somerset," which ended with the show's demise on December 31, 1976.

In April 1977 she made her motion picture debut in an unbilled bit part in Woody Allen's New York–made ANNIE HALL. She next appeared in the Israeli-lensed MADMAN (1977), featuring F. Murray Abraham and Michael Beck. Beginning October 27, 1977, for eight episodes on PBS-TV, she was Laura Wheeler in the drama "The Best of Families," set in America during the late nineteenth century. The series was narrated by John Houseman, and its large cast featured another rising talent, William Hurt. From March 19 to April 2, 1978, she appeared in *Conjuring an Event* at the American Place Theatre in New York City. During the spring of 1978, wearing a T-shirt, jeans, boots, and an air of indifference, Weaver brazenly auditioned for a screen role written originally for a man, reportedly for Paul Newman. The project was ALIEN (1979). In being selected by the producers and director Ridley Scott for the lead role of Ripley, Sigourney received her big break in movies. ALIEN opened in theaters across the United States in May 1979 to enthusiastic reviews. By year's end, the feature had grossed more than $100 million domestically. It was a forerunner of the space-ace horror genre, loaded with carnage and shock effects. Within its gripping plot, Ripley is left alone after the other six crew members have fallen victim to the alien creature. It is up to her, caught in bra and panties, to finish the creature off. The *Washington Post* rated her as "the most courageous and resourceful heroine seen on the screen in years." Called "the thinking man's sex symbol" and "the perfect contemporary heroine," she graced the cover of *Newsweek* magazine in June 1979 and was heralded as "the new Jane Fonda." Much was made of the fact that within ALIEN, it was a female, not a male, who proved to be the ultracourageous, resourceful survivor.

In January–February 1979, Sigourney starred off-Broadway in *New Jerusalem*, during which time she became involved romantically with actor/writer James McClure. Beginning February 16, 1980, she and Christopher Durang had a good time on stage at New York's Chelsea Theatre Center in a two-character cabaret act they had written. Titled *Das Lusitania Songspiel,* it was a spoof of the works of Bertolt Brecht. Both stars were nominated for Drama Desk Awards for acting and writing, and the *New York Times* called her "a fine, loose, knockout comedienne." On October 24, 1979, Sigourney appeared in "The Sorrows of Gin," on PBS-TV's "Great Performances." In this adaptation of John Cheever's story, she played the preoccupied, drink-happy socialite wife of Edward Herrmann, too busy for her precocious youngster (Mara Hobel). *Variety* reported that although the "adaptation never catches fire," Herrmann and Weaver offered "solid performances." (She would appear later in "O Youth and Beauty," another PBS-TV adaptation of a John Cheever story.) Weaver was in Chicago during the autumn of 1980 in James McClure's comedy *Lone Star*, presented at the Travel Light Theatre. At one point, Twentieth Century–Fox planned to turn the play into a movie starring Sigourney; however, the project was later dropped. It was Debra Winger who won the female lead in URBAN COWBOY (1980) after Sigourney was rejected as being too old (at thirty-one) to co-star with twenty-six-year-old John Travolta.

As her second major film, she chose the New York–filmed EYEWITNESS (1981), in which she played an aloof television newswoman adored from afar by the janitor (William Hurt) of a building in which an Asian businessman has been murdered. This shiny, slick production, directed by Peter Yates, had a screenplay, written by Steve Tesich, that was cluttered with unsatisfactory red herrings. Although slow to generate box-office interest, its appeal increased after the release a few months later of BODY HEAT (1981), with moviegoers intrigued to see more of William Hurt. She was on stage off-Broadway in Durang's *Beyond Therapy* and *The Nature and Purpose of the Universe.* Wanting badly to be directed by veteran Fred Zinnemann, she flew to England in 1981 to talk to him about co-starring in his FIVE DAYS ONE SUMMER (1983), but she was persuaded that she was not right physically for the part of a female mountain climber. (It was Betsy Brantley who was hired to co-star opposite Sean Connery.) Simultaneously, Weaver decided that YES,

GIORGIO (1982) was not for her and turned down the offer to appear with Luciano Pavarotti. Kathryn Harrold accepted the unchallenging assignment in what proved to be a critical and box-office flop.

In January 1983 *People* magazine predicted, "It hardly seems premature to predict this film will rank among the year's best." With Mel Gibson, she starred in THE YEAR OF LIVING DANGEROUSLY (1983), filmed in the Philippines and Australia. The steamy love scenes caused *Playgirl* magazine to applaud "the combined heat of these two new sexual icons." Within this well-regarded political drama filled with romantic interludes, Sigourney was cast as an American Embassy attaché with access to secret documents who is in love with and is used by an Australian journalist (Mel Gibson) during the period of political unrest in Indonesia in the mid-1960s. Diminutive Linda Hunt (playing a man!) won a Best Supporting Actress Oscar for her role as the wily native who befriends Gibson.

At Equity scale of $375 per week, Weaver joined the Williamstown Theatre Festival on the campus of Williams College in Massachusetts in its August 1983 production of *Old Times*. There, she met Jim Simpson, a dimpled, pixie-faced theater director. On movie screens in November 1983, Sigourney co-starred with Chevy Chase in DEAL OF THE CENTURY, hustling weapons in Latin America. Intended as a comedy, it fell far short of its goal and was her first unsuccessful movie. When her father was honored with the Governor's Award at the 1983 Emmy Awards for his pioneering work at NBC, Sigourney proudly beamed from the audience. "He's the man of the hour," she said. "He's the *star*."

In the spring of 1984 she premiered on stage in Chicago with William Hurt and Christopher Walken in David Rabe's *Hurlyburly*, concerning the drug scene in Hollywood. She had the role of Darlene, a wacky photojournalist. In June the production

Gregory Hines, Chevy Chase, and **Sigourney Weaver** in DEAL OF THE CENTURY (1983).

moved to off-Broadway and then to Broadway where, under Mike Nichols's direction, Hurt, Weaver, and Judith Ivey were all nominated for Tony Awards, the latter two competing in the same category. Ivey won the trophy. Also in June, GHOSTBUSTERS (1984) premiered with Sigourney as Manhattanite Dana Barrett, whose body is inhabited by spirits from another time. However, a team of zany exorcists (Bill Murray, Dan Aykroyd, Harold Ramis, Ernie Hudson) finally get the better of the slimy devils. The *New York Post* singled her out with, "As usual, the calm, collected, and always sexy Sigourney Weaver makes the thankless role of female foil something special indeed." GHOSTBUSTERS ranked #2 for the year—behind BEVERLY HILLS COP—with domestic grosses of $220.8 million. In October 1984 Sigourney left the cast of *Hurlyburly* to marry Jim Simpson in a simple ceremony at the Long Island Yacht Club, where her father was a member. Sigourney was thirty-five and her husband was twenty-nine. They took up residence on Manhattan's Upper West Side.

Traveling to France in February 1985, she co-starred with popular French film star Gérard Depardieu in the comedy UNE FEMME OU DEUX, not released in the United States until 1987 (as ONE WOMAN OR TWO). For the most part, critics were not kind and Sigourney herself refers to it as "that French film." Later in 1985, with Christopher Durang, she spoofed OUT OF AFRICA (1985) in a photo spread in *Esquire* magazine. On Christmas Eve 1985 she starred in CBS-TV's "An American Portrait," in the episode "Clement Clark Moore."

ALIENS (1986) established Sigourney Weaver as a major screen star. Reprising the role of Warrant Officer Ripley (whose first name was never revealed), she awakens from a fifty-seven-year sleep aboard the same ship on which she had won the battle against the ugly reptilian creature. She discovers that the planet Archeron that birthed the monster has been colonized during her absence by unsuspecting humans. Now, contact with them has been lost. Reluctantly, she agrees to return with a squadron of marines. Filmed in London at the Pinewood Studios, ALIENS had a more realistic look than its predecessor. It was less glossy and audiences could better respond to the story. The sequel realized domestic grosses in excess of $81.4 million, making it the #7 box-office hit of the year. Sigourney was nominated for a Best Actress Academy Award, but lost to Marlee Matlin (CHILDREN OF A LESSER GOD). In describing her macho heroine role she said, "I felt like 'Ramboline.' I lugged around all those heavy guns—I detest guns." Weaver would later become an outspoken member of the Handgun Control Lobby.

Toward the end of 1986, Jim Simpson directed her as Portia in *The Merchant of Venice* for the Classic Stage Company of New York. "We got killed," she admitted later. "I didn't even read the reviews, but I know we got killed." She was right. The *New York Times*, for example, reported that "in all candidness, this is not Ms. Weaver's finest three and one-quarter hours."

After completing ALIENS, she had remained in London to film HALF-MOON STREET (1986), an interesting but not totally believable story of an intelligent scholar (Sigourney) who supplements her low-paying job with funds derived from prostitution. *Variety* gave the spy movie, which co-starred Michael Caine, its deepest cut by labeling it "a half-baked excuse for a film." Weaver, hosting NBC-TV's "Saturday Night Live" in mid-October 1986, participated in a parody of ALIENS that was less than sparkling.

Absent from movie screens for nearly two years, she returned resoundingly on September 23, 1988, in GORILLAS IN THE MIST, based on the life of the late primatologist Dian Fossey. The role had been offered to Jessica Lange, who rejected the assignment. Sigourney's audition hinged on whether or not the gorillas inhabiting the Virunga Mountains of Central Africa would accept her. They did, and she undertook the grueling characterization. Sigourney gave a brilliant portrayal of the driven researcher who becomes obsessive in her quest to save the vanishing breed. A week before the movie's general release, she starred in the syndicated special "Making *Gorillas in the Mist*" (September 16, 1988).

Initially she turned down Mike Nichols's offer to take a less-than-starring role in WORKING GIRL (1988), but he talked her into it with: "As your friend, you really have to play this part because nobody knows you're funny." At a reported salary of $1.4 million, she was Katharine Parker, a well-tailored, smartly coiffed New York City bitch who is very successful in big business mergers and acquisitions. Although she received second billing, after Harrison Ford, her memorable role was much smaller than the third-billed Melanie Griffith's.

For the December 1988 issue of *Vanity Fair* magazine, Sigourney stood for a photo session by Helmut Newton wearing a silver satin gown and a blonde wig in the style of Louise Brooks's famous cut. (Weaver was among those, including Charlotte Rampling, Catherine Deneuve, and Faye Dunaway, who appeared in the West German–French documentary HELMUT NEWTON: FRAMES FROM THE EDGE, 1989.) She also created Goat Cay Productions, her own company, while *US* magazine, in its wrap-up issue of 1988, selected her as one of the screen's top twenty stars. On January 28, 1989, nominated for Golden Globe Awards as both Best Supporting Actress in a Comedy for WORKING GIRL and Best Actress in a Drama for GORILLAS IN THE MIST, she won the latter award in a three-way tie with Jodie Foster (THE ACCUSED) and Shirley MacLaine (MADAME SOU-SATZKA). "I'll probably never work again," she quipped after being handed the award. A month later, she was honored in two Academy Award categories as well, one of four times in Oscar history that this had occurred. All the previous double nominees had won the Best Supporting Actress statue. However, on the evening of March 29, 1989, Sigourney lost to Jodie Foster (Best Actress) and to Geena Davis (Best Supporting Actress for THE ACCIDENTAL TOURIST).

There was some question whether or not Sigourney would return in GHOSTBUST-ERS II (1989). She demanded a $3 million salary, which was rejected. However, after reading the script, she decided to do it anyway. This time around, however, it was not she whom the slime creatures of ancient Babylon were after, but her baby boy (twins William and Henry Deutschendorf). Genevieve Robert, the wife of director Ivan Reitman, noted of Weaver, "She takes this character and gives it dignity and intelligence." Co-star Bill Murray teased, "You know, you're not such a *big* deal when you're working with actors as tall as you are. You can't work with Mel Gibson forever." Not-easy-to-please Pauline Kael

(*The New Yorker* magazine) had to concede that the movie "has a nice, lazy, unforced rhythm. I found it much more enjoyable than the first. . . ." Audiences liked it, too, but not as much as its more inventive and spontaneous predecessor. Costing $40 million to make, the sequel grossed $112 million domestically, a respectable yet disappointing sum.

In July 1989 Weaver announced that she now charged $1.00 for her autograph, with the proceeds donated to AIDS research, an idea she had picked up from Celeste Holm, who for twenty years had been charging fifty cents for her autograph and contributing the money to UNICEF. In January 1990 Sigourney was paid somewhere between $200,000 and $1 million to appear on posters for Japan's Nippon Steel with the caption, "To every part of life, we are committed," referring to the company's diversification in electronics and leisure parks. She had joined the elite Hollywood crowd consisting of Eddie Murphy, Sylvester Stallone, Arnold Schwarzenegger, Kevin Costner, and others who advertised Japanese products in Japan.

On April 14, 1990, she became a mother for the first time at the age of forty with the birth in Manhattan of daughter Charlotte. When initially informed that she might have twins, she was not terribly happy: "One is plenty to start with," she said.

By mid-year Sigourney was publicly making known her displeasure over salary inequities paid in male-dominated Hollywood. Considering herself a victim of sexism at the $2 million salary mark, along with Jessica Lange and Melanie Griffith, she said, "It's a scandal. I certainly feel I'm well paid—but compared to the guys I work with? Forget it. . . . I have this intense desire to get all the actresses together on this. It would be interesting to see what would happen if we all boycotted."

David Twohy had written two scripts for ALIEN III (1991), one without Sigourney, the second with her. Meanwhile, in August 1990, she, the writer/director (James Cameron), and producers of ALIENS sued Twentieth Century–Fox Films, insisting the studio improperly withheld their shares of the net profits from ALIENS. (Weaver claims to be entitled to 10 percent of the film's net profits, Cameron to 10.5 percent.) Reportedly at a salary of $4 million, Sigourney went to London in September 1990 to film ALIEN III, set for release in late 1991.

Sigourney Weaver has been described by director Michael Apted (gorillas in the mist) as having "a devastating combination: she's good-looking and she's smart. She can carry and dominate a movie. I don't think she could act the sort of power that she has on film if she didn't have it in life." However, Sigourney has admitted that the appearance of power can create a problem in offers of film roles. "I'd love to be given something that people don't think I can play," she says. "A dumb blonde, something like that." Regarding her looks and intelligence and abilities, what it boils down to is that filmmakers have not yet tapped Weaver's full potential. As in the case of Rosalind Russell, who was wasted in dramatic roles at the beginning of her career, Sigourney Weaver could work wonders with eccentric characters such as Mame Dennis (AUNTIE MAME, 1958) or Aunt August (TRAVELS WITH MY AUNT, 1972).

Filmography

Annie Hall (UA, 1977)
Madman (Israeli, 1977)
Alien (20th–Fox, 1979)
Eyewitness [The Janitor] (20th–Fox, 1981)
The Year of Living Dangerously (MGM/UA, 1983)
Deal of the Century (WB, 1983)
Ghostbusters (Col, 1984)
Aliens (20th–Fox, 1986)
Half-Moon Street (20th–Fox, 1986)
One Woman or Two [Une Femme ou Deux] (Orion Classics, 1987) [made in 1985]

Gorillas in the Mist (Univ, 1988)
Working Girl (20th–Fox, 1988)
Helmut Newton: Frames from the Edge (West German–Fr, 1989)
Ghostbusters II (Col, 1989)

Future Releases

Alien III (20th–Fox, 1991)

Television Series

Somerset (NBC, 1976)

The Best of Families (PBS, 1977)

Broadway Plays

The Constant Wife (1974) (revival) (understudy)

Hurlyburly (1984)

ROBIN WILLIAMS

"I can barely talk to one person, but when I'm performing for 4,000
people, I'm on. The audience is my high. I could snort them."
—*Los Angeles Times*, May 9, 1990

ROBIN WILLIAMS HAS BEEN COMPARED TO EVERYONE WHO HAS MADE
people laugh since the invention of celluloid, from Charles Chaplin to *all* the Marx
Brothers, to Danny Kaye and Sid Caesar, to Steve Martin and John Belushi, and, adding a
dash of international flair, to Marcel Marceau. No one, however, past or present, can
match his rapid-fire mind and mouth or his physical dexterity. When "on," which is most
of the time, he is a superactive volcano of inventiveness and unpredictability. "You're only
given a little spark of madness," he once confided to *Cue* magazine, "you mustn't lose that
madness." Restrained except when on a comedy club stage, he proved a disappointment in
movies, both to his public and to himself, until a certain vehicle came along in 1987. The
role of the kinetic G.I. radio disc jockey of GOOD MORNING, VIETNAM was tailor-made
for him: loud, fast, improvisational, and *funny*.

He was born on Monday, July 21, 1952, in Chicago, where his parents were living
at the moment. Robert Williams, his fifty-year-old father, was a vice-president of the Ford
Motor Company as well as Midwest regional manager of its Lincoln-Mercury division,
with duties that required frequent relocation. During one eight-year period, Robert
moved his family six times. Robin's mother, Laurie Smith Williams, was involved in
society events during her son's early years, leaving him largely in the care of housekeepers.
Although Laurie had had aspirations toward an acting career, she never pursued them. Yet
Robin credits her and his television idol, Jonathan Winters, as major influences in his
professional life. Two half brothers from his parents' previous marriages, McLaurin Smith-
Williams and Todd Williams, were grown men by the time Robin was born and did not
live at home.

Home to Robin, for possibly the longest period of his childhood, was a thirty-room
house situated on twenty acres in Bloomfield Hills, Michigan, an exclusive suburb of
Detroit. There, in the basement, his stern, disciplinarian father, whom he called "sir," had
a sandbox built for him in which he kept his two thousand toy soldiers, creating voices for
the soldiers and sound effects for their battles. "My imagination was my friend," Robin
once remembered. In his loneliness, he invented characters, using television comedians,
especially Winters, as models. Laurie Williams has claimed that he "wasn't funny around
the house," but Robin remembers performing for his parents as a way of saying "love me."
He attended six different private schools during his formative years, before ending at the

exclusive Detroit Country Day School in Birmingham, Michigan. A fat boy, he was abused verbally by classmates who called him "dwarf" or "leprechaun." He soon learned that they would become friendly with him only by his making them laugh. He began entertaining them with comedy routines he made up himself.

Robert Williams retired in 1969 and moved his small family to Tiburon, California, overlooking San Francisco Bay. For the first time, Robin attended a public school, Redwood High School. He quickly adapted to its relaxed atmosphere by losing thirty pounds and getting involved in sports. His senior class of 1970 voted him the "most humorous" and the "least likely to succeed." This sobriquet did not deter him from enrolling at Claremont Men's College in Claremont to study political science. Unable to focus on his studies because his mind kept concocting comedy routines, he told his father that he wanted to become an actor. "Fine," Robert replied, "but study welding just in case."

After studying the works of Shakespeare at the College of Marin in Kentfield, California, he was granted a full scholarship as an advanced drama student at the Juilliard School in New York City under the directorship of the great John Houseman. It was not long before Houseman realized that his new student did not know the rudiments of acting, so he re-directed Robin into the first-year class. "He was a cutup," Houseman was to recall years later, "but not to the point of unbearableness." During the three years Robin spent at Juilliard, his roommate was Christopher Reeve, who would become a lifelong friend. During their free time, Williams and a friend performed mime in whiteface near the Metropolitan Museum of Art, often collecting as much as $150 a day.

In 1975, having fallen in love, Robin chose not to graduate from Juilliard and instead followed his inamorata to San Francisco where he tried unsuccessfully to obtain dramatic stage parts with the American Conservatory Theatre. Within a short time he had joined a comedy workshop, performing in small San Francisco nightclubs (the Intersection, the Great American Music Hall, the Boardinghouse, and the Holy City Zoo). He also worked in an organic ice cream parlor and tended bar in a Mill Valley club where he also performed. There, having already abandoned any romantic hopes with his "love," he met a modern dancer named Valerie Velardi, who was filling in as a waitress.

Williams realized that Los Angeles presented more opportunities for stand-up comedy. Thus, the bearded comedian with shoulder-length hair moved there in the summer of 1976. He was accepted at the Hollywood Comedy Workshop headed by Harvey Lembeck before he went on stage at "open mike night" at the Comedy Store. He found this club on Sunset Boulevard to be a "terrorizing combination of the Roman Arena and 'The Gong Show.'" "My stomach was in my shoes," he recalled of that first night. "I was so scared." Nevertheless, he went on to become a regular improvisationalist at both the Comedy Store and the Ice House before being recruited—minus the long hair and beard—by television producer George Schlatter for a revival of "Laugh-In." NBC-TV's new "Laugh-In" was first seen on September 12, 1977, followed by five more presentations at irregular intervals. It was last telecast on February 8, 1978, but would be rerun from June 6, 1979, through July 4, 1979, after Robin had gained popularity. Beginning

September 13, 1977, he was a regular on NBC-TV's "The Richard Pryor Show," but this program failed to garner a following and went off the air on October 20, 1977. His motion picture debut, if it can be termed that, consisted of about sixty seconds in CAN I DO IT 'TIL I NEED GLASSES? (1977), a conglomeration of antiquated jokes about sex. A couple of years later it was rereleased and Robin sued to keep his name out of the credits. Williams was among those who appeared in NBC-TV's "The Great American Laugh-Off" (October 22, 1977).

In the February 28, 1978, segment of ABC-TV's "Happy Days," the zany character of Mork from the planet Ork was introduced. Both Jonathan Winters and Dom DeLuise had rejected the part; it was offered to Robin after he sat on his head during his audition. So much fan mail was received after the February showing that ABC decided to create a sitcom series revolving around Mork. With his next five years secure (he had signed a contract with Paramount Pictures from which he would realize $3 million), Robin was married in June 1978 to Valerie Velardi in Marin County, California. A few months later, they rewed in a second ceremony with her East Coast Italian relatives in attendance. They moved into a small eight-room house in the Topanga Canyon area of Los Angeles.

During the summer of 1978 he parodied himself in a guest spot on "America 2-Night," a syndicated TV program. The misfit Mork officially touched down on earth (in Boulder, Colorado) to study a primitive human society on September 14, 1978, in "Mork & Mindy" with Pam Dawber as Mindy, his new-found earth friend and foil. Baffled by earthly things, the innocent alien, sporting rainbow-colored suspenders, wore his watch around an ankle, got drunk on soda pop, talked to plants, and spoke English with a wacky accent punctuated by Orkian phrases such as "Na-noo, na-noo" for "hello." *Variety* enthused, "Williams, who specializes in wild gibberish in a trick voice, seemed completely in control of the required contrasts necessary to make Mork likeable along with being nuttily funny. . . ." An instant hit, the premiere received an astounding 46 percent share of the viewing audience, according to the A. C. Nielsen Company. The sole TV comic permitted to ad-lib during a show, Robin soared to further celebrity heights through Mork T-shirts, dolls, and bubble gum sold in a plastic egg. In December 1978 he was presented with a Golden Apple award as the Male Discovery of the Year by the Hollywood Women's Press Club. He also won Golden Globe and People's Choice Awards. While he continued to perform on weekends at the Comedy Store at no salary, he politely refused offers to appear on network talk or game shows.

Williams's per episode salary was doubled for the 1979–1980 season, from $15,000 to $30,000, but for inexplicable reasons Paramount and ABC-TV tampered with their success by moving the show from Thursday to Sunday and, later, by writing out and replacing well-known, accepted characters. On September 9, 1979, Robin guest-starred as Mork in an ABC-TV pilot, "Out of the Blue," in which Mork helped series lead Jimmy Brogan (playing an angel) who is sent to earth to help five orphaned kids. Robin's comedy album *Reality . . . What a Concept* sold over one million copies during 1979–1980, ensuring its status as a platinum landmark. He was honored with a Grammy for his efforts. In April 1979 he had appeared in a six-day engagement at the Copacabana club in New

York City, and then did a short tour of his one-man show, which was taped and shown on HBO–Cable as "Robin Williams: Off the Wall." Robin, who purchased his customary baggy trousers and loud Hawaiian shirts at used-clothing stores, could, it seemed, do no wrong professionally. "When you're creating," he said, "you just become a vehicle. It seems to come from a divine source, a sense of wonder of God." Publicly, he was involved in various causes, such as the Human/Dolphin Foundation, the March of Dimes, and benefits for the Los Angeles Children's Museum, and was active in anti-nuclear rallies. Privately, during this period he developed a strong proclivity for alcohol and cocaine. "I was on everything but skates," he has said of the next three years, but never imbibed any drug while working.

In January 1980 he traveled to Malta to film his first major motion picture, POPEYE, released that December. At a salary of $500,000, he brought America's beloved spinach-eating strongman sailor to life on the big screen. Once intended for Dustin Hoffman, POPEYE was scorned by critics for its dreary songs, uninventive plotline, and stagnant direction. However, audiences, eager to see what else one of their TV favorites could do, bought tickets to the tune of $50 million, establishing POPEYE as the #10 moneymaker of the year.

With the ratings of "Mork & Mindy" sagging, a new character, Mork's son Mearth, was introduced on October 29, 1981. After a return trip to Ork, Mork discovers that he is pregnant when, from his navel, a giant egg issues. From the egg emerges Jonathan Winters, Robin's long-time idol and television mentor. On Ork, babies are born mature, then age backward to infancy. The delightfully bizarre idea was initially enjoyed by viewers, but interest soon waned. "Mork & Mindy" went off the air with its episode of June 10, 1982. A cartoon version of the series debuted in September 1982 using Robin's voice for Mork's, but lasted only a few months. Also in 1982, Paramount Home Video released *An Evening with Robin Williams*. According to *TV Guide* magazine, "Freud would have loved to listen to this guy free-associate" as "the master motormouth ricochets from gay burglars who redecorate to white sharks off black beaches."

The events of the night of March 4–5, 1982, marked an important, decisive period in Robin's life. Ten minutes before John Belushi died from a drug overdose, Robin had been with his friend at the Chateau Marmont and because of this Robin was ordered to testify at a grand-jury probe into the comedian's death. A few months later, Valerie became pregnant. Robin, on the threshold of fatherhood, abandoned both drink and drugs. "I couldn't imagine being fried and being a father," he was to say later.

THE WORLD ACCORDING TO GARP (1982), a distillation of John Irving's quirky best-selling novel, cast Robin as the adult Garp making his bizarre odyssey through life. *People* magazine complained, "Casting Robin Williams as the sanity-seeking Garp can hardly be called inspired. He plays so hard against his Morky, zonked-out image, it's like watching an actor in a straitjacket." Much better cast were Glenn Close (in her screen debut) as his unmarried, feminist mother, and John Lithgow as a former pro football player turned transsexual. Soon after the release of GARP, Robin starred on Showtime–Cable in the "Faerie Tale Theatre" episode "The Tale of the Frog Prince" (September 11,

1982) as a royal frog showing a selfish princess (Teri Garr) that love exists.

Both Robin and co-star Walter Matthau tried hard to breathe life into THE SURVIVORS (1983) as unemployed men who witness a robbery and then become involved in a militaristic self-survival training program. The black comedy had its rare good moments, along with ample degrees of vulgarity and violence. In 1983 Valerie gave birth to son Zachary, with Christopher Reeve named as the child's godfather. April 1984 saw the release of MOSCOW ON THE HUDSON, a fun movie that gave Robin ample opportunity to use his Russian accent as a musician who defects in Bloomingdale's perfume department. On February 19, 1984, he was one of the masters of ceremonies of Showtime–Cable's hour-long special "An Evening at the Improv," honoring the twentieth year of the Los Angeles comedy nightclub.

Off movie screens for almost two years, Robin returned, against the advice of his manager, co-starring with Kurt Russell as an over-the-hill athlete in THE BEST OF TIMES (1986), a critical and financial disappointment. His career slump was solidified by the Jamaican-filmed CLUB PARADISE (1986). He starred as a Chicagoan who retires early to a Caribbean isle only to become involved in a revolution which he helps to abort. He turned dramatic in an adaptation of Saul Bellow's novella *Seize the Day*, presented at the Toronto Festival of Festivals on September 9, 1986, and later aired on PBS-TV (May 1, 1987). It dealt with a man who discovers at age forty that he is a failure in life. Robin's one-man comedy show filmed at the Metropolitan Opera House in New York City earned him the distinction of being the first comic to perform there. Called *Robin Williams Live*, it was later released on home video. (The album from the event, called *A Night at the Opera*, won him a Grammy Award.) In 1986, in conjunction with HBO–Cable, he, Whoopi Goldberg, and Billy Crystal organized and presented the first "Comic Relief," a fundraiser on behalf of the nation's homeless. The charity special became a major annual event.

Robin Williams in THE WORLD ACCORDING TO GARP (1982).

Back in 1984 Valerie Williams had hired painter/waitress/nanny Marsha Garces, an attractive young woman of Filipino and Finnish extraction, to care for her son. Two years later, when Marsha left the Williamses' home, Robin admitted, "My marriage fell apart." Early in 1987 he made a private out-of-court separation settlement with Valerie. Thereafter, he and Marsha became live-in companions. On February 10, 1987, Robin joined Carol Burnett,

Whoopi Goldberg, and Carl Reiner for ABC-TV's "A Carol Burnett Special." He hosted "Saturday Night Live" in 1987 and was among many stars providing voiceovers in DEAR AMERICA: LETTERS HOME FROM VIETNAM.

Mitch Markowitz might have written the screenplay for GOOD MORNING, VIET-NAM (1987) with Robin in mind, since the film finally enabled him to be as outrageous on screen as he is in real life. In the comedy, set in 1965 Saigon, Airman Adrian Cronauer (Robin) has just been transferred from Greece to become the new morning disc jockey of the Armed Forces Radio network in Vietnam to help boost morale. Opening his show with a rousing "Gooooood Mooooooorning, Vietnaaammm," he presented his own brand of frenetic humor with pell-mell monologues on political matters. Thanks to Williams's energy-packed performance, GOOD MORNING, VIETNAM grossed $123.9 million domes-tically, becoming the #4 box-office hit of the year. After he received an Academy Award nomination as Best Actor (he lost to Michael Douglas of WALL STREET), Robin's per film salary escalated from $2 million to $4 million. For his appearance on "ABC Presents a Royal Gala" (May 28, 1988), Robin won an Emmy for Best Individual Performance in a Variety or Music Program.

In November 1988, under the direction of Mike Nichols, Robin co-starred on stage with Steve Martin at the 299-seat Mitzi E. Newhouse Theatre in New York City's Lincoln Center in a limited-run revival of *Waiting for Godot*, described by *Newsweek* magazine as "electrifying." On December 14, 1988, on ABC-TV's "Free to Be . . . a Family," Robin used a bag of props to show children of the United States and Russia "what is funny for two cultures." The Hasty Pudding Theatricals of Harvard University honored him as their Man of the Year on February 21, 1989. On April 30, 1989, at Lake Tahoe, Williams was married to Marsha Garces. She was five years his junior and five months pregnant.

As a picture, DEAD POETS SOCIETY (1989) received mixed reviews. Gene Shalit (TV's "The Today Show") decided it was "One of the most magnificent motion pictures I have ever seen." On the other hand, *People* magazine reported, "[They] seem to have had in mind a substantial movie; they ended up making *Goodbye, Mr. Chips Meets Revenge of the Nerds*." But almost everyone agreed that as the freethinking, good-hearted prep school teacher, Robin was superb, albeit in a rather small role. He received his second Oscar nomination, but lost the Best Actor Academy Award to Daniel Day-Lewis (MY LEFT FOOT). Nevertheless, DEAD POETS SOCIETY emerged the #9 hit of 1989, with worldwide receipts totaling $170 million. It was during this period that Robin lost out both on playing The Joker in BATMAN (1989) to Jack Nicholson and being the voice of the baby in LOOK WHO'S TALKING (1989) to Bruce Willis. He did take the small, but funny, uncredited part of the Moon King in THE ADVENTURES OF BARON MUNCHAUSEN (1989), one of the decade's biggest box-office disasters. (It lost an estimated $43 million.)

In mid-1989, in a two-part interview on ABC-TV's "Good Morning America," he told viewers that comedy was his shield: "It's a great way to keep people out. Comedy is a defense and also a weapon. You can use it to decimate people and to hold people back to defuse them . . . if they laugh, they won't hurt you." In Manhattan, on July 31, 1989, Marsha Garces Williams gave birth to a baby girl, whom the couple named Zelda. "The

Barbara Walters Special" (September 26, 1989) included an eager Robin Williams, wife, and baby in an effort to correct misimpressions given in the tabloid press. Robin, on December 15, 1989, narrated, on Showtime–Cable, "Legend of Pecos Bill," the children's story of the cowboy raised by coyotes. (The Windham Hill album version won a Grammy Award.)

In March 1990 Robin moved his growing family and his collection of lead soldiers to a six hundred-acre ranch in northern California's Napa Valley. On April 22, he joined a host of celebrities for ABC-TV's "Earth Day Special," while the dynamic trio of "Comic Relief IV" drummed up $4.7 million for the homeless. "Comic Relief" I, II, and III were made available as albums on the Rhino label, while *Comic Relief—The Best of Comic Relief* was issued by Rhino on compact disc as well as in cassette and home video format, with the proceeds from sales going to Comic Relief, Inc. to benefit the homeless. Opening in May 1990, CADILLAC MAN was soundly trashed by the *Hollywood Reporter* as "a lemon" and by *Variety* as "dilapidated" with "the distinction of being the loudest film of 1990 so far and one of the worst." Even the *San Francisco Chronicle* columnist Herb Caen, not a movie critic, was unable to contain himself when he called it "a clunker that gets about two smiles per gallon." Robin was cast as a womanizing car salesman who suddenly finds himself the savior of a group of hostages being held at gunpoint by a crazed man (Tim Robbins). However, it was reported by *People* magazine that "the French apparently have gone gaga over CADILLAC MAN"; in September 1990 it was the #3 box-office attraction for Parisians.

Robin was a last-minute addition to the cast of the Bread and Roses Acoustic Music Festival on September 8, 1990, at the University of California at Berkeley's Greek Theatre, where he delivered "fresh comedic bits" about birth control, abortion, oil and Iraq, Jim and Tammy Bakker, "and other topics of morality" (*Oakland Tribune*). To benefit the California environment and Proposition 128, called "Big Green," on the November 1990 ballot, Robin provided comedy on stage at the Greek Theatre in Los Angeles on September 13; the event was televised by ABC-TV as "An Evening with . . ." (September 19, 1990). On December 12, 1990, Robin was the recipient of the 1,926th star on the Hollywood Walk of Fame.

AWAKENINGS (1990) presented Williams as a psychiatrist (based on real-life neurologist Dr. Oliver Sacks) who in the mid-1960s encountered a group of extreme catatonics, including Robert De Niro, who are actually victims of a post–sleeping sickness syndrome. Determined to prove that these people are still alive inside, Williams tests a new drug on them, which temporarily alleviates their trance-like condition. During the long shooting schedule in Manhattan, Robin accidentally broke De Niro's nose. The feature, directed by Penny Marshall, ran four hours and twenty minutes in its first cut. (When released in mid-December 1990, the medical drama was shorn to 121 minutes, with *Variety* enthusing, "Robin Williams finds another role perfectly suited to his gifts. . . . Enacting the shy, fidgety doctor, Williams extends the extraordinary dramatic gifts he displayed in DEAD POETS SOCIETY. . . . He's also very funny. . . .") THE FISHER KING (1991) found Williams playing a radio show personality, with Jeff Bridges as a disc jockey. In the course of the story, the two men are reduced to street persons searching for the Holy Grail.

Forthcoming for Robin Williams in 1991 is HOOK, directed by Steven Spielberg, described as "a 1990s 'Peter Pan,'" with Robin as Pan's great-grandson and Dustin Hoffman as the dastardly Captain Hook. Robin will also star in MOSCOW ON THE HUDSON II for producer-director Paul Mazursky, in which Williams's character returns to Russia to visit his pal (Elya Baskin) and, while there, falls in love with a Russian woman. In TOYS, to be directed by Barry Levinson, Robin will play the son of a famous toy manufacturer. Other possible projects for the comedian star include the long-discussed GOOD MORNING, CHICAGO, a sequel to GOOD MORNING, VIETNAM. Williams would reprise his successful role of Adrian Cronauer, this time in civilian togs. Robin, who has been said to resemble Lech Walesa, Poland's Solidarity leader, has for some years wanted to portray this present-day European hero in a musical movie or play.

Having sworn to slow down after making THE FISHER KING, Robin apparently has either forgotten his pledge or has been offered projects he finds far too intriguing to dismiss. Ideas come from all areas; he once told of a Los Angeles policeman who stopped him for speeding but who first told him, "Oh, Mr. Williams, before I give you a ticket, I'd like to show you my script." Having found the power of fantasy, Williams refuses to let it go, since it, along with comedy, provides the shield necessary to cloak his innate shyness. "Comedy is a great way to keep people out," This would be an empty world, indeed, if it were robbed of Williams's mimicking of a Japanese rabbi, or Jonathan Winters in a hot tub, or Timothy Leary on acid. Robin credits his wife and his San Francisco–area neighbors with imbuing with a touch of normalcy what might easily otherwise be for him a super-hyper existence. "Fame can be like a drug," he says, "there's an exhilaration to it, but you can come crashing down hard."

Filmography

Can I Do It 'Til I Need Glasses? (National-American, 1977)
Popeye (Par, 1980)
The World According to Garp (WB, 1982)
The Survivors (Col, 1983)
Moscow on the Hudson (Col, 1984)
The Best of Times (Univ, 1986)
Club Paradise (WB, 1986)
Dear America: Letters Home from Vietnam (HBO–Couturie, 1987) (voice only)
Good Morning, Vietnam (BV, 1987)

Dead Poets Society (BV, 1989)
The Adventures of Baron Munchausen (Col/Tri-Star, 1989)
Cadillac Man (Orion, 1990)
Awakenings (Col, 1990)
Dead Again (Par, 1991)
The Fisher King (Tri-Star, 1991)

Future Releases

Hook (Tri-Star, 1991)

Television Series

Laugh-In (NBC, 1977–78)
The Richard Pryor Show (NBC, 1977)

Mork & Mindy (ABC, 1978–82)
Mork & Mindy (ABC, 1982–83) (cartoon series; voice only)

Album Discography

The Best of Comic Relief 2 (Rhino R11H-
70707)

Comic Relief '90 (Rhino R215-71010)

Comic Relief—The Best of Comic Relief (Rhino
RNIN-70704)

Comic Relief 3 (Rhino R21K-70893)

A Night at the Opera (Columbia FCT-40541)

Pecos Bill (Windham Hill WH-0709)

Popeye (Boardwalk SW-36880) [ST]

Reality . . . What a Concept (Casablanca 7162)

Throbbing Python of Love (Casablanca 811150-
1)

TREAT WILLIAMS

"I'm a character actor and I like to work on pieces that are challenging and different. Those kinds of pieces usually go to another actor who's already got clout in Hollywood, if they go to anybody at all."
—*Video Review* magazine, April 1990

ALL THE INGREDIENTS OF A PROMINENT LEADING MAN IN SHOW BUSIness are there: talent, brooding good looks, and muscles. But motion picture fame remains an elusive commodity for Treat Williams. Although his stage, film, and television performances regularly receive critical acclaim, he has no big-grossing motion picture on his résumé. Thus, in the eyes of an industry that focuses closely on box-office receipts, Williams is not a bankable actor. Too, by his own admission, Treat lacks sufficient goal orientation. Another factor that has deterred him on the path to full stardom is his resemblance to many other contemporary celebrities. With the square jaw, chiseled features, and bushy brows, he is a composite of Tom Berenger, Mark Harmon, Jeff Bridges, Robert De Niro, Al Pacino, and others. What this resourceful performer needs is a strong role that captures his comedic talents along with his ability to sing and dance—anything to remove him from the buddy-cop mold.

An ancestor of Robert Treat Paine, a signer of America's Declaration of Independence, Richard Treat Williams was born on Saturday, December 1, 1951, in Rowayton, Connecticut, on Long Island Sound. The only son of a New York City corporate executive, Richard Williams, and his wife, Treat—as he was called—grew up in a sheltered atmosphere from which he longed to escape. An unruly boy imbued with Welsh stubbornness, he survived several private preparatory schools before discovering football at Rowayton High School. Through the sport he was able to unleash his rebellious fury. Airplanes and flying were also of major interest and he dreamed of becoming a pilot.

At Franklin & Marshall College in Lancaster, Pennsylvania, in 1969, he played freshman football. Then he found an alternative outlet for his creative juices—the theater. He quit the football squad to work with a little theater group, joined the school's drama department, took voice classes with an opera singer, and took dance lessons as well. Ostracized by his former gridiron friends for having abandoned them for what were considered effeminate endeavors, he became moody and withdrawn. However, he stuck with his chosen curriculum. In 1971 he added flying instructions to his list of studies, aiming for a commercial pilot's license.

Williams dropped out of college after three years to go to New York City in search of stage work, helped by Broadway-associated friends of his family. For nine months he played a minor role in the touring company of *Grease*, opening in Boston on December 23, 1972. During the trek he became friendly with fellow cast member John Travolta, with whom he shared a passion for airplanes. Returning to New York, and now being represented by the prestigious William Morris Agency, he understudied Travolta on Broadway in *Grease*. Next both he and Travolta obtained chorus roles in *Over Here!*, the 1940s-set musical starring Patty and Maxene Andrews. That production opened on March 6, 1974, and ran for 348 performances. Treat then returned to *Grease* for a short time, playing the lead part of Danny Zuko, which, he says, "was like getting paid to go to high school." This was followed by co-starring in the Equity Library Theatre's February 1975 revival of *Bus Stop* as the love-smitten cowboy, which he played for fourteen performances.

His first motion picture role was in dramatic support of Don Murray (as a psychotic cop) and others in DEADLY HERO (1976), a low-budget feature shot in New York City. The suspense picture was hardly noticed by the public. In THE RITZ (1976), adapted for the screen by Terrence McNally from his Broadway comedy, Treat received seventh billing as blond-haired Michael Brick, the often partially nude prepubescent-voiced straight private detective summoned to a notorious Manhattan gay bathhouse. He went to England for the filming of the big-budgeted THE EAGLE HAS LANDED (1977), taken from the engrossing best-selling novel by Jack Higgins about a fictional attempt to capture and assassinate Winston Churchill. Williams was the gung-ho, by-the-book American Army officer in this suspenseful entry, which most critics liked but which had low box-office returns.

In 1978 he starred in Broadway's Circle in the Square Theatre revival of George S. Kaufman and Moss Hart's satirical comedy (*Once in a Lifetime*) about Hollywood's new invention, the talkies. On August 25, 1978, he sang at Leonard Bernstein's sixtieth birthday party held at Virginia's Wolf Trap farm outside Washington, D.C., and a few days later obtained a commercial pilot's license. "Flying is the way I get high," he said, "and I am spaced. It's a natural reaction." He purchased a Cherokee 180 plane. Treat was chosen by Czech director Miloš Forman to star in the screen version of HAIR (1979) after Forman saw him on stage in *Grease*. As hippie leader Berger (complete with a wild hair style courtesy of a painful hair weave), he performed with gusto in this "tribal love rock musical." In the course of the musical, he skinny-dipped in Central Park's lake, did a wild dance number with Charlotte Rae, and easily slid into drugs, sex, and the peace movement as expressions of distaste for the situation in Vietnam. The show had been a Broadway megahit in 1968, but a decade later, movie audiences had perhaps overdosed on the plot and songs and did not attend as expected. Williams ruefully recalled of his sudden burst of fame, "I've had a taste of celebrity. And it left a bad taste. I got a lot of [celebrity party] invitations after HAIR, but after the film flopped, the invitations stopped."

In Steven Spielberg's overly ambitious comedy 1941 (1979), boasting a large cast and good special effects depicting hysteria in Los Angeles after the attack on Pearl Harbor on December 7, 1941, Treat was eleventh-billed as a soldier named Sitarski. This was one of the few Spielberg endeavors that failed to attract moviegoers. In the economy production WHY WOULD I LIE? (1980), Treat had top billing as a compulsive liar involved with an ex-convict (Lisa Eichhorn). *Variety* pinpointed the movie's problem: "[this] is another one of those pictures . . . that assembles a good cast to struggle with a bad script."

With six feature films to his credit, none of which made enough money to qualify him for stardom, Treat deserted the industry and his friends (who included Warren Beatty, Diane Keaton, and Miloš Forman) to take a co-pilot's job with a small Los Angeles–based airline. Confused about his career, he said that he wanted "to do something more solid" than make movies. From his point of view, "I felt so out of control. I wasn't working with people I wanted to work with. I was very frustrated." When asked about marriage, he questioned the ideals of monogamy and fidelity. "I don't think I'd want to be married to someone who just depended on me," he said. "Meeting somebody new can be exciting."

After about six months away from the industry, he was contracted by director Sidney Lumet for the lead in PRINCE OF THE CITY (1981); he first had to read for the part three times because of Lumet's doubt that a song-and-dance man could handle such a somber, complex role. (Because he played the role so well, he was forever after placed squarely in the category of dramatic actor.) PRINCE OF THE CITY is drawn from Robert Daley's book (based on real events) about a dirty New York City cop who cooperated with a 1971 investigation of police corruption and, in the harrowing process, earned the enmity of his peers. In this stark drama, Treat, as that policeman, was required to be on camera— and in an intense mode—for most of its 167 minutes. To prepare for his grueling characterization, Williams spent more than a month at a Manhattan precinct (including going on drug busts) and staying for a time with the man (police detective Robert Leuci) whom he was to portray on screen. Critics like Roger Ebert applauded Treat's powerhouse performance and the total film as "a very good movie," yet it was too overwhelmingly depressing to gain wide audience attention.

While awaiting public reaction to PRINCE OF THE CITY, Treat (a tenor) replaced Kevin Kline as the bearded pirate king in the award-winning *The Pirates of Penzance* at Broadway's Uris Theatre when Kline acquired the male lead in SOPHIE'S CHOICE (1982). When asked about his next screen project, THE PURSUIT OF D. B. COOPER (1981), Treat cracked, "It ain't gonna be CASABLANCA." In the film he portrayed the real-life skyjacker who parachuted from a plane and was never seen again. In his first television movie, DEMPSEY, shown on CBS-TV on September 28, 1983, he portrayed the "Manassa Mauler," Jack Dempsey, a man whose existence was filled with turbulence and no humor. The telefilm was based on the fighter's autobiography. Meanwhile, he starred in the first of several Italian-made features, STANGATA NAPOLETANA—LA TRASTOLA [Something About the Sting] (1983).

Newsweek magazine's appraisal of Treat's characterization of Stanley Kowalski in ABC-TV's presentation of A STREETCAR NAMED DESIRE (March 4, 1984) referred to his having to battle a celluloid ghost: "It would require an awesomely gifted actor to override our memories of Marlon Brando's Kowalski, and Williams has not been so blessed." Nevertheless, he held his own against the dramatic talents of Ann-Margret as Blanche

DuBois and was given ample opportunities to display his bare torso. Other actors given early consideration for the TV role were Richard Gere, Nick Nolte, and Mickey Rourke. For ONCE UPON A TIME IN AMERICA (1984), a panorama of American gangsterism filmed in Italy by Sergio Leone, Treat was reduced to a minor supporting role as an Irishman dabbling in crimes committed by a Jewish gang. Shown in America at various lengths, the home video version ran 227 minutes but was still lacking a scene or two (included in European release versions) thought to be too explicit for American eyes. FLASHPOINT (1984), an underrated action picture, paired Treat and Kris Kristofferson as Texas border patrolmen who find a skeleton and a cache of money in a long-abandoned jeep.

In 1984 he returned to Manhattan to star off-Broadway with Philip Bosco as an executive drowning his sorrows after the loss of his wife in John Ford Noonan's two-character play *Some Men Need Help*. Taped for PBS-TV's "American Playhouse," the eighty-minute drama was shown February 18, 1985. Joyce Chopra, director of SMOOTH TALK (1985), credited Treat as "a gifted comic" who "really cared about the film and was very helpful to the other actors." As a drifter who edges teenager Laura Dern toward adulthood, he gave one of the best screen performances of his career. He was the doctor member of THE MEN'S CLUB (1986), a therapy group, then portrayed J. EDGAR HOOVER (Showtime–Cable, January 11, 1987) through his fifty-five year FBI career. Joining Shelley Duvall's "Faerie Tale Theatre" ensemble, he co-starred in "The Little Mermaid" episode (April 6, 1987) on Showtime–Cable. The next month, on May 18, 1987, he was given a chance to sing and dance in the "Movie-Musical Nostalgia" portion of ABC's "Happy Birthday, Hollywood," honoring Tinsel Town's centennial celebration. He was again, but briefly, a member of the FBI in the CBS-TV movie ECHOES IN THE DARKNESS (November 1–2, 1987), investigating a 1979 suburban Philadelphia homicide. Joseph Wambaugh's adaptation of his own novel was shown in two parts, but Treat appeared only in the concluding episode. *TV Guide* magazine rated him "outstanding," along with Gary Cole and Peter Boyle.

Treat Williams in DEAD HEAT (1988).

By 1988 Treat had made three movies and a television comedy in

Italy, only one of which (RUSSICUM I GIRONI DEL DIAVOLO, 1988) made it briefly to American theatrical release. "It's been a wonderful kind of second home over there," he told the *Los Angeles Times* in May 1988. "Whether or not the films I did will be translated to English, I don't know . . . you don't have to worry quite so much about the success or failure. They don't give so much weight to success and failure. If a film fails, it doesn't mean the actor's career is over. It's not a disgusting thing if somebody falls on their face." (He would later make more films in Italy: BURRO [1989] and OLTRE L'OCEANO [1990], the latter with Jill Clayburgh and Ben Gazzara, who also directed.)

DEAD HEAT (1988) was a different type of police partnership film in that Treat's character, aptly named Roger Mortis, killed in a decompression chamber, was brought back to life for twelve hours by means of reanimation in order to help his buddy (Joe Piscopo) clear up a mystery. Filmed in Paris, SWEET LIES (1989) was a silly romantic comedy, with Treat as an insurance investigator sent abroad to track a case of fraud. Two women (Joanna Pacula, Julianne Phillips) make a wager as to who will be the first to seduce him.

In September 1988 Treat was married to model/actress and former Texarkana waitress Pamela Van Sant in New York City. They chose rural Vermont as their home. Williams was scheduled to star as Elvis Presley in the whimsical HEARTBREAK HOTEL (1988), but it was David Keith who ended up playing "The King" who, in 1972, is kidnapped by the offspring of a disgruntled single mother (Tuesday Weld) who has a long-time crush on Elvis.

Williams replaced John Heard, who had walked off the Seattle, Washington, set of HBO–Cable's THIRD DEGREE BURN (May 28, 1989), as a divorced private detective with an eye for the ladies. Removing his shirt a lot, he attracts Virginia Madsen, who attempts to frame him for the murder of her husband (Richard Masur). "Passion in the first degree. Murder in the second," read the advertisements in *TV Guide*, but in its review, the magazine labeled it "a low-voltage knockoff of BODY HEAT."

HEART OF DIXIE (1989) grossed a paltry $1.1 million in regional release and was declared the year's biggest flop. For fear of connecting it controversially with the studio's MISSISSIPPI BURNING (1988), Orion Pictures chose not to publicize the movie and did not release it nationwide. Made at a cost of $8 million, the drama was set on a southern university campus in 1957 during the growing civil rights unrest, with Treat as a photojournalist involved with a co-ed (Ally Sheedy). In reviewing the picture, Peter Stack (*San Francisco Chronicle*) termed Williams "an underused actor who always gives his character a convincing toughness and yet a powerful sense of the loner looking for love."

Love Letters, the popular A. R. Gurney two-character dramatic reading play, was presented in New York, Los Angeles, San Francisco, and other cities by rotating pairs of name performers. Treat and Kate Nelligan read the "letters" at New York's Promenade Theatre for the week of October 3–8, 1989, and would repeat their performance at Gotham's Edison Theatre from January 9 to 14, 1990.

On December 3, 1989, for a limited run through December 31 at the Mitzi E. Newhouse Theatre at New York's Lincoln Center, Treat starred in the second half of a double bill (*Oh, Hell*) of one-act plays, dealing with man's conscience and the Devil. In his showcase—David Mamet's *Bobby Gould in Hell*—Williams was the movie executive chastised by Mr. Scratch (W. H. Macy) for seducing and abandoning a woman (Felicity Huffman). Mimi Kramer (*The New Yorker* magazine) applauded the "brilliant casting" of Treat who has "a look of dumb suffering and the demeanor of a dog who can't understand why he's been put out for the night."

Returning to television, he was once again an investigator, this time for the U.S. Drug Enforcement Administration, in "Drug Wars: The Camarena Story," a fact-based NBC-TV miniseries shown in January 1990. As Ray Carson, he appeared in only the second and third installments, involved in the hunt for culprits in Mexico after the disappearance of a U.S. undercover agent (Steven Bauer). *TV Guide* magazine called Treat and Craig T. Nelson, "the avenging angels" who take over in Parts 2 and 3, "stick figures," while the *San Francisco Examiner*'s Joyce Millman claimed that the latter two parts of the miniseries were "driven by a handful of fine performances," including Treat's. The TNT–Cable movie MAX AND HELEN (January 8, 1990) was filmed in Budapest and Paris. It co-starred Treat and Alice Krige as World War II concentration camp survivors who find each other after a twenty-year search through Europe. The *Los Angeles Times* credited both actors with "affecting portrayals," while *TV Guide* magazine found that Treat's "unaffected acting style works beautifully." When it was released in videocassette form, *Video Review* magazine enthused of MAX AND HELEN, "the screenplay is a quiet triumph of construction. . . . Williams is impassioned as Max. . . ."

By 1990 Treat was part-owner, with actor Peter Weller and nonprofessional Larry McIntyre, of the Chelsea Central restaurant in Manhattan. In the spring of the year, Treat reprised his rendition of *Love Letters* for the week starting April 17, 1990, at the Canon Theatre in Beverly Hills, paired with Christine Lahti. The *Los Angeles Times* described Treat as growing "comfortably (and in the end movingly) into the nice-guy, suburban senator with feelings."

Beginning March 12, 1991, Treat took on his first television series, ABC's hour-long "Eddie Dodd," as a counter-cultural lawyer with a yuppie associate (Corey Parker). It was adapted for TV from the 1989 motion picture TRUE BELIEVER, which starred James Woods and Robert Downey, Jr. In reviewing the series, John Carman (*San Francisco Chronicle*) pointed out, "it's hard to discern any real difference between Eddie Dodd and the lawyer played by Michael O'Keefe on Fox's floundering 'Against the Law' series. . . . In its favor, 'Eddie Dodd' has strong performances from Williams. . . ." Miles Beller (*Hollywood Reporter*) decided, "Williams as the relentless attorney creates a memorable character, a bit predictable perhaps but nonetheless compelling." *Daily Variety* admitted that "Eddie Dodd" has "the advantage of solid production values" and that the lead is "played with assurance by Williams." Shown as a spring filler in ABC-TV's "thirtysomething" Tuesday night time spot. The show went on permanent hiatus after two aired episodes. In FINAL VERDICT (forthcoming, 1991), a TNT-cable movie, Treat plays legendary 20th century attorney Earl Rogers.

Even after two decades as an acting professional, Williams admits, "Acting is pretty frightening; you never know if you're going to get it right." Regarding his future, he says, "I always felt it was limiting to do what you could do easily. I'm beginning to want to do some light comedy and a little more normal people. . . . I'm not avoiding playing classical leading men anymore." He does admit that flying remains his first love. "Flying gives me an incredible sense of accomplishment. . . . And, of course, being up there is like a religious experience for me . . . there's no critic who's going to say you stunk!"

Filmography

Deadly Hero (Avco Emb, 1976)
The Ritz (WB, 1976)
The Eagle Has Landed (Col, 1977)
Hair (UA, 1979)
1941 (Univ/Col, 1979)
Why Would I Lie? (UA, 1980)
Prince of the City (Orion/WB, 1981)
The Pursuit of D. B. Cooper (Univ, 1981)
Stangata Napoletana—La Trastola [Something About the Sting] (It, 1983)
Dempsey (CBS-TV, 9/28/83)
A Streetcar Named Desire (ABC-TV, 3/4/84)
Once Upon a Time in America (WB, 1984)
Flashpoint (Tri-Star, 1984)
Smooth Talk (Spectrafilm, 1985)
The Men's Club (Atlantic, 1986)

J. Edgar Hoover (Showtime–Cable, 1/11/87)
La Notte degli Squali [The Night of the Sharks] (It, 1987)
Echoes in the Darkness (CBS-TV, 11/1/87–11/2/87)
Russicum i Gironi del Diavolo (Col, 1988)
Dead Heat (New World, 1988)
Burro [Butter] (It, 1989)
Sweet Lies (Island, 1989)
Third Degree Burn (HBO–Cable, 5/28/89)
Heart of Dixie (Orion, 1989)
Max and Helen (TNT–Cable, 1/8/90)
Oltre l'Oceano [Beyond the Ocean] (It, 1990)

Future Releases

Final Verdict (TNT-Cable, 1991)

Broadway Plays

Grease (1974) (understudy)
Over Here! (1974)
Grease (1975) (replacement)
Once in a Lifetime (1978) (revival)

The Pirates of Penzance (1981) (revival) (replacement)
Love Letters (1990) (alternating cast)

Television Series

Drug Wars: The Camarena Story (NBC, 1/7/90–1/9/90) [miniseries]

Eddie Dodd (ABC, 1991–)

Album Discography

Hair (RCA CBL 2-3274 [ST]

Over Here! (Columbia KS-32961) [OC]

BRUCE WILLIS

> "I know, now, too much about the business of show business to have
> any misconceptions about what it's really about. It's all about money;
> it's all about selling tickets."
>
> —on "Face to Face with Connie Chung,"
> CBS-TV, July 23, 1990

PRIOR TO 1985, BRUCE WILLIS WAS AN UNKNOWN SOMETIME ACTOR
and constant party person. He could swagger along big city sidewalks on either coast
without a second glance from any passersby—except, perhaps, from one who might
fleetingly consider the cool, earringed, oddly dressed macho stranger good looking or sexy.
But after 1985, in just three years, the smirking, highly paid toast of Hollywood had his
privacy shattered and coped with his new notoriety in the manner of Sean Penn. He struck
back, a move that prompted even more attention from the tabloid press. He became
Hollywood's newest high-living "bad boy," a substance abuser with an ego of incredible
proportions and an oversized temper to boot. Like Kathleen Turner and Mickey Rourke,
Willis claims that he owes nothing to the public or to the press because "nobody put me
here but me." Branded an arrogant loudmouth, he bases his comedy style on a combination of Bob Hope, Jerry Lewis, and Curly of The Three Stooges. However, his acting in
blockbuster action movies comes straight from within himself, maybe with a touch of
Arnold Schwarzenegger and Sylvester Stallone thrown into the mix. "Yeah, that's why I'm
here," he told TV's Connie Chung with his disarming grin. "I'm just here for the dough."

Bruce Walter Willis was born on Saturday, March 19, 1955, in West Germany, the
eldest of four children parented by U.S. serviceman David Willis and his German-born
wife, Marlene. In 1957, after completing his Army tour of duty, David returned to the
United States with his growing family. They settled in Carneys Point, New Jersey, where
he obtained work as a mechanic at the Camden, New Jersey, shipyard.

Bruce's childhood was fairly typical: he liked to play soldier and climb trees. He
described himself as having been a "happy-go-lucky kid." At the age of eight, he developed
a stutter; as a result, he learned to make people laugh so they would not notice it or with
the hope they might forget it. (To this day, the stutter disappears whenever he is acting or
in front of a live audience.) He claims to have lost his virginity at age fourteen in the
laundry room of a local Holiday Inn. He attended Penns Grove High School in the nearby
town of Penns Grove, New Jersey. There the prankster was popular with schoolmates,
who called him Bruno. However, teachers considered him undisciplined. During a period

of racial unrest at the school, Bruce was expelled for instigating a fracas. Policemen with dogs patrolled the school corridors while David Willis, with the assistance of an attorney, got Bruce reinstated. The teenager became a member of the school's drama club, learned to play the harmonica, and was elected president of the student council. During the streaking craze of the early 1970s, he ran naked, except for sunglasses and sneakers, through the streets of Carneys Point.

In mid-1973, after graduation from high school, he got a job at the E. I. Du Pont plant in Deepwater, New Jersey, driving work crews around the enormous plant grounds. This ended, however, when another driver was killed in an explosion of mixed chemicals and Bruce decided his work assignment was too hazardous. Taking a job as night security guard at a nuclear generating station, Bruce also played harmonica with a local blues band called Loose Goose. Finally setting his sights on stage work, he enrolled at Montclair State College, where tuition fees were low for New Jersey residents. There, in Upper Montclair, the six-foot, blue-eyed student made a handsome Brick in *Cat on a Hot Tin Roof,* after which he increasingly took time from classes to seek off-Broadway stage roles in New York City. In January 1977 he landed a role in *Heaven and Earth.* He quit college and moved to a flat on West 49th Street, beyond Ninth Avenue, in the rough New York City area known as Hell's Kitchen. Even now, years later, he still holds the lease to that apartment.

When Bruce was not aggressively bombarding casting offices with his photograph and slight resumé, he worked as a bartender at various Manhattan locations, most notably at the Cafe Central, an Upper West Side spa frequented by show business people. Willis provided entertainment behind the bar by singing, playing his harmonica, and traveling the length of the bar on roller skates. Ahead of his time, he wore baggy trousers, a headband, earrings, and torn T-shirts. In the summer of 1979 he became the sixth and final cast member of the First Amendment Comedy Theatre, a workshop repertory group operating from a theater on West 22nd Street. He made lucrative TV commercials for Levi Strauss's 501 blue jeans and obtained a coveted Screen Actors Guild card through a small part in Frank Sinatra's New York–lensed THE FIRST DEADLY SIN (1980). Also during this time he acted off-off-Broadway in *Bullpen,* a play in which he portrayed the sole white prisoner in the holding pen of a New York jail. He also had bits in other features, including the low-budget IN SEARCH OF THE GURU (1980) and Paul Newman's THE VERDICT (1982). (His scene was cut from THE VERDICT, as it had been from PRINCE OF THE CITY (1981).)In 1981, at the off-off-Broadway Labor Theatre, he played in *Railroad Bill,* then won his first off-Broadway stage lead in *Bayside Boys.*

While bartending at the popular downtown Manhattan disco Kamikaze, Bruce replaced Will Patton in the long-running Sam Shepard play *Fool for Love* off-Broadway. There he was spotted by a casting director for NBC-TV's "Miami Vice." In the 1985 episode "No Exit," he was featured as a wife-beating weapons smuggler. With this newly acquired taste for acting, Bruce went to Los Angeles where he appeared in a segment of ABC-TV's "Hart to Hart." He auditioned for but did not get the role of Aidan Quinn's buddy in DESPERATELY SEEKING SUSAN (1985). Wearing triple earrings in his left earlobe and battle fatigues, he was one of the last of some three thousand actors to interview with producer Jay Daniel for the male lead of David Addison, opposite the already cast Cybill Shepherd, in the upcoming ABC-TV series "Moonlighting." Meanwhile, he was offered a lead role in Stanley Kubrick's Vietnam drama FULL METAL JACKET, but turned it down after being chosen for the television series. Meanwhile, Adam Baldwin took the FULL METAL JACKET role, but the film was not released until 1987 in order not to follow too closely in the wake of the Oscar-winning PLATOON (1986), another war movie set in Vietnam.

It was during 1984, initially on a social level, that Bruce fell victim to heavy consumption of alcohol and drugs. Claiming to be only "fun seeking," he was, during a three-year period, a wild man ever in search of parties with his buddies, one of whom was actor John Goodman (whom he had met in his Cafe Central days).

"Moonlighting," an atypical detective series in which the characters frequently provided asides to the audience and engaged in oddly structured plotlines, premiered as a TV movie on March 3, 1985. However, it did not catch on immediately with audiences, who were confused by the innovative structure. Nonetheless, with its refreshing sense of humor, the offbeat program soon developed solid word-of-mouth acceptance. Increasingly large numbers of viewers appreciated the very modern, very funny couple (Willis, Shepherd) maneuvering their bodies and sensual dialogue in this show about a former fashion model who takes over the Blue Moon Detective Agency in Los Angeles, joined in her capers by cocky employee Willis. Shepherd told reporters, "The first time Bruce and I were in a room together, there was a reaction. Sparks flew. . . . It's chemistry, baby. Either you got it or you don't, and David and Maddie have it." *Newsweek* magazine, in a cover story, rated Willis and Shepherd the "freshest characters on any television show." In its first season, the program was nominated for sixteen Emmy Awards, including one for Bruce as Outstanding Lead Actor in a Drama Series, which he won not that year, but the following season. "I always knew that I was going to be successful one day," he said, immodestly. "So when it happened, I just said, 'Good. There it is.'" After his Emmy win, his salary escalated from $15,000 to $25,000 per episode.

In January 1987 Bruce signed a multi-year contract, reportedly worth between $5 million and $7 million, with The House of Seagram to promote its Golden Wine Cooler in television commercials. He received a different type of exposure in the January 14, 1987, segment "The Ronnie and Nancy Show" on NBC-TV's "Spitting Image," where his likeness was depicted in marionette form with hollow head and cloth body. He sang "Jackpot" on ABC-TV's telecast of the fourteenth annual American Music Awards (January 26, 1987) and introduced his saloon-singing alter ego, Bruno Radolini, in HBO–Cable's special "Bruce Willis: The Return of Bruno" (February 24, 1987). It was a prelude to his upcoming record album of the same name. On February 24, 1987, he was a presenter on CBS-TV's telecast of the twenty-ninth annual Grammy Awards. Also in 1987, on the "Shatterday" episode of syndicated television's "Twilight Zone," he surprised viewers by turning in a superlative dramatic performance as a man who discovers that he has been cloned.

Scheduled to film BURGLAR (1987) with Whoopi Goldberg, he backed out of the project at the last minute in order to star with Kim Basinger in Blake Edwards's BLIND DATE (1987), a project formerly slated for Madonna and Sean Penn. In BLIND DATE, considered by many to be his motion picture debut, he played an ambitious business executive warned not to let his blind date (Basinger) imbibe strong drink. He of course ignores the warning, and the inebriated miss leads him on an unexpectedly wild excursion. Regarding Bruce's essentially subordinate role, critic Roger Ebert analyzed, "Willis plays a nerd so successfully that he fades into the shrubbery and never really makes us care about his fate." Considered a disappointment, the wacky comedy grossed $39 million at domestic box offices.

His Motown album of soul and rhythm and blues songs, *Bruce Willis: The Return of Bruno*, was released on May 21, 1987, and sold over 500,000 copies. For eight weeks it was on *Rolling Stone* magazine's chart of the top fifty albums, and it was #6 on the British charts. In addition, his single (from the album) of "Under the Boardwalk" was #3 on the British charts in August 1987. A second single from the album, "Respect Yourself," was simultaneously a hit in the United States.

Willis spoke of his personal life as a "monastic" existence in a large home situated in Nichols Canyon between the hills of Hollywood, surrounded by a six-foot-high wall to keep out probing members of the press. Although he dated Sherry Rivera, the ex-wife of Geraldo Rivera, he was enchanted by actress Demi Moore, whom he had met at a screening of STAKEOUT in 1987. Meanwhile, problems erupted on the "Moonlighting" set, with reports of disenchantment between Willis and Shepherd, with the latter complaining that his drinking interfered with production. At 10 p.m. on Memorial Day 1987, Bruce and friends gained nationwide headlines when neighbors summoned police to his home because of loud music reverberating throughout the neighborhood amid a general aura of over-partying. Healing from a collarbone fracture in a recent skiing accident, Bruce was removed from his home by police. During the ruckus, the actor rebroke the bone, and he and five of his pals were taken to jail. This explosive incident was given extensive coverage by the tabloids, who dubbed him "Hollywood's Bad Boy," a tag that would be his for several years. The charges against him, including drug possession, were later dropped. His contract with The House of Seagram was not

Bruce Willis in BLIND DATE (1987).

renewed (he claimed that it was his decision not to continue the contract). By October 1987 he had turned away from drugs and alcohol.

At one minute before midnight on November 21, 1987, at the Golden Nugget Hotel in Las Vegas, Bruce was married to Demetria (Demi) Moore. Born on November 11, 1962, the actress had been wed previously to musician Freddy Moore, and in her teen years had posed for nude photographs, which were republished in 1987 in *Celebrity Sleuth*, called the "Nude Stars" magazine. A few days after their marriage, they were remarried by rock 'n' roll singer/ordained minister Little Richard at a large party held at the Burbank Studios. "Demi has made me laugh at things a lot more," he confided. "My life is now full of love and warmth." However, their quarrels, largely over his jealousy concerning her past involvement with Emilio Estevez and her on-screen love scenes with younger, better-looking actors, would be constantly featured in the tabloids.

His second major motion picture was SUNSET (1988), also directed by Blake Edwards and co-starring veteran James Garner as Wyatt Earp. Wearing oversized western hats, Bruce appeared as silent screen legend Tom Mix, in this comedy-drama combination of fact and fiction set in early Hollywood. With brilliant sets and costumes and utilizing fantastic vintage automobiles, the movie ends with the words, "And that's the way it really happened—give or take a lie or two." Young moviegoers who had never heard of Tom Mix or Wyatt Earp stayed away from theaters in droves. Willis's fans from "Moonlighting" were put off by reviews such as *Variety*'s, which judged, "Despite the tough guy charm he has exhibited elsewhere, Bruce Willis is one of the least likely choices imaginable to play Mix. . . ." Consequently, the expensively produced movie was a financial bomb, with domestic box-office grosses of only $6 million.

"I'm going to get work after this, regardless if [it] is a big hit or doesn't do well," Willis stated emphatically prior to the July 1988 release of DIE HARD. The movie industry, shocked at the $5 million salary afforded an actor with no prior track record, sat back and watched and waited. Turned down by Clint Eastwood and Richard Gere, the exciting, nonstop action thriller made a true movie star of Bruce Willis, who earned his salary by doing much of his own stunt work. Bruce played New York police officer John McClane, on Christmas holiday in Los Angeles to visit his wife (Bonnie Bedelia) and his two children (Taylor Fry, Noah Land). As fate and the script would have it, he single-handedly repels a gang of enterprising European terrorists, headed by Hans Gruber (superbly played by Alan Rickman), who are after the millions of dollars worth of negotiable bearer bonds locked within the corporate safe of the international Nakatomi Corporation, headquartered in a thirty-four-story high-rise (actually Century City's Fox Plaza tower). According to *People* magazine, Bruce's methods of operation were "sprinkled with self-mocking humor" as he "gleefully strips down the action movie to a pretend game for children who like to fire guns and shoot bad guys. Machismo may never be the same." Peter Stack (*San Francisco Chronicle*), calling it a "fun" movie, also observed that Willis "gains real credibility this time as a star of the big screen." The suspenseful adventure epic, with its spectacular special effects, became the year's #7 hit, with domestic box-office earnings of $80.7 million.

Opting, because of his stutter, not to make talk-show appearances, Bruce was nevertheless quoted regularly in magazines. *US* magazine had him boasting in 1988, "Ladies have often said I'm funny, sexy and personable—and fortunately, a few million people I've met agree with that estimation." In Paducah, Kentucky, the location site of his next movie, Demi Moore gave birth on August 15, 1988, to a daughter, Rumer Glenn Willis. The baby was named in part for Glenn Gordon Caron, executive producer of "Moonlighting," one of Bruce's best friends.

THAT'S ADEQUATE, referring to the make-believe Adequate Studios founded by a B-budget Hollywood mogul (James Coco), was previewed as a "mockumentary" at the Park City, Utah, U.S. Film Festival in January 1989. In a cameo role, Bruce was one of the Adequate pioneers interviewed on screen. Judged by *Variety* as "rarely original and sometimes surprisingly imitative of what's already been done," the movie failed to find a theatrical distributor and was shunted into home video distribution.

"Moonlighting" left the air on May 14, 1989, a victim of continuing production problems involving personality clashes, inefficiencies on the set, and the absences of both stars, resulting in rerun after rerun during what should have been the first-run season. *TV Guide* magazine in December 1989 listed the late series as one of the twenty top shows of the 1980s.

Turning to drama as Emmett in IN COUNTRY (1989), filmed in Kentucky, Bruce gained weight, tobacco-stained his teeth, let his hair grow, and sported a Fu-Manchu type moustache. Within the drama, he helps his niece (Emily Lloyd) unravel the mystery of her father's death in Vietnam. *Time* magazine credited Bruce with employing "his alert reserve to better effect" than ever before. His fans, however, refused to accept him as a serious actor and ignored the vehicle. Bruce's enthusiasm for the role had induced him to work for union scale, $1,511 per week, while Warner Bros.'s enthusiasm at this uncalled-for generosity, plus his performance, prompted the studio to encourage an Academy Award nomination for him as Best Supporting Actor. However, he was not nominated.

On September 30, 1989, he hosted the fifteenth season opener of NBC-TV's "Saturday Night Live," in which the *Hollywood Reporter* found him "more effective performing musically than comedically."

By taking 25 percent of the gross receipts in lieu of salary for LOOK WHO'S TALKING (1989), Bruce had a financial windfall. Third in consideration, after Steve Martin and Robin Williams, as the voice of baby/child Mikey, Bruce was thought to have a "perfect" voice by director Amy Heckerling, because it is "airy, quiet," and "sophisticated, and the baby is very knowing." With John Travolta and Kirstie Alley as the nominal stars, LOOK WHO'S TALKING opened in October 1989 and by the spring of 1990 had grossed over $133.1 million domestically.

Having increased security measures at both his Los Angeles and Sun Valley, Idaho, homes after the birth of his daughter, Bruce became even more resentful of the paparazzi who followed him everywhere. On one occasion he rammed one of their vehicles with his Mercedes. He formed his own production company in 1989 and in December of that year, his second Motown album, *If It Don't Kill You, It Just Makes You Stronger*, was released. No longer referring to Bruno, he talked about himself between songs and referred to the studio band as Jimmy and the Termites. Collectively, his record sales totaled 1.5 million by July 1990. "I realize now," he said, "that my career will pretty much go forward whether I explain myself or not. And, I'd much rather not explain myself."

In April 1990 he and Demi purchased producer Robert Stigwood's San Remo triplex on Manhattan's Central Park West for $8 million. On April 22, 1990, he joined other celebrities on ABC-TV's "Earth Day Special," while the announcement was made that he had arranged a deal with producer/friend Jay Daniel to guest-star on TV's "Roseanne" (starring pal Roseanne Barr) during the 1990–1991 season at the union minimum of $2,500.

During the filming of DIE HARD II (1990) at various locations in Colorado, Washington, and Michigan while waiting for snow, Bruce had clauses added to the contracts of all the production extras forbidding them to attempt to socialize with him. As had been the custom of eccentric billionaire Howard Hughes, Willis was now surrounded at all times by bodyguards who helped ensure his privacy. DIE HARD II was in general release in July 1990. According to a count made by Vincent Canby (*New York Times*), 264 people meet their deaths within this gory action sequel. Sheila Benson (*Los Angeles Times*) warned that the film "is a lively three-ring circus; just don't be fussy about logic or timing." Gene Siskel (*Chicago Tribune*) gave thanks "to all involved" with the movie because "I sat there aghast with pleasure." Although DIE HARD II was not as spontaneous, inventive, or believable as its predecessor, it grossed over $101.1 million in its first five weeks of domestic distribution. After this blockbuster hit, Bruce's per-picture salary was said to have increased from $7.5 million to $10 million.

Bruce joined John Travolta, Dan Aykroyd, John Candy, and Vanessa Williams as guests on CBS-TV's Phil Collins special (September 8, 1990) as the rock star spent an hour showing excerpts from his recent concert tour.

Eager to take advantage of his enormous salary potential, Willis continues to make film after film. Playing the type of real-life person he detests, a sleazy tabloid reporter, in THE BONFIRE OF THE VANITIES (1990), a flop film of Tom Wolfe's best-selling novel, he was directed by Brian De Palma in a cast that included Tom Hanks and Melanie Griffith. LOOK WHO'S TALKING TOO (1990) allowed Willis to repeat his voiceover role as Mikey, with Roseanne Barr cast as the voice of Mikey's baby sister, Julie. In conjunction with the release of the sequel, a T-shirt was readied for retail sale, with 50 percent of all profits going to Bruce. The shirt bore the face of the movie's boy-child, Mikey, and when his nose was pressed, out came Bruce's voice. For his production company, Flying Heart Films, in conjunction with Silver Pictures, Bruce starred in HUDSON HAWK (1991) as a man permitted to leave his jail cell to force his way into European art galleries to retrieve stolen paintings. The film was shot in Rome, Budapest, London, and New York. Next, he took a supporting role, requiring him to work only eight days, in MORTAL THOUGHTS (1991), starring Demi Moore and Glenne Headly. In THE LAST BOY SCOUT (1991), yet another comic book hero brought to the screen, Bruce was cast as the fighting hero lead. Willis also co-stars with Dustin Hoffman in the gangster yarn BILLY BATHGATE (1991), an adaptation of the E. L. Doctorow novel.

Forthcoming for Bruce is THREE RIVERS, a police suspense mystery set against the background of Pittsburgh's three rivers (Allegheny, Monongahela, Ohio), about which producer Arnon Milchan has said, "I don't remember the last time I read such a good thriller with such incredible texture" (the script is by Rowdy Harrington).

Despite his heavy moviemaking schedule, Bruce insists he would like to return to stage work, specifically in New York City. He credits his popularity and success to the fact that "I'm not like anybody else."

Bruce Willis loves his work. "It's a good job being an entertainer," he has said. "It's a good job, I think, taking people's minds off what they do." Distrustful of the press, which, he feels, will resort to any means to gain a story, he insists, "I don't think that because I am a public figure that people are allowed to come to my house, climb over my fence, and try and take pictures of my wife and family. . . . It just makes me so mad. I hate it." He simply wants to be a happy person, and toward that end enjoys the movie business. "I like being in [movies] and I like going to see them. . . . I mean I want to see *all* of [the] blockbusters."

As to the future, Bruce, whose wife, Demi, is expecting their second child in 1991, says he is not certain if he and his family will live in Los Angeles or that he will remain in the film industry: "there is very little in terms of being a movie star, in terms of being a famous person, that I have yet to explore. The novelty has really worn thin for me. . . . I used to wonder why so many people quit at the height of their career. But, you know, Hollywood has always had this kind of ugly thing about it that is hidden. I once heard somebody say that Hollywood is like a beautiful woman with the clap."

Filmography

The First Deadly Sin (Filmways, 1980)
In Search of the Guru (Unk, 1980)
Prince of the City (Orion/WB, 1981) (scene cut)
The Verdict (20th–Fox, 1982) (scene cut)
Moonlighting (ABC-TV, 3/3/85)
Blind Date (Tri-Star, 1987)
Sunset (Tri-Star, 1988)
Die Hard (20th–Fox, 1988)
That's Adequate (That's Adequate, 1989)
In Country (WB, 1989)

Look Who's Talking (Tri-Star, 1989) (voice only)
Die Hard II (20th–Fox, 1990)
Look Who's Talking Too (Tri-Star, 1990) (voice only)
The Bonfire of the Vanities (WB, 1990)
Mortal Thoughts (Col, 1991)
Hudson Hawk (Tri-Star, 1991)
Billy Bathgate (BV, 1991)
The Last Boy Scout (WB, 1991)

Television Series

Moonlighting (ABC, 1985–89)

Album Discography

Bruce Willis: The Return of Bruno (Motown)
If It Don't Kill You, It Just Makes You Stronger
   (Motown MOT-6290)

Moonlighting (MCA 6214) [ST/TV]

OPRAH WINFREY

"I do everything to the absolute ultimate. I grow until I can't grow
anymore in a certain position. And then another door opens for me.
That's been the pattern for as long as I can remember."
—*Ladies Home Journal* magazine, May 1990

ALTHOUGH OVERWEIGHT, BLACK, AND A WOMAN—THREE STRIKES
against her professionally—Oprah Winfrey in the late 1980s became the phenomenon of
national talk television as well as the reigning queen of Chicago's four million inhabitants.
She reached her status through eloquence, spontaneity, intelligence, and a very warm,
earthy manner. With her dancing hazel eyes and oversized empathy (she frequently cries
along with her TV guests when they are distressed about what they are telling her and the
audience), Winfrey generously shares her wealth with less fortunate others.

"I've always known that I was born for greatness," she admitted in all modesty in a
recent interview with her one-time mentor, Barbara Walters. "Dishing the dirt and
meddling in other folks' business is what I do best." Repeatedly hurt by accusations that
she is an "Oreo" (black on the outside, white on the inside) and that she is striving to be
another Mae West, Oprah denies that she is nicer to whites in her audiences than to blacks.
To her, all people need a sympathetic hug now and again.

Oprah Gail Winfrey was born on Friday, January 29, 1954, in Kosciusko, Mississippi, to unmarried parents, Vernon Winfrey, a barber, and Vernita Lee, a domestic
worker. Her mother had chosen "Orpah," a biblical name, for her child. But the midwife,
in entering the name on the birth certificate, transposed two letters. Within a year the
child was relegated to the care of her maternal grandmother on a farm in rural Mississippi
with chickens, cows, and corncob dolls as her friends. From her grandmother, an outgoing
person, she learned to read and write and developed her gregarious personality. At the age
of three she gave her first recitation, "Jesus Rose on Easter Day," at the country church.
Not only was she eager to learn, she was quick. On her first day in kindergarten, she wrote
to her teacher, "Dear Miss New: I don't think I belong here." Miss New was obliged to
agree and promoted her immediately to the first grade. Her boredom during that first year
of schooling, from being intellectually more advanced than her classmates, prompted a
second skip, to the third grade.

In 1960, at the age of six, Oprah was sent north to live with her mother in a
Milwaukee, Wisconsin, housing project, along with her younger half brother, Jeffrey, and
her half sister, Patricia. Alone much of the time while her mother worked two jobs (as a
maid and a clothing store clerk), Oprah read vociferously, recited poetry aloud, and

collected cockroaches in a jar. In the summer of 1963, her ninth year, she was raped by a nineteen-year-old cousin at a relative's home. He later plied her with ice cream to keep her from telling about the incident, but "I knew it was bad. I knew it." Blaming herself for the rape, she told no one. At the age of ten, while watching Sidney Poitier receive his Academy Award on television for LILIES OF THE FIELD (1963), she vowed to herself, "I'm going to be there!" Two years later, on a visit to her father, who had moved to Nashville, Tennessee, Oprah earned $500 for giving a speech at a community gathering. That job confirmed her goal to be "paid to talk."

On returning to Milwaukee, she was subsequently raped two more times, by an uncle and by the boyfriend of a cousin, traumatic experiences that "made me a sexually promiscuous teenager." When her mother was not at home, which was often, she took men to her bedroom, where the walls were festooned with magazine pictures of white girls. She has admitted that at that point in her life she wanted to be white because white girls received more love and attention. Bused to an otherwise all-white school in a suburb of Milwaukee because of her advanced scholastic abilities, she felt that her butterfly-framed glasses did not fit in, so she broke them. When her mother refused to replace them, she faked a robbery of their apartment by smashing glass and telling the story that she had been hit on the head but could remember nothing else. Later, she began stealing money from her mother's purse and pawning jewelry to buy records. On one occasion she obtained $100 from singer Aretha Franklin by telling her a hard-luck story as she emerged from a taxi. With her money, she ran away to a hotel for several days, until the money ran out. Then, upon going to a church minister, she was taken home. Considered an uncontrollable delinquent, she was faced with the alternative of either being sent to a juvenile detention home or going to live with her father. It was agreed that Vernon Winfrey and his wife, Zelma, would provide a home for her with them in Nashville. Unknown to the family, fourteen-year-old Oprah was pregnant. She gave birth prematurely to a baby boy who died, an experience she has described as "the most emotional, confusing and traumatic of my young life."

Her father, in exercising parental discipline, established a midnight curfew for his daughter and provided her with books, guidance, and long discussions. He would not allow her dinner unless she had learned five new words each day and demanded weekly report cards from school. As a consequence, she excelled at East Nashville High School in oratory, debate, and drama. At the age of sixteen she won the local Elks Club Oratorical Contest, which guaranteed her a full scholarship to Tennessee State University in Nashville. She planned to study to be a journalist like her role model, Barbara Walters. A year later, she attended a White House Conference on Youth in Washington, D.C., and won the "Miss Fire Prevention" contest sponsored by Nashville radio station WVOL. Winfrey was the first black woman so honored, and her prizes included a Longines wristwatch as well as the job of reading newscasts over the air.

Oprah graduated from high school in 1971 as the class's most popular student. She entered Tennessee State University in the autumn of 1972 and in her freshman year was named "Miss Black Nashville." This entitled her to compete in the Miss Black America" pageant. Thereafter, she was twice offered a position by WTVF-TV, the local CBS affiliate. She turned the offers down until an instructor reminded her that the reason she was in college was to earn just such offers. At nineteen, she became the station's first black woman co-anchor on the evening news. "Sure I was a token," she would admit later, "but, honey, I was one happy token." She was earning $15,000 a year while a college sophomore, but her father still enforced the midnight curfew.

After attaining a B.A. in speech and drama in 1976, Winfrey accepted a position in Baltimore with ABC's WJZ-TV as reporter and co-anchor on the six o'clock newscast and would often be seen sobbing while interviewing victims at the scene of a tragedy. The assistant news director decided to change her name to Cindy Winfrey, along with altering her ethnicity to Hispanic rather than black. He sent her to a Manhattan beautician because your "hair is too thick, your nose too wide, your chin too big." The first step in transforming Winfrey left her completely, but temporarily, bald, because the hairdresser was inexperienced with black hair. Returning to WJZ-TV, she retained her own name while trying to cover her head with scarves. She cried a lot and turned to food for solace. Her weight shot up to 190 pounds. In 1977 the station demoted her, switching her to the 7:25 a.m. "cut-ins" or updates on ABC's "Good Morning America." Later, having shown resiliency, she was given the task of co-hosting, with Richard Sher, the morning talk show "Baltimore Is Talking." "This is what I was born to do," she said. "*This* is really breathing." She would remain in this job for the next seven years, during which time she fell in love with a married man. The affair ended badly, with her even contemplating suicide at one point. In 1978, in Baltimore's Black Theater Festival, she appeared on stage as a cast of one in *The History of Black Women Through Drama and Song.*

In September 1983 she was spotted in a videotape by Dennis Swanson, the general manager of WLS-TV, the ABC affiliate in Chicago. Oprah was offered and accepted the position of hosting "A.M. Chicago," the lowest-rated talk show in that city. In the four-month interim before she could leave Baltimore, she studiously planned the changes she intended to make in the Chicago program. When she began her new assignment in January 1984, the Chicago-based, nationally syndicated "Phil Donahue Show" had been the number one talk show in Chicago for sixteen years. Within a month, "A.M. Chicago" received equal ratings; after three months it was unmistakably ahead, as a result of Oprah's selection of topical guests whom she interviewed without a script. *People* magazine described hers as "a mind as quick as any in television, yes, [Johnny] Carson and [David] Letterman included." Viewers considered her a friend. In September 1985 the show was expanded from thirty minutes to an hour and was retitled "The Oprah Winfrey Show." It was perhaps coincidental that Phil Donahue abandoned his Chicago headquarters in favor of New York City, where his wife, actress Marlo Thomas, resided. Oprah's on-air guests varied from Ku Klux Klansmen to nudists (shown from the waist up) to Tom Selleck. When asked about her own love life, her response was, "Mr. Right is on the way, walking from Africa."

During her first year in Chicago, musician Quincy Jones saw her show and immediately relayed to producer-director Steven Spielberg the news that he had found the person to portray the important role of Sofia in the film adaptation of Alice Walker's novel THE COLOR PURPLE (1985). Oprah was delighted with the movie offer from Spielberg inasmuch as Walker's book was one of her favorites and "I've known all those women" depicted in the story. Always trying to keep down her weight, which had been a problem since the mid-1970s, she was asked to *gain* twenty pounds for the screen role. She proved to be marvelous on screen as the young, independent Sofia, keeping her husband (Willard Pugh) in line; she was stellar as the disfigured older Sofia, forced to abide by the rules of the whites. Critic Gene Siskel (*Chicago Tribune*) called her "Shockingly good," while David Ansen (*Newsweek* magazine) credited her as "a brazen delight." She received a nomination for a Golden Globe Award as Best Supporting Actress along with an Academy Award nomination in the same category. In competition for eleven Oscars, THE COLOR PURPLE failed to win a single statue. However, with domestic grosses of $94.1 million, THE COLOR PURPLE was the #4 moneymaker of 1985.

In August 1986 she formed Harpo Productions, Inc., through which she planned to make films, videos, and TV movies. Later in the month, *Playgirl* magazine named Oprah as one of America's ten most admired women. On September 8, 1986, "The Oprah Winfrey Show" was launched in syndication on 139 U.S. television stations, and received a 31 percent share of all viewers watching television during its time period. King World Productions, responsible for the show, projected revenue as high as $150 million by the 1988–1989 season, with Oprah to receive 25 percent of the earnings. Since 1986 her annual salary has been estimated at between $30 million and $70 million. In December 1986 she signed a five-year contract with King World, at about the same time that she met 6' 6" public relations executive Stedman Graham of North Carolina. (He was a former basketball player.) In the ensuing years, she and Stedman would reportedly be on the verge of marriage several times, and at one point she refurbished a 2,100-seat church in Chicago just for the nuptials. However, on May 2, 1990, she made a public announcement that she was "not ready for marriage."

In December 1986, one year after the release of THE COLOR PURPLE, she played another character role. This time, in NATIVE SON, she was the mother of a young man (Victor Love) hired as a chauffeur to a white family. Later in the film, he kills the family's daughter (Elizabeth McGovern) and is placed on trial. Based on Richard Wright's 1940 novel and a co-production of PBS-TV's "American Playhouse," the somber movie did not fare well with audiences, although Oprah received respectable reviews.

Continuing to ask relevant questions of her show's guests, with sexual subjects a staple, she interviewed her guests from a small stage, later leaving the stage to answer questions from the studio audience or from telephone callers. Don Merrill (*TV Guide* magazine) endorsed, "If you haven't yet treated yourself to 'The Oprah Winfrey Show,' we suggest that you do so soon." Merrill described her with: "Beneath a homey personality that invites confidences, there is a confident, talented journalist digging for truth." In 1987 the show was honored with a daytime Emmy Award as Outstanding Talk/Service Program; at the same time she received a statuette as Outstanding Talk/Service Show Host.

During 1987 Winfrey bought an $800,000 condominium on Chicago's prestigious "Gold Coast," overlooking Lake Michigan. The following year, she added a 160-acre Indiana farm to her real estate holdings. She played herself briefly (as a talk show host) in THROW MOMMA FROM THE TRAIN (1987), a dark comedy patterned after Alfred Hitchcock's STRANGERS ON A TRAIN (1951). She was interviewed on ABC-TV on Barbara Walters's Oscar-night special on April 11, 1988. Among many things, Oprah told Barbara, whom she had admired for years, "I don't regret being born illegitimately. . . . It has made me exactly who I am." Hoping to star in a thirty-minute TV sitcom series during the 1988–1989 season, she had filmed an ABC-TV pilot, tentatively titled "The Oprah Winfrey Show" or "Natalie," in 1987 playing a talk show host. She took a lengthy look at the results and concluded that it was terrible. It was never aired.

In 1988 Oprah, who won the Broadcaster of the Year Award from the International Radio and TV Society, embarked on a much-publicized Optifast liquid diet and proudly managed to lose sixty-seven pounds from her 5' 7" frame. The diet, a frequent topic on her show, was also endorsed by Winfrey in various advertisements. Meanwhile, Oprah unselfishly concerned herself with several causes: she donated $50,000 a year to the hungry of Africa, gave $500,000 to the Chicago Academy for the Performing Arts, wrote a $1 million check to Atlanta's all-black Morehouse College, contributed $250,000 to Tennessee State University, and gave $200,000 to the Chicago Corporate/Community College fund. She also organized benefits for underprivileged children, took her show to the scene of racial violence in Cumming, Georgia, and raised $1 million for Charleston, South Carolina, victims of Hurricane Hugo in 1989. Also in 1989 she did magazine ads for Revlon nail polish and lipsticks, asking that the $100,000 fee be given to a fund for inner-city schools. She became a limited partner in Chicago's The Eccentric Restaurant, was honored by *Ebony* magazine with its Dramatic Arts Award, and bought a $350,000 home in Brentwood, Tennessee, a suburb of Nashville, for her father. However, he refused to live in it.

In the ABC-TV movie THE WOMEN OF BREWSTER PLACE (March 19–20, 1989), adapted from Gloria Naylor's novel about seven black women in an unnamed urban ghetto, she starred as Mattie Michael, striving to make a decent life

Oprah Winfrey in THE WOMEN OF BREWSTER PLACE (1989).

for herself. The show depicted men as shiftless and brutal, with women suffering at their hands. Co-executive produced by Oprah, the four-hour-long program, shown over two nights, did well in the ratings. *TV Guide* magazine credited Winfrey with being "triumphant, turning in the strongest of the film's several fine performances." On June 3, 1989, for TV's syndicated "Just Between Friends," she spent an hour in a change-of-pace media format, first simply chatting with her close pal Gayle King Bumpus, a Connecticut news anchor, then exploring bonds of friendship between six other "sets of boon companions." The program was later telecast on ABC-TV (June 8, 1989). In June 1989 the *Wall Street Journal* named Oprah one of twenty-eight rising stars in the business world, with an estimated net worth of $250 million. The next month, she was a guest speaker in Detroit at the eightieth annual convention of the NAACP. She was unwittingly involved in one of the most publicized faux pas in the publishing world when *TV Guide* magazine, on its cover of August 26/September 1, 1989, featured a painting of Oprah's face resting atop the 1979 body of Ann-Margret, depicted in a Bob Mackie–designed gown, wearing Ann-Margret's ring on the right hand, and appearing extremely slim and sexy. Only the figure's face and skin tone had been altered. Both women smilingly denied any connection with the ploy. On December 9, 1989, at the twenty-second annual NAACP Image Awards, televised on ABC-TV on January 6, 1990, Oprah won four Hall of Fame Awards as the best in the areas of acting, producing, entertaining, and journalism. In 1989 her show won the daytime Emmy Award as Outstanding Talk/Service Program.

By early 1990 "The Oprah Winfrey Show" was seen nationwide on 213 TV stations, averaging a 9.8 rating, while Phil Donahue's talk show from New York appeared on 226 stations and averaged a 6.6 rating. Oprah was now seen in Canada, Bermuda, England, The Netherlands, and, later during 1990, in Poland. Oprah continued with topics of a sexual nature, including "Sex Before the Wedding Night" and "When You Have a Crush on Someone Other Than Your Spouse." In mid-year she was awarded an honorary Doctor of Humane Letters degree by Morehouse College in appreciation for her financial assistance, and it was reported that King World Productions had insured her life for between $50 million and $70 million. Part-owner of three television stations, she bought an 88,000-square-foot TV-movie studio in Chicago, which she remodeled at a cost of $30 million, with plans to produce a TV series and at least four TV movies, in two of which she would star.

"Brewster Place," the ABC-TV series spin-off of the successful TV movie, debuted on May 1, 1990. In her first thirty-minute prime-time series, Oprah reprised her role of Mattie who, in the opener, has been fired from her job. Having regained about seventeen of the pounds she had lost in her famous diet, she was the matronly centerpiece and narrator of the proceedings. *Variety* reviewed the uneven premiere episode by stating that "there's plenty of work ahead," but wondered, "will this show get the kind of time it needs to develop a following?" Oprah continued her daily talk show while filming eight of the thirteen optioned segments of "Brewster Place," which was shot at Harpo Productions in Chicago. Never gaining a sufficient following, "Brewster Place" was cancelled on May 22, 1990, after four episodes had aired.

On June 28, 1990, in New York City, Oprah hosted the seventeenth annual daytime Emmy Awards ceremony, telecast on ABC-TV. Nominated in the best talk/ service host category, she lost to Joan Rivers. *Forbes* magazine reported that Oprah was the third highest wage earner in America's entertainment industry during 1990, with an income of $68 million (behind New Kids on the Block with $78 million and Steven Spielberg with $87 million).

In July 1990 *U.S. News and World Report* magazine selected Oprah as the nation's best talk show host, outdistancing Johnny Carson and Arsenio Hall. ABC-TV aired an "All-Star Tribute to Oprah Winfrey" on September 18, 1990, in "recognition of her generosity and humanity," with First Lady Barbara Bush on hand along with Lily Tomlin, Whoopi Goldberg, M.C. Hammer, Bob Hope, and others. During the telecast Oprah received the Hope Award (named for Bob Hope) and a check for A Better Chance, a charitable organization that Winfrey founded. Winfrey was quoted in *Ladies Home Journal* magazine as saying, "I am a live-for-the-moment, do-the-best-you-can-this-day kind of person. I never think of what's going to happen a year from now, two years from now, five years from now. I don't know. I really only worry about today." On another occasion, she noted, "I believe in the God-force that lives inside all of us, and once you tap into that you can do anything." Yet not to be ignored are her words in a *People* magazine interview of 1985, "My idea of heaven is a great big baked potato and someone to share it with." These beliefs probably still hold true, although another well-publicized passion has earned her the nickname "Oprah Spend-free." Not only does Winfrey provide financially for her closest friends and family, but she also indulges herself with extravagant shopping sprees of costly antiques, thoroughbred horses (which she cannot ride), Bob Mackie–designed gowns, designer shoes and purses, jewelry and furs. Her friend Gayle King Bumpus has said, "If you check the dictionary under the word 'generosity,' you'll find Oprah Winfrey's name."

Filmography

The Color Purple (WB, 1985)
Native Son (Cinecom, 1986)

Throw Momma from the Train (Orion, 1987)
The Women of Brewster Place (NBC-TV, 3/19/ 89–3/20/89) (also co-executive producer)

Television Series

Baltimore Is Talking (WJZ, 1977–1984) (Baltimore local)
A.M. Chicago (WLS, 1984–1985) (Chicago local)

The Oprah Winfrey Show (WLS, 1985–1986) (Chicago local)
The Oprah Winfrey Show (Synd, 1986-)
Brewster Place (ABC, 1990)

DEBRA WINGER

"I don't want to be an actress at any cost. I only want to act if I can
do it great."   —*Los Angeles Times*, August 28, 1988

ASK ALMOST ANY PERSON ABOUT DEBRA WINGER AND THE RESPONSE
is likely to be: "She's good. I love her voice. Why hasn't she done more? Why isn't she a big
star?" Her destiny in Hollywood seems to parallel that of Suzanne Pleshette: she has
tremendous talent, beauty, and intelligence, but her career has thus far been marked more
by good notices from emoting in mediocre screen fare than by a list of hits.

A former wild youth, with a vocabulary heavily punctuated with four-letter exple-
tives, Debra has frequently irritated film directors with her anger, volatile nature, and
continual nit-picking. Yet filmmakers also admire the tough-talking, aggressive woman
whose ideas sometimes benefit the finished product. More often compared with male
actors like Robert De Niro than to her female contemporaries, Winger has not always
shown sound judgment in selecting or rejecting film properties. Yet she ranks as one of
filmdom's highest-paid actresses.

Mary Debra Winger was born on Tuesday, May 16, 1955, in Cleveland, Ohio, the
youngest of three offspring of Robert Winger, general manager of Winger Brothers, a
kosher frozen-food enterprise, and his wife, Ruth. The parents gave all their children first
names that began with the letter "M" (brother Marc, sister Marla). Ruth Winger selected
her baby daughter's middle name for actress Debra Paget, who at the time was smoldering
on theater screens in diaphanous costumes in semi-biblical epics. Hungarian-Russian
Jews, the Wingers were a closely knit family. The grandparents doted on the grandchildren, especially the youngest—an excitable child with imaginary illnesses that garnered
even further attention from her elders. "I was a brat," Debra was to admit years later. If the
term "Jewish American Princess" had been known in that era, it would certainly have been
applied to her.

On Labor Day 1960, at the age of five, she arrived in Van Nuys, California, with the
family in their 1957 Chevrolet; she once likened their trip to that taken by the Joad family
in *The Grapes of Wrath*. In Van Nuys, Robert Winger joined his brother's firm, which sold
and installed burglar alarm systems. Mary Debra encountered no problems in adjusting to
the California weather or schools, but was sent back to Cleveland each year to spend the
summer months with her maternal grandparents. As a member of the local Temple youth
group, she participated in hayrides and dances, but particularly enjoyed acting in school
plays. In 1969, at the age of fourteen and overweight, she begged her father to speak with

noted Hollywood film director George Cukor about the possibility of her becoming an actress. Cukor, who had had his residential alarm system installed by Winger, agreed to meet her. He was forced to admit that she showed no promise. After graduating from high school in 1971, she went to Israel, where she lived and worked on a kibbutz and was so enthralled by the nation that she applied for citizenship. However, she took back the application following three months of strenuous training with the Israeli Defense Forces.

Upon returning to California, Mary Debra enrolled at California State University, studying sociology and criminology and hoping for a career in rehabilitating juvenile delinquents. Meanwhile, she worked part-time as a costumed troll at the nearby Magic Mountain Amusement Park. On December 31, 1973, she was thrown from the back of a moving pickup truck at Magic Mountain and suffered a cerebral hemorrhage, which resulted in temporary paralysis, blindness in one eye (from a damaged optic nerve), and a punctured eardrum. She was near death, but slowly regained her health after a year of periodic hospitalization. Her eyesight was restored, but she would forever have chronic back problems and would experience discomfort in traveling by air because of the ear impairment. During her convalescence, she made the decision to change the course of her life. "Poetically," she has said, "I look at my accident as a huge hunk of grace, which propelled me into doing what I wanted to do." She turned to acting, quitting college and taking drama lessons with actor Michael V. Gazzo. She was on stage in repertory in San Fernando Valley theaters billed as Debra, while also doing TV commercials for Metropolitan Life Insurance, American Dairy Milk products, and Sani-Flush, a toilet bowl cleaner. For the latter alone she was paid $9,000. During this time she also acted in a Los Angeles Police Department safety film showing what not to do as a hitchhiker, and was seen in commercials for the fast-food chains McDonald's and Burger King.

Managing to obtain assignments without benefit of an agent, she says, she auditioned for and won the part of Drusilla, the "Wonder Girl," younger sister of "Wonder Woman" Lynda Carter, in two episodes of the ABC-TV series "The New Original Wonder Woman." The first segment, "Feminine Mystique," aired in two parts on November 6 and 8, 1976; the second, "Wonder Woman in Hollywood," aired on February 16, 1977. She also was seen in "The Runaway" episode (September 5, 1977) of the short-lived series "Szysznyk"; the title was the difficult-to-pronounce last name of a retired Marine (Ned Beatty) turned playground supervisor. She made her motion picture debut as one of several high school girls reminiscing about their first sexual encounters in SLUMBER PARTY '57 (1977). In this forgettable entry, her character says, "Violence gets me hotter than a pistol!," which may account for Vestron Video's billing the cassette edition of the picture as "the sexiest film ever made for adults about teenagers."

On CBS-TV, Debra supported Charles Durning and Mare Winningham in SPECIAL OLYMPICS (February 22, 1978), subsequently entitled A SPECIAL KIND OF LOVE. Winger was engaged in police drama in the "Battered Teachers" episode (March 1, 1978) of NBC-TV's "Police Woman" and was one of those amazed at the precocity of "James at 16" on NBC-TV in June 1978. Her second theatrical film was as a disco dancing attendee of a Los Angeles nightspot in THANK GOD IT'S FRIDAY (1978), performing in the background to stars Donna Summer and Valerie Landsburg. In FRENCH POSTCARDS (1979), a cute comedy about American college students in Paris, Debra exhibited star potential as a sexy woman.

In aligning herself with one of Hollywood's biggest talent agencies, Creative Artists Agency (CAA), Debra won the lead female role in URBAN COWBOY (1980) opposite John Travolta, despite the studio's wanting Sissy Spacek for the part. Showing no signs of baby fat, Winger's figure on screen was neatly embraced by jeans and skirt as the woman picked up at Gilley's Bar in Pasadena, Texas, by hard-hat refinery worker Travolta. Her riding of a mechanical bull set the scene for future sensual/sexual on-screen action. *The New Yorker* magazine critic Pauline Kael observed, "She's naked all through the movie, though she never takes her clothes off." Production on the film was shut down on several occasions, sometimes because of Debra's insistence that dialogue be altered or that lighting or costumes be changed. Director James Bridges, often annoyed with his leading lady, said, "If you expect a normal working relationship with her . . . well, don't." Nevertheless, he liked her professionally. (Co-star Travolta publicly called her "very, very sexy and sensuous and funny and smart.") The much-touted feature was not a financial success, nor did it shore up Travolta's slipping star. However, it made a star of Debra, who received only favorable reviews. Off screen, though, the sudden success caused her to brag, swagger, and to be generally loud-mouthed.

Now considering herself above auditioning, Debra refused to read for George Lucas and Steven Spielberg for what would have been an impressive addition to her resumé, RAIDERS OF THE LOST ARK (1981). She rejected the feminine lead in ARTHUR (1981) as a role too secondary to Dudley Moore's star part, and made the mistake of refusing BODY HEAT (1981), an assignment that catapulted Kathleen Turner to sexy stardom. Instead, she chose to replace Raquel Welch, who had been fired, as a wisecracking prostitute in CANNERY ROW (1982), set in 1940s Monterey, California. With first-time director David S. Ward at the helm, the movie, described by one writer as "bland as farina," did not pass audience muster. But again Debra's reviews were solid. For example, Richard Schickel (*Time* magazine) called her "the best thing in a bad movie." She was uncredited in E.T. THE EXTRA-TERRESTRIAL (1982), in which her husky voice was mixed electronically with that of an older woman's to create the sound of the lovable E.T.

"How can you resist me?" she purred from the lap of Richard Gere in AN OFFICER AND A GENTLEMAN (1982), "I'm like candy." Later, in a motel scene in the drama, she bared it all while straddling him with tears streaming down her face from projected joy. (Actually, she would later admit, she was crying because she was so unhappy from the combination of the rainy Seattle, Washington, locale; director Taylor Hackford, whom she referred to as "an animal"; and Gere, whom she termed "a brick wall.") The final scene of the movie, in which Gere, realizing his emotional need for her, literally carries her away from her boring factory job, earned cheers and applause from audiences. With worldwide box-office grosses of $129.7 million, AN OFFICER AND A GENTLEMAN was the #3 moneymaker of 1982. Regarding her performance in this popular picture, David Ansen (*Newsweek* magazine) praised Debra as "one of those rare actresses who seems to open herself totally to the camera: every moment is raw, honest, freshly discovered." Winger was nominated for an Oscar as Best Actress. Apparently sensing that she would not win, she did not attend the ceremonies the night of April 11, 1983, when Meryl Streep was declared the winner for SOPHIE'S CHOICE. Ruth Winger told *People* magazine that AN OFFICER AND A GENTLEMAN was not the "easiest [movie] for a parent to sit through" because "the nude scenes . . . were a bit cringy . . . more for my husband than for me." She said that Streep deserved to win the Academy Award because "Debra's career is new—she has time yet."

Early in 1983, while on location in Lincoln, Nebraska, for TERMS OF ENDEARMENT (1983)—a role originally intended for Sissy Spacek—Debra met Nebraska governor Robert Kerrey, a Vietnam veteran who had lost his lower right leg in a 1969 grenade explosion. The populace of Lincoln, gossiping that she had booked bed-and-breakfast at the governor's mansion, did not take kindly to her because of her continual swearing. "Here comes l.c. [low class]," they murmured whenever she appeared. When the governor was asked about the romance, he replied, "Fluff up your pillow and dream about it," a

remark that a political opponent had print-ed on $3 posters. Forced to leave her new-found love when the location shooting moved to Houston, Texas, Debra wore the pregnancy padding used in her movie role all over town, reportedly even to basketball games in the company of her film co-star Jack Nicholson. By now, her romance with Kerrey was over.

Debra Winger in AN OFFICER AND A GENTLEMAN (1982).

TERMS OF ENDEARMENT, released in November 1983, was an instant winner, with a cast that was nothing short of bril-liant. As Emma, the rebellious daughter of age-conscious Aurora (Shirley MacLaine), Debra hit her professional peak, as her role spanned a period of fourteen years, ending with the young mother's death from can-cer. The tearjerker's worldwide grosses to-taled $108.4 million, making it the #2 financial success of the year. Although Winger was honored as Best Actress by the National Society of Film Critics, she lost her second Academy Award bid to five-time nominee and co-star Shirley Ma-cLaine. The latter, in her Oscar acceptance speech, made reference to Debra's "turbu-lent brilliance." Debra has credited James

Brooks, the director of TERMS OF ENDEARMENT, with having done the most to mold her burgeoning acting career. Jack Nicholson would judge that Winger is "a metamorphic actress. . . . I think she's a great actress—a genius."

During 1984 she campaigned on behalf of Democratic senator Gary Hart in Ohio in his bid for the Democratic presidential nomination, met actor Timothy Hutton for the first time, and purchased a hideaway "cabin" in New Mexico. She starred in MIKE'S MURDER (1984), written especially for her by director James Bridges. The mystery picture, plagued by production problems, was completed in 1983 but went through extensive reediting, rescoring, etc., and was not released until after TERMS OF ENDEARMENT. As a Los Angeles bank employee in MIKE'S MURDER, she falls in love with a tennis bum (Mark Keyloun). When he is killed, she sets out to investigate his murder, only to discover that he had led a double life. It was not a distinguished follow-up to her 1983 on-screen accomplishment.

Debra was a replacement for both Cher and Diane Keaton in Jack Nicholson's proposed feature film ROAD SHOW, a project that was to co-star Timothy Hutton. However, the production never materialized. In various stages of pre-production, Penny Marshall was scheduled to direct PEGGY SUE GOT MARRIED (1986) and wanted Debra as the matron who travels back in time to her high school days. However, when Francis Ford Coppola took over the reins, the choice role went to Kathleen Turner. Winger turned down MARIE (1985), which went to Sissy Spacek, as well as CRIMES OF THE HEART (1986), with Jessica Lange accepting that role. In 1985, returning to Seattle, Washington, to film LEGAL EAGLES (1986), she shot what was called "an extended music video" with Tom Robbins. On March 16, 1986, after having lived together for three months, she and Timothy Hutton were married in romantic Big Sur on the California coast. She was thirty; he was twenty-five.

Ostensibly a comedy, LEGAL EAGLES was originally set to star Robert Redford and Bill Murray. When Murray had to drop out over a schedule conflict, Debra was asked to step in. Director Ivan Reitman (whom she later said was "crude") promised the actress that the script would be an updated version of the immensely popular ADAM'S RIB (1949), which had starred Katharine Hepburn and Spencer Tracy. What emerged on movie screens in June 1986, however, was a virtual mess in which Debra was cast as an offbeat attorney whose latest client (Daryl Hannah) is very bizarre. In addition, she (Debra) has an unlikely romance with an assistant district attorney (Robert Redford). The anemic situations within LEGAL EAGLES did not make any sense because of the studio's last-minute pressure to change the ending. When the "comedy" aired on television, months later, Reitman reverted to the original ending, which made the film more comprehensible but scarcely more enjoyable. Complaining that LEGAL EAGLES had been edited with a chain-saw, Debra also blamed her agents for involving her in the project. She was the first star to walk out on CAA. A year later, though, she returned to them.

In 1986 she suffered a miscarriage while filming Bob Rafelson's BLACK WIDOW (1987), a slick, elegant movie that falls apart at the end. Debra's character, Alexandra, an undercover Justice Department investigator, is obsessed with capturing a serial killer

(Theresa Russell) who specializes in eliminating her wealthy husbands. The two actresses played well together, including scenes that smacked of lesbianism. However, as in LEGAL EAGLES, where Daryl Hannah had the more interesting role, in BLACK WIDOW it was Theresa Russell who captured the bulk of attention from reviewers and audiences. On March 30, 1987, Debra was interviewed by Barbara Walters on ABC-TV, and her performance confirmed that she was a very independent, self-directed person.

In MADE IN HEAVEN (1987), starring Debra's husband, Timothy Hutton, Winger had a cameo as Emmett, a male guardian angel. Debra had to forego starring in BROADCAST NEWS (1987) due to her pregnancy. The pivotal female role in this hit movie went instead to soundalike Holly Hunter. Winger became a mother in April 1987 with the birth of son Emanuel Noah. Within six months after the child's arrival, it was clear to observers that all was not well in the Huttons' Malibu household. While Timothy was a laid-back introvert, Debra was a loud, almost militantly outspoken woman who did not like his friendship with actor Sean Penn. In May 1988 the couple separated, with Hutton moving to quarters in the Hollywood Hills. In December of that year he filed for divorce, requesting joint custody of their son. "I fell deeply in love and got married," Debra would say, "but the fact is that the system doesn't work for me." She found being a single mother to be "very hard emotionally," and also "very isolating." She admitted, "I get very sad," a state of mind she shared with Bob Kerrey of Nebraska, with whom she had rekindled a friendship. She donated $2,000 to his successful campaign as a Democrat for the U.S. Senate. Upon taking office in January 1989 he was publicized as possible presidential material, which led to speculation that Debra just might follow in the footsteps of former actress Nancy Davis Reagan. Kerrey insisted that he and Debra were now no more than friends and co-partners in Kerrey's Prairie Life fitness center in Omaha, Nebraska.

Debra had rejected the leads in both BULL DURHAM (1988) and THE GOOD MOTHER (1988)—roles taken respectively by Susan Sarandon and Diane Keaton—in order to accept another undercover agent role in BETRAYED (1988). She vowed that "This is my swan song to cops." Cast as a federal agent, she is sent to America's Midwest to investigate a farmer (Tom Berenger) suspected of heading a white supremacy cult. In the process, she falls in love with this brooding, sensual family man. Later, he takes her into his confidence and she learns that the initial suspicions concerning him are true. Jack Kroll (*Time* magazine) asked, "who could resist the vital Winger in her best role since TERMS OF ENDEARMENT?" Television critic Rex Reed termed both stars "simply *magnificent.*" However, BETRAYED had too many plot loopholes and its somber subject matter did not attract filmgoers. It was not a financial success.

Tantalizing advertisements for EVERYBODY WINS (1990) read: "Everybody knows. Everyone's guilty. No one pays." However, those few people who saw the feature film concluded that no one cares. In the story, Debra hires a retired Boston cop (Nick Nolte) to investigate the murder of her former psychiatrist because she feels that the man imprisoned for the deed is innocent. The cop soon decides that she is schizophrenic. Of this film, shot from Arthur Miller's ambiguous screenplay, *Variety* noted, "this big-budget prestige picture is obscure and artificial, with appeal only for a handful of film buffs." Reunited with Nick Nolte, with whom she had co-starred in CANNERY ROW eight years earlier, Debra seemed uncomfortable with Miller's dialogue as well as with her co-star. Again she was playing a prostitute—one with secrets. *People* magazine's Ralph Novak conceded that Debra "flounces and curls her lip with a vengeance yet never seems crazy so much as just tired," while *Daily Variety* concluded that the "film founders immediately due to the miscasting of Winger as a schizo femme fatale."

In March 1990 Debra sold her apartment on New York City's Central Park West, which she had bought soon after her divorce. The buyer was actor Harrison Ford, who paid more than $2 million for the property. Although Winger had not had a box-office smash in seven years, her per-film salary was in league with those of Jane Fonda, Cher, Sally Field, Michelle Pfeiffer, and Kim Basinger in the $2 million to $3 million range. Debra's reaction to this is "I'm shocked that I get this price," but unlike Sigourney Weaver or Meryl Streep, she is not complaining. It had been reported in late 1988 that Winger would star in the screen adaptation of Susan Isaacs's novel *Shining Through*, as a secretary joining the OSS during World War II. However, the project would later be assigned to Melanie Griffith. Winger rejected the lead roles in both MUSIC BOX (1989) (Jessica Lange took it) and THE FABULOUS BAKER BOYS (1989) (it went to Michelle Pfeiffer), but Debra did star in THE SHELTERING SKY (1990), the screen adaptation of Paul Bowles's semi-autobiographical 1949 novel. Directed in Tangier, Morocco, and Rome by Italian film-maker Bernardo Bertolucci, the feature starred Debra and John Malkovich as an alienated American couple wandering through post–World War II North Africa hoping to find answers to their problems, but instead discovering deep despair. When the arty film opened in the highly competitive Christmas season of 1990, Sheila Benson (*Los Angeles Times*) cautioned that the 138-minute film was "querulous and exhausting" but that "John Malkovich and Debra Winger are superb at suggesting a couple quiveringly attuned to each other's needs and neuroses after a decade of marriage, yet tragically unable to connect." Duane Byrge (*Hollywood Reporter*) rated the offering a "flat and distended cinematic trek," although he acknowledged, "Winger brings an appropriately manic and moody intensity to her performance as the prickly traveler. . . ."

RADIO FLYER (forthcoming, 1991) was written by David Mickey Evans with actress Rosanna Arquette in mind. However, when Columbia Pictures replaced Evans as director of the project with Richard Donner, Arquette was out and Debra was in as the movie's female star. However, Debra, too, dropped out, leaving producer Michael Douglas without a leading lady until Lorraine Bracco was hired to fill the vacancy. Instead, Winger signed to co-star with Tom Hanks in SIGNIFICANT OTHER, to have been directed by Alan J. Pakula, in which she would have played Hanks's alcoholic girlfriend. This project fell into an abyss when Pakula became unavailable. Debra Dropped out of the Penny Marshall-directed film A LEAGUE OF THEIR OWN (forthcoming, 1992), the story of an all-female baseball team in the 1940s, and was replaced by Geena Davis. Next, Debra announced she would star in Tri-Star's WILDER NAPALM (forthcoming, 1991), to be directed by Glenn Caron.

An actress who literally lives each role she plays, Debra is content to limit her screen appearances. She reasons, "I need time for my life. I don't have the stuff to go from one film to another. That's like lining up your life, and it doesn't work. If you know what you are going to do next year, you become that." Regarding her recurring contretemps with the directors on her motion pictures, she says, "I'm a director's actress. That's why I have such turmoil when I don't get along with them." As she turned thirty-five, Debra stopped using four-letter words and gave up chain-smoking. She explained the lifestyle changes with, "Once you're a mother, man, once you've carried this kid around, and given birth to it, you pretty much never feel the same."

Filmography

Slumber Party '57 (Cannon–Happy, 1977)
Special Olympics [A Special Kind of Love] (CBS-TV, 2/22/78)
Thank God It's Friday (Col, 1978)
French Postcards (Par, 1979)
Urban Cowboy (Par, 1980)
Cannery Row (MGM/UA, 1982)
E.T. the Extra-Terrestrial (Univ, 1982) (voice only)

An Officer and a Gentleman (Par, 1982)
Terms of Endearment (Par, 1983)
Mike's Murder (WB, 1984)
Legal Eagles (Univ, 1986)
Black Widow (20th–Fox, 1987)
Made in Heaven (Lorimar, 1987)
Betrayed (MGM/UA, 1988)
Everybody Wins (Orion, 1990)
The Sheltering Sky (WB, 1990)

JAMES WOODS

"The only thing I strive for is perfection, absolute greatness.
I don't always succeed, but the few great shining moments I have
will be with me the rest of my life."
— *Fame* magazine, September–October 1989

BETTE DAVIS, JAMES GARNER, AND DUSTIN HOFFMAN HAVE EACH
named the very intense James Woods the best actor of his generation. But for Woods, a
man of evident abilities, talent is not enough. He longs to be a leading man—a romantic
star. However, by conventional Hollywood standards, his angular, offbeat looks (like those
of Willem Dafoe, Robert Davi, and Scott Glenn) do not qualify him as handsome enough
for traditional movie hero roles. Thus, the very frustrated, very outspoken Woods has been
forced to depend on the bankable reputations of co-stars like Glenn Close and Michael J.
Fox rather than content himself with playing second leads. Once he is on the set, the
actor's high-voltage energy and ambition can make him exasperatingly argumentative and
meddlesome (as director Oliver Stone found during the making of SALVADOR [1986]), but
he always turns in a driven, gripping performance.

James Howard Woods was born on Friday, April 18, 1947, in Rangely, Colorado,
to Gail, a multi-decorated World War II naval hero working for Standard Oil as a pipe
fitter, and his wife, Martha Ann. Short on money and furniture, the parents made a bed for
their newborn in a dresser drawer. They talked to him as an adult, not in baby talk, and at
the age of eight months James spoke his first word, "cookie." By the age of twelve months
he was carrying on conversations with his parents, who took turns reading to him or
reciting passages from the works of Shakespeare. Prior to the outbreak of the Korean
conflict, Gail accepted an officer's commission with the U.S. Army, leading to his being
stationed on the island of Guam, where the family joined him. With the outbreak of
hostilities between North and South Korea in June 1950, Martha Ann and her son were
sent to live with her mother in Greenup, Illinois. At the end of the Korean war, Gail was
stationed at Fort Lee, Virginia, with his small family joining him in nearby Hopewell.
However, within two years they moved again, to Warwick, Rhode Island, where Gail had
been transferred. Hoping for a permanent assignment there, he bought a home, but would
leave one more time to fulfill an assignment in Asia.

Despite the many changes in locale and the absences of his father, James has
remembered the family as close and "Norman Rockwell-esque." He had a newspaper route
in Warwick, but spent most of his time studying or reading in his room with the door shut.

In 1957, when James was ten, his brother, Michael, was born. When he was twelve, his father, who had returned from the Orient, underwent routine surgery for a blood clot, but died during the operation. He was given a military hero's funeral with a twenty-one-gun salute, but he left little for his widow and sons. Forced to find work, Martha started "Lad 'n Lassie," a preschool for young children, which proved successful. Meanwhile, James engaged in odd jobs, including his paper route, and later worked on an assembly line at the Speidel Watch Company.

At Pilgrim High School, Woods became proficient on the classical guitar, was an honor student with a straight-A average, and played fifty-year-old Oscar Hubbard in a school production of *The Little Foxes*. At age seventeen he scored 180 (above genius level) on the Stanford-Binet IQ Test, and achieved a perfect score of 800 on the verbal part of the Scholastic Aptitude Test (SAT) and 779 on the math segment of the test, the highest in Rhode Island. In the summer of 1965, between his junior and senior years, he was one of thirty-five students awarded a National Science Foundation grant to study linear algebra at the University of California at Los Angeles in a high school exchange program. His professional goal of becoming an eye surgeon was further whetted by scholarship offers from several top universities, including an appointment at the Air Force Academy at Colorado Springs, partially arranged by Rhode Island Senator John O. Pastore.

Woods's dream of a life in medicine, along with his guitar-strumming, came to an end at UCLA when he accidentally thrust his right arm through a plate-glass door. He severed the radial artery, all the tendons in the arm, and the median nerve. He was in surgery for ten hours and required more than two hundred stitches. Changing his career path, he accepted a full scholarship at the Massachusetts Institute of Technology at Cambridge, majoring in political science. In his freshman year, he joined the drama workshop, appearing in experimental plays as well as in productions at the Harvard Summer Theatre, the Theatre Company of Boston, and the Provincetown Playhouse. By his senior year he had acted in thirty-six plays and was spending as much time as possible in New York City auditioning at off-Broadway theaters.

After spending only a few days in senior classes, he quit college in September 1969 to seek an acting career. He insisted that he would much rather pursue this type of work than spend even one day as a "policy wonk" for the U.S. State Department or the Central Intelligence Agency. He refrained from taking acting classes because "I saw no reason to pay some failed actor a lot of money so that thirty other nonactors could sit around and tell me what was wrong with the way I acted." He claimed to know enough already about doing accents, age, comedy, and drama because "I'd been out on the front lines." His first professional acting job was at the Paramus Playhouse on the Mall in New Jersey in *There's a Girl in My Soup*. This was followed by faking an accent as a Britisher from Liverpool in order to obtain a part in the otherwise all-English cast of Brendan Behan's *Borstal Boy*, which opened March 31, 1970, on Broadway and won a Tony Award and the New York Drama Critics Award as best dramatic play of the 1969–1970 season. Stating that he would have a Tony Award by the time he was twenty-five, he was honored with an Obie and a Theatre World Award, as well as the Clarence Derwent Award as "most promising actor," for his performance in *Saved* at the Brooklyn Academy of Music, which began on October 20, 1970, and ran into 1971 off-Broadway. On December 1, 1971, James was seen in the "Hallmark Hall of Fame" production of "All the Way Home," taped by NBC-TV in Toronto and starring Joanne Woodward, Richard Kiley, and Pat Hingle. That same year he was off-Broadway in *The Trial of the Catonsville Nine, Finishing Touches, Green Julia*, and on Broadway in *Conduct Unbecoming*. He had hoped that *Moonchildren*, which *Show* magazine called "one of the best plays to have opened all season," would propel him to the top. However, it closed after only thirteen performances on Broadway after its opening on February 21, 1972.

Since Woods spent every afternoon in movie theaters and because he claimed to be disenchanted with New York theater, he obtained an agent, Todd Smith, to help him get screen roles. His film debut was as a Vietnam veteran turned stoolie in THE VISITORS (1972), a low-budget film directed by Elia Kazan on 16-millimeter film. It was based on a *New Yorker* magazine article by Daniel Lang. During its very limited release, it received negative reviews. THE VISITORS was based on the same story as the later CASUALTIES OF WAR (1989). This was followed by a small part in HICKEY AND BOGGS (1972), an action picture starring Robert Culp and Bill Cosby. Then James played a reporter in the CBS-TV movie FOOTSTEPS (October 3, 1972) and supported George Kennedy and Vera Miles in the ABC-TV movie A GREAT AMERICAN TRAGEDY (October 18, 1972). In THE WAY WE WERE (1973), a project he fought hard to obtain, he was the nerd boyfriend/disciple of political activist Barbra Streisand. He had the small role of a bank officer in James Caan's THE GAMBLER (1974). In Los Angeles in September 1974, Woods played Paula Kelly's love-struck boyfriend in the Center Theatre Group's stage production of *The Charlatan* at the Music Center's Mark Taper Forum.

Continuing in supporting roles, James was on TV in a segment of "The Streets of San Francisco," on the theatrical screen in NIGHT MOVES (1975) and DISTANCE (1975), and in the CBS-TV movie FOSTER & LAURIE (November 13, 1975) as a dope addict. He received third billing in Jack Lemmon's misfire, ALEX AND THE GYPSY (1976) and was next involved in the Hollywood of the 1920s in F. SCOTT FITZGERALD IN HOLLYWOOD, an ABC-TV movie broadcast on May 16, 1976. In NBC-TV's THE DISAPPEARANCE OF AIMEE (November 17, 1976), he played an assistant district attorney. While making this project he became a friend of Bette Davis, who advised him to improve his craft by listening to what others had to say. He was Dr. Robert Styles in the January 4, 1977, episode of "Family," the ABC-TV drama series, and portrayed an Israeli army officer in NBC-TV's RAID ON ENTEBBE (January 9, 1977).

In its March 29, 1977, edition, the *Hollywood Reporter* announced that production had begun on "the movie event of 1977," which would present "The funniest, wildest, toughest bunch to ever hit the screen—and we promise . . . you'll never forget them." The movie was THE CHOIRBOYS (1977), adapted for the screen by Joseph Wambaugh from his best-selling novel about a group of Los Angeles policemen who relieve the pressure of their job by heavy partying and playing. It was one of the most foul-mouthed films to come out of Hollywood up to that time, and Wambaugh later disavowed it. In an ensemble cast,

James played Harold Bloomguard, a vice squad cop, who has great difficulty in attempting to arrest two whores at once. On August 31, 1977, James starred in the sixty-minute NBC-TV presentation "Billion Dollar Bubble," a dramatization of two billion dollar insurance embezzlements, filmed in London and shown on the BBC television network in 1976.

"Holocaust" (1978), a nine-and-a-half-hour miniseries televised in four parts, reportedly captured the attention of 120 million Americans. A saga of two German families, one Jewish, the other members of the Nazi Party, it induced both sobs and shock from viewers. James was the Jewish Karl Weiss in the drama, which received sixteen Emmy nominations. James followed that prestigious production by wearing 1890s costumes in support of Marie Osmond in ABC-TV's fluffy THE GIFT OF LOVE (December 8, 1978) as well as playing an eerie Appalachian in CBS-TV's THE INCREDIBLE JOURNEY OF DOCTOR MEG LAUREL (January 2, 1979). Having long since paid his professional dues, on January 28, 1979, he was seen in his first co-starring role. He and Sally Struthers played a New York couple who discover that their son (Jeff Bravlin) is deaf, rather than mentally retarded, as originally diagnosed, in CBS-TV's AND YOUR NAME IS JONAH (1979).

THE ONION FIELD (1979), James's second film with writer Joseph Wambaugh, did not come about easily. Having nothing but disgust for the way Hollywood had handled THE CHOIRBOYS, Wambaugh made sure he had full creative control of this new project. He personally chose Harold Becker to direct the venture, and Becker insisted on being faithful to Wambaugh's book. Thus, in casting the role of Gregory Powell, the director wanted a blue-eyed blond to play the real-life small-time hood. Because Woods did not fit this description, it was only because of his agent's incredible persistence that the actor was given a screen test (paid for by agent Smith's selling his car). Wambaugh, who wrote the screenplay from his best-selling book, had good reason to be proud of the movie version of THE ONION FIELD, partly because of James's intense portrayal of the terrifying, unpredictable psychopathic killer. THE ONION FIELD is a haunting film, one that exposes the way that America's judicial system wastes taxpayers' dollars and often makes the policeman, doing his duty, the victim in the case. *Variety* endorsed, "Woods . . . is chillingly effective, creating a flakiness in the character that exudes the danger of a live wire near a puddle." However, in a reunion with Wambaugh and Becker in THE BLACK MARBLE (1980), a little-seen film in which he supported Robert Foxworth and Paula Prentiss, James was reasonably normal as a Gypsy fiddler who provides string music while the leads romance.

By 1980 Woods had taken up residence full time in Los Angeles. There he met model Kathryn Greko, ten years his junior. During a whimsical moment, the couple went to Las Vegas where they were married at 2 a.m. on Labor Day, September 8, 1980. This marriage ended in divorce three years later with the ex-Mrs. Woods saying, "He loved the way I looked, but he never really trusted me. Jim thinks his way is the only way. That drove me crazy."

In his only 1981 release, the New York–lensed EYEWITNESS, Woods had the relatively small part of William Hurt's persistent, odd friend. However, he was seen in two features in simultaneous release in October 1982. In FAST-WALKING, a quirky low-budget prison drama shot in 1980, he starred as a mercenary, amoral prison guard hired to assassinate a jailed black political figure (Robert Hooks). In SPLIT IMAGE, his character was not much nicer: a demonic deprogrammer of young adults kidnapped by religious cultists. Because of his prior commitment to SPLIT IMAGE, James lost the opportunity to take the role of the drill sergeant in one of the year's biggest box-office champions, AN OFFICER AND A GENTLEMAN. That role went to Louis Gossett, Jr., who won an Academy Award for his performance. James desperately wanted the part of Nathan (played by Kevin Kline) in SOPHIE'S CHOICE (1982), but was refused even an unofficial interview for the job. Instead, VIDEODROME (1983), filmed in Canada, had him in a starring role as a cable-channel TV operator mind-warped by a secret TV system with hallucinatory capabilities involving sex and gore. *Playgirl* magazine noted that James "is wonderful but the rest is inferior." A second role that he coveted was Meryl Streep's boyfriend in SILKWOOD (1983), but the better-looking Kurt Russell got it.

As ex–New Yorker Jake Wise, the bookie/owner of a Sunset Strip club in AGAINST ALL ODDS (1984), Woods was particularly snaky in his efforts to earn respect from the wealthy men who control Los Angeles. Third-billed, after Jeff Bridges and Rachel Ward as the couple whose passion sizzled on the screen, James played the role originated by Kirk Douglas in the earlier 1947 version (OUT OF THE PAST) of Geoffrey Homes's novel. ONCE UPON A TIME IN AMERICA (1984), directed by Italian filmmaker Sergio Leone in several locales, was the epic telling of fifty years in the lives of New York Jewish gangsters. James was Max, sneakier and smarter than the rest, while Robert De Niro was the partner he betrayed. Shown at the Cannes Film Festival in its full length (more than 227 minutes), the picture made sense, but when released in the United States at an abbreviated 139 minutes, it proved to be a jumbled, inexplicable mess. As a result, it was a failure in distribution.

People magazine credited CAT'S EYE (1985), based on three macabre stories by Stephen King, with being the perfect film for "those who like to have their funnybones tickled and chilled at the same time." James was in the first episode, a serio-comic tale of a man who joins Quitters, Inc., to stop smoking and of the terrible consequences he undergoes if he takes so much as one further puff of nicotine. He was a sympathetic character, a successful Jewish novelist, in JOSHUA THEN AND NOW (1985), filmed in Canada as a television miniseries but edited, instead, to the customary length of a theatrical release. CBS-TV's BADGE OF THE ASSASSIN (November 2, 1985) starred James as a Manhattan assistant district attorney, a role that was the forerunner of many such roles to come. The methodical story derived from a novel written by Robert Tanenbaum, the real-life attorney who in May 1971 prosecuted the case of the self-styled Black Liberation Army.

James talked his way into starring in SALVADOR (1986) as the lying hustler freelance photojournalist who gained personal redemption in civil war–torn El Salvador in 1980–1981. Photographed in Mexico with funds raised from British and Mexican sources, it was directed by Oliver Stone, who later described Woods as a lunatic. "He always knows better, which is very irritating." However, Stone also expressed admiration for the actor, who earned a Best Actor Academy Award nomination for his performance. James lost the award to Paul Newman (THE COLOR OF MONEY). He did, however, win the Independent Film Project Spirit Award. After SALVADOR, James was promoted to starring or co-starring status, both in feature films and TV movies. The title of PROMISE (December 14, 1986), a "Hallmark Hall of Fame" presentation on CBS-TV, referred to the oath made by an older brother (James Garner) to his dying mother that he would care for his schizophrenic younger sibling (Woods). The television movie, which Garner co-executive produced, won five Emmy awards, including one for James Woods as Outstanding Lead Actor in a Mini Series or a Special. He was also honored with a Golden Globe Award and a Golden Apple.

In NBC-TV's LOVE AND WAR (March 16, 1987), co-starring Jane Alexander, Woods portrayed real-life Commander James B. Stockdale, a Navy pilot imprisoned and tortured for eight years in Vietnam while his wife fought for his release through Washington, D.C., sources. For his convincing performance he received a Golden Globe nomination as best actor. BEST SELLER (1987), although a very intriguing story, was not popular with moviegoers. James, in a sensationally intense, quirky performance, was a professional hit man who sought revenge on his past employer (Paul Shenar), a wealthy businessman. The film's producer, Carter De Haven, found that James "can be a real irritant" because "if Jimmy could, he would do wardrobe, music, the grip's job and work the camera." However, like Stone, De Haven had to evaluate him honestly, adding, "Actually, I'd do it again in a minute. There are certain actors you put up with because you get something for it."

James Woods in BEST SELLER (1987).

In 1985, while hoping to reconcile with his ex-wife, Kathryn, James met Sarah Marie Owen at a Chevron station on Sunset Boulevard, where both were filling their gas tanks. A boutique owner and an equestrian, Owen said, "At first, I couldn't get a word in at all." Nevertheless, the pair began a love affair that included, in November 1987, her filing a report with the Los Angeles Police Department that he had held her at gunpoint. The charge was later dropped. In January 1988 he proposed marriage to her in a restaurant by dropping a glittering diamond engagement ring into her champagne glass, a gesture that was approved and applauded by onlookers.

Pre-release ads screamed "When a Cop Cares Too Much, How Far Is Too Far?" Co-producing with writer/director

James B. Harris, James was COP (1988), obsessed with finding a serial killer, but interrupting his search occasionally to sleep with female witnesses. *Premiere* magazine's disapproval of the feature suggested that Woods had seen "too many James Woods movies" and that "the only redeeming moment . . . comes when he does an imitation of his own tough-guy character." Despite a lack of true box-office hits, his per-film salary was now at $1 million, which, he hoped, would escalate following THE BOOST (1988). The author described this movie as "a story about two people with black holes in their souls." Playing opposite him as his wife was Sean Young, whose character followed his lead to become a cocaine addict after his financially successful real estate career in Los Angeles began to nose-dive. Dismissed by *US* magazine as giving an "overwrought performance," James was credited by the *San Francisco Chronicle*, on the other hand, as being "brilliant" in "a good picture."

During the shooting of THE BOOST, Woods and Young embarked on a love affair that he was forced to end at the demand of Sarah Owen. However, their home life was shattered by hate mail, anonymous phone calls, mutilated baby dolls placed on their doorstep (in reference to an abortion Owen had had), destruction of garden flowers, and other vandalism. James filed a $6 million suit against Young, the alleged culprit, and the parties settled out of court in August 1989 for an undisclosed amount. Thereafter, James declared, "If anybody tries to hurt me, they better be willing to do it until the day they die, because I will never forget."

Pauline Kael (*The New Yorker* magazine), long a fan of James Woods, wrote of his "sensational" performance in TRUE BELIEVER (1989), "it's the impression he gives of hyperbolic self-regard that makes him seem perfectly cast here." His Eddie Dodd, a lawyer with a graying ponytail and a former counterculture hero of the 1960s, becomes obsessed with obtaining another trial for an Asian (Yuji Okumoto) whom he feels has been unjustly imprisoned for eight years. Although Woods once again received favorable reviews, the film, which co-starred Robert Downey, Jr., as his idealistic young lawyer assistant, was not a box-office blockbuster. In 1991, ABC-TV presented a TV series version of TRUE BELIEVER called "Eddie Dodd," with Treat Williams cast in James's big-screen role.

Woods's second collaboration with James Garner was in the title role of MY NAME IS BILL W. (April 30, 1989), another "Hallmark Hall of Fame" presentation for ABC-TV. As Bill Wilson, the co-founder, with Dr. Robert Smith (Garner), of Alcoholics Anonymous, Woods won his second Emmy Award as Outstanding Lead Actor. He accepted his award by saying "This is beyond belief" and gave credit to Garner as "a good-luck charm." Garner showed his respect for James by saying, "Jimmy is utterly hyper. He's going all the time—a brilliant young man, a great mind, very well read. He can speak on any subject and *will*."

His marriage to Sarah Owen on July 2, 1989, was kept secret until the last minute because, referring to Sean Young, "We didn't want any demented people to know where." Following a ceremony at Greystone Mansion in Beverly Hills, the couple resided in their home near the Beverly Hills post office with their two terrier dogs. Four months later, on November 6, they separated. On November 30, 1989, James filed for a legal separation, citing irreconcilable differences. Sarah stated, "he can be volatile and combative, and everyone knows he's intense. Before I met him, I wasn't used to the fact that buying the wrong length shoe-laces could be reason to contemplate suicide." A few weeks later, their home was sold for just under $2 million. Meanwhile, James appeared as a presenter at the MTV Music Video Awards on September 6, 1989, at the Universal Amphitheater in Los Angeles. Out of place in a conservative gray suit among the more outlandish costumes of other presenters, he said, "I look like George Bush!"

Having aligned his services with Columbia Pictures, then headed by Dawn Steel, an executive James felt cared more about talent than beauty, he and Glenn Close co-starred as a married couple who adopt a baby in IMMEDIATE FAMILY (1989). With makeup covering his acne scars and well-groomed hair, James looked handsome in his portrayal of the anxious husband. *Variety* noted that the unique casting gave him "a chance to apply his considerable talents to a different kind of character than those that occupy most of his résumé." Another box-office disappointment, the film realized a gross of just $1.6 million during its first week of domestic release. On October 11, 1989, at the Mill Valley, California, Film Festival, James was given a standing-room-only tribute at the Sequoia II Theatre, where he made frequently witty but stinging references to his struggles to overcome typecasting. "I loathe the word 'star,'" he told the crowd from behind horn-rimmed glasses, "unless, of course, I'm negotiating my contract, and then I use it as often as possible."

On August 19, 1990, he starred with Melanie Griffith, whom he had first met when she was seventeen, during the filming of NIGHT MOVES, on HBO–Cable in one of three American short stories dealing with love, lovers, and their problems in WOMEN AND MEN: STORIES OF SEDUCTION. In the third segment, Ernest Hemingway's "Hills Like White Elephants," James was a writer who encouraged his wealthy lover (Griffith) to have an abortion. Filmed in Spain under the direction of Tony Richardson, their segment was, according to *Time* magazine, "a haunting brief encounter frozen in time by good acting and writing." On September 7, 1990, James was one of many stars from all media to participate in the AIDS Project Los Angeles's fundraiser *Commitment to Life IV* at the Wiltern Theatre in Los Angeles.

In THE HARD WAY (1991), co-starring Michael J. Fox, Woods has the role of John Moss, a seasoned New York Police Department homicide detective who is shadowed by Nick Lang (Fox), Hollywood's top male star, who is studying the tough cop to prepare for a movie role. James said that he wanted the part (a lighter one than usual) "just for fun" in order to spoof his many intense portrayals. Next on Woods's acting agenda was THE BOYS (April 15, 1991), an ABC-TV movie dealing with two TV writers, one a cigarette smoker (John Lithgow), the other a nonsmoker (Woods), with the latter contracting lung cancer. Next, Woods is set to co-star with Dolly Parton in STRAIGHT TALK (forthcoming, 1992).

In June 1990, while seen around Hollywood in the company of beautiful companions such as blonde Elizabeth Hilden and the attractive Julie Tesh (ex-wife of TV personality John Tesh), James told of his talks with filmmaker Oliver Stone about producing, while James directed, a movie about the life of Harvey Milk, the slain San Francisco gay city supervisor. So far that project has not come to fruition. Meanwhile, he was chosen by the National Academy of Cable Programming (ACE) to be the sole host of its twelfth annual ACE Awards show on January 13, 1991.

With his burning creative passions and his seemingly inexhaustible energy, Woods once told *Esquire* magazine, "everyone in this business is scared to death of me . . . because they're all morons and I'm not." Perhaps his goal in life should be to form his own independent movie studio where his energetic genius can be put to work in all areas of filmmaking—a latter-day Orson Welles in a Howard Hughes environment.

Filmography

Footsteps (CBS-TV, 10/3/72)
A Great American Tragedy [Man at the Crossroads] (ABC-TV, 10/18/72)
The Visitors (UA, 1972)
Hickey and Boggs (UA, 1972)
The Way We Were (Col, 1973)
The Gambler (Par, 1974)
Foster & Laurie (CBS-TV, 11/13/75)
Night Moves (WB, 1975)
Distance (Cine Bright, 1975)
F. Scott Fitzgerald in Hollywood (ABC-TV, 5/16/76)
The Disappearance of Aimee (NBC-TV, 11/17/76)
Alex and the Gypsy (20th–Fox, 1976)
Raid on Entebbe (NBC-TV, 1/9/77)
The Choirboys (Univ, 1977)
The Gift of Love (ABC-TV, 12/8/78)
The Incredible Journey of Doctor Meg Laurel (CBS-TV, 1/2/79)
And Your Name Is Jonah (CBS-TV, 1/28/79)
The Onion Field (Avco Emb, 1979)
The Black Marble (Avco Emb, 1980)
Eyewitness [The Janitor] (20th–Fox, 1981)
Fast-Walking (Pickman, 1982)

Split Image [Captured!] (Orion, 1982)
Videodrome (Univ, 1983)
Against All Odds (Col, 1984)
Once upon a Time in America (WB, 1984)
Badge of the Assassin (CBS-TV, 11/2/85)
Cat's Eye (MGM/UA, 1985)
Joshua Then and Now (20th–Fox, 1985)
Promise (CBS-TV, 12/14/86)
Salvador (Hemdale, 1986)
Love and War (NBC-TV, 3/16/87)
Best Seller (Orion, 1987)
Cop (Atlantic, 1988) (also co-producer)
The Boost (Hemdale, 1988)
My Name Is Bill W. (ABC-TV, 4/30/89)
True Believer (Col, 1989)
Immediate Family (Col, 1989)
Women and Men: Stories of Seduction [episode: Hills Like White Elephants](HBO–Cable, 8/19/90)
The Hard Way (Univ, 1991)
The Boys (ABC-TV, 4/15/91)

Future Releases

Straight Talk (BV, 1992)

Television Series

Holocaust (NBC, 4/16/78–4/19/78) [miniseries]

Broadway Plays

Borstal Boy (1970)
Conduct Unbecoming (1971)

Moonchildren (1972)

INDEX

INDEX

Boldface page references at the end of entries indicate photographs. Titles of films and made-for-television movies are in italics; radio and television titles and titles of short stories are in quotation marks and are indicated as such in parentheses; titles of books, stage productions, and record albums are in italics and are indicated as such in parentheses.

"A.D." (TV) 470, 473
"A.M. America" (TV) 57
"A.M. Chicago" (TV) 609, 613
Aaron, Paul 329, 330
"ABC Presents a Royal Gala" (TV) 587
"ABC's Silver Anniversary Celebration—25 and Still the One" (TV) 502
"ABC's Wide World of Sports" (TV) 477
Abdul, Paula 233, 545
Abdul-Jabbar, Kareem 187
Abraham, F. Murray 73, 575
Abry, Jonas 348
Absence of Malice 160, 164
Absent-Minded Professor, The 453, 458
"Absolute Monarch of Ward C" (TV) 202
Absolutely Mahvelous (book) 109
"Academy of Country Music Awards" (TV) 67
Accidental Tourist, The 206, 280, 281, 282, 380, 382, 562, 565, 579
Accused, The 94, 387, 388, 537, 579
Ackerman, Harry 158
Ackland, Joss 332
Acrobats (stage) 151
Act of Love 445, 451
Act of Vengeance 24, 26
"Adam-12" (TV) 251, 567
Adams, Brooke 167, 350
Adams, Jane 512

Adam's Rib 618
Addams Family, The 85
Adjani, Isabelle 93
Adler, Luther 99
Adler, Matt 264
Adler, Stella 216, 217, 437
Adventurers, The 56, 61, 501, 506
Adventures of Baron Munchausen, The 587, 589
Adventures of Buckaroo Banzai, The: Across the 8th Dimension 24, 26, 116, 118, 203, 207
Adventures of Huckleberry Finn, The (book) 209
Aesop (stage) 151
"After George" (TV) 464
"After Midnight" (TV) 211
"After-School Special" (TV) 225
After the Promise 255, 258
Against All Odds 73, 76, 626, 630
"Against Her Will" (TV) 387
"Age of Steel, The" (statue) 528
Agutter, Jenny 495
AIDS: Everything You Should Know 195
Aiello, Danny 83, 155
Air America 100, 180, 181, 394
Ajaye, Franklin 211, 230
Alamo, The 17
Alamo, The: 13 Days to Glory 17, 21
Albert, Eddie 16, 424; **493**
Albert, Edward 64
Alda, Alan 417, 535
Aldrich, Robert 559
Alex and the Gypsy 624, 630

Alexander, Jane 627
Alfie 79, 86
Alfred Hitchcock Presents 217, 220
"Alfred Hitchcock Presents" (TV) 570
Ali, Muhammad 445
Alias Smith and Jones 461, 465
"Alias Smith and Jones" (TV) 159, 164, 501
Alice 20, 21, 282, 498, 499
"Alice at the Palace" (TV) 535
Alice in Wonderland (1985) 294, 296
Alice in Wonderland (stage) 534
Alien 576, 581
Alien Nation 401, 403
"Alien Nation" (TV) 401
Alien III 580
Aliens 578–579, 581
Aliens Return, The 494
Alison, Charles Gary 260
All I Ever Need Is You (album) 86
All I Really Want to Do (album) 87
"All in the Family" (TV) 108, 320, 454
"All My Children" (TV) 509
All Night Long 423, 427
"All-Star Party for Lucille Ball, An" (TV) 363
"All-Star Pro Sports Award Show" (TV) 147, 481
"All-Star Salute to the President" (TV) 488
"All-Star Spectacular" (TV) 496
"All-Star Tribute to Kareem Abdul-Jabbar, The" (TV) 195

All That Jazz 354, 359
All the Marbles 559
"All the Way Home" (TV) 161, 278, 624
"All You Need Is Cash" (TV) 8
Allen, Brian 553
Allen, Irwin 252
Allen, Karen 73
Allen, Nancy 516, 551, 553
Allen, Thomas 132
Allen, Woody 20, 129, 130, 201, 282, 312, 313, 314, 315, 316, 322, 373, 381, 498, 534, 575
Alley, Kirstie 49, 138–139, 140, 254, 255, 325, 363, 555, 603; **137**
"Allison Sidney Harrison" (TV) 138
Allman, Elijah Blue 81, 85
Allman, Gregg 80, 81
Allman Brothers, The 299
"All's Fair" (TV) 321, 326
Almendros, Nestor 167
Altered States 277, 282
Altman, Robert 81, 201, 204, 516, 517
Always 154, 156, 212, 214
Alyn, Kirk 430
Amadeus 73
Amadeus (stage) 486
Amants, Les 58
Amateur Night at the Dixie Bar and Grill 300, 304, 422, 427
"Amazing Falsworth, The" (TV) 271
Amazing Grace and Chuck 116, 118
Amazing Howard Hughes, The 307, 310
"Amazing Stories" (TV) 100, 271, 287, 544
Amazon Women on the Moon 226, 228, 231, 234, 417, 420
Amber Waves 455, 458
Ameche, Don 225
"America 2-Night" (TV) 584
"American Chronicles" (TV) 155
American Dream 377, 382
"American Experience, The" (TV) 93–94
American Flyers 100, 105
American Gigolo 168, 173, 431
"American Girls, The" (TV) 300
American Graffiti 151, 156
"American Playhouse" (TV) 99, 186, 203, 371, 377, 379, 470, 594, 610
"American Portrait, An" (TV) 363, 464, 470, 487, 561, 570, 578
"American Red Cross Emergency Test" (TV) 241, 303, 442

"American Short Story, The" (TV) 308
American Sportsman 104
American Success Company, The 72, 76
"America's Dance Honors" (TV) 546
Americathon 439, 443
"Amerika" (TV) 348, 351
Amos, John 273
Amurri, Eva Maria Livia 470
Amurri, Franco 470
And Baby Makes Six 285, 290
. . . And Justice for All 346, 351; **346**
And Whose Little Boy Are You? (stage) 151
And Your Name Is Jonah 625, 639
Anderson, Kevin 171
Anderson, Loni 291, 332
Anderson, Louie 211
Anderson, Richard Dean 1–6, 242; **4**
Anderson, Stuart 1
Andress, Ursula 237, 239
Andrews, Anthony 487
Andrews, Dana 421
Andrews, Julie 198
Andrews, Maxene 550, 592
Andrews, Patty 550, 592
Andy Warhol Diaries, The (book) 100, 168
Andy Warhol's Bad 330, 334
Angel Heart 448, 451
Angel in Green 66, 68
Angel of Death 266, 267, 488–489, 490
Angel on My Shoulder (stage) 354
"Angels in Chains" (TV) 40
Angry Housewives 85, 86
Animalympics 108, 112
Animalympics (album) 112
"Animalympics: Winter Games" (TV) 108
"Ann Jillian Show, The" (1982) (TV) 293
"Ann Jillian Show, The" (1989) (TV) 295, 296
Ann Jillian Story, The 295, 296; **294**
Ann-Margret 56, 469, 477, 533, 593–594, 612
Anna Karenina (1985) 432, 435
Annie Hall 201, 207, 314, 315, 318, 469, 575, 581
"Annie Oakley" (TV) 116
Anniversary Waltz (stage) 70, 292
"Another World" (TV) 135, 509
"Antonia Stone" (TV) 570
Antony and Cleopatra (stage) 210

"Anything But Love" (TV) 117, 118, 441, 442
Apple Tree, The (stage) 107
"Apple's Way" (TV) 329
Apprenticeship of Duddy Kravitz, The 155, 156, 345
April Morning 309, 311
Apted, Michael 580
Arachnophobia 131, 133, 212–213, 214
Archer, Anne 50, 93, 316
"Arctic Refuge: A Vanishing Wilderness" (TV) 538
Arden, Eve 291
Are You in the House Alone? 422, 427
Ariane 447
Ariano (stage) 509
Arkin, Alan 73, 130, 183, 225
Arms and the Man (stage) 339, 343, 378, 383
Armstrong, Bess 252
Arnaz, Desi, Jr. 216
Arness, James 62, 63, 66, 126, 265
Arnold (book) 480
Arnold, Tom 34, 35, 36, 37, 211, 214
Arnold: The Education of a Bodybuilder (book) 476
Arnold's Bodyshaping for Women (book) 477
Arost, Lynn 359
Arquette, Patricia 411
Arquette, Rosanna 226, 368, 423, 620
Arrive Alive 124
"Arsenio Hall Show, The" (TV) 180, 232, 234, 235, 497
Arthur 616
Arthur, Bea 320, 321
Arthur, Jean 215, 491
Arthur the King 59, 61
As Summer Dies 116, 118
Ashbrook, Daphne 67
Ashcroft, Peggy 92, 347
Ashes (stage) 376
Ashley, Elizabeth 357, 564
Asner, Ed 163, 197, 206, 261
"Aspen" (TV) 330, 335
Aspern Papers, The (stage) 432
Assante, Armand 329, 488, 504, 570
Astaire, Fred 268, 270
Astin, John 114
Astor, Mary 557
At Close Range 374, 408, 411
At Long Last Love 494, 499
At Long Last Love (album) 499
At Play in the Fields of the Lord 50, 51

Atlantic City 469, 473
Atlantic City, U.S.A. 473
Attack Force Z 176, 181
Attenborough, Michael 484
Attenborough, Richard 58, 330, 484
Auntie Mame 580
Austin, Karen 331
Autry, Gene 421
Aviator, The 432, 435
Avildsen, John G. 528
Aviles, Rick 546
Awake and Sing! (stage) 166, 238, 242
Awakening, The (book) 388
"Awakening Land, The" (TV) 485, 489
Awakenings 588, 589
Aykroyd, Dan 7–13, 116, 118, 205, 246, 247, 389, 392, 578, 604; **10**
Aykroyd, Daniella Alexandra 11
Aykroyd, Lloyd 8
Aykroyd, Lorraine Gougeon 7
Aykroyd, Mark 8
Aykroyd, Oscar 8
Aykroyd, Samuel Cuthbert Peter Hugh 7
Aznavour, Charles 460

"B.A.D. Cats" (TV) 414, 420
"B. L. Stryker" 505
Babe 213–214
Babenco, Hector 50
Babes in Toyland (1961) 291, 296
Babes in Toyland (album) 296
Babies 572, 573
Baby Blue Marine 167, 173
Baby Boom 316, 318
"Baby Boom" (TV) 316
Baby Don't Go (album) 86
Baby Songs Presents John Lithgow's Kid-Size Concert 441
"Baby Talk" (TV) 147, 148
Bacall, Lauren 504, 557, 566
Bacchae, The (stage) 284
Bach, Barbara 362
"Bachelor-at-Law" (TV) 437
Bachelor Party 246, 248
Bachman, Richard 479
Back Roads 160, 164, 308, 310
Backdraft 457, 458
Backfield in Motion 38
Backstage (album) 87
Bacon, Kevin 17, 118, 222, 224, 381, 407, 446
Bad Boys 406–407, 411
Bad Company 71, 76
Bad Day 101, 105
Bad Medicine 225, 228

Badge of the Assassin 626, 630
Badham, John 180
Badlands 515–516, 520
Bagdad Cafe 196
"Bagdad Cafe" (TV) 196, 198, 199
Baggetta, Vincent 295
Bagnold, Enid 429
Bailey, Shane **178**
Baio, Scott 240
Baker, Carroll 330
Baker, Diane 461
Baker, Joe Don 468
Baker, Kathy 206
Bakula, Scott 322
Balanchine, George 501
Baldwin, Adam 248, 600
Baldwin, Alec 14–21, 102, 155, 282, 289, 385, 417, 442, 472; **18**
Baldwin, Alexander Rae, Jr. 14
Baldwin, Alexander Rae, III 14
Baldwin, Beth 14
Baldwin, Carol Martineau 14
Baldwin, Daniel 14
Baldwin, Jane 14
Baldwin, Stephen 14, 19, 20
Baldwin, William "Billy" 14, 20, 457
Bale, Christian 379
Ball, Lucille 321, 360, 438, 440, 476, 503
Ball, Randall 567
Ball, Ted 566, 567
Ballad of Soapy Smith, The (stage) 509
Balm in Gilead (stage) 377
Baltimore Bullet, The 64, 68
"Baltimore Is Talking" (TV) 609, 613
Bananas 522, 529
Bancroft, Anne 519, 566
"Banzai Pipeline, The" (TV) 328
"Barbara Walters Special, The" (TV) 480, 588
Barbarsh, Uri 386
Barbeau, Adrienne 115
Barber, Mary Beth 4
Barbone, Camille 367
Bardot, Brigitte 39
Bare Essence 65, 68
Bare Essentials 266, 267
Barefoot Executive, The 437, 443, 453–454, 458
"Baretta" (TV) 63, 144
Barfly 448, 451
Barkin, Ellen 22–27, 212, 224, 288, 334, 387, 424, 446, 512; **25**
Barkin, George 22

"Barnaby Jones" (TV) 261, 299, 306, 406
Barnes, Priscilla 438
Barnum (stage) 90, 96
Barnum (album) 96
Barnum, Phineas T. 90
Barone, Sal 32
Barr, Ben 28
Barr, Geraldine 28, 31, 32, 33
Barr, Helen Davis 28
Barr, Jerry 28
Barr, Roseanne 28–38, 85, 211, 212, 234, 531, 538, 604; **33**
Barr, Stephanie 28
Barrows, Sydney Biddle 59
Barry, Gene 151, 461
Barry, John 430, 431, 486
Barrymore, Drew 336, 362
Bartel, Paul 523
Bartlett, Bonnie 480
Barton Fink 213, 214
Baryshnikov, Alexandra 354
Baryshnikov, Mikhail 271, 354, 393
Basinger, Ann 39
Basinger, Ashley 39
Basinger, Barbara 39
Basinger, Donald 39
Basinger, Kim 11, 20, 39–44, 73, 146, 300, 323, 324, 370, 442, 448, 565, 601, 620; **41**
Basinger, Mick 39
Basinger, Skip 39
Baskin, Elya 589
Bastard, The 300
Bat 21 186, 189
Bates, Alan 55, 95, 180, 206
Bates, Kathy 50
Batman (1989) 42, 43, 44, 324, 326, 373, 393, 402, 587
Batman II 43
Batman III 43
"Battered Teachers" (TV) 615
"Battle of the Network Stars" (TV) 262, 293, 485, 502
Battlestar Galactica 485, 489
"Battlestar Galactica" (TV) 485
Bauer, Alexander 217
Bauer, Steven 217, 236, 596
Baum, L. Frank 442
Baxter, Meredith 435
"Bay City Blues" (TV) 253
Bayside Boys (stage) 599
Beach Blanket Babylon (stage) 527
Beacham, Stephanie 572
Beaches 317
Beasley the Dog 247
Beat Goes On, The (album) 86
Beatles, The 79
Beatty, Ned 278, 615

Beatty, Warren 78, 282, 312, 315, 366, 372, 373, 402, 485, 523, 593
"Beauty and the Beast" (TV) 470
Beck, Michael 333–334, 575
Becker, Harold 625
Bedelia, Bonnie 519, 602
Bedroom Window, The 225, 228
Bee Gees 552
Beery, Noah, Jr. 331
Beetlejuice 17, 21, 323, 326
"Beetlejuice" (TV) 323
Before and After Edith 388
Beggar's Opera, The (stage) 337
Begley, Ed, Jr. 34, 538
Behan, Brendan 623
Bel Geddes, Barbara 564
Belafonte, Harry 387
Believers, The 510, 513
Belkin, Alan 329, 330
Bell, Mike 222
Bellamy, Ralph 14
Bellisario, Don 49
Bellow, Saul 586
Belushi, James "Jim" 196, 321, 440, 479, 498
Belushi, John 8, 9, 10, 11, 361, 390, 391, 392, 582, 585
Belzer, Richard 211
Benefactors (stage) 92, 96
Bening, Annette 94, 219
Benjamin, Richard 407
Benny, Jack 29
Benny & Barney: Las Vegas Undercover 485, 489
"Benson" (TV) 322
Benson, Robby 216
Bent (stage) 168, 173
Benton, Robert 161, 184, 531
Berenger, Allison 46
Berenger, Barbara 46
Berenger, Chelsea 48
Berenger, Chloe 48
Berenger, Patrick 46
Berenger, Tom 45–51, 91, 101, 121, 510, 591, 619; 47
Bergen, Candice 52–61, 558, 564; 55
Bergen, Edgar 52, 53, 54, 55, 57
Bergen, Frances Westerman 52, 53, 60
Bergen, Kris 53
Bergen, Polly 124, 359
Berghof, Herbert 46
Bergman, Ingrid 489, 575
Bergman, Sandahl 477
Berle, Milton 111, 118, 197, 442, 481
Berlin, Jeannie 314, 493
Bernhard, Sandra 370, 409

Bernsen, Corbin 40, 50, 239, 508
Bernstein, Carl 399, 536
Bernstein, Jay 64, 65, 67
Bernstein, Leonard 592
Bertinelli, Valerie 5, 285, 362, 509
Bertolucci, Bernardo 253, 380–381
Best, Jim 566, 567
Best, Joby 566
"Best of Arsenio Hall, The" (TV) 231
Best of Cher, The (album) 87
Best of Cher, Vols. 1–2, The (album) 87
Best of Comic Relief 195
Best of Comic Relief '90, The (album) 196, 199
Best of Comic Relief 2, The (album) 38, 112, 199, 589, 590
"Best of Families, The" (TV) 276–277, 282, 575, 581
Best of the Best, The 410
Best of the Blues Brothers (album) 9, 13
Best of Times, The 456, 458, 586, 589
Best Place to Be, The 262, 266, 285, 290
Best Seller 627, 630; 627
Best Short Plays of 1968, The (book) 55
Betrayed 49, 51, 101, 288, 290, 619, 621
Betsy, The 307, 310; 307
Better Dead Than Sorry (stage) 575
Betts, Dickey 299
"Beulah Land" (TV) 300, 304
Beverly Hills Cop 447, 527, 578
Beyond Obsession 51
Beyond the Door 48, 51
Beyond the Limit 170, 173
Beyond the Ocean 597
Beyond the Poseidon Adventure 160, 164, 252, 257; 161
Beyond Therapy 204–205, 207
Beyond Therapy (stage) 576
Biehn, Michael 241, 288
Big 246–247, 248
Big Chill, The 45, 48, 51, 91, 95, 99, 104, 202, 207, 278, 282, 339, 343
Big Clock, The 101
Big Deal on Madonna Street 407
Big Easy, The 18, 24, 26, 210, 214, 421, 424–425, 427
Big Fix, The 152, 156, 397, 403; 153
"Big Hawaii" (TV) 299
Big Mack and Poor Clare 328, 334
Big River (stage) 209, 210, 214
Big River (album) 214

Big Town, The 309, 310
Big Trouble in Little China 456, 458; 456
"Big Valley, The" (TV) 150
Bigelow, Kathryn 120
Bill 423, 427
Bill: On His Own 423, 427
"Billion Dollar Bubble" (TV) 625
"Billy" (TV) 223, 228
Billy Bathgate 605
"Billy Crystal Comedy Hour, The" (TV) 108, 112
Billy Liar 223
Bionic Showdown, The: The Six Million Dollar Man and the Bionic Woman 571, 573
"Bionic Woman, The" (TV) 568, 573
Bird, Sarah 227, 365
Bird on a Wire 180, 181
Birds, The 215
Bishop, Joey 150
Bishop, Larry 150
Bishop, Troy 129
Bishop's Wife, The 157
Bisset, Jacqueline 58, 432, 463
Bite the Bullet 57, 61
Bittersweet White Light (album) 87
Bixler, Denise 226
Black, Cilla 79
Black, Karen 571
Black Broadway (stage) 270
Black Marble, The 625, 630
Black Moon Rising 309, 310
Black Rose 81
Black Rose (album) 87
"Black Tide" (TV) 434
Black Widow (1987) 83, 288, 618–619, 621
Blackboard Jungle, The 331
Blackwell, Earl 43, 80, 496
Blades, Ruben 187, 317, 350
Blake, Eubie 269, 270
Blake Street Hawkeyes 192
Blakeley, Donald 166
Blanc, Mel 196
Blessing in Disguise 373
Blind Date 44, 370, 601, 605; 601
Blond Ambition (stage) 371–372, 373
"Blood Brothers" (TV) 543
Blood Knot (stage) 183
Blood Money 25, 27
"Blood Money" (TV) 328
Bloodbrothers 167, 173; 167
Bloodhounds of Broadway 371, 374
Bloom, Claire 237
Bloom, Michael 15
Bloom, Rick 381
Blow Out 556
Blue Angel, The (1989) 317, 370

Blue Boys (stage) 306
"Blue Knight, The" (TV) 201
Blue Skies Again 238, 242
Blue Sky 310, 311, 359
Blue Steel 117, 118
Blues Brothers, The 9, 12
Blues Brothers—Made in America, The (album) 9, 13
Blues in the Night (stage) 270
Blum, Mark 256
"Bob Hope's Super Bowl Party" (TV) 364
"Bob Hope's USO Christmas in Beirut" (TV) 294
Bobby Gould in Hell (stage) 596
Bochco, Steven 238, 508
Bochner, Hart 115, 488
Body Double 217, 220
Body Heat 136, 137, 141, 278, 280, 282, 445–446, 451, 559, 562, 565, 576, 616
Bogart, Humphrey 119, 450
Bogdanovich, Peter 71, 72, 439, 492, 493, 494, 495, 497
"Bold Ones, The: The Lawyers" (TV) 567
Bon Jovi 84
"Bonanza" (TV) 436, 452
Bonet, Lisa 448
Bonfire of the Vanities, The 102, 220, 248, 249, 604, 605
Bonham-Carter, Helena 95, 449
Bono, Chastity 79, 80, 84
Bono, Salvatore "Sonny" *see:* Bono, Sonny
Bono, Sonny 78, 80, 83, 84, 85, 86, 87
Bonsall, Brian 488
Book of Daniel, The (book) 287, 398
Boone, Richard 72
Boost, The 628, 630
Booth, Connie 379
Booth, Shirley 292
Boothe, Powers 310, 359, 560
Bootleggers 501, 506
Bootlegger's Angel 506
Born on the Fourth of July 51, 123–124, 125, 410
Born Yesterday 194
Borstal Boy (stage) 623, 630
Bosco, Philip 594
"Bosom Buddies" (TV) 245, 249
Bostonians, The 92, 432, 435
Bostwick, Barry 66, 166, 332, 361, 468, 503
Bottoms, Timothy 64, 74, 492, 497, 567
Bounty, The 177, 181
Bourke-White, Margaret 54, 58

Bourne Identity, The 504–505, 507
Bowles, Paul 620
Boxleitner, Bruce 62–68, 135, 265; 167
Boxleitner, Kathryn "Kitty" 63, 64, 65, 66
Boxleitner, Lee Davis 64
Boxleitner, Sam 64
Boy and His Dog, A 299, 304
Boy Friend, The (stage) 558
Boy in the Plastic Bubble, The 551
Boy Meets Girl 110
Boyce, Christopher 287
Boyfriend School, The (book) 227, 365
Boyle, Peter 324, 594
Boys, The 629, 630
Boys from Brazil, The 223, 228
Boys Next Door, The (stage) 227, 228
Bozos, The 279–280
Bracco, Lorraine 248, 620
"Bracken's World" (TV) 159
Bradford, Barbara Taylor 571, 572
"Brady Bunch, The" (TV) 114
Brander, Richard 98
Brando, Marlon 177, 305, 314, 375, 405, 422, 430, 444, 471, 593
Brandon, Michael 462, 568
Brandt, Robert 113
Brantley, Betsy 576
Brauner, Asher 414
Bravlin, Jeff 625
Bray, Steve 367
Bray, Thom 331
Break-Up (stage) 438
Breakaway 67, 68
Breakfast Club 367
Breakfast in Bed 439, 443
Breaking Away 423, 427
Breaking Up Is Hard to Do 108, 112
Breathless (1983) 169, 173
Brecht, Bertolt 135, 532
Breed Apart, A 560, 565
Brennan, Eileen 74, 469, 492, 497
Brennan, Walter 151, 159
"Br'er Rabbit and the Wonderful Tar Baby" (TV) 188
Br'er Rabbit and the Wonderful Tar Baby (album) 190
"Brewster Place" (TV) 612, 613
"Brian and Sylvia" (TV) 2
Brice, Fanny 28
Brickman, Marshall 314
Bridger 159, 164
Bridges, Beau 69, 70, 72, 73, 74, 118, 238, 418, 468, 498
Bridges, Dorothy Simpson 69, 70

Bridges, Isabelle 73
Bridges, James 616, 618
Bridges, Jeff 42, 64, 69–76, 93, 100, 418, 452, 476, 492, 497–498, 588, 591, 626; 72
Bridges, Jordan 73
Bridges, Lloyd 16, 69, 70, 73, 247
Bridges, Lucinda 69
Briefcase Full of Blues, A (album) 9, 13
Briggs, Bunny 273
Brimley, Wilford 92, 225
"Bring 'Em Back Alive" (TV) 65, 68
Bringing Up Baby 370
Britton, Ron 41, 42
Broad Abroad, A (stage) 193
Broadcast News 280, 282, 348, 619
Broderick, Matthew 161
Brogan, Jimmy 584
Broken Vows 309, 310
Brolin, James 137
Bronson, Charles 24, 411, 430, 437
Brontosaurus (stage) 127
Brooks, Albert 150, 539
Brooks, James L. 143, 280, 617–618
Brooks, Mel 106, 270
Brooks, Richard 315
Brosnan, Pierce 266
Brothers, Dr. Joyce 371
Brown, Barry 70
Brown, Blair 238
Brown, Brandi 30, 35
Brown, David 99
Brown, Gail 30
Brown, Johnny 269
Brown, Stanley 30
"Bruce Willis: The Return of Bruno" (TV) 600
Bruce Willis: The Return of Bruno (album) 600, 601, 606
Bubbles, John W. 270
Buck, Frank 65
"Buck Rogers in the 25th Century" (TV) 114
Buddy Boys 20
Buddy System, The 153, 156, 470, 473
"Bugs Bunny/Looney Tunes All-Star 50th Anniversary" (TV) 204, 393
Bujold, Genevieve 432
Bull Durham 101–102, 105, 471, 473, 619
Bullock, Sandra 219
Bullpen (stage) 599
Bump in the Night 434–435
Bumpus, Gayle King 612, 613

Bundy, Ted 254
'Burbs, The 247, 248
Burglar 194, 198, 214, 600
Burke, Delta 397
Burn This (stage) 342, 379, 380, 382
Burnett, Carol 183, 194, 264, 285, 586–587
Burro 595, 597
Burrows, James 137
Burstyn, Ellen 388
Burton, Richard 98, 294
Burton, Tim 323, 324
Bus Stop (stage) 255, 422, 551, 592
Busey, Gary 547
Busfield, Timothy 149
Bush, Barbara 613
Bush, President George 36, 333, 479, 480, 488
But, Seriously . . . (stage) 151, 156
Butch and Sundance: The Early Years 47, 51
Butch Cassidy and the Sundance Kid 47
Butcher's Wife, The 132, 133
Butler, George 476
Butter 597
Butterflies Are Free 224
Butterflies Are Free (stage) 114, 437
Butterscotch Kid, The 232
"By Hooker, By Crook" (TV) 218
Bye Bye Birdie (stage) 312, 501, 550
Byrne, David 210
Byrne, Gabriel 25, 26
Byrne, Jack 26
Byron, David 441

C.H.U.D. 209, 214
Caan, James 73, 252, 314, 430, 523, 624
Caccialanza, Lorenzo 512
Cacoyannis, Michael 55
Cactus Flower (stage) 70
Cactus Jack 482
Caddyshack 391, 395
Caddyshack II 11, 13
Cadillac Man 588, 589
Cadorette, Mary 440
Caesar, Sid 306, 582
Caesar and Cleo 78
Cage, Nicolas 83, 101, 124, 310
Cagney, James 24, 149
Cahn, Sammy 292
Cain, Dean 92
Cain, James M. 241
Caine, Michael 49, 55, 121, 160, 162, 170, 226, 314, 393, 394, 431, 488, 525, 578
Caine Mutiny Court-Martial, The 131, 133

Caine Mutiny Court-Martial, The (stage) 390
Caldwell, Taylor 329
"California Girl" (TV) 158
California Split 201, 207
California Suite 534
"Callahan" (TV) 115
Callahan, John 281
Callas, Maria 487
Callie & Son 415, 419, 569, 572
"Calucci's Department" (TV) 467
Cameron, Dean 406
Cameron, James 580
Cameron, Nina 558
Camille (stage) 563
"Camille" (TV) 194
Camilletti, Robert 82–83
Camino Real (stage) 166
Campbell, Glen 566
Can I Do It 'Til I Need Glasses? 584, 589
Candida (stage) 431
Candy, John 11, 12, 247, 393, 401, 498, 604
Cannery Row 355, 616, 621
"Cannon" (TV) 328
Cannon, Dyan 238
Cannonball 523, 529
Cannonball Run II 144, 148
Can't Let You Go (album) 556
Can't Stop the Music 224, 228
Can't Stop the Music (album) 228
Canton, Neil 417
Cape Fear (1991) 359
Capone 523, 529
Capshaw, Kate 93
"Captain Planet and the Planeteers" (TV) 197, 199, 206
"Captains and the Kings" (TV) 329–330, 335, 484, 490
Carbon Copy 463, 465
Caretaker, The (stage) 378
Carlisle, Belinda 317
Carlito's Way 401
Carlson, Karen 439
Carlyle, Phyllis 380
Carnal Knowledge 52, 56, 61
Carnal Knowledge (stage) 265
Carney, Art 24, 516
"Carol Burnett Special, A" (TV) 194, 587
Caron, Glenn Gordon 323, 497, 620
Carpenter, John 85, 114, 307, 455
Carpenter, Karen 79
Carr, Allan 370
Carradine, Keith 74, 93, 516
Carradine, Robert 115, 216, 223
Carrera, Barbara 171
Carreras, José 400

Carrey, Jim 205
Carrie 516, 520, 551, 556
Carroll, Beeson 519
Cars, The 287, 288
Carsey, Marcy 32
Carson, Johnny 109, 161, 230, 232, 234, 313, 613
Carter, Amy 552
Carter, President Jimmy 552
Carter, Lynda 615
Carter, Nell 270, 273
"Carter Country" (TV) 217, 221
Carvey, Dana 106
Case of the Beautiful Beggar, The (audio cassette) 334
Cassavetes, John 470
Cassidy, David 114
Cassidy, Patrick 16, 545
Casualties of War 370, 409–410, 412, 624
Cat Chaser 387, 388
Cat on a Hot Tin Roof 357, 564
Cat on a Hot Tin Roof (stage) 346, 563–564, 565, 599
"Cat on a Hot Tin Roof" (TV) 308–309, 357
"Catalina C-Lab" (TV) 128
"Catch-22" (TV) 151
Cates, Joseph 341
Cates, Phoebe 339, 341
Cat's Eye 626, 630
Cattrall, Kim 456
Caulfield, Maxwell 415
Caveman 321, 362, 365, 423, 427
Cavett, Dick 89
Cazale, John 533
Cazenove, Christopher 572
Cease Fire 301, 304
Cedoona (stage) 175
"Celebrity Challenge of the Sexes" (TV) 462
"Centennial" (TV) 252, 258, 261, 267
Certain Sacrifice, A 367, 374
Chadwick Family, The 63, 68
Chains of Gold 556
"Challenge of the Seas" (TV) 140, 141
Chamberlain, Richard 432, 467, 486, 504, 560
Chambers, Everett 414
Chances Are 497, 499
Channing, Carol 306
Channing, Stockard 498
Chaplin, Charles 57, 524, 582
Chaplin, Geraldine 516
Character and Confession: New Experience in Narrative Theatre (stage) 193
Charlatan, The (stage) 624

Charleston 397, 403

Charley and the Angel 454, 458

Charlie Chan and the Curse of the Dragon Queen 415, 419

Charlie's Angels 306, 310, 506

"Charlie's Angels" (TV) 40, 114, 502, 503, 507

Chase, Chevy 7, 8, 10, 12, 204, 247, 271, 390, 391, 486, 577; 577

"Chase and Sanborn Hour, The" (radio) 52

Chasing Dreams 99, 105

Chastity 79, 86

Chastity (album) 87

Chavez, Ingrid

Chayefsky, Paddy 277

Checkered Flag or Crash 468, 473

Checking Out 131, 133

"Cheers" (TV) 134, 137, 138, 139, 140, 141, 246, 360, 362, 363, 364, 365; 137

Cheever, John 576

Chekhov, Anton 244, 386

Chelsea *see:* Basinger, Kim

Chenoweth, Ellen 23

Cher 77–87, 93, 162, 194, 195, 366, 417, 425, 470, 537, 538, 618, 620; 82

"Cher" (TV) 80, 86

Cher (album) 83, 87

"Cher—A Celebration at Caesar's Palace" (TV) 81

"Cher and Other Fantasies" (TV) 81

Cher Backstage (album) 87

Cher Superpak, Vols. 1–2 (album) 87

Cherilyn *see:* Cher

Cherished (album) 87

Cherry Orchard, The (stage) 244, 431, 533, 540

Cherry 2000 218, 220

Chetwynd, Lionel 46

Chèvre, La 189

Chicken Chronicles, The 223, 228

"Chiefs" (TV) 184, 189, 209, 214

Childe Byron (stage) 277

Children Nobody Wanted, The 415, 419

Children of a Lesser God 279, 282, 562, 578

Child's Cry 570, 572

Child's Play (stage) 265, 328

"China Beach" (TV) 317–318

China Blue 565

China Moon 104

Chinatown 386

"CHiPs" (TV) 262

Chivers, Colin 430

Choirboys, The 330, 334, 624–625, 630

Chopin, Kate 388

Chopra, Joyce 594

Chorus Line, A 554

"Christine Cromwell" (TV) 505–506, 507; 505

"Christmas Carol, A" (story) 270, 393

Christmas Coal Mine Miracle, The 454, 458

Christmas Miracle in Caufield, U.S.A. 454, 458

Christopher, Dennis 442

Chu Chu and the Philly Flash 183, 189

Churchill, Caryl 17

Ciccone, Madonna Louise Veronica *see:* Madonna

Ciccone, Sylvio "Tony" 366, 367

Cimino, Michael 72, 447, 450

Cinderella (stage) 484

"Circus of the Stars" (TV) 114, 198

City, The 299, 304

City in Fear 330–331, 334, 445, 451

City Slickers 111, 112

City Sugar (stage) 201

Claessen, David 194, 195

Clairvoyant, The 331, 334

Clancy, Tom 18

Clara's Heart 195, 198

Clark, Candy 71

Clark, Andrew Dice 234

Clayburgh, Jill 58, 160, 352, 354, 595

Clean and Sober 323, 325, 326

Clear and Present Danger 20

Cleese, John 117, 341

"Clement Clark Moore" (TV) 578

Clifford, Graeme 355

Clift, Montgomery 66, 264, 405

Cline, Patsy 210, 357

Clinton and Nadine 25, 27

Close, Bettine 88, 89

Close, Glenn 48, 73, 88–96, 99, 138, 180, 278, 280, 281, 339, 348, 380, 399, 487, 514, 585, 622, 629; 92

Close, Dr. William 88, 89

Close Encounters of the Third Kind 151–152, 156

Cloughley, Kimberlea Gayle 308

Club Paradise 586, 589

Coal Miner's Daughter 308, 309, 310, 517, 519, 520

Coal Miner's Daughter (album) 520

Coates, Casey 135

Cobb, Lee J. 375

Cobra 526, 530

Coburn, David 197

Coburn, James 64, 206, 469

Coca, Imogene 108, 393

Coco, James 329, 467, 603

Cocoon 225, 228; 225

Cocoon: The Return 226, 228

Cody, Kathleen 454

Coen, Ethan 213

Coen, Joel 213

Colasanto, Nick 138

Colbert, Claudette 191, 388

Cold Feet 74, 76

Cold Heaven 256, 258

Cole, Dennis 502, 503

Cole, Gary 594

Cole, Joseph 503

Coleman, Cy 338

Coles, Honi 268, 270

Colicos, John 354

Collins, Jackie 59

Collins, Joyce 74

Collins, Phil 604

Collins, Stephen 65, 273, 469

Colomby, Harry 321, 322, 323

Color of Money, The 279, 627

Color Purple, The 185, 189, 193, 198, 610, 613; 185

Colors 409, 412; 408

Colours of the Heart 318, 359, 520

"Columbo" (TV) 505

Columbu, Francesco 475

"Combatants, The" (TV) 299

Comden, Betty 338

Come Back to the 5 & Dime, Jimmy Dean, Jimmy Dean 81, 86

Come Back to the 5 & Dime, Jimmy Dean, Jimmy Dean (stage) 81, 86

Come See the Paradise 426, 427

Comeback Kid, The 439, 443, 543, 547

Comedy Jam 107

"Comedy Salute to Baseball, A" (TV) 109

"Comedy Theater" (TV) 136

Comes a Horseman 252, 257

"Comic Relief" (TV) 109, 194, 586

"Comic Relief 4" (TV) 111, 588

Comic Relief '90 (album) 112, 589, 590

Comic Relief—The Best of Comic Relief (album) 112, 199, 589, 590

"Comic Relief 3" (TV) 84, 110, 195

Comic Relief 3 (album) 84, 87, 110, 112, 199, 589, 590
Comin' Uptown (stage) 270, 274
Coming Attractions 391, 395
Coming to America 231–232, 234; 232
"Coming Up Rosie" (TV) 8, 13
Commando 478, 482
Commitment to Life IV (stage) 197, 333, 350, 373, 512, 547, 629
Company She Keeps, The 70, 75
Competition, The 152, 156
Compromising Positions 470, 473
Computer Wore Tennis Shoes, The 453, 458
Conan Doyle, Arthur 90
Conan the Barbarian 477, 482
Conan the Destroyer 478, 482
Conaway, Jeff 143
Concrete Cowboys, The 406, 411
Condos, Steve 273
Conduct Unbecoming (stage) 624, 630
"Coneheads, The" (TV) 9
Conjuring an Event (stage) 575
Connelly, Jennifer 303
Connery, Sean 18, 41, 57, 101, 155, 255, 419, 576
Constant Wife, The (stage) 575, 581
Conti, Tom 384, 554
Conundrum 163, 164
Converse, Frank 166
Convicted 570, 572
Convicted: A Mother's Story 294, 296
Convy, Bert 440
Cook, Barbara 400, 402
Cool Blue 410, 412
Cooper, Gary 97
Cooper, Jackie 430
Cooper, Wilhelmina 353
Cop 627–628, 630
Copley, Teri 144
Copperfield, Sandra Jean 478
Coppola, Francis Ford 73, 170, 313, 447, 543, 561
Cops (stage) 120
Corbett, Glenn 453
Cordobes, El 450
Corey, Jeff 78
Cornell, Katharine 393
Cosby, Bill 106, 182, 269, 624
"Cosby Show, The" (TV) 32, 448
Cosell, Howard 390
Costa-Gavras, Constantin 358, 517
Costner, Annie 100
Costner, Bill 97
Costner, Cindy 98

Costner, Dan 97
Costner, Joe 100
Costner, Kevin 14, 18, 97–105, 155, 185, 203, 471, 472, 505, 580; **103**
Costner, Lily 100
Cotton Club, The 170, 173, 270–271, 274
Couch Trip, The 10–11, 13
Country 161, 171, 177, 357, 359, 377, 518
Coupla White Chicks Sitting Around Talking, A (stage) 459
Cousin, Cousine 139
Cousins 139, 141
Cover Girls 304
Coward, Noël 347
Cowboy 137–138, 141
Cox, Courteney 66, 324
Cox, Ronnie 481
Coyote, Peter 186, 363
Coyote Ugly (stage) 378
Cracker Factory, The 330, 334, 361, 365
Crackers 407, 411
Craig, David 159
Craig, Elijah 159
Craig, Peter 159
Craig, Sally *see:* Field, Sally
Craig, Steven 159
Crain, Jeanne 413
Crane, Bob 454
Crane, Cheryl 370
Craven, Matt 288
Crawford, Cindy 173
Crawford, Joan 49, 344, 483, 500, 531
Crazy from the Heart 350, 351
Crazy Mama 422, 427
Crazy Monkey's Dream, The 207
Crazy People 380
Creamer, Robert 213
Creepshow 137, 141
Crenna, Richard 138, 321, 559, 570
Crichton, Charles 341
"Crime Victims" (TV) 387
Crimen 498
Crimes of Passion 560, 565
Crimes of the Heart 316, 318, 358, 359, 519, 520, 618
"Criminal Justice System, The" (TV) 387
Crocker, James 67
Cromwell, John 70
Cronley, Jay 394
Cronyn, Hume 225
"Crossings" (TV) 487, 490
Crow, Ashley 227
Crucible, The (stage) 120

Crucifer of Blood, The (stage) 90, 96
Cruise, Tom 102, 123, 286, 325, 362, 386, 410, 441, 543; **385**
Cry-Baby 124, 125
Cry for Help, A 63, 68
Cry Freedom 340, 343; **340**
Cry in the Dark, A 537, 540
Cryer, Jon 161
Crystal, Billy 60, 106–112, 181, 194, 203, 272, 436, 509, 554, 586; **110**
Crystal, Helen Gabler 106
Crystal, Jack 106
Crystal, Janice 107
Crystal, Jennifer 107
Crystal, Joel 106
Crystal, Lindsay 107
Crystal, Richard 106
Crystal, William *see:* Crystal, Billy
Crystals, The 78
Cukor, George 615
Culkin, Macaulay 12
Cullum, John 338
Culp, Robert 146, 624
Cummings, Quinn 152
Curry, Tim 468, 486
Curse of the Starving Class (stage) 376–377
Curtin, Jane 8, 12, 354, 463, 464
Curtis, Jamie Lee 12, 82, 113–118, 140, 197, 232, 341, 381, 419, 442, 543, 554, 564; **10, 116**
Curtis, Keene 346
Curtis, Kelly Leigh 113
Curtis, Tony 113, 114, 115, 325, 502
Cusack, Joan 401
Cusack, John 403
Cutter and Bone 72, 76
"Cutter to Houston" (TV) 15, 21
Cutter's Way 72, 76
"Cutting Edge, The" (TV) 523
Cybill Does It . . . to Cole Porter (album) 493, 499
Czack, Sasha *see:* Stallone, Sasha

"D.C. Follies" (TV) 487
"D.H.O." (TV) 166
D.O.A. (1988) 425, 427
Da Grande 471, 473
Dad 139, 141
Daddy, I Don't Like This 216, 220
"Dade County Fast Lane" (TV) 301
Dafoe, Willem 49, 101, 119–125, 189, 272, 282, 305, 375, 381, 622; **123**
Daisy Miller 493, 499
Dalai Lama 171

Dale, Jim 90
Daley, Robert 593
"Dallas" (TV) 252
Dallas Cowboys Cheerleaders, The 485, 489
Dalton, Liam 218
Daly, Timothy 446
"Dan August" (TV) 437
Dance on a Country Grave (stage) 338
Dances with Wolves 103, 105
D'Angelo, Beverly 517
Dangerfield, Rodney 31, 391
Dangerous Affection 510, 513
Dangerous Liaisons 94, 96, 172, 379, 380, 382, 418, 420, 487
Dangerous Pursuit 265, 267
Daniel 24, 26, 287, 290, 398, 403
Daniel, Benjamin 128
Daniel, Jay 35, 600, 604
"Daniel Boone" (TV) 453
Danielle Steel's Kaleidoscope 333, 335, 506, 507
Daniels, Jeff 126–133, 213, 218, 277, 322, 350, 386, 427; **129**
Daniels, Jeffery *see:* Daniels, Jeff
Daniels, John 130
Daniels, Kathleen 128
Daniels, Lucas 128
Daniels, Robert 126
Danilova, Alexandra 388
Danner, Blythe 332, 467
Danson, Alexis 138
Danson, Casey 135, 136, 138, 139
Danson, Edward Bridge, III *see:* Danson, Ted
Danson, Katherine MacMaster 136
Danson, Ted 63, 91, 118, 134–141, 154, 197, 226, 348, 362, 363; **137**
Danza, Gina 144
Danza, Katharine Anne 146
Danza, Marc Anthony 143, 144, 146
Danza, Rhonda 143, 144
Danza, Tony 43, 142–148, 259, 415; **145**
Danza, Tracy 145
D'Arbanville, Patti 216, 299, 300, 301
Dark, O'Lan Johnson 356
"Dark Fury" (TV) 567
Dark Half, The 289, 290
Dark Lady (album) 87
Dark Mirror (1984) 487, 489
Darnell, Linda 413
Daviau, Allen 185
Davidson, John 159
Davidson, Martin 519
Davis, Altovise 224

Davis, Bette 58, 116, 294, 344, 483, 498, 622, 624
Davis, Bill C. 254
Davis, Brad 131
Davis, Geena 17, 204, 205, 206, 280, 380, 394, 419, 472, 562, 579, 621
Davis, Jim 299
Davis, Judy 175
Davis, Robert 622
Davis, Roger 501, 502
Davis, Sammy, Jr. 268, 272, 273
Davis, Susan *see:* Dreyfuss, Jeramie Rain
Davis, Willie 464
Dawber, Pam 254, 257, 584
Dawson, Richard 479
Day, Doris 55, 56
Day After, The 224, 228
Day in Hollywood/A Night in the Ukraine, A (stage) 90
Day-Lewis, Daniel 587
Day the Fish Came Out, The 55, 61
Dayne, Taylor 212
Days of Heaven 167, 168, 173, 552
"Days of Our Lives" (TV) 16
Days of Thunder 539, 546
De Haven, Carter 627
De Havilland, Olivia 487, 544
De Jesus, Wanda 510
De Laurentiis, Dino 177, 329, 353, 354, 358, 477, 481
De Niro, Robert 71, 152, 165, 359, 393, 405, 410, 457, 494, 536, 588, 591, 614, 626
De Palma, Brian 101, 217, 220, 248, 515, 516
Dead Again, 589
Dead-Bang 302, 304; **302**
Dead Heat 595, 597; **594**
"Dead Lifts" (TV) 477
Dead Man Out 186–187, 189
Dead Poets Society 18, 394, 587, 589
Dead Ringer 294
Deadliest Season, The 533, 539
Deadline Salonika (book) 179
Deadly Hero 592, 597
Deadly Intentions . . . Again? 241–242
Deadly Tower, The 454, 458
Deal of the Century 271, 274, 577, 581; **577**
Dean, James 405, 422, 444, 549
"Dean Jones Show, The" (TV) 292
Dear America: Letters Home from Vietnam 49, 51, 122, 125, 255, 258, 409, 411, 562, 565, 587, 589
"Dear Teacher" (TV) 136

Dearden, James 93
Death Dreams 435
Death of a Centerfold: The Dorothy Stratten Story 115, 118
Death of a Salesman (1985) 378, 382
Death of a Salesman (stage) 177, 377, 382, 522
Death Race 2000 523, 529
Death Wish 201, 207
Deathbed 26
Deathtrap 431, 435
Deathwatch (stage) 445
"Debbie Allen Special, The" (TV) 195
Deceptions 241, 242
DeCroux, Etienne 353
Dee, Sandra 158, 459
Deer Hunter, The 534, 536, 539
Defending Your Life 539, 540
DeGuerre, Phil 67
Deja Vu 504, 507
Delany, Dana 317
Deliberate Stranger, The 254, 256, 257
"Delta House" (TV) 414, 420
DeLuise, Dom 584
Demme, Jonathan 18, 19, 217
DeMornay, Rebecca 100, 457
Dempsey 593, 597
Dempsey, Jack 593
Deneuve, Catherine 120, 470, 579
Dennehy, Brian 185, 226, 464
Dennis, John 1
Dennis, Sandy 330, 411
Deodato, Kennya 19
Depardieu, Gérard 275, 578
Depp, Johnny 266
Dern, Bruce 238
Dern, Laura 124
Desert Bloom 24, 26
Desire Under the Elms (stage) 437
Desperate Hours, The (1955) 450
Desperate Hours (1990) 450, 451
Desperate Women 463, 465
Desperately Seeking Susan 34, 368, 372, 374, 595
Detour (book) 370
Deuel, Peter 501
Deutschendorf, Henry 579
Deutschendorf, William 579
Devane, William 137, 307, 467
Devil's Rain, The 550, 556
DeVito, Danny 109, 143, 154, 479–480, 560, 563
"Devlin Connection, The" (TV) 202
Devore, Gary 257
deVries, Peter 384
Dewhurst, Colleen 285

DeWitt, Joyce 438
Dey, Susan 239
Diamante, Rene 288–289
Diamond, Legs 447
Diamond, Selma 28
Dick, Philip K. 480
Dick Tracy (1990) 197, 366, 372, 374, 402, 403
Dickens, Charles 270, 393
Dickinson, Angie 59, 415, 502
"Die Before They Wake" (TV) 292
Die Hard 497, 602, 605
Die Hard 2 196, 539, 546, 604, 605
Different Story, A 330, 334
"Different World, A" (TV) 147
Dillinger (1973) 151, 156
Dillinger (1991) 257, 258
Dillman, Bradford 71
Dillon, Matt 309, 447, 543
"Dinah!" (TV) 108
Diner 23, 26, 222, 224, 228, 446, 451
Dinesen, Isak 536
Dinner at Eight (1933) 241
Dinner at Eight (1989) 241, 242
"Dinosaur!" (TV) 432
Diplomatic Immunity 68
Dirty Dancing 541, 544–545, 547
"Dirty Dancing" (TV) 545
Dirty Dancing (album) 545, 547
Dirty Dancing II 546
Dirty Rotten Scoundrels 393
Disappearance of Aimee, The 624, 630
Disaster at Silo 7 332, 334
Disney, Walt 53, 452, 453
"Disney Sunday Night Movie" (TV) 570
"Disneyland's 35th Anniversary Celebration" (TV) 147
Distance 624, 630
Distant Shores 512
Diversion 93
"Divine Garbo, The" (TV) 95
Division Street (stage) 346, 351
Dixon, Donna 9, 10, 12
"Do You Mean There Are Still Real Cowboys?" (TV) 94
Dobson, Kevin 16, 385
"Doc" (TV) 223
Doctor, The 282, 350, 351, 403
Doctor Detroit 9, 12
Dr. Scorpion 346, 351
Doctorow, E. L. 287, 398, 605
"Doctors, The" (TV) 15, 21, 559, 565
Dog and Cat 44
"Dog and Cat" (TV) 40, 44
Dog Day Afternoon 126

Dogs of War, The 48, 51; 47
Doing Life 145–146, 148
Dominick and Eugene 116, 118
Domino Principle, The 57, 61
"Don Kirshner's Rock Concert" (TV) 551
Doña Flor and Her Two Husbands 73, 161, 362
Donahue, Phil 609, 612
Donahue, Troy 124
"Donald Duck's 50th Birthday" (TV) 440
Donen, Joshua 82
Donen, Stanley 237
Donner, Richard 620
D'Onofrio, Vincent P. 513
Don't Cry, It's Only Thunder 464, 465
"Don't Get Me Started" (TV) 109
Don't Tell Her It's Me 227, 228, 365
Don't Worry, He Won't Get Far on Foot (book) 281
"Dooley Brothers, The" (TV) 361
Doors, The 125
Doors, The 125
Double Fault 547
Double Indemnity 241, 559
"Doug Henning's World of Magic" (TV) 293
Douglas, Kirk 151, 529, 626
Douglas, Michael 84, 93, 218, 220, 280, 434, 560, 561, 563, 587
Douglas, Michael see also: Keaton, Michael
Dowling, Vincent 244
Down and Out in Beverly Hills 154, 155, 156
Down by Law 24, 26
"Down Home" (TV) 140, 141
Downey, Robert, Jr. 497, 596, 628
Doyle-Murray, Brian 390, 391, 393
Dracula (stage) 430
Dragnet (1987) 10, 13, 246, 248
Dragonfly 473
Dream Merchants, The 252, 257
Dream Team, The 324, 326
Dreamer of Oz, The: The L. Frank Baum Story 442, 443
Dreamers 386, 388
Dreamscape 424, 427
Dress Gray 16, 21
Dreyfuss, Benjamin 153
Dreyfuss, Emily 153
Dreyfuss, Harry Spencer 155
Dreyfuss, Jeramie Rain 153, 155
Dreyfuss, Lorin 149
Dreyfuss, Norman 149

Dreyfuss, Richard 149–156, 194, 212, 322, 345, 347, 394, 397, 470, 481, 552; **153**
Driving Miss Daisy 11, 13, 358, 418
Drowning Pool, The 216, 220
Dru, Joanne 66
"Drug Wars: The Camarena Story" (TV) 595, 597
Drum 329
Dry White Season, A 471, 473
Dryer, Fred 137
Du Maurier, Daphne 487
Dudek, Les 81
Duff, Howard 253
Duffy, Julia 137, 147
Duffy, Patrick 262
Duguay, Ron 81
Dukakis, Michael 171, 479
Dukakis, Olympia 139, 162, 555, 572
Dukes, David 168, 329, 504
"Dumb Waiter, The" (TV) 554
"Dummy" (story) 57
Dun, Dennis **456**
Dunaway, Faye 160, 294, 307, 448, 531, 579
Duncan, Arthur 273
Duncan, Sandy 333
Dunlop, Frank 166
Dunne, Irene 154, 312
Dunnock, Mildred 262
Durang, Christopher 575, 576, 578
Durning, Charles 358, 378, 563–564, 615
Duvall, Robert 92, 161, 309, 310, 409
Duvall, Shelley 73, 203, 432, 517, 594
Dying Young 163, 164
"Dynasty" (TV) 3

E., Sheila 212
E.T. The Extra-Terrestrial 616, 621
Eagle Has Landed, The 592, 597
Earp, Wyatt 602
"Earth Day Special" (TV) 104, 140, 324, 538, 588, 604
Earth Girls Are Easy 205, 207
"Earthbeat" (TV) 139
Earthright 494, 499
Earthworms (stage) 167, 405
Eastwood, Clint 81, 183, 430, 602
Ebersol, Charles 464
Ebersol, Dick 463, 464, 465
Ebersol, Edward Bright 465
Ebersol, Willie 464
Eccentricities of a Nightingale (stage) 330

Echoes in the Darkness 594, 597
Eclectics, The 425, 426
"Ed Sullivan Show, The" (TV) 29, 269
Eddie and the Cruisers 24, 26, 48, 51
"Eddie Dodd" (TV) 596, 597, 628
Eddie Macon's Run 209, 214
Eden Court (stage) 24
Educating Rita 399
Edwards, Blake 26, 42, 138, 224–225, 370, 387, 436, 441, 512, 601, 602
Edwards, Willis 232
Eichhorn, Lisa 137, 168, 593
8 Million Ways to Die 73, 76
Eikenberry, Jill 314
Eisner, Michael 552
Eleanor and Franklin 252
Eleanor and Franklin: The White House Years 252, 257
Electra (stage) 46
Eleni 378–379, 382
11 Harrowhouse 57, 58, 61
Eliza's Horoscope 306, 310
Ellerbee, Linda 59
Ellington, Duke 270
Elliott, Sam 100, 194, 497
"Ellis Island" (TV) 294, 296
Elvidge, Jamison "Jamie" 332, 333
Elvis 300, 455, 458
Elvis and the Beauty Queen 300, 304
"Emerald Point N.A.S." (TV) 3, 6
"Emergency" (TV) 251–252
Emperor & the Nightingale, The (album) 96
Empire of the Sun 379–380, 382
Encyclopedia of Modern Bodybuilding, The (book) 479
End, The 160, 164
End as a Man (stage) 46
End of the World in Our Usual Bed in a Night Full of Rain, The 57–58, 61
Enemy Mine 424, 427
English, Diane 59
Enlightened Rogues (album) 299, 304
Enola Gay: The Men, the Mission, the Atomic Bomb 108, 112, 262, 266–267
Enormous Changes at the Last Minute 24, 26
"Entertainment Tonight" (TV) 147, 153, 411
Ephron, Nora 110, 130, 399, 536
Epstein, Julius J. 384
Equus (stage) 237
Erikson, Erik H. 533

Ernest Hemingway's "The Sun Also Rises" 487, 489
Ernie Kovacs: Between the Laughter 203, 207
Erwin, Elaine 411
Escape from Alcatraz 183, 189
Escape from Bogen County 502, 506
Escape from New York 455, 458
Escape to Victory 525, 529
Esper, William 345
Estevez, Emilio 154, 543, 602
Eubie! (stage) 269–270, 274
Eubie! (album) 274
"Eunice Kennedy Shriver" (TV) 464
Eureka 446, 451
Evans, Bob 553
Evans, David Mickey 620
Evans, Denny 397
Evans, Linda 500, 544
Evans, Robert 271
Eve of Destruction 273, 274
"Evening at the Improv, An" (TV) 109, 586
"Evening Magazine" 102
"Evening with . . ., An" (TV) 85, 538, 588
Evening with Richard Nixon, An (stage) 467
Evening with Robin Williams, An 585
Every Time We Say Goodbye 246, 248
"Everybody Rides the Carousel" (TV) 533
Everybody Wins 619–620, 621
Everybody's All-American 20, 101, 211, 214, 288, 358, 359, 425, 427; *425*
Everything in the Garden (stage) 166
Evil in Clear River 570, 572
Evil Roy Slade 437, 443
Evita 373, 401, 537, 545
Evita (stage) 377, 397–398, 403
Evita (album) 403
Ex Mrs. Winfield, The 359
Execution of Charles Horman, The (book) 517
Executioner's Song, The 308, 310, 347, 351
Experts, The 554, 556
Exton, Gae 431, 433
Extremities (stage) 24, 470
Eyes of Laura Mars 307, 310
Eyewitness 277, 282, 576, 581, 625, 630

F.I.S.T. 524, 529
F. Scott Fitzgerald and "The Last of the Belles" 467, 473

F. Scott Fitzgerald in Hollywood 624, 630
Fabulous Baker Boys, The 74, 75, 76, 372, 418, 420, 620
Fabulous Baker Boys, The (album) 420
Face in the Crowd, A 172
Face of Rage, The 184, 189, 209, 214
"Face to Face with Connie Chung" (TV) 234, 497, 512
"Facts of Life, The" (TV) 2
Fade to Black 445, 451
"Faerie Tale Theatre" (TV) 24, 73, 109, 203, 272, 432, 470, 585
Fairbanks, Douglas 336
Falcon, Ellen 211
Falcon and the Snowman, The 287, 290, 407, 411
"Falcon Crest" (TV) 238, 265, 267
Falk, Peter 505, 559
Falling in Love 536, 539
Falling in Love Again 415, 419
Fame 22
Fame Is the Name of the Game 460, 461, 465
"Family" (TV) 361, 624
"Family Man, The" (TV) 265–266, 267
"Family Ties" (TV) 245
Fandango 100, 104, 105
Fantastic Voyage 424
Fantasticks, The (stage) 260
"Fantasy Island" (TV) 414, 495
Far North 358, 359
Farewell, My Lovely (1975) 523, 529
Farina, Richard 166
Farm, The (stage) 127, 166
Farmer, Frances 355
Farrell, James T. 237
Farrell, Mike 384, 463
Farrow, Mia 20, 70, 73, 282, 373, 381
Fast, Howard 155
"Fast Lane Blues" (TV) 143
"Fast Times" (TV) 406
Fast Times at Ridgemont High 406, 411
Fast-Walking 625–626, 630
Fat City 71, 76
Fatal Attraction 88, 93, 96, 348
Fatal Beauty 83, 198
"Fatal Witness" (TV) 306
Father Figure 286, 290
Father Sky (book) 286
Fauci, Dan 135, 138, 140
Faustus in Hell (stage) 237
Favor, the Watch and the Very Big Fish, The 206, 207

"Favorite Son" (TV) 240, 242
Fawcett, Farrah 65, 72, 74, 497, 502
"FBI, The" (TV) 313
Fear City 48, 51, 217, 220
Fedders, Charlotte 571
Feedlot (stage) 127
Fehmiu, Fakim 56
Feiffer, Jules 348
Feldman, Randy 527
Feldshuh, Tovah 24
Fell, Norman 438
Fellow Travelers 20
"Feminine Mystique" (TV) 615
Fernandez, José 328
"Ferret, The" (TV) 224
Ferrigno, Lou 474
Ferrin, Bran 90
"Festival of Lively Arts for Young People" (TV) 338
"Festival of the Stars: Mexico" (TV) 114
Feuer, Debra 446–447
Feury, Peggy 406, 414
"Fever" (TV) 317–318
Few Good Men, A (stage) 334, 335
Field, The 50, 51
Field, Margaret 157
Field, Richard 157
Field, Sally 72, 73, 157–164, 184, 197, 198, 208, 211, 226, 247, 278, 279, 308, 342, 357, 364, 378, 476, 518, 547, 620; **161**
Field of Dreams 102, 105, 240; **103**
Fields, Freddie 168
Fields, Totie 29
Fifth [5th] of July, The (stage) 127, 133, 277
"50 Years on Television" (TV) 488
Fighter, The 263, 267
Final Analysis, The 172, 173
Final Payments 315
Final Verdict 596, 597
Fine Mess, A 138, 141
Fingernails, The Group with Polish, The 89
Finishing Touches (stage) 624
Fire Birds 310, 311
Fire in the Dark 572, 573
Fires Within 125, 512–513
First Blood 525
First Deadly Sin, The 599, 605
"First Nine Months Are the Hardest, The" (TV) 80
First You Cry 300, 304
Fish Called Wanda, A 117, 118, 340–341, 343
Fisher, Carrie 152, 172, 198, 538
Fisher, Eddie 392
Fisher King, The 75, 76, 588, 589

Fisk, Jack 515, 516, 517, 519
Fisk, Schuyler Elizabeth 518
Fisk, Virginia Madison 519
Fitzgerald, Ella 273
Fitzgerald, F. Scott 327, 575
Five Days One Summer 576
Flag for Sunrise, A (book) 564
Flamingo Road (1949) 252–253
Flamingo Road (1980) 252–253, 257
"Flamingo Road" (TV) 253, 258
Flash Gordon 477
Flashdance 99
Flashpoint 594, 597
Flaubert Dreams of Travel But the Illness of His Mother Prevents It 122
Flavin, Jennifer 527
Flesh and Blood 47, 51
Fletcher, Dexter 206
Flight of the Dragons 440, 443
Flight of the Intruder 125, 188–189
Flintstones, The 213
"Flipside" (TV) 303
Florence Nightingale 504, 506
Fly, The (1958) 204
Fly, The (1986) 204, 207
Fly Away Home (1981) 64, 68
Fly Away Home (1991) 198, 199
"Flying Nun, The" (TV) 158, 164
Fly II, The 205
Flynn, Christopher 367
Flynn, David 485, 486, 489
Flynn, Errol 165, 177, 336, 421
Flynn, Katherine 486
Flynn, Sean 487
Foch, Nina 437
Fog, The 114, 118
Follies (stage) 77, 400
Follies in Concert 400
"Follies in Concert" (TV) 400, 401
Follies in Concert (album) 403
Follow Me, Boys 453, 458
Fonda, Henry 151, 174, 283, 286
Fonda, Jane 73, 82, 160, 162, 252, 271, 355, 357, 360, 511–512, 533, 576, 620
Fonda, Peter 462, 567
Fool for Love 42, 44
Fool for Love (stage) 599
"Fools, Females and Fun" (TV) 501
Fools' Parade 454, 458
Foote, Shelby 498
Footsteps 624, 630
For Ladies Only 262, 267
Ford, Betty 57
Ford, Clementine 494, 495
Ford, David 494, 495
Ford, Eileen 40

Ford, Faith 60
Ford, President Gerald 57
Ford, Glenn 430
Ford, Harrison 11, 101, 102, 385, 456, 539, 579, 620
Ford, John 494
Ford, Paul 401, 402
Forestieri, Lou 74
Forever Fit (book) 85
Forever Lulu 17, 21
Forman, Miloš 94, 398, 592, 593
Forrest, Steve 59
Forsythe, John 502
Fortune and Men's Eyes (stage) 298
Fosse, Bob 354
Fossey, Dian 579
Foster, Jodie 255, 387, 419, 494, 537, 579
Foster, Meg 330
Foster & Laurie 329, 334, 524, 630
"Four Alarm Family" (TV) 265
Four Feathers, The (1978) 485, 489
Four on a Garden (stage) 306, 311
Four Past Midnight (audio cassette) 124
"Fourth Annual American Comedy Awards" (TV) 212
Fourth Story, The 257, 258
Fox, Huckleberry **129**
Fox and the Hound, The 455, 458
Foxworth, Robert 625
Foxy Lady (album) 87
Foy, Eddie, III 158
Framed 205–206, 207
Frances 99, 104, 352, 355, 357, 359
Francesco 448–449, 451
Franciosa, Tony 461
Francis, Anne 331
Francis, Genie 2
Franciscus, James 503
Franco, Giuseppe 445, 448
Frank, Robert 353
Frank Dell's The Temptation of Saint Antony 124
Frankenberg, Dr. John 483
Frankenberg, Joyce Penelope Wilhelmina *see:* Seymour, Jane
Frankenberg, Mieke 483
Frankenheimer, John 308
Frankenstein: The True Story 484, 489
Frankie and Johnny 419, 420
Frankie and Johnny in the Clair de Lune (stage) 419
Franklin, Aretha 608
Franklin, Howard 394
Frann, Mary 231
Fraternity Row 261, 266
Frayn, Michael 92

"Free to Be . . . a Family" (TV) 195
Freedom Fighter 146, 148
Freeman, Morgan 104, 248, 342, 432, 564
Freezer, The (stage) 55
French Connection, The 121
French Lieutenant's Woman, The 535, 539
French Postcards 397, 403, 616
French Revolution, The 488, 490
"Fresno" (TV) 264, 267
Frida and Diego 373
"Friday Night Videos" (TV) 33
Friedkin, William 121
Friedman, Dana 233
Friendly Fire 285, 290
From Here to Eternity 41
"From Here to Eternity" (TV) 41, 44, 300, 304
From the Dead of Night 66, 68, 571, 572
Front Page, The (1974) 467, 473; 467
Front Page, The (stage) 431, 433
Front Runner, The 50
Frost, Mark 155
Frost, Robert 529
"Frozen Smoke" (TV) 550
Fry, Taylor 435, 602
Fugard, Athol 183, 184, 185
Fugitive, The 20
"Fugitive, The" (TV) 2, 453
Full Metal Jacket 600
"Fun in the Mexican Sun" (TV) 295
Funny About Love 350, 351
Funny Thing Happened on the Way to the Forum, A (stage) 292
"Funny, You Don't Look 200" (TV) 154, 194
Furst, Stephen 203, 324

G.I. Joe—The Movie 301, 304
Gabbard, Lucy 376
Gable, Clark 97, 174, 177
"Gabriel Kaplan Presents the Small Event" (TV) 551
Gage, Martin 40
Gagnier, Holly 16
Gaines, Charles 476
Gallipoli 176, 181
Gambler, The 624, 630
Gambler III, The—The Legend Continues 68
Gandhi 58, 61
Gandhi, Mahatma 58
"Gandy" (TV) 299
"Gangs" (TV) 225
Garces, Marsha 586, 587

Garcia, Andy 18, 25, 171
Garden, The 216
Gardner, Ava 46, 413
Gardner, Erle Stanley 334
Garfield, John 5, 165, 237
Garfunkel, Art 56
Garland, Judy 53, 84
Garlin, Christopher 489
Garner, James 162, 238, 433, 567, 602, 622, 626, 628
Garr, Teri 322, 586
Garrett, Betty 69, 278
Garrett, Leif 240
Garroway, Dave 574
Gaslight (1991) 489, 490
Gastineau, Mark 527
Gathering, The 261, 266
Gathering II, The 261
Gatlin, Larry 546
Gaynor, Janet 314
Gazzara, Ben 439, 506, 545, 595
Gazzo, Michael V. 615
Geary, Anthony 2, 253
Geffen, David 80
Gellis, Danny 153
Gemignani, Paul 401
Gemini (stage) 559, 565, 575
"General Hospital" (TV) 6, 21
"Generation" (TV) 3
Gentlemen Prefer Blondes (stage) 500
George, Susan 329
"George Washington" (TV) 503, 507
Gere, Dolores 165
Gere, Homer 165
Gere, Richard 42, 46, 165–173, 198, 315, 380, 432, 470, 549, 552, 553, 594, 602, 616; 167
Geston, Susan 72
"Get Christie Love" (TV) 501
Getting Married 252, 257
Getting Out (stage) 192
Getting Straight 56, 61
Getting Straight (album) 61
Ghost 196–197, 198, 199, 546, 547
"Ghost of a Chance" (TV) 361–362
Ghost of Flight 401, The 40, 44
Ghostbusters 9–10, 12, 392, 395, 578, 581
Ghostbusters II 11, 13, 393, 395, 579–580, 581; 394
Ghostley, Alice 108
Giannini, Giancarlo 58, 429, 498
Gibb, Barry 552
Gibb, Maurice 552
Gibb, Robin 552
Gibons, Ann 174

Gibson, Buck *see:* Quaid, Dennis 427
Gibson, Christian 176
Gibson, Edward 176
Gibson, Hannah 176
Gibson, Hutton 174
Gibson, Louis 176
Gibson, Mel 14, 95, 100, 102, 134, 174–181, 186, 187, 189, 236, 250, 255, 316, 417, 457, 518, 574, 577; 178
Gibson, Milo 180
Gibson, Robyn 176, 177
Gibson, Will 176
Gidget 158
"Gidget" (TV) 158, 164
Gielgud, Sir John 488
Gift of Love, The 504, 625, 630
Gilbert, Kenneth C. 406
Gilbert, Sara 32
Gillette, William 533
"Gilligan's Island" (TV) 453
Gilmore, Gary 308
Gilroy, Dan 367
Gimbel, Roger 571
Ginger in the Morning 515, 520
Giorgi, Eleonora 48
Giovanni, Paul 90
Giraud, Roland 206
Girl in Pink Tights, The (stage) 269, 274
"Girl in the Night" (TV) 460
Girl on the Via Flamina, The (stage) 407
"Girl with Something Extra, The" (TV) 159, 164
"Girl with the Crazy Brother, The" (TV) 317
Girls in the Office, The 463, 465
Girls of Huntington House, The 515, 520
Girls of the White Orchid 294, 296
Givens, Robin 273
Glass Menagerie, The (1987) 379, 382
Glass Menagerie, The (stage) 437
Gleason, Jackie 214, 246
Glenn, Scott 100, 116, 177, 185, 288, 339, 379, 457, 622
Glennon, Judge Bert 35
Gless, Sharon 440
Glitz 511, 513
Glover, Asaka 183
Glover, Danny 125, 179, 182–190, 273; 185
Glover, Mandisa 183
"Go, Go Goldblum" (TV) 205
Godfather, The 313–314, 318
Godfather, Part II, The 71, 314, 318

Godfather, Part III, The 18, 317, 318, 527, 552
Goin' South 354
Going Ape! 144, 148
Golchan, Frederic 394
Gold, Eddie 195
Gold, Joe 479
Goldberg, Whoopi 83, 109, 111, 118, 140, 163, 172, 185, 189, 191–199, 210, 280, 342, 347, 363, 442, 519, 546, 586, 587, 600, 613; **194**
Goldblum, Jeff 11, 23, 24, 48, 91, 197, 200–207, 273, 417, 418; **203**
Golden Gate 217, 220, 331, 334
Golden Greats (album) 87
Golden Voyage of Sinbad 485
Goldfinger, Janice 107
"Goldie Hawn Special, The" (TV) 439
Goldman, William 400
Goldthwait, Bob 198, 224, 225–226
Goliath Awaits 253, 257
Golina, Valeria 289
Golub, Richard 281
Gone with the Wind 488, 500
"Good Morning America" (TV) 587, 609
Good Morning, Chicago 589
Good Morning, Vietnam 582, 587, 589
Good Mother, The 316–317, 318, 619
Good Times 79, 86
Good Times (album) 86
Good Woman of Setzuan, The (stage) 244
Goodall, Jane 57, 574
Goodbye Columbus 501, 506
Goodbye Girl, The 151, 152, 156, 552
GoodFellas 410
Goodman, Anna Elizabeth 212, 214
Goodman, Betty 208
Goodman, John 32, 127, 131, 162, 208–214, 421, 423, 427, 558, 600; **33, 210**
Goodman, Leslie 208
Goodman, Leslie, Jr. 208
Goodman, Molly Evangeline 214
Goodman, Virginia 208
Goodnight Ladies (stage) 292,
Goodtime Charley (stage) 542, 544, 548
Goodtime Charley (album) 548
Goose and Tomtom (stage) 369, 408
Goranson, Lecy 32

Gorillas in the Mist 579, 581
Gorky Park 278–279, 282; 278
Gorman, Cliff 166
Gorney, Karen Lynn 551
Gorp 423, 427
Gossett, Louis, Jr. 169, 424, 626
Gotham 309, 311
Gottlieb, Hildy 19
Gould, Elliott 56, 314, 415, 494
Gould, Harold 437
Goulet, Robert 230
Grable, Betty 413
Graduate, The 150, 156
Graffiti Bridge 43
Graham, Heather 555
Graham, Martha 367
Graham, Stedman 610
Grand Isle 388
Grand Tour, The 132, 133
Grande, Paco 353, 355
Grande de Coca-Cola, El (stage) 201
Grandview, U.S.A. 82, 116, 118, 543, 547
Grant, Cary 114, 126, 157
Grant, Lee 131, 350, 415
Grapes of Wrath, The (book) 614
Grass Is Greener, The (stage) 192
Gray, Spalding 210
Gray Lady Down 429, 435
Grazer, Brian 245
Grease 552, 556
Grease (stage) 166, 173, 542, 548, 550, 553, 556, 592, 597
Grease (album) 552, 556
Grease 2 415, 419
Grease 2 (album) 420
"Great American Laugh-Off, The" (TV) 584
Great American Tragedy, A 624, 630
Great Balls of Fire! 18, 21, 425–426, 427
Great Escape, The 433
Great Escape II, The: The Untold Story 433, 435
Great Gatsby, The (book) 575
Great God Brown, The (stage) 166
Great Grandson of Jedediah Kohler, The (stage) 278
Great Outdoors, The 11, 13
"Great Performances" (TV) 417, 533, 576
Great Smoky Roadblock, The 468, 473
Great Waldo Pepper, The 468, 473
Greatest Hits (Cher; album) 87
Greatest Hits (Sonny and Cher; album) 86

"Greed" (TV) 8
Greeks, The (stage) 431
Green, Adolph 338
Green Berets, The 283
Green Julia (stage) 624
Greenburg, Michael 5
Greene, Graham 170
Greenwald, Robert 131, 471
Greer, Jane 70
"Gregory Harrison Show, The" (TV) 265
Gregory Hines (album) 272, 274
"Gregory Hines' Tap Dance in America" (TV) 273
Greisman, Alan 161, 162
Greisman, Sam 162
Greko, Kathryn 625
Grey, Jennifer 371, 544, 546
Grey, Joel 542, 544
Greystoke: The Legend of Tarzan, Lord of the Apes 92, 95–96
Grieco, Richard 266
Griffin, Mary 132
Griffin, Merv 364, 476
Griffith, Andy 172
Griffith, Kristin 47
Griffith, Melanie 12, 18, 115, 130, 215–221, 248, 299, 301, 302, 303, 325, 471, 579, 580, 604, 620, 629; **218**
Griffith, Peter 215
Griffith, Tom 604
Grifters, The 219
Grimes, Scott 504
Grimes, Tammy 73
Grizzard, George 286
Grodin, Charles 72, 85, 314, 493
Grody, Kathryn 314, 317, 397
Groomes, Gary 11
Gross Anatomy 349, 351
Group, The 54–55, 60
Guardino, Harry 460
Guare, John 201, 347
Guber, Peter 417, 489
Guc, David 23, 550
Guest, Christopher 72, 116
Guest, Judith 285
Guest, Nicholas 72
Guide for the Married Woman, A 494, 499
"Guiding Light, The" (TV) 467, 509
Guinness, Alec 197, 336, 341
Gummer, Donald 534
Gummer, Grace 534
Gummer, Henry 534
Gummer, Louisa Jacobson 534
Gummer, Mary Willa "Mamie" 534, 537

Gung Ho (1986) 322, 326
"Gung Ho" (TV) 322
Gunrunner, The 100, 105
Guns in the Heather 453, 458
Guns of Diablo 453, 458
"Gunsmoke" (TV) 62, 63, 453, 454
Gurney, A. R. 442, 595
Guttenberg, Ann Iris Newman 222
Guttenberg, Denise 226
Guttenberg, Jerome Stanley 222
Guttenberg, Steve 139, 140, 162, 222–228, 365, 446; **225**
Guy Named Joe, A 154, 212
Guys and Dolls (stage) 142, 284
Gwaltney, Jack 512
Gypsies, Tramps & Thieves (album) 80, 87
Gypsy 291, 296, 372–373, 550
Gypsy (album) 296

Haapaniemi, Lisa *see:* Niemi, Lisa
Haas, Lukas 385
Habeas Corpus (stage) 166, 173
Hackett, Joan 54
Hackford, Taylor 271, 616
Hackman, Gene 56, 57, 123, 155, 186, 310, 430, 432, 446, 543
Hagen, Uta 46, 345
Hagerty, Julie 130, 155, 434
Haines, Randa 282
Hair 592, 597
Hair (stage) 166, 192, 199, 313, 318
Hair (album) 597
Hale, Teddy 268
Half-Breed (album) 87
"Half-Hour Comedy Hour, The" (TV) 231, 235
Half-Moon Street 578–579, 581
"Half 'n' Half" (TV) 332–333
Halfway to Hell 187
Hall, Annie 229, 230
Hall, Arsenio 36, 102, 182, 195, 229–235, 373, 613; **232**
Hall, Diane *see:* Keaton, Diane
Hall, Dorothy Keaton 312
Hall, Dorrie 312, 315
Hall, Rev. Fred 229
Hall, Jack 312
Hall, Juanita 400
Hall, Randy 312
Hall, Robin 312
"Hallmark Hall of Fame" (TV) 309, 397, 624, 626, 628
Halloween 114, 118
Halloween II 115, 118
Halls of Anger 70, 75
Halyalkar, Johnathon 147
Hamilton, George 463

Hamilton, Linda 445, 478
Hamlet (1990) 95, 96, 180–181
Hamlet (stage) 238, 277, 340, 342, 397, 509
"Hamlet" (1990) (TV) 342
Hamlin, Bernice 236
Hamlin, Chauncey Jerome, Jr. 236
Hamlin, Chauncey Jerome, III 236
Hamlin, Dimitri 237, 239
Hamlin, Harry 154, 236–242; **239**
Hamlin, Laura *see:* Johnson, Laura
Hammer, M.C. 613
Hampton, Christopher 94, 172
Handman, Wynn 166
Hands of Its Enemies, The (stage) 154
Handy, John 188
Hangin' Up My Heart (album) 520
Hanks, Amos 243
Hanks, Colin 244
Hanks, Elizabeth 245
Hanks, Jimmy 243
Hanks, Larry 243
Hanks, Rita 246
Hanks, Samantha, 244, 245, 246
Hanks, Sandra 243
Hanks, Steve 414
Hanks, Tom 10, 12, 102, 162, 243–249, 319, 322, 323, 363, 554, 604, 620; **245**
Hannah, Daryl 58, 162, 226, 245, 618, 619; **446**
Hannah and Her Sisters 49, 121
Hansberry, Lorraine 186
Happily Ever After 64, 68
"Happy Anniversary and Goodbye" (TV) 476
"Happy Birthday, Bob" (TV) 364
"Happy Birthday, Bugs" (TV) 196
"Happy Birthday, Hollywood" (TV) 504, 594
"Happy Days" (TV) 245, 523, 584
Happy End (stage) 532, 533, 540
Hard Country 41, 44; **41**
Hard Driver 76
Hard Promises 520, 629, 630
Hardboiled 563
Hardy, Oliver 214
"Hardy Boys/Nancy Drew Mysteries, The" (TV) 502
Harewood, Dorian 333
Hargitay, Mickey 477
Harlem Nights 233, 234
Harley Davidson and the Marlboro Man 303, 304, 450, 451
Harling, Robert 162
Harlow, Jean 215
Harmon, Elyse Knox 250
Harmon, Estelle 260
Harmon, Kelly 250

Harmon, Kristin 250, 251
Harmon, Mark 102, 236, 250–258, 259, 591; **256**
Harmon, Sean Thomas 255
Harmon, Tom 250, 251, 256
Harnick, Sheldon 90
Harper, Tess 558
Harper, Valerie 128
Harrad Experiment, The 216, 220, 260, 266, 299, 304
Harrelson, Woody 138, 410
Harrington, Rowdy 605
Harris, Ed 104, 410
Harris, James B. 628
Harris, Jeff 35, 211
Harris, Julie 159
Harris, Mel 441
Harris, Neil Patrick 195
Harris, Richard 50
Harrison, Chris 259, 262
Harrison, Donna 259
Harrison, Ed 259
Harrison, Emma Lee 264
Harrison, George 369,
Harrison, Gregory 66, 250, 259–267, 331, 455, 488, 496; **263**
Harrison, Kate La-Priel 266
Harrison, Lily Anne 264
Harrold, Kathryn 478, 577
Harry, Deborah 17
Harry & Son 24, 26
Harry and Walter Go to New York 314, 318
"Harry O" (TV) 454
Harryhausen, Ray 237
Hart, Gary 618
Hart, Mary 527
Hart, Moss 592
Hart, Roxanne 346
"Hart and Lorne Terrific Hour, The" (TV) 8
"Hart to Hart" (TV) 599
Hartman, Lisa 16, 266
Hartsfield, Gaston 500
Hartzog, Anna Elizabeth 211
Harvey (stage) 284
Harvey, Laurence 17
"Harvey Korman Show, The" (TV) 346, 351
Hasty Heart, The (stage) 262–263, 455
"Hasty Heart, The" (TV) 263, 331
Hauck, Charlie 320
Hauer, Rutger 47, 416, 455, 525, 560
Haufrecht, Marcia 15, 23
Haunting Passion 489
"Have Faith" (TV) 441
Havens, Annette 217
Havoc, June 224

"Hawaii Five-O" (TV) 63, 328, 329, 437, 438
Hawn, Goldie 162, 180, 347, 348, 355, 357, 453, 455, 456, 485, 536, 538
Haysbert, Dennis 419
Hayward, Susan 413, 557
Hayworth, Rita 413, 418
"Hazel" (TV) 292, 296
He Knows You're Alone 244, 248
Head Office 487, 489
"Headliners" (TV) 552
Headly, Glenne 376–377, 378, 380, 388, 604
Heard, John 81, 248, 517, 595
Hearn, George 399, 400
Hearst, Patty 124
Heart Beat 517, 520
Heart of Dixie 595, 597
Heart of Steel 209, 214
Heart of Stone (stage) 84
Heart of Stone (album) 87
"HeartBeat" (TV) 239, 301
Heartbeat (album) 301, 304
Heartbreak Hotel 595
Heartbreak Kid, The 314, 492, 499; **493**
Heartbreak Kid, The (album) 499
Heartburn 130, 133, 399–400, 536, 540
Heartland (stage) 406, 412
Hearts of the West 72, 76
Heatherton, Joey 124
Heaven 316, 318
Heaven and Earth (stage) 599
"Heaven on Earth" (album) 316
Heaven's Gate 72, 76, 120, 125, 445, 451
"Hec Ramsey" (TV) 454
Hecht, Ben 433, 467
Heckerling, Amy 406, 603
Hedaya, Dan 478
Hedison, David 204
Hedren, Nathalie *see:* Hedren, Tippi
Hedren, Tippi 215, 216, 217, 219, 220, 299
Heidi Chronicles, The (stage) 349, 350, 351
Heiferman, Marvin 315
Heiress, The (stage) 431
Helen Keller: The Miracle Continues 332, 334
Helgenberger, Marg 435
Hell Hath No Fury (book) 303
"He'll See You Now" (TV) 471
Heller, Paul 381
Hellinger's Law 406, 411
Hello Again 364, 365
Hello Down There 150, 156

Hell's Kitchen 523
Helmond, Katherine 142, 144
Helmut Newton: Frames from the Edge 579, 581
Help Save Planet Earth 118, 140, 197, 442
Hemingway, Ernest 629
Hemingway, Margaux 329
Hemingway, Mariel 329, 435, 456
"Hemingway Play, The" (TV) 329
Henderson, Heidi 280
Henderson, Skitch 280
Henderson Monster, The 346, 351
Henley, Beth 350
Henley, Don 287, 564
Henner, Marilu 143, 550, 555
Henry, Justin 535
Henry IV, Part I (stage) 175, 397
Henry V (stage) 166, 276, 339, 533
Hepburn, Audrey 439
Hepburn, Katharine 89, 318, 429, 469, 535, 618
Herbert, Victor 291
Hercules Goes Bananas 482
Hercules in New York 476, 482
Hercules: The Movie 482
"Hero, The" (TV) 177
Hero at Large 439, 443; **439**
Heroes 160, 164
Herrman, Edward 576
Hershew, Michael **153**
Hershey, Barbara 93, 317, 339, 350
Hesse, Hermann 376
Hesseltine, Stark 434
Heston, Charlton 41, 53, 295, 429, 434
"Hey, Landlord!" (TV) 158
Hickey, William 480
Hickey and Boggs 624, 630
Hicks, Catherine 293
Higgins, Jack 592
High Risk 572
High Road to Health, The (book) 571–572
High Spirits 226, 228
Highwayman, The 510, 513
Hilden, Elizabeth 629
Hill, George Roy 90
Hill, Steven 349
"Hill Street Blues" (TV) 184, 238
Hiller, Wendy 432
"Hills Like White Elephants" (TV) 219, 220, 629
Hines, Alma Iola Lawless 268
Hines, Daria 269
Hines, Gregory 109, 122, 268–274, 418, 509; **272, 577**
Hines, Maurice, Jr. 268, 269–270, 271

Hines, Maurice, Sr. 268, 269
Hines, Ora 270
Hines, Pamela 270
Hines, Patricia 269
Hines, Zachary Evan 270
Hines, Hines and Brown 269
Hines, Hines and Dad 269
Hines Kids, The 268–269
Hingle, Pat 624
Hirsch, Judd 143, 348
History of Black Women Through Drama and Song, The (stage) 609
History of the World: Part I 270, 274
Hitchcock, Alfred 114, 180, 215, 217, 516, 611
Hitched 159, 164
"Hitchhiker, The" (TV) 240
Hobel, Mara 576
Hoffman, Dustin 70, 123, 247, 325, 355, 377, 378, 392, 395, 405, 531, 535, 585, 589, 605, 622; **356**
Hogan, Paul 179
Hogestyn, Drake 3
Holbrook, Hal 16, 338
Holcomb, Kathryn 63
Hold-Up 394
Holden, William 264
Holiday, Billie 106
Holliday, Judy 39, 194, 215, 366
Holliday, Polly 278
Hollis, Carey, Jr. 517
Hollywood Knights, The 144, 148, 414, 419
"Hollywood Palace, The" (TV) 54
"Hollywood Squares" (TV) 114
"Hollywood Tribute to Arnold Schwarzenegger, A" (TV) 481
"Hollywood Wives" (TV) 59, 61
"Hollywood's Diamond Jubilee" (TV) 315
Holm, Celeste 580
Holm, Ian 95
"Holocaust" (TV) 533, 540, 625, 630
Holt, Georgia 77, 78, 79, 83, 84
Holvoe, Maria 256; **256**
Home for the Holidays 159, 163
Home Is Where the Heart Is 353, 359
Homeboy 448, 451
Homeless 131
Homer & Eddie 196, 198
Homes, Geoffrey 626
Honey, I Shrunk the Kids 394
Hong, James 456
Honorary Consul, The 170, 173
"Honoring a Show-Business Legend" (TV) 273

Hook 589
Hooks, Robert 626
Hooper 160, 164
"Hooperman" (TV) 441, 443
Hope, Bob 294, 295, 325, 364, 598, 613
Hopkins, Anthony 450, 572
Hopkins, Miriam 58
Hopper, Dennis 303, 409
Horne, Geoffrey 15
Horse in the Gray Flannel Suit, The 453, 458
Horsley, Lee 266, 487
Horton, Peter 2, 414, 417
Hoskins, Bob 50, 85, 197, 206, 448, 483
"Hot Hero Sandwich" (TV) 431
"Hot Number Affair, The" (TV) 79
Hot Paint 265, 267
Hot Spot, The 219, 303, 304
Hot to Trot 225–226
Hotchner, A. E. 332
House on Carroll Street, The 130, 133, 386–387, 388, 401, 403
Householder, The 329
Housekeeping 348, 351
Houseman, John 223, 328, 330, 337, 429, 567
"How the Leopard Got His Spots" (TV) 187
How the Leopard Got His Spots (album) 190
How the West Was Won 64, 97
"How the West Was Won" (TV) 64, 68
How to Beat the High Cost of Living 354, 359, 463, 465
Howard, Cheryl 439
Howard, Ken 328, 504
Howard, Richard 53
Howard, Ron 245, 321, 322, 362, 439, 445, 457
Howell, C. Thomas 543
Hoxie, Richmond 505
Hryharrow, Karen 328
Hubley, Season 455
Hudson, Bill 455
Hudson, Ernie 11, 578
Hudson, Katie 455
Hudson, Oliver 455
Hudson, Rock 202, 461, 462
Hudson Hawk 604, 605
Hugh-Kelly, Daniel 24
Hughes, Barnard 19, 289
Hughes, Howard 604, 630
Hulce, Tom 116
"Hullabaloo" (TV) 79
Human Feelings 108, 112
Hunger, The 120, 125, 470, 473

Hunt, Helen 138
Hunt, Linda 81, 91, 577
Hunt for Red October, The 14, 18–19, 21, 102
Hunter, Holly 154, 155, 348, 349, 488, 619
Hunter, Ross 262
Hunting Party, The 56, 61
Hurlyburly (stage) 59, 279, 282, 370, 409, 577–578, 581
Hurt, Alexander Devon 278
Hurt, Claire McGill 275
Hurt, Heidi 280
Hurt, James 275
Hurt, John 50
Hurt, Kenneth 275
Hurt, Mary Beth 90, 92, 276, 277, 280, 281, 339
Hurt, McChord, 275
Hurt, Samuel 280
Hurt, William 20, 48, 90, 91, 92, 99, 101, 127, 136, 161, 275–282, 288, 299, 341, 350, 403, 498, 517, 559, 562, 575, 576, 577, 625; 278
Huston, John 71, 72, 217
Hutton, Daniel 398
Hutton, Emanuel Noah 288, 619
Hutton, Heidi 283, 284
Hutton, Jim 283, 284, 285
Hutton, Lauren 168, 171, 332, 447, 516
Hutton, Maryline 283, 284
Hutton, Timothy 19, 262, 280, 283–290, 386, 407, 618, 619; 286
Hyland, Diana 551

I Enjoy Being a Girl (album) 38
"I Love Liberty" (TV) 271
I Love My Wife (stage) 293
I Love You to Death 281–282, 341, 343, 537
I Married Wyatt Earp 65, 68
I Never Promised You a Rose Garden 422, 427
I Paralyze (album) 87
I Take These Men 464, 465
I Want to Live (1983) 569, 572
I Will, I Will . . . For Now 314, 318
Iadanza, Ann 142, 144
Iadanza, Anthony *see*: Danza, Tony
Iadanza, Matty 142, 144
Iadanza, Matty, Jr. 142
Ibsen, Henrik 345
Iceman 184, 189, 287, 290
Iceman Cometh, The 71, 76
Iceman Cometh, The (stage) 244
I'd Rather Believe in You (album) 87

If It Don't Kill You, It Just Makes You Stronger (album) 604, 606
"If Tomorrow Comes" (TV) 48, 51
Iglesias, Julio 31
"I'll Take Manhattan" (TV) 332, 335
I'm Breathless: Music from and Inspired by the Film "Dick Tracy" (album) 372, 373, 374, 402, 403
Imagining Argentina 172
Immaculate Collection, The (album) 373, 374
Immediate Family 94, 96, 629, 630
Impromptu 403
In Case You're in Love (album) 86
In Country 603, 605
In Love with an Older Woman 439, 443
In Mama's House (stage) 150
In Our Hands 470, 473, 536, 539
In Praise of Older Women 46–47, 51
In Search of America 71, 75
In Search of the Guru 599, 605
In the Spirit 219, 220
Incident at Vichy (stage) 150
Incredible Journey of Doctor Meg Laurel, The 569, 572, 625, 630
Indian Runner, The 411, 412
Indiana Jones and the Last Crusade 393
Indiana Jones and the Temple of Doom 10, 12
Inge, William 415
Initiation, The (stage) 166
Inmates: A Love Story 331, 334
Innaurato, Albert 167, 575
Innerspace 424, 427
Innocent, The 429, 435
Insana, Tino 12
Inserts 156
"Inside the Summer Blockbusters" (TV) 43
"Insight" (TV) 439
"Interceptor" (TV) 66
Interiors 315, 318
Internal Affairs 171, 173
Intimate Agony 253, 257
Into the Night 12, 203, 207, 417, 420
Introducing Ann Jillian the Singer (album) 294, 296
Invasion of Privacy, An 128, 133
Invasion of the Body Snatchers (1978) 201–202, 207
Ireland, John 265
Irish Coffee (stage) 23
Irons, Jeremy 92, 94, 103, 535

"Ironside" (TV) 144, 460
Ironweed 448, 536–537, 540
Irreconcilable Differences 362–363, 365
Irving, Amy 154, 216, 239, 516
Irving, John 90
Isaacs, Susan 620
Island, The (stage) 183
It Came from Hollywood 9, 12
It Happened at the World's Fair 453, 458
It Happened One Night 191–192
"It Takes a Thief" (TV) 460, 461
Italian Stallion, The 522, 529
"It's a Living" (TV) 293, 296
Ivanov (stage) 282
Ivey, Dana 342
Ivey, Judith 132, 364, 578
Ivory, James 329

J. Edgar Hoover 594, 597
Jack the Ripper (1988) 488, 489
Jacker, Corinne 127, 276
Jackson, Jesse 188, 232
Jackson, Kate 66, 316, 331, 502; 65
Jackson, Latoya 234
Jackson, Michael 154
Jackson County Jail 306–307, 310
Jaclyn Smith Beauty Book, The (book) 504
Jacobi, Derek 186
Jacobson, Danny 35
Jacoby, Laura 504
Jacoby, Scott 422
Jacqueline Bouvier Kennedy 503, 506
Jacqueline Susann's Once Is Not Enough 484
Jagged Edge 73, 75, 76, 93, 95, 96, 100
Jamaica Inn (1985) 487, 489
James, Henry 432, 493
James, Judith 155
"James A. Michener's 'Space'" (TV) 238, 242
"James at 16" (TV) 615
Jane Seymour's Guide to Romantic Living (book) 487
Janitor, The 581, 630
January Man, The 341, 343, 471, 473
Jaws 151, 156
Jaws 3-D 423, 427
Jayne Mansfield Story, The 477, 482
Jeanmaire 269
Jenner, Bruce 224, 430, 440
"Jennifer Slept Here" (TV) 293–294, 296

Jennings, Sandra 278, 279, 281
Jerk, The 391, 395
Jerome, Timothy 202
Jerosa, Vincent 170
"Jessie" (TV) 569, 573
Jesus Christ Superstar (stage) 192, 199
Jewel of the Nile, The 561, 565
Jewison, Norman 346
Jigsaw (1968) 460–461, 465
Jillian, Ann 291–296; 294
Jillian and Shulman 292
Jilliann, Ann *see:* Jillian, Ann
"Jim Henson Hour, The" (TV) 139
Jim, the World's Greatest 260, 266
Joan of Arc at the Stake (stage) 92
Joe 467, 473
Joe Versus the Volcano 247, 249
"John Alexander" (TV) 487
John and Mary 70, 75
John and Mary (album) 76
"John Denver in Australia" (TV) 462
"John Steinbeck's 'East of Eden'" (TV) 64, 68, 483, 486, 490
John Travolta (album) 551, 556
Johnny Belinda (1982) 423, 427
Johnny Dangerously 322, 326
Johnny Got His Gun (stage) 128
Johnny Handsome 25, 27, 449, 451; 25
Johnny, We Hardly Knew Ye 46, 51
Johnson, Ben 64, 70, 492
Johnson, Beverly 154
Johnson, Brad 125, 189
Johnson, Caryn *see:* Goldberg, Whoopi
Johnson, Dakota Mayi 219
Johnson, Darlene 298
Johnson, Don 12, 131, 216, 217, 218, 219, 220, 297–304, 450, 457, 471, 496, 509, 565; 302
Johnson, Emma 191
Johnson, Jesse Wayne 300
Johnson, Laura 66, 232, 238, 239, 240
Johnson, Magic 232
Johnson, Nell Wilson 297
Johnson, Van 131
Johnson, Wayne Fred 297, 298
Jones, Austin 306
Jones, Clyde L. 305
Jones, Dean 453
Jones, Grace 478
Jones, James 300
Jones, Kimberlea 308
Jones, Leonard 306
Jones, Lucille Marie Scott 305
Jones, Quincy 185, 609

Jones, Sam J. 477, 510
Jones, Shirley 70
Jones, Spike 106
Jones, Tom 230
Jones, Tommy Lee 160, 218, 305–311, 347, 357, 359, 471, 502, 517; 307
Jordan, Richard 555
Joshua Then and Now 626, 630
Journey to the Day (stage) 150
Joyride 216, 220
"Judd for the Defense" (TV) 150
Judgment in Berlin 409, 412
Julia 533, 539
Julia, Raul 279, 338, 378, 470, 534
Julia and Julia 562, 565
Julius Caesar (stage) 152
Jumpin' Jack Flash 193–194, 198, 363; 194
"June Moon" (TV) 467
Just Between Friends 138, 141, 348, 351
"Just Between Friends" (TV) 612
"Just the Facts" (TV) 246

K2 288
Kahn, Madeline 270, 494
Kamins, Mark 367–368
Kane, Bob 324
Kane, Carol 314, 317, 470
"Kane and Abel" (TV) 154
Kanew, Jeff 18
Kania, Cynthia 99
Kaplan, Gabriel "Gabe" 550
Kaprisky, Valerie 169
"Karen" (TV) 150, 156
Kasdan, Lawrence 91, 99, 100, 104, 185, 200, 202, 203, 278, 280, 281, 339, 341, 559
Kasdan, Mark 339
Kastner, Elliott 448
"Kate & Allie" (TV) 464, 465, 570
"Kate Loves a Mystery" (TV) 136
Katherine 516, 520
Katie: Portrait of a Centerfold 40–41, 44, 300, 304
Katt, William 46, 47, 308, 516
Kaufman, George S. 592
Kava, Caroline 447
Kaye, Danny 582
Kaye, Judy 202
Kazan, Elia 624
Kazantzakis, Nikos 122
Keach, James 116
Keach, Stacy 115
Keaton, Buster 129
Keaton, Caroline 322, 323, 324
Keaton, Diane 46, 83, 128, 167, 177, 313–318, 320, 348, 355,

358, 370, 519, 593, 618, 619; **316**

Keaton, Michael 17, 43, 99, 129, 219, 242, 245, 293, 319–326, 362, 553; **323**

Keaton, Sean 322, 324

Keats, Steven 362

Keel, Howard 2

Keeler, Ruby 270

Keitel, Harvey 471, 516

Keith, Brian 57

Keith, David 177, 595

Keller, Mary Page 147

Kellerman, Sally 197, 516

Kellogg, Lynn 313

Kelly, David Patrick 478

Kelly, Fred 549

Kelly, Gene 268, 543, 544, 549

Kelly, Grace 215, 500

Kelly, Margaret "Mickey" 391–392

Kelly, Paula 624

Kemp, Elizabeth 331

Kennedy, Edward "Ted" 463

Kennedy, George 624

Kennedy, John 476

Kennedy, Robert 437, 476

Kennedy, William 447, 537

Kennedy's Children (stage) 533

Kenny Rogers as "The Gambler" 64, 68

Kenny Rogers as "The Gambler"— The Adventure Continues 66, 68

Kent State 23, 26

Kerkorian, Kirk 529

Kerns, Joanna 242

Kerrey, Robert "Bob" 617, 619

Kerwin, Brian 417, 519

Kestner, Boyd 543

Key Exchange (stage) 253

Keyloun, Mark 618

Keys to Freedom 488, 490

Kid from Nowhere, The 464, 465

Kidder, Margot 138, 430, 431, 463

Kiley, Richard 315, 624

Killer in the Mirror 294, 296

Killer on Board 485, 489

Killer's Head (stage) 166

Killing Fields, The 378, 382

Killing Hour, The 331, 334

"Killing in a Small Town, A" (TV) 350

Killing of Randy Webster, The 406, 411

Killings on the Last Line (stage) 23

Killjoy 44

Kilmer, Val 24, 81, 263, 416

Kimbrough, Charles 60

Kindergarten Cop 481–482

King, Alan 110, 111

King, Jamison "Jamie" 333

King, Karen 328

King, Louise 328, 330, 332

King, Rev. Martin Luther, Jr. 154, 272, 437

King, Perry 26, 64, 327–335, 506, 512, 523; **331**

King, Stephen 137, 289, 479, 516, 551, 626

King, Zalman 449

King David 170, 173

King Kong (1976) 72, 76, 353–354, 359

King Lear (stage) 89, 575

King of the Gypsies 469, 473

King of the Mountain 237, 242

King Ralph 213, 214

King Solomon's Mines (1985) 560

Kingi, Alex Nathan 569

Kingi, Dorian Henry 569

Kingi, Henry 569

Kingsley, Ben 58

Kingston, Kenny 541

Kinski, Klaus 470

Kirby, Bruno 111

Kirkland, Douglas 563

Kiss 81

Kiss Me Goodbye 73, 76, 161, 164

Kiss Me, Kill Me 63, 68

"Kiss Me, Petruchio" (TV) 535

Kiss of the Spider Woman 279, 282

Kiss Shot 195, 198

"Kissing Bandit, The" (TV) 108

Klein, Ellie 353

Kline, Kate 336

Kline, Kevin 48, 90, 91, 99, 161, 185, 203, 209, 280, 281, 336–343, 346, 378, 471, 518, 535, 538, 564, 593, 626; **340, 518**

"Knife and Gun Club, The" (TV) 333

Knight, Gladys 273

Knight, Shirley 54, 533

Knight, Ted 391

Knock Wood (book) 59

"Knots Landing" (TV) 16, 21, 240, 242, 252

Knox, Elyse *see:* Harmon, Elyse Knox

Knuckle (stage) 329

Koch, Howard W. 484

"Kojak" (TV) 144, 166, 276, 292, 505, 523

Korman, Harvey 346

Korsmo, Charlie 358

Koslow, Pamela 269, 270

Kovacs, Ernie 106, 525

Kozlowski, Linda 240

Kramer Vs. Kramer 58, 535, 536, 539

Krane, Jonathon 66, 554, 568, 569

Krantz, Judith 66, 568, 569

Krents, Harold 223

Krige, Alice 74, 596

Kristofferson, Kris 348, 594

Kubrick, Stanley 527–528, 600

"Kung Fu" (TV) 299

Kurosawa, Akira 172

Kurt Russell (album) 454, 458

Kurtz, Swoosie 90, 130

Kuttner, Henry 132

"L.A. Law" (TV) 238–239, 240, 241, 242, 508, 509–510, 511, 512, 513

L.S.D. (stage) 120

LaBelle, Patti 231

Laclos, Pierre Choderlos de 94

Lacombe Lucien 58

LaCroix, Christian 487

Ladd, Cheryl 263, 502

Ladies and Gentlemen, The Fabulous Stains 347, 351

Lady Liberty 467, 473

Lady Vanishes, The (1980) 494, 499

Ladyhawke 416, 420, 455

Ladykillers, The 197

Laguna Heat 239, 242

Lahr, Bert 303

Lahti, Christine 90, 131, 138, 145, 344–351, 433, 596; **346**

Lahti, Elizabeth Tabar 344

Lahti, Paul Theodore 344

Lamas, Fernando 508

Lambert, Mary 388

Lamour, Dorothy 53, 413

Lancaster, Burt 138, 271, 469

Land, Noah 602

Landis, John 9, 203, 529

Landsburg, Valerie 616

Landscape of the Body (stage) 347

Lane, Diane 285, 512

Lang, Pearl 367

Lang, Stephen 334

Lange, Albert 352

Lange, Jessica 41, 42, 91, 95, 99, 161, 162, 288, 308, 310, 316, 352–359, 463, 518, 519, 580, 618; **356**

Lansbury, Angela 339, 557–558

LaPaglia, Anthony 325

LaPiere, Gilbert 78

Lapine, James 399, 403

Lardner, Katherine 306, 308

Lardner, Ring, Jr. 306

LaRocca, John 414, 415

Larroquette, John 265, 570

Laskey, Kathleen 37

Lassiter 486–487, 489

Last American Hero, The 71, 76
Last Boy Scout, The 604–605
"Last Chance" (TV) 223
"Last Convertible, The" (TV) 64, 68, 330, 335
Last Detail, The 550
Last Embrace 397, 403
Last Fling, The 443
Last Minstrel Show, The (stage) 269
Last of the Cowboys, The 473
Last Picture Show, The 71, 74, 76, 492, 497, 499
Last Rites 49, 51
Last Temptation of Christ, The 119, 122–123, 125
Last Tenant, The 346, 351
Last Unicorn, The 73, 76
Last Wave, The 176
"Late Night America" (TV) 387
"Late Night with David Letterman" (TV) 83, 496
"Late Show, The" (TV) 231, 235
Latham, Aaron 575
Latzen, Ellen Hamilton 93
"Laugh-In" (TV) 583, 589
Lauper, Cyndi 205
Laurents, Arthur 372
Laurie, Piper 176, 516
Lavender Hill Mob, The 341
"Laverne and Shirley" (TV) 202, 252
Law, John Phillip 252
Law of the Land 299, 304
Lawrence, Matthew 442
Lawrence, Susan 346
Lawrence of Arabia 282
Le Carré, John 316, 419
Leachman, Cloris 74, 492, 497
League of Their Own, A 621
Lear, Norman 107
Leave It to Beaver Is Dead (stage) 397
Leave Yesterday Behind 439, 443
LeCompte, Elizabeth 120
Leda and Swan 373
Lee, Andrew Daulton 287
Lee, Gypsy Rose 372
Lee, Spike 191, 233, 234
Lee, Vernita 607
Legal Eagles 393, 618, 619, 621
"Legend of Pecos Bill" (TV) 588
Legend of Pecos Bill (album) 588
Legend of Sleepy Hollow, The (1980) 202, 207
Legend of Sleepy Hollow, The (album) 93, 96
Lehne, Fredric 415
Lehne, John 512
Leigh, Janet 113, 114, 115, 117
Leigh, Jennifer Jason 413, 457

Leigh, Vivien 95, 358
Leigh, Wendy 480
Lelouch, Claude 55
Lembeck, Harvey 437, 583
Lemmon, Jack 139, 285, 325, 517, 624
Lemon Sisters, The 317, 318
LeMond, Bob 550
Lennon, John 515
Lennon, Julian 232
Leonard, Elmore 59, 511
Leone, Sergio 594, 626
Lesson from Aloes, A (stage) 185
Let It Ride 154, 156
LeTang, Henry 269
Lethal Weapon 179, 181, 185–186, 189, 457
Lethal Weapon 2 179, 181, 189, 287
Lethal Weapon 3 189
Let's Get Harry 254, 257
Letterman, David 31, 232
Lettice and Lovage (stage) 198, 564
Letting Go 440, 443
Leuci, Robert 593
Levi, Stephen 354
Levine, Ted 50
Levinson, Barry 224, 446, 589
Levy, Franklin 262, 264
Lewes, Samantha 244
Lewis, Bruce 463
Lewis, Charlotte 266
Lewis, Huey 55
Lewis, Jenny 364, 598
Lewis, Jerry Lee 18, 425
Lewis, Maureen 8
Lewis, Richard 117, 211, 442, 498
Liaisons Dangereuses, Les (stage) 380
Liberian Girl 154
Liddy, G. Gordon 301, 510
Lies Before Kisses 506, 507
Life Force 205, 207
"Life of Python" (TV) 12
"Life on Death Row" (TV) 544
Life Study 306, 310
"Life with Lucy" (TV) 440
Light, Judith 144, 147, 253, 510
Light Years 93, 96
Like a Prayer (album) 371, 374
Like a Virgin (stage) 368
Like a Virgin (album) 368, 374
Li'l Abner (stage) 532
Lilies of the Field 608
Limato, Ed 417
Lindfors, Viveca 516
Lindley, Audra 438; **493**
"Lindsay Wagner—Another Side of Me" (TV) 568
Lindsey, Robert 407

Line (stage) 151
Linn-Baker, Mark 266
Linson, Art 101
Lion in Winter, The (stage) 223
Liotta, Ray 116, 130, 218, 240, 393, 401, 410
Lipstick 329, 334
Lithgow, John 50, 90, 91, 128, 239, 346, 585, 629
Little Drummer Girl, The 316; **316**
Little Foxes, The (stage) 623
Little Havana 512
Little Mary Sunshine (stage) 312
"Little Mermaid, The" (TV) 594
Little Mo 252, 257
Little Murders (stage) 348
Little Richard 213, 602
"Little Rosey" (TV) 37
Little Shop of Horrors 393, 395
Little Treasure 138, 141
Little White Lies 295, 296
Live and Let Die 484, 489
Live for Life 55, 61
"Live Theatre" (TV) 161
Living on the Edge of Chaos (stage) 195
Lloyd, Christopher 143, 324
Lloyd, Emily 603
"Lloyd Bridges Show, The" (TV) 70
Lloyd Webber, Andrew 397
Lo Bianco, Tony 295, 569
Lock Up 527, 530
Locke, Sondra 151
Lockhart, Anne 216
Loden, Barbara 415
Loeffler, John 81
"Logan's Run" (TV) 261, 267
Loggia, Robert 416
Lolly-Madonna XXX 71, 76
Lombard, Carole 191, 352
Lone, John 184, 287, 447
Lone Star (stage) 576
Lonesome Cowboys 515, 520
"Lonesome Dove" (TV) 186, 189, 309–310, 311
Long, Shelley 113, 137, 138, 193, 227, 360–365, 566; **364**
Long Day's Journey into Night, A (stage) 276
Long Goodbye, The 476, 482
Long Hot Summer, The (1958) 308
Long Hot Summer, The (1985) 301, 304, 496, 499
Long Riders, The 72, 423, 427
Long Road Home, The 257, 258
Long Time Coming and a Long Time Gone (stage) 166
Long Walk Home, The 197, 199, 519, 520

Long Way Home, A 286, 290
Look at Us (album) 86
Look Who's Talking 147, 549, 554–555, 556, 587, 603, 605
Look Who's Talking Too 37, 38, 555, 556, 604, 605
Looking for Mr. Goodbar 45, 46, 51, 167, 173, 315, 318
Looking for Someone 405
Loon 411
Loose Cannons 11, 13
Loose Ends (stage) 209, 214, 338, 343, 346, 351
Loose Goose 599
Loose Shoes 391, 395
Loot (stage) 17, 21
Lopez, Priscilla 90
Lords of Discipline, The 177
Lords of Flatbush, The 327, 328–329, 334, 523, 529
Loren, Sophia 467
Losin' It 362, 365
"Lost in Space" (TV) 453
"Lou Grant" (TV) 184
Louis L'Amour's "Down the Long Hills" 66, 68
Louzil, Eric 98
"Love, American Style" (TV) 80, 313, 461, 515
Love and Death 314, 318
"Love and the Sack" (TV) 80
Love and War 627, 630
Love at First Bite 463, 465
Love at First Sight 8, 12
Love at Large 50, 51
"Love Boat, The" (TV) 108, 114, 144, 245, 252, 253, 293, 361, 439, 502
"Love Boat Fall Preview Party, The" (TV) 569
Love Field 419, 420
Love for Love (stage) 89, 96, 384
Love Hurts 131–132, 133
Love Letters (stage) 116, 118, 281, 290, 333, 365, 434, 442, 595, 596, 597
Love Lives On 347–348, 351
"Love of Life" (TV) 429, 435
"Love on Instant Replay" (TV) 136
Love on the Run 16, 21
Love Story 57, 306, 310
Love Thy Neighbor 440, 443
"Love with a Twist" (TV) 67
Loveless 125
Loveless, The 120, 125
Lovell, Dyson 310
Lovely, Dr. Thomas 441
Lover, The (stage) 376
Lovers (stage) 558

Lovers, The 58
Lovers and Other Strangers 313, 318
Love's Dark Ride 485, 489
Love's Savage Fury 330, 334
Lovin' Molly 467, 473
Loving Couples 469
"Loving the Rock" (TV) 560
Loving You 455
Lowe, Chad 309
Lowe, Rob 263, 543, 544
Lower Depths, The (stage) 337
Loy, Myrna 95, 113, 491, 564
Lucas, Craig 19, 289
Lucas, George 616
Lucas, Harmony 461
Lucas, Sunshine 461
Lucas, Tom 461
Lucci, Susan 145
Luce, Claire 275
Luce, Henry, III 275, 276
Luckinbill, Laurence 397
Lucky Star (album) 374
"Lucy Makes a Hit with John Ritter" (TV) 440
Ludlum, Robert 504
Lumbly, Carl 188
Lumet, Sidney 54, 170, 593
Lunch Power (stage) 495
Lundgren, Dolph 474, 526
Lunghi, Cherie 332
Lupino, Ida 550
LuPone, Patti 337, 397–398
Lusitania Songspiel, Das (stage) 576
Lynch, David 124, 155
Lynch, Kelly 545
Lynde, Paul 108
Lyne, Adrian 93
Lynn, Loretta 517
Lyttle, Lawrence 213

"M*A*S*H" (TV) 260, 261, 361, 543
"M & W—Men & Women" (TV) 487
Macahans, The 63, 64, 68
MacArthur, Charles 433, 467
Macbeth (stage) 183
Macchio, Ralph 543
MacDermot, Galt 201
MacDowell, Andie 92, 381
MacGraw, Ali 52, 223, 488
"MacGyver" (TV) 1, 3, 4, 5, 6; 4
Macht, Stephen 377
Mackie, Bob 80, 84, 612
MacLachlan, Kyle 172, 198
MacLaine, Shirley 128, 155, 162, 329, 469, 535, 538–539, 579, 617

MacMurray, Fred 63, 265, 453
Macon County Line 299
Mad About the Boy (album) 494, 499
"Mad, Mad, Mad World of the Superbowl, The" (TV) 502
Mad Max 175, 178, 181
Mad Max Beyond Thunderdome 178, 181
Mad Max II 176, 181
Mad Max III 178, 181
Mad Monkey, The 207
Madame Sousatzka 579
Made in Heaven 24–25, 26, 288, 290, 386, 388, 619, 620
Madman 575, 581
Madonna 34, 39, 84, 86, 234, 360, 366–374, 381, 402, 407–408, 409, 527, 537, 601; 369
Madonna (album) 368, 374
"Madonna Ciao Italia: Live from Italy" (TV) 370
Madsen, Virginia 303, 309, 595
Mae West 293, 296
Magic Carpet 462, 465
Magic Garden of Stanley Sweetheart, The 298, 304
"Magic of Christmas, The" (TV) 229
"Magic with the Stars" (TV) 503
"Magical World of Disney, The" (TV) 147
"Magnum P.I." (TV) 136
Magus, The 55, 61; 55
Mahoney, Jock 157
Mahoney, Maggie 157, 158
Mailer, Norman 308
Main, Marjorie 28
Major Barbara (stage) 152
Major League 49–50, 51
Majors, Lee 568, 570
"Making a Living" (TV) 293, 296
Making Love 48, 238, 242
Making Mr. Right 379, 382
Malden, Karl 224, 377
Malibu 293, 296
Malibu Hot Summer 98, 104
Malkovich, Daniel 375, 376
Malkovich, Jo Anne 375
Malkovich, John 94, 118, 125, 339, 342, 375–382, 418, 620; 378
Malle, Chloe 59
Malle, Louis 58, 407, 469
Malmuth, Bruce 525
Mame (stage) 558
Mamet, David 345–346, 370, 595
"Man About the House, A" (TV) 438

Man and Superman (stage) 276
"Man and the City, The" (TV) 567
Man at the Crossroads 630
Man Called . . . Rainbo, A 523, 529
Man for All Seasons, A (stage) 63
"Man from the South" (TV) 217, 220
"Man from U.N.C.L.E., The" (TV) 79, 453
Man in Love, A 116, 118
Man to Man (book) 295
Man Who Came to Dinner, The 187
Man Who Came to Dinner, The (stage) 158, 376
Man Who Lived at the Ritz, The 332, 334
Man Who Loved Women, The 41–42, 44
Man Who Wasn't There, The 224, 228
Man with One Red Shoe, The 246, 248
Man with Two Brains, The 518, 520, 560, 565
Mancuso, Nick 346
Mandan, Robert 440
Mandel, Howie 138, 232
Mandela 186, 189
Mandela, Nelson 171
Mandingo 329, 334
Mandrake, The (stage) 244
Mandrell, Barbara 325
Mandy Patinkin (album) 401, 403
Mandy Patinkin—Dress Casual (album) 403
Mandy Patinkin in Concert: Dress Casual (stage) 401–402
Manhattan 315, 318, 534, 539; 534
"Mannix" (TV) 313, 438
Manoff, Dinah 285, 572; 286
Manson, Charles 56
Mantegna, Joe 282, 370, 381, 452
Mantle, Mickey 452
Marceau, Marcel 353, 582
March, Fredric 71, 450
March (album) 410
"Marcus Welby, M.D." (TV) 159, 567
Maria's Lovers 209, 214
Marie 130, 133, 518, 520, 618
Marilyn: The Untold Story 293
Marin, Cheech 442
Maris, Roger 452
Mark, Mary Ellen 54
Markham, Monte 515
Markowitz, Mitch 587
Marnie 215

Marriage of Bette and Boo, The (stage) 575
Marriage: Year One 159, 163
Married to It 498, 499
Married to the Mob 18, 21, 417, 420
Marrying Man, The 20, 21, 43, 44, 442
Marsalis, James 92, 93, 95
Marsh, Jean 347
Marshall, Clay 215
Marshall, E. G. 315
Marshall, Garry 172, 419
Marshall, Noel 215
Marshall, Penny 440, 561, 588, 618, 621
Marshall, Tracy 215
Martin, Alexandrea 192, 195
Martin, Amarah Skye 195
Martin, Mary 388, 400
Martin, Steve 7, 204, 393, 518, 560, 582, 587, 603
Martinez, A. 512
Martins, Sylvia 168, 171
Martin's Day 570, 572
Marvin, Lee 57, 71, 278–279, 281
"Mary" (TV) 321, 326
"Mary Hartman, Mary Hartman" (TV) 320
"Mary Henton Vorse" (TV) 561
Mary Stuart (stage) 277, 387
"Mary Tyler Moore Hour, The" (TV) 321, 326
"Mary Tyler Moore Show, The" (TV) 63
Mask 82, 100; 82
Maslansky, Paul 227
Mason, Bonnie Jo *see:* Cher
Mason, James 329
Mason, Marsha 152
Mason, Marshall 46, 127
"Masquerade" (TV) 495
Master Harold . . . and the Boys (stage) 184, 190
"Master of the Game" (TV) 238, 242
Masters of Menace 12, 13
Masterson, Mary Stuart 94, 257, 347–348, 350, 407, 497
Mastrantonio, Mary Elizabeth 104
Mastroianni, Marcello 48
Masur, Richard 138, 595
"Match Game, The" (TV) 114
"Matchmaker, A" (TV) 453
Matheson, Tim 295, 365, 454, 487
Matlin, Marlee 257, 279, 280, 281, 562, 578
"Matt Houston" (TV) 301
Matter of Gravity, A (stage) 429, 435

Matters of the Heart 489, 490
Matthau, Walter 586
Mature, Victor 165, 521
"Maude" (TV) 320
Maugham, W. Somerset 575
Max and Helen 596, 597
Maxie 88, 92–93, 96, 242, 399, 403
May, Elaine 219, 314
Maybe I'll Come Home in the Spring 159, 163
Mayflower Madam 59, 61
Mayron, Melanie 131
Mays, Willie 464
Mazursky, Paul 154, 201, 470, 589
McAlary, Michael 20
McBride, Jim 18
McCambridge, Mercedes 151
McCarthy, Charlie 52, 53, 54
McCarthy, Mary 54
McCartney, Paul 538
McCashin, Constance 440
McClanahan, Rue 163
"McCloud" (TV) 461, 501
McClure, James 576
McCormick, Kevin 163
McCovey, Willie 464
McCrea, Joel 69, 126
McCullers, Carson 89
McCullough, Colleen 176
McDermott, Patrick 467
McDonnell, Mary 103
McDowall, Roddy 334, 456
McDowell, Malcolm 59
McDowell, Ronnie 300, 455
McGillis, Kelly 16, 130, 288, 383–388; 385
McGinnis, Scott 3
McGovern, Elizabeth 17, 286, 289, 407, 610
McGreevey, Michael 455
McGuire Sisters, The 196
McIntyre, Larry 596
McKellen, Ian 486
McLaglen, Andrew 158
"McMillan" (TV) 462
"McMillan and Wife" (TV) 40, 461–462, 465; 461
McMurtry, Larry 186, 492, 496, 498
McNally, Terrence 419, 592
McNichol, Kristy 286, 423
McQueen, Steve 54, 297, 430
McRaney, Gerald 486
McWilliams, Caroline 322, 324
Mean Season, The 455–456, 458
Measure for Measure (stage) 533
Meatballs 391, 392, 395
"Medical Center" (TV) 329, 550
Medoff, Mark 253, 279

Meeker, Ralph 264
Meeks, Clare 140
Meeting Venus 95, 96
Mega Hits (Don Johnson album) 304
Meisner, Sanford 313
Melanie 300, 304
Melcher, Marty 56
Melcher, Terry 55, 56
Member of the Wedding, The (stage) 89, 96
Memories Never Die 569, 572
Memories of Me 110, 112
Memory of Two Mondays, A (stage) 533, 540
Memphis 498, 499
Memphis All-Stars, The 495
Men Don't Leave 358, 359
Mengers, Sue 237, 495
Men's Club, The 594, 597
Merchant of Venice, The (stage) 386, 578
Meredith, Burgess 71, 237
"Merlin and the Dragons" (TV) 342
Merlin and the Dragons (album) 343
Mermaids 85, 86
Mermaids (album) 87
Merrick, David 328
Merrill, Dina 403
Merry Wives of Windsor, The (stage) 387
"Merv Griffin Show, The" (TV) 80
Metaphors (stage) 550
Meyers, Patrick 288
Miami Blues 19, 21
"Miami Vice" (TV) 218, 297, 301, 302, 304, 509, 599
Michaels, Lorne 7, 8, 11, 390, 391, 392, 393
Michan, Arnon 605
Michener, James 261
Mick 104, 105
Mickelson, Marty 364
Middle Ages, The (stage) 440
Midler, Bette 28, 154, 212, 317, 347, 363, 369
"Midnight Caller" (TV) 211
Midnight Run 85
"Midnight Special" (TV) 398
Midnight Spy 435
Midsummer Night's Dream, A (stage) 15, 166, 560
Migrants, The 515, 520
Mike's Murder 618, 621
Milagro Beanfield War, The 218, 220
Milano, Alyssa 144, 147, 478

Miles, Vera 453, 624
Miles from Home 171, 173, 380, 382
Milford, Penelope 168
Milius, John 477
Millay, Edna St. Vincent 529
Miller, Ann 293
Miller, Arthur 120, 375, 377, 378, 619
Miller, Barry 279
Miller, George 175, 176, 417
Miller, Jason 346
Miller, Marilyn Suzanne 401
Miller, Susan Jane *see:* Saint James, Susan
"Million Dollar Bluff" (TV) 567
Mimieux, Yvette 307
Mineo, Sal 298
Minnelli, Liza 53
Miracle on Ice 224, 228
Miracle Worker, The (stage) 158
Mirage 461
Mishkin, Meyer 150
Mishkin, Phil 150
Miss Firecracker 349, 351
Miss Julie (stage) 532
Missing 517–518, 520
"Mississippi, The" (TV) 301
Mississippi Burning 101, 123, 125, 595
Missouri Breaks, The 422
Mr. Blandings Builds His Dream House 363
Mr. Frost 206, 207
Mr. Mike's Mondo Video 9, 12, 391, 395
Mr. Mom 17, 293, 296, 322, 326
"Mr. Mom" (TV) 322
"Mister Rogers' Neighborhood" (TV) 320
Mr. Saturday Night 111
Mr. T 182
Mitchum, Robert 359, 503, 523, 544
Mix, Tom 602
"Mod Squad, The" (TV) 150, 543
Modine, Matthew 177, 219, 325, 349
Molina, Alfred 163
Moment by Moment 552–553, 556; 553
Mommie Dearest 531
Money on the Side 115, 118
Money Pit, The 246, 248, 363, 365
Mongo's Back in Town 159, 163
Monk, Thelonious 321
Monroe, Marilyn 41, 215, 293, 325, 366, 413, 549
Monsignor 431–432, 435
Montalban, Ricardo 508

Montand, Yves 55
Montgomery, Elizabeth 485
Montgomery, Monty 120
Moon for the Misbegotten, A (stage) 350
Moon Over Parador 154, 156
Moonchildren (stage) 630
Mooney, Paul 233
Moonglow 162
Moonlighting 499, 605
"Moonlighting" (TV) 194, 254, 495, 496, 497, 498, 499, 600, 601, 603, 606
Moonlighting (album) 499, 606
Moonstruck 77, 83, 86, 93, 162, 537
Moony Shapiro Songbook, The (stage) 202, 207
Moore, C. L. 132
Moore, Demetria *see:* Moore, Demi
Moore, Demi 12, 132, 161, 196, 373, 546, 601, 602, 603, 604, 605
Moore, Dudley 30, 616
Moore, Mary Tyler 138, 283, 285, 300, 321, 348, 360, 437, 461
Moore, Roger 484
Moorman, Elizabeth 306
More, Robyn 176
Moreau, Jeanne 282
Morgan, Debbi 329
Morgan, Nancy 438, 439
Moriarty, Michael 533
"Mork & Mindy" (TV) 584, 585, 589
Morning After, The 73, 76
Morosini, Dana 433
Morris, Eric 476
Morris, Garrett 8, 198
Morris, Megan 129
Morrison, Tommy 528
Morse, David 411
Mortadella, La 473
Mortal Thoughts 604, 605
Mortoff, Lawrence 571
Morton, Gary 476, 503
"Mosby Raiders, The" (TV) 453
Moscow, David 247
Moscow on the Hudson 586, 589
Moscow on the Hudson II 589
Mostel, Zero 306
Mother Courage (stage) 192
Mother Lode 41, 44
Motolanez, Evi 426
"Motown Returns to the Apollo" (TV) 271
"Motown Revue" (TV) 231, 235
Mount, Thom 411
Mountain King 49

Mouse That Roared, The (stage) 165

Movie, Movie 237, 242

Mrs. Caliban 85

Mrs. Soffel 100, 177–178, 181, 316, 318

"MTV Cops" (TV) 301

"MTV Video Music Awards" (TV) 371

Much Ado About Nothing (stage) 2, 341

Mueller-Stahl, Armin 358

Muggs, J. Fred 574

Muktananda, Swami 70

Muppets Take Manhattan, The 271, 274

Murcia, Andrew 292, 295

Murder at the World Series 63, 68

Murder: By Reason of Insanity 59, 61

Murder Can Hurt You! 144, 148

Murder in Los Angeles (audio cassette) 334

"Murder, Ink" (TV) 24

Murderous Visions 67, 68

Murmur of the Heart 58

Murphy, Danny 182

Murphy, Eddie 9, 111, 116, 230–231, 232, 233, 234, 389, 527, 580; **10, 232**

"Murphy Brown" (TV) 52, 59, 60, 61

Murphy Brown: Anatomy of a Sitcom (book) 60

Murphy's Romance 162, 164

Murray, Bill 7, 9, 10, 11, 155, 204, 319, 324, 336, 361, 389–395, 410, 578, 579, 618; **394**

Murray, Brian 342

Murray, Brian *see:* Doyle-Murray, Brian

Murray, Don 592

Murray, Ed 389, 390

Murray, Homer Bank William 392

Murray, Lucille 389

Murray, Luke 392

Music Box 358, 359, 620

Music Man, The (stage) 390, 532

Mussolini and I 473

Mussolini: The Decline and Fall of Il Duce 470, 473

Muti, Ornella 498

Mutiny on the Bounty 177

"My Brother, My Enemy" (TV) 523

My Brother's Wife 441, 443

My Darling Clementine 494

My Fair Lady (stage) 40, 62–63

My Father Grew Up 442–443

My Left Foot 587

My Life (stage) 276, 430

My Name Is Bill W. 628, 630

"My Past Is My Own" (TV) 195

"My Three Sons" (TV) 265

Mylott, Eva 175

Myman, Robert 440

Myrer, Anton 64

"Mystery of the Fallen Angels" (TV) 114

Nadine 42, 44, 73, 76

Naifeh, Gary 254

Naked Tango 282

Namath, Joe Willie 464

"Name of the Game, The" (TV) 461, 465

"Nancy Drew Mysteries, The" (TV) 114, 252

Nash, Ogden 95

Nashville 201, 207, 552

"Natalie" (TV) 611

Nate and Hayes 308, 310

"Natica Jackson" (TV) 417

National Anthems (stage) 50

"National Driving Test" (TV) 188, 333, 434

"National Lampoon Radio Hour, The" (radio) 390, 395

National Lampoon Show, The (stage) 390

Native Son (1986) 610, 613

Native Speech (stage) 509

Natural, The 42, 44, 92, 95; **92**

Nature and Purpose of the Universe, The (stage) 576

Naughton, James 568

Nauseda, Ann Jura *see:* Jillian, Ann

Nauseda, Joseph 291

Nauseda, Margaret 291

Nayatt School (stage) 120

Naylor, Gloria 611

"NBC All-Star Hour" (TV) 293

NBC's Saturday Night Live (album) 13

"NBC's 60th Anniversary Celebration" (TV) 363

Neeson, Liam 83, 220, 226, 316

Neighbors 9, 12

Neill, Sam 282

Nelligan, Kate 595

Nelly, Richard 50

Nelson, Barry 501

Nelson, Craig T. 364, 596

Nelson, David 124

Nelson, Harriet 251

Nelson, Kristin 255

Nelson, Ozzie 251

Nelson, Rick 250, 255

Network 524

Neubert, Richard 460

Neufeld, Mace 18

Nevada (stage) 437

Never Say Never Again 41, 44

New Breed, The (book) 124

New Face in Hell 465

New Jerusalem (stage) 576

New Kids on the Block 613

"New Land, The" (TV) 454, 458

"New Original Wonder Woman, The" (TV) 615

"New Year's Wedding" (TV) 108

New York Nights 120, 125

New York Times 350

Newborn, Phineas, Jr. 495

Newman, Laraine 8, 443

Newman, Paul 47, 57, 149, 216, 255–256, 279, 297, 301, 308, 309, 379, 576, 599, 627

Newton, Helmut 579

Newton-John, Olivia 415, 434, 552, 554

Next of Kin 545–546, 547

Next Stop, Greenwich Village 201, 207, 390, 395

Ngor, Dr. Haing S. 378

Nicholas, Harold 273

Nichols, Jenny 398

Nichols, Mike 18, 56, 59, 81, 92, 193, 279, 399–400, 426, 536, 538, 578, 579, 587

Nichols, Nichelle 195

Nicholson, Jack 43, 56, 83, 128, 130, 151, 287, 319, 324, 354, 359, 386, 400, 417, 422, 448, 470, 531, 536, 587, 618; **561**

Nickelodeon 438, 439, 443, 494

Nielsen, Brigitte 478, 526–527

Niemi, Lisa 542, 543, 544, 545, 547

Night at the Opera, A (album) 586, 590

Night Cries 462, 465

"Night Gallery" (TV) 159, 313, 567

'Night, Mother 519, 520

Night Moves 216, 220, 624, 629, 630

Night of Great Movie Music, A (stage) 562

Night of the Juggler 398, 403

Night of the Sharks, The 597

Night Ride to Osaka 296

Night Shift 98–99, 104, 321–322, 326, 362, 365, 553

Night That Panicked America, The 438, 443

Night the Lights Went Out in Georgia, The 423, 427

Night the Lights Went Out in Georgia, The (album) 427

Night They Saved Christmas, The 504, 506

Nighthawks 525, 529, 569, 572; **569**

Nightkill 503, 506

Nightmare at Bitter Creek 570–571, 572

Nimoy, Leonard 139, 226, 316–317, 350

9 1/2 Weeks 42, 43, 44, 447–448, 451

9/30/55 422, 427

1941 9, 12, 445, 451, 592, 597

"99 Ways to Attract the Right Man" (TV) 145

Niven, David 53

"No Exit" (TV) 599

No Man's Land (stage) 377

No Mercy 42, 44, 170–171, 173

No Place Like Home 131, 133, 350, 351

No Place to Hide 522–523, 529

No Small Affair 161

"No Soap, Radio" (TV) 224, 228

No Way Out (1987) 101, 105

Nolte, Nick 102, 275, 299, 359, 517, 594, 619

Noonan, John Ford 594

Noonan, Tom 470

Norma Rae 160, 164

Normal Heart, The (stage) 154

Norman, Marsha 519

Norris, Christopher 260, 261

Norris, Chuck 457

North, Sheree 108

"North and South" (TV) 544, 548

"North and South, Book II" (TV) 544, 548

North by North Wells (stage) 361

North by Northwest 180

North Shore 264, 267

Not Now, Darling (stage) 484

Not Without My Daughter 163, 164

Nothing But Trouble 12, 13

Nothing in Common 246, 248

Nothing Lasts Forever 10, 12, 392, 395

Notre Dame de Paris (book) 125

Notte degli Squali, La 597

Nouri, Michael 64, 99, 504

Novak, Kim 217, 366

Novarro, Ramon 317, 508

Now You See Him, Now You Don't 454, 458

"Nurses, The" (TV) 261

Nuts 154, 156

"O Youth and Beauty" (TV) 576

Oakes, Randi 262, 263–264, 266

Oates, Warren 285, 309, 329, 425

Oberon, Merle 483

Object of Beauty, The 381, 382

O'Brien, Edmond 425

Obsessed with a Married Woman 487

Ocasek, Ric 287, 288

Oceans of Fire 264, 267

Ochs, Bobby 547

O'Connor, Glynnis 252, 300

Odd Couple, The (stage) 320

Odd Jobs 3, 6

Odets, Clifford 166, 379

O'Donnell, Chris 358

Oedipus (stage) 175

Of Mice and Men (stage) 509

Off Limits 122, 125, 272, 274; **123**, **272**

Off Sides 543, 547

"Off We Go" (TV) 292

Officer and a Gentleman, An 169, 173, 553, 616–617, 621, 626; **617**

Official Rocky Scrapbook, The (book) 524

Oh, Brotherhood 261, 266

Oh, Heavenly Dog 486, 489

Oh, Hell (stage) 595–596

Oh! What a Lovely War 484, 489

O'Hara, John 417

O'Hara, Maureen 504

Ojeda, Manuel 560

O'Keefe, Michael 308, 332

Oklahoma! (stage) 532

Oktober-Dage 484, 489

Okumoto, Yuji 628

Old Acquaintance 58

Old Gringo 511–512, 513; **511**

Old Times (stage) 577

Oldest Living Graduate, The (stage) 286

Oldman, Gary 155, 388, 410

Oley, Prof. Claude 441

Olin, Ken 381

Oliver, Jane 328

Oliver, Michael 443

Oliver, Susan 462, 515

Oliver's Story 57, 61, 558

Olivier, Laurence 237, 307

Olmos, Edward James 508

Olsen, Dana 247

Olson, James 398

Oltre la Porta 51

Oltre l'Oceano 595, 597

On Golden Pond 469, 535

"On Location: Rodney Dangerfield—It's Not Easy Bein' Me" (TV) 32

"On Location: The Roseanne Barr Show" (TV) 32

On the Twentieth Century (stage) 338, 343

On the Twentieth Century (album) 343

Onassis: The Richest Man in the World 487, 489

"Once an Eagle" (TV) 216, 221

Once Around 155, 156

Once in a Lifetime (stage) 166, 592, 597

Once Upon a Dead Man 461, 465

Once Upon a Spy 136, 141

Once Upon a Time in America 177, 594, 597, 626, 630

"Once Upon Her Time" (TV) 571

Once We Were Dreamers 386, 388

One and Only Genuine Original Family Band, The 453, 458

One and Only Genuine Original Family Band, The (album) 458

One Flew over the Cuckoo's Nest 323

One Flew over the Cuckoo's Nest (stage) 337

One Good Cop 325, 326, 394

"One Life to Live" (TV) 46, 51, 306, 311, 509, 510

One Million B.C. 362

One More Saturday Night 10, 13

One on One 216, 220

One Summer Love 468, 473

"One Too Many Lives" (TV) 416

One Woman or Two 578, 581

O'Neal, Patrick 3

O'Neal, Ryan 57, 306, 362, 496, 523, 558

O'Neal, Tatum 286, 447

"Onedin Line, The" (TV) 484

O'Neill, Ed 147

O'Neill, Eugene 71, 166, 276, 350

O'Neill, Michael **210**

Onion Field, The 135–136, 141, 625, 630

Only One Survived 333–334, 335

Only Way, The 484, 489

Ono, Yoko 515

Ontkean, Michael 48, 238

Operation Petticoat 114, 118

"Operation Petticoat" (TV) 114, 118

Operation Scotland Yard 227

Operation Undercover 167, 173

Oppenheim, Bruce 496, 497

Oppenheim, Cyrus Zachariah 496

Oppenheim, Molly Ariel 496

"Oprah Winfrey Show, The" (TV) 609, 610, 611, 612, 613

"Oracle, The" (TV) 177

Orbach, Jerry 544

Ordinary Heroes 4, 6

Ordinary People 283, 285, 286, 289, 290; **286**
Ordinary People (book) 285
Original Sin 295, 296
Orphan Train 90, 95
Orpheus Descending (stage) 284
Ortiz, Freddie 479
Osborne, Madolyn Smith 434
Oscar 529, 530
Osmond, Marie 625
Othello (stage) 152, 244, 509
Other, The 437, 443
Other Lover, The 570, 572
Other Side of Midnight, The 468, 473
"Other Side of the Border, The" (TV) 510
Otis, Carré 449
O'Toole, Annette 216, 442
Our Family Business 136, 141
Our Late Night (stage) 201
"Our Man Higgins" (TV) 453
"Our Mutual Friend" (TV) 485, 490
Our Town (stage) 120, 376
Our Winning Season 422, 427
Out 186, 189
Out of Africa 487, 536, 539, 578
"Out of the Blue" (TV) 584
Out of the Past 73, 626
Outlaw Blues 462, 465
Outrageous Fortune 363, 365
Outside Chance 307
Outsiders, The 447, 543, 547
"Outsiders, The" (TV) 543
Over Here! (stage) 550, 556, 592, 597
Over Here! (album) 556, 597
Over the Top 526, 530
Overboard 456, 458
Ovitz, Mike 101
Owen, Sarah Marie 627, 628–629
"Owen Marshall, Counselor at Law" (TV) 550, 567
"Oxbridge Blues" (TV) 471
"Ozzie's Girls" (TV) 251

P.J. 460, 465
Pacific Heights 219–220, 325, 326
Pacino, Al 25, 126, 212, 312, 313, 314, 316, 317, 346, 370, 401, 416, 521, 591; **210, 416**
Package, The 310, 311
Page, Geraldine 193, 255–256, 315, 349, 357, 514, 536
Paget, Debra 614
Pai, Suzee **456**
Paine, Robert Treat 591
Pakula, Alan J. 338, 620
Pale Rider 410

Paley, Grace 24
Palin, Michael 341
Panella, Patricia 269
Paper Chase, The 567, 572
Papp, Joseph 17, 201, 205, 342, 345–346, 397, 401, 434, 532, 535, 564
"Parade of Stars" (TV) 271
Paradise 220, 303, 304
Paradise Alley 525, 529
Paradise Alley (book) 524
Paradise Found 227
Pare, Michael 48, 121
Paretsky, Sara 564
Parisot, Dean 206
Park, Reg 475
Parker, Alan 448
Parker, Corey 596
Parker, Eleanor 136, 413
Parker, Jameson 67, 415
Parker, Julie 505
Parker, Mary-Louise 19, 289
Parks, Larry 69
Parole 23, 26
Parton, Dolly 162, 440, 525, 630
"Partridge Family, The" (TV) 114, 292, 501
"Party, The" (TV) 439
Party at Kitty and Stud's, A 522, 529
Pasdar, Adrian 388, 512
Passage to India, A 92, 347
Passion Flower 66, 68
Passions 570, 572
Pastore, Senator John O. 623
"Pat Sajak Show, The" (TV) 234
Pate, Michael 176
Patinkin, Doris Sinton 396
Patinkin, Gideon 397
Patinkin, Isaac 397
Patinkin, Lester 396
Patinkin, Mandel *see:* Patinkin, Mandy
Patinkin, Mandy 92, 314, 372, 393, 396–403, 434, 536, 537; **400**
Patinkin, Marsha 396
Patric, Jason 411
Patrick, Dennis 467
Patriot for Me, A (stage) 306, 311
Patriot Games 20
Patton, Will 599
Pavarotti, Luciano 577
"Peaceable Kingdom, The" (TV) 571, 573
Peale, Norman Vincent 503
Peck, Gregory 134, 359, 461, 511
Peckinpah, Sam 425
Pecos Bill (album) 590
"Pecos Bill: King of the Cowboys" (TV) 225

"Pee-wee's Playhouse Christmas Special" (TV) 84, 195
Peg (stage) 501
Peggy Sue Got Married 561–562, 565, 618
Penn, Arthur 277
Penn, Christopher "Chris" 405, 410
Penn, Dylan Frances 411
Penn, Eileen Ryan 405, 410
Penn, Leo 405, 406, 409
Penn, Michael 405, 410
Penn, Sean 283, 286, 287, 288, 289, 360, 366, 368, 369–370, 371, 393, 405–412, 531, 598, 601, 619; **369, 408**
Penny, Joe 327, 331
Pentland, Bill 30, 32, 33, 34, 35, 211
Pentland, Jake 30, 35
Pentland, Jennifer 30, 35
Pentland, Jessica 30, 34, 35
People Need People (stage) 150
Peppard, George 460, 462
Perfect 116, 118, 554, 556; **116**
Perfect People 332, 334
Perkins, Elizabeth 50, 131
Perkins, Maxwell 327
Perkins, Tony 72
Perlman, Ron 334
Perrine, Valerie 224
Perry, John Bennett 440
"Perry Como's Easter in Guadalajara" (TV) 293
Perry Mason: The Case of the Murdered Madam 294–295, 296
Pesci, Joe 179
Peter and the Wolf (stage) 188, 465
"Peter Rabbit and Mr. Jermey Fisher" (TV) 538
Peters, Bernadette 321, 399, 403
Peters, Jon 42, 324, 417, 489
Petersen, William 519
Petersen, Wolfgang 50
Petrie, Daniel J. 243
"Petrocelli" (TV) 438
"Peyton Place" (TV) 150
Pfeiffer, Dedee 419
Pfeiffer, Donna 413
Pfeiffer, Lori 419
Pfeiffer, Michelle 18, 26, 39, 74, 83, 94, 179, 203, 205, 273, 323, 372, 380, 413–420, 457, 470, 487, 620; **416**
Pfeiffer, Richard 413
Phantom of the Opera (1983) 486, 489
Phantom of the Opera (stage) 400
Phantom of the Paradise 515, 520

"Phil Collins" (TV) 12
"Phil Donahue Show, The" (TV) 609
Phillips, Chynna 333
Phoenix, River 2, 348–349
"Phyllis" (TV) 438
Piaf, Edith 460
Picnic (stage) 264, 495
"Picnic" (TV) 264
Picnic at Hanging Rock 176
"Piece of God, A" (TV) 550
Pierpoint, Eric 401
Pin Cushion 85
Pinchot, Bronson 163
Pintauro, Danny 144
Pinter, Harold 376, 378, 535, 554
Pinza, Ezio 400
Pippin (stage) 192, 199
Pirandello, Luigi 89
Pirates of Penzance, The 339, 343
Pirates of Penzance, The (stage) 81, 338, 343, 593, 597
Pirates of Penzance, The (album) 343
Piscopo, Joe 595
Pisier, Marie-France 468
Place, Mary Kay 91
"Place at the Table, A" (TV) 184
Places in the Heart 161, 164, 171, 177, 184, 189, 357, 377–378, 382, 518; **378**
Planer, Geoffrey 484, 485
Platoon 45, 49, 50, 51, 100–101, 121, 122, 125, 600
Platt, Polly 492
Play It Again, Sam 314, 319
Play It Again, Sam (stage) 313, 318
Playboy of Seville, The (stage) 532
Players 223, 228
Playground in the Fall (stage) 415
Pleasence, Donald 455
Plenty 536, 539
Pleshette, Suzanne 47, 614
Plimpton, Martha 309
Plowright, Joan 281, 341
Poe, Edgar Allan 523, 528
Point Break 547
Pointer Sisters, The 31, 196
"Pointer Sisters ('Pointers on L.A. Nightlife')" (TV) 196
Poitier, Sidney 49, 186, 608
Polanski, Roman 56
Police Academy 224, 228
Police Academy 2: Their First Assignment 224, 228
Police Academy 3: Back in Training 225, 228
Police Academy 4: Citizens on Patrol 225, 228
"Police Story" (TV) 223, 251, 299, 454, 523, 571

Police Story: Burnout 571, 572
"Police Woman" (TV) 63, 251, 502, 615
Pollack, Sydney 531
Poor Clare 328, 334
Pop, Iggy 124
Pope of Greenwich Village, The 447, 451; **446**
Popeye 585, 589
Popeye (album) 590
"Popular Neurotics" (TV) 203
Popwell, Albert 252
Porter, Cole 198
Posse, The 232
Possession of Joel Delaney, The 328, 334
Post, Markie 441, 511
Postcards from the Edge 155, 426, 427, 531, 538–539, 540
Postman Always Rings Twice, The (1946) 354
Postman Always Rings Twice, The (1981) 41, 354–355, 359
"Postpartum: Beyond the Blues" (TV) 471
Potter, Madeleine 432
Potts, Annie 74, 498
Potts, Cliff 485
Pouget, Ely 410
Powell, Jane 2
Power 170, 173
Power, Tyrone 165, 257, 305, 392
Powers, Alexandra 265
Powers, Stefanie 59
Pratt, Robert 462
Pray TV 439, 443
Prayer for the Dying, A 448, 451
Predator 479, 482
Predator 2 188, 189
Prelude to a Kiss 20, 21
Prelude to a Kiss (stage) 19, 227, 228, 289, 290
Prentiss, Paula 625
Preppie Murder, The 20
Present Laughter (stage) 347, 351
Presidio, The 255, 258
Presley, Elvis 300, 319, 453, 459, 492, 541, 549
Pressman, Lawrence 261
Presson, Jason 92
Preston, Kelly 480, 556
Presumed Innocent 102
Pretty Baby 58, 468–469, 473
Pretty Maids All in a Row 492
Pretty Woman 171–172, 173, 539
Pretty Woman (album) 172
Pride of the Marines 4–5
Primary English Class, The (stage) 314
Prime Cut 515, 520

Prince 20, 42
Prince, Harold "Hal" 89, 338, 398
Prince of Bel-Air 254, 257
Prince of the City 553, 591, 593, 597, 605
Prince of Tides 102
Princess and the Cabbie, The 362, 365
Princess Bride, The 109, 112, 403; **400**
Princess Daisy 569, 572
"Princess Who Never Laughed, The" (TV) 24
"Prism" (TV) 570
Prison for Children 440, 443
Prisoner (album) 87
Prisoner of Second Avenue, The 523, 529
Private Conversations 378, 382
Private Sessions 384–385, 388
Prizzi's Honor 565; **561**
Probe 501, 506
Problem Child 442, 443
Problem Child II 443
Prochnow, Jurgen 59
Prom Night 115, 118
Promise 627, 630
Promise, The (stage) 260, 337
Promise of Love, The 362, 365
Proud and the Free, The 155, 156
Pryor, Rain 198
Pryor, Richard 270, 271
"Pryor's Place" (TV) 440
Psycho 114
Psychocalisthenics with Lindsay Wagner 570
Public Enemy 234
Pugh, Willard 610
Pumping Iron 476, 482
Pumping Iron: The Art and Sport of Bodybuilding (book) 476
Punchline 162, 164, 208, 211, 214, 247, 248
Purcell, Lee 257
Pure Luck 189
Purlie Victorious (stage) 230, 509
Purple Rain 42
Purple Rose of Cairo, The 129, 131, 322
Pursuit of D. B. Cooper, The 593, 597
"Puss in Boots" (TV) 272
Puzo, Mario 313

Q & A 289, 290
Quadrille 494
Quaid, Dennis 18, 24, 83, 101, 155, 209, 210, 211, 212, 288, 321, 358, 421–427; **425**
Quaid, Nita 421, 422

Quaid, Randy 74, 394, 421–422, 423, 424, 426, 550
Quaid, William "Buddy" 421, 422
"Quantum Leap" (TV) 309
Quarterback Princess 138, 141
"Queen of the Beasts, The" (TV) 571
Queens Logic 118, 381, 382
Quest, The 454, 458
"Quest, The" (TV) 331, 335, 454, 458
Quick (book) 394
Quick Change 394, 395
Quigley, Lee 430
Quigley, Linnea 113
"Quincy, M.E." (TV) 114
Quinlan, Kathleen 115, 422
Quinn, Aidan 50, 122, 599
Quinn, Anthony 55, 102, 508, 555

Rabal, Francisco 280, 288
Rabbit Test 108, 112
Rabe, David 279, 369, 408, 577
Raboy, Marc 563
Race for the Double Helix, The 205, 207
"Race to Save the Planet" (TV) 539, 540
Racing with the Moon 407, 411
Radio Days 130, 133, 316, 318
Radio Flyer 248, 249, 620
Radner, Gilda 8, 28, 108, 361, 390, 391, 401
Rae, Charlotte 592
Rafelson, Bob 354, 618
Raffin, Deborah 484
Rage in Harlem, A 189, 273, 274
Rage of Angels 503, 505, 506
Rage of Angels: The Story Continues 504, 507
Raggedy Man 517, 520
Ragtime 128, 133, 398, 403
Raid on Entebbe 624, 630
Raiders of the Lost Ark 616
Railroad Bill (stage) 599
Railsback, Steve 300
Rain (stage) 522, 550
Rain, Jeramie *see:* Dreyfuss, Jeramie Rain
Rain Man 123, 247, 280
Rainbo 515
"Rainbow Girl, The" (TV) 293
Raines, Cristina 253
Rainmaker, The (stage) 160
"Rainmaker, The" (TV) 308
"Raisin in the Sun, A" (TV) 186
Raising Arizona 101, 210, 213, 214
Raitt, Bonnie 426
Rake's Progress, The (stage) 298

Ralph, Sheryl Lee 155
Ralston, Vera Hruba 413
"Rambo and the Force of Freedom" (TV) 527
Rambo: First Blood Part II 526, 529
Rambo III 527, 530
Rambo IV 528
Ramis, Harold 9, 11, 390, 392, 578
Rampling, Charlotte 579
Rancho Deluxe 71–72, 76
Randall, Tony 543
Randall & Juliet 155
Randolph, John 227
Ransom, Tim 512
Rape and Marriage—The Rideout Case 445, 451
Raposo, Joe 94
"Rapunzel" (TV) 73
Ratzenberger, John 197
Raw Deal 478–479, 482
"Ray Bradbury Theatre" (TV) 204
Raye, Martha 28
Razorback 263, 267
Razor's Edge, The (1946) 392
Razor's Edge, The (1984) 392, 393, 395
Read, James 544
Reagan, Nancy Davis 301, 619
Reagan, Patti 286
Reagan, Ronald 331, 477
"Real Ghostbusters, The" (TV) 235
Real Inspector Hound, The (stage) 135
Real Men 440–441, 443
Real Thing, The (stage) 88, 92, 96
Reality . . . What a Concept (album) 584, 590
Rear Window 217
"Reasonable Doubts" (TV) 257, 258
Rebel 529
Rebel Without a Cause (stage) 352
Rebel Women (stage) 397
Rebels, The 300, 304
Red Dawn 543–544, 547; *543*
Red Heat (1988) 479, 482
"Red, Hot & Blue" (TV) 172, 198
Red River (1948) 264
Red River (1988) 66, 68, 264–265, 267
Red Sonja 478, 482, 526
Redford, Robert 42, 47, 92, 218, 275, 285, 286, 393, 430, 468, 536, 618, 649
Redgrave, Lynn 202
Redgrave, Vanessa 432
Redgrave, Wendy 432
Redmond, Marge 158

Reds 315, 318
Reed, Donna 41, 262
Reed, Jerry 406
Reed, Oliver 56
Reed, Pamela 281
Rees, Roger 139
Reeve, Barbara Johnson 428, 429
Reeve, Benjamin 428
Reeve, Christopher 127, 179, 255, 280, 349, 401, 428–435, 472, 479, 481, 486, 562, 583, 586; **433**
Reeve, Franklin 428, 429
Reeves, Alexandra 431
Reeves, George 430
Reeves, Keanu 281, 341, 547
Reeves, Matthew 431
Reeves, Steve 475
Regalbuto, Joe 60
Rehearsal for Murder 202, 207
Reiner, Carl 150, 163, 194, 197, 560, 587
Reiner, Rob 107, 108, 110, 111, 150, 154, 396, 400–401
Reinhold, Judge 121
Reinking, Ann 542
Reiser, Paul 3
Reitman, Ivan 390, 391, 393, 481, 579, 618
Remember My Name 201, 207
Remick, Lee 136, 262, 400
Renegades, The 543, 547
"Renegades, The" (TV) 543, 549
"Report to Murphy" (TV) 321, 326
Report to the Commissioner 167, 173
Reporters, The 169, 173
"Reporters, The" (TV) 387
Reservations (book) 315
Respectful Prostitute, The (stage) 158
Return, The 494, 499
Return of Mickey Spillane's Mike Hammer, The 66, 68
"Return of the Bionic Woman, The" (TV) 568
Return of the Rebels 542, 547
Return of the Six Million Dollar Man and the Bionic Woman 570, 572
Return to Macon County 299, 304
Returning Napoleon 498, 499
Reuben, Reuben 384, 388
Revenge 102, 105
Revenge of the Nerds 209, 214
Revenge of the Stepford Wives, The 300, 304
Revere, Anne 151
Reversal of Fortune 94–95, 96

Rex (stage) 90, 96
Rex (album) 96
Reynolds, Burt 42, 58, 59, 160, 161, 170, 433, 437, 494, 505, 506, 523, 562
Reynolds, Kevin 104
Reynolds, Ramona 567
Rhapsody in August 172, 173
Rhinestone 525–526, 529
Rhinestone (album) 530
"Rhoda" (TV) 438
Rice, Tim 397
Rich, Allan 355
Rich, John 3, 5
Rich and Famous 58, 61
"Richard Pryor Show, The" (TV) 584, 589
Richard II (stage) 277
Richard III (stage) 339
Richards, Lloyd 23
Richardson, Natasha 206
Richardson, Tony 310, 629
Richmond, Anthony "Tony" 503, 504, 505
Richmond, Gaston Anthony 503, 506
Richmond, Spencer-Margaret 503, 506
Richter, W. D. 203
Rickman, Alan 380, 602
Rickman, Tom 309
Ricochet 572, 573
Rider, Alan 567
Rieffel, Lisa 295
Riegert, Peter 294
Right Stuff, The 202–203, 207, 423, 427
Righteous Brothers, The 78
Riley, John 262
"Riptide" (TV) 327, 331–332, 334, 335; **331**
Ritt, Martin 160, 161, 162, 308
Ritter, Dorothy Fay Southworth 436, 437, 438
Ritter, Jason 439
Ritter, John 118, 140, 197, 241, 435–443, 543; **439**
Ritter, Maurice Woodward *see:* Ritter, Tex
Ritter, Nancy 438, 439
Ritter, Tex 436, 437–438
Ritter, Thomas 436, 438
Ritter, Tyler 439
Ritz, The 592, 597
Ritz, The (stage) 550
River, The 162, 171, 177, 181, 377, 518, 520; **178**
River Rat, The 309, 310
Rivera, Chita 399
Rivera, Geraldo 601

Rivera, Sherry 601
Rivers, Joan 108, 111, 231, 614
Road Games 115, 118
Road House 545, 547
Road Raiders, The 66, 68
Road Show 85, 287, 618
Road to Immortality, The (stage) 122
Road Warrior, The 176, 181
Roadhouse 66 121, 125
Roadrunners, The 313
Roar 220
Robards, Jason 224, 239, 260
Robber Bridegroom, The (stage) 209, 337
Robbins, Harold 56, 501
Robbins, Jack Henry 471
Robbins, Tim 104, 471, 472, 588, 618
Roberts, Eric 379, 447; **446**
Roberts, Julia 43, 162, 163, 172, 413
Roberts, Pernell 261
Roberts, Rachel 415
Roberts, Tony 313
Robin Hood: Prince of Thieves 104, 105
Robin Williams Live (stage) 586
"Robin Williams: Off the Wall" (TV) 585
Robinette, Dale 40
Robinson, Bill "Bojangles" 268
Robinson, Tracy 145
Robocop 481, 539
Robocop 2 197, 546
Rockabye 509, 513
"Rocket to the Moon" (TV) 379
Rockford Files, The 567, 572
Rocky 143, 523–524, 529; **524**
Rocky (book) 524
Rocky II 525, 529
Rocky III 525, 529
Rocky III (album) 530
Rocky IV 526, 529
Rocky V 528–529, 530
Rocky Horror Picture Show, The 468, 472, 473
Rocky Horror Picture Show, The (album) 473
Roddenberry, Gene 195
Rodgers, Richard 90
Roe Vs. Wade 488
Rogers, Earl 596
Rogers, Kenny 64, 66, 300
Rogers, Mimi 93, 257, 441
Rogers, Wayne 261
Roland, Gilbert 508
Rolle, Esther 186, 198
Roller Boogie 81, 86
Roller Boogie (album) 87

Rollercoaster 223, 228
"Rolling Stone: The 10th Anniversary" (TV) 517
Rolling Thunder 307, 310
Rollins, Howard E. 128
Romancing the Stone 470, 560, 561, 565
Romero, George 289
Romero, Cesar 293
Rona Jaffe's "Mazes and Monsters" 245, 248
Ronettes, The 78
"Ronnie and Nancy Show, The" (TV) 600
Ronstadt, Linda 338, 339
"Rookies, The" (TV) 299, 501, 515, 550
"Room 222" (TV) 150
Rooney, Ann 293
Rooney, Mickey 292, 423
"Ropers, The" (TV) 439
Rose, George 152
Rose, Jamie 439
Rose and the Jackal, The 434, 435
Rose Tattoo, The (stage) 46, 89–90
"Roseanne" (TV) 32, 33, 34, 35, 36, 37, 38, 211–212, 213, 214, 604; **33**
"Roseanne Barr Live from Trump Castle" (TV) 37
Roseanne: My Life as a Woman (book) 34
Rosen, Gary 206
Rosenberg, Ethel 287, 398
Rosenberg, Julius 287, 398
Rosenberg, Stuart 178
Rosencrantz and Guildenstern Are Dead 155, 156
Rosencrantz and Guildenstern Are Dead (stage) 166, 376
Rosenzweig, Barney 486
Ross, Diana 171
Rossellini, Isabella 139
Rossilli, Paul 486
Roth, Tim 155
Rourke, Mickey 23, 25, 43, 222, 224, 373, 425, 444–451, 527, 594, 598; **25, 446**
Rourke, Philip Andre, Jr. *see:* Rourke, Mickey
Routes 1 & 9 (stage) 120
Rover, The (stage) 433
Roving Boy 102
Rowlands, Gena 155, 470, 495
Roxanne: The Prize Pulitzer 333, 335
"Roy Orbison Tribute" (TV) 546
Rubini, Michel 342
Rubinstein, John 464
Rudolph, Alan 50, 516

Rules of the Game, The (stage) 89, 96
Rumble Fish 410, 447, 451
Rumor of War, A 128, 133
Rumpelstiltskin (stage) 98
"Runaway, The" (TV) 615
Runner Stumbles, The (stage) 277
Running Man, The 178, 432, 479, 482
Running on Empty 348–349, 351
Running Scared 109, 112, 272, 274, 509, 513, 554
Runyon, Damon 371
Rush, Barbara 501
Russell, Bing Oliver 452, 454, 455
Russell, Boston 455
Russell, Bryan 452
Russell, Jamie 452
Russell, Jane 413
Russell, Jill 452
Russell, Jody 452
Russell, Ken 277, 560
Russell, Kurt 179, 300, 303, 347, 387, 389, 417, 452–458, 527, 541, 586, 626; **456**
Russell, Louise "Lulu" Julia Crone 452
Russell, Nipsey 230
Russell, Pee Wee 106
Russell, Rosalind 460, 580
Russell, Theresa 83, 256, 619
Russia House, The 419, 420
Russicum i Gironi del Diavolo 595, 597
Rustlers' Rhapsody 48, 51
Ruthless People 369
Ryan, Meg 60, 110, 197, 206, 247, 255, 424, 425, 426; **110**
Ryan, Mitchell 502
Ryder, Winona 85, 132
Ryerson, Ann 360, 361

S.O.S. Titanic 463, 465
SST—Death Flight 108, 112
Sabrina Fair (stage) 55
Sacks, Dr. Oliver 588
Safe at Home 452
"Saga of a Star World" (TV) 485
Sahl, Mort 392
Sahlins, Bernie 361
Saint, Eva Marie 397, 437
"St. Elsewhere" (TV) 253, 254, 258
St. Ives 201, 207
Saint James, Susan 354, 424, 459–465, 572; **461**
Saint-Saëns Carnival of the Animals 95
St. Thomas Boys' Choir 402
Sajak, Pat 232

Salkind, Alexander 430, 435
Salkind, Ilya 430, 435
Sally Field (album) 158, 164
"Sally Field Show, The" (TV) 159
"Sally Jessy Raphaël Show, The" (TV) 36
Salt, Jennifer 263
Salvador 622, 626–627, 630
"Sam" (TV) 252, 258
"Samantha" (TV) 146
Sambora, Richie 84
Samms, Emma 231
Samuels, Ron 568
"San Pedro Beach Bums" (TV) 502
Sand, Paul 151
Sand Pebbles, The 54, 55, 58, 61
Sanders, George 79
Sands, Julian 388
"SantaBear's First Christmas" (TV) 386
SantaBear's First Christmas (album) 388
"SantaBear's Highflying Adventure" (TV) 380, 386
Sarah Plain and Tall 95, 96
Sarandon, Chris 346, 466, 467, 469, 570
Sarandon, Susan 58, 83, 101, 104, 120, 131, 153, 302, 417, 466–473, 619; **467**
"Sarge" (TV) 299, 567
Sarkisian, Cherilyn *see:* Cher
Sarkisian, Georgia *see:* Holt, Georgia
Sarkisian, Jan 353
Sarkisian, John 77
Saroyan, William 338
Saturday Night Fever 525, 549, 551–552, 554, 555, 556
"Saturday Night Live" (TV) 7, 8, 11, 13, 19, 57, 106, 107, 109, 112, 180, 212, 218–219, 246, 255, 369, 380, 389, 390, 391, 392, 401, 463, 464, 516, 547, 563, 587, 603
"Saturday Night Live 15th Anniversary" (TV) 11, 393
"Saturday Night Live with Howard Cosell" (TV) 107, 390
"Saturday's Child" (TV) 550
Savage, John 136
Savage Islands 310
Savages (stage) 397
Savalas, Telly 159, 505
Saved (stage) 624
Sawyer, Diane 59
Scacchi, Greta 50, 513
Scalia, Jack 202, 444, 570
Scandalous John 437, 443

"Scandals" (TV) 571
"Scarecrow and Mrs. King" (TV) 65–66, 68; **65**
Scarface (1983) 416, 419; **416**
Scarlet Pimpernel, The (1982) 486, 489
Scavenger Hunt 477, 482
Scenes and Revelations (stage) 346, 351
Schaffer, Peter 197–198
Schechner, Richard 120
Scheider, Roy 152, 354, 392, 400, 535
Schein, David 192
Schell, Maximilian 306, 486
Schepisi, Fred 537
Schiebel, Diana 281
Schiller, Tom 392
Schlamme, Thomas 347, 349, 350, 351
Schlamme, Wilson 349, 350, 351
Schlatter, George 583
Schlesinger, John 315, 325
Schmidt, Michael 84
Schneider, Alan 338
Schneider, Bert 57
School for Scandal, The (stage) 337
"Schoolbreak Special" (TV) 195, 317
Schrader, Paul 168
Schroder, Rick 569
Schulman, Tom 394
Schuman, William 388
Schwarzenegger, Arnold 72, 188, 432, 434, 474–482, 525, 527, 580; **480**
Schwarzenegger, Aurelia 474, 477
Schwarzenegger, Gustav 474, 475, 477
Schwarzenegger, Meinhard 474, 477
Schwarzenegger, Peter Knapp 480
Schygulla, Hanna 17
Scofield, Paul 95, 180
Scolari, Peter 245
"Scooby-Doo Where Are You" (TV) 292
Score (stage) 522
Scorsese, Martin 107, 122, 359, 494
Scott, Campbell 163, 380–381
Scott, George C. 347
Scott, Lizabeth 413, 557
Scott, Ridley 576
Scott, Tony 102, 526
Scott, Zachary 253
Scott Free 462, 465
Scrooged 393, 395
"Scruples" (TV) 568–569, 573
Scudder, Susan 15

Sea Gull, The (stage) 385
Sea Horse, The (stage) 376
"Sea Hunt" (TV) 70
Sea of Love 25, 27, 212, 214; **210**
"Sea World Summer Night Magic" (TV) 295
"Sea World's All-Star Celebration" (TV) 505
Seacat, Sandra 445
"Sealab 2020" (TV) 292, 296
Seales, Franklyn 136
"Search" (TV) 501
Search and Destroy 331, 334
Search for the Gods 454, 458
"Search for Tomorrow" (TV) 23, 27, 338, 343, 467, 473
"Second Annual American Comedy Awards" (TV) 194–195
"Second Annual Circus of the Stars, The" (TV) 114, 462
"Second City 25th Anniversary Special" (TV) 363
Second Coming of Suzanne, The 151, 156
Second Wind 568, 572
Secret Garden, The (stage) 403
Secret Service (stage) 533, 540
"Secret Service" (TV) 533
"Secret Tragedy, A" (story) 480
"Secret World of the Very Young, The" (TV) 440
Secrets of a Married Man 495, 499
"Secrets of Midland Heights" (TV) 252
"Secrets Women Never Share" (TV) 364
Seduced 264, 267, 496, 499; **263**
Seduction of Joe Tynan, The 535, 539
See You in the Morning 74, 76
Sefano, Joey 474
Segal, George 45, 463
Seidelman, Susan 368
"Seize the Day" (TV) 586
Selassie, Haile 57
Self Portrait (book) 503
Sellecca, Connie 147, 440
Selleck, Tom 134, 139, 140, 226, 266, 406, 487, 488, 609
Sellers, Peter 197, 436
Seltzer, David 243
Selznick, Joyce 293
Seniors, The 422, 427
"Sensational, Shocking, Wonderful, Wacky '70s, The" (TV) 315
Sentimental Journey (1984) 503–504, 506
Sentinel, The 46, 51, 201, 207
September, September 496, 498
Sgt. Rock 481, 605

Serious Money (stage) 17, 21
Serpent, The (stage) 383
"Sesame Street" (TV) 117
"Sesame Street Remembers Joe Raposo" (TV) 94
Session, The 150
"Set Up for Romance" (TV) 253
Settle the Score 505, 507
Seurat, Georges 399
Seven Brides for Seven Brothers 2
"Seven Brides for Seven Brothers" (TV) 2, 6, 415
1776 (stage) 209
"Seventh Annual MTV Music Video Awards" (TV) 234
"Seventh Avenue" (TV) 485, 490
"75th Anniversary of Beverly Hills, The" (TV) 195
Severance, Joan 435
Severence 269
Sex and the Single Parent 463, 465
Seymour, Danny 353
Seymour, Jane 64, 266, 431, 483–490, 566; **486**
Shadow Box, The (stage) 397, 403
Shadow of a Doubt (1942) 257
Shadow of a Doubt (1991) 257, 258
Shadows and Fog 373, 374, 381, 382
Shadows Run Black 98, 105
Shakedown on the Sunset Strip 332, 334
Shakespeare, William 339
Shakespeare Wallah 329
Shame of the Jungle 391, 395
Shane 107
Shange, Ntozake 188
Shanghai Surprise 369, 374, 408–409, 411; **369**
Shapiro, Esther 3
Shapiro, Mel 201
Shapiro, Richard 3
Sharif, Omar 64
Sharkey, Ray 329, 444, 537
Sharp, Thom 231
Shatner, William 550
"Shatterday" (TV) 600
Shattered 50, 51
Shattered Dreams 571, 573
Shaud, Grant 60
Shaw, George Bernard 151, 339, 345
She-Devil 33–34, 38, 85, 531, 538, 540
She Stoops to Conquer (stage) 337
Shea, John 64, 386, 517
Shearer, Norma 88
Sheedy, Ally 595
Sheen, Charlie 50, 544

Sheen, Martin 197, 206, 397, 510, 516
Sheldon, Sidney 48, 503, 504
"Shelley Duvall's Tall Tales & Legends" (TV) 116
Sheltering Sky, The 380–381, 382, 620, 621
Shenar, Paul 627
Shepard, Hannah 357
Shepard, Sam 42, 167, 183, 316, 355, 356–357, 358, 359, 376, 377, 423, 424, 517, 519, 599
Shepard, Samuel 357
Shepherd, Cybill 20, 74, 254, 264, 316, 491–499, 600, 601; **263, 493**
Shepherd, Patty Shobe 491, 496
Shepherd, William "Bill" Jennings 491
Sher, Richard 609
Sheridan, Jim 50
Sheridan, Nicollette 240, 241, 242
"Sheriff and the Astronaut, The" (TV) 16
Sherlock, Jr. 129
Sherwood, Madeleine 158
She's Da Lovely 411
She's Having a Baby 17, 21
She's in the Army Now 115, 118, 217, 220
She's Out of Control 146, 148
Sheslow, Stuart 143
Shields, Brooke 58, 232, 468
"Shindig" (TV) 79
Shining Through 220, 282, 620
Shining Through (book) 620
Shink, Heidi 84
"Shirley MacLaine's Illusions" (TV) 271
Shoot the Moon 128, 315, 318
Shoot to Kill 49, 51
Shore, Dinah 230
Shore, Mitzi 31
Short, Bobby 270
Short, Martin 189, 273, 389, 424
Short Circuit 225, 228
Short Circuit II 225
Shortchanged Review, The (stage) 127
Shot in the Dark, A (stage) 495
Shout 555, 556
Shout Across the River (stage) 23
Shout and Twist (stage) 117
Shriver, Eunice Kennedy 476
Shriver, Katherine Eunice 480
Shriver, Maria 476, 478, 480
Shue, Elisabeth 342
Shukovsky, Joel 59
Shulman, Debra 292
Siesta 25, 27

Signature (stage) 350
Significant Other 620
Sikes, Cynthia 132
Silbermann, Judge Jacqueline 281
Silence of the Lambs, The 419
Silent Night, Lonely Night 70, 75
Silkwood 81, 455, 457, 458, 535–536, 539, 626
Silva, Cindy 98
Silver, Ron 472, 498
"Silver Anniversary Celebration" (TV) 439
Silver Bears 494, 499
Silverado 100, 101, 104, 185, 189, 203–204, 207, 339, 343
Silverman, Fred 438
Silvers, Phil 223
Silvinha *see:* Martins, Sylvia
Simmons, Gene 81
Simon, Neil 20, 314, 493
Simpson, Charlotte 580
Simpson, Jim 577, 578
Simpson, Wallis 487
Sims, Sandman 268, 273
Sinatra, Frank 273, 599
Sinbad and the Eye of the Tiger 485, 489
Singer, Marc 569
Single Bars, Single Women 145, 148, 347, 351
Singular Life of Albert Nobbs, The (stage) 91
Sinise, Gary 376, 380
Six Characters in Search of an Author (stage) 384
"Six Million Dollar Man, The" (TV) 40, 568
Six Pack 300–301, 304
Six-Pack Annie 63, 68
Sizwe Bansi Is Dead (stage) 183
Sizzle Beach, U.S.A. 104
Skatetown, U.S.A. 542, 547
Ski Lift to Death 300, 304
Skin Deep 441, 443
Skin of Our Teeth, The (stage) 150
Skolimowski, Jerzy 289
Slab Boys, The (stage) 407, 412
Slater, Christian 104
Slaughterhouse-Five 328, 334
Sleeper 314, 318
"Sleeping Beauty" (TV) 432
Sleeping with the Enemy 43
Slumber Party '57 615, 621
Slyde, Jimmy 273
Small Circle of Friends, A 361, 365
Smash Up on Interstate 5 307, 310
Smile 216, 220
Smith, Alexis 16
Smith, Frank 497
Smith, Jack 500

Smith, Jacklyn 333, 483, 500–507, 566; **505**
Smith, Kate 28
Smith, Madolyn 48
Smith, Maggie 237, 534, 564
Smith, Margaret Ellen 50
Smith, Martin Cruz 278
Smith, Thomas "Tommy" 500
Smith, Todd 624
Smits, Barbara 509, 510
Smits, Emelina 508, 509
Smits, Jimmy 26, 239, 272, 334, 508–513; **511**
Smits, Joaquin 509, 510
Smits, Taina 509, 510
Smokey and the Bandit 160, 164
Smokey and the Bandit II 160, 164
Smoky Mountain Christmas, A 440, 443
Smolinski, Aaron 430
Smooth Talk 594, 597
Smothers, Tom 494
Snodgress, Carrie 485
Snyder, Allan "Whitey" 41
"So Nice to Come Home To" (TV) 564
"Soap" (TV) 108, 112, 322
Soapdish 163, 164, 197, 199, 342, 343
Social Change and the Fruits of Culture (stage) 188
Soggy Bottom U.S.A. 300, 304
Soldier Blue 56, 61
Soles, P. J. 422, 423, 424
"Solid Gold" (TV) 231, 235
Solitary Man, The 414, 419
Some Like It Hot 325
Some Men Need Help (stage) 594
"Some Men Need Help" (TV) 594
Somebody Killed Her Husband 72
Someone to Watch Over Me 45, 49, 51, 510
Somers, Suzanne 59, 64, 438
"Somerset" (TV) 135, 141, 575, 581
Something About Amelia 91, 95, 138, 141
Something About the Sting 593, 597
Something for Joey 223, 228
Something Short of Paradise 469, 473
Something Wild 130, 133, 217–218, 220
Somewhere in Time 431, 435, 486, 489; **486**
Sommer, Josef 342
Sondheim, Stephen 77, 396, 399
Sonny and Cher 77, 78, 79, 80, 86–87

"Sonny and Cher Comedy Hour, The" (TV) 80, 86
Sonny and Cher Live (album) 87
Sonny and Cher Live in Las Vegas, Vol. 2 (album) 87
Sonny Side of Cher, The (album) 87
Soon (stage) 166
Sophie's Choice 338–339, 343, 355, 356, 518, 535, 539, 593, 617, 626
Sophisticated Ladies (stage) 270, 274
Sophisticated Ladies (album) 274
"Sorrows of Gin, The" (TV) 576
"Sorting It Out" (TV) 361, 365
Souffle au Coeur, Le 58
Sounds of Murphy Brown, The (album) 60, 61
Soutendijk, Renee 273
Souter, David 497
South Pacific (stage) 142, 400
South Pacific (album) 403
Southall, Georgeanne 77
Southall, John 77
"Space" (TV) 238
Spacek, Ed 514
Spacek, Edwin 514
Spacek, Mary Elizabeth *see:* Spacek, Sissy 514
Spacek, Robert "Robbie" 514, 515
Spacek, Sissy 130, 161, 177, 197, 277, 308, 316, 340, 357, 358, 514–520, 551, 616; **178, 518**
Spacek, Virginia 514
Spade, Ariane 572
Spader, James 403, 472
"Sparrow" (TV) 397
Special Delivery 201, 207, 494, 499
Special Kind of Love, A 615, 621
Special Olympics 615, 621
Spector, Phil 78
Speed-the-Plow (stage) 370
Spelling, Aaron 332
Spielberg, Steven 9, 100, 131, 151, 154, 185, 193, 212, 213, 279, 363, 379, 445, 589, 592, 609, 616
Spies Like Us 10, 12
Spiner, Brent 195–196
Spittin' in the Wind 257, 258
"Spitting Image" (TV) 600
Splash 245–246, 248, 322, 554; **245**
Splash, Too 246
Splendor in the Grass (1981) 415, 419
Split (stage) 397
Split Image 626, 630
Spook Show, The (stage) 192
"Sporting Chance" (TV) 67

"Sportworld" (TV) 145
Spottiswoode, Roger 247
Springfield, Rick 179
Springsteen, Pamela 406
Square One (stage) 402
Squeeze, The 322, 326; **323**
Stack, Robert 247, 461, 543
Stacking 348, 351
Stacy, James 334
Stacy's Knights 99, 104
Stairway to Heaven 553
Stakeout 154, 155, 156, 322, 601
Stallone, Frank 521, 522
Stallone, Frank, Jr. 521
Stallone, Jacqueline LaBeau 84, 521, 522, 523
Stallone, Sage Moonblood 523, 529
Stallone, Sasha 522, 523, 526
Stallone, Sergeoh Joseph 525
Stallone, Sylvester 327, 328–329, 430, 457, 474, 478, 480, 521–530, 535, 553–554, 569, 580; **524, 569**
Stand by Me 154, 156
Stand-In, The 184–185, 189
Stangata Napoletana—La Trastola 593, 597
Stanley, Kim 355
Stanwyck, Barbara 291, 483, 557, 559
Stapleton, Jean 196, 198, 437
Stapleton, Maureen 315
Star Maker, The 217, 220
"Star Trek: The Next Generation" (TV) 195
Starke, Annie Maude 93
Starke, John 91, 93
Starman 73, 76
Starpower: An Astrological Guide to Supersuccess (book) 527
Starr, Ringo 362
Stars (album) 87
"Starsky and Hutch" (TV) 40, 216, 438
Starting Over 52, 58, 61
State of Grace 410–411, 412
Status Quo Vadis (stage) 63, 68, 135, 141
Stay Hungry 72, 76, 159, 164, 476, 482
Staying Alive 525, 529, 553–554, 556
Stealing Home 255, 258
Steel, Alan 475
Steel, Dawn 629
Steel Cowboy 217, 220
Steel Dawn 545, 547
Steel Magnolias 162–163, 164
"Steel Magnolias" (TV) 163

Steenburgen, Mary 132, 349, 354, 398
Steiger, Rod 341
Stein, Seymour 368
Stella 212, 214
Stephen King's It 443
Stern, Daniel 23, 111
"Steve Martin's Best Show Ever" (TV) 9
Stevens, Andrew 224, 300
Stevens, Fisher 418
Stewart, James 454, 544
Stewart, Marlene 84
Stick 59, 61
Stigwood, Robert 551, 604
Still Life (book) 315
Still of the Night 535, 539
Stills, Stephen 463
Sting 218, 562
Sting, The 49
Stockwell, Dean 18, 197, 309
Stoltz, Eric 82, 204
Stone, Oliver 18, 49, 100–101, 121, 123, 125, 263, 401, 410, 447, 537, 545, 626
Stone, Robert 564
Stone, Sharon 481
Stone Boy, The 91–92, 95
Stone Killer, The 437, 443
Stones for Ibarra 93, 96
Stoppard, Tom 135
Stormy Monday 218, 220, 309, 311
Story of a Teenager 260
Story of David, The 484, 485, 489
"Storybook Classics" (TV) 187, 188
Stowe, Madeleine 104, 256; **256**
Straight Talk 630
Stranded 332, 334
Stranger in My Bed 570, 572
Stranger on My Land 309, 310
Strangers, The 166
Strangers on a Train 611
Strasberg, Lee 158, 346, 515
Strassman, Marcia 5
Strauss, Peter 56, 154, 327
Streep, Harry, II 531
Streep, Harry, III 534
Streep, Mary 531
Streep, Mary Louise *see:* Streep, Meryl
Streep, Meryl 33, 46, 58, 81, 85, 130, 155, 312, 339, 352, 354, 355, 356, 373, 387, 396, 399, 401, 426, 448, 455, 469, 514, 518, 531–540, 545, 616, 620, 626; **534**
Street Smart 432, 435; **433**
Streetcar Named Desire, A (1984) (TV) 469, 533, 593–594, 597

Streetcar Named Desire, A (stage) 46, 90, 532
Streets of Fire 120–121, 125
"Streets of San Francisco, The" (TV) 299, 438, 477, 624
Streisand, Barbra 154, 162, 271, 302, 314, 357, 398–399, 423, 624
Strickland, Gail 63, 135
Strike Force 166, 173
Striking Back 334
Stripes 392, 395
Strong, Arnold *see:* Schwarzenegger, Arnold
Strongest Man in the World, The 454, 458
Struthers, Sally 625
Student Exchange 570, 572
Studs Lonigan (1960) 237
"Studs Lonigan" (TV) 237, 242
Study in Scarlet, A (stage) 15
Styne, Jule 373
Styron, William 338
Success 72, 76
Suddenly Last Summer (stage) 158
Sueno del Mono Loco, El 207
Sugar Babies (stage) 293
Suicide in B-Flat (stage) 183
Sullivan, Ed 508
Sullivan, Susan 504
"Sullivans, The" (TV) 177
Summer, Donna 366
Summer and Smoke (stage) 54, 127, 349, 433
Summer City 175, 181
Summer School 255, 258
Summers, Cathleen 426
Summertree (stage) 15
Sunday in the Park with George (stage) 399, 403
Sunday in the Park with George (album) 403
Sunset 602, 605
Sunset Limousine 439, 443
"Super Force" (TV) 547
Superdad 454, 458
Superman (1978) 430–431, 435
Superman II 430, 431, 435
Superman III 432, 435
Superman IV: The Quest for Peace 432, 435
Superman V 435
Superman in the Bones (stage) 2
"Superstars and Their Moms" (TV) 83, 117, 219, 496
Supinger, Mary Beth 276
Surrender 162, 164, 226, 228
Surtees, Robert 492
"Survival" (TV) 300
Survive! 429, 435

Survivors, The 209, 214, 585, 589
Suspect 83, 86, 427, 425
Sutherland, Donald 285, 527
Svenson, Bo 494
Swaggart, Jimmy 18
Swanson, Dennis 609
Swayze, Bambi 541
Swayze, Don 541
Swayze, Jesse Wayne "Buddy" 541,
542
Swayze, Lisa *see:* Niemi, Lisa
Swayze, Patrick 196, 198, 255,
452, 381, 541–548; **543**
Swayze, Patsy 541, 542
Swayze, Sean 541
"Sweathog Back-to-School Special"
(TV) 551
Sweet Bird of Youth (1962) 255–
256
Sweet Bird of Youth (1989) 255–
256, 258
Sweet Dreams 210, 214, 357, 359
Sweet Hearts Dance 131, 133, 302,
304, 471, 473
Sweet Liberty 417, 420
Sweet Lies 595, 597
Sweet Revenge 16, 21, 385, 388
Swindlehurst, Joe 426
Swing Shift 347, 351, 455, 456,
458
Switch (1975) 501, 506
Switch (1991) 26, 27, 334, 335,
387, 512, 513
"Switch" (TV) 501
"Switch, The" (TV) 480
Switching Channels 433, 435, 562,
565
Sybil 159–160, 164, 364–365
"Szysynyk" (TV) 615

T. R. Baskin 57, 61
Table for Five 99, 104
Tabloids 85, 86
Tailor of Gloucester, The (album)
540
Take Me Home (album) 87
Taken in Marriage (stage) 535
*Taking of Flight 847, The: The Uli
Derickson Story* 570, 572
*Tale of Peter Rabbit with The Tales
of Mr. Jeremy Fisher and Two
Bad Mice, The* (album) 540
"Tale of the Frog Prince, The"
(TV) 585–586
"Tales from the Crypt" (TV) 480
"Tales from the Whoop" (TV) 197
"Tales of the Gold Monkey" (TV)
65
Talk Radio 18, 21; **18**

*Talked to Death: The Life and
Murder of Alan Berg* (book) 18
*Tall Blond Man with One Black
Shoe, The* 246
Tall Guy, The 205, 207
Taming of the Shrew, The (stage)
166, 244, 534
"Taming of the Shrew, The" (TV)
535
Tandy, Jessica 225, 358, 418
Tanenbaum, Robert 626
Tango and Cash 457, 458, 527,
530
Tap 272–273, 274
Tap (album) 274
Taps 286, 287, 290, 406, 407, 411
Tarnowski, Adam 435
Tarquin, Tim 284
Tartikoff, Brandon 234
Tate, Sharon 56
"Tattinger's" (TV) 464
"Taxi" (TV) 137, 143, 144, 148,
235, 397
Taxi Driver 494, 499
Taylor, Dub 361
Taylor, Elizabeth 151, 255, 357,
544, 564
Taylor, Renee 472
Taylor, Robert 305
Te Kanawa, Kiri 95, 400
Telephone, The 194, 198
"Television's Greatest Commer-
cials" (TV) 503
Tempest 470, 473
Tempest, The (stage) 345, 387
Temptations, The 230
Tender, The 555, 556
Tender Mercies 24, 26
"Tenspeed and Brown Shoe" (TV)
202, 207
Tenth Man, The (stage) 151
"Tenth Man, The" (TV) 186
Tequila Sunrise 179, 417–418,
420, 457, 458
Terminal Choice 24, 26
Terminator, The 478, 482, 539
Terminator 2: Judgment Day 482
Terms of Endearment 126, 128,
133, 518, 536, 617–618, 621;
129
Terrible Jim Fitch (stage) 405–406
Terrible Joe Moran 24, 26
"Terror on the Trail" (TV) 453
Terror Train 115, 118
Tesh, John 629
Tesh, Julie 629
Tesich, Steve 402, 576
Testament 99–100, 104
"Texas 150: A Celebration" (TV)
504, 519

Texasville 74–75, 76, 497–498,
499
Thank God It's Friday 201, 207,
615–616, 621
Thanksgiving Promise, The 73, 76
"That Second Thing on ABC"
(TV) 361, 397
"That Thing on ABC" (TV) 361,
397
That's Adequate 603, 605
That's Dancing! 554
"That's What Friends Are For"
(TV) 196, 219
Thaxter, Phyllis 430
"Theatre in America" (TV) 467
Thelma & Louise 472, 473
"Then Came Bronson" (TV) 453
There's a Girl in My Soup (stage)
623
They All Laughed 439, 443
Thicke, Alan 231
"Thicke of the Night" (TV) 231,
235
Thing, The (1982) 455, 458
"Thing Called Love" (music video)
426
Third Degree Burn 595, 597
3614 Jackson Highway (album) 87
"Thirtysomething" (TV) 415
This Child Is Mine 570, 572
This Is Cher (album) 87
This Is Spinal Tap 109, 112
"This Morning" (TV) 196
This Park Is Mine 309, 310
This Property Is Condemned (stage)
566
This Wife for Hire 294, 296
This Will Kill That 125
Thomas, Danny 204
Thomas, Henry 517
Thomas, Kristin Scott 206
Thomas, Marlo 609
Thomas, Philip Michael 302
Thomas, Richard 127, 298, 402,
422, 442
Thompson, Larry 65
"Thorn Birds, The" (TV) 432, 486
"Three Little Pigs, The" (TV) 109,
203
Three Men and a Baby 139, 141,
226, 227, 228
Three Men and a Little Lady 140,
141, 227, 228
Three Rivers 605
Three Sisters, The (stage) 128, 166,
384
Three Stooges, The 174, 598
Three Women 517, 520
"Three's a Crowd" (TV) 440, 443

"Three's Company" (TV) 107, 438, 439, 443

Threshold 202, 207

Throbbing Python of Love (album) 590

Through the Wire 473

Throw Momma from the Train 109, 112, 611, 613

"Thumbelina" (TV) 387

Thumbelina (album) 388

Thunderbolt and Lightfoot 71, 72, 76

Thundering Ho Down Under, The (stage) 196

Thursday's Child 263

Ticking Man, The 605

"Tickled Pink" (TV) 177

Tierney, Gene 603

Tiger Warsaw 545, 547

Till I Loved You (album) 302, 304

Till There Was You 256, 258

Till We Meet Again 66–67, 68

Tillman, Fred 387

Tilly, Meg 48, 91, 386

Tim 176, 181

Time of Destiny, A 280, 282, 288, 290

Time of Your Life, The (stage) 151

"Time of Your Life, The" (TV) 338, 406

"Timebomb: Mother Earth" (TV) 434

Tin Men 154, 155

Tiny Alice (stage) 244

Titanic (stage) 575

To Be the Best 572, 573

To Live and Die in L.A. 119, 121, 122, 125

To Race the Wind 223, 228

To Sleep with Anger 187–188, 189

"Today Makes Me Nervous" (TV) 8

"Today Show, The" (TV) 57, 402, 574

Tolstoy, Leo 432

"Tom & Jerry's 50th Bash" (TV) 213

"Tom Snyder's Celebrity Spotlight" (TV) 81

Tomalin, Marie Criscioni 466

Tomalin, Phillip Leslie 466

Tomalin, Susan Abigail *see:* Sarandon, Susan

Tomlin, Lily 46, 552–553, 613

"Tonight Show Starring Johnny Carson, The" (TV) 109, 231, 269, 515

"Tony Randall Show, The" (TV) 320

Too Far to Go 90, 95

Tootsie 91, 355–356, 359, 392, 395; **356**

Top Gun 385–386, 388; **385**

Torn, Rip 194, 514

Torrents of Spring 289, 290

Total Abandon (stage) 153, 156

Total Recall 197–198, 481, 482, 546

Touch 570

Touch and Go 322, 326

"Touch the Sky" (TV) 432

Tough Dreams 427

Tough Enough 423, 425, 427

Tough Guys Don't Dance 496

Towering Inferno, The 457

Town Bully, The 66, 68

"Town Where No One Got Off, The" (TV) 204

Towne, Robert 174

Townsend, Robert 3, 233

Toys 589

Tozer, Geoffrey 419

Tracy, Spencer 149, 154, 618

Trading Places 9, 12, 116, 118; **10**

Transylvania 6–5000 204, 207; **203**

"Trapper John, M.D." (TV) 259, 261, 262, 264, 267, 361

Trash 515, 520

"Travels of Jaimie McPheeters, The" (TV) 453, 458

Travels with My Aunt 580

Travolta, Anne 549

Travolta, Ellen 549

Travolta, Helen Burke 549

Travolta, Joey 549

Travolta, John 12, 116, 168, 414, 431, 521, 525, 549–556, 576, 592, 603, 604, 616; **116, 553**

Travolta, Margaret 549

Travolta, Salvatore "Sam" 549

Travolta, Sam 549

Travolta Fever (album) 556

Treado, Kathleen 128

Treas, Terri 2

Trelawny of the Wells (stage) 532, 540

Trial of the Catonville Nine, The (stage) 624

"Triangle" (TV) 67

Tricks of the Trade 441, 443

Trilogy of Terror 266

Trip to Bountiful, The 193, 357, 536

Triumph of the Spirit 124, 125

Trois Hommes et un Couffin 226

Tron 64, 68, 72–73, 76

Troop Beverly Hills 364, 365; **364**

Troppo 426

True Believer 596, 628, 630

True Blue (album) 369, 408

True Colors 403

"True Detectives" (TV) 266

True Stories 210, 214

True West (stage) 377, 424

"True West" (TV) 377

Trumbo, Dalton 128

Trump, Donald 67, 303

"Truth About Teachers, The" (TV) 195

Truth or Dare 373, 374

"Trying Times" (TV) 130

Tuareg, the Desert Warrior 253, 257

Tubb, Barry 386

Tucker, Tanya 300

Tucker: The Man and His Dream 73–74, 76

"Tucker's Witch" (TV) 137

Tummy Trouble 563

Tunel, El 487, 490

Tunnel, The 490

Turgenev, Ivan 289

Turk 182 287, 290

Turner, Allen Richard 557

Turner, Kathleen 57, 84, 95, 136, 198, 278, 280, 342, 383, 419, 433, 557–565, 598, 616, 618; **561**

Turner, Lana 84, 354, 370, 413

Turner, Patsy Magee 557, 558

Turner, Tina 196, 230

Turner & Hooch 247, 249

"Turner & Hooch" (TV) 248

Twain, Mark 209

Twelfth Night (stage) 163, 205, 273, 298, 387, 418

25-Cent Romance 426

27 Wagons Full of Cotton (stage) 533, 540

"Twilight Zone, The" (TV) 291–292, 600

Twilight Zone—The Movie 9, 12

"Twin Peaks" (TV) 155

Twins 479–480, 482; **480**

Twisted Obsession 206, 207

Two-Five, The 300, 304

Two for the Money 151, 156

"240-Robert" (TV) 252 258

Two Gentlemen of Verona, The (stage) 201, 207, 244

Two Jakes, The 386

Two Kinds of Love 569, 572

Two Lives of Carol Letner 300, 304

Two of a Kind 554, 556

Two of a Kind (album) 556

Two of Us, The (album) 87

Two People 567, 572

Two the Hard Way (album) 87

Two Virgins (album) 515
Two Worlds of Jennie Logan, The 569, 572
Twohy, David N. 132, 580
Tyson, Bruce 362, 364
Tyson, Juliana 363
Tyson, Richard 481

U.S.A. (stage) 150
"USSR, Midnight Train to Moscow" (TV) 111
Ugly Duckling, The 85
Ugly Duckling, The (album) 87
Ullman, Tracey 212, 281, 341
Ulysses in Nighttown (stage) 306, 311
Ulysses in Traction (stage) 277
Uncommon Valor 543, 547
Uncommon Women and Others (stage) 90
"Uncommon Women and Others" (TV) 533–534
Undercover 273
Underground Aces 217, 220
Une Femme ou Deux 578, 581
Unnatural Causes 440, 443
Unsettled Land 386, 388
Until the End of the World 282
Untouchables, The 101, 105
Up with People 89
Updike, John 90, 417
"Upward Mobility" (TV) 201
Urban Cowboy 541, 553, 556, 576, 616, 621
Ure, Mary 89
Urich, Robert 134, 287, 333, 570
"Us Against the World II" (TV) 485
Used Cars 455, 458
Users, The 502, 506
Ustinov, Peter 328, 415, 488

V. I. Warshawski 564, 565
Vadim, Roger 492
Valdez, Luis 450
Valentine, Scott 265
Valkenvania 12
Valley of the Dolls 150, 156
Valmont 94
Van Damme, Jean-Claude 474
Van Dyke, Barry 322, 362
Van Dyke, Dick 277, 321
Van Kamp, Merete 569
Van Sant, Gus 125, 381
Van Sant, Pamela 595
Vandross, Luther 272
Vanilla (album) 495, 499
Vanities (stage) 495
"Variety '77—The Year in Entertainment" (TV) 315

Vaughan, Sarah 400
Vaughn, Robert 3
Velardi, Valerie 583, 584
"Velveteen Rabbit, The" (TV) 536
Velveteen Rabbit, The (album) 540
Venora, Diane 170, 342
Verdict, The 599
Vereen, Ben 202, 272
Verhoeven, Paul 481
Verna: U.S.O. Girl 277, 282, 517, 520
Vernon, Jackie 29
Very Best of Cher, The (album) 87
Vest Pocket Players, The 337
Vibes 11, 205, 207
Victor, Don 192
Victory 525, 529
Victory at Entebbe 151, 156
Videodrome 626, 630
Vieira, Asia 316
View from the Bridge, A (stage) 98
Vigoda, Abe 555
Villa, Pancho 511
Village People, The 224
Villain, The 477, 482
Vincent, Jan-Michael 41, 167, 494
Vinnie the Giver 547
Vintage Season (book) 132
Violets Are Blue 340, 343, 518–519, 520; **518**
"Virginia's Story" (film episode) 24, 26
Vision Quest 368, 374
Vision Quest (album) 374
Visitors, The 624, 630
"Visitors in Paradise" (TV) 114
Vital Signs 512, 513
Vitte, Ray 331
Viva Detroit (stage) 188
"Vivien Leigh: Scarlett and Beyond" (TV) 358–359
Vivre pour Vivre 55, 61
Voice of the Heart 571, 573
Voices Within: The Lives of Trudi Chase 364–365
Voight, Jon 99, 275
Volunteers 246, 248
Von Furstenberg, Diane 171

Wachs, Robert 234
Wade, Cabot 89
Wager, The (stage) 15, 253
Wagner, Billy Nowels 566
Wagner, Jane 552
Wagner, Lindsay 66, 415, 566–572; **569**
Wagner, Marilyn Louise Thrasher 566
Wagner, Robert 434, 504
"Wagon and the Elephant, The" (TV) 261

Wahl, Ken 241, 266
Waiting for Godot (stage) 587
Waiting for Lefty (stage) 98, 376
Walcott, Derek 188
Walesa, Lech 589
Walk, Don't Run 283
Walken, Christopher 48, 95, 408, 410, 470, 577
Walker, Alice 188, 193, 610
Walker, Marcy 572
Walker, Nancy 108, 159, 321
Wall Street 218, 280, 587
Wallace, Marjorie 216, 299
Walsh, M. Emmet 210
Walsh, Phil 42
Walters, Barbara 110, 134, 181, 541, 545, 563, 607, 608, 611, 619
Walters, James 555
"Waltons, The" (TV) 437, 443, 515
Wambaugh, Joseph 135, 330, 594, 624, 625
Wanamaker, Sam 136
"War and Remembrance" (TV) 488, 490
"War and Remembrance: The Final Chapter" (TV) 490
War of the Roses, The 83–84, 240, 563, 565
"War of the Worlds" (radio) 438
Ward, David S. 616
Ward, Fred 19
Ward, Rachel 69, 73, 486, 626
Ward, Sela 3
Ward, Tony 373
Warden, Jack 407, 443
Warfield, Marsha 36
Warhol, Andy 125, 170, 285, 312, 316, 368, 381, 405, 440, 515
Waring, Todd 246
Warren, Lesley Ann 256; **256**
Warren, Patricia Nell 50
Warrick, Lee 306
"Warriors, The" (TV) 143
Wars of the Roses (stage) 337
Washington, Denzel 340, 572; **340**
Wasserman, Edie 113
Wasserman, Lew 113, 114
"Watch the Fur Fly" (TV) 202
Waterston, Sam 92, 378
Watson, Rev. Bob 438
Way We Were, The 549, 624, 630
Way West, The 158, 163
Wayans, Damon 205
Wayans, Keenen Ivory 233, 234
Wayne, John 17, 62, 64, 66, 174, 264, 528
Wayne, Patrick 485
We Are the Children 138, 141

"We Can Remember It for You Wholesale" (story) 481
We the People 107
Weathers, Carl 182
Weaver, Dennis 332
Weaver, Elizabeth Inglis 574
Weaver, Sigourney 59, 174, 176, 219, 271, 277, 574–581, 620; **394, 577**
Weaver, Susan Alexandra *see:* Weaver, Sigourney
Weaver, Sylvester "Pat" 574, 577, 578
Weaver, Trajan 574
Weaver, Winston "Doodles" 574
Webb, Jack 251, 252
Webb, Jimmy 2
"Weekend Special" (TV) 386
Weider, Joe 475
Weill, Kurt 532
Weinberger, Ed. 144
Weintraub, Jerry 537
Weir, Peter 18, 176, 386
Weisman, Robin 140, 227
Weiss, Jay 560–561
Weiss, Rachel Ann 562
Weissmuller, Johnny, Jr. 391
Weitz, Bruce 128
Welch, Raquel 329, 355, 616
Welch, Tahnee 226
"Welcome Back, Kotter" (TV) 549, 550–551, 552
Welcome Home, Roxy Carmichael 132, 133
Welcome to L.A. 516–517, 520
Weld, Tuesday 171, 308, 355, 595
Weller, Peter 128, 203, 387, 596
Welles, Orson 438, 493, 495, 524, 630
We're Fighting Back 23, 26
We're No Angels (1989) 410, 412
Werner, Tom 32, 36
Wertmuller, Lina 57
Wessex 488, 490
West, Adam 464
West, Mae 28, 291, 366, 607
West Side Story (stage) 298, 500, 542
Westcott, Frances 52
Westheimer, Dr. Ruth 17, 232
Whale Song 140
What About Bob? 155, 156, 394, 395
What Does Dorrie Want? 315, 318
"What Really Happened to the Class of '65" (TV) 299–300
What's So Bad About Feeling Good? 465, 468
When Harry Met Sally . . . 110, 112; **110**

When the Bough Breaks 138, 141
Where Angels Go . . . Trouble Follows 460, 465
Where the Buffalo Roam 391, 395
Whereabouts of Jenny, The 147, 148
Which Way Home 498, 499
Whitaker, Forest 273
White, Betty 262
White, Vanna 527
White Lies, The (stage) 166
White Nights 271–272, 274
White Palace 472, 473
Whitmore, James 240
Whitney, Ruth 492
Whitton, Margaret 443
"Whiz Kid and the Carnival Caper, The" (TV) 501
"Who Am I This Time?" (TV) 470
Who Framed Roger Rabbit 562, 565
Wholly Moses! 439, 443
Whoopi Goldberg 195
Whoopi Goldberg (stage) 193, 199
"Whoopi Goldberg—Direct from Broadway" (TV) 193
Whoopi Goldberg—Direct from Broadway (album) 199
"Whoopi Goldberg Live" (TV) 195
Whoopi Goldberg Variations (stage) 193
Who's Afraid of Virginia Woolf? (stage) 45
Who's Minding the Mint 283
Who's That Girl 370, 374
Who's That Girl (stage) 370
Who's That Girl (album) 374
"Who's the Boss?" (TV) 144, 145, 146, 147, 148; **145**
Whose Life Is It Anyway? 152, 156, 347, 351
Why Am I Straight? (album) 199
Why Would I Lie? 593, 597
Widmark, Richard 119, 403
Wiest, Dianne 209
Wild at Heart 124, 125
Wild on the Beach 79, 86
Wild on the Beach (album) 87
Wild Orchid 449–450, 451
Wild Party, The 329, 334
Wild Times 64, 68
Wilder, Gene 350
Wilder, James 240
Wilder, Thornton 120
Wilder Napalm 621
Will There Really Be a Morning? (book) 355
Willard, Fred 203
Williams, Charles 303
Williams, Cindy 163, 441
Williams, Esther 39, 109

Williams, JoBeth 26, 48, 224
Williams, Laurie Smith 582
Williams, Lisa 48
Williams, Marsha 587, 588
Williams, Matt 32, 33, 211
Williams, R. J. 504
Williams, Richard 591
Williams, Richard Treat *see:* Williams, Treat
Williams, Robert 538, 582, 583
Williams, Robin 18, 75, 90, 106, 109, 111, 191, 194, 198, 280, 336, 436, 437, 456, 582–590, 603; **586**
Williams, Tennessee 287, 330, 469, 515
Williams, Todd 582
Williams, Treat 550, 553, 591–597; **594**
Williams, Valerie 584, 586
Williams, Vanessa 12, 604
Williams, Zachary 586
Williams, Zelda 587, 588
"Willie and the Yank" (TV) 453
Willis, Bruce 12, 35, 37, 42, 194, 196, 209, 210, 212, 248, 323, 370, 411, 481, 495, 497, 531, 539, 555, 587, 598–605; **601**
Willis, David 598, 599
Willis, Marlene 598
Willis, Rumer Glenn 603
Wilson, Bill 628
Wilson, Flip 230
Wilson, Jim 104
Wilson, Lanford 127, 379
Wilson, Nancy 230
Wilson, Rita 246
Wilson, Tom 248
"Wilton North Report, The" (TV) 231
Wimmer, Brian 265
Wind and the Lion, The 57, 61
Windmills of the Gods 504, 507
"Windows, Doors & Keyholes" (TV) 568
"Winds of War, The" (TV) 488
Wine Untouched (stage) 90
Winfrey, Cindy 608
Winfrey, Oprah 193, 233, 607–613; **611**
Winfrey, Vernon 607, 608, 611
Winfrey, Zelma 608
Winger, Debra 93, 128, 169, 287–288, 355, 375, 380–381, 393, 515, 561, 576, 614–621; **129, 617**
Winger, Marc 614
Winger, Marla 614
Winger, Robert 614
Winger, Ruth 614

Winkler, Henry 3, 5, 99, 110, 160, 247, 321, 328–329, 523, 552
Winningham, Mare 243, 332, 615
Winter Dancers, The (stage) 90
Winter Kills 72, 76; *72*
Winter People 387, 388, 457, 458
Winters, Jonathan 582, 584, 585
Winter's Tale, The (stage) 384, 401, 433–434
Wired 11
Wise, Robert 54, 567
"Wiseguy" (TV) 241
Witches of Eastwick, The 83, 86, 417, 420, 470–471, 473
"Witches of Eastwick, The" (TV) 417
With Love (album) 87
Without a Word (stage) 543
Witness 184, 189, 385, 388
Witt, Paul Junger 233
Wittman, Ricky 464
"Wolcott" (TV) 346
Wolfe, Thomas 327
Wolfe, Tom 238, 604
Wolfen 270, 274
Wolff, Art 406
Wolff, Michael 232, 497
Wolinski, David 369, 408
Woman He Loved, The 487–489
Women and Men: Stories of Seduction 219, 220, 629, 630
Women in Revolt 515, 520
Women of Brewster Place, The 611–612, 613; **611**
Women of Valor 470, 473
"Women Who Rate a '10'" (TV) 293
Women's Room, The 136, 141, 262, 266
"Wonder Woman in Hollywood" (TV) 615
Wonderful Wizard of Oz, The (book) 442
"Wonderful World of Disney, The" (TV) 291, 453
Wondrous World of Sonny and Cher, The (album) 87
Wood, John 416
Wood, Natalie 330, 357, 361, 565
Woodard, Alfre 186
Woods, Gail 622, 623

Woods, James 73, 94, 119, 136, 177, 219, 596, 622–630; **627**
Woods, Kathryn 625, 627
Woods, Martha Ann 622, 623
Woods, Michael 623
Woods, Sarah 628–629
Woods, The (stage) 345–346
Woodward, Bob 11
Woodward, Joanne 24, 379, 570, 624
Woolgatherer, The (stage) 362
Wopat, Tom 571
Word of Honor 377, 382
Words and Music (stage) 292
Working Girl 18, 21, 218, 219, 220, 579, 581; **218**
"Working Girl" (TV) 219
"Working Stiffs" (TV) 321, 326
World According to Garp, The 90–91, 95, 128, 585, 589; **586**
World According to Garp, The (book) 90
"World Apart, A" (TV) 467, 473
"World of Disney" (TV) 501
"World of Jewish Humor, The" (TV) 111
"World's Greatest Stunts, The" (TV) 179, 255, 545
World's Greatest Stunts, The! A Tribute to Hollywood Stuntmen 434, 481
Worth Winning 256, 258; **256**
Wray, Fay 353
Wrestlers (stage) 254
Wright, Richard 610
Wright, Robin 411
Wrong Guys, The 211, 214
Wyatt, Jane 516
Wyman, Jane 265

Yanks 168, 173
Yarbrough, Janice 547
Yates, Peter 576
Year of Living Dangerously, The 81, 91, 176–177, 181, 574, 577, 581
Year of the Dragon 447, 451
Yefremov, Oleg 282
"Yellow Rose, The" (TV) 495, 498, 499
Yentl 398–399, 403

Yentl (album) 403
"Yentl, the Yeshiva Boy" (story) 398
Yes, Giorgio 576–577
Yesso, Don 386
Yin and Yang of Mr. Go, The 70–71, 76
Yolen, Jane 342
York, Michael 238
York, Susannah 415, 430
Yorkin, Bud 131
You Can Dance (album) 374
"You Can't Tell by Looking" (TV) 371
You Look Mahvelous! (album) 109, 112
Young, Loretta 157, 312
Young, Neil 50
Young, Sean 42, 324, 498, 628
Young Again 570, 572
Young Doctors in Love 2
"Young Guy Christian" (TV) 361
Young Hollywood 53, 61
Young Love, First Love 285, 290
"Young Riders, The" (TV) 20
Young Runaways, The 150, 156
Young Winston 484, 489
Youngblood 544, 547
Youngman, Henny 29, 231
Your Own Thing (stage) 298
You're a Good Man, Charlie Brown (stage) 107
"You're Not a Hero Until You're Sung" (TV) 568
Yuri Nosenko, KGB 309, 310

Zachariah 299, 304
Zachary, Bohden 83
Zagone, Robert N. 185
Zaks, Jerry 402
Zal, Roxana 91, 138
Zapata, Carmen 512
Zeffirelli, Franco 95
Zeller, Lois 550
Zieff, Howard 118
Zimbalist, Stephanie 16
Zinnemann, Fred 576
Zoli 353
Zorba! (stage) 555
Zorba the Greek 555
Zuma Beach 284, 290
Zuniga, Daphne 49